D1433486

Advanced Parallel Computing

PARALLEL COMPUTING: FROM MULTICORES AND GPU'S TO PETASCALE

Advances in Parallel Computing

This book series publishes research and development results on all aspects of parallel computing. Topics may include one or more of the following: high-speed computing architectures (Grids, clusters, Service Oriented Architectures, etc.), network technology, performance measurement, system software, middleware, algorithm design, development tools, software engineering, services and applications.

Series Editor:
Professor Dr. Gerhard R. Joubert

Volume 19

Recently published in this series

Vol. 18.   W. Gentzsch, L. Grandinetti and G. Joubert (Eds.), High Speed and Large Scale Scientific Computing

Vol. 17.   F. Xhafa (Ed.), Parallel Programming, Models and Applications in Grid and P2P Systems

Vol. 16.   L. Grandinetti (Ed.), High Performance Computing and Grids in Action

Vol. 15.   C. Bischof, M. Bücker, P. Gibbon, G.R. Joubert, T. Lippert, B. Mohr and F. Peters (Eds.), Parallel Computing: Architectures, Algorithms and Applications

Volumes 1–14 published by Elsevier Science.

ISSN 0927-5452 (print)
ISSN 1879-808X (online)

Parallel Computing: From Multicores and GPU's to Petascale

Edited by

Barbara Chapman
University of Houston, USA

Frédéric Desprez
INRIA, France

Gerhard R. Joubert
TU Clausthal, Germany

Alain Lichnewsky
GENCI, France

Frans Peters
Philips Research, The Netherlands

and

Thierry Priol
INRIA, France

IOS
Press

Amsterdam • Berlin • Tokyo • Washington, DC

© 2010 The authors and IOS Press.

All rights reserved. No part of this book may be reproduced, stored in a retrieval system, or transmitted, in any form or by any means, without prior written permission from the publisher.

ISBN 978-1-60750-529-7 (print)
ISBN 978-1-60750-530-3 (online)
Library of Congress Control Number: 2010923473

Publisher
IOS Press BV
Nieuwe Hemweg 6B
1013 BG Amsterdam
Netherlands
fax: +31 20 687 0019
e-mail: order@iospress.nl

Distributor in the USA and Canada
IOS Press, Inc.
4502 Rachael Manor Drive
Fairfax, VA 22032
USA
fax: +1 703 323 3668
e-mail: iosbooks@iospress.com

LEGAL NOTICE

The publisher is not responsible for the use which might be made of the following information.

PRINTED IN THE NETHERLANDS

Parallel Computing: From Multicores and GPU's to Petascale
B. Chapman et al. (Eds.)
IOS Press, 2010
© 2010 The authors and IOS Press. All rights reserved.

Preface

Parallel Computing technologies brought dramatic changes to mainstream computing. This trend is accelerating as the end of the development of hardware following Moore's law looms on the horizon. The majority of standard PC's and even notebooks today incorporate multiprocessor chips with up to four processors. This number is expected to soon reach eight and more.

These standard components, COTS (Components Off The Shelf), are increasingly combined with powerful parallel processors originally designed for high-speed graphics processing, GPU's (Graphics Processing Units), and FPGA's (Free Programmable Gate Arrays) to build heterogeneous parallel computers that offer a wide spectrum of high speed processing functions. The number of processors incorporated in such systems are today of the order of up to 10^4 to 10^6. This vast number of processors allows the construction of high speed computers in the petascale range, and even the exascale range, at a reasonable cost. The limiting factor for constructing more powerful hardware is the energy consumption and thermal control of such systems. Many research efforts concentrate on reducing the overall energy consumed.

In addition to the hardware design and build limitations, the practical use of petascale or exascale machines is hampered by the difficulties of developing software that efficiently and effectively run on such architectures. This holds for system as well as application software. The ParCo conference aimed at addressing many of these issues through contributed papers as well as the various mini-symposia presentations.

In this book, which includes selected and refereed papers presented at the international Parallel Computing conference (ParCo2009) held from 1–4 September 2009 at ENS (École Normale Supérieure), Lyon, France, problems associated with the development of high speed parallel systems using new hardware concepts and the associated software development issues are considered. The papers were presented as keynote papers, in regular sessions, an industrial session and various mini-symposia covering specialised topics. Overall these give a snapshot of the state-of-the-art of parallel computing technologies, both in hardware as well as application and software development.

This year's highlight is no doubt the increasing number of papers addressing the programming of general-purpose graphics processing units. Considering the main track of the conference, as well as the mini-symposium dedicated to GPU's, ParCo2009 turned into one of the main scientific venues covering this important research topic in 2009.

The editors wish to express their sincere gratitude for all persons who supported this venture and lastly made it feasible. In particular we wish to thank the many reviewers who, as members of the international Program Committee, not only assessed papers, but also acted as session chairmen during the conference.

Sincere thanks is due to the members of the Organising Committee, and in particular to Laurent Lefèvre, Eddy Caron and Jean-Christophe Mignot, who spent many hours assisting in organising a very successful event. We are also very grateful for work done by Virginie Mahdi from Genci, Paris in attracting a considerable number of sponsors as well as participants in the Industrial Session.

Please note that versions of papers with colour images and diagrams are available in the electronic version of the book on http://www.booksonline.iospress.nl/ under Advances in Parallel Computing.

Barbara Chapman, *University of Houston, USA*
Frédéric Desprez, *INRIA, France*
Gerhard Joubert, *TU Clausthal, Germany*
Alain Lichnewsky, *GENCI, France*
Frans Peters, *Philips Research, Netherlands*
Thierry Priol, *INRIA, France*

31 December 2009

Conference Organization

Conference Committee
Gerhard Joubert (Germany/Netherlands) (Conference Chair)
Barbara Chapman (USA)
Frédéric Desprez (France)
Alain Lichnewsky (France)
Virginie Mahdi (France)
Frans Peters (Netherlands)
Thierry Priol (France)

Advisory Committee
Jean-Yves Berthou (France)
Jack Dongarra (USA)
Alain Lichnewsky (France)
Thomas Lippert (Germany)

Minisymposium Committee
Gerhard Joubert (Germany/Netherlands)
Frans Peters (Netherlands)

Organising Committee
Frédéric Desprez (France)
Laurent Lefèvre (France)
Eddy Caron (France)
Jean-Christophe Mignot (France)

Exhibition Committee
Alain Lichnewsky (France)
Virginie Mahdi (France)

Finance Committee
Frans Peters (Netherlands)

Conference Program Committee
Thierry Priol (France) (Chair)
Barbara Chapman (USA) (Co-Chair)

David Abramson (Australia)
Sadaf Alam (USA)
Gabrielle Allen (USA)
Rosa Badia (Spain)
Dirk Bartz (Germany)
Jean-Yves Berthou (France)
Petter Bjørstad (Norway)
Arndt Bode (Germany)
Marian Bubak (Poland)
Mark Bull (UK)
H. Calandra (France)
Arun Chauhan (USA)
Andrea Clematis (Italy)
Pasqua D'Ambra (Italy)
Luisa D'Amore (Italy)
Erik H. D'Hollander (Belgium)
Michel Dayde (France)
Frank Dehne (Canada)
Luiz DeRose (USA)
Anne Elster (Norway)
Edgar Gabriel (USA)
Efstratios Gallopoulos (Greece)
Lei Huang (USA)
Kevin Huck (USA)
Emmanuel Jeannot (France)
Hai Jin (China)
Christoph Kessler (Sweden)
Dieter Kranzlmüller (Austria)

Herbert Kuchen (Germany)
Alexey Lastovetsky (Ireland)
Pierre Leca (France)
Thomas Ludwig (Germany)
Emilio Luque (Spain)
Federico Massaioli (Italy)
Satoshi Matsuoka (Japan)
Wolfgang Nagel (Germany)
Kengo Nakajima (Japan)
Raymond Namyst (France)
Christian Pérez (France)
Serge Petiton (France)
Nicolai Petkov (Netherlands)
Oscar Plata (Spain)
Jean Roman (France)
Ullrich Rüde (Germany)
Gudula Rünger (Germany)
Marie-Chr. Sawley (Switzerland)
Martin Schulz (USA)
Tor Sørevik (Norway)
Erich Strohmaier (USA)
Frédéric Suter (France)
Domenico Talia (Italy)
Paco Tirado (Spain)
Denis Trystram (France)
Marco Vanñeschi (Italy)
Zhiwei Xu (China)
Albert Zomaya (Australia)

Program Committees of Mini-Symposia

Adaptive parallel computing: latency toleration, non-determinism as a form of adaptation, adaptive mapping
Chris Jesshope (Netherlands)

DEISA: Extreme Computing in an Advanced Supercomputing Environment
Hermann Lederer (Germany)
Gavin Pringle (UK)
Wolfgang Gentzsch (Germany)

EuroGPU 2009
Anne C. Elster (Norway)
Stephane Requena (France)
Guillaume Colin de Verdière (France)

ParaFPGA-2009: Parallel Computing with FPGA's
Erik D'Hollander (Belgium)
Dirk Stroobandt (Belgium)
Abdellah Touhafi (Belgium)

Parallel Programming Tools for Multi-Core Architectures
Bernd Mohr (Germany)
Bettina Krammer (France)
Hartmut Mix (Germany)

Programming Heterogeneous Architectures
Lei Huang (USA)
Eric Stotzer (USA)
Eric Biscondi (USA)

ParCo2009 Sponsors

Contents

Preface   v
Barbara Chapman, Frédéric Desprez, Gerhard Joubert,
Alain Lichnewsky, Frans Peters and Thierry Priol

Conference Organization   vii

ParCo2009 Sponsors   x

Invited Talks

Exascale Computing: What Future Architectures Will Mean for the User
Community   3
Alan Gara and Ravi Nair

Making Multi-Cores Mainstream – From Security to Scalability   16
Chris Jesshope, Michael Hicks, Mike Lankamp, Raphael Poss and Li Zhang

Numerical Algorithms

Efficiency and Scalability of the Parallel Barnes-Hut Tree Code PEPC   35
Robert Speck, Paul Gibbon and Martin Hoffmann

Combining Numerical Iterative Solvers   43
Yanik Ngoko and Denis Trystram

A Comparative Study of Some Distributed Linear Solvers on Systems Arising
from Fluid Dynamics Simulations   51
Désiré Nuentsa Wakam, Jocelyne Erhel, Édouard Canot and
Guy-Antoine Atenekeng Kahou

Gradient Projection Methods for Image Deblurring and Denoising on Graphics
Processors   59
Thomas Serafini, Riccardo Zanella and Luca Zanni

Parallel Simulations of Seismic Wave Propagation on NUMA Architectures   67
Fabrice Dupros, Christiane Pousa Ribeiro, Alexandre Carissimi
and Jean-François Méhaut

Aitken-Schwarz and Schur Complement Methods for Time Domain
Decomposition   75
Patrice Linel and Damien Tromeur-Dervout

Performance Modeling Tools for Parallel Sparse Linear Algebra Computations   83
Pietro Cicotti, Xiaoye S. Li and Scott B. Baden

Narrow-Band Reduction Approach of a DRSM Eigensolver on a Multicore-Based
Cluster System   91
Toshiyuki Imamura, Susumu Yamada and Masahiko Machida

Parallel Multistage Preconditioners by Extended Hierarchical Interface
Decomposition for Ill-Conditioned Problems   99
    Kengo Nakajima

A Comparison of Different Communication Structures for Scalable Parallel
Three Dimensional FFTs in First Principles Codes   107
    A. Canning, J. Shalf, L.-W. Wang, H. Wasserman and M. Gajbe

Parallelization Strategies for ODE Solvers on Multicore Cluster Systems   117
    Thomas Rauber and Gudula Rünger

Evaluation of Parallel Sparse Matrix Partitioning Software for Parallel Multilevel
ILU Preconditioning on Shared-Memory Multiprocessors   125
    José I. Aliaga, Matthias Bollhöfer, Alberto F. Martín and
    Enrique S. Quintana-Ortí

A Parallel Implementation of the Davidson Method for Generalized
Eigenproblems   133
    Eloy Romero and Jose E. Roman

Bio-Informatics

A Data-Flow Modification of the MUSCLE Algorithm for Multiprocessors and
a Web Interface for It   143
    Alexey N. Salnikov

A Parallel Algorithm for the Fixed-Length Approximate String Matching
Problem for High Throughput Sequencing Technologies   150
    Costas S. Iliopoulos, Laurent Mouchard and Solon P. Pissis

Computing Alignment Plots Efficiently   158
    Peter Krusche and Alexander Tiskin

Image Processing & Visualisation

Parallelizing the LM OSEM Image Reconstruction on Multi-Core Clusters   169
    Philipp Ciechanowicz, Philipp Kegel, Maraike Schellmann,
    Sergei Gorlatch and Herbert Kuchen

Hierarchical Visualization System for High Performance Computing   177
    Oxana Dzhosan, Nina Popova and Anton Korzh

Real Time Ultrasound Image Sequence Segmentation on Multicores   185
    D. Casaburi, L. D'Amore, L. Marcellino and A. Murli

GRID & Cloud Computing

Processing Applications Composed of Web/Grid Services by Distributed
Autonomic and Self-Organizing Workflow Engines   195
    Giuseppe Papuzzo and Giandomenico Spezzano

LPT Scheduling Algorithms with Unavailability Constraints Under Uncertainties 205
    Adel Essafi, Amine Mahjoub, Grégory Mounié and Denis Trystram

Parallel Genetic Algorithm Implementation for BOINC   212
  Malek Smaoui Feki, Viet Huy Nguyen and Marc Garbey

RPC/MPI Hybrid Implementation of OpenFMO – All Electron Calculations of
a Ribosome   220
  *Yuichi Inadomi, Toshiya Takami, Jun Maki, Taizo Kobayashi
  and Mutsumi Aoyagi*

When Clouds Become Green: The Green Open Cloud Architecture   228
  Anne-Cécile Orgerie and Laurent Lefèvre

A Versatile System for Asynchronous Iterations: From Multithreaded
Simulations to Grid Experiments   238
  Giorgos Kollias, Konstantinos Georgiou and Efstratios Gallopoulos

Programming

Exploiting Object-Oriented Abstractions to Parallelize Sparse Linear Algebra
Codes   249
  *Christian Terboven, Dieter An Mey, Paul Kapinos,
  Christopher Schleiden and Igor Merkulow*

Handling Massive Parallelism Efficiently: Introducing Batches of Threads   257
  Ioannis E. Venetis and Theodore S. Papatheodorou

Skeletons for Multi/Many-Core Systems   265
  Marco Aldinucci, Marco Danelutto and Peter Kilpatrick

Efficient Streaming Applications on Multi-Core with FastFlow: The Biosequence
Alignment Test-Bed   273
  *Marco Aldinucci, Marco Danelutto, Massimiliano Meneghin,
  Massimo Torquati and Peter Kilpatrick*

A Framework for Detailed Multiphase Cloud Modeling on HPC Systems   281
  *Matthias Lieber, Ralf Wolke, Verena Grützun, Matthias S. Müller
  and Wolfgang E. Nagel*

Extending Task Parallelism for Frequent Pattern Mining   289
  *Prabhanjan Kambadur, Amol Ghoting, Anshul Gupta and
  Andrew Lumsdaine*

GPU & Cell Programming

Exploring the GPU for Enhancing Parallelism on Color and Texture Analysis   299
  *Francisco Igual, Rafael Mayo, Timothy D.R. Hartley, Umit Catalyurek,
  Antonio Ruiz and Manuel Ujaldón*

Generalized GEMM Kernels on GPGPUs: Experiments and Applications   307
  Davide Barbieri, Valeria Cardellini and Salvatore Filippone

Comparison of Modular Arithmetic Algorithms on GPUs   315
  Pascal Giorgi, Thomas Izard and Arnaud Tisserand

Fast Multipole Method on the Cell Broadband Engine: The Near Field Part 323
Pierre Fortin and Jean-Luc Lamotte

The GPU on the Matrix-Matrix Multiply: Performance Study and Contributions 331
José María Cecilia, José Manuel García and Manuel Ujaldón

Performance Measurement of Applications with GPU Acceleration Using CUDA 341
Shangkar Mayanglambam, Allen D. Malony and Matthew J. Sottile

Compilers & Tools

Conflict Analysis for Heap-Based Data Dependence Detection 351
Rosa Castillo, Francisco Corbera, Angeles Navarro,
Rafael Asenjo and Emilio L. Zapata

Adaptive Parallel Matrix Computing Through Compiler and Run-Time Support 359
Jorge Buenabad-Chávez, Miguel Alfonso Castro-García,
Rosa Angélica Rosales-Camacho, Santiago Domínguez-Domínguez,
Julio C. Peralta and Manuel Aguilar-Cornejo

Parallel I/O

High-Throughput Parallel-I/O Using SIONlib for Mesoscopic Particle Dynamics
Simulations on Massively Parallel Computers 371
Jens Freche, Wolfgang Frings and Godehard Sutmann

Tracing Performance of MPI-I/O with PVFS2: A Case Study of Optimization 379
Yuichi Tsujita, Julian Kunkel, Stephan Krempel and Thomas Ludwig

Communication Runtime

A Historic Knowledge Based Approach for Dynamic Optimization 389
Saber Feki and Edgar Gabriel

Evaluation of Task Mapping Strategies for Regular Network Topologies 397
Sebastian Rinke, Torsten Mehlan and Wolfgang Rehm

Benchmark & Performance Tuning

Automatic Performance Tuning of Parallel Mathematical Libraries 407
Ihab Salawdeh, Anna Morajko, Eduardo César, Tomàs Margalef
and Emilio Luque

Automatic Performance Tuning Approach for Parallel Applications Based
on Sparse Linear Solvers 415
Vasiliy Yu. Voronov and Nina N. Popova

A Flexible, Application- and Platform-Independent Environment for
Benchmarking 423
Wolfgang Frings, Alexander Schnurpfeil, Stefanie Meier,
Florian Janetzko and Lukas Arnold

Fault Tolerance

Optimized Checkpointing Protocols for Data Parallel Programs   433
Carlo Bertolli and Marco Vanneschi

Constructing Resiliant Communication Infrastructure for Runtime Environments   441
*George Bosilca, Camille Coti, Thomas Herault, Pierre Lemarinier
and Jack Dongarra*

Industrial Papers

Optimizing Performance and Energy of High Performance Computing
Applications   455
*Luigi Brochard, Raj Panda, Don Desota, Francois Thomas
and Rob Bell Jr.*

Mini-Symposium "Adaptive Parallel Computing: Latency Toleration, Non-Determinism as a Form of Adaptation, Adaptive Mapping"

An Operational Semantics for S-Net   467
Frank Penczek, Clemens Grelck and Sven-Bodo Scholz

Mini-Symposium "DEISA: Extreme Computing in an Advanced Supercomputing Environment"

DEISA Mini-Symposium on Extreme Computing in an Advanced
Supercomputing Environment   477
Wolfgang Gentzsch and Hermann Lederer

DEISA Extreme Computing Initiative (DECI) and Science Community Support   482
Alison Kennedy and Hermann Lederer

Application Oriented DEISA Infrastructure Services   492
*Andrew P.J. Emerson, Giovanni Erbacci, Juha Fagerholm,
Denis Girou, Gavin J. Pringle and Mariano Vázquez*

Chemical Characterization of Super-Heavy Elements by Relativistic
Four-Component DFT   501
Francesco Tarantelli, Leonardo Belpassi and Loriano Storchi

Direct Numerical Simulation of the Turbulent Development of a Round Jet
at Reynolds Number 11,000   513
Christophe Bogey and Olivier Marsden

EUFORIA: Exploring E-Science for Fusion   520
D.P. Coster, P. Strand and Contributors to the EUFORIA Project

Mini-Symposium "EuroGPU 2009"

Parallel Computing with GPUs   533
Anne C. Elster and Stéphane Requena

Porous Rock Simulations and Lattice Boltzmann on GPUs 536
Eirik O. Aksnes and Anne C. Elster

An Efficient Multi-Algorithms Sparse Linear Solver for GPUs 546
Thomas Jost, Sylvain Contassot-Vivier and Stéphane Vialle

Abstraction of Programming Models Across Multi-Core and GPGPU
Architectures 554
Thomas H. Beach, Ian J. Grimstead, David W. Walker and Nick J. Avis

Modelling Multi-GPU Systems 562
Daniele G. Spampinato, Anne C. Elster and Thorvald Natvig

Throughput Computing on Future GPUs 570
Rune J. Hovland and Anne C. Elster

Mini-Symposium "ParaFPGA-2009: Parallel Computing with FPGA's"

ParaFPGA: Parallel Computing with Flexible Hardware 581
Erik H. D'Hollander, Dirk Stroobandt and Abdellah Touhafi

Software vs. Hardware Message Passing Implementations for FPGA Clusters 584
Eoin Creedon and Michael Manzke

RAPTOR – A Scalable Platform for Rapid Prototyping and FPGA-Based Cluster
Computing 592
Mario Porrmann, Jens Hagemeyer, Johannes Romoth,
Manuel Strugholtz and Christopher Pohl

Speeding up Combinational Synthesis in an FPGA Cluster 600
César Pedraza, Javier Castillo, José Ignacio Martínez, Pablo Huerta,
José Luis Bosque and Javier Cano

A Highly Parallel FPGA-Based Evolvable Hardware Architecture 608
Fabio Cancare, Marco Castagna, Matteo Renesto and Donatella Sciuto

Applying Parameterizable Dynamic Configurations to Sequence Alignment 616
Tom Davidson, Karel Bruneel, Harald Devos and Dirk Stroobandt

Towards a More Efficient Run-Time FPGA Configuration Generation 624
Fatma Abouelella, Karel Bruneel and Dirk Stroobandt

ACCFS – Virtual File System Support for Host Coupled Run-Time
Reconfigurable FPGAs 632
Jochen Strunk, Andreas Heinig, Toni Volkmer, Wolfgang Rehm
and Heiko Schick

Mini-Symposium "Parallel Programming Tools for Multi-Core Architectures"

Parallel Programming Tools for Multi-Core Architectures 643
Bernd Mohr, Bettina Krammer and Hartmut Mix

Parallel Programming for Multi-Core Architectures 645
Jean-Marc Morel for the ParMA Project Partners

An Approach to Application Performance Tuning 653
Andres Charif-Rubial, Souad Koliai, Stéphane Zuckerman,
Bettina Krammer, William Jalby and Quang Dinh

How to Accelerate an Application: A Practical Case Study in Combustion
Modelling 661
Benedetto Risio, Alexander Berreth, Stéphane Zuckerman, Souad Koliai,
Mickaël Ivascot, William Jalby, Bettina Krammer, Bernd Mohr and
Thomas William

From OpenMP to MPI: First Experiments of the STEP Source-to-Source
Transformation Tool 669
Daniel Millot, Alain Muller, Christian Parrot and
Frédérique Silber-Chaussumier

Using Multi-Core Architectures to Execute High Performance-Oriented
Real-Time Applications 677
C. Aussagues, E. Ohayon, K. Brifault and Q. Dinh

Performance Tool Integration in a GPU Programming Environment: Experiences
with TAU and HMPP 685
Allen D. Malony, Shangkar Mayanglambam, Laurent Morin,
Matthew J. Sottile, Stephane Bihan, Sameer S. Shende and Francois Bodin

An Interface for Integrated MPI Correctness Checking 693
Tobias Hilbrich, Matthias Jurenz, Hartmut Mix, Holger Brunst,
Andreas Knüpfer, Matthias S. Müller and Wolfgang E. Nagel

Enhanced Performance Analysis of Multi-Core Applications with an Integrated
Tool-Chain – Using Scalasca and Vampir to Optimise the Metal Forming
Simulation FE Software INDEED 701
Thomas William, Hartmut Mix, Bernd Mohr, René Menzel and
Felix Voigtländer

Mini-Symposium "Programming Heterogeneous Architectures"

Mini-Symposium on Programming Heterogeneous Architectures 711
Lei Huang, Eric Stotzer and Eric Biscondi

Parallelization Exploration of Wireless Applications Using MPA 712
Martin Palkovic, Praveen Raghavan, Thomas J. Ashby, Andy Folens,
Hans Cappelle, Miguel Glassee, Liesbet Van der Perre and
Francky Catthoor

Prototyping and Programming Tightly Coupled Accelerators 720
Eric Stotzer, Ernst L. Leiss, Elana Granston and David Hoyle

Simplifying Heterogeneous Embedded Systems Programming Based on OpenMP 728
Lei Huang and Barbara Chapman

Author Index 737

Invited Talks

Parallel Computing: From Multicores and GPU's to Petascale
B. Chapman et al. (Eds.)
IOS Press, 2010
© 2010 The authors and IOS Press. All rights reserved.
doi:10.3233/978-1-60750-530-3-3

Exascale computing: What future architectures will mean for the user community

Alan Gara and Ravi Nair

IBM T.J. Watson Research Center, P.O. Box 218, Yorktown Heights, NY 10598

Abstract. Exascale computing platforms will soon emerge over the horizon. Architectures for such platforms are already on drawing boards. This paper will focus on some of the key drivers of the technology that will be needed on exascale platforms along with the impact that these new technology drivers will have on system architecture. The important implications for users of such exascale systems will also be discussed.

Keywords. Exascale, exaflops

Introduction

Exascale computing, meaning computing at a scale almost 1000x of what was available in 2008, will present many challenges. System architects are now grappling with the realities offered by future technologies with the goal of providing usable, energy-efficient systems. Some of the directions that these future machines will take are becoming clearer. In all cases, the user community will be asked to adapt to a different system balance than what is currently available. This will be most evident to users who will be seeking orders of magnitude more performance from future machines. Here we will investigate some of the key technical challenges on the road to exascale systems along with their implications on system architecture. Topping the list of key technical challenges are energy, optics, packaging and power delivery. These technologies will drive and motivate a system architecture where the levels of concurrency will far exceed what is common today. Much of this additional concurrency will be contained within a single chip because of continued increases in component density on chip. However, such extremely high chip performance will also call for interfaces providing high bandwidth along with low latency to allow this performance to be practically utilized.

Without a doubt, the most severe constraint we will face in the future is that of energy. This constraint will significantly impact system architectures; it will also have an impact on how users will achieve the most out of a system. The way that algorithms are optimized and deployed on machines is likely to undergo change. We will explore the likely directions that these optimizations will take.

1. Technology Challenges

1.1. Silicon Scaling Challenges

It is well known that silicon technology, while continuing to achieve density improvements, will not offer the energy efficiency and performance boost that was traditionally offered by CMOS scaling. This disruption will make the task of achieving exascale computing at current energy levels extremely difficult.

The historic Top500 curve shows an annual performance increase of 1.9x for the highest performing system. Extrapolating from this curve we can expect a system delivering one exaflops to be available in 2018. The target total power consumption of this exascale system (as well as that of an intermediate 300 petaflops system to be available in 2015) is no more than 20 MW.

Historically we have enjoyed a new CMOS generation only every 2 years. Thus, even without disruption in CMOS scaling, the power, performance and schedule targets mentioned above are especially challenging.

1.2. Energy Efficiency in Perspective

As of June 2009, the most energy efficient system as determined by the Green500 list achieved 534 MFlops/Watt. It takes approximately 2 Gigawatts, 100x more than what is targeted, to power an exascale system at this energy efficiency. Using the historical trend of 2.5x improvement in energy efficiency over 4 years, we can expect no better than an 8x improvement in energy efficiency from process technology alone. Thus in order to stay on track for the targeted power efficiency we would need a further improvement of approximately 12x.

1.3. Technology extrapolation

It is instructive to investigate where a simple extrapolation of the BlueGene/L machine to 2018 would get us. Such an extrapolation is shown in Table 1.

A number of interesting characteristics emerge from Table 1. One of the most dramatic items is the power, which will exceed our targets if we simply follow evolutionary design practices and advances in technology. This is evident at all levels -- in the chip power, I/O power, and network power. Any one of these would use our entire power budget.

Once the technology factors are accounted for, the compute chip emerges as the biggest consumer of power, but this is mainly due to a quirk of circumstances. Packaging constraints, especially limitations in the number of signal pins to connect the compute chip to memory and to the network will force much lower network and memory bandwidth than is desirable. This, in turn, will limit the power required in the these parts of the system.

One can of course reduce the performance delivered by each node and use more nodes/chips in the system to overcome the bandwidth limitation but this will increase both cost and power. For reasonable number of nodes in the system, the performance that needs to be delivered in each node is such that the memory bandwidth would need to drop by a factor of 20x, even after accounting for likely higher signaling rates.

Adjusting to this reduced memory bandwidth will prove to be a fundamental challenge for users of an exascale system.

	BlueGene/L	Exaflops (Directly scaled)	Exaflops (with scaling realities)
Node peak performance	5.6 GF	20 TF	20 TF
Hardware concurrency per node	2	8000	1600
System power in compute chip	1 MW	3.5 GW	40 MW
Link bandwidth (each unidirectional 3-D link)	1.4 Gbps	5 Tbps	1 Tbps
Wires per unidirectional 3-D link	2	400	80
Network pins per node	24	5,000	1,000
Power in network	100 KW	20 MW	4 MW
Memory bandwidth per node	5.6 GB/s	20 TB/s	1 TB/s
L2 cache per node	4 MB	16 GB	500 MB
Data pins associated with memory per node	128	40,000	2000
Power in memory I/O (not DRAM)	12.8 KW	80 MW	4 MW
QCD CG single iteration time	2.3 msec	11 usec	15 usec

Table 1: Scaling system attributes from BlueGene/L to those of an exaflops machine in 2018. Two cases are shown, the first where a naïve scaling is used (essentially scaling a BlueGene/L machine to 1 exaflops), and the second is what we would get after accounting for scaling limitations

1.4. Components of Power Scaling

In evaluating power scaling we must consider the contribution of all components in the system, each of which has its own scaling laws. There is often a mistaken focus on the power consumed by the floating point unit or even just the processing core. While these are often large contributors to power in current systems, they are unlikely to continue to dominate in the future. For example, even today, the floating point unit represents only a tiny fraction (typically less that 10%) of the total system power.

One key characteristic of scaling has been that the capacitance per unit length for chip wiring has been nearly constant over the previous five generations of technology. This trend is expected to continue. Thus, unless we lower the voltage enormously (not a practical reality), or dramatically reduce wire lengths, the power associated with a wire over a given distance will not change significantly. This can pose a challenge for the future in areas of the chip with large structures having high density of wires. This power problem will therefore make it unattractive to devote large areas of the chip real estate to a single processor. While large local caches also present a similar problem, their disadvantage is offset by the power savings resulting from reduced cache misses and hence reduced power-hungry accesses to the next level of the hierarchy.

1.5. Variability of power usage for applications

Different applications consume different amounts of power. There is some correlation between the efficiency of an algorithm and the power that it consumes. In the past when the total power was largely determined by the power in the processor, applications which demonstrated high computational efficiency generally consumed high power. In the future, memory power will constitute a higher proportion and hence applications which saturate the memory system in terms of bandwidth are likely to be the higher power applications.

Figure 1 shows that even though the range of supported power consumption for processors is increasing, the actual range for typical applications is not. This disparity will likely have interesting consequences as we move to exascale systems. One likely consequence is that applications which utilize less power will likely get more relative machine time as the cost of running these applications will be relatively lower. This could then temper the value of extreme application tuning – tuning that does not reduce power through reduced memory system activity will not be as valuable as in the past when costs were not dominated by power.

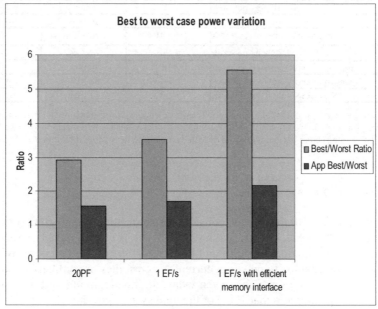

Figure 1: Comparison of best-to-worst power consumption for any workload (blue) vs. best-to-worst consumption for typical set of applications (magenta)

1.6. Power allocation trends for the Exascale

There has been enormous attention paid in recent years to streamlining processor cores from an energy point of view. Throughput-oriented applications perform well on a mix consisting of a large number of small cores rather than a small number of large cores. These smaller cores save power not only by being less complex, but also because wire lengths are shorter. As mentioned in section 1.4 shorter wire distances are critical to saving power in future technologies. Unfortunately similar improvements are harder to come by for caches and memory systems. The result of these successful efforts in saving processor power is that a higher fraction of the total energy in a system is moving towards memory. Advances on these other fronts, especially in external memory technology, will be critical to achieving the energy targets set down by the community.

1.7. Cost factors

Another key area for systems is of course cost. When we study scaling behavior for different system components we find that relative costs change substantially as we move to the exascale domain. This shift occurs without any fundamental change in technology and in fact motivates and justifies the need for significant investment in certain new technologies. The return on investment in optical links, for example, is large – without such technology the industry will not have a solution that meets exascale needs at a reasonable price. Optical technology evolving solely from commodity market needs would neither be cost effective nor result in a package suitable to the needs of supercomputing.

1.8. Reliability

The reliability of future systems is of great concern. On some existing systems, it is proving to be difficult to achieve a system level mean time between failures of even a few days. This leads to the need to frequently checkpoint the application state and, in turn, to include a high bandwidth file system for checkpointing. The cost of the system is thus driven up higher than what it would otherwise have been.

Silicon technology will continue to be less reliable in future. This, combined with the expected increase in silicon area in the largest future systems due to the annual doubling of performance, will cause both raw hard and soft fail events to be significantly higher. A rough estimate is for such events to be somewhere between 5x to 10x higher for an exascale system in 2018 compared to current petaflop-scale systems.

One important note on this is that while this raw rate will be significantly higher, it does not necessarily result in less reliable systems. There are well known methods to handle both hard and soft errors that have been employed in high end server systems for many years. While these techniques can be expensive in terms of power and cost, they can successfully improve system reliability by orders of magnitude. What is important for the future is to balance the desired reliability of machines with the additional cost needed to get to this level of reliability. Large systems already pay a cost of 10%-20% for achieving their present reliability through the addition of error correcting memory, redundant power supplies, and the like.

1.9. Processor and storage memory

Memory will play an increasingly important role in future systems. The "memory wall" will be less of a problem for two reasons. Higher system performance will be obtained through higher level of concurrency at the node level, which will help in hiding memory system latency. In addition, with processor frequencies leveling off, memory system cycle latencies will also level off.

However, there will be bigger challenges with respect to bandwidth, density, power and cost. Future systems will demand high performance from the compute chip which must be balanced with an appropriately large memory system. This balanced memory system must provide high bandwidth along with continued higher bits/cost. Commodity roadmaps do not provide such a solution at this time and innovations in memory design are certainly needed. 3-dimensional stacked memory is one such innovation, offering the hope for higher memory density along with improved bandwidth.

Another exciting direction is the emergence of new memory technologies such as phase change memory. These technologies carry the promise of significantly higher bit density and hence better price performance. As with Flash technology today, these technologies will likely be exploited first as storage replacement. Bandwidth and reliability requirements tend to be higher for processor main memory compared to storage. We will discuss more about this in Section 2.2.

1.10. Packaging

As we move forward to the 1000x performance boost needed for exascale computing we will be forced to consider improvements, however small, in all components of the system. The card and connector technology used in current high end systems is fairly mature and it would be unreasonable to expect more than perhaps 50% to 100% improvement here. At the same time, the number of racks in a large system is already in the few hundreds and it is unreasonable to expect this number to get significantly higher.

This reality will drive us to continue toward higher levels of integration but with optics rather than copper at the boundary of small building blocks. These building blocks will need to be significantly smaller than a rack for the above stated reasons. This re-emphasizes the need for cost effective, dense optics – a technology that we consider one of the key enablers for exascale computing.

1.11. Software

Software represents one of the key challenges to exploiting the exascale machine of the future. The level of concurrency will need to be approximately 1000x the current level of concurrency. This will impose a challenge for nearly all layers of the system software stack and to the end user. This topic requires a much more detailed investigation than can be given here.

New program models are likely to emerge but the successful models will be those that can be supported by multiple platforms. Ideally these program models would be a result of collaboration between developers and users. It is however unrealistic to expect all applications to migrate to a new program model. Important legacy applications will remain and these need to be satisfactorily supported by future exascale systems.

1.12. Energy Distribution

The last area where technology could play an important role is in energy distribution. There are significant energy losses that accumulate as we transfer and transform the 480 VAC customarily available at the computing facility to the 1 VDC or so that is needed by the processor and memory chips. The losses can be dramatically reduced by investing in highly efficient power components that also meet the reliability needs for supercomputing. It is estimated that one could save over $170M by reducing losses over an aggregate 400 MW-year power environment. This represents another area where a return on investment of more than 10x could be easily achieved.

2. Architectural Characteristics of Future Systems

The last section outlined the important technology trends that will shape exascale systems of the future. In this section we examine system architecture trends. We start by looking at the system interconnect requirements and its implication on the optics components that will be needed. We will also look at the roles of new storage-class memory that appear to be on the horizon. Finally, we will examine the power issue again, but this time from the point of view of system architecture.

2.1. System Interconnect Options

The main requirement from the network topologies of large-scale scientific systems is that they provide high total memory bandwidth and high bisection bandwidth. (Bisection bandwidth refers to the minimum bandwidth between two partitions each having exactly half the total number of nodes in the system.) The cost of the interconnect network, on the other hand, is determined not only by these bandwidth requirements, but also by the number of physical links connecting the nodes of the system. This link cost comes not only from the cost of the wires comprising the links, but also the cost of router chips and special adapters that may be needed.

One method for containing such costs in a large system is through higher levels of integration. By putting more processors on a single node, the number of links interconnecting the nodes can be reduced, though the bandwidth needed by each of the links may increase in order to maintain the desired bisection bandwidth for the system. However, the more important ways to contain interconnect costs are (a) by selecting the right topology for the interconnection network, and (b) by exploiting low-cost commodity components.

Complex factors come into play in determining the right topology for a network. Fat-tree topologies [1] have the property that the latency of communication is reasonably independent of which pair of nodes is communicating. The cost of this topology is roughly proportional to the number of stages in the fat-tree network because both the total bandwidth and the number of optical components increase linearly with the number of stages. Countering this is the fact that it is virtually impossible to implement a single-stage fat-tree for a very large number of nodes. Reasonable multi-stage fat-trees can be built though for systems with tens of thousands of nodes as envisioned in the exascale machine.

The availability of low-cost components, on the other hand, is determined by the extent of commoditization of optical components, including transmitters and cables. The most prevalent, low-cost technology solutions are based on VCSELs and optical fibers, mainly to interconnect boards at a higher level. Interconnecting nodes at a lower level in an optical manner, though, will have to await commoditization of silicon photonics, which has the potential to lower power consumptions while providing far greater bandwidth capacity. Silicon waveguides are emerging from the labs and could be in production soon. The biggest excitement though is around integrated photonics [2], which is still in the labs but which has the potential for further dramatically lowering power requirements and improving density of packaging, while satisfying the enormous bandwidth needs of future systems.

The graph below shows estimates of the cost of various levels of optics integration for different topologies. The analysis is provided just as an example. It compares commonly know topologies, a multi-stage crossbar switch, three different types of fat-trees, and a 4-dimensional torus network. What we observe from the graph is that there is a tradeoff between the ease of implementation of a topology option and either its cost or its symmetry of communication. The torus network, for example, incurs low latency of communication for neighbors and high latency for remote nodes, but has the lowest cost for any of the optics options. The power curve in the same figure shows the tremendous benefit that newer photonics technology can provide in reducing the overall energy consumption in the system.

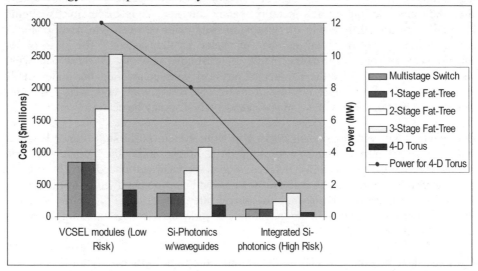

Figure 2: Estimates of the cost of various levels of optics integration for different topologies. This comparison is communication pattern dependent. Here we have chosen nearest neighbor exchange as a reasonable communication pattern. Therefore the costs are for equal performance for nearest neighbor exchange.

2.2. Storage-Class Memory Technology

Recent developments in storage-class memory technology [3] appear to indicate a growing realization that movement of data is increasingly the bottleneck in most systems. Flash memory, with its low latency, higher reliability and lower power is increasingly replacing spinning disks, although still at a higher cost per bit. Among the newer non-volatile memory technologies the one that appears to be most promising is the chalcogenide phase-change memory technology that promises densities comparable to flash with significantly lower read access latencies and higher write endurance. These solid-state technologies will not only replace disks, but will change the way storage is organized in systems. It no longer becomes necessary to place large non-volatile only at the periphery of the system. They can be distributed throughout the system, with significant chunks located close to or even internal to each node in the system.

There are interesting developments also in the area of using storage-class memory technology in main memories [4]. The principal challenges here are to overcome the long write latencies associated with these non-volatile technologies and to carefully manage the limited number of writes that cells in these technologies can be subjected to.

There is little debate that advances in process technology have provided us with higher integration densities which have been exploited well through changes in the microarchitecture of processors comprising large scale supercomputing systems. The same cannot be said about the memory hierarchy. Cost considerations have led supercomputers to adopt commodity components that cater largely to low-end systems and that have no incentive to provide data to processors at high bandwidth rates. There is a window of opportunity now with the new storage-class memories for a new memory architecture designed for the needs of the ubiquitous hand-held devices, but that can provide adequate bandwidth for supercomputing when accompanied by advanced packaging technologies.

2.3. System Power

We have already emphasized the role of power in the design of processors. Management of power assumes even greater importance at the system level. It is no longer possible to simply add up the worst-case power needs of the different parts of a system and then provide a power supply capable of delivering that amount of power. That amount is just too large to provide exascale capability today, and will remain large for at least a couple more technology generations. Power requirements of large systems are getting to a point where special power plants need to be designed to feed power into the system and where care must be taken in selecting the location of the system to meet cooling needs, A significant cost of the maintenance and running of the system will go into power distribution and delivery. We are getting into a regime where the amount of power available is going to determine the highest performance that can be delivered by a system.

Fortunately, the power needed by most applications is much lower than the sum of the component worst-case power. It is less important to be able to deliver the maximum worst case power, and more important to be able to manage an amount of power closer to the average. This brings with it the challenges of monitoring usage of power in various parts of the system and throttling each part of the system dynamically in order to ensure that the total power of the system is contained. It calls for new architectures that treat power as a principal resource, with greater emphasis on the monitoring, controlling and consumption of power in all parts of the system. A system may be able to save power at the network level and direct it towards the processors during the execution of an application that is compute-intensive. Thus system-level management of power treats power as a limited resource that must be apportioned to the various parts of the system in a dynamic manner.

Power is becoming such an important factor that it is likely to be a key metric used in the acquisition of systems in the future. Unlike today, the cost of a new product is going to be determined not simply by the cost of acquiring the product, but by its total ownership cost, an increasing component of which will be the cost of energy spent during the lifetime of the system.

3. Implication of Technology and Architecture for Users

We are at an inflection point in computing. Applications are not going to be able simply to ride the technology curve to enjoy the benefits of continuously decreasing costs of computing because of the slowing technology trends that we have already described. Power and reliability considerations are driving changes in the architecture of systems. These aspects are going to force fundamental changes also in the way computers are programmed and in the way applications are deployed in future. Let us examine this in some more detail.

3.1. Power Implications

We have already discussed how power constraints are going to force the mindset of consumers to think of power as their currency. In effect the question which will be asked will not be "How can I solve this problem in the fastest manner?" but rather "How can I solve this problem within my power and energy budget?" Tuning of code in traditional ways may in some cases be counterproductive, for example if the speedup enjoyed by the code through tuning requires the expenditure of additional resources and hence more power than budgeted or causes the total energy expended (power x delay product) to be higher. Listed in the table below are various optimization techniques and a qualitative description of whether they will be beneficial in the old realm of computing where performance was the key metric and in the new realm where performance/power will be the important metric.

Optimization	Effect	
	On Performance	On Performance/Power
Reorder instructions to maximize cache reuse at all levels	Helps in reducing both latency and bandwidth	Helps in reducing power for memory accesses
Pack data structures to maximize cache reuse	Helps in reducing both latency and bandwidth	Helps in reducing power for memory accesses
Using Newton's method to optimize mathematical functions (e.g. exp)	Reduces latency	Generally unhelpful; memory access energy outweighs computation energy
Exploiting SIMD instructions	Helps	Helps inside the processor
Prefetching within a node	Helps with latency hiding	Could hurt
Software controlled power gating of units	Does not help	Helps
User tagging of critical paths through code	May help compilers in some circumstances	Helps direct energy to performance-critical regions

Overlapping compute with communication	Helps	Helps by slowing non-critical component, but could exceed combined power limits

Table 2: Effect of various optimizations with performance and performance/power as figures of merit

It is not uncommon for code to have identifiable domains, a parallel domain which can take advantage of the power-efficient part, and a serial domain that will benefit from the core providing strong single-thread performance. This is the basic principle behind heterogeneous processors [5] which consist of a mix of cores, some providing high single-thread performance and others providing high power-efficiency. Domain-specific accelerators [6] are a form of heterogeneous processors where the hardware is customized to the needs of a specific domain of computing. An important aspect in the design of heterogeneous processors in general is that of transferring control and data from one type of processor to another. In a power-constrained world, such a transfer should ideally also be accompanied by a reallocation of available power from the original processor to the other. It would be ideal if the system autonomously took care of such transfers. Yet, the more knowledgeable user can exploit the system to its fullest either by providing hints to the system, or by writing code in a manner that helps a compiler with such transitions.

3.2. Reliability Implications

The vast increase in the number of components from today's petaflops-scale systems to future exascale systems is going to increase the rate of failures of the system in a significant way. It is going to be virtually impossible to design a system in which the mean time between failures is longer than the expected longest-running job. This implies that the combination of hardware and software must be capable of (a) detecting the occurrence of such failures, (b) reconfiguring the system and the application to avoid the failed component, if it is a hard failure, (c) recovering the state of the application at a point before the failure, and (d) restoring the application to this point to resume execution. Moreover, in order to ensure forward progress, all these steps must be completed before another failure occurs.

In the past, most of these functions were provided by the hardware, the firmware, or by the system software. Application programmers did not have to think about structuring programs specifically to overcome reliability problems. It is interesting to ask whether this model can continue in the exaflops regime. On the one hand, the productivity of the application programmer is improved if these issues are taken care of by the system. On the other, a system that expects nothing from the user tends to be over-designed to take care of all possible situations, potentially adding to its cost both in dollars and in energy.

It is likely therefore that programming models will change and that middleware and compilers will take on more of the responsibility of adding reliability aspects to the application. But as in the case of heterogeneous processors, the application developer who understands the real costs and tradeoffs between performance and resilience will be able to exploit the system better. We have been here before. Programming model developments aimed at reducing the complexity of hardware is not unknown in computer architecture. For example, as the scale of multiprocessor systems grew and the cost of providing system-wide memory coherence became prohibitive, message-passing programming models like MPI became popular. More recently, the cluster community embraced the Map-Reduce model to hide the complexity of parallel deployment and unreliability of very large distributed cluster systems.

4. Concluding Remarks

We are at the cusp of a new age of computing. The phenomenal advances that have been made in technology over the past few decades have brought us to a point where our ability to move, consume, and archive data are not keeping up with our ability to produce data. This is forcing us to rethink all levels of computing, most of which have not changed significantly almost since the dawn of computing. This includes not only the architecture of systems and programming models used by application developers, but the way in which users interact with computing systems and the way in which computation is delivered to the users.

The main forces that are driving this upheaval are the massive increase in the scale of computing systems that will be needed in the future, and the energy needs of such large systems in a world that is growing more conscious of the limited sources of energy and the effect of energy consumption on our ecosystem.

Energy-efficiency will be central in design decisions of all types of computing systems in the future. It has already caused a shift in the focus of achieving greater performance through parallelism, rather than through greater single-thread performance. It is causing users, compilers, and middleware to embrace heterogeneity in computing structures, to utilize different types of energy-appropriate computational nodes for different phases in an application.

At the same time, the definition of performance is being changed. No longer is performance measured by the time it takes to complete a single task. The cost of systems, the power needed in the system, and increasingly, the ease of programming, are all being included in the performance equation. It is clear however that parallelism will be central to performance improvements in the future. In the transition from petascale systems to exascale systems, high-performance computing machines will embrace more parallelism not as much by increasing the number of nodes in the system, but by great increases in the level of parallelism at the lower node level. This then will require innovations at the programming model level in order to make such systems easy to use.

At the system level, energy considerations are going to dictate the topology of interconnection between components in the system. At the lower levels, interesting options are emerging. Energy efficiency is driving innovation in memory technology, packaging technology, and 3-d integration technology. Without corresponding innovation and commoditization at the higher interconnect levels, the current gap between local and global communication will only increase and add burden on application programmers.

All this implies a rich field of research and innovation in the areas of computer architecture and computer science in general. It is incumbent on the community to rethink all options carefully and fundamentally. The exascale generation of computing systems could be setting the stage for architectures, system software, programming models, and tools for several decades to come.

References

[1] C.E. Leiserson, "Fat-trees: universal networks for hardware-efficient supercomputing," *IEEE Transactions on Computers*, **34** (1985) 892-901.

[2] L.Tsybeskov, D.J. Lockwood, and M. Ichikawa, "Silicon Photonics: CMOS Going Optical," *Proceedings of the IEEE*, **97** (2009), 1161-1165.

[3] R.F. Freitas and W.W. Wilcke, "Storage-Class Memory: The Next Storage System Technology," *IBM Journal of Research and Development*, **52** (2008), 439-447.

[4] M. Qureshi, V. Srinivasan, and J.A. Rivers, "Scalable High-Performance Main Memory System Using Phase-Change Memory Technology," *Proceedings of the International Symposium on Computer Architecture (ISCA-2009)*, Austin, TX, 2009.

[5] R. Kumar, K.I. Farkas, N.P. Jouppi, P. Ranganathan, and D.M. Tullsen, "Single-ISA Heterogeneous Multi-Core Architectures: The Potential for Processor Power Reduction," *Proceedings of the 36th annual IEEE/ACM International Symposium on Microarchitecture (MICRO-36)*, San Diego, CA, 2003.

[6] S. Patel, and W.W. Hwu, "Accelerator Architectures," *IEEE Micro*, **28** (2008), 4-12.

Parallel Computing: From Multicores and GPU's to Petascale
B. Chapman et al. (Eds.)
IOS Press, 2010
© *2010 The authors and IOS Press. All rights reserved.*
doi:10.3233/978-1-60750-530-3-16

Making multi-cores mainstream – from security to scalability

Chris JESSHOPE, Michael HICKS, Mike LANKAMP, Raphael POSS and Li ZHANG
Institute for Informatics, University of Amsterdam, The Netherlands

Abstract. In this paper we will introduce work being supported by the EU in the Apple-CORE project (http://www.apple-core.info). This project is pushing the boundaries of programming and systems development in multi-core architectures in an attempt to make multi-core go mainstream, i.e. continuing the current trends in low-power, multi-core architecture to thousands of cores on chip and supporting this in the context of the next generations of PCs. This work supports dataflow principles but with a conventional programming style. The paper describes the underlying execution model, a core design based on this model and its emulation in software. We also consider system issues that impact security. The major benefits of this approach include asynchrony, i.e. the ability to tolerate long latency operations without impacting performance and binary compatibility. We present results that show very high efficiency and good scalability despite the high memory access latency in the proposed chip architecture.

Keywords. Concurrency model, multi-core, multi-threading, resource deadlock.

Introduction

One of the principle research goals in parallel computing is the ability to write code once, or to take legacy sequential code, and to execute it on any parallel computer with a high efficiency and with scalable speedup. This need only be constrained by the concurrency exposed in the algorithm and the characteristics of the target parallel computer. Problems arise because these characteristics vary significantly and that most developments in tools target a particular architecture rather than a generic parallel execution model. The characteristics that vary include synchronisation and scheduling overhead, which determine the granularity of the units of concurrency that can be executed efficiently and the ratio of computation to communication rates, which determines whether it is worthwhile distributing code at a given level of granularity.

Whether this goal of general-purpose parallel computing can be achieved across a wide range of targets is still an open question but one that we are working towards. Our first steps have focused on the narrower field of achieving genericity of target when programming many-core processors. Here we see the same issues affecting different generations of the same processor or dynamic partitions of a multi-core chip. We want to be able to compile code once and execute it on any number of cores, anywhere on chip and to deal with systems issues such as scalability and security in a multi-user environment. Our execution model, SVP [1], provides concurrent composition by default. This invited paper describes an implementation of that model in the ISA of a conventional, in-order issue RISC core. More details on various aspects of this EU-funded project can be found at (http://www.apple-core.info/).

1. Motivation

That there is a practical urgency in this matter is common knowledge. On the one hand, there is an inescapable requirement to manage power dissipation on chip, which requires many simple cores rather than fewer, more complex ones. On the other hand, a many-core approach requires tools supporting massive explicit concurrency, which are difficult to implement and error prone to use. In embedded and special purpose systems, e.g. picoChips [2], NVIDIA [3, 4], Intel [5, 6, 7] and ClearSpeed [8], this is common. However, here the focus is on a limited set of applications, where skilled effort can be applied to find and map the applications' concurrency. Moore's law still predicts that the number of cores on chip will double every 18 to 24 months (for at least for another decade [9]) and this raises compatibility issues even in a specific processor.

In a more general market, the labour-intensive approach of hand mapping an application is not feasible, as the effort required is large and compounded by the many different applications. A more automated approach from the tool chain is necessary. This investment in the tool chain, in turn, demands an abstract target to avoid these compatibility issues. That target or concurrency model then needs to be implemented on a variety of platforms to give portability, whatever the granularity of that platform.

Our experience suggests that an abstract target should adopt concurrent rather than sequential composition, but admit a well-defined sequential schedule. It must capture locality without specifying explicit communication. Ideally, it should support asynchrony using data-driven scheduling to allow for high latency operations. However, above all, it must provide safe program composition, i.e. guaranteed freedom from deadlock when two concurrent programs are combined.

Our SVP model is designed to meet all of these requirements. Whether it is implemented in the ISA of a conventional core, as described here or encapsulated as a software API will only effect the parameters described above, which in turn will determine at what level of granularity one moves from parallel to sequential execution of the same code. The work presented in this paper describes the execution model, its implementation as an extension to the Alpha ISA and its core compiler that compiles the language µTC, which captures SVP in an architecture neutral form, to a *Microgrid* of SVP-enabled cores. Compilers to this model, emitting µTC, are also being developed from the functional, data-parallel language SAC [10, 11], the high-level coordination language and component technology S-Net [12, 13] as well as an automatically parallelising compiler for legacy C code [14].

2. The Self-adaptive Virtual Processor - SVP

SVP is a hierarchical thread-based model developed in the EU AETHER project (http://www.aether-ist.org/) to support adaptive computing. It provides a complete separation of concerns between the two most important aspects of concurrent programming. The first is the description of an application's functionality expressed concurrently and the second is the mapping of that program onto a set of resources. This separation is achieved by binding processing resources to units of work dynamically using opaque, implementation-defined objects called *places*. In this paper, a place is a ring of SVP-enabled cores but it could just as easily be a conventional core or cluster of cores or even dynamically configured logic (e.g. an FPGA), as was implemented in the AETHER project.

In its resource-neutral form, SVP provides an abstract target for high-level language compilation, which need not be concerned with mapping and scheduling. The code generated is highly concurrent and guaranteed to be free from deadlock [15]. Mapping is performed by the core-compiler (i.e. the μTC compiler) and a run-time system that provides dynamic allocation of places in a manner similar to memory allocation. Scheduling is controlled using synchronising communication. SVP defines *shared* and *global* objects giving pair-wise and collective, one-way synchronisation channels respectively. These are implemented with i-structures [16]. They are written once in one thread and are read-only in one or more other threads. I-structures provide the data-driven scheduling in an SVP implementation. An i-structure suspends a thread attempting to read it in an empty or unwritten state and stores these continuations until data is written, at which point it must reschedule the suspended threads.

Currently SVP is described by the language μTC [17], for which we have a core compiler tool chain based on GCC [18]. This has multiple targets that currently include:

- a sequential implementation for program validation;
- a cycle-accurate multi-core chip emulation, where SVP is implemented directly in the core's ISA [19, 20] - a *Microgrid* of SVP cores; and
- a POSIX-thread-based SVP API [21] for general use, developed in the EU AETHER project.

SVP programs are composed concurrently, at all levels, from the smallest threads (maybe a few instructions) up to complete systems. This means that there is always an appropriate level of granularity that will map to a given target at some point in the concurrency tree. Hence, when a target is selected, the SVP program is transformed to that level of granularity using its sequential schedule. In the Microgrid of SVP cores, no code transformation is required. Places are selected at run time and the hardware provides support for the automatic sequencing of SVP binary code, if too few concurrent contexts are available. This is described in more detail in Section 3.

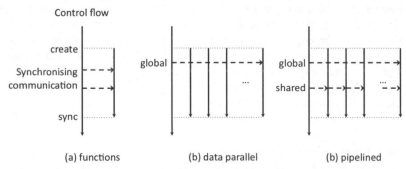

Figure 1. Three variants of an SVP create showing synchronisations: (a) concurrent function execution with synchronising parameters; (b) concurrent loop execution (n.b. each thread is created with a unique index in a specified range); and (c) concurrent loop execution with loop-carried dependencies (linear pipelines).

2.1. SVP concurrency controls

SVP provides concurrency controls to *create* and terminate (*kill* and *break*) a named unit of work. That unit is a family of identical indexed threads and any subordinate families that those threads may create. The index is specified on create by a triple of (*start, step, limit*) or (*start, step*) for unbounded families. Unbounded families must be terminated dynamically with a *break* instruction executed in one of the family's threads.

The parent thread may execute and communicate asynchronously with the family it creates. SVP provides a barrier (*sync*), which signals the completion of a family to the parent thread. Communication between the parent and its children may occur anywhere in the parent from create to sync, using shared and/or global objects.

The create/sync pair is used to compose both functions and loops as concurrently executing threads, including loops with dependencies. This is shown in Figure 1. As can be seen, we allow communication only between parent and first child and between adjacent children defined on the thread's index value. For shared objects, an association is made between a local in the creating thread and the shared object defined in the thread's parameters. A write in the parent thread is only seen by the first child thread and, with more than one thread created in the family, a write to a shared in one thread will be seen by its successor in index sequence. For global objects, a similar association is made between a local in the parent thread and the global object defined in the thread's parameters. Global objects may be read by all threads. The write to a shared object in the last thread in index sequence will update (on sync) the initialising variable in the creating thread. This restriction on communication has a threefold advantage:

- it provides a well defined sequential schedule for any SVP program;
- it guarantees freedom of deadlock in the abstract model, although failure to write to synchronising objects where visible and dealing with finite resource can still cause deadlock; and
- it provides an abstract notion of locality to the high-level compiler, which must transform dependencies to conform to this restriction.

So, what appears as a restriction in the model has advantages. The obvious question that follows is whether the model is still sufficiently general. Work on the C-to-SVP compiler [14] has shown that such transformations are possible in loops for all regular dependencies. Moreover, irregular dependencies can be made regular by a gather and/or scatter stage.

2.2. SVP memory model

We wish to support a very relaxed memory consistency model in SVP that would map naturally onto shared memory but, at the same time, ease any implementation on distributed memory. Consider a branch of the SVP concurrency tree (at any level); then for any memory location used anywhere in that branch and known not to be accessed concurrently by other (unrelated) branches while this branch is running, SVP provides Gao and Sakar's Location Consistency (LC) semantics, but without the synchronising *acquire* and *release* operations described in [22]. Instead, the synchronising operations that establish partial order on memory accesses are SVP's create and sync operations, which have different semantics to LC's acquire and release.

Thus, SVP's concurrency model provides support for non-synchronising, competing shared memory accesses (using the terminology proposed by Mosberger [23]) from different threads in a family, but exposes memory state from one thread to all its subordinate threads. Location consistency is then resolved for a thread on termination of a subordinate concurrency tree. In the hierarchy proposed by Mosberger [23], this model is a hybrid of LC (between parent threads and child families) and a weaker model without any synchronisation (between sibling threads).

Communication via memory is not defined in SVP between sibling threads. The only guaranteed synchronisation is through shared objects, which have different semantics, as described in Section 2.1, and which can be of arbitrary size. Whether these shared objects are supported by a specific SVP implementation using a shared-memory architecture with more constrained consistency semantics, via explicit communication channels or via some other mechanism, is not specified in the abstract SVP model.

In some circumstances it is necessary to provide consistency between global objects used in unrelated threads. We support this through the use of SVP's *exclusive place*. Exclusive place are shared between threads and sequence requests to create families of threads at that place. SVP's exclusive places in effect implement Dijkstra's "secretary" concept [24], where communication can occur between independent sequential processes by means of changing the secretary's local (private) state.

3. The SVP core

We have implemented SVP's concurrency controls and shared object semantics for basic types (integer and floats) as extensions to the ISA of an in-order Alpha core. Support is also provided in the form of memory barriers for arbitrary shared objects using pointers to objects stored in memory. This implementation is a full software emulation of the extended instruction set. It is supported by a set of tools to compile, assemble, link, load and execute μTC programs. This implementation takes account of all internal processor state in each of the six stages of the Alpha pipeline. It also restricts concurrent reads to an implementable number of ports on memory structures and hence provides a cycle-accurate simulation of the execution time of SVP programs.

As an example, consider the register file. This is the largest memory structure in the core and if silicon layout constraints were not taken into account, the core could not be implemented in a reasonable area and with a reasonable clock frequency; the area of a memory cell grows as the square of the number of its ports. Single instruction issue requires two reads and one write to the register file to support the pipeline's operation. However, the register file is also written with a thread's index value by the thread create process (potentially once every cycle). The register file must also be accessed for shared-register communication between threads that are mapped to adjacent processors and for operations that terminate asynchronously (described below). To support all of this, we provide 5 ports to the register file: 3 for pipeline operation and one read and one write port with arbitration for all other uses. Static analysis predicted this to be sufficient [24] and subsequent emulation has shown that while some processes may stall for a few cycles, overall progress is assured.

3.1. Synchronising registers

In SVP (unlike pure dataflow), constraints in a program are captured using two mechanisms, namely program sequence and by capturing dependencies. The latter uses SVP's synchronising objects, as described in Section 2.1. Ideally each should be implemented at the same level of granularity and hence we implement synchronising communication in the register file of the SVP core. By synchronising at this level, threads mapped to the same core can synchronise in a single cycle using the pipeline's bypass bus and between cores in a time not much longer than the pipeline's length.

Each register can be used either as an i-structure or as a conventional register. A state transition diagram for the i-structure is given in Figure 2. It will block any thread attempting to read in the *empty* state (i.e. before it the location has been written), continue to suspend thread continuations while it is *waiting* and reschedule those threads for execution upon being made *full* (i.e. when the location has been written). In the waiting state therefore, a register-file location contains a link to all threads that have attempted to read that location before its value was defined.

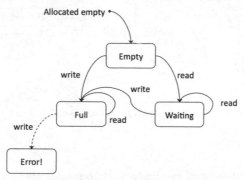

Figure 2. I-structure state-transitions

SVP instructions		
Family/thread management		**Family parameter setting**
allocate	Takes a place at which a family will execute, allocates a family table entry and returns a family table index - FTid (asynchronous).	*setstart* — Sets a *start* index value for the given family – threads start from this index
create	Takes an FTid and creates threads described by the parameters stored there and returns a termination code, the *sync* (asynchronous).	*setlimit* — Sets a *limit* index value for the given family.
break	Terminates a thread's family and all subordinate families and returns a break value. Only one thread in a family may succeed in breaking its family (asynchronous).	*setstep* — Sets a *step* index value for the given family
		setblock — Sets the maximum number of threads created on a given core.
kill	Terminates a family identified by a family table index and all subordinate families.	*setbreak* — Nominates the register that will be used to return the break value

Table 1. SVP instructions.

3.2. Family and thread management

In the SVP core, only a finite number of families and threads may be defined and these are stored in dedicated tables. This information is managed by instructions added to the Alpha ISA, which are listed in Table 1. Family state is stored in the *family table* and thread state is stored in the *thread table*. Both families and threads are identified by their index into these respective tables. Instructions in Table 1: allocate a family table entry, which comes with a default set of parameters; overwrite the default parameters where required; and initiate thread creation. The latter takes a single pipeline cycle to create an unlimited number of threads at a rate of one per cycle until resources are exhausted or the block size has been reached. Kill terminates a family based on its index in the family table and is fully recursive, i.e. all subordinate families are also killed. From a program's perspective only the family table index is visible, however, all instructions executed in an SVP core are tagged with their family and thread indices. This allows us to suspend and resume threads using the i-structures, which maintain linked lists of suspended thread indices.

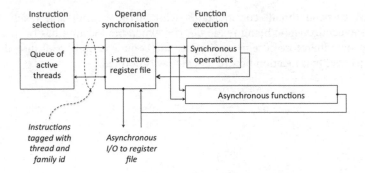

Figure 3. SVP pipeline phases

3.3. Instruction execution

The SVP pipeline is illustrated in Figure 3. It comprises three phases, each of which may comprise multiple pipeline stages. Instructions are issued from the head of the queue of active threads, where threads that can make progress are stored. These threads are not suspended and have their next instruction in the I-cache. Context switching (selecting the next thread from the active list) occurs on branches, when the current program counter increments over a cache-line boundary and, for efficiency, on instructions tagged by the compiler that are dependent on asynchronous instructions. In the latter case, this avoids flushing the pipeline if that instruction finds one of its operands empty at the register-file read. Thus, the core only executes sequences of statically schedulable instructions without context switching and then only when it can be guaranteed that instruction fetch will hit the I-cache. This makes for a very efficient instruction execution. In the limit, threads can context switch on each cycle and thread creation or wakeup can meet this rate.

In the next phase, instructions read their operands from the synchronising register file. Only when both operands are available can the instruction be dispatched for execution. The thread is suspended if either of the instruction's source registers is empty. A suspended thread will be rescheduled and re-execute the same instruction when the register it is suspended on is written to. This differs from dataflow execution where an instruction is only issued when all of its operations are available. The benefit is that statically scheduled instructions from multiple threads can be executed with RISC-like efficiency.

At execution, all instructions write back to the register file in their allocated pipeline slot, however, at this stage, asynchronous instructions simply set the target register's i-structure state to *empty*. Data is written when the operation completes. This may be the completion of a family, i.e. create writing a return code, or other long-latency operation (including memory fetches, floating point operations and any instructions labeled asynchronous in Table 1). In this way, no dependent instruction can execute until the asynchronous operation completes.

3.4. Thread-to-thread communication

Most of the bandwidth for thread-to-thread communication in a Microgrid of SVP cores is provided by the implementation of shared memory on-chip. We adopt an on-chip COMA memory that has already been reported elsewhere [26]. This uses a hierarchy of cache-line-wide ring networks to implement an attraction memory with a large aggregate bandwidth. In this memory, cache lines have no home. They can be copied and invalidated anywhere on chip so that data always migrates to the point of last update. A token-based cache-coherence protocol implements the memory consistency model described in Section 2.2.

An *inter-place* network provides low-latency communication between clusters of cores on a chip (the implementation of SVP's place). The place at which a family is created is defined on allocating its family table entry and if this is neither the core nor the cluster on which the parent thread is executing, then the inter-place network is used to implement the instructions listed in Table 1. The remote execution of a subordinate family on another place is called a *delegation* and requires a proxy family table entry on the creating core, which identifies the remote place. It also requires a family table entry at the remote place that controls thread creation in the normal manner. Parameters that define the family of threads are communicated across this network using these instructions. The Proxy must also manage communication of global and shared parameters between parent and child, which need not have been defined prior to create.

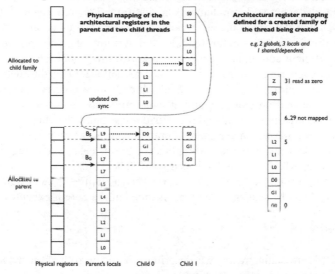

Figure 4. Mapping of the overlapping register windows on creating a family of two threads with three local, two global and one shared/dependent defined in its register context. Shared register communication is illustrated with dashed arrows. The base addresses for the mapping of globals (B_G) and shareds (B_S) to the parent's locals is shown. N.b. this picture is repeated for ints and floats in the Alpha architecture.

An *intra-place* network manages communication between cores in a cluster. This includes the distributed implementation of create and sync actions that result in the distribution of the threads in a family to a multi-core place. It also implements a distributed-shared register file between the cores. This network is a word-wide ring network between adjacent cores in a cluster. To understand how this communication is specified it is necessary to understand the mapping of SVP's four classes of variables onto the distributed-shared register file. Register variables are divided into a number of overlapping windows, these are:
- *local* - visible only to one thread;
- *global* - written in a parent thread and read only in all threads in a family;
- *shared* - written once and visible to the next thread in index sequence;
- *dependent* - read-only access to the previous thread's shareds.

When a thread function is compiled, a partition is made of the architectural register context between these classes and this is defined in a header to its binary code, e.g. N_L, N_G, N_S, where: $N_G + N_L + 2 * N_S \leq 31$, n.b. not all registers need be mapped. To create n threads on a single core, n*(N_L+ N_S) registers are dynamically allocated from its register file, where n is determined by the number of threads in a family, a limit on the number of contexts available for a given core or by the block size defined in *setblock* (see Table 1). In Figure 4, eight registers are allocated on the creation of a family of two threads, with N_L=3 and N_S=1.

In order to pass parameters between parent and child threads the creating thread identifies offsets into its local variables to map to the globals (B_G) and shareds (B_S) of the created threads. These registers are written in the parent thread and are visible to all threads for globals and to the first thread only for shareds. Between siblings, a write to a shared in one thread can be read as a dependent in the subsequent thread. In the last thread, the shared write is visible to the parent thread in its locals via B_S, i.e. on sync, the location used as the parent's shared is updated.

The intra-place network implements a distributed-shared register file over the windowing scheme described above, so that the register files of all cores in a place provide a uniform mechanism for reading and writing registers regardless of their location. For efficient communication between cores, the global registers are replicated with a copy in each core's register file. These are allocated in the distributed create operation over the intra-place network. When threads on a core read an empty global, they will be suspended on that core and at most one read request is sent to the parent thread, which eventually responds with a broadcast around the ring, rescheduling any waiting threads. Similarly, when a shared communication is mapped between two cores the shared/dependent registers are also replicated. In this case, a read request is made to the adjacent core, which is eventually satisfied. The latter requires an additional N_S registers to be allocated per family, per core when a family is distributed. Again the dependent thread can be suspended and rescheduled at the core it executes on.

3.5. SVP security

To make multi-core mainstream, we described in the introduction a requirement to execute binary programs on an arbitrary number of cores (i.e. on one or more places of various sizes) by automating whether families of threads execute concurrently or sequentially. However, we also need to guarantee freedom from deadlock when finite resources are applied to an abstract SVP program and to guarantee this in the presence of potentially many different jobs competing for those resources in a multi-user environment. Note that we have to consider the situation where some of those programs may be hostile. It is not only deadlock that is an issue; programs can execute very powerful instructions in an open environment (for example to kill a family of threads and its descendants, see Table 1). We do have solutions to most of these problems although some are not yet implemented in our emulation environment. We deal with each of these issues in turn starting with the latter.

To protect a family from being the subject of an accidental or even malicious kill instruction, we protect families with capabilities. When a family is created, a key of arbitrary entropy is generated, which is stored in the family table and combined with the family table index to comprise a *family identifier*. This can be made arbitrarily secure. In order to issue an asynchronous kill on a family, the thread issuing the kill instruction must provide a family identifier that matches the security key stored in the family table, otherwise the instruction is ignored. In practical terms, this means that it must have been passed the capability by the creator of that family.

To protect a program from resource deadlock we have two strategies. The first is to analyse the resource requirements of a µTC program and to ensure that those resources are exclusively allocated to that program. The issue at hand is not the breadth of the concurrency tree, since a single context on one core is sufficient to execute any family regardless of its breadth. The problem is recursion of creates in the presence of finite concurrency resources. If that can be bounded, then deadlock freedom can be guaranteed by restricting the number of contexts allocated to families using *setblock* and to allocate places at appropriate points in the concurrency tree. At what point in the execution of a family those resources are guaranteed is an issue requiring further research. However, at present we can assume that they are allocated prior to the execution of the program, in which case we have a static solution, although not necessarily the most efficient one. To provide a more dynamic mapping, some guarantee of obtaining minimal resources in a finite time is required.

We must also consider how to ensure that if a program is allocated a place, then no other thread is allowed to create a family at the same place. This could consume those resources required to guarantee freedom from deadlock. This is achieved by including a capability in the *place identifier,* in the same way as described above for securing against kill. If the place identifier used in a create does not match the one-time key stored at that place when it was allocated, then the create will be ignored. Note that the only guarantee we can give on sharing the concurrency resources on a processor is when legacy code is executed. Here a single processor place can be shared between a number of legacy programs, where each is guaranteed to run in a single SVP thread.

Where it is not possible to statically analyse resource usage, we provide a software solution with an instruction that allows the code to determine whether any contexts remain. The procedure is to request a family table entry and then to check whether a context is still available. If so it continues its recursion concurrently. If it has the last context, it is obliged to use it to execute its recursion sequentially using the thread's memory stack. In this way we can guarantee progress, even if every other thread may have suspended in attempting to obtain a new context, as eventually that context will be released and the same procedure will be followed by the other suspended threads. Of course there must be a guarantee that the recursion terminates.

4. Results and analysis

We have configured our Microgrid emulator to implement the following chip design, which will be used in obtaining the results on scalability presented in this paper.

- A 64-bit Alpha core with 1Kbyte, 4-way set associative L1 I- and D-caches, 1024 integer registers, 512 floating-point registers, supporting a maximum of 256 threads. The clock rate is assumed to be 1.6 GHz.
- A pipelined floating point unit shared between two cores with 3, 8 and 10 cycles latency for *add/mult, division* and *sqrt* respectively.
- An on-chip COMA memory with two-levels of ring network and two DDR3 2400 channels off chip. At the top level are four COMA directories each supporting rings of eight 32 Kbyte, 4-way, set-associative L2 caches (i.e. 128 sets of 64-Byte cache lines) This gives a modest 1 MByte of L2 cache on chip.

- 128 cores configured with an inter-place cross-bar network as nine places comprising the following number of cores: {64, 32, 16, 8, 4, 2, 1, 1}.

Figure 5 is a schematic illustration of this chip. Prior work indicates that such a chip is feasible in current technology [20].

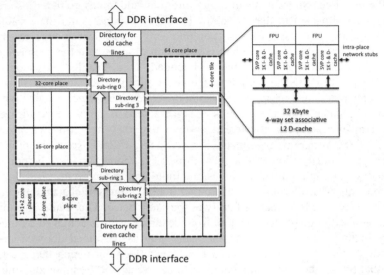

Figure 5. The Microgrid of 128 SVP cores and 32 by 32 KByte L2 caches.

The results presented here use code compiled from μTC versions of the Livermore loop kernels. We have verified this tool chain by comparing the execution of the same μTC code on both the emulator platform and on conventional processors, by applying SVP's sequential schedule. The specific kernels are not chosen to highlight the best results but rather to stress various aspects of the architecture and to illustrate the three different programming patterns found in loop-based code.

Each benchmark creates one or more families of threads on places of size 1 to 64 cores and measures the time to create, execute and synchronise the threads. For each kernel, we execute and time the code twice, the first execution with cold-caches, i.e. all code and data loaded from off-chip memory. The second execution (labeled warm) is run with whatever data remains in the caches and hence we would expect temporal locality when the problem fits into on-chip cache. As the COMA memory injects evicted cache lines into other caches on the same ring, when possible, the maximum cache is 256KBytes for places up to 32 cores and 512KBytes for 64 cores. We evaluate three different problem sizes: n=1K stressing concurrency overheads and limiting virtual concurrency in large places (1K threads is just 16 threads per core at 64-cores); n=8K where at least four arrays of this size map to the on-chip cache; and n=64K where the cache would accommodate at most one array of this size (only on 64 cores).

4.1. Data-parallel loops

The results for the data parallel benchmarks are shown in Figure 6. The *hydro fragment* executes the following simple expression n times, once per thread created.

```
x[k] = q + y[k]*(r*z[k+10] + t*z[k+11]);
```

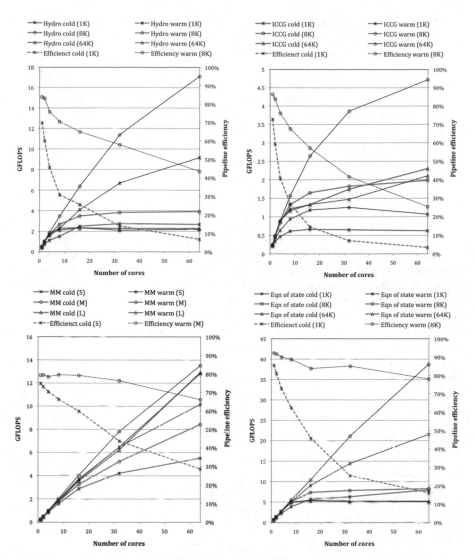

Figure 6. Data-parallel kernels: *hydro fragment* (top left), *ICCG* (top right), *Matrix Multiplication* (bottom left) and *equation of state* (bottom right), showing performance in GFLOPS and upper and lower bounds on pipeline efficiencies averaged over all cores. Execution is on places of size 1 to 64 cores.

The best execution times for the different problem sizes are 0.55μs, 2.4μs and 150μsec on 64 cores. For n=8K warm we get the best speedup, with a factor of 33 over the single core result and an average pipeline efficiency of 42-85%. For n=1K warm, the speedup drops to 17 on 64 cores. Here the total execution time is 893 processor cycles of which 208 are required to execute the 16 threads on one core. The remainder arise from distributing and synchronising the family of threads over a given number of cores and from pipeline stalls due to fewer threads to hide memory access latency. Even so, 1024 threads are created, executed and synchronised across 64 cores in less than one cycle per thread. This demonstrates the efficiency of our heavily overlapped process of thread creation and distribution.

The results for cold caches and for the 64K problem, where the caches are also effectively cold (they will hold the high index array values), we see saturation due to memory-bandwidth limitation between 8 and 32 cores. The peak memory bandwidth is 38.4 GBytes/sec and the peak bandwidth required by the code is 4 GBytes/sec per core at full pipeline efficiency, so these results are not unexpected.

ICCG shows a similar overall pattern but the performance is lower and for n=8K warm the maximum speedup is only 19 on 64 cores. However, ICCG has more steps and less concurrency. A total of $\log_2 n$ families are created, where at each step the number of threads varies from 2 to n/2. Thus, like the smaller problem size above, we have fewer threads and more concurrency-management overhead. Best execution times for ICCG are 2, 3.5 and 57 μsecs for 1K, 8K and 64K respectively.

Matrix multiplication is shown for sizes of n=20 (S), 32 (M), 90 (L). This gives array sizes of 400, 1K and 8K, i.e. n^2 elements, however the algorithm performs $O(n^3)$ operations for n^2 results. The simplest algorithm was implemented, where n^2 threads each compute one element of the result by performing an inner product. It can be seen that the results scale well for both warm and cold caches, due to the amount of computation required in obtaining the result for a single element. This problem stresses the on-chip cache organisation, as although it has temporal on-chip locality, accesses to columns have no spatial locality. This can be seen in the results for the large problem, where both cold and warm performance is reduced due to capacity misses. Maximum speedup is a factor is 53 (warm) and 34 (cold) for n=32 on 64 cores. The best execution times were *1.6, 5 and 90* μsecs, respectively for three problem sizes.

Equation of state is also a single family of n threads, although the thread in this instance are more complex than hydro and give a better overall performance. We have near perfect speedup for n=8K warm, 54 fold speedup on 64 cores. Even allowing for concurrency overheads, the pipelines are still operating at over 78% on 64 cores, i.e. less than 1 bubble in 4 cycles. The best execution times are 1.6, 4.8 and 113 μsecs for the three problem sizes.

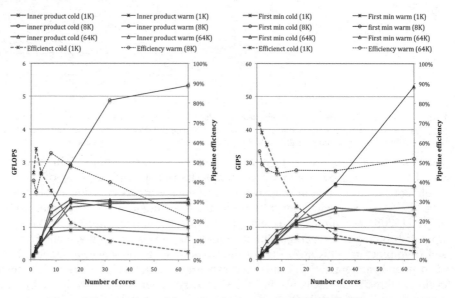

Figure 7. Inner product and first min reductions for 1k, 8K and 64K points.

4.2. Reductions

We implemented two reductions from the Livermore loops, *inner product* and *first min.* The code for both is quite general although they require the system to provide the number of cores, in order to implement four partial reductions on each core before completing the reductions across the cores. As can be seen in Figure 7, we get a similar pattern of performance to the data-parallel loops. Efficiencies overall are lower due to the higher concurrency overheads and the sequential reduction between the cores. For the warm caches we get speedups of 7, 12 and 34 for the different problem sizes.

4.3. Parallel prefix sum

The prefix sum operation is one of the simplest and most useful building blocks for designing parallel algorithms. It appears to be inherently sequential but has an efficient parallel implementation that requires $\log_2 n$ steps. For example, linear recurrences, including many of the sequential Livermore loops can be expressed in parallel using it. Blelloch in [28] lists a range of applications, including parsing, sorting, variable precision arithmetic, regular expression searching, etc. The same algorithm is also used in hardware in most ALUs to perform binary addition (carry look-ahead adders). Parallel prefix sum can be generalised to any binary associative operation and is also known as the scan operation.

Scan takes a binary associative operator $\oplus$, and an ordered set of n elements:

$$[a_0, a_1, ..., a_{n-1}],$$

and returns the ordered set:

$$[a_0, (a_0 \oplus a_1), ..., (a_0 \oplus a_1 \oplus ... \oplus a_{n-1})].$$

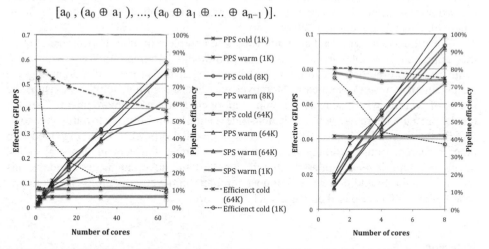

Figure 8. Parallel prefix sum (PPS) and sequential prefix sum (SPS) for 1K, 8K and 64K points respectively. The same results are plotted at two different scales.

Because of its importance, we have investigated the implementation of this algorithm using floating-point addition. We have implemented both parallel (PPS) and sequential (SPS) versions in μTC and compared the results. The sequential version also generates threads but implements the algorithm with a thread-to-thread dependency. The parallel algorithm requires $\log_2 n/2$ more operations than the sequential one, i.e. a factor of 5, 6.5 and 8 for the 1K, 8K and 64K problem sizes. Figure 8 compares the relative performance of both algorithms, i.e. effective GFLOPS are computed using the sequential operation count in both sets of performance curves. The sequential algorithm shows a speedup of 1.1 at 64 cores. The parallel version has a speedup of 18, 38 and 46 on 64 cores (warm caches) compared to its single core performance and 7.2, 8.2. and 8.5 when compared to the performance of the single-core sequential code. Note also, that the cold- and warm-cache performance is very similar due to the locality over the algorithm's $\log_2 n$ stages. The exception is the small problem size, where only 8 threads are created per core, on the 64-core place, which is insufficient to tolerate the latency of off-chip memory accesses.

5. Conclusions

This paper presents a significant amount of work, which spans more than a decade of research and engineering effort. It is exciting to see the fruition of this work, made possible with the support of the EU funded Apple-CORE project, which we gratefully acknowledge. We have demonstrated here results obtained from our core compiler and a realistic emulation of a processor chip that could be implemented in today's technology. We have only just begun to investigate the characteristics of this disruptive approach to many-core computing but these initial results are very encouraging. We have evaluated the performance of a range of common, loop-based programming paradigms and have shown speedup on every one. Although performance saturates due to memory bandwidth constraints in these simple benchmarks, distributing them as concurrent components of a larger application, executing at different places on chip, will minimise this problem. What we have shown is arguably the worst case scenario, where very simple kernels are executed from start to finish where all data and code is sourced off chip.

We still have a significant amount of work to complete in order to demonstrate that this approach is viable in the context of commodity computing. We have started evaluating more complex algorithms and have begun the process of automating the management of resources on chip. Moreover we have shown that solutions exist to the issues of security when using such a chip in an open, many-user environment. Thus the results presented here, we believe, demonstrate a significant first step towards this goal.

Furthermore, the Apple-CORE project has enabled this work to be extended into other research groups working in complimentary areas. Partners in this project are developing high-level compilers from both standard and novel languages targeting this core tool chain. In addition work is almost complete in developing an FPGA prototype based of an SVP core based on the LEON 3 soft core.

References

[1] C.R. Jesshope, A model for the design and programming of multi-cores, in (L. Grandinetti, ed.), *High Performance Computing and Grids in Action, Advances in Parallel Computing*, **16**, IOS Press, 2008, 37–55.

[2] A. Duller, G. Panesar, and D. Towner. Parallel processing—the picoChip way, in (J.F. Broenink and G.H. Hilderink, eds.) *Communicating Process Architectures 2003, Concurrent Systems Engineering Series*, **61**, IOS Press, 2003, 1-14.

[3] D. Kirk, NVIDIA CUDA software and GPU parallel computing architecture, in Proc. *6th international symposium on Memory management, ISMM '07*, ACM, 2007, 103–104.

[4] NVIDIA Corporation, *CUDA Zone - the resource for CUDA developers*, http://www.nvidia.com/cuda, 2009.

[5] J. Held, J. Bautista and S. Koehl, *From a few cores to many: a Tera-scale computing research overview*, Intel Corporation technical report, http://download.intel.com/research/platform/ terascale/terascale_overview_paper.pdf, 2006.

[6] Intel Corporation, *Tera-scale computing research programme*, http:// techresearch.intel.com/articles/Tera-Scale/1421.htm.

[7] Intel Corporation, *Teraflops research chip*. http://techresearch. intel.com/articles/Tera-Scale/1449.htm.

[8] Clearspeed, *CSX Processor Architecture*. Whitepaper, Clearspeed Technology plc, Bristol, UK, 2007.

[9] ITRC, International Technology Roadmap for Semiconductors. http://public.itrs.net, 2007.

[10] C. Grelck and S-B. Scholz. SAC: A functional array language for efficient multithreaded execution, *International Journal of Parallel Programming*, **34**(4), 2006, 383–427.

[11] C. Grelck and S-B. Scholz. SAC: off-the-shelf support for data-parallelism on multicores, in Proc. 2007 workshop on *Declarative aspects of multicore programming, DAMP '07*, ACM, 2007, 25-33.

[12] C. Grelck, S-B Scholz, and A. Shafarenko. Streaming networks for coordinating data-parallel programs, in (I. Virbitskaite and A Voronkov, eds), *Perspectives of System Informatics, 6th International Andrei Ershov Memorial Conference (PSI'06)*, Novosibirsk, **4378** LNCS, Springer-Verlag, 2007, 441–445.

[13] C. Grelck, S-B Scholz, and A. Shafarenko. A gentle introduction to S-Net: Typed stream processing and declarative coordination of asynchronous components, *Parallel Processing Letters*, **18**(1), 2008, 221- 237.

[14] D. Saougkos, D. Evgenidou, and G. Manis. Specifying loop transformations for C2µTC source-to-source compiler, in *14th Workshop on Compilers for Parallel Computing (CPC'09)*, 2009.

[15] T.D Vu and C. R. Jesshope, Formalizing SANE virtual processor in thread algebra, in (M. Butler, M. G. Hinchley and M. M. Larrondo-Petrie, eds.) *Proc. ICFEM 2007*, **4789** LNCS, Springer-Verlag, 2007, 345-365.

[16] Arvind, R.S. Nikhil, and K.K. Pingali, I-structures: data structures for parallel computing, *ACM Trans. Program. Lang. Syst.*, **11**(4), 1989, 598-632.

[17] C.R. Jesshope, µTC - an intermediate language for programming chip multiprocessors, in *Asia-Pacific Computer Systems Architecture Conference*, **4186** LNCS, 2006, 147-160.

[18] GCC, *the GNU compiler collection*. http://gcc.gnu.org.

[19] T. Bernard, K. Bousias, L. Guang, C.R. Jesshope, M. Lankamp, M.W. van Tol and L. Zhang, A general model of concurrency and its implementation as many-core dynamic RISC processors, in (W. Najjar and H. Blume Eds.) *Proc. Intl.Conf. on Embedded Computer Systems: Architecture, Modeling and Simulation, SAMOS-2008*, 2008, 1-9.

[20] K. Bousias, L. Guang, C.R. Jesshope, M. Lankamp, Implementation and Evaluation of a Microthread Architecture, *Journal of Systems Architecture*, **55**(3) 2009, 149-161.

[21] M.W. van Tol, C.R. Jesshope, M. Lankamp and S. Polstra, An implementation of the SANE Virtual Processor using POSIX threads, *Journal of Systems Architecture*, 55(3), 2009,162-169.

[22] G. R. Gao and V. Sarkar, Location consistency – a new memory model and cache consistency protocol. *IEEE Transactions on Computers*, 1998.

[23] D. Mosberger, Memory consistency models. *SIGOPS Oper. Syst. Rev.*, **27**(1), 1993, 18–26.

[24] E. W. Dijkstra, Hierarchical ordering of sequential processes. *Acta Informatica*, **1**(2), 1971, 115-138.

[25] K. Bousias, N. M. Hasasneh and Jesshope C R (2006) Instruction-level parallelism through microthreading - a scalable Approach to chip multiprocessors, *Computer Journal*, **49** (2), 211-233.

[26] C. Jesshope, M. Lankamp and L Zhang, Evaluating CMPs and their memory architecture, in (Eds. M Berekovic, C. Muller-Schoer, C. Hochberger and S. Wong) Proc. *Architecture of Computing Systems, ARCS 2009*, **5455** LNCS, 2009, pp246-257.

[27] J. Masters, M. Lankamp, C.R. Jesshope, R. Poss, E. Hielscher, Report on memory protection in microthreaded processors, Apple-CORE deliverable D5.2, http://www.apple-core.info/wp-content/apple-core/2008/12/d52.pdf.

[28] G. E. Blelloch, Prefix Sums and Their Applications, in *Synthesis of Parallel Algorithms*, (J. H. Reif, ed.) Morgan Kaufmann, 1991.

Numerical Algorithms

Parallel Computing: From Multicores and GPU's to Petascale
B. Chapman et al. (Eds.)
IOS Press, 2010
© 2010 The authors and IOS Press. All rights reserved.
doi:10.3233/978-1-60750-530-3-35

Efficiency and scalability
of the parallel Barnes-Hut tree code PEPC

Robert SPECK [a], Paul GIBBON [a] and Martin HOFFMANN [b]

[a] *Jülich Supercomputing Centre*
Forschungszentrum Jülich GmbH
D–52425 Jülich, Germany
[b] *Martin-Luther-Universität Halle-Wittenberg*
Institut für Physik
D–06120 Halle, Germany

Abstract. We present scaling results of the parallel tree code PEPC on an IBM
BlueGene/P and identify performance bottlenecks and intrinsic algorithmic issues.
Using more than 8192 processors the tree code is capable of simulating more than
100 million particles, but as our analysis shows, fundamental changes will be necessary for porting this code to petaflop systems. However, an efficiency examination
reveals a very good ratio between communication and computation in the traversal
process. Furthermore, we present a library version of the code, which may act as a
'black box' for front-end users.

Keywords. Tree codes, BlueGene/P, Scaling, Efficiency, Petaflop challenges

Introduction

Even in the era of Petaflop computing, the naive approach of solving the N-body problem directly by an $\mathcal{O}(N^2)$-algorithm is simply impractical for the vast majority of physical systems. Despite the high accuracy and scalability of these algorithms, they are in-
effective for problems where statistically significant results can only be obtained by simulating the presence of more than a few thousand particles.

In the mid-1980s two techniques – the hierarchical Tree Code [1] and the Fast Multipole Method (FMM) [2], with respective algorithmic scalings of $O(N \log N)$ and $O(N)$
– revolutionized long-range N-body simulation for scientists across a wide range of
disciplines [3]. These methods reduce the number of direct particle-particle interactions
through the systematic use of multipole expansions up to a given degree. For many dynamical systems, there is no need to compute potentials and forces to higher accuracy
than the error incurred by the time-differencing scheme used to integrate the equations of
motion. In such cases tree codes and the FMM make it possible to perform significantly
fast simulations with many millions of particles (see also [4]). A further advantage is
that these methods are absolutely mesh-free: they do not require underlying grids for the
field solver and are therefore intrinsically adaptive.

In [5] Gibbon et. al. demonstrated the performance and scalability of the parallel tree code PEPC – Pretty Efficient Parallel Coulomb-solver [6] – on the former Jülich IBM p690 and BlueGene/L machines. This highly portable code was designed primarily for mesh-free modeling of nonlinear, complex plasma systems [7], but has since been adapted for gravitational problems and vortex fluid methods, even with different potentials. Based on the original Warren-Salmon 'hashed oct-tree' scheme [8] with a fixed multipole expansion up to $p = 2$ (quadrupole), PEPC provides a flexible, highly accurate and fully parallelized tool for $O(N \log N)$ tree code simulations. It is now part of the ScaFaCoS project [9] and the DEISA Benchmark Suite [10].

The structure of this paper is as follows: Focusing on the classical electrostatic front-end PEPC-E we present our library version of the code as an introduction to the PEPC kernel routines. After the performance and scaling analysis on a BlueGene/P system we analyze the efficiency of the tree traversal and conclude with a review of emerged problems and possible solutions concerning further scalability.

1. A 'black box' for Library Usage

For using PEPC in many different applications its components are split into two parts: The kernel routines LPEPC and a user-dependent front-end application. The kernel routines provide user-independent functionality such as building the oct-tree and computing forces. It is essential that these routines are well-separated from any front-end: a user should not have to care for the tree structure nor should the kernel routines make use of variables which were introduced by a front-end. That is, the LPEPC library is designed as a 'black box'.

The controlling routine in LPEPC is `fields`, which acts as a gateway to the user. Figure 1 shows the main steps of this function called by an user application with an initial set of particles:

```
begin fields
   (1) copy particles to local arrays
   (2) domain decomposition
   (3) construct local trees and multipole moments
   (4) build interaction lists
   (5) compute forces and potential
   (6) return forces and potential
end fields
```

Figure 1. `fields` routine

Although each of these steps are already implemented in parallel, this routine carries an intrinsic handicap. The domain decomposition in step (2) redistributes the initial set of particles according to their computed unique keys. Note that with step (1) they are only redistributed 'virtually', without touching the original particle order the user provides prior to calling `fields`. But now step (5) computes the forces and potential for these redistributed particles, while step (6) passes them back to the front-end. Inside `fields` the mapping of particles and forces is correct, but these forces no longer belong to the initial particle set outside `fields`. The mapping which is now visible to the user is defective and any further computation will fail unless a remedy is supplied for this reordering.

Our first approach focuses on usability and preserved black box behavior. Inside `fields` a routine `restore` is inserted between steps (5) and (6), which redistributes the *computed forces* according to the initial particle order. Therefore, it is necessary to modify the domain decomposition routine in such a manner that it now provides the sorting information which was used to redistribute the particles. With this information the routine `restore` performs the inverse operation of the domain decomposition by swapping the corresponding forces instead of the particles. Therefore the user retains the initial particle order with a correct force mapping computed by `fields`. With this approach the tree code conforms to a black box behavior which is highly convenient for users. A disadvantage of this approach is that the sorting information is lost outside `fields`, although it may be useful for users as well as for a subsequent domain decomposition in the next time step.

The second variant tries to make use of the provided sorting information more efficiently. Here, we have modified the domain decomposition and `fields` itself so that the user may access the redistribution vectors. In return `fields` does not care about the 'wrong' force assignment, the responsibility is passed back to the user. A front-end application using this version of `fields` has to provide its own remedy for handling this problem. This behavior is of course a clear breach of the black box idea. While this is initially a drawback, it has the major benefit of preserving the sorting information for the next time step.

2. Performance Analysis on BlueGene/P

To show the capabilities of our tree code PEPC we tested the pure black box algorithm at the Juelich Supercomputing Centre on the IBM BlueGene/P system JUGENE. This system is a 72-rack supercomputer with 73728 4-way SMP compute nodes. Each of them has 2 GB of main memory, which gives 512 MB per single processors in virtual node (VN) mode. In this mode we have tested our code using up to 16384 processors for the first time. For these simulations we set up a homogeneous cube ("homogen") and two distant spheres ("inhomogen"), both with 25.600.000 particles. Furthermore, we tested the difference between the point-to-point version ("p2p") of the information exchange and its collective alternative ("coll."). The results for strong and weak scaling are presented in Figures 2 and 3. For a better comparison we provide the execution times next to the plots.

The first thing we notice is the clear inferiority of the collective approach in both scalings. Especially for large numbers of processors the overlap of communication and computation is exploited heavily in the point-to-point algorithm, which makes the col-

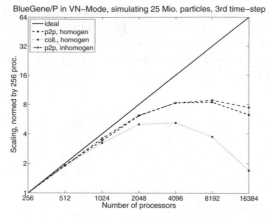

Figure 2. Strong scaling speedup

Execution time per time step for 256 / 16384 proc. in seconds:

p2p, homogen: 95.1 / 15.1
coll., homogen: 94.4 / 55.4
p2p, inhomogen: 105.7 / 14.2

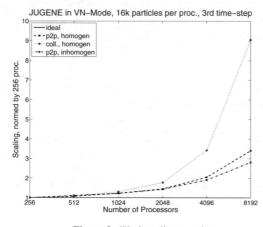

Figure 3. Weak scaling speedup

Execution time per time step for 256 / 8192 proc. in seconds:

p2p, homogen: 13.7 / 46.8
coll., homogen: 13.6 / 123.1
p2p, inhomogen: 15.1 / 43.6

lective variant much less attractive. This observation is supported by the fact, that the results in the weak scaling are similar: Again, the point-to-point version is already superior at 1024 processors. While a slight increase of execution time is due to the $\log N$ dependency of the algorithm, the collective routine becomes impractical at 8192 processors.

But concentrating now on the strong scaling behavior we see a clear saturation at large systems. The code almost stops profiting from the usage of more than 4096 processors. To analyze this behavior we take a more detailed look inside the homogeneous scaling results in Figure 4.

Here we can identify two major problems: First, the construction of local trees becomes more expensive at higher numbers of processors. This is partly due to our current sorting routine, which does not handle large, inhomogeneous systems very well, but for which a more efficient alternative will soon be available. Second, the generation of the interaction lists and therefore the main communication part stops scaling at around 4096 processors. This is basically the reason for the observed saturation and simultaneously

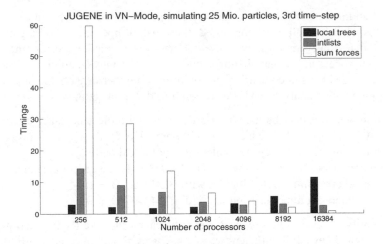

Figure 4. Detailed scaling analysis – homogeneous case

the most demanding issue of the algorithm. The explanation is simple: the more processors which share a fixed problem like in the strong scaling situation, the smaller the local trees become. On the one hand, this fact is part of our first identified problem, since the overhead of organizational tree structure becomes evident. But smaller local trees also imply fewer local interactions, so that for obtaining the same result as before, the processors need more time (and memory) for requesting and fetching particle or node data. Even by using the efficient and robust point-to-point communication scheme this issue cannot be avoided.

However, in its present version the tree code PEPC is capable of utilizing 8192 processors for simulations with many million particles, regardless of their distribution. We are able to simulate 2^{28} particles for many time steps for real world problems. Tackling the sorting issue and optimizing the memory usage of the code we expect to increase these numbers significantly.

3. Efficiency Analysis

As we have seen in the previous section the most demanding and fragile part of our tree code is the generation of the interaction lists within the tree traversal routine. Its underlying concept is the data-shipping paradigm: In contrast to function-shipping [11], each processor gathers the corresponding data (multipole moments, center-of-charge, keys and so on), which is needed for its particles interaction lists. While function-shipping means gathering the already computed partial multipole expansion from non-local particles our choice has clear positive and negative consequences: The incoming data multipole moment information needs an unpredictable and large amount of memory on the requesting processor, but in return recurring requests do not produce recurring communication. Already gathered data is integrated into the local tree so that following accesses are then local operations.

Now, the question in this context is whether this strategy produces an overhead which consumes the advantage of buffering and leaves us with the need for excessive amount of additional memory. Since the integration into the local tree on a certain level requires knowledge of all overlying nodes, these parent nodes have to be gathered and integrated first. However, they may be used directly for interaction lists of other particles on the same processor. We may therefore classify our strategy as efficient if the ratio of gathered and used keys in comparison to the overall number of gathered keys is near to 100%. For a detailed analysis we have chosen four different settings:

1. Homogeneous distribution with Barnes-Hut multipole acceptance criterion (BH-MAC, [1]) $\Theta = 0.0$, which yields a pure $\mathcal{O}(N^2)$ algorithm as every pseudo-particle in the tree is rejected unless it is not a real particle
2. Homogeneous distribution with BH-MAC $\Theta = 0.6$, a common choice
3. One-sphere Plummer distribution with BH-MAC $\Theta = 0.0$
4. One-sphere Plummer distribution with BH-MAC $\Theta = 0.6$

To identify the usage of a key we compare on each processor the interaction list with the list of fetched keys. It is sufficient when a key is used only once in an arbitrary inter-action list on the same processor. In Tables 1 and 2 we present details for 32 processors and 8192 particles, averaged over processors.

Table 1. Simulation with $P = 32$, $N = 8192$, $\Theta = 0.0$

	Homogeneous			Plummer model		
	average	max	min	average	max	min
fetches	11050.53	11071	11036	10921.69	10938	10903
found	7709.31	7713	7709	7661.84	7663	7660
efficiency %	69.76	69.66	69.85	70.15	70.06	70.26

Table 2. Simulation with $P = 32$, $N = 8192$, $\Theta = 0.6$

	Homogeneous			Plummer model		
	average	max	min	average	max	min
fetches	946.81	1370	525	1057.78	1755	429
found	946.68	1369	525	1057.53	1752	429
efficiency %	99.99	99.92	100	99.84	99.82	100

These tables show two main results of our analysis: Firstly, our efficiency values are much higher than expected and secondly, there is no significant difference in efficiency between a homogeneous and a non-homogeneous simulation. The results for $\Theta = 0.0$ are as expected: Since each processor has to fetch and integrate every non-local particle, but also receives the corresponding parent nodes, the overhead must be coupled to the size of every non-local tree.

We are aware that these examples are simplified regarding their amount of particles. To verify our conclusion we evaluated the ratio for 524288 particles on 32 processors with two time steps (see Table 3).

Besides the fact that there is no difference regarding the time steps, this simulation reveals, that for increasing problem sizes per processor the gap between received and used keys may become significantly higher. But this is reasonable: The local tree size on every processor has increased and with this higher degree of "bookkeeping" more

Table 3. Simulation with $P = 32$, $N = 524288$, $\Theta = 0.6$

	Time step 2			Time step 3		
	average	max	min	average	max	min
fetches	22545.23	36614	7391	22545.12	36615	7391
found	19186.06	27431	7368	19186.2	27433	7368
efficiency %	85.10	74.91	99.68	85.10	74.92	99.68

information is needed for accessing the nodes belonging to the interaction lists. However, we still have obtained an efficiency of 85% on average, which underlines the advantage of buffering in the data-shipping paradigm. Especially for the common usage as a tree code with $\Theta = 0.6$ nearly every communication for generating the interaction lists is necessary, which is an outstanding result regarding our choice of data-shipping. However, further analyses are necessary to understand the communication structure, efficency and potential of our tree code more deeply.

4. Towards Petaflop Systems

Although our results are promising and better than expected, there are strong indications that we may not proceed with simple bugfixes or patches in our development of PEPC. Especially the saturation of scaling at 4096 processors seems to be a genuine barrier which may not be resolved without fundamental changes to the algorithm. In its current version the code is not capable of running on more than 16384 processors due to a number of issues, which we discuss in the following.

Memory requirements. With larger systems (particle and processors) the costs for the organization of the local and non-local trees grows in relation to the simulated number of particles. This disproportional ratio complicates the internal bookkeeping structure significantly. Especially the need for arrays with $\mathcal{O}(P)$ size, as used in the global branch node management [8], defines an upper limit for the usability of PEPC on larger systems. Therefore, one open question is the search for an alternative to the branch nodes: How can a global domain covering on each processor be accomplished without a dependency of P?

Global communication. Since we have no a priori estimation of the length and members of the interaction lists the particle assignment to the processors according to Morton ordering leads to a significant amount of non-local, i.e. non-neighborship communication. Although the code is capable of using point-to-point communication strategy for interaction list generation the non-blocking send and receive patterns to and from physically distant processors is inevitable in the present version. This disadvantage is of course intensified when using even more processors. As we have seen before, the saturation of scaling makes the adaption of the code to larger systems impractical.

Load balancing. As a direct consequence of the need for global communication we have applied a load balancing strategy to avoid highly varying latencies. Taking the length of the interaction lists in the previous time step the sorting routine in the domain decomposition is able to alter the local number of particles, aiming at a well-balanced work load on the processors but restricted by the particle Morton ordering. However, this approach seems to fail for larger systems [12,13]: The balancing integrator is not always able to avoid the appearance of processors with a constantly high and even growing work load, especially in sparsely populated areas of the simulation region. The more processors we use, the often this effect may occur, since increasing the number of processors by fixing the problem size always leads to more non-local communication.

Consequently, we are aware that fundamental changes in our algorithm are inevitable for moving to Petascale hardware. Besides a fix for the load imbalance problem (provided, this can be fixed) our attention will be focused on a better communication scheme. Since the data is already structured in a hierarchical manner, our next step is to implement an adequate hierarchical communication pattern. Based on the idea of an information broker and therefore of a distinction between computation and communication tasks we may ease the memory problem by a separation of particle/multipole data on the one hand and local trees/branch nodes on the other. Despite the implicit risk of a communication bottleneck in information broker concepts this strategy may lead to a way of handling the problem of global communication, too: As a group of physically local processors share one broker, the information transfer between these local processors is already a more or less local operation, because it is basically performed by the broker. Therefore, global communication might be only needed between different brokers, who "serve" different processor groups.

References

[1]   J. E. Barnes and P. Hut: A hierarchical O(NlogN) force-calculation algorithm, *Nature* **324** (1986), 446–449.
[2]   L. Greengard and V. Rokhlin: A fast algorithm for particle simulations, *Journal of Computational Physics* **73** (1987), 325–348.
[3]   S. Pfalzner and P. Gibbon: Many-Body Tree Methods in Physics, Cambridge University Press (1996).
[4]   V. Springel, N. Yoshida, and S.D.M. White: GADGET: A code for collisionless and gasdynamical cosmological simulations, astro-ph/0003162 (2000).
[5]   P. Gibbon, W. Frings and B. Mohr: Performance analysis and visualization of the N-body tree code PEPC on massively parallel computers, *Proceedings of Parallel Computing* (2005).
[6]   P. Gibbon: PEPC: Pretty Efficient Parallel Coulomb-solver, Technical Report **IB-2003-05** (2003), Research Centre Jülich
[7]   P. Gibbon, F. N. Beg, R. G. Evans, E. L. Clark and M. Zepf: Tree code simulations of proton acceleration from laser-irradiated wire targets, *Physics of Plasmas* **11** (2004).
[8]   M. S. Warren and J. K. Salmon: A portable parallel particle program, *Computer Physics Communications* **87** (1995), 266–290.
[9]   ScaFaCoS - Scalable Fast Coulomb Solvers, a German network project, supported by the German Ministry of Education and Science, BMBF, 01 IH 08001 A-D.
[10] DEISA - Distributed European Infrastructure for Supercomputing Applications, Website: www.deisa.eu.
[11] A. Grama, V. Kumar and A. Sameh: Scalable parallel formulations of the Barnes-Hut method for n-body simulations, *Parallel Computing* **24** (1998), 797–822.
[12] Z. Szebenyi, B.J.N Wylie and F. Wolf: Scalasca Parallel Performance Analyses of PEPC, Euro-Par 2008 Workshops - Parallel Processing (2009).
[13] M. Hoffmann in: M. Bolten, Technical Report **IB-2008-07** (2008), Research Centre Jülich

Parallel Computing: From Multicores and GPU's to Petascale
B. Chapman et al. (Eds.)
IOS Press, 2010
© 2010 The authors and IOS Press. All rights reserved.
doi:10.3233/978-1-60750-530-3-43

Combining Numerical Iterative Solvers

Yanik NGOKO [a,b] and Denis TRYSTRAM [b]

[a] *University of Yaoundé I, Cameroon; E-mail: ngoko@uy1.uninet.cm.*
[b] *LIG, Grenoble University, France; E-mail: yanik.ngoko@imag.fr,*
denis.trystram@imag.fr.

Abstract We are interested in this work by the combination of iterative solvers
when solving linear systems of equations in an on-line setting. Our study targets
users who may not be able to choose the best solvers for solving a set of linear systems while minimizing the total execution time. We propose a framework and algorithms in which the combination of solvers depends on informations gathered at
runtime. The framework is assessed by extensive experiments using 5 SPARSKIT
solvers over more than 70 matrices. The results show that the proposed approach
is robust for solving linear sytems since we were able to solve more linear systems
than each individual solver with an execution time nearly two times equal to those
of the worst individual solver. Morever, we were able to predict a set of two solvers
containing the best solver on more than 80% cases.

Keywords. Iterative solvers, algorithm portfolio, algorithm selection

1. Introduction

With the great diversity of new computational platforms and algorithms to solve a given
problem, it is hard nowadays for a simple user to choose the most suitable algorithm.
Indeed, the behaviour of algorithms may change depending on the computational platform or the problem instance to solve. It is then interesting in such a context to build
mechanisms for helping the users on choosing the most suited algorithm for their favorite
applications.

In this work, we are interested by such mechanisms for solving sparse linear systems that can be written as follows: $Ax = b$ where $A \in R^{p \times p}, x, b \in R^p$. We target
on iterative methods [10] which are known to be a good compromise with a low cost
and good quality of the solution. However, there exist many iterative solvers that can be
used. According to some general theoretical properties of the matrices (symmetry, diagonal dominance), various solvers may have different convergence speeds, or may even
not converge at all depending on the considered matrices. Nevertheless, it is usually difficult to verify these properties in practice [10,6]. This situation has lead in practice to
detailed studies of different matrices such as to identify elements which determine the
convergence of an iterative solver on them. Even if such studies have some interests, we
believe that the great diversity of matrices structures that can be observed in sparse linear systems [10] motivate a specific study of more generic approaches for determining a
convenient way for combining iterative solvers.

There are many studies that aim at proposing a framework for selecting the solver
which converges with the shortest execution time in a practical point of view. Most of

them explore machine learning techniques such as statistical analysis [7], or reinforcement learning [8]. These works generally intent to identify structural characteristics of linear systems that can affect their convergence speeds with iterative solvers. With these characteristics, some rules are deduced (like indicating which solver is the fastest). However, this characterization is not easy to establish since many elements have to be taken into account. Moreover, one can notice that even "small" changes on structural characteristics between two linear systems can lead in practice to different behaviours as stated in [6].

We propose in this work to investigate another direction for determining the most suited iterative solver using informations gathered at runtime. This study is based on algorithm portfolio [4,3]. Similar directions have been studied in [6], where three iterative solvers are combined or in [9] where the choice of the best preconditioner for solving Partial Differential Equation is chosen from runtime informations. The main difference between these works and the solution proposed in this work is on the runtime prediction framework for combining the solvers.

The main result of this work is to propose a framework for combining Krylov subspace methods based on the idea of starting the execution of all available solvers on the linear system and reducing progressively the set of considered solvers. The proposed framework distinguishes two phases. The first one is an *exploration phase* which aims at gathering informations and suggests a measure of the convergence of the linear system for each solver. In this phase, all the solvers are executed and the convergence of the different solvers is estimated using our benchmark. The second phase is an *execution phase* where only the most suited solvers are executed.

2. Combination model

We base our combining approach on algorithm portfolio [3,4,1] and task switching scheduling. For describing the model, let us consider a set of k iterative solvers $\mathcal{H} = \{h_1, \ldots, h_k\}$. We also introduce a given real number B which corresponds to the maximal amount of times that we allow when executing a solver. This bound will be needed in the case when an iterative solver does not converge or when its convergence can stall.

2.1. Task switching scheduling for solver combination

We define a task switching scheduling as a function $\sigma : \{1, \ldots, k \times B\} \longrightarrow \mathcal{H}$.

Let suppose that given a solver h and an instance I (here a linear system defined by its matrix and right hand side), the resolution time of h requires $C(h, I)$ time units. Given a task switching function σ the execution time of an instance I can be defined as the smallest t such that for a solver h, $C(h, I) = |\{t_1 < t : \sigma(t_1) = h\}|$. In the time switching schedule, we assume that the resources are shared between the available solvers during the execution time. The task switching model is similar to the composite solvers model proposed in [9]. Using the task switching combination model, one can consider the combination of solvers in using the on-line task switching problem described as follows.

The on-line task switching scheduling problem [4] can be described as an adversarial game with N successive rounds with N instances representing the linear systems to solve. At the beginning of the game, the adversary fixed a cost $C(h_i, I_j) > 0$ for each $i \in \{1, \ldots, k\}$, $j \in \{1, \ldots, n\}$. At the beginning of round j, the player chooses a task switching schedule σ^j. After this choice, he-she gets in return the associated payoff $C(\sigma^j, I_j)$. When choosing σ^j, the player has not the knowledge of the fixed cost $C(h_i, I_j), 1 \leq i \leq k$. The objective of the player is to minimize the sum of observed payoffs $\sum_{j=1}^{N} C(\sigma^j, I_j)$. In this problem, the value $C(h_i, I_j)$ corresponds to the execution time of solver h_i, on the instance I_j. The on-line task swithcing scheduling problem can also be described in a parallel context as done in [2]. It is also important to notice that this problem generalizes the selection of the most suited algorithms for solving instances in an on-line setting.

There are some details that have to be taken into account while defining a task switching combination of iterative solvers. For instance, it may not always be interesting to switch the execution from a solver to another if the first solver was executing an iteration that is not ended. To manage this, we assume that we do not switch through the time but only at the end of solver iterations. Another detail to take into account is the fact that switching between iterations can really increase the execution time since some data may be lost in the caches (in our case, the vectors of the Krylov basis). To manage this, we will define a minimum number of iterations before switching between solvers. This later consideration is reasonnable since our solvers will nearly be executed as restarted Krylov based solvers which in some cases have the same convergence properties as non-restarted ones. In what follows, we propose existing approaches for addressing the on-line task switching problem.

2.2. The Constant Rebalanced Approach

The Constant Rebalanced Algorithm ($CBAL$) is a well-used approach for solving the portfolio problem [2,1]. In context of linear solvers, this approach can be considered as choosing a fixed task switching schedule σ and applying it for solving each instance. Given a set of solvers $\mathcal{H}$ and a set of instances $\mathcal{I}$, one interesting property here is that the optimal solution using the $CBAL$ is always at least as good as the best solver $h^{opt} \in \mathcal{H}$ executed on the set of instances in $\mathcal{I}$.

A particular case using the $CBAL$ approach consists in considering the MA (Mean Allocation) algorithm defined in [2] in a more general context. In the task switching model, the MA consist to interleave the execution of algorithms through the time such that each of them been executed during a nearly same amount of time before we obtain a solution. For our context, the MA algorithm can be defined as a fixed schedule σ_{MA} such that $\sigma_{MA}(t) = h_{st}$ where $st = t \mod k+1$. A such schedule fairly share the resources between the available solvers. This algorithm is interesting since it is k competitive for the on-line task switching scheduling problem [3].

MA can be adapted to iterative solver combination in switching between solvers at the frontier of iterations. It is important to remark that it is hard to obtain a better approximation ratio than the MA algorithm for the on-line task switching scheduling problem if we do not have more informations on the problem [2].

To build better task switching schedules in pratice, most existing studies consider the existence of a benchmark for the target problem. Mainly, in [3,4] the authors consider the off-line task switching scheduling problem in which we are looking for a fixed task switching schedule such as to minimize the mean execution time obtained while solving the instances of a given benchmark $\mathcal{I}$. Being given a problem, a set of algorithms and a representative set of instances for the problem, the main idea here is to build a task switching schedule using available algorithms which minimize the mean execution time for solving representative instances for the problem. The interest of such an off-line task switching schedule is that even in an on-line setting, the built schedule may minimize the mean execution time of incomming instances since each on-line instance is "close" to one representative instance.

The $CBAL$ approach is an interesting approach for combining solvers. However, one main drawback is that we do not try to improve the schedule with informations related to the particular instance to solve. Indeed, even if it is hard to determine which instances of the benchmark are close to the instance to solve, we can deduce such an information while observing the convergence after some iterations. We will describe such an approach in the following section.

3. A Framework for task switching with iterative solvers

3.1. General description

The proposed framework distinguishes two phases when executing each instance. Namely, an exploration phase followed by an execution phase. In both phases, the solvers are executed following the MA algorithm (but algorithms are switched here not depending on fixed time intervals but at the frontier of iterations). The role of the exploration phase is to gather informations that will later be used to reduce (in the execution phase) the number of solvers that will be used in task switching.

Let us suppose that we have a set $\mathcal{H}$ of numerical solvers. We consider two bounds T and m. The first bound T gives the number of iterations that may be used by each solver in the exploration phase. The second bound serves to deduce the maximal number of solvers that are required to execute in task switching after T iterations of each solver. More precisely, if k solvers are considered, after T iterations of each solver, we should have only $\lceil \frac{k}{m} \rceil$ solvers that are executed in task switching during the execution phase.

The key point in this approach is in the selection of an adequate subset of solvers. We will describe in what follows, how we will proceed.

3.2. Reducing the set of solvers by monitoring

Given an instance, we select a subset of solvers by comparing the behaviour of the different solvers on the instance that we are executing with instances in the benchmark. For this, we let first assume that all the linear systems to solve have a same right hand side $b = [1, \ldots, 1]^T$ (we could have used any other right hand side). With this consideration, a problem instance for us is given only by a matrix.

Given a set of benchmark matrices, we first record in an off-line setting the distribution of execution of each instance given each method. Such a distribution is characterized here by the evolution of the convergence rate of the instance on a method. For a benchmark matrix A and a numerical solver, we build a convergence rate vector ρ^A of $T - 1$ components such that if $r^A(q)$ is the residual when solving the system $Ax = b$ with the numerical solver at iteration q, $(q < T)$, then $\rho^A(q) = \frac{\|r^A(q) - r^A(q-1)\|}{\|r^A(q-1)\|}$. When having another instance to solve (with matrix A'), we believe that if A' is close to A, then when applying a Krylov method on matrices A and A' with the same initial approximation and stopping criteria, we could expect a similar convergence rate distribution for both matrices. Thus, the best solver on A may also be the best on A'.

These two informations are important here. The first information (comparable rate convergence) serves to deduce in observing a set of iterations of and unknown matrices, the benchmark matrices from which it is near. The second information serves to then deduce the restricted set of potential solvers (since we know the best solver in the benchmark) that first gives a solution of the linear system to solve. In the following, we give a detailed description of our algorithms.

3.3. Algorithm

In the proposed algorithm, the two first steps (denoted as steps 1 and 2) are executed in a off-line setting and the other in an on-line setting.

1. Given a benchmark of matrices $\mathcal{I}$ and a set of iterative solvers $\mathcal{H}$, one builds a function $\varrho : \mathcal{I} \times \mathcal{H} \longrightarrow \mathbf{R}^T$ which gives for each instance $I_j \in \mathcal{I}$, and solver $h_i \in \mathcal{H}$ the convergence rate vector $\varrho(I_j, h_i)$ obtained from the benchmark instance I_j when executed with the solver h_i on the T first iterations. This result is obtained through execution of each benchmark instance with different solvers.
2. One also build a function $Best : \mathcal{I} \longrightarrow \mathcal{H}$ which gives for each benchmark instance its best solver (the one which minimize the execution time).
3. When having an instance I to solve, it is executed on all solvers in $\mathcal{H}$ using the MA algorithm. One stops the execution when all the solvers are executed during T iterations. During the execution, the convergence rate vector $\rho_i^I = [\rho_i^I(1), \dots, \rho_i^I(T)]^T$ obtained during the sucessive iterations $1, \dots, T$ for each solver h_i is gathered.
4. The vectors $\rho_i^I, \forall i$ are compared with the vectors $\varrho(I_j, h_i)$ and then one selects the k/m distinct benchmark instances($\mathcal{I}_s$) that are close to I.
5. Then the execution of I continues with the MA algorithm only with the best solvers (deduced from the function $Best$) on instances in $\mathcal{I}_s$.

The k/m solvers here are selected in taking the best solver for instances I_j on which $v(j) = \sum_{i=1}^{k} \|\rho_i^I - \varrho(I_j, h_i)\|_2$ is minimized.

Let us denote by $MA(x, T)$ the above algorithm where $x = k/m$. Let consider now the complexity of $MA(x, p)$. This complexity mainly depends on the costs $v(j)$ for $I_j \in \mathcal{I}$. The computation of a value $\|\rho_i^I - \varrho(I_j, h_i)\|_2$ can easily been done in $O(T)$ since one has vectors of size T. Thus, the computation of all values $v(j)$, for all I_j can be done in $O(nkT)$. Since one has to take giving each value $v(j)$ the smallest one (in order to deduce the k/m solvers), one can sort the vector v and this can be done in $O(n \log n)$ with the Merge Sort algorithm. Thus the total computation cost for restricting the set of solver is in $O(n(\log n + kT))$. This result indicates that the complexity of $MA(x, T)$ can be large when having many instances, many solvers or a long observation phase. In such cases however, one can hope that the prediction framework is more precise.

4. Experimental results

To assess the proposed algorithm, we did several experiments using the SPARSKIT library [11] and the Matrix Market database [12].

4.1. Selecting a benchmark and a set of Solvers

For selecting a convenient set of benchmark and solvers, we chose a set of 76 matrices in matrix market issued of 14 Harwell/Boeing Matrix Collection (each collection refered to a specific problem and we verified that each martices was solved by at least one solver). The chosen collections contained: symmetric and positive definite matrices, symmetric matrices and unsymmetric matrices. We executed on these matrices 8 SPARSKIT solvers using the ilut preconditionning where the fill-in was setted to the values, 0, 9 and 15. The drop tolerance (for ilut) here was setted to $1E - 5$. If r is the residual vector obtained at a step, tol_r and tol_a are the relative and absolute tolerance that we authorized, the stopping criteria for all solvers was $\|r\| \leq tol_r * \|b\| + tol_a$ (here $tol_r = 10^{-6}$ and $tol_a = 10^{-10}$). All solvers were executed with at most 4000 iterations. From these executions we observed that in varying the fill-in the behaviour of solvers changed. For instance, the BICGSTAB solver with ilut(0) (BICGSTAB(0)) was unable to converge on some matrices of the *GRENOBLE* matrices collection where the BICGSTAB(9) converges. From obtained results, we extracted a set of 5 solvers and a set of 15 matrices used as benchmark. The set of solvers was chosen such as to have complementaries behaviours on instances. We eliminated instances on which solvers on them have similar behaviour in the convergence point of view and execution time. As final solvers, we considered: The BICGSTAB with ilut(lfil) and $lfil = 0, 9, 15$, the FOM solver restarted after 5 iterations and preconditionned with ilut(9), the FGMRES solver restarted after 5 iterations and preconditionned with ilut(15).

4.2. Combining Solvers

To build the MA algorithm, we first executed, all solvers on the set of instances (76 matrices) such as to obtain a ratio between the mean execution time taken for each iteration with the chosen solvers. From these executions, we decided to execute in a cycle of MA: 8 iterations of BICGSTAB (for any fill-in) for, 5 iterations of the FOM solver and 5 iterations of FGMRES. These iterations were executed in the order: BICGSTAB(9) and then BICGSTAB(0), BICGSTAB(15), FOM, and FGMRES. This ordering was chosen from benchmark execution such as to have a minimal execution time and to solve the greatest number of linear systems. We also built an $MA(2, T)$ (Two solvers are selected in the execution phase) based on the MA algorithm in taking different values for T (mainly 8, 10 and 12).

4.3. Experimental results

The Table 1 depicts the mean execution time obtained from the considered solvers and the MA on the chosen benchmark. These times are obtained on a an Intel(R) Core(TM)2 Duo CPU 2.26 GHz /2Gbytes of memory

One can notice here that the MA has the greatest execution time. However, MA here is the only solver which converges on all benchmark instances when giving at most

Table 1. Execution time on the 15 matrices chosen as benchmark

BICGSTAB(0)	BICGSTAB(9)	BICGSTAB(15)	FOM	FGMRES	MA
6.30	9.76	11.32	10.25	14.527	41.18

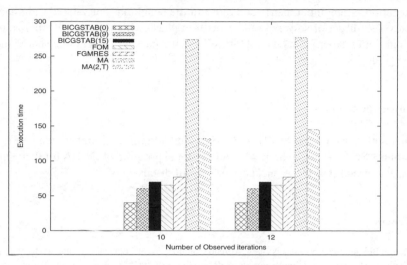

Figure 1. Total execution time on 76 matrices.

Table 2. Proportion of solved linear systems

BICGSTAB(0)	BICGSTAB(9)	BICGSTAB(15)	FOM	FGMRES	MA	MA(2,10)
0.79	0.88	0.88	0.64	0.67	1	0.92

4000 iterations to each solver that it contains. We report in Figure 1 the mean execution time obtained by $MA(2,T)$ in a set of 76 matrices with $T = 10$ and $T = 12$. The execution time of $MA(2,T)$ here is nearly two times equal to those the worst individual solver. However, this overhead is compensated by the proportion of instances solved by $MA(2,T)$. Indeed we report in Table 2 the proportion of solved instances for different solvers. This table shows that MA is the most robust algorithm. The $MA(2,T)$ is not as robust as the MA solver but is better than the remaining ones. This is due to the fact that in some cases, the observation phases was enough to solve the set of instances and in other cases, it chooses the best solver after the observation phase. We also point out that the $MA(2,T)$ has been able to select a set of two solvers containing the best solver on 83.5% of the available linear systems (for $T = 10$ or $T = 12$).

5. Conclusion

We presented in this work a framework for combining iterative solvers in order to help users in choosing the best compromise for solving linear systems in an on-line setting. Preliminary experiments using academic solvers showed that we were able to obtain a better mean execution time than MA while solving more instances than each individual solver. Morever, we were able to predict on more than 80% linear systems a set of two solvers containing the best solver after an observation phase. We would like to emphazise that the proposed framework can be easily adapted to other domains, for instance those where there are iterative algorithms in combinatorial optimization. There are many perspectives for continuing this work. One can generalize the proposed framework to take into account other right hand side in using the result of the comparison between the execution of any input matrix and those in the benchmark on a fixed right hand side to reduce the subset of solvers in the execution phase. One can also parallelize our approach in doing experiments with $MA(x, T)$ using parallel solvers in a shared memory context [13].

Acknowledgements

The first author would like to thank "Le Service Culturel de l'Ambassade de France au Cameroun"(SCAC) and the SARIMA international program of INRIA for their supports. We are also grateful to Dr. Atenekeng for helpful discussions.

References

[1]   Marin Bougeret Pierre-François Dutot, Alfredo Goldman, Yanik Ngoko and Denis Trystram, *Combining Multiple Heuristics on Discrete Resources*, Proceedings of the 2009 Workshop on Advance in Parallel and Distributed Computing. Roma, 2009.

[2]   Yanik Ngoko and Denis Trystram, *Combining SAT solvers On Discrete Resources*, Proceedings of the 2009 International Conference on High Performance Computing and Simulation, 2009 , 153–160

[3]   T. Sayag, S. Fine and Y. Mansour, *Combining multiple heuristics*, Proceedings of the 23rd International Symposium on Theoretical Aspects of Computer Science, 2006, 242–253

[4]   M. Streeter, D. Golovin and S. Smith, *Combining multiple heuristics on-line*, Proceedings of the 22rd Conference on Artificial Intelligence, 2007, pp 1197-1203

[5]   Allan Borodin and Ran El-Yaniv, *on-line computation and competitive analysis*, Cambridge University Press, 2005

[6]   Richard Barrett , Michael Berry , Jack Dongarra , Victor Eijkhout and Charles Romine *Algorithmic Bombardment for the Iterative Solution of Linear Systems: A Poly-iterative Approach*, Journal of Computational and Applied Mathematics, **74** (1996), 91–110

[7]   Jim Demmel, Jack Dongarra, Victor Eijkhout, Erika Fuentes, Antoine Petitet, Richard Vuduc, R. Clint Whaley and Katherine Yelick, *Self adapting linear algebra algorithms and software*, Proceedings IEEE 93, **2** (2005) 293–312

[8]   Erik Kuefler and Tzu-Yi Chen, *On Using Reinforcement Learning to Solve Sparse Linear Systems*, Procedings of International Conference on Computational Science, 2003, 955–964

[9]   S. Bhowmick, L. McInnes, B. Norris and P. Raghavan, *The role of multi-method linear solvers in PDE-based simulations*, Lectures Notes in Computer Science, **2667** (2003), 828–839

[10] Yousef Saad, *Iterative Methods for Sparse Linear Systems*, PWS Publishing Company, 1995.

[11] SPARSKIT's Web Page, http://www.cs.umn.edu/ saad/software/SPARSKIT/sparskit.html.

[12] Matrix Market's Web Page, http://math.nist.gov/MatrixMarket/.

[13] TAUCS's Web page http://www.tau.ac.il/ stoledo/taucs/

Parallel Computing: From Multicores and GPU's to Petascale
B. Chapman et al. (Eds.)
IOS Press, 2010
© 2010 The authors and IOS Press. All rights reserved.
doi:10.3233/978-1-60750-530-3-51

A comparative study of some distributed linear solvers on systems arising from fluid dynamics simulations

Désiré NUENTSA WAKAM [a,1] Jocelyne ERHEL [a] Édouard CANOT [b]
Guy-Antoine ATENEKENG KAHOU [c]

[a] *INRIA-Rennes, Campus de Beaulieu, 35042 Rennes Cedex*
[b] *CNRS-IRISA, Campus de Beaulieu, 35042 Rennes Cedex*
[c] *INRIA-Saclay, Parc Orsay Université, 91893 Orsay Cedex*

Abstract. This paper presents a comparative study of some distributed solvers on a set of linear systems arising from Navier-Stokes equations and provided by an industrial software. Solvers under consideration implement direct, iterative or domain decomposition methods and most of them are freely available packages. Numerical tests with various parameters are made easier by developing a unified toolbox that links with interface functions provided by these libraries. The intensive numerical tests performed on various sets of processors reveal the good performance results achieved by the recently proposed parallel preconditioner for Krylov methods based on an explicit formulation of multiplicative Schwarz [1].

Keywords. Fluid dynamics simulation, large linear systems, distributed solvers, parallel preconditioning, Multiplicative Schwarz, Additive Schwarz.

1. Problem Definition

In this paper, we are interested in finding a good solver for a class of large linear systems

$$Ax = b \tag{1}$$

where $A \in \mathbb{R}^{n \times n}$ is a real and unsymmetric sparse matrix, $x, b \in \mathbb{R}^n$ are respectively solution and right hand side vectors. The matrix A corresponds to the global jacobian matrix resulting from the partial first-order derivatives of the Reynolds-averaged Navier-Stokes equations. The derivatives are done with respect to the conservative fluid variables. There are various linear solvers libraries freely available and a task of finding a good one among them (for our set of linear systems) is not easy by itself. Although a theoretical analysis of the problem can suggest a class of solver, it is necessary to consider numerical comparisons on the problem being solved. These comparisons include, but are not limited to, memory usage, reliability, parallel efficiency, CPU time and accuracy in the final solution. So in this work, we present a comparative study of some

---

[1]Corresponding Author: Désiré NUENTSA WAKAM, IRISA, Campus de Beaulieu, 35042 Rennes cedex, e-mail address: desire.nuentsa_wakam@irisa.fr

distributed linear solvers on the above-mentioned set of linear systems. We do not have the pretension to consider all existing distributed solvers in this short study neither all aspects in the solvers as in [2,3]. At least, we expect this numerical study to suggest which method is appropriate for this problem. This study is also motivated by the performance achieved on these systems using the parallel preconditioned GMRES with the explicit formulation of multiplicative Schwarz [4]. As this kind of study needs many tests with various parameters, we have found useful to design a unified interface that helps us to link uniformly to the interfaces provided by the solvers. However, we should stress on the fact that our main goal in this work is not to offer a generic framework such as Trilinos [5] or Numerical Platon [6] but to test and compare each method suitable for our set of linear problems; so the toolbox is designed primarily to switch between all the solvers under study in some easy and uniform way. The paper is organized as follows. In the next section, the distributed solvers we used in this study are listed. The third part gives an overview of the toolbox. The section 4 is the major part of this work: it is devoted to the experimental comparisons. Concluding remarks are given at the end.

2. Distributed Linear Solvers

Traditionally speaking, the solvers suitable for the system (1) are based either on sparse direct or iterative methods. But with the actual state-of-art, the separation between these two classes is tight. Presently, techniques from the first class are used as preconditioners into the second class. Even in the second class, there are a variety of techniques based on Krylov subspace methods or multilevel methods (Multigrid, Domain decomposition). We first consider the solution with two distributed direct solvers, namely SuperLU_DIST [9] and MUMPS [10]. They are representative of two widely-used techniques in this class. Almost all aspects in both packages have been thoroughly compared [2] using a collection of matrices of reasonable size. Our guess is that the need of memory will become a bottleneck with our present collection of matrices. In fact, this memory usage can be reduced significantly when direct methods are used in incomplete form as preconditioner for iterative methods. So, in this work, we consider EUCLID [11], the recommended ILU preconditioner in HYPRE [12] library. Secondly, we focus on domain decomposition methods. Acting as preconditioners for the Krylov subspace methods (essentially GMRES method), they make use of previous methods to solve (more or less) the local problems induced by the decomposition.

When using Domain Decomposition methods to solve PDE equations, a classical scheme is to consider the splitting from the computational domain. Here, we consider rather a load balancing partitioning based on the adjacency graph of the matrix. Schur complement approaches use a partitioning without overlap while Schwarz methods are applied to partitions that are allowed to overlap. First, we consider the pARMS [8] package based on the first group. In the second group, we use the additive Schwarz preconditioner in the PETSc package.

The convergence of the Schwarz methods is better with a successive correction of the residual vector over the subdomains. This is the case in the Multiplicative Schwarz. However, it leads to an inefficient preconditioner in parallel environment due to the high dependencies of data between the subdomains. In a recent work [1], the authors proposed an explicit formulation of this preconditioner in order to dissociate the computation of the residual vector from the preconditioner application. This explicit form is used in conjunction with the parallel version of GMRES proposed in [13]. Hence, the preconditioned Newton-basis is first constructed in a pipeline over all processors [4]; then, a parallel version of QR factorization [14] is called to get an orthogonal basis. In this study, we use the result of that work which is expressed in the PETSc format and available in a library named as GPREMS (Gmres PREconditioned by Multiplicative Schwarz)[2].

3. Environment of Tests

Our main goal here is to build a ready-to-use interface toolbox such that we can uniformly test any method presented above. The PETSc installer tool is used to build compatible libraries of some of the solvers under study. Figure 1 gives a simplified overview of this architecture. The *routines for sparse matrix format* are provided to read data of systems from files (matrices and right hand side). These data can be in compressed Harwell Boeing format, in Coordinate Matrix Market format, or in compressed block sparse row. The *parameter routines* define *classes* that are used to select options for solvers as well as other parameters either from XML files or PETSc-style database options. At the top level, the test routines define interface functions to all solvers under consideration. So, we need only to choose a solver, edit or generate parameter file and give it to the test routine along with matrix and right hand side file. At the end of execution, the main statistics are returned in html (XML) or text file via the *statistics routines*. As our toolkit has a capability to switch between solvers transparently, it can be used to select automatically a particular solver given some properties of the linear system being solved such as the size of the matrix or its structural symmetry. However, as we shall see shortly with the results, this decision making is not easy.

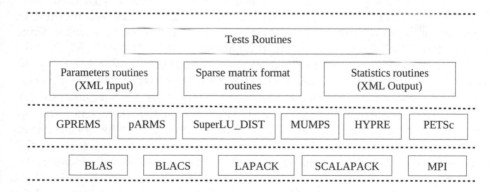

Figure 1. Architecture of our toolbox

---

[2]This library will be soon available for public use

4. Experimental Comparisons

Tests are carried out using the Grid'5000 experimental testbed, on *paradent* cluster in the Rennes site. Each compute node is a dual-cpu and each cpu is a quadricore Carri System CS-5393B (Intel Xeon L5420 at 2.5GHz) with a 32 GB shared memory. In the following, only one cpu is working in each node as no shared-memory programming paradigm was used. All nodes are connected through a Gigabyte Ethernet switch.

4.1. Test Matrices

All the matrices presented here are freely available upon request at [15]. In table 1, we list the characteristics of some of them. Integers n and nnz are respectively the size and

Table 1. Matrices of test

Idx	Matrix	n	nnz	origin
1	CASE_05	161,070	5,066,996	2D linear cascade turbine
2	CASE_07	233,786	11,762,405	2D linear cascade compressor
3	CASE_10	261,465	26,872,530	3D hydraulic gate case
4	CASE_17	381,689	37,464,962	3D jet engine compressor

the number of the nonzeros of the matrix.

4.2. Numerical Behavior, Parallel Efficiency and Fill-in with Direct Solvers

We consider the minimum degree (MD) and the nested dissection (ND) ordering. As the two direct packages (MUMPS and SuperLU_DIST) accept any pivotal sequence, any ordering method can be used. So we have used METIS as nested dissection ordering in both solvers. With approximate minimum degree (AMD) in SuperLU_DIST, we have observed that the fill-in produced was less than that in multiple minimum degree (MMD); however the factorization time is larger. So we have preferred to use the default ordering provided, *i.e.* MMD in SuperLU and AMD in Mumps.

First, the accuracy in the computed solution is considered. In table 2, we give the relative residual norm in the solution, *i.e.* $||b - Ax||/||b||$. Tests are done on 4 processors but the results are roughly the same on 8 or 16 processors. We have observed that in some cases, depending on the use of HSL-MC64 routine to permute large elements on diagonal, the computed solution could be wrong. With CASE_05 for instance, when MC64 is used after a nested dissection ordering, both methods do not achieve a good accuracy. With CASE_07, the situation is more complicated. Either with minimum degree or nested dissection ordering, the solution produced with SuperLU_DIST is not accurate. On the other side, without MC64 permutation, all systems are solved somehow accurately with both methods.

After the accuracy, we look at the increasing of memory needed during the factorization. So in table 3, the ratio of fill-in in factored matrices is given with respect to the nonzeros in the initial matrix i.e $fill = nnz(L + U - I)/nnz(A)$. The fill-in is larger when the permutation is performed to obtain large diagonal elements, particularly with the nested dissection ordering. As a result, it takes much more time to factorize the matrix, particularly for the largest case. In table 4, this preordering effect is shown for the

Table 2. Numerical behavior : Relative residual norm (4 processors)

Matrix	Ordering	SuperLU_DIST		MUMPS	
		No MC64	MC64	No MC64	MC64
CASE_05	MD	3.6e-14	3.5e-14	1e-13	9.4e-14
	ND	3.6e-14	1.3e-02	8e-14	29.9e-01
CASE_07	MD	1.8e-16	9.9e-01	4.7e-16	1.2e-13
	ND	3.6e-14	7.05e-01	3.6e-16	5.1e-10
CASE_10	MD	8.1e-13	8.8e-13	1.2e-12	1.5e-12
	ND	6.3e-16	8.3e-13	1.2e-12	1.4e-12
CASE_17	MD	7.3e-14	9e-12	6.3e-13	1.3e-10
	ND	7.5e-14	4.4e-13	8.2e-13	2.3e-10

overall CPU time on 16 processors. Observe that it takes twice CPU time with MC64 preordering in both methods. Surprisingly with METIS, the time in SuperLU_DIST is ten times larger when this preordering step is performed despite the fact that the fill-in is not so large as shown in table 3. For the MUMPS solver, these results confirm the advices that the maximum transversal should not be applied on matrices with nearly symmetry structure[2]

Table 3. Ratio of fill-in $(fill = nnz(L + U - I)/nnz(A))$: 4 processors

Matrix	Ordering	SuperLU_DIST		Mumps	
		No MC64	MC64	No MC64	MC64
CASE_05	MD	13	17	12	20
	ND	10	64	10	15
CASE_07	MD	30	32	30	34
	ND	22	126	21	27
CASE_10	MD	21.8	23.8	20.9	25.1
	ND	17.6	95.4	17.4	21.8
CASE_17	MD	115	138	100	119
	ND	61	74	58	77

Table 4. CASE_17: Effect of preprocessing on the CPU time (16 processors)

	SuperLU_DIST		MUMPS	
Ordering	No MC64	MC64	No MC64	MC64
MMD/AMD	3050	4045	4228	8229
METIS	1098	17342	1960	3605

The last aspects of interest are the overall time and the parallel efficiency. In table 5, we consider these aspects on the matrix CASE_17. T is the time in seconds while Acc and Eff are respectively the acceleration and the efficiency with respect to the time on 4 nodes. In this part, all tests are done without the permutation by MC64 as it leads in some cases to huge fill-in and consequently, large CPU factorization time. Note that MUMPS is slightly better than SuperLU_DIST on 4 processors. However, SuperLU_DIST performs better when we increase the number of processors. Moreover, it scales better than MUMPS. This result may come from the relatively slow network interconnecting the nodes [16]. Also in SuperLU_DIST, the amount of communication is reduced during the numerical factorization by using the static pivoting.

Table 5. Parallel efficiency with CASE_17

Ordering	Solver	P=4	P=8			P=16		
		T	T	Acc	Eff	T	Acc	Eff
METIS	SuperLU_DIST	3923	2073	1.89	0.94	1098	3.57	0.89
	MUMPS	3598	2969	1.21	0.6	1960	1.83	0.45

4.3. Parallel Behavior of Preconditioners

In the following, we strike to see the convergence of GMRES with the preconditioners mentioned in section 2; namely the parallel ILU preconditioner (EUCLID) in HYPRE, the restricted additive schwarz(ASM) available in PETSc, the Explicit Form of Multiplicative Schwarz(EFMS) used in GPREMS and the left Schur complement (SC) associated with the flexible GMRES in pARMS. To solve the local systems, we have used MUMPS in the case of ASM and EFMS while ILUK is used as approximate solver in the case of SC. The maximum number of iterations allowed is 4000 and the relative tolerance for the convergence is 10^{-9}. The size of the Krylov basis is 64 for the CASE_05 and CASE_07 cases and 128 for the largest ones.

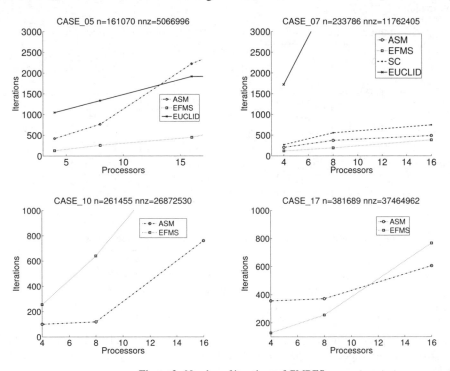

Figure 2. Number of iterations of GMRES

In figure 2 the number of iterations is given as a function of the computing nodes. On small systems (CASE_05, CASE_07) with all preconditioners, this number of iterations grows very fast with the number of processors. In many cases, the maximum number of iterations is reached before convergence. See for instance the CASE_07 with EUCLID on 8 nodes or more. For the largest cases, CASE_10 and CASE_17, GMRES with SC or EUCLID does not converge, whatever the number of nodes used. Thus, only ASM and EFMS are taken into account. On a small number of processors, with all cases but the CASE_10, EFMS gives less number of iterations than ASM. With the CASE_10, ASM performs better than EFMS. However, for more than 8 processors, the number of iterations increases very fast.

Figure 3 gives the time needed to converge to the right solution with respect to the number of processors. For the smallest case and the largest case, we compare direct solvers to preconditioned GMRES. METIS ordering is used in the two direct solvers without MC64 ordering. For the CASE_05, SuperLU_DIST and MUMPS are clearly faster than preconditioned GMRES. Also, the CPU time with ASM and EFMS tends to increase in CASE_05 and CASE_10. For the largest case, GMRES with ASM or EFMS performs better than direct solvers. However, ASM is better than EFMS with more than 4 processors. The main reason is that in EFMS, the residual vector is corrected in a pipeline through the subdomains whereas this correction is done almost simultaneously in ASM. On the other side, GPREMS do perform well regarding the number of iterations as shown in fig. 2.

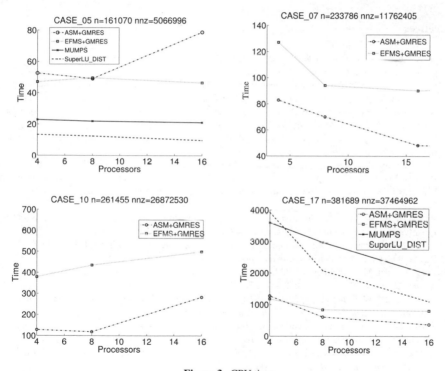

Figure 3. CPU time

5. Concluding Remarks

In this paper, we are interested in the numerical solution of some sparse linear systems issued from actual industrial CFD cases. The distributed solvers we have used are based either on direct, iterative or hybrid techniques. Usually direct solvers are robust, but we have observed here that they could fail to solve some of these systems with some non-obvious parameters. However, on small cases, they are markedly more efficient than other methods used in this study. Also, we have tested the ILU-EUCLID and the left Schur Complement preconditioner in pARMS library but on our set of linear systems, Schwarz-based preconditioners should be preferred. So, in this last category, the restricted additive Schwarz preconditioner performs well when it is associated with a direct solver on subdomains. However, we still need to take a very large Krylov basis which could be a bottleneck in the case of larger systems. Finally, one motivation in this work was to show the significant performance achieved by the parallel GMRES when it is preconditioned by one iteration of the multiplicative schwarz method. The results prove that this preconditioner is competitive among other domain decomposition methods. However, it still suffers from poor scalability. So we are investigating ways to improve this aspect by using some multilevel techniques.

Acknowledgment This work was supported by ANR-RNTL under the LIBRAERO contract. Experiments were carried out using the Grid'5000 experimental testbed (https://www.grid5000.fr).

References

[1]   G.-A. Atenekeng Kahou, E. Kamgnia, B. Philippe. An explicit formulation of the multiplicative Schwarz preconditioner. *Applied Numerical Mathematics*, 57:1197-1213, 2007

[2]   P. Amestoy, I. S. Duff, J-Y, L'Exclellent, X. S. Li, Analysis and Comparison of Two General Sparse Solvers for Distributed Memory Computers, *ACM Trans. Mathematical Software*, 27(4):388-421, 2001

[3]   A. Gupta, Recent Advances in Direct Methods for Solving Unsymmetric Sparse Systems of Linear Equations. *ACM Trans. Mathematical Software*, 28(3):301-324, 2002

[4]   G.-A. Atenekeng-Kahou. Parallélisation de GMRES préconditionné par une itération de Schwarz multiplicatif, *PhD thesis, University of Rennes 1 and University of Yaounde I*, December 2008.

[5]   M.A. Heroux, R.A Bartlett, V.E. Howle, R.J. Hoekstra, J.J. Hu, T.G. Kolda, R.B. Lehoucq, K.R. Long, R.P. Pawlowski, E.T. Phipps, A.G. Salinger, H.K. Thornquist, R.S. Tuminaro, J.M. Willenbring, A. Williams, K.S. Stanley, An overview of the Trilinos project, *ACM Trans. Mathematical Software*, 31(3), 397-423, 2005

[6]   B. Secher, M. Belliard, C. Calvin Numerical Platon: A unified linear equation solver interface by CEA for solving open foe scientific applications. *Nucl. Eng. Des. (2008)*, doi:10.1016/j.nucengdes.2008.06.025

[7]   S. Balay, K. Buschelman, W.D. Gropp, D. Kaushik, M.G. Knepley, L.C. McInnes, B.F. Smith, H. Zhang, PETSc Web page. *http://www.mcs.anl.gov/petsc*, 2008

[8]   Z. Li, Y. Saad, M. Sosonkina. *pARMS* : A parallel version of the algebraic recursive multilevel solver. *Numer. Linear Algebra Appl.*, 10:485-509, 2003

[9]   X. S. Li and J. W. Demmel. SuperLU_DIST : A Scalable Distributed-Memory Sparse Direct Solver for Unsymmetric Linear Systems *ACM Trans. Mathematical Software*, 29(2):110-140, 2003

[10] P. Amestoy, I. Duff, J.-Y. L'Excellent, J. Koster, A fully asynchronous multifrontal solver using distributed dynamic scheduling, *SIAM J. on Matrix Analysis and Applications,* 23(1):15-41, 2001

[11] D. Hysom, A. Pothen. A scalable parallel algorithm for incomplete factor preconditioning. *SIAM J. on Scientific Computing*, 27:1689-1708, 2006

[12] R. Falgout, U. Yang, HYPRE: a Library of High Performance Preconditioners. *C.J.K.Tan, J.J. Dongarra, A.G. Hoekstra (Eds.), Lectures Notes in Computer Science*, 2331:632-641, Springer-Verlag, 2002

[13] J. Erhel, A parallel GMRES version for general sparse matrices. *Electronic Transaction on Numerical Analysis*, 3:160-176, 1995.

[14] R.B. Sidje, Alternatives for parallel subspace basis computation. *Numerical Linear Algebra with Applications*, 4:305-331, 1997.

[15] FLUOREM, The Fluorem Matrix Collection, *http://www.fluorem.com* LIB0721 2.0 / FP-SA, 2009

[16] É. Canot, C. de Dieuleveult, J. Erhel, A parallel software for a saltwater intrusion problem. *G. Joubert, W. Nagel, F. Peters, O. Plata, P. Tirado, E. Zapata (Eds.), Parallel Computing: Current and Future Issues of High-End Computing*, 33:399-406, NIC, 2006.

Parallel Computing: From Multicores and GPU's to Petascale
B. Chapman et al. (Eds.)
IOS Press, 2010
© 2010 The authors and IOS Press. All rights reserved.
doi:10.3233/978-1-60750-530-3-59

Gradient projection methods for image deblurring and denoising on graphics processors

Thomas SERAFINI [1], Riccardo ZANELLA and Luca ZANNI

Department of Mathematics,
University of Modena and Reggio Emilia, Italy

Abstract. Optimization-based approaches for image deblurring and denoising on Graphics Processing Units (GPU) are considered. In particular, a new GPU implementation of a recent gradient projection method for edge-preserving removal of Poisson noise is presented. The speedups over standard CPU implementations are evaluated on both synthetic data and astronomical and medical imaging problems.

Keywords. Image deblurring, image denoising, gradient projection methods, graphics processing units

Introduction

Image deblurring and denoising have given rise to interesting optimization problems and stimulated fruitful advances in numerical optimization techniques. Nowadays several domains of applied science, such as medical imaging, microscopy and astronomy, involve large scale deblurring problems whose variational formulations lead to optimization problems with millions of variables that should be solved in a very short time. To face these challenging problems a lot of effort has been put into designing effective algorithms that have largely improved the classical optimization strategies usually applied in image processing. Nevertheless, in many large scale applications also these improved algorithms do not provide the expected reconstruction in a suited time. In these cases, the modern multiprocessor architectures represent an important resource for reducing the reconstruction time. Among these architectures we are considering the Graphics Processing Units (GPUs), that are non-expensive parallel processing devices available on many up-to-date personal computers. Originally developed for 3D graphics applications, GPUs have been employed in many other scientific computing areas, among which signal and image reconstruction [7,9]. Recent applications show that in many cases GPUs provide performance up to those of a medium-sized cluster, at a fraction of its cost. Thus, also the small laboratories, which cannot afford a cluster, can benefit from a substantial reduction of computing time compared to a standard CPU system. Here, we deal with the GPU implementation of an optimization algorithm, called Scaled Gradient Projection (SGP) method, that applies to several imaging problems [3,11]. A GPU version of

---

[1]Corresponding Author: Thomas Serafini, Department of Mathematics, University of Modena and Reggio Emilia, Via Campi 213/B, I-41100 Modena, Italy; E-mail: thomas.serafini@unimore.it.

Algorithm 1 Scaled Gradient Projection (SGP) Method

Choose the starting point $x^{(0)} \geq \eta$, set the parameters $\beta, \theta \in (0,1), 0 < \alpha_{min} < \alpha_{max}$ and fix a positive integer M.

FOR $k = 0, 1, 2, \dots$ DO THE FOLLOWING STEPS:

    STEP 1. Choose the parameter $\alpha_k \in [\alpha_{min}, \alpha_{max}]$ and the scaling matrix $D_k \in \mathcal{D}$;

    STEP 2. Projection: $y^{(k)} = P(x^{(k)} - \alpha_k D_k \nabla f(x^{(k)}))$;

    STEP 3. Descent direction: $\Delta x^{(k)} = y^{(k)} - x^{(k)}$;

    STEP 4. Set $\lambda_k = 1$ and $f_{max} = \displaystyle\max_{0 \leq j \leq \min(k, M-1)} f(x^{(k-j)})$;

    STEP 5. Backtracking loop:

           IF $f(x^{(k)} + \lambda_k \Delta x^{(k)}) \leq f_{max} + \beta \lambda_k \nabla f(x^{(k)})^T \Delta x^{(k)}$ THEN

                go to Step 6;

           ELSE

                set $\lambda_k = \theta \lambda_k$ and go to Step 5.

           ENDIF

    STEP 6. Set $x^{(k+1)} = x^{(k)} + \lambda_k \Delta x^{(k)}$.

END

---

this method has been recently evaluated in case of deblurring problems [9], while a new parallel implementation for facing denoising problems is presented in this work.

1. A scaled gradient projection method for constrained optimization

We briefly recall the SGP algorithm for solving the general problem

$$\min \quad f(x)$$
$$\text{sub. to} \quad x \geq \eta, \tag{1}$$

where $\eta \in \mathbb{R}$ is a constant and $f : \mathbb{R}^n \to \mathbb{R}$ is a continuously differentiable function, we need some basic notation. We denote by $\| \cdot \|$ the 2-norm of vectors and we define the projection operator onto the feasible region of the problem (1) as

$$P(x) = \arg\min_{y \geq \eta} \|y - x\|.$$

Furthermore, let $\mathcal{D}$ be the set of the $n \times n$ symmetric positive definite matrices D such that $\|D\| \leq L$ and $\|D^{-1}\| \leq L$, for a given threshold $L > 1$. The main SGP steps can be described as in Algorithm 1. At each SGP iteration the vector

$$y^{(k)} = P(x^{(k)} - \alpha_k D_k \nabla f(x^{(k)}))$$

is defined by combining a scaled steepest descent direction with a projection onto the feasible region; it is possible to prove that the resulting search direction $\Delta x^{(k)} = y^{(k)} - x^{(k)}$ is a descent direction for $f(x)$ in $x^{(k)}$, that is $\Delta x^{(k)^T} \nabla f(x^{(k)}) < 0$. The global convergence of the algorithm is obtained by means of the nonmonotone line-search procedure described in the Step 5, that implies $f(x^{(k+1)})$ lower than the reference value f_{max}. We observe that this line-search reduces to the standard monotone Armijo rule when $M = 1$ ($f_{max} = f(x^{(k)})$). In the following, we describe the choice of the steplength α_k and the scaling matrix D_k, while we refer to [3] for a convergence analysis of the method. It is worth to stress that any choice of the steplength $\alpha_k \in [\alpha_{min}, \alpha_{max}]$ and of the scaling matrix $D_k \in \mathcal{D}$ are allowed; then, this freedom of choice can be fruitfully exploited for introducing performance improvements. An effective selection strategy for the steplength parameter is obtained by adapting to the context of the scaling gradient methods the Barzilai-Borwein (BB) rules [1], widely used in standard non-scaled gradient methods. When the scaled direction $D_k \nabla f(x^{(k)})$ is exploited within a step of the form $(x^{(k)} - \alpha_k D_k \nabla f(x^{(k)}))$, the BB steplength rules become

$$\alpha_k^{(1)} = \frac{r^{(k-1)^T} D_k^{-1} D_k^{-1} r^{(k-1)}}{r^{(k-1)^T} D_k^{-1} z^{(k-1)}}, \quad \alpha_k^{(2)} = \frac{r^{(k-1)^T} D_k z^{(k-1)}}{z^{(k-1)^T} D_k D_k z^{(k-1)}},$$

where $r^{(k-1)} = x^{(k)} - x^{(k-1)}$ and $z^{(k-1)} = \nabla f(x^{(k)}) - \nabla f(x^{(k-1)})$. The recent literature on the steplength selection in gradient methods suggests to design steplength updating strategies by alternating the two BB rules. We recall the adaptive alternation strategy used in [3], that has given remarkable convergence rate improvements in many different applications. Given an initial value α_0, the steplengths α_k, $k = 1, 2, \ldots$, are defined by the following criterion:

IF $\alpha_k^{(2)} / \alpha_k^{(1)} \leq \tau_k$ THEN
$$\alpha_k = \min \left\{ \alpha_j^{(2)}, \ j = \max \left\{ 1, k - M_\alpha \right\}, \ldots, k \right\}; \qquad \tau_{k+1} = \tau_k * 0.9;$$
ELSE
$$\alpha_k = \alpha_k^{(1)}; \qquad \tau_{k+1} = \tau_k * 1.1;$$
ENDIF

where M_α is a prefixed non-negative integer and $\tau_1 \in (0, 1)$.

Concerning the choice of the scaling matrix D_k, a suited updating rule generally depends on the special form of the objective function and then we discuss this topic separately for image deblurring and denoising.

2. Optimization-based approaches for image deblurring and denoising

2.1. Image deblurring

It is well-known that the maximum likelihood approach to image deblurring in the case of Poisson noise gives an approximation of the image to be reconstructed by solving the following nonnegatively constrained minimization problem [2]:

$$\min \ \sum_{i=1}^{n} \left(\sum_{j=1}^{n} A_{ij} x_j + bg - b_i - b_i \ln \frac{\sum_{j=1}^{n} A_{ij} x_j + bg}{b_i} \right), \tag{2}$$
$$\text{sub. to} \ \ x \geq 0$$

where $b \in \mathbb{R}^n$ is the observed noisy image, $bg > 0$ denotes a constant background term and $A \in \mathbb{R}^{n \times n}$ is the blurring operator. Due to the ill-posedness of this convex problem, a regularized solution can be obtained by early stopping appropriate iterative minimization methods. Among these iterative schemes, the most popular is the Expectation Maximization (EM) method [10] that, under standard assumption on A, can be written as:

$$x^{(k+1)} = X_k A^T Y_k^{-1} b = x^{(k)} - X_k \nabla J(x^{(k)}), \qquad x^{(0)} > 0, \tag{3}$$

where $X_k = \text{diag}(x^{(k)})$ and $Y_k = \text{diag}(Ax^{(k)} + bg)$. The EM method is attractive because of its simplicity, the low computational cost per iteration and the ability to preserve the non-negativity of the iterates; however, it usually exhibits very slow convergence rate that highly limits its practical performance. When SGP is equipped with the scaling

$$D_k = \text{diag}\left(\min\left[L, \ \max\left\{\frac{1}{L}, \boldsymbol{x}^{(k)}\right\}\right]\right),$$

it can be viewed as a generalization of EM able to exploit variable steplengths for improving the convergence rate. The computational study reported in [3] shows that the fast convergence allows SGP to largely improve the EM computational time on the standard serial architectures. In Section 4.1 we report some numerical results showing that the same holds when these algorithms are implemented on GPU.

2.2. Image denoising

In order to develop a GPU implementation of SGP also for denoising problems, we follow the optimization-based approach recently proposed in [11] for the edge-preserving removal of Poisson noise. This approach consists in the minimization of a functional obtained by penalizing the Kullback-Leibler divergence by means of a special edge-preserving functional (we remark that for removing different kinds of noise, other approaches, simple and suited to parallelization, are also available [5]). Let $\boldsymbol{y} \in \mathbb{R}^n$ be the detected noisy image and x_i be the value associated to the i-th pixel of the image x; we denote by x_{i+} and x_{i-} the values associated to the pixels that are just below and above the i-th pixel, respectively; similarly, x_{i_+} and x_{i_-} denote the values associated to the pixels that are just after and before the i-th pixel, respectively. Then, an estimate of the noise-free image can be obtained by solving the problem

$$\min_{\text{sub. to } \ \boldsymbol{x} \geq \eta} F(\boldsymbol{x}) = \sum_{i=1}^n \left(x_i - y_i - y_i \ln \frac{x_i}{y_i}\right) + \tau \left(\frac{1}{2}\sum_{i=1}^n \psi_\delta\left(\Delta_i^2\right)\right), \tag{4}$$

where $\Delta_i^2 = (x_{i_+} - x_i)^2 + (x_{i+} - x_i)^2$ and $\psi_\delta(t) = 2\sqrt{t + \delta^2}$, δ being a small quantity tuning the discontinuities into the image, $\eta > 0$ is a small positive constant smaller than the background emission and $\tau > 0$ is a regularization parameter. In the feasible region the objective function of the problem (4) is continuously differentiable, thus the SGP method can be applied. In particular, following the gradient splitting idea presented in [6], a diagonal scaling matrix for SGP can be defined as

$$(D_k)_{i,i} = \min\left(L, \ \max\left[\frac{1}{L}, \frac{x_i^{(k)}}{1 + \tau V_i(\boldsymbol{x}^{(k)})}\right]\right), \tag{5}$$

where $V_i(\boldsymbol{x}^{(k)}) = \left\{2\psi_\delta'(\Delta_i^2) + \psi_\delta'(\Delta_{i_-}^2) + \psi_\delta'(\Delta_{i-}^2)\right\} x_i^{(k)}$.

In the numerical experiments described in [11], the SGP equipped with the scaling matrix (5) largely outperformed other popular gradient approaches in terms of reconstruction time. Here we propose a GPU implementation of SGP and we evaluate its performance on a simulated test problem and on a denoising problem arising in medical imaging.

3. A GPU implementation of the SGP algorithm

Our GPU implementation is developed on NVIDIA graphics adapters using the CUDA (Compute Unified Device Architecture) framework for programming their GPUs [8]. By means of CUDA it is possible to program a GPU using a C-like programming language. A CUDA program contains instructions both for the CPU and the GPU. The CPU controls the instruction flow, the communications with the peripherals and it starts the single computing tasks on the GPU. The GPU performs the raw computation tasks, using the problem data stored into the graphics memory. The GPU core is highly parallel: it is composed by a number of streaming multiprocessors, which depend on the graphics adapter model. Each streaming multiprocessor is composed by 8 cores, a high speed ram memory block, shared among the 8 cores and a cache. All the streaming multiprocessors can access to a global main memory where, typically, the problem data are stored. For our numerical experiments we used CUDA 2.0 [8] and a NVIDIA GTX 280 graphics card, which has 30 streaming multiprocessors (240 total cores) running at 1296 MHz. The total amount of global memory is 1GB and the connection bus with the cores has a bandwidth of 141.7 GB/sec. The peak computing performance is 933 GFLOPS/sec. The GPU is connected to the CPU with a PCI-Express bus, which grants a 8GB/sec transfer rate. It should be noted that this speed is much slower than the GPU-to-GPU transfer so, for exploiting the GPU performances, it is very important to reduce the CPU-GPU memory communications and keep all the problem data on the GPU memory. Besides, the full GPU-to-GPU bandwidth can be obtained only if a coalesced memory access scheme (see NVIDIA documentation [8]) is used; so, all our GPU computation kernels are implemented using that memory pattern. For the implementation of SGP, two kernel libraries of CUDA are very important: the CUFFT for the FFT computations required by the deblurring application and the CUBLAS for exploiting the main BLAS subroutines. The use of these libraries is highly recommended for maximizing the GPU performances. For the image deblurring problem, the main computational block in the SGP iteration consists in a pair of forward and backward FFTs for computing the image convolutions. We face these task as follows: after computing a 2-D real-to-complex transform, the spectral multiplication between the transformed iterate and PSF is carried out and the 2-D inverse complex-to-real transform is computed. For the image denoising problem, one of the most expensive task is the computation of the regularization term in (4). In the C implementation, the ghost cell technique is used for computing more efficiently the regularizer: according to this technique, the computational domain is extended by adding null cells on the borders. In this way, all the corner and border points can be treated as if they were interior points: this ensures a more regular instruction flow on a standard CPU. On a GPU this approach can add a computational penalty: in fact, working with a regularizer which have a domain size different than the image size, leads to a memory unalignment, and the memory accesses may not be coalesced. Bad memory accesses yield a performance loss much greater than the introduction of conditional instructions into the GPU kernels, for checking if each point is a border or a corner point; then, as usually done on a GPU, we prefer to add more cpu cycles for optimizing memory accesses. Both the deblurring and denoising cases need a division and a logarithm computation for each pixel in the image. These tasks are particularly suited for a GPU implementation: in fact there is no dependency among the pixels and the computation can be distributed on all the scalar processors available on the GPU. Besides, divisions and logarithms require a higher number of clock cycles than a simple floating point operation, thus the GPU memory bandwidth is not a limitation for these operations. Finally, we must discuss a critical part involved by the SGP: the scalar products for updating the steplength. The "reduction" operation necessary to compute a scalar product implies a high number of communications among the processors and there are dependencies that prevent a straight parallelization. In [4], NVIDIA reports an analysis of 7 different strategies for computing a reduction and suggests which is the best one for a high volume of data. In our experiments, the CUBLAS function for scalar product (cublasSdot) generally achieves the best

Original image   Blurred noisy image   Reconstructed image

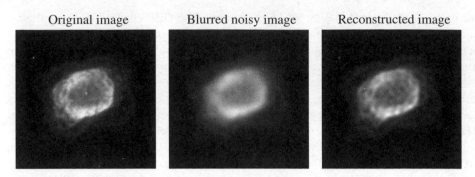

Figure 1. Image for the deblurring test problem.

performance and then we exploit the kernel libraries provided by NVIDIA also for this task. Apart from the above analysis on the reduction operation, the GPU development of SGP has not required particular coding techniques since the main computational tasks of the algorithm are well suited to the architectural features of a GPU.

4. Computational results

We show the practical behaviour of the GPU implementation of SGP on the considered deblurring and denoising problems. We evaluate the speedups provided by the GPU implementations in comparison to a standard CPU implementation of the algorithm written in C. The test platform consists in a personal computer equipped with an AMD Athlon X2 Dual-Core at 3.11GHz, 3GB of RAM and the graphics processing unit NVIDIA GTX 280 described in the previous section; the codes are developed within the Microsoft Visual Studio 2005 environment. Double precision is used in the CPU version of SGP, while the mixed C and CUDA implementation exploits the single precision. The SGP parameter settings are as described in the computational study reported in [3] and [11]; in particular, the monotone version of SGP ($M = 1$) is used.

4.1. Numerical results for deblurring problems

A deblurring test problem is obtained by considering an astronomical image corrupted by Poisson noise: the original image of the nebula NGC5979 sized 256×256 is convolved with an ideal PSF, then a constant background term is added and the resulting image is perturbed with Poisson noise. The original image, the blurred noisy image and a reconstruction obtained by solving the problem (2) with SGP are shown in Figure 1. Test problems of larger size are generated by expanding the original images and the PSF by means of a zero-padding technique on their FFTs. For both the SGP and EM methods, we evaluate the relative reconstruction error, defined as $\|x^{(k)} - x\|/\|x\|$, where x is the image to be reconstructed and $x^{(k)}$ is the reconstruction after k iterations; then we report the minimum relative reconstruction error (err.), the number of iterations (it.) and the computational time in seconds (time) required to provide the minimum error. The results in Table 1 show that the GPU implementations allow us to save time over the CPU implementation for more than one order of magnitude. Furthermore, SGP largely outperforms EM also on graphics processors, even if the additional operations required in each SGP iteration (in particular the scalar products involved in the steplength selection) make this algorithm less suited than EM for a parallel implementation on GPU. We

Table 1. Behaviour of EM and SGP on deblurring problems

	SGP (it. = 29)				EM (it. = 500)				
	CPU (C-based)		GPU (C_CUDA-based)			CPU (C-based)		GPU (C_CUDA-based)		
n	err.	time	err.	time	Speedup	err.	time	err.	time	Speedup
256^2	0.070	0.72	0.071	0.05	14.7	0.070	4.41	0.071	0.19	23.2
512^2	0.065	2.69	0.065	0.16	16.8	0.064	19.91	0.064	0.89	22.4
1024^2	0.064	10.66	0.064	0.58	18.4	0.063	97.92	0.063	3.63	27.0
2048^2	0.064	49.81	0.063	2.69	18.5	0.063	523.03	0.063	23.05	22.7

Table 2. Behaviour of SGP on denoising problems.

		CPU (C-based)			GPU (C_CUDA-based)			
Test problem	n	it.	err.	time	it.	err.	time	Speedup
	256^2	83	0.025	1.27	79	0.025	0.06	21.2
Phantom	512^2	97	0.018	5.89	73	0.018	0.16	36.8
	1024^2	60	0.015	15.13	85	0.014	0.53	28.5
	2048^2	62	0.012	64.45	87	0.011	1.88	34.3
Dental radiography	512^2	28	0.020	1.86	25	0.029	0.06	31.0

refer to [3] for more details on the comparison between EM, SGP and other well known deblurring methods; furthermore, other examples of deblurring problems solved by the GPU implementation of SGP can be found in [9].

4.2. Numerical results for denoising problems

Two denoising test problems are considered: the former is generated from the phantom described in [11], consisting in circles of intensities 70, 135 and 200, enclosed by a square frame of intensity 10, all on a background of intensity 5; the latter is derived from a dental radiography (gray levels between 3 and 64). The corresponding images corrupted by Poisson noise are shown in Figure 2, together with the original images and the reconstructions obtained by applying SGP to the problem (4) with $\eta = 10^{-3}$. The reconstructions are obtained by a careful tuning of the parameters τ and δ: the values $\tau = 0.25$, $\delta = 0.1$ for the phantom image and $\tau = 0.3$, $\delta = 1$ for the dental radiography are used. The SGP behaviour on both CPU and GPU is described in Table 2. Here the number of iterations refers to the number of SGP steps required to satisfy the criterion $|F(x^k) - F(x^{k-1})| \leq 10^{-6}|F(x^k)|$; the differences between the CPU and GPU iterations are due to the different precision and organization of the computations used in the two environments. However, it is important to observe that the relative reconstruction errors are very similar on the two architectures. The speedups are significantly better than in the case of the deblurring problems since now the computation of the denoising objective function and of its gradient are dominated by simple pixel-by-pixel operations (no image convolutions are required) that are well suited for an effective implementation on the graphics hardware.

5. Conclusions

GPU implementations of a gradient projection method for image deblurring and denoising have been discussed. For both the imaging problems a time saving of more than one order of magnitude over standard CPU implementations has been observed. In particular, the GPU implementation presented in this work for denoising problems achieves very

Original images   Noisy images   Reconstructed images

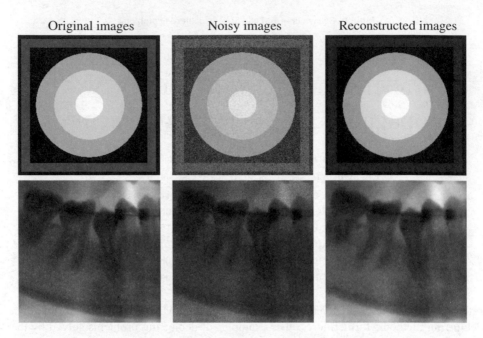

Figure 2. Images for the denoising test problems.

promising speedups and confirms that the considered optimization-based approaches are well suited for facing large imaging problems on graphics processors. Work is in progress about the extension of the proposed algorithms and their GPU implementations to related optimization problems in signal and image restoration (compressed sensing, blind deconvolution, multiple image restoration).

References

[1]   J. Barzilai, J. M. Borwein: Two point step size gradient methods, IMA J. Num. Anal. 8, 141–148, 1988.

[2]   M. Bertero, P. Boccacci: Introduction to Inverse Problems in Imaging. IoP Publishing, Bristol (1998)

[3]   S. Bonettini, R. Zanella, L. Zanni: A scaled gradient projection method for constrained image deblurring, Inverse Problems 25, 015002, 2009.

[4]   M. Harris: Optimizing parallel reduction in CUDA. NVidia Tech. Rep. (2007). Available: http://developer.download.nvidia.com/compute/cuda/1_1/Website/projects/reduction/doc/reduction.pdf

[5]   O. Kao: Modification of the LULU Operators for Preservation of Critical Image Details, International Conference on Imaging Science, Systems and Technology, Las Vegas, 2001.

[6]   H. Lanteri, M. Roche, C. Aime: Penalized maximum likelihood image restoration with positivity constraints: multiplicative algorithms, Inverse Problems 18, 1397–1419, 2002.

[7]   S. Lee, S.J. Wright: Implementing algorithms for signal and image reconstruction on graphical processing units. Submitted (2008). Available: http://pages.cs.wisc.edu/ swright/GPUreconstruction/.

[8]   NVIDIA: NVIDIA CUDA Compute Unified Device Architecture, Programming Guide. Version 2.0 (2008). Available at: http://developer.download.nvidia.com/compute/cuda/2_0/docs/NVIDIA_CUDA_ Programming_Guide_2.0.pdf

[9]   V. Ruggiero, T. Serafini, R. Zanella, L. Zanni: Iterative regularization algorithms for constrained image deblurring on graphics processors. J. Global Optim., to appear, 2009. Available: http://cdm.unimo.it/home/matematica/zanni.luca/ .

[10] L. A. Shepp, Y. Vardi: Maximum likelihood reconstruction for emission tomography, IEEE Trans. Med. Imaging 1, 113–122, 1982.

[11] R. Zanella, P. Boccacci, L. Zanni, M. Bertero: Efficient gradient projection methods for edge-preserving removal of Poisson noise. Inverse Problems 25, 045010, 2009.

Parallel Computing: From Multicores and GPU's to Petascale
B. Chapman et al. (Eds.)
IOS Press, 2010
© 2010 The authors and IOS Press. All rights reserved.
doi:10.3233/978-1-60750-530-3-67

Parallel simulations of seismic wave propagation on NUMA architectures

Fabrice DUPROS [a,1], Christiane POUSA RIBEIRO [b], Alexandre CARISSIMI [c] and
Jean-François MÉHAUT [b]

[a] *BRGM, BP 6009, 45060 Orléans Cedex 2, France*
[b] *LIG, Grenoble, France*
[c] *UFRGS, Porto Alegre, Brazil*

Abstract. Simulation of large scale seismic wave propagation is an important
tool in seismology for efficient strong motion analysis and risk mitigation. Being
particularly CPU-consuming, this three-dimensional problem makes use of parallel computing to improve the performance and the accuracy of the simulations.
The trend in parallel computing is to increase the number of cores available at
the shared-memory level with possible non-uniform cost of memory accesses. We
therefore need to consider new approaches more suitable to such parallel systems.
In this paper, we firstly report on the impact of memory affinity on the parallel performance of seismic simulations. We introduce a methodology combining efficient
thread scheduling and careful data placement to overcome the limitation coming
from both the parallel algorithm and the memory hierarchy. The MAi (Memory
Affinity interface) is used to smoothly adapt the memory policy to the underlying architecture. We evaluate our methodology on computing nodes with different
NUMA characteristics. A maximum gain of 53% is reported in comparison with a
classical OpenMP implementation.

Keywords. seismic wave propagation, NUMA, multicore architecture

1. Introduction

One of the most widely used techniques for the numerical simulation of seismic wave
propagation is the finite-difference method because of its simplicity and numerical efficiency. A review can be found for instance in [1]. Recent advances in high-performance
computing make realistic three-dimensional simulations feasible at large scale. Most of
the parallel implementations routinely used in the scientific community are based on
cluster architectures and rely on the MPI library. The increasing number of cores per
processor and the effort made to overcome the limitation of classical symmetric multiprocessors (SMP) systems make available a growing number of NUMA (Non Uniform
Memory Access) architecture as computing node. However, the different memory levels
in these NUMA nodes lead to differences between the access times to local and remote
memories. Thus, the degradation of the performance of parallel applications could be
severe depending not only on the hardware but also on the characteristics of the prob-

---

[1]Corresponding Author: BRGM, BP 6009, 45060 Orléans Cedex 2, France; E-mail: f.dupros@brgm.fr.

lem under study (i.e. data access pattern, potential cache effects, memory consumption) [2,3]. We therefore need to consider efficient thread scheduling and memory mapping on such hierarchical architectures. In [4] a methodology based on intensive multithreading for parallel simulation of seismic wave propagation has been introduced. This strategy takes full advantage of the shared-memory at the node level and outperforms classical MPI implementation limited by the load imbalance between the distributed subdomains of the three-dimensional problem. The efficiency of this approach relies on domain over-loading and self-scheduling algorithm at the thread level to handle without significant overhead, more than a thousand threads on a computing node with 16 cores for example. The PM2 software package is used at this level providing an efficient user-level thread library (Marcel threads) described in [5]. In this study, we consider the impact of hierar-chical architectures on this algorithm. In a first part, we propose a detailed evaluation of the NUMA factor[2] with classical OpenMP approach or explicit Marcel threads program-ming. The MAi (Memory Affinity interface) library ([6]) allows us to smoothly change the Linux first-touch memory allocation strategy for our application and we therefore report on the benefits on the parallel performance. The document is organized as follows : Section 2 introduces the numerical problem under study and classical strategy for its implementation on parallel architectures. We underline the load-balancing bottlenecks and briefly recall the impact of the algorithms introduced in [4] on the memory access pattern. Section 3 gives an overview of related works on memory mapping on hierar-chical architectures. We therefore introduces the MAi software package and the associ-ated mechanisms. In sections 4 and 5 we describe the parallel architectures used for the experiments and we analyze the results.

2. Numerical modeling of seismic wave propagation

2.1. Governing equations

The seismic wave equation in the case of an elastic material is:

$$\rho \frac{\partial v_i}{\partial t} = \frac{\partial \sigma_{ij}}{\partial j} + F_i \tag{1}$$

and the constitutive relation in the case of a isotropic medium is:

$$\frac{\partial \sigma_{ij}}{\partial t} = \lambda \delta_{ij} \left(\frac{\partial v_x}{\partial x} + \frac{\partial v_y}{\partial y} + \frac{\partial v_z}{\partial z} \right) + \mu \left(\frac{\partial v_i}{\partial j} + \frac{\partial v_j}{\partial i} \right) \tag{2}$$

where indices i, j, k represent a component of a vector or tensor field in Cartesian co-ordinates (x, y, z), v_i and σ_{ij} represent the velocity and stress field respectively, and F_i denotes an external source force. ρ is the material density and λ and μ are the elastic coefficients known as Lamé parameters.

A time derivative is denoted by $\frac{\partial}{\partial t}$ and a spatial derivative with respect to the i-th di-rection is represented by $\frac{\partial}{\partial i}$. The Kronecker symbol δ_{ij} is equal to 1 if $i = j$ and zero otherwise. A scheme that is fourth-order accurate in space and second-order in time is used to discretize the equations. Another requirement in the case of unbounded physical

---

[2]NUMA factor is the ratio between latency on remote memory access and latency on local memory access

domain is the definition of a finite computational domain with artificial conditions to absorb the outgoing energy. Several approaches are available. We select the Convolutional Perfectly Matched Layer (CPML) [7] which is an improvement of the PML method .A common feature of these formulations is to introduce different computational loads in the computing domain, especially at the lateral and bottom edges of the three-dimensional geometry. A fixed size of ten grid points is chosen for the thickness of this layer.

2.2. Computational flowchart and Parallel implementation

The implementation of the numerical method described in the previous section leads to a computational flowchart with two phases described in Figure 2. The first part includes the

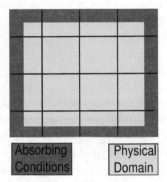

Figure 1. Top view of the computational domain. A Cartesian-based decomposition is represented

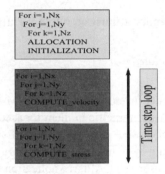

Figure 2. Computational flowchart of a classical seismic wave propagation simulation based on finite-differences method.

allocation and the initialization of the three-dimensional arrays used for the computation. The second part of the implementation is the time dependent loop with successive update of the stress and velocity components. A classical strategy for the parallelization of this simulation relies on MPI library and a Cartesian-based decomposition [8] as observed on Figure 1. Unfortunately this approach leads to an imbalance partitioning as the workload between the physical domain and the absorbing boundary condition layer is rather different (typically a ratio of three is observed). Even a quasi-static methodology could hardly solve this problem, especially with a large number of cores. In [4] we have introduced an algorithm to alleviate this drawback by using a hybrid decomposition (MPI+thread) with massive multithreading and self-scheduling at the shared-memory level. One of the main differences with classical hybrid approaches, for example using OpenMP, is coming from the memory access pattern that is dramatically changed between the initialization and the computational phase.

2.3. Memory access pattern

Many scientific applications on NUMA architecture are built under the assumption of using a parallel initialization (each thread allocates and initializes data corresponding to its own subdomain) in order to place the data close to the computing threads and then rely on threads binding to force the affinity [9]. Considering OpenMP implementation, some applications simply assume that the library will automatically replay the same mapping during initialization and computation phases, this could be wrong depending on the implementation used or the operating system running on the computer. Unfortunately, the introduction of a dynamic thread scheduling for the application breaks the relation between the allocation and the computation phase and makes the previously described strategy inefficient. This dynamical workload sharing could be mandatory to maximize the parallel performance, this is the case for our application. The use of the dynamic loop scheduling feature of OpenMP or the intensive multithreading implementation with Marcel threads library make impossible any bind of threads and underlines the importance of the choice of the memory mapping policy.

3. Memory affinity on NUMA Platforms

3.1. Related works

Managing memory affinity in NUMA platforms is an important issue due to the factor NUMA (asymmetric in memory access costs) of this platforms. In the last years, many researches were done in this field for different NUMA platforms [2]. Regarding Linux operating system, most solutions are proposals of new memory policies in kernel/user space, user-level APIs (Application Programming Interface) and tools [10,11,12]. In Linux operating system the default memory policy used to obtain a good memory placement is *first-touch*. This memory policy allocates a memory page in the node that first caused the page-fault. *First-touch* presents great performance results in parallel applications with regular memory access patterns. In these applications, a parallel data initialization allows *first-touch* to place threads and data in the same node. However, in applications with irregular memory access patterns, *first-touch* can not assure affinity since it does not perform any page migration [10,11]. *Next-touch* is another memory policy that can be used on Linux based NUMA platforms. This memory policy is not a integral part in such operating system but, some implementation proposals were already presented. In this memory policy, data migration is allowed when threads touch memory pages, that are not local for them, in future time. *Next-touch* showed great performance gains with highly-dynamic applications, as presented in [10,11]. However, the migration overheads can sometimes be higher than the gains obtained with such policy. NUMA API is a user-level solution for memory affinity on cache-coherent NUMA (ccNUMA) platforms. This solution is composed of different sub components: system calls, library and a command line tool. The system calls approach allow programmers to manage memory affinity using low level functions to control placement of memory pages and threads. The second approach is an interface called *libnuma* that is composed of high level functions. In such interface, there are only two sets of memory policies and the shared library *libnuma* must be linked with applications. The last approach is a command line tool called *numactl*. This tool allows users to set a memory policy for a whole process without modifications to the application source code [12].

3.2. MAi Library

The solutions presented in the last section have showed different ways to manage memory affinity in Linux ccNUMA platforms, introducing important ideas and results. However, they do not be used systematically in Linux operating system and do not allow the use of different memory policies in the same application. Another problem is that they do not have a fine affinity control of application variables (considering access patterns). MAi[3] is a user-level API to manage memory affinity on Linux ccNUMA platforms. It lessens memory affinity management issues, since it provides the developer with simple and high level functions to optimize bandwidth and latency. MAi allows the use of different policies in different phases of the application. Furthermore, with MAi, developers can set memory policies for each variable of an application. Due to this, memory management is easier for developers, since they do not have to care about pointers and page addresses. The library has three sets of memory policies, bind, random and cyclic. In bind policies, memory pages are placed in memory banks specified by the developer. These memory policies try to optimize latency, since data and threads are placed closer as possible. The second set of memory policies places memory pages randomly across memory banks of the ccNUMA platform. In cyclic policies, the memory pages are placed following a round-robin strategy. The random and cyclic policies optimize bandwidth of ccNUMA platforms (the main goal in Opteron machines). In MAi there are two cyclic policies, *cyclic* and *cyclic_block*. In *cyclic* memory policy, memory pages are spread in th memory banks in a round-robin fashion. The granularity used in this policy is a memory page. A page i is allocated in the memory bank $i \bmod N$, where N is the total number of memory banks. Whereas in *cyclic_block*, although the same placement strategy is used, the granularity is a block of memory pages. The block size is defined by the developer (number of rows or columns) and must be power of two.

4. Results

4.1. Experimental platforms and methodology

The target architecture is based on AMD Opteron dual core processors with 2 MB of cache memory for each processor. It is organized in eight NUMA nodes corresponding to the eight processors with a total 32 GB of main memory (4 GB of memory per node) and the system page size is 4 KB. Each node has three connections with other nodes or with input/output controllers (NUMA factor between 1.2 and 1.5). Figure 3 gives an overview of the experimental platform. In order to illustrate the imbalance effects on the parallel performance, we have also used a bi-quadcore system based on Intel Xeon processor. This machine (phoebus) exhibits no memory hierarchy. Three different memory policies have been considered for our experiments. In the first case, we rely on the default first-touch policy of Linux operating system with no control over the mapping of the allocated memory over the NUMA nodes. The second case corresponds to the explicit binding of threads during memory allocation and computation. Finally, MAi cyclic memory policy is considered. Preliminary experiments have demonstrated better results for cyclic policy rather than cyclic_block on Opteron architecture. We have selected two different sizes

---

[3]MAi can be download from http://mai.gforge.inria.fr/

of problem. The first problem size is 2.6 GB and it is based on a computational domain of 14 millions of grid points (grid_2.6). The second example is based on a much larger mesh (110 millions of grid points) and the memory usage is 18 GB (grid_18). This allows us to evaluate the effect of our strategy for problems size at the numa node level or at the machine level.

4.2. Numerical experiments

As described in the previous sections, the application under study is unbalanced and part of the final gain will come from the improvement of this aspect. As a first set of experiments, we have modified our 3D finite differences code to suppress the imbalance. In this

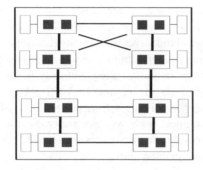

Figure 3. Idkoiff NUMA architecture.

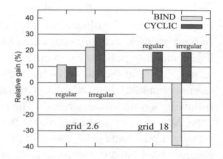

Figure 4. Different memory policies with OpenMP implementation - The first-touch default policy is used as reference - <u>Balanced situation</u>

case we only evaluate the impact of the memory hierarchy regarding the parallelization strategy. Figure 4 presents the results using OpenMP implementation with static (regular memory access) or dynamic (irregular memory access) worksharing. Bind and cyclic memory policies are compared with the default first-touch Linux policy. If we consider the smallest example, we observe a gain in all cases with a maximum of 31%. The cyclic policy is more efficient for irregular memory accesses than the bind policy, whereas the results are quite similar for regular pattern. Considering the dynamic thread scheduling, the scattering of the memory pages in a cyclic way allows us to maximize the usage of the bandwidth. For the grid_18 example, we are close to saturate the memory available on Idkoiff machine and the memory usage involves several NUMA nodes. The maximum gain is lower (18%) as the first-touch policy places the memory on almost all the nodes. As the size of the problem is increased, optimizations of the memory mapping is more critical and the difference between the results obtained with the bind or the cyclic policy is more significant. We observe a ratio of more than a factor two between these two strategies for irregular pattern. The regular memory access results underline the impact of the optimization of bandwidth on Opteron processors. The situation could be rather different on Itanium-based NUMA machine on which latency in crucial to consider. In the case of irregular pattern, the bind policy is particularly inefficient as we maximize accesses of all computing threads on the same NUMA node. This is coming from the static initial distribution of the variables across the memory blocks and from the Opteron architecture more efficient when data are scattered. We have performed the same experiments with the PM2 implementation and intensive multithreading, we have observed an

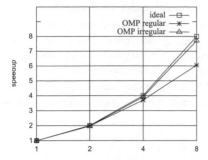
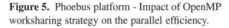

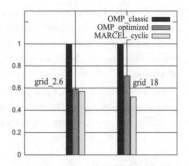

Figure 5. Phoebus platform - Impact of OpenMP worksharing strategy on the parallel efficiency.

Figure 6. Idkoiff platform - Impact of the memory policy with different multithreading strategies - Complete modeling.

average gain of 30% for both examples with cyclic memory policy. We now consider the complete version of our code with the absorbing conditions responsible for the imbalance. On phoebus platform, we have run the grid_18 example to illustrate the effects of the boundary conditions on the parallel scalability (figure 5). Using 8 processors, the maximum speedup is 6.06 for the naive implementation whereas we reach respectively 7.71 and 7.82 for OpenMP dynamic implementation and the PM2 version. Figure 6 summarizes the results for the complete simulation on Idkoiff NUMA platform. OMP_classic denotes the naive implementation without any optimizations. OMP_optimized version combine MAI cyclic policy and dynamic worksharing. Marcel_cyclic implementation is based on PM2/marcel lightweight threads and cyclic memory policy. At this level we hope to combine the gain from the load balancing improvement and from the numa-aware memory allocation. For both test case, the PM2 version outperforms the OpenMP implementation. The difference is more impressive for the grid_18 test case as we increase the number of numa-miss. First of all the marcel threads library provides very good performance in terms of thread management in comparison with OpenMP library. We use more than a thousand threads on sixteen cores without significant overhead. The dynamicity is also higher with PM2 implementation as we can divide the 3D domain of computation into tiny 2D or 3D blocks. The OpenMP parallelization is only applied on the external dimension of the nested loop leading to 2D slices. Finally we have also benefit from cache effects coming from the very small size of the subdomains. We have evaluated this improvement between 5% and 10% of the initial elapsed time.

5. Conclusion and future works

In this paper we have underlined the impact of memory hierarchy on finite differences simulation of seismic wave propagation. Considering static memory access pattern classical memory policies provide rather good results and OpenMP parallel implementation could be efficient. Advanced implementations designed to tackle load-balancing problems or to enhance data-locality lead to a dynamic memory access pattern and new strategies are therefore required to maximize the parallel performance on NUMA architecture. We have demonstrated the efficiency of our approach combining MAI library for the flexibility in the choice of the memory policy and massive multithreading with PM2 threads library. This allows us to obtain a speedup of 53% over a naive OpenMP implementation. We have also underlined the limitation of advanced OpenMP implementation in terms flexibility and extraction of the parallelism of the application. We intend to investigate the possibility to use MAI as a preprocessor and simply identify in the code the significant variables in terms of size and access frequency. Another direction is to consider the timespace implementation [13] of the finite differences time domain algorithm and explore the advantages of using the methodology described in this paper as the algorithm is therefore much more imbalanced and irregular.

Acknowledgements

This research was supported in part by the French ANR under grant NUMASIS ANR-05-CIGC, CAPES under grant number 4874-06-4 and INRIA Associate Teams - DIODE. We acknowledge the Computing Center of Region Centre (CCSC) for providing us access to the Phoebus computing system.

References

[1]   P. Moczo, J. Robertsson, and L. Eisner, "The finite-difference time-domain method for modeling of seismic wave propagation," in *Advances in Wave Propagation in Heterogeneous Media*, ser. Advances in Geophysics.   Elsevier - Academic Press, 2007, vol. 48, ch. 8, pp. 421–516.

[2]   J. Antony, P. P. Janes, and A. P. Rendell, "Exploring Thread and Memory Placement on NUMA Architectures: Solaris and Linux, UltraSPARC/FirePlane and Opteron/HyperTransport," in *Proceedings of HiPC 2006*, Bangalore, India, pp. 338–352.

[3]   M. Castro, L. G. Fernandes, C. Pousa, J.-F. Méhaut, and M. S. de Aguiar, "NUMA-ICTM: A Parallel Version of ICTM Exploiting Memory Placement Strategies for NUMA Machines," in *Proceedings of the 23rd IEEE International Parallel and Distributed Processing Symposium - PDSEC '09 (to appear)*, Rome, Italy, 2009.

[4]   F. Dupros, H. Aochi, A. Ducellier, D. Komatitsch, and J. Roman, "Exploiting Intensive Multithreading for the Efficient Simulation of 3D Seismic Wave Propagation," in *Proceedings of the 11th IEEE International Conference on Computational Science and Engineering*, Sao Paolo, Brazil, 2008, pp. 253–260.

[5]   R. Namyst and J.-F. Méhaut, "PM2: Parallel multithreaded machine. a multithreaded environment on top of PVM," in *Proceedings of the 2nd Euro PVM Users' Group Meeting*, Lyon, France, 1995, pp. 179–184.

[6]   C. Pousa and J.-F. Méhaut, "MAI: Memory Affinity Interface," INRIA, Tech. Rep. RR-5191, Dec. 2008.

[7]   D. Komatitsch and R. Martin, "An unsplit convolutional Perfectly Matched Layer improved at grazing incidence for the seismic wave equation," *Geophysics*, vol. 72, no. 5, pp. SM155–SM167, 2007.

[8]   M. Chavez, E. Cabrera, R. Madariaga, N. Perea, C. Moulinec, D. Emerson, M. Ashworth, and A. Salazar, "Benchmark Study of a 3D Parallel Code for the Propagation of Large Subduction Earthquakes," in *Proceedings of the 15th Euro PVM/MPI Users' Group Meeting*, Dublin, Ireland, 2008, pp. 303–310.

[9]   M. Faverge and P. Ramet, "Dynamic Scheduling for sparse direct Solver on NUMA architectures," in *Proceedings of PARA'2008*, Trondheim, Norway, 2008.

[10] C. Terboven, D. A. Mey, D. Schmidl, H. Jin, and T. Reichstein, "Data and Thread affinity in OpenMP programs," in *Proceedings of the 2008 workshop on Memory access on future processors*, Ischia, Italy, pp. 377–384.

[11] B. Goglin and N. Furmento, "Enabling High-Performance Memory Migration for Multithreaded Applications on Linux," in *Proceedings of the 23rd IEEE International Parallel and Distributed Processing Symposium - MTAAP'09 (to appear)*, Rome, Italy, 2009.

[12] A. Kleen, "A NUMA API for Linux," Tech. Rep. Novell-4621437, April 2005.

[13] K. Datta, S. Kamil, S. Williams, L. Oliker, J. Shalf, and K. Yelick, "Optimization and performance modeling of stencil computations on modern microprocessors," *SIAM Review*, vol. 51, no. 1, pp. 129–159, 2009.

Parallel Computing: From Multicores and GPU's to Petascale
B. Chapman et al. (Eds.)
IOS Press, 2010
© 2010 The authors and IOS Press. All rights reserved.
doi:10.3233/978-1-60750-530-3-75

Aitken-Schwarz and Schur complement methods for time domain decomposition

Patrice LINEL [a] and Damien TROMEUR-DERVOUT [a]

[a] *Université de Lyon, Université Lyon1, CNRS, Institut Camille Jordan,*
43 Bd du 11 Novembre 1918, F-69622 Villeurbanne Cedex

Abstract. New parallel methods, based on the Schwarz and Schur domain decomposition technique, are proposed for time domain decomposition of Cauchy problem. Firstly, the initial value problem is transformed in a time boundary values problem. Then the demonstration of the pure linear divergence/convergence of the Schwarz algorithm, applied to systems of linear ODE, allows us to accelerate the convergence of the solution at the time slices boundaries with the Aitken's acceleration technique of the convergence. Secondly, a Schur complement method is developed for linear problem. Numerical results show the efficiency of the proposed method on the linear system of ODEs modeling the harmonic oscillator problem.

Keywords. Schwarz Domain Decomposition, reversible time integration, Aitken's acceleration of convergence, parallel method, Schur complement

1. Introduction

As the domain decomposition in space is often limited by the practical size of the computational domain, the time domain decomposition is becoming an issue to obtain parallelism with the development of computing capacities with several thousand of processors/cores. This paper focuses only on the time domain decomposition for system of ordinary differential equations. The benefits of parallelism in space usually present in the space discrete scheme of partial differential equations is not available for ODE. The development of a parallel method to solve ODE or DAE is a challenging problem because usual time integrators are sequential (i.e. the solution at the previous time steps are required in the time advancing scheme). The proposed methodology is based on domain decomposition into slices of the the time interval. Then the problem is tried to be solve in parallel on each time slice with imposed transmission conditions (Schwarz iterative) or matching conditions (Schur complement method) at the boundaries of time slices.

Related works in time domain decomposition have been done with the Parareal algorithm [1] or Pita algorithm [2], where a coarse time grid is used to correct the fine time grid solution. For Pita, the linearized correction problem on the coarse grid is more stiff than the original problem and is computationally more expansive for the time integrator. In Parareal, for stiff problems the constraint on the time step for the coarse time integrators limits the parallelism gain. The PAWSAR algorithm [3] is the first attempt to solve time dependent heat equation in parallel. Several time steps are solved in parallel by integrating in space with an Aitken-Schwarz domain decomposition method. This time and space domain decomposition is mainly a space domain decomposition, as the time stepping is windowing with several time steps.

In this paper, only ODE or DAE are under consideration, so no advantage with the space decomposition is available. Let us consider the Cauchy problem for the first order ODE $\{\dot{y} = f(t, y(t)), \; t \in [0, T], \; y(0) = \alpha_0 \in \mathbb{R}^d$. The time interval $[0, T]$ is split into p time slices $S_i = [T_{i-1}^+, T_i^-]$, with $T_0 = 0$ and $T_p = T$. The goal is to break the sequentiality of the time integration process present in the numerical time integrators. The difficulty is to match the solutions $y_i(t)$ defined on S_i at the boundaries T_{i-1}^+ and T_i^-. Most of time domain decomposition are shooting methods where the jump $y_i(T_i^-) - y_{i+1}(T_i^+)$ is corrected by a Newton method with a sequential propagation of the corrections. The no knowledge of the solution at the final time T does not allow to link these corrections. Under some hypothesis on the flow $f(t, y(t))$, the proposed approach consists to transform the initial value problem (IVP) into a boundary values problem (BVP). The problem is symmetrized in order to have well defined boundary conditions. The ρ-reversibility property of partitioned systems justifies the reversible integration with symmetric schemes on the time symmetric part of the problem. We show how to build explicitly the block tri-diagonal system satisfy by the boundary conditions of the time slices for linear system of ODE solved by the explicit Störmer-Verlet scheme.

2. Transformation of IVP to BVP on a symmetric time interval

Let $f(t, y(t))$ be derivable in t, the IVP with a system of first order ODE is transformed into a BVP with a system of second order ODE.

$$\begin{cases} \ddot{y}(t) = g(t, y(t)) \stackrel{def}{=} \dfrac{\partial f}{\partial t}(t, y) + f(t, y(t)) \dfrac{\partial f}{\partial y}(t, y(t)), \; t \in]0, T[, \\ y(0) = \alpha_0, \qquad\qquad \dot{y}(0) = f(0, \alpha_0). \end{cases} \tag{1}$$

Notice that the complexity of the computation increases and there is no interest to proceed like this in a sequential computing on one processor. This transformation is not sufficient to break the sequentiality of the integration process on to S_{i+1} i.e. the result of the time integration on to S_i is needed to define the boundary condition on to S_{i+1}. The main idea is to make the time interval symmetric and to applied a reverse time integration on to the symmetric interval in order to have a Neumann boundary condition at $T = 0$ of the symmetric time interval. The justification of this symmetrization is back on to the ρ-reversibility of the partitioned system $(\dot{y}, \dot{v})^t = \Phi(y, v) \stackrel{def}{=} (v, g(y))^t$ [4]. Indeed, the linear application $\rho : (y, v) \rightarrow (y, -v)$ allows to write $\rho \circ \Phi = -\Phi \circ \rho$. We need of a symmetric time integrator in order to integrate backward on to the symmetric time interval and to come back to the initial state.

Then the boundary conditions can be distributed between time slices S_i of $[0, T]$ and the p time slices $S_{i+p} = \overline{S}_i = [T_i^-, T_{i-1}^+]$ of $[T, 0]$ with Dirichlet-Neumann transmission conditions:

$$\begin{cases} 1 \leq j < p, \\ \dot{y}_j(T_j^-) = \dot{y}_{j+1}(T_j^+), \\ y_{j+1}(T_j^+) = y_j(T_j^-) \end{cases} , \; \begin{cases} j = p, \\ \dot{y}_p(T_p^-) = -\dot{\overline{y}}_p(T_p^-), \\ \overline{y}_p(T_p^-) = y_p(T_p^-). \end{cases} , \; \begin{cases} p > j \geq 1, \\ \dot{\overline{y}}_{j+1}(T_j^+) = \dot{\overline{y}}_j(T_j^-), \\ \overline{y}_j(T_j^-) = \overline{y}_{j+1}(T_j^+) \end{cases} . \tag{2}$$

We have two ways to satisfy the matching of solutions:

1. An additive (or multiplicative) Schwarz algorithm without overlap for which we can accelerate the convergence to the solution [3].
2. A Newton algorithm that solves a block tri-diagonal system for systems of linear ODE.

Notice, that classical shooting methods for time domain decomposition such as [2] are only based on the Dirichlet matching between time slices because Neumann matching is not available as the condition at the final time is not known.

3. The iterative Schwarz time domain decomposition method

For sake of simplicity let us consider only two domains S_1 and $\bar{S}_1$. The matching conditions reduce to the case $j = p$ in cq. (2). Starting from an initial guess $\dot{\bar{y}}_1^0(T^-)$, the iterative Schwarz domain decomposition method at the continuous level writes :

$$
❶ \begin{cases} \ddot{y}_1^{2k+1} = g(t, y_1^{2k+1}) & t \subset S_1 \text{(forward integration)} \\ y_1^{2k+1}(0) = \alpha \\ \dot{y}_1^{2k+1}(T^-) = -\dot{\bar{y}}_1^{2k}(T^-) \end{cases}
$$

$$
❷ \begin{cases} \ddot{\bar{y}}_1^{2k+2} = g(t, \bar{y}_1^{2k+2}) & t \in \bar{S}_1 \text{(backward integration)} \\ \dot{\bar{y}}_1^{2k+2}(0) = -f(0, \alpha) \\ \bar{y}_1^{2k+2}(T^-) = y_1^{2k+1}(T^-) \end{cases}
$$

Then the algorithm writes:

Algorithm 1 Multiplicative Schwarz Algorithm

1: **while** $||y_1^{2k+1}(T^-) - y_1^{2k-1}(T^-)||_2 + ||\dot{y}_1^{2k+1}(T^-) - \dot{y}_1^{2k-1}(T^-)||_2 \geq eps$ **do**
2:     Solve problem ❶ for iterate $2k + 3$
3:     Exchange the Dirichlet boundary condition $y_1^{2k+3}(T^-)$
4:     Solve problem ❷ for iterate $2k + 4$
5:     Exchange the Neumann boundary condition $\dot{\bar{y}}_1^{2k+4}(T^-)$
6: **end while**

For $2p$ time slices case, a red-black coloring of time slices occurs. Solving red time slices problems gives the Dirichlet boundary condition to the right neighbor black time slices and the Neumann boundary condition to the left neighbor black time slices. The same exchanges between black and red time slices happen after solving black time slices problems.

At the discrete level, let us consider the Störmer-Verlet implicit symmetric scheme : $y_{i,n+1} - 2y_{i,n} + y_{i,n-1} = h^2 g(t_n, y_{i,n})$, where $y_{i,n}$ is an approximation of the solution $y(t_n) = y_i(t_n)$ at $t_n \in S_i$ and h the constant time step of the integration on S_i taken with a size constant and discretized with $N + 1$ time steps.

The next stage of the methodology is to save computing amount by reducing the iterations of the Schwarz algorithm. In case of systems of linear ODE, we can demonstrate the pure linear convergence or divergence of the Schwarz method:

Theorem 3.0.1. *Let $\dot{y} = Ay + b, y(0) = \alpha_0 \in \mathbb{R}^d$ be a system of ODE with A diagonalizable, then the Schwarz algorithm with the Neumann-Dirichlet boundary conditions applied to the problem symmetrized exhibits a pure linear converge or diverge. Its convergence toward the exact boundary conditions can be accelerated with the Aitken's acceleration of the convergence technique.*

Proof. Let us consider first the two time slices S_1 and $\bar{S}_1 = S_2$ case. Using the diagonalizable property of A there exists an unitary matrix U such that $U^{-1}AU = \Lambda \overset{def}{=} diag(\lambda_1, \ldots, \lambda_d)$. Then the original system is transformed in a system of d ODE (3) where $y = T\tilde{x}, c = U^{-1}b, \gamma = U^{-1}\alpha, \beta = -U^{-1}g(0, \alpha)$.

$$\tilde{x}_{j,p}^{i+1,2k+p} + \lambda_j \tilde{x}_{j,p}^{i,2k+p} + \tilde{x}_{j,p}^{i-1,2k+p} = c_j, 1 \leq i \leq N - 1, 1 \leq j \leq d, p = \{1,2\} \quad (3)$$

associated to the boundary conditions:

$$\begin{cases} \tilde{x}_{j,1}^{0,2k+1} = \gamma_j \\ \tilde{x}_{j,1}^{N,2k+1} - \tilde{x}_{j,1}^{N-1,2k+1} = -\tilde{x}_{j,2}^{0,2k} + \tilde{x}_{j,2}^{1,2k} \end{cases} , \begin{cases} \tilde{x}_{j,2}^{0,2k+2} = \tilde{x}_{j,1}^{0,2k+1} \\ \tilde{x}_{j,2}^{N,2k+2} - \tilde{x}_{j,2}^{N-1,2k+1} = \beta_{j,2} \end{cases} \quad (4)$$

For the sake of simplicity, a first order discrete scheme is used for the Neumann boundary conditions. A high order discretization will change the calculus but not the pure linear property of the convergence. Let $X_{1,2}$ be the solutions of the characteristic equation of the linear recurrence (3): $X^2 + \lambda_j X + 1 = 0$. Then the error for the time slice S_1 at iteration $2k + 1$ with regard of the error at $2k - 1$ writes:

$$e_{j,1}^{N,2k+1} = \underbrace{\frac{(X_1^N - X_2^N)}{(X_1^N - X_1^{N-1}) - (X_2^N - X_2^{N-1})}}_{\rho_{j,1}} k_j \, e_{j,1}^{N,2k-1} \quad (5)$$

with $k_j = \left(1 - \dfrac{(X_1^N - X_1^{N-1})X_2^1 - (X_2^N - X_2^{N-1})X_1^1}{(X_1^N - X_1^{N-1}) - (X_2^N - X_2^{N-1})}\right)$. The amplification factor $\rho_{j,1}$ does not depend on the Schwarz iterate, consequently the convergence or the divergence of the error at end boundary T^- is purely linear and the Aitken acceleration of the convergence (6) can be applied component by component.

$$\tilde{x}_{j,1}^{N,\infty} = (1 - \rho_{j,1})^{-1}(\tilde{x}_{j,1}^{N,2k+1} - \rho_{j,1}\tilde{x}_{j,1}^{N,2k-1}) \quad (6)$$

Equation (5) can be generalized in $e_j^{2k+1} = \mathbb{P}_j\tilde{e}_j^{2k-1}$ where e_j is the error for mode j at the $p - 1$ Dirichlet boundary conditions of the black time slices and $\mathbb{P}_j$ does not depend of the Schwarz iterate. In practice, the system of ODE is not diagonalized and the acceleration is performed with a $\mathbb{P}$ matrix linking all the solution components at the Dirichlet boundaries of black time slices. The matrix $\mathbb{P}$ is independent of the Schwarz iterate and is numerically computed from $d + 2$ Schwarz iterates. The relation $e^{2k+1} = \mathbb{P}\tilde{e}^{2k-1}$ holds where e is the error of the solution components at the $p - 1$ boundaries with Dirichlet condition of the black time slices. $\qquad \square$

In order to illustrate numerically the pure linear convergence of the Aitken-Schwarz method, it is applied to the linear systems of ODE (7) with the Störmer-Verlet implicit scheme and appropriated initial conditions.

$$
\begin{cases}
\dot{y}_1 = ay_1 + by_2 + cy_3, \\
\dot{y}_2 = by_1 + ay_2 + cy_3, \\
\dot{y}_3 = cy_1 + cy_2 + dy_3, \\
\dot{y}_4 = -k_2 y_4.
\end{cases}
\quad \text{with} \quad
\begin{aligned}
& k_1 = 20, && k_2 = 200 \\
& a = -\tfrac{1}{4}(3k_1 + k_2), && b = \tfrac{1}{4}(k_1 - k_2) \\
& c = \tfrac{1}{2\sqrt{2}}(k_1 - k_2), && d = -\tfrac{1}{2}(k_1 + k_2).
\end{aligned}
\tag{7}
$$

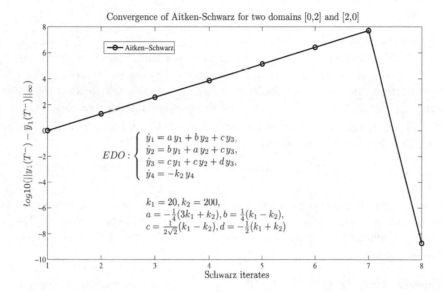

Figure 1. Convergence of the Aitken-Schwarz for two time slices S_1 and $\bar{S}_1$ for a linear system of ODE modeling a harmonic oscillator

Figure 1 exhibits the pure linear divergence of the Schwarz method for the linear system of ODE (7). Starting with an error of 1 at first iterate, the Aitken's acceleration of convergence gives the solution with an accuracy greater than 10^{-8} after 6 Schwarz iterates for this system of ODE with 4 components.

When nonlinear system of ODE are under consideration, the Aitken's acceleration stills available but it must be iterated as there is no guarantee to accelerate in one time.

4. The Schur complement time domain decomposition

Consider integrating (1) with the partitioned system $(\dot{y}, \dot{v})^t = (v, g(t, y(t)))^t$ and the Störmer-Verlet explicit scheme with time step h that writes:

$$
\begin{cases}
y_{n+1} = y_n + hv_n + h^2/2 g(t_n, y_n) \\
v_{n+1} = v_n + h/2 g(t_n, y_n) + h/2 g(t_{n+1}, y_{n+1})
\end{cases}
\tag{8}
$$

As it is a symmetric scheme we can integrate forward (subscript F) or backward (subscript B) until the middle of S_i (respectively $\overline{S}_i$) (see Figure 2).

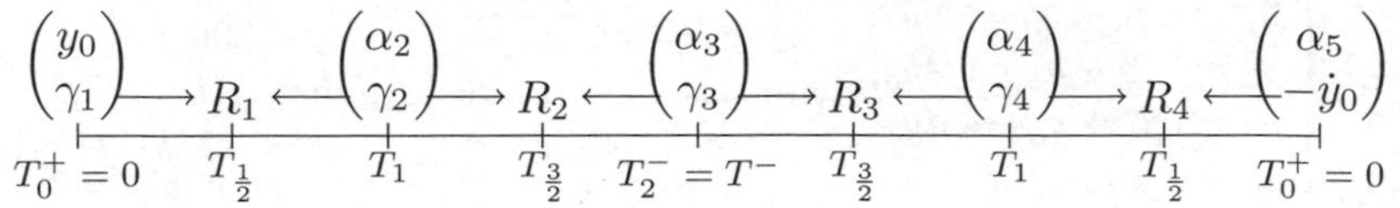

Figure 2. Forward and backward time integration schedule and matching conditions localizing for 4 times slices over the symmetric time interval

The matching R_i of these two solutions at $T_{i-\frac{1}{2}} = (T_{i-1}^{+} + T_i^{-})/2$ links the boundary Dirichlet conditions $\alpha_i, i = 2, \ldots 2p$ and Neumann boundary conditions $\gamma_i, i = 1, \ldots, 2p-1$ as the root of a non linear function $F(\gamma_1, \alpha_2, \gamma_2, \ldots, \alpha_{2p-1}, \gamma_{2p-1}, \alpha_{2p})$. Starting from the boundary conditions γ_i and α_i at T_i^{+}, the forward integration toward $T_{i+\frac{1}{2}}$ gives $H_F^i(T_{i+\frac{1}{2}}, \gamma_i, \alpha_i)$ while the backward integration toward $T_{i-\frac{1}{2}}$ gives $H_B^i(T_{i-\frac{1}{2}}, \gamma_i, \alpha_i)$. The ith vectorial component of F can be computed independently from the other components and writes for $i = 1, \ldots, 2p-1$:

$$F_i(\alpha_{i-1}, \gamma_{i-1}, \alpha_i, \gamma_i) = H_F^{i-1}(T_{i-1+\frac{1}{2}}, \gamma_{i-1}, \alpha_{i-1}) - H_B^i(T_{i-\frac{1}{2}}, \gamma_i, \alpha_i). \quad (9)$$

F represents the matching condition and can be assimilated to the Schur complement method as we have to solve a (nonlinear) system on the boundary condition. The zero of F can be obtained by a Newton method. For system of linear ODE we have the result that follows:

Theorem 4.0.2. *Let $\dot{y} = Ay + b, y(0) = \alpha_0 \in \mathbb{R}^d$ be a system of ODE with A diagonalizable, then the Schur complement algorithm reduces to solve a block tri-diagonal linear system linking the Dirichlet and Neumann time slices boundary conditions.*

Proof. Without loss of generality, let us consider the IVP $\dot{y} = \lambda y, y(0) = \alpha_0, \lambda \in \mathbb{R}$. The system of ODE $\{\dot{y}_i = v_i, \dot{v}_i = \lambda^2 y_i, t \in S_i, y_i(T_{i-1}^{+}) = \alpha_i, v_i(T_{i-1}^{+}) = \gamma_i\}$ admits the continuous solution $(y_i(t), v_i(t))^T = \alpha_i G_F^i(t) + \gamma_i H_F^i(t)$ where

$$H_F^i(t) = \frac{1}{2|\lambda|} \begin{pmatrix} e^{|\lambda|(t-T_{i-1}^{+})} - e^{-|\lambda|(t-T_{i-1}^{+})} \\ e^{|\lambda|(t-T_{i-1}^{+})} + e^{-|\lambda|(t-T_{i-1}^{+})} \end{pmatrix}, \quad (10)$$

$$G_F^i(t) = \frac{1}{2} \begin{pmatrix} e^{|\lambda|(t-T_{i-1}^{+})} + e^{-|\lambda|(t-T_{i-1}^{+})} \\ e^{|\lambda|(t-T_{i-1}^{+})} - e^{-|\lambda|(t-T_{i-1}^{+})} \end{pmatrix} \quad (11)$$

Then the $2p-1$ matching conditions on the solution link the boundary conditions by the block tri-diagonal system that follows for $i = 1, \ldots, 2p-1$:

$$G_F^{i-1}(T_{i-\frac{1}{2}})\alpha_{i-1} + H_F^{i-1}(T_{i-\frac{1}{2}})\gamma_{i-1} - G_B^i(T_{i-\frac{1}{2}})\alpha_i - H_B^i(T_{i-\frac{1}{2}})\gamma_i = 0. \quad (12)$$

$\square$

$$
\begin{pmatrix}
H_F^0 & -G_B^1 & -H_B^1 & 0 & 0 & 0 & 0 & 0 \\
0 & G_F^2 & H_F^2 & -G_B^3 & -H_B^3 & 0 & 0 & 0 \\
0 & 0 & 0 & G_F^4 & H_F^4 & -G_B^5 & -H_B^5 & 0 \\
0 & 0 & 0 & 0 & 0 & G_F^6 & H_F^6 & -G_B^7
\end{pmatrix}
\begin{pmatrix}
\gamma_1 \\ \alpha_2 \\ \gamma_2 \\ \alpha_3 \\ \gamma_3 \\ \alpha_4 \\ \gamma_4 \\ \alpha_5
\end{pmatrix}
=
\begin{pmatrix}
-y_0 G_F^0 \\ 0 \\ 0 \\ 0 \\ 0 \\ 0 \\ 0 \\ v_0 H_B^7
\end{pmatrix}
$$

Figure 3. Block tri-diagonal structure of the linear system of the matching conditions that links the boundary values of time slices

Omitting the time $T_{i\pm\frac{1}{2}}$ in the notation , Figure 3 exhibits the block tridiagonal structure of (12).

Numerically, matrices $G_F^i(T_{i-\frac{1}{2}}), H_F^i(T_{i-\frac{1}{2}}), G_B^{i+1}(T_{i+\frac{1}{2}}), H_B^{i+1}(T_{i+\frac{1}{2}})$ are built approximately by using the Störmer-Verlet explicit scheme and by differentiating two values of one boundary condition the other being constant.

5. Parallel performances

Let us discuss the parallel performance of the Aitken-Schwarz and the Schur complement methods for solving systems of linear ODE (7) $t \in [0, 40]$ and (13) that follows:

$$
\{\dot{y}_1 = 2y_1 + y_2, \dot{y}_2 = -4y_1 - 3y_2, t \in [0, 5] \text{ with initial values} \tag{13}
$$

The global number of time steps on $[0, T]$ to solve problem (13) for the implicit Störmer-Verlet scheme of the Schwarz is 10^5 and for the explicit Störmer-Verlet of the Schur is 10^7 (respectively $2\,10^7$ for problem (7)). The parallel target computers are computer A: SGI-Altix 350 with 16 IA64 1.5Ghz/6Mo and with a Numalink communication network and computer B: rack of SGI Altix ICE with 16 lames of 2 Intel Quad-Core E5472 processors (Harpertown 3 GHz) and 4Go per core. The communication network is performed by dedicated Intel Quad-Core X5472.

Computer A								
Schwarz Eq (13) / # process	1	2	4	8	16	-	-	-	-
cputime(s)	-	8.3	2.72	1.4	1.1	-	-	-	-
Schur Eq (13) / # process	1	2	4	8	16	-	-	-	-
cputime(s)	1.74	17	5.25	2.7	1.34	-	-	-	-
Schur Eq (7) / # process	1	2	4	8	16	-	-	-	-
cputime(s)	5.4	61	22.5	12.2	5.7	-	-	-	-
Computer B								
Schwarz Eq (13) / # process	1	2	4	8	16	32	64	-	-
cputime(s)	-	6.28	1.82	3.4	10	13	170	-	-
Schur Eq (13) / # process	1	2	4	8	16	32	64	128	256
cputime(s)	0.54	2.63	1.60	1.36	0.7	0.35	0.18	0.084	0.04
Schur Eq (7) / # process	1	2	4	8	16	32	64	128	256
cputime(s)	1.63	13.9	9	8.7	4.4	2.2	1.11	0.6	0.3

Table 1. cputime(s) with respect to the number of time slices/processors for the Aitken-Schwarz and the Schur complement methods for system of linear ODE .

One processor case of table 1 gives the time of the explicit Störmer-Verlet scheme on $[0, T]$. This table 1 exhibits

- Aitken-Schwarz algorithm has a good parallel efficiency on computer A until 16 processors. On computer B, the parallelism efficiency for problem (13) decreases drastically and there is no gain to use more than 8 processors. We expect that the global communications used to gather the $\mathbb{P}$ matrix on this network is the bottleneck. Nevertheless, on both computer the Aitken-Schwarz method is not enough performing to be competitive with the direct solve.
- Schur complement algorithm has very good parallel performances until 256 process. It becomes competitive with the classical IVP solve after 16 process on computer B. On 256 process on computer B a 14 times acceleration is obtained for problem (13) while it is 5 for (7). It must be noticed, a 14 speed-up is obtained with respect to the 2 processes case but the extra work paid with solving the second order ODE deteriorates the overall parallel performances compared to the original IVP resolution.

6. Conclusion

An adaptation of the Aitken-Schwarz method to time integration, by symmetrization of the time interval and transforming the IVP into a BVP, has been presented. The pure linear convergence or divergence of the Schwarz method is demonstrated. Nevertheless, to be competitive the classic integration scheme, a method based on Schur complement method is developed. A such method is really interesting, when a large number of processors is available. Our current work addresses the problem of accelerating the Newton method involved in this method when systems of nonlinear ODE have to be solved.

Thanks

First author is backed by the région Rhône-Alpes through the project CHP of cluster ISLE.This work was supported by the french National Agency of Research through the project ANR-06-TLOG-26 01 PARADE.It was granted access to the HPC resources of [CCRT/CINES/IDRIS] under the allocation 2009- [x2009066099] made by GENCI (Grand Equipement National de Calcul Intensif) and CDCSP.

References

[1] J.-L. Lions, Y. Maday, and G. Turinici, C. R. Acad. Sci. Paris Sér. I Math. **332**, 661 (2001).
[2] C. Farhat and M. Chandersis, Int. J. for Num. Methods in Engineering 1397 (2003).
[3] M. Garbey, *Domain decomposition methods in science and engineering XVII*, Vol. 60 of *Lect. Notes Comput. Sci. Eng.* (Springer, Berlin, 2008), pp. 501–508.
[4] E. Hairer, C. Lubich, and G. Wanner, *Geometric numerical integration*, Vol. 31 of *Springer Series in Computational Mathematics*, 2nd ed. (Springer-Verlag, Berlin, 2006), pp. xviii+644, structure-preserving algorithms for ordinary differential equations.
[5] M. Garbey and D. Tromeur-Dervout, Internat. J. Numer. Methods Fluids **40**, 1493 (2002), IMS Workshop on Domain Decomposition Methods in Fluid Mechanics (London, 2001).
[6] U. M. Ascher, R. M. M. Mattheij, and R. D. Russell, *Numerical Solution of Boundary Value Problems for Ordinary Differential Equations* (SIAM, Philadelphia, 1995).

Parallel Computing: From Multicores and GPU's to Petascale
B. Chapman et al. (Eds.)
IOS Press, 2010
© 2010 The authors and IOS Press. All rights reserved.
doi:10.3233/978-1-60750-530-3-83

Performance Modeling Tools for Parallel Sparse Linear Algebra Computations

Pietro Cicotti [a] Xiaoye S. Li [b] and Scott B. Baden [a]

[a] *Department of Computer Science and Engineering University of California, San Diego La Jolla, CA 92093-0404. {pcicotti,baden}@cse.ucsd.edu.*

[b] *Corresponding Author: Computational Research Division, Lawrence Berkeley National Laboratory, Berkeley, CA 94720. xsli@lbl.gov.*

Abstract. We developed a Performance Modeling Tools (PMTOOLS) library to enable simulation-based performance modeling for parallel sparse linear algebra algorithms. The library includes micro-benchmarks for calibrating the system's parameters, functions for collecting and retrieving performance data, and a cache simulator for modeling the detailed memory system activities. Using these tools, we have built simulation modules to model and predict performance of different variants of parallel sparse LU and Cholesky factorization algorithms. We validated the simulated results with the existing implementation in SuperLU_DIST, and showed that our performance prediction errors are only 6.1% and 6.6% with 64 processors IBM power5 and Cray XT4, respectively. More importantly, we have successfully used this simulation framework to forecast the performance of different algorithm choices, and helped prototyping new algorithm implementations.

Keywords. Performance modeling, linear algebra, parallel sparse factorizations

1. Introduction

Developing accurate performance models for parallel sparse linear algebra algorithms becomes increasingly important because the design space of parallelization strategies is large and implementing each strategy is labor-intensive and requires significant amount of expertise. Accurate performance modeling and prediction of different algorithms could narrow down the design choices and point to the most promising algorithms to implement. It is intractable to derive closed form analytical models for most sparse matrix algorithms because performance of such algorithms depends on both the underlying computer system and the input characteristics. In many parallel sparse matrix algorithms, computations often alternate between "memory-bound" phases and "CPU-bound" phases [3]. In addition, the sparsity and the nonzeros locations determine the amount and the granularity of communication as well as load distribution. This also presents a significant challenge for accurate performance modeling. On the other hand, *simulation-based performance models* offer the potential for taking into account details of the input and reproduce the relevant system behaviors. We propose a methodology for creating performance models where the computation is represented by a sequence of interleaved memory operations, the calls to the BLAS routines, and the inter-process communications. Our model simulates the steps of the algorithm as driven by the input and charges for the cost of memory accesses, local arithmetic calculations, and communications.

Our simulation framework consists of two components. The first component is a low level library of Performance Modeling Tools, PMTOOLS, which is based on our previous work in modeling parallel sparse LU factorization [1]. The PMTOOLS library can be generally useful for modeling any parallel linear algebra algorithms, dense or sparse. With slight modification, PMTOOLS can also be used to study performance of larger application codes. The second component is application-specific simulation module, which depends on the specific algorithm to be modeled and which consults PMTOOLS to obtain the running times of the low level operations. In the following sections, we will describe each component in more detail, and show the simulation results with validations.

Our objective is twofold: 1) we would like to predict performance of existing implementations on different architectures, including hypothetical machines that do not exist yet. To this end, we build the application-specific simulation module by mimicking computations and communications in the actual implementation including software/hardware interactions. 2) We would like to use this simulation framework to help design and prototype new algorithms, and eliminate bad algorithm choices. This is an even more valuable and novel use of this predictive framework, which distinguishes our work from the others in the area of performance evaluation and benchmarking.

2. Performance Modeling Tools

PMTOOLS is a collection of tools intended to calibrate performance of the machine's individual components. It contains the micro-benchmarks, the data structures and management routines for storing and retrieving the data collected by the micro-benchmarks, and a cache simulator to represent the memory hierarchy at runtime. Each micro-benchmark is run off-line and measures the times taken by a basic operation, such as the execution of a BLAS routine, over a parameter space of interest and the data are collected into the tables once and for all. These data represent the cost functions of the relevant operations at the simulation time. Since the configuration space can be extremely large, some configurations are omitted. The omitted values are later estimated using various interpolation or curve-fitting algorithms [5,12]. Currently, PMTOOLS contains the following three models.

1) Memory model. PMTOOLS provides a cache simulator capable of combining several cache instances. Each instance is parameterized according to the cache characteristics (e.g. capacity and associativity) of the target system. Thus, we can compose an entire memory hierarchy simulator that also includes the TLBs. The simulator has two functions: to maintain the state of the memory hierarchy throughout a simulation and to estimate the cost of each operation. We designed a memory micro-benchmark to measure the latency and bandwidth of each level of the cache. The latencies are measured by timing the updates at various memory locations. Each level in the memory hierarchy is measured in isolation by choosing the locations of the updates in a controlled operational regime, so that each access hits the desired cache level. The latency for this level is derived accurately [9]. The bandwidth is measured by timing sequential memory accesses. The measured bandwidth is applicable as long as the number of consecutive memory locations transferred is greater than a threshold that triggers hardware prefetching.

2) Model of linear algebra kernels. Most high level linear algebra algorithms can be expressed as a number of calls to the BLAS routines, which provide a nice abstract interface between the high level algorithms and the low level arithmetic engine. In PM-TOOLS, we use micro-benchmarks to measure performance of the BLAS kernels of interest, with varying matrix/vector dimensions. The timings are measured off-line and stored in the lookup tables, and will be retrieved later during the application's simulation. Since the parameters space can be very large, timing each possible point is both time-consuming and requires large tables. Instead, we benchmark the routines of all the small dimensions which are sensitive to timings, but only for a subset of the other larger dimensions. During simulation, the probing function first searches the tables for the given dimensions; if such dimension is not found, an estimate is obtained by linear interpolation using the closest times available in the table (or extrapolation if the dimensions are outside the bounds). We note that this simple interpolation/extrapolation can be improved by a more sophisticated scheme to improve prediction accuracy [12].

3) Communication model. The communication model is based on point-to-point message passing. The other communication primitives such as collective communication are modeled as a sequence of point-to-point transfers. We perform the measurement of varying message sizes off-line, store the timings in a lookup table, and retrieve the timings during the actual simulation. The cost of a transfer is measured using a ping-pong micro-benchmark, and again, the probing function either consults the lookup table for the cost of a given message size, or does interpolation for the message sizes not directly measured. Our table includes the ping-pong timings between two processors, as well as the timings with simultaneous ping-pongs among all pairs of processors. We also support the SMP or multicore CMP nodes in that the micro-benchmark is run to measure both intra-node and inter-node communication. The probing function can take the information about the number of nodes and the two processes involved, and return the appropriate measured cost.

3. Application-specific Simulation Modules

To demonstrate the effectiveness of PMTOOLS for achieving our first objective, we consider an existing implementation of sparse LU factorization in SuperLU_DIST [6]. The LU factorization algorithm uses supernodal block structure in the kernel. The factored matrices L and U are stored in compressed format and distributed with block cyclic layout on a 2D processor grid. Each unit of work (or a vertex in the dataflow graph) is defined as a block column/row factorization in a right-looking fashion, and the factorization proceeds sequentially along the outer K-dimension. A single level of pipelining (i.e. one step look-ahead) was implemented by hand across the kth and $(k + 1)$st iterations to shorten the critical path. Figure 1 illustrates such a block distribution. The highlighted block column and row correspond to the kth step of outer factorization.

We developed a simulation module which is a close mimic of the factorization algorithm except that we do not perform the actual operations, but only advance the simulated runtime. This is done by charging the times for each BLAS function and MPI function, using the probing function provided by PMTOOLS. The memory system is also closely simulated as if the algorithm is run on a real machine. The simulation module first instantiates the memory state for the cache simulator in PMTOOLS. During simulation, whenever the algorithm involves a memory access, the module consults the cache simu-

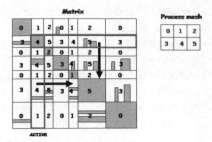

Figure 1. Sparse LU block cyclic distribution.

Algorithm 1 SuperLU_DIST: simulated update of the kth block row of U.

1: **for all** $p \in Processors \wedge UBLOCKS\_OF\_P(p, k) \neq \varnothing$ **do**
2:      $time[p] = time[p] + memory\_update(p, stack)$
3:      $time[p] = time[p] + memory\_read(p, index)$
4: **end for**
5: **for all** $b \in UBLOCKS(k)$ **do**
6:      $p \leftarrow OWNER(b)$
7:      $time[p] = time[p] + memory\_read(p, b)$
8:      **for all** $j \in b$ **do**
9:          **if** column j is not empty **then**
10:             $time[p] = time[p] + lookup(dtrsv, sizeof(j))$
11:         **end if**
12:     **end for**
13: **end for**
14: **for all** $p \in Processors \wedge UBLOCKS\_OF\_P(p, k) \neq \varnothing$ **do**
15:     $time[p] = time[p] + memory\_update(p, stack)$
16: **end for**

---

lator to obtain the access time and to trigger an update to the state of the memory. As an illustration, Algorithm 1 shows the simulated procedure that corresponds to the update of a block row of U. The procedure shows how the cost of each simulated operation is collected. Memory access functions (e.g., *memory_update* and *memory_read*) take a parameter p to indicate the instance of the simulated memory system that belongs to processor p.

We validated the model on eight unsymmetric matrices selected from the University of Florida Sparse Matrix Collection [2]: **bbmat, ecl32, g7jac200, inv-extrusion, mixing-tank, stomach, torso1, and twotone**. We used up to 64 processors with two different machines at NERSC, one is an IBM Power5 (`bassi`) and another is a Cray XT4 with quad-core AMD Opteron nodes (`franklin`). Figure 2 shows the percentage absolute errors of the predicted times versus the actual times for the eight matrices (shown in the legend). In most cases, our simulated time is accurate within 15% error. The average absolute prediction errors among all matrices and processor configurations are only 6.1% and 6.6% for the IBM Power5 and the Cray XT4, respectively. This level of accuracy is remarkable for such complicated sparse matrix calculations.

In addition to analyzing performance of the existing implementation, we have used this simulation model to forecast the performance of different algorithm choices, and successfully improved the parallel efficiency.

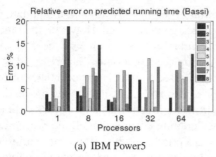 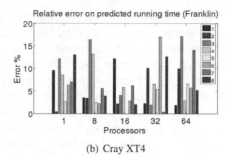

(a) IBM Power5   (b) Cray XT4

Figure 2. Accuracy of the simulated factorization times compared to the actual times. Each bar represents one matrix.

1) Shape of the processor grid.   For a fixed processor count, the shape of the 2D processor grid can affect the factorization speed. We used our model to predict the optimal shape of the processor grid with 16 processors. Figure 3 shows the actual running times and the simulated times for the eight matrices. The model was able to correctly sort the grid shapes using the simulated execution times, and the processor grid shape 2×8 is the best in most cases.

2) Latency-reducing panel factorization.   The panel factorization at each step of the outer loop usually lies on the critical path. The original algorithm performs a series of broadcasts for each rank-1 update. An alternative design is to use asynchronous point-to-point communication, reducing the latency cost. We ran the simulation with different strategies, and then chose the best simulated one to implement. This optimization led to 20-25% improvement for the entire factorization on 64 processors.

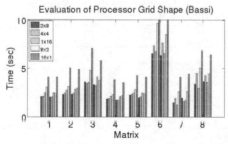

Figure 3. Choices of the shapes of the processor grid with 16 processors. Each matrix has 10 bars, divided into 2 groups of 5 each. The left group is from the actual runs, and the right group is from simulation. For each matrix, the two bars of the same color represent the same shape.

4. Prototyping New Factorization Algorithms by Simulation

We have been designing and prototyping parallel sparse Cholesky factorization using the SuperLU_DIST code base. Cholesky factorization works for symmetric positive definite matrices, which requires half of the operations and half of the memory compared to LU factorization. That is, after factorization, the upper triangular matrix is equal to the transpose of the lower triangular matrix, and so the algorithm only needs to compute the lower triangular matrix.

In a symmetric factorization, the computation of the block rows and the update of the upper triangular part of the trailing submatrices are not required. However, the block rows are still needed for updating the lower triangular part. By symmetry, these blocks reside only in the symmetric block column. A simple adaptation of SuperLU_DIST's sparse data layout and communication is as follows (see Figure 1). At each step of the outer factorization the block column of L is aggregated and replicated on the processors that own the block column. Then, each of these processors sends the entire block column along its processor row. Sending the entire block column ensures that all the processors involved in the update of the trailing submatrix are provided with all the data required. Like the LU factorization in SuperLU_DIST, we implemented a single level of pipelining scheme for better overlapping communication with computation and shortening the critical path. The implementation in the SuperLU_DIST framework is straightforward, but the drawbacks are that it sends more data than necessary and imposes synchronization of the processors along each block column.

We built a simulation module to analyze performance of this algorithm. For our experiments we used a suite of 8 matrices (**2cubes_sphere, boneS01, ship_001, smt, bmw7st_1, hood, nd3k, and thread**) and ran on an IBM Power5, and a Cray XT4. Our simulation predicts that collective communication becomes a performance bottleneck and seems to hinder scalability. In fact, it can be observed that comparing the timings of Cholesky factorization and LU factorization, when the increased communication cost outweighs the reduction in computation time, there is almost no speedup and sometimes there is even a slowdown. This effect is most noticeable for small matrices and when scaling up the number of processors, see Figure 4. However, in some cases we observed very large discrepancy between predicted and measured time where the actual running time is unexpectedly high (e.g. on 64 processors the factorization is 3 times slower that on 1 processor); we are currently investigating the causes of what appears to be a performance bug in the Cholesky algorithm.

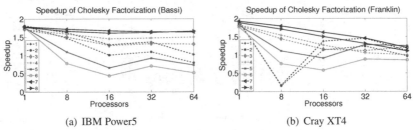

(a) IBM Power5   (b) Cray XT4

Figure 4. Speedup achieved by Cholesky factorization relative to LU factorization applied to the same problem. Each line represents one matrix.

An alternative parallelization is block-oriented in which the sparse factor is represented by blocks (in contrast to block column in SuperLU_DIST). Each block is sent to only those processors that need it, and the communication will not be restricted along each processor row. This eliminates the need for synchronization of each column processors but may involve transferring more messages of smaller size. This was shown to work reasonably well on earlier machines [8], but it is not clear on the newer machines which have much faster processors relative to interconnect speed. Since a block-oriented approach requires different ad-hoc data structures, we plan to develop a new simulation module in order to compare the two strategies before engaging in the costly implementation.

5. Related Work

Performance modeling efforts range from developing synthetic benchmarking suites for measuring raw performance of the machines' individual components to developing high level tools and application-specific cost models for performance prediction [11,4,10,12].

Our micro-benchmarking approaches to measuring the raw latencies and bandwidths of the memory and interconnect systems are based on the widely adopted methodology of Saavedra et al. [9]. By systematically accessing memory locations with varying range and stride, it is possible to derive the latency, line size and associativity of each cache level. Similarly is done in STREAM [7] and MultiMAPS [10], with the difference that our micro-benchmarks combine multiple tests in order to estimate a larger set of parameters. Our MPI ping-pong benchmarking is similar to IMB [4], but we consciously perform the ping-pong tests with single pair and all pairs, as well as intra-node and inter-node. This covers most scenarios of the point-to-point communications occurred in real applications.

A major difference between our framework and many others appears in the way how the application performance profile is collected. A popular approach is trace-based, such as [12], which captures the addresses of the program during execution, and feed the trace to the memory simulator to derive runtime with different cache configurations. The drawbacks of this approach are that it can only predict performance for the existing applications and analyze codes that are purely memory-bound. We chose to use simulation-based approach at the application level mainly because we would like to use this framework for faster prototyping of new algorithms, in addition to analyzing existing implementations. Writing the simulation code with different algorithm choices is much easier than implementing the actual algorithms (see Algorithm 1), since we can avoid dealing with the details of the complicated sparse matrix data structures. Furthermore, an important characteristic of sparse matrix factorization algorithms is that they consist of a mixture of memory-bound and CPU-bound phases, hence any method simply based on memory-bound characteristic would likely overestimate runtime. That is why we developed a separate benchmark model for the BLAS kernels, which captures most of the CPU-bound phases. Thus, our combined memory simulator and BLAS benchmarks can predict performance of this workload mixture more accurately. Our simulation framework is also more flexible in that once we create an application module, the inputs (e.g., different sparse matrices) and the processor configurations are arguments of a simulation run, whereas a trace-based method needs a re-run of the code when the input changes.

Previously, Grigori et al. made a first attempt for developing a realistic simulation model to study the sparse factorization algorithm implemented in SuperLU_DIST [3]. Their framework is also simulation-based, containing memory simulator, detailed models of BLAS kernels, and a communication bandwidth model for varying message sizes. The model has greatly improved the prediction accuracy, but it is tailored for a specific algorithm-implementation and requires estimation of the instructions involved in the BLAS routines. Therefore, it is very difficult to adapt to different algorithms and to achieve our Goal 2).

6. Conclusions

Performance models based on simulations are very useful in several cases: to enable rapid prototyping of new algorithms, to evaluate systems design, and to model performance that heavily depends on complex characteristics of the input. With PMTOOLS we modeled parallel sparse LU factorization and we observed errors within 15% in most cases and an average of less than 7% error across two different architectures for up to 64 processors. More importantly, the model proved to be useful for our goal of new algorithm design.

Our results indicate that the approach is promising and is applicable in modeling different and perhaps more complex applications. While the achieved accuracy in the work presented seemed sufficient for our goals, it exposed some weaknesses of the framework, namely the inaccuracy that might arise in presence of contention. To improve the robustness of our framework we plan to model the effect of resources contention as it is becoming a crucial aspect of multi-core systems. To this end we will investigate two types of contention: contention of memory resources, and contention of network resources.

Acknowledgement

This research was supported in part by the NSF contract ACI0326013, and in part by the Director, Office of Science, Office of Advanced Scientific Computing Research, of the U.S. Department of Energy under Contract No. DE-AC02-05CH11231. It used resources of the National Energy Research Scientific Computing Center, which is supported by the Office of Science of the U.S. Department of Energy under Contract No. DE-AC02-05CH11231.

References

[1]   P. Cicotti, X. S. Li, and Scott B. Baden. LUSim: A framework for simulation-based performance modeling and prediction of parallel sparse LU factorization. Technical Report LBNL-196E, Lawrence Berkeley National Laboratory, May 2008.

[2]   Timothy A. Davis. University of Florida Sparse Matrix Collection. http://www.cise.ufl.edu/research/sparse/matrices.

[3]   L. Grigori and X. S. Li. Towards an accurate performance modeling of parallel sparse factorization. *Applicable Algebra in Engineering, Communication, and Computing*, 18(3):241–261, 2007.

[4]   Intel® MPI Benchmarks 3.2. http://software.intel.com/en-us/articles/intel-mpi-benchmarks/.

[5]   Raj Jain. *The Art of Computer Systems Performance Analysis*. John Wiley & Sons, New York, 1991.

[6]   Xiaoye S. Li and James W. Demmel. SuperLU_DIST: A scalable distributed-memory sparse direct solver for unsymmetric linear systems. *ACM Trans. Mathematical Software*, 29(2):110–140, June 2003.

[7]   John D. McCalpin. Memory bandwidth and machine balance in current high performance computers. IEEE Computer Society Technical Committee on Computer Architecture (TCCA) Newsletter, December 1995.

[8]   Edward Rothberg and Anoop Gupta. An efficient block-oriented approach to parallel sparse cholesky factorization. *SIAM J. Scientific Computing*, 15(6):1413–1439, November 1994.

[9]   Rafael H. Saavedra and Alan J. Smith. Measuring cache and tlb performance and their effect on benchmark run times. Technical report no. usc-cs-93-546, University of Southern California, 1993.

[10]   Allan Snavely, Laura Carrington, Nicole Wolter, Jesus Labarta, Rosa Badia, and Avi Purkayastha. A framework for application performance modeling and prediction. In *Supercomputing (SC02)*, Baltimore, MD, November 16-22, 2002.

[11]   E. Strohmaier and H. Shan. Architecture independent performance characterization and benchmarking for scientific applications. In *International Symposium on Modeling, Analysis and Simulation of Computer and Telecommunication Systems*, Volendam, The Netherlands, Oct. 2004.

[12]   Mustafa M Tikir, Laura Carrington, Erich Strohmaier, and Allan Snavely. A genetic algorithms approach to modeling the performance of memory-bound computations. In *Supercomputing (SC07)*, Reno, California, November 10-16, 2007.

Parallel Computing: From Multicores and GPU's to Petascale
B. Chapman et al. (Eds.)
IOS Press, 2010
© 2010 The authors and IOS Press. All rights reserved.
doi:10.3233/978-1-60750-530-3-91

Narrow-band reduction approach of a DRSM eigensolver on a multicore-based cluster system

Toshiyuki IMAMURA [a,c] Susumu YAMADA [b,c] Masahiko MACHIDA [b,c]

[a] *The University of Electro-Communication, Japan*
[b] *Japan Atomic Energy Agency, Japan*
[c] *CREST, Japan Science and Technology Agency, Japan*

Abstract. This paper presents a performance review and reconsideration of the conventional algorithm for the eigenvalue problem for dense-real-symmetric matrices (DRSM's) on multicore parallel computer systems. We examine a narrow-band reduction approach on a multicore based cluster system.

Keywords. multicore and multiprocessors, eigenvalue problem, peta-scale parallel computer, narrow band-reduction algorithm.

1. Introduction

Recently, the trend in microprocessor architecture has been to increase the number of cores; thus we are moving into the multicore architecture age. Usually, multiple cores are being installed on a single processor. A high end server may have more than four or six cores. We imagine that future PC-cluster systems will comprise thousands of multi-socket and multicore processors. Consequently, it will become difficult to obtain scalable performance and speed up for such highly advanced processors.

There appear to be two factors causing this situation. The first concerns difficulties with utilizing multicore architecture. An illustration of the deep and complex hierarchy of cache and memory structures in such processors is shown in Figure 1. The processor cores are situated at the top of this memory hierarchy but the data stored in main memory is distant from them. To access the data with low latency, it must be pre-fetched into cache memory, and dealt with carefully. In fact, we have to consider the problem of cache conflicts and memory traffic. Since many cores also share the cache or memory bus, we also need to allow for cache reuse among the multiple cores, which is a problem that does not occur for a single core processor. The second factor is the failure to achieve a breakthrough improvement in memory bandwidth or throughput. Improvement in memory bandwidth is extremely gradual in semiconductor technology. This results in the absolute bandwidth being reduced while the number of cores is increasing, even though it consumes from one third to half of the frequency of the processor.

In the field of numerical linear algebra, especially for numerical libraries, matrix-vector multiplication is adversely affected by poor memory bandwidth in combination

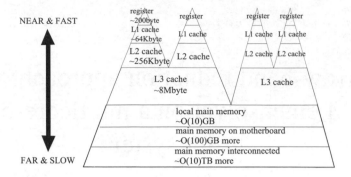

Figure 1. Memory hierarchy of a modern multicore multi-processor system

with higher processor frequencies. Specifically, theoretical analysis indicates that matrix-vector multiplication, which is categorized as a Level 2 BLAS, requires $O(1)$ data per single floating point operation. This implies that matrix-vector multiplication has a data requirement of $O(1)$ Byte/flop (B/F; this indicates the memory bus potential). B/F also represents the bus speed required to transfer data from main memory to the processor core per single floating point operation in a specific part of the program. Even for the improved implementations that currently exist, matrix-vector-multiplication subroutines are still performance-limited by the memory bandwidth. What is more, it is hard to take advantage of the capabilities of multicore processors. On the other hand, the matrix-matrix product, which is included in the Level 3 BLAS category and which is often used for performance benchmarking of systems, demands asymptotically $O(1/n)$. This product can be calculated very efficiently on multicore systems using various optimization techniques, as was stated in the top 500 report [1].

To make use of the full capabilities of multicore processors, replacing Level 2 BLAS by Level 2.5 or 3 is definitely a suitable strategy. In this paper, we focus on the advantages of using Level 2.5 BLAS with regard to the Householder transform, and present surprising performance improvements due to this strategy. As a result, a distinct approach involving narrow-band reduction will be introduced into the eigenvalue solver. In this the current multicore and upcoming peta-scale computing era, there are some suggestions that conventional approaches must be altered and in some cases a return to older methods may be required.

2. Performance of Level 2.5 BLAS

Let us use a principal Level 2.5 BLAS operator, whose formulation is similar to Level 3 BLAS but whose performance does not reach that of Level 3. For instance, a matrix-skinny matrix product or matrix-multiple vector multiplication is a typical operation in Level 2.5 BLAS, where the number of vectors to be multiplied is smaller than 8 or 16.

Table 1 shows the performance of a hand-coded Level 2.5 BLAS. The routine is tuned as much as possible, and it performs at least as well as the vendor development code. When $k = 1$, i.e. the unit is equivalent to Level 2 BLAS, our routine can use less than 25% of the processor potential. The performance scalability is saturated in the utilization of only two cores. This has its origin in the memory

Table 1. Performance of a hand-coded Level 2.5 BLAS routine, Matrix-multiple vector multiplication (unit in GFLOPS); the matrix dimension (N) is 5000, and the number of vectors agglomerated is given by the parameter k. This is measured on an Intel Xeon E5345 (2.33 GHz, Quad-core) dual sockets (total 8 cores, theoretical peak of 74.6 GFLOPS) with FB-DIMM 533 MHz.

#cores	parameter k							
	1	2	3	4	5	6	7	8
1	1.7	3.1	3.6	3.8	4.2	4.4	4.5	4.3
2	2.1	4.2	5.7	6.6	7.4	7.8	8.2	8
4	2.1	4.2	6.1	7.9	9.4	10.7	11.4	12
8	2.1	4.2	6.1	7.6	9.3	10.7	12	13.1

bandwidth. It coincides perfectly with the B/F value, which is easily calculated as $533[\text{MHz}] \times 16[\text{Byte}] \times (2[\text{flop}]/8[\text{Byte}]) = 2133\text{MFLOPS}$. Increasing the value of the parameter k results in the required B/F being reduced by a factor of k, since matrix elements are shared by the core for the k-vectors' loop calculation. The required B/F value decreases satisfactorily, and higher performance can be achieved without considering the effect of the memory bandwidth. In fact, Table 1 shows that the performance upper bound increases in proportion to k. Besides, we make use of a larger number of cores when we use large enough k to reduce the required B/F. This result suggests that the strategy to replace Level 2 BLAS by Level 3 BLAS is appropriate for multicore computing.

3. Eigenvalue computation scheme

The standard eigenvalue calculation algorithm for a DRSM (Dense Real Symmetric Matrix) can be neatly divided into three stages. Conventionally, the first stage is preprocessing of the Householder Tridiagonalization. The second stage is the eigenvalue computation for the tridiagonal matrix, using methods such as Cuppen's divide and conquer method (DC)[2], and the Multiple Robust Relative Representive (MRRR) method proposed by Dhillon etc.[3]. The last stage is back-transformation of the computed eigenvectors to the original matrix.

Figure 2 illustrates the results of a performance study of our eigensolver carried out on the Earth Simulator, and reported in [4]. In that study, we confirmed that the standard approach works without major problems, even if the matrix dimensions are above three hundred thousand. We also found that the code we developed performs remarkably well with 4096 or more processors. None the less it was established that the cost of Householder tridiagonalization, which is the preprocessing step indicated by 'Red' in Figure 2, is quite huge in comparison with the computational complexity. We should recognize that this result can only be attained by a hardware configuration of a vector processor system having high memory bandwidth and high interconnection speed (in this case the Earth Simulator has a single-step switch). Modern microprocessors do not have such elaborate hardware. Thus, it is easy to predict that the performance and scalability issues discussed above for Level2 BLAS will exist not only on a large-scale system but also on a medium class system.

3.1. Narrow-band reduction algorithm (Block version Householder tridiagonalization)

As mentioned above, the tridiagonal matrix approach is believed to be a standard or universal method. There are some excellent implementations such as `dstedc` and

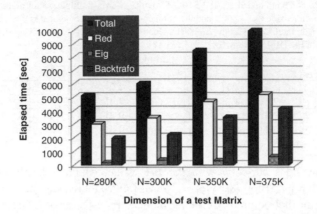

Figure 2. Results for huge eigenproblems on a **vector-parallel** computer, *Earth Simulator* with 4096 vector units in a flat-MPI configuration. Calculation of all eigenpairs (eigenvalues and corresponding eigenvectors) required about three hours, especially in the largest case of a 375-thousand-dimension matrix.

`pdstedc` in LAPACK[5] and ScaLAPACK[6], respectively. However, as shown above, this process dominates the computational cost, and therefore affects the total performance. In addition, internal analysis of the algorithm reveals that the cost of Level 2 BLAS is remarkably high.

Figure 3 shows the block version of the Householder tridiagonalization algorithm. Since the output matrix is a narrow band matrix, we call it the 'Narrow-band reduction' algorithm. This algorithm was originally proposed by Bischof, and Wu, et al.[7,8], and it is used as the first step of the multistep tridiagonalization technique. If $k = 1$, this is equivalent to the conventional Householder tridiagonalization algorithm. Though some variations were developed in the calculation of the block reflector in stage (1) such as in [9,10], no large differences exist for other stages. In our study, we adopted the compact

$$
\begin{aligned}
&\textbf{for } j = N, \ldots, 1 \textbf{ step } -M \\
&\quad U \leftarrow \emptyset, \, V \leftarrow \emptyset, \, W \leftarrow A_{(*,j-M+1:j)} \\
&\quad \textbf{for } k = 0, \ldots, M-1 \textbf{ step } K \\
&\qquad (1) \text{ Householder block reflector: } (C, U^{(k)}) := H(W_{(*,j-k)}) \\
&\qquad (2) \text{ Matrix-Vectors multiplication (BLAS2.5)} \\
&\qquad\quad V^{(k-\frac{2}{3})} \leftarrow A_{(1:j-k-1,1:j-k-1)} U^{(k)} \\
&\qquad (3) \, V^{(k-\frac{1}{3})} \leftarrow V^{(k-\frac{2}{3})} - (UV^T + VU^T) U^{(k)} \\
&\qquad (4) \, V^{(k)} \leftarrow V^{(k-\frac{1}{3})} C^T - U^{(k)} S, \, S = \tfrac{1}{2} C U^{(k)T} V^{(k-\frac{1}{3})} C^T \\
&\qquad\quad U \leftarrow [U, U^{(k)}], \, V \leftarrow [V, V^{(k)}]. \\
&\qquad (5) \, W_{(*,j-k:j)} \leftarrow W_{(*,j-k:j)} - (U^{(k)} V^{(k)T} + V^{(k)} U^{(k)T})_{(*,j-k:j)} \\
&\quad \textbf{endfor} \\
&\quad A_{(*,j-M+1:j)} \leftarrow W \\
&\quad (6) \text{ 2M rank-update (BLAS3)} \\
&\qquad A_{(1:j-M,1:j-M)} \leftarrow A_{(1:j-M,1:j-M)} - (UV^T + VU^T)_{(1:j-M,1:j-M)} \\
&\textbf{endfor}
\end{aligned}
$$

Figure 3. Narrow-band reduction algorithm (block-version Householder reduction). Basically, capital letters refer to square matrices or tall-skinny matrices (except for N and M).

WY representation, $I - UCU^T$, composed of a block reflector U and a coefficient matrix C. Assuming that $h(w)$ returns the reflector u and the parameter c corresponding to w, the simplest way to obtain U and C is as follows.

$$(u_i, c_i) = h((I - UCU^T)w_i), \ U := [U|u_i], \ C := \left[\begin{array}{c|c} C & 0 \\ \hline c_i u_i^T UC & c_i \end{array}\right] \ \text{for} \ i = 1, 2 \ldots M$$

Since most of the algorithm consists of the multiplication of a matrix and a skinny-matrix, Level 2.5 BLAS governs the performance. Performance results for this algorithm are presented in Section 4.

3.2. Divide and Conquer approach for Band matrices

The part of the algorithm that computes eigenpairs of a band matrix is not the main concern of this paper but several algorithms have already been proposed. Let us discuss the basic idea of the algorithm based upon the divide and conquer algorithm due to [11].

1. First, the band matrix B (the width of the B is $2k + 1$) is rewritten as a direct sum of two band matrices and k pieces of rank one perturbations;

$$B = B_1 \oplus B_2 + u_1 u_1^T + \cdots u_k u_k^T.$$

2. Next, either the proposed algorithm or another parallel algorithm is used for the diagonalization of a particular pair of B_1 and B_2.
3. Then, the original matrix B is transformed by a similarity transform Q derived from the eigenvectors of B_1 and B_2 into the form of $D_1 + v_1 v_1^T + \cdots v_k v_k^T$; here $D_1 = Q(B_1 \oplus B_2)Q^T$ is a diagonal matrix, and $v_j = Qu_j$.
4. Then, the eigenvalue and eigenvector of $D_1 + v_1 v_1^T$ are computed by Cuppen's original divide and conquer algorithm.
5. Finally, by means of a similarity transform, the diagonal $D_2 = Q_1(D_1 + v_1 v_1^T)Q_1^T$ is obtained. $D_2 + v_2' v_2'^T$ $(v_2' - Q_1 v_2)$ is then solved by a similar approach to that shown in step 4.
6. The above steps are repeated for all k-perturbations.

By using the algorithm shown above, all the eigenvalues and the corresponding eigenvectors of the band matrix can be calculated. This algorithm basically consists of a recurrent or consecutive application of Cuppen's divide and conquer method. Therefore, it uses only calculation principles based on Cuppen's algorithm. It exhibits a large degree of parallelism, as does Cuppen's original algorithm.

4. Multicore parallel implementation

We have already described the development of a high-speed eigenvalue solver that executes on the Earth Simulator. We parallelized the solver in a flat-MPI fashion, where all the processors correspond to one process, even though 8 vector processors share main memory. For more details, please refer to our previous report[4].

In a multicore multiprocessor environment, we need to select a programming style to reduce the number of processes and increase the number of threads for each process. It is also necessary to reduce inter-process communication and to rely mainly on com-

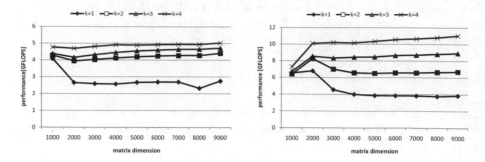

Figure 4. Preliminary performance test of a Narrow-band reduction routine on a dual Intel Xeon E5345. Left and right graphs show the result of one thread with one core and eight threads with eight cores, respectively.

munication between threads. We actually use a hybrid parallel programming style with MPI and OpenMP, for inter-node and inter-process parallelism, and thread parallelism, respectively. Our newly developed code is an enhancement of the old version used on the Earth Simulator, and it enables us to control the number of threads and processes arbitrarily. Thus, we can also optimize thread-process-processor mappings from the viewpoints of communication and data locality by using it with an affinity control tool.

4.1. Preliminary test on a multicore processor

Figure 4 plots a graph of the performance (GFLOPS) of the Narrow-band reduction routine for various values of the parameter k. We set up two configurations, one with a single core and one with eight cores. As already shown in Section 2, the performance of the code substituted by Level 2.5 BLAS improves as the parameter k increases. If we compare the cases for which $k = 1$ and 4, the performance improvement of our solver on a single core reaches only 1.8. For a larger value of k, the speed-up ratio is saturated instantly. On the other hand, it is excellently scalable with respect to the parameter k on eight cores. Parallelism efficiency between a single thread up to eight threads also increases as the value of k increases. The performance trends indicated in Table 1 and Figure 4, are almost analogous. This guarantees the marked superiority of the Narrow-band reduction approach for a multiple core environment.

4.2. Performance result and prediction of Narrow-band-reduction for a multicore multiprocessor system

Figure 5 demonstrates the elapsed time of our solver on a single node of the T2K super-computer housed in the information technology center at the University of Tokyo. Each node has 4 sockets, and has installed AMD Barcelona quad core processors, with a frequency of 2.3 GHz. Total performance throughput is up to 36.2 GFLOPS. Each process with four threads is mapped to one socket in this test.

In Figure 5, we plot only the execution time of Level 2.5 BLAS denoted in MV, and the total time. Another major computational part of the Narrow-band reduction algorithm is the rank-2k update routine, and its computational cost is a constant 7.98 seconds in

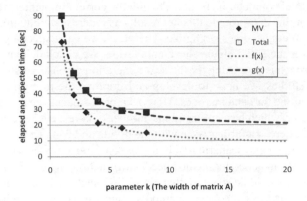

Figure 5. Performance test on *the T2K supercomputer* housed at Tokyo University. Each node has 4 sockets for AMD Barcelona quad core 2.3 GHz processors. The dimension of the matrix to be diagonalized is 10000.

this case. We can roughly build a performance model function such as $a + b/k$, and fit it to the observations. The two broken curves in Figure 5 represent fits to $f(x) = 6.1 + 66.6/k$, $g(x) = 17.5 + 70.8/k$. From the observations, we can save about 35 seconds, when $k = 2$. The calculation time is reduced by approximately 1/3, with an increase for only the off-diagonal element line. Furthermore, $k = 6$ and $k = 16$ can reduce the time by nearly 2/3 and 3/4, respectively. Even though this model does not consider blocking and parallelization overhead, the performance improvement is quite remarkable.

The remainder of this problem, which is not described in this paper, concerns the cost of the divide and conquer method. We can estimate the worst cost of the method for band matrices $T(k) = (2k-1)T(1)$; here $T(1)$ refers to the cost of the original Cuppen's divide and conquer method for a tridiagonal matrix. In the case of $k = 2$, the total cost becomes smaller, if $T(1) < 35/2 = 17.5$ seconds. The current implementation of pdstedc in ScaLAPACK takes 17.8 seconds for this dimension. From our experience on larger scale eigenproblems, the ratio of the computational cost for pdstedc decreases compared with the Householder transform as in Figure 2.

Furthermore, this approach can reduce the number of communications, since the Narrow-band reduction agglomerates not only the vectors' computation but the vectors' communications such as broadcast and all_reduce. This effect is unclear for a low dimensional matrix and using a small number of processes. However, it can reduce parallel overhead on a large configuration. Thus, it appears that Narrow-band reduction can be a promising approach.

5. Conclusion

In this paper, we have discussed the Narrow-band reduction approach to diagonalize a DRSM. Replacing a blocking scheme is quite suitable for cases of relatively low memory bandwidth, and we can take advantage of the full potential of multiple cores. The approach yields a good performance improvement for the pre-processing stage of matrix diagonalization. Furthermore, it can avoid an increase in communication overheads, as the size of the parallel computer increases. Though the current implementation of the divide and conquer routine does not yield better results as regards computational time, the cost for a larger problem becomes negligible. Therefore, we can expect a good performance improvement for the entire eigenvalue computation. We conclude that the Narrow-band reduction approach is promising for the next generation eigensolvers.

In future studies, we hope to develop and improve the performance of the divide and conquer routine for band matrices. Moreover, performance measurement on a highly parallel computer, which has a tremendous number of cores, e.g., exceeding 10000, will be carried out. There is a further issue with the divide and conquer routine. In most large scale problems, the major scenario is solving for some eigenmodes which lie in a specific region. The divide and conquer method needs information on all the eigenmodes of sub-problems during the middle stages. Other algorithms such as the bisection method might be better than the divide and conquer method in such a situation. Studying the calculation pattern demanded by real applications is also one of our future aims. The results obtained here are expected to play a part in the construction of the next generation numerical library for the next generation supercomputer system.

Acknowledgment

This research was supported in part by the Ministry of Education, Science, Sports and Culture, Grant-in-Aid for Scientific Research (B), 21300013, 21300007, 20300007, 20500044, and Scientific Research on Priority Areas, 21013014.

References

[1]   Top 500 Homepage, http://www.top.org/.
[2]   J.J.M. Cuppen. A divide and conquer method for the symmetric tridiagonal eigenproblem. *Numer. Math.* **36** (1981), 177–195.
[3]   I.S. Dhillon, Beresford N. Parlett, and Christof Vëmel, The design and implementation of the MRRR algorithm. *ACM Trans. Math. Softw.* **32**(4) (2006), 533–560.
[4]   S. Yamada, T. Imamura, T. Kano, and M. Machida, High-performance computing for exact numerical approaches to quantum many body problems on the earth simulator. In Proc. of the 2006 ACM/IEEE Conf. on Supercomputing SC|06 (2006).
[5]   See, for example. http://www.netlib.org/lapack/.
[6]   See, for example, http://www.netlib.org/scalapack/.
[7]   C.H. Bischof, B. Lang, and X. Sun, The SBR Toolbox – Software for Successive Band Reduction, *ACM TOMS* **26**(4) (2000), 602–616.
[8]   Y.J. Wu, P.A. Alpatov, C.H. Bishof, and R.A. Geijn, A Parallel Implementation of Symmetric Band Reduction Using PLAPACK, In Proc. Scalable Parallel Library Conference (1996).
[9]   H. Murakami, An Implementation of the Block Householder Method, *IPSJ Digital Courrier* **2** (2006), 298–317.
[10] R. Shreiber, and B. Pearlett, Block Reflectors: Theory and Computation, *SIAM J. Numer. Anal.* **25**(1) (1988), 189–205.
[11] W.N. Gansterer, R.C. Ward, R.P. Muller, and W.A. Goddard III, Computing approximate eigenpairs of symmetric block tridiagonal matrices, *SIAM J. Sci. Comput.* **25** (2003), 65-85.

Parallel Computing: From Multicores and GPU's to Petascale
B. Chapman et al. (Eds.)
IOS Press, 2010
© 2010 The authors and IOS Press. All rights reserved.
doi:10.3233/978-1-60750-530-3-99

Parallel Multistage Preconditioners by Extended Hierarchical Interface Decomposition for Ill-Conditioned Problems

Kengo NAKAJIMA

Information Technology Center, The University of Tokyo

Abstract. In this work, extended version of "Hierarchical Interface Decomposition (HID)" for parallel preconditioning method has been developed. Extension of overlapped elements between domains and effect of thicker separators were considered. Proposed method has been implemented to finite-element based simulations of linear elasticity problems for simple cubic geometries with heterogeneous distribution of distortion angle of elements. The developed code has been tested on the "T2K Open Supercomputer (T2K/Tokyo)" using up to 512 cores. Extended HID provides more robust and scalable performance than original HID and localized-block-Jacobi-type BILU with extension of overlapped elements.

Keywords. Parallel Iterative Solver, Preconditioning Method, HID

Introduction

Localized-block-Jacobi-type preconditioners are widely used for parallel iterative solvers [1]. They provide excellent parallel performance for well-defined problems, although the number of iterations required for convergence gradually increases according to the number of processors. However, this preconditioning technique is not robust for ill-conditioned problems with many processors, because it ignores the global effect of external nodes in other domains [1]. The generally used remedy is the extension of overlapped elements between domains [2]. In [3], new parallel preconditioning methods for ill-conditioned matrices, derived from finite-element applications for contact problems, have been proposed. The *selective overlapping* method was the one of the proposed methods, which extends the layers of overlapped elements according to the information of the special elements used for contact conditions. In addition, robustness and efficiency of *"Hierarchical Interface Decomposition* (HID)" [4] were also evaluated in [3]. HID provides a method of domain decomposition with robustness and scalability for parallel preconditioners based on the incomplete lower-upper (ILU) and incomplete Cholesky (IC) factorization. Generally speaking, *extension of overlapping* and HID are competitive, but HID cannot consider the effects of *fill-ins* of higher order for *external* nodes. Therefore, HID is not necessarily suitable for ill-conditioned problems. In the present work, effects of *external* nodes on fill-ins of higher order are introduced to HID with ILU/IC type preconditioners by the following ideas:

- Extension of depth of overlapped elements between domains
- *Thicker* separators

Developed methods were tested by a finite-element based simulation code for 3D linear elasticity problems in media with heterogeneous material properties developed in [5] on the "T2K Open Supercomputer (T2K/Tokyo)" at the University of Tokyo [6] using up to 512 cores.

The rest of this paper is organized as follows: In section 1 we outline the details of the present application, and describe the linear solvers and HID procedures. In section 2 preliminary results of the computations are described, while related work is described in section 3 and some final remarks are offered in section 4.

1. Implementations

1.1. Finite-Element Application

In the present work, linear elasticity problems in simple cube geometries of media with heterogeneous material properties (Fig.1(a)) are solved using a parallel finite-element method (FEM). Tri-linear hexahedral (cubic) elements are used for the discretization. Each of Young's modulus and Poisson's ratio is set to 1.00 and 0.25, respectively, for all elements, while a heterogeneous distribution of intensity of distortion in each element is calculated by a sequential Gauss algorithm, which is widely used in the area of geostatistics [7]. Distortion around z-axis of each element is applied to each cubic element. The maximum distortion angle is set to 200-deg. The boundary conditions are described in Fig.1(b). The GPBi-CG (Generalized Product-type methods based on Bi-CG) [8] solver with BILU(2,t,m-d) (Block ILU preconditioner with second order fill-ins by three types of parameters for threshold (t) [9], method of domain decomposition (m) and depth of overlapping (d)), where three components of (u,v,w) on each vertex are processed simultaneously with block-wise manner in matrix operations. The code is based on the framework for parallel FEM procedures of GeoFEM [10], and the GeoFEM's local data structure is applied. The local data structures in GeoFEM are node-based with overlapping elements [11]. In this work, idea of *normal extension of overlapping* [2,3] without *selective* operations is applied.

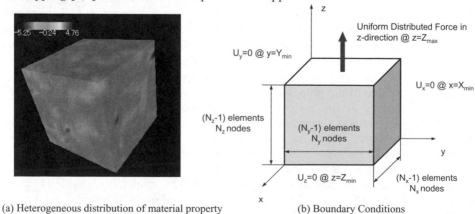

(a) Heterogeneous distribution of material property   (b) Boundary Conditions

Figure 1. Simple cube geometries with heterogeneity as domains for 3D linear elasticity problems

1.2. Hierarchical Interface Decomposition (HID)

The HID process starts with a partitioning of the graph into sub-graphs, where there is no overlapping between sub-graphs. These sub-graphs are called *connecters with level-1* (C^1). Because each C^1 connector corresponds to each domain in parallel computation with domain decomposition, C^1 connectors are called *sub-domains*. The "levels" are defined recursively from this partitioning, with each level. Each vertex group of a given level is a *separator* for vertex groups of a *lower* level. In [4], the concepts of *connectors* of different *levels* (C^k) are introduced, where C^k connectors are adjacent to k *sub-domains*. Figure 2(a) shows the example of the partition of a 9-point grid into 4 domains. Note that different connectors of the same level are not connected directly, but are separated by connectors of higher levels. If the unknowns are reordered according to their level numbers, from the lowest to highest, the block structure of the reordered matrix is as shown in Fig.2(b). This block structure leads to a natural parallelism if ILU/IC factorization or forward/backward substitution processes are applied. Details of algorithms for the construction of independent connectors are provided in [4]. Thus, HID-based ILU/IC type preconditioners can consider the global effect in parallel computations, and are expected to be more robust than localized-block-Jacobi-type ones. In [5], original partitioner of GeoFEM for domain decomposition was modified so that it could create a distributed hierarchical data structure for HID.

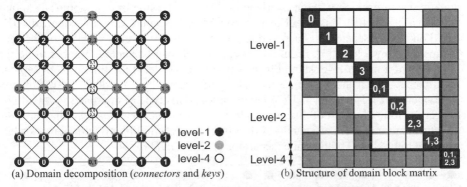

(a) Domain decomposition (*connectors* and *keys*)   (b) Structure of domain block matrix

Figure 2. Domain/block decomposition of the matrix according to the HID reordering

```
do lev= 1, LEVELtot
   do i0= LEVELindex(lev-1)+1, LEVELindex(lev)
      i= OtoN(i0)
      SW1= WW(3*i-2,R); SW2= WW(3*i-1,R); SW3= WW(3*i  ,R)
      isL= INL(i-1)+1; ieL= INL(i)
      do j= isL, ieL
         k= IAL(j)
         X1= WW(3*k-2,R); X2= WW(3*k-1,R); X3= WW(3*k  ,R)
         SW1= SW1 - AL(9*j-8)*X1 - AL(9*j-7)*X2 - AL(9*j-6)*X3
         SW2= SW2 - AL(9*j-5)*X1 - AL(9*j-4)*X2 - AL(9*j-3)*X3
         SW3= SW3 - AL(9*j-2)*X1 - AL(9*j-1)*X2 - AL(9*j  )*X3
      enddo
      X1= SW1; X2= SW2; X3= SW3
      X2= X2 - ALU(9*i-5)*X1
      X3= X3 - ALU(9*i-2)*X1 - ALU(9*i-1)*X2
      X3= ALU(9*i  )* X3
      X2= ALU(9*i-4)*( X2 - ALU(9*i-3)*X3 )
      X1= ALU(9*i-8)*( X1 - ALU(9*i-6)*X3 - ALU(9*i-7)*X2)
      WW(3*i-2,R)= X1; WW(3*i-1,R)= X2; WW(3*i  ,R)= X3
   enddo

   call SOLVER_SEND_RECV_3_LEV(lev,…):     Communications using
                                           Hierarchical Comm. Tables.
enddo
```

Figure 3. Forward substitution process of preconditioning written in FORTRAN and MPI, global communications using hierarchical communication tables occur at the end of the computation of each level

Figure 3 shows *forward substitution* process of preconditioning, written in FORTRAN and MPI. Global communications using hierarchical communication tables for HID procedures occur in the end of the computation at each level. HID is more expensive than *localized-block-Jacob-type* ILU/IC type preconditioners due to these additional communications.

1.3. Extended HID

Feature of HID is suitable for parallel iterative solvers with ILU/IC type preconditioners. Generally speaking, HID is competitive with *selective overlapping*, but *selective overlapping* is more robust if the coefficient matrices are more ill-conditioned, because HID cannot consider the effects of *fill-ins* of higher order for *external* nodes. In the present work, effects of *external* nodes are introduced to HID by the following ideas:

- Simple extension of depth of overlapped elements between domains
- *Thicker* separators

Each plate of Fig.4 briefly describes idea of the *extended HID* for two domains. In original local data set (Fig.4(a)), effect of vertex A cannot be considered as off-diagonal components of *vertex B* for ILU(2) factorization, because HID is based on domain decomposition without overlapping [3]. If extension of overlapping is applied, as shown in Fig.4(b), this effect can be considered. Second idea for extended HID is based on *thicker* separators. Each vertex group of a given level is a separator for vertex groups of a lower level [3]. From the view point of load-balancing, number of vertices in groups of a higher level should be as small as possible. If the thickness of separator is larger as shown in Fig.4(c), effect of *vertex A* can be considered as off-diagonal components of *vertex B* for ILU(2) factorization. This type of approach is called *HID-new* in the following part of this paper. *HID-new* with *thicker separators* may introduce effect of external nodes efficiently in ILU/IC type preconditioning with higher order of fill-ins. Original HID with thinner separator is called *HID-org*.

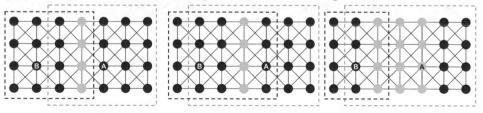

(a) Original local data set   (b) Extension of overlapping   (c) *Thicker* separator (*HID-new*)

Figure 4. Extended HID for 2 domains with 2 levels (black circles: level-1 connectors, gray circles: level-2 connectors, dashed lines: range of local data set for each domain)

2. Preliminary Results

2.1. Hardware Environment

Proposed methods were applied to the parallel FEM code with preconditioned GPBi-CG solver. The developed code has been tested on the "T2K Open Supercomputer

(T2K/Tokyo)" at the University of Tokyo [6]. The "T2K/Tokyo" was developed by Hitachi under "T2K Open Supercomputer Alliance". T2K/Tokyo is an AMD Quad-core Opteron-based combined cluster system with 952 nodes, 15,232 cores and 31TB memory. Total peak performance is 140.1 TFLOPS. Each node includes four "sockets" of AMD Quad-core Opteron processors (2.3GHz), therefore 16 cores are on each node. Each node is connected via Myrinet-10G network. In the present work, 32 nodes (512 cores) of the system have been evaluated.

2.2. Problem Setting

Performance of the developed code has been evaluated using between 2 and 32 nodes (32 and 512 cores) of the T2K/Tokyo. In this work, strong scaling test, where the entire problem size is fixed at 2,097,152 ($=128^3$) elements and 6,440,067 DOF, has been conducted.

Flat MPI parallel programming model has been applied using 16 cores of each node. BILU(2,t,m-d) factorization has been applied to all cases. Effect of *thickness* of level-2 layers is evaluated in HID. In original HID (*HID-org*), thickness of level-2 layer is one, but in the *HID-new*, this thickness is set as *three*, as shown in Fig.5. Moreover, effect of extension of overlapping is also evaluated. Comparisons with *localized-block-Jacobi-type* BILU(2,t) are also conducted. Table 1 summarizes these cases.

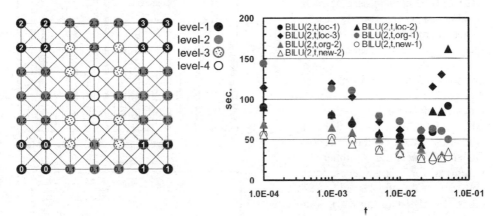

Figure 5. Extended HID (*HID-new*), thicker level-2 separators

Figure 6. Relationship between computation time of linear solvers of BILU(2,t,m-d)/GPBi-CG and threshold parameter *t* on the T2K/Tokyo for the 3D linear elasticity model with 2,097,152 elements and 6,440,067 DOF, with 512 cores

Table 1. Summary of Test Cases

Name	Description	Optimum "*t*" at 512 cores
BILU(2,t,loc-1)	Localized-block-Jacobi-type BILU(2,t), depth of overlapping=1	0.02
BILU(2,t,loc-2)	Localized-block-Jacobi-type BILU(2,t), depth of overlapping=2	0.02
BILU(2,t,loc-3)	Localized-block-Jacobi-type BILU(2,t), depth of overlapping=3	0.02
BILU(2,t,org-1)	BILU(2,t) with *HID-org*, depth of overlapping=1 (Fig.4(b))	0.05
BILU(2,t,org-2)	BILU(2,t) with *HID-org*, depth of overlapping=2 (Fig.4(b))	0.03
BILU(2,t,new-1)	BILU(2,t) with *HID-new*, depth of overlapping=1 (Fig.4(c))	0.03
BILU(2,t,new-2)	BILU(2,t) with *HID-new*, depth of overlapping=2 (Fig.4(c))	0.02

In BILU(2,t,m-d), *t* provides value of threshold parameter and *m-d* means method of domain decomposition (*m*) and depth of overlapping (*d*). In BILU(2,t,m-d), components of factorized matrix for preconditioning, which is smaller than *t*, are ignored in preconditioning process of iterative solvers. Therefore *t*=0.00 means full BILU(2) preconditioning. We have three types of methods for domain decomposition, *loc* (localized-block-Jacobi-type), *org* (HID-org) and *new* (HID-new), as shown in Table 1. Generally speaking, more iterations are required for convergence if the threshold parameter *t* is larger. But cost of a single iteration is less expensive for larger *t*, therefore trade-off between robustness and cost should be considered. Figure 6 shows relationship between *t* and computation time for linear solver using 512 cores for each method. Optimum value of *t* for each method with 512 cores, shown in the last column of Table 1, has been applied in the strong scaling test in the next part.

2.3. Strong Scaling Tests

Each plate of Fig.7 shows performance of seven types of preconditioners and domain decomposition methods with overlapping, described in Table 1. *Relative performance* is relative computation time for linear solvers normalized by that of correspond BILU(2,0.03,new-1) case at each number of cores, where value larger than 1.0 means that the method is more efficient than BILU(2,0.03,new-1), which provides the best performance at 384 and 512 cores. Localized-block-Jacobi-type BILU(2,0.02,loc-2/loc-3) did not converge in some cases. Generally speaking, number of iterations for convergence kept constant between 32 and 512 cores for BILU(2,t,new-d), but convergence of other methods, such as BILU(2,t,loc-d) and BILU(2,0.05,org-1), is getting worse with more than 192 cores. This is especially significant for BILU(2,0.05,org-1), but convergence is improved for BILU(2,0.03,org-2) with extension of overlapped elements. BILU(2,0.05,org-1) is rather faster than BILU(2,0.03,new-1) if the number of core is less than 128, but at 384 and 512 cores, it's worse than BILU(2,t,loc-d). Effect of *thicker separator* shown

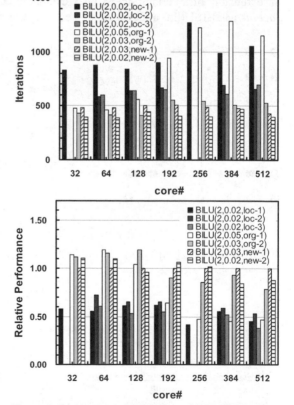

Figure 7. Performance of BILU(2,t,m-d)/GPBi-CG on the T2K/Tokyo for the 3D linear elasticity model with 2,097,152 elements and 6,440,067 DOF, up to 512 cores, *relative performance* is performance of linear solvers of normalized by computation time of BILU(2,0.03,new-1) at each number of cores

in Fig.4(c) provides robustness of BILU(2,t,new-d). BILU(2,0.02,new-2) with 2-layers of overlapped elements is slightly more robust than BILU(2,0.03,new-1), but BILU(2,0.03,new-1) is the most efficient, especially if the number of cores is larger. Figure 8 shows scalability from 32 cores up to 512 cores. Computation time of linear solvers for each case is normalized by that of BILU(2,0.03,new-1) with 32 cores. Figure 9 shows minimum and maximum number of internal nodes at 512 cores for BILU(2,t,loc-d), BILU(2,t,org-d), and BILU(2,t,new-d), respectively. Load imbalance is more significant in BILU(2,t,new-d). The standard deviation for each of BILU(2,loc-d), BILU(2,t,org-d), and BILU(2,t,new-d) is 85, 155 and 289, respectively.

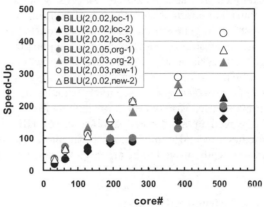

Figure 8. Strong Scalability of BILU(2,t,m-d) /GPBi-CG on the T2K/Tokyo for the 3D linear elasticity model with 2,097,152 elements and 6,440,067 DOF, from 32 cores up to 512 cores, according to computation time for linear solvers of BILU(2,0.03,new-1) with 32 cores

3. Related Work

There are many research works related to robust and efficient parallel preconditioned iterative solvers and domain decomposition, because they are critical issues for large-scale scientific computations. Iwashita et al. proposed *block red-black ordering* for parallel ILU preconditioning method [11]. The idea is very similar to that of HID, where *red blocks* correspond to *sub-domains* and *black blocks* are *separators* in structured three-dimensional geometries for finite-difference type applications. Generally speaking, performance is improved as *block size* increases, especially for ill-conditioned problems. Larger block size corresponds to *thicker separator* in *HID-new*. Finally, the results in [11] provide similar conclusions with those of this paper, although only structured grids were considered.

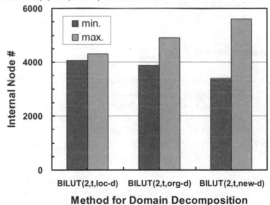

Figure 9. Minimum and maximum number of internal nodes at 512 cores, standard deviation: BILU(2,t,loc-d)=85, BILU(2,t,org-d)=155, and BILU(2,t,new-d)=289

4. Summary and Future Works

In this work, extended version of "Hierarchical Interface Decomposition (HID)" for parallel preconditioning method has been developed. Extension of overlapped elements between domains and effect of thicker separators were considered in the *extended HID*.

Proposed method has been implemented to finite-element based simulations of linear elasticity problems for simple cubic geometries with heterogeneous distribution of distortion angle of elements, where the maximum distortion angle is set to 200-deg. The developed code has been tested on the T2K/Tokyo using up to 512 cores. Extended HID provides more robust and scalable performance than original HID and *localized-block-Jacobi-type* BILU with extension of overlapped elements. Especially, effect of *thicker separator* is very significant if the number of core is larger. BILU with extended HID and *thicker separator* may be the effective choice as preconditioners for robust and efficient convergence of large-scale ill-conditioned problems. In the present work, only very simple geometry is considered. Therefore, it is very easy to define *thicker* separators. Development of sophisticated domain partitioner for complicated geometries is a key technology for practical application of extended HID to real applications. In the present work, *thickening* of separators is considered for only level-2 layers. *Thickening* of separator should be considered at every level for robust convergence. Moreover, load-balancing for extend HID is another big technical issue to be solved in the future. Application of HID for scalable solver such us multigrid methods in real computations is an interesting area for future works, while HID has been already proved to be effective for multigrid-type algorithms [12].

Acknowledgments

This work is supported by *Core Research for Evolutional Science and Technology, Japan Science and Technology Agency (JST)*. Author would like to thank Professor Takeshi Iwashita (Kyoto University) for his helpful suggestions and advices.

References

[1] K. Nakajima, Parallel Iterative Solvers of GeoFEM with Selective Blocking Preconditioning for Nonlinear Contact Problems on the Earth Simulator, *ACM/IEEE Proceedings of SC2003* (2003) .

[2] T. Washio, T. Hisada, H. Watanabe and T.E. Tezduyar, A Robust and Efficient Iterative Linear Solver for Strongly Coupled Fluid-Structure Interaction Problems, *Computer Methods in Applied Mechanics and Engineering* **194** (2005) 4027-4047.

[3] K. Nakajima, Strategies for Preconditioning Methods of Parallel Iterative Solvers in Finite-Element Applications in Geophysics, *Advances in Geocomputing, Lecture Notes in Earth Science* **119** (2009), 65-118.

[4] P. Henon and Y. Saad, A Parallel Multistage ILU Factorization based on a Hierarchical Graph Decomposition, *SIAM Journal for Scientific Computing* **28** (2007), 2266-2293.

[5] K. Nakajima, Parallel Multistage Preconditioners based on a Hierarchical Graph Decomposition for SMP Cluster Architectures with a Hybrid Parallel Programming Model, *Lecture Notes in Computer Science* **4782** (2007) 384-395.

[6] Information Technology Center, the University of Tokyo: http://www.cc.u-tokyo.ac.jp/

[7] C.V. Deutsch and A.G. Journel, *GSLIB Geostatistical Software Library and User's Guide, Second Edition*, Oxford University Press, 1998.

[8] S.L. Zhang, GPBi-CG: Generalized Product-type methods based on Bi-CG for solving nonsymmetric linear systems, *SIAM Journal of Scientific Computing* **18** (1997) 537-551.

[9] Y. Saad, Y., *Iterative Methods for Sparse Linear Systems (2nd Edition)*. SIAM, 2003.

[10] GeoFEM: http://geofem.tokyo.rist.or.jp/

[11] T. Iwashita, Y. Nakanishi and M. Shimasaki, Comparison Criteria for Parallel Ordering in ILU Preconditioning, *SIAM Journal on Scientific Computing* **26-4** (2005) 1234-1260.

[12] K. Nakajima, Parallel multigrid method based on a hierarchical graph decomposition, *IPSJ Proceedings of HPCS 2008* (2008) 115-122 (in Japanese).

Parallel Computing: From Multicores and GPU's to Petascale
B. Chapman et al. (Eds.)
IOS Press, 2010
© 2010 The authors and IOS Press. All rights reserved.
doi:10.3233/978-1-60750-530-3-107

A Comparison of Different Communication Structures for Scalable Parallel Three Dimensional FFTs in First Principles Codes

A. Canning, [a,1], J. Shalf, [a] L-W. Wang, [a] H. Wasserman, [a] and M. Gajbe [b]

[a] *Lawrence Berkeley National Laboratory, Berkeley, California, USA*
[b] *Georgia Institute of Technology, Atlanta, Georgia, USA*

Abstract. Plane Wave based first principles electronic structure calculations are the most widely used approach for electronic structure calculations in materials science. In this formulation the electronic wavefunctions are expanded in plane waves (Fourier components) in three dimensional space and 3d FFTs are used to construct the charge density in real space. Many other scientific application codes in the areas of fluid mechanics, climate research and accelerator design also require efficient parallel 3d FFTs. Due to the large amount of communications required in parallel 3d FFTs the scaling of these application codes on large parallel machines depends critically on having a 3d FFT that scales efficiently to large processor counts. In this paper we compare different implementations for the communications in a 3d FFT to determine the most scalable method to use for our application. We present results up to 16K cores on the Cray XT4 and IBM Blue Gene/P as well as compare our implementations to publicly available 3d FFTs such as P3DFFT and FFTW. In our application our 3d FFTs significantly outperform any publicly available software. Our 3d FFT has been implemented in many different first principles codes used for research in materials science, nanoscience, energy technologies etc. as well as being a stand alone benchmark code used for the procurement of new machines at the Department of Energy NERSC computing center.

Keywords. Fast Fourier Transform, Parallel Computing, Materials Science

Introduction

In electronic structure calculations in materials science first-principles methods based on Density Functional Theory (DFT) in the Kohn-Sham (KS) formalism [1] are the most widely used approach. In this approach the wave functions of the electrons are usually expanded in plane waves (Fourier components) and pseudopotentials replace the nucleus and core electrons. This implementation requires parallel 3d FFTs to transform the electronic wavefunctions from Fourier space to real space to construct the charge density.

---

[1]Corresponding Author: A. Canning, Lawrence Berkeley National Laboratory, Berkeley, CA94720, USA.
E-mail: ACanning@lbl.gov

This gives a computationally very efficient approach with a full quantum mechanical treatment for the valence electrons, allowing the study of systems containing hundreds of atoms on modest-sized parallel computers. Taken as a method DFT-based codes are one of the largest consumers of scientific computer cycles around the world with theoretical chemists, biologists, experimentalists etc. now becoming users of this approach. Parallel 3d FFTs are very demanding on the communication network of parallel computers as they require global transpositions of the FFT grid across the machine. The ratio of calculations to communications for 3d FFTs is of order $\log N$ where N is the grid dimension (compared to a ratio of N for a distributed matrix multiply of matrix size N) which makes it one of the most demanding algorithms to scale on a parallel machine. A scalable parallel 3d FFT is critical to the overall scaling of plane wave DFT codes. Many papers have been written discussing in more detail these issues of scalability of parallel 3d FFTs (see for example [2,3]). In this work we have implemented six different versions of the communications routines used in the 3d FFT to determine which is the most efficient for different processor counts and different grid sizes.

In plane wave first principles codes we have many electronic wavefunctions where each one is represented in Fourier space so unlike spectral type codes we are typically performing many moderate sized 3d FFTs rather than one large 3d FFT. This has the disadvantage from the scaling point of view that it is difficult to efficiently scale up a moderate sized 3d FFT on a large number of processors but it has the advantage that for all-band codes we can perform many 3d FFTs at the same time to aggregate the message sizes and avoid latency issues. The wavefunctions are also represented by a sphere of points in Fourier space and a standard grid in real space where the sphere typically has a diameter about half the size of the grid as the charge density is proportional to the square of the wavefunctions. This means we can also reduce the amount of message passing and calculations required compared to using a standard 3d FFT where the number of grid points is the same in Fourier and real space. We have therefore written our own specialized 3d FFTs for plane wave codes that is faster than using any public domain 3d FFT libraries such as FFTW [7] or P3DFFT [8] and have no restrictions on what grid sizes can be run on any number of processors. Our specialized 3d FFTs are used in many widely used materials science codes such as PARATEC, PeTOT, and ESCAN [6].

DFT using the Local Density Approximation (LDA) for the exchange-correlation potential requires that the wavefunctions of the electrons $\{\psi_i\}$ satisfy the Kohn-Sham equations

$$[-\frac{1}{2}\nabla^2 + \sum_R v_{ion}(r - R) + \int \frac{\rho(r')}{|r - r'|}d^3r' + \mu_{xc}(\rho(r))]\psi_i = \varepsilon_i\psi_i \qquad (1)$$

where $v_{ion}(r)$ is the ionic pseudopotential, $\rho(r)$ is the charge density and $\mu_{xc}(\rho(r))$ is the LDA exchange-correlation potential. We use periodic boundary conditions, expanding the wavefunctions in plane waves (Fourier components),

$$\psi_{j,\mathbf{k}}(\mathbf{r}) = \sum_g a_{j,\mathbf{k}}(g)e^{i(\mathbf{g}+\mathbf{k})\cdot\mathbf{r}} . \qquad (2)$$

The selection of the number of plane waves is determined by a cutoff E_{cut} in the plane wave kinetic energy $\frac{1}{2}|\mathbf{g} + \mathbf{k}|^2$ where $\{g\}$ are reciprocal lattice vectors. This means that the representation of the wavefunctions in Fourier space is a sphere or ellipsoid with each **g** vector corresponding to a Fourier component (see Figure 1). The **k**'s are vectors sampling the first Brillouin Zone (BZ) of the chosen unit cell (or supercell). The Kohn-Sham equations are usually solved by minimizing the total energy with an iterative scheme, such as conjugate gradient (CG), for a fixed charge density and then updating the charge density until self-consistency is achieved (for a review of this approach see reference [4]). Some parts of the calculation are done in Fourier space and some in real space transforming between the two using 3d FFTs. Parallelization of plane wave type codes was first studied in reference [5].

1. Parallel Data Decomposition and Communication Structure for 3d FFT

A 3d FFT consists of three sets of 1d FFTs in the x,y and z directions with transpositions of the data between each set of 1d FFTs to make x,y and z the first dimension of the array for the sets of 1d FFTs. Only two transposes are needed if the final data layout is not required to have the same x,y,z order in both spaces. Since the **g** vectors, corresponding to the Fourier coefficients, are distributed across the processors these two transposes can require global communications across the parallel computer.

As mentioned in the previous section the data for a given wavefunction forms a sphere of points in Fourier space and a standard grid in real space (see Figure 1). The parallel data distribution for the sphere is driven by 1) the need to have complete columns of data on a given processor to perform the first set of 1d FFTs 2) other parts of the code require intensive calculations related to the number of Fourier components each processor holds so to load balance those parts of the calculation we require a similar number of Fourier components on each processor. The data layout we use in Fourier space is to order the columns of the sphere in descending order and then to give out the individual columns to the processors such that each new column is given to the processor with the fewest number of Fourier components. In this way each processor holds sets of complete columns and approximately the same number of Fourier components (see Figure 1 for an example of the layout on three processors). In real space we consider the grid as a one dimensional set of columns with (x,y,z) ordering and then give out contiguous sets of columns to each processor giving as closely as possible the same number of columns to each processor. In this way each processor will hold complete planes or sections of planes of the three dimensional grid (see Figure 1). With this data layout we have no restrictions, other than memory limits, on the number of processors that can be used for a given sphere or grid size. The size of the sphere is determined by the size of the supercell and energy cutoff. With this data layout the first transpose in the 3d FFT typically requires all processors communicating with every other processor while the second transpose may require no communications (if each processor has complete planes) or limited local communications if each processor has a section of a plane. In the case of SMP nodes complete planes can still reside on a node even if each processor is performing calculations on sections of the planes. In terms of the data layout at each of the x,y,z, 1d sets of FFTs we go from a cylinder to a slab to the full grid. One of the major savings of our 3d FFT compared to a standard 3d FFT is that we only perform 1d FFTs on the cylinder and slab in the x and y direction 1d FFTs and we only perform the parallel transpose operation on the cylinder. Since the sphere in Fourier space typically has a diameter half that of the full grid dimension this is a large saving in communications

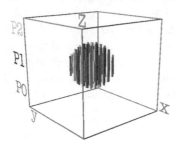 

Figure 1. Three processor example of the parallel data layout for the wavefunctions of the electrons in Fourier space (left) and real space (right). The different colors correspond to the data held by processors P0, P1 and P2.

compared to a parallel transpose of the full grid. A more detailed description of each step in our specialized 3d FFT can be found in reference [9].

It is also possible for a parallel 3d FFT to use a so called two dimensional mapping of processors to the FFT grid where the processors are divided into a two dimensional grid mapped onto two of the three dimensions of the full FFT grid. This layout can have superior performance on large processor counts but is not appropriate for our first principles code. This issue will be discussed in more detail in the section comparing our 3d FFT to the publicly available P3DFFT and FFTW 3d FFT libraries.

In order to have a scalable parallel 3d FFT we need to have as efficient as possible an implementation of the communications in the two parallel transposes. As mentioned above it is the first transpose that typically involves almost all the processors communicating with each other while the second transpose will typically involve limited local communications. We have implemented two basic types of MPI communications in our transposes. The first one uses MPI_ISEND and MPI_RECV or MPI_IRECV and the second uses MPI_ALLTOALLV which is a collective operation allowing all processors to send distinct messages of different lengths to all the other processors. In the case of the SEND and RECV versions we have implemented different communication structures. In the first case all the processors send to processor one then processor two etc. at the same time while in the second case each processor sends to its processor number plus one, then plus two etc. as if in a ring, to avoid contention in communications. We also have what we will refer to as blocked versions of these 3d FFTs where we perform a number of 3d FFTs at the same time (40 in our results) and so can aggregate the message sizes to avoid latency problems. In our particular application we are performing a large number of moderate sized 3d FFTs (our strong scaling tests will be for a 512^3 grid) so it is important to take advantage of this blocking to avoid latency issues on large processor counts.

2. Results on the Cray XT4 and IBM Blue Gene/P platforms

Our 3d FFT codes are written in Fortran 90 and use MPI libraries for the communications and calls the FFTW package [7] to perform the one dimensional FFTs in each of the three

Proc	isendrecv	isendrecv_s	isendirecv_all	alltoallv	alltoallv_bl	isendrecv_bl	weak scale
128	0.4139	0.2994	0.3082	0.3605	0.3663		0.0945
256	0.2730	0.1707	0.1899	0.2123	0.1921	0.2132	0.0996
512	0.3176	0.1181	0.1725	0.1743	0.1004	0.1168	0.1004
1024	6.2567	0.2722	0.2499	0.1969	0.0558	0.1310	0.1102
2048	7.9659	0.5982	0.4469	0.2808	0.0370	0.2355	0.1169
4096	8.0062	0.7872	0.4726	0.3077	0.0312	0.3862	0.1301
8192		0.4652	0.2514	0.2375	0.0221	0.3263	0.1680
16384		0.2533		0.1715	0.0136		0.2262

Table 1. Strong and weak scaling test for our 3d FFT on the Cray XT4. Time given in seconds is the sum of a forward and reverse 3d FFT on a 512^3 grid. The isendrecv versions use MPI_ISENDs and MPI_RECVs or MPI_IRECVs for the communications while the alltoall versions use MPI_ALLTOALLV. The bl versions block together 40 3d FFTS to aggregate the message sizes. The weak scaling test is the same as alltoallv_bl except that the grid size is chosen to be 512x512x(number of processors). A fuller explanation of the different implementations is presented in the main text. The Cray XT4 has quad core 2.3GHz Opteron processors, where each node is one quad core processor and the nodes are connected in a 3d torus. The Cray XT4 (named Franklin) has 38,640 compute node cores with a peak speed of 356 TFlops and is situated at the Department of Energy NERSC computing center [10].

Proc	alltoallv_bl(4cores)	alltoallv_bl(2cores)	alltoallv_bl(1core)
128	0.3663	0.2544	0.2120
256	0.1921	0.1301	0.1124
512	0.1004	0.0699	0.0596
1024	0.0558	0.0379	0.0325
2048	0.0370	0.0235	0.0232

Table 2. Strong Scaling for different core counts per node on the Cray XT4, 512^3 grid. All results are for the alltoallv blocked version of the code (see Table 1 caption plus text for more details)

Proc	isendrecv	isendrecv_s	isendrecv_bl	alltoallv	alltoallv_bl
512	0.2413			0.1768	
1024	0.1911	0.1232	0.1377	0.0929	0.1150
2048	0.9008	0.0636	0.0843	0.0396	0.0646
4096	6.5026	0.0758	0.1611	0.0346	0.0303
8192	41.4946	0.0979	1.0962	0.0342	0.0257
16384		0.1175	5.1327	0.0295	0.0124

Table 3. Strong scaling test for our 3d FFT on the IBM Blue Gene/P system. Annotations are the same as Table 1. The IBM Blue Gene/P system (named Intrepid) has 40,960 quad-core compute nodes (163,840 processors) and is situated at Argonne National Laboratory. Peak performance is 557 teraflops. Nodes are each connected to multiple inter-node networks, including a high-performance, low-latency 3D-torus, a highly scalable collective network, and a fast barrier network [11].

dimensions. Tables 1 and 2 show scaling on the Cray XT4 and Table 3 the scaling on the IBM Blue Gene/P for the different MPI and blocking implementations (for details on the Cray XT4 and IBM BG/P see figure captions plus references [10,11]). For the strong scaling results we have chosen a grid size in real space of 512^3. The sphere diameter in Fourier space was chosen to be half the grid size (256) giving a sphere with about 51400 columns in Fourier space. These dimensions were chosen to reflect what would be typical for a state-of-the-art calculation on of the order of a thousand atoms with a first principles electronic structure code. We would have obtained better scaling with a larger grid size but the results would not have had direct relevance to our application code. Other studies of 3d FFTs typically involve larger grid sizes. Since the number of columns in our sphere is about 51400 we present scaling results up to 16K processor cores as this corresponds to each processor having only about three columns in Fourier space. Above this number of processors we will have bad load balancing and scaling in other parts of our first principles code due to the small number of columns per processor. For the weak scaling results (last column in Table 1) we chose a grid size of 512x512x(number of processor cores). We should note that since the number of operations in an FFT scales as $N log N$ there is an increase in the number of flops performed in the z direction one dimensional FFTs so we do not expect perfect scaling (even if communications took no time). In this test the number of flops per processor increases by about 30% in going from 256 to 16384 processor cores which in part accounts for the increase in time in going from 256 to 16384 processors but the main contribution comes from the increased communication costs.

The different versions of the code correspond to the following implementations of the communication schemes. For the isendrecv version of the code each processor uses MPI_ISEND to post all its sends to all the other processors starting with processor one to processor *nproc* where *nproc* is the total number of processor cores. Each processor then posts all its MPI_RECVs in the same order followed by an MPI_WAIT on all the MPI_ISEND requests. The isendrecv_bl version is the original method used in our first principles code that was found to be near optimal for the early IBM SPs with small processor counts. As mentioned previously, in our application we wish to perform a 3d FFT for each electron state so our code typically performs hundreds to thousands of 3d FFTs for a large system of hundreds of atoms allowing us to easily block the 3d FFTs. In isendrecv_s communications are staggered (each processor sends to its nearest neighbor then next nearest neighbor etc. in a ring structure) rather than all just sending to the same processor at the same time. Also only one MPI_ISEND is posted by each processor before the corresponding MPI_RECV is posted followed by MPI_WAIT. isendirecv_all corresponds to an implementation using MPI_ISEND and MPI_IRECV that performs as closely as possible the communications in the same way as the implementation of MPI_ALLTOALLV in MPICH2 [12]. The communication structure in isendirecv_all is similar to isendrecv_s except that blocks of MPI_IRECVs are posted followed by the corresponding blocks of MPI_ISENDs followed by MPI_WAITs for the nonblocking sends and recvs. The default block size is set to four in the MPICH2 implementation. In our implementation the block size for the sends and recvs is given as an input. The motivation for this implementation in MPICH2 is probably to post as many messages as possible to exploit all the links in the network without posting too many that may cause contention in the network or exhaust the number of outstanding messages that can be handled by the hardware. The alltoallv implementation in the table uses the Cray implementation of the MPI_ALLTOALLV for communications which is a modified form of the MPICH2 implementation. We were not able to obtain from Cray the details of the modifications they have made to the MPICH2 version to optimize it for the XT4. alltoallv_bl is a blocked version performing 40 3d FFTs at the same time, aggregating the message sizes by 40 to avoid latency issues on larger processor counts. Similarly isendrecv_bl is a blocked verion of isendrecv. The isendrecv_bl version is the original method used in our first principles code that was found to be optimal for the early IBM

SPs with small processor counts. The weak scaling test is the same code as alltoallv_bl except that the grid size is chosen to be 512x512x(number of processors).

Overall the results show that on the Cray XT4 the best scaling to high processor counts is achieved by using the blocked version alltoallv_bl, with reasonable scaling up to 16K processors. As mentioned previously, in our implementation of the first parallel transpose in the 3d FFT, all processors are essentially communicating with each other and for the strong scaling tests the message size decreases as the inverse squared of the number of processors. To avoid latency issues on large processor counts it is there-fore crucial to perform blocks of 3d FFTs so that we can aggregate the messages by the block size. For the non-blocked implementations we can see in the tables that on smaller processor counts (below 512) they perform as well as the blocked versions and in some cases faster but on larger processor counts they are much slower. In particular the isendrecv version becomes very slow on lager processor counts (above 512) probably due to the limits on the number of outstanding messages that can be stored in hardware in the portals implementation on the Cray SeaStar interconnect [16]. The isendirecv_all version of our code is based closely on the MPICH2 implementation and was written to determine if we could gain any improvements over using the Cray MPI_ALLTOALLV for our particular application. With our version of the code we tried varying the num-ber of MPI_IRECVs that were preposted per processor before the MPI_ISENDs, from four to 128 but found little variation in the performance. The default value for this is four in the MPICH2 implementation. The results for isendirecv_all in table 1 are for the MPI_IRECVs preposted in blocks of 64 before the MPI_ISENDs and MPI_WAIT calls. Overall the performance of isendirecv_all compared to alltoallv (which calls the Cray MPI_ALLTOALLV routine) is very similar, with isendirecv_all being slightly faster on lower processor counts and a similar speed on 8K processors. The main difference is on 1K and 2K processor counts where alltoallv is about 35% faster. Since we do not have access to Crays source code for MPI_ALLTOALLV we do not know exactly what mod-ifications they have made to the MPICH2 version that could explain these differences in timing. Table 2 shows the results for the alltoall_bl version of the code on one to four cores per node. On smaller processor counts where most of time is spent on performing 1d FFT calls to FFTW, we can clearly see the contention for memory on the node for the four processor cores case. The single core run being about 1.7 times faster than the four core run for these cases. It should also be noted that we found large time variations of up to 30% from run to run on the same processor count on the Cray XT4. The data in the tables is for the fastest run. We attribute these differences mainly to the fact that on the XT4 the geometry of nodes obtained varies from run to run depending on what nodes are free. The nodes for one job can therefore be well separated physically on the machine compared to another job leading to higher communication costs. When we ran the same run many times from the same job script (so the nodes used would be the same) we saw little variation in the timings.

Table 3 shows results for similar tests on the IBM BG/P architecture. The IBM BG/P has a much lower latency for communications than the Cray XT4 so the blocking of communications gives a smaller gain in time for the alltoallv although the gain is still large on the isendrecv implementation. The isendrecv implementation clearly results in major contention as well as latency issues on higher processor counts as can be seen by the drop-off in performance on the Cray XT4 and even more so on the IBM BG/P architecture. Overall while the timings on the Cray XT4 are faster than the IBM BG/P architecture due to the faster processor the scaling to large processor counts is better on the IBM BG/P due to the better communication network. As on the Cray XT4 by far the best performance on the IBM BG/P at large processor counts is with the alltoallv_bl version of our code which scales well to 16K processors and runs faster than the Cray XT4 on 16K processors.

3. Comparison to P3DFFT and 3d FFTW

The specialized complex to complex 3d FFT we have written for our first principles code has many features that are not available in 3d FFT libraries. Usind a one dimensional based data layout it can perform a 3d FFT of any grid size on any number of processors and in Fourier space accepts the load balanced sphere data distribution as input. Even if we remapped our sphere data distribution to a more standard grid distribution, which would require significant communications, we are not aware of any 3d FFTs libraries that work for any grid size on any number of processors. Our 3d FFT can also perform many 3d FFTs at the same time to aggregate the message size and avoid latency issues. Again we are not aware of any 3d FFT libraries having this feature. One of the most flexible, in terms of data layout, and highest performance parallel 3d FFTs is P3DFFT [8]. At present P3DFFT is only available in real to complex form which makes it difficult to compare directly to our complex to complex 3d FFT. Using the same grid size a complex to complex 3d FFT has a data set that is twice the size of a real to complex and performs twice as many flops as a real to complex 3d FFT. In the case of a parallel version it will also communicate twice as much data as a real to complex 3d FFT. Two real to complex 3d FFTs can be performed with a complex to complex 3d FFT by packing the two real space grids into complex form. Therefore to a first approximation a complex to complex 3d FFT takes twice the time as a real to complex for the same grid size although complex to complex typically can run faster than this since the flop rate can be higher on a complex dataset and latency in communications can be less of an issue since the messages are twice the size. In Table 4 we present a comparisons of our 3d FFT with P3DFFT and FFTW where the times in brackets for P3DFFT are the measured times for a forward plus reverse real to complex 3d FFT and to give a reasonable comparison to our 3d FFT we have doubled those timings in the table. The times for 3d FFTW are for a complex to complex 3d FFT. Both P3DFFT and FFTW use the MPI_ALLTOALLV routine for communications in a similar way to our alltoallv routine.

The data layout for P3DFFT is specified by giving a two dimensional processor grid layout which maps onto two of the three dimensions of the FFT grid. The 3d FFTW can only accommodate complete planes of data on each processor. For small processor counts the best data layout for P3DFFT is a one dimensional layout where we have complete planes of data on each processor as shown in the 1d layout column in Table 4. In the case of our 512^3 grid this means we can have this data layout with up to 512 processors. As we go to larger processor counts where latency becomes an issue then a two dimensional data layout as shown in the 2d layout column becomes the most efficient. With a two dimensional data layout in each of the transposes we are only communicating the data set on each processor with of order $\sqrt{nproc}$ processors while with the one dimensional layout in one of the transposes we communicate with all $nproc$ processors. The one dimensional layout does have the advantage on smaller processor counts, where we have complete planes of the grid on each processor, that in the second transpose there are no communications to perform the transpose. So basically there is a crossover point as we go to larger processor counts where the two dimensional layout becomes faster than the one dimensional layout. In our case this occurs at about 512 processors as above this number we do not have complete planes on each processor and latency becomes more of an issue. Since in our implementation of the 3d FFT, even though we use a one dimensional type data layout, we are aggregating the message sizes for many 3d FFTs we do not have this same latency issue at larger processor counts. Also since our first transpose which involves communications between all the processors is only on the smaller cylinder of data rather than the full grid we have savings in the amount of data communicated compared to using P3DFFT. Since the diameter of the cylinder is 256 compared to the grid size of 512 the ratio of data in the cylinder to the full grid is $\frac{\pi}{16}$ so we have a large saving in communications and we also perform fewer 1d FFTs in the x and y directions than P3DFFT. All these factors explain why our specialized 3d FFT is much faster than P3DFFT and 3d FFTW at all processor counts and also scales well to large processor counts (16K) while P3DFFT does not scale well past 2K processors.

Proc	alltoallv_bl	P3DFFT [1d proc. layout]	P3DFFT [2d proc layout]	3d FFTW
128	0.3663	0.4988 (0.2494) [1x128]	1.0498 (0.5249) [8x16]	1.1275
256	0.1921	0.3228 (0.1614) [1x256]	0.5450 (0.2725) [16x16]	0.6235
512	0.1004	0.2938 (0.1469) [1x512]	0.2824 (0.1412) [16x32]	1.4063
1024	0.0558	0.3050 (0.1525) [2x512]	0.1236 (0.0618) [32x32]	
2048	0.0370	0.2370 (0.1185) [4x512]	0.0766 (0.0383) [32x64]	
4096	0.0312	0.2154 (0.1077) [8x512]	0.0698 (0.0349) [64x64]	
8192	0.0221	0.1659 (0.0829) [16x512]	0.0874 (0.0437) [64x128]	
16384	0.0136		0.0958 (0.0479) [128x128]	

Table 4. Comparison on the Cray XT4 of our 3d FFT (alltoallv_bl) to P3DFFT and 3d FFTW for a 512^3 grid. Our 3d FFT performs a complex to complex 3d FFT while the P3DFFT software performs a real to complex 3d FFT. The times for P3DFFT are double the measured time (which is shown in brackets) to give a fairer comparison to our 3d FFT. The last entry in the columns corresponds to the mapping of the processor grid to the FFT grid. The results for 3d FFTW are for a complex to complex 3d FFT and the only allowed data layout is complete planes of the FFT grid on each processor. See the main text for a fuller discussion.

4. Discussion and Future Work

Overall in this paper we have shown that by exploiting the specific features of our 3d FFTs in our specialized code for our first principles application we can achieve very good performance and scaling to large processor counts. At present in our materials science codes that use our 3d FFT, such as PARATEC [6] we have only implemented the blocked isendrecv version of the 3d FFTs but we are in the process of implementing the blocked alltoall version as well to allow it to scale to larger processor counts. This also requires modification of many other parts of the code to allow them to scale to larger processor counts. It should be noted that in the full code the number of operations scales as N^3 where N is the number of atoms while the 3d FFT part only scales as $N^2 log N$ so that as we go to larger numbers of atoms the FFT part takes a smaller percentage of the overall run time. In the full code the ratio of calculations to communications scales as N rather than $log N$ for the 3d FFT part which can allow the full code to scale up much better than the 3d FFT. Scaling results for the full PARATEC code have previously been published up to 2048 cores on the Cray XT4 where good scaling was achieved [13].

Other similar plane wave DFT codes such as QBOX [14] and CPMD [15] have achieved high levels of scalability (up to 64K nodes on the IBM BG/L in the case of QBOX) by having multiple levels of parallelism over k points, bands and the 3d FFTs rather than having a high level of parallelism in the 3d FFT. As we move to larger systems with more atoms the number of k points required typically decreases (often we just run at one k point for large systems, particularly for insulators and semi-conductors) so that to scale to larger processor counts for these codes requires a higher level of parallelism in the 3d FFTs. In the QBOX code they typically only parallelize the 3d FFT over at most 512 processors. Our new alltoallv blocked approach to the parallelization of the 3d FFT can allow these codes to scale to larger processor counts. Another area of research we are exploring to increase the level of parallelization in our 3d FFTs is to use a two level parallelization using MPI between nodes and OPENMP on the node. Since each node performs many one dimensional FFTs in each of the three dimensions we can thread these 1d FFTs over the processor cores on the node to increase the level of parallelization.

Acknowledgements

This research used resources of the National Energy Research Scientific Computing Center at the Lawrence Berkeley National Laboratory and the Argonne Leadership Computing Facility at Argonne National Laboratory, which are supported by the Office of Science of the U.S. Department of Energy under contracts DE-AC02-05CH11231 and DE-AC02-06CH11357.

References

[1]   W. Kohn and L.J. Sham, Phys. Rev. **140**, A1133 (1965).
[2]   A. Gupta and V. Kumar, In proceedings of the the third symposium on the frontiers of massively parallel computation, (1990).
[3]   D.H. Bailey The Journal of Supercomputing, 4:23-35, (1990).
[4]   M. Payne, M.P. Teter, D.C. Allan, T.A. Arias and J.D. Joannopoulos, Rev. Mod. Phys. **64**, 1045 (1992).
[5]   L.J. Clarke, I. Stich and M.C. Payne, Comput. Phys. Comm. 72 p14 (1992)
[6]   PARATEC (PARAllel Total Energy Code) www.nersc.gov/projects/paratec/
       PEtot, https://hpcrd.lbl.gov/ linwang/PEtot/PEtot.html
[7]   Matteo Frigo and Steven G. Johnson, "The Design and Implementation of FFTW3," Proceedings of the IEEE 93 (2), 216-231 (2005). http://www.fftw.org/
[8]   www.sdsc.edu/us/resources/p3dfft.php
[9]   A. Canning, L.W. Wang, A. Williamson and A. Zunger, J. of Comput. Phys. **160**, 29 (2000).
[10]   www.nersc.gov
[11]   http://www.alcf.anl.gov/
[12]   http://www.mcs.anl.gov/research/projects/mpich2/
[13]   A. Canning, Springer, J.M.L.M Palma et. al. (Eds.) proceedings of VECPAR 2008, p280 (2008).
[14]   F. Gygi et. al. Proceedings of the 2006 ACM/IEEE conference on Supercomputing Tampa, Florida, Gordon Bell prize winner, No. 45 (2006).
[15]   http://www.cpmd.org/
[16]   Ron Brightwell, Kevin T. Pedretti, Keith D. Underwood, Trammell Hudson, "SeaStar Interconnect: Balanced Bandwidth for Scalable Performance," IEEE Micro, vol. 26, no. 3, pp. 41-57, (2006).

Parallel Computing: From Multicores and GPU's to Petascale
B. Chapman et al. (Eds.)
IOS Press, 2010

© 2010 The authors and IOS Press. All rights reserved.

doi:10.3233/978-1-60750-530-3-117

Parallelization Strategies for ODE Solvers on Multicore Cluster Systems

Thomas RAUBER [a,1] Gudula RÜNGER [b]

[a] *University Bayreuth, Germany*
[b] *Chemnitz University of Technology, Germany*

Abstract. Mathematical models involving ordinary differential equation (ODEs) arise in many diverse applications, such as fluid flows, physics-based animation, mechanical systems, mathematical finances, or chemical reaction. The realistic simulation of these applications depends on fast methods for the numerical solution of ODEs as well as adequate parallel computation schemes exploiting the potential parallelism in an optimal way. Due to the advent of multicore technology, parallel resources are now widely available in form of multicore processors or clusters. It is required to revisit parallel computation schemes of ODE solvers for the use on these multicore platforms. The objective of this article is a survey and classification of computational techniques for the numerical integration of ODE systems. The emphasis lies on a computational model which captures the specifics of ODE codes as well as a hierarchical architectural model of multicore systems.

Keywords. multicore cluster, ordinary differential equation, parallelization

1. Introduction

Many scientific and engineering problems lead to systems of ordinary differential equations (ODEs). The numerical solution of such ODEs often requires a lot of computational resources, especially for large ODE systems as they typically occur when applying the method of lines to time-dependent partial differential equations (PDEs) using a fine-grain spatial discretization.

In this article, we consider parallelization strategies for one-step solution methods for initial value problems of ODEs. These methods are often used in practice because of their numerical stability and their efficiency. One-step methods perform a large number of consecutive time steps where the result of one time step κ is used for the execution of the next time step $\kappa + 1$. Parallelization strategies for these methods have to consider the parallelism available within one time step. Often, parallelism across the method and parallelism across the system can be exploited for task and data parallel formulations, respectively. Examples are stage-vector based solution methods, like iterated Runge-Kutta (RK) methods [10] or general linear methods [1], which compute a fixed number of in-

---

[1] Corresponding Author: Thomas Rauber, University Bayreuth, Germany; E-mail: rauber@uni–bayreuth.de.

dependent stage vectors in each time step and combine these stage vectors to compute the final solution vector of the time step.

For an efficient parallelization, the characteristics of the execution platform also have to be taken into consideration. Modern multicore cluster systems provide a hierarchy of computing resources consisting of nodes, processors, and cores, as well as different interconnections between the cores of the same processors, between processors of the same node, and between different nodes. Often, cores of the same processor or node can exchange data faster than cores of different processors or nodes. These differences have to be taken into consideration for the mapping of the computations of ODE methods to resources of the execution platform.

The main contribution of this paper are (i) a detailed analysis of the computational structure of task and data parallel execution schemes of typical ODE solvers, (ii) a discussion of the resulting communication requirements and, based on this, (iii) an exploration and discussion of the suitability of different mapping strategies for ODE-tasks to the resources of modern multicore cluster systems. The investigations are performed by considering two representative ODE solvers. The results can be extended to a larger class of computation schemes for ODE solvers that are based on stage vector computations.

The rest of the paper is structured as follows. Section 2 describes the computational structure of the ODE solvers considered and discusses parallelization strategies. Section 3 investigates mapping strategies for ODE-tasks, which are then evaluated in Section 4 concerning their parallel efficiency on selected execution platforms. Section 5 concludes.

2. Parallelization Strategies for ODE solvers

During the last years, several parallel solution methods for first-order ODEs have been proposed [2,3,5,8]. Many of these ODE solvers are based on multistage methods, including RK methods and their parallel variants. Another class of solution methods are general linear methods with their parallel variants Parallel Adams-Bashforth (PAB) and Parallel Adams-Bashforth-Moulton (PABM) methods [1,9]. All these methods provide potential task and data parallelism. However, they have different communication requirements between the resulting tasks.

We consider a system of initial-value problems (IVPs) of first order ODEs of the form

$$\mathbf{y}'(t) = \mathbf{f}(t, \mathbf{y}(t)), \quad \mathbf{y}(t_0) = \mathbf{y}_0 \tag{1}$$

with initial vector $\mathbf{y}_0 \in \mathbb{R}^d$ at start time $t_0 \in \mathbb{R}$, system size $d \geq 1$, and right hand side function $\mathbf{f} : \mathbb{R} \times \mathbb{R}^d \to \mathbb{R}^d$. The unknown solution function is $\mathbf{y} : \mathbb{R} \to \mathbb{R}^d$. One-step methods for solving ODE systems of the form (1) start with $\mathbf{y}_0$ and generate a sequence of approximations $\mathbf{y}_n$, $n = 1, 2, ...$, for the solution $\mathbf{y}(t_n)$ at time t_n, $n = 1, 2, ...$ Parallelism can only be exploited within the computations of each time step, since the time steps depend on each other.

In this section, we discuss parallelization strategies for ODE solvers that are based on mixed task and data parallel execution. We consider the following stage-based ODE methods as examples: (i) Iterated RK methods (IRK), (ii) Parallel Adams-Bashforth (PAB) methods, and (iii) Parallel Adams-Bashforth-Moulton (PABM) methods [9,7]. IRK and PAB methods are explicit solution methods; PABM methods are implicit solution methods. PAB and PABM methods are examples for general linear methods.

2.1. Iterated Runge-Kutta methods

Iterated RK methods are derived from s-stage implicit RK methods with stage vectors

$$\mathbf{k}_l = \mathbf{f}(x_\kappa + c_l \cdot h_\kappa, y_\kappa + h_\kappa \sum_{i=1}^{s} a_{li}\mathbf{k}_i), \quad l = 1, \ldots, s. \tag{2}$$

They iterate the implicit equation system (2) for a fixed number of times m producing approximations $\mu_{(j)}^l$, $j = 1, \ldots, m$, of the stage vectors $\mathbf{k}_l$, $l = 1, \ldots, s$. The last approximations $\mu_{(m)}^l$ are used for the computation of the next approximation of the solution function (denoted by $y_{\kappa+1}^{(m)}$) according to the corresponding computation scheme:

$$\mu_{(0)}^l = \mathbf{f}(y_\kappa), \qquad l = 1, \ldots, s,$$

$$\mu_{(j)}^l = \mathbf{f}(y_\kappa + h_\kappa \sum_{i-1}^{s} a_{li}\mu_{(j-1)}^i), \qquad l = 1, \ldots, s, \qquad j = 1, \ldots, m, \tag{3}$$

$$y_{\kappa+1}^{(m)} = y_\kappa + h_\kappa \sum_{l=1}^{s} b_l \mu_{(m)}^l.$$

The order of the approximation $y_{\kappa+1}^{(m)}$ is $min\{r, m+1\}$ where r is the order of the underlying implicit RK method. Embedded solutions result when using approximations $\mu_{(j)}^l$ of the stage vectors $\mathbf{k}_l$ with $j < m$.

For a parallel implementation with mixed task and data parallelism, s disjoint groups $G_1, \ldots, G_s$ of symbolic processors are used with about the same number of processors $g_l = \lceil p/s \rceil$. In each time step, the initialization of $\mu_{(0)}^l$ is performed by each of these groups in parallel such that each processor of each group G_l initializes about $\lceil d/g_l \rceil$ components of $\mu_{(0)}^1, \ldots, \mu_{(0)}^s$ where d is the size of the ODE system. These components are needed for the first iteration step. Each processor initializes exactly those components that it later needs for the iteration steps. To do so, each processor evaluates $\lceil d/g_l \rceil$ components of $\mathbf{f}$. In each iteration step $j = 1, \ldots, m$ of the fixed point iteration (3), group G_l is responsible for the computation of one subvector $\mu_{(j)}^l$, $l \in \{1, \ldots, s\}$. This computation can be considered as a parallel task (also called M-task) which is executed by all processors of G_l in parallel. The parallel task consists of the computation of the argument vector $\tilde{\mu}(l, j) = y_\kappa + h \sum_{i=1}^{s} a_{li}\mu_{(j-1)}^i$ and the evaluation of $\mathbf{f}(\tilde{\mu}(l, j)) = (f_1(\tilde{\mu}(l, j)), \ldots, f_n(\tilde{\mu}(l, j)))$. In the following, we call this an ODE-task $ODE_{IRK}(l, j)$. In order to achieve an even distribution of the computational work among the processors, each processor $q \in G_l$ computes about $\lceil d/g_l \rceil$ components of $\tilde{\mu}(l, j)$ and executes about $\lceil d/g_l \rceil$ function evaluations $f_i(\tilde{\mu}(l, j))$. Between these steps, processor q

communicates its local elements of $\tilde{\mu}(l, j)$ to the other members of the same group using a group-internal multi-broadcast operation. After each iteration step, each processor sends its local elements of $\mu^l_{(j)}$ to all other processors. Thus, the vectors $\mu^1_{(j)}, \ldots, \mu^s_{(j)}$ are available on all processors for the next iteration step. The computation of $y_{\kappa+1}$ is performed in parallel by all processors and the result is broadcast such that $y_{\kappa+1}$ is available on all processors for the next time step. Stepsize control is based on the computation of $y^{m-1}_{\kappa+1}$ in the same way, see [6] for details.

An analysis of the resulting communication pattern shows that a significant amount of communication is performed between the ODE tasks because of the global multi-broadcast operation after each fixed point iteration step. Thus, for a multicore platform, both ODE-task-internal and communication between the ODE-tasks is important.

2.2. PAB and PABM methods

General linear methods compute several stage values $\mathbf{y}_{ni}$ (vectors of size d) in each time step, corresponding to numerical approximations of $\mathbf{y}(t_n + a_i h)$ with abscissa vector (a_i), $i = 1, \ldots, k$ and stepsize $h = t_n - t_{n-1}$. The stage values of one time step are combined in the vector $\mathbf{Y}_n = (\mathbf{y}_{n1}, \ldots, \mathbf{y}_{nk})$ of length $d \cdot k$ and the computation in each step is given by:

$$\mathbf{Y}_{n+1} = (\mathbf{R} \otimes \mathbf{I})\mathbf{Y}_n + h(\mathbf{S} \otimes \mathbf{I})\mathbf{F}(\mathbf{Y}_n) + h(\mathbf{T} \otimes \mathbf{I})\mathbf{F}(\mathbf{Y}_{n+1}), \quad n = 1, 2, \ldots \quad (4)$$

The matrices $\mathbf{R}$, $\mathbf{S}$ and $\mathbf{T}$ have dimension $k \times k$ and $\mathbf{R} \otimes \mathbf{I}$, for example, denotes the Kronecker tensor product, i.e. the $d \cdot k \times d \cdot k$ dimensional block matrix with $d \times d$ blocks $r_{ij} \cdot \mathbf{I}$ for $i, j = 1, \ldots, k$. $\mathbf{I}$ denotes the $d \times d$ unit matrix. Typical values for k lie in the range 2 to 8. The PAB and PABM methods result from (4) by specific choices for $\mathbf{R}$, $\mathbf{S}$, and $\mathbf{T}$ [7]: The PAB method results from setting $\mathbf{T} = 0$ and $\mathbf{R} = \mathbf{e} \cdot \mathbf{e_k}^T$ where $\mathbf{e} = (1, \ldots, 1)$ and $\mathbf{e_k} = (0, \ldots, 0, 1)$. The PAM method results by using a diagonal matrix $\mathbf{T}$ with suitable diagonal entries δ_i and $\mathbf{R} = \mathbf{e} \cdot \mathbf{e_k}^T$, leading to an implicit method. The PABM method results by using the PAB method for a predictor step and the PAM method as corrector in form of a fixed point iteration, see [7,9] for more details.

A mixed task and data parallel computation scheme for the PAB method results by employing k disjoint groups $G_1, \ldots, G_k$ of symbolic processors of approximately equal size $g = \lceil p/k \rceil$ where p is the total number of cores. In each time step n, processor group G_i is responsible for computing stage value $y_{n+1,i}$, $i = 1, \ldots, k$. This is referred to as ODE-task $\text{ODE}_{PAB}(i)$ in the following. The computation of $y_{n+1,i}$ requires accesses to $\mathbf{f}(y_{n1}), \ldots, \mathbf{f}(y_{nk})$ for $i = 1, \ldots, k$ which are computed independently. Thus, by data exchange, each processor gets exactly those components that it needs for its local computation. This can, for example, be implemented by first collecting the components of $\mathbf{f}(y_{ni})$ on a specific processor, q_{ij}, of G_i, $i = 1, \ldots, k$, using a group-local gather operation and then broadcasting them to the processors of all other groups. The group-local gather operations can be performed concurrently by the different groups, whereas the single-broadcast operations have to be performed one after another because all processors are involved, thus leading to k single-broadcast operations. Since the right-hand side function $\mathbf{f}$ is different for every specific ODE problem, no specific access property of $\mathbf{f}$ can be assumed. Thus, $y_{n+1,i}$ has to be distributed among all the processors of G_i by a multi-broadcast operation to ensure a group-replicated distribution of the stage values and to enable a group internal evaluation of $\mathbf{f}(y_{n+1,i})$ in the next time step. In addition, the last stage vector y_{nk} has to be sent to all other groups G_i, $i = 1,\ldots,k$, by a single-broadcast operation involving all processors for the computation of the PAB step in the next time step.

Considering the resulting communication pattern, it can be seen that most of the communication is performed within the specific ODE-tasks $\text{ODE}_{PAB}(i)$ for $i \in \{1,\ldots,k\}$. Only the last stage vector must be communicated to processors outside the processor group. This suggests that this ODE method can benefit significantly from a mixed task and data parallel implementation. For multicore processors, it is important to minimize the group-local communication by a suitable mapping.

Based on a parallel implementation of the PAB method, the PABM method performs a fixed number of corrector steps with the same communication pattern as the PAB method. The communication pattern of both the PAB and PABM methods can be further improved towards group-local communication by exploiting orthogonal structures of communication based on the definition of orthogonal processor groups. This can be used to replace the global communication by local communication within the orthogonal processor groups, see [7] for more details.

For multicore processors, the mapping of the symbolic processor groups to the cores provided by the hardware is important. This is investigated in the next section.

3. Mapping Strategies for ODE solvers

Even for homogeneous parallel platforms, the scheduling of ODE-tasks to sets of processors has an influence on the performance of the ODE solver. For such homogeneous schedules, the exploitation of parallelism across the method by parallel ODE-tasks and of parallelism across the system within ODE-tasks can lead to notable variations in the performance. Due to the diversity of the problem concerning, e.g., size of the ODE system, number of internal ODE-tasks in each time step due to the basic solution method, varying ODE methods and different characteristics of the ODE problem, different schedules may lead to the best performance for different parallel platforms [6,7]. Even for the same ODE problem and the same solution method, a varying size of the ODE system may require a change of the schedule to get the best performance.

Considering multicore systems with homogeneous cores, but heterogeneous interconnections introduces a new dimension for the scheduling problem of the ODE-tasks to execution units (cores). The specific selection of physical cores for the execution of ODE-tasks can have a large influence on the resulting communication time, since different communication costs for internal task communication and re-distributions between tasks can result for different selections. Multicore clusters considered in this article consist of a hierarchy of computing resources. We assume that the cores are of the same type but different interconnections exist between (i) cores of the same processor, (ii) processors of the same compute node, and (iii) nodes of a partition or the entire machine.

The assignment of ODE-tasks to cores should take the task structure and the hierarchical architectural structure of the execution platform into account in order to achieve a good

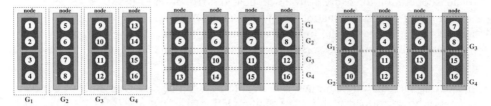

Figure 1. Ordering of the 16 cores of a cluster system with four nodes of two dual-core processors each. The different orderings consecutive (left), scattered (middle), and mixed (right) are illustrated by the numbers 1, ..., 16. The cores are arranged in four groups $G_1, \ldots, G_4$.

overall performance of the ODE solver. In this paper, we adopt a two-step approach consisting of a scheduling step and a mapping step. For ODE solution methods, an ODE-task-oriented scheduling and mapping mechanism is reasonable to maintain the inherent potential parallelism across the method and across the system. For the scheduling, the ODE-tasks are assigned to groups of homogeneous symbolic cores, as described in the previous section, without considering varying communication costs. Thus, the scheduling step mainly realizes a load balancing step on the mixed task and data parallel level. The ODE-tasks are assigned to symbolic cores in such a way that the ODE-tasks finish each time step of the solution method at the same time.

The symbolic cores are then mapped to physical cores in the mapping step taking communication costs into account. As starting point of the mapping step, we assume that s independent ODE-tasks are executed concurrently to each other using a group partitioning $G = (G_1, \ldots, G_s)$ of symbolic cores such that group G_i executes one ODE-task. The mapping maintains the ODE-task-oriented scheduling and maps an entire group of symbolic cores to a set of physical cores. To investigate different mappings, we consider different linearizations of the physical cores of the system: (i) A *consecutive ordering* enumerates the cores in the order of the nodes, i.e., in this ordering, the cores of the first node come first, then the cores of the second node etc. Within the nodes, there is no specific order of the cores. (ii) A *scattered ordering* enumerates the cores such that the first cores of each node come first, then the second cores etc. No specific order of the cores of a node is assumed. (iii) A *mixed ordering* mixes both orderings in a regular way, e.g., by using the first two cores of each node first. The mappings assign the cores to the ODE-tasks such that a contiguous set of cores executes one ODE-task. Figure 1 gives an illustration. Due to the different enumerations of the cores, different mappings result: For the consecutive mapping, symbolic cores of one group are mapped consecutively to physical cores, such that as few nodes as possible are used for a group. The scattered mapping tries to use one core per node only, thus using as many nodes as possible for a group. The mixed mapping mixes these two strategies by using a fixed number of cores per node.

Which of these mappings leads to the smallest execution times depends on the communication pattern of the ODE-tasks. If the ODE-tasks perform mainly internal communication, it can be expected that a consecutive mapping leads to the best results, since it can use node-internal communication. On the other hand, if the communication between different ODE-tasks is dominating, other mappings can be beneficial.

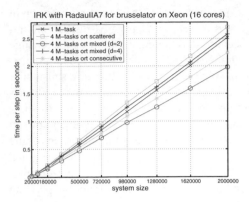
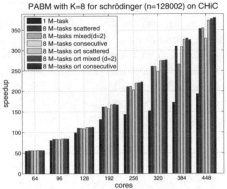

Figure 2. Left: Execution times of one time step of IRK using the four-stage RadauIIA7 method on the Xeon cluster for one M-task (data parallel) and four M-tasks (task parallel) with different mappings. Right: Speedups of PABM method with $K = 8$ stages using the Schrödinger equation on the CHiC system.

4. Experimental evaluation

For the runtime experiments, we use the following two platforms: A Xeon cluster which consists of two nodes with two Intel Xeon E5345 quad-core processors each. The processors run at 2.33 GHz. An infiniband network with a bandwidth of 10 GBit/s connects the nodes. MVAPICH2 1.0bcta is used. The Chemnitz High Performance Linux (CHiC) cluster is built up of 538 nodes each consisting of two AMD Opteron 2218 dual core processors with a clock rate of 2.6 GHz. The nodes are interconnected by a 10 GBit/s infiniband network. For the benchmark tests, the MVAPICH 1.0beta MPI library is used.

The evaluation cost of the components of the right-hand side function of the ODE system to be solved has a large influence on the resulting performance. We consider two classes of ODE systems: (i) For *sparse* ODE systems, each component of the right-hand side function **f** has fixed evaluation time independent of the size of the ODE system. (ii) For *dense* ODE systems, each component of **f** has an evaluation time that increases linearly with the system size. An example for (i) is an ODE system that results from the spatial discretization of a 2-dimensional PDE describing the reaction with diffusion of two chemical substances (Brusselator equation) [4,6]. An example for (ii) is a spectral decomposition of a time-dependent Schrödinger equation [6].

Figure 2 (left) shows the execution times of one time step of an IRK method with four stages on the Xeon cluster with 16 cores. In this configuration each M-task is executed by four cores. As discussed in Section 2, communication between the ODE-tasks is important for the IRK methods, and therefore the task-parallel versions do not have a clear advantage over the data parallel version. The orthogonal data exchange is carried out by the processes with the same rank within an M-task. The scattered and the mixed ($d = 2$) mappings make sure that these processes run on the same cluster node. The mixed ($d = 2$) mapping additionally allows shared memory optimizations for intra M-task communication and therefore leads to the smallest execution times. This example shows that the mapping of M-tasks to cores has to be selected carefully depending on the target application to reach an optimal performance.

Figure 2 (right) compares the different execution schemes of a PABM method with eight stage vectors on the CHiC cluster. As discussed in Section 2, intra M-task communication is important in the PABM methods because only a single global data exchange is required in each time step. For the task-parallel versions, intra M-task communication can be performed concurrently on disjoint subsets of cores leading to a substantial speedup of task parallelism compared to pure data parallelism. A comparison of the different mappings shows that for a smaller number of cores, all mappings lead to similar speedups for the standard version with some advantages for the scattered and mixed mappings for a larger number of processors caused by the global communication for the last stage vector. This global communication can be avoided by exploiting an orthogonal communication pattern as discussed in Section 2. By doing so, the speedup can be further increased, especially for a larger number of cores, and the consecutive mapping perform best because of the dominating role of intra-task communication.

5. Conclusions

This paper demonstrates that mixed task and data parallel computation schemes for ODE solvers can be exploited for scheduling and mapping strategies for parallel algorithms with a good scalability behavior. In particular, it is possible to exploit the structure of modern multicore architectures by suitable mappings of ODE-tasks to execution cores of the platform. Because of the communication structure of multicore cluster systems, it is typically beneficial to assign ODE-tasks to cores such that the cores of one processor or node are used for a single ODE-task. Comparing data-parallel implementations with mixed parallel versions, it can be observed that the mixed parallel versions lead to faster execution times, if most of the communication is performed within the ODE-tasks. This becomes especially important if the number of cores increases.

References

[1]   J.C. Butcher. *The Numerical Analysis of Ordinary Differential Equations, Runge-Kutta and General Linear Methods*. Wiley, New York, 1987.
[2]   N. Cong and L. Xuan. Twostep-by-twostep PIRK-type PC methods with continuous output formulas. *J. Comput. Appl. Math.*, 221(1):165–173, 2008.
[3]   E. Hairer, S.P. Nørsett, and G. Wanner. *Solving Ordinary Differential Equations I: Nonstiff Problems*. Springer–Verlag, Berlin, 2000.
[4]   E. Hairer and G. Wanner. *Solving Ordinary Differential Equations II*. Springer, 2002.
[5]   M. Korch and T. Rauber. Optimizing locality and scalability of embedded Runge-Kutta solvers using block-based pipelining. *Journal of Parallel and Distributed Computing*, 66(3):444–468, March 2006.
[6]   T. Rauber and G. Rünger. Parallel Iterated Runge–Kutta Methods and Applications. *International Journal of Supercomputer Applications*, 10(1):62–90, 1996.
[7]   T. Rauber and G. Rünger. Mixed task and data parallel executions in general linear methods. *Scientific Programming*, 15(3):137–155, 2007.
[8]   B. A. Schmitt, R. Weiner, and K. Erdmann. Implicit parallel peer methods for stiff initial value problems. *Appl. Numer. Math.*, 53(2):457–470, 2005.
[9]   P.J. van der Houwen and E. Messina. Parallel Adams Methods. *J. of Comp. and App. Mathematics*, 101:153–165, 1999.
[10]   P.J. van der Houwen and B.P. Sommeijer. Iterated Runge–Kutta Methods on Parallel Computers. *SIAM Journal on Scientific and Statistical Computing*, 12(5):1000–1028, 1991.

Parallel Computing: From Multicores and GPU's to Petascale
B. Chapman et al. (Eds.)
IOS Press, 2010

© 2010 The authors and IOS Press. All rights reserved.

doi:10.3233/978-1-60750-530-3-125

Evaluation of Parallel Sparse Matrix Partitioning Software for Parallel Multilevel ILU Preconditioning on Shared-Memory Multiprocessors [1]

José I. ALIAGA [a]   Matthias BOLLHÖFER [b]   Alberto F. MARTÍN [a]
Enrique S. QUINTANA-ORTÍ [a]

[a] *Dept. of Computer Science and Engineering, Universidad Jaume I, Castellón, Spain*
e-mail: {aliaga,martina,quintana}@icc.uji.es
[b] *Inst. of Computational Mathematics, TU-Braunschweig, Braunschweig, Germany*
e-mail: m.bollhoefer@tu-braunschweig.de

Abstract In this paper we analyze the performance of two parallel sparse matrix partitioning software packages, ParMETIS and PT-SCOTCH. We focus our analysis on the parallel performance of the nested dissection partitioning stage as well as its impact on the performance of the numerical stages of the solution of sparse linear systems via multilevel ILU preconditioned iterative methods. Experimental results on a shared-memory platform with 16 processors show that ParMETIS seems to be the best choice for our approach.

Keywords. large sparse linear systems, factorization-based preconditioning, nested dissection, parallel partitioning software, shared-memory multiprocessors

1 Introduction

The solution of linear systems of the form $Ax = b$ is one of the key computational tasks in many problems arising from chemistry, physics, and engineering applications. Furthermore, solving the linear system often consumes most of the total computation time of the application problem and, therefore, the development for fast and efficient numerical solution techniques becomes crucial. When A is a *large* and *sparse* matrix, Krylov subspace iteration algorithms accelerated via approximate factorization-based preconditioners often result in an attractive solution technique [9]. Among these preconditioning methods, ILUPACK (Incomplete LU decomposition PACKage, `http://ilupack.tu-bs.de`) is a software package which computes an approximate LU factorization of A and solves linear systems via preconditioned Krylov subspace methods.

In an earlier work [1], we presented an OpenMP parallelization of ILUPACK for shared-memory multiprocessors. The approach considered there relies on a initial parti-

---
[1] This research has been supported by the CICYT project TIN2008-06570-C04, and the DAAD D-07-13360/*Acciones Integradas Hispano-Alemanas* programme HA2007-0071

tioning step of A which exposes parallelism for the numerical stages of the solver. Currently, this preprocessing step only exploits the (naive) type of parallelism based on re-ordering in parallel the independent subgraphs resulting from the nested dissection process. One of the main conclusions derived from our initial results is that, for large-scale problems arising from discretized partial differential equations in three-spatial dimensions (3D), this partitioning stage dominates the overall execution time when the number of processors is large. Therefore the computational cost for this stage has to be reduced using more efficient algorithms which exploit additional types of parallelism during the partitioning phase. In this paper we evaluate two different state-of-the-art parallel sparse matrix partitioning software packages: ParMETIS[2] and PT-SCOTCH[3]. We focus our analysis on the parallel performance of the nested dissection partitioning stage as well as its impact on the performance of the numerical stages of the iterative solution of the linear system. We believe that the analysis of these techniques in the context of preconditioned iterative solvers together with a fully-parallel approach for the solution of large and sparse linear systems are two significant contributions of this paper.

The paper is organized as follows. In Section 2 we present the general framework for the iterative solution of linear systems with ILUPACK. Section 3 briefly discusses our approach to parallelization, focusing on the initial preprocessing step and the state-of-the-art parallel partitioning software: ParMETIS and PT-SCOTCH. In Section 4 we demonstrate experimentally the effectiveness of our method for several large-scale examples which reveal that ParMETIS seems to be the best choice for our approach. A few concluding remarks close the paper in Section 5.

2. Iterative solution of sparse linear systems with ILUPACK

The iterative solution of linear systems with ILUPACK is based on preconditioning the original linear system with an approximate factorization of A. In particular, ILUPACK implements a multilevel variant of the ILU factorization which is based on the so-called inverse-based approach. This type of multilevel preconditioners have been successfully applied to large-scale 3D application problems with up to millions of equations [1,3,10]. In the rest of the paper, we assume A to be s.p.d. because this is the class of linear systems currently targeted by the parallel version of ILUPACK.

We introduce the computation of the Multilevel Incomplete Cholesky (MIC) decomposition in ILUPACK next. Initially, A is scaled by means of a diagonal matrix D, which balances the size of its entries, and permuted by a fill-in reducing permutation matrix P.

$$Ax = b \quad \rightarrow \quad \left(P^T DADP\right)\left(P^T D^{-1}x\right) = \left(P^T Db\right) \quad \rightarrow \quad \hat{A}\hat{x} = \hat{b}. \tag{1}$$

The approximate factorization process of $\hat{A}$ essentially avoids the factorization of "bad" diagonal pivots by moving these to the end of the system. Formally this is done by applying a sequence of permutations, $\hat{P}$. In order to compute this factorization efficiently, the Crout formulation [9] of the IC decomposition is used, and the following steps are performed at each iteration:

---

[2]http://glaros.dtc.umn.edu/gkhome/views/metis.
[3]http://www.labri.fr/perso/pelegrin/scotch.

1. Compute the row/column of the (approximate) Cholesky factor corresponding to this iteration. This is done by considering the current row/column of $\hat{A}$ and updating it using that part of the Cholesky factor which has already been computed.
2. If the current diagonal pivot is "bad", move the current row and column to the bottom and right-end part of the system rejecting the updates of the previous step.
3. Otherwise, apply certain "dropping techniques" to the row/column of the approximate Cholesky factor computed at the first step (essentially entries below a given relative threshold τ are dropped [4]).

This process finally results in a partial IC decomposition of a permuted matrix $\hat{P}^T \hat{A} \hat{P}$. The approximate Schur complement corresponding to this partial decomposition must be computed for that part of the system that was not factored, leading to

$$\hat{P}^T \hat{A} \hat{P} = \begin{pmatrix} B & F^T \\ F & C \end{pmatrix} = \begin{pmatrix} L_B & 0 \\ L_F & I \end{pmatrix} \begin{pmatrix} D_B & 0 \\ 0 & S_C \end{pmatrix} \begin{pmatrix} L_B^T & L_F^T \\ 0 & I \end{pmatrix} + E, \tag{2}$$

where E refers to some error matrix which contains those "small" entries which have been dropped during the approximate factorization. The whole method (scaling, fill-reducing permutation and partial IC factorization) is then restarted on the approximate Schur complement S_C, turning this computation into a multilevel procedure. The computation is finished when, at a given level, S_C is void or "dense enough" to be handled by a dense Cholesky solver.

A theoretical analysis along with numerical observations reveals that, for robustness, a diagonal pivot will be considered "bad" whenever the norm of the scaled inverse Cholesky factor exceeds a given moderate bound. This property improves the numerical performance of the method as the iterative solution of the preconditioned linear system involves inverting the approximate Cholesky factor [3,4].

3. Partitioning techniques for parallel iterative solution of linear systems

Our approach for the computation of the parallel MIC employs nested dissection partitioning algorithms. These algorithms use a heuristic partitioning strategy which is based on the recursive application of vertex separator-finding algorithms. Let G_A refer to the adjacency graph of A. Nested dissection starts by finding a *small* subset of G_A, called vertex or node separator, which splits G_A into two independent subgraphs of roughly *equal size*. These graphs are then partitioned recursively using the same strategy, until the desired number of independent subgraphs are obtained. As a result of this process, a permuted coefficient matrix $A \to \Pi^T A \Pi$ is obtained, and because of its structure, concurrency can be easily exploited for the computation of the preconditioner. In Figure 1, G_A is split into four subgraphs (1,1), (1,2), (1,3), and (1,4) (in a two-level recursion of nested dissection) by separators (3,1), (2,1), and (2,2). The graph resulting from the dissection procedure exhibits the property that disconnected subgraphs or separators can be factorized independently. This property is captured in the task dependency tree in Figure 1, which also identifies a certain ordering of the elimination process imposed by the dependencies. For the computation of the parallel preconditioner, essentially the multilevel approach of ILUPACK is applied within the nodes of the task tree, taking care of the dependencies during the computation. The parallelization of the operations involved in the preconditioned iteration is done conformally with the logical structure built during the computation of the parallel MIC. For details, see [1,2].

$$G_A \qquad\qquad A \qquad\qquad A \to \Pi^T A \Pi \qquad\qquad \text{Task dependency tree}$$

Figure 1. Nested dissection partitioning. From left to right: nested dissection, natural ordering, nested dissection (re)ordering, and task dependency tree.

For the computation of the vertex separators we currently employ the fast and efficient multilevel [6] variants implemented, e.g., in the METIS and SCOTCH partitioning packages. The procedure underlying these multilevel variants can be sketched into the three following stages:

1. In the coarsening stage, a hierarchy of coarser graphs is constructed from the initial graph by computing matchings which collapse vertices and edges.
2. In the partitioning stage, a separator is computed for the coarsest graph.
3. In the uncoarsening stage, the initial separator is projected back and refined through the hierarchy of graphs up to the initial graph using local refinement optimization heuristics such as the KL or FM algorithms; see, e.g, [6].

In METIS, the nested dissection procedure enters the recursion until the independent subgraphs are "small", switching to minimum-degree-like orderings on these small graphs. (Fill-reducing is the guiding principle for such a deep recursive partitioning.) As our main motivation for using nested dissection is to reveal parallelism for the computation of the numerical stages of our solver, reordering the independent subgraphs recursively by nested dissection is not necessary as long as enough parallelism has been revealed during the process. We can instead switch to cheaper fill-in reducing orderings on the subdomains such as AMD-like heuristics. This can already be done in parallel by exploiting the parallelism exposed by partitioning A. We have observed that this partitioning stage consumes a relative significant amount of time, which needs to be reduced (without degrading the performance of the parallel numerical stages). In this sense, SCOTCH is a more flexible software because the nested dissection procedure can be truncated as soon as the desired number of independent subgraphs have been obtained.

Although we significantly benefit in terms of overall execution time from truncating the nested dissection procedure and reordering the independent subgraphs in parallel, the computational cost of the partitioning stage still increases when the number of processors gets larger. A larger number of processors translates into additional levels of recursion of the nested dissection procedure, and therefore implies larger computational costs. This can clearly limit the parallel efficiency of the approach. Furthermore, for 3D problems the initial levels of the dissection procedure usually consume a significant amount of time with respect to the overall nested dissection process, and therefore the degree of concurrency which can be exploited by reordering the independent subgraphs in parallel drops rapidly. These are the main motivations for considering parallel solutions for the initial partitioning step.

ParMETIS and PT-SCOTCH are, respectively, the parallel versions of METIS and SCOTCH, designed both for distributed-memory multiprocessors. ParMETIS exploits parallelism in the whole multilevel framework by means of distributed matching, contraction and refinement algorithms. Note that FM-like refinement heuristics are inherently sequential and therefore difficult to parallelize efficiently. In [7], a parallel FM-like algorithm was proposed and included in ParMETIS but, in order to reduce communication overheads, only moves from the separator to the subdomains that strictly improve the quality of the separator are allowed if the vertex to be moved has neighbours in other processors. This relaxation hinders the ability of the FM algorithm to escape from local minima of its cost function, and leads to severe loss of quality when the number of processors (and thus of potential remote neighbours) is large. This is why it is frequently observed that the fill-in and the number of operations to compute the direct sparse factorization of $\Pi^T A \Pi$ increases as the number of processors involved in the computation increases. On the other hand, PT-SCOTCH includes a semi-parallel solution for the multilevel framework, where refinement is performed by means of multi-sequential optimization. At every uncoarsening step, a distributed band graph is created, which is then replicated on all participating processors. Each processor executes an independent instance of the sequential FM algorithm, and the best refined separator is then projected back to the original distributed graph. By sacrificing optimal parallel scalability, this approach computes similar quality partitions as the state-of-the-art sequential algorithms [5].

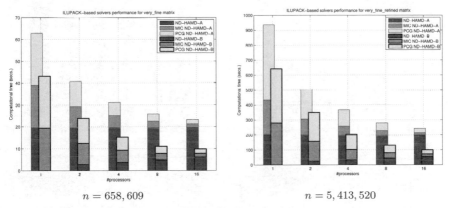

$$n = 658,609 \qquad\qquad n = 5,413,520$$

Figure 2. Computational time of the three stages in our solver using SCOTCH when the number of recursion levels in the nested dissection partitioning algorithm is truncated (ND-HAMD-B) or not (ND-HAMD-A).

4. Experimental Results

In this section we compare the influence of PT-SCOTCH (version 5.0.6RC16) and ParMETIS (version 3.1.1) on the overall solution process. The target platform is a SGI Altix 350 CC-NUMA shared-memory multiprocessor consisting on 8 nodes with 32 GBytes of RAM connected via a SGI NUMAlink network. Each node is composed of two Intel Itanium2@1.5 GHz processors (256 KBytes level-2 and 6 MBytes level-3 cache) with 4 GBytes of local memory. We linked both partitioning softwares with an optimized MPI library included in the SGI Message Passing Toolkit, version 1.12. The test problems are derived from the linear finite element discretization of the irregular $3D$ PDE problem $[-\mathrm{div}\,(A\,\mathrm{grad}\,u) = f]$ in a $3D$ domain, where $A(x, y, z)$ is chosen with positive random coefficients. The size and number of nonzero elements of the resulting

sparse s.p.d. linear systems depend on the initial mesh refinement level of the computational domain and the number of additional mesh refinements. We have tested several
benchmarks matrices from this problem [1], but for ease of presentation we only report
results for two large-scale cases.

In Figure 2 we show the computational cost of the three stages of our current solution: partitioning (MLND), computation of the preconditioner (MIC), and iterative solution of the preconditioned linear system (PCG) for varying number of processors. The
partitioning step is done sequentially with SCOTCH for both options shown in Figure 2.
In particular, in ND-HAMD-A nested dissection goes through recursion until the subgraphs are "small", while in ND-HAMD-B nested dissection is truncated and the independent subgraphs reordered in parallel by HAMD-like [8] fill-in reducing heuristics.
For ND-HAMD-A, we can observe that the computational cost of the preprocessing step
is maintained and its weight is significantly high. This cost is reduced for ND-HAMD-B,
but again the computational time of this step starts dominating the overall execution time
when the number of processors is large. The results for METIS and ND-HAMD-A were
similar to those shown in Figure 2, while the results for ND-HAMD-B could not be obtained; see Section 3.

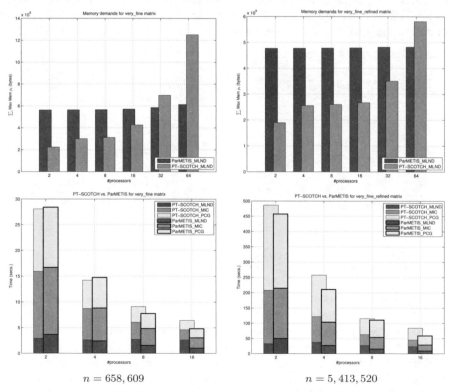

$n = 658,609$ $n = 5,413,520$

Figure 3. Memory demands (top) and computational time of the three stages in our solver (bottom) using
PT-SCOTCH and ParMETIS for parallel truncated nested dissection.

Figure 3 compares the performance, i.e., memory demands and computational time
for ParMETIS and PT-SCOTCH. Now the partitioning step is performed in parallel and
we consider the truncated version of the nested dissection procedure for both packages.

In order to obtain the results in Figure 3 (top), we instrumented both libraries so that each processor traces the amount of memory it requires (i.e., it has allocated) at any given time. At the end of the parallel partitioning stage, each processor determines the maximum memory locally required, and the addition of these quantities across all the processors is reported in Figure 3 (top). As can be observed, ParMETIS shows linear memory scalability, as the memory required is maintained. On the other hand, PT-SCOTCH initially requires significantly less memory, although the amount increases with the number of processors and finally exceeds the memory required by ParMETIS. In particular, the size of the distributed band graph that PT-SCOTCH creates in order to refine the separator on the finest (initial) graph becomes relatively high. This explains the results of Figure 3 (top), as the memory consumed for multi-sequential optimization increases linearly with the number of processors (due to distributed band graph replication on all participating processors).

The first remark regarding the results in Figure 3 (bottom) is that the computational time for ParMETIS is reduced when the number of processors increases, while for PT-SCOTCH it remains almost constant. As mentioned in Section 3, PT-SCOTCH essentially refines separators sequentially. For the matrices in our benchmark, the computational cost of the uncoarsening stage is significant, and therefore becomes a bottleneck for large number of processors. Although the computational time for ParMETIS with 2 processors is larger than for PT-SCOTCH, ParMETIS is faster for 16 processors. Furthermore, the weight of the partitioning step on the overall execution time is maintained for ParMETIS, while it is increased for PT-SCOTCH and, finally, it dominates the overall execution time. With respect to the numerical stages (MIC and PCG), the behavior for both partitioning solutions is similar, which serves as a practical demonstration that the MIC factorization of ILUPACK is not sensitive to the relaxations made for ParMETIS. For direct methods, it is known the impact of these relaxations on the performance of the solution of large and sparse linear systems [5]. For the benchmark examples considered, a symbolic factorization of $\Pi^T A \Pi$ reveals that the number of floating point operations required to compute the sparse direct Cholesky factorization is increased (with respect to sequential METIS) by 64% (smaller matrix), and 67% (larger matrix), when 16 processors are used to compute Π with the parallel nested dissection included in ParMETIS. In contrast to sparse direct methods, approximate factorization techniques such as those from ILUPACK accommodate less optimal orderings This is because for typical choices of drop tolerances, e.g. $\tau = 10^{-2}$, many entries can be dropped from the approximate Cholesky factor. In particular this is the case when the underlying problem arises from 3D elliptic PDEs, where the fill-in of an ILU factorization is several orders of magnitude smaller than that of direct solvers. For this kind of problems the multilevel method in ILUPACK mimics the behavior of AMG [3]. As further evidence of this last statement, Table 1 analyses thoroughly the multilevel hierarchy of the MIC preconditioner. The last level is not considered because its size is relatively negligible. The MIC preconditioner was computed by the sequential method in ILUPACK, and the matrix A was reordered using parallel nested dissection with PT-SCOTCH and ParMETIS. As can be observed in the table, the size of the successively coarser systems constructed by the numerical method is almost insensitive to the number of processors involved in the computation of the initial partitioning and to the library used, as well is the fill-in. We stress that, for the rest of the benchmark matrices, and for reasonable choices for the drop tolerances, i.e., $\tau = 10^{-1}, 10^{-2}, 10^{-3}$, behavior similar to that summarized in the table was observed.

$n = 658,609 \wedge nnz(A) = 4,976,665$							
	ParMETIS				PT-SCOTCH		
lev	$p = 2$	$p = 4$	$p = 8$	$p = 16$	$p = 2$	$p = 4$	$p = 8$	$p = 16$
0	100 1.02	100 1.02	100 1.02	100 1.02	100 1.07	100 1.07	100 1.07	100 1.07
1	35 0.87	35 0.87	35 0.87	35 0.87	36 0.88	36 0.88	36 0.88	36 0.88
2	7 0.09	7 0.09	7 0.09	7 0.09	7 0.09	7 0.09	7 0.09	7 0.10

$n = 5,413,520 \wedge nnz(A) = 42,174,347$							
	ParMETIS				PT-SCOTCH		
lev	$p = 2$	$p = 4$	$p = 8$	$p = 16$	$p = 2$	$p = 4$	$p = 8$	$p = 16$
0	100 1.07	100 1.07	100 1.07	100 1.07	100 1.14	100 1.14	100 1.14	100 1.14
1	37 1.11	37 1.11	37 1.08	37 1.13	37 1.07	37 1.07	37 1.06	37 1.07
2	11 0.20	12 0.20	11 0.17	12 0.21	11 0.17	11 0.17	11 0.16	11 0.17

Table 1. Multilevel hierarchy for the MIC preconditioner using ParMETIS and PT-SCOTCH. The left value on each cell reports the percentage of A which remains to be factorized on the level, and the right value is the fraction of the fill-in ratio produced by the partial factorization (2), i.e., $[(nnz(L_B) + nnz(L_F))/nnz(A)]$.

5. Conclusions

In this paper we have reviewed the stages involved in our approach for the parallel solution of sparse linear systems via preconditioned iterative methods on shared-memory multiprocessors, and we have analyzed the state-of-the-art software for parallelizing the partitioning step. We compared the performance of ParMETIS and PT-SCOTCH, observing that the influence on the numerical stages of the solver from the relaxations made by ParMETIS have a minor effect in our method.

References

[1]   José I. Aliaga, Matthias Bollhöfer, Alberto F. Martín, and Enrique S. Quintana-Ortí. Exploiting thread-level parallelism in the iterative solution of sparse linear systems. 2008. submitted to Parallel Comput.

[2]   José I. Aliaga, Matthias Bollhöfer, Alberto F. Martín, and Enrique S. Quintana-Ortí. Parallelization of multilevel preconditioners constructed from inverse-based ILUs on shared-memory multiprocessors. In *Parallel Computing: Architectures, Algorithms and Applications*, volume 38, pages 287–294. C. Bischof, M. Bücker, P. Gibbon, G.R. Joubert, T. Lippert, B. Mohr, F. Peters, John von Neumann Institute for Computing, Jülich, NIC Series, 2008.

[3]   Matthias Bollhöfer, Marcus Grote, and Olaf Schenk. Algebraic multilevel preconditioner for the helmholtz equation in heterogeneous media. *SIAM J. Scientific Computing*, 2009. accepted to appear.

[4]   Matthias Bollhöfer and Yousef Saad. Multilevel preconditioners constructed from inverse–based ILUs. *SIAM J. Sci. Comput.*, 27(5):1627–1650, 2006.

[5]   Cédric Chevalier and François Pellegrini. PT-SCOTCH: A tool for efficient parallel graph ordering. *Parallel Comput.*, 34(6-8):318–331, 2008.

[6]   George Karypis and Vipin Kumar. A fast and high quality multilevel scheme for partitioning irregular graphs. *SIAM J. Sci. Comput.*, 20(1):359–392, 1998.

[7]   George Karypis and Vipin Kumar. A parallel algorithm for multilevel graph partitioning and sparse matrix ordering. *J. Parallel Distrib. Comput.*, 48(1):71–95, 1998.

[8]   François Pellegrini, Jean Roman, and Patrick Amestoy. Hybridizing nested dissection and halo approximate minimum degree for efficient sparse matrix ordering. volume 1586/1999 of *Lecture Notes in Computer Science*, pages 986–995.

[9]   Yousef Saad. *Iterative Methods for Sparse Linear Systems*. SIAM Publications, 2003.

[10] Olaf Schenk, Matthias Bollhöfer, and Rudolf A. Römer. On large scale diagonalization techniques for the Anderson model of localization. *SIAM Review*, 50:91–112, 2008.

Parallel Computing: From Multicores and GPU's to Petascale
B. Chapman et al. (Eds.)
IOS Press, 2010
© 2010 The authors and IOS Press. All rights reserved.
doi:10.3233/978-1-60750-530-3-133

A Parallel Implementation of the Davidson Method for Generalized Eigenproblems

Eloy ROMERO [1] and Jose E. ROMAN

Instituto ITACA, Universidad Politécnica de Valencia, Spain

Abstract. We present a parallel implementation of the Davidson method for the numerical solution of large-scale, sparse, generalized eigenvalue problems. The implementation is done in the context of SLEPc, the Scalable Library for Eigenvalue Problem Computations. In this work, we focus on the Hermitian version of the method, with several optimizations. We compare the developed solver with other available implementations, as well as with Krylov-type eigensolvers already available in SLEPc, particularly in terms of parallel efficiency.

Keywords. Generalized eigenvalue problem, Davidson-type methods, Message-passing parallelization

1. Introduction

Let A and B be large, sparse Hermitian matrices of order n. We are concerned with the partial solution of the generalized eigenvalue problem defined by these matrices, i.e., the computation of a few pairs (λ, x) that satisfy

$$Ax = \lambda Bx, \tag{1}$$

where the scalar λ is called the eigenvalue, and the n-vector x is called the eigenvector. If B is a positive definite matrix, the eigenvalues and the eigenvectors are real. Otherwise the eigenpairs could be complex even if the matrices are real. This problem arises in many scientific and engineering areas such as structural dynamics, electrical networks, quantum chemistry, and control theory.

Many different methods have been proposed for solving the above problem, including Subspace Iteration, Krylov projection methods such as Lanczos, Arnoldi or Krylov-Schur, and Davidson-type methods such as Generalized Davidson or Jacobi-Davidson. Details of these methods can be found in [1]. Subspace Iteration and Krylov methods achieve good performance when computing extreme eigenvalues, but usually fail to compute interior eigenvalues. In that case, the convergence is accelerated by combining the method with a spectral transformation technique, i.e., to solve $(A - \sigma B)^{-1} Bx = \theta x$ instead of Eq. 1. However this approach adds the high computational cost of solving

---

[1]Corresponding Author: Instituto ITACA, Universidad Politécnica de Valencia, Camino de Vera s/n, 46022 Valencia, Spain; E-mail: eromero@itaca.upv.es.

large linear systems at each iteration of the eigensolver and very accurately (usually with direct methods). Davidson-type methods try to reduce the cost, by solving systems only approximately (usually with iterative methods) without compromising the robustness. This kind of methods are reaching increasing popularity due to their good numerical behaviour. Among the benefits of these methods, we can highlight (1) their good convergence rate in difficult problems, e.g. when internal eigenvalues are to be computed, (2) the possibility of using a preconditioner as a cheap alternative to spectral transformations, and (3) the possibility to start the iteration with an arbitrary subspace, so that good approximations from previous computations can be exploited.

Parallel Davidson-type eigensolvers are currently available in the PRIMME [11] and Anasazi [2] software packages. However, currenly PRIMME can only cope with standard eigenproblems, and Anasazi only implements a basic block Davidson Method. Our aim is to provide robust and efficient parallel implementations of the Generalized Davidson Method in the context of SLEPc, the Scalable Library for Eigenvalue Problem Computations [8], that can address both standard and generalized problems. In this work, we focus on the case of symmetric-definite generalized eigenproblems, although some attention will be devoted to the case of semi-definite or indefinite B.

Section 2 describes the different variants of the method that we have considered. In sections 3 and 4 we provide details related to the implementation. Section 5 presents some performance results comparing the developed implementation with other solvers.

2. Generalized Davidson Method

The Generalized Davidson (GD) method is an iterative subspace projection method for eigenproblems. It is a generalization of the original Davidson's method [4] that allows using an arbitrary preconditioner. In its variant for symmetric-definite generalized eigenproblems, in each iteration the GD method performs a Rayleigh-Ritz procedure for selecting the most relevant approximate eigenpairs (θ, x) in the search subspace represented by a matrix with B-orthonormal columns, V. Then it computes a correction to x and expands the search subspace by adding this correction.

Many optimizations have been proposed with respect to the basic algorithm. The following are the most important ones considered in this work:

- The block version (originally called Liu-Davidson method [9,5]) updates several eigenpairs simultaneously. Besides accelerating the convergence, this technique is useful for finding more than one eigenpair. However, the block size s should be kept small to avoid a cost blow-up. In this section, X denotes a matrix with s columns, the approximate eigenvectors x_i. A similar notation is used for the corrections, D, and the residuals, R.
- Restarting combined with locking strategies allows the computation of more eigenpairs without enlarging the search subspace's maximum dimension.
- Olsen's variant [10] consists in computing the correction vector d_i as

$$d_i \leftarrow K^{-1}(I - x_i(x_i^* K^{-1} x_i)^{-1} x_i^* K^{-1}) r_i, \qquad (2)$$

being K^{-1} a preconditioner.
- Thick restart [12], in particular the GD(m_{min}, m_{max}) variant, restarts with the best m_{min} eigenvectors when the size of V reaches m_{max}.

Algorithm 1 (Block symmetric-definite generalized GD with B-orthogonalization)

Input: matrices A and B of size n, preconditioner K, number of wanted eigenpairs p, block size s, maximum size of V m_{max}, restart with m_{min} vectors

Output: resulting eigenpairs $(\widetilde{\Theta}, \widetilde{X})$

Choose an $n \times s$ full rank matrix V such that $V^* B V = I$

While size$(\widetilde{\Theta}) < p$

    1. Compute $H \leftarrow V^* A V$

    2. Compute the eigenpairs (Θ, U) of H and sort them

    3. Compute the first s Ritz vectors, $X \leftarrow V U_{1:s}$

    4. Compute the residual vectors, $r_i \leftarrow A V u_i - B V u_i \theta_i$

    5. Test for convergence

    6. Compute the corrections, $d_i \leftarrow K^{-1}[I - x_i(x_i^* K^{-1} x_i)^{-1} x_i^* K^{-1}] r_i$

    7. If size$(V) \geq m_{max}$, $V \leftarrow V U_{1:m_{min}}$

        Else if k pairs are converged

            Add eigenvalues $\theta_1, \ldots, \theta_k$ to $\widetilde{\Theta}$

            $\widetilde{X} \leftarrow [\widetilde{X} \quad V U_{1:k}]$

            $V \leftarrow V U_{k+1:k'}$, where $k' = $ size(V)

        Else, $V \leftarrow [V \quad B\text{-orthonormalize}([\widetilde{X} \quad V], D)]$

End while

Algorithm 1 details the GD method for symmetric-definite eigenproblems, including the optimizations mentioned above. The subspace basis V grows in each iteration with s new vectors, except in the case of a restart or when some eigenpairs have converged in the last iteration. Note that most operations involving V, such as the computation of H, can be optimized to reuse values obtained in previous iterations.

From the numerical point of view, maintaining a B-orthonormal basis of subspace V is beneficial because exact eigenvectors satisfy a B-orthogonality relation. However, enforcing B-orthogonality may be too expensive, and if B is numerically singular the method may suffer from instability. As an alternative, we propose another variant that works with an orthonormal basis V, as shown in Algorithm 2. This algorithm is an adaptation of GD for non-Hermitian generalized problems [6], where we maintain the searching subspace basis V orthogonal with respect to the left invariant subspace corresponding to the converged vectors, spanned by $Y = B\bar{X}$. With these changes, the method becomes valid for problems with B being indefinite and nonsingular, and $B^{-1}A$ being non-defective.

As a result, the new method does not work with eigenvectors, but with Schur vectors that are always orthonormal.

There are differences in the cost of both methods. On the one hand, Algorithm 2 has to compute two projected matrices H and G (step 1), whereas Algorithm 1 needs only one, and it also needs to orthogonalize the residual vector against the columns of Y (step 4). On the other hand, if the B-orthonormalization of step 7 is implemented with Iterative Gram-Schmidt, then Algorithm 1 may perform more than one B-inner product per vector.

Algorithm 2 (Block symmetric-indefinite generalized GD with orthonormalization)

Input: matrices A and B of size n, preconditioner K, number of wanted eigenpairs p,
          block size s, maximum size of V m_{max}, restart with m_{min} vectors
Output: resulting eigenvalues $\widetilde{\Theta}$ and Schur vectors $\widetilde{X}$

Choose an $n \times s$ full rank matrix V such that $V^*V = I$
While size$(\widetilde{\Theta}) < p$
    1. Compute $H \leftarrow V^*AV$ and $G \leftarrow V^*BV$
    2. Compute the eigenvalues Θ and Schur vectors U associated to the pencil (H, G)
    3. Compute the first s approximate Schur vectors, $X \leftarrow VU_{1:s}$
    4. Compute the residual vectors, $r_i \leftarrow \text{orthonormalize}(Y, AVu_i - BVu_i\theta_i)$
    5. Test for convergence
    6. Compute the correction, $d_i \leftarrow K^{-1}[I - x_i(x_i^*K^{-1}x_i)^{-1}x_i^*K^{-1}]r_i$
    7. If size$(V) \geq m_{max}$, $V \leftarrow VU_{1:m_{min}}$
        Else if k pairs are converged
            Add eigenvalues $\theta_1, \ldots, \theta_k$ to $\widetilde{\Theta}$
            $\widetilde{X} \leftarrow [\widetilde{X} \quad VU_{1:k}]$
            $Y \leftarrow [Y \quad B\overline{V}U_{1:k}]$
            $V \leftarrow \text{orthonormalize}(Y, VU_{k+1:k'})$, where $k' = \text{size}(V)$
        Else, $V \leftarrow [V \quad \text{orthonormalize}([Y \quad V], D)]$
End while

3. Implementation Details

In this section, we describe the context in which the algorithms have been implemented, and we compare it with existing related software efforts for solving large-scale eigenvalue problems with Davidson methods [7], in particular Anasazi and PRIMME.

Anasazi [2] is part of Trilinos, a parallel object-oriented software framework for large-scale multi-physics scientific applications. It was designed for being independent of the choice of the underlying linear algebra primitives, in order to facilitate its incorporation into larger libraries and application codes. The Anasazi framework contains a collection of independent eigensolvers that includes Block Davidson as described in Algorithm 1, among others.

PRIMME implements a parametrized Davidson method general enough to include algorithms ranging from Subspace Iteration to Jacobi-Davidson with several options about the correction equation. It uses its own distributed vectors with the solely support of BLAS, LAPACK and a sum reduction operation. Currently, it only supports standard eigenproblems, but the interface is prepared for a non-trivial matrix B.

The implementation of the algorithms that we are presenting here is being integrated as a solver in SLEPc, the Scalable Library for Eigenvalue Problem Computations. SLEPc's design goals lie between Anasazi and PRIMME. SLEPc eigensolvers use vectors, matrices and linear algebra primitives of PETSc (Portable, Extensible Toolkit for Scientific Computation, [3]), a parallel framework for the numerical solution of partial differential equations, whose approach is to encapsulate mathematical algorithms using object-oriented programming techniques in order to be able to manage the complexity of efficient numerical message-passing codes. However, the PETSc-dependence does not reduce the software interoperability because PETSc objects allow user implementation.

The stopping criteria and the computation of the correction vectors D (step 6) are encapsulated and decoupled from the eigensolvers, as in Anasazi, because they are the most application dependent components. The orthonormalization is also encapsulated in order to be possible to select any routine that SLEPc offers.

4. Parallel Implementation

The parallelization of the Davidson method can be done easily by parallelizing the operations with multivectors (such as V and X) and matrices (such as A and B), i.e., the matrix-vector products (such as $W \leftarrow AV$), the inner vector products (such as $H \leftarrow W^*V$) and the vector updates (such as $V \leftarrow VU$). The multivectors are dense rectangular matrices stored as a collection of vectors. One advantage of using a multi-vector data structure, instead of performing the operations column by column, is to improve the ratio of floating-point operations to memory references thus better exploiting the memory hierarchy.

Anasazi provides an interface to these operations, and has wrappers to employ the Epetra and Thyra (also Trilinos packages) multivectors and matrices. In PRIMME the user must provide the matrix-vector product, and the sum reduction operation (typically implemented by calling MPI_Allreduce) used by the hard-coded multivector routines.

PETSc supports MPI parallel sparse matrix computations by providing parallel matrix storage formats (distributed by blocks of contiguous rows), along with parallel vectors (distributed in a compatible way) and vector scattering operations for efficient communication among processes. If the matrix nonzero pattern is reasonably arranged (e.g. coming from an unstructured mesh discretization partitioned in compact subdomains), then the matrix-vector product operations scale well.

PETSc does not provide support for multivectors. In order to develop an optimized version of a block Generalized Davidson it is necessary to implement AXPY and dot product multivector operations, using BLAS to perform the local calculations.

In addition, some optimizations are applied in our implementations to improve the parallel performance. It is possible to mitigate the latency of communication primitives by joining several reductions together. For instance, the residual norm is commonly needed by the convergence test routine. Instead of performing the summation of the residual norms vector by vector, all the local results are considered in a unique call. This technique is also used in our eigensolver for updating the matrices H and G with a single communication operation. It is also possible to reduce the communication time by avoiding transfering unnecessary data. For instance, since V^*AV is symmetric only the upper triangular part is taken into account in the parallel operation.

5. Testing and validation

This section summarizes the experiments carried out in order to evaluate the convergence behaviour and the parallel performance of our implementations versus Anasazi and PRIMME. The preconditioner and the matrix-vector product may have a great im-

Table 1. Sequential results for computing on Odin the 10 largest magnitude eigenpairs over the symmetric-definite generalized eigenproblems testbed of 37 problems with Anasazi, SLEPc Davidson Algorithm 1, and SLEPc Krylov-Schur and ARPACK with a MUMPS direct solver and the GMRES solver. The iterations and accumulated time only include the problems solved by all eigensolvers.

Solver	Solved problems	Accumulated Iterations	Accumulated Time (s)	Accumulated Time/Iterations
SLEPc Davidson Algorithm 1	22	5923	13.54	0.0353
Anasazi	20	6251	17.40	0.0398
SLEPc Krylov-Schur MUMPS	37	–	5.23	–
SLEPc Krylov-Schur GMRES	35	–	5.81	–
ARPACK MUMPS	36	–	7.18	–

Table 2. Sequential results for computing on Odin the 10 largest magnitude eigenpairs over the symmetric-indefinite generalized eigenproblems testbed of 12 problems with SLEPc Davidson Algorithm 2 and SLEPc Krylov-Schur with a MUMPS direct solver. The iterations and accumulated time only include the problems solved by both eigensolvers.

Solver	Solved problems	Accumulated Iterations	Accumulated Time (s)	Accumulated Time/Iterations
SLEPc Davidson Algorithm 2	8	209	11.63	0.406
SLEPc Krylov-Schur MUMPS	12	–	55.90	–

pact on the global performance, especially on parallel performance. For that reason, the parallel test problems were selected to have an efficient parallel matrix-vector product. All tests use the Jacobi preconditioner (matrix K) because it is appropriate for $A - \sigma B$ operators with variable σ and its setup time is negligible.

The tests were executed on two clusters: Odin, made up of 55 bi-processor nodes with 2.80 GHz Pentium Xeon processors, arranged in a 2D torus topology with SCI interconnect, and CaesarAugusta, consisting of 256 JS20 blade computing nodes, each of them with two 64-bit PowerPC 970FX processors running at 2.2 GHz, interconnected with a low latency Myrinet network. In this machine, only 64 processors were employed due to account limitations.

The eigensolvers were configured for computing the 10 largest magnitude eigenvalues with a relative tolerance of 10^{-7}, with an m_{max} of 40, and up to 5000 iterations. The Davidson eigensolvers start with 5 vectors and restart with 8 eigenvectors. The default convergence test labels an eigenpair as converged if $||Ax - Bx\theta||_2/\theta \leq$ tol, with $||x||_B = 1$ for Algorithm 1, and $||x||_2 = 1$ for Algorithm 2. The Krylov eigensolvers, which work on the operator $B^{-1}A$, were tested using a direct (MUMPS) and an iterative (GMRES) linear system solvers (both available in PETSc) with the default options.

The matrices used in the tests are from the University of Florida Sparse Matrix Collection. The symmetric-definite testbed used in Table 1 includes 37 eigenproblems with dimension up to 15,439. All matrices are real symmetric, and B positive definite. The tested Davidson eigensolvers solve around 21 problems of the testbed and in a comparable time (although Anasazi is slightly slower), with respect to Krylov eigensolvers. That may be due to the already commented limitation of the Jacobi preconditioner.

Table 2 summarizes the performance solving 12 indefinite B problems of size as the ones above. In that case, the Davidson eigensolver is faster than Krylov-Schur.

Figure 1 shows the speedup in both clusters solving the Boeing/pwtk matrix (standard problem), a 217,918 size matrix with 11,524,432 nonzero elements. The PRIMME performance is significantly better compared with SLEPc and Anasazi implementations.

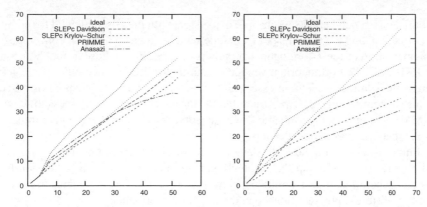

Figure 1. Speedup for the solution of the problem pwtk on Odin (left) and CaesarAugusta (right).

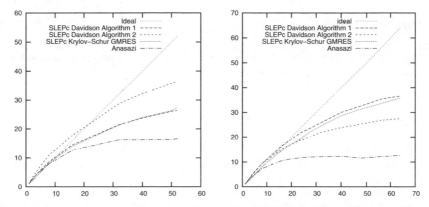

Figure 2. Speedup for the solution of the problem qa8f on Odin (left) and CaesarAugusta (right).

The generalized problem used in Figure 2 is formed by the Cunningham group matrices qa8fk and qa8fm. Its size is 66,127 and each matrix has 1,660,579 nonzero elements. SLEPc Algorithm 1 shows similar speedup as Krylov-Schur with GMRES, maybe dominated by the B-orthonormalization, and has the best speedup in CaesarAugusta. But on Odin, SLEPc Algorithm 2 has the best speedup. That may be due to the different performace of the B matrix-vector product and the multivector inner product (the core operation of orthonormalization) in both clusters, as well as the different use of these operations by the Algorithms 1 and 2 (see the end of section 2). In both platforms, the performance of Anasazi in generalized problems is not good.

6. Conclusions

In this work, we have presented a parallel implementation of the Generalized Davidson method for the solution of generalized eigenproblems. The methods have been implemented in SLEPc and constitute the basis for a future solver covering a number of Davidson-type methods, including Jacobi-Davidson. For the moment, only symmetric problems have been addressed, both definite and indefinite.

We have evaluated two algorithms, one with B-orthonormal basis and another one with orthonormal basis, the latter being able to solve indefinite problems. Both variants are based on a block Davidson subspace expansion, with the Olsen method for computing the correction, and the thick restart technique with locking. In terms of convergence, our implementation of the B-orthogonal version is comparable to those available in Anasazi and PRIMME. The orthonormal version is unique to SLEPc since other packages only address the symmetric-definite case, and has proven to be faster than Krylov-Schur in our tests. From the perspective of parallel performance, our solver is less efficient than PRIMME, but among the available Davidson solvers for generalized eigenproblems it is the one that achieves better speedup.

Future works will include the development of different options for the computation of the correction, including the Jacobi-Davidson one, as well as the extension to standard and generalized non-Hermitian eigenvalue problems. It also remains to analyze the impact of different preconditioners on the overall performance.

Acknowledgements

The authors thankfully acknowledge the computer resources and assistance provided by the Barcelona Supercomputing Center (BSC).

References

[1]   Z. Bai, J. Demmel, J. Dongarra, A. Ruhe, and H. van der Vorst, editors. *Templates for the Solution of Algebraic Eigenvalue Problems: A Practical Guide*. Society for Industrial and Applied Mathematics, Philadelphia, PA, 2000.

[2]   C. G. Baker, U. L. Hetmaniuk, R. B. Lehoucq, and H. K. Thornquist. Anasazi software for the numerical solution of large-scale eigenvalue problems. *ACM Trans. Math. Software*, 36(3):13:1–13:23, July 2009.

[3]   Satish Balay, Kris Buschelman, Victor Eijkhout, William Gropp, Dinesh Kaushik, Matt Knepley, Lois Curfman McInnes, Barry Smith, and Hong Zhang. PETSc users manual. Technical Report ANL-95/11 - Revision 3.0.0, Argonne National Laboratory, December 2008.

[4]   Ernest R. Davidson. The iterative calculation of a few of the lowest eigenvalues and corresponding eigenvectors of large real-symmetric matrices. *J. Comput. Phys.*, 17(1):87–94, 1975.

[5]   Ernest R. Davidson. Monster matrices: Their eigenvalues and eigenvectors. *Comput. Phys.*, 7(5):519–522, 1993.

[6]   Diederik R. Fokkema, Gerard L. G. Sleijpen, and Henk A. van der Vorst. Jacobi–Davidson style QR and QZ algorithms for the reduction of matrix pencils. *SIAM J. Sci. Comput.*, 20(1):94–125, January 1999.

[7]   V. Hernandez, J. E. Roman, A. Tomas, and V. Vidal. A survey of software for sparse eigenvalue problems. Technical report, D. Sistemas Informáticos y Computación, Universidad Politécnica de Valencia, 2007. Available at http://www.grycap.upv.es/slepc.

[8]   V. Hernandez, J. E. Roman, and V. Vidal. SLEPc: A scalable and flexible toolkit for the solution of eigenvalue problems. *ACM Trans. Math. Software*, 31(3):351–362, September 2005.

[9]   B. Liu. The simultaneous expansion method for the iterative solution of several of the lowest eigenvalues and corresponding eigenvectors of large real-symmetric matrices. Technical Report LBL-8158, Lawrence Berkeley National Laboratory, 1978.

[10] Jeppe Olsen, Poul Jørgensen, and Jack Simons. Passing the one-billion limit in full configuration-interaction (FCI) calculations. *Chem. Phys. Lett.*, 169(6):463–472, 1990.

[11] Andreas Stathopoulos and James R. McCombs. PRIMME: PReconditioned Iterative MultiMethod Eigensolver: Methods and software description. Technical Report WM-CS-2006-08, College of William & Mary, November 2006.

[12] Andreas Stathopoulos and Yousef Saad. Restarting techniques for the (Jacobi-)Davidson symmetric eigenvalue methods. *Electron. Trans. Numer. Anal.*, 7:163–181, 1998.

Bio-Informatics

Parallel Computing: From Multicores and GPU's to Petascale
B. Chapman et al. (Eds.)
IOS Press, 2010
© 2010 The authors and IOS Press. All rights reserved.
doi:10.3233/978-1-60750-530-3-143

A data-flow modification of the MUSCLE algorithm for multiprocessors and a web interface for it [1]

Alexey N. Salnikov (salnikov@cs.msu.su)

Faculty of Computational Mathematics and Cybernetics, Lomonosov Moscow State University, 2-nd educational building, Leninskie Gory, Moscow, 119992, Russia

Abstract. Nucleotide and amino acid sequences research is actual for molecular biology and bioengineering. An important aspect of analysis of such sequences is multiple alignment. This article discusses the implementations of the MUSCLE and ClustalW programs on multiprocessors and a web interface to them. The modification of the MUSCLE algorithm realize a data-flow manner of sequence alignment. It uses the PARUS system to build a data-flow graph and execute this graph on one multiprocessor as a MPI-program. The data-flow algorithm has been tested on the sequences of human Long Terminal Repeats class five (LTR5) and several other examples.

Keywords. sequence alignment, data-flow, clusters

Introduction

Nucleotide and amino acid sequences research is actual for molecular biology and bio-engineering. An important aspect of analysis of such sequences is multiple alignment. Its purpose is to arrange the sequences of DNA, RNA, or protein to identify regions of similarity that may be a consequence of functional, structural, or evolutionary relationships between the sequences. Aligned sequences are typically represented as rows within a matrix. Gaps are inserted between the residues so that residues with identical or similar characters are aligned in successive columns. There are several algorithms of multiple sequence alignment: ClustalW [1], MUSCLE [3], DIALIGN-TX [8]. The most popular method for multiple sequence alignment of nucleotides and amino acids is ClustalW. But ClustalW has several disadvantages and now there is available a new algorithm MUSCLE that tries to solve some disadvantages of the ClustalW.

Unfortunately on a large number of sequences or on long sequences originally non-parallel algorithms can consume rather long time for the execution — up to several days, and can demand a large amount of memory. It should be noted that several algorithms has parallel implementation (for example: ClustalW-MPI [2], DIALIGN P [9]).

For the pairwise alignment the dynamic programming method [4] allows to get the precise result in a reasonable time, but for the multiple alignment the time complexity of

---
[1] This work was supported by grants RFBR-08-07-00445-a and MK-1606.2008.9.

the multidimensional analog of dynamic programming is an exponential function with respect to the number of sequences. Usually heuristic algorithms are used, which do not give precise solution in the terms of optimization of some score function, but have a less complexity and give an eligible result in the context of biology. We will consider the algorithm described in the article [3]. It is realized in the MUSCLE software product available at http://www.drive5.com/muscle.

A web interface has been developed to facilitate availability of multiprocessor for researcher. The web interface requires creating the task by researcher. Each task binds the source data represented as sequences in FASTA format, algorithm (ClustalW-MPI, modified MUSCLE) and multiprocessor resources.

1. The MUSCLE algorithm

The MUSCLE algorithm is divided into several stages.

On the first stage the algorithm calculates the degrees of similarity between all aligned sequences and aggregates them into a matrix. Then the sequences are clustered by their similarities, and a binary cluster tree is built from the similarity matrix using the UPGMA[5] algorithm.

The similarity degree of sequences is calculated by the following method: all sequences are divided into sets of fragments with the length of k (k-mers), then the occurrence of each k-mer in all the sequences is calculated. Similarity calculation uses this formula:

$$similarity(S_i, S_j) = \sum_{m=1}^{M} \frac{min(frequency(S_i, \tau_m), frequency(S_j, \tau_m))}{min(length(S_i), length(S_j)) - k + 1}$$

where τ_m is one of the k-mers distinguished from the sequences, $frequency(S_i, \tau_m)$ is the number of times τ_m was met in sequence S_i, M — the number of all different revealed k-mers for all sequences in alignment.

After similarity calculating, the alignments for pairs of leaves having a common parent in the tree are built. The alignments for the pairs of sequences are built using a modification of the dynamical programming method. Then we get sub-alignments (alignments of sequences subset) for the all interior tree nodes that is done by pairwise alignment of two sub-alignments. Sequences that are involved in such sub-alignment cannot be shifted, so gaps are inserted simultaneously into all lines of sub-alignment. Quality of such sub-alignment are calculated by the following formula:

$$score(R_x, R_y) = \sum_{i=1}^{L} \sum_{\alpha} \sum_{\beta} f(\alpha, R_{x,i}) f(\beta, R_{y,i}) substitute(\alpha, \beta) -$$
$$- \sum_{j=1}^{G} gap\_penalty(g_j), \tag{1}$$

$$\alpha \in column\_symbols(R_{x,i}),$$
$$\beta \in column\_symbols(R_{y,i}).$$

where $column\_symbols(R_{x,i})$ determines the set of all the different symbols of a column i of sub-alignment R_x, and $f(\alpha, R_{x,i})$ calculates the frequency of α symbol occurrences in the column i of sub-alignment R_x. The function $gap\_penalty(g_j)$ calculates the penalty for one individual gap where G is a number of all gaps which are inserted into the entire column, for either all rows of R_x or R_y.

On the second stage the tree is refined using the Kimura distance [3], a more accurate metric than the k-mer distance used on the first stage. Then the alignment is rebuilt by the method similar the first stage. Practically, algorithm needs to realign the sub-alignments that corresponds to the vertices which have been changed in tree.

The third stage is iterative. The alignment is "refined".

2. The data-flow algorithm for multiple sequence alignment

For using the MUSCLE algorithm on multiprocessor systems, the original method has been modified on the stage of building sub-alignments using the cluster tree. We build a parallel program as a graph-program by means of PARUS [7](PARUS is a parallel programming language that allows to build parallel programs in a data-flow graph notation (http://parus.sf.net)).

2.1. Brief PARUS description

PARUS allows the user to create a file with a text which describes vertices, edges, user defined C++ declarations and C++ code of prologue and epilogue. Then this file will be converted automatically to the MPI/C++ source code using the PARUS utility called graph2c++. Once the source code is compiled to a binary executable file, this action is performed by using the standard MPI utility called mpicxx, then this code becomes ready for running on any multiprocessor system or cluster (including cluster of multicore processors).

The Edges and vertices are described in the text file. They implement the data-flow abstraction. There are source vertices which do not contain any incoming edges and drain vertices which do not contain any outgoing edges. Other vertices could be connected by edges with each other. All vertices are converted to the C++ functions. Each function contains a code of vertex and automatically generated service MPI-code. The edges correspond to data dependencies and implements mapping of arrays used by function of one vertex to arrays used by function of another vertex. The edges are converted to operations of memory coping or to the data transfer through the multiprocessor communications that is performed by call to the MPI_Isend function.

The first action performed by all the MPI-process when the binary file is executing, is the call to the prologue routine. The prologue routine corresponds to the prologue code that is specified in the graph-program source file. Then the code for all internal vertices will be executed in the order defined by edges, from the source vertices to the drain vertices. Vertices send MPI-messages each to other if they are connected by edge and appointed on executing to the different MPI-processes. Vertices are balanced between the MPI-processes to minimize execution time of vertex accordingly to the messages passing delays and processor performance. After all the drain vertices are finished the epilogue code will be executed by all the MPI-processes. Then the MPI-program is finished.

```
                                              <EDGE_BEGIN>
                                                number 17
                                                weight 1
                                                type GRAPH_NONE
                                                num_var 1
                                                num_send_nodes 1
                                                send_nodes ( 18 )
                                                num_recv_nodes 1
        <NODE_BEGIN>                            recv_nodes ( 17 )
          number 17                            <SEND_BEGIN>
          type 0
          weight 1000                            <CHUNK_BEGIN>
          layer 150                                name "fictitious_var"
          num_input_edges 2                        type GRAPH_CHAR
          edges (   17   18 )                      left_offset  "0"
          num_output_edges 1                       right_offset "1"
          edges ( 16 )                           <CHUNK_END>
          head ""
          body "body_node_17.cpp"             <SEND_END>
          tail ""                             <RECEIVE_BEGIN>
        <NODE_END>
                                                 <CHUNK_BEGIN>
                                                   name "fictitious_var"
                                                   type GRAPH_CHAR
                                                   left_offset  "0"
                                                   right_offset "1"
                                                 <CHUNK_END>
                                               <RECEIVE_END>
                                              <EDGE_END>
```

Figure 1. The Examples of vertex and edge recorded in the PARUS notation for the MUSCLE data-flow program.

2.2. A data-flow program

Developed data-flow algorithm is split into several stages. On the first stage the original MUSCLE algorithm is used to calculate similarities between sequences and to build the cluster tree. On the second stage a graph-program is built and source file in FASTA format is split into many files with individual sequences. For any file there is available to contain a little group of sequences. Number of sequences in the group is defined by one of the algorithm's parameters. Third stage concentrates on multiprocessor execution of the graph-program.

A graph-program is built from the cluster tree in the following way: each source vertex in a PARUS graph-program corresponds to one or several aligning sequences. Graph-program edges are directed from the source vertices to the inner ones. Inner vertices align pairs of sub-alignments to create a new sub-alignment that can be sent to a next inner vertex or to a drain vertex of the graph-program. Figure 1 illustrates an examples of vertex and edge. The edge and vertex are recorded in the PARUS notation.

The algorithm goes to the drain vertex when the number of sequences in the current sub-alignment of global alignment is equal to the whole number of sequences to be aligned. The code of vertex induces the original muscle function to align a pair of sub-alignments. The code is analogous to the following string: *"muscle -profile -in1 data_node_18.fasta -in2 data_node_19.fasta -out data_node_17.fasta"*.

Therefore, graph-program is built from the leaves of the cluster tree to the root vertex. To improve the efficiency of the parallel program the bottom (closer to leaves) layers of the cluster tree are compressed into one layer of graph-program. To do that, a special parameter is introduced into the algorithm. It defines a number of layers of the cluster tree to be compressed. As a result of the compression, the source vertices of the graph-program can contain more than one sequence, unlike the leaves in the cluster tree. For such source vertices the original MUSCLE algorithm is used to build a sub-alignments.

The time of program execution for the modified MUSCLE algorithm is reduced due to the possibility to execute each vertex of graph-program on a different processor. The maximal number of concurrently handled vertices is limited by the number of vertices in one layer of the graph-program and the number of processors accessible for running the parallel program.

3. Web interface

The Web interface has been developed to bind needs of the researcher to align the sequences in a shortest time with a multiprocessor and job scheduling system on it (for example LoadLeveler).

The Web interface is provided by simultaneous work of several programs: Python-script, bash-script, php-application. The php-application performs an interaction with user. The python script is automatically called by UNIX utility cron regularly (every hour for example). It looks for changes in user data or changes on one of the multiprocessors then it performs an actual actions. If one requires some interaction with multiprocessor, the python-script calls to the bash-script on a remote machine via the SSH. The bash-script performs following actions: it submits a task to a queue on the multiprocessor, it returns an information on the submitted task status and it terminates the task on user's request.

Now, an abstraction of the user's task in the Web interface will be introduced. For each task, a researcher should chose one of the multiprocessors, then for the chosen multiprocessor he specifies desired amount of time and number of processors or processor cores. Once created task does not contain any sequences to align them. Such tasks have status 'new'. User should upload sequences to the web-server via web interface, then is allowed to change task status on 'ready'. After marking the task as 'ready', during one hour the sequences will be transmitted to the multiprocessor and the task will be submitted to the multiprocessor's queue. Then, the user's task abstraction will be implemented as the MPI-application executing on many processors of one multiprocessor.

Once per hour the task on the multiprocessor is automatically checked by means of Python-script. If the task finished it's work, then the researcher will be notified by email on success or errors. There are two task statuses 'finished' and 'refused' in accordance with described situation on the multiprocessor. In any case, the result on success and the temporary data on error will be transferred back to the Web site. Relations between the task statuses are illustrated on the figure 2.

The web interface is available at: *http://angel.cs.msu.su/aligner*.

4. Testing results

The data-flow algorithm has been tested on sequences of LTR's class five in human genome. LTR (Long Terminal Repeat) is a family of so-called repeats (sequences occurring in the genome in a number of nearly identified copies); there are several classes of LTR. The class 5 (LTR5) contains approximately 1500 sequences approximately with 1200 nucleotides each. The LTR5 collection has been described in article [6]. Also, a multiple sequence alignment of 1088 protein sequences of globins approximately with 300 amino acids each has been constructed.

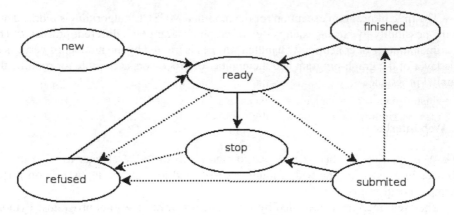

Figure 2. The graph of task statuses and rules how to change status for one task. The actions for rules denoted by solid arrows are performed by user. The actions for rules denoted by breaking arrows are performed automatically by the Python-script.

Table 1. Delay values for LTR5

computer	single processor (min)	12 procs	16 procs
IBM pSeries 690	up to 420	21	24
PrimePOWER 850	68	28	-

Table 2. Delay values for protein sequences on mvs100k cluster

sequential code (sec)	16 cores	100 cores	500 cores
420	28	21	245

Table 3. Speedup values

number of procs (cores)	12	16	100	500
speedup	2.4	17.5	20	1.7

Several multiprocessor computers to build alignments has been used. There are one cluster and two SMP machines:

- PrimePOWER 850 is a SUN SMP machine with 12 processors
- IBM pSeries 690 "Regatta" is a SMP machine in 16 processors configuration (maximum is 32 processors).
- mvs100k is a cluster of 470 nodes with four Intel Xeon 5160 processors which are connected via Infiniband network.

Results of tests are concentrate in tables: 1 and 2. The averaged over all machines and all types of input data values of algorithm speedup are concentrate in the table 3. We use a work time of the original one-processor MUSCLE algorithm with imposed limit of 3 iterations to estimate a speedup for parallel algorithm. Maximum speedup value (20x) has been achieved on 100 processors of mvs100k machine for the sequences of LTR class 5. But, speedup value in 1.7x has been achieved on 500 processors, see table 3. This result shows a bad scalability of the algorithm and how does it important choose an optimal number of processors required for task. Scalability of the algorithm is discussed in the next section of the article.

5. Conclusion

The execution time of MPI-program that implements a data-flow algorithm of multiple sequence alignment appreciably depends on several parameters. At first, it is very important for a cluster tree to be well balanced for maximizing parallel program efficiency. But cluster trees for biological sequences usually are rather imbalanced. Balanced tree provides maximum number of sub-alignments which could be aligned in parallel, because maximum number of vertices per level of cluster tree is achieved. Execution time depends on processors performance and volume of primary memory. For example DI-ALIGN and ClustalW-MPI has crash during they align LTR5 sequences on mvs100k cluster because 4Gb primary memory per cluster node is not enough for these algorithms. So, the scalability of algorithm is limited by number of sequences and structure of the cluster tree.

Further scalability improvement will be based on deep review of the MUSCLE algorithm stages implementation. The maximal time complexity has an implementation of modified Needelman–Wunsch algorithm where quality of alignment is calculated by the formula (1). Parallel implementation of the Needelman–Wunsch algorithm is a very difficult task due to the type of dependencies for current step of algorithm on the previous steps. So, probably, a dynamic programming step in MUSCLE algorithm for all stages will be parallelled. If there will be difficulties with Needelman–Wunsch then an other method for pairwise alignment building will be developed and parallelled.

References

[1] Julie D. Thompson, Desmond G. Higgins, Toby J. Gibson CLUSTAL W: improving the sensitivity of progressive multiple sequence alignment through sequence weighting, position-specific gap penalties and weight matrix choice //Nucleic Acids Research, 1994, vol. 22 No. 22 , pp. 4673-4680. ISSN: 0305-1048 (Print), ISSN: 1362-4962 (Electronic).

[2] Kuo-Bin Li ClustalW-MPI: ClustalW analysis using distributed and parallel computing //Bioinformatics Vol. 19, No. 12, 2003, pp. 1585-1586. ISSN: 1460-2059 (Electronic),ISSN: 1367-4803 (Print)

[3] Robert C. Edgar MUSCLE: a multiple sequence alignment method with reduced time and space complexity //BMC Bioinformatics 2004, 5:113, ISSN: 1471-2105 (Electronic).

[4] Saul B. Needleman and Christian D. Wunsch A general method applicable to the search for similarities in the amino acid sequence of two proteins //Journal of Molecular Biology Volume 48, Issue 3, 1970, pp. 443-453, ISSN: 0022-2836.

[5] P.H.A. Sneath, Robert R. Sokal Numerical Taxonomy //Nature 193, pp. 855-860 (03 March 1962), ISSN: 0028-0836, EISSN: 1476-4687.

[6] Alexeevski A.V., Lukina E.N., Salnikov A.N., Spirin S.A. Database of long terminal repeats in human genome: structure and synchronization with main genome archives //Proceedings of the fours international conference on bioinformatics of genome regulation and structure, Volume 1. BGRS 2004, pp. 28-29 Novosibirsk.

[7] Alexey N. Salnikov PARUS: A Parallel Programming Framework for Heterogeneous Multiprocessor Systems //Lecture Notes in Computer Science (LNCS 4192) Recent Advantages in Parallel Virtual Machine and Message Passing Interface, Volume 4192, pp. 408-409, 2006, ISBN-10: 3-540-39110-X ISBN-13: 978-3-540-39110-4.

[8] Amarendran R Subramanian, Michael Kaufmann and Burkhard Morgenstern DIALIGN-TX: greedy and progressive approaches for segment-based multiple sequence alignment // Algorithms for Molecular Biology, 2008, 3:6, ISSN: 1748-7188 (electronic).

[9] Martin Schmollinger, Kay Nieselt, Michael Kaufmann and Burkhard Morgenstern DIALIGN P: Fast pair-wise and multiple sequence alignment using parallel processors // BMC Bioinformatics, 2004, 5:128, ISSN: 1471-2105 (Electronic).

Parallel Computing: From Multicores and GPU's to Petascale
B. Chapman et al. (Eds.)
IOS Press, 2010
© 2010 The authors and IOS Press. All rights reserved.
doi:10.3233/978-1-60750-530-3-150

A Parallel Algorithm for the Fixed-length Approximate String Matching Problem for High Throughput Sequencing Technologies

Costas S. ILIOPOULOS [a,b], Laurent MOUCHARD [a,c], Solon P. PISSIS [a]

[a] *King's College London, Dept. of Computer Science, London WC2R 2LS, UK*
[b] *Curtin University, Digital Ecosystems & Business Intelligence Institute, GPO Box U1987 Perth WA 6845, Australia*
[c] *University of Rouen, LITIS (EA 4108), 76800 Saint-Etienne-du-Rouvray, France*

Abstract. The approximate string matching problem is to find all locations at which a query of length m matches a substring of a text of length n with k-or-fewer differences. Nowadays, with the advent of novel high throughput sequencing technologies, the approximate string matching algorithms are used to identify similarities, molecular functions and abnormalities in DNA sequences. We consider a generalization of this problem, the *fixed-length approximate string matching problem*: given a text t, a pattern ρ and an integer ℓ, compute the optimal alignment of all substrings of ρ of length ℓ and a substring of t. We present a practical parallel algorithm of comparable simplicity that requires only $\mathcal{O}(\frac{nm\lceil \ell/w \rceil}{p})$ time, where w is the word size of the machine (e.g. 32 or 64 in practice) and p the number of processors, by virtue of computing a bit representation of the relocatable dynamic programming matrix for the problem. Thus the algorithm's performance is independent of k and the alphabet size $|\Sigma|$.

Keywords. parallel algorithms, string algorithms, approximate string matching, high throughput sequencing technologies

Introduction

The approximate string matching problem is of great interest in many computational biology applications. These applications are strongly related to the technology that generates the data they are considering. The algorithms, and the application parameters, are tuned in such a way they abolished intrinsic limitations of the technology. Among the large number of equipment that produce data, the DNA sequencers play a central role. DNA sequencing is the generic term for all biochemical methods that determine the order of the nucleotide bases in a DNA sequence.

Very recent advances, based either on sequencing by synthesis or on hybridization and ligation, are producing millions of short reads overnight. Depending on the technology (454 Life Science, Solexa/Illumina or Polony Sequencing, to name a few), the size of the fragments can range from a dozen of base pairs to several hundreds. These advances, and the way they will crucially impact tomorrow's biology, have been presented in several articles [4,9,11,14]. The authors are commenting on the existing gap between this new promising biomechanical technology and existing algorithms for handling this high-throughput stream of data, that small labs will be able to generate on a daily basis.

One of the most common variants of the approximate string matching problem is that of finding substrings that match the pattern with at most k-differences. The first algorithm addressing exactly this problem is attributable to Sellers [12]. Sellers algorithm requires $\mathcal{O}(mn)$ time, where m is the length of the query and n is the length of the text. A thread of practice-oriented results exploited the hardware word-level parallelism of bit-vector operations. Wu and Manber in [15] showed an $\mathcal{O}(nkm/w)$ algorithm for the k-differences problem, where w is the number of bits in a machine word. Baeza-Yates and Navarro in [1] have shown a $\mathcal{O}(nkm/w)$ variation on the Wu/Manber algorithm, implying $\mathcal{O}(n)$ performance when $mk = \mathcal{O}(w)$.

We consider the following versions of the sequence comparison problem: given a solution for the comparison of A and $B = b\hat{B}$, can one incrementally compute a solution for A versus $\hat{B}$? and given a solution for the comparison of A and B, can one incrementally compute a solution for A versus $\hat{B}c$? where b and c are additional symbols. By solution we mean some encoding of a relevant portion of the traditional dynamic programming matrix D computed by comparing A and B.

The above ideas are the bases of the *fixed-length approximate string matching problem*: given a text t of length n, a pattern ρ of length m and an integer ℓ, compute the optimal alignment of all substrings of ρ of length ℓ and a substring of t. Iliopoulos, Mouchard and Pinzon in [6] presented the MAX-SHIFT algorithm, a bit-vector algorithm that requires $O(nm\lceil \ell/w \rceil)$ time and its performance is independent of k. As such, it can be used to compute blocks of dynamic programming matrix as the 4-Russians algorithm (see [16])

There has been ample work in the literature for devising parallel algorithms for different models and platforms, for the approximate string matching problem [2,3,5,7,13]. In this paper, we design and analyze a practical parallel algorithm for addresing the fixed-length approximate string matching problem in $\mathcal{O}(\frac{nm\lceil \ell/w \rceil}{p})$ time. Thus the algorithm's performance is independent of k and the alphabet size $|\Sigma|$. Since the length of the high throughput sequences depends on the technology they were derived from, an algorithm independent of k is of great importance. The proposed algorithm makes use of message passing parallelism model, and word-level parallelism for efficient approximate string matching.

The rest of the paper is structured as follows. In Section 1, the basic definitions that are used throughout the paper are presented. In Sections 2 and 3, we present the sequential and the parallel algorithm, respectively. In Section 4, we present the experimental results of the proposed algorithm. Finally, we briefly conclude in Section 5.

1. Basic Definitions

Consider the sequences x and y with $x[i], y[i] \in \Sigma \cup \{\epsilon\}$. If $x[i] \neq y[i]$, then we say that $x[i]$ *differs* from $y[i]$. We distinguish among the following three types of differences:

1. A symbol of the first sequence corresponds to a different symbol of the second one, then we say that we have a *mismatch* between the two characters, i.e., $x[i] \neq y[i]$.
2. A symbol of the first sequence corresponds to "no symbol" of the second sequence, that is $x[i] \neq \epsilon$ and $y[i] = \epsilon$. This type of difference is called a *deletion*.
3. A symbol of the second sequence corresponds to "no symbol" of the first sequence, that is $x[i] = \epsilon$ and $y[i] \neq \epsilon$. This type of difference is called an *insertion*.

Figure 1. Types of differences: mismatch, insertion, deletion

As an example, see Figure 1; in positions 1 and 3 of t and ρ we have no differences (the symbols "match") but in position 2 we have a "mismatch". In position 4 we have a "deletion" and in position 5 we have a "match". In position 6 we have an "insertion", and in position 7 and 8 we have "matches". Another way of seeing this difference is that one can transform the t sequence to ρ by performing insertions, deletions and replacements of mismatched symbols.

Let $t = t[1...n]$ and $\rho = \rho[1...m]$ with $m \leq n$. We say that ρ occurs at position q of t with at most k-differences (or equivalently, a *local alignment of ρ and t at position q with at most k differences*), if $t[q] \ldots t[r]$, for some $r > q$, can be transformed into ρ by performing at most k of the following operations: inserting, deleting or replacing a symbol. Furthermore we will use the function $\delta(x, y)$ to denote the minimum number operations (deletions, insertions, replacements) required to transform x into y.

Our aim is to construct a matrix $D'[0...m, 0...n]$, which contains the best scores of the alignments of all substrings of ρ of length ℓ and any contiguous substring of the text t. Table 1 shows the matrix D' for $t = \rho = GGGTCTA$ and $\ell = 3$.

2. The MAX-SHIFT Algorithm

One can obtain a straightforward $\mathcal{O}(nm\ell)$ algorithm for computing matrix D' by constructing matrices $D^{(s)}[1...\ell, 1...n]$, $1 \leq s \leq m - \ell + 1$, where $D^{(s)}[i, j]$ is the minimum number of differences between the prefix of the pattern $\rho_s, ..., \rho_{s+\ell-1}$

		0	1	2	3	4	5	6	7
		ϵ	G	G	G	T	C	T	A
0	ϵ	0	0	0	0	0	0	0	0
1	G	1	0	0	0	1	1	1	1
2	G	2	1	0	0	1	2	2	2
3	G	3	2	1	0	1	2	3	3
4	T	3	2	1	1	0	1	2	3
5	C	3	2	2	2	1	0	1	2
6	T	3	3	3	3	2	1	0	1
7	A	3	3	3	3	2	2	1	0

Table 1. Matrix D' for $t = \rho = GGGTCTA$ and $\ell = 3$.

		0	1	2	3	4	5	6	7
		ϵ	G	G	G	T	C	T	A
0	ϵ	0	0	0	0	0	0	0	0
1	G	1	0	0	0	1	1	1	1
2	G	11	10	00	00	01	11	11	11
3	G	111	110	100	000	001	011	111	111
4	T	111	101	001	001	000	0001	110	111
5	C	111	011	011	011	001	000	0001	101
6	T	111	111	111	111	110	001	000	0001
7	A	111	111	111	111	101	101	001	000

Table 2. The bit-vector matrix B for $t = \rho = GGGTCTA$ and $\ell = 3$.

and any contiguous substring of the text ending at $t[j]$; its computation can be based on the Dynamic-Programming procedure presented in [8]. We can obtain D' by collating $D^{(1)}$ and the last row of the $D^{(s)}$, $2 \leq s \leq m - \ell + 1$.

The MAX-SHIFT algorithm makes use of word level parallelism in order to compute matrix D' more efficiently, similar to the manner used by Myers in [10]. The algorithm is based on the $\mathcal{O}(1)$-time computation of each $D'[i,j]$ by using bit-vector operations, under the assumption that $\ell \leq w$, where w is the number of bits in a machine word, or $\mathcal{O}(\ell/w)$-time for the general case. We maintain the bit-vector $B[i,j] = b_\lambda...b_1$, where $b_r = 1$, $1 \leq r \leq \lambda$, $\lambda < 2\ell$, If there is an alignment of a contiguous substring of the text $t[q...j]$ (for some $1 \leq q < j$) and $\rho[i - \ell + 1...i]$ with $D'[i,j]$ differences such that

- The leftmost $r-1$ pairs of the alignment have $\Sigma_\lambda^{\lambda-r-2} b_j$ differences in total.
- The r-th pair of the alignment (from left to right) is a difference: a deletion in the pattern, an insertion in the text or a replacement.

Otherwise we set $b_r = 0$. In other words $B[i,j]$ holds the binary encoding of the path in D' to obtain the optimal alignment at i, j with the differences occurring as leftmost as possible.

Example. Let the text $t = \rho = GGGTCTA$ and $\ell = 3$. Table 2 shows the bit-vector matrix B.

Given the restraint that the integer ℓ is less than the length of the computer word w, then the bit-vector operations allow to update each entry of the matrix B in constant time (using "shift"-type of operation on the bit-vector). The maintenance of the bit-vector is done via operations defined as follows:

- *shift*: moves the bits one position to the left and enters zero from the right
- *shiftc*: shifts and truncates the leftmost bit
- *bitminmax(x,y,z)*: given integers x, y, z this function returns one of the integers $\{x, y, z\}$ with the property that it has the least number of 1's (bits set on). If there is a draw then the algorithm returns the maximum of the two when viewed as decimal integers.
- *leftmostbit*: returns the leftmost bit
- *ones(v)*: returns the number of 1's in the bit-vector v

The MAX-SHIFT algorithm for computing the bit-vector matrix B and matrix D' is outlined in Figure 2.

Max-Shift
▷Input: t, n, ρ, m, ℓ
▷Output: B, D'

  1 **begin**
  2   ▷ Initialization
  3     $B[0...m, 0] \leftarrow \min(i, \ell)$ 1's; $B[0, 0..n] \leftarrow 0$
  4     $D'[0...m, 0] \leftarrow \min(i, \ell)$; $D'[0, 0..n] \leftarrow 0$
  5   **for** $i \leftarrow 1$ **until** m **do**
  6   **for** $j \leftarrow 1$ **until** n **do**
  7   **if** $i \leq \ell$ **then**
  8   ▷ Normal-DP
  9            $B[i, j] \leftarrow bitminmax\{shift(B[i-1, j])$ OR $1, shift(B[i, j-1])$ OR $1,$
                              $shift(B[i-1, j-1])$ OR $\delta(\rho[i], t[j])\}$
10   **else**
11   ▷ Max-Shift
12            $B[i, j] \leftarrow bitminmax\{shiftc(B[i-1, j])$ OR $1, shift(B[i, j-1])$ OR $1,$
                              $shiftc(B[i-1, j-1])$ OR $\delta(\rho[i], t[j])\}$
13        $D'[i, j] \leftarrow ones(B[i, j])$
14 **end**

Figure 2. MAX-SHIFT algorithm

3. The PARALLEL-MAX-SHIFT **Algorithm**

The proposed parallel algorithm makes use of the message-passing parallelism model by using p processors. The following assumptions for the model of communications in the parallel computer are made. The parallel computer comprises a number of nodes. Each node comprises one or several identical processors interconnected by a switched communication network. The time taken to send a message of size n between any two nodes is independent of the distance between nodes and can be modelled as $t_{comm} = t_s + nt_w$, where t_s is the latency or start-up time of the message, and t_w is the transfer time per data. The links between two nodes are full-duplex and single-ported.

We will use the *functional* decomposition, in which the initial focus is on the computation that is to be performed rather than on the data manipulated by the computation. We assume that both text t and pattern ρ are stored locally on each processor. This can be done by using a *one-to-all* broadcast operation in $(t_s + t_w(n + m)) \log p$ communication time, which is asymptotically $\mathcal{O}(n \log p)$.

The key idea behind parallelising the MAX-SHIFT algorithm, is that cell $B[i, j]$ can be computed only in terms of $B[i, j-1]$, $B[i-1, j]$ and $B[i-1, j-1]$. Based on this, if we partition the problem of computing matrix B (and D') into a set of diagonal vectors $\Delta_0, \Delta_1, ..., \Delta_{n+m}$, as shown in Equation 1, the computation of each one of these would be independent, and hence parallelisable.

$$\Delta_\nu[x] = \begin{cases} B[\nu - x, \ x] & : \ 0 \le x \le \nu, & \text{(a)} \\ B[m - x, \ \nu - m + x] & : \ 0 \le x < m + 1, & \text{(b)} \\ B[m - x, \ \nu - m + x] & : \ 0 \le x < n + m - \nu + 1, & \text{(c)} \end{cases} \tag{1}$$

where,
(a)   if $0 \le \nu < m$
(b)   if $m \le \nu < n$
(c)   if $n \le \nu < n + m + 1$

It is possible that in a certain diagonal Δ_ν, $\nu > 0$, a processor will need a cell or a pair of cells, which were not computed on its local memory in diagonal $\Delta_{\nu-1}$. We need a communication pattern in each diagonal Δ_ν, for all $0 \le \nu < n + m$, which minimises the data exchange between the processors. It is obvious, that in each diagonal, each processor needs only to communicate with its neighbours.

An outline of the PARALLEL-MAX-SHIFT algorithm in each diagonal Δ_ν, for all $0 \le \nu < n + m + 1$, is as follows.

Step 1. Each processor is allocated with $|\Delta_\nu|/p$ cells (without loss of generality).
Step 2. Each processor computes each allocated cell using the MAX-SHIFT.
Step 3. Processors communication involving point-to-point boundary cells swaps.

Theorem 1. Given the text $t = t[1...n]$, the pattern $\rho = \rho[1...m]$, the motif length ℓ, the size w of the computer word, and the number of processors p, the PARALLEL-MAX-SHIFT algorithm computes the matrix B in $\mathcal{O}(\frac{nm\lceil \ell/w \rceil}{p})$ units of time.

Proof. We partition the problem of computing matrix B into a set of $n + m + 1$ diagonal vectors, thus $\mathcal{O}(n)$ supersteps. In step 1, the allocation procedure runs in $\mathcal{O}(1)$ time. In step 2, the cells computation requires $\mathcal{O}(\frac{m\lceil \ell/w \rceil}{p})$ time. In step 3, the data exchange between the processors involves $\mathcal{O}(1)$ point-to-point message transfers. Hence, asymptotically, the overall time is $\mathcal{O}(\frac{nm\lceil \ell/w \rceil}{p})$.   □

Also, the space complexity is reduced to $\mathcal{O}(n)$ by noting that each diagonal vector Δ_ν depends only on $\Delta_{\nu-1}$, for all $1 \le \nu < n + m + 1$.

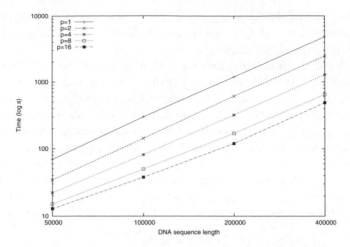

Figure 3. Execution time for $t = \rho$ and $\ell = 20$

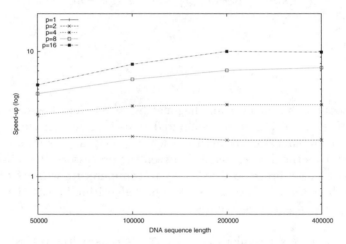

Figure 4. Measured speed-up for $t = \rho$ and $\ell = 20$

4. Experimental Results

In order to evaluate the parallel efficiency of our algorithm, we implemented the MAX-SHIFT algorithm in ANSI C language and parallelised it with the use of the MPI library. Experimental tests were run on 1 up to 16 processing nodes (2.6 GHz AMD Opteron) of a cluster architecture. As an input, DNA sequences of the mouse chromosome X were used, retrieved from the *Ensembl* genome database. Experimental results regarding the execution time and measured speed-up are illustrated in Figures 3 and 4, respectively. The speed-up is calculated as the ratio of elapsed time with p processors to elapsed time with one processor.

The presented experimental results demonstrate a good scaling of the code. The proposed algorithm scales well even for small problem sizes. As expected in some cases, when increasing the problem size, the algorithm achieves a linear speed-up, confirming our theoretical results. Further tests were conducted for different values of fixed-length ℓ, with no difference observed, regarding the execution time.

5. Conclusion

We have presented a practical parallel aglorithm that solves a generalization of the approximate string matching problem, motivated by the new high through-put sequencing technologies in biology. In particular, the proposed parallel algorithm solves the fixed-length approximate string matching problem in $\mathcal{O}(\frac{nm\lceil \ell/w \rceil}{p})$ time, which is $\mathcal{O}(\frac{nm}{p})$, in practical terms. It is considerably simple and elegant, it achieves a theoretical and practical linear speed-up, it does not require text preprocessing, it does not use/store look up tables and it does not depend on the number of differences k and the alphabet size $|\Sigma|$.

References

[1] R. A. Baeza-Yates and G. Navarro, A faster algorithm for approximate string matching, *Proceedings of the 7th Symposium on Combinatorial Pattern Matching*, LNCS, Vol. 1075, Springer-Verlag, New York, 1996, pp. 1–23.

[2] A. A. Bertossi, F. Luccio, L. Pagli and E. Lodi, A parallel solution to the approximate string matching problem, *The Computer Journal*, Vol. 35, Issue 5, 1992, pp. 524–526.

[3] A.R. Galper and D.R. Brutlag, Parallel similarity search and alignment with the dynamic programming method, *Technical Report KSL 90-74*, Stanford University, 1990, 14pp.

[4] N. Hall, Advanced sequencing technologies and their wider impact in microbiology, *J. Exp. Biol.*, 2007, pp. 1518-1525.

[5] X. Huang, A space-efficient parallel sequence comparison algorithm for a Message-Passing Multiprocessor, *International Journal of Parallel Programming*, Vol. 18, n. 3, 1990, pp. 223–239.

[6] C. S. Iliopoulos, L. Mouchard and Y. J. Pinzon, The Max-Shift algorithm for approximate string matching, *WAE '01: Proceedings of the 5th International Workshop on Algorithm Engineering*, 2001, pp. 13–25.

[7] G.M. Landau and U. Vishkin, Fast parallel and serial approximate string matching. *Journal of Algorithms*, Vol. 10, 1989, pp. 157–169.

[8] G.M. Landau and U. Vishkin, Fast string matching with k differences, *Journal of Computer and Systems Sciences*, Vol. 37, 1900, pp. 63–78

[9] E. H. Margulies and E. Birney, Approaches to comparative sequence analysis: towards a functional view of vertebrate genomes, *Nat. Rev. Genet.*, 2008, pp. 303–313.

[10] E. W. Myers, A Fast Bit-Vector Algorithm for Approximate String Matching Based on Dynamic Programming, *Journal of the ACM*, Vol. 46, 1999, pp. 395–415.

[11] S. C. Schuster, Next-generation sequencing transforms today's biology, *Nat. Methods*, 2008, pp. 16–18.

[12] P. H. Seller, The theory and computation of evolutionary distances: Pattern recognition, *Journal of Algorithms*, Vol. 1, 1980, pp. 359–373.

[13] C.C.T. dos Reis, Approximate string matching algorithm using parallel methods for molecular sequence comparisons, *Artificial intelligence, 2005. epia 2005. portuguese conference on*, 2005, pp. 140–143.

[14] B. Wold and R. Myers, Sequence consensus methods for functional genomics, *Nature Methods*, 2008, pp. 19–21.

[15] S. Wu and U. Manber, Fast text searching allowing errors, *CACM*, Vol. 35, 1992, pp. 83–91.

[16] S. Wu, U. Manber and G. Myers, A subquadratic algorithm for approximate limited expression matching, *Algorithmica*, Vol. 15, 1996, pp. 50–67.

Parallel Computing: From Multicores and GPU's to Petascale
B. Chapman et al. (Eds.)
IOS Press, 2010
© 2010 The authors and IOS Press. All rights reserved.
doi:10.3233/978-1-60750-530-3-158

Computing alignment plots efficiently

Peter Krusche and Alexander Tiskin*,

Dept. of Computer Science, University of Warwick, Coventry, CV4 7AL, UK

Abstract. Dot plots are a standard method for local comparison of biological sequences. In a dot plot, a substring to substring distance is computed for all pairs of fixed-size windows in the input strings. Commonly, the Hamming distance is used since it can be computed in linear time. However, the Hamming distance is a rather crude measure of string similarity, and using an alignment-based edit distance can greatly improve the sensitivity of the dot plot method. In this paper, we show how to compute alignment plots of the latter type efficiently. Given two strings of length m and n and a window size w, this problem consists in computing the edit distance between all pairs of substrings of length w, one from each input string. The problem can be solved by repeated application of the standard dynamic programming algorithm in time $O(mnw^2)$. This paper gives an improved data-parallel algorithm, running in time $O(mnw/\gamma/p)$ using vector operations that work on γ values in parallel and p processors.

1. Introduction

Dot plots are a standard method for local comparison of two biological sequences introduced by Gibbs/McIntyre [6] and Maizel/Lenk [10]. When creating a dot plot, a substring to substring distance is computed for all pairs of fixed-size windows in the input strings. The result can be visualized by a plot showing a dot for each pair of windows that achieves a distance below a fixed threshold. Commonly, the Hamming distance is used [10,9], since it can be computed very efficiently. However, the Hamming distance is a rather crude measure of string similarity. Using a string edit distance or alignment score (see e.g. [7]) for dot plot filtering can greatly improve the sensitivity of the method. In the context of biological sequence comparison, this idea has been implemented by Ott et al. [12], where a sequential algorithm is given which creates an alignment plot for two strings of lengths m and n using a fixed window length w in time $O(mnw^2)$.

In this paper, we give an improved data-parallel algorithm, running in time $O(mnw/\gamma)$ using vector operations that work on γ values in parallel, and show experimental speedups from an implementation using MMX [8]. Furthermore, we demonstrate that the algorithm can be parallelized to run on multiple processors using MPI [14].

* Research supported by the Centre for Discrete Mathematics and Its Applications (DIMAP), University of Warwick, EPSRC award EP/D063191/1. Computational resources were provided by the Centre for Scientific Computing at the University of Warwick.

2. Computing longest common subsequences and string alignments

Let $x = x_1 x_2 \ldots x_m$ and $y = y_1 y_2 \ldots y_n$ be two strings over an alphabet Σ of size σ. We distinguish between contiguous *substrings* of a string x, which can be obtained by removing zero or more characters from the beginning and/or the end of x, and *subsequences*, which can be obtained by deleting zero or more characters in any position. The *longest common subsequence* (LCS) of two strings is the longest string that is a subsequence of both input strings; its length (the LLCS) is a measure for the similarity of the two strings. Substrings of length w are called *w-windows*. For a given w, the length of the LCS of two w-windows $x_i \ldots x_{i+w-1}$ and $y_j \ldots y_{j+w-1}$ will be denoted as $WLCS(i,j)$. An *alignment plot* for x and y consists of all values $WLCS(i,j)$ with $i \in \{1, 2, \ldots, m-w\}$, $j \in \{1, 2, \ldots, n-w\}$.

Although the LCS is more accurate than the Hamming score, more general similarity measures are of interest in practice. A standard interpretation of LCS is *string alignment* [7, p. 209 ff.]. An alignment of strings x and y is obtained by putting a subsequence of x into one-to-one correspondence with a (not necessarily identical) subsequence of y, character by character and respecting the index order. The corresponding pairs of characters, one from x and the other from y, are said to be *aligned*. A character not aligned with a character of another string is said to be aligned with a *gap* in that string. Finding the LCS corresponds to computing a maximum alignment when assigning the scores $w_= = 1$ to aligning a matching pair of characters, $w_- = 0$ to inserting a gap, and $w_{\neq} = 0$ to aligning two mismatching characters. More general alignments than the LCS can be obtained using the standard dynamic programming algorithm [17,11], which allows for gap penalties as well as different scores for each individual pair of matching/mismatching characters, forming a *pairwise score matrix*. Any algorithm for LCS computation can be generalized to pairwise score matrices with small rational scores at the price of a constant factor blow up of the input strings [16]. In this paper, we will consider alignments with match score $w_= = 1$, mismatch score $w_{\neq} = 0$ and gap penalty $w_- = -0.5$. To compute these alignments, we modify the input strings by adding a new character $ to the alphabet, which we insert before every character in both input strings such that e.g. abab transforms into abab. For input strings x and y of length m and n, the alignment score $S(x, y)$ can be retrieved from LLCS of the modified strings x' and y' as $S(x, y) = LLCS(x', y') - 0.5 \cdot (m + n)$. We expect the running time of the seaweed algorithm to increase by a factor of four by this reduction, as both input strings double in size.

Our new algorithms are based on semi-local sequence alignment [15], for which we now give the necessary definitions. Throughout this paper, we will denote the set of integers $\{i, i+1, \ldots, j\}$ by $[i : j]$, and the set of odd half-integers $\{i + \frac{1}{2}, i + \frac{3}{2}, \ldots, j - \frac{1}{2}\}$ by $\langle i : j \rangle$. We will further mark odd half-integer variables by a "^" symbol. When indexing a matrix M by odd-half integer values $\hat{i}$ and $\hat{j}$, we define that $M(\hat{i}, \hat{j}) = M(i, j)$ with $i = \hat{i} - 1/2$ and $j = \hat{j} - 1/2$. Therefore, if a matrix has integer indices $[1 : m] \times [1 : n]$, it has odd-half integer indices $\langle 1 : m+1 \rangle \times \langle 1 : n+1 \rangle$. We also define the *distribution matrix* D^{Σ} of an $m \times n$ matrix D as $D^{\Sigma}(i, j) = \sum D(\hat{i}, \hat{j})$ with $(\hat{i}, \hat{j}) \in \langle i : m+1 \rangle \times \langle 1 : j \rangle$.

Let the *alignment dag (directed acyclic graph)* $G_{x,y}$ for two strings x and y be defined by a set of vertices $v_{i,j}$ with $i \in [0 : m]$ and $j \in [0 : n]$ and edges as follows. We have horizontal and vertical edges $v_{i,j-1} \to v_{i,j}$ and $v_{i-1,j} \to v_{i,j}$ of score 0. Further, we introduce diagonal edges $v_{i-1,j-1} \to v_{i,j}$ of score 1, which are present only if $x_i = y_j$. Longest common subsequences of a substring $x_i x_{i+1} \ldots x_j$ and y correspond to highest-scoring paths in this graph from $v_{i-1,0}$ to $v_{j,m}$. When drawing the alignment dag in the plane, its horizontal and vertical edges partition the plane into rectangular *cells* each of which, depending on the input strings, may contain a diagonal edge or not. For every pair of characters x_i and y_j, we define a corresponding cell $(i - \frac{1}{2}, j - \frac{1}{2})$. Cells corresponding to a matching pair of characters are called *match cells*, and cells corresponding to mismatching characters are called *mismatch cells*.

Solutions to the *semi-local LCS problem* are given by a *highest-score matrix* which we define as follows. In a highest-score matrix $A_{x,y}$, each entry $A_{x,y}(i,j)$ is defined as the length of the highest-scoring path in $G_{x,y}$ from $v_{i-1,0}$ to $v_{j,m}$. Each entry $A_{x,y}(i,j)$ with $0 < i < j < n$ gives the LLCS of x and substring $y_i \ldots y_j$.

Since the values of $A_{x,y}(i,j)$ for different i and j are strongly correlated, it is possible to derive an implicit, space-efficient representation of matrix $A_{x,y}(i,j)$. This implicit representation of a semi-local highest-score matrix consists of a set of *critical points*. The critical points of a highest-score matrix A are defined as the set of odd half-integer pairs $(\hat{i}, \hat{j})$ such that $A(\hat{i} + \frac{1}{2}, \hat{j} - \frac{1}{2}) + 1 = A(\hat{i} - \frac{1}{2}, \hat{j} - \frac{1}{2}) = A(\hat{i} + \frac{1}{2}, \hat{j} + \frac{1}{2}) = A(\hat{i} - \frac{1}{2}, \hat{j} + \frac{1}{2})$. Consider a highest-score matrix A. The matrix D_A with $D_A(\hat{i}, \hat{j}) = 1$ if $(\hat{i}, \hat{j})$ is a critical point in A, and $D_A(\hat{i}, \hat{j}) = 0$ otherwise, is called the *implicit highest-score matrix*.

Tiskin [15] showed that in order to represent a highest-score matrix for two strings of lengths m and n, exactly $m + n$ such critical points are sufficient.

Theorem 2.1 (see [15] for proof). *A highest-score matrix A can be represented implicitly using only $O(m+n)$ space by its implicit highest-score matrix D_A, which is a permutation matrix. We have: $A(i,j) = j - i - D_A^\Sigma(i,j)$, where D_A^Σ is the distribution matrix of the implicit highest-score matrix D_A.*

The set of critical points can be obtained using the *seaweed algorithm* (by Alves et al. [3], based on Schmidt [13], adapted by Tiskin [15]) which computes critical points by dynamic programming on all prefixes of the input strings. This method is graphically illustrated by tracing *seaweeds* that start at odd half-integer positions between two adjacent vertices $v_{0,\hat{i}-\frac{1}{2}}$ and $v_{0,\hat{i}+\frac{1}{2}}$ in the top row of the alignment dag, and end between two adjacent vertices $v_{m,\hat{j}-\frac{1}{2}}$ and $v_{m,\hat{j}+\frac{1}{2}}$ in the bottom row. Each critical point is computed as the pair of horizontal start and end coordinates of such a seaweed (see Algorithm 1). Two seaweeds enter every cell in the alignment dag, one at the left and one at the top. The seaweeds proceed through the cell either downwards or rightwards. In the cell, the directions of these seaweeds are interchanged either if there is a match $x_k = y_l$, or if the same pair of seaweeds have already crossed. Otherwise, their directions remain unchanged and the seaweeds cross. By Theorem 2.1, the length of the highest-scoring path in $G_{x,y}$ from $v_{i-1,0}$ to $v_{j,m}$ can be computed by counting the number of seaweeds which both start and end within $\langle i : j \rangle$.

3. Data-parallel window-window comparison using seaweeds

The seaweed algorithm can be used to compute the LCS of all pairs of w-windows simultaneously in time $O(wn)$ for two strings of respective lengths w and n (i.e. one of the strings consists of only one w-window). By Theorem 2.1, the LCS of x and any w-window $y_i \ldots y_{i+w-1}$ is computed as the number of seaweeds starting and ending within the odd half-integer range $\langle i : i + w \rangle$. By keeping track of only these seaweeds in a sliding window, our algorithm can compute the LLCS for all w-windows in a single pass over all columns of cells in the alignment dag. We obtain an improved algorithm for comparing all pairs of w-windows.

Theorem 3.1. *Given two strings x and y of lengths m and n, the LLCS for all pairs of w-windows between x and y can be computed in time $O(mnw)$.*

Proof. We apply the seaweed algorithm for computing the implicit highest-score matrices for y and all substrings of x that have length w. Each application of the seaweed algorithm therefore runs on a strip of height w and width n of the alignment dag corresponding to $x_i \ldots x_{i+w-1}$ and y. A column of cells in this strip can be processed in time $O(w)$. In each column j, exactly one new seaweed starts at the top of the alignment dag, and exactly one seaweed ends at the bottom. We track seaweeds ending within $\langle j - w : j \rangle$. To count the seaweeds that have reached the bottom of the alignment dag, we maintain a priority queue B. In each step, one seaweed reaches the bottom of the alignment dag. Furthermore, in each step, we have to delete at most one seaweed from B. We use a priority queue of $\lceil \log n \rceil$-bit integers to represent B. For each seaweed that reaches the bottom, we compute its starting point and add it to the queue. We delete the minimum value from the queue if it is smaller than the starting position of the current w-window in string y. By using a min-heap [4], both operations can be implemented in $O(\log w)$. The number d of seaweeds which start within $\langle j - w : j \rangle$ is then given by the size of queue B. The LLCS of $y_{j-w+1} \ldots y_j$ and $x_i \ldots x_{i+w-1}$ can then be calculated as $w - d$. In total, we have to process n columns using time $O(w)$ in every strip. Overall, $m - w$ strips exist, therefore we obtain running time $O(mnw)$. $\qquad\square$

Algorithm 1 The Seaweed Algorithm

input: Strings x and y
output: The critical points for x against y
Initialise $J[i] = i + m$ for $i \in \langle -m, n \rangle$
for $r \in [1, m]$ **do**
  $l \leftarrow -\infty$
  for $c \in [1, n]$ **do**
    $t \leftarrow J[c + \frac{1}{2}]$
    if $x_r = y_c$ **or** $l > t$ **then**
      Swap l and t
    end if
    $J[c + \frac{1}{2}] \leftarrow t$
  end for
  $J[n + r - \frac{1}{2}] \leftarrow t$
end for
return the points $\{(i, J[i]) \mid i \in \langle -m, n \rangle$ with $J[i] \neq -\infty\}$

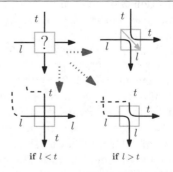

if $l < t$ if $l > t$

While this direct application of the seaweed method gives an asymptotic improvement on the method of computing the LCS independently for every pair of windows by dynamic programming, it is not necessarily more practical. The dynamic programming method can exploit the fact that we are only interested in windows with an alignment score above a given threshold. More importantly, the dynamic programming method allows one to improve performance by introducing a step size h, and only comparing w-windows starting at positions that are multiples of h. We will now show how to improve the practical performance of the algorithm.

Algorithm 1 requires $O(\log(m+n))$ bits to represent the start and endpoints of a single seaweed. We first show that for computing alignment plots with a fixed window length w, $O(\log w)$ bits are sufficient for tracing seaweeds, independently of the size of the input strings. To show this, we define the *span* of a seaweed as the horizontal distance it covers in the alignment dag. A seaweed corresponding to a critical point $(\hat{i}, \hat{j})$ has span $\hat{j} - \hat{i}$. Seaweeds that have a span greater than the window length w are not relevant for computing the alignment plot, since they will not start and end within a single window. Furthermore, we are only interested in values with index pairs (i, j) having $i \bmod r = j \bmod r = 0$, where r is the constant blowup induced by the alignment score (for the scoring scheme described in the previous section, we have $r = 2$). This is equivalent to computing the semi-local LCS for substrings restricted to length w, starting and ending at positions 0 mod r.

Definition 3.2. Let A be a highest-score matrix. The (w, r)-*restricted highest-score matrix* $A^{w,r}$ is defined as $A^{w,r}(i, j) = A(i, j)$ if $j - i \leq w$ and $i \bmod r = j \bmod r = 0$, and $A^{w,r}(i, j) = undefined$ otherwise.

This restriction on the highest-score matrices allows us to reduce the number of critical points we need to store, and also to reduce the number of bits required to represent seaweeds in our computation.

Proposition 3.3. *To represent a (w, r)-restricted highest-score matrix implicitly, we only need to store the critical points $(\hat{i}, \hat{j})$ of the corresponding unrestricted highest score matrix for which $\hat{j} - \hat{i} < w$.*

Proof. Straightforward from Theorem 2.1 and Definition 3.2. □

Proposition 3.4. *We can represent a single critical point in a (w, r)-restricted highest-score matrix for comparing strings x and y using $O(\log(w/r))$ bits.*

Proof. We store the seaweeds in a vector S of size $m + n$, where each vector element stores $\lceil \log_2(w/r + 1) \rceil$ bits. For each critical point $(\hat{i}, \hat{j})$, we have one vector element $S(\hat{i} + 1/2) = \min(2^{w/r+1} - 1, (\hat{j} - \hat{i})/r)$. Each vector element stores the span of the seaweed starting at $\hat{i}$.

It is straightforward to see that we only need $O(\log w)$ bits for a vector element: seaweeds in a (w, r)-restricted highest-score matrix become irrelevant once their span is larger than w, since these critical points will not affect any LCS for a substring of length w (see Theorem 2.1). In order to reduce the number of bits to $O(\log w/r)$, we use the fact that we only need to answer LCS queries correctly if $i \bmod r = j \bmod r = 0$. We therefore do not need to distinguish between the individual r seaweeds starting within $[k : k + r - 1]$ with $k \bmod r = 0$: once they reach the bottom, we only need to know their starting position within a window of size r. We can therefore divide the distance values by r, which gives the claimed number of required bits. □

We now show how to use vector instructions for improving Algorithm 1 to trace multiple seaweeds in parallel. A practical example for vector parallelism are Intel's MMX instructions [8] for integer vector arithmetic and comparison (it would also be possible to implement our algorithm using floating point vector processing, e.g. using SSE [8]). In our algorithm, we assume that all elements $V(j)$ in a vector V are v-bit values. If an element of a vector has all bits set, then this represents the value of $+\infty$, having $INF \equiv 2^v - 1$. When carrying out the seaweed algorithm on columns of the alignment dag, the result of every comparison in a cell of the column depends on the comparison result from the cell above it. To be able to process multiple cells in parallel, we need to process cells by antidiagonals. We can then use vector operations to implement each step in the the seaweed algorithm, as each cell can be processed only using data computed in the previous step. We need to track seaweeds only if they are within the window of interest. In order to keep the required value of bits per seaweed as small as possible (and hence allow a high degree of vector parallelism), we identify seaweeds by the distance of their starting points to the current column. This distance can be represented using $v = \lceil \log_2 2w + 1 \rceil$ bits (see Proposition 3.4). When advancing to the next column, we use saturated addition to increment all distances in parallel (i.e. saturated addition of one to vector element $V(k)$ gives $V(k) + 1$ if $V(k) < 2w$, and INF otherwise). In each step, we compare the characters corresponding to the cells in the current antidiagonal using vectorised mask generation. Given two vectors V and W, we generate a mask vector which contains the value INF at all positions k, where $V(k) = W(k)$ and zero otherwise. The seaweed behaviour in mismatch cells is implemented by a compare/exchange operation which, given two vectors V and W, exchanges $V(k)$ and $W(k)$ only if $V(k) > W(k)$. To combine the results from the mismatch cells and the match cells, we require an operation to exchange vector elements conditionally using the mask vector M generated earlier. Given two vectors V and W), this operation returns vector elements $V(k)$ if $M(k) = INF$, and $W(k)$ otherwise. All these operations can be vectorized efficiently using MMX. Using these operations, we can implement the seaweed operations from Algorithm 1 by storing all seaweeds on the current antidiagonal in a vector V if they enter the respective cell from the left, and a vector W if they enter the respective cell from the top. We use a v-bit shift operation on vector W in each step to advance the seaweeds leaving cells at the bottom downwards.

4. Experimental Results

We have implemented the algorithm from the previous sections for allowing its application to actual biological sequences. The implementation uses C++ with and Intel MMX assembly code. As input data for our tests, we used different biological sequence data sets and a fixed window size of 100 (the nature of the sequences does not affect the running time of our algorithm, but may affect the impact of the heuristic speedup employed by the heuristic method we compare the results to). In all experiments, we used a vertical step size of 5, i.e. we only compare every fifth window in the first input to all windows in the other string. Using the scoring scheme as described in Section 2 induces a window size of 200 due to the constant-size blowup of the alignment dag. For comparing the results to existing methods, we implemented an alternative fast method for bit-parallel LCS computation [5] to compute the pairwise alignment scores ("BLCS") – our 64-bit implementation of this algorithm achieves a speedup of 32 over the standard dynamic programming algorithm for inputs of length 200. Furthermore, we compared our results to the code used in [12] ("Heur") which uses the standard dynamic programming algorithm [17,11] and a heuristic to speed up computation when a minimum alignment score for a window pair is specified. In the Sea-16, vectors of 16-bit values were used. Using the results from Section 3, we can improve this to use 8-bit values, by computing (200, 2)-restricted highest-score matrices. The results of our experiments are shown in Table 1. We see that the seaweed-based algorithm is fastest for all data sets. We also see that the heuristic employed by Heur makes this algorithm more effective than the BLCS method for long sequences. However, we note that it would be possible to adapt BLCS to make use of the same heuristic speedup. Overall, these results show that the seaweed algorithm is highly competitive against the repeated dynamic programming approach, and that particularly the byte vector version (Sea-8) is more than seven times faster than the best existing method.

We further conducted experiments to study the scalability on larger numbers of processors using MPI. Input sequence x is broadcast to all nodes, and input sequence y is split into chunks of equal size using MPI_Scatterv. Each node produces a local output file, these are merged in a postprocessing step. We obtained good speedup especially for the large datasets both on small and larger parallel systems. Note that our sample datasets are still rather small. We plan to apply the algorithm to whole-genome comparison, which involves much larger input sequences, and hence better speedup on more processors.

Table 1. Execution times in seconds and speedups

Data Set	Mikey (2712×628)	Berti (2712×2305)	Jimmy (15k×97k)	Henry (80k×80k)
MMX vector speedup on Linux/x86_64/1.83GHz Core2-duo (non-MPI), gcc 4.3.1				
Heur	5.1 (÷ 1.0)	41.1 (÷ 1.0)	2677 (÷ 1.0)	11708 (÷ 1.0)
BLCS	3.6 (÷ 1.4)	37.3 (÷ 1.1)	3680 (÷ 0.7)	16191 (÷ 0.7)
Sea-16	1.4 (÷ 3.6)	10.8 (÷ 3.8)	1026 (÷ 2.6)	4514 (÷ 2.6)
Sea-8	0.5 (÷ 10.2)	3.8 (÷ 10.8)	368 (÷ 7.3)	1614 (÷ 7.3)
Linux desktop system, Core2-quad 2.66GHz, 64-bit, MPI, gcc 4.3.1				
1 core	0.4 (÷ 1.0)	2.9 (÷ 1.0)	271 (÷ 1.0)	1199 (÷ 1.0)
4 cores	0.7 (÷ 0.6)	1.3 (÷ 2.2)	70 (÷ 3.9)	307 (÷ 3.9)
IBM Cluster [1], 2×dual-core Xeon 3GHz/node, QLogic InfiniPath network, MPI, gcc 4.1.2				
1 core	0.67 (÷ 1.0)	3.1 (÷ 1.0)	225 (÷ 1.0)	991 (÷ 1.0)
4 cores	0.57 (÷ 1.2)	1.4 (÷ 2.2)	58 (÷ 3.9)	251 (÷ 3.9)
16 cores	1.26 (÷ 0.5)	1.6 (÷ 1.9)	20 (÷ 11.5)	66 (÷ 14.9)
64 cores	–	–	11 (÷ 20.5)	23 (÷ 42.4)

5. Conclusions and Outlook

In this paper, we present a practical algorithm for local string comparison by edit distance filtered dot plots which uses vector-parallelism and recent algorithmic results to achieve both improved asymptotic cost and performance over applying optimized standard methods. We have further shown results from a coarse-grained parallel implementation of the algorithm, which achieved good speedup on different parallel systems. Further performance could be gained by using SSE [8] or newer vector architectures like Larrabee [2] for implementing our code. A few algorithmic improvements are possible as well. In [16], a tree approach is proposed to avoid recomputing all seaweeds in each strip of height w, which allows to perform the computation in time $O(mn)$. We are currently investigating a practical variation of this theoretical method which further reduces the dependency on the window size, and may improve the algorithm shown here. Moreover, we believe that it is possible to use a similar heuristic to the one applied in [12] to further improve performance.

References

[1] Centre for Scientific Computing, University of Warwick, http://www.csc.warwick.ac.uk.
[2] M. Abrash. A First Look at the Larrabee New Instructions (LRBni). *Dr. Dobb's Journal*, 2009.
[3] C.E.R. Alves, E.N. Caceres, and S.W. Song. An all-substrings common subsequence algorithm. *Discrete Applied Mathematics*, 156(7):1025–1035, April 2008.
[4] T.H. Cormen, C.E. Leiserson, R.L. Rivest, and C. Stein. *Introduction to Algorithms, Second Edition*. MIT Press/McGraw-Hill Book Company, 2001.
[5] M. Crochemore, C.S. Iliopoulos, Y.J. Pinzon, and J.F. Reid. A fast and practical bit-vector algorithm for the longest common subsequence problem. *Inf. Proc. Lett.*, 80(6):279–285, 2001.
[6] A.J. Gibbs and G.A. McIntyre. The diagram: A method for comparing sequences. its uses with amino acids and nucleotide sequences. *Eur. J. Biochem.*, 16:1–11, 1970.
[7] D. Gusfield. *Algorithms on Strings, Trees, and Sequences*. Cambridge Univ. Press, 1997.
[8] Intel Software Developer's Manuals, http://www.intel.com/products/processor/manuals, 2009.
[9] J. Krumsiek, R. Arnold, and T. Rattei. Gepard: a rapid and sensitive tool for creating dotplots on genome scale. *Bioinformatics*, 23(8):1026–1028, 2007.
[10] J. V. Maizel and R. P. Lenk. Enhanced graphic matrix analysis of nucleic acid and protein sequences. *Proc. Nat. Academy of Sciences of the USA*, 78(12):7665–7669, 1981.
[11] S. B. Needleman and C. D. Wunsch. A general method applicable to the search of similarities in the amino acid sequence of two proteins. *J. Mol. Biology*, 48:443–453, 1970.
[12] S. Ott, S. Gunawardana, M. Downey, and G. Koentges. Loss-free identifcation of alignment-conserved CRMs. *In preparation*, 2009.
[13] J. P. Schmidt. All highest scoring paths in weighted grid graphs and their application to finding all approximate repeats in strings. *SIAM J. Computing*, 27(4):972–992, 1998.
[14] M. Snir, S. W. Otto, D. W. Walker, J. Dongarra, and S. Huss-Lederman. *MPI: The Complete Reference*. MIT Press, Cambridge, MA, USA, 1995.
[15] A. Tiskin. Semi-local longest common subsequences in subquadratic time. *J. Discrete Algorithms*, 6(4):570–581, 2008.
[16] A. Tiskin. Semi-local string comparison: Algorithmic techniques and applications. *Mathematics in Computer Science*, 1(4):571–603, 2008. See also arXiv: 0707.3619.
[17] R. A. Wagner and M. J. Fischer. The string-to-string correction problem. *J. ACM*, 21(1):168–173, 1974.

Image Processing & Visualisation

Parallel Computing: From Multicores and GPU's to Petascale
B. Chapman et al. (Eds.)
IOS Press, 2010
© 2010 The authors and IOS Press. All rights reserved.
doi:10.3233/978-1-60750-530-3-169

Parallelizing the LM OSEM Image Reconstruction on Multi-Core Clusters

Philipp CIECHANOWICZ, Philipp KEGEL, Maraike SCHELLMANN,
Sergei GORLATCH, and Herbert KUCHEN

University of Münster, Germany

Abstract. In this paper we present four different parallel implementations of the popular LM OSEM medical image reconstruction algorithm. While two of them use libraries such as MPI, OpenMP, or Threading Building Blocks (TBB) directly, the other two implementations use algorithmic skeletons of the Münster Skeleton Library *Muesli* to hide the parallelism. We compare the implementations w.r.t. runtime, efficiency, and programming style and show the resulting benchmarks which have been conducted on a multi-processor, multi-core cluster computer.

Keywords. algorithmic skeletons, Muesli, MPI, OpenMP, TBB, medical imaging

Introduction

Writing a parallel program for a multi-processor computer can be a complicated task. When using communication libraries such as MPI directly, the abstraction level is rather low. The programmer has to think about decomposing the problem, integrating the partial solutions, and bother with communication problems. More recently, multi-core processor architectures have evolved. While this provides additional parallelism, this also increases the complexity of writing efficient programs. Although it is comparatively clear how to make use of multi-processor architectures, this is not yet the case for multi- and especially many-core architectures. In this paper we evaluate four different parallel implementations of the popular LM OSEM image reconstruction algorithm and compare them w.r.t. to runtime, efficiency, and programming style. While tow of our implementations use MPI, OpenMP, and TBB directly, the other two use the Münster Skeleton Library *Muesli* as a framework for hiding the parallelism.

The remainder of this paper is structured as follows: Section 1 introduces some fundamentals. The LM OSEM image reconstruction algorithm is presented in detail in Section 2. Then, Section 3 discusses our four parallel implementation alternatives. The resulting benchmarks are shown in Section 4. Finally, Section 5 concludes with related work and gives an outlook to future work.

1. Fundamentals

Hybrid MPI-OpenMP programming is a popular approach to exploit parallelism on clusters with multiple processors per node. MPI facilitates inter-node communication and synchronization, OpenMP is used to exploit (particularly) data parallelism on each node. While OpenMP can also exploit parallelism in recent multi-core clusters, newer approaches exist that have been developed with multi-core processors in mind. Threading Building Blocks (TBB) is a novel C++ library for parallel programming introduced by Intel [1]. TBB extends C++ with higher-level, task-based abstractions for parallel programming. In TBB, a program is described in terms of fine-grained tasks, such that threads are completely hidden from the programmer. Tasks are more light-weight than threads, because they cannot be preempted, such that no context switching is needed. TBB also provides a sophisticated task scheduling mechanism including load-balancing.

The Münster Skeleton Library *Muesli* [2] is a program library written in standard C++ making use of MPI 1.2 and OpenMP 2.5 to efficiently support both multi-processor and multi-core computer architectures. It has been developed to relieve programmers of parallel applications from low-level programming problems by offering predefined parallel computation and communication patterns, so-called *algorithmic skeletons* [3]. These skeletons can roughly be divided into task and data parallel ones. Task parallel skeletons can be used to construct skeleton topologies and are offered as separate classes in our library. Currently, Muesli provides task parallel skeletons such as `Pipe`, `Farm` [4], `BranchAndBound` [5], and `DivideAndConquer` [6]. Data parallel skeletons such as *fold*, *map*, *zip*, and their variants are offered as member functions of a distributed data structure. Currently, Muesli provides distributed data structures for arrays, matrices, and sparse matrices [7]. Analogously to P^{3}L [8], all task and data parallel skeletons of our library can be combined and nested arbitrarily. Additionally, all skeletons offer at least one template parameter to flexibly define the data type used by the skeleton. As a unique feature, Muesli provides an automated serialization mechanism inspired by [9], such that arbitrary data types can be exchanged between the skeletons.

2. PET-based Medical Imaging

Positron emission tomography (PET) is a crucial, non-invasive medical imaging technology. For using PET, a radioactive substance, the so-called *tracer*, is injected into a specimen (mice or rats in our case). As the tracer particles decay, two positrons are emitted in opposite directions. The positrons and thus the "decay events" are recorded. The actual image reconstruction is made upon the processing of the recorded events. Several methods for 2D and 3D image reconstruction exist. One of them is *ListMode Ordered Subset Expectation Maximization* (LM OSEM) [10] which is a block-iterative algorithm for 3D image reconstruction. It takes a set of recorded events and splits it into s equally sized subsets. For each subset $l \in \{0, \ldots, s - 1\}$, the following computation is performed:

$$f_{l+1} = f_l c_l \quad \text{with} \quad c_l = \frac{1}{A_N^t \mathbf{1}} \sum_{i \in S_l} (A_i)^t \frac{1}{A_i f_l}. \tag{1}$$

Here, $f \in \mathbb{R}^n$ is a 3D image in vector form with dimensions $n = (X \times Y \times Z)$. Row A_i, $A \in \mathbb{R}^{m \times n}$, is called a *path*, whose elements a_{ik} give the length of intersection of the line between the two detectors of event i with voxel k of the reconstruction region, computed using Siddon's algorithm [11]. Each subset's computation takes its predecessor's output image as input and produces a new, more precise image. A simplified sequential implementation of LM OSEM is shown in Listing 1.

```
1   for (l=0; l<numberOfSubsets; l++) {
2     events = readEvents(numberOfEvents);     // read subset
3     for (i=0; i<numberOfEvents; i++) {       // compute c_l
4       path = computePath(events[i]);           // compute A_i
5       fp = 0;                                   // compute fp = A_i f_l
6       for (m=0; m<path.length; m++)
7         fp += f[path[m].coord] * path[m].length;
8       for (m=0; m<path.length; m++)            // add (A_i)^t fp^-1 to c_l
9         c[path[m].coord] += path[m].length / fp;  }
10    for (j=0; j<imageSize; j++)                // compute f_{l+1}
11      if (c[j] > 0.0) f[j] *= c[j];   }
```

Listing 1. Sequential implementation of the LM OSEM algorithm.

A typical reconstruction of a $150 \times 150 \times 280$ PET image processes about 6×10^7 events and takes more than two hours on a single-core computer. Therefore, parallelization is mandatory to reduce the runtime of the algorithm. The subsets cannot be processed in parallel because of the data dependency between the subset's computations (implied by $f_{l+1} = f_l c_l$). Therefore, we developed two parallelization approaches for a single subset:

With the first approach, we parallelize the loop that computes c_l (lines 5–9), such that each event is processed independently. However, this forces us to prevent race conditions when $(A_i)^t c^{-1}$ is actually added to c_l (line 9). Since this approach results in splitting up a subset between processes, it is called *Projection Space Decomposition* (PSD).

The second approach, called *Image Space Decomposition* (ISD), is based on a distributed representation of image-related data structures like f_l and c_l. Each part of these data structures is handled by another process. Since f_l is also distributed, a single process can only compute a fraction of $A_i f_l$. Thus, for each event, the processes have to perform a global reduction to retrieve $A_i f_l$.

3. Implementation Details

The following subsections show some details of our parallelized implementations of the LM OSEM algorithm. Except for the data parallel implementation with Muesli, all implementations use PSD while the former uses ISD. All implementations have been tested on a multi-core cluster to evaluate their runtime performance.

3.1. MPI and OpenMP

Our MPI-based implementations of the LM OSEM algorithm (cf. Listing 2) employ the PSD approach. Therefore, we have to divide the subset into equal fractions and specify the fraction that each MPI process should read. We compute a fraction size and an offset value for each process. The offset value specifies the number of events that the process should skip when reading the subset. The read subset fraction is then processed as described in the sequential implementation (cf. Listing 1) by each process to compute a *local* result for c_l. Afterwards, a global reduce is performed to retrieve the *global* c_l (line 10) which refers to the whole subset. Finally, each process computes f_{l+1} independently. While this implementation causes redundant computations on each process, communication between processes is minimized.

Provided that the MPI processes run on separate nodes, we can further increase the level of parallelism by exploiting multi-core architectures. For this, we augment the loops for computing c_l (local) and f_{l+1} with the OpenMP `for` construct. Thus, the loops are processed in parallel by one thread per core on each node. Possible race conditions during the computation of the local c_l are prevented by OpenMP's `critical` construct [12]. Note that parallelizing the computation of f_{l+1} in the last loop (line 12) resembles the ISD parallelization approach on each node.

```
1    for (l=0; l<numberOfSubsets; l++) {
2        events = readEvents(numberOfEvents,      // read fraction of subset
3                            offset);
4        #pragma omp parallel for private(path)
5        for (i=0; i<numberOfEvents; i++) {       // compute local cl
6            ...
7            #pragma omp critical
8            for (m=0; m<path.length; m++)                  // add (Ai)^t fp^-1 to local cl
9                local_c[path[m].coord] += path[m].length / fp;  }
10       MPI_Allreduce(local_c, c, imageSize,     // compute global cl
11                     MPI_DOUBLE, MPI_SUM, MPI_COMM_WORLD);
12       #pragma omp parallel for
13       for (j=0; j<imageSize; j++) {...}  }     // compute fl+1
```

Listing 2. Parallel implementation of LM OSEM (PSD) using MPI and OpenMP.

3.2. MPI and TBB

TBB provides similar features for multi-core programming as compared to OpenMP but uses a task-based scheduling mechanism. To compare both programming models w.r.t. programming effort and runtime performance, we have created a second implementation for the PSD approach using MPI and TBB. While the MPI-related program modifications remain unchanged, we have replaced the OpenMP constructs by their TBB counterparts. With TBB, the loops are embedded into separate classes and replaced by the `parallel_for` template in the main program (cf. Listing 3). Thus, TBB fosters a slightly improved programming style which reduces the amount of code within the main program. OpenMP's `critical` construct is replaced by one of TBB's mutex implementations. The details of loop parallelization with TBB are explained in [1,13].

```
1    /* compute local cl */
2    parallel_for(blocked_range<size_t>(0, numberOfEvents, GRAIN_SIZE),
3                 ProcessEvents(f, c, imageSize, events));
4    ...
5    /* compute fl+1 */
6    parallel_for(blocked_range<size_t>(0, imageSize, GRAIN_SIZE),
7                 UpdateImage(f, c));
```

Listing 3. Loop parallelization in the parallel implementation of LM OSEM (PSD) using MPI and TBB.

3.3. Muesli with Data Parallel Skeletons

Listing 4 shows the most important part of the LM OSEM implementation using data parallel skeletons from Muesli. Here, `f` and `c` are global variables of type `DistributedArray<double>`. While `f` corresponds to f_l from Eq. (1), `c` corresponds to the summation part on the right-hand side. For each event, the resulting A_i is stored in the global structure `path` (line 4). Using this `path`, we can compute $A_i f_l$ (`fp`) by applying the `foldIndex` skeleton and passing the function `computeFp` as an argument (line 5). Finally, we can update `c` by using the `mapIndexInPlace` skeleton (line 6). After having processed all events of a subset, the new image is computed by calling the `mapIndexInPlace` skeleton on `f` and passing the function `updateImage` as an argument (line 7). This procedure is repeated for all subsets.

```
1    for (l=0; l<numberOfSubsets; l++) {
2      events = readEvents(numberOfEvents);     // read subset
3      for (i=0; i<numberOfEvents; i++) {       // compute c_l
4        path = computePath(events[i]);         // compute A_i
5        fp = f.foldIndex(&computeFp);          // compute fp = A_i f_l
6        c.mapIndexInPlace(&updateC);  }        // add (A_i)^t fp^{-1} to c_l
7      f.mapIndexInPlace(&updateImage);  }      // compute f_{l+1}
```

Listing 4. Implementation of the LM OSEM algorithm using data parallel skeletons.

Using data parallel skeletons from Muesli the important part of the LM OSEM algorithm reduces to a few lines of code which makes it more legible and easier to maintain. The computation details are hidden inside the argument functions, the parallelism is hidden inside the skeletons. The abstraction level is clearly higher compared to the implementations using MPI, OpenMP, or TBB directly (cf. Section 3.1).

3.4. Muesli with Task Parallel Skeletons

To reconstruct the image in a PSD manner, a skeleton topology is built as depicted in Figure 1a. The outermost skeleton is a `Pipe` consisting of three stages. In the first stage, the `Initial` skeleton is responsible for reading all events from a file and sending them to the second stage. Here, the farm skeleton is responsible for computing the summation part of Eq. (1) and sending the result to the third stage. In this stage, the `Final` skeleton computes the new image and either sends it back to the `Farm` skeleton or writes the final result to a file depending on the current subset. Taking a closer look at the `Farm` skeleton we see that the farm itself is merely a container for multiple `Filter` skeletons (cf. Figure 1b). In fact, the `Filter` skeletons are responsible for computing the summation part depending on the events they receive from the `Initial` skeleton.

Listing 5 shows the most important part of the LM OSEM implementation using task parallel skeletons from Muesli. It is clear that the abstraction level is even higher than the one when using data parallel skeletons. The source code is divided into three separate functions, namely `getNextEvent`, `processEvent`, and `updateImage` (lines 1, 2, and 4). The parallelism is hidden inside the skeletons and is therefore completely transparent to the programmer. While the class `EventPacket` is used to send multiple events to a filter, the class `Image` is used as a container to serialize an image.

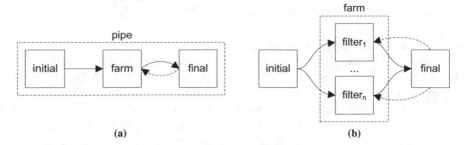

Figure 1. (a) Coarse and (b) fine-grain view of the skeleton topology used with the task parallel implementation of the LM OSEM algorithm. Arrows indicate the communication direction.

```
1  Initial<EventPacket> initial(getNextEvent);
2  Filter<EventPacket, Image> filter(processEvent);
3  Farm<EventPacket, Image> farm(filter, numberOfFilters);
4  Final<Image> final(updateImage);
5  Pipe pipe(initial, farm, final);
6  pipe.start();
```

Listing 5. Implementation of the LM OSEM algorithm using task parallel skeletons.

4. Results

Figure 2 shows the runtimes of our implementations on a multi-core cluster. The test system comprises 20 nodes with two quad-core processors (AMD Opteron 2352, 2.1 GHz) and 32 GB of main memory each. The operating system is Scientific Linux 5.2.

In our experiments, all implementations process a test file that contains about 6×10^7 events retrieved from scanning a mouse. To limit the overall reconstruction time, we process only about 10^6 of these events. The events are divided into ten subsets of one million events each. Thus, we get subsets that are large enough to provide a reasonable intermediate image (c_l) while the number of subsets is sufficient for a simple reconstruction. From at least five executions we calculate the average runtime for a complete PET image reconstruction of each program.

The implementations that use MPI directly show an identical scaling behaviour. With up to 8 nodes, the average relative speedup is 1.8 when doubling the number of nodes, from 8 to 16 nodes the speedup drops to 1.5. Regarding the overall runtime, the OpenMP-based implementation slightly outperforms the TBB-based one. However, when using 8 threads, both implementations provide a speedup of only 2.4. We attribute this poor speedup on each node to the mutual exclusion of threads from the local computation of c_l. With Muesli, we run multiple processes per node which is an alternative method to fully exploit the multi-core architecture. This avoids the drawback of mutual exclusion, but also increases the application's memory and communication requirements.

The results of the parallelization approaches using Muesli are twofold. The data parallel implementation suffers from communication overhead when $A_i f_l$ is computed using the foldIndex skeleton (cf. Listing 4, line 5). For each event, all collaborating processes compute a part of $A_i f_l$, exchange their local results, and update the summa-

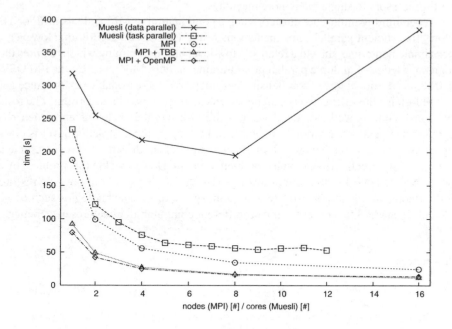

Figure 2. Runtimes of a complete PET image reconstruction on a multi-core cluster.

tion. An alternative would be to store the local results of $A_i f_l$ and postpone the update of the summation part to a point after the inner loop. However, exchanging the local results using Muesli would require some sort of stateful skeletons which are able to store temporary results and broadcast them only under certain conditions. The task parallel implementation also suffers from synchronization overhead. As indicated by the dashed lines in Figure 1, the `Pipe` skeleton is not constructed to send data back from the `Final` skeleton. However, the LM OSEM algorithm requires this behaviour such that this communication step has been implemented manually using the `MPI_Bcast` routine. While this shows that our library is flexible and can be adopted if needed, this also creates a synchronization point which reduces scalability.

5. Related Work and Conclusion

The original OSEM algorithm has also been parallelized using a hybrid MPI-OpenMP implementation [14]. On a dual core processor this implementation provides a 17% improvement as compared to an MPI only implementation.

Besides Muesli, there are other skeleton libraries. Among the most prominent ones are eSkel [3], P^{3}L [8], and muskel [15]. They focus on task parallel skeletons. An overview of all skeleton projects can be found on [16]. In contrast to Muesli, data parallelism is not introduced by operations handling a distributed data structure in parallel but by simulating it by task parallel constructs. None of the mentioned libraries addresses the portability across completely different architectures ranging from single-core multi-processors to single many-core machines.

Programming multi-core clusters using a combination of MPI and OpenMP or TBB allows for efficient parallel implementations of the LM OSEM algorithm. However, all these implementations stick to a relatively low level of programming which requires thorough knowledge of multiple parallel programming models. Moreover, for the LM OSEM algorithm, additional thread parallelism does not provide a reasonable performance gain.

Muesli is able to effectively parallelize an existing sequential algorithm. The resulting source code is well structured when using task parallel skeletons and much more legible when using data parallel skeletons. In both cases the abstraction level is clearly higher compared to versions which implement parallelism directly. However, efficiency and scalability greatly depend on the problem domain. How to tackle this problem by either providing new skeletons or optimizing existing ones is part of our ongoing research. Furthermore, we plan to investigate how to make use of new technologies such as MPI 2.0 and OpenMP 3.0 in order to support different computer architectures even better.

References

[1]   J. Reinders. *Outfitting C++ for Multi-core Processor Parallelism - Intel Threading Building Blocks.* O'Reilly, July 2007.

[2]   P. Ciechanowicz, M. Poldner, and H. Kuchen. The Münster Skeleton Library Muesli - A Comprehensive Overview. Technical report, University of Münster, 2009.

[3]   M. Cole. *Algorithmic Skeletons: Structured Management of Parallel Computation.* MIT Press, 1989.

[4]   M. Poldner and H. Kuchen. Scalable Farms. In *Proceedings of the International Conference ParCo*, volume 33, pages 795–802, 2006.

[5]   M. Poldner and H. Kuchen. Algorithmic Skeletons for Branch & Bound. In *Proceedings of the 1st International Conference on Software and Data Technology (ICSOFT)*, pages 291–300, 2006.

[6]   M. Poldner and H. Kuchen. Skeletons for Divide and Conquer Algorithms. In *Proceedings of the IASTED International Conference on Parallel and Distributed Computing and Networks (PDCN)*, pages 181–187, 2008.

[7]   P. Ciechanowicz. Algorithmic Skeletons for General Sparse Matrices on Multi-Core Processors. In *Proceedings of the 20th IASTED International Conference on Parallel and Distributed Computing and Systems (PDCS)*, pages 188–197, 2008.

[8]   B. Bacci, M. Danelutto, S. Orlando, and S. Pelagatti. P³L: A Structured High Level Programming Language and its Structured Support. In *Concurrency: Practice and Experience*, volume 7(3), pages 225–255. John Wiley & Sons, 1995.

[9]   A. Alexandrescu. *Modern C++ Design: Generic Programming and Design Patterns Applied.* Addison-Wesley, 2001.

[10]   A. J. Reader, K. Erlandsson, M. A. Flower, and R. J. Ott. Fast accurate iterative reconstruction for low-statistics positron volume imaging. *Physics in Medicine and Biology*, 43(4):823–834, April 1998.

[11]   R. L. Siddon. Fast calculation of the exact radiological path for a three-dimensional CT array. *Medical Physics*, 12(2):252–255, March 1985.

[12]   B. Chapman, G. Jost, and R. van der Pas. *Using OpenMP - Portable Shared Memory Parallel Programming.* MIT Press, October 2007.

[13]   P. Kegel, M. Schellmann, and S. Gorlatch. A case study on multi-core programming using threading building blocks. In *22th International Conference in Architecture of Computing Systems - Workshop Proceedings*, pages 39–46, Delft, NL, March 2009. VDE.

[14]   M. D. Jones, R. R. Yao, and C. P. Bhole. Hybrid MPI-OpenMP programming for parallel OSEM PET reconstruction. *IEEE Transactions on Nuclear Science*, 53(5):2752–2758, October 2006.

[15]   M. Aldinucci, M. Danelutto, and P. Dazzi. Muskel: A Skeleton Library Supporting Skeleton Set Expandability. In *Scalable Computing: Practice and Experience*, volume 8(4), pages 325–341, 2007.

[16]   M. Cole. The skeletal parallelism homepage. http://homepages.inf.ed.ac.uk/mic/Skeletons, 2008.

Parallel Computing: From Multicores and GPU's to Petascale
B. Chapman et al. (Eds.)
IOS Press, 2010
© 2010 The authors and IOS Press. All rights reserved.
doi:10.3233/978-1-60750-530-3-177

Hierarchical Visualization System for High Performance Computing

Oxana DZHOSAN[a], Nina POPOVA[a], Anton KORZH[b]

[a] *Moscow State University, Moscow, Russia*
[b] *NICEVT, Moscow, Russia*

Abstract. The article proposes a scientific data visualization system for high performance computing. Suggested system has hierarchical architecture where software modules of the system are implemented on the different hardware modules. Supercomputer IBM Blue Gene /P is used as the main test system. Visualization system includes parallel modules for video rendering, video enhancement, video compression and video up-sampling. System proposes visualization for 2D displays, 3D displays, multidisplay complexes. The results of using proposed visualization system for 3D torus network simulation are presented.

Keywords. Scientific data visualization, high performance computing, Blue Gene /P, parallel video processing, communication network simulation.

Introduction

High quality data visualization plays an important role in high performance computing. Large scale data processing is used for different tasks in most of research areas. Main problem in such processing is how to store and analyze terabytes of produced information. One way of data size decreasing is to make its visualization and to analyze data as visualized image or video sequence. Using such approach it is not required to store large amount of data. The size of data transferred to local work station for displaying is strongly decreased.

Different systems for scientific data visualization already exist. They provide wide range of visualization possibilities. As the most frequently used general visualization systems Visualization Toolkit (VTK) [1], ParaView system [2], VisIt [3] can be mentioned. They can produce good results in most cases of processing data on local work station. But when applying them to high performance complexes such as Blue Gene /P they loose their effectiveness. Strong modifications and adaptations are required.

The task of visualization of large scale scientific data produced on Blue Gene /P was studied in [4]. There were proposed four different strategies for parallel visualization on Blue Gene /P and their effectiveness was analyzed. In Argonne National Laboratory [5] Blue Gene /P system was added with installation of NVIDIA Quadro Plex S4 external graphics processing units for fast data visualization.

This paper proposes visualization system architecture and parallel video processing methods for supercomputer Blue Gene /P. A hierarchical distribution of visualization system modules according to the hardware parts of computing system is used. The proposed system includes parallel method of video rendering in different formats that are used for displaying information on different types of display systems such as 3D displays and multi display complexes. Also the system includes parallel methods for video enhancement based on jagged edges correction, block based video compression method and real time method for high quality video up-sapling to optimize video for display resolution.

Realization of proposed methods and visualization system architecture was done for supercomputer IBM Blue Gene/P installed at Moscow State University. This high performance complex includes 2048 computational nodes, each node has four PowerPC 450 processors with 850Mhz, system includes 2GB DRAM per each node and 16 I/O nodes. IBM pSeries 55A is connected as front-end.

Effectiveness of suggested system was tested on different types of large scale scientific data such as molecular dynamic simulation, turbulent combustion, biometrics data processing. In current paper the results of using proposed system for 3D torus network simulation research are presented.

1. Visualization system architecture

In visualization system different subtasks are performed: rendering video in different output formats, video enhancement, video compression and so on. In case of different cost of computational time on different hardware part of high performance system it is required to minimize the time of processing on computing nodes and realize some operations outside of computing nodes, for example on frontend. So it was analyzed the computational complexity and scalability of subtasks in visualization system and these subtasks were rearranged for hierarchical structure of Blue Gene /P system. On the Fig.1 it is illustrated a principal scheme of suggested visualization system architecture.

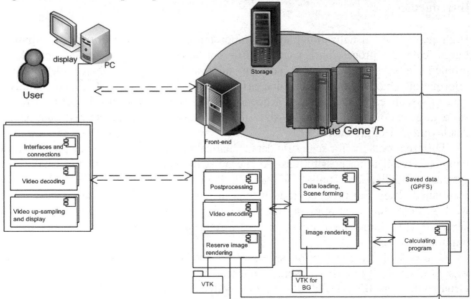

Figure 1. A scheme of the main blocks of visualization system for Blue Gene /P.

The module with the most computational complexity in the visualization system is the parallel image or video rendering method. We have suggested a parallel rendering strategy based on VTK volume rendering methods. It is performed on the computational nodes of Blue Gene /P. Rendering strategy includes method for input data parsing, decimation and its transformation to the set of volumes to form the rendering scene. Rendering produces video and images in different formats that can be displayed on different types of screens: for a 2D display – general 2D format, for a 3D display – a stereo video, multi-view video, video in texture and depth format, for a multi-screen display – up to 9 streams can be generated [6].

Next level of hierarchy in the hardware system is frontend. On this part we suggest to perform video postprocessing tasks and video compression. Video post processing includes parallel jagged edge removal algorithm for visual quality enhancement. Video compression part performs encoding of video in different formats. Compression algorithm is based on block encoding and uses fast method of block complexity estimation for distributing processing blocks between processors using the information about block processing time that depends on block visual complexity. That is used for processors load balancing. In suggested compression algorithm bit-rate is not fixed, compression ration in this case is between 4 and 30 times.

The third level of visualization system is performed on the user terminal – workstation that is connected to the display. On this level a decompression of transmitted sequence with fast decoding method is applied. And then the video is processed with up-sampling method to make video in the same format as display resolution is. Also suggested up-sampling method allows decreasing a resolution of frame during rendering on Blue Gene /P and this leads to rendering time decreasing and data size decreasing. Currently PC stations can use GPU for data processing. So it is realized Nvidia CUDA based version of decompression and up-sizing.

During system architecture development different aspects of method effectiveness and scalability were tested. Effectiveness can be measured with two main parameters: ratio of data size decrease and time required for data processing. Both parameters were analyzed and there were shown dependence between data size and time of processing. System has shown acceptable time of processing for the most experiments. Scalability of video producing and video post processing methods was also tested and recommendation for optimal number of processors were given. Optimal criteria were based on processing time minimization and decreasing of computational time cost. More details of suggested system architecture and the details of its realization are discussed in [6].

Such a hierarchical structure of the visualization system can be generalized on different computation complexes where processing units have different productivity and different cost of computations.

2. Parallel video compression method

A compression method is used for decreasing size of video sequence that is transmitted to the local workstation. Structure of suggested compression algorithm is shown on the Fig.2. The method includes the following steps: video preprocessing, blocks visual complexity estimation, calculation of block distribution according to the processors for load balance optimization, parallel blocks encoding, palettes optimization, statistical encoding of stream (optionally). Bellow these steps are described in details.

Block complexity is estimated using the information of spatial block structure. Set of parameters is calculated to estimate the complexity value. First is average value and values of dispersion that are calculated by the following equations:

$$\bar{x} = \frac{1}{k}\sum_{i=1}^{k} x_i, \quad \sigma = \frac{1}{k}\sum_{i=1}^{k} (x - x_i)^2, \quad a = \bar{x} - \sigma \times \sqrt{\frac{q}{k-q}}, \quad b = \bar{x} + \sigma \times \sqrt{\frac{k-q}{q}} \quad (1)$$

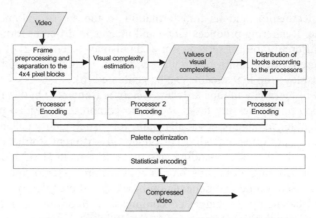

Figure 2. Main blocks of parallel compression method.

Where k is the number of pixels in block and q is the number of pixels that are more then average value. *a* and *b* are the two values that are optimal for block color representation. Also in the set of parameters it is included the values about edges in the block. This information can be obtained by calculation values according equations (2)-(5). $I_Y(i,j)$ – is a luminance channel of the center pixel of a block.

$$D_X = \frac{1}{12} \sum_{\substack{k=-1..1 \\ l=-1..2}} \left| I_Y(i+k+1, j+l) - I_Y(i+k, j+l) \right|$$

(2)

$$D_Y = \frac{1}{12} \sum_{\substack{k=-1..2 \\ l=-1..1}} \left| I_Y(i+k, j+l+1) - I_Y(i+k, j+l) \right|$$

(3)

$$D_{d1} = \frac{1}{9} \sum_{\substack{k=-1..1 \\ l=-1..1}} \left| I_Y(i+k+1, j+l+1) - I_Y(i+k, j+l) \right|$$

(4)

$$D_{d2} = \frac{1}{9} \sum_{\substack{k=-1..1 \\ l=-1..1}} \left| I_Y(i+k+1, j+l) - I_Y(i+k, j+l+1) \right|$$

(5)

Additionally it is checked if current block belongs to "chess" area. So it is calculated the following values for all three channels:

$$A_T = \frac{1}{4} \sum_{\substack{h \in \{-1,1\} \\ g \in \{-1,1\}}} \left| I_T(i, j) - I_T(i+h, j+g) \right|$$

,

(6)

$$B_T = \frac{1}{4} \left(\left| I_T(i, j-1) - I_T(i-1, j) \right| + \left| I_T(i-1, j) - I_T(i, j+1) \right| + \left| I_T(i, j+1) - I_T(i+1, j) \right| + \left| I_T(i+1, j) - I_T(i, j-1) \right| \right)$$

(7)

where T is a channel, $T \in \{Y, Cb, Cr\}$, $I_T(i,j)$ – is a luminance channel of the center pixel of a block.

Then if $A_T <$ CHESS_TR and $B_T <$ CHESS_TR, where T is at least one of the channels and CHESS_TR is a threshold for very frequency areas, and $\left| I_T(i, j) - I_T(i, j-1) \right| >$ CHESS_UP_TR then this pixel is considered to belong to chess area. Then for block complexity estimation it is calculated as integral value of the values of estimated parameters and then this integral value is used for distribution of blocks to the processing unit to optimize the loading of processors. Distribution scheme is described in work [7].

After complexity estimation for each block it is calculated optimal palette for block representation. Number of colors in palette depends on block complexity. Palette is estimated using iterative method of deleting zero intervals from block histogram. On each iteration it is selected the longest zero interval and colors with zero values are excluded from histogram. Process stops when there are no zero intervals or number of iterations is more then number of colors in palette. Colors of palette are estimated as middle values of histogram intervals that were not excluded.

3. Video postprocessing and up-sampling methods

A lot of image interpolation methods of have already been developed. There is a wide variety of interpolating kernels, such as sinc, Lanzcos, linear, B-spline, Gauss, Hermite, etc. Comprehensive description of generalized interpolation and choice of convolution kernel functions is presented in [8, 9]. But for scientific data visualization system it was required a method that produces good visual result for content of specific type. Method should have low computational complexity and be optimized for realization on GPU.

Proposed method uses the combination of wavelets and edge preserving triangulation interpolation method for image and video up-sampling task. Algorithm consists of three main steps: directions and frequency type estimation, interpolation, edge post-processing. First, prevailing edge direction is determined. For this purpose absolute values of difference between neighboring pixels are used. For determination of diagonals absolute values of differences between pixels are utilized, which are located in 5x5 neighborhood of the pixel being interpolated.

Then frequency area type is estimated using wavelets. Wavelet 5-3 is used in horizontal and vertical direction to calculate area frequency number. Wavelet value W_{HH} is calculated using the following equation:

$$w(T,k,l) = I_T(i+k, j+l) - \frac{1}{2}\sum_{h\in\{-1,1\}} I_T(i+k, j+l+h) + \frac{1}{2}\sum_{h\in\{-1,1\}} I_T(i+k+h, j+l)+$$

$$\frac{1}{4}\sum_{h\in\{-1,1\}} I_T(i+k-1, j+l+h) + \frac{1}{4}\sum_{h\in\{-1,1\}} I_T(i+k+1, j+l+h)$$

$$W_{HH} = \max_{T\in\{Y,Cb,Cr\}} \max_{\substack{k=-1..1 \\ l=-1..1}} |w(T,k,l)| \qquad (8)$$

On the input of this step we have two values: possible edge direction and wavelet value. Pixel interpolation type is set to 9 if wavelet value is less then predefined thresholds. Otherwise interpolation type is set equal to the number of pixel direction (8 possible directions).

For interpolation two types of processing are used. If pixel interpolation type is 9 then pixel is interpolated using simple bi-cubic kernel. If interpolation type is less then 9 then interpolation is done using the following equations.

$$C_{s,1} = y_{s,3} - 2y_{s,2} + y_{s,1}, \quad s = 1,2$$

$$C_{s,2} = y_{s,4} - 2y_{s,3} + y_{s,2}, \quad s = 1,2$$

$$P_s = y_{s,2} + \Delta_{s,1}(y_{s,3} - y_{s,2}) - \frac{2}{30}(\Delta_{s,1} - 1)(5\Delta_{s,1}(C_{s,1} - C_{s,2}) + 5C_{s,2} - 7(C_{s,1} + C_{s,2}))), \quad s = 1,2$$

$$Out = \Delta_2(P_2 - P_1) + P_1 \qquad (9)$$

Where $\Delta_{s,1}$ and Δ_2 are determined using the Table 1. Let δ_x be the distance from current pixel to the nearest left column of source image, where the distance between the two nearest columns of source image is assumed to be 1. Let δ_y be the distance from current pixel to the nearest upper row of source image, where the distance between the two nearest rows of source image is assumed to be 1. $y_{s,k}$ are estimate using the following equation, where $I(i,j)$ – the nearest left top pixel of source image to the interpolated pixel:

$$y_{s,k} = I(i+t_{s,k}, j+p_{s,k}), \ s=1,2, \ k=1,..,4, \tag{10}$$

where parameters $t_{s,k}$ and $p_{s,k}$ are assumed using the Table 2. So *Out* is the output pixel of up-sampling method.

Table 1. $\Delta_{s,1}$ and Δ_2 determination

T/P	1	2	3	4	5	6	7	8
$\Delta_{1,1}$	δ_y	δ_x	$\lvert\delta_y-\delta_x\rvert$	$\begin{cases}\delta_x+\delta_y, \delta_x+\delta_y \le 1 \\ \delta_x+\delta_y-1, \delta_x+\delta_y > 1\end{cases}$	$\dfrac{\delta_y-\delta_x}{2}$	$\dfrac{\delta_y+\delta_x}{2}$	$\dfrac{\delta_x-\delta_y}{2}$	$\dfrac{\delta_y+\delta_x}{2}$
$\Delta_{2,1}$	δ_y	δ_x	$1+\lvert\delta_y-\delta_x\rvert$	$\begin{cases}\delta_x+\delta_y, \delta_x+\delta_y \le 1 \\ \delta_x+\delta_y-1, \delta_x+\delta_y > 1\end{cases}$	$\dfrac{1-\delta_x}{2}+\delta_y$	$\dfrac{\delta_x-1}{2}+\delta_y$	$\dfrac{1-\delta_y}{2}+\delta_x$	$\dfrac{\delta_y-1}{2}+\delta_x$
Δ_2	δ_x	δ_y	$\begin{cases}\dfrac{\delta_x}{1+\delta_y-\delta_x}, \delta_x>\delta_y \\ \dfrac{\delta_y}{1+\delta_x-\delta_y}, \delta_x\le\delta_y\end{cases}$	$\begin{cases}\dfrac{\delta_y}{\delta_y+\delta_x}, \delta_x+\delta_y \le 1 \\ \dfrac{1-\delta_x}{2-\delta_x-\delta_y}, \delta_x+\delta_y > 1\end{cases}$	δ_x	δ_x	δ_y	δ_y

Table 2. $t_{s,k}$ and $p_{s,k}$ determination, where 3.1 is case when $\delta_y < \delta_x$, 3.2 is case when $\delta_y \ge \delta_x$, 4.1 is case when $\delta_y+\delta_x \le 1$, and 4.2 is case when $\delta_y+\delta_x > 1$

T/P	1	2	3.1	3.2	4.1	4.2	5	6	7	8	T/P	1	2	3.1	3.2	4.1	4.2	5	6	7	8
$t_{1,1}$	0	-1	-1	0	-1	1	0	0	-1	-1	$p_{1,1}$	-1	0	0	-1	0	-1	-1	-1	0	0
$t_{1,2}$	0	0	0	0	0	1	0	0	0	0	$p_{1,2}$	0	0	0	0	0	0	0	0	0	0
$t_{1,3}$	0	1	1	0	1	1	0	0	1	1	$p_{1,3}$	1	0	0	1	0	1	1	1	0	0
$t_{1,4}$	0	2	2	0	2	1	0	0	2	2	$p_{1,4}$	2	0	0	2	0	2	2	2	0	0
$t_{2,1}$	1	-1	1	-1	0	-1	1	1	-1	-1	$p_{2,1}$	-1	1	-1	1	-1	1	-1	-1	1	1
$t_{2,2}$	1	0	1	0	0	0	1	1	0	0	$p_{2,2}$	0	1	0	1	0	1	0	0	1	1
$t_{2,3}$	1	1	1	1	0	1	1	1	1	1	$p_{2,3}$	1	1	1	1	1	1	1	1	1	1
$t_{2,4}$	1	2	1	2	0	2	1	1	2	2	$p_{2,4}$	2	1	2	1	2	1	2	2	1	1

A new algorithm of jagged edges removal for visual quality of output video enhancement is suggested. The algorithm analyses two adjacent lines of an image and finds the parts of these lines where the colors of adjacent pixels are in the defined ratio. For jaggies modification it is suggested an algorithm based on linear press procedure. Method has good scalability and can be effectively parallelized.

4. Visualization of 3D torus network simulation

The proposed visualization system was applied to the problem of simulating interconnection network with 3D torus topology. Actual goal was to provide network developers with graphical representation of network load, packet routing and fault-tolerance. This helped routing algorithms and arbitration logic to be tuned aiming minimal network congestion on different communication patterns. The resulting algorithms obtained with help of simulation and visualization were tested on real network routers built with use of FPGA with integrated multi-gigabit links connected to commodity x86 processors. We consider a parallel communication network simulator for a massive parallel machine with shared memory. For simplicity of visualization scheme topology is supposed to be a 3D torus, although toruses with any number of dimensions are supported as well as the Clos topology and some Caley graph based topologies. Routing is packet-based and virtual-cut-through. Each packet consists from several flow control units - flits. The bandwidth of external links is simulated to be one flit per cycle. Trying to follow actual networks [10,11] we have chosen to use two virtual channels, one for adaptive and one for deterministic minimal routing. Deterministic routing is based upon bubble rule and direction-order for avoiding multidimensional deadlocks. Livelocks are avoided with use of minimal routing.

The architecture of router is input-queued and consists of link control blocks maintaining per-link data integrity,crossbar, injection and ejection units with integrated routing table and several virtual channels with routing units. All units were simulated to run at the same clock frequency, although real hardware uses several unsynchronized clocks. Network simulator can be used in connection to simple pattern-based packet generator written in C++, or to a full-weight simulator of processing unit. The network simulator is highly parallel itself and is written using a Charm++ parallel language scaling up to thousand of cores for large simulated networks.

Experiments were done for 3D torus 8x8x8 size. As simulator works simulator collects and writes to file some statistical information about channels load average by user defined period. Based on this data we are able to make a image visualizing channel load using volume rendering. For this purpose the best was 3D torus topology, visualized as 3D-mesh. Each node corresponds to a cube of points colored according collected load information for each period of time. Red color corresponds to 100% load and nontransparent, whereas green corresponds to 50% channel load, and black transparent to 0%. Intermediate values get their colors and transparency value using linear approximation. For each period of time mesh of load based colored cubes is rendered, and we have a movie showing changing network load in details. This mode helped analyzing congestion situations for different communication patterns. Another visualization mode is using statistics collection period equal to one clock thus showing us packet as a wormhole and providing ability of visual profiling pipeline stalls and adaptive routing algorithms while simulating arbiter conflicts. For this mode best pattern are those having small number of packets in flight like ping-pong modified by increasing number of packets send to common destination.

Also we are forced to set latency of external links (including serialization and deserialization (SerDes) latency) equal to one cycle, thus allowing packet to occupy several router, what is impossible in modern communication networks using serialized external links due to enormous SerDes latency. This mode was also used to test the fault tolerance subsystem which maintains data integrity on packet level and has ability of recalculating the route table in hardware in case of link failure. In this situation packet is restored from internal router buffers and is resent using new recalculated route. Examples of visualization with proposed system are shown on the Fig.3.

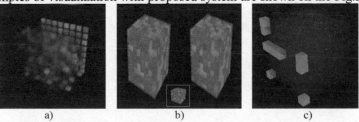

a)   b)   c)

Figure 3. a) Ejector channel load for each router in a 3D-torus 8x8x8 network for an adaptive hotzone pattern; b) Stereo visualization, frame in side-by-side stereo format; c) Data routing visualization in a 3D-torus.

Conclusions

This paper presents a system for scientific data visualization that is simulated on high performance computers. The main objective of the system is its hierarchical structure that is developed in accordance with optimization of computational costs and time of video producing. The main goal of the system is to provide for users of high performance system an instrument of decreasing the size of data that is transmitted from computational complex to local PC workstation.   Proposed system was implemented on IBM Bleu Gene /P. Visualization system was tested on 3D torus network simulation task. Visualization in 3D format shows informative visual representation of results and helps to analyze simulation process. Proposed system provides strong decreasing of the size of data: for 80Gb data pattern result video size is approximately 1Mb.

The work was done with support of the following grants: RFFI 08-07-12081, RFFI 09-07-12068, RFFI 09-07-13596.

References

[1] Marcio Dutra, Paulo Rodrigues, Gilson Giraldi, Bruno schulze, Distributed visualization using VTK in Grid Environments, *pros. conf. Seventh IEEE International Symposium on Cluster Computing and Grid* (CCGrig'07), 2007

[2] Moreland K., Avila A., Fisk L.A., Prallel Unstructured Volume Rendering in ParaView, *Proceedings of IS&T SPIE Visualization and Data Analysis 2007*, San Jose, 2007

[3] Childs H., Duchaineau M., Ma K.L., A Scalable, Hybrid Scheme for Volume Rendering Massive Data Sets, *Proceedings of EurographicsSymposium on Parallel Graphics and Visualization 2006*, Braga, Portugal, 2006

[4] Tom Peterka, Hongfeng Yu, Robert Ross, Kwan-Liu Ma, Parallel Volume Rendering on the IBM Blue Gene/P, *pros. conf. Eurographics Symposium on Parallel Graphics and Visualization*, 2008

[5] Installation of leading-edge data analytics, visualization set for world's fastest open science supercomputer http://www.anl.gov/Media_Center/News/2008/news080722.html

[6] Dzhosan O., Scientific Data Visualization for High Performance Parallel Applications. *Pros. conf. PAVT2009*, Nijniy Novgorod, Russia, 2009

[7] Dzhosan, O.,Mishourovsky, M., Analysis of methods for visually lossless colour image compression with low complexity, *Proceedings of "Television: Images Transmitting and Processing" Conference*, Russia, St.-Petersburg, 2008

[8] Blu, T., Thvenaz, T., Unser M., Generalized interpolation: higher quality at no additional cost. *Proc. Int. Conf. Image Process.1999, vol. III*, 1999

[9] Yu, X., Morse, B., Sederberg, T., Image Reconstruction Using Data-Dependent Triangulation. *IEEE Computer Graphics and Applications*, vol. 21 No. 3, 2001, pp. 62-68

[10] M. Blumrich et al. Design and Analysis of the BlueGene/L Torus Interconnection Network, *IBM Research Report*, December 3, 2003

[11] V. Puente, C. Izu, R. Beivide, J.A. Gregorio, F. Vallejo and J.M. Prellezo, The Adaptive Bubble Router , *Journal of Parallel and Distributed Computing*. Vol 61 - №9, 2001

Parallel Computing: From Multicores and GPU's to Petascale
B. Chapman et al. (Eds.)
IOS Press, 2010
© *2010 The authors and IOS Press. All rights reserved.*
doi:10.3233/978-1-60750-530-3-185

Real time ultrasound image sequence segmentation on multicores

D. Casaburi [a], L. D'Amore [a], L. Marcellino [b] and A. Murli [a]

[a] *Department of Mathematics and Applications, Federico II University, Naples, Italy*
[b] *Department of Applied Sciences, Parthenope University, Naples, Italy*

Abstract. Echography (ultrasound imaging of the heart) is one of the driving application areas of medical imaging. Our focus is to track the motion of endocardium during a complete cardiac cycle to allow clinicians for estimating the left ventricle and atrium (LVA) area deformations. The main challenge is to do this in a suitable response time. We describe a PETSc-based parallel software designed to detect and delineate the LV contour during a complete cardiac cycle. LV segmentation is performed by applying a three steps algorithm: speckle reduction, optic flow computation and spatio-temporal level-set segmentation. Using a scale-space approach each step is mathematically described by nonlinear time dependent PDE. Experiments on real data are obtained on a parallel computing platform made of 16 blades Dell PowerEdge M6000 each one consisting of 2 processors quad-core (Intel Xeon E5410@2.33GHz (64 bit)) connected by high performance network InfiniBand and located at the University of Naples Federico II.

Keywords. medical imaging, parallel software, level-set equations, multicore.

Introduction

High performance computing (HPC) technologies is having a huge impact in a number of applications in medical imaging enabling compute intensive algorithms to execute very fast. Moreover, parallel platforms based on multicore chips are becoming dominant systems in HPC. This will heavily benefit health care and medical imaging applications. The recent proliferation of embedded systems tuned for medical imaging applications developed by processor vendors (such as Intel and IBM) are a proof of this activity [10,11,12]. To harness the power of advanced high performance systems parallel algorithms have to be designed in order to extract concurrency from both the distributed and the multithreaded architecture of these computing systems.

We focus on segmentation and tracking of left ventricle and atrium (LVA) deformations on a sequence of 2D ultrasound images. We describe a PETSc-based parallel software performing a motion-aided segmentation. We parallelize the computational kernels by distributing workload among multicore progessor.

Segmentation model is a level set equation where the edge indicator is obtained using information provided by the optic flow. An automatic markers-controlled evolution of the segmentation level set surface is used as a prior knowledge about the shape of the LVA chamber. Moreover, a preliminary speckle noise reduction is performed.

The paper is organized as follows. In section 1, we recall the mathematical models we are using for segmentation and we show how these models were integrated with the optic flow and the speckle reduction. In section 2, we describe the numerical approach, starting from discretization schemes until to the analysis of main computational kernels. In section 3, we describe the parallel software. Finally, in section 4, experiments on real data are presented and they are discussed together with performance analysis.

1. Motion-aided image sequence segmentation

To mathematically define this problem, let us give the following:

Definition [The image sequence brightness function]: *Let $J \subset \Re$ be a bounded interval. Given $t \in J$, let $P(t) \equiv (x(t), y(t)) \in \Omega$, where $\Omega = \Omega_x \times \Omega_y \subset \Re^2$ is the image plane[1]. The image sequence is defined as the piecewise differentiable function:*

$$I: \quad t \in J \longrightarrow P(t) \in \Omega \longrightarrow I(t) \equiv I(P(t), t) \in [0, 255]$$

Due to the presence of speckle-noise, instead of $I(t)$ we deal with the noisy brightness function: $I_S(t) = \eta_M \cdot I(t) + \eta_A$, where η_M, η_A are multiplicative and additive noise, respectively. Hence, a preliminary speckle-noise reduction is necessary.

1.1. The de-speckle task

Following [2], $\forall t \in J$, we consider the PDE:

$$\frac{\partial I(\tau, t)}{\partial \tau} = \nabla \left(D(|\nabla I(\tau, t)|) |\nabla I(\tau, t)| \right), \quad \tau \in [0, T], P(t) \in \Omega, t \in J \quad (1)$$

with zero Neummann boundary conditions:

$$\frac{\partial I(\tau, t)}{\partial n} = 0, \quad \tau \in [0, T], \quad P(t) \in \partial\Omega$$

and $I_0(t) = I_S(t)$ as initial condition ($\tau = 0$). The *diffusion matrix* is:

$$D = (w_1 w_2) \begin{pmatrix} \lambda_1 & 0 \\ 0 & \lambda_2 \end{pmatrix} \begin{pmatrix} w_1^T \\ w_2^T \end{pmatrix}, \quad \lambda_1 = \begin{cases} \alpha \left(1 - \frac{(\mu_1 - \mu_2)^2}{s^2} \right) & (\mu_1 - \mu_2)^2 \le s^2 \\ 0 & otherwise \end{cases}$$

---

[1]The image plane Ω should depend on the acquisition time t. In practice, it is the same at each t because it refers to the rectangular plane of the image acquisition. Then, for simplicity of notations, we omit the dependence of Ω on t.

and $\lambda_2 = \alpha$ (s and α are constants). The diffusion reaction matrix is obtained by the eigenvectors of the structure matrix:

$$J = G_\sigma \star \left(\nabla I \nabla I^T \right) = \begin{pmatrix} G_\sigma \star I_x^2 & G_\sigma \star I_x I_y \\ G_\sigma \star I_x I_y & G_\sigma \star I_y^2 \end{pmatrix}$$

where G_σ is the Gaussian function and $\star$ is the convolution operator.

1.2. The segmentation task

The starting point is the level set equation based on Riemannian mean curvature flow [7]. At each $t \in J$, the segmentation function:

$$u : t \in J \longrightarrow (P(t), t) \in \Omega \times J \longrightarrow u(t) \equiv u(P(t), t, \tau) \in \Re^2$$

is obtained by solving the PDE:

$$\frac{\partial u(t)}{\partial \tau} = \sqrt{\epsilon + |\nabla u(t)|^2} \, \nabla \cdot \left(g(|\nabla G_\sigma \ast \tilde{I}(t)|) \frac{\nabla u(t)}{\sqrt{\epsilon + |\nabla u(t)|^2}} \right) \qquad (2)$$

$\varepsilon > 0$ is the regularization parameter, $g(s) = 1/\left(1 + Ks^2 \right)$ $(K > 0)$ is the Perona-Malik edge-indicator function, G_σ is the Gaussian function, $\ast$ is the convolution operator. In our experiments we select $K = 0.01$ and $\varepsilon = 0.001$. The PDE is equipped with zero Dirichlet boundary conditions.

A key challenge in many applications is the definition of the initial function $u_0(t)$ (the so-called *point-of-view surface*). We use a set of peak centered functions, located inside the interesting region, as specified in the following:

Definition [initial condition]: *Let $t = t_0$ be the acquisition time of first frame. Let $D_i, i = 1, ..., n$ be a set of cycles, located inside the interesting region, each one having center $C_i = (x_i(t_0), y_i(t_0))$ (also denoted as* focus-points*) and radius R. Given D_i, $i = 1, ..., n$, we set:*

$$u_0(t_0) = \max_{i=1,n} \omega_i \left(x(t_0), y(t_0) \right)$$

where:

$$\omega_i \left(x(t_0), y(t_0) \right) = \begin{cases} \frac{1}{|(x(t_0), y(t_0)) - (x_i(t_0), y_i(t_0))| + 1} & if (x(t_0), y(t_0)) \in D_i \\ \\ \frac{1}{R+1} & if \, (x(t_0), y(t_0)) \in \Omega - D_i \end{cases}$$

In subsequent frames, u_0 is obtained in automatic way using functions ω_i previously introduced. More precisely, $\forall t > t_0$, and $\forall i = 1, ..., n$ to calculate u_0 are considered only those ω_i such that: $\forall (x(t), y(t)) \in D_i$, $\quad I(x(t), y(t)) \leq H$ where $H = \alpha |max_\Omega I(t) - min_\Omega I(t)| + min_\Omega I(t), \alpha \in \Re$ (see figure 1).

The key feature of the segmentation model that we employ for LVA border detection is the definition of $\tilde{I}$ in (2) inside the edge indicator function g. We combine the image to segment at each time with the contour obtained at previous time, by computing the **motion trajectory** of the LVA border.

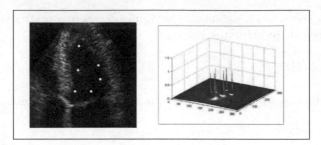

Figure 1. Definition of initial condition.

1.3. Motion computation and subjective contours

Let $t_1, t_2 \in J$, where $t_2 > t_1$, and $\Delta t = t_2 - t_1$, be two consecutive frames of the sequence. If $\Gamma(t_1)$ is the LVA border obtained at t_1, we consider $\widetilde{I}(t_2) = I(t_2) + I_\Gamma(t_2)$, where: $I_\Gamma(t_2) = \{(x_\Gamma(t_2), y_\Gamma(t_2)) : (x(t_1), y(t_1)) \in \Gamma(t_1)\}$.
In other words, we supply the subjective contours of LVA border by combining the frame to segment with the contour obtained at previous time.
To define $I_\Gamma(t_2)$, we first compute Γ at time t_1 then, using the motion trajectory, we predict the position of the LVA border at a subsequent time as follows:

$$(x_\Gamma(t_2), y_\Gamma(t_2)) = (x(t_1) + v_1(t_1)\Delta t, y(t_1) + v_2(t_1)\Delta t),$$

$\forall (x(t_1), y(t_1)) \in \Gamma(t_1)$, $v_1(t_1)\Delta t, v_2(t_1)\Delta t$ are obtained by the *motion trajectory* of $P(t)$.

[**Motion trajectory**]: *The motion trajectory of a point* $P(t) = (x(t), y(t)) \in \Omega$ *is the line (or the arc of line)* **L**, *defined by the successive positions of* $P(t)$, *as* t *moves from* t_1 *towards* t_2. *The parametric equation for L is*:

$$L : \begin{cases} \Delta x = x(t_2) - x(t_1) = \Delta t \cdot v_1(t_2) \\ \Delta y = y(t_2) - y(t_1) = \Delta t \cdot v_2(t_2) \end{cases},$$

where $(v_1(t), v_2(t)) = (\frac{d}{dt}x(t), \frac{d}{dt}y(t))$ are the components of the **motion field**, at $P(t) \in \Omega$.

Following [8], we find the apparent motion field (the so-called *optical flow*), by imposing that the spatial brightness gradient does not change along motion trajectory. We get a system of two non linear parabolic (diffusion-reaction) PDE equations:

$$\begin{cases} \frac{\partial u}{\partial \tau} = \alpha \cdot div \left[\phi' \left(\nabla u \nabla u^T + \nabla v \nabla v^T \right) \nabla u \right] - 2 \left[I_{xx} u + I_{yx} v + I_{tx} \right] \cdot I_{xx} + \\ \qquad\qquad\qquad\qquad\qquad\qquad -2 \left[I_{xy} u + I_{yy} v + I_{ty} \right] \cdot I_{xy} \\ \frac{\partial v}{\partial \tau} = \alpha \cdot div \left[\phi' \left(\nabla u \nabla u^T + \nabla v \nabla v^T \right) \nabla v \right] - 2 \left[I_{xx} u + I_{yx} v + I_{tx} \right] \cdot I_{yx} + \\ \qquad\qquad\qquad\qquad\qquad\qquad -2 \left[I_{xy} u + I_{yy} v + I_{ty} \right] \cdot I_{xy} \end{cases} \quad (3)$$

with zero initial conditions and Dirichlet boundary conditions, $\alpha > 0$ the regularization parameter and $\phi'(s^2) = \varepsilon + (1 - \varepsilon)/2\sqrt{1 + s^2/\lambda^2}$ as edge-indicator function.

2. Numerical Model

In image analysis it is required that numerical models satisfy fundamental properties of images, i. e., to be invariant with respect to transformations such as gray level shift, translations, rotations [1]. Semi-implicit schemes meet these requirements as well as *consistency, convergency* and *stability* properties [9].

Semi-implicit discretization scheme: *Let* $\Delta\tau$ *denote the scale-space stepsize, and let* $\tau_n = n \cdot \Delta\tau$, $n = 1, 2, \ldots, N scale$, *the uniform discretization grid of the scale interval* $[0, T]$. *Given a 2D* $N \times N$ *image, semi-implicit scheme for scale-space discretization and forward finite difference for time discretization, of nonlinear PDEs such the (1), (2) and (3), gives rise to a linear system of* $N^2 \times N^2$ *equations, to solve at each step* τ_n:

$$\frac{u^{\tau_n} - u^{\tau_{n-1}}}{\Delta\tau} = M\left(u^{\tau_{n-1}}\right) u^{\tau_n}, \quad u^{\tau_n} \in \Re^{N^2}$$

Moreover, for space-scale discretization we use finite differences for PDE in (1) and (3) and (complementary) finite volumes for (2). Both schemes are widely use in image processing because of the intrinsic nature of images, the latter are more appropriate than the first one for discretization of (2) because it is a level set equation where discontinuities in the evolving surface are allowed: we need discrete non oscillatory conservative schemes converging to the weak solution.

Concerning the solution of such discrete problems, we use the Additive Operator Scheme (AOS) for solving the linear system arising from (1). Indeed, the accuracy requirements of the despeckling task (about the 2%) allows to take fully advantage of the efficiency of the AOS by choosing a step size sufficiently big (we choose the scale step size equals to 2.2). In this case M is a *block-diagonal* matrix, with tridiagonal blocks. We employ the LU factorization without pivoting because of the diagonal dominance of the matrix coefficients.

Regarding (2) and (3), M is a *tridiagonal-block matrix*, with diagonal blocks tridiagonal matrices, while lower and upper diagonals are diagonal matrices. These last two discrete problems have been solved by using GMRES equipped with *algebric multi grid* preconditioner. Multigrid methods are one of the most promising methods for solving large scale problems that arise in the numerical solution of PDEs. In particular, algebraic multigrid is very robust in presence of discontinuous coefficients, which is our case. As coarse grid selection we consider FALGOUT-CLJP. Regarding the problem (3), only 1 scale step is needed to get the accuracy of about 1% (scale step size is equal to $\Delta\tau = 0.05$). Finally, for the segmentation problem, the maximum number of scale steps allowed is $N scale = 46$, with a scale step size equals to $\Delta\tau = 0.1$. Our experiments confirm that the algebraic multigrid preconditioner is algorithmically scalable: both for problem (2) and for problem (3) the convergence factor of the algebraic multigrid preconditioner (per cycle) is very stable at approximately 0.04 for all scales. The setup time averages roughly 1% of cycle time. Finally, the computational work is O(1) per scale step.

2.1. Semi-automatic stopping criterion

For each $t \in J$, an automatic stopping criterion of the segmentation surface evolution as $n \to +\infty$, has been employed by using a set of **marker points**, $P_1(x_1(t), y_1(t)), \ldots, P_m(x_m(t), y_m(t)) \in \Omega$. Let

$$\delta_i = \{P(x(t), y(t)) \in \Omega : |(P - P_i| \leq r\}, \quad i = 1, \ldots, m$$

be the m neighborhoods of P_i. The evolution of the segmentation surface $u(\tau_n, x(t), y(t), t)$, stops at step n if

$$\exists(\bar{x}(t), \bar{y}(t)) \in \delta_i : u(\tau_n, \bar{x}(t), \bar{y}(t), t) < c, \quad \forall i = 1, \ldots, m$$

Marker points are manually selected on the first frame ($t = t_0$): they are used as prior knowledge about the shape of the LV chamber. On subsequent frames, i.e. $\forall t > t_0$, their position is automatically updated using their motion trajectory (see figure 2):

$$\forall i = 1, \ldots, m, \quad P_i\left(x\left(t + \Delta t\right), y\left(t + \Delta t\right)\right) = P_i\left(x(t) + u(t)\Delta t, y(t) + v(t)\Delta t\right)$$

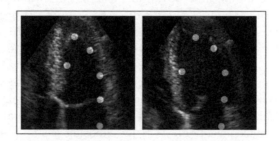

Figure 2. Markers points at frame 1 and at frame 15.

3. Parallel Software

It is worth noting that there is a strong relationship among the three tasks. Actually, such dependence synchronizes the execution of these tasks on each frame. In other words, tasks do not act independently of each other, instead, they operate following a prescribed order: despeckle, optical flow and segmentation. The execution of each task is strictly linked to the availability of results from the previous one. This assumption is quite natural in sequence analysis because of the high temporal correlations that exist between frames. As a consequence, the achievable overall performance of this application depends on deep interactions among computations, memory accesses and communications. This means that due to the fixed size of the application, there exists an *optimal configuration* of the parallel computing platform that delivers least achievable turnaround time. Let us briefly describe how this is obtained. We parallelize each task by distributing both the workload and I/O among multicore processors; for each task the most suitable number of cores was determined according to workload and I/O of each task. This allows us both to synchronize the task execution for each frame and to balance communications and computations. To determine the most suitable number of core, each task was monitored in terms of floating point and I/O operations. We find that, with respect floating point operations, de-speckle is the cheapest task and segmentation is the most time-consuming (see Fig. 3). On the other hand, in terms of communication time (mainly I/O, i.e. read/write on files) the optic flow task is the most expensive. We get a good tradeoff between communications and computations by allocating 2 core for despeckle, 6 core for optic flow and 24 for segmentation. By this way, for each task the overall execution time is the same (see Fig. 4).

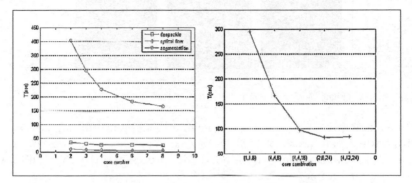

Figure 3. Execution times: on the left the execution time of each task versus the cores number; on the right the execution time of the full process versus the cores number combination.

The parallel software has been developed using PETSc parallel objects [14] and the BoomerAMG library [4]. Linear systems have been solved using as KSP solver the GMRES iterative method equipped with algebraic multigrid parallel preconditioner.

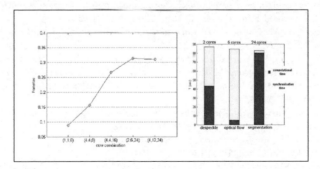

Figure 4. On the left, frames/sec versus core number; on the right I/O and computation time, for each task.

4. Results

Experiments on real data (a sequence of $26 \times 300 \times 300$ images) are carried out using 16 blade Dell PowerEdge M6000 each made of 2 processor quad core Intel

Xeon E5410@2.33GHz (64 bit) connected by the high performance network InfiniBand [13] and located at the University of Naples Federico II. Some results are shown in figure 5.

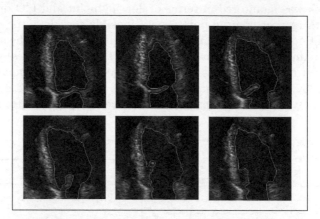

Figure 5. Some final results: frame 1, 5, 9, 13, 17 and 21.

On a single processor computing machine this application requires about 13 minutes with a bandwidth of 0.03 frame/sec. The execution time on a multicore parallel computing platform (8 quad core processors) is 1.23 minutes with a bandwidth of 0.3 frame/sec.

References

[1] L. Alvarez, P. L. Lions, J. M. Morel - *Image Selective Smoothing and Edge Detection by nonlinear Diffusion II*. SIAM J. Numerical Analysis **29**, (1992) 845–866

[2] K. Z. Bbbd-Elmoniem, A. M. Youssef, Y. M Kadah - *Real-Time Speckle Reduction and Coherence Enhancement in Ultrasound Imaging via Nonlinear Anisotropic Diffusion*. IEEE Trans on Biomedical Engineering, **49** (9), (2002) 997–1012.

[3] Y. Gousseau, J. M. Morel - *Are natural images of bounded variation*. SIAM jurnal of Mathematical Analysis, **33**, (2001) 634–648.

[4] Henson V.E.; Yang U.M., *BoomerAMG: A parallel algebraic multigrid solver and preconditioner*, Applied Numerical Mathematics, Volume 41, **1**, (2002) , 155–177.

[5] J.A. Noble - *Ultrasound Image Segmentation: A survey*. IEEE Trans. on Medical Imaging, **25** (8), (2006) 987–1010.

[6] N. Paragios, *A Variational Approach for the Segmentation of the Left Ventricle*, International Journal of Computer Vision, (2002) 345–362.

[7] A. Sarti, G. Citti - *Subjective surface and Riemannian mean curvature flow graphs*, Acta Math. Univ. Comeniamae, **70**(1) (2001) 85–104.

[8] J. Weickert, C. Shnorr - *A Theoretical Framework for Convex Regularizeds in PDE-Based Computation of Image Motion* TR 13/2000, Computer Science Series, (2000)

[9] J. Weickert, B. M. ter Haar Romeny - *Efficient and Reliable Schemes for Nonlinear Diffuzion Filtering*, IEEE Trans. on Image Processing, **7**(3) (1998), 398–409.

[10] http://www.ibm.com/technology/cell

[11] http://www.ti.com/medical

[12] http://www.intel.com/go/embedded

[13] http://scopedma-wn.dma.unina.it/

[14] http://www.msc.anl.gov/petsc/petsc-as

GRID & Cloud Computing

Parallel Computing: From Multicores and GPU's to Petascale
B. Chapman et al. (Eds.)
IOS Press, 2010
© 2010 The authors and IOS Press. All rights reserved.
doi:10.3233/978-1-60750-530-3-195

Processing Applications Composed of Web/Grid Services by Distributed Autonomic and Self-organizing Workflow Engines

Giuseppe PAPUZZO [a] and Giandomenico SPEZZANO [a,1]

[a] *CNR-ICAR, Via P. Bucci 41C, 87036 Rende(CS), Italy*

Abstract.

The dynamic and decentralized nature of Grids requires new approaches to make reliable and self-managing the service-oriented workflow management systems. Self-organization, like proposed by the autonomic computing concept, might be the key to design and develop systems/applications that can adapt themselves to meet requirements of performance, fault tolerance, reliability, security etc. without manual intervention. This paper describes Sunflower an innovative P2P agent-based framework for configuring, enacting, managing and adapting workflows on the Grid. The novel aspect of Sunflower is that key functions, include resource allocation, are decentralized and use a bio-inspired approach. This facilitates scalability and robustness of the overall system. Decentralized compositions is implemented by coordinating BPEL processes running on different organizational domains through a choreography model. A bio-inspired virtual shared space is concurrently accessed by workflow engines to discovery and select the appropriate services. Agents manage the workflow at runtime and adapt the workflow proactively to address the dynamism of the Grid execution environment and QoS requirements of the applications.

Keywords. Autonomic workflow, choreography, Petri nets, Swarm intelligence

Introduction

Workflows today play a very important role in the scientific and business communities. Grid applications are now evolving from monolithic entities to complex service-oriented workflows that need to be distributed and executed efficiently in a highly heterogeneous and dynamic environment like the Grid. Grid workflows must be dynamic and adaptive as Web/Grid services periodically can become unavailable and/or the resources availability can change over time while the workflow is executing. Self-managing and autonomic mechanisms are necessary to allow to workflows to adapt quickly and efficiently to change in the Grid environment. To support autonomic behavior [6], the workflow

---

[1]Corresponding Author: CNR-ICAR, Via P. Bucci 41C, 87036 Rende(CS), Italy; E-mail: spezzano@icar.cnr.it.

execution engine must feature self-configuration, self-tuning and self-healing capabilities. We take inspiration from models of social insect collective behavior [2] to achieve autonomic management of Grid workflows [1]. Bio-inspired algorithms based on self-organizing agents that locally interact and with the environment can be used to achieve the desirable characteristics for the dynamic workflow management such as autonomy, robustness, scalability, adaptability.

1. Sunflower framework

This paper describes Sunflower a bio-inspired framework for self-managing service-based Grid workflows. Sunflower is an adaptive p2p agent-based framework for configuring, enacting, managing and adapting Grid workflows [5]. The novel aspect of Sunflower is that key functions, including resource allocation, are decentralized, which facilitates scalability and robustness of the overall system. The framework dynamically and effectively self-configures the workflow engine in response to changes in load patterns and server failures. Workflows are described in Sunflower by the BPEL language in order to exploit existing design tools. Sunflower replaces the standard BPEL engine with a new decentralized engine able to exploit the dynamic information available in the Grid and respond to the dynamic nature of the Grid. Decentralized compositions is implemented by coordinating BPEL processes runing on different organizational domains through a *choreography* model. Sunflower supports service-level parallelism using a QoS-aware service-level schedule algorithm and flow-level parallelism by partitioning a workflow into sub-flows and running the sub-flows in multiple peers in parallel. BPEL programs are translated into a Petri Net for the coordination of the concurrent activities. This representation is then structurally decomposed into a set of distributed sub-flow schemas. On the basis of these schemas, Sunflower enacts a set of autonomic self-organizing workflow engines (*SWFE*) as a federation of agents that interact with each other and with So-Grid [3], a P2P self-organizing Grid information system, to adapt the workflow to unforeseen circumstances. So-Grid provides a global virtual shared space that can be concurrently and associatively accessed by the *SWFE* agents to discovery and select the appropriate services. So-Grid uses bio-inspired algorithms to organize the construction of a Grid information system in which content, specifically metadata descriptors that describe the characteristics of Grid services, is disseminated and logically reorganized on the Grid. Sunflower connects, in a transparent and fully automated manner, the *SWFE* agents with Web/Grid services to manage the invocation of the service and the execution of the workflow task assigned to that service. In Grid each Web/Grid service is bound to a single node for its entire lifetime and, moreover, the binding between grid service and its body is generally static. Sunflower assumes that multiple copies of a Web/Grid service, with different performance profiles and distributed in different locations, co-exist. During the execution of the workflow, if a service fails or becomes overloaded, a self-reconfiguring mechanism based on a *binding adaptation* model is used to ensure that the running workflow is not interrupted but its structure is adapted in response to both internal or external changes. *SWFE* agents adapt their structure moving over the grid to position themselves in the nodes with low workload and where are available the Web/Grid services with the best performance. The framework provides support for the migration-transparent of the agents and instructs the agents, by a migration policy, to migrate in order to achieve goals like load balancing, performance optimization or guaranteeing QoS. *Self-healing* execution of a Grid workflow is achieved through service replacement in case of Web services failures. Furthermore, a backward recovery mechanism is used to bring the system from its erroneous state back into a previously correct state.

The remainder of this paper is organized as follows. Section 2 presents a general overview of the Petri nets and BPEL language and the partitioning rules for a decomposition of the workflow model. Section 3 provides a description of the architecture for the decentralized execution of workflows in Sunflower. Section 4 draws some conclusions.

2. Partitioning of the workflow model

Before to start the distributed execution of a workflow, modeled by BPEL language, is necessary that the workflow model be divided into small partitions, that we call sub-workflows, and that the single partitions be allot to different engines to be executed. A BPEL program can be partitioned into an equivalent set of cooperating sub-workflows in an exponential number of ways. The partitioning depends on how the language constructs are aggregated into the partitions. To define a correct and efficient schema of partitioning of a BPEL workflow a rigorous approach based on a formal method must be adopted. We adopt the well-known Petri net formalism for the partitioning of a workflow model. Petri nets can also be used to validate properties on the workflow level, e.g. soundness, reachability and correctness. Our approach requires the mapping of an BPEL program onto a Petri-net and the application, to this abstract representation, of partitioning rules to create the set of decentralized sub-workflows. This approach allows to increase the parallelism in the execution and to automatize the partitioning phase. Before to show how the workflow model can be partitioned we briefly introduce the BPEL language and the Petri nets model.

2.1. BPEL

The WS-BPEL (Web Service Business Process Execution Logic) [7] language, approved as an OASIS Standard, was a result of the combined efforts of many companies for supplying a standardized way to compose web service.

Table 1. Summary of BPEL constructs

BPEL construct	Description
sequence	sequential flow
switch	conditional flow
while	iterative flow
pick	non-deterministic conditional flow
flow	concurrent flow similar cobegin-coend
link	wait-notify type of synchronization
variable	variables
invoke	synchronous (blocking) invocation on a Web service
receive	blocking receive of data from a Web service P into a variable *var*
reply	send response to a Web Service P from a variable *var*
assign	assignment

The language consists of standard flow constructs for *sequential, conditional* and *concurrent* execution of activities such as invoking a service or standard assignment and arithmetic operations.The BPEL language constructs under consideration are summarized in table 1. An example of a BPEL workflow modeled using the Eclipse BPEL Designer and the XML-BPEL code generated are illustrated in figure 1.

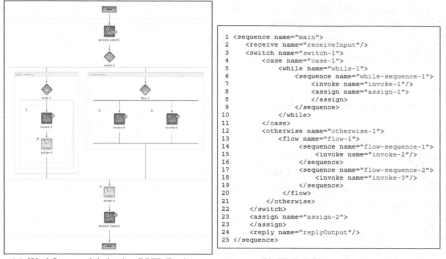

```
1 <sequence name="main">
2     <receive name="receiveInput"/>
3     <switch name="switch-1">
4         <case name="case-1">
5             <while name="while-1">
6                 <sequence name="while-sequence-1">
7                     <invoke name="invoke-1"/>
8                     <assign name="assign-1">
8                     </assign>
9                 </sequence>
10            </while>
11        </case>
12        <otherwise name="otherwise-1">
13            <flow name="flow-1">
14                <sequence name="flow-sequence-1">
15                    <invoke name="invoke-2"/>
16                </sequence>
17                <sequence name="flow-sequence-2">
18                    <invoke name="invoke-3"/>
19                </sequence>
20            </flow>
21        </otherwise>
22    </switch>
23    <assign name="assign-2">
23    </assign>
24    <reply name="replyOutput"/>
25 </sequence>
```

   (a) Workflow modeled using BPEL Designer   (b) XML-BPEL code generated

Figure 1. Example of a BPEL Process.

2.2. Petri nets

A Petri net (also known as a place/transition net) is a very useful formalism to represent discrete distributed systems. It is constituted by two kinds of nodes, *places* and *transitions*, and by directed *arcs* connecting places with transitions. It can be modeled as a directed bipartite graph. Places can be marked by *tokens*. A transition from a place to another is enabled (i.e. can *fire*), when tokens are present in all its input places. The fire operation, performed atomically, consists in performing some processing operations and putting tokens in all the output places. In addition, boolean conditions can be used to decide whether an enabled transition can fire or not. Note that non determinism is one of their main properties and this is really useful for representing the behavior of distributed systems. In fact, using petri nets, the topological structure of a distributed system can be represented and so the events and their order can be easily visualized. Petri nets are well suited for modeling workflow processes.

2.3. Mapping BPEL workflows on Petri Nets

A workflow described in BPEL details the flow control and any data dependencies among a collection of Web services being composed. We build every process in a BPEL workflow by plugging language constructs together; we thus can translate each construct of the language into a Petri net (PN). Each primitive or structured activity can be easily modeled as a Petri Net as illustrated in figure 2.

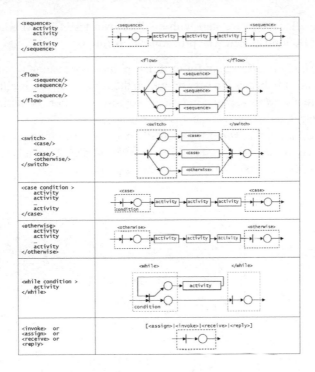

Figure 2. Example of BPEL constructs (left) converted to Petri nets (right).

BPEL based workflows are converted to a Petri net applying the rules defined by the Van der Aalst methodology [8] that generate a PNs via the repetitive replacement of elemental PNs with other PNs. Figure 3(a) shows the conversion of the BPEL workflow described in figure 1 to a PN form using the replacement property.

2.4. Petri nets partitioning

A workflow written as a single BPEL program must be decomposed in an equivalent set of decentralized processes to implement the choreography model. Our strategy is to construct a PN for the workflow and then apply partitioning rules operate on such an abstract representation to create the set of cooperating sub-workflows. Our PN partitioning algorithm is based on the idea of merging tasks starting from the *invoke* activities along the control dependence edges.

An informal description of the partitioning algorithm is as follow:

- The begin and end portions of PN concerning the *main sequence* must be assigned to the same peer, named Peer Collector (PC). *Reply* and *receive* activities must be also executed on the PC.
- The portion of PN concerning the *invoke* is assigned to the peer handling the web service called by the invoke itself.
- All the other constructs are assigned by means of two subsequent visits (*top down* and *bottom up*) of the PN graph. The visits of the PN graph start from the invoke activities. Constructs between two invoke activities can be assigned to one of the two peers where are executed the invokes in order to balance the load.

After the initial allocations, we start with an TopDown visit of the PN graph and then continue with a BottomUp visit. The procedure is as follow:

1. *TopDown initial allocation*: for each PN portion concerning the invoke activity, the label that indicates the peer on which the invoke activity is allocated is propagated to all the *successors*; in case of controversy (more activities going to the same place), only the *right* label is propagated.

2. *BottomUp final allocation*: for each PN portion concerning the invoke activity, the label of the peer assigned to this activity is propagated to all the *predecessors*; in case of controversy, only the *left* label is propagated.

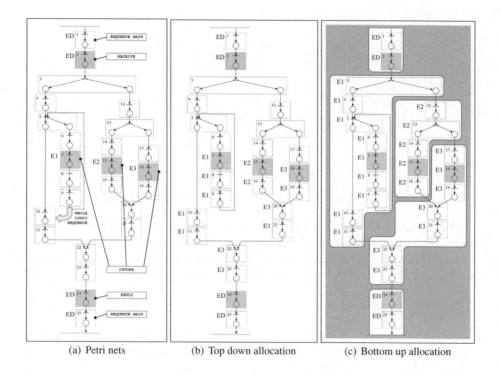

(a) Petri nets   (b) Top down allocation   (c) Bottom up allocation

Figure 3. Petri nets partitioning.

In order to better describe the entire process, the PN graph shown in figure 3(a) will be used to illustrate the partitioning procedure. Figure 3(b) shows as the activities are allocated to the peers through the TopDown procedure. Following the above partitioning algorithm, the activities 1, 2 (*main sequence, begin and receive*) and 24, 25 (*reply and main sequence end*) are assigned to the Peer Collector. Then, starting from the invoke activities marked as 7, 15 and 18 the activities 7-11, with the E1 label, are assigned to the Peer1, the activities 15 and 16, with E2 label, are assigned to the Peer2 and the activities 18-23, with E3 label, are assigned to the Peer3. Then, applying the BottomUp procedure, the activities 3-6 are assigned to the Peer1, 12-14 to the Peer2, 17 to the Peer 3 as shown in figure 3(c).

3. Sunflower decentralized execution

The Sunflower framework applies key biological concepts and mechanisms to design an autonomic service-oriented Grid workflow that allows to workflow enactment engine to autonomously adapt to dynamic environment changes in the Grid and fulfill QoS requirements for Web/Grid services. Figure 4 shows the architecture of the framework Sunflower. The workflow process is enacted by a dynamic group of bio-inspired mobile *SWFE* agents that can migrate from node to node while the workflow is being executed to adapt it to environment variations and QoS requirements of the application (self-configuring). The *SWFE* agents use simple local rules to govern their actions and via the interactions of the entire group, the swarm achieves the objective to deploy the workflow in an optimal configuration.

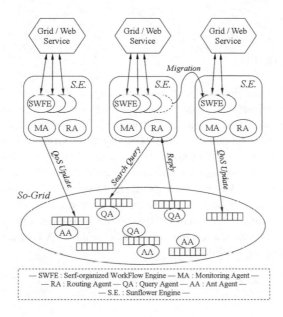

Figure 4. The Sunflower architecture.

The decentralized execution of the workflow is coordinate by tokens exchanged among the *SWFE* agents that perform the fragments of the Petri net and invoke the services. Each *SWFE* agent performs the portion of workflow assigned and determine which agent should be activated next.

To support workflow adaptation the *SWFE* agents are assisted by *router* agents and monitoring/analizing *MA* agents that interact with the So-Grid information system. The MA agent collects details about the performance metrics and workload of Grid service and when detects a change, due to external events, it inserts a new Web/Grid service descriptor with the new information in the So-Grid virtual space and notify the change to the *router* agent. When the *router* agent receives a notification about a modification of the class of QoS, it sends a query to So-Grid to discovery and select a descriptor of an equivalent optimal service. Then, So-Grid returns a reference to an end point handler for the selected service. The activities of the *MA* and *router* agents are performed continuously. Before to execute the sub-workflow, the *SWFE* agent contacts the *MA* agent to verify if the class of QoS of the service to invoke is respected. In the affirmative case, the *SWFE* invokes the service and performs the workflow task, otherwise it uses its migration-policy to decide its actions looking up the *router* agent.

So-Grid uses a number of ant-like agents (*AA*) that autonomously travel through P2P interconnections and use biased probability functions to: (i) replicate resource descriptors in order to favor resource discovery; (ii) collect resource descriptors with similar characteristics in nearby Grid hosts; (iii) foster the dissemination of descriptors corresponding to fresh (recently updated) resources and to resources having high Quality of Service (QoS) characteristics. Moreover, as descriptors are progressively reorganized and replicated, The So-Grid discovery algorithm allows query-ant agents (*QA*) ro reach Grid hosts that store information about a larger number of useful resources in a shorter amount of time.

4. Experimental results

We implemented and deployed a Java based prototype of the Sunflower framework on Linux. A set of experiments have been conducted to validate the proposed QoS oriented framework for adaptive management of Web/Grid Service based workflows. In these preliminary experiments actual services available on our Grid were used. We evaluated our system according to two criteria: *efficiency* and *adaptability*. The efficiency of the system was evaluated in order to compare the execution times of a standard BPEL engine with those of Sunflower. We assessed the system efficiency for various intensities of the external load. Figure 5 shows that the execution time of Sunflower (SF) is slower than that of Oracle BPEL (OB). This is due to the communication overheads that are introduced by the synchronization mechanisms among the JXTA peers that perform the various fragments of the workflow.

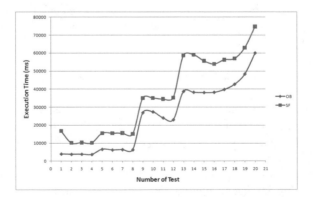

Figure 5. Comparison of the execution times of BPEL engine (OB curve) with those of Sunflower (SF curve).

Adaptability captures the capability of the system to respond to a change in the operating conditions by reconfiguring and converging to a new steady state. We evaluated the Sunflower adaptability for the case where additional load is added to a system with three machines having a different CPU speed and running the same service on each node. Initially the system is in steady state providing the same service with three different values of QoS. In figure 6, the curves labeled P800, P1500 and P2200 show the values of the QoS for the service during the execution on an Intel machine with 800, 1500 and 2200 MHz. The PN portion, concerning the invoke activity, is delivered on P800 in point A. However, the QoS threshold defined for the correct execution of the service is 1500, so the router agent looks for to individuate a substitute. QoS negotiation is carried out during workflow execution. At the point B the service request for a service with QoS of 1500 is routed toward the available service on the 1500 MHz machine (point C). The service is invoked at the D point and used until the E point. Then, at the F point, the workflow is terminated. As you can see Sunflower quickly adapts to new situations while maintaining the QoS requirements of the service.

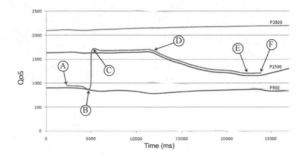

Figure 6. Adaptive behavior of Sunflower.

5. Conclusions

In this paper, we have presented a decentralized and cooperative strategy for the execution of autonomic workflows on Grids. A bio-inspired cross-layer approach is used to support the self-adaptation of the workflow enactment engines to changes in the Grid and fulfill QoS requirements for Web/Grid services.

Acknowledgements

This work is partially funded by the MIUR project DM21301, "OpenKnowTech: Laboratory of Technologies for the Integration, Management and Distribution of Data, Processes and Knowledge".

References

[1]   M. Rahman and R. Buyya : An Autonomic Workflow Management System for Global Grids, *Proceedings of the 8th IEEE International Symposium on Cluster Computing and the Grid (CCGrid 2008)*, IEEE CS Press, pp.578-583, 2008.

[2]   Bonabeau E., Dorigo M., Theraulaz G. : Swarm Intelligence: From Natural to Artificial Systems New York, *NY: Oxford University Press*, Santa Fe Institute Studies in the Sciences of Complexity 1999.

[3]   Forestiero A., Mastroianni C., and Spezzano G. : So-Grid: A Self-organizing Grid Featuring Bio-inspired Algorithms, *ACM Transactions on Autonomous and Adaptive Systems*, vol. 3 n. 2, 2008.

[4]   Brazier, F.M.T., Kephart, J.O., Van Dyke Parunak, H. Huhns M.N. : Agents and Service-Oriented Computing for Autonomic Computing: A Research Agenda, *IEEE Internet Computing*, vol. 13 n. 3, pp. 82-87 2009.

[5]   Vidal, J.M., Buhler, P., Stahl, C.: Multiagent systems with workflows, *IEEE Internet Computing*, vol. 8 n. 1, pp. 76-82 2004.

[6]   Kephart Jeffrey O., Chess David M. : The Vision on Autonomic Computing, IEEE Computer, vol. 36, n. 1, pp.41-50, 2003.

[7]   Web Services Business Process Execution Language Version 2.0 - Committe Specification. Technical Report, OASIS, Jan. 2007.

[8]   W. van der Aalst and K.M. van Hee: Workflow Management: Models, Methods, and Systems, *MIT Press*, Cambridge, MA, 2002.

Parallel Computing: From Multicores and GPU's to Petascale
B. Chapman et al. (Eds.)
IOS Press, 2010
© 2010 The authors and IOS Press. All rights reserved.
doi:10.3233/978-1-60750-530-3-205

LPT scheduling algorithms with unavailability constraints under uncertainties

Adel ESSAFI [a,b], Amine MAHJOUB [a], Grégory MOUNIÉ [b] and Denis TRYSTRAM [b]

[a] *Unité de Recherche en Technologies de l'Information et de la Communication, Ecole Supérieure des Sciences et Techniques de Tunis 5, Avenue Taha Hussein, BP 56, Bab Menara, 1008 Tunis, Tunisia*
[b] *Laboratoire d'Informatique de Grenoble, 51, avenue Jean Kuntzmann 38330 Montbonnot Saint Martin, France*

Abstract. Cluster of computers are more and more popular for running applications. Such computing architectures are composed of collections of processors that are not always continuously available over time. Usually, the corresponding unavailabilities are not precisely known in advance because they are often subject to disturbances.

We propose in this paper to study the impact of disturbances on the performance of the well-known LPT scheduling algorithm (Largest Processing Time) with unavailability periods. We establish new approximability bounds for this algorithm and we discuss several variants that allow to absorb the disturbances on the dates of perturbations.

Keywords. list scheduling, LPT algorithm, availability constraints, uncertainties

1. Introduction

A large amount of work of studies has been devoted to the parallel execution of sequential jobs on clusters (collection of homogeneous computing units interconnected by a fast local network [4,1]). The jobs correspond to independent applications that are submitted in a front-end machine and executed in successive batches. The jobs are transferred to local queues of the computing resources. An important issue is the situation where the resources (processors) are not continuously available over time. It is common that these unavailability periods are not known precisely in advance because they are often subject to disturbances on starting and finishing times. To our knowledge, the problem of studying the impact of disturbances on scheduling algorithms with unavailabilities has never been addressed before.

The main contribution of this work is to propose a new scheduling algorithm based on the well-known LPT list algorithm (Largest Processing Time) [5] for scheduling independent jobs in the presence of unavailability periods and disturbances. Then, we compare its behaviour to several variants of LPT on adequate scenarii.

2. Preliminaries

2.1. Basic Definitions and Notations

A set $J = \{J_1.....J_n\}$ of n sequential jobs have to be executed on a parallel platform (cluster) composed of m identical processors denoted by $P_1...P_m$. Each job J_i has a processing time p_i. C_i denotes the completion time of job J_i. The objective is to minimize the makespan, defined as the maximum completion time and denoted by C_{max}. C_{max}^* denotes the optimal value of the makespan. There are k fixed disjoint unavailability periods and no more than one unavailability period can be scheduled on the same processor. We restrict this study to this case for the theoretical analysis. The unavailability period on processor q starts at time s_q and ends at time e_q. Let e_{max} denote the maximum value of the e_q. Without loss of generality, the processors are ordered by decreasing order of starting unavailability time. Thus, the processors $P_1..P_k$ are such that $s_1 \leq .. \leq s_k$ and the remaining processors are completely available.

We consider the off-line version of the problem in which all informations about the jobs to execute are known *a priori*. According to the usual execution in batches, we consider that all the jobs and unavailability intervals are known. This problem has been proved to be NP-hard in [9].

2.2. Motivations

Most results on scheduling assume that the informations about the problem are perfectly known. Unfortunately, this is not always true, particularly, in new versatile distributed platforms and clusters of identical processors. Indeed, some values of the problem such as event dates, their duration, structure of the problem, costs, etc. can be partially unknown or estimated when designing the schedule.

Two main disturbances may occur in such environments: the starting times of the unavailabilities and their duration. It is obvious that if the starting time of the unavailabilities is delayed or if the duration of the unavailabilities is shorter that expected, the disturbances will have no big impact on the scheduling. It is also easy to see that if the end of the unavailability is delayed, then, we can simply delay the execution of all the jobs scheduled after the end of the unavailability period. Thus, the impact of such disturbances is limited in this case. The most interesting situation is when the starting time of the unavailability is disturbed in such a way that in the disturbed instance, the unavailability period would start before the expected date and then, may affect some jobs. For instance, an academic cluster may be planned to be available during the night between 8 p.m, and 10 a.m., but for some reason (a session that have been re-scheduled), it may be taken back at 8 a.m. Formally, we consider the disturbed instances such that $\forall q \leq k, \tilde{s}_q \leq s_q$.

2.3. Dealing with Disturbances

There exist several possible approaches for solving a scheduling problem with uncertainties [2]. Fundamentally, the main difference between these approaches is the moment when the schedule is fully computed. In dynamic or purely on-line approaches, the solution is computed at execution time using simple priority rules when the actual data are known. However, in static or robust approaches, the schedule is fully computed before the beginning of the execution. This schedule is calculated by taking into account a possible disturbance, and it is designed to be as good as possible for all the possible disturbances. Between the robust and the purely on-line approaches, it is possible to consider an intermediate approach: *the partially on-line* approach. It consists in computing an initial schedule with the estimated data and, depending of the disturbances, to adjust the schedule on-line.

In the literature [8], [2] some measures or criteria of robustness have been proposed. One of the possible criteria consists to measure the difference between the makespan of the schedule computed with the estimated data and the actual makespan obtained after the execution, this measure is called *stability*. Thus, a schedule is stable, if the actual makespan remains close to the initial makespan estimated without disturbances.

In this work, we adopt a robust approach with the stability criteria. We consider the hypothesis, that if the beginning of the unavailability period causes the interruption of a job, then, the job is entirely restarted immediately after the end of the unavailability period. This hypothesis does not contradict the static approach, because we will not re-optimize the schedule on-line, we will just adapt it.

Let $\tilde{\sigma}$ be the actual executed schedule. Notice that the order of the executed jobs on the processors remains the same in σ and in $\tilde{\sigma}$. Let $\tilde{C}_{max}$ be the makespan of the disturbed schedule $\tilde{\sigma}$.

As we have mentioned before, we focus on the case where the uncertainties are relative to the beginning of the unavailability period. Such uncertainties are due to the fact that the knowledge about these unavailabilities is not complete and disturbances may affect the predicted dates. We aim at measuring the impact of these disturbances on the performance of the schedule.

Definition 1. *The stability ratio of an algorithm is the maximum for all the possible instances between the disturbed makespan over the initial one :* $max(\frac{\tilde{C}_{max}}{C_{max}})$

A schedule is as stable as its stability ratio is close to 1, i.e, the disturbances have no effect on the makespan.

3. Review of Related Works

First, notice that most of the approaches used to solve the problem of scheduling with unavailabilities are based on the LPT rule. In [10], Lee studied the problem of scheduling independent jobs with non-simultaneous available times. This corresponds to the problem of scheduling jobs when all the unavailabilities are at the beginning ($\forall q, s_q = 0$). The main result in this case is to show that the performance of LPT is bounded by $\frac{3}{2}$. He also proposed a modified version of LPT with an improved performance ratio of $\frac{4}{3}$. A more general problem was studied by Lee in [9], and consists in scheduling jobs under any pattern of availability. He showed that the problem cannot be polynomially approximated if no restrictions are done on the availabilities. He also proved that the performance of LPT is bounded by $\frac{m+1}{2}$ when at least one machine is always available and at most one unavailability period per machine is allowed.

In [6], the authors analysed the problem when no more than half of the machines are allowed to be unavailable simultaneously. Under this condition, the performance of LPT is bounded by 2. This result was generalized in [7] by Hwang et al. as follows: if at most λ (ranging from 1 to $m - 1$) processors are allowed to be unavailable simultaneously, then LPT generates a schedule whose performance is bounded by $1 + \frac{1}{2} \lceil \frac{m}{m-\lambda} \rceil$.

In [3], the authors analysed the problem where one machine is always available and with an arbitrary number of unavailabilities on another processor. It is shown that the problem admits no FPTAS, however, it is possible to design a PTAS based on the multiple knapsack problem. Such an approach is too costly for being used in practical scheduler.

4. Variants of LPT

In this section, we develop four variants of the well known LPT algorithm. Recall that this algorithm is a list algorithm that sorts the jobs by decreasing order of job processing times. Then, the algorithm schedules one of ready jobs to the first available processor.

The first variant is called LPT top-down in which the list of jobs is ordered in decreasing order of size. Then, the job at the head of the list is scheduled to the first available resource. If there exist many processors available at the same time, the job is scheduled to the one with the largest index.

The second variant is LPT bottom-up. In this version, the processors are considered by increasing order of their index. Thus, If there exist many processors available at the same time, the job at the head of the list is scheduled to the one with the smallest index.

We have also implemented a third variant, called restricted LPT, which aims absorb the effect of the disturbances. In this version, a fixed free space is kept free besides each unavailability. Then, we restrict the scheduling of the jobs to the remaining available area using LPT.

The last version aims also to minimize the effect of the disturbances by placing the small jobs besides the unavailabilities. This version is called adapted LPT-SPT backwards. Let λ be a positive integer smaller than s_1. The list of the jobs is built as follows:

- select a subset of the jobs starting from the smallest one to the largest until the sum of all the jobs becomes greater than $k\lambda$. Let J_s denote the name this subset of jobs.
- put the subset of the jobs at the head of the list. The jobs are sorted by increasing order of size.
- the remaining jobs are inserted to the list and sorted by decreasing order of size.

The scheduling algorithm is described as follows:

- schedule the job at the head of the list to job to the first available processor having an index between 1 and k (i.e, with an unavailability). Stop when all the jobs in J_s are scheduled.
- schedule the remaining jobs using LPT algorithm
- re-order the jobs that were scheduled before the unavailabilities by decreasing order of job processing time.

5. Simulation results

5.1. simulation scenarii

To evaluate the performance and the stability of the algorithms described above, we simulated their behaviour for clusters with small and medium size.

For the k first processors, we schedule an unavailability period with size 350 and we generate jobs with processing time between 40 and 100. The sum of all the jobs processing times and reservation duration is equal to 1000. For the remaining processors, we generate jobs with processing times between 40 and 100 such that the sum of all the processing times of the jobs is equal to 1000. This way, the optimal makespan for the considered instance is equal to 1000.

We have simulated the behaviour of the designed algorithms for clusters with number of processors from ten to two hundreds. This corresponds to small and medium cluster size. Each simulation returns four makespan of the four variants of LPT and their disturbed makespan. For each value of m we run 100 simulations and we consider the mean value. In each instance, we consider that 75% of the processors have an unavailability constraint and that the remaining processors are entirely available. Note that we have considered a disturbance of size 75 on the starting time of all the unavailabilities. The length of the free intervals in restricted-LPT algorithm and λ in the LPT-SPT backwards algorithm is equal to 150.

5.2. results

Figure 1 shows that performance of LPT top-down and LPT bottom-up is almost optimal. Although adapted LPT-SPT backwards achieves worst performance than the former algorithms, it remains very efficient since the degradation does not exceed 8% of the optimal performance. Finally, restricted LPT is the less efficient algorithms between the considered ones. The fact is due to the forbidden area kept free before the availability intervals.

However, as figure 2 shows, the stability of restricted LPT algorithm is optimal, i.e, the disturbances have no impact on the makespan. LPT top-down and LPT bottom-up algorithms have an opposite behaviour since the disturbances cause the degradation of the expected makespan. The best compromise is achieved by adapted LPT-SPT backwards. Indeed, as it is shown in the figures above, both the performance and the stability of this algorithm remain near the optimal value. Compared to restricted LPT, the performance is improved by using the available area before the availability. From another side, the stability ratio is better that LPT top-down and LPT bottom-up since no big jobs will be scheduled before the reservation. Then, any disturbance on the beginning of the unavailability intervals will eventually cause some small jobs to be re-scheduled after the end of these unavailability periods. Consequently, the impact of the disturbances is limited on the makespan.

6. Summary of the Results and Perspectives

In this paper, we considered the problem of scheduling a set of n independent jobs on a cluster of m identical processors when they are not always available over time. Our

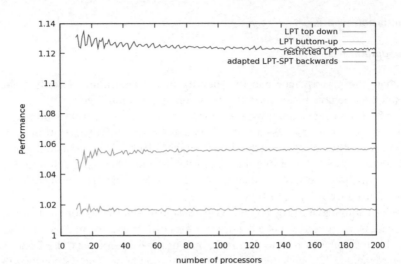

Figure 1. Performance of the variants of LPT algorithms: LPT top-down and LPT bottom-up achieve almost optimal performance

objective was to study the impact of disturbances on the beginning of the unavailability periods on the classical LPT list scheduling algorithm.

Our main contribution was to design a new scheduling algorithm called adapted LPT-SPT backwards which achieves a good compromise between performance and stability. This result is assessed by simulations run on typical scenarii which show that the makespan of LPT top-down and LPT bottom-up is almost optimal whereas the stability is worst. Contrary to these two variants, restricted LPT achieves an optimal stability but worst performance. Finally, adapted LPT-SPT backwards has the best compromise between both performance and stability.

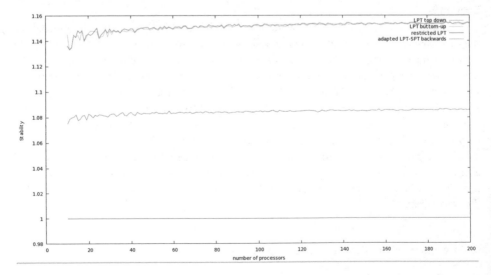

Figure 2. Stability of the variants of LPT algorithms: adapted LPT-SPT backwards achieves nearly optimal stability

We are currently extending and implementing this analysis for more general cases with any number of unavailability periods. The analysis reported in this paper is a good starting point.

References

[1]   M. Baker and R. Buyya. *High Performance Cluster Computing: Architectures and Systems*, chapter Cluster Computing at a Glance. Prentice Hall PTR, NJ, USA, 1999.

[2]   J.C Billaut, A. Moukrim, and Eric Sanlaville, editors. *Flexibility and Robustness in Scheduling*. Wiley-ISTE, 2008.

[3]   F. Diedrich, K. Jansen, F. Pascual, and D. Trystram. Approximation algorithms for scheduling with reservations. *Algorithmica*, 2009.

[4]   D. G. Feitelson, L. Rudolph, and U. Schwiegelshohn. Parallel job scheduling - a status report. pages 1 16. Springer Verlag, 2004.

[5]   R.L. Graham. Bounds on multiprocessing timing anomalies. *SIAM J. Appl. Math*, 17:263–269, 1969.

[6]   H.-C. Hwang and S.Y. Chang. Parallel machines scheduling with machine shutdowns. *Computers and Mathematics with Applications*, 36:21–31(11), August 1998.

[7]   H.C. Hwang, K. Lee, and S.Y. Chang. The effect of machine availability on the worst-case performance of lpt. *Discrete Applied Mathematics*, 148:49 – 61, 2005.

[8]   P. Kouvelis and G. Yu. *Robust Discrete Optimization and its Applications*. Kluwer Academic Publishers, 1997.

[9]   C. Y. Lee. Machine scheduling with an availability constraint. *Journal of global optimization*, 9:363–382, 1996.

[10]   C.Y. Lee. Parallel machines scheduling with nonsimultaneous machine available time. *Discrete Appl. Math.*, 30(1):53–61, 1991.

Parallel Computing: From Multicores and GPU's to Petascale
B. Chapman et al. (Eds.)
IOS Press, 2010
© 2010 The authors and IOS Press. All rights reserved.
doi:10.3233/978-1-60750-530-3-212

Parallel Genetic Algorithm Implementation for BOINC

Malek SMAOUI FEKI [a] Viet Huy NGUYEN [a] and Marc GARBEY [a]

[a] *Department of Computer Science, University of Houston, 4800 Calhoun rd, Houston, Texas, 77004*

Abstract. In this paper we present our implementation of a Genetic Algorithm on the BOINC volunteer computing platform. Our main objective is to construct a computational framework that applies to the optimum design problem of prairies. This ecology problem is characterized by a large parameter set, noisy multi-objective functions, and the presence of multiple local optima that reflects biodiversity. Our approach consists in enhancing the iterative (synchronous) master-worker genetic algorithm to overcome the limitations of volatile and unreliable distributed computing resources considering a sufficiently large number of volunteer computers. Though volunteer computing is known to be much less performing than parallel environments such as clusters and grids, our GA solution turns to exhibit competitive performance.

Keywords. Genetic Algorithms, Volunteer Computing, Prairie Optimization, Ecology, Clonal plants

Introduction

Parallel Genetic Algorithms

Evolutionary algorithms (EA), namely Genetic Algorithms (GA), have been proved to be efficient optimization methods. GA's were clearly formalized in the late 80's and beginning of the 90's with the works of D. E. Goldberg and J. R. Koza[1,2]. Since then, they have been successfully applied to complex optimization problems [3,4,5,6]. GA's are inspired from nature. They use the principals of reproduction and natural selection ensuring the dominance of individuals of the most fit species. The GA starts with an initial population of potential solutions of the optimization problem (individuals) that are represented as strings of genes. This population evolves to a better fit population by crossover and mutation of some of the candidate solutions (reproduction process). The individuals participating in the reproduction process are selected according to their fitness to the problem i.e. how close they are to the optimization solution.

According to the objective function computation needs, a GA may require a considerable amount of computation. Thus, one of the most important extensions in GA's was their parallelization. The simplest parallelization scheme is a Global Master-worker distribution of fitness function evaluations [7]. However, Parallel GA's (PGA) models represent a broader class of algorithms with enhanced search strategies [8,9]. These PGA's have been implemented for networks of heterogeneous workstations, parallel mainframes and cluster grids [10].

Volunteer Computing

Nowadays, volunteer computing [11,12] is recognized as a viable and cost-effective parallel framework. Indeed, the access to High Performance Computing (HPC) facilities such as parallel mainframes, grids, elastic clouds, etc ... is not affordable by every scientist. Volunteer computing, however, is an arrangement between the scientist or the team of scientists and a group of volunteers in which computing resources are donated to a research project to satisfy its computation needs. Computing resources are mainly idle cpu cycles of Internet connected PC's owned by individuals or institutions. Obviously, such an arrangement cuts significantly the computation expenses of the project but offers limited freedom of use of the computing resources and lower performance. BOINC [13] is a well known middleware which enables the utilization of such volunteered computing resources. BOINC has a server/client architecture and is project based. In other words, clients running on the volunteered PC's can be attached to different projects running on different, independently administrated, servers. This feature allows resource sharing between projects. However, the main limitation of BOINC is that distributed tasks should be completely independent (embarrassing parallelism). This is due to the fact that commercial Internet is the only available and affordable communication medium between the computing entities.

The master-worker PGA has an obvious embarrassing parallelism and a structure that coincides with BOINC architecture. The main difficulty however is that the hosts of a BOINC project can be extremely volatile and perhaps unreliable. Provided that the project is attracting few thousands of volunteers and these issues are overcome, this framework could be ideal for applications having a large search domain dimension and high fitness evaluation computation requirements.

Target application: the Virtual Prairie project

The Virtual Prairie (ViP) project is a study of the dynamics of clonal plant populations and which goals are guiding engineering of prairies and helping biodiversity preservation [14,15,16]. The application simulates the growth of prairies of clonal plants (c.f. figure 1) using a parametric Individual Based Model (IBM) for each plant and a set of rules defining the interactions between the different plants. The model may take more than 16 variable parameters per species, and the dimension of the search space for a prairie with half a dozen of species end up with about 100 parameters to optimize! The model is highly stochastic: two runs with the same set of parameter values would produce different outcomes. Thus, each simulation outputs a number of prairie performance metrics. These are averaged over multiple runs of the simulation for the same parameter set. So, the actual outputs of the application are averages of prairie performance metrics which can be optimized using GA's. The choice of the objective function (performance metric) depends on the goals of the study which is not often completely known. In order to study the model and investigate its emerging properties, parameter space browsing have been carried out for isolated plants and for competing plants within prairies thanks to the ViP BOINC project [16,15]. More simulations are still in progress on this project. Detailed information can be found at the web site http://vcsc.cs.uh.edu/virtual-prairie/. The computation requirements of a prairie simulation ranges from few minutes to few hours depending on the problem size and the time scale. Once the objective function is

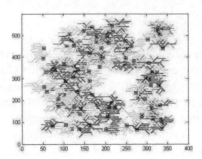

Figure 1. Example of a single run prairie simulation output.

clear, the ViP project can make good use of a PGA implementation on top of BOINC to fine tune the optimization process.

This paper aims at describing the methods used for PGA implementation on BOINC and the challenges that faced this work. While we have carried out optimizations using the virtual prairie application, we have set up a simplified benchmark application with multiple competitive maximum that can be better used for evaluation purposes.

1. Genetic Algorithm Library

The intuitive way to tackle this project is to leverage an open source GA library such as PGAPACK [17], a Parallel Genetic Algorithm library developed at Argonne National Lab by David Levine in 1995. We used this library to write a master-worker GA code optimizing the Virtual Prairie application with 16 parameters. We tested this code on a 72 cores SiCortex machine. The GA converged in less than 100 generation to the global maximum. The result was confirmed by the space browsing already carried out on BOINC (described above). However, using this library, we recognized the complexity and constraints that this tool would impose, when combining it with BOINC components. So, we decided to write our own GA library (MCS_GA) to gain more control over the data structures. MCS_GA offers a multitude of different GA operators: selection methods, crossover and mutation operators. In addition, it provides MPI implementations of multiple parallel genetic algorithm models including master-worker, multi-deme (multi-population) and steady-state.

2. PGA Model for BOINC

2.1. How does BOINC operates?

As mentioned previously, BOINC [13] has a server/client architecture. The main components of the server are (c.f. figure 2) work handling daemons and scripts, a data base, a file repository and a web interface. The vital work handling daemons for most projects are the work generator, the feeder, the scheduler, the validator and the assimilator. BOINC uses abstractions namely workunits and results for work handling. A workunit is a reference to an application and one or a set of input files. A result is a reference to a workunit and one or a set of output files. Workunits and results are manipulated through the data

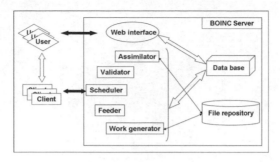

Figure 2. BOINC architecture.

base. Typically, the work generator creates or retrieves input files and creates corresponding workunits in the data base. The feeder creates results for the unprocessed workunits found in the data base. The scheduler will send the unprocessed results to clients requesting work. The validator verifies the correctness of output files returned by the clients after the computation is done. The assimilator aggregates and post processes these outputs.

2.2. GA model design

2.2.1. Implementation and challenges

The design of a master-worker GA using BOINC work handling daemons consists in incorporating the generational loop in the work generator. This latter would create input files containing each the gene string of one or a set of individuals of the population. It would create the corresponding workunits and leave the floor to the feeder and scheduler to scatter the jobs. Knowing that the assimilator is the unit responsible for assimilating computation results, it should then notify the work generator of the availability of current generation fitness results as soon as they are ready.

BOINC uses redundancy to deal with the volatility of clients and unreliability of their results. Thus, for each workunit (in our case fitness evaluation(s)), multiple replicas of the same task (result) are produced and sent to different clients. The validation process will ensure that, for each workunit, the output produced by the different hosts match. The replication and validation process may lead to multiple scenarios:

- The optimal situation is that initially two results are sent out to performing hosts. The two clients immediately process the tasks and send back the data, right away. The two outputs match and the evaluation is done.
- In most cases, clients do not start computation immediately because they might be busy doing other computations for other projects. That is why each task has a deadline and the client should return the results before the deadline is met. In case the deadline is passed, the server will issue another job replica. The server creates another job replica also in case the output of the first ones do not match. These situations can significantly slow down the whole process since the above described synchronous master-worker PGA has to wait for them to continue with the next generation.

2.2.2. Iterative versus steady-state algorithms

To overcome the above limitation, there are two possible solutions:

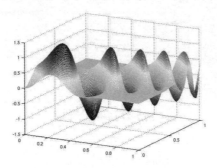

Figure 3. Plot of the benchmark function g

- One can use a master-worker steady-state algorithm where there is no iterations: the population is continuously updated by creating new individuals when clients request work and replacing old individuals by the new ones when clients return the new fitness values. Desell et al. described their implementation of this algorithm in [18] (where they call it Asynchronous Genetic Search)
- An alternative solution is to conserve the iterative character of the master-worker model while tweaking the algorithm and the BOINC project configuration.

We adopted the second solution here for two main reasons. First, for our target application, the optimization purpose is not to find the absolute optimum but rather end up with a sample population that represents regions of the domain around a number of significant maxima: multimodal optimization. Niching techniques in GAs allow such procedure. However, all the known niching techniques have been designed for iterative GAs. Thus, we need to prepare the ground for such addition to the algorithm. Besides, although earlier studies showed that steady-state PGAs may work as well as (or even outperform) iterative GAs, our experience with steady-state was not as successful. Indeed, using the MPI implementation of the steady-state algorithm and the iterative master-worker algorithms in MCS_GA we carried out some performance and robustness comparison through benchmark optimizations. We ran 20 instances of the maximization of the benchmark function g (c.f. figure 3):

$$g : [0, 1] \times [0, 1] \rightarrow R$$

$$g(x, y) = \frac{\sin(\mu^2(x^2+y^2)) \exp^{-\lambda(x-y)^2}}{\log(\theta+x^2+y^2)} \ where \ \mu = 4, \ \lambda = 12 \ and \ \theta = 2$$

with the same selection, crossover and mutation operators and GA parameters using the iterative master-worker and the steady-state master-worker algorithms. We chose this benchmark function because several local maximum of the same order coexist, which is typical of our prairie model. Our comparison (c.f. Table 1) on the benchmark showed that though steady-state requires less fitness evaluations, it is less robust: results quality was much poorer.

GAs are not parameter-free methods, so we decided not to tune the GA parameter to our specific target application, but rather to use commonly used mutation and crossover rates. It would be difficult to optimize the parameter set of a GA for complex models such that of the Virtual Prairie application.

	Iterative master-worker	Steady-state master-worker
average nbr of evaluations	5615.2	2335.45
result average	1.330928	1.235792
result standard deviation	0.057996	0.177931
best result obtained	1.350497	1.350497

Table 1. Iterative versus steady-state comparative study

2.2.3. The iterative solution

We present here the heuristic rules that we added to the GA running on top of BOINC. These heuristics aim mainly at controlling the time required for the evaluation of the objective values of the population at each generation.

As soon as jobs for one generation are created, a deadline is fixed for the assimilator to report their outcome to the work generator. This deadline is initialized by an experimental estimation which depend (1) on the average execution time of the objective function evaluation and (2) the average time needed for the scheduler to scatter the jobs (depending on the population size). When, the assimilator meets this deadline two scenarios are possible:

- All the results were already received and sent to the work generator.
- Some results are still missing. In which case, the assimilator would notify the work generator of the end of computation if it already received at least 90% of the populations individuals fitness values or will extend the deadline if this threshold is not yet met.

• To lower the risk of missing some critical information in the remaining 10% individuals, the work generator tries to ensure that the 90% individuals that have been evaluated would be the best fit ones of the generation. So, at creation time, the work generator favors some individuals by assigning higher priorities to their corresponding jobs. Higher priorities are assigned to individuals with higher probability of being more fit. This probability is inversely proportional to the distance between each new individual and the best individuals of the past generation. Such probability can be also computed according to other similarity criteria between new and old individuals.

• To speed up the processing of each generation, jobs with higher priorities are sent only to reliable hosts which have a short turnaround time and low error rate. Besides, these jobs see their initial deadline reduced by a given ratio according to their priority level. That is why these jobs will have a very good chance of being returned before the generation deadline fixed for the assimilator.

• Finally all the jobs are replicated more than twice while their outputs are assimilated as soon as the two first matching results are received. This reduces the effect of late and erroneous results. This technique is affordable only with BOINC because the computing resources are abundant and cheap.

The job deadline, the priority of the job, and the redundancy factor of the job can be dynamically adjusted according to the behavior of the first generations. A statistical model that can be dynamically fitted on the run would be presented in a companion journal paper.

2.3. Tests and results

The ViP BOINC project served as a testbed for our GA. We ran maximizations of the benchmark function g described in section 2.2.2 using a population of 100 individuals, proportional selection and two-point crossover. The GA converges, when for 10 generations, the maximum obtained remains unchanged. The computation of the benchmark function is very fast which is not the case of real applications. So, we added 200 GFLOP of dummy cpu usage in the objective function to simulate a real application.

We ran the same maximizations using the master-worker MPI version of MCS_GA on:

- SiCortex computer using 100 cores (700 MHz).
- Beowulf cluster using 34 Opteron processors (2 GHz).

	BOINC	SiCortex	Beowulf
objective function computation time (avg)	variable	1270 s	365 s
GA execution time (avg)	63988 s	71305	67384
average result obtained	1.350497	1.350497	1.350497

Table 2. Performance of GA on different platforms

Table 2 details the results and performance obtained. It shows that the techniques used in our GA solution on BOINC allowed to obtain a comparable performance to that of a medium size SiCortex or a small size Beowulf cluster, when we imposed relatively short deadlines for the jobs (2 hours). However, BOINC offers two more advantages:

- the costs of acquiring, powering and maintaining clusters is much higher than those of a BOINC server setup and maintenance. So, BOINC becomes a viable solution for scientists who can not afford access to parallel computers.
- with the abundance of the computing resources offered by BOINC (the ViP project has more than 2000 hosts), we can perform optimizations with large population sizes without dramatically increasing the overall execution time. The only overhead that will be added is the time needed for scattering the jobs and which is much lower than the objective function computation cost. Large populations are much needed for multimodal optimizations.

3. Conclusion

In a quest for exploiting a cheap and abundant computation resource, that is volunteer computing, this paper describes the implementation of a genetic algorithm on top of BOINC. Though the iterative master-worker parallel genetic algorithm fits the distributed character of this environment, the volatility and unreliability of the resources offered by BOINC slows down significantly the process. The enhancements added to this algorithm combined to the proper use of BOINC features (like priorities) provided execution times competitive with those of much more expensive parallel computing resources. We expect that a single optimization of a virtual prairie with 5 species would require a dedicated Beowulf cluster with a thousand processor during several month. Because in our continuous dialogue with the interdisciplinary team of ecologists, we keep improving our model as more experimental result in the field come, we view volunteer computing as the best solution to our ViP project.

Acknowledgements

We would like to thank K. Crabb for supporting the ViP BOINC project at the University of Houston Research Computing Center as well as D. Anderson, the principal investigator of BOINC from University of California at Berkeley.

References

[1] D. E. Goldberg. *Genetic Algorithms in Search, Optimization, and Machine Learning*. Addison-Wesley Professional, January 1989.

[2] J. R. Koza. *Genetic Programming: On the Programming of Computers by Means of Natural Selection.* The MIT press, Cambridge, MT, December 1992.

[3] L. Dumas and L. El Alaoui. How genetic algorithms can improve a pacemaker efficiency. In *GECCO '07: Proceedings of the 2007 GECCO conference companion on Genetic and evolutionary computation*, pages 2681–2686, New York, NY, USA, 2007. ACM.

[4] Y. Gao, H. Rong, and J. Z. Huang. Adaptive grid job scheduling with genetic algorithms. *Future Generation Computer Systems*, 21(1):151–161, 2005.

[5] S. Karungaru, M. Fukumi, and N. Akamatsu. Automatic human faces morphing using genetic algorithms based control points selection. *International Journal of Innovative Computing, Information & Control*, 3(2):247–256, April 2007.

[6] M. Olhofer, T. Arima, T. Sonoda, and B. Sendhoff. Optimisation of a stator blade used in a transonic compressor cascade with evolution strategies. In I. Parmee, editor, *Adaptive Computing in Design and Manufacture (ACDM)*, pages 45–54. Springer Verlag, 2000.

[7] E. Cantu-Paz. Designing efficient master-slave parallel genetic algorithms, 1997. Available online at: ftp://ftp-illigal.ge.uiuc.edu/pub/papers/IlliGALs/97004.ps.Z.

[8] E. Cantu-Paz. A survey of parallel genetic algorithms. *Calculateurs Paralleles, Reseaux et Systems Repartis*, 10(2):141–171, 1998.

[9] M. Nowostawski and R. Poli. Parallel genetic algorithms taxonomy. In *Proceedings of the third international conference on Knowledge-based information Engineering Systems*, pages 88–92, August 1999.

[10] D. Lim, O. Y.S, Y. Jin, B. Sendhoff, and L. B. A. Efficient hierarchical parallel genetic algorithms using grid computing. *Future Generation Computer Systems*, 23(4):658–670, 2007.

[11] D. P. Anderson, J. Cobb, E. Korpela, M. Lebofsky, and D. Werthimer. Seti@home: an experiment in public-resource computing. *Communications of the ACM*, 45(11):56–61, 2002.

[12] D. P. Anderson and G. Fedak. The computational and storage potential of volunteer computing. In *CCGRID '06: Proceedings of the Sixth IEEE International Symposium on Cluster Computing and the Grid*, pages 73–80, Washington, DC, USA, 2006. IEEE Computer Society.

[13] D. P. Anderson. Boinc: A system for public-resource computing and storage. In *GRID '04: Proceedings of the 5th IEEE/ACM International Workshop on Grid Computing*, pages 4–10, Washington, DC, USA, 2004. IEEE Computer Society.

[14] M. Garbey, C. Mony, and M. Smaoui. Fluid flow - agent based hybrid model for the simulation of virtual prairies. In *to appear soon in the proceedings of the 20th Parallel Computational Fluid Dynamics Conference*, May 2008.

[15] M. Smaoui, M. Garbey, and C. Mony. Virtual prairie: going green with volunteer computing. In *2008 IEEE Asia-Pacific Services Computing Conference*, pages 427–434. IEEE Computer Society, December 2008.

[16] C. Mony, M. Garbey, M. Smaoui, and M. Benot. Optimal profiles for clonal plant growth: a modelling approach. submitted to a journal in ecology, 2009.

[17] D. Levine. Users guide to the pgapack parallel genetic algorithm library, technical report anl-991 8, 1995. Technical report, Argonne National Laboratory, 1995. PGAPACK is available via anonymous ftp at ftp.mcs.anl.gov or from URL http://info.mcs.anl.gov/pub/pgapack/pgapack.tar.Z.

[18] T. Desell, B. Szymanski, and C. Verla Asynchronous genetic search for scientific modeling on large-scale heterogeneous environments In *IEEE International Symposium on Parallel and Distributed Processing, 2008*, pages 1–12, Miami, Florida. April 2008.

Parallel Computing: From Multicores and GPU's to Petascale
B. Chapman et al. (Eds.)
IOS Press, 2010
© 2010 The authors and IOS Press. All rights reserved.
doi:10.3233/978-1-60750-530-3-220

RPC/MPI Hybrid Implementation of OpenFMO

— *All Electron Calculations of a Ribosome* —

Yuichi INADOMI [a], Toshiya TAKAMI [b], Jun MAKI [a], Taizo KOBAYASHI [b], and Mutsumi AOYAGI [b]

[a] *Next-Generation Supercomputer Development Partnership, ISIT,*
3-8-33-711 Momochihama, Sawara-ku, Fukuoka 814-0001, JAPAN
[b] *Research Institute for Information Technology (RIIT), Kyushu University,*
6-10-1 Hakozaki, Higashi-ku, Fukuoka 812-8581, JAPAN

Abstract. Robust and effective implementations for large-scale realistic application programs are analyzed under the assumption that they are executed on the next-generation supercomputer system. In order to estimate performance of all-electron calculations of a ribosome, a discrete-event simulation for the parallel program is introduced, in which execution of program components and communications between them is emulated. Through the analysis, it is realized that middleware developed for Grids is still valid and useful even for massively-parallel supercomputer systems since they have a huge number of cores and full stability over weeks is not guaranteed.

Keywords. fragment molecular orbital method, fault tolerant, RPC/MPI, ribosome, quantum biology

1. Introduction

In July 17, 2009, Riken announced a new system configuration only with a scalar processing architecture for its next-generation supercomputer (NGS) [1] toward peta flops computing, which is modified from a former hybrid one with two different architectures: an interconnected vector unit and an interconnected scalar unit. Riken and Fujitsu also disclosed that the scalar processor is based on SPARC64 (8 cores, 128 giga flops).

When we consider realistic applications in science and engineering, robustness becomes one of the most important factors. If you implement a program by a flat parallelization scheme using Message Passing Interface (MPI), all the calculation will be aborted by a trouble in one process. Since large-scale applications often require a continued execution over several days or a week, it is apparent that simple use of the flat MPI implementation is dangerous unless fault-tolerant properties are available [2].

Over the last decade, various middleware has been developed for Grid computing systems, some of which implement fault-tolerant properties to manage thousands of computers distributed over wide-area networks. When we take notice of robustness, their software heritage must be used even for massively parallel supercomputers. One such software is Ninf-G [3] known as a reference implementation of GridRPC, an RPC mechanism tailored for the Grid, which has been used to perform large-scale simulations [4,5,6]

One of the application areas gathering public interests is quantum biology which studies quantum mechanical properties of bio-molecules in a cell, where large-scale electronic state calculations are required. One of the drawbacks in the calculation of large molecules is $O(N^4)$ computations to a problem size N, e.g., the number of atoms. The Fragment Molecular Orbital (FMO) method [7,8,9] solves this problem by dividing a molecule into many fragments, each of which consists of several tens of atoms. A self-consistent field calculation is performed on each single fragment under quantum mechanical interactions between surrounding fragments, and a fragment-pair correction is applied after convergence of all the single-fragment calculations. Through these refinements, FMO provides useful information on a total energy and electron densities of the molecule.

This paper is arranged as follows. In Section 2, the RPC/MPI hybrid implementation of OpenFMO [10,11] is introduced, which enables us to plan the all-electron calculation of a ribosome. In Section 3, an application simulator is used to estimate performance of the program on massively parallel computers, where preliminary calculations of a ribosome are analyzed from the viewpoints of robustness and performance. In Section 4, we conclude this article by considering appropriate structures of applications for the next-generation massively parallel systems.

2. RPC/MPI hybrid implementation of FMO

FMO is one of the prominent methods which provides electronic-states of large bio-molecules, i.e., proteins, nuclear acids, etc. The electronic states of a molecule are approximated by electronic states of each fragment (Monomer) and each pair of fragments (Dimer). According to the standard FMO flow in Fig. 1(a), calculations for Monomers and Dimers are executed in parallel (coarse-grained parallel) as well as each electronic-state calculation within a Monomer or a Dimer can also be parallelized (fine-grained parallel). Through this implementation, FMO has been effectively executed in distributed parallel computers up to a thousand of processors [4,5].

Existing parallel implementations of the FMO method, found in ABINIT-MP [9] and GAMESS [12], are based on parallel APIs such as MPI or GDDI [13] because of simplicity and performance in relatively small systems. Since the purpose of these programs are stable and reliable execution on current mainstream

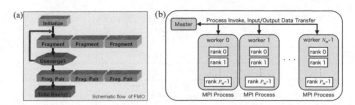

Figure 1. (a) Flow of FMO calculations, and (b) master-worker implementation of OpenFMO.

machines, it is almost impossible to apply them to the next-generation massively parallel computers without modification.

For relatively small systems, two implementations has been analyzed in OpenFMO [14]: one uses collective communications and synchronous transfers based on the MPI-1 standard; the other uses one-sided communications based on the MPI-2 standard. In addition to these, the third implementation of OpenFMO, the RPC/MPI hybrid model, is introduced in this paper. Because of the intrinsic hierarchical structure of the FMO method, it is naturally implemented in a master-worker type programming model. The master process assigns computational tasks (Monomer or Dimer calculations) to workers (logical groups of processors), where the electronic-states calculations for a Monomer/Dimer are also parallelized by MPI (see Fig. 1(b)). It is expected that this implementation retains both of robustness and performance.

When we construct the FMO calculation according to the RPC/MPI hybrid model, it is required that the RPC middleware supports invocations of MPI processes and communications between the master and workers. Such property is provided by Ninf-G [3] which is implemented so as to use many distributed computers on Grid environments with fault-tolerant functions such as a heartbeat function for checking status of remote jobs.

2.1. All electron calculations of a ribosome

All electron calculation of a ribosome on NGS is planned using OpenFMO. Ribosomes are one of the structures in a cell. For examples, eukaryotes have 80S ribosomes consisting of a small (40S) and large (60S) sub-unit. They contain thousands of amino-acids and nucleotides, and their geometric information has been published in Protein Data Bank (PDB) [15] (ID:1s1h and 1s1i). All electron calculation of the ribosome is executed by the FMO method after it is divided into tens of thousands of fragments including water molecules.

In order to prepare geometric information of the ribosome with surrounding water molecules, however, it is necessary to execute further molecular modeling procedures which include making up for missing residues or atoms, arranging water molecules according to statistical distribution functions, and so forth. In this contribution, only preliminary calculations of each sub-unit, 40S and 60S, without water molecules are analyzed as benchmark studies.

Table 1. Parameters of inputs for the OpenFMO emulator.

	40S sub-unit	60S sub-unit
PDB ID	1s1h	1s1i
Number of fragments	4121	7024
Number of atoms / average	88843 / 21.6	159973 / 22.8
Number of basis sets / average	856373 / 207.8	1566982 / 223.1
Data size / average (bytes)	891,678,996 / 216,374	1,718,917,504 / 244,721

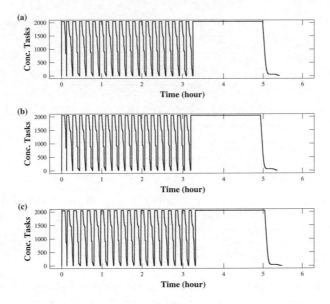

Figure 2. Simulated time series for OpenFMO calculations of the smaller sub-unit (40S, PDB:1s1h). The number of concurrent tasks are shown for implementations by the use of (a) MPI-1 (collective communications), (b) MPI-2 (one-sided communications), and (c) RPC.

3. Emulation of OpenFMO by a Discrete-Event Simulator

There are various kinds of simulator in every area of science and engineering. Continuous simulators emulate real-world dynamics or microscopic objects according to differential equations given by physics, chemistry, and biology, where the OpenFMO is also a simulator based on quantum chemistry. On the other hand, discrete-event simulators [16], describing dynamics of objects in waiting queues, are often used to emulate events in computers: instruction set simulators are used to design and develop new computers; network simulators [17] analyze packet transfers over distributed environments.

By combining these simulators for instruction executions and packet transfers [18], an application simulator for parallel computers can be constructed theoretically. However, it is easily realized that, even if it might be executed on large computers with huge resources, it takes much time to analyze the result to extract useful information. Fortunately, since the FMO method has layered structure, we can construct a reliable emulator on the coarse-grained level without requiring large-scale resources.

The analysis of the OpenFMO in the present paper is performed by a discrete-event simulator instead of actual execution of OpenFMO programs on NGS. The procedure of the emulation is as follows: (1) a fragment file for simulator is created from geometry information of the molecule, where missing atoms and hydrogen atoms are supplemented according to the standard structure database for residue and nucleotide; (2) input files for specification are defined from machine parameters and benchmark executions in smaller systems; (3) parallelization scheme definition files are written according to the implementations of the OpenFMO (see below); (4) execution of the simulator, and analysis of the result.

PDB:1s1h

MPI-1	calc: 66.5%	comm: 1.8%	idle: 31.7%	3:15:28.8
MPI-2	calc: 67.7%	(comm: 12.9%)	idle: 32.3%	3:11:54.8
RPC	calc: 65.5%	(comm: 12.4%)	idle: 31.8%	3:18:23.6

PDB:1s1i

MPI-1	calc: 79.2%	comm: 1.2%	idle: 19.6%	9:20:48.1
MPI-2	calc: 80.2%	(comm: 7.7%)	idle: 19.8%	9:13:31.9
RPC	calc: 79.6%	(comm: 7.6%)	idle: 19.7%	9:18:07.4

Figure 3. Predicted rates for calculation, communication, and idle time are shown for the smaller sub-unit (40S, PDB:1s1h) and the larger sub-unit (60S, PDB:1s1i) of a ribosome. Note that communications and calculations are executed concurrently in implementations by the MPI-2 (one-sided communication) and the RPC/MPI hybrid method. Times shown in the right of the bar graph are elapsed time of the Monomer calculations.

It is assumed that the OpenFMO is executed on a massively parallel machine which consists of 2048 computational units with 256 cores in each. Only communications between these units (10Gbps) are emulated while fine-grained communications within a unit over 256 cores are ignored. In the actual programming of OpenFMO, `MPI_Comm_split` and other communicator handling functions are used to realize hierarchical communications over and within those units in the implementations by MPI-1 and MPI-2 [14], and separate MPI jobs are invoked at each computing unit in the RPC/MPI hybrid implementation. Three different parallelization schemes are introduced:

MPI-1: All the density data are distributed over all units through collective communications such as `MPI_Bcast` synchronously. Therefore, all the calculations of fragments wait throughout the data transfer.

MPI-2: One-sided communications in the MPI-2 standard are used, where asynchronous transfer of the density data is minimized by `MPI_put` and `MPI_get`. In this implementation, waiting time for communication is ignored.

RPC: The RPC/MPI hybrid implementation requires a master process other than the computational ones. The density data required in computational units are transferred through the master process. Conflicts occur at the master when the data transfers are concentrated.

The CPU time estimated for i-th fragment can be written by a sum of 2-centered integrals and 4-centered integrals,

$$T_i \approx C_2 \left(N_b^{(i)} \right)^2 \sum_{\text{far}} N_a^{(k)} + C_4 \left(N_b^{(i)} \right)^2 \sum_{\text{near}} \left(N_b^{(k)} \right)^2, \tag{1}$$

where $N_b^{(i)}$ and $N_a^{(i)}$ are the number of basis functions and the number of atoms in i-th fragment, respectively. The sums are taken over the fragments far from the i-th fragment and ones near the i-th fragment. The coefficients C_2 and C_4 can be estimated by benchmark executions of FMO calculations on smaller machines. The number of fragments near a fragment is relatively small (≈ 20) compared

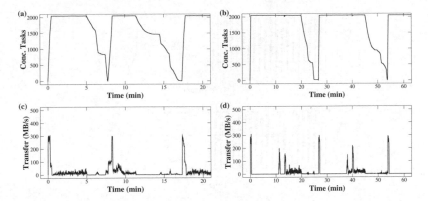

Figure 4. Simulated time series for OpenFMO calculations: (a) the numbers of concurrent tasks for 40S sub-unit (PDB:1s1h); (b) ones for 60S sub-unit (PDB:1s1i); (c) the effective transfer rates through an RPC-master process for the 40S sub-unit; (d) ones for the 60S sub-unit.

to the all the number of fragment even in the spherical molecule, and only the density data near the fragment is necessary in each fragment calculation. Thus, the transferred data size in MPI-2 and RPC implementations is small compared to one in the MPI-1 implementation.

3.1. Performance Simulation in the Ideal Environment

In Fig. 2, simulated results are shown under the idealized situation in which no breakdown occurs. The total execution times are 5.41, 5.35, and 5.48 hours for MPI-1, MPI-2, and RPC implementations, respectively. Though almost no difference is found, the highest performance is the MPI-2 case, since data transfers are minimum and the communication time is hidden by the use of MPI_Put/MPI_Get.

Problem-size dependency is also analyzed in Fig. 3 by comparing time consumption for 40S and 60S sub-units. The ratio for communication becomes smaller when the number of fragments is larger. This is explained by the ratio of the computational cost $O(N_f{}^2)$ and the density data size $O(N_f)$. Figure 4 is a magnified view of Monomer calculations in the RPC model to show how data transfers block the calculations.

3.2. Robustness and Performance in a Realistic Environment

In parallel applications with the standard MPI, breakdown of only one core aborts the whole calculation. In order to ensure stable executions, the use of FT-MPI [2] or other fault-tolerant implementation of MPI is necessary. Unfortunately, it has not been announced that fault-tolerant functions are implemented in the officially supported MPI in NGS. Since it is difficult to assume the fault-tolerant properties of MPI in NGS, only the RPC/MPI hybrid implementation is analyzed in this subsection. However, once we have an application written in RPC/MPI, it is not difficult to rewrite them only by MPI with fault-tolerant properties, and the performance of them can be guaranteed by the analysis of the RPC model.

Three cases are analyzed under the random breakdown of cores in Fig. 5, where the mean time to failure (MTTF) of a core is set to 100 years, 10 years, and

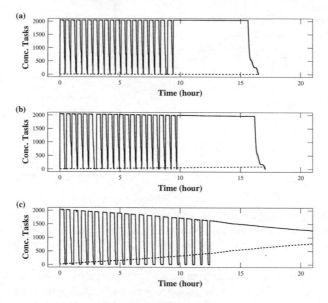

Figure 5. Simulated time series of the number of concurrent tasks for the RPC/MPI hybrid OpenFMO. This emulation is performed for the larger sub-unit (60S, PDB:1s1i) under the value of MTTF of each core: (a) 100 years (876,000 hours); (b) 10 years (87,600 hours); (c) 1 year (8,760 hours). The dashed curves represent the numbers of broken workers.

1 year. In this simulation, the numbers of units broken during the calculations were 9, 89, and 813, respectively. The total execution times predicted were 16.51 hours for the case of 100 years and 17.07 hours for the case of 10 years, which is comparable to the case of no breakdown (16.37 hours, not shown in Fig. 5), while the total time is 23.04 hours for the case of 1 year. Thus, the RPC/MPI hybrid model for OpenFMO shows both of robustness and performance even if the random breakdown of cores is inevitable.

4. Conclusion

Implementations and executions of a realistic large-scale application were studied. Through discrete-event simulations of the program execution, it was shown that the RPC/MPI hybrid implementation is safely and effectively introduced for OpenFMO calculations. It is interesting that some of middleware developed for Grids are still useful even for the massively parallel computers.

It is important to tell what program structure is applicable to the next-generation supercomputer. The application emulator for the OpenFMO was easily constructed and effectively used to predict performances because of the hierarchical structure of the FMO calculations. The point is whether such well-formed application structures are realized or not. The program emulator on massively parallel computers can be combined with well-designed integrated tools for application developments by which the hierarchical programming style is naturally introduced. Conversely, without such tools, it is difficult to develop large-scale applications with both robustness and performance.

Acknowledgments

This work is supported by the next-generation supercomputer project, Riken.

References

[1] Next-generation supercomputer, Riken, http://www.nsc.riken.jp/index-eng.html
[2] FT-MPI, http://icl.cs.utk.edu/ftmpi/
[3] Y. Tanaka, H. Nakada, S. Sekiguchi, T. Suzumura, and S. Matuoka, "Ninf-G: A Reference Implementation of RPC-based Programming Middleware for Grid Computing," J. Grid Comp. **1**, 41–51 (2003).
[4] T. Ikegami, T. Ishida, D. G. Fedorov, K. Kitaura, Y. Inadomi, H. Umeda, M. Yokokawa, and S. Sekiguchi, "Full electron calculation beyond 20,000 atoms: Ground electronic state of photosynthetic proteins," SC05 Tech. Paper, Proc. ACM/IEEE Supercomputing 2005.
[5] T. Ikegami, J. Maki, T. Takami, Y. Tanaka, M. Yokokawa, S. Sekiguchi, and M. Aoyagi, "GridFMO — Quantum chemistry of proteins on the grid," Proc. GRID 2007, pp.153–160 (IEEE Conf. Proc. 2007).
[6] H. Takemiya, Y. Tanaka, S. Sekiguchi, S. Ogata, R. K. Kalia, A. Nakano, and P. Vashishta, "Sustainable adaptive grid supercomputing: Multiscale simulation of semiconductor processing across the pacific," SC06 Tech. Paper, Proc. ACM/IEEE Supercomputing 2006.
[7] K. Kitaura, T. Sawai, T. Asada, T. Nakano, and M. Uebayasi, "Pair interaction molecular orbital method: an approximate computational method for molecular interactions," Chem. Phys. Lett. **312**, 319–324 (1999).
[8] K. Kitaura, E. Ikeo, T. Asada, T. Nakano, and M. Uebayasi, "Fragment molecular orbital method: an approximate computational method for large molecules," Chem. Phys. Lett. **313**, 701–706 (1999).
[9] T. Nakano, T. Kaminuma, T. Sato, Y. Akiyama, M. Uebayasi, and K. Kitaura, "Fragment molecular orbital method: application to polypeptides," Chem. Phys. Lett. **318**, 614–618 (2000).
[10] OpenFMO project, http://www.openfmo.org/OpenFMO/
[11] T. Takami, J. Maki, J. Ooba, Y. Inadomi, H. Honda, R. Susukita, K. Inoue, T. Kobayashi, R. Nogita and M. Aoyagi, "Multi-physics Extension of OpenFMO Framework," AIP Conf. Proc. **963** (vol.2, Part A), 122–125 (2007).
[12] M. W. Schmidt, K. K. Baldridge, J. A. Boatz, S. T. Elbert, M. S. Gordon, J. J. Jensen, S. Koseki, N, Matsunaga, K. A. Nguyen, S. Su, T. L. Windus, M. Dupuis, and J. A. Montgomery, "General Atomic and Molecular Electronic Structure System," J. Comput. Chem. **14**, 1347–1363 (1993).
[13] jD.G. Fedorov, R. M. Olson, K. Kitaura, M. S. Gordon, and S. Koseki, "A New Hierarchical Parallelization Scheme: Generalized Distributed Data Interface (GDDI), and an Application to the Fragment Molecular Orbital Method (FMO)," J. Comput. Chem. **25**, 872–880 (2004).
[14] J. Maki, Y. Inadomi, T. Takami, R. Susukita, H. Honda, J. Ooba, T. Kobayashi, R. Nogita, K. Inoue, and M. Aoyagi, "One-sided Communication Implementation in FMO Method," Proc. HPCAsia 2007, pp. 137–142 (2007).
[15] Protein Data Bank, http://www.pdb.org/pdb
[16] Discrete-event simulation language based on Python, http://simpy.sourceforge.net/
[17] Open Source Network Simulator, http://nsnam.isi.edu/nsnam/
[18] R. Susukita, H. Ando, M. Aoyagi, H. Honda, Y. Inadomi, K. Inoue, S. Ishizuki, Y. Kimura, H. Komatsu, M. Kurokawa, K. J. Murakami, H. Shibamura, S. Yamamura, and Y. Yu, "Performance prediction of large-scale parallell system and application using macro-level simulation," SC08 Tech. Paper, Proc. ACM/IEEE Supercomputing, Art. No. 20 (2008).

Parallel Computing: From Multicores and GPU's to Petascale
B. Chapman et al. (Eds.)
IOS Press, 2010
© *2010 The authors and IOS Press. All rights reserved.*
doi:10.3233/978-1-60750-530-3-228

When Clouds become Green: the Green Open Cloud Architecture

Anne-Cécile ORGERIE [a] and Laurent LEFÈVRE [a]

[a] *INRIA RESO - Université de Lyon - LIP (UMR CNRS, INRIA, ENS, UCB)*
École Normale Supérieure - 46, allée d'Italie - 69364 LYON Cedex 07 - FRANCE
annececile.orgerie@ens-lyon.fr, laurent.lefevre@inria.fr

Abstract. Virtualization solutions appear as alternative approaches for companies to consolidate their operational services on a physical infrastructure, while preserving specific functionalities inside the Cloud perimeter (e.g., security, fault tolerance, reliability). These consolidation approaches are explored to propose some energy reduction while switching OFF unused computing nodes. We study the impact of virtual machines aggregation in terms of energy consumption. Some load-balancing strategies associated with the migration of virtual machines inside the Cloud infrastructures will be showed. We will present the design of a new original energy-efficient Cloud infrastructure called Green Open Cloud.

Keywords. Energy Efficiency, Large-Scale Systems, Cloud Infrastructures, Migration

Introduction

Cloud infrastructures have recently become a center of attention. They can support dynamic operational infrastructures adapted to the requirements of distributed applications. Cloud systems provide on-demand computing power and storage, so they can perfectly fit the users' requirements. But as they reach enormous sizes in terms of equipments, energy consumption becomes one of the main challenges for large-scale integration.

This paper deals with the support of energy-efficient frameworks dedicated to Cloud architectures. Virtualization is a key feature of the Clouds, since it allows high performance, improved manageability, and fault tolerance. In this first step of our work, our infrastructure is focusing its action on this essential aspect. It also uses migration, which brings the benefit of moving workload between the virtual machines (VMs).

The remainder of this paper is organized as follows. Section 1 reviews related works. This is followed by an evaluation of the electric cost of a virtual machine in Section 2. Section 3 outlines the architecture and the components of the energy-aware Cloud infrastructure that we propose. The conclusion and future works are reviewed in Section 4.

1. Related Works

Innovative technologies have broadly contributed to the expansion of Clouds. They differ from Grids as explained in [2] and can be part of the next-generation data centers with virtualized nodes and on-demand provisioning. Clouds are already used by numerous companies. For instance, Salesforce.com handles 54,000 companies and their 1.5 million employees via just 1,000 servers [18]. Different manufacturers, like IBM [1], also support and provide Clouds infrastructures and services for customers companies. Cloud computing is, by nature, dynamically scalable and virtualized resources are often provided as a service over the Internet [7]. This opens up wide new horizons where everything is considered as a service (infrastructure, platform, software, computing, storage). Among the other advantages of the Clouds are scalability, cost, and reliability. Cloud providers such as Amazon[1] should however face doubts on security and loss of control over sensitive data. The other main issue is the accounting.

Virtualization is the key feature of the Clouds, which allows improving the efficiency of large-scale distributed systems [15]. This technology needs powerful resource-management mechanisms [6] to benefit from live migration and suspend/resume mechanisms that allow moving a virtual machine from a host node to another one, stopping the virtual machine and starting it again later. The design of resource-management policies is a challenging (NP-hard) and dynamic problem.

Live migration [5] greatly improves the capacities and the features of Cloud environments: it facilitates fault management, load balancing, and low-level system maintenance. Migration operations imply more flexible resource management: when a virtual machine is deployed on a node, we can still move it to another one. It offers a new stage of virtualization by suppressing the concept of locality in virtualized environments.

However, this technique is complex and more difficult to use over the MAN/WAN [16] than in a cluster. IP addressing is a problem since the system should change the address of the migrated virtual machine which does not remain in the same network domain. Moreover, it impacts the performances of the virtual machines by adding a non negligible overhead [17].

With virtualization came some ideas concerning energy management [15,8]. Indeed, large-scale distributed systems are always increasing in size, and thus in power consumption. Each node can be virtualized and host several virtual machines.

So, at the same time, virtualization addresses the limitations in cooling and power delivery. This leads to the design of new techniques of energy management in virtualized systems. In [10], the authors propose a management system that uses different power management policies on the virtualized resources of each virtual machine to globally control power consumption.

The emerging concept of consolidation is directly linked with energy management in Clouds. The consolidation techniques aim to manage the jobs and combine them on the physical nodes. These techniques can be used to optimize energy usage [14].

2. Energy Cost of Virtual Machines

Cloud computing seems to be a promising solution to the increasing demand of computing power needed by more and more complex applications. We have seen that virtualization is promoted by several researches to decrease the energy consumption of large-scale distributed systems. However, the studies often lack real values for the electric consumption of virtualized infrastructures.

---

[1] http://aws.amazon.com

Our experimental Cloud consists of HP Proliant 85 G2 Servers (2.2 GHz, 2 dual core CPUs per node) with XenServer 5.0[2] installed on them.

Each Cloud node is linked to an external wattmeter that logs the power consumption of the node every second.

The measurement precision of our experimental platform is 0.125 watts and the maximum frequency is one measure per second.

On Xen, the VM live migration consists in transferring its memory image from the host Cloud node to the new one. If the VM is running, it is stopped for a period of time during the copy of the last memory pages (the ones that are often modified).

So when a migration occurs, the end of the job which is in the migrated VM is delayed by a certain amount of time (the period during which the VM is stopped): we denote that time T_m. This time does not include the whole duration of the migration process. Indeed, we have the same phenomenon as in the previous paragraph: competition at the hypervisor level. If several migrations are required at the same time on the same node, they are queued and processed one by one by the hypervisor (this can also be influenced by the network bandwidth).

On Figure 1 we have launched six *cpuburn*[3], one by one in six different VMs on Cloud node 1. The first starts at $t = 10$; we see that consumption increases to reach 219 watts. Then the second starts and consumption reaches 230 watts. The third starts and the node consumes 242 watts. The fourth leads to 253 watts. The appearance of the fifth and the sixth jobs does not increase consumption.

Indeed, since the jobs are CPU intensive (*cpuburn* uses 100 % of a CPU's capacity) and since there are only four cores on the node (2 dual core CPUs), they are fully used with the first four VMs. The fifth VM is free in terms of energy cost because it should share resources that would have been fully used without it too.

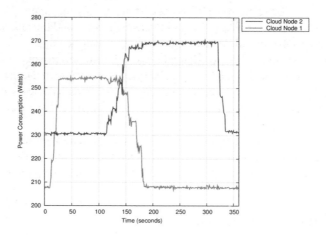

Figure 1. Migration of virtual machines

---

[2]XenServer is a cloud-proven virtualization platform that delivers the critical features of live migration and centralized multi-server management (http://citrix.com/English/ps2/products/product. asp?contentID=683148).

[3]cpuburn is a software designed to apply a high load to the processor (http://pages.sbcglobal. net/redelm/).

Each *cpuburn* job lasts 300 seconds (Figure 1). At $t = 110$, we launch the migration of the 6 VMs from Cloud node 1 to Cloud node 2. The migration requires sustained attention from the hypervisor that should copy the memory pages and send them to the new host node. For this reason, it cannot handle 6 migrations at the same time, they are done one by one.

The competition occurs and we see with the power consumption of Cloud node 2 that the VMs arrived one by one. The consumption of Cloud node 1 begins to decrease during the migration of the third VM. At that time, only three VMs are still running on the node.

Each job ends 5 seconds late, this is T_m. The competition that occurs during the migration request does not affect the jobs running on the last migrated VMs more than the others, since they are still running while waiting for a migration.

Among the components of a Cloud architecture, we have decided to focus on virtualization, which appears as the main technology used in these architectures. Our future works will include algorithms employing other Cloud components, like accounting, pricing, admission control, and scheduling. We also use migration to dynamically unbalance the load between the Cloud nodes in order to shut down some nodes, and thus to save energy.

3. Green Open Clouds

Some previous work on operational large-scale systems show that they are not utilized at their full capacity [9]. Resources (computing, storage, and network) are not used in a constant way by applications and users of large-scale distributed systems (e.g., clusters, grids, clouds). Some inactivity periods can be observed, monitored, and predicted. During these periods, some energy-aware frameworks can reduce energy consumption at a global level.

By generalizing the EARI framework (Energy Aware Resource Infrastructure) proposed for energy-efficient experimental Grids [12,13], we designed the Green Open Cloud architecture (GOC): an energy-aware framework for Clouds (Fig. 2). The described solution supports the "do the same for less" approach, dealing with efficient ON/OFF models combined with prediction solutions.

3.1. Green Open Cloud Architecture

The GOC architecture supports the following facilities:

- switching OFF unused computing, networking, and storage resources;
- predicting computing resources usage in order to switch ON the nodes which are required in a near future;
- aggregating some reservations to avoid frequent ON/OFF cycles;
- green policies which allow users to specify their requests in terms of energy targets.

The GOC infrastructure is added to the usual resource manager of the Cloud as an overlay. We do not modify the job scheduling policies (for example) in order to be adaptable to all the resource managers (such as Eucalyptus [11]).

The GOC infrastructure embeds (Figure 2): a set of electrical monitoring sensors providing dynamic and precise measurements of energy consumption, an energy data collector, a trusted proxy for supporting the network presence of switched-OFF cloud nodes, and an energy-aware resource manager and scheduler.

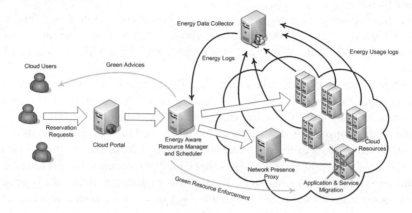

Figure 2. The Green Open Cloud (GOC) Infrastructure

The electrical sensors are connected to each node and they send their consumption measurements to the energy collector. The resource manager has access to this collector and requests for the energy logs when needed. It sends them to the Cloud portal in a well presented manner so that users can see them and see their impact on the power consumption of the nodes. The Cloud portal is responsible for providing some web services to the users and it is the access point for the outside.

The first idea to save energy is to switch off unused nodes because, as we have seen in Section 2, an idle node consumes a lot. We will thus develop our prediction algorithms, which aim to switch on the nodes when required. The energy-aware resource manager makes the decisions concerning the shutdown and the boot of the nodes (green resource enforcement).

The energy-aware resource manager also provides users with "green" advice in order to increase their energy awareness. This consists in proposing several solutions to the user when he submits a job: running it now if possible, or running it later and aggregate it with others (on the same nodes), or allowing migration decisions for running jobs. These green policies would increase resource sharing and so decrease the energy consumption of the Cloud. If the job is urgent, it can still be run immediately if there are available nodes.

3.2. GOC Resource Manager Architecture

The resource manager is the key element that concentrates the energy-efficient functionalities in the GOC architecture. Figure 3 presents the detailed architecture and features of this resources manager, including its interactions with the other components. The green boxes shows the energy-efficient parts.

The user's access portal is directly linked with the admission control module that is responsible for the security. Then, the job acceptance module determines if the user's

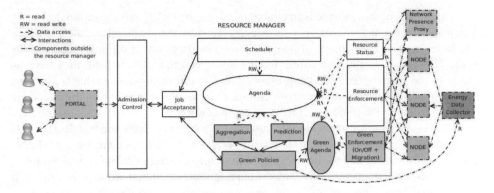

Figure 3. Architecture of the GOC Resource Manager

submission is acceptable according to management policies (for example, the system administrator can put a limit on the resources for a single user). If the submission is accepted, it is sent to the scheduler and the green policies module. The scheduler looks at the agenda to see if the submission can be put into this agenda (enough resources at the date wished by the user). According to the green policies defined by the admin and by using aggregation, the green policies module computes other possible slots for this job which are more energy efficient (the job will consume less energy because it will be aggregated with other ones).

The answers of the scheduler and the green policies module are sent back to the user who picks out one solution between the one he has submitted and the energy-efficient solutions proposed by the green policies module. Afterward, the solution chosen by the user is returned to the scheduler which puts it into the agenda.

At the end of each reservation, if there is totally or partially free nodes (with few VMs), the green policies use prediction to anticipate the next use of the freed resources. If they will be used in a short time, we do not switch them off or migrate their remaining VMs. We switch them off if they are totally free. If they are partially free and if their jobs will not end in a short time, we try to migrate their VMs on other nodes to minimize the number of nodes that are powered on. Otherwise, if they are partially free and if their jobs will end in a short time, we do not change anything. It will indeed cost more energy to migrate the VMs for such a short time. This process is described in Algorithm 1.

Algorithm 1 At the end of each job

    ForEach totally or partially free resource M **Do**
      Predict the next use of M.
      If M will be used in less than T_s **Then**
        Nothing to do for M.
      Else
        If M is totally free **Then**
          Switch off M.
        Else
          If the job(s) of M will end in more than T_m **Then**
            Try to migrate the remaining VMs of M on other partially free resources to minimize the number
            of used resources.
          Else
            Nothing to do for M.

The green policies module is in charge of taking the on/off and migration decisions, then it inscribes it in the green agenda, which is read by the green enforcement module. The latter module is in charge of switching the resources on an off and migrating the VMs. This part is totally transparent for the non-green modules. Indeed, they have no access to the green agenda and the presence proxy is informed when a node is switched off and so can answer for it. The green enforcement module has access to the agenda in order to switch on the resources at the beginning of a job.

The resource enforcement module launchs the jobs and creates and installs the VMs of the users. It reads the agenda to know the reservations features (start time, VM configuration). It ensures that the user will not take more resources than he is allowed to.

The resource status module checks if the nodes are dead (not working properly). If the node has been switched off by the green enforcement module, the presence proxy answers instead. If a node is dead, the module writes it in the agenda.

As we switch off unused nodes, they do not answer to the Cloud resource manager. So they can be considered dead (not usable). This is a problem that we solve by using a trusted proxy. When we switch off a Cloud node, we migrate its basic services (such as ping or heartbeat services for example) on this proxy, which will answer for the node when asked by the resource manager. The key issue is to ensure the security of the infrastructure and to avoid the intrusion of malicious nodes. Our trust delegation model is described in [4].

3.3. Queue and Predictions

As we have seen in Section 2, there is competition between the VMs and between the jobs. Another level of competition appears in the resource manager. The Cloud portal transmits the user's jobs to the resource manager which schedules them on the different Cloud nodes. But it treats user requests one by one. So the requests are first queued.

A key feature of our infrastructure consists in switching off unused nodes. But, we need to boot them before a burst of jobs. Otherwise, if there are no more available host nodes, we should switch on the sleeping nodes when the requests arrive and we will delay them by the booting time.

Our prediction algorithms are based on the average values of the last submissions' inter-arrival times. When we have idle nodes (because they have finished their jobs or because we have migrated their VMs to free them), we need to know if we can switch them off. So we have defined a period of time denoted T_s.

This time is such that the node consumes as much power when it is idle as when we switch it off and on again during that time. So T_s is defined by:

$$T_s = \frac{E_s - P_{OFF}(\delta_{ON \to OFF} + \delta_{OFF \to ON}) + E_{ON \to OFF} + E_{OFF \to ON}}{P_{idle} - P_{OFF}}$$

where P_{idle} is the idle consumption of the node (power in watts), P_{OFF} the power consumption when the node is off (power in watts), $\delta_{ON \to OFF}$ the duration of the node's shutdown (in seconds), $\delta_{OFF \to ON}$ the duration of the node's boot, $E_{ON \to OFF}$ the energy consumed to switch off the node (in Joules), $E_{OFF \to ON}$ the energy consumed to switch on the node (in Joules), and E_s an energy threshold (a few Joules) that represents the amount of energy we save by switching the node off and on during T_s.

When a node is free, we predict when the next job will occur. If it is in less than T_s seconds and if this node is required for this predicted job, we leave it on. Otherwise we switch it off. Our prediction is computed as follows: at a given time t, the submission times of the $(n + 1)$ previous jobs are denoted $t_0, \ldots, t_n$ where t_n is the most recent. So the next predicted job submission t' is:

$$t' = t + 1/n[(t_1 - t_0) + \cdots + (t_n - t_{n-1})] + t\_feedback = t + 1/n[t_n - t_0] + t\_feedback$$

where $t\_feedback$ is a feedback computed with the previous predictions: it represents an average of the errors made by computing the previous few predictions. The error is the difference between the true value and the predicted one.

We have seen in [12] that even with a small n (5 for example) we can obtain good results (70% of good predictions on experimental Grid traces). This prediction model is simple but it doesn't need a lot of disk accesses and is really fast to compute. These are crucial features for real-time infrastructures.

3.4. Comparison between GOC and EARI

GOC infrastructure is an adaptation of our Energy-Aware Reservation Infrastructure [13] that deals with Grids environments. This infrastructure is quite different from our previous work. Indeed, in EARI, we only handle the reservations: each user that wants to submit a job should precise its length in time, its size in number of nodes, and a wanted start time. With GOC, we just need the size in terms of number of VMs and there is no reservation nor agenda. For this reason, it greatly modifies the specifications of the elementary entity: the job in our case, the reservation for EARI. It implies different management algorithms for the jobs (to act live and not in the future) and different prediction algorithms since we want to predict the next submission and not the next reservation (in EARI, the user does a submission for a reservation that is in the future).

In both infrastructures, we guarantee the performance: we do not impact on the resources wanted by the user nor on the end time if the user does not agree.

We have validated EARI by using real usage traces of an experimental Grid. It is not possible with GOC since we do not have access to Cloud usage logs, so the GOC infrastructure is validated with some usage scenarios.

4. Conclusion and Perspectives

This paper presents our first step in designing a Green Open Cloud architecture by taking into account the energy usage of virtualization frameworks.

Based on the EARI model, we have experimentally measured and analyzed the electric cost of migrating virtual machines. We have proposed original software frameworks able to reduce the energy usage of Cloud infrastructure. These frameworks embed load balancing solutions with migration facilities and an ON/OFF infrastructure associated with prediction mechanisms. The GOC architecture is customizable, to include any green policy. For example, an admin can increase energy awareness by using a green accounting (the users who accepts to delay their jobs can be rewarded). The GOC architecture can be adapted to any Cloud infrastructure: we are currently implementing and experimenting our GOC architecture with Eucalyptus [11] in large-scale distributed systems (i.e. the Grid5000 platform [3]) to fully validate it.

References

[1]   G. Boss, P. Malladi, D. Quan, L. Legregni, and H. Hall. Cloud Computing. Technical report, IBM, 8 October 2007.

[2]   Rajkumar Buyya, Chee Shin Yeo, Srikumar Venugopal, James Broberg, and Ivona Brandic. Cloud Computing and Emerging IT Platforms: Vision, Hype, and Reality for Delivering Computing as the 5th Utility. *Future Generation Computer Systems*, 25(6):599–616, June 2009.

[3]   F. Cappello et al. Grid'5000: A large scale, reconfigurable, controlable and monitorable grid platform. In *6th IEEE/ACM International Workshop on Grid Computing, Grid'2005*, Seattle, Washington, USA, Nov. 2005.

[4]   Georges Da-Costa, Jean-Patrick Gelas, Yiannis Georgiou, Laurent Lefèvre, Anne-Cécile Orgerie, Jean-Marc Pierson, Olivier Richard, and Kamal Sharma. The green-net framework: Energy efficiency in large scale distributed systems. In *HPPAC 2009 : High Performance Power Aware Computing Workshop in conjunction with IPDPS 2009*, Roma, Italy, May 2009.

[5]   Christopher Clark, Keir Fraser, Steven Hand, Jacob Gorm Hansen, Eric Jul, Christian Limpach, Ian Pratt, and Andrew Warfield. Live migration of virtual machines. In *NSDI'05: Proceedings of the 2nd conference on Symposium on Networked Systems Design & Implementation*, pages 273–286, Berkeley, CA, USA, 2005. USENIX Association.

[6]   Laura Grit, David Irwin, Aydan Yumerefendi, and Jeff Chase. Virtual machine hosting for networked clusters: Building the foundations for "autonomic" orchestration. In *VTDC '06: Proceedings of the 2nd International Workshop on Virtualization Technology in Distributed Computing*, page 7, Washington, DC, USA, 2006. IEEE Computer Society.

[7]   Brian Hayes. Cloud computing. *Communication of the ACM*, 51(7):9–11, 2008.

[8]   Fabien Hermenier, Nicolas Loriant, and Jean-Marc Menaud. Power management in grid computing with xen. In *XEN in HPC Cluster and Grid Computing Environments (XHPC06)*, number 4331 in LNCS, pages 407–416, Sorento, Italy, 2006. Springer Verlag.

[9]   A. Iosup, C. Dumitrescu, D. Epema, Hui Li, and L. Wolters. How are real grids used? the analysis of four grid traces and its implications. In *7th IEEE/ACM International Conference on Grid Computing*, September 2006.

[10] Ripal Nathuji and Karsten Schwan. Virtualpower: coordinated power management in virtualized enterprise systems. In *SOSP '07: Proceedings of twenty-first ACM SIGOPS symposium on Operating systems principles*, pages 265–278, New York, NY, USA, 2007. ACM.

[11] Daniel Nurmi, Rich Wolski, Chris Grzegorczyk, Graziano Obertelli, Sunil Soman, Lamia Youseff, and Dmitrii Zagorodnov. The eucalyptus open-source cloud-computing system. In *Proceedings of Cloud Computing and Its Applications*, Chicago, Illinois, USA, October 2008.

[12] Anne-Cécile Orgerie, Laurent Lefèvre, and Jean-Patrick Gelas. Chasing gaps between bursts : Towards energy efficient large scale experimental grids. In *PDCAT 2008 : The Ninth International Conference on Parallel and Distributed Computing, Applications and Technologies*, Dunedin, New Zealand, December 2008.

[13] Anne-Cécile Orgerie, Laurent Lefèvre, and Jean-Patrick Gelas. Save watts in your grid: Green strategies for energy-aware framework in large scale distributed systems. In *14th IEEE International Conference on Parallel and Distributed Systems (ICPADS)*, Melbourne, Australia, December 2008.

[14] Shekhar Srikantaiah, Aman Kansal, and Feng Zhao. Energy aware consolidation for cloud computing. In *Proceedings of HotPower '08 Workshop on Power Aware Computing and Systems*. USENIX, December 2008.

[15] Richard Talaber, Tom Brey, and Larry Lamers. Using Virtualization to Improve Data Center Efficiency. Technical report, The Green Grid, 2009.

[16] Franco Travostino, Paul Daspit, Leon Gommans, Chetan Jog, Cees de Laat, Joe Mambretti, Inder Monga, Bas van Oudenaarde, Satish Raghunath, and Phil Yonghui Wang. Seamless live migration of virtual machines over the man/wan. *Future Gener. Comput. Syst.*, 22(8):901–907, 2006.

[17] W. Voorsluys, J. Broberg, S. Venugopal, and R. Buyya. Cost of Virtual Machine Live Migration in Clouds: A Performance Evaluation. Technical report, Technical Report, Grid Computing and Distributed Systems Laboratory, The University of Melbourne, Australia, 5 April 2009.
[18] Business Week.   With Sun, IBM Aims for Cloud Computing Heights, 26 March 2009 `http://www.businessweek.com/magazine/content/09\_14/b4125034196164.htm?chan=magazine+channel\_news`.

Parallel Computing: From Multicores and GPU's to Petascale
B. Chapman et al. (Eds.)
IOS Press, 2010
© 2010 The authors and IOS Press. All rights reserved.
doi:10.3233/978-1-60750-530-3-238

A versatile system for asynchronous iterations: From multithreaded simulations to Grid experiments

Giorgos Kollias [a,1] Konstantinos Georgiou [a,2] and Efstratios Gallopoulos [a,3]

[a] *Computer Engineering and Informatics Department (CEID)*
University of Patras, Greece

Abstract. We present a system for asynchronous iterations, integrated in a portable environment for interactive computations. This system facilitates both the simulation of asynchronous computations in a multithreading context and their execution within a relatively complex platform such as the Grid. Numerical experiments with the PageRank algorithm are also given to demonstrate the practicality of our approach.

Keywords. parallel asynchronous iterations, PageRank, multicore, Grid, multithreading

1. Introduction

Many challenging applications in our "Web era" are by nature very large scale and distributed. Moreover, they necessitate the application of iterative numerical techniques; Google's PageRank is the most prominent problem in this category. In order to address such applications effectively requires the use of distributed and parallel computing infrastructure and the software and algorithmic framework to harness it. In fact, standard numerical techniques on commodity clusters may not suffice to handle problems of this size. Several researchers have been studying the suitability of the asynchronous iterations model [2,4,7,6], for some of these problems. This model relaxes or completely eliminates the synchronization requirement that is the source of performance limitations in iterative computations.

In very loosely coupled and highly heterogeneous computational platforms, that are natural vehicles for deploying Web-scale problems (e.g. Grid and P2P systems), synchronization can become a prohibitive bottleneck. In the asynchronous model, each computing node proceeds by incorporating whatever remotely processed data happen to be available at the time the local update is to take place; no delays for ensuring that all nodes have reached the same phase are introduced, each processor computes at its own pace. We have already shown in [12] that the PageRank vector can be computed asynchronously on a commodity cluster.

---

[1] E-mail: gdk@hpclab.ceid.upatras.gr (Corresponding Author)
[2] E-mail: georgiu@ceid.upatras.gr
[3] E-mail: stratis@ceid.upatras.gr

Even though the asynchronous framework is attractive, it introduces some theoretical and practical difficulties:

- The mathematical analysis of the convergence properties of the original sequential or synchronous parallel iterative schemes no longer applies. Alternative techniques are necessary; some exist, some remain to be discovered.
- By eliminating synchronization, the virtual global clock controlling the iteration steps is removed too. Consequently, local convergence does not imply global convergence. Methods for detecting global convergence in this asynchronous setting are needed.
- Communication libraries typically used in parallel computations do not fully support this class of algorithms. Although the latest data from peers is needed at the application level, the programmer is distracted by having to explicitly receive and reject any messages delivered in between.

Even though there is extensive literature on the mathematical properties of asynchronous algorithms, there are few implementations and experimental studies regarding their behaviour.

Overall the differences between the synchronous and asynchronous frameworks are many and make the learning curve for a scientist accustomed to message passing APIs like MPI, quite steep. Problem Solving Environments (PSEs) like MATLAB and Mathematica, that could lower such usability barriers, have only recently added support for parallel computation, mostly aiming at feeding the multiple cores of modern CPU processors; not surprisingly, asynchronous iterations are not yet supported. Moreover, these environment do not expose the threading capabilities of the underlying platform, that could be used for simulating the asynchronous computation under study prior to porting on a real heterogeneous platform.

In this paper, we address the above obstacles by means of Jylab [10], our portable PSE, that enables the rapid prototyping of the asynchronous computations. The PageRank calculation is used as a proof-of-concept of our approach.

We experiment within two different contexts: In Section 3 we explore a multi-threaded version of this asynchronous computation [11] while in Section 4 we present its implementation on the EGEE Grid platform. Our results demonstrate the versatility of Jylab as a simulation engine as well as an exploratory tool for the asynchronous model. It is worth noting that Jylab provides a uniform programming environment: Everything is written in Python [4], a scripting language which is frequently termed "executable pseudo-code".

2. Computing PageRank and beyond

The ranking of web pages is today a critical component of most search engines. Indeed, it is widely acknowledged that much of Google's success is due to the invention by the company's founders of PageRank [5]. In particular web pages are ranked based on a value assigned to each of them in the, so called, PageRank vector x. This vector is commonly interpreted as the dominant eigenvector of the *Google matrix*, $G = \alpha S + (1 - \alpha) v e^T$, where S depends on the webgraph adjacency matrix, e is the n-dimensional vector of

---

[4]More specifically, Jylab uses Jython, an implementation of the Python programming language

all 1's, v is a stochastic vector encoding web surfing preferences and α is a relaxation parameter in the $[0, 1)$ interval.

To make the computation of x feasible for the problem sizes that occur in practice, it becomes necessary to deploy an iterative scheme of the form:

$$x(t + 1) = G\,x(t), \quad x(0) \text{ given.} \tag{1}$$

where in our parallel settings, matrix G, which is not explicitly formed, is partitioned by rows across the communicating peers and fragments of vector x are asynchronously computed and exchanged. This is the well-known power method for finding the eigenvector of G corresponding to the eigenvalue of largest magnitude [13].

Note, that we have applied the asynchronous model, at least adapting its multithreaded implementation described in Section 3 in other cases as well. We have recently explored the behavior of Gossip algorithms [9], i.e. inherently asynchronous algorithms for the distributed computation of statistical quantities. However due to lack of space we focus only on the asynchronous PageRank computations within more or less identical software contexts.

3. Multithreaded Experiments

3.1. Setup

In these experiments we used a core-2 quad Intel processor (2.66 GHz per core, 4GB RAM) running Java Virtual Machine (JVM, v1.6), hosting Jylab's scripting component, Jython (v2.5); multithreaded code was conveniently developed in Python syntax making extensive use of webmatrix class library separately coded also in Java. The link matrix used in the experiments was mainly the Stanford Web matrix [1], generated from an actual web-crawl ($n = 281,903$ pages, $2,312,497$ non-zero elements, 172 dangling nodes); in a few cases our experiments were baseed on, synthetic Barabasi-Albert [3] graphs. The local convergence threshold was set to 10^{-4} (one-norm was used in all experiments). Note that in each case, blocks of consecutive $[n/p]$ rows were distributed among p computing peers (executing on a thread each). Termination detection was determined by checking special global flags, set whenever "converged" status *persisted* locally (i.e. within a peer's execution context).

3.2. Results

Various configurations of up to 192 concurrently executing asynchronous peers were tested and convergence to the PageRank vector was observed at all cases. All experiments are controlled by two parameter vectors:

startdelays[] contains values of time delays (in secs) for the respective peer to join the computation. A value of None at its ith position simply states that peer with $ID = i$ started with no delay. This is very useful since it permits us to investigate the behavior of asynchronous PageRank under dynamic changes in the computation; when a delayed peer starts it brings along its corresponding part of the web link structure. Therefore this parameter can determine the timing of massive and abrupt changes in the processed data.

stepdelays[] contains values of delays (in secs) synthetically injected at each step of the iteration performed by the peer with corresponding ID. This allows us to parameterize heterogeneous machines in terms of their speed: thus large values simulate slow machines. It follows that None lets the underlying (fair) thread scheduler decide.

Output vector iterations[] contains the total number of iterations performed by each asynchronously executing peer to reach convergence. Although large numbers are sometimes recorded here (in cases of either large heterogeneity or late startup peers) the decisive comparison metric (relative to the synchronous parallel case), would be the smallest value in the aforementioned vector, because in a synchronous setting, execution ends when the last UE converges (typically the slowest) and it begins when the last UE in the group joins the computation. Of course, in a synchronous setting all peers would be simultaneously available at the start.

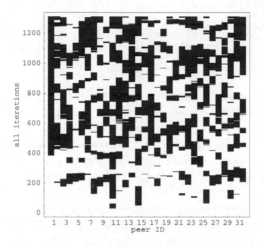

Figure 1. Asynchronous convergence patterns: Each vertical column represents the timeline of convergence status for a specific peer, black denoting non-convergence, while the white that convergence has been reached. Global time runs downwards starting when less than half of the total number of peers were left in non-convergent state for the first time. This experiment is for 32 peers (synthetic Barabasi-Albert Web matrix, 100k pages) startdelays=None, stepdelays=None.

Figure 1 shows a distinctive feature of asynchronous computations compared to their synchronous counterparts: In the course of an asynchronous iterative process a peer can enter and exit 'converged' status multiple times quite independently from other UEs. This happens as a possibly 'converged' process receives data -completely out of sync- from either asynchronous 'futures' or 'pasts' (i.e. other processes respectively having performed more or less iterations). Convergence is eventually attained by all peers which confirms the general theoretical predictions (see e.g. [15,4]. Predicting the exact number of iteration steps per peer is generally impractical.

Tables 1 and 2 summarize our experiments with 4 peers. In particular Table 2 focuses on the scenario that one peer starts computing long after the others. Note that this late processor needs less than 39 iterations (this is for the sequential-synchronous case for the same error threshold). In the extreme case when this peer also happens to be the slowest, we can also draw an important conclusion: Because this processor decides results delivery time, it seems advantageous to start up computation immediately in the absence of

startdelays[]	stepdelays[]	iterations[]
None	[None, 1., 2., 3.]	[561, 29, 20, 12]
None	[None, 2., 4., 6.]	[860, 29, 16, 12]
None	None	[15, 16, 17, 15]
[10.,None,20.,None]	None	[62, 124, 23, 122]

Table 1. Experiments (4 peers, Stanford Web matrix) for a variety of startdelays[] and stepdelays[] (in secs). Number of iterations to convergence for each peer (iterations[] vector) is given.

startdelays[]	stepdelays[]	iterations[]
[3 x None, 15.]	None	[73, 74, 78, 16]
[3 x None, 15.]	[3 x None, 1.]	[96, 101, 103, 11]
[3 x None, 15.]	[3 x None, 2.]	[121, 128, 130, 11]
[3 x None, 15.]	[1., 1., 1., None]	[28, 25, 29, 141]
[3 x None, 15.]	[2., 2., 2., None]	[22, 22, 24, 271]

Table 2. Experiments (4 peers, Stanford Web matrix) for a variety of stepdelays[] when one of the peers joins the computation after it has started. Number of iterations to convergence for each peer (iterations[] vector) is given.

slow machines to be available later on, rather than deferring calculation launch. Other results (some also from Table 1) generally suggest that it is preferable to start computing asynchronously as early as possible rather than wait all peers to be ready. Even though the gain towards convergence per iteration is expected to be small it certainly does no harm (note the large iteration numbers at 'fast' machines); on the contrary it helps to critically reduce the number of iterations of the slow peers (fewer than 39 iterations in some cases).

In Figure 2, on the other hand, peers are homogeneous but started at different times. We observe that the introduction of 'new' computing threads is clearly sensed by 'old' ones in the form of abrupt changes in their error profile (these points of change can also be used for translating iteration steps to real time intervals). The important thing here is that although severely perturbed, no special treatment is needed for the computation (e.g. no need to restart or checkpoint it); asynchronous computing seems to automatically adapt to dynamic changes (here more peers and drastic changes in link structure) and find its way to convergence.

4. Grid Experiments

4.1. Enabling parallel programming on the Grid (without MPI)

In the official gLite [14] middleware documentation[5], which is the software stack of choice for "Enabling Grids for e-science" (EGEE) [6], the largest multi-disciplinary Grid infrastructure in the world, also being the platform used in our experiments, it is clearly stated that MPI is only supported experimentally, not including the genuine "parallel processing" scenario, in which processes executing in WNs of *different* CEs need to communicate.

---

[5]https://edms.cern.ch/file/722398/1.2/gLite-3-UserGuide.pdf
[6]http://www.eu-egee.org/

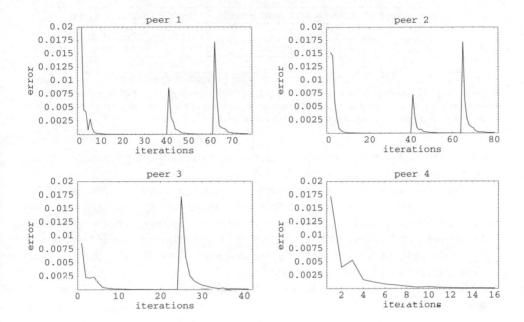

Figure 2. The effect of massive changes in the underlying Web matrix during the computation: Error vs number of iterations for 4 asynchronous peers computing with the Stanford Web matrix. Peers 3 and 4 join the computation 10 and 20 secs respectively later than peers 1 and 2 (which start computing simultaneously), i.e. startdelays=[None,None,10.,20.]. Note that iterations=[77,80,41,16] and stepdelays=None.

In order to alleviate such a limitation we adopted and experimented with an alternative approach, based on the Ibis communication framework [16]. Specifically, in order to perform a parallel computation over the Grid, we first launch a special process, the ibis-server, in a machine with fixed, publicly visible IP. Then we submit to the Grid several identical jobs (Single Program Multiple Data model) carrying as an extra parameter the communication endpoint of the ibis-server. The jobs drive the execution of corresponding processes, featuring an initialization phase for communication clique establishment (discover local communication endpoints, register them with the ibis-server, query it for the endpoints of the remote peer processes and connect to them). As soon as this phase completes, the processes can exchange messages and thus participate in a parallel computation.

4.2. Setup and Results

To conveniently capture all these steps we implemented special IbisParallelRank computation objects. Then, an asynchronous mode calculation of PageRank over the Grid, amounts to only one line of code in the Grid job executable:

```
rank = IbisParallelRank(properties,capabilities,configuration,mode)
rank.execute()
```

In the argument list, **properties** contain parameters for the underlying JVM, while **configuration** collects information for the computation itself e.g. location of input/output data, number of iterations, stopping criterium, calculation method and its parameters.

Parallel ranker ID	t_1(sec) = Job execution time	t_2(sec) = Computation time
0	62	55
1	49	30
2	36	26

Table 3. IbisParallelRank for 3 Grid jobs and $\alpha = 0.6$ after 30 iterations. Here t_1 includes the time taken for downloading and installing Jylab as well as the time t_2 spent in "computation", which includes times for the communication clique establishment and fetching suitable input data (webgraph fragment) from the SE. Note that in all cases Jylab image download times were minimal (just over 3 seconds).

Also **capabilities** identify low-level preferences for the underlying messaging system and **mode** was always set to "asynchronous"

Code files were typically the library containing our framework specification together with the implementation of the computation objects for the target calculations (in our case, **pageranks.py**). and the application itself, of minimal size (essentially the two lines of code mentioned earlier). Output data (e.g. the PageRank vector) would typically be sent -as part of the job cycle- to some SE; we can retrieve it locally using facilities either of our **grid** package [8] or the framework library.

Results from parallel asynchronous computations of PageRank over the Grid are tabulated in Table 3.

5. Conclusions and future work

We have demonstrated the effectiveness of enhancing a PSE, Jylab, with components facilitating the exploration of the asynchronous computation model.

Our approach is twofold: An algorithm can be both simulated and executed, even over a complex platform such as the Grid, under the asynchronous model, from within the same environment. In this paper we focused on presenting our experience gained from porting the PageRank algorithm over to this model, making use of a common software infrastructure.

We emphasize the fact that with the many-core processors to come, our multi-threaded implementations can eventually serve not only as simulators, but also as the final target execution contexts. On the other hand it has been shown that the parallel asynchronous model can also be supported across clusters in a Grid environment.

We are currently extending our methodology on algorithms of an inherently asynchronous nature, naturally occuring in distributed settings. Our future work includes the unification of software modules now separately developed for addressing porting of the same asynchronous iterative algorithms over different platforms.

References

[1] Stanford Web Matrix. http://nlp.stanford.edu/~sdkamvar/data/stanford-web.tar.gz.
[2] J. M. Bahi, S. Contassot-Vivier, and R. Couturier. *Parallel Iterative Algorithms: From Sequential to Grid Computing.* Chapman & Hall/CRC, Nov. 2007.
[3] A. L. Barabási and R. Albert. Emergence of scaling in random networks. *Science*, 286(5439):509 – 512, 1999.

[4] D. P. Bertsekas and J. N. Tsitsiklis. *Parallel and Distributed Computation*. Prentice Hall, Englewood Cliffs, NJ, 1989.

[5] S. Brin and L. Page. The anatomy of a large-scale hypertextual web search engine. *Computer Networks and ISDN Systems*, 33:107–117, 1998.

[6] D. de Jager. PageRank: Three Distributed Algorithms. Master's thesis, Imperial College of Science, Technology and Medicine, Sept. 2004.

[7] A. Frommer and D. B. Szyld. On asynchronous iterations. *J. Comput. Appl. Math.*, 123(1-2):201–216, 2000.

[8] K. Georgiou, G. Kollias, and E. Gallopoulos. Grid-enabling a problem solving environment: Implementation and everyday use. In M. Danelutto, P. Fragopoulou, and V. Getov, editors, *Making Grids Work*, pages 129–138. Springer US, 2008.

[9] D. Kempe, A. Dobra, and J. Gehrke. Gossip-based computation of aggregate information. In *Foundations of Computer Science, 2003. Proceedings. 44th Annual IEEE Symposium on*, pages 482–491, 2003.

[10] G. Kollias and E. Gallopoulos. Jylab: A System for Portable Scientific Computing over Distributed Platforms. In *2nd IEEE Int'l. Conf. on e-Science and Grid Computing(e-Science 2006): Session on Innovative and Collaborative Problem Solving*, Amsterdam, December 2006. IEEE.

[11] G. Kollias and E. Gallopoulos. Asynchronous computation of pagerank computation in an interactive multithreading environment. In A. Frommer, M. W. Mahoney, and D. B. Szyld, editors, *Web Information Retrieval and Linear Algebra Algorithms*, number 07071 in Dagstuhl Seminar Proceedings, Dagstuhl, Germany, 2007.

[12] G. Kollias, E. Gallopoulos, and D. B. Szyld. Asynchronous iterative computations with web information retrieval structures: The PageRank case. In *Parallel Computing: Current and Future Issues of High-End Computing (Proceedings of Parco05)*, volume 33 of *NIC Series*, pages 309–316, 2006.

[13] A. Langville and C. Meyer. *Google's Pagerank and Beyond: The Science of Search Engine Rankings*. Princeton University, 2006.

[14] E. Laure, S. M. Fisher, A. Frohner, C. Grandi, P. Kunszt, A. Krenek, O. Mulmo, F. Pacini, F. Prelz, and J. White. Programming the grid with gLite. *Computational Methods in Science and Technology*, 12(1):33–45, 2006.

[15] B. Lubachevsky and D. Mitra. A Chaotic, Asynhronous Algorithm for Computing the Fixed Point of a Nonnegative Matrix of Unit Spectral Radius. *J. ACM*, 33(1):130–150, January 1986.

[16] R. V. van Nieuwpoort, J. Maassen, G. Wrzesinska, R. Hofman, C. Jacobs, T. Kielmann, and H. E. Bal. Ibis: a Flexible and Efficient Java based Grid Programming Environment. *Concurrency and Computation: Practice and Experience*, 17(7-8):1079–1107, June 2005.

Programming

Parallel Computing: From Multicores and GPU's to Petascale
B. Chapman et al. (Eds.)
IOS Press, 2010

249

© *2010 The authors and IOS Press. All rights reserved.*
doi:10.3233/978-1-60750-530-3-249

Exploiting Object-Oriented Abstractions to parallelize Sparse Linear Algebra Codes

Christian TERBOVEN [a] Dieter AN MEY [a] Paul KAPINOS [a]
Christopher SCHLEIDEN [a] Igor MERKULOW [a]

[a] *JARA, RWTH Aachen University, Center for Computing and Communication*
Seffenter Weg 23, 52074 Aachen, Germany
{terboven, anmey, kapinos, schleiden, merkulow}@rz.rwth-aachen.de

Abstract. Object-oriented (OO) programming conquered mainstream in the 1990s but the procedural programming languages Fortran and C are still dominating in the High-Performance-Computing (HPC) community. However in recent years, compute kernels or even whole applications have been migrated from C to object-oriented C++ and Fortran has been retrofitted with OO capabilities as well. In this work we illustrate how OO abstractions can be used to introduce Shared-Memory parallelization into existing applications by using the concepts of encapsulation and modularity. For the important domain of sparse linear algebra routines, we discuss several parallel implementation strategies and data type design considerations. We aim to maximize performance and scalability while hiding the implementation details as much as possible.

Keywords. OpenMP, Object-Oriented, Linear Algebra, Parallelization, C++, Fortran, cc-NUMA, Abstraction

1. Introduction

Although object-oriented (OO) programming is commonly used since the 1990s, the High-Performance-Computing (HPC) community still uses the procedural programming languages C and Fortran over the last decades primarily. New HPC projects often employ the C++ programming language instead of C, and several compute kernels or even whole parts of applications have been rewritten in C++ to handle increased code complexity much better. With the advent of Fortran 95/2003 - although not yet fully implemented by commercial compilers - this programming language has been retrofitted with OO capabilities, too.

In this work we explore and compare techniques for Shared-Memory parallelization with OpenMP [ARB08] by exploiting object-oriented data type design. We concentrate on the domain of sparse linear algebra kernels, but believe that the results are applicable to other scenarios as well. The C++ Navier-Stokes Solver DROPS [GPRR02] employs an abstract data type design which allows the developers to write numerical algorithms resembling mathematical text book notation, which then allows very good readability and maintainability of the resulting code. By exploiting this design to introduce Shared-

Memory parallelization, we aim to maximize performance and scalability while minimizing the impact on the elegance of the OO code, that algorithmic modifications will not be complicated by parallelization. Particular attention is paid on how the topology of the hardware architecture can be efficiently exploited with minimal care required by the algorithm developer, since cc-NUMA architectures are getting more widespread and respecting the memory hierarchy is crucial for performance. Since Fortran 95/2003 introduces many OO features [MRC04], we explored how far the techniques discussed in this work can be applied to Fortran as well.

The rest of this paper is structured as follows: The following subsection discusses related work and highlights the new concepts presented herein. Chapter 2 presents our application cases and the methodology we used to develop and compare the OO parallelization techniques that are examined in chapter 4. In the chapter 3 we discuss the resulting data type design we propose to build parallel sparse linear algebra codes. Chapter 5 presents performance and scalability experiments of our implementation. Finally we conclude and propose future work in chapter 6.

1.1. Related Work

Blitz++ [Vel98] is a C++ class library employing Template Expressions to provide performance on par with Fortran. It is limited to dense linear algebra and serial optimization. Based on the concepts mainly pioneered by Blitz++, other libraries providing parallel domain-specific abstractions have been developed, for instance POOMA [RHC+96] to write parallel PDE solvers using finite-difference and particle methods. Other frameworks, such as STAPL [RAO98], allow parallelization based on the algorithmic concepts introduced with the C++ Standard Template Library (STL).

Our approach differs from those in putting the focus on the Shared-Memory parallelization of existing code. While also developing a library, we describe a methodology to exploit OO for parallelization of (sparse) linear algebra codes. We also provide abstractions to optimize for cc-NUMA architectures.

2. Case Study and Methodology

The excerpt in code 1 is taken from the C++ Navier-Stokes solver DROPS. The abstractions of a matrix (class `MatrixCL`) and a vector (class `VectorCL`) allow to write numerical algorithms closely resembling the notation found in mathematical text books. The expression in line 6 implements a sparse matrix-vector-multiplication (SMXV) with matrix A being stored in compress row storage (CRS) format, a dot-product can be found in line 7, lines 8 and 9 are vector operations.

Implementing numerical algorithms on the abstraction level as shown in code 1 allows algorithmic modifications with little effort, thus increasing the overall productivity. In parallelizing such a code with OpenMP, where a significant part of the compute intense code is found in operator functions, one would typically break up the OO coding style by restructuring it to allow loop-level parallelization. This has been done in the past with the DROPS code [TSaM+05] and lead to the expected performance, but the code modifications were not well-accepted by the application developers. Maintenance and algorithmic modifications often lead to errors such as race conditions when the programmers were not fully aware of the OpenMP subtleties.

Code 1 Iteration loop of a CG-type solver in C++.

```
 1 MatrixCL A(rows, cols, nonzeros);
 2 VectorCL q(n), p(n), r(n);
 3 for (int i = 1; i <= max_iter; ++i)
 4 {
 5     [...]
 6     q = A * p;
 7     double alpha = rho / (p*q);
 8     x += alpha * p;
 9     r -= alpha * q;
10     [...]
```

In order to improve the acceptance of the parallelization and make it more robust, we aimed to exploit the OO data type design to hide the parallelization from the user. None of the parallelization paradigms we explored for the DROPS [TSaM09] has explicit support for writing parallel software components that can be put together without worrying about correctness. This had to be respected in choosing the right implementation approach, as will be discussed in chapter 4.

Adding more cores on a processor increases its compute power, but especially for sparse linear algebra the memory bandwidth is the factor delimiting the performance of an application. Since multiple cores on the same socket have to share the memory bandwidth, even the vendors of x86-based commodity processors are nowadays implementing non-uniform memory access (NUMA) architectures to increase the aggregated memory bandwidth in multi-socket systems. In such an architecture, each processor is connected to a local memory that can be accessed with lower latency and higher bandwidth than remote memory attached to a different socket, although remote accesses are completely transparent to the programmer because of cache coherency (cc). Beside hiding the parallelization from the user, we also aimed at hiding the architectural details without decreasing the performance, as will be discussed in chapter 3. In order to split the process of further application / algorithm development and the parallelization and tuning efforts, we created a generic C++ class template library named *laperf* [TSaM09] that provides the data types needed for DROPS and other applications as well.

Code 2 shows that the Fortran version of the sparse matrix-vector-multiplication looks very similar to a loop-based rewrite of code 1. Hence we aimed to transfer the benefits of parallelization via OO abstractions to Fortran as well.

3. Data Type Design

The laperf library provides data types for sparse and dense matrix and vector operations ready to be plugged into application kernels such as DROPS, while still allowing to independently experiment with parallelization strategies. It currently consists of three generic data types:

- `vector`: one-dimensional vector.

Code 2 Excerpt of an iteration loop of a CG-type solver in Fortran.

```fortran
1  double precision a(nz_num), irow(n+1), icol(nz_num), q(n)
2  do iter=1, max_iter
3      [...]
4          do i = 1, n
5              q(i) = 0.0d0
6              do j=irow(i), irow(i+1)-1
7                  q(i)=q(i)+a(j)*p(icol(j))
8              end do
9          end do
10         [...]
```

- `matrix_crs`: sparse matrix in compressed row storage (CRS).
- `matrix_dense`: dense matrix.

Each of these data types accepts the following template parameters:

- `T`: element data type, default is `double`.
- `ParallelizationType`: flag to select implementation strategy.
- `MemoryPolicy`: flag to select thread binding and memory allocation strategy.

With that, all matrix and vector operations are implemented with our parallel data types, the user of our library has to provide the template parameters `ParallelizationType` and `MemoryPolicy` to enable and optimize the parallelization. This is achieved by using a policy-based class design [GHJV95] allowing to influence the functionality of a class from the outside via compile-time parameters.

On cc-NUMA architectures, the `MemoryPolicy` parameter is of high importance. Although parallel programming has become ubiquitous for simulation software, the adaption to a given hardware architecture is still a manual process executed by domain experts. By using our library, the user can choose between several policies that implement best practice approaches on recent architectures [NVDY04], [TaMS+08]. A typical policy is to partition the nonzeros of a matrix into as many chunks as there are cc-NUMA nodes used by the program, while taking care that all chunks are of approximately the same size to prevent a load imbalance. This can automatically be done in the constructor of the matrix class and the distribution pattern can be stored along with the matrix to exploit that knowledge in the computation to optimize the memory access pattern. We found that simplifying the task of cc-NUMA optimization to merely selecting a template argument is a great relief to the programmer.

Figure 1a shows the influence of the memory hierarchy on the scalability of an interative solver, chapter 5 contains a discussion of the actual implementation. The *compact* binding scheme puts the threads as close together as possible, while the *scatter* scheme spreads the threads over the whole machine. The latter provides the best memory bandwidth to the application and makes use of all caches.

The *default* scheduling scheme does not take the memory hierachy into account at all. The *distributed* scheme distributes the data in the same fashion as the OpenMP loop scheduling used in the computation. The *chunked* scheme delivers the best performance

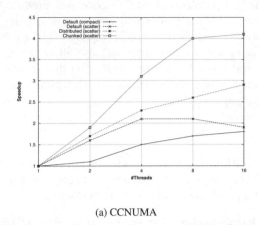

(a) CCNUMA

Figure 1. Comparison of cc-NUMA strategies for a CG-style algorithm.

by explicitly distributing the nonzeros over the numa nodes (as described above), when combined with the *scatter* binding scheme.

4. Implementation

In this section we discuss strategies to parallelize OO codes in C++ and Fortran.

4.1. C++

Loop-level Parallelization. As mentioned above, the obvious approach of refactoring the C++ kernel as shown in code 1 breaks the object-oriented paradigm and therefore it was not considered as a valid final result, but nevertheless we created this version for performance comparison and it will be referred as *C++ (loop)* in chapter 5.

Parallel Operations on Data Types. If the OO paradigm has to be preserved, the obvious place to introduce the parallelization are the operator calls of the matrix and vector classes. In order to make this approach safe to use and robust in terms of correctness against code changes, each operator call has to host a self-contained parallel region. The authors discussed this approach for several different parallelization paradigms for C++ in [TSaM09] and two problems arise:

- *Temporaries in compound expressions*: In case of a compound expression, such as x = (a * 2.0) + b; where x, a and b are vector data types, the compiler is allowed to introduce temporaries. Temporaries impose not only some sequential overhead, they also can drastically decrease the performance on cc-NUMA architectures and therefore should be avoided if possible.
- *Overhead in compound expressions*: Since each operator call contains a complete parallel region, a compound expression such as x = (a * 2.0) + b; could lead to up to five parallel regions in this single expression: The computation of a * 2.0 and the assignment of the result to a temporary t1, the computation of t1 + b and the assignment of the result to a temporary t2, and finally the assignment of t2 to x.

In order to overcome both problems of the C++ code, we introduced an Expression Template [Vel95] framework for our matrix and vector classes. Using this framework, the right hand side of any compound expression is only evaluated in the assignment operator. This avoids the creation of any temporaries and also allows for an efficient parallelization with OpenMP worksharing constructs. Following this approach, the parallelization can be completely hidden from the application or algorithm developer. We refer to this version as *C++ (datatype)* in chapter 5.

4.2. Fortran

Loop-level Parallelization. The Fortran code version is already well-prepared for applying the OpenMP FOR worksharing constructs, no code changes would be necessary. In section 5 we will refer to this version as *Fortran (loops)*.

Workshare-based Parallelization. The Fortran 90 language revision introduced the array syntax allowing to express operations on arrays without explicit loops, which greatly enhances the readability of the code and can be considered as a basic OO abstraction. In order to support the parallelization of such constructs, OpenMP offers the WORKSHARE construct. We will refer to this approach as *Fortran (workshare)* in chapter 5.

Parallel Operations on Data Types. Although the array syntax already provides some sort of abstraction that can be applied to some parts of the linear algebra kernel, it still has to be considered basic. While the vector operations contained in the code can be parallelized, the sparse matrix-vector-multiplication cannot be completely hidden. In order to overcome this limitation, we introduced matrix and vector classes and defined appropriate operators to encapsulate the parallelization, but had to address several limitations induced by the language and its current implementations:

- Using native arrays to represent the vector is not possible since the Fortran 95 language does not allow to override the pre-defined operators for intrinsic data types.
- In order to represent the array to hold the data of a vector or a sparse matrix, respectively, we had to use ALLOCATABLE arrays. Using Fortran pointers would allow for more flexibility, but that turned out to be significantly slower.
- The problem of temporaries exists in Fortran as well. In each operator call, a check has to occur whether the left hand side is already allocated and in case it is not, is has to be allocated explicitly. Because of that, a compound operation such as x = (a * 2.0) + b always has to consist of multiple parallel regions.
- As Fortran does not offer any language construct providing the capabilities of a C++ class constructor, hiding the cc-NUMA architecture as has been discussed in chapter 3 is not possible. We decided to implement an initialization function that should be called whenever a matrix or vector data type has been instantiated.

5. Evaluation

All performance measurements discussed in this section were carried out on Sun Lynx blade systems equipped with two Intel Xeon X5570 processors (Nehalem) with a clock speed of 2.93 GHz running Linux. We used the Intel C/C++/Fortran 11.0 compiler suite.

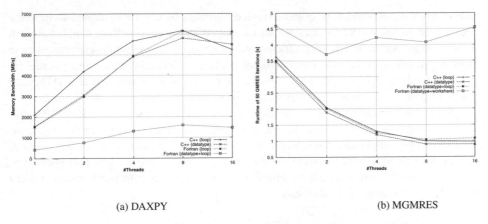

(a) DAXPY   (b) MGMRES

Figure 2. Comparison of implementation strategies for DAXPY and MGMRES.

5.1. DAXPY-operation from STREAM

In order to evaluate the approaches discussed above, we first looked at the performance of STREAM-like [McC99] operations, because exploiting the memory bandwidth is a critical issue for sparse solvers. Especially the DAXPY part of that benchmark is of interest, since it represents a compound expression. Figure 2a shows the memory bandwidth [MB/s] with up to 16 threads for the loop versions in C++ and Fortran and the data type version in C++. All arrays have a dimension of 300 MB.

For up to four threads, the C++ loop version outperforms both the Fortran loop version and the C++ data type version. Since we used allocatable arrays the Fortran compiler was not able to carry out all optimizations, while in the C++ loop version we used the `restrict` keyword to explicitly enable these optimizations and because of that the C++ loop version is the fastest version of the three. Using eight threads, all versions deliver approximately the same performance, since the memory bandwidth is exhausted. We did not plot the performance of the Fortran `WORKSHARE` version, since the Intel 11.0 compiler currently does not support the parallelization of this construct.

5.2. MGMRES Iterative Solver

Figure 2b shows the runtime comparison [s] of the MGMRES solver as used in DROPS for 50 iterations on a matrix with approximately 20,000,000 nonzero elements. As can be seen clearly, the performance difference is very small as all versions reside in the same range of scalability. The C++ data type version is the fastest one, because of the efficient implementation of compound expressions. Fortran's disadvantage into that respect is not of high significance here, since the runtime of that solver is dominated by the sparse matrix-vector-multiplication, which can be implemented efficiently with Fortran as well.

For this algorithm, the OO abstractions are for free in terms of runtime when implemented correctly.

6. Conclusion and Future Work

In this work we showed how object-oriented abstractions can be exploited to hide the parallelization and its details. In C++ we employed an Expression Template framework to implement our approach very efficiently. We achieved the same programmability in Fortran, but since compound expressions cannot be parallelized with a single parallel region the overhead is higher than for C++. The approach of using self-contained OpenMP parallel regions inside operator calls turned out to be very elegant and safe to use.

Subject to current work is the elimination of implicit barriers of the OpenMP work-sharing constructs. In order to achieve this, we aim to have just one parallel region spanning the whole solver and using orphaned worksharing constructs inside the operator calls. If the distribution of work onto threads could be taken into account in the data type operations, most barriers could be eliminated while still providing robustness against code changes in terms of correctness.

References

[ARB08]   ARB. OpenMP Application Program Interface, version 3.0, May 2008.
[GHJV95]   E. Gamma, R. Helm, R. Johnson, and J. Vlissides. *Design Patterns: Elements of Reusable Object-Oriented Software*. Addison-Wesley Professional, 1995.
[GPRR02]   S. Gross, J. Peters, V. Reichelt, and A. Reusken. The DROPS Package for Numerical Simulations of Incompressible Flows using Parallel Adaptive Multigrid Techniques. In *IGPM-Report*, volume 211, 2002.
[McC99]   J. McCalpin. Stream: Sustainable Memory Bandwidth in High Performance Computers, 1999.
[MRC04]   M. Metcalf, J. Reid, and M. Cohen. *fortran 95/2003 explained*. Oxford University Press, 2004.
[NVDY04]   R. Nishtala, R. Vuduc, J. Demmel, and K. Yelick. When Cache Blocking of Sparse Matrix Vector Multiply Works and Why. In *Proceedings of the PARA'04 Workshop on the State-of-the-art in Scientific Computing*, 2004.
[RAO98]   L. Rauchwerger, F. Arzu, and K. Ouchi. Standard Templates Adaptive Parallel Library (STAPL). In *Proc. of the 4th International Workshop on Languages, Compilers and Run-Time Systems for Scalable Computers (LCR'98)*, pages 402–409. Springer-Verlag, 1998.
[RHC+96]   J. V. W. Reynders, P. J. Hinker, J. C. Cummings, S. R. Atlas, S. Banerjee, W. F. Humphrey, K. Keahey, M. Srikant, and M. Tholburn. POOMA: A Framework for Scientific Simulation on Parallel Architectures, 1996.
[TaMS+08]   C. Terboven, D. an Mey, D. Schmidl, H. Jin, and T. Reichstein. Data and Thread Affinity in OpenMP Programs. In *Workshop Memory Access on future Processors: A solved problem?, ACM International Conference on Computing Frontiers*, Ischia, Italy, May 2008.
[TSaM+05]   C. Terboven, A. Spiegel, D. an Mey, S. Gross, and V. Reichelt. Parallelization of the C++ Navier-Stokes Solver DROPS with OpenMP. In G. R. Joubert, W. E. Nagel, F. J. Peters, O. Plata, P. Tirado, and E. Zapata, editors, *Parallel Computing (ParCo 2005): Current & Future Issues of High-End Computing*, volume 33 of *NIC Series*, pages 431 – 438, Spain, September 2005.
[TSaM09]   C. Terboven, C. Schleiden, and D. an Mey. Comparing Programmability and Scalability of Multicore Parallelization Paradigms with C++. In E. Ayguade, R. Gioiosa, P. Stenstrom, and O. Unsal, editors, *Second Workshop on Programmability Issues for Multi-Core Computers (MULTIPROG-2)*, Paphos, Cypress, January 2009.
[Vel95]   T. Veldhuizen. Expression Templates. *C++ Report*, 7(5):26–31, June 1995. Reprinted in C++ Gems, ed. Stanley Lippman.
[Vel98]   T. L. Veldhuizen. Arrays in Blitz++. In *ISCOPE '98: Proceedings of the Second International Symposium on Computing in Object-Oriented Parallel Environments*, pages 223–230, London, UK, 1998. Springer-Verlag.

Parallel Computing: From Multicores and GPU's to Petascale
B. Chapman et al. (Eds.)
IOS Press, 2010
© 2010 The authors and IOS Press. All rights reserved.
doi:10.3233/978-1-60750-530-3-257

Handling Massive Parallelism Efficiently: Introducing Batches of Threads

Ioannis E. Venetis, Theodore S. Papatheodorou

Department of Computer Engineering & Informatics
University of Patras, Rion 26500, Greece
http://www.ceid.upatras.gr

Abstract. Emerging parallel architectures provide the means to efficiently handle more fine-grained and larger numbers of parallel tasks. However, software for parallel programming still does not take full advantage of these new possibilities, retaining the high cost associated with managing large numbers of threads. A significant percentage of this overhead can be attributed to operations on queues. In this paper, we present a methodology to efficiently create and enqueue large numbers of threads for execution. In combination with advances in computer architecture, this reduces cost of handling parallelism and allows applications to express their inherent parallelism in a more fine-grained manner. Our methodology is based on the notion of *Batches of Threads*, which are teams of threads that are used to insert and extract more than one objects simultaneously from queues. Thus, the cost of operations on queues is amortized among all members of a batch. We define an API, present its implementation in the NthLib threading library and demonstrate how it can be used in real applications. Our experimental evaluation clearly demonstrates that handling operations on queues improves significantly.

1. Introduction

Multi-core processors are an emerging technology in the field of high-performance computing. They are already extensively used and it is predicted that it will soon be possible to fit more than 1000 cores on a single chip [2]. In some cases, this technology is combined with *Simultaneous MultiThreading (SMT)* [13], which creates the illusion that there exist even more cores per processor. Due to this large number of available execution units, these architectures start to include improvements that allow faster handling of parallelism at the hardware level. Barriers [3], context-switching and faster implementations of mutual exclusion [13] in hardware are some examples. These advances are designed to allow software to reduce the cost of handling parallelism, in order for it to exploit all available execution units of a processor. To achieve this, however, the task to be performed has to be divided into an increasing number of smaller tasks, i.e., more fine-grained parallelism has to be exploited.

Typically, a run-time system is employed to handle tasks that can be executed in parallel by means of threads. Such run-time systems rely on queues to perform most of their operations. For example, a newly created thread is enqueued into a ready-queue, in order to be selected by the scheduler of the run-time system for execution on a processor. After execution, the data structure describing a thread (descriptor) is usually enqueued into a recycling-queue, in order for new threads to be created faster. Such run-time systems have already started exploiting the aforementioned hardware techniques [11]. However, the goal in these cases is to reduce the time required to perform "traditional" operations of threading run-time systems. Threads are still enqueued, with the only difference being that faster synchronization methods provided by the hardware are exploited by the run-time system to gain access to queues. We believe that software can do better to exploit the possibilities provided by new hardware to handle fine-grained parallelism.

A well known category of applications that could easily take advantage of fine-grained parallelism is the one that includes embarrassingly parallel and irregular applications. In other words, there are no dependencies between tasks and each data point does not require the same amount of time to be calculated. Although simple, this category includes some important applications like ray-tracing, fractals calculations and stock option pricing. In theory, the best method to execute such an application in parallel is to create a thread for each data point. If a processor requires more time to calculate a data point, there are numerous other threads that can be executed on all other processors. This automatically leads to a load-balanced execution of the application. However, assigning each data point to a separate thread requires the creation of a large number of threads. The cost to create and handle such an amount of parallelism becomes extremely high on most threading run-time systems and execution time actually worsens, despite good load-balancing. The solution adopted to this problem, until now, is to pack multiple data points together and assign them to a single thread. Statically assigning multiple data points to threads usually leads to bad load-balancing, degrading performance significantly. Dynamic schemes, like *Guided Self-Scheduling* [10] and *Factoring* [5], perform better in these cases, but are usually far from optimal.

Several ideas have been proposed to reduce the amount of time required to complete basic operations in threading run-time systems. An important methodology is recycling of used objects, in order to avoid expensive allocations of memory. Others include lazy techniques [4,12], memory aware creation of parallel tasks and self-adapting techniques for applications [1,3,8]. Due to the importance of this problem, even hardware solutions have been proposed, like queues implemented in hardware [6]. However, this limits the number of threads that can be simultaneously present in a queue.

In this paper we present a novel approach that allows fast creation of large numbers of threads. Our approach is based on the notion of *Batches of Threads*, which are defined as teams of threads that are handled together, with respect to operations on queues. This, in conjunction with the fact that modern parallel architectures are able to handle such a number of threads, allows us to significantly reduce cost of handling parallelism and allows applications to express their parallelism at a more fine-grained level. We define an API for Batches of Threads in the context of NthLib [7], a threading library that implements the Nano-Threads programming model [9], and demonstrate how the idea can be used in real applications. We further improve on this by exploiting the hardware provided aids to reduce overhead of mutual exclusion inside NthLib.

2. Defining Batches of Threads

Operations on queues take up a significant percentage of the time required to handle parallelism in a threading model. An obvious thought would be to use lock-free mecha-

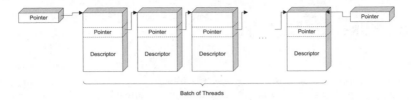

Figure 1. Representation of a Batch of Threads.

nisms to insert into and extract objects from queues. However, this is not always possible. For example, if it is required to access a queue from both the head and the tail, the data structure that represents a queue must maintain two pointers. Insertion or extraction of an object implies that both pointers must be updated together atomically. Hence, the underlying hardware must provide the necessary instructions to allow this kind of operations, which is not always the case. There are other solutions to tackle this problem, which however have other inefficiencies associated with them, like the ABA problem.

The observation that leads us to a more general solution, is the fact that the associated cost for operations on queues is always measured *per thread*. This observation reveals an obvious way that allows us to reduce this cost. If an operation on a queue is performed on a team of threads, the cost of the operation can actually be amortized among the threads of the team. This allows us to introduce the notion of a *Batch of Threads* (BoT), which can be defined as a team of threads, that are handled as an indivisible entity with respect to operations on queues. Accordingly, the services provided by a threading library can be extended to include creation of BoTs and their insertion into ready-queues.

The above definition is very general and does not include any details about how to implement BoTs. One possibility would be to use the pointer already present in each descriptor, that is used to manage threads in queues. As can be seen in Figure 1, each member of a BoT uses this pointer to keep track of the next member, except of the last one that terminates the BoT. In order to be able to efficiently insert a BoT into a queue, it is necessary to use two pointers, that point to the first and the last member of it. Under this scheme, a BoT is actually a queue of its own, which has not yet been inserted into a predefined queue of a library, like the ready and the recycling queues. Obviously, an important parameter for a BoT is it's size, i.e., the number of threads that constitute it.

Probably the easiest way to exploit BoTs is for loop-level parallelism, although their applicability is not limited to this domain. The regularity of loops in most programming languages allows easy integration of BoTs into threaded applications and allows the programmer to easily express parallelism in a natural way, as will be demonstrated shortly.

2.1. Defining the API for Batches of Threads

In order to demonstrate that BoTs can actually be used in threading libraries, we implemented an API in the context of NthLib. More specifically, the addition of the API for BoTs has been carried out on a newer implementation of the library, which has been optimized with respect to memory requirements [14,15]. This allows creation of a greater number of threads, compared to the original implementation of NthLib. In addition, we took into account the methods provided by each hardware architecture that is supported to improve mutual exclusion to access queues. Thus, we combined these methods with our software based improvements. Our main concerns while designing the API were

```
void nth_func(long Arg1, long Arg2) {
    /* Work performed by each thread */
}

void nth_main() {
    long    i;
    struct nth_desc *nth, *nth_myself = nth_self();

    nth_depadd(nth_myself, NumOfThreads + 1);
    for (i = 0; i < NumOfThreads; i++) {
        nth = nth_create_1s(nth_func, 0, nth_myself, 2, Arg1, Arg2);
        nth_to_lrq(i % kthreads, nth);
    }
    nth_block();
}
```

Figure 2. Creating threads with the original API of NthLib. 'kthreads' is the number of processors.

simplicity and ease of use. In order to achieve these goals, the API has been designed to be as similar as possible to existing and widely used APIs. Moreover, the design allows both, the original and the new API for creating threads to be used simultaneously in an application, if the programmer decides that this would benefit the application.

Carefully analyzing an example that uses the current interface of NthLib to create threads, reveals important aspects of the procedure and helps us define the interface for BoTs. Figure 2 presents the simplest method to create parallelism using NthLib. The function nth_self() returns a pointer to the descriptor of the running thread, which is stored in nth_myself. Using the last value, a number of dependencies is added to the current thread (nth_depadd()), which equals the number of threads that will be created (NumOfThreads). The additional dependency is added for internal use of the library. Consequently, all threads are created one by one in a loop through the function nth_create_1s(), which returns a pointer to the descriptor of the newly created thread. Through this value, the thread is inserted into a ready-queue (nth_to_lrq()). Finally, the main thread suspends itself by calling the function nth_block(), hence calling the user-level scheduler to select a new thread to run on the processor.

A thread is interested only on the number of dependencies it has, and not on the method used to create those threads. Hence, the function nth_depadd() does not need any modifications in the API for BoTs, which is also true for the function nth_block(). As a result, new functions must be added only to create and enqueue threads. Defining the latter ones poses no special problems. If the first and the last member of a BoT are known, insertion either in front or at the end of a queue can be performed easily. However, defining the functions to create BoTs seems to be more demanding. Creation of a thread can be divided into two stages. First, a descriptor has to be found in a recycling queue. If that fails, a new object must be allocated. Secondly, the descriptor must be initialized. The goal in using BoTs is to minimize references to queues. Therefore, finding objects in the recycling queues should also be done using BoTs. Each time a processor locks a queue, in order to create a BoT, it should return from that queue as many objects as possible, without surpassing the requested size of the BoT. Initializing each descriptor in this step would increase the time that each processor remains in a critical section. Therefore, it would be more efficient to initialize each descriptor of a BoT, after the latter has been created. Due to this fact, creating a BoT and initializing each descriptor of it have been defined to be separate operations in the current implementation. As a result, the API that we defined is as follows:

```
void nth_main () {
    long    i , nth_batch , nth_batch_remainder;
    struct nth_desc *first_nth , *last_nth , *temp_nth, *nth_myself = nth_self ();

    nth_batch = NumOfThreads / BatchSize;
    nth_batch_remainder = NumOfThreads % BatchSize;

    nth_depadd (nth_myself , NumOfThreads + 1);

    for (i = 0; i < nth_batch; i++) {
        first_nth = nth_batch_get_desc(&last_nth , BatchSize );
        temp_nth = first_nth ;
        while (temp_nth != NULL) {
            nth_batch_create_1s (temp_nth , nth_func , 0, nth_myself , 2, Arg1 , Arg2);
            temp_nth = nth_batch_get_next (temp_nth );
        }
        nth_batch_to_lrq (i % kthreads , first_nth , last_nth );
    }

    first_nth = nth_batch_get_desc(&last_nth , nth_batch_remainder );
    temp_nth = first_nth ;
    while (temp_nth != NULL) {
        nth_batch_create_1s (temp_nth , nth_func , 0, nth_myself , 2, Arg1 , Arg2);
        temp_nth = nth_batch_get_next (temp_nth );
    }
    nth_batch_to_lrq (0, first_nth , last_nth );
    nth_block ();
}
```

Figure 3. Creating threads with the new API of NthLib.

- `struct nth_desc *nth_batch_get_desc (struct nth_desc **last_nth, long num_of_nths):`
  Create a BoT of size `num_of_nths`. A pointer to the first member of the BoT is returned, whereas a pointer to the last member is stored in `last_nth`.
- `void nth_batch_create_1s (struct nth_desc *nth, void (*nth_func)(), int ndep, struct nth_desc *succ, int narg, ...):`
  Initializes the descriptor `nth`, which belongs to a previously created BoT. The thread will execute the function `nth_func()` and will depend on thread `succ`. The parameter `narg` is the number of arguments to `nth_func`. Finally, the actual parameters of the function are mentioned.
- `struct nth_desc *nth_batch_get_next (struct nth_desc *nth):`
  Returns the thread that follows `nth` in the BoT or `NULL`, if there are no other threads.
- `void nth_batch_to_lrq (int which, struct nth_desc *first_nth, struct nth_desc *last_nth):`
  Insert the BoT with first member `first_nth` and last member `last_nth` into the local ready-queue of processor `which`.

Having defined the new API, we will demonstrate its use by changing accordingly the example of Figure 2. The new program is depicted in Figure 3. We assume that each BoT will have a size of `BatchSize` and that the total number of threads will be again `NumOfThreads`. Firstly, we compute the total number of BoTs that will be created (`nth_batch`) and the possible remainder (`nth_batch_remainder`). In the next step, we update the dependencies of the current thread, as in the previous example. At this point, we observe that instead of the loop that creates threads, there is a loop over all BoTs. In each iteration, a BoT of size `BatchSize` is allocated, using the function `nth_batch_get_desc()`. An important difference is that in addition to the pointer

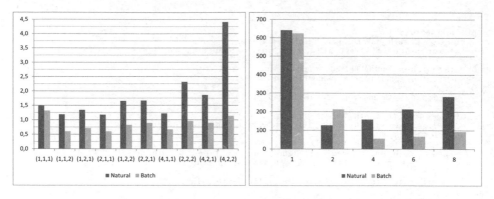

Figure 4. Execution time for the synthetic benchmark on the Intel and SMTSIM platforms.

that is returned (`first_nth`), another pointer to the last member of the BoT is also updated (`last_nth`). At this point, the descriptors in the BoT have not yet been initialized. Using the temporary variable `temp_nth` and a second loop, we initialize the first descriptor (`nth_batch_create_1s()`) and move to the next descriptors in the BoT (`nth_batch_get_next()`). Finally, using the pointers to the first and last member of the BoT, we insert the latter into the local ready-queue of a processor. If there are any remaining threads, they are handled in the same way, as a BoT of a smaller size. The last step, as in the original example, is to suspend the main thread.

A last remark about the newly defined API is the fact that it can be used together with the previous approach, due to the fact that both create and enqueue threads using the same ready and recycling queues. A possible scenario, where this could be useful, would be an application that needs to create a small number of threads per processor in some parallel regions, whereas a larger number of threads in the remaining regions. In the first case, the original API could be used, whereas in the second case the new one.

3. Experimental Evaluation

In order to evaluate our approach, we implemented the proposed API for BoTs in the context of NthLib. The version of NthLib that has been used, is the one that implements a *Direct Stack Reuse* scheme, which allows the library to drastically reduce memory requirements to represent parallelism, without sacrificing performance [14,15].

Our experiments were run on two hardware platforms. The first one contains 4 dual-core Intel Xeon processors, clocked at 3.0 GHz. Each core supports HyperThreading and features a 32KB L1 and a 2MB L2 data cache. The operating system is Linux 2.6.24. The second one is SMTSIM [13], a simulator that implements an Alpha processor with 8 execution contexts (EUs) and features a 32KB L1 and a 256KB L2 data cache. The compiler used is gcc 4.3.1 at the highest optimization level (-O3). We present results for one synthetic benchmark and low-level measurements of basic thread operations.

The synthetic benchmark follows the fork/join model. The master thread creates one million empty nano-threads, whereas the slave processors dispatch and execute them. The master thread blocks after it has created all threads, hence calling the user-level scheduler and joining the other processors to execute threads. This benchmark is appropriate for estimating the pure run-time overhead of thread management in NthLib. In the

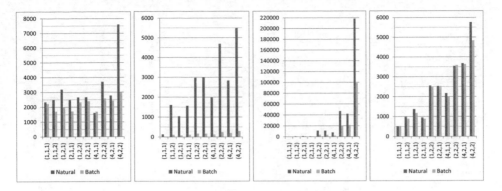

Figure 5. Time in clock cycles to create, enqueue, lookup and start a thread on the Intel platform.

original version of the benchmark, which we will refer to as *Natural*, all threads are created one-by-one. We also implemented a version, which we will refer to as *Batch*, that creates threads using BoTs with a size of 16.

Figure 4 summarizes the results for this benchmark on both platforms. Execution times are given in seconds for the Intel based system and in millions of simulated clock cycles for SMTSIM. For the latter, the horizontal axis represents the number of EUs used. For the Intel based system, the numbers of physical processors, cores and EUs used are mentioned. For example, (4, 2, 1) means that 4 physical processors, both cores on each processor and one EU on each core were used. Creating threads using BoTs is from 11,9% (case (1,1,1)) up to 74,2% (case (4,2,2)) faster on the Intel platform, with the average gain being 53,0%. For SMTSIM, the range is between 2,6% (1 EU) up to 68,3% (6 EUs) and the average gain is 25,8%.

In order to better understand these large differences, we include Figures 5 and 6, where the time required for basic operations of NthLib is presented. To obtain these results, we run the same benchmarks as above and used the Time Stamp Counter on both hardware platforms to measure such small time intervals. All results presented are per thread, meaning that the measured times for *Batch* have been divided by the size of each BoT. With respect to the Intel platform, creation time of a thread improved from 4,9% (case (1,1,1)) up to 60,8% (case (4,2,2)) when BoTs are used. The average gain in thread creation time is 30,1%. The time to start a thread after it has been selected to run did not change significantly, since the steps required to do so are almost identical in both cases. However, the time to enqueue a thread into a ready-queue has dropped significantly, from 86,5% (case (1,1,1)) up to 94,7% (case (2,2,2)). Finally, the time required to find the next thread that will be executed on a processor improved significantly, from 5,2% (case (1,1,1)) up to 71,5% (case (4,1,1)), the average gain being 55,2%. With respect to SMTSIM, we observe that the time to create a thread is worse when only one EU is used. However, if two or more EUs are used, the improvement is from 17,7% (2 EUs) up to 72,5% (4 EUs). The average improvement, including the 1 EU case, is 33,2%. As with the Intel platform, time to enqueue a thread again improves significantly, from 88,2% (2 EUs) up to 97,1% (1 EU).The time required to find the next thread to be executed is slightly worse when up to two EUs are used, but improves significantly in all other cases, ranging from 73,0% (8 EUs) up to 80,9% (6 EUs). The average improvement, including the 1 and 2 EUs cases, is 74,3%.

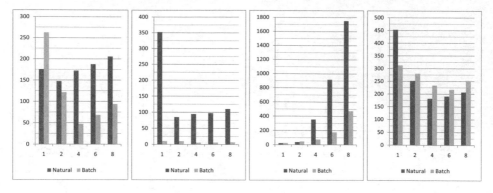

Figure 6. Time in clock cycles to create, enqueue, lookup and start a thread on SMTSIM.

References

[1]   C. D. Antonopoulos, D. S. Nikolopoulos, and T. S. Papatheodorou. Scheduling Algorithms with Bus Bandwidth Considerations for SMPs. In *Proceedings of the 32nd International Conference on Parallel Processing*, pages 547–554, Kaohsiung, Taiwan, October 2003.

[2]   K. Asanovic, R. Bodik, B. Catanzaro, J. Gebis, P. Husbands, K. Keutzer, D. Patterson, W. Plishker, J. Shalf, S. Williams, and K. Yelick. The Landscape of Parallel Computing Research: A View from Berkeley. Technical Report UCB/EECS-2006-183, University of California, December 2006.

[3]   J. del Cuvillo, W. Zhu, Z. Hu, and G. R. Gao. TiNy Threads: a Thread Virtual Machine for the Cyclops64 Cellular Architecture. In *Proceedings of the 5th Workshop on Massively Parallel Processing*, Denver, Colorado, April 2005.

[4]   S. C. Goldstein, K. E. Schauser, and D. E. Culler. Lazy Threads: Implementing a Fast Parallel Call. *Journal of Parallel and Distributed Computing*, Volume 37, Issue 1:5–20, August 1996.

[5]   S. Hummel, E. Schonberg, and L. Flynn. Factoring: a Practical and Robust Method for Scheduling Parallel Loops. In *Proceedings of Supercomputing 1991*, pages 610–632, Albuquerque, USA, 1991.

[6]   S. Kumar, C. J. Hughes, and A. Nguyen. Architectural Support for Fine-Grained Parallelism on Multicore Architectures. *Intel Technology Journal*, Volume 11, Issue 3, August 2007.

[7]   X. Martorell, J. Labarta, N. Navarro, and E. Ayguade. A Library Implementation of the Nano-Threads Programming Model. In *Proceedings of the 2nd International EuroPar Conference*, pages 644–649, Lyon, France, August 1996.

[8]   D. S. Nikolopoulos, T. S. Papatheodorou, C. D. Polychronopoulos, J. Labarta, and E. Ayguadé. Is Data Distribution Necessary in OpenMP? In *Proceedings of Supercomputing'2000: High Performance Computing and Networking Conference*, Dallas, TX, November 2000.

[9]   C. Polychronopoulos, N. Bitar, and S. Kleiman. Nanothreads: A User-Level Threads Architecture. Technical Report 1297, CSRD, University of Illinois at Urbana-Champaign, 1993.

[10] C. Polychronopoulos and D. Kuck. Guided Self-Scheduling: A Practical Scheduling Scheme for Parallel Supercomputers. *IEEE Transactions on Computers*, 36(12):1485–1495, December 1987.

[11] B. Saha, A.-R. Adl-Tabatabai, R. L. Hudson, V. Menon, T. Shpeisman, M. Rajagopalan, A. Ghuloum, E. Sprangle, A. Rohillah, and D. Carmean. Runtime Environment for Tera-scale Platforms. *Intel Technology Journal*, Volume 11, Issue 3, August 2007.

[12] K. Taura, K. Tabata, and A. Yonezawa. Stackthreads/MP : Integrating Futures into Calling Standards. Technical Report TR 99-01, University of Tokyo, 1999.

[13] D. Tullsen, S. Eggers, and H. Levy. Simultaneous Multithreading: Maximizing On-Chip Parallelism. In *Proceedings of the 22nd Annual International Symposium on Computer Architecture*, pages 392–403, S. Margherita Ligure, Italy, 1995.

[14] I. E. Venetis and T. S. Papatheodorou. A Time and Memory Efficient Implementation of the Nano-Threads Programming Model. Technical Report HPCLAB-TR-210106, High Performance Information Systems Laboratory, January 2006.

[15] I. E. Venetis and T. S. Papatheodorou. Tying Memory Management to Parallel Programming Models. In *Proceedings of the 2006 European Conference on Parallel Computing (EuroPar 2006)*, pages 666–675, Dresden, Germany, August 2006. Springer Verlag, LNCS Vol. 4128.

Parallel Computing: From Multicores and GPU's to Petascale
B. Chapman et al. (Eds.)
IOS Press, 2010
© 2010 The authors and IOS Press. All rights reserved.
doi:10.3233/978-1-60750-530-3-265

Skeletons for multi/many-core systems

Marco ALDINUCCI [a] Marco DANELUTTO [b] Peter KILPATRICK [c]

[a] *Dept. Computer Science – Univ. of Torino – Italy*
[b] *Dept. Computer Science – Univ. of Pisa – Italy*
[c] *Dept. Computer Science – Queen's Univ. Belfast – UK*

Abstract. We discuss how algorithmic skeletons (and structured parallel program-ming models in general) can be used to efficiently and seamlessly program multi-core as well as many-core systems. We introduce a new version of the `muskel` skeleton library that can be used to target multi/many-core systems and we present experimental results that demonstrate the feasibility of the approach. The experi-mental results presented also give an idea of the computational grains that can be exploited on current, state-of-the-art multi-core systems.

Keywords. algorithmic skeletons, multi-core, many-core, multithreading

1. Introduction

It is evident that multi/many-core systems (M^2C, from now on) are going to replace single core systems in the immediate future. At the moment, dual/quad core chips al-ready provide the same aggregated performance as single core chips at a fraction of the frequency (and therefore of power) [10]. At the same time, many-core chips have been demonstrated that reach performances in the Teraflop range with power consump-tion which is orders of magnitude smaller than that of clusters with comparable process-ing power [11]. Unfortunately, M^2C systems do not implement the same architectural model as single core ones: single core systems basically present the user/compiler with a Von Neumann architecture. M^2C systems present instead a (possibly, but not necessarily, shared memory) multiprocessor architecture. Therefore *parallel programs* are needed to exploit their power. It is not possible to take a current, sequential program and run it twice as fast on a dual core without modifying it, unless it is already multithreaded. Even if the code has already been implemented as multithreaded, it is not clear whether it could be run on high-end multi-core chips, those hosting tens to hundreds of cores, with decent performance and scalability.

The main issue related to M^2C system exploitation consists in being able to feed these processing elements with a large number of independent threads [9]. A fundamental principle underpinning pursuit of high performance from parallel systems is to always have a thread ready to be scheduled any time one of the independent cores is available to execute a new task. However, this is not the only issue. In the case of the M^2C systems

This work has been partially supported by EU FP6 NoE CoreGRID, EU FP6 STREP GridCOMP and Italian FIRB Insyeme projects.

with a traditional, hierarchical memory subsystem–e.g. those systems where each core accesses memory through one or more levels of local caches–the threads should be such that the memory hierarchy works effectively. The number and the kind of accesses of the different threads should not impair locality in the accesses to the memory subsystem. When the number of threads is large, this might not be so easy. If the M^2C cores do not have access to a traditional cache/memory system–for example, as in the Cell synergic processing elements–or the interconnection network used on the chip is not uniform–e.g. it is a mesh, as in the 80 core Intel experimental chip–more problems arise, leading either to the necessity of being able to identify the memory block transfers needed to execute a thread or to the necessity to move from threads to processes and, moreover, to map the resulting (possibly internally multithreaded) processes in such a way that locality at the process level is preserved at the interconnection level.

Algorithmic skeletons have been presented for many years as an effective means of supporting parallel computing, in contrast with the traditional one where programmers intervene at the source code level to handle all the details related to parallelism exploitation. Many skeleton programming environments have been developed, either as libraries with bindings in well-known sequential languages ([12,5,13] in C/C++, [7,1,8,4] in Java, to name but a few) or as new languages, perhaps providing the possibility to reuse existing sequential portions of code [3,16].

Recently, skeleton system designers have developed versions of their systems effectively targeting multithreaded systems. Calcium [4] allows the programmer/user to choose one of three different "execution environments" via a very simple library call. These execution environments basically represent optimized run times relative to different types of target architectures. One of them targets exactly those architectures capable of running a number of independent threads, such as symmetric multi-processors (SMPs) or M^2C. However, there is as yet no possibility of having different run time systems (execution environments) coexisting and cooperating during the same program execution to target, for example, a network of SMP/M^2C processing elements. Muesli [15] exploits both MPI and openMP to achieve efficient implementation of skeletons on clusters of multi-core processing elements. However, the openMP pragmas affect only data parallel skeletons (distributed arrays and map/reduce/gather operations), as evinced from the source code (see code at [15]). The stream parallel skeleton implementation–e.g. the implementation of pipelines and farms–appears not to take any advantage of the multi-core potentialities.

Here we propose an evolution of the `muskel` skeleton programming environment that seamlessly supports networked M^2C and single core processing elements (Sec. 2). The new `muskel` version (nmc_{muskel}, **n**etworked **m**ulti-**c**ore `muskel`) will be used to assess the feasibility of using skeletons as a programming model for M^2C and networked M^2C systems (Sec. 3). It will also be used to assess (once again) the principle that structuring parallel activities at a high level of abstraction removes much of the burden from the programmer by allowing the compiler and run time system of the skeleton framework to implement very effective policies and strategies.

2. Skeletons going multi/many-core

`muskel` is a full Java skeleton library implementing skeletons according to the macro data flow model [6]. It currently provides a subset of stream parallel skeletons (pipeline

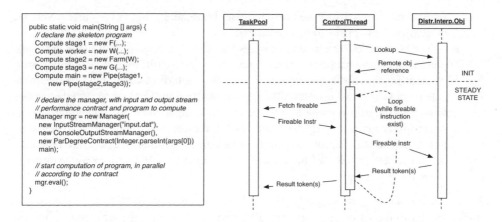

Figure 1. Sample muskel code (*left*). Structure of a muskel ControlThread (*right*).

and task farm) and a simple data parallel skeleton (map). Furthermore, it allows users to extend the skeleton set by defining new entries in the skeleton library and providing a macro data flow implementation of these new skeleton entries. Originally, muskel targeted clusters and networks of workstations, provided the processing elements support Java and RMI accesses.

A muskel program has the form depicted in Fig. 1, left (this is a three stage pipeline, with parallel second stage, computing $G(W(F(x_i)))$ for each input task x_i). First, the code to be executed is defined as a composition of available skeletons and sequential portions of code subclassing the Compute class. This class assumes only the existence of a method sequentially computing the result relative to the input data passed as parameter(s), without any side effect. All the details relative to the parallel execution of the program defined by the user are hidden in the muskel application Manager. The user instantiates a Manager and then uses the manager's eval() method to execute the skeleton program. When the eval() method terminates, the parallel execution of the skeleton program is terminated and its results can be processed. The parallelism degree for the execution of the *whole* program is passed to the Manager (in this case taking it from the command line parameters). An input and an output stream manager should be given to the Manager to handle skeleton program I/O. The InputStreamManager is basically a Java Iterator providing input tasks, while the OutputStreamManager provides a deliver(Object res) method handling (post-processing, storing, etc.) a single item of the result stream. Programmers should instantiate a manager and provide a program, an input and an output stream and then request computation of the program. When the eval() method of the Manager is called

- The program is compiled into a macro data flow graph (a data flow graph where instructions compute sequential, side effect free portions of code modelled by Compute subclasses).
- Then each item on the input stream is used to instantiate an input token of a new graph instance in the muskel TaskPool. The TaskPool is the repository of macro data flow instructions processed by the muskel distributed interpreter. It is a logically centralized data structure. Its implementation may obviously be

implemented in a distributed way to avoid bottlenecks, but in the current version of `muskel` it happens to be centralized.

- A set of `ControlThreads` (set up by the `Manager`, according to the user supplied `PerformanceContract`[1], each managing a different remote processing element hosting a distributed macro data flow interpreter instance) fetches fireable macro data flow instructions from the instruction `TaskPool` and dispatches them for execution on remote interpreters, ensuring load balancing and fairness in remote interpreter usage. The results of the remote executions are dispatched as new tokens to the instructions in the `TaskPool` (if intermediate) or to the output stream (in the case of final results). The operation of a `ControlThread` is shown in Fig. 1 right.

The computation of a `muskel` program therefore consists in the execution of the `Manager` (with the associated `ControlThreads`) on the local user machine and on the execution of distributed macro data flow interpreter instances (`RemoteInterpreter` objects) on remote resources. The exact number of remote interpreters required by the `Manager` according to the user supplied `PerformanceContract` are dynamically recruited through a multicast based discovery protocol run by the `Manager` and by the `RemoteInterpreters`. Interactions between the `Manager` and the remote interpreter instances use plain Java RMI. In the initial phase of a `muskel` program execution the `Compute` subclasses used to execute the different macro data flow instructions are staged to the remote computing elements before program execution actually starts. Then, each time an instruction has to be executed, only the input tokens are serialized to the remote node for execution of the macro data flow instruction. Fig. 2 shows the Orc [14] model of the `muskel` skeleton interpreter, as introduced in [2][2].

Moving to M^2C we decided to perform two different sets of experiments with `muskel`: i) modify the `muskel` `Manager` in such a way that a single M^2C resource is efficiently targeted, and ii) modify the `muskel` `Manager` and the `RemoteInterpreter` in such a way that a cluster of M^2C resources can be efficiently targeted. The resulting prototype is nmc$_{\text{muskel}}$. Both the modifications required a minimal set of changes in the current version of the `muskel` interpreter:

i) in order to have a `Manager` targeting a single M^2C resource, we modified the way `ControlThreads` are paired with the remote resources. Instead of passing the `ControlThread` a resource name obtained from the discovery service, we simply passed the `ControlThread` a new instance of the RMI `Remote` object run by the `RemoteInterpreter` in the original version of `muskel`. In terms of the Orc model of Fig. 2, this means the $discovery(G, pgm, t)$ definition is substituted by

$$discovery(G, pgm, t) \triangleq$$
$$(|_{i=1, n_{core}} let(worker.new())) > w > rmworkerpool.add(w)$$

where $worker.new()$ is the instantiation of a new local object of the same class as the one instantiated by the remote interpreter on remote resources in the original `muskel`. The rest of the interpreter is left unmodified.

---

[1] `ParDegree` is a subclass of `PerformanceContract`

[2] The reader not familiar with Orc may refer to the Orc web site http://orc.csres.utexas.edu/index.shtml for tutorials and documentation

$system(pgm, tasks, contract, G, t) \triangleq$
  $taskpool.add(tasks) \mid discovery(G, pgm, t) \mid manager(pgm, contract, t)$

$discovery(G, pgm, t) \triangleq$
  $(\mid_{g \in G} (\text{ if } remw \neq \text{false} \gg rworkerpool.add(remw)$
        $\text{where } remw \in (g.can\_execute(pgm) \mid Rtimer(t) \gg let(false))))$
                                $\gg discovery(G, pgm, t)$

$manager(pgm, contract, t) \triangleq$
  $\mid_{i\ 1 \leq i \leq contract}(rworkerpool.get > remw > ctrlthread_i(pgm, remw, t))$
  $\mid monitor$

$ctrlthread_i(pgm, remw, t) \triangleq taskpool.get > tk >$
  $(\text{ if } valid \gg resultpool.add(r) \gg ctrlthread_i(pgm, remw, t)$
   $\mid \text{if } \neg valid \gg (taskpool.add(tk)$
                        $\mid alarm.put(i) \gg c_i.get > w > ctrlthread_i(pgm, w, t)))$
    $\text{where } (valid, r) \in$
       $(remw(pgm, tk) > r > let(true, r) \mid Rtimer(t) \gg let(false, 0))$

$monitor \triangleq alarm.get > i > rworkerpool.get > remw > c_i.put(remw)$
        $\gg monitor$

Figure 2. muskel interpreter modelled: Orc modelling/specification

ii) in order to target M^2C remote resources, instead, we changed the discovery service in such a way that remote resources publish their number of cores in response
to the discovery protocol messages. Then, the Manager is free to recruit multiple
instances of RemoteInterpreters on the remote resources hosting multiple
cores. The original multithreaded implementation of RMI servers in Java guarantees that multiple execution requests of macro data flow instructions directed to
the same remote object are executed concurrently. Referring to the Orc model of
Fig. 2, this means the portion

$\mid_{g \in G} (\text{ if } remw \neq \text{false} \gg rworkerpool.add(remw)$
    $\text{where } remw \in (g.can\_execute(pgm) \mid Rtimer(t) \gg let(false))$

Is changed to

$(\mid_{g \in G} (\text{ if } remw \neq \text{false} \gg (\mid_{i \in 1, \#ncore} rworkerpool.add(remw))$
    $\text{where } (remw, \#ncore) \in$
        $(g.can\_execute(pgm) \mid Rtimer(t) \gg let(false))))$

The result is that for each remote resource declaring #ncores available, up to
#ncore ControlThreads will eventually be forked, if needed according to the
PerfConctract. The rest of the interpreter is left unmodified.

We modified the muskel prototype in accordance with i) and ii) above to get the
first version of the nmc$_{muskel}$ interpreter. Using nmc$_{muskel}$, we are able to demonstrate
that heterogeneous workstation networks, hosting different CPUs, single or multi-core,
can be efficiently exploited using skeletons. In the general case, and provided the average
computational grain of the macro data flow instructions executed after compiling the
skeleton application is not too fine, a network with k processing elements and a total
number of M cores can achieve a speedup proportional to M ($speedup = \alpha \times M$) rather
than k (values of α depend on the processing power of the single cores involved).

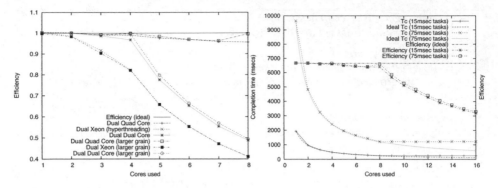

Figure 3. nmc$_{\texttt{muskel}}$: synthetic (floating point) benchmark on different SMP configurations (left) and effect of computational grain on completion time and efficiency of a synthetic (floating point) benchmark on a dual quad core (length of the tasks varied through command line parameters) (right)

3. Experimental results

With the nmc$_{\texttt{muskel}}$ prototype we performed a set of experiments aimed at validating our M^2C targeting strategy. The experiments were run on a network of multi-core systems in Pisa, including dual quad core, dual dual core and dual core Linux systems and dual core Mac OS X systems. The interconnection network used is a (shared) 100Mbit Fast Ethernet.

    Fig. 3 shows results achieved running nmc$_{\texttt{muskel}}$ on a single M^2C system. In this case, the user program, the **Manager** and the distributed macro data flow interpreter instances all run on a single SMP target machine. The left part of this Figure shows the results achieved when executing a synthetic floating point benchmark on different kinds of single M^2C configurations: a dual Xeon machine, a dual dual core and a dual quad core machine, all running Linux (kernel 2.6). As expected, the dual (single core) Xeon stops scaling at 2, while keeping efficiency higher than 80% up to 4 threads, the dual dual core scales up to 4 and the dual quad core scales up to 8. The right part of the same Figure shows completion times and efficiency in relation to average computational grain in the macro data flow instructions derived from the skeleton code according to the **muskel** semantics. Larger grain values present better efficiency than computations whose grain is smaller. These results have been accomplished on a single dual quad core Linux 2.6 system.

    Fig. 4 shows the results achieved using nmc$_{\texttt{muskel}}$ targeting a cluster of multi-core machines interconnected by a Fast Ethernet and running either Linux (kernel 2.6, different distributions) or Mac OS X (10.5.7). All the machines used were running Java 1.6. The left part of the Figure plots completion time and efficiency relative to synthetic applications with quite coarse grain macro data flow instructions. Each macro data flow instruction executed to compute the program took around 0.8 secs to execute on the different machines, after receiving a small number of bytes representing the input data (less that the Fast Ethernet MTU) and delivering a comparable sized result. Both ideal curve and efficiency consider normalized weight for the different cores in the systems used. The numbers shown as n_p in the Figure caption represent the relative speed of the processors, taking into account both the processor speed *and* the time spend to "ping" the machine, as a raw measure of its "network speed". The right part of the Figure shows effects of computational grain on efficiency. Here we used a synthetic program gener-

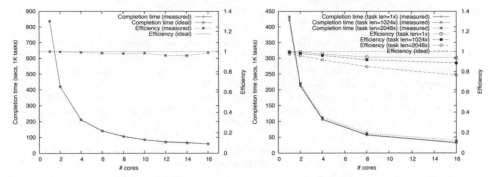

Figure 4. nmc$_{\texttt{muskel}}$: efficiency (left) and effect of computational grain (right) relative to the execution of skeleton programs on a cluster of multi core machines (1 dual quad core (Xeon E5420, 2.5GHz, Linux RedHat, kernel 2.6, $n_p = 1$), 1 dual dual core (Xeon E5150, 2.66GHz, Linux Debian, kernel 2.6, $n_p = 1.1$), 1 dual core hyperthreading (Xeon, 2.80GHz, Linux RedHat, kernel 2.6, $n_p = 0.48$), 1 dual core (Core 2 duo 2.0GHz, Mac OS 10.5.7, $n_p = 0.85$))

ating smaller grain macro data flow instructions and we varied the amount of data consumed (input token(s)) and produced (output token(s)) by the instructions. It is clear that as soon as the computational grain decreases, the efficiency also decreases consistently. We should point out that the decrease in efficiency is partially due to the high serialization penalty incurred when sending input tokens (retrieving output tokens) to (from) the remote interpreters with standard Java RMI.

Last but not least, we compared the execution times achieved using nmc$_{\texttt{muskel}}$ with the times achieved using a dedicated, hand coded implementation programmed using plain TCP/IP sockets. For the synthetic benchmarks used in the experiments relative to Fig. 3 and 4 we measured a constant initialization overhead of about 2 seconds, but then the time spent executing the application with nmc$_{\texttt{muskel}}$ does not exceed the time of the hand coded implementation by more than 8%.

4. Conclusions

We discussed how a macro data flow based skeleton framework conceived to target workstation clusters can be transformed in such a way that multi/many core clusters may be efficiently targeted. The proposed implementation uses only standard Java mechanisms and, this notwithstanding, achieves respectable performance in medium to coarse grain skeleton programs. This is due to the structure of the distributed macro data flow used to implement skeleton programs in `muskel`.

We did not consider targeting heterogeneous multi/many-core systems at the moment, such as those including GPUs or FPGAs. GPUs, in particular, are efficient in executing data parallel (structured) code and we are investigating how to accelerate data parallel skeleton execution when GPUs are available. This research area is being investigated using `muskel`-like C-based prototypes and we will soon have results to present in this area.

References

[1]   Marco Aldinucci, M. Danelutto, and Patrizio Dazzi. Muskel: an expandable skeleton environment. *Scalable Computing: Practice and Experience*, 8(4):325–341, December 2007.

[2]   Marco Aldinucci, Marco Danelutto, and Peter Kilpatrick. Management in distributed systems: a semi-formal approach. In A.-M. Kermarrec, L. Bougé, and T. Priol, editors, *Proc. of 13th Intl. Euro-Par 2007 Parallel Processing*, volume 4641 of *LNCS*, pages 651–661, Rennes, France, August 2007. Springer.

[3]   Bruno Bacci, Marco Danelutto, Salvatore Orlando, Susanna Pelagatti, and Marco Vanneschi. P^3L: a structured high level programming language and its structured support. *Concurrency Practice and Experience*, 7(3):225–255, May 1995.

[4]   Denis Caromel and Mario Leyton. Fine tuning algorithmic skeletons. In *13th International Euro-par Conference: Parallel Processing*, volume 4641 of *Lecture Notes in Computer Science*, pages 72–81, Rennes, France, 2007. Springer-Verlag.

[5]   Murray Cole. Bringing skeletons out of the closet: A pragmatic manifesto for skeletal parallel programming. *Parallel Computing*, 30(3):389–406, 2004.

[6]   Marco Danelutto. Efficient support for skeletons on workstation clusters. *Parallel Processing Letters*, 11(1):41–56, 2001.

[7]   Marco Danelutto. QoS in parallel programming through application managers. In *Proc. of Intl. Euromicro PDP: Parallel Distributed and network-based Processing*, pages 282–289, Lugano, Switzerland, February 2005. IEEE.

[8]   J. Dünnweber and S. Gorlatch. HOC-SA: A grid service architecture for higher-order components. In *IEEE International Conference on Services Computing, Shanghai, China*, pages 288–294. IEEE, September 2004.

[9]   Antonio Gonzales. Elastic Parallel Architectures, 2008. Invited talk at Euro-Par 2008, Las Palmas, Gran Canaria (E), available at http://europar2008.caos.uab.es/documentos/presentation_gonzalez.pdf.

[10] Empowering Advancement with revolutionary energy-efficient performance, 2007. http://www.intel.com/technology/computing/dual-core/index.htm.

[11] TeraFLOPS Research Chip, 2008. http://techresearch.intel.com/articles/Tera-Scale/1449.htm.

[12] Herbert Kuchen. A skeleton library. In B. Monien and R. Feldman, editors, *Proc. of 8th Intl. Euro-Par 2002 Parallel Processing*, volume 2400 of *LNCS*, pages 620–629, Paderborn, Germany, August 2002. Springer.

[13] Kiminori Matsuzaki. Sketo home page, 2009. http://www.ipl.t.u-tokyo.ac.jp/sketo/.

[14] Jayadev Misra and William R. Cook. Computation orchestration: A basis for a wide-area computing. *Software and Systems Modeling*, 2006. DOI 10.1007/s10270-006-0012-1.

[15] The muesli home page, 2006. http://www-wi.uni-muenster.de/pi/personal/kuchen.php.

[16] Marco Vanneschi. The programming model of ASSIST, an environment for parallel and distributed portable applications. *Parallel Computing*, 28(12):1709–1732, December 2002.

Parallel Computing: From Multicores and GPU's to Petascale
B. Chapman et al. (Eds.)
IOS Press, 2010
© 2010 The authors and IOS Press. All rights reserved.
doi:10.3233/978-1-60750-530-3-273

Efficient streaming applications on multi-core with FastFlow: the biosequence alignment test-bed[1]

Marco ALDINUCCI [a,2], Marco DANELUTTO [b], Massimiliano MENEGHIN [b], Massimo TORQUATI [b], and Peter KILPATRICK [c]

[a] *Computer Science Dept., University of Torino, Italy*
[b] *Computer Science Dept., University of Pisa, Italy*
[c] *Computer Science Dept., Queen's University Belfast, U.K.*

Abstract. Shared-memory multi-core architectures are becoming increasingly popular. While their parallelism and peak performance is ever increasing, their efficiency is often disappointing due to memory fence overheads. In this paper we present FastFlow, a programming methodology based on lock-free queues explicitly designed for programming streaming applications on multi-cores. The potential of FastFlow is evaluated on micro-benchmarks and on the Smith-Waterman sequence alignment application, which exhibits a substantial speedup against the state-of-the-art multi-threaded implementation (SWPS3 x86/SSE2).

Keywords. Lock-free queues, multi-threading, multi-core, stream parallel programming, software pipeline, SCM, Smith-Waterman, local sequence alignment, bioinformatics.

Introduction

The success of future multi- and many-core chips depends mainly on advances in system software technologies (compilers, run-time support, programming environments) in order to utilise fully the on-chip parallelism. The tighter coupling of on-chip resources changes the communication to computation ratio that influences the design of parallel algorithms. Modern Single Chip Multiprocessor (SCM) architectures introduce the potential for low overhead inter-core communications, synchronisations and data sharing due to fast path access to the on-die caches. These caches, organised in a hierarchy, are also a potential limiting factor of these architectures since access patterns which are not carefully optimised may lead to relevant access contention for shared cache and invalidation pressure for replicated caches. In fact SCM and, especially, shared-cache multi-core

---

[1]This work was partially funded by the project BioBITs ("Developing White and Green Biotechnologies by Converging Platforms from Biology and Information Technology towards Metagenomic") of Regione Piemonte, by the project FRINP of the "Fondazione della Cassa di Risparmio di Pisa", and by the WG Ercim CoreGrid topic "Advanced Programming Models".

[2]Corresponding Author: Computer Science Department, University of Torino, Corso Svizzera 185, Torino, Italy; E-mail: aldinuc@di.unito.it

architectures are showing, even at the current scale, severe scalability limitations when programmed in the traditional way (e.g. using threads and monitors).

Performance on SCM is limited by the same factors as those that arise in shared-memory parallel architectures. Some of these limitations stem from the use of atomic memory transactions, which exhibit a rather high latency and tend to pollute the shared memory hierarchy. In reality, those operations are not strictly required when concurrent threads operate in a pipeline fashion, because data can be streamed from one stage to the next using fast lock-free queues. In this paper we show that this lock-free approach can be extended from simple pipelines to any *streaming network*. Such networks can be used directly to build efficient applications working on data streams; and, indirectly, to realise the implicit parallelisation of a wide class of algorithms. In fact a parallel Macro Data-Flow interpreter can be designed as a (cyclic) streaming network (e.g. according to the *farm* or *master-worker* paradigms/skeletons) [2,4,16,3].

FastFlow streaming networks are build upon two lower-level companion concepts: lock-free Multiple-Producer-Multiple-Consumer (MPMC) queues and a parallel lock-free memory allocator (MA). Both are realised as specific networks of threads connected via lock-free Single-Producer-Single-Consumer (SCSP) queues, which admit a very efficient implementation on cache-coherent SCM [9]. These concepts are implemented as a C++ template library.

Here we discuss how the FastFlow library can be used to build a widely used parallel programming paradigm (a.k.a. skeleton), i.e. the streaming stateful farm; and we compare its raw scalability against a hand-tuned Pthread-based counterpart on a dual quad-core Intel platform. The FastFlow farm skeleton can be rapidly and effectively used to boost the performance of many existing real-world applications, for example the Smith-Waterman local alignment algorithm [18]. In the following we show that a straightforward porting of the multi-threaded x86/SSE2-enabled SWPS3 implementation [19] onto FastFlow is twice as fast as the SWPS3 itself, which is a hand-tuned high-performance implementation.

1. Related Work

The stream programming paradigm offers a promising approach for programming multi-core systems. Stream languages are motivated by the application style used in image processing, networking, and other media processing domains. Many languages and libraries are available for programming stream applications. Some are general purpose programming languages that hide the detail of the underlying architectural. Stream languages enable the explicit specification of producer-consumer parallelism between coarse grain units of computation; examples include *StreamIt* [20], *S-Net* [17], *Brook* [6], and *CUDA* [11]. Some other languages, such as the *Intel Threading Building Block* (TBB), provide explicit mechanisms for both streaming and other parallel paradigms, while others, such as *OpenMP* and *Cilk*, although targeted particularly at data parallelism, can with greater programming effort be used to implement streaming applications.

StreamIt is an explicitly parallel programming language based on the Synchronous Data Flow (SDF) programming model. A StreamIt program is represented as a set of autonomous actors that communicate through first-in, first-out (FIFO) data channels. StreamIt contains syntactic constructs for defining programs structured as task graphs, where each task contains Java-like sequential code. The interconnection types provided are: Pipeline for straight task combinations, SplitJoin for nesting data parallelism and FeedbackLoop for connections from consumers back to producers. The communications are implemented either as shared circular buffers or message passing for small amounts of control information.

S-Net [17] is a coordination language to describe the communications of asynchronous sequential components (a.k.a. boxes) written in sequential language (e.g. C, C++, Java) through typed streams. S-net boxes are entirely stateless, they are connected to other boxes by one single input and one single output typed streams and operate only in a input-process-output cycle. Complex stream networks are inductively defined using a set of four network combiners, which can express serial and parallel composition of two different networks as well as serial and parallel replication of a single network.

Brook [6] provides extensions to the C language with single program multiple data (SPMD) operations that work on streams. User defined functions operating on stream elements are called kernels and can be executed in parallel. Brook kernels feature blocking behaviour: the execution of a kernel must complete before the next kernel can execute. This is the same execution model as is available on graphics processing units (GPUs). CUDA [11], which is an infrastructure from NVIDIA, presents features similar to those of Brook, but programmers are required to use low-level mechanisms to manage memory hierarchies.

Streaming applications are also targeted by TBB [10] through the *pipeline* construct. FastFlow is methodologically similar to TBB, since it aims to provide a library of explicitly parallel constructs (a.k.a. parallel programming paradigms or skeletons) that extends the base language (e.g. C, C++, Java). This approach is fully aligned with those traditionally followed within the skeleton research community [7,16,1,4,5,15,3]. However, TBB does not support any kind of non-linear streaming network, which therefore has to be embedded in a pipeline. This results in a non-trivial programming and performance drawback since pipeline stages must bypass data that they are not interested with.

Giacomini et al. [9] highlight the fact that traditional locking queues feature a high overhead on today's multi-core. Revisiting Lamport's work [12], which proves the correctness of lock-free mechanisms for concurrent Single-Producer-Single-Consumer (SPSC) queues on systems with memory sequential consistency commitment, they proposed a set of lock-free cache-optimised protocols for today's multi-core architectures. They also prove the benefit of those mechanisms on pipeline applications. Exploiting a lock-free SPSC, FastFlow substantially extends the work of Giacomini et al., from simple pipelines to *any streaming network*.

2. Fast Streaming Networks on Multi-core

FastFlow aims to provide a set of low-level mechanisms capable of supporting low-latency and high-bandwidth data flows in a network of threads running on a cache-coherent SCM. These flows, which are typical of streaming applications, are assumed to be mostly unidirectional and asynchronous. On these architectures the key issues concern memory fences, which are required to keep the various caches coherent.

FastFlow currently provides the programmer with two basic mechanisms: MPMC queues and a memory allocator. The memory allocator is build on top of MPMC queues

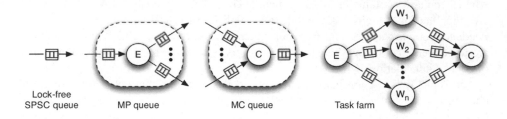

Figure 1. FastFlow concepts: Lock-free SPSC queue, MP queue, MC queue, Emitter (E) and Collector (C), and a streaming network implementing a task farm.

and can be substituted by either an OS standard allocator or a third-party allocator (e.g. TBB scalable allocator [10]). The FastFlow memory allocator substantially boosts Fast-Flow applications that use dynamic memory allocation but it does not have any impact on applications using static memory allocation, and thus is not discussed in this paper.

The key intuition behind FastFlow is to provide the programmer with lock-free MP queues and MC queues (that can be used in pipeline to build MPMC queues) to support fast streaming networks. Traditionally, MPMC queues are build as passive entities: threads concurrently synchronise (according to some protocol) to access data; these synchronisations are usually supported by one or more atomic operations (e.g. CAS: Compare-And-Swap) that behave as memory fences. The FastFlow design follows a different approach: to avoid any memory fence, the synchronisations among queue readers or writers are arbitrated by an active entity (e.g. a thread), as shown in Fig. 1. We call these entities *Emitter* (E) or *Collector* (C) according to their role; they actually read an item from one or more lock-free SPSC queues and write to one or more lock-free SPSC queues. This requires a memory copy but no atomic operations (this is a trivial corollary of lock-free SPSC correctness [9]). FastFlow networks do not suffer from the ABA problem [14] since MPMC queues are built by explicitly linearising correct SPSC queues using Emitters and Collectors.

The performance advantage of this solution derives from the relative speed of the copy with respect to the memory fence, and its impact on cache invalidation. This also depends on the size and the memory layout of copied data. The former point is addressed by using data pointers instead of data and enforcing that data is not concurrently written: in many cases this can be derived from the semantics of the skeleton that has been implemented using MPMC queues (for example, this is guaranteed in a stateless farm and many other cases). The latter point is addressed by using a suitable memory allocator (not presented in this paper).

3. Experimental Evaluation

We evaluate the performance of FastFlow with two families of applications: a synthetic micro-benchmark and the Smith-Waterman local sequence alignment algorithm. All experiments are executed on a shared memory Intel platform with two quad-core Xeon E5420 Harpertown 2.5GHz 6MB L2 cache and 8 GBytes of main memory.

```
void Emitter () {                    void Worker() {                      int main () {
  for ( i=0;i<streamLen;++i){          while (!end_of_stream){              spawn_thread(Emitter);
    task = create_task () ;              myqueue−>POP(&task);              for ( i=0;i<nworkers;++i){
    queue=                               do_work(task);                     spawn_thread(Worker);
      SELECT_WORKER_QUEUE();        }                                    }
    queue−>PUSH(task);             }                                     wait_end () ;
  }                                                                    }
}
```

Figure 2. Micro-benchmark pseudo-code.

3.1. Micro-benchmarks

Micro-benchmarks mock a parallel filtering application via a farm skeleton with a parametric synthetic load in the worker; by varying this load it is possible to evaluate the speedup for different computation grains, and therefore the overhead of the communication infrastructure. The pseudo-code of the micro-benchmark is sketched in Fig.2. A task is a pointer to a pre-allocated array of data, whereas the *do_work()* function just modifies the data pointed to by the task and then spends a fixed amount of time. Notice that the analysis of communication latency and bandwidth among a linear pipeline (through a lock-free SPSC queue) is beyond the scope of this paper (see related works [9]).

As is clear from the comparison of the two families of curves in Fig. 3, the standard implementation based on Pthread exhibits no speedup at all with fine grain tasks, while the proposed implementation exhibits a reasonable speedup, even for very fine computation grains (e.g. 5 μS and even finer grains such as 0.5 μS), and almost ideal speedup for medium to coarse grains. The communication overhead between successive stages is the most important limiting factor for fine-grain streaming networks. On the tested architecture we experienced that a put/get operation on a lock-based queue exhibits at least a threefold cost with respect to the same operation on a lock-free implementation (0.09 − 0.11 μs vs 0.03 − 0.04 μs).

3.2. Smith-Waterman Algorithm

In bioinformatics, sequence database searches are used to find the similarity between a query sequence and subject sequences in the database, in order to discover similar regions between two nucleotide or protein sequences, encoded as a string of characters in an alphabet (e.g. {A,C,G,T}). The sequence similarities can be determined by computing their optimal local alignments using the Smith-Waterman (SW) algorithm [18]. SW is a dynamic programming algorithm that is guaranteed to find the optimal local alignment with respect to the scoring system being used. Instead of looking at the total sequence, the SW algorithm compares segments of all possible lengths and optimises the similarity measure. The cost of this approach is fairly expensive in terms of memory space and computing time ($\mathcal{O}(mn)$, where n and m are the lengths of the two sequences), which is increasingly significant with the rapid growth of biological sequence databases.

For SW and similar algorithms, the emerging multi- and many-core architectures represent a concrete opportunity to cut computation time to acceptable figures, even for large datasets.

Moreover, it provides an ideal test-bed to evaluate the FastFlow performance on a real-world algorithm because:

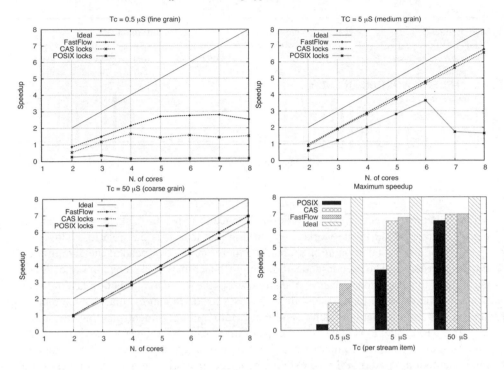

Figure 3. The speedup of different implementations of farm for different computation grains.

- SW features several efficient parallel hand-tuned implementations to be used as reference implementations;
- it works on a long stream of independent tasks;
- it makes possible variation of the computational grain from very fine to coarse by simply changing the query length.

Recent works in this area focus on the implementation of the SW algorithm on many-core architectures like GPUs [13] and Cell/BE [8] and on multi-core architectures exploiting the x86/SSE2 instruction set [8]. From them we selected the SWPS3, which has been extensively optimised to run on Cell/BE and on x86/64 CPUs with SSE2 instructions [19]. SWPS3 is an extension of Farrar's work for the Striped Smith-Waterman algorithm described in [8].

The original SWPS3 version is designed as a master-worker computation where the master process distributes the workload to a set of worker processes. The master process handles file I/O and communicates with the worker processes over bidirectional pipes to supply them with database sequences and to collect alignment scores. Every worker computes the alignment of the query sequence with a separate database sequence. We modified the original code to turn it into a FastFlow application by simply (almost syntactically) substituting processes with threads and pipes with FastFlow queues. The master thread (emitter) reads the sequence database and produces a stream of pairs: *<query sequence, subject sequence>*. The query sequence remains the same for all the subject sequences contained in the database. The worker threads compute the Smith-Waterman

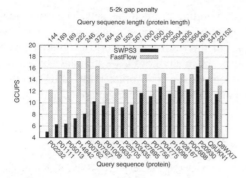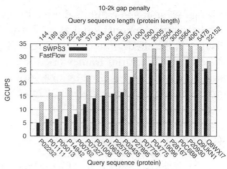

Figure 4. Smith-Waterman sequence alignment algorithm: FastFlow against SWPS3 implementation for $(5 - 2k)$ and $(10 - 2k)$ gap penalties evaluated on Release 57.5 of 07-Jul-09 of UniProtKB/Swiss-Prot (contains 471472 sequence entries, comprising 167326533 amino-acids abstracted from 181042 references). The two implementations share exactly the same sequential (x86/SSE2 vectorised) code.

algorithm on the input pairs using the SSE2 instructions set. The collector thread gets the resulting score and produces the output string (score and sequence name).

Figure 4 reports the performance comparison between SWPS3 and the FastFlow version of the SW algorithm for x86/SSE2 executed on the test platform described above. The scoring matrix BLOSUM50 is used for the tests with a gap penalty of 10-2 k and 5-2 k respectively. All the other parameters in the SWPS3 implementation are used with their default values. As can be seen from the figures, the FastFlow implementation outperforms the original SWPS3 x86/SSE2 version for all the sequences tested. SWPS3 achieves a peak performance of up to 16.31 and 29.19 GCUPS with a gap penalty of 5-2 k and 10-2 k, respectively, whereas the FastFlow version reaches a peak performance of up to 18.94 GCUPS with a gap penalty of 5-2 k and 34.38 GCUPS with a gap penalty of 10-2 k. The GCUPS (Giga-Cell-Updates-Per-Second) is a commonly used performance measure in bioinformatics and is calculated by multiplying the length of the query sequence by the length of the database divided by the total elapsed time.

The smaller the query sequences are, the bigger is the performance gain. This is mainly due to the lower overhead of the FastFlow communication channels with respect to the standard POSIX channels exploited by SWPS3. Other results, not shown here due to space limitations, demonstrate the further performance gain obtained by the FastFlow implementations when multiple query sequences are tested in a single FastFlow run. In fact, in this case, contrary to the SWPS3 implementation, FastFlow does not require the flushing of farm queues when the query changes.

4. Conclusions

FastFlow extends the use of lock-free SPSC queues from the implementation of the linear pipeline to any streaming network, including task farming. FastFlow networks make it possible to build very fast streaming applications on commodity multi-core architectures even for very fine-grained tasks. As an example, the FastFlow version of the Smith-Waterman algorithm, obtained from a third-party high-performance implementation by simply substituting communication primitives, is always faster when compared to the original version and exhibits double its speedup on fine-grained datasets. The presented results should be considered as a "feasibility study" of the proposed approach. We envisage, in the medium term, FastFlow as part of the run-time support of a higher-level skeletal programming framework for a multi- and many-core C++ template-based library that will be released as open-source. Comparison with other multi-core-specific programming frameworks such as Intel TBB and OpenMP is among planned activities.

References

[1]   M. Aldinucci, S. Campa, P. Ciullo, M. Coppola, S. Magini, P. Pesciullesi, L. Potiti, R. Ravazzolo, M. Torquati, M. Vanneschi, and C. Zoccolo. The implementation of ASSIST, an environment for parallel and distributed programming. In *Proc. of 9th Intl Euro-Par 2003 Parallel Processing*, volume 2790 of *LNCS*, pages 712–721, Klagenfurt, Austria, Aug. 2003. Springer.

[2]   M. Aldinucci and M. Danelutto. Stream parallel skeleton optimization. In *Proc. of PDCS: Intl. Conference on Parallel and Distributed Computing and Systems*, pages 955–962, Cambridge, Massachusetts, USA, Nov. 1999. IASTED, ACTA press.

[3]   M. Aldinucci, M. Danelutto, and P. Kilpatrick. Towards hierarchical management of autonomic components: a case study. In *Proc. of Intl. Euromicro PDP 2009: Parallel Distributed and network-based Processing*, pages 3–10, Weimar, Germany, Feb. 2009. IEEE.

[4]   M. Aldinucci, M. Danelutto, and P. Teti. An advanced environment supporting structured parallel programming in Java. *Future Generation Computer Systems*, 19(5):611–626, July 2003.

[5]   H. Bischof, S. Gorlatch, and R. Leshchinskiy. Dattel: A data-parallel c++ template library. *Parallel Processing Letters*, 13(3):461–472, 2003.

[6]   I. Buck, T. Foley, D. Horn, J. Sugerman, K. Fatahalian, M. Houston, and P. Hanrahan. Brook for gpus: stream computing on graphics hardware. In *ACM SIGGRAPH '04 Papers*, pages 777–786, New York, NY, USA, 2004. ACM Press.

[7]   M. Cole. *Skeletal Parallelism home page*, 2009. http://homepages.inf.ed.ac.uk/mic/Skeletons/.

[8]   M. Farrar. Striped Smith-Waterman speeds database searches six times over other SIMD implementations. *Bioinformatics*, 23(2):156–161, 2007.

[9]   J. Giacomoni, T. Moseley, and M. Vachharajani. Fastforward for efficient pipeline parallelism: a cache-optimized concurrent lock-free queue. In *Proc. of the 13th ACM SIGPLAN Symposium on Principles and practice of parallel programming (PPoPP)*, pages 43–52, New York, NY, USA, 2008. ACM.

[10] Intel Corp. *Threading Building Blocks*, 2009. http://www.threadingbuildingblocks.org/.

[11] D. Kirk. Nvidia cuda software and gpu parallel computing architecture. In *Proc. of the 6th Intl. symposium on Memory management (ISM)*, pages 103–104, New York, NY, USA, 2007. ACM.

[12] L. Lamport. Specifying concurrent program modules. *ACM Trans. Program. Lang. Syst.*, 5(2):190–222, 1983.

[13] Y. Liu, D. Maskell, and B. Schmidt. CUDASW++: optimizing Smith-Waterman sequence database searches for CUDA-enabled graphics processing units. *BMC Research Notes*, 2(1):73, 2009.

[14] M. M. Michael and M. L. Scott. Nonblocking algorithms and preemption-safe locking on multiprogrammed shared memory multiprocessors. *J. of Parallel and Distributed Computing*, 51(1):1–26, 1998.

[15] M. Poldner and H. Kuchen. Scalable farms. In *Proc. of Intl. PARCO 2005: Parallel Computing*, Malaga, Spain, Sept. 2005.

[16] J. Serot. Tagged-token data-flow for skeletons. *Parallel Processing Letters*, 11(4):377–392, 2001.

[17] A. Shafarenko, C. Grelck, and S.-B. Scholz. Semantics and type theory of S-Net. In *Proc. of the 18th Intl. Symposium on Implementation and Application of Functional Languages (IFL'06)*, TR 2006-S01, pages 146–166. Eötvös Loránd University, Faculty of Informatics, Budapest, Hungary, 2006.

[18] T. F. Smith and M. S. Waterman. Identification of common molecular subsequences. *J Mol Biol*, 147(1):195–197, March 1981.

[19] A. Szalkowski, C. Ledergerber, P. Krähenbühl, and C. Dessimoz. *SWPS3 – fast multi-threaded vectorized Smith-Waterman for IBM Cell/B.E. and x86/SSE2*, 2008.

[20] W. Thies, M. Karczmarek, and S. P. Amarasinghe. StreamIt: A language for streaming applications. In *Proc. of the 11th Intl. Conference on Compiler Construction (CC)*, pages 179–196, London, UK, 2002. Springer.

Parallel Computing: From Multicores and GPU's to Petascale
B. Chapman et al. (Eds.)
IOS Press, 2010
© 2010 The authors and IOS Press. All rights reserved.
doi:10.3233/978-1-60750-530-3-281

A framework for detailed multiphase cloud modeling on HPC systems

Matthias LIEBER [a,1], Ralf WOLKE [b], Verena GRÜTZUN [b], Matthias S. MÜLLER [a], and Wolfgang E. NAGEL [a]

[a] *Center for Information Services and High Performance Computing (ZIH), TU Dresden, Germany*
[b] *Leibniz Institute for Tropospheric Research (IfT), Leipzig, Germany*

Abstract. Cloud processes are appreciated to be of increasing importance to the comprehension of the atmosphere. Therefore, weather models have recently been extended by detailed spectral descriptions of cloud processes. However, the high computational costs hinder their practical application. This paper introduces the novel framework FD4 (Four-Dimensional Distributed Dynamic Data structures), which is developed to parallelize and couple cloud models to atmospheric models in an efficient way and to enable a higher scalability on HPC systems. Results of first tests with the regional forecast model COSMO are presented.

Keywords. multiphase cloud modeling, spectral microphysics, high performance computing, parallelization framework, load balancing, model coupling

Introduction

Clouds are of significant importance to the atmosphere due to their influence on the radiation budget, the hydrological cycle, scavenging, and wet deposition processes, as well as aqueous-phase chemical reactions [9,24]. Nevertheless, cloud processes represent one of the major uncertainties in current weather forecast, air quality, and climate models [18]. Most of today's weather models incorporate cloud microphysical processes based on the *bulk* approach. Each of the hydrometeor classes (e.g. water droplets, graupel, and snow) is represented by its bulk mass only, while neglecting the size distribution of the particles. However, several studies emphasize the importance of a size-resolving approach [5,15]. Such *spectral* microphysical models explicitly characterize the size distribution of the hydrometeors by applying a bin discretization. These models have been applied for process studies only, but not for operational applications because of very high computational costs. However, the next generation of atmospheric model systems has to incorporate more detailed descriptions of cloud processes in order to achieve more realistic forecasts, for example in air quality modeling [8]. This is only possible by taking the space-time heterogeneity of cloud processes into account in order to focus computation time and

---

[1]Corresponding Author: Matthias Lieber, Center for Information Services and High Performance Computing (ZIH), TU Dresden, 01062 Dresden, Germany; E-mail: matthias.lieber@tu-dresden.de

This work has been funded by the German Research Foundation (DFG), grant No. NA 711/2-1.

memory on interesting (cloudy) regions. To our knowledge, such dynamic techniques have not yet been used for spectral cloud models.

This paper presents first results of our efforts to overcome this deficiency and enable the practical application of such complex model systems. We are developing the software framework FD4 (Four-Dimensional Distributed Dynamic Data structures), which provides an efficient coupling of detailed cloud models to existing atmospheric models. It matches the specific requirements of cloud models in terms of data structures and load balance to achieve better performance on HPC systems than previous approaches. Furthermore, FD4 is designed to be generally applicable to multiphase modeling in the geosciences and chemical engineering [3].

1. Related work

Spectral bin microphysics have been introduced in the 3D atmospheric models MM5 [15], WRF [14], and COSMO [6]. In all three cases, the weather model's framework was used for storage and static domain decomposition of the hydrometeor size distributions. Due to the high computational costs, these detailed cloud models have been used only for process studies until now.

The space-time heterogeneity of cloud processes demands adaptive simulation methods to limit the computational costs. Today, space-time heterogeneity is handled with adaptive mesh refinement (AMR). Several frameworks for parallel structured AMR [4] have been developed in the last years, e.g., PARAMESH [16], CHOMBO [21], and ALPS [2]. In the structured AMR approach, the grid is decomposed into blocks which are refined hierarchically depending on solution features. These blocks are also used for dynamic load balancing [22], which is typically based on space-filling curves (SFC) or graph repartitioning methods. Our framework handles spatial adaptivity not by refinement, but by allocating blocks of a fixed resolution only where clouds exist. However, there are many common problems like dynamic data structures, domain decomposition, load balancing, as well as the need for a flexible user interface.

Coupling models of different disciplines is an important approach to more detailed simulations, especially in the Earth Sciences. Therefore, different coupling frameworks for parallel models have been developed. OASIS [23] and PALM [1] focus on coupling independent models whose grids may have a different structure and decomposition. They use a coupler process as intermediate instance for data transformation with a potential trade-off on performance, but benefits in flexibility when assembling a complex system of many models. A direct and thus tighter coupling is provided by MCT [13]. MESSy [10] is a special infrastructure to couple various fine-grained submodels to a general circulation model. Like MESSy, FD4 is focused on a special application domain which allows us to realize specific optimizations of data structures and parallel algorithms. In contrast to OASIS and PALM, our approach favors performance even if this compromises flexibility. This is motivated in the following section.

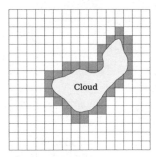

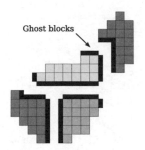

1.1 Grid adaption to clouds: Only those blocks are allocated which are required to capture the clouds.

1.2 Hilbert SFC partitioning: Allocated blocks are ordered by the SFC and divided into partitions for parallelization.

1.3 Ghost blocks: Ghost cells are allocated at the partition boundaries only, not at every block, to reduce memory consumption.

Figure 1. Illustration of FD4 concepts for a 2D grid with an exemplary cloud.

2. The multiphase cloud modeling framework FD4

Our experiences with the detailed cloud modeling system COSMO–SPECS [6] influenced the design process of the new framework FD4. From the computational point of view, COSMO–SPECS is a straightforward implementation: the microphysics parameterization of the mesoscale forecast model COSMO [19] has been replaced by the spectral cloud model SPECS [20]. The microphysics computation and related boundary communication take up more than 90% of the total runtime of COSMO-SPECS (measured with 100 processes on an SGI Altix 4700). The high computational costs of the spectral bin microphysics model are further degraded by poorly balanced workload. We observed that grid cells within clouds consume more than six times of the calculation time than grid cells in cloudless areas.

Future applications of detailed cloud models demand a high scalability which is only possible by introducing a dynamic load balancing of the microphysics computations. This requires the separation of the cloud data structures from the usually static domain decomposition of the basic meteorological model. Our new framework FD4 handles this separation along with further optimizations which utilize specific properties of spectral cloud models: The data structures are optimized for huge amounts of data per grid cell and the microphysics variables are only allocated where clouds exist to save memory. This unique combination of features will help making detailed cloud modeling more applicable for practical cases.

The framework FD4 is implemented in Fortran 95 and uses MPI for parallelization, which allows a smooth integration in present weather codes. In its current state, the following basic services for multiphase cloud modeling are provided:

- Block-based decomposition and parallelization of a rectangular numerical grid
- Dynamical adaption of the grid to spatial cloud structure
- Dynamic load balancing
- Coupling interface to embed cloud models into meteorological models
- NetCDF4 and Vis5D output

Important features are described in the following subsections.

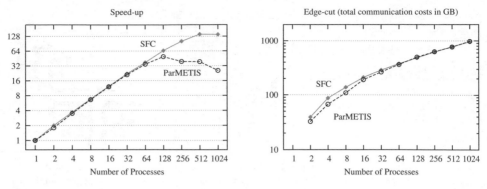

Figure 2. Performance comparison of SFC partitioning and ParMETIS on an SGI Altix 4700 system. The Edge-cut is shown as the total communication volume of the boundary data exchange.

2.1. Adaption to spatial cloud structure

The spectral approach as applied in COSMO-SPECS requires in the order of 1000 variables per grid cell, which potentially results in substantial quantities of wasted memory for cloudless grid cells. FD4 provides a dynamic adaption of the grid to the cloud structure, which means that only the parts of the grid are present where clouds exist and *empty* blocks claim no memory, see Figure 1.1. *Empty* can be defined via a threshold for selected variables, such as, e.g., cloud water concentration. The framework ensures that appropriate data are provided for the numerical stencil around non-*empty* cells. The removal of blocks may cause mass loss, which can be avoided by setting the threshold to zero. However, due to the numerical diffusion of advection schemes, this can lead to a large number of allocated blocks, which limits the advantage of the approach. Therefore, less diffusive advection schemes or volume-of-fluid methods [7] should be applied. In our application, the microphysics reduces the effect of the cloud diffusion by the evaporation of hydrometeors to water vapor.

2.2. Dynamic load balancing

By separating data structures of the cloud model and the atmospheric model, it is possible to apply an individual decomposition with dynamic load balancing for the cloud model. Repartitioning is triggered either when the load balance decreases below a certain limit or when the block structure needs to readapt to the cloud structure, i.e. blocks are added or removed. Two methods of partitioning have been implemented in FD4: partitioning based on the Hilbert space-filling curve (see Figure 1.2) and graph repartitioning using the library ParMETIS [11]. To compare the performance of both approaches, a benchmark simulating the transport of an 'abstract cloud' using a 2nd order advection scheme has been implemented. 1000 variables per grid cell are transported to replicate the memory demands of a detailed spectral model. The parallel block structure dynamically adapts to the cloud structure. Consequently, permanent rebalancing of the blocks is required. Note, that this benchmark is relatively communication-bound, as the advection calculation is computationally inexpensive. The results presented in Figure 2 show that both methods provide comparable partition quality. However, the SFC-based load balancing scales much better. The reason is the faster calculation of the new partitioning in comparison to ParMETIS. A detailed analysis using the Vampir tool-set [12] revealed that ParMETIS spends most of the time performing global MPI communication, which becomes more expensive at higher processor numbers.

2.3. Ghost block implementation

Since we are confronted with hundreds of variables per grid cell, only small blocks (in terms of grid cells) will not exceed the processor cache. Additionally, only such small blocks can adapt efficiently to the spatial cloud structure. With a large number of small blocks it is also possible to achieve a more fine-grained load balancing. For these reasons we optimized the framework for blocks containing only a few grid cells but a large amount of variables. First of all, this means that the typical way to allocate blocks with additional so-called ghost cells to store data from neighbor blocks is too costly in terms of memory requirements. For example, in a three-dimensional decomposition with blocks of 4^3 grid cells, 87.5 % of the storage is consumed for ghost cells when applying two rows of them. Instead of allocating all blocks with ghost cells, FD4 provides only additional ghost blocks at the processor boundaries as shown in Figure 1.3. To access local blocks and ghost cells in the same manner as in the usual approach, the data are copied to a work array before performing stencil computations. This approach of reducing memory requirements has also been implemented as an option in the PARAMESH framework [16].

2.4. Coupling to meteorological models

FD4 features a coupling interface to send variables from a parallel meteorological model to the data structures of the framework and vice versa. As both have different domain decompositions, the geometrically overlapping areas between the partitions of all senders and the partitions of all receivers are determined by the library. The data of these intersections are then exchanged directly between the meteorological model's data fields and the FD4 data structures.

3. Test applications

We have developed exemplary test applications of the framework in order to demonstrate its applicability and analyze its performance. For this purpose, FD4 has been coupled to the weather forecast models COSMO [19] and WRF [17].

3.1. Adaption to the cloud structure of a real-life scenario in COSMO

This test is based on a COSMO real-life scenario covering Saxony, Germany. The computational grid has a horizontal resolution of 1 km and consists of 249×174 cells in 50 vertical layers. The cloud describing variables (cloud water and cloud ice) of the COSMO model are transmitted to the FD4 framework using its coupling interface. There, the block structure adapts to the cloud structure and is partitioned as depicted in Figure 3. No computations are carried out on the FD4 data structures. The overhead of the framework for block adaption, partitioning, and coupling data transfer has been measured for a one hour forecast with a time step of 10 s. The framework performs basically three tasks for each of the 360 time steps:

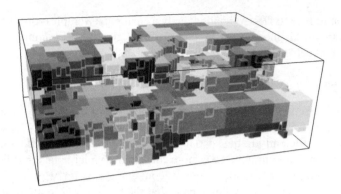

Figure 3. Visualization of the FD4 cloud partitioning for a real-case simulation. The blocks are 4^3 grid cells in size and the partitioning for 64 processes is calculated using the Hilbert space-filling curve.

1. Determine required blocks: Find out which blocks are required to cover all grid cells for which cloud water or cloud ice concentration is not zero in COSMO. Additionally, ensure that a boundary of two grid cells around each of the 'cloudy' cells is present in the block structure.
2. SFC partitioning: Calculate a balanced partitioning of these blocks using the Hilbert SFC.
3. Coupling: Transfer cloud variables from COSMO's partitions to the FD4 block structure.

Note, that the clouds show such high dynamics that the block structure needs to readapt every time step. The benchmark has been run with different block sizes: medium sized blocks with 4^3 grid cells and very small blocks with 2^3 grid cells. In the first case, 11 427 blocks were present in average over the runtime compared to 63 597 blocks in the latter case. Figure 4 shows the results measured on an AMD Opteron cluster with SDR Infiniband interconnect. The determination of required blocks scales only little, as the algorithm's speed depends on the partition size as well as on the total number of blocks. At high processor numbers, collective communication with `MPI_Allgatherv` becomes very costly. The SFC partitioning time depends only on the number of blocks and does not scale. However, in comparison to ParMETIS, the SFC partitioning is much faster. The coupling transfer, which is mainly communication-bound, scales well to 256 processes. Further tuning of the partition matching algorithm is necessary to enable a higher scalability. In summary, the framework's overhead highly depends on the number of blocks, which is a critical issue since we are aiming to apply relatively small blocks.

3.2. Tracer simulation with WRF

As a proof of concept demonstration, FD4 has been coupled to the Weather Research and Forecasting Model (WRF). The WRF model provides an API for I/O and model coupling, which is used to write model output in various formats as well as for coupling of, e.g., ocean models to WRF. Based on this API, we implemented a new coupling package to transfer data fields from WRF to the data structures of FD4. As an exemplary application, the wind fields computed by WRF are used to transport a passive tracer which represents the prospective cloud variables. The tracer is transported with an advection scheme implemented and parallelized with FD4. FD4 adapts the block structure dynamically to

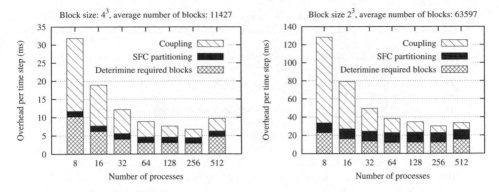

Figure 4. Performance of FD4 in the COSMO test application. The overhead of FD4 components is shown as average time per process and time step for different block sizes.

the propagation of the tracer. This example is already very close to the application of the framework for the coupling of a detailed cloud model to an atmospheric model.

4. Conclusion and outlook

In this paper, we introduced the computational barriers which hinder the operational application of spectral cloud models in three-dimensional atmospheric models. Current approaches use the static framework of their basic weather code to couple the cloud processes and, thus, do not take the heterogeneity of cloud processes into account. The new parallelization and coupling framework FD4 adapts the grid's memory and partitioning dynamically to the cloud structure, to enable a more efficient coupling of the cloud processes than current implementations. As a next step, we will upgrade COSMO–SPECS to use FD4 for the parallelization and coupling of the cloud model. We expect substantial performance gain due to the dynamic load balancing and the more efficient boundary communication provided by FD4. Further, we will add the ability to perform parallel I/O, which is required to efficiently cope with large amounts of data, as in spectral cloud models. Finally, the most challenging task in developing such dynamic frameworks is to keep the balance between adaptivity in the data structures (aiming at saving memory and computations) and the overhead that comes along with this adaptivity.

References

[1] S. Buis, A. Piacentini, and Damien Déclat.   PALM: a computational framework for assembling high-performance computing applications. *Concurrency and Computation: Practice and Experience*, 18(2):231–245, 2006.

[2] C. Burstedde, O. Ghattas, M. Gurnis, G. Stadler, E. Tan, T. Tu, L. C. Wilcox, and S. Zhong. Scalable Adaptive Mantle Convection Simulation on Petascale Supercomputers. In *SC 08*, 2008.

[3] A. Caboussat. Numerical Simulation of Two-Phase Free Surface Flows. *Arch. Comput. Meth. Engng.*, 12:165–224, 2005.

[4] L. F. Diachin, R. D. Hornung, P. Plassmann, and A. M. Wissink. Parallel Adaptive Mesh Refinement. In *Parallel processing for scientific computing*. Cambridge University Press, 2006.

[5] K. M. Fahey and S. N. Pandis.   Size-resolved aqueous-phase atmospheric chemistry in a three-dimensional chemical transport model. *J. Geophys. Res.*, 108(D22):4690, 2003.

[6] V. Grützun, O. Knoth, and M. Simmel. Simulation of the influence of aerosol particle characteristics on clouds and precipitation with LM–SPECS: Model description and first results. *Atmos. Res.*, 90:233–242, 2008.

[7] D. Hinneburg and O. Knoth. Non-dissipative cloud transport in Eulerian grid models by the volume-of-fluid (VOF) method. *Atmos. Environ.*, 39:4321–4330, 2005.

[8] IGAC. *Science Plan and Implementation Strategy.* IGBP Secretariat, 2006. http://www.igac.noaa.gov.

[9] IPCC. *Climate Change 2007: The Physical Science Basis. Contribution of Working Group I to the Forth Assessment Report of the Intergovernmental Panel on Climate Change (IPCC).* Cambridge University Press, Cambridge, UK and New York, USA, 2007.

[10] P. Jöckel, H. Tost, A. Pozzer, C. Brühl, J. Buchholz, L. Ganzeveld, P. Hoor, A. Kerkweg, M. G. Lawrence, R. Sander, B. Steil, G. Stiller, M. Tanarhte, D. Taraborrelli, J. van Aardenne, and J. Lelieveld. The atmospheric chemistry general circulation model ECHAM5/MESSy1: consistent simulation of ozone from the surface to the mesosphere. *Atmos. Chem. Phys.*, 6(12):5067–5104, 2006.

[11] G. Karypis, K. Schloegel, and V. Kumar. *ParMETIS: Parallel graph partitioning and sparse matrix ordering library (Version 3.1)*, 2003. University of Minnesota.

[12] A. Knüpfer, H. Brunst, J. Doleschal, M. Jurenz, M. Lieber, H. Mickler, M. S. Müller, and W. E. Nagel. The Vampir Performance Analysis Tool Set. In *Tools for High Performance Computing*, pages 139–155. Springer, 2008.

[13] J. Larson, R. Jacob, and E. Ong. The Model Coupling Toolkit: A New Fortran90 Toolkit for Building Multiphysics Parallel Coupled Models. *Int. J. High Perf. Comput. Appl.*, 19:277–292, 2005.

[14] B. Lynn, A. Khain, D. Rosenfeld, and W. L. Woodley. Effects of aerosols on precipitation from orographic clouds. *J. Geophys. Res.*, 112:D10225, 2007.

[15] B. H. Lynn, A. P. Khain, J. Dudhia, D. Rosenfeld, A. Pokrovsky, and A. Seifert. Spectral (Bin) Microphysics Coupled with a Mesoscale Model (MM5). Part I: Model Description and First Results. *Mon. Weather Rev.*, 133:44–58, 2005.

[16] P. MacNeice, K. M. Olson, C. Mobarry, R. de Fainchtein, and C. Packer. PARAMESH: A parallel adaptive mesh refinement community toolkit. *Comput. Phys. Comm.*, 126:330–354, 2000.

[17] J. Michalakes, J. Dudhia, D. Gill, T. Henderson, J. Klemp, W. Skamarock, and W. Wang. The Weather Research and Forecast Model: Software Architecture and Performance. In *Proceedings of the 11th ECMWF Workshop on the Use of High Performance Computing In Meteorology*, 2004.

[18] P. Monks, P. Borrell, M. Kanakidu, K. Law, M. Millan, and N. Moussiopoulos. Frontiers in the Transport and Transformation of Pollutants. In *The Report of the Barnsdale Expert Meeting 2004*, 2005. http://www.accent-network.org/portal/project-description/project-archive.

[19] U. Schättler, G. Doms, , and C. Schraff. *A Description of the Nonhydrostatic Regional COSMO-Model, Part VII: User's Guide.* Deutscher Wetterdienst, 2008. http://www.cosmo-model.org.

[20] M. Simmel and S. Wurzler. Condensation and activation in sectional cloud microphysical models. *Atmos. Res.*, 80:218–236, 2006.

[21] B. Van Straalen, J. Shalf, T. Ligocki, N. Keen, and W. Yang. Scalability challenges for massively parallel AMR applications. In *IPDPS 2009*, 2009.

[22] J. D. Teresco, K. D. Devine, and J. E. Flaherty. Partitioning and Dynamic Load Balancing for the Numerical Solution of Partial Differential Equations. In *Numerical Solution of Partial Differential Equations on Parallel Computers*, pages 55–88. Springer, 2006.

[23] S. Valcke and R. Redler. *OASIS4 User Guide (OASIS4_0_2)*. CERFACS, Toulouse, 2006.

[24] V. Wulfmeyer, A. Behrendt, Ch. Kottmeier, U. Corsmeier, et al. The Convective and Orographically-induced Precipitation Study: A Research and Development Project of the World Weather Research Program for Improving Quantitative Precipitation Forecasting in Low-mountain Regions. *Bull. Amer. Meteor. Soc.*, 89(10):1477–1486, 2008.

Parallel Computing: From Multicores and GPU's to Petascale
B. Chapman et al. (Eds.)
IOS Press, 2010
© 2010 The authors and IOS Press. All rights reserved.
doi:10.3233/978-1-60750-530-3-289

Extending Task Parallelism For Frequent Pattern Mining

Prabhanjan Kambadur [a], Amol Ghoting [b], Anshul Gupta [b] and
Andrew Lumsdaine [a]

[a] *Open Systems Lab, Indiana University, Bloomington, IN - 47408*
[b] *IBM T J Watson Research Center, Yorktown Heights, NY - 10598*

Abstract. Algorithms for frequent pattern mining, a popular informatics application, have unique requirements that are not met by any of the existing parallel tools. In particular, such applications operate on extremely large data sets and have irregular memory access patterns. For efficient parallelization of such applications, it is necessary to support dynamic load balancing along with scheduling mechanisms that allow users to exploit data locality. Given these requirements, task parallelism is the most promising of the available parallel programming models. However, existing solutions for task parallelism schedule tasks implicitly and hence, custom scheduling policies that can exploit data locality cannot be easily employed. In this paper we demonstrate and characterize the speedup obtained in a frequent pattern mining application using a custom clustered scheduling policy in place of the popular Cilk-style policy. We present PFunc, a novel task parallel library whose customizable task scheduling and task priorities facilitated the implementation of our clustered scheduling policy.

Keywords. task parallelism, frequent pattern mining, data locality.

Introduction

Algorithms for frequent pattern mining (FPM), a popular informatics application, exhibit certain distinct characteristics that distinguish them from traditional high-performance computing applications. Typically, FPM applications operate on large, irregular and dynamic data sets. The data (and corresponding computations) cannot be partitioned *a priori*, making these applications extremely sensitive to load balancing and scheduling. Memory access patterns are often data-dependent, requiring one data object's location in memory to be resolved before the next can be fetched. Finally, safe parallelization of FPM applications requires fine-grained synchronization. For all of these reasons, popular parallel programming models such as the data parallel and the single process multiple data (SPMD) models are not well-suited to FPM applications. Of the variety of alternative parallel programming models available, task parallelism is the most promising when it comes to meeting the challenges posed by FPM applications. The task parallel programming model is sufficiently high-level and general purpose to be able to parallelize both regular and irregular applications. However, existing solutions for task parallelism have shortcomings that prevent efficient parallelization of FPM applications. Specifically, FPM applications require custom task scheduling policies that can exploit data locality between tasks that are not always related by the parent-child relationship. In most existing solutions for task parallelism, not only are tasks scheduled transparently from the users, but also, data locality between tasks is exploited only if there is a parent-child relationship between those two tasks.

In this paper, we demonstrate the speedup obtained in a task parallel Apriori-based FPM implementation by switching from the popular Cilk-style [8] task scheduling policy to a customized "clustered" task scheduling policy. Furthermore, we collect various hardware metrics to characterize the factors that resulted in the speedup. To implement these two (Cilk-style and clustered) scheduling policies, we use PFunc, a novel library-based implementation of task parallelism, that allows users to customize parameters such as task scheduling policy and task priority. Unlike most other parallelization tools, PFunc provides a natural interface that enables facile implementation of our clustered scheduling policy. Through this study, we highlight the need to incorporate support for efficient parallelization of FPM applications in the task parallel model.

1. Background

Murphy and Kogge [23] demonstrated the differences in memory access patterns of informatics applications when compared to those of traditional scientific computing applications. Berry et al. [7] and Lumsdaine et al. [22] have shown that current techniques applied to high performance computing are inadequate for informatics applications. Since FPM was introduced as a relevant problem in informatics, its memory characteristics and parallelization have been extensively researched [3,4,9,16,18,19,21,24,26,29]. Zaki and Parathasarathy [31] were the first to explore the idea of clustering to aid in fast discovery of frequent patterns.

Many solutions have been implemented to facilitate dynamic task parallelism. Fortran M [13], Cilk [14] and OpenMP 3.0 [25] implement task parallelism as extensions to stock programming languages. Other solutions such as Intel's Threading Building Blocks (TBB) [27], Microsoft's Parallel Patterns Library (PPL) and Task Parallel Library (TPL), and Java Concurrency Utilities are library-based. All of the three HPCS languages (Chapel [10], Fortress [6] and X10 [11]) offer task parallelism as language features. Scheduling of tasks has received wide attention in the programming community. Cilk's *depth-first work* [8] model, the X10 Work Stealing framework's (XWS) *breadth-first* [12] model and Guo et al.'s *hybrid* model [17] are notable examples of work stealing schedulers. Each of the three above mentioned scheduling policies exploit data locality under different circumstances. For example, Cilk's scheduling policy exploits data locality only when the applications are deeply nested. All of the task parallel solutions discussed above schedule tasks implicitly, thereby disallowing customization of task scheduling policies. In this paper, we demonstrate the importance of customizing the task scheduling policy in parallelization tools when parallelizing FPM applications. We also describe the features of PFunc that enable FPM applications to employ custom scheduling strategies that help them outperform other implementations that employ default scheduling policies provided by existing solutions for task parallelism.

2. Problem Description

In this section, we describe FPM and comment on important aspects of its implementation that influence performance. Briefly, the problem description is as follows: Let $I = \{i_1, i_2, .., i_n\}$ be a set of n items, and let $D = \{T_1, T_2, .., T_m\}$ be a set of m transactions, where each transaction T_i is a subset of I. An itemset $i \subseteq I$ of size k is known as a k-itemset. The support (that is, frequency) of i is $\sum_{j=1}^{m}(1 : i \subseteq T_j)$, or informally speaking, the number of transactions in D that have i as a subset. The FPM problem is to find all $i \in D$ that have support greater than a user supplied minimum value. For our FPM implementation, we choose the *Apriori* [5] algorithm. Due to its efficiency, robustness and guaranteed main memory footprint, the Apriori algorithm is widely used in FPM implementations including those in commercial products such as IBM's InfoSphere Warehouse [30]. Apriori traverses the itemset search space in breadth-first order. Its efficiency stems from its use of the anti-monotone property: If a size k-itemset is not frequent, then any size $(k+1)$-itemset containing it will not be frequent. The algorithm first finds all frequent 1-items in the data set, and then iteratively finds all frequent k-itemsets using the frequent $(k-1)$-itemsets discovered previously. For example, let A, B, C and D be individual items (1-itemsets) that are frequent in a transaction database. Then, for stage 2, AB, AC, AD, BC, BD, and CD are the candidate 2-itemsets. If at stage 2, after counting, 2-itemsets AB, AC and AD were found to be frequent, then ABC, ABD, and ACD are the candidates for stage 3. The frequency of a candidate k-itemset is counted by performing a join ($\bowtie$) operation on the transaction-ID lists of each individual item in that particular itemset. In our task parallel implementation of the Apriori algorithm, the counting operations required for each k-itemset are executed as a separate task.

Requirements for efficient parallelization: The Apriori algorithm is highly dependent on memory reuse for its performance [16]. As tasks mine for itemsets, they access overlapping memory regions as many itemsets share transaction-ID lists. For example, if we were mining for 2-itemsets AB, AC, and AD, then the transaction-ID list of A would be common in the mining operations. The greater the overlap of items in the itemsets, the greater the potential for memory reuse between their respective tasks. Exploiting such inter-task data localities through locality-aware scheduling of tasks is the key for efficient parallel execution of Apriori-based FPM applications.

Shortcomings of current solutions: Existing task parallel solutions schedule tasks implicitly using different flavors of the Cilk-style work stealing [8] task scheduler and hence, do not support custom task scheduling policies that can exploit data localities between user-specified tasks. Furthermore, in the Cilk-style scheduling policy, there is little or no contention when a thread executes tasks that are on its own task queue, but stealing a task from another thread's task queue is an expensive operation. Cilk-style work stealing benefits applications that are deeply nested (that is, recursive) in nature. Nested tasks, by definition, spawn other tasks. Therefore, when a thread steals a nested task, it implicitly gains all the tasks that will be generated by the stolen task–thereby minimizing task stealing. However, in the Apriori algorithm, tasks are non-nested as we traverse the search space in breadth-first order. Hence, once a thread runs out of work, it must steal tasks repeatedly from other *victim* threads' task queues in order to keep itself busy. Such work stealing is detrimental to Apriori-based FPM implementations' performance both because of the increased contention on victim threads' task queues and the lack of data locality among stolen tasks.

3. PFunc: A new tool for task parallelism

PFunc [20] is a lightweight and portable task parallel library for C and C++ users, which has been designed using the generic programming paradigm [15] to overcome some of the shortcomings of existing solutions for task parallelism. Due to space constraints, we describe only those features of PFunc that affect Apriori-based FPM implementations. PFunc allows users to choose the task scheduling policy at compile time. Users can either choose from built-in scheduling policies such as Cilk-style, first-in first-out (FIFO), last-in first-out (LIFO) and priority-based, or they can supply their own scheduling policy. All scheduling policies are "models" of the scheduler "concept". This generic design enforces a uniform interface across the different scheduling policies and enables compile time plug-and-play capabilities with no runtime penalty. By default, PFunc follows the work stealing model in which each thread has its own task queue and tasks are enqueued on the task queue of the thread that spawned the task. Users have the option to override this default setting at runtime and place tasks onto a particular thread's task queue (that is, change the task's *affinity*). PFunc also provides *task attributes* that can be attached to each individual task when spawning the task. Task attributes, such as task priority, are an important tool in the implementation of many scheduling policies. For example, when using priority-based scheduling, users specify a task's priority using the task attribute mechanism. Like the scheduler, task attributes can be customized to suit the task scheduling policy. To enable hardware profiling, PFunc is fully integrated with the Performance Application Programming Interface (PAPI) [1].

4. Clustered task scheduling

To efficiently parallelize our Apriori-based FPM implementation using the task parallel programming model, we have designed a clustered scheduling policy. In this policy, tasks are clustered together such that there is a greater likelihood of memory reuse between the clustered tasks (for example, tasks mining for 3-itemsets ABC and ABD) as they are executed by the same thread. Furthermore, we employ a custom task stealing policy in which clusters of tasks are stolen instead of a single task. Such clustered stealing not only reduces contention on the thread-local task queues by minimizing the number of required steals, but also maintains data locality between the stolen tasks.

Implementation: In our FPM implementation, each task performs the mining operations required for one k-itemset. Each k-itemset is stored as a *sorted* set of individual items. To cluster tasks that have significant memory overlap, we use a common prefix of length (k-1). For example, the 3-itemsets ABC and ABD share the 2-prefix AB and hence, their respective tasks are clustered together. For efficient execution of our FPM application, it is necessary to ensure that such clusters of tasks have a high likelihood of being executed by the same thread. To this end, we use a hash table (std :: hash_map) as the task queue for each thread. This is a departure from the Cilk model [14], in which each thread's task queue is a deque. With the hash table structure in place, clustering of tasks is achieved by placing all k-itemsets that have a common (k-1) prefix into the same bucket. To achieve such clustering, we used the following hash function to compute the hash of a k-itemset. First, the hash of each of its first (k-1) items is computed using C++ Standard Library's [28] std :: hash function object. Then, these individual hashes are XOR'ed together to produce one final hash. For example, the hash for the 3-itemset ABC is computed by XOR-ing the results of applying std :: hash to A and B separately. The hashes thus computed for the 3-itemsets ABC and ABD are equal and hence, their respective tasks are placed in the same bucket. Each thread executes the tasks placed in its task queue (that is, hash table) by iterating through its task queue's buckets starting from the first non-empty bucket. When a thread runs out of tasks on its own task queue, it randomly selects a victim thread to steal tasks. Then, it steals the first non-empty bucket from the victim thread's task queue. This stealing policy is better equipped than the Cilk-style stealing policy to avoid repeated stealing in our FPM implementation as potentially, more than one task can be stolen during each steal. Furthermore, by stealing an entire bucket of tasks, data locality between stolen tasks is preserved.

Integrating with PFunc: Realizing our customized clustered task scheduling policy in PFunc is achieved in two steps. First, the entire scheduling policy is implemented to model PFunc's **scheduler** concept. This enables us to pick our clustered scheduling policy as the task scheduling policy of choice at compile time. Second, we customize PFunc's task attributes (again, at compile time) such that we can attach a *reference* to the k-itemset that needs to be mined as the respective task's priority. When a task is spawned, our hash function uses its priority (that is, the associated k-itemset's reference) to determine the appropriate bucket (that is, cluster) for this task in the spawning thread's task queue.

5. Results

In this section, we present the results of running our Apriori-based FPM implementation using the Cilk-style and the clustered scheduling policies. PFunc was used for parallelization of our FPM implementation and the scheduling policy for a particular run was chosen at compile time. Minimal code modifica-

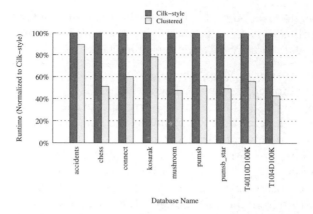

Figure 1. Graph showing the normalized runtimes of different datasets when using the Cilk-style and Clustered task scheduling policies in our Apriori-based FPM implementation with 8 threads. Support (that is, frequency) for each of the datasets is given in Table 1.

Dataset	Support	IPC		DTLB L1M/L2H		DTLB L1M/L2M	
		Cilk	Cluster	Cilk	Cluster	Cilk	Cluster
accidents	0.25	0.595689	0.603959	0.000048	0.000046	0.000161	0.000110
chess	0.6	0.560538	0.668965	0.000797	0.000242	0.001006	0.000032
connect	0.8	0.543099	0.809308	0.000249	0.000112	0.001204	0.000141
kosarak	0.0013	0.692103	0.717599	0.000400	0.000185	0.000659	0.000123
pumsb	0.75	0.494539	0.719072	0.000230	0.000114	0.001276	0.000126
pumsb_star	0.3	0.527659	0.698358	0.000315	0.000145	0.001082	0.000113
mushroom	0.10	0.570390	0.705003	0.000477	0.000267	0.000950	0.000022
T40I10D100K	0.005	0.627272	0.727288	0.000368	0.000305	0.000900	0.000021
T10I4D100K	0.00006	0.555330	0.716282	0.000218	0.000144	0.000876	0.000044

Table 1. Instructions-per-cycle (IPC), L1 data TLB misses (L1M/L2H) and L2 data TLB misses (L1M/L2M) when using the Cilk-style and Clustered task scheduling policies in our Apriori-based FPM implementation with 8 threads for different datasets from the FIMI repository [2].

tion was required to attach the k-itemset reference as task priority when spawning the tasks for the clustered scheduling policy. We ran our experiments on a four socket, quad-core (total 16 cores) AMD 8356 processor running Linux Kernel 2.6.24. For compilation, we used GCC 4.3.2 with: "-O3 -fomit-frame-pointer -funroll-loops". To collect hardware metrics, we used PFunc's integration with PAPI. The benchmarks were run on data sets from the FIMI repository [2].

Figure 1 depicts the runtimes of our FPM implementation for both the Cilk-style and the clustered task scheduling policies. Runtimes were recorded with hardware profiling turned off and were averaged after 5 runs. The clustered scheduling policy runs significantly faster (more than 50%) for most of the data sets, with the accidents.dat data set being the only exception. To test our hypothesis that our clustered scheduling policy exploits data locality better than the Cilk-style policy, we collected various hardware metrics. Table 1 summarizes some of the important metrics. Our clustered scheduling policy delivers more instructions per clock cycle than the Cilk-style scheduling policy for all data sets. Also, our clustered scheduling policy incurs far fewer L2 data TLB misses than the Cilk-style scheduling policy. This is because the benefits of clustering tasks that have a significant memory overlap outweigh the additional operational costs incurred due to using hash tables in our clustered scheduling policy. When results from Figure 1 and Table 1 are taken together, we can conclude that the clustered scheduling policy exploits data locality better than the Cilk-style scheduling policy for our Apriori-based FPM implementation.

6. Conclusion and Future Work

We have demonstrated that our custom clustered scheduling policy performs better than the popular Cilk-style scheduling policy for an Apriori-based FPM implementation. This was made possible by PFunc, which provides better support for parallelization of FPM applications than existing solutions for task parallelism by allowing facile customization of task scheduling policy and task attributes. An interesting topic for future research is to implement a dynamic task scheduling policy that utilizes a multi-dimensional index structure as task queues. This would enable a thread to dynamically pick the "nearest-neighbor" of the previously executed task as its next task to execute.

Acknowledgments: We thank Melanie Dybvig for her help in improving the quality of this paper. Our work was supported by IBM, King Abdullah University of Science and Technology (KAUST), National Science Foundation grants EIA-0202048 and CCF-0541335, and a grant from the Lilly Endowment.

References

[1] *Performance Application Programming Interface.* ICL, Knoxville, TN.

[2] *Datasets of the workshops on Frequent Itemset Mining Implementations (FIMI).* University of Helsinki, 2004.

[3] R. Agrawal, T. Imielinski, and A. Swami. Mining association rules between sets of items in large databases. In *SIGMOD '93: Proceedings of the 1993 ACM SIGMOD international conference on Management of data*, pages 207–216, New York, NY, USA, 1993. ACM.

[4] R. Agrawal and J. C. Shafer. Parallel Mining of Association Rules. *IEEE Trans. on Knowl. and Data Eng.*, 8(6):962–969, 1996.

[5] R. Agrawal and R. Srikant. Fast Algorithms for Mining Association Rules in Large Databases. In *VLDB '94: Proceedings of the 20th International Conference on Very Large Data Bases*, pages 487–499, San Francisco, CA, USA, 1994. Morgan Kaufmann Publishers Inc.

[6] E. Allen, D. Chase, J. Hallett, V. Luchangco, J.-W. Maessen, S. Ryu, G. L. S. Jr., and S. Tobin-Hochstadt. The Fortress Language Specification, Version 1.0. Technical report, Sun Microsystems, Inc., 2008.

[7] J. W. Berry, B. Hendrickson, S. Kahan, and P. Konecny. Software and Algorithms for Graph Queries on Multithreaded Architectures. *Parallel and Distributed Processing Symposium, 2007. IPDPS 2007. IEEE International*, 2007.

[8] R. D. Blumofe and C. E. Leiserson. Scheduling Multithreaded Computations by Work Stealing. In *Proceedings of the 35th Annual Symposium on Foundations of Computer Science (FOCS*, pages 356–368, 1994.

[9] G. Buehrer, S. Parthasarathy, and Y.-K. Chen. Adaptive Parallel Graph Mining for CMP Architectures. *Data Mining, IEEE International Conference on*, 0:97–106, 2006.

[10]   B. L. Chamberlain, D. Callahan, and H. P. Zima. Parallel Programmability and the Chapel Language. *International Journal of High Performance Computing Applications*, Jan 2007.

[11]   P. Charles, C. Grothoff, V. Saraswat, C. Donawa, A. Kielstra, K. Ebcioglu, C. von Praun, and V. Sarkar. X10: an object-oriented approach to non-uniform cluster computing. In *OOPSLA '05: Proceedings of the 20th annual ACM SIGPLAN conference on Object-oriented programming, systems, languages, and applications*, pages 519–538, New York, NY, USA, 2005. ACM.

[12]   G. Cong, S. Kodali, S. Krishnamoorthy, D. Lea, V. Saraswat, and T. Wen. Solving Large, Irregular Graph Problems Using Adaptive Work-Stealing. In *ICPP '08: Proceedings of the 2008 37th International Conference on Parallel Processing*, pages 536–545, Washington, DC, USA, 2008. IEEE Computer Society.

[13]   I. Foster, D. R. Kohr, Jr., R. Krishnaiyer, and A. Choudhary. A Library-based Approach to Task Parallelism in a Data-parallel Language. *J. Parallel Distrib. Comput.*, 45(2):148–158, 1997.

[14]   M. Frigo, C. E. Leiserson, and K. H. Randall. The implementation of the Cilk-5 multithreaded language. In *Proceedings of the ACM SIGPLAN '98 Conference on Programming Language Design and Implementation*, pages 212–223, Montreal, Quebec, Canada, June 1998. Proceedings published in ACM SIGPLAN Notices, Vol. 33, No. 5, May, 1998.

[15]   R. Garcia, J. Järvi, A. Lumsdaine, J. Siek, and J. Willcock. An extended comparative study of language support for generic programming. *Journal of Functional Programming*, 2005.

[16]   A. Ghoting, G. Buehrer, S. Parthasarathy, D. Kim, A. Nguyen, Y.-K. Chen, and P. Dubey. Cache-conscious frequent pattern mining on modern and emerging processors. *The VLDB Journal*, 16(1):77–96, 2007.

[17]   Y. Guo, R. Barik, R. Raman, and V. Sarkar. Work-First and Help-First Scheduling Policies for Async-Finish Task Parallelism. In *Proceedings of the 23rd IEEE International Parallel and Distributed Processing Symposium*, May 2009.

[18]   E.-H. S. Han, G. Karypis, and V. Kumar. Scalable Parallel Data Mining for Association Rules. *IEEE Trans. on Knowl. and Data Eng.*, 12(3):337–352, 2000.

[19]   J. Han, J. Pei, and Y. Yin. Mining frequent patterns without candidate generation. In *SIGMOD '00: Proceedings of the 2000 ACM SIGMOD international conference on Management of data*, pages 1–12, New York, NY, USA, 2000. ACM.

[20]   P. Kambadur, A. Gupta, A. Ghoting, H. Avron, and A. Lumsdaine. PFunc: Modern Task Parallelism For Modern High Performance Computing. In *SC '09: Proceedings of the 2008 ACM/IEEE conference on Supercomputing*, Portland, Oregon, November 2009.

[21]   J.-S. Kim, X. Qin, and Y. Hsu. Memory characterization of a parallel data mining workload. In *WWC '98: Proceedings of the Workload Characterization: Methodology and Case Studies*, page 60, Washington, DC, USA, 1998. IEEE Computer Society.

[22]   A. Lumsdaine, D. Gregor, B. Hendrickson, and J. W. Berry. Challenges in parallel graph processing. *Parallel Processing Letters*, 17(1):5–20, 2007.

[23]   R. C. Murphy and P. M. Kogge. On the Memory Access Patterns of Supercomputer Applications: Benchmark Selection and Its Implications. *IEEE Trans. Comput.*, 56(7):937–945, 2007.

[24]   S. Nijssen and J. N. Kok. A quickstart in frequent structure mining can make a difference. In *KDD '04: Proceedings of the tenth ACM SIGKDD international conference on Knowledge discovery and data mining*, pages 647–652, New York, NY, USA, 2004. ACM.

[25]   OpenMP Architecture Review Board. *OpenMP Application Program Interface, v3.0*. May 2008.

[26]   S. Parthasarathy, M. J. Zaki, M. Ogihara, and W. Li. Parallel data mining for association rules on shared memory systems. *Knowl. Inf. Syst.*, 3(1):1–29, 2001.

[27]   J. Reinders. *Intel Threading Building Blocks*. O'Reilly, 2007.

[28]   A. A. Stepanov and M. Lee. The Standard Template Library. Technical Report X3J16/94-0095, WG21/N0482, ISO Programming Language C++ Project, May 1994.

[29]   C. Wang and S. Parthasarathy. Parallel algorithms for mining frequent structural motifs in scientific data. In *ICS '04: Proceedings of the 18th annual international conference on Supercomputing*, pages 31–40, New York, NY, USA, 2004. ACM.

[30]   M. J. Zaki. Parallel and Distributed Association Mining: A Survey. *IEEE Concurrency*, 7(4):14–25, 1999.

[31]   M. J. Zaki, S. Parthasarathy, M. Ogihara, and W. Li. New Algorithms for Fast Discovery of Association Rules. Technical report, Rochester, NY, USA, 1997.

GPU & Cell Programming

Parallel Computing: From Multicores and GPU's to Petascale
B. Chapman et al. (Eds.)
IOS Press, 2010
© 2010 The authors and IOS Press. All rights reserved.
doi:10.3233/978-1-60750-530-3-299

Exploring the GPU for Enhancing Parallelism on Color and Texture Analysis

Francisco IGUAL [a] Rafael MAYO [a] Timothy D. R. HARTLEY [b]
Umit CATALYUREK [b] Antonio RUIZ [c] Manuel UJALDÓN [c]

[a] *Department of Computer Engineering and Computer Science,*
University Jaume I, Castellon (Spain)
[b] *Departments of Biomedical Informatics and Electrical and Computer Engineering,*
The Ohio State University, Columbus, OH (USA)
[c] *Computer Architecture Department, University of Malaga, Malaga (Spain)*

Abstract. Textural features are quite effective in pattern recognition and image analysis algorithms, but their use comes with high computational cost. In this work, we present novel implementations on graphics processors (GPUs) for fast calculations of a set of basic operations for color and texture analysis. Our approach focuses on CUDA programming for exploiting the inherent parallelism and computational power of GPUs from different perspectives, as our target operations possess diverse features: streaming operators favoured on GPUs, recursive procedures easier on CPUs, memory intensive kernels with assorted access patterns (requiring considerable programming effort to fully exploit the memory hierarchy), matrix operators demanding sustainable bandwidth, and mathematical functions with remarkable arithmetic intensity on ALUs and FPUs. Experimental results are compared among different GPU strategies and versus a multicore CPU implementation, leading to varying amounts of execution time speedup up to 500x on a low cost platform recruited for high-performance computing like the commodity GeForce 8 from Nvidia.

Keywords. High Performance Computing, Graphics Processors (GPUs), Texture Analysis, Emerging Architectures, CUDA Programming

1. Introduction

The properties of an image are usually divided into color and texture features. While color features get significant attention in image retrieval because of their powerful discriminating abilities, they are complex to handle because color is not invariant to the imaging conditions. Meanwhile, texture is the most important visual cue in identifying homogeneous regions within an image, and is usually characterized by a set of features which are distorted due to the imaging process and the perspective projection, influencing the surface orientation and shape.

The selection of the color space is a paramount issue for subsequent texture analysis, and often requires conversion from the native image format as retrieved from file or captured by a device. Local shape analysis is then performed through a set of neighborhood operators using patterns, masks and convolutions. Finally, texture analysis methods extend globally the study to the entire image, typically through matrix operators.

In this work, our goal is to demonstrate how one can benefit from the computational diversity present in a representative set of image analysis kernels to study trade-offs of implementing those in CPU vs GPU. Our ultimate goal is to identify properties that a given kernel requires to be attractive to the GPU platform, and provide some guidance to the CUDA developer for the optimization of kernels according to its nature.

2. Kernels for GPU implementation

Color-space Conversions.   The formulas used for color-space conversion are linear transformations, with a 3x3 matrix containing the weights connecting input and output color channels and the operation being expressed as a matrix-vector product. We use float data types and **streaming operators** for our implementation within the GPU, which converts the features of each declared pixel from its native color format (e.g. RGB, coming from an imaging device) into the most convenient color space required by a particular image processing application.

Texture Analysis Kernels.   Among the variety of methods used in texture analysis, we selected three **matrix operator** techniques which range from local to global scope:

1. The **uniform local binary pattern (LBP)** studies the closest neighborhood to capture micro-structures [10,19].
2. Convolution operators extract micro-features using spatial domain filters and can be extended with **Zernike moments** [1,13].
3. Second-order statistics perform a macro-level characterization based on **co-occurrence matrices** and aim to provide a more global image analysis [2,12].

3. Experimental setup

Hardware.   Table 1 provides detailed hardware specifications for the CPU and GPU we have used during our experiments. The Nvidia GeForce 8800 GPU has 128 stream processors (cores) running at 1.35 GHz (instead of the main 575 MHz GPU clock speed), leading to a peak processing power exceeding 500 MFLOPS.

Software tools.   The CPU was programmed using C++ with multimedia extensions enabled directly through HAL layer without any specific library in between. Pthreads were not used during the parallelization process. CUDA compilation tools, release 1.1, were used for GPU programming.

Input images.   Our input data set consisted of real biomedical images used for cartilage and bone regeneration. The tissue in these images is stained with different protocols in order to highlight certain physical features in the tissue. Since the workload of our image processing kernels was strongly affected by image resolution and loosely affected by image contents, we therefore run our experiments on a single image of 1024x1024 pixels.

Kernels.   The set of kernels we have considered here have a wide spectrum of characteristics (see Table 2). We believe this set of kernels will be sufficient to define the API for subsequent implementation as a library of CUDA procedures.

Table 1. Summary of hardware features for our CPU (Intel) and GPU (Nvidia).

Processor	CPU	GPU		Memory	CPU side	GPU side
Model	Core 2 Duo	GeF. 8800 GTX		Speed	2 x 333 MHz	2 x 900 MHz
Codename	Conroe E6400	G80		Bus width	64 bits	384 bits
Speed	2.13 GHz	575 MHz		Bandwidth	10.8 GB/sec.	86.4 GB/sec.
Peak power	20 GFLOPS	520 GFLOPS		Size/type	2 GB DDR2	768 MB GDDR3

Table 2. Characterization of our image processing kernels implemented on GPUs.

	Color conversions	Uniform LBP	Zernike moments	Co-occurrence matrices
Input	Pixel	3x3 window	Full image	Variable size window (centered on pixel in question)
Output	Pixel	Ten histogram bins (values)	Var. array of tens of floats	Variable size matrix (depending on color discretization)
Color channels	Three	One	One	One

4. Implementation on the GPU and performance evaluation

4.1. Color conversions

We have implemented 9 color conversion kernels listed in Table 3. The first three conversions we present are more computationally demanding because they actually require an additional conversion to sRGB as an intermediate step in order to achieve better color fidelity. These transitive operations are faster on the GPU, because they can be implemented as a sequence of in-place filters or typical streaming operators where the output of an operation passes as input to the next one without accessing main GPU memory.

Experimental results shown in Table 3 for a 1024x1024 image reveal that the strong streaming behaviour of an operator is translated into impressive GPU execution time speedups compared to a CPU implementation.

Table 3. Execution times (in milliseconds) for different color format conversions on the CPU and the GPU for a 1024x1024 pixels image. Inverse conversions have a similar cost.

Color format conversion	CPU time	GPU time	Speedup on GPU	GPU rating
1. RGB to XYZ	140.01	0.435	321.86x	Faster
2. RGB to Luv	273.83	0.529	517.63x	Fastest
3. RGB to L*A*B*	267.92	1.769	151.45x	Fast
4. RGB to CMYK	16.37	0.452	36.21x	Good
5. RGB to HSV	16.60	0.489	33.94x	Good
6. RGB to sRGB	123.51	0.394	313.47x	Faster
7. sRGB to XYZ	16.50	0.364	45.32x	Good
8. sRGB to Luv	150.31	0.451	333.28x	Faster
9. sRGB to L*A*B*	144.41	1.158	124.70x	Fast

4.2. LBP operator

The computation of the LBP operator entails a convolution with a 3x3 mask, followed by a binary to decimal conversion. All the LBP patterns are accumulated into a histogram

Table 4. Execution times (in milliseconds) for the LBP operator on a single color channel under different image sizes, programming tools and hardware platforms. Results include the time for computing a histogram for accumulating the number of pixels having the same LBP value. CPU speedup refers to C++ vs. Matlab, GPU speedup quantifies CUDA vs.Cg, comparison across platforms reflects the best GPU time (CUDA) vs. the best CPU time (C++).

Image	CPU using		GPU using		Speedup across:		
size	Matlab	C++	Cg	CUDA	CPU	GPU	Platforms
128x128	31.25	3.95	1.01	0.07	7.91	14.42x	54.86x
256x256	62.50	17.83	1.09	0.14	3.50	7.78x	127.35x
512x512	218.75	76.70	1.92	0.41	2.85	4.68x	184.81x
1024x1024	859.37	310.65	6.88	1.56	2.76	4.41x	198.62x
2048x2048	3390.62	1234.96	23.91	6.11	2.74	3.91x	201.98x

(similarly to a CUDA library histogram kernel [16]) with ten bins; nine bins for uniform rotation-invariant patterns and one bin collecting non-uniform patterns ([9]).

Overall, we have implemented four different versions of the LBP operator: two on the CPU using Matlab and the C++ programming language, and another two on the GPU using Cg [3] and the CUDA programming model. For our experiments, a single color channel was computed and no vector processing was performed by the CPU. Since the LBP operator is a local feature, it is performed once for each pixel of the image.

Table 4 shows the execution times for different image sizes. Since the limited resources (8,192 registers and 16 KB of shared memory in GeForce 8) of one of the GPU's multiprocessors are shared by all of the threads assigned to that multiprocessor, optimizing the use of those resources greatly improves the execution time of the operator by increasing the number of concurrent executions that can be done in the GPU. In the CUDA implementation, each thread requires 10 registers and each block of threads uses 296 bytes of shared memory. Computational threads are arranged in rectangular *blocks* in the CUDA model, with increasing thread ids in up to three dimensions. Since the LBP kernel is a very regular 2-D computation, we can select different sizes of thread deployments, provided a square block is used. After investigating the effect of different thread/block ratios, we gathered values for blocks of threads of sizes 20x20, 18x18, 16x16, 14x14, 12x12, 10x10, and 8x8, finding a 16x16 block yielded the minimum execution time by around 20%. This result justifies why a block of 16x16 threads is a popular choice among expert programmers to maximize performance in CUDA.

4.3. Zernike moments

The computation of Zernike moments has been extensively improved over the years. We highlight the three following methods which summarize all major optimizations:

1. Mukundan et al. [14] use a recursive algorithm for the calculation of Zernike polynomial coefficients through a square-to-circular image transformation which minimizes the computation involved in Zernike moment functions.
2. Hwang et al. [11] have developed a fast recursive computation that depends on the symmetry properties of a point in the first octant, where the reduction in operations is accomplished by making use of similar terms derived for the symmetrical points in the remaining seven octants.

Table 5. Execution times (in milliseconds) for computing Zernike moments of several orders for three different methods on the CPU compared to the direct method on the GPU. All moments of a given order are shown in the upper table for a 1024x1024 image resolution (the total number of moments computed are given between parenthesis). The lower table shows the time for a single moment on a smaller image, where the slowest method on the CPU has been replaced by its direct computation on the first column for an illustrative comparison between processors.

All mo-ments of an order	Times on a 1024x1024 image				Speedup on GPU versus:		
	MUKUNDAN (1995)	HWANG (2006)	AL-RAWI (2008)	Direct on GPU	MUKUNDAN (1995)	HWANG (2006)	AL-RAWI (2008)
$A_{4,*}$ (3)	1 391.0	258.0	62.5	10.98	126,68x	23.49x	5.69x
$A_{8,*}$ (5)	3 820.5	859.0	54.5	20.74	184.18x	33.89x	2.62x
$A_{12,*}$ (7)	7 703.0	1 969.0	62.5	32.74	235.27x	60.14x	1.90x
$A_{16,*}$ (9)	13 187.5	3 836.0	78.0	46.99	280.63x	81.63x	1.66x
$A_{20,*}$ (11)	20 109.5	6 586.0	93.5	63.42	317.08x	103.84x	1.47x
$A_{24,*}$ (13)	28 719.0	10 617.0	117.5	82.76	347.01x	128.28x	1.42x

A single moment of an order	Times on a 256x256 image				Speedup on GPU versus:		
	DIRECT on CPU	HWANG (2006)	AL-RAWI (2008)	DIRECT on GPU	DIRECT on CPU	HWANG (2006)	AL-RAWI (2008)
$A_{6,2}$	225	26	4.00	0.55	409.09x	47.27x	7.27x
$A_{12,0}$	282	30	7.75	0.74	381.08x	40.54x	10.47x
$A_{25,13}$	408	46	7.75	1.17	348.71x	39.31x	6.62x

3. Al-Rawi [1] recently implemented on a Pentium 4 CPU a wide range of Zernike moment orders via geometric moments which clearly outperforms the best methods based on Zernike polynomials.

In other work, we developed a scalable GPU cluster-based implementation for an end-to-end biomedical application [9] which dealt with large-scale images decomposed into 1024x1024 tiles. Within this context, Zernike moments up to order 25 are useful as features for further classification of biological tissues [17]. Table 5 shows the execution times on a 1024x1024 image size for our GPU implementation using CUDA as compared to existing CPU implementations. Due to the peculiar way in which the GPU processes data through rendering passes and its huge raw computational power, the direct method is faster than any other recursive method on the GPU platform. This also introduces the advantage of a much higher degree of parallelism when running on multiprocessors, together with promising scalability in future graphics platforms.

In addition to being faster, our method allows for the computation of a single order moment and a single repetition within an order; these computations can be used as an isolated feature for an image, something that the recursive methods are unable to perform without calculating all previous orders and repetitions. Hwang et al. [11] developed individual formulas to avoid this extra computation, and the lower portion of Table 5 shows these results for an image of 256x256 pixels, where the slowest recursive method has also been replaced by the direct method computed on the CPU for a comparison with the GPU. The GPU is around 300-400 times faster than the CPU when processing the same non-recursive kernel on both sides. Differences versus the method proposed by Hwang et al. [11] are maintained, whereas margins with the remaining recursive method widens.

Table 6. Execution times on the GPU (in milliseconds) for the computation of a 256x256 co-occurrence matrix (non-discretized version) on a single pixel and a single color channel under different window sizes centered on the pixel in question.

Window size	4x4	8x8	16x16	32x32	64x64	128x128	256x256
CPU time	1.36	2.82	2.82	3.04	3.08	2.94	2.96
GPU time	7.61	7.62	7.58	7.63	7.76	8.54	9.19

Table 7. Execution times on the GPU (in milliseconds) for the computation of the co-occurrence matrix on a single pixel and a single color channel under different discretization levels. The window size is 16x16 pixels, and the CPU time is 2.82 msc. in all cases, against which the GPU speedup is calculated.

Co-occurrence matrix size	16x16	32x32	64x64	128x128	256x256
GPU time (msc.)	0.23	0.31	0.67	2.09	7.58
GPU speedup	12.26x	9.09x	4.20x	1.34x	0.37x

4.4. Co-occurrence matrices

Several statistical features based on co-occurrence matrices were previously implemented on the GPU using the Cg language [18]. Under this approach, each element of the co-occurrence matrix was computed by a single GPU rendering pass, thus making the GPU slower even for highly discretized matrices. Our goal now is to accelerate the code using CUDA to provide at least some scenarios in which the GPU runs faster.

Our implementations are based on Argenti's method ([2]), when either conducted on multi-core CPUs or many-core GPUs using CUDA. This method exploits the observation that co-occurrence matrices extracted from windows centered on adjacent pixels overlap most of their computations. For example, the co-occurrence matrix for each pixel in a row can be derived from the matrix associated to the neighbor pixel on its left, just by replacing the contribution to the matrix of the first column of pixels by those of the new column entering the computational domain on the right.

In our CUDA implementation, for the first co-occurrence matrix, pixels are equally distributed among threads and local co-occurrence matrices are simultaneously computed by each thread. Finally, partial results are accumulated through a reduction operation. The more discretized the co-occurrence matrix, the more reduction stages that can be carried out using shared memory. However, it was found to be challenging to avoid conflicts accessing the 16 banks of the shared memory during the initial computation of co-occurrence matrices. With a block of 256 threads arranged in a 16x16 block, the naive thread deployment would force the 32 threads in a warp to access only 8 shared-memory banks, which would severely limit parallelism and performance. We found that by intelligently shuffling the active threads combined into a warp, the local matrix computation and the subsequent global matrix aggregation operation can proceed without forcing threads to wait for bank access. This complex optimization solves all conflicts when accessing memory banks, reducing the execution time by around 40%.

Table 6 shows the impact on execution time of the input window size, whereas Table 7 shows the impact of the matrix discretization. This discretization reduces the workload and memory requirements, as it determines the size of the output matrix given the rounding applied to the color intensities acting as matrix coordinates. For example, when discretizing into 4x4 matrices, all color intensities between 0 and 63 are mapped into level 0, and similarly, color intensities between 192 and 255 are mapped into level 3.

From those results shown in Table 6, we can tell that this particular operation, with its irregular nature and high data reuse, is better-suited to a standard CPU. Further, the GPU is hampered in current system architectures by the transfer of data down to the GPU device, and worse, back from the GPU device. Still, the GPU is well within striking distance of becoming a viable general purpose processor, even for operations which may not fit the traditional uses for streaming, many-core architectures.

5. Related Work

In parallel with the development of our image processing kernels on GPUs, several efforts have been carried out by the scientific community. The CUDA Web site [5] makes a good compilation of them, among which we may highlight three as particularly close to our work: OpenVIDIA [6] was the first library implemented to make use of parallel GPUs within the computer vision context. OpenCV [15] is an open source library for real-time computer vision developed by Intel, and GpuCV [7] offers GPU-accelerated replacement routines that are fully compatible with their OpenCV counterpart.

J. L. T. Cornwall et al. [4] implement a C++ source-to-source translator that automatically seeks parallelizable code fragments and replaces them with code for a graphics co-processor, showing results on an industrial image processing library.

More recently, GPU VSIPL is an implementation of Vector Signal Image Processing Library that targets Graphics Processing Units (GPUs) supporting CUDA platforms.

6. Conclusions and Future Work

This work presents methods for computing a set of image processing kernels on graphics processors (GPUs). Our approach focuses on CUDA programming techniques for exploiting parallelism and the computational power of GPUs, leading to extraordinary acceleration factors which are summarized in Table 8.

Up to a 500x performance gain is achieved for the case of streaming-like operators, whereas modest gains are attained by kernels exposing high data reuse (where CPUs perform well due to cache memory). We also only see modest gains, or indeed losses on the GPU for low arithmetic intensity and recursive algorithms, even when we focus our optimizations on the memory hierarchy.

Overall, this effort is part of the development of an image processing library oriented to biomedical applications and accelerated using the GPU as co-processor. Future achievements include the implementation of each step of our image analysis process so that it can be entirely executed on GPUs without incurring data transfers to/from the CPU. Our plan also includes porting the code to CPU/GPU clusters and TESLA nodes, where we intend to make use of recently released double-precision hardware.

Acknowledgements

This work was partially supported by the US National Science Foundation (CNS-0643969, CNS-0403342, CNS-0615155, CFF-0342615), by the NIH NIBIB BISTI (P20EB000591), by US Department of Energy (ED-FC02-06ER25775), by the Min-

Table 8. Characterization of our image processing kernels on large-scale images implemented on GPUs, together with the the range of speedup achieved (see last row).

Computational issue	Color conversion	Uniform LBP	Zernike moments	Co-occurrence matrices
Computational weight	Very light	Light	Strong	Heavy
Operator type	Streaming	Streaming	Recursive	Recurrence
Data reuse	None	Little	Heavy	Strong
Locality access	None	Little	Strong	Heavy
Arithmetic intensity	Heavy	Average	Strong	Low
Memory access	Low	Average	Strong	Heavy
GPU speedup	**30-500x**	**50-200x**	**1-5x**	**0.3-12x**

istry of Education of Spain (TIC2003-06623, PR-2007-0014, TIN2008-06570-C04-01), by the Junta de Andalucía of Spain (P06-TIC-02109), and by Fundación Caixa-Castellón/Bancaixa and the University Jaume I (P1-1B2007-32).

References

[1]   M. Al-Rawi. *Fast Zernike moments.* J. Real-Time Image Processing. Vol. 3, No. 1-2, pp. 89-96 (2008).

[2]   F. Argenti, L. Alparone, G. Benelli. *Fast Algorithms for Texture Analysis Using Co-occurrence Matrices.* IEE Proceedings F, vol. 137, n. 6, pp. 443-448, Dec. 1990.

[3]   The Cg language. Home Page maintained by Nvidia. http://developer.nvidia.com/page/cg_main.html.

[4]   J. L. T. Cornwall, O. Beckmann and P.H.J. Kelly. *Accelerating a C++ Image Processing Library with a GPU.* Procs. 19th IEEE IPDPS Workshop on Performance Optimization for High-Level Languages and Libraries, 2006.

[5]   A CUDA repository of applications maintained by Nvidia. http://www.nvidia.com/object/cuda_home.html.

[6]   J. Fung and S. Mann. *OpenVIDIA: Parallel GPU Computer Vision.* Proceedings 13th Ann. ACM Intl. Conf. Multimedia (MULTI-MEDIA?05), pp. 849-852, 2005.

[7]   *GpuCV: GPU-accelerated Computer Vision.* http://picoforge.int-evry.fr/cgi-bin/twiki/view/Gpucv/Web.

[8]   *GPU-VSIPL. A Vector Signal Image Processing Library.* http://gpu-vsipl.gtri.gatech.edu. August, 2009.

[9]   T. Hartley, U. Catalyurek, A. Ruiz, M. Ujaldon, F. Igual, R. Mayo. *Biomedical Image Analysis on a Cooperative Cluster of GPUs and Multicores.* Procs. 22nd ACM Intl. Conf. on Supercomputing (2008).

[10] L. He, C. Zou, and D. Hu. *An enhanced LBP feature based on facial expression recognition.* Proceedings IEEE Engineering in Medicine and Biology, 2005.

[11] S.K. Hwang, W.Y. Kim. *A novel approach to the fast computation of Zernike moments.* Pattern Recognition, vol. 39, no. 11, pp. 2065-2076 (2006).

[12] V. Kovalev and M. Petrou. *Multidimensional Co-occurrence Matrices for Object Recognition and Matching.* Graphical Models and Image Processing, vol. 58, no. 3, pp. 187-197 (1996).

[13] S.X. Liao, M. Pawlak. *On the Accuracy of Zernike Moments for Image Analysis.* IEEE Transactions on Pattern Analysis and Machine Intelligence, vol. 20, no. 12, dec., 1998.

[14] R, Mukundan and K.R. Ramakrishnan. *Fast Computation of Legendre and Zernike moments.* Pattern Recognition, vol. 28, no. 9, pp. 1433-1442 (1995).

[15] The OpenCV library developed by Intel. http://software.intel.com/en-us/articles/intel-integrated-performance-primitives-intel-ipp-open-source-computer-vision-library-opencv-faq/.

[16] V. Podlozhnyuk. *Histogram calculation in CUDA.* NVIDIA CUDA SDK Code Samples, 2007.

[17] A. Ruiz, J. Kong, M. Ujaldón, K. Boyer, J. Saltz and M. Gurcan. *Pathological Image Segmentation for Neuroblastoma Using the GPU.* Procs. IEEE Intl. Symposium on Biomedical Imaging: From Nano to Macro. Paris (France). May, 2008.

[18] A. Ruiz, O. Sertel, M. Ujaldón, U. Catalyurek, J. Saltz and M. Gurcan. *Stroma Classification for Neuroblastoma on Graphics Processors.* Intl. Journal of Data Mining and Bioinformatics (2009).

[19] V. Takala, T. Ahanen, and M. Pietikainen. *Block-based methods for image retrieval using local binary patterns.* Lecture Notes in Computer Science, vol. 3540, pp. 882-891 (2005).

Parallel Computing: From Multicores and GPU's to Petascale
B. Chapman et al. (Eds.)
IOS Press, 2010
© 2010 The authors and IOS Press. All rights reserved.
doi:10.3233/978-1-60750-530-3-307

Generalized GEMM Kernels on GPGPUs: Experiments and Applications

Davide BARBIERI Valeria CARDELLINI Salvatore FILIPPONE [1]

Università di Roma "Tor Vergata", 00133 Roma, Italy

Abstract. General purpose computing on graphics processing units (GPGPU) is fast becoming a common feature of high performance computing centers. In this paper we discuss some implementation issues related to dense linear algebra computations on GPUs, such as the GEneral Matrix-Matrix product, as well as other kernels sharing the same computational pattern, such as the matrix form of the All-Pairs Shortest-Path problem. Our CUDA implementation has shown a significant improvement on the NVIDIA processing units over the vendor's software. We review the optimization techniques that can be employed to implement such operations, as well as outline further development work in connected application domains.

Keywords. Software and architectures, GPU programming, performance evaluation.

1. Introduction

Efficient matrix-matrix multiplication routines in the BLAS lie at the heart of linear algebra computations as implemented in modern computational libraries such as LA-PACK [1,3]. The road to maximal performance is influenced by architectural characteristics of the graphics processing unit (GPU). Indeed, many techniques that were developed over the years for optimal exploitation of vector and RISC processing units have a counterpart in the GPU world, including stride one accesses, bank-conflict avoidance techniques, padding to optimal length, and copy-in/copy-out.

Adapting these techniques to suit GPU devices programming allowed us to obtain excellent results in both memory management and GPU exploitation; in particular,

- gains of orders of magnitude in GPU performance compared to CPU results on matrix operations;
- smooth behavior of the optimized code over many input configurations (up to 59% faster than the vendor's original version).

Indeed, the code developed at our institution is now included in the latest version of the CUBLAS software distribution [8]. Concentrating on GEneral Matrix-Matrix (GEMM) computations is not overly restrictive; it is well known that it is possible to implement efficiently the BLAS standard by reusing the GEMM routine with some additional software [6].

---

[1]Corresponding author e-mail: salvatore.filippone@uniroma2.it

We also consider the All-Pairs Shortest-Path (APSP) problem on general graphs. An implementation based on a matrix representation of the graph shares most features of the matrix-multiply code, once we make the algebraic substitution of using the sum in place of the product and the maximum in place of the sum. Therefore, we can reuse the implementation techniques adopted for the matrix-matrix multiplication routine, leading to a "brute-force" algorithm that can outperform the "smart" sequential algorithms: algorithms implementing better patterns of problem decomposition scale better than the optimal solution for legacy architectures, despite having worse sequential bounds. This is the case for two APSP algorithms, the original Floyd-Warshall one for general graphs, and a modified *GPU-friendly* version; our results show that there is a significant range of problems where the suboptimal algorithm actually gives the best time to solution on the GPU platform.

A significant number of research efforts has recently focused on GPGPU, among which [5,10] are more related to our work. In our GEMM kernel, we have applied some of the optimization strategies discussed by Volkov et al. in [10]; with respect to their work, which is included in the CUBLAS library from version 2.0, our kernels for single-precision and double-precision matrix multiplication (SGEMM and DGEMM, respectively) obtain a significant improvement for transposed matrices in input. Harish et al. [5] report results for the implementation of some APSP algorithms on GPUs. Differently from them, we tackle the APSP problem by developing an algorithm entirely based on our efficient matrix multiplication routine.

The rest of this paper is organized as follows. Section 2 gives an overview of the main features of the NVIDIA GPU architecture we used and its programming environment. Section 3 presents the performance optimization techniques for the GEMM kernel and discusses the performance results of the matrix multiplication for both single and double precision computations. Section 4 presents the application of the same techniques to the APSP problem and evaluates their performance. Section 5 discusses our current investigation of other kinds of linear algebra operations. Finally, Section 6 concludes the paper with some final remarks.

2. The Architecture of NVIDIA GPU and its Programming Environment

The NVIDIA GPU architectural model is based on a scalable array of *multi-threaded streaming multi-processors* (SMs), each composed by eight *scalar processors* (SP), one instruction fetch unit, one on-chip shared memory plus additional special-function hardware; a scheme is depicted in Fig. 1(a). Each multiprocessor is capable of creating and executing concurrent threads in a completely autonomous way, with no scheduling overhead, thanks to the hardware support for thread synchronization; threads are created, scheduled, and executed in groups called *warps*.

A warp (a group of 32 threads) is the minimum execution unit, because each compute element has 8 processors sharing a single instruction fetch unit, running at 1/4 of the processor speed; it is also quite common to concentrate on a half-warp when considering accesses to shared memory (both on-chip, and on DRAM), because in this case read and write operations are executed in separate halves. The GPU is capable of hosting a maximum number of warps (and hence, threads) at any given time; the GPU occupancy is defined as the ratio between the actual number of threads and this theoretical maximum.

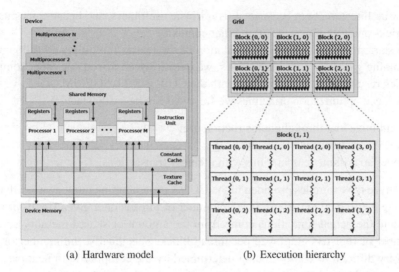

        (a) Hardware model   (b) Execution hierarchy

Figure 1. NVIDIA GPU architectural model.

To the hardware hierarchy there corresponds a software hierarchy of threads, blocks and grids, as shown in Fig. 1(b). Threads in a given block may synchronize, share data, and be executed on a given multiprocessor with essentially zero overhead. The dimension of blocks and grids is specified by the programmer to match the problem size with the available execution hardware. The CUDA programming environment specifies a set of facilities to create, identify, and synchronize the various threads involved in the computation.

The device memory is divided into global, local, and on-chip shared memory areas. The efficient exploitation of the available global memory bandwidth depends critically on two basic code features: data structure alignment and coalesced accesses.

The alignment issue is quite clear, because of the additional overhead of unaligned accesses; its implementation is aided by the use of compilation directives. Coalesced accesses to global memory involve all threads in a half-warp, and enable completion of read accesses in a single memory transaction. Optimal access patterns for coalescing may vary among different GPU models, but so far they have done so in a backward compatible manner.

Local memory is private to each thread; it is not directly available to the programmer, and is only used by the compiler to handle register spill.

Shared memory is actually local to each multiprocessor; it is shared among threads and it is interfaced to the cores with a crossbar of 16 elements, so it is organized in 16 banks. Given this structure, threads in a half-warp can access the memory with no overhead provided that there are no back conflicts.

3. Performance Optimization Techniques for the GEMM Kernels

The GEMM multiply that computes $C = \alpha A \times B + \beta C$ is one of the best known computational kernels in common scientific applications, and lies at the heart of the BLAS and LAPACK software packages. It is usually among the first kernels to be implemented on a new architecture, both because of its intrinsic usefulness, and because its study can reveal tricks and techniques useful in other contexts.

We started from a naive implementation of the matrix multiply, and following the programming guide [7, p. 71] guidelines, we iteratively improved our code, comparing our timing results with those obtained with the CUBLAS 2.0 SGEMM.

The basic optimization principles we followed can be easily stated:

- minimize low-throughput instruction use;
- maximize memory bandwidth usage, for each memory subsystem;
- overlap arithmetic operations with memory transactions.

If we analyze the examples provided in the CUDA programming guide, we see that even though the theoretical maximum for the number of threads on a given (multi)processor is constant, the actual limitations come from the amount of shared memory and from the number of registers employed per thread block. Specifically, the number of registers is very difficult to control, being determined by the compiler optimizations. However, it is possible to force the maximum number of registers of a kernel, passing some special parameters to the compiler. Even in this case, it is still necessary to check the compiler output for register occupancy, employing some tools provided in the CUDA environment or from third parties, such as the binary code disassembler *decuda* [9].

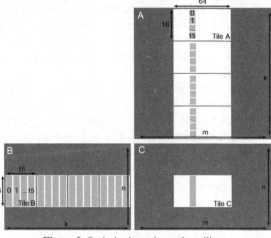

Subsequent tests showed that ensuring maximum GPU occupancy is not the most important factor in the GEMM kernel. Indeed, we adopted the large tiling technique presented in [10], consisting of:

- computing a tile of matrix C of size 64×16 per thread block, where each thread computes a column within the tile (see Fig. 2);
- using shared memory just for tiles from matrix B, whereas tiles from matrix A are loaded from global memory.

Figure 2. Optimized matrix product tiling
(A, B, and C matrices are stored in Fortran memory layout).

This implied a drop in occupancy down to 33%; nevertheless, it shows better performance due to better memory transactions hiding, more efficient calculation of the element offsets, and less use of shared memory (i.e., a lower number of total thread block synchronizations).

The offset computation reduction is achieved by properly sequencing the accesses to tile B by columns (rather than by rows), and by doing explicitly the pointer arithmetic needed to update the base addresses of the individual columns. However, care must be taken to avoid bank conflicts; in our case, it is sufficient to adopt the time-honored trick of increasing by one the leading dimension of the buffer in shared memory that will hold the (transposed) tile.

Further performance improvements were gained through the *prefetching* of elements from tile A, within the multiplication loop; this was enough to reach CUBLAS 2.0 SGEMM performance level.

Variations of the above scheme apply for the other combinations of transpose/no-transpose of the input matrices A and B that have to be supported to conform to the BLAS standard. In particular, we succeeded in exploiting the same optimizations in a version of the SGEMM routine for transposed matrices in input; our version computes the $A^T B^T$ product by first calculating BA and then transposing the result on-the-fly without using additional shared memory. The performance results in Fig. 3 show an improvement of up to 59% with respect to the 2.0 version of the CUBLAS library on the NVIDIA GeForce 9800GTX+ in the innermost kernel, and up to 50% when considering host-device-host memory transactions; overall this achieves approximately 40% of the available peak performance. Note that NVIDIA has included some of our code in its 2.1 version of the CUBLAS library, and therefore the performance gap has now disappeared.

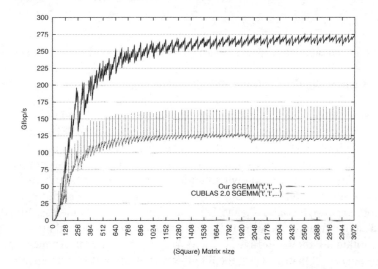

Figure 3. Performance of transpose-transpose SGEMM on NVIDIA GeForce 9800GTX+ (kernel only).

The last technique we employed to achieve maximum performance stems from the need to handle matrix sizes that are not necessarily multiples of tile size, causing the need of additional control and the misalignment of matrix rows (and so uncoalesced accesses); The obvious solution is to pad with zeroes the various involved matrices during the copy-in/copy-out between host and device memory; strictly speaking, this technique is external to the GEMM kernel, but affects the user anyway.

Newer NVIDIA GPUs offer native support for double precision computations. As shown in Fig. 4, for DGEMM we obtained nearly 100 % of peak performance (versus 42% of SGEMM), proving that the optimization techniques are essentially the same as in the single precision version, modulo the obvious adjustments to the memory allocations and address computations. The main difference is that DGEMM does not need to use the prefetching technique, because the new hardware seems to improve the double precision pipeline throughput when operands are in shared memory (i.e., it does not need to move all operands first from shared memory to registers).

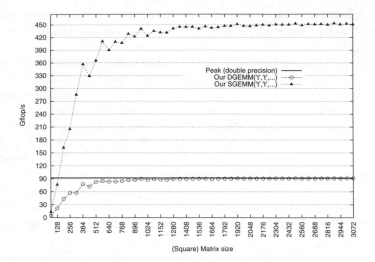

Figure 4. Performance of transpose-transpose DGEMM on NVIDIA GeForce GTX285 (kernel only).

4. Performance Results for the APSP Problem

An interesting application of the same performance optimization techniques we have analyzed so far is in the context of the All-Pairs Shortest-Path (APSP) problem. Given a weighted graph $G = (V, E, W)$, with non negative weights, the aim is to find out the distance matrix between all possible pairs of vertices. In the serial context, the Floyd-Warshall algorithm is a well-known solution characterized by time-complexity $O(V^3)$ and space complexity $O(V^2)$. If the graph is quite sparse, the algorithm turns out to be much more expensive than, e.g., the Dijkstra algorithm. Nevertheless, Floyd-Warshall has a redeeming feature: its formal structure is that of a generalized matrix "multiplication" algorithm, as shown in Fig. 5, where Ms is the matrix of distance estimates and Ma is the adjacency matrix. Thus, the Floyd-Warshall algorithm is amenable to the same optimization techniques we have discussed above.

$$Ms \leftarrow Ma$$
for $k = 1, \dots$ **do**
    for $D(i, j) \in Ms$ **do**
        $D(i, j) \leftarrow \min\left(D(i, j), D(i, k) + D(k, j)\right)$
    end for
end for

Figure 5. Floyd-Warshall algorithm for APSP.

The only significant difference between the Floyd-Warshall algorithm and the Matrix-Multiply based one is that Floyd-Warshall is sequentially bounded by the outer loop, that prevents the algorithm to be execute entirely on a kernel launch, due to the grid synchronization. For this reason, it is harder to gain the same GEMM code efficiency. Therefore, we have developed an algorithm entirely based on the matrix multiply code, that determines, after N iterations, the 2^N-shortest paths for all pairs of nodes. Every

Table 1. APSP kernel timing on random graphs for NVIDIA GeForce GTX285 (time values are in msec).

nodes	Floyd-Warshall			Matrix-Multiply based		
	#edges/#nodes ratio			#edges/#nodes ratio		
	1/10	1/1	10/1	1/10	1/1	10/1
64	1.28	1.3	1.4	**0.49**	**0.72**	**0.74**
128	2.49	2.53	2.81	**0.75**	**1.13**	**1.27**
256	5.5	5.6	8	**1.45**	**2.12**	**3**
512	14	14	40	**5.73**	**8.45**	**15**
1024	41	**42.6**	275	**30**	43	**102**
2048	**136**	**157**	1525	191	262	**816**
4096	**508**	**659**	8514	1480	1896	**6877**
8192	**2067**	**3012**	**51949**	13901	19661	58736

iteration has the same time complexity of the Floyd-Warshall algorithm, so it totally has $O(V^3 \cdot \log(\min(E, V - 1)))$ time complexity, where $\min(E, V - 1)$ is the maximum length of all shortest paths in a graph. Table 1 compares the performance results of the Floyd-Warshall algorithm vs. the matrix-multiply based one, which represents the "GPU-friendly but theoretical worse" approach. The graphs with a number of nodes varying from 64 up to 8192 (and three different values for the ratio between the number of edges and the number of nodes) have been generated using the GTgraph-random tool [2]. In Table 1 the values reported in bold represent the better performing solution for each graph size. The results show that for graphs of large sizes and not too dense the Floyd-Warshall algorithm outperforms the matrix-multiply based one, while the latter turns out to be the better solution when the graph density increases.

5. New Developments

The usage of the GPU programming model is spreading throughout the scientific computing world because of the very appealing price/performance ratio. However, the successful applicability of these computing devices is far from universal; in particular, applying the GPU programming techniques to sparse linear algebra computations is not an obvious proposition.

The bane of sparse matrix computations is the need to perform indexed addressing; this is well known in the scientific computing community, and is also recognized by (at least some in) the hardware design community, as recently highlighted in [4]. Unfortunately, the GPU architecture does not offer specialized support for indexed addressing, and thus the performance level that can be achieved falls quite short of the theoretical peak supported by the hardware. In preliminary results, we have found that the performance ratio between single precision and double precision kernels is just near to 2x (although peak ratio is more than 10x). This proves as our first sparse matrix-vector multiply kernel implementation still holds a significant memory bottleneck, due to the difficulty of providing coalesced accesses in such algorithms, and thus to the impossibility of hiding memory transactions with ALU operations.

6. Conclusions

In this paper we have shared our programming experience on the NVIDIA CUDA environment and devices, showing as it is possible to take advantage of this cheap architecture for high performance computing. Besides an evident benefit from using GPU for embarrassingly parallel algorithms, there are some perplexities on using CUDA for algorithms that have several sequential constraints or, more in general, for algorithms that do not provide a large ratio of arithmetic operations per memory accesses, like sparse numerical computing. Despite the GPU inefficiency to suit these algorithms compared to the peak performance, it is still convenient compared to other general purpose solutions. Nevertheless, GPU manufacturers promise to increment the already large on-board GDDR bandwidth and to improve the double precision support of future devices and this could imply interesting implications in scientific computing.

As discussed in Section 5, our current research direction is to investigate other kinds of linear algebra operations, such as the sparse matrix-vector product involved in many types of computations, specifically in explicit time-marching schemes for fluid dynamics based on the Lattice-Boltzmann model. Our future work will also focus on the best exploitation of further evolutions of the newer GPUs generations.

References

[1]   E. Anderson, Z. Bai, C. Bischof, J. Demmel, J. Dongarra, J. Du Croz, A. Greenbaum, S. Hammarling, A. McKenney, S. Ostrouchov, and D. Sorensen. *LAPACK's user's guide*. Society for Industrial and Applied Mathematics, Philadelphia, PA, USA, 1992.

[2]   D. A. Bader and K. Madduri. *GTgraph: A suite of synthetic graph generators*. http://hpcrd.lbl.gov/~kamesh/GTgraph/

[3]   J. Dongarra, J. Du Croz, S. Hammarling, and I. S. Duff. A set of level 3 basic linear algebra subprograms. *ACM Trans. Math. Softw.*, **16**(1):1–17, 1990.

[4]   J. Gebis and D. Patterson. Embracing and extending 20-th century instrucion set architectures. *IEEE Computer*, **40**(4):68–75, 2007.

[5]   P. Harish and P. J. Narayanan. Accelerating large graph algorithms on the GPU using CUDA. *Proc. of HiPC 2007*, LNCS Vol. 4873, Springer, 2007.

[6]   B. Kågström, P. Ling, and C. van Loan. GEMM-based level 3 BLAS: High-performance model implementations and performance evaluation benchmark. *ACM Trans. Math. Softw.*, **24**(3):268–302, 1998.

[7]   NVIDIA Corporation. *NVIDIA CUDA Compute Unified Device Architecture Programming Guide, Edition 2.0*, 2008. http://www.nvidia.com

[8]   NVIDIA Corporation. *CUBLAS Library, Programming Guide, version 2.1*, Sept. 2008.

[9]   W. J. van der Laan. Cubin utilities. http://www.cs.rug.nl/~wladimir/decuda/

[10] V. Volkov and J. W. Demmel. Benchmarking GPUs to tune dense linear algebra. *Proc. of 2008 ACM/IEEE Conf. on Supercomputing*, Austin, TX, Nov. 2008.

Parallel Computing: From Multicores and GPU's to Petascale
B. Chapman et al. (Eds.)
IOS Press, 2010
© 2010 The authors and IOS Press. All rights reserved.
doi:10.3233/978-1-60750-530-3-315

Comparison of Modular Arithmetic Algorithms on GPUs

Pascal GIORGI [a], Thomas IZARD [a] and Arnaud TISSERAND [b]

[a] *LIRMM, CNRS – Univ. Montpellier 2, 161 rue Ada, F-34392 Montpellier, France*
[b] *IRISA, CNRS – INRIA Centre Rennes Bretagne Atlantique – Univ. Rennes 1,
6 rue Kérampont, F-22305 Lannion, France*

Abstract. We present below our first implementation results on a modular arithmetic library for cryptography on GPUs. Our library, in C++ for CUDA, provides modular arithmetic, finite field arithmetic and some ECC support. Several algorithms and memory coding styles have been compared: local, shared and register. For moderate sizes, we report up to 2.6 speedup compared to state-of-the-art library.

Keywords. Multiple precision arithmetic, mathematical library, CUDA.

Introduction

Modular operations on large integers are used in many applications such as cryptography, coding and computer algebra. Efficient algorithms and implementations are required for $a \pm b \bmod p$, $a \times b \bmod p$ where a, b and p are multiple precision integers and p is prime. Those operations are required in finite field arithmetic over $\mathbb{F}_p$ and in elliptic curve cryptography (ECC) where sizes are about 200–600 bits. Graphic processor units (GPUs) are used in high-performance computing systems thanks to their massively multithreaded architectures. But due to their specific architecture and programming style, porting libraries to GPUs is not simple even using high-level tools such as CUDA [8].

This paper presents our first implementation results on modular arithmetic for large integers, arithmetic over $\mathbb{F}_p$ and ECC scalar multiplication application on GPUs. This work is a part of a software library called PACE [5]. This library is aimed at providing a very large set of mathematical objects, functions and algorithms to facilitate the writing of arithmetic applications. Below, we only deal with the use of GPUs as accelerators for parallel computations with different sets of data. In asymmetric cryptography applications, this kind of parallelism level is required for servers on which cyphering and/or digital signatures are computed for parallel sessions. This paper presents sequential arithmetic operations (one thread per operation) but for massively parallel computations on independent data sets. We compare our code with $\mathrm{mp}\mathbb{F}_q$ library[3] and the work from [9].

1. Large Integers on GPU

We consider modular arithmetic for arbitrary values of the modulo (i.e. p) and size N of numbers in the range 160–384 bits. The operands a and b are integers in the range $[0, p-1]$ (reduced values). Standard modular arithmetic algorithms and some implementation guidelines on standard processors may be found in good books such as [4]. But this is not the case for GPU implementation. The design and optimization of arithmetic operations is done using a complex trade-off between: *number representation* (width, radix), the *algorithm(s)* and some *architecture constraints* (type and number of functional units and memory latencies). Our goal is to define an efficient layer which can be used on a single thread, since our parallelism is only on the data. We will see that the memory mapping of the integers into various memories is a key element for this kind of GPU implementation.

1.1. Integers Representation and Memory

Large integers are usually stored into an array of words such as depicted below.

$$a = \boxed{\begin{array}{|c|c|c|c|} a_{n-1} & a_{n-2} & \cdots & a_0 \end{array}} = \sum_{i=0}^{n=-1} a_i \beta^i$$

The word size depends on the functional units characteristics. This size leads to various values for the radix β. The choice of β and the word's datatype is clearly related to GPUs capabilities. According to NVIDIA CUDA programming guide [8], the possible native datatype for a word can be either 32-bit integer, 32-bit or 64-bit floating-point (FP) numbers. Considering current lower[1] throughputs of the 64-bit FP numbers compare to 32-bit datatype on newest GPU (GT200 core), one can avoid for the time being the use of 64-bit FP number as word.

Considering 32-bit arithmetic units on GPU, one can issue one of the following operations in 4 clock cycles on a GPU multiprocessor: one exact multiply-and-add (MAD) operation on 10-bit operands with `float`, one exact multiplication on 16-bit operands with `int` and one exact addition with carry on 16-bit operands with `int`.

Looking at the school book multiplication[2] on N-bit integers this gives the following theoretical clock cycle counts:

	160-bit	192-bit	224-bit	256-bit	384-bit
# cycle with float, $\beta = 2^{10}$	1024	1600	2116	2704	6084
# cycle with int, $\beta = 2^{16}$	724	1252	1460	1924	4420

It seems clear from this comparison that 32-bit integers with $\beta = 2^{16}$ is a better choice than 32-bit FP numbers. Moreover, a smaller word number saves memory. Furthermore, bit manipulations remain easier with integer representation.

The main difficulty with GPU is to fully benefit from high memory bandwidth within the global memory (the RAM of the GPU). In particular, one needs to design code such that many concurrent memory accesses from many concurrent threads of a multiprocessor can be coalesced into a single transaction. The basic idea is that the i-*th* thread of a multiprocessor needs to read/write the i-*th* data in a particular segment of memory. See [8, Chapter 5] for further details.

In our computational model, integers are not gathered between threads and using linear array to store integer's words leads to non-coalesced memory patterns. To fulfill this requirement, we provide functionality to load (resp. store) integer from (resp. to) global memory. These functions change the words order to ensure coalesced access. We define the following rule to reorder words of a same variable across all threads:

---

[1]Throughput of 64-bit float is barely equal to 1/8 of 32-bit float throughput.
[2]School book multiplication requires N^2 multiplications and $(N-1)^2$ additions or N^2 MAD

$$i\text{-}th \text{ thread} \quad a = \boxed{\; a_0 \;}\;\cdots\;\boxed{\; a_{n-2} \;}\boxed{\; a_{n-1} \;}$$

$$(i+1)\text{-}th \text{ thread} \quad a = \boxed{\; \bar{a}_0 \;}\;\cdots\;\boxed{\; \bar{a}_{n-2} \;}\boxed{\; \bar{a}_{n-1} \;}$$

$$\text{Global memory reordering} \quad \boxed{a_0}\boxed{\bar{a}_0}\;\cdots\;\boxed{a_{n-2}}\boxed{\bar{a}_{n-2}}\boxed{a_{n-1}}\boxed{\bar{a}_{n-1}}$$

Figure 1. Global memory organization for coalesced integer access

To ensure memory alignment, two consecutive words of one integer of one thread are distant of i word addresses, where i is the minimal power of 16 greater or equal to the total number of threads launched on the GPU.

Global memory accesses are quite costly and must be avoided. Therefore, one would prefer to store integers in a non-coalesced form in another memory region (local memory or shared memory). Fetching all data in local or shared memory at the beginning of a GPU kernel function will ensure that all reads from global memory are coalesced.

1.2. Large Integer in GPUs Registers

For efficiency reason it would be interesting to map large integers directly into GPU registers. This should save at least the latency of memory load/store instructions. However, as all hardware registers, GPU's registers are not indexable. This means that no arrays can be mapped into registers. The only way to map large integers into registers is to design specific structures with one variable per integer word. This approach is feasible but not used for generic and portable code.

Fortunately, C++ and template metaprogramming [1] can help. In particular, one can design a generic structure which defines fixed number of variables with compile time indexable access.

```
template <uint N>  struct IntegerReg : IntegerReg <N-1> {
    uint word;
    IntegerReg() : IntegerReg<N-1>() {word=0;}};
  template<> struct IntegerReg <1> {
    uint word;
    IntegerReg() {word=0;}};
#define AT(x,i)  x.IntegerReg<i+1>::word
```

Figure 2. A register-compliant structure for large integer with indexable access.

`IntegerReg` structure defined in Figure 2 uses C++ recursive inheritance to define a proper number of variables to store an N-word integer. One can access a particular variable from this structure by using the index given within the template parameter. The macro `AT` defines the proper accessor to the $(i+1)\text{-}th$ word of the integer x. The only drawback of this structure is that all indices need to be known at compile time, meaning no runtime loop can be executed. Here again C++ templates come to rescue to define compile time loop as illustrated in Figure 3.

Compile time loop consists of completely unrolling loops by duplicating code with proper register values. This technique can be very efficient if the compiler is able to discover registers reusability. In case of GPU, `nvcc` compiler (the CUDA compiler)

```
template<uint beg, uint end>
struct IntegerLoop {
   template<uint N>
   static bool egal(const IntegerReg<N>& a, const IntegerReg<N>& b)
   {return  AT(a,beg)==AT(b,beg) && IntegerLoop<beg+1,end>::egal(a,b);}};
template<uint end>
struct IntegerLoop<end,end> {
   template<uint N>
   static bool egal (const IntegerReg<N>& a, const IntegerReg<N>& b)
   {return AT(a,end)==AT(b,end);}};
```

Figure 3. C++ compile time loop for register-compliant integers comparison.

seems to not be very friendly with such a technique. In particular, with quite simple code nvcc might ran out of registers when it tries to compile code for the GPU. This comes from GPUs code generation which uses intermediate PTX code in SSA form (Single Static Assignement) before to call open64 compiler[3] to generate code for GPU. The SSA forms of compile time loops are usually quite large and discovering registers mapping from this form is not well handled by nvcc. To reduce SSA code and register usage, we change the base β value to 2^{32} whenever register-compliant integers are used.

2. Modular Arithmetic on Large Integers

We investigate GPU implementation of the 3 basic modular arithmetic operations on large integers: addition, subtraction and multiplication. We do not investigate division since it can be avoided in most of our target applications. Memory accesses within GPU can be very costly depending where data are localized. For instance one access to global memory costs around 400–600 cycles while one register or one shared memory access cost around 10 cycles. Minimizing data access and intermediate variables is thus critical.

For the modular addition/subtraction the basic algorithm can suffice since it requires only an integer addition (potentially with a carry) and a conditional subtraction. Moreover, this operation can be done inplace (a += b mod p) with only one extra register for the carry propagation. We use classical integer algorithm with carry propagation along limbs as described at [4, pp.30].

In the case of register version of integers, we have $\beta = 2^{32}$ and no instruction is available to get the carry of addition or subtraction of words. Thus, we need to calculate explicitly the carry using the following trick: the carry of $a + b$ is equal to the result of the test $a + b < a$. A similar trick is available for subtraction.

Separated operation and reduction become too costly for multiplication. The product $a \times b$ is $2n$ words long. Then the reduction to a single n words number is close to a division by p. In that case, the operation and the reduction are interleaved using a bit-serial scan of one operand (usually, the multiplier a). At each step, the partial product $a_{i,j} \times b$ (where $a_{i,j}$ is the jth bit of the word a_i) a is accumulated and reduced modulo p. We use the well known Montgomery's algorithm to avoid the use of multi-precision division [7]. In order to reduce memory usage we use an interleaved Montgomery's method which consists of doing multiplication and reduction at the same time. Our implementation is

---

[3]http://www.open64.net/

based on the Finely Integrated Operand Scanning (FIOS) method described in [6] which required only 3 extra words. Using $\beta = 2^{16}$ with 32-bit integers, we do not suffer from carry propagation along word additions.

We compare our arithmetic layer performance when data are localized in the different memory regions: local memory, shared memory and registers. In Table 1, we report computation times of modular operations for N in 160–384 bits. Operands are chosen randomly with full limb occupancy and the GPU kernel function consists in 1024 threads within 64 blocks. Each thread loads its two operands from the global memory to the chosen memory space (local, shared, register) and then compute a loop of 10 000 operations (using result in the loop as a new operand for the next operation). We perform our GPU computation on a Geforce 9800GX2 card.

N	addition			multiplication		
	local	**shared**	**register**	**local**	**shared**	**register**
160	9	2.3	0.7	88	40	22
192	11	2.3	0.7	125	51	33
224	23	5.0	1.1	172	107	55
256	26	3.1	1.5	214	80	81
384	38	7.4	3.9	673	221	261

Table 1. Computation times in ns for modular addition and multiplication.

One can see from this table that GPU data location in memory is important, and register usage can improve speed. One can also remark that multiplication for $N > 256$ registers version becomes less efficient than shared version. This comes from the CUDA compilation chain which is not able to handle code with large register usage. Note that each thread can use at most 128 registers of 32-bit integers.

In order to demonstrate benefits of GPU for multiprecision modular arithmetic, we compare our layer with the $\mathrm{mp}\mathbb{F}_q$ library [3] which is currently the best library to perform modular arithmetic on CPU with modulo of moderate size (i.e. less than 600 bits). In Table 2 we report the comparison of our best GPU modular arithmetic implementation (register version) with $\mathrm{mp}\mathbb{F}_q$ library. Benchmarks are identical as in previous section, except that $\mathrm{mp}\mathbb{F}_q$ handles sequentially the 1024 threads on a Core(TM)2 Duo E8400 3GHz processor. For N less than 384 bits GPU beats CPU calculation. However, speedup factors are moderate since CPU processor has higher frequency than GPU multiprocessor. Moreover, $\mathrm{mp}\mathbb{F}_q$ uses well tuned code with SIMD SSE-2 instructions, which allows to be more efficient implementation of large integers than our GPU implementation.

N	addition mod p			multiplication mod p		
	our impl.	**mpfq**	**speedup**	**our impl.**	**mpfq**	**speedup**
160	0.7	15	×21	22	64	×2.9
192	0.7	16	×22	33	70	×2.1
224	1.1	21	×19	55	105	×1.9
256	1.5	21	×14	81	109	×1.3
384	3.9	30	×7	261	210	×0.8

Table 2. Time comparison in ns of software library $\mathrm{mp}\mathbb{F}_q$ and our best GPU implementation.

3. ECC Application

In order to evaluate our library in a realistic application, we use it for scalar multiplications. This is the main operation required in ECC. For instance, servers performing many digital signatures have to compute parallel and independent scalar multiplications. Below, we consider an elliptic curve (EC) $E(\mathbb{F}_p)$ defined over the prime finite field $\mathbb{F}_p$ (a is the parameter of the curve). See [4] for background, details and notations. In order to avoid modular inversions, we use the Jacobian coordinates system ($P = (X, Y, Z)$ where X, Y and Z are in $\mathbb{F}_p$). Montgomery representation is used for fast multiplications. All threads share p and a parameters but points P and Q are different.

All operations presented in this section are used in the same way. Data are sent to the GPU global memory in coalesced form. The GPU kernel loads the selected memory (local, shared or registers) from the global memory, converts necessary values to the Montgomery form, performs the curve operation, and converts back to standard form. Then results are sent from the GPU to the CPU.

3.1. Point Addition and Doubling

Two basic operations are used for points P and Q on $E(\mathbb{F}_p)$: *point addition $P + Q$* (for $P \neq Q$) and *point doubling $2P$* (specific addition for $P = Q$). Those point operations are defined using several additions, multiplications over $\mathbb{F}_p$. Point addition and doubling require respectively 2 and 3 extra integers (and 6 for P and Q). These intermediate values are stored in same memory than the other data.

Timings are reported in Table 3 for the three considered memory schemes: local, shared and registers. The computation was launched on 1024 threads (64 blocks of 16 threads) and 100 operations for each thread. Due to the limited number of registers for one thread, the CUDA compiler was unable to build the code for N greater than 192 bits (*ror* is reported for compilation aborted due to "run out of register" compiler error).

N	point addition			point doubling		
	local	**shared**	**register**	**local**	**shared**	**register**
160	2.57	0.78	0.70	1.64	0.50	0.54
192	3.51	1.01	1.13	2.30	0.58	0.70
224	4.41	1.95	*ror*	2.73	1.01	*ror*
256	5.89	1.56	*ror*	3.71	1.09	*ror*
384	13.9	7.50	*ror*	13.3	2.42	*ror*

Table 3. Computation timings in μs for point addition and doubling.

For both operation, local memory is the worst due to its high latency. Except for point addition with $N = 160$, the shared memory implementation is the best. One drawback of shared memory is the fact it limits the number of threads per block to 16. In the shared memory version, the huge timing gap between $N = 256$ and $N = 384$ is due to the card occupancy which is twice for $N = 256$ (or less) than for $N = 384$. For point doubling, occupancy is the same for all N and the factor 2 is due to the computations. We notice that register version is slower than shared version due to the fact that the compiler was unable to use correctly all the registers it has and put data in local memory.

In Table 4, we compare our best implementation with the PACE library coupled to $\text{mp}\mathbb{F}_q$ running on the CPU for the same data. The shared memory version is at least twice faster than the CPU version for point doubling, but is no more than twice for addition. The difference comes from the number of Montgomery multiplications required in each operation: 9 for point doubling and 16 for point addition and the fact that the speedup factor for one Montgomery multiplication is small.

N	point addition			point doubling		
	our impl.	**mpfq+pace**	*speedup*	**our impl.**	**mpfq+pace**	*speedup*
160	0.78	1.52	*1.9*	0.50	1.99	*4.0*
192	1.01	1.91	*1.9*	0.58	1.99	*3.4*
224	1.95	2.65	*1.3*	1.01	2.69	*2.6*
256	1.56	2.65	*1.7*	1.09	2.65	*2.4*
384	7.50	5.11	*0.7*	2.42	5.01	*2.0*

Table 4. Time [μs] for our GPU implementation and (PACE+mp$\mathbb{F}_q$) on CPU.

3.2. Scalar Multiplication

Scalar multiplication $Q = [k]P = P + \cdots + P$ (with k additions of point P) where k is an N-bit integer and P a point of $E(\mathbb{F}_p)$, is the main operation in ECC protocols (see [4] for details and algorithms). We use a right-to-left double-and-add algorithm since it does not require pre-computations and additional storage. It uses point addition and point doubling for each step of a loop over the bits of k. Furthermore, it allows some threads to follow the same execution pattern as the base point is doubled at each step of the loop.

Table 5 reports times and operation throughput (in $[k]P/s$) for our best implementation (i.e., the shared version) and $\text{mp}\mathbb{F}_q$+PACE implementations. Our tests use the same N for k and $\mathbb{F}_p$ and the Hamming weight of k equal to $N/2$. For $N = 384$, our scalar multiplication on GPU is slower than the CPU version (computed with $\text{mp}\mathbb{F}_q$+PACE). We noticed that the speedup factor decreases for larger numbers. This is mainly due to the small factor between the $\text{mp}\mathbb{F}_q$+PACE version and our shared memory version of the Montgomery multiplication (1.6 for $N = 160$ and 1.3 for $N = 256$).

N	computation time in μs		operation throughput in [k]P/s		
	our impl.	**mpfq+pace**	**our impl.**	**mpfq+pace**	*speedup*
160	179	464	5586	2155	*2.6*
192	304	550	3289	1818	*1.8*
224	507	878	1972	1138	*1.7*
256	617	1003	1620	997	*1.6*
384	4609	2941	216	340	*0.6*

Table 5. Scalar multiplication result for our GPU implementation and (PACE+mp$\mathbb{F}_q$) on CPU.

In [9], a seminal GPU implementations of $[k]P$ is provided with $N = 224$. Their throughput is about 1412.6 $[k]P/s$ using mixed affine-Jacobian coordinates and left-to-right double-and-add algorithm. Our implementation is a little better than this result.

3.3. *w-NAF Implementation of Scalar Multiplication*

Some signed-digit representations are used for recoding k in the $[k]P$. This is motivated by the fact that point subtraction on an EC is just as efficient as addition. Among these representations, w-digit windows non-adjacent forms (w-NAF) are frequently used in ECC [4]. Using w-NAF, $k = \sum_{i=0}^{l-1} k_i'2^i$ where non-zero digits k_i' are odd, $|k_i'| < 2^{w-1}$ and at most one digit of any w-digit window is non-zero. Thus w-NAF recoding decreases the number of point additions/subtractions ($\approx 1/(w+1)$ w.r.t. 0.5 for binary). It is also used as a simple countermeasure against side channel attacks [2].

Several versions have been implemented: $w \in \{2, 3\}$ as well as basic and optimized storage. The basic storage uses a complete word for each w-NAF digit. The optimized storage uses the minimal number of bits for a w-NAF digit (i.e., 2 bits for $w = 2$ and 3 bits for $w = 3$) through a dedicated multiple precision storage. For $w = 3$, $3P$ is precomputed and stored. Addition of $-P$ and $-3P$ are obtained by subtracting respectively P and $3P$. Recoding from integer k into w-NAF is performed on the GPU.

Due to `nvcc` compiler limitations, it was not possible to compile more than $N = 256$ bits with $w = 2$ and $N = 160$ for $w = 3$. Using a $w = 3$ leads to 10% speed improvement compared to $w = 2$. The number of operations is reduced, but the additional internal value $3P$ puts a too high pressure on scheduling. Surprisingly, basic and optimized storage of the w-NAF recoding gives very close results.

Conclusion and Future Prospects

In this work we report our first implementation results on modular arithmetic for large integers on GPUs which achieves a speedup of 2.6 compared to state-of-the-art library. We show that porting modular arithmetic algorithms on GPUs is not direct. Our long term goal is to design a high-performance arithmetic library for cryptography.

Acknowledgments

The authors are grateful to the Nvidia donation program for its support with GPUs cards.

References

[1] Andrei Alexandrescu. *Modern C++ design: generic programming and design patterns applied.* Addison-Wesley Longman Publishing Co., Inc., Boston, MA, USA, 2001.

[2] A. Byrne, N. Meloni, A. Tisserand, E. M. Popovici, and W. P. Marnane. Comparison of simple power analysis attack resistant algorithms for an ECC. *Journal of Computers,* 2(10):52–62, 2007.

[3] P. Gaudry and E. Thomé. The mpFq library and implementing curve-based key exchanges. In *Proc. Software Performance Enhancement for Encryption and Decryption Workshop,* pages 49–64, 2007.

[4] D. Hankerson, A. Menezes, and S. Vanstone. *Guide to Elliptic Curve Cryptography.* Springer, 2004.

[5] L. Imbert, A. Peirera, and A. Tisserand. A library for prototyping the computer arithmetic level in elliptic curve cryptography. In F. T. Luk, editor, *Proc. Advanced Signal Processing Algorithms, Architectures and Implementations XVII,* volume 6697, pages 1–9, San Diego, California, U.S.A., August 2007. SPIE.

[6] Cetin Kaya Koc, Tolga Acar, and Jr. Burton S. Kaliski. Analyzing and comparing montgomery multiplication algorithms. *IEEE Micro,* 16(3):26–33, 1996.

[7] P. L. Montgomery. Modular multiplication without trial division. *Mathematics of Computation,* 44(170):519–521, April 1985.

[8] NVIDIA. *NVIDIA CUDA Programming Guide 2.0.* 2008.

[9] R. Szerwinski and T. Güneysu. Exploiting the power of gpus for asymmetric cryptography. In Springer, editor, *Proc. Cryptographic Hardware and Embedded Systems,* volume 5154, pages 79–99, 2008.

Parallel Computing: From Multicores and GPU's to Petascale
B. Chapman et al. (Eds.)
IOS Press, 2010
© 2010 The authors and IOS Press. All rights reserved.
doi:10.3233/978-1-60750-530-3-323

Fast Multipole Method on the Cell Broadband Engine: the Near Field Part

Pierre FORTIN, Jean-Luc LAMOTTE

Université Pierre et Marie Curie, LIP6 UMR 7606,
4 place Jussieu, F-75252 Paris Cedex 05, France
E-mail: {Pierre.Fortin, Jean-Luc.Lamotte}@lip6.fr

Abstract. The implementation of the near field part of the Fast Multipole Method, which solves hierarchically N-body problems, is presented for the Cell Broadband Engine. Algorithmic and hardware issues, as well as code specific optimizations, are detailed for this first step towards the first full implementation of a hierarchical N-body method on the Cell processor. We compute up to more than 8.5 billion interactions per second (115.8 Gflop/s) on the Cell Processor, and up to more than 17 billion interactions per second on the IBM QS20 blade (230.4 Gflop/s), for both uniform and non-uniform distributions of particles.

Keywords. Cell processor, N-body problem, Fast Multipole Method, direct computation

1. Introduction

In June 2008, the petaflop barrier has been broken by the IBM *Roadrunner* computer located at Los Alamos National Laboratory. Over 96% of the 1.3 Pflop/s theoretical peak performance is contributed by the Cell Broadband Engine [1,2]. This Cell processor is composed of a general-purpose PowerPC core (PPE) and of eight Synergistic Processing Elements (SPEs) specialized for high performance computing. Each SPE has an independant fast local store (LS) managed through explicit direct memory access (DMA) instructions from/to the Cell main memory. The overall Cell architecture presents thus 3 level of parallelism: MPI multi-process parallelism among several Cell processors, multi-thread parallelism among the eight SPEs of each Cell processor and finally SIMD (Single Instruction on Multiple Data) parallelism by using the vector units of each SPE. Along with graphics processing units (GPUs), these hardware accelerators are increasingly used in the scientific computing community. Their specific architectures may however not be suitable for all applications and all algorithms.

In [3], 13 scientific kernels (the 13 "dwarfs") have been described as representative of the computational characteristics and data movement patterns of all scientific applications. The N-body problem is one the these 13 dwarfs: it describes the computation of all pairwise interactions among N bodies. In astrophysics or in molecular dynamics for example, the interactions between two bodies A and B are the gravitational or Coulomb force vectors which can be written as

$$\mathbf{F}_{A \to B} = -\mathbf{F}_{B \to A} = C \frac{v_A v_B}{r_{AB}^2} \mathbf{u}_{AB}, \tag{1}$$

where C is a physical constant, v_A and v_B are either the masses or the charges of A and B, r_{AB} is the distance between A and B, and $\mathbf{u}_{AB}$ is the unitary vector between A and B, defined as $\mathbf{u}_{AB} = \frac{\mathbf{r}_B - \mathbf{r}_A}{r_{AB}}$, where $\mathbf{r}_A$ and $\mathbf{r}_B$ are the position vectors of A and B.

The direct computation of all these pairwise interactions in $\mathcal{O}(N^2)$ is prohibitive. Therefore, cut-off radius methods [4] with $\mathcal{O}(N)$ runtime, or hierarchical methods with $\mathcal{O}(N \ln N)$ or $\mathcal{O}(N)$ runtime [9], have been introduced. Compared to the cut-off radius method, the hierarchical methods are more precise especially for long-range interactions like the Coulomb and gravitational ones. According to [5], the N-body methods have not yet been fully investigated for the Cell processor. In molecular dynamics, N-body simulations with cut-off radius have already been performed on the Cell processor [6,7] and on the Roadrunner [2]. Astrophysical $\mathcal{O}(N^2)$ direct computations have also been performed [8]. Depending on the considered forces and on the number of particles, the performance results in single precision for one Cell processor vary between 45 Gflop/s [6], 60 Gflop/s (for 6 SPEs) [7] and 83 Gflop/s [8]. [2] presents 34 Gflop/s performance for double precision computations on the PowerXCell8i processor. But to our knowledge, no hierarchical N-body method has already been efficiently implemented for the Cell processor, either in astrophysics or in molecular dynamics.

We will focus in this paper on the hierarchical Fast Multipole Method (FMM) [9], where the potential field is decomposed in a near field part, directly computed, and a far field part approximated with multipole and local expansions. An octree is used for this decomposition, and the algorithm requires both an upward pass and a downward pass of this octree. The FMB (Fast Multipole with BLAS) code [10] relies on a matrix formulation of the most time consuming operator of the far field computation. By using the BLAS (Basic Linear Algebra Subprograms) routines, which are highly efficient routines performing matrix operations, this code offers substantial runtime speedup for the targeted precisions in astrophysics and in molecular dynamics (between 10^{-2} and 10^{-7}). Thanks to the BLAS portability, the far-field computation in FMB will be directly ported to the Cell processor as soon as optimized level 3 BLAS routines for complex numbers (CGEMM/ZGEMM) will be available: the current IBM Software Development Kit (SDK 3.1 [1]) provides complex BLAS routines that run only on the PPE, not on the SPEs, yielding to limited performance.

Therefore, this article presents the first step of the FMB implementation of the Cell processor, namely the near field part. This near field computation corresponds to the direct computation of all particles among nearest neighbors at the last level of the octree. More precisely, for each octree leaf L, we have first to compute all the interactions between each particle contained in L and each particle contained in each of its 26 nearest neighbors[1] in the 3D octree: these are the *pair* computations. Interactions between each pair of particles contained in L must then also be performed: this is the *own* computation.

An hybrid MPI-thread parallelization of FMB has been proposed in [11], where the multi-thread parallelization is based on POSIX threads. The data locality and the load balancing among these threads are ensured by an octree decomposition. This octree decomposition is based on Morton ordering and appropriate cost functions: see [11]. Because of the mutual interaction principle, write/write conflicts can sometimes occur between two threads. These conflicts are treated through mutual exclusion mechanisms for all particles of an octree leaf at the same time: a single bit per leaf (named *lock bit*

---

[1]26 neighbors or less thanks to the mutual interaction principle.

afterwards) is used to detect conflicts, and FIFO (*First In First Out*) data structures enable to postpone the conflicting operation.

In this paper, we plan to adapt this multi-thread parallelization in order to implement the near field part on the Cell processor. The key features of this near-field implementation of the FMM will be described in section 2, and we will present in section 3 performance results of our implementation on various particle distributions.

2. Near Field Part Implementation Key Features

The first step is the design of efficient computation kernels for both the pair and own computations while exploiting at most the mutual interaction principle. We will consider here only the force computation (no potential computation) in single precision.

2.1. Efficient Code for Computation Kernels

At first, as we may have to treat low numbers of particles per leaf, we have chosen not to divide one pair or own computation among several SPEs. Secondly, SIMD vectorization for the SPE code requires a "structure of arrays" (SOA) data layout [2] which had to be implemented in the whole FMB code. The SPE vector registers lead us to compute together blocks of 4 bodies: this implies array padding with zero mass bodies so that the array sizes are multiples of 4. The key insight here is to have enough instructions in the body of the internal loop. The compiler can then reorder instructions in order to fill at best the two SPE pipelines and achieve the best dual-issue rate [5].

For the pair computation code between 2 leafs, this is accomplished thanks to the numerous SPE vector registers which enable us to compute together all the 16 interactions among the 2×4 bodies in the two leaf blocks. The required quadword rotates are dual-issued with floating point instructions, and we hence obtain 8 body loads (from local store to registers) for 16 computations. The internal loop has also been unrolled manually, and the instructions of the 2 iterations have been interleaved in the C code.

The own computation requires special treatment when computing interactions among the same 4 bodies (*own* block computation): only 12 interactions are then performed without the mutual interaction principle. Interactions between distinct blocks are treated with the pair computation code and with the mutual interaction principle.

Finally, we use the IBM _rsqrtf4 vector function for the square root reciproqual which uses a floating-point reciprocal square root estimate (dual-issued with floating point instructions) and one Newton-Raphson iteration to match floating point single precision. For each interaction in the pair computation, the final code requires hence 27 flops[2]. Since we use the mutual interaction principle in this pair computation, this results in 13.5 flops per interaction. As these 27 floating point instructions are written with 7 fused multiply-add (FMA), the theoretical peak performance of such computation, obtained when the floating point pipeline is always filled, is thus 67.5% of the SPE hardware peak performance, namely 17.28 Gflop/s on one SPE. It can be noticed that an own block computation leads to 24 flops per interaction since no mutual interaction is computed in this case.

---

[2]Following [2], we do not count the reciprocal square root estimate which is performed on the non floating point instruction pipeline of the SPE.

2.2. Data Flow and Communication Overlapping with Computation

With such computation kernels for pair and own computations, we now have to set efficient data DMA transfers for the bodies of a given leaf (the *target*) and of all its nearest neighbors (the *sources*).

First of all, DMA transfers are simpler and more efficient when all bodies of a given leaf are contiguous in main memory. Discontiguous locations in memory would indeed imply random memory accesses which may impact DMA transfer performance. In this respect, the FMB octree data structure was already suitable for DMA transfers. Then, the set of bodies of a leaf has to be transfered chunk by chunk since all bodies may not fit into the SPE 256KB local store. The maximum chunk size is set to 2048 bodies, for both target and source bodies, which corresponds to the allocated buffer size on the SPE. With the SOA data layout, 7 DMA commands are thus required to transfer the masses, position vectors and force vectors of all bodies of a given chunk.

The external loop applies to the target chunks, and we have the following data flow for each target chunk. The first chunk c_0 is transfered to the SPE local store, and following [2] we then start with the c_0 own computation, which overlaps the transfer of the target chunk c_1. Thanks to double buffering, we then transfer the target chunk c_2 while performing the pair computation between c_0 and c_1; and so on with all target chunks c_n with $n > 0$. When all target chunks have been treated, we continue with all chunks of all source neighbors. When all neighbors have been treated, this whole data flow is restarted with c_1 instead of c_0. The own computation of the target leaf and the pair computations with all its source neighbors is over when this data flow has been executed for all target chunks c_n.

This algorithm requires only 3 buffers which are always used as shared I/O buffers, where the next `get` operation is synchronized (*fenced*) with the previous `put` operation on the same buffer. All DMA transfers are thus overlapped with computation, except for the first target chunk read as well as for the last target and source chunk writes.

2.3. Load Balancing, Conflict Management and Synchronization Overhead

The multi-thread parallelization at the PPE level ensures a static load balancing determined by cost functions: for the near field part the cost function is based on the number of particles in the target leaf and in all neighboring source leafs. Since the PPE computation unit (PPU) is known to deliver poor computation power, this PPU being for example renamed "Poorly Performing Unit" in [2], no interaction computation is expected to be performed on the PPE. This static load balancing is therefore also suitable for balancing computations among the homogeneous SPEs.

In order to maintain the performance of our computation kernels on the overall near field computation part of the FMM, for 1 to 16 SPEs, we have to minimize the time where the SPEs are idle, waiting for their next computation. This requires a responsive PPE code and fast notifications between the PPE and the SPE.

In the previous multi-thread parallelization at the PPE level [11], the lock bits were set and unset for each pair or own computation. This resulted in fine-grained locks and fined-grained computations which may imply too strong synchronisation overhead for our Cell implementation. We have thus changed our locking strategy: we now set together the lock bits of the current leaf and of all its required nearest neighbors. All the corresponding pair and own computations will form one elementary *task* for the SPE (treated as presented in section 2.2). If some lock bits are already set for another SPE, meaning that the force vectors of these bodies are currently being updated, we use the same FIFO data structures as in [11] to postpone the whole conflicting task. This increases the computation grain but may lead to deadlocks. We have thus moved the PPE code from a multi-thread execution to a single thread one. The deadlocks are now easily avoided, no mutexes are required to set or unset the lock bits and this also avoids costful context switches between the different PPE threads. All this results in a fast single thread code which will help the PPE to be more responsive to all SPEs. In addition, this saves the PPE SMT feature for inter process communications of a future implementation over multiple Cell processors.

Besides, a given task availability is determined by the PPE thread, depending on the the value of the current lock bits, and notified to the SPE thanks to a mailbox message. By using several slots on both the PPE and the SPE sides, we can have several tasks assigned to each SPE at any time. As soon as the SPE ends a task, a new task will therefore already be available on the next slot. Since there are 4 entries in the inbound SPE mailbox, up to 4 slots can be used.

Moreover, at the end of each task a notification has to be sent by the SPE to the PPE to unset the corresponding lock bits (unless these are used by another task in another slot of the same SPE). DMA writes in the Cell main memory issued by the SPE are the fastest notification approach [5,12]: the PPE thread does not then use the next slot of a given SPE before having been notified of the slot previous task ending. These DMA writes also allow new notifications to overwrite safely the previous ones without blocking.

In order to show how our implementation attributes at best the computation work to the SPEs and the conflict management to the PPE, we have also implemented a *lock-free* version. Pair computations are here performed without the mutual interaction principle if the two leafs are attributed to two different threads in the octree decomposition. This minimizes the PPE management but increases the SPE work due to redundant computations.

3. Performance Benchmarks

We now present results with up to 16 SPEs on one IBM QS20 Cell blade located at the CINES (Centre Informatique National de l'Enseignement Supérieur, France).

3.1. Computation Kernels

Figures 1(a) and 1(b) present performance results for our own and pair computation kernels on one SPE depending on the number N of bodies in the leafs. These kernels are also compared to scalar code running on the PPE and on a standard CPU core (Intel Xeon 5150, running at 2.66GHz); we have 12 flops per (mutual) interaction in this scalar code when considering the reciprocal square root as 2 flops. As expected the PPE performs poorly, whereas the SPE outperforms the CPU core, being 10 times faster for high enough N values. The SPE code reaches 14.6 Gflop/s for the pair computation (more than 10^9 interactions per second) and 12.4 Gflop/s for the own computation. This shows very good performance compared to the theoretical 17.28 Gflop/s maximum performance of this computation (see section 2.1).

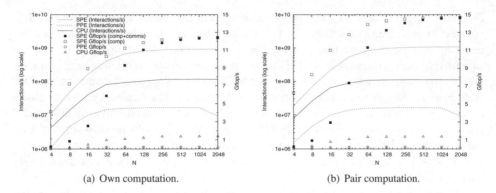

(a) Own computation.   (b) Pair computation.

Figure 1. Number of interactions computed per second and Gflop/s rate for own and pair computation of leafs with N bodies. comp denotes the SPE computation part only whereas comp+comms includes the DMA times.

The required DMA transfers are not costful for high enough N values since the DMA time grows like $\mathcal{O}(N)$, while the computation time grows like $\mathcal{O}(N^2)$.

3.2. Single SPE Computation

We now present results of full FMM near field part computations on one single SPE. From now on, the Gflop/s rate G is merely indicative since it is directly computed from the number of interactions per second N as $G = N \times 13.5$ according to section 2.1. This underestimates the flops used in the own block computations, but these become minority in the overall computation for increasing number of particles.

Figure 2(a) shows the overall Gflop/s rate for the near field computation on one SPE with different numbers of possible slots for the task mailbox notification of the PPE to the SPE (see section 2.3). This figure also details the Gflop/s rates of the pure computation kernel (without DMA time) running on the SPE as well as the reference pair computation kernel Gflop/s rate of figure 1(b) (comp+comms). Despite the fact that all numbers of bodies are not multiple of 4 anymore, the overall rate is better than the reference pair rate thanks to the DMA overlapping presented in section 2.2. Using 2 slots increases the computation rate for low and medium average number of bodies N_{avg}, but using 4 slots give almost identical results. We will therefore use 2 slots in all the following tests.

Finally, the overall Gflop/s rate is close to the pure computation one for $N_{avg} \geq 64$. This performance rate is also maintained when N_{avg} exceeds the sizes of the SPE buffers (2048 bodies). All this validates our data flow and synchronization mechanism between the PPE and the SPE. Besides, it can be noticed that, according to additional tests, buffer sizes smaller than 2048 do not improve the overall computation rate for low N_{avg} values, since this does not change the number of DMA commands per chunk (see section 2.2).

3.3. Multiple SPEs Computation

Uniforms distributions of particles, distributions on the surface of a cylinder, and astrophysical distributions based on the Plummer model [11] are respectively presented in figures 2(b), 2(c) and 2(d) for full FMM near field part computations with up to 16 SPEs. The Plummer model presents only low average number of particles per leaf N_{avg} since low precisions are required in astrophysics.

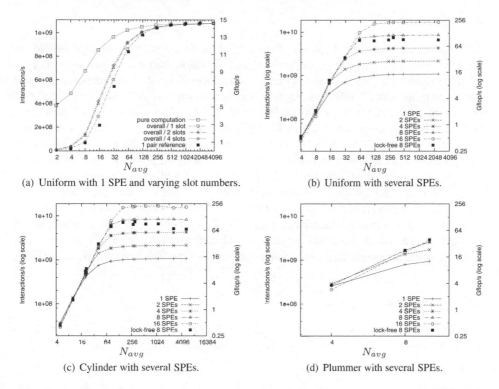

(a) Uniform with 1 SPE and varying slot numbers.

(b) Uniform with several SPEs.

(c) Cylinder with several SPEs.

(d) Plummer with several SPEs.

Figure 2. Neaf field computation for increasing average number of particles per leaf (N_{avg}) with various distributions. We use several distributions with different number of particles (from 100 000 to 10 millions) and different octree heights in order to obtain various N_{avg} values. The number of interactions computed per second by the lock-free version with 8 SPEs is also plotted on figures 2(b), 2(c) and 2(d).

For $N_{avg} \geq 128$ we have very good parallel accelerations up to 16 SPEs on figures 2(b) and 2(c), which validates our load balancing for both uniform and non-uniform distributions. This also shows that our single thread PPE code is responsive enough to handle 16 SPE threads. With N_{avg} close to 64, our implementation is still very efficient on one single Cell processor. We finally obtain up to 115.8 Gflop/s on one Cell processor (more than 8.5 billion interactions per second) and up to 230.4 Gflop/s on one QS20 blade (more than 17 billion interactions per second). This compares favorably with published results on direct computation, where the maximum performance is 83 Gflop/s on a Cell.

Too low N_{avg} values do not yield to good parallel efficiencies: the computation grain is here too small and the PPE is not responsive enough so that all SPEs can not be kept always busy during the overall near field computation. Likewise the highly concentrated Plummer model offers too many almost empty leafs with very low computation grain. The lock-free version is hardly faster here which proves that this bottleneck at the PPE level is due to the PPE hardware, which is not powerful enough to handle such low computation grain for all SPEs. Furthermore, for high values of N_{avg} this lock-free version can not reach the performance rate of our main implementation because of its redundant computations. Very good performance is therefore obtained with our main implementation on one QS20 blade, even for non-uniform distributions, as long as N_{avg} is high enough.

4. Conclusion

This first implementation of the near field part of the Fast Multipole Method (FMM) on the Cell processor calculates up to more than 8.5 billion interactions per second (up to 115.8 Gflop/s with 13.5 flops per interaction thanks to the mutual interaction principle), and up to more than 17 billion interactions per second (up to 230.4 Gflop/s) on the QS20 blade. On a NVIDIA Tesla C1060 GPU located at Polytech'Paris-UPMC, the CUDA SDK 2.3 N-body code [13] reaches 17.9 billion interactions per second for the direct computation within a set of 16 384 bodies (359.0 Gflop/s with 20 flops per interaction computed on the GPU without use of the mutual interaction principle), 8.6 billion interactions per second for 1024 bodies (171.1 Gflop/s) and 1.8 billion interactions per second for 128 bodies (35.5 Gflop/s). Our code compares thus favorably with previous results in the literature for direct N-body computation on the Cell processor as well as on GPU.

Moreover, our high performance rates on the Cell are obtained for an average particle number close to 128 or more. Similar results with such low average particle number seem thus to require important algorithmic improvements for the FMM near field part on GPU.

Acknowledgements

The authors are very grateful to the CINES for the QS20 blade access, and to B. Cirou (CINES) and C. Augonnet (INRIA - Runtime) for helpful discussions on the Cell.

References

[1]   IBM, Cell B.E. resource center, http://www.ibm.com/developerworks/power/cell
[2]   S. Swaminarayan, K. Kadau, T.C. Germann, G.C. Fossum, 369 Tflop/s molecular dynamics simulations on the Roadrunner general-purpose heterogeneous supercomputer, *SC '08: Proceedings of the 2008 ACM/IEEE conference on Supercomputing*, pp. 1-10.
[3]   K. Asanovic, R. Bodik, B. Catanzaro, J. Gebis, P. Husbands, K. Keutzer, D. Patterson, W. Plishker, J. Shalf, S. Williams, K. Yelik, The Landscape of Parallel Computing Research: A View from Berkeley, EECS Department, University of California at Berkeley, UCB/EECS-2006-183, December 2006.
[4]   M.P. Allen, D.J. Tildesley, Computer Simulation of Liquids, Oxford University Press, 1989.
[5]   A. Arevalo, R.M. Matinata, M. Pandian, E. Peri, K. Ruby , F. Thomas, C. Almond, Programming the Cell Broadband Engine Architecure, Examples and Best Practices, IBM Redbook SG24-7575, 2008.
[6]   G. De Fabritiis, Performance of the Cell processor for biomolecular simulations, *Computer Physics Communications*, 176, pp. 660-664, 2007.
[7]   E. Luttmann, D. Ensign, V. Vaidyanathan, M. Houston, N. Rimon, J. Øland, G. Jayachandran, M. Friedrichs, V. Pande, Accelerating molecular dynamic simulation on the cell processor and Playstation 3, *Journal of Computational Chemistry*, 30(2), pp. 268-274, 2009.
[8]   T.J. Knight, J.Y. Park, M. Ren, M. Houston, M. Erez, K. Fatahalian, A. Aiken, W.J. Dally, P. Hanrahan, Compilation for Explicitly Managed Memory Hierarchies, *PPoPP* 2007.
[9]   H. Cheng, L. Greengard, V. Rokhlin, A Fast Adaptive Multipole Algorithm in Three Dimensions, *Journal of Computational Physics*, 155, pp. 468-498, 1999.
[10] O. Coulaud, P. Fortin, J. Roman, High performance BLAS formulation of the multipole-to-local operator in the Fast Multipole Method, *Journal of Computational Physics*, 227(3), pp. 1836-1862, 2008.
[11] O. Coulaud, P. Fortin, J. Roman, Hybrid MPI-thread parallelization of the Fast Multipole Method, *6th International Symposium on Parallel and Distributed Computing (ISPDC)*, pp. 391-398, 2007.
[12] Maik Nijhuis, Herbert Bos, Henri Bal, Cédric Augonnet, Mapping and synchronizing streaming applications on Cell processors, *HiPEAC*, 2009.
[13] Lars Nyland, Mark Harris, Jan Prins, Fast N-Body Simulation with CUDA, *GPU Gems 3*, chapter 31, pp. 677-695, 2007.

Parallel Computing: From Multicores and GPU's to Petascale
B. Chapman et al. (Eds.)
IOS Press, 2010
© 2010 The authors and IOS Press. All rights reserved.
doi:10.3233/978-1-60750-530-3-331

The GPU on the Matrix-Matrix Multiply: Performance Study and Contributions

José María CECILIA [a] José Manuel GARCÍA [a] Manuel UJALDÓN [b]

[a] *Computer Engineering and Technology Dept., Univ. of Murcia (Spain)*
[b] *Computer Architecture Department, University of Malaga, Malaga (Spain)*

Abstract.
Modern graphics processing units (GPUs) have been at the leading edge of increasing chip-level parallelism over the last ten years, and the CUDA programming model has recently allowed us to exploit its power across many computational domains. Within them, dense linear algebra algorithms emerge like a natural fit for CUDA and the GPU because they are usually inherently parallel and can naturally be expressed as a blocked computation. In this paper, we extensively analyze the GPU programming and performance of one of the fundamental building blocks in numerical lineal algebra algorithms: The Matrix-Matrix Multiply. Different programming approaches and optimization techniques have already been published in the literature, which we review and analyze to pursue further optimizations and unveil the potential of some hardware resources when programming the GPU under CUDA. Experimental results are shown on a GeForce 8800 GTX and a Tesla C870 GPU with a performance peak of 43 GFLOPS.

Keywords. Graphics Processors, Linear Algebra, High-Performance Computing, CUDA Programming.

1. Introduction

Driven by the demand of the game industry, Graphics Processing Units (GPUs) have completed a steady transition from mainframes to workstations to PC cards, where they emerge nowadays like a solid and compelling alternative to traditional computing, delivering extremely high floating point performance at a very low cost. This fact has attracted many researchers and encouraged the use of GPUs in a broader range of applications, where developers are required to leverage this technology with new programming models which ease the developer's task of writing programs to run efficiently on GPUs.

Nvidia and ATI/AMD, manufacturers of the popular GeForce and Radeon sagas of graphics cards, have released software components which provide simpler access to GPU computing power. CUDA (Compute Unified Device Architecture) [4] is Nvidia's solution as a simple block-based API for programming; AMD's alternative is called Stream Computing [8]. Those companies have also developed hardware products aimed specifically at the scientific General Purpose GPU (GPGPU) computing market: The Tesla products are from NVIDIA, and Firestream is AMD's product line.

Between Stream Computing and CUDA, we chose the latter to program the GPU for being more popular and providing more mechanisms to optimize general-purpose applications. More recently, the Apple's OpenCL framework [9] emerges as an attempt to unify those two models with a superset of features, but since it is closer to CUDA and inherits most of its mechanisms, we are confident on an eventual portability for the methods described throughout this paper without loss of generality.

The Matrix-Matrix Multiply has traditionally been chosen as benchmark for scoring the highest rates of performance on standard CPU architectures and parallel machines, reporting a number of GFLOPS close to the machine's peak. In GPUs, however, this was not that straightforward, and using shaders and Cg we saw a disappointing period where CPU outperformed most GPU implementations, with only the ATI X800XT producing comparable results to those 12 GFLOPS achieved by a 3 GHz Pentium 4. The advent of CUDA as programming model in 2007 quickly reversed this situation, and significantly faster GPU implementations started to see the light in early 2008.

For example, Ryoo et al. [6] reported 91 GFLOPS, followed by 125 GFLOPS achieved by Nvidia in their CUBLAS library. More recently, Volkov et al. [10] reported 180 GFLOPS in their implementation using a block algorithm similar to those used for vector computers, enabling GPU registers and per-block shared memory to store the data blocks. As the GPU has an unusually large register file, this can be used as the primary scratch space for the computation.

While writing a basic dense Matrix-Matrix Multiply kernel is a fairly simple exercise (see [5] for details), achieving this high level of performance requires much more dedication. This paper tries to illustrate the basic development cycle to achieve this goal while providing the keys for the success.

This paper is structured as follows. Section 2 introduces into CUDA programming model and hardware interface on GPUs. Section 3 constitutes the core of our work, where different experimental studies and performance numbers are shown. Finally, Section 4 ends with a summary and the conclusions we draw from this work.

2. The CUDA programming model and hardware interface

Modern GPUs are powerful computing platforms recently devoted to general-purpose computing using CUDA (Compute Unified Device Architecture) [4]. As a hardware interface, CUDA started by transforming the G80 microarchitecture related to the GeForce 8 series from Nvidia into a parallel SIMD architecture endowed with up to 128 cores where a collection of threads run in parallel. Figure 1.a outlines the block diagram of this architecture. From the CUDA perspective, G80 cores are organized into 16 multiprocessors, each having a set of 32-bit registers, constants and texture caches, and 16 KB of on-chip shared memory as fast as local registers (one cycle latency). At any given cycle, each core executes the same instruction on different data (SIMD), and communication between multiprocessors is performed through global memory.

As a programming interface, CUDA consists of a set of C language library functions, and the CUDA-specific compiler generates the executable for the GPU from a source code where the following elements meet (see Figure 1.b):

1. A program is decomposed into **blocks** that run *logically* in parallel (physically only if there are resources available). Assembled by the developer, a block is a group of threads that is mapped to a single multiprocessor, where they can share 16 KB of memory.

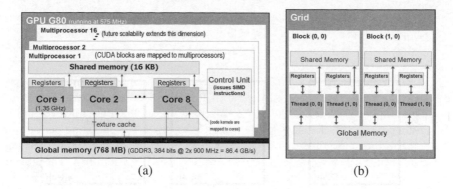

Figure 1. CUDA highlights: (a) Hardware interface for the Nvidia G80 GPU. (b) Programming model.

2. All **threads** of concurrent blocks on a single multiprocessor divide the resources available equally amongst themselves. The data is also divided amongst all of the threads in a SIMD fashion with a decomposition explicitly managed by the developer.
3. A **warp** is a collection of threads that can actually run concurrently (with no time sharing) on all of the multiprocessors. The developer has the freedom to determine the number of threads to be executed (up to a limit intrinsic to CUDA), but if there are more threads than the warp size, they are time-shared on the actual hardware resources.
4. A **kernel** is the code to be executed by each thread. Conditional execution of different operations can be achieved based on a unique thread ID.

In the CUDA model, all of the threads can access all of the GPU memory, but, as expected, there is a performance boost when threads access data resident in shared memory, which is explicitly managed. In order to make the most efficient usage of the GPU's computational resources, large data structures are stored in global memory and the shared memory should be prioritized for storing strategic, often-used data structures.

3. Benchmarking GPUs to Tune Matrix Matrix Multiply

3.1. Our metrics

We have used several metrics to evaluate real performance and bandwidth attained on the GPU when running the Matrix-Matrix Multiply.

For performance, we use **FLOPS (Floating-Point Operations Per Second)**, by taking the operations from the PTX code generated by the NVCC compiler with the -ptx flag. This is an internal representation later used by the back-end to produce the actual binary code on a particular platform, so it should be taken as an estimation. Another useful metric we use is **throughput**, calculated as the product between the peak performance and the ratio of FLOPS per instruction, again taken from the PTX code.

For bandwidth with off-chip video memory, we use **GB/sc. (Gigabytes per second)**, calculated by multiplying four magnitudes: the number of accesses to device memory (from the PTX code), the amount of bytes transferred on each access, the actual number of cores the GPU has, and the core clock frequency.

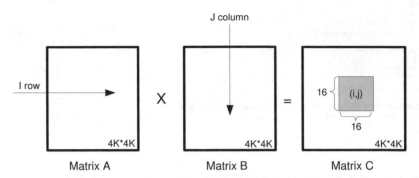

Figure 2. Threads organization for the initial version of our Matrix-Matrix Multiply.

3.2. Departure point

Our first version of the Matrix-Matrix Multiply does not exploit the benefits of the shared memory. One thread is created to produce each output result, loading a row from source matrix A and a column from source matrix B (see Figure 2). Products are performed on pairs of elements from device memory, accumulating them on and on (see Figure 2).

Figure 3 outlines this version, where indexes are calculated based on thread and block coordinates. We use 9 registers per thread, and each block contains 256 threads. Thus, each multiprocessor holds 3 blocks, reaching its maximum of 768 threads and being fully utilized.

```
#define MATRIX_SIZE 4096
#define WA MATRIX_SIZE
#define WB MATRIX_SIZE
#define WC MATRIX_SIZE
__global__ void matrixMul (float* C, float* A, float* B)
{
  int bx = blockIdx.x;
  int by = blockIdx.y;
  int tx = thredIdx.x;
  int ty = threadIdx.y;
  int indexA = by*BLOCK_SIZE*WA + ty*WA;

  int indexB = bx*BLOCK_SIZE + tx;
  float Csub = 0.0;
  for (int i=0; i<WA; i++)
  {
    Csub += A[indexA] * B[indexB];
    indexA++;
    indexB += WB;
  }
  int indexC = by*BLOCK_SIZE*WC + bx*BLOCK_SIZE;
  C[indexC+WB*ty+tx] = Csub;
}
```

Figure 3. Kernel code for the initial version of our Matrix-Matrix Multiply.

Table 1 shows the performance for this kernel depending on the matrix size and the platform used, where we see how GeForce 8800 GTX slightly outperforms Tesla C870. On a 4Kx4K matrix size, GeForce delivers 64 GFLOP and 36.36 secs., for a total of 1.76 GFLOP per second (that is, 1.76 GFLOPS). By examining the PTX code, there are eight instructions in the inner loop where the kernel spends most of its execution time. One of these instructions is a floating-point fused multiply-add (madd). The peak performance for this code is then 43.2 GFLOPS (128 cores * 2 instructions per core* 1.35 GHz * 1/8 FLOP), far from our achievements and also from those 10.58 GFLOPS reported in [6,7].

The PTX code also reveals two loads in the inner loop, so this kernel has 2/8 load operations for a total bandwidth required of 173 GB/sc. (128 SPs * 1/4 instructions * 4

Matrix size	1024x1024	2048x2048	4096x4096
GFLOPS on Tesla C870	1.51	1.60	1.72
GFLOPS on GeForce GTX 280	1.75	1.86	1.76

Table 1. Performance in GFLOPS for the initial version of our Matrix-Matrix Multiply.

Matrix size	1024x1024	2048x2048	4096x4096
Time for accessing A uncoalesced	0.59 msc.	4.42 msc.	35.02 msc.
Time for accessing B coalesced	0.07 msc.	0.54 msc.	4.25 msc.

Table 2. Performance comparison when accessing to matrix A uncoalesced and matrix B coalesced in device memory. We provide overall accessing time for each matrix on the Tesla C870 GPU.

bytes/instruction * 1.35 GHz). This is twice the bandwidth available on GeForce 8800 GTX, so access to device memory becomes the actual bottleneck for this kernel, which also explains why Tesla C870 is slower (its DDR memory is clocked at 2x800 MHz, versus 2x900 MHz on the GeForce).

To reduce the bandwidth requirements, we first use coalesced accesses and then shared memory, also reorganizing computations to exploit tiling.

3.3. Coalescing accesses to device memory

The goal for coalescing is to organize 16 data accesses in a way suitable for being recovered simultaneously from device memory in a half-warp, so that all threads within it can compute in parallel. The condition for a coalesced access (see [5]) is that each of these 16 threads accesses to the following address: *HalfWarpBaseAddress + N*, where N is the thread id. In our case, threads of the same half-warp access to the same elements in the same row of matrix A, so the access to device memory is fully uncoalesced [5]. At the same time, threads of the same half-warp get the data from different columns in matrix B, leaving accesses fully coalesced [5]. We have created a couple of micro kernels to compare the performance of these two access patterns when accessing to device memory. Table 2 shows the execution times, where the access to B is almost ten times faster on large matrices.

These results encourage us to provide coalesced access for matrix A, and to do so, all threads have to access different elements in a way that thread 0 should access the HalfWarpBaseAddress+0 address, thread 1 should access to the HalfWarpBaseAddress + 1 address, and so on. This fulfillment will be combined with the use of shared memory and tiling in what constitutes our next optimization step.

3.4. Tiled version using shared memory

At this point of our work, the bottleneck is the device memory bandwidth. In order to alleviate the pressure on this device memory, we will perform *tiling* [2] to reuse data located in a lower level of the memory hierarchy. This faster level in CUDA is represented by the shared memory.

Three main steps are needed to implement the tiling technique in CUDA:

1. Copy from device to shared memory all the data used by all the threads in a block. These threads cooperate with each other to load the data efficiently, that is, accesses to device memory are coalesced.

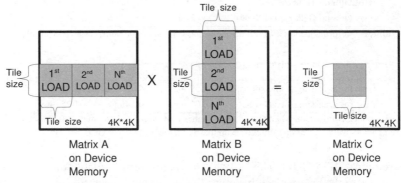

Figure 4. Computing the tiled version of our Matrix-Matrix Multiply.

```
#define  MATRIX_SIZE  4096
#define  WA  MATRIX_SIZE
#define  WB  MATRIX_SIZE
#define  WC  MATRIX_SIZE

__shared__ float As[BLOCK_SIZE][BLOCK_SIZE];
__shared__ float Bs[BLOCK_SIZE][BLOCK_SIZE];

int indexA = WA*BLOCK_SIZE*by + ty*WA + tx;
int indexB = bx*BLOCK_SIZE + ty*WB + tx;

float Csub = 0.0;
```

```
for (int i=0; i<WA/BLOCK_SIZE; i++)
{
    As[ty][tx] = A[indexA];
    Bs[ty][tx] = B[indexB];
    indexA += BLOCK_SIZE;
    indexB += WB*BLOCK_SIZE;
    __syncthreads();
    for (int k=0; k<BLOCK_SIZE; k++)
        Csub += As[ty][k] * Bs[k][tx];
    __syncthreads();
}
int indexC = WB*BLOCK_SIZE*by + BLOCK_SIZE*bx;
C[indexC+WB*ty+tx] = Csub;
```

Figure 5. Tiled version for the code of our Matrix-Matrix Multiply.

2. Perform the actual computation in shared memory, trying to avoid conflicts when accessing memory banks [5].
3. Copy the results back to device memory.

Figure 4 illustrates how tiling is performed on the Matrix-Matrix Multiply. The result matrix C is decomposed in blocks where each thread of a block calculates a single element. Considering the block size as *tile_size * tile_size* according to shared memory limitations, this kernel is required to load *tile_size* entire rows from matrix A and *tile_size* entire columns from matrix B, with those rows and columns coordinates matching those of the target block. Figure 5 shows the code for this tiled version.

A major constraint for this tiling technique is imposed by the size of the shared memory, which is 16 KB. in the G80 architecture, and that has to be shared by all the blocks within a multiprocessor. Therefore, depending on the *tile size*, this multiprocessor can execute more or less blocks in parallel. Another upper bounds to account for are described in [5], among which we highlight the 768 threads that may run in parallel on a multiprocessor, and the 8192 registers they are allowed to use.

Table 3 shows the performance we obtain when varying the tile size in our code version. The smaller tile considered, 4x4, has 16 threads per block and uses only 64 bytes per block (16 threads x 4 bytes/thread). Since a maximum of eight blocks may run in

Tile size	No tiling	4x4	8x8	12x12	16x16
GFLOPS for the MxM kernel	1.72	3.76	7.73	11.34	22.10

Table 3. Performance in GFLOPS for different tile sizes of our Matrix-Matrix Multiply using kernels that require 14 registers running on the Tesla C870 GPU.

parallel on a multiprocessor, the shared memory usage is just 512 bytes out of 16 KB. (3.125%) and the amount of extracted parallelism is 128 threads out of 768 (16.7%).

As we increase the tile size, performance improves due to a better use of shared memory together with the cooperation of a higher number of threads in parallel. 16x16 is the largest tile size for the G80 platform, which may reach 256 threads per block as long as the kernel uses ten or less registers. But our kernel requires 14 registers, so only two blocks can be scheduled on a single multiprocessor (2 blocks x 256 threads/block x 14 registers/thread require 7168 registers out of the 8192). Even with this constraint, the 16x16 tiled version improves performance more than any other tile size because it uses more shared memory.

In addition, memory accesses are coalesced in all these tiled versions as computations are rearranged, so device memory bandwidth is fully exploited and data movement between device and shared memory is greatly amortized.

3.5. Increasing arithmetic intensity

An important issue to consider when optimizing codes on graphics processors is *arithmetic intensity*, defined as the percentage of instructions executed on ALUs from a total including branches, memory address calculation, data accesses and so on. One way to greatly improve this parameter through CUDA code transformations is to apply *loop unrolling* [6].

By default, the nvcc compiler performs this transformation on small loops like the innermost one in Figure 5. When this is applied, the PTX file shows 63 instructions, and 16 of them are MADD (25.4%). However, without unrolling, the PTX file shows 19 instructions, but only one is MADD (5.2%).

3.6. Optimizing registers usage

Each multiprocessor in our G80 architecture contains 8192 registers which are dynamically partitioned among the threads running on it. When a kernel uses at most ten registers for each of the threads, a maximum of 768 threads can be scheduled per multiprocessor (768 x 10 = 7680 < 8192).

For the 16*16 tiled version of our code with a 4K * 4K matrix size (see Figure 5), we use 14 registers per thread. The PTX code for this kernel also reports that the innermost loop is totally unrolled.

Figure 6 illustrates the development cycle we have followed to minimize the registers usage. With the help of the PTX and .cubin files, we can extract valuable information. For example, the .cubin file shows the number of registers per thread used by the kernel and the local memory consumed by the kernel, together with some other magnitudes. On the other hand, the PTX code shows an estimation for the registers used by the kernel. The problem with the PTX file is that it uses more registers than those reported by the cubin file, so it is difficult to have an idea about the registers usage with only those files. We complement that information with the Decuda application [4],

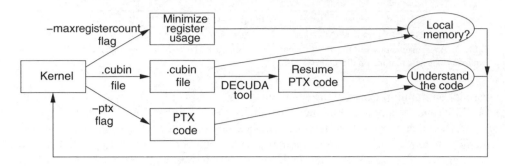

Figure 6. The development cycle we have followed to minimize the registers usage.

which uses the binary code in the .cubin file to provide a more comprehensive version for the code generated for the GPU G8x and G9x architectures, including the use of the same number of registers that the .cubin file says.

Another useful tool to reduce the number of registers is the compiler flag -*maxregistercount*, which reduces the number of registers used by the kernel at the expense of mapping them onto local memory, which is slower than the registers. However, it is also possible that extra registers can be removed due to compiler optimizations instead of being sent to local memory. So, there is a tradeoff between occupancy and memory speed. Based on our experience, we provide the following heuristics to minimize the number of registers in a CUDA code:

1. Try to use preprocessing instructions instead of instantiate kernel parameters so that the compiler may map those as constants rather than registers.
2. Array indices do not use extra registers, neither block nor thread indices.
3. The tile size has a strong influence on the registers usage. For instance, the 4*4 tiled version uses 9 registers in its unrolling version, whereas 16*16 tiled version uses 14 registers.

3.7. Performance evaluation

Figure 7 shows the results for the experiments we have conducted on different tile sizes and hardware platforms: The Tesla C870 and the Geforce 8800GTX. We also compare them with those published in [6].

Our performance peak is 43 GFLOPS, scored by the 16*16 tiled version unrolled and running on a GeForce 8800GTX (the Tesla C870 performs slightly worse because of a slower memory clock). The registers usage for this version is 10 registers, allowing the maximum of 768 threads to be scheduled per multiprocessor. The PTX code for the 16*16 tiled and unrolled version shows 16 fused multiply-add out of 63 instructions in the main loop. This produces a potential throughput of 87.77 GFLOPS (345.6 Peak * 16/63 MADDs) In terms of device memory bandwidth, 2/63 operations executed during the loop are loads from off-chip memory, which would require a bandwidth of 21.94 GB/s (128 SPs * 2/63 load instructions * 4 bytes/instructions * 1.35 GHz), which is almost 4 times less than GeForce 8800 GTX can deliver. This leads us to conclude that the device memory bandwidth has successfully been removed as a serious bottleneck in the underlying architecture.

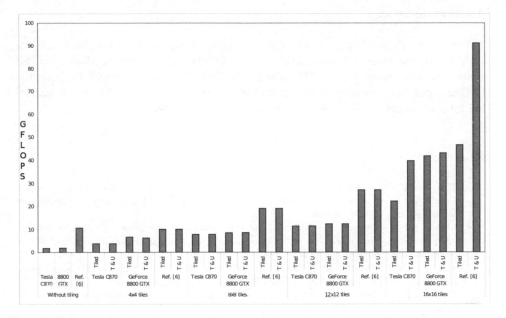

Figure 7. Performance comparison for the Matrix-Matrix Multiply using CUDA in our GPU platforms and with respect to results published in [6] (T & U stands for tiled and unrolling).

4. Summary and conclusions

This work presents a guide for the CUDA implementation of kernels and applications on the GPU using CUDA, taking a typical Matrix-Matrix Multiply as a driving example. This code has been extensively used as benchmark on virtually any existing platform, so we wanted to explore the CUDA capabilities on an emerging and successful architecture like the GPU. Two different hardware platforms were chosen in this respect: The GeForce 8800 GTX and the Tesla C870. The aim was to evaluate the influence of three issues: the clock frequency for the cores, and the speed and size of the video memory. Our results show that the cores frequency is more relevant to performance than the speed of the video memory, and that the video memory size is less important.

The optimization process was also described as a guideline to tune dense linear algebra codes. Starting from a naive version, we show how to use the shared memory, exploit it efficiently by coalescing accesses and solving conflicts to memory banks, and rearrange the code to increase arithmetic intensity and reduce registers usage. As a result, we reach 43 GFLOPS as performance peak, with the device memory bandwidth being removed as the actual bottleneck for the code. We also learn that the optimization process is a daunting task where many parameters are involved in a non-linear fashion.

Using CUDA to implement scientific applications on the GPU we can fully exploit SIMD programming to populate with work the hundreds of cores the GPU possesses. These gains will extend in the future thanks to the promising scalability and larger number of cores that GPU architectures are bringing to the marketplace at a commodity cost. In fact, this trend is continuing in 2008 with the GTX280 GPU consisting of 240 cores or stream processors, and the recently announced Fermi by Nvidia, which will be endowed with 512 cores by the year 2010.

Acknowledgements

This work was partially supported by the Fundación Séneca (Agencia Regional de Ciencia y Tecnología, Región de Murcia) under grant 00001/CS/2007, by the Ministry of Education of Spain under project TIN2006-15516-C04-03, by the European Commission FEDER funds under grant "Consolider Ingenio-2010" (project CSD2006-00046) and by the Junta de Andalucía of Spain under project P06-TIC-02109.

References

[1]   T. Hartley, U. Catalyurek, A. Ruiz, M. Ujaldon, F. Igual, R. Mayo. *Biomedical Image Analysis on a Cooperative Cluster of GPUs and Multicores.* Proceedings 22nd ACM International Conference on Supercomputing, 2008 (submitted).

[2]   M.D. Lam, E.E. Rothberg, M.E. Wolf. *The cache performance and optimizations of blocked algorithms.* ASPLOS-IV: Proceedings of the Fourth International Conference on Architectural Support for Programming Languages and Operating Systems, 1991, pages 63-74.

[3]   W.R. Mark, R.S. Glanville, K. Akeley and M.J. Kilgard. *Cg: A System for Programming Graphics Hardware in a C-like Language.* Proceedings SIGGRAPH 2003, pages 896-907.

[4]   Nvidia CUDA. *Home Web Page maintained by Nvidia.* http://developer.nvidia.com/object/cuda.html (accessed, March, 15th, 2009).

[5]   Nvidia. CUDA Programming Guide 2.0, 2008.

[6]   S. Ryoo, C. Rodrigues, S. Baghsorkhi, S. Stone, D. Kirk, W. Hwu. *Optimization Principles and Application Performance Evaluation of a Multithreaded GPU using CUDA.* Proceedings 13th ACM SIGPLAN Symposium on Principles and Practice of Parallel Programming. ACM Press, pp. 73-82. February, 2008.

[7]   S. Ryoo, C. Rodrigues, I. Christopher, S. Stone, J. Stratton, S. Ueng, S. Baghsorkhi, W. Hwu. *Program optimization carving for GPU computing.* J. Parallel Distributed Computing, Special Issue on General-Purpose Parallel Processing Using GPUs, vol. 68, no. 10, pp. 1389-1401.

[8]   Stream Computing. *Home Web Page maintained by AMD.* http://ati.amd.com/technology/streamcomputing/index.html (accessed, January, 31st, 2009).

[9]   The Khronos Group. *The OpenCL Core API Specification, Headers and Documentation.* http://www.khronos.org/registry/cl (accessed, March, 15th, 2009).

[10] V. Volkov and J.W. Demmel. *Benchmarking GPUs to tune dense linear algebra.* Proceedings of the 2008 ACM/IEEE conference on Supercomputing. Austin, Texas. November, 2008.

Parallel Computing: From Multicores and GPU's to Petascale
B. Chapman et al. (Eds.)
IOS Press, 2010

© 2010 The authors and IOS Press. All rights reserved.

doi:10.3233/978-1-60750-530-3-341

Performance Measurement of Applications with GPU Acceleration using CUDA

Shangkar MAYANGLAMBAM [1] and Allen D. MALONY and Matthew J. SOTTILE

Dept. of Computer and Information Science, University of Oregon
Eugene, OR 97403
{smeitei,malony,matt}@cs.uoregon.edu

Abstract. Multi-core accelerators offer significant potential to improve the performance of parallel applications. However, tools to help the parallel application developer understand accelerator performance and its impact are scarce. An approach is presented to measure the performance of GPU computations programmed using CUDA and integrate this information with application performance data captured with the TAU Performance System. Test examples are shown to validate the measurement methods. Results for a case study of the GPU-accelerated NAMD molecular dynamics application application are given.

1. Introduction

There is growing interest in the use of multi-core accelerators to improve the performance of parallel applications, with GPU computing devices gaining the most traction. Achieving the performance potential of accelerators is challenging due to complexity of the multi-core hardware and their operational/programming interface. In the case of general purpose GPUs (GPGPUs), CUDA was created to support program development targeting GPU-based accelerators. However, few tools exist to help the parallel application developer measure and understand accelerator performance. Performance analysis tools for GPGPU developers to date have been largely oriented towards aiding developers on individual workstation-class machines with limited parallelism present within the GPU host. When used in large-scale parallel environments, it is important to understand the performance of accelerators (such as with a CUDA measurement library when GPUs are used) in the context of whole parallel program's execution. This will require the integration of accelerator measurements in scalable parallel performance tools.

This paper describes our approach to performance measurement of GPGPU execution using CUDA in the context of a larger parallel performance measurement environment. We consider the problem from the point of view of a parallel application where host (CPU-side) performance measurement already has robust support, in our case from the TAU Performance System [3]. The goal is to measure the performance of GPU com-

---

[1] Corresponding E-Mail: smeitei@cs.uoregon.edu

putational kernels, wherever they are invoked in the application, and integrate the measurements with the TAU parallel performance data. Methods developed for CUDA performance measurement are presented and the TAU CUDA measurement interface is described. Test examples are shown to validate the measurement model. Results for a case study of a GPU-accelerated molecular dynamics application are given.

2. CUDA Performance Model and TAUcuda Approach

The CUDA programming environment enables easy development of applications with GPU acceleration of certain components. Computationally intensive parts of applications can be launched as tasks into the GPU device. Measuring performance of CUDA application would appear straightforward for simple usages. However, the concurrent and asynchronous model of CUDA programs relative to the GPU host makes it problematic to create an accelerator performance view in general with respect to the performance of the parallel application as a whole. Programmers can use multiple concurrent CUDA streams to queue independently executable sequences of GPU tasks. Furthermore, different strategies can be used to overlap CPU and GPU execution, as well as CPU-GPU data transfers. There can also be multiple GPU devices accelerating different parts of the application for different CPU threads. To understand and optimize GPU-accelerated parallel applications using CUDA, all these scenarios are of interest and important performance factors should be measured, such as GPU utilization and CPU waiting time, but standard parallel performance tools can not be applied directly.

There are two general approaches to GPU performance measurement. First, we could consider making the measurement on the CPU (host) side. If the GPGPU is used in a *synchronous* manner (the CPU immediately waits for GPGPU execution to finish), we could just place measurement points before and after launching the GPU kernel to determine performance. If the GPGPU is used in an *asynchronous* (the CPU does not immediately wait), the measurements could still be done in this way, but it would be difficult to determine exactly when the GPGPU completed execution. In CUDA, a GPU *kernel* is launched on a *stream* and multiple kernels on the same stream run sequentially. However, multiple streams can be concurrently active and multiple GPU devices can be used. In such cases, the performance measurement becomes even more complex. For instance, consider the four simple scenarios shown in Figure 1. The top row shows the synchronous cases for one and two streams. The bottom row shows the asynchronous cases. Notice in the synchronous case for two streams, it will be difficult to extract the performance for each stream independently.

We initially considered the use of NVIDIA profiling tools to address the performance measurement problems. NVIDIA has a rich performance SDK known as *PerfKit* [4] for profiling the GPU driver interface. It provides access to low-level performance counters inside the driver and hardware counters inside the GPU itself. However, PerfKit is limited for use with the CUDA programming environment. We need different measurement semantics to capture the CUDA program performance and integrate the data with parallel application performance. NVIDIA also provides the *CUDA Profiler* [5] which includes performance measurement in the CUDA runtime system and a visual profile analysis tool. While the CUDA Profiler provides extensive stream-level measurements, it collects the data in a trace and does not provide access until after the program terminates.

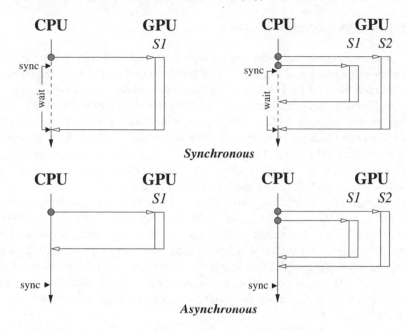

Figure 1. Scenarios of Host-GPGPU use.

We want to be able to produce profiles that show the distribution of accelerator performance with respect to application events. This performance view is difficult to produce with the CUDA Profiler trace data.

On the other hand, CUDA provides an *event* interface that can be used to obtain performance data for a particular stream's execution, including each kernel's precise termination. The performance data is measured by the CUDA runtime system. We developed a CUDA performance measurement library based the stream event interface called *TAUcuda*. The TAUcuda approach is described below and the library API is presented in section §3.

Consider the execution of a single GPU kernel execution on a stream. We can use a CUDA *begin* event and *end* event placed around the CUDA statement to measure the begin time and end time of the kernel's execution in the GPU. When the begin and end events are retrieved from the CUDA runtime system, TAUcuda can calculate the kernel's elapsed execution time. In addition, TAUcuda can calculate the *waiting* time from when it requested the CUDA events to when they were delivered and the *finalize* time from the beginning. The integration with the TAU measurement system occurs with the begin event when the *TAU context* (most recent TAU performance event) is sampled and stored.

Of course, many GPU kernels can be executed during an application on multiple streams and GPU devices. TAUcuda events are kept per stream and per GPU device. In addition, TAUcuda events can be nested. At the end of execution, the TAUcuda measurement library creates performance profiles for each event showing the *event_name*, *tau_context*, *device_id*, *stream_id*, *#_calls*, *inclusive_time*, *exclusive_time*, *wait_time*, and *finalize_time*.

3. TAU CUDA Measurement Interface

The TAUcuda measurement library implements a versatile interface for the application programmer to measure performance for GPGPU computations. A TAUcuda object is created for each block of CUDA code to be measured. At the core of the library, CUDA event objects play a vital role in tracking GPGPU computation time. Internally the TAUcuda objects map to two CUDA event objects which record *begin* and *end* execution times for the code block, as measured by the GPU clock. The CUDA event objects are scheduled in the GPGPU by calling the *cudaEventRecord* interface and specifying the corresponding stream of execution. However, it is imperative that the two events are scheduled immediately before and after the CUDA code block.

CUDA provides both blocking and non-blocking interfaces to check the event status. Correspondingly, TAUcuda also exposes both blocking and non-blocking interfaces to gather the event data and compute performance profiles. The TAUcuda data structures are managed for every CPU thread independently in thread local memory. This avoids the overhead of ensuring thread safety and also works the around limitations of CUDA event objects. CUDA event objects are not reliably accessible outside the scope of their originating thread lifetime. Hence, the profile data needs to be processed and written out before each thread exits.

The TAUcuda library interface shown in Table 1. The initialization interface *tau_cuda_init* should be called at the start of the application. It initializes data structures and sets up the initialization time for both CPU and GPGPU. To process and write TAUcuda profiles, each thread must call *tau_cuda_exit* before exiting. TAUcuda enables programmers to choose the granularity of CUDA code block observation. The *tau_cuda_stream_begin* and *tau_cuda_stream_end* interfaces are used to mark the begin and end TAUcuda events in application source code. The *event* name token passed to the begin call identifies the TAUcuda object associated with the GPGPU computations enclosed. The library also provides an interface, *tau_cuda_update*, which returns a vector of completed event statistics for a single stream or all streams at any time. The call to this interface returns without blocking. On the other hand, *tau_cuda_finalize* performs the similar action except that it waits for outstanding events to complete. Both interfaces free up the CUDA event objects after processing them. Frequent use of these interfaces is recommended in experiments with large number of profile events.

4. Examples

4.1. Computational Scenarios

We evaluated the TAUcuda measurement library with scenarios of computation varying the interactions between CPU, CUDA streams, and GPGPU devices. All experiments were performed on a NVIDIA Tesla S1070 GPU server. The single stream experiment in Table 2 illustrates how a TAUcuda profile can detect CPU cycles wasted in waiting for GPGPU computations to complete. We observe decreases in wait time with more utilization of CPU in parallel with the GPGPU computation. Similar results are observed for experiments in Table 3 with two CUDA streams executing on a single GPGPU device. We can also see the proportional inclusive computation time for variations of the computation loads in the streams.

void tau_cuda_init(int argc, char **argv)
o To be called when the application starts
o Initializes data structures and checks GPU status
void tau_cuda_exit()
o To be called before any thread exits at end of application
o All CUDA profile data is output for each thread of execution
void* tau_cuda_stream_begin(char *event, cudaStream_t stream)
o Called before CUDA statements to be measured
o Returns handle which should be used in the end call
o If event is new or the TAU context is new for the event, a new CUDA event profile object is created
void tau_cuda_stream_end(void * handle)
o Called immediately after CUDA statements to be measured
o Handle identifies the stream
o Inserts a CUDA event into the stream
vector<Event> tau_cuda_update()
o Checks for completed CUDA events on all streams
o Non-blocking and returns # completed on each stream
int tau_cuda_update(cudaStream_t stream)
o Same as tau_cuda_update() except for a particular stream
o Non-blocking and returns # completed on the stream
vector<Event> tau_cuda_finalize()
o Waits for all CUDA events to complete on all streams
o Blocking and returns # completed on each stream
int tau_cuda_finalize(cudaStream_t stream)
o Same as tau_cuda_finalize() except for a particular stream
o Blocking and returns # completed on the stream

Table 1. TAUcuda measurement interfaces.

CPU Load	GPU Load	Event	Inclusive Time	Wait Time
0	X	Interpolate (C-[mainl]#D-0#S-0)	75222.4922	75134.7656
0	2X	Interpolate (C-[mainl]#D-0#S-0)	150097.7031	149995.6094
0	3X	Interpolate (C-[mainl]#D-0#S-0)	225034.2031	224915.5312
Y	X	Interpolate (C-[mainl]#D-0#S-0)	74985.6953	64097.1680
2Y	X	Interpolate (C-[mainl]#D-0#S-0)	75058.5234	42563.9648
10Y	X	Interpolate (C-[mainl]#D-0#S-0)	75032.9609	0.0000

Table 2. TAUcuda profiles for a single stream (time measured in milliseconds).

In multi-GPU experiments, individual CPU threads launch computations on corresponding devices. Table 4 shows experiments with two GPGPU devices. *D-0* and *D-1* are device identifiers and are included in the TAUcuda event names to identify the corresponding CPU threads using the device. We observe meaningful results for inclusive time as well as the wait time appropriate to the computational size.

More sophisticated profile results are shown in Table 5, demonstrating how TAUcuda can capture the CPU context (from the concurrent TAU measurement layer) in which the GPGPU computation is launched. The information is again encoded in the

	GPU Load		Time Measured (in milliseconds)		
CPU Load	S-1	S-2	Event	Inclusive Time	Wait Time
0	2X	X	Interpolate (C-[mainl]#D-0#S-1)	149982.8750	149858.8906
0	2X	X	Interpolate (C-[mainl]#D-0#S-2)	74929.6953	74909.6719
0	X	2X	Interpolate (C-[mainl]#D-0#S-1)	74993.2188	74869.6250
0	X	2X	Interpolate (C-[mainl]#D-0#S-2)	150055.8750	150019.0469
Y	X	X	Interpolate (C-[mainl]#D-0#S-1)	75054.0156	53687.0117
Y	X	X	Interpolate (C-[mainl]#D-0#S-2)	74989.4688	53708.9844
2Y	X	X	Interpolate (C-[mainl]#D-0#S-1)	74899.1406	32293.9453
2Y	X	X	Interpolate (C-[mainl]#D-0#S-2)	74948.7344	32429.6875
5Y	X	X	Interpolate (C-[mainl]#D-0#S-1)	75007.4219	0.0000
5Y	X	X	Interpolate (C-[mainl]#D-0#S-2)	75008.5469	0.0000

Table 3. TAUcuda profiles for two streams.

CPU Load		GPU Load		Time Measured (in milliseconds)		
D-0	D-1	D-0	D-1	Event	Inclusive Time	Wait Time
0	0	X	2X	Interpolate (C-[mainl]#D-0#S-0)	75068.2500	74855.4688
0	0	X	2X	Interpolate (C-[mainl]#D-1#S-0)	149795.0156	149698.7344
0	0	2X	X	Interpolate (C-[mainl]#D-0#S-0)	150171.8750	150054.6875
0	0	2X	X	Interpolate (C-[mainl]#D-1#S-0)	74969.5625	74892.5781
2Y	Y	X	X	Interpolate (C-[mainl]#D-0#S-0)	75121.7266	53530.7617
2Y	Y	X	X	Interpolate (C-[mainl]#D-1#S-0)	75864.0938	18769.0430
Y	2Y	X	X	Interpolate (C-[mainl]#D-0#S-0)	75119.8750	53557.1289
Y	2Y	X	X	Interpolate (C-[mainl]#D-1#S-0)	75123.8984	18204.1016

Table 4. TAUcuda profiles for two devices.

Event	Calls	Inclusive Time	Exclusive Time
All-Interpolate (C-[FirstWrapperl]#D-0#S-0)	1	300019.9375	65.3992
InterpolateA (C-[FirstWrapperl]#D-0#S-0)	10	150013.6250	150013.6250
InterpolateB (C-[FirstWrapperl]#D-0#S-0)	10	149940.8750	149940.8750
All-Interpolate (C-[SecondWrapperl]#D-0#S-0)	1	300111.6250	65.0635
InterpolateA (C-[SecondWrapperl]#D-0#S-0)	10	150018.1719	150018.1719
InterpolateB (C-[SecondWrapperl]#D-0#S-0)	10	150028.3750	150028.3750

Table 5. TAUcuda profiles with two tau contexts and nested events.

TAUcuda event name by *[FirstWrapper]* and *[SecondWrapper]*, representing two different CPU function contexts. We also see here the calls field which accounts for the repetitive access of the TAUcuda object for the stream, device, and context. Again, CUDA computation can be profiled at the level of the programmer's choice of granularity and nesting of TAUcuda profile events. The exclusive time measure is included only in this table as it is meaningful with nested events.

To verify the TAUcuda performance values, we turned on the *CUDA Runtime Profiler* [5] functionality to dump elapsed time measures for all the kernels and other memory related GPGPU tasks. The profiling feature is integrated in CUDA runtime system

Measurement Scenarios		Inclusive Time (in milliseconds)	
Event	GPU Load	TAUcuda	CUDA Profiler
Interpolate (C-[main]#D-0#S-0)	X	75065.9844	75045
Interpolate (C-[main]#D-0#S-0)	2X	150012.6094	150067
Interpolate (C-[main]#D-0#S-0)	3X	225058.2500	224950
Interpolate (C-[main]#D-0#S-0)	4X	300173.8438	299928
Interpolate (C-[main]#D-0#S-0)	5X	374917.5625	374887

Table 6. TAUcuda versus CUDA Runtime Profiler.

and a visual profile analysis tool is provided. Table 6 shows CUDA Profiler values together with the TAUcuda data. The results are seen to be very close.

4.2. Profiling Inside CUDA Kernels

We have also prototyped measurement interfaces for use inside a CUDA kernel. However, the performance data managed by these interfaces is not yet fully integrated to the TAUcuda system. Collecting profile data from device address space requires a good approach to limit the profiler memory usage. Our approach transmits out chunks of performance data from device to the host CPU. The kernel profile data is managed with a data structure called the *TAU Data Unit* (TDU) frame. The TDU frame has a header segment which contains fields to communicate with the device. The host CPU can inform the device about the frame structure and the device can inform the status of profiling to the host. Due to the high cost of writing out profile records in the GPGPU global memory, we manage a cache buffer of shared memory for manipulating the profile records. Further details of kernel measurement will be produced after fully integrating it into the TAUcuda system.

4.3. Application Case Study

To demonstrate TAUcuda with a realistic parallel application that utilizes GPGPU acceleration, we considered the NAMD [2] application. NAMD is a parallel molecular dynamics simulation built with the Charm++ framework. The TAU measurement system has recently been integrated with Charm++ to enable profiling of Charm++ events [1]. NAMD has been programmed for GPGPU acceleration using CUDA. We use the *tau_cuda_stream_begin* and *tau_cuda_stream_end* interfaces to capture TAUcuda profiles for certain CUDA code in NAMD, namely *dev_nonbonded* and *dev_sum_forces* GPU kernels. We ran NAMD on four MPI processes each using a Tesla GPU on our S1070 server.

The TAUcuda profiles generated are displayed shown in Figure 2 together with the TAU profile for the four MPI processes. We can see that the GPGPU computation time for each event is almost uniform across all 4 processes. However, *dev_nonbonded* inclusive time is much higher than that of *dev_sum_forces*. These two events maps to two different CUDA kernels and both kernels are launched from the same CPU function context *WorkDistrib::enqueCUDA*. In this experiment, the performance is improved by about 4 times compared to the computation without GPGPU acceleration.

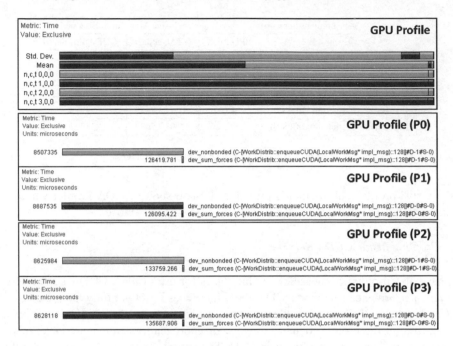

Figure 2. TAUcuda profiles for NAMD.

5. Conclusion

We have developed a profiling system for measuring and integrating performance data on both the host CPU and the GPU kernel components of a CUDA application. This work describes and demonstrates performance measurement techniques for parallel programs using acceleration technologies such as GPUs. With the increased presence of accelerator technologies in conventional parallel computers such as clusters, integration of performance measurement on acceleration devices within the overall parallel application is critical for maintaining a complete picture of large scale parallel program performance. Our initial work described in this paper forms the basis for accelerator performance measurement being integrated into current and future versions of the TAU performance analysis framework.

References

[1]   S. Biersdorff, C.W. Lee, A. Malony, and L. Kale. Integrated Performance Views in Charm++: Projections Meets TAU. In *International Conference on Parallel Processing*, September 2009. To appear.
[2]   J. Phillips el al. Scalable molecular dynamics with namd. In *Journal of Computational Chemistry*, pages 1781 – 1802, October 2005.
[3]   A. Malony, S. Shende, A. Morris, S. Biersdorff, W. Spear, K. Huck, and Aroon Nataraj. Evolution of a Parallel Performance System. In M. Resch, R. Keller, V. Himmler, B. Krammer, and A. Schulz, editors, *2nd International Workshop on Tools for High Performance Computing*, pages 169–190. Springer-Verlag, July 2008.
[4]   NVIDIA Corporation. *NVIDIA Performance Toolkit*, da-01800-001v03 edition, May 2006.
[5]   NVIDIA Corporation. *NVIDIA CUDA Visual Profiler*, 1.1 edition, 2007.

Compilers & Tools

Parallel Computing: From Multicores and GPU's to Petascale
B. Chapman et al. (Eds.)
IOS Press, 2010
© 2010 The authors and IOS Press. All rights reserved.
doi:10.3233/978-1-60750-530-3-351

351

Conflict Analysis for heap-based Data Dependence Detection [1]

Rosa Castillo [a], Francisco Corbera [a], Angeles Navarro [a] Rafael Asenjo [a] and
Emilio L. Zapata [a]

[a] *Dept. of Computer Architecture, University of Malaga, Spain*

Abstract. In this paper we address the problem of detecting carried data dependences on loops or recursive functions for codes that create and traverse dynamic data structures. We propose a data dependence detection test based on a new conflict analysis algorithm. This algorithm requires two pieces of information: i) abstract shape graphs that represent the state of the heap at the code section under analysis and ii) path expressions that collect the traversing information for each statement. Our algorithm projects the path expressions on the shape graphs and checks over the graph if one of the sites reached by a write statement matches one of the sites reached by another statement on a different iteration, in which case a conflict between the two statements is reported. The proposed approach may improve other previous works by some orders of magnitude.

Keywords. Heap-based dynamic data structures, conflict analysis, shape analysis, data dependence test

1. Introduction

The detection of data dependences between program statements is essential for important compiling optimizations such as reordering of the statements, determination of invariant values in basic blocks, loops or methods. In particular, we focus in detecting the presence of *carried data dependences - CDD*, on loops or recursive call functions that traverse heap-based dynamic data structures. In a loop, two statements induce a CDD, if a memory location accessed by one statement in a given iteration, is accessed by the other statement in a future iteration, with one of the accesses being a write access. In the case of recursive call functions, we say that two (recursive) call instances in the body of a function induce a CDD, if a memory location accessed by one of the call istances is accessed by the other call, with one of the accesses being a write access.

Several research works have been devoted to develop compilation techniques for computing CDDs between scalar or, even pointer variables, but not for memory heap accesses. The main reason for the small number of techniques targeted to the problem of carried dependence detection for heap accesses is the lack of heap analysis to support them. Previous work focused on two approaches for identifying possible CDDs due to heap accesses: points-to analysis [12], [10], and shape analysis [4]. The former just deals with stack directed pointers, whereas the later tries to capture objects dynamically allocated in the heap. We focus our research in the latter. Our research group has developed

---

[1]This work was supported in part by the Ministry of Education of Spain under contract TIN2006-01078 and Junta de Andalucia's grant P08-TIC-3500.

a powerful shape analysis framework [11] based on abstract interpretation of the program statements. Our shape analysis captures, quite accurately, in the form of an abstract bounded graph, the program heap storage. On top of this shape analysis we developed, on a previous work, a client data dependence test [1] that annotates the read and write accesses in the graph's nodes. This process allows us to accurately detect flow, anti and output data dependences in C-codes that traverse and modify complex heap data structures. Other data dependence tests for heap access based on shape analysis have been developed, but fail to disambiguate heap references when the structure contain cycles or there are structure modifications [4,7]. In other recent work the underlying shape analysis has been targeted to Java manually-tuned collection libraries [8]. Summarizing, the applicability of these other related techniques is not as general as our work.

However, the experimental results of our previous approach have shown us that the computational cost of the data dependence test as a client analysis of a shape analysis is an expensive approach, due to the high cost of abstract interpretation [1]. In fact, the algorithms have an exponential complexity (which depends on the number of live pointer variables). So till now, we have restricted our experimental studies to small benchmarks with some hundred of lines. We are aware that we have to be able to address bigger programs to demonstrate the feasibility of our techniques. This is the goal of the new approach for detecting heap CDDs that we present in this paper. For such task, we have modified our analysis approach, incorporating a new preprocessing stage, and a new conflict detection algorithm. The preprocessing stage [9] performs a pruning of the program statements. The goal of this stage is to select only the statements that create or modify the data structures. Next, our shape analysis tool is fed with the output of this preprocessing stage, so the shape analysis only performs abstract interpretation for a subset of the program statements. Following, for each interval where we want to perform the data dependence analysis (a loop or a recursive function call), our framework collects, at the header of the interval, the shape graphs that represent the heap for that interval, as well as the access paths for all the statements that access the heap in the interval. Precisely, these paths and shape graphs are the input of our new conflict detection algorithm. This new algorithm is the focus of the paper.

One original contribution of our work, is that the checking of conflicts is not based in the identification of common subpath expressions as [6,5]. Instead, for each pair of potential conflictive paths, we decompose each path in a sequence of subpaths (entry, navigation and tail components) and use the accurate information that the shape graphs provide us, to identify the sites visited by each subpath. The sites are graph's nodes that are reached by a pointer or a selector that belongs to the subpath. We carry out, recursively, a conflict detection between the sites reached by each subpath, starting the checking for the entry subpaths, next for the navigation and finally for the tail subpaths. We have conducted some experiments and the results have demonstrated that our new data dependence approach spends significantly less time, mainly due to the polynomial complexity of our new algorithms, that clearly outperforms the exponential complexity of our previous work.

2. Data Dependence Method

2.1. Background

Our data dependence test needs to know the shape of the heap storage and how the statements traverse it, for the code section under analysis (typically a loop or the body of a recursive function). For instance, in the code of Fig. 1(b) we see two statements in the body of a loop (SR and SW), that access to the same field, index, on the elements of a linked list (see the concrete domain in Fig. 1(a)). One of the statements represents a write access (statement SW). These two statements could provoke a CDD if the same element is visited by the two statements in two different iterations of the loop. Looking at the code, we see that both statements traverse (through selector nxt) the elements of a data structure, starting at the element pointed to by A. Inspecting the data structure, we see that there is not a CDD in that loop because each iteration, advancing through nxt, visits different elements. This is the kind of information we need to extract from our data dependence test.

In our research, we use *shape graphs* as the abstract representation of the heap. The shape graphs are constructed using a shape analysis tool [11] that works by symbolically executing the pointer statements in the program. The shape analysis algorithm is designed as an iterative data-flow analysis, that continues analyzing the pointer statements in the program until a fixed point is reached. A **shape graph** sg^k contains important information about the dynamic objects and how they are connected. In Fig. 1(a), we see the linked list of our example in the concrete domain and the abstraction of such list in the abstract domain: the shape graph sg^1. This shape graph comprises nodes, N_k, that represent one or several memory locations; edges that represent pointer links, named PL_k, or selector links, named SL_k; and, finally, especial tuples named CLS (*Coexistent Link Sets*), which capture the connectivity and aliasing information that can coexist in an abstract node. As typically the size of the graph is not known at compile time, the graph must be bounded during the analysis. The strategy we use to perform the bounding is named *summarization* [11]. Our shape analysis carries out a summarization operation that limits the number of nodes and edges by representing in a single node all the memory locations not pointed to by any pointer variable. For instance, the node N1 in the shape graph of Fig. 1(a) represents the first element (memory location) in the list, whereas node N2 represents all the other ones. In the same way, some selector links are represented by one edge, for instance the edge named SL2 represents all the nxt links, but the first one which is represented by edge SL1 and the last one which is represented by edge SL3.

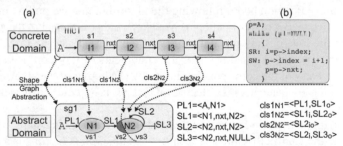

Figure 1. (a) A list in the concrete domain and in the abstract domain; (b) Code sample traversing the list.

Other piece of information that our dependence test needs is how the pointer statements traverse the data structures in the code section under analysis. For it, we need to collect the *paths* associated to each pointer statement. Our algorithms use interval analysis to collect the paths. A **path** is a tuple that contains a statement id si, and an expression, named the *path expression*. It is defined as: $path_{si} = < si, entry : navigation : tail >$. The path expression is composed by three subpath expressions: *entry*, *navigation* and

$tail$. A subpath expression consists in a pointer instance followed by a string of selectors connected by the component operator ".", or just a string of selectors connected by "." . The operators "*" or "+" can be used to indicate multiple occurrences of the same selector. The $entry$ subpath represents the entry point to the current interval. The $navigation$ subpath represents how the statement advances along the data structure, from one iteration to the next one in the current loop or recursive call. The $tail$ subpath is the expression that represents the subpath that can be traversed after the navigation. For example, at the loop header of the code of Fig. 1(b) we collect, among others, the paths for statements SR and SW: $path_{SR} = < SR, A : (nxt)^* : - >$ and $path_{SW} = < SW, A : (nxt)^* : - >$.

One important operation that we need to introduce before presenting the conflict detection analysis (the key algorithm in our data dependence test) is the $projection\ of$ $a\ path\ expression\ over\ a\ shape\ graph$. This operation consists in identifying, in the abstract shape graph, the $sites$ visited by each subpath component of the path expression. We define a **site** as a tuple $vs_i = < link_j, N_k >$, where $link_j$ is the edge (a pointer link PL_j, or a selector link SL_j) used to reach the node N_k, and N_k is the reached node. For instance, when projecting the path expression $< A : (nxt)^* : - >$ over the shape graph of Fig. 1(a) we reach the following sites: the entry subpath component A, visits the site $vs1 = < PL1, N1 >$. From that site, we use now the navigation subpath component $(nxt)^*$ to find the sites visited during the navigation (the iterations of the loop): $vs2 = < SL1, N2 >$ and $vs3 = < SL2, N2 >$. As in our path example the tail subpath component is empty, our path does not reach new sites. In the memory configuration $mc1$ shown in Fig. 1(a), we can see the elements visited by the path expression associated to SR, in the concrete domain: $s1$, $s2$, $s3$ and $s4$. In the graph sg^1 in the same figure, we find the sites visited by the same path expression, but in the abstract domain: $vs1$, $vs2$ and $vs3$. The correspondence between the elements visited in the concrete data structure and the sites visited in the abstract shape graph is as follows: $vs1$ represents $s1$, whereas $vs2$ represents $s2$ and $vs3$ represents $s3$ and $s4$.

2.2. Conflict Detection Algorithm

Our data dependence test tries to identify if there is any CDD in an interval (which is a loop or a recursive function body) following the algorithm that we outline in Fig. 2. Our method needs two pieces of information: i) $SG^{\bullet header}$, that is the set of the shape graphs that represent the state of the heap at the entry of the interval, and ii) $Path^{\bullet header}$, that is the set of the upward exposed paths of the statements of the loop or function body, that reaches the entry of the corresponding interval. The output of the algorithm is TRUE if a conflict (a data dependence) is detected or FALSE if no conflict (or dependence) is found.

Summarizing, our algorithm can be divided into the following steps: 1) In the first step, we create the **Conflict Groups**. A Conflict Group, $ConfGroup_g$, is a set of paths, that represent statements in the interval that may potentially lead to a CDD, which happens if there is one or several statements accessing to the same field (g) and one of the accesses is a write. The output of the function `Create_Conflict_Groups` is the set of all the Conflict Groups, named $CONFGROUP$. For instance, for the code example of Fig. 1(a) there is one $ConfGroup_{index} = \{path_{SR}, path_{SW}\}$; 2) Once the Conflict Groups have been created, our next step will look for conflicts between each pair of path expressions in a Conflict Group, $path_i, path_j \in ConfGroup_g$, and for each graph sg^n that belongs to the set of graphs available at the entry of the in-

```
fun Dependence_Detection (SG•header, Path•header)
1. CONFGROUP = Create_Conflict_Groups(Path•header);
2. foreach ConfGroupg ∈ CONFGROUP
       foreach pathi =< si, entryi : navigationi : taili >∈ ConfGroupg | si is a write stm.
         foreach pathj =< sj, entryj : navigationj : tailj >∈ ConfGroupg
           foreach sgn ∈ SG•header
             level = entry; VS1 = VS2 = null; ComEst = TRUE
             Conflictg(i,j)=Check_Conflict_subpath(level, sgn, pathi, pathj, VS1, VS2, ComEst)
             if (Conflictg(i,j) == TRUE ) return TRUE
           endfor
         endfor
       endfor
     endfor
  return FALSE
end
```

Figure 2. Our data dependences detection algorithm.

terval. When no conflict for any pair of paths on any graph is found, then function `Dependence_Detection` returns FALSE. The function that looks for the conflicts is named `Check_Conflict_subpath` and is the key function of our approach. The output of this function will be TRUE, when a definitive conflict for the two paths in graph sg^n is detected, indicating that a dependence exists. Otherwise, the function will return FALSE. In more detail, function `Check_Conflict_subpath` starts a process in which, basically, we check recursively the conflicts between the set of sites visited by each subpath component of the path expressions. We start by checking the conflicts for the *entry* subpaths, next for the *navigation* subpaths and finally for the *tail* subpaths. We use the input parameter *level* to identify in the ordered set {*entry, navigation, tail*} the subpath component where the current conflict checking is performed. The set of sites that are visited by each subpath level, VS_1 and VS_2, are input parameters of `Check_Conflict_subpath`. From these sites we will start the checking of conflicts for each subpath level. Initially, when function `Check_Conflict_subpath` is called for the first time (i.e. before the entry level checks, see Fig. 2), the VS sets only contain the null value. Other input parameter of `Check_Conflict_subpath` is $ComEst$, which is a boolean variable that for each level represents if the current subpaths have reached a common site. Initially $ComEst$ is TRUE. Later, during each level checking, this variable is recalculated as $ComEst'$ using the helper function `Check_ComEst` (that is called by function `Check_Conflict_subpath`). The input parameters of this helper function are: sg^n (the shape graph), $vs_i \in VS_1$ and $vs_j \in VS_2$ (the input sites from which the current subpaths $path_i.level$ and $path_j.level$ are projected over the graph), and variable $ComEst$ that informs if a potential conflict was detected in the previous level. Basically, function `Check_ComEst` projects over the graph sg^n, the current subpath components $path_i.level$ and $path_j.level$, starting from the input sites vs_i and vs_j, respectively. When projecting the subpaths over the graph, our algorithm marks over the graph the sites that are visited during the projection. This sequence of sites is a list that we call UP_1 and UP_2 (*Unrolled subPaths*), for the projection of $path_i.level$ and $path_j.level$, respectively. Once we have the list of sites visited by each projected subpath, we have to check if there is a conflict among them. This checking is a process that starts at the last site of each list. See in [3] the rules that function `Check_ComEst` applies to guess if the last site reached by the two unrolled subpaths, is the same or not and therefore may be a conflict or not.

For instance, when checking the conflicts for the $path_{SR}$ and $path_{SW}$ expressions of the code of Fig. 1(a), the first `Check_Conflict_subpath` call is for the entry level, with $VS_1 = VS_2 = \{null\}$. Here, when calling the helper function `Check_ComEst`, it projects the entry subpaths $path_{SR}.entry = A$ and $path_{SW}.entry = A$, over the shape graph that represents the heap at this point, getting the site $vs_{SR} = vs_{SW} = vs1 =< PL1, N1 >$ (Fig. 1(a)). Therefore the unrolled subpaths are $UP_{SR_1} = UP_{SW_1} = [vs1]$. The rules in [3] instruct that since the site reached is the same and there are not a previous site on each unrolled subpath, then we need to use the initial input $ComEst$ value to disambiguate if there is conflict or not. In this example, that value is TRUE, therefore we get the output $ComEst' = TRUE$. This is a trivial case of a common entry, where both subpaths reaches the same site and thus there is a potential conflict at this level. Next, we assign $level = navigation$, we initialize $VS_1 = \{vs1\}$ and $VS_2 = \{vs1\}$ as the new input sites, we assign $ComEst = ComEst' = TRUE$ (from the entry level checking) and call again function `Check_Conflict_subpath` for the checking of conflicts at the navigation level. Now, when calling the helper function `Check_ComEst` we use the navigation subpaths $path_{SR}.navigation = (nxt)^*$ and $path_{SW}.navigation = (nxt)^*$. We get that the helper function projects these subpath components over the shape graph, starting from $vs1 \in VS_1$ (for SR) and $vs1 \in VS_2$ (for SW). We get the following unrolled subpaths (Fig. 1(a)): $UP_{SR_1} = UP_{SW_1} = [vs1]$ - just the initial site, $UP_{SR_2} = UP_{SW_2} = [vs1, vs2]$ - the initial site plus one advance through selector nxt, and $UP_{SR_3} = UP_{SW_3} = [vs1, vs2, vs3^+]$ - the initial site plus one advance, plus more than one advance through selector nxt. In our example, our helper function checks if there are conflicts for the following cases (we only show the true dependences checking cases): $UP_{SW_1} \times UP_{SR_2}, UP_{SW_1} \times UP_{SR_3}, UP_{SW_2} \times UP_{SR_3}$. For these cases our helper function infers that there is not conflict (because the last reached site is different on each unrolled subpath). Therefore, there is not conflict at this level, and the output value for $ComEst' = FALSE$. As there is not tail component in the path expressions of SR and SW, function `Check_Conflict_subpath` would end up returning this last $ComEst' = FALSE$ value, and finally function `Dependence_Detection` would return that there is no CDD in this loop.

3. Experimental results

We have implemented the compilation algorithms described in this paper, within our shape analysis framework [11], and have conducted experiments over six benchmark codes. `Matrix x Vector` and `Matrix x Matrix` codes are the product of a sparse matrix-vector and a sparse matrix-matrix, being the matrices and vectors doubly-linked lists; they represent typical kernels of sparse matrices libraries with traversal and creation of dynamic data structures. The rest of benchmarks are from the Olden suite [2]: `TreeAdd` and `Bisort` creates and traverse binary trees, `Power` creates and recursively traverses multilevel structures of single linked-lists and `Em3d` creates and traverses a bipartite graph.

Our experimental framework performs the data dependence analysis following three steps: first a preprocessing pruning step ("Prune"). The input of this step is the original code in which we have annotated with pragmas the intervals of interest where we want to perform the dependence detection. In the experiments, we annotated the computationally most intensive loops or recursive call functions for each benchmark as intervals of interest. In this preprocessing step we run a code pruning algorithm (see [9]) to select the pointer statements related to the dynamic data structures traversed or modified in the interval of interest. During this step we collect and compute the paths of the pointer statements for the corresponding intervals. Next, using as input the pruned code, our framework carries out a shape analysis based on symbolic execution (abstract interpretation) where we compute the shape graphs ("ShapeA", more details in [11]). As a last step, our framework, using as inputs the paths and shape graphs previously computed, performs the Dep_Detection or dependence detection test ("DepDet"), which is the algorithm presented in Fig. 2. One first result is that our dependence detection algorithm detects no CDDs in the intervals of interest of our benchmarks. Table 1 summarizes the times that our algorithms spent in our experiments for the 6 selected benchmarks. The testing platform is a 3GHz Pentium 4 with 1 GB RAM. The first column identifies the codes; the next three columns show the break down of times to perform the complete dependence analysis process: the "Prune", "ShapeA" and the "DepDet" steps. The next column, "DepNew" is the sum of the three previous ones and represents the whole time that our framework needs to compute the data dependences. The next column, "DepOld" represents the times required by our old dependence test [1]. Let's recall that this old test was designated as a client analysis that annotated the read and write accesses in the graph nodes during the abstract interpretation process of the shape analysis. Other important remark is that in the old analysis, the code pruning was performed by hand, so the pruning times are not accounted for the "DepOld" column. Finally, the "Speedup" column represents the "DepOld" vs. "DepNew" times ratio.

Table 1. The running Times of our algorithms: DepNew and DepOld are the times of the new dependence analysis presented here vs. our old dependence analysis based on abstract interpretation.

Bench.	Prune	ShapeA	DepDet	DepNew	DepOld	Speedup
Matrix x Vector	2.96s	0.79s	6.3ms	3.77s	139.80s	37.1
Matrix x Matrix	7.62s	1.35s	15.8ms	8.93s	553.38s	61.9
TreeAdd	1.31s	1.62s	3.6ms	2.94s	31.42s	10.6
Bisort	7.68s	1.80s	7.5ms	9.49s	2706.88s	285.3
Power	16.69s	0.48s	2.3ms	17.17s	12.91s	0.8
Em3d	50.53s	7.36s	6.4ms	57.89s	125.88s	2.1

The table shows us that the most important contribution to the whole "DepNew" process is due to the preprocessing step, where the code pruning and collection of paths take place. Although the shape analysis is a costly approach [11], in column "ShapeA" we see that for the analyzed codes, thanks to the pruning step, we have substantially limited its cost. On the other hand, the contribution of the "DepDet" step is negligible (only some msec.). Precisely, this is the part of the algorithm that performs basically the conflict detection, that is the main contribution of this paper. Other result that the table shows is that, in all the cases, our new dependence analysis based on conflict detection ("DepNew"), significantly outperforms the times required by the old dependence analysis based on abstract interpretation ("DepOld"), in fact in some orders of magnitude as the last column of the table shows. The only exception is for the Power code, where the times are similar (although the pruning was not taken into account in the "DepOld" times). We could remark that Power is a code with a small number of live pointer variables, which translates into a small number of generated shape graphs, what makes the abstract interpretation process in the "DepOld" test less expensive than in the other codes.

4. Conclusions

In this paper we contribute with a new data dependence test for dynamic data structures based codes. We can analyze general C-codes that create, traverse and modify complex dynamic data structures, differently to other related works, uncovering parallelism that could not be efficiently detected till now. Our test relies in: i) a shape graph static analysis that captures the topological information about the connectivity between the memory locations, and ii) a path representation based on expressions that describes how the statements access the memory locations. The distinguish feature of our test is that performs a conflict analysis of the sites (the memory locations in our abstract shape domain) reached by the projection of the path expressions over the graphs. Avoiding abstract interpretation of the statements for which the conflict analysis is performed, we have significantly reduced the data dependence times of our previous approach. Actually, the complexity of the new dependence test is polynomial whereas the previous one had an exponential one, which makes the new algorithm suitable for analyzing larger codes.

References

[1]   R. Asenjo, R. Castillo, F. Corbera, A. Navarro, A. Tineo, and E. Zapata. Parallelizing irregular C codes assisted by interprocedural shape analysis. In *2nd IEEE International Parallel & Distributed Processing Symposium (IPDPS'08)*, Miami, Florida, USA, April 2008.

[2]   M. C. Carlisle and A. Rogers. Software caching and computation migration in Olden. In *ACM Symposium on Principles and Practice of Parallel Programming (PPoPP)*, July 1995.

[3]   F. Corbera, A. Navarro, R. Castillo, R. Asenjo, and E. L. Zapata. Conflict analysis for heap-based data dependence detection. In *Technical Report at http://www.ac.uma.es/~asenjo/research/*, Dpt. Computer Architecture, Univ. of Malaga, Spain, July 2009.

[4]   R. Ghiya and L. J. Hendren. Putting pointer analysis to work. In *Proc. 25th Annual ACM SIGPLAN-SIGACT Symposium on Principles of Programming Languages*, pages 121–133, San Diego, California, January 1998.

[5]   B. Hackett and R. Rugina. Region-based shape analysis with tracked locations. In *Proceedings of the ACM SIGPLAN Symposium on Principles of Programming Languages (POPL'05)*, pages 310–323, Long Beach, California, USA, 12-14 January 2005.

[6]   L. Hendren and A. Nicolau. Parallelizing programs with recursive data structures. *IEEE Transactions on Parallel and Distributed Systems*, 1(1):35–47, January 1990.

[7]   Y. S. Hwang and J. Saltz. Identifying parallelism in programs with cyclic graphs. *Journal of Parallel and Distributed Computing*, 63(3):337–355, 2003.

[8]   M. Marron, D. Stefanovic, D. Kapur, and M. Hermenegildo. Identification of heap-carried data dependence via explicit store heap models. In *Languages and Compilers for Parallel Computing (LCPC'08)*, Alberta, Canada, 2008.

[9]   R.Castillo, F. Corbera, A. Navarro, R. Asenjo, and E. Zapata. Complete DefUse analysis in recursive programs with dynamic data structures. In *Workshop on Productivity and Performance (PROPER 2008) Tools for HPC Application Development*, Las Palmas de Gran Canaria (Spain), August 2008.

[10] M. Shapiro and S. Horwitz. Fast and accurate flow-insensitive points-to analysis. In *Proc. 24th Annual ACM SIGPLAN-SIGACT Symposium on Principles of Programming Languages*, pages 1–14, Paris, France, January 1997.

[11] A. Tineo. *Compilation techniques based on shape analysis for pointer-based programs.* PhD thesis, Department of Computer Architecture, University of Malaga, Spain, 2009. Available at http://www.ac.uma.es/~compilacion/publicaciones/phd_tineo_final.pdf.

[12] R. P. Wilson and M. S. Lam. Efficient context-sensitive pointer analysis for C programs. In *Proc. ACM SIGPLAN'95 Conference on Programming Language Design and Implementation*, pages 1–12, La Jolla, California, June 1995.

Parallel Computing: From Multicores and GPU's to Petascale
B. Chapman et al. (Eds.)
IOS Press, 2010
© 2010 The authors and IOS Press. All rights reserved.
doi:10.3233/978-1-60750-530-3-359

Adaptive Parallel Matrix Computing through Compiler and Run-time Support

Jorge BUENABAD-CHÁVEZ [a,1], Miguel Alfonso CASTRO-GARCÍA [b],
Rosa Angélica ROSALES-CAMACHO [c], Santiago DOMÍNGUEZ-DOMÍNGUEZ [a],
Julio C. PERALTA [d], and Manuel AGUILAR-CORNEJO [b]

[a] *Departamento de Computación, CINVESTAV-IPN, México D.F.*
[b] *Departamento de Ingeniería Eléctrica, UAM-Iztapalapa, México D.F.*
[c] *Facultad de Informática Mazatlán, Universidad Autónoma de Sinaloa, México*
[d] *IRISA Campus de Beaulieu 35042 Rennes, France*

Abstract. This paper presents compiler and run-time support that simplifies the programming of adaptive parallel matrix computing. Matrices are declared with special keywords and can be referred to in high-level matrix operations specifying only their names, e.g., A=B*C, or in statements specifying individual matrix elements. Both types of references are translated into calls to procedures in a library. Procedures that carry out matrix operations are adaptive, currently in two ways: i) in selecting a parallel algorithm based on a cost model that considers various run-time conditions, and ii) in adapting to load imbalance.

Keywords. Adaptive Computing, Parallel Computing, Load Balancing, Compiling, Run-time Support

Introduction

Parallel computing is now mainstream on various architectures including multicores, Cell processors, GPUs and clusters of these. While application performance is most likely to keep improving, parallel programming has become more specialised, having to consider the characteristics of each target architecture and, in clusters, combining intra- and inter-node parallelism. In addition, good performance and efficient use of resources also depend on applications being adaptive, e.g., to load imbalance and hardware failure.

This paper presents an approach to matrix computing wherein parallelism and adaptivity issues are hidden from programmers through compiler and run-time support. Our compiler allows the use both of high-level matrix operations and of typical C language references to individual elements in a matrix, translating both into calls to procedures which comprise the run-time support as a libray. The use of high-level matrix operations simplifies coding; translating into calls to procedures gives freedom of choice to implement matrix operations in different ways transparently to the programmer. An implementation could use a single parallel algorithm for each matrix operation, or could

---

[1]Corresponding Author: Jorge Buenabad-Chávez, Departamento de Computación, CINVESTAV-IPN, Av. Instituto Politécnico Nacional 2508, D.F., 07360, México; E-mail: jbuenabad@cs.cinvestav.mx.

also include mechanisms for fault tolerance, load balance, or run-time selection of an algorithm or a platform configuration on account of various characteristics of the target architecture and the problem to be solved.

Using matrix multiplication as example, we present performance empirical results of an implementation that is adaptive in two ways: i) in selecting one of two algorithms based on a cost model that considers problem size, parallelism level and synchronisation overhead; and ii) in adapting to load imbalance. Our results show substantial performance gains through both forms of adaptivity.

Our implementation is based on two middlewares: an all-software distributed shared memory (DSM) [1] and the data list management library (DLML) [2]. Both run under the single program multiple data (SPMD) parallel computing model. Our DSM is partly based on the message passing interface (MPI), using MPI functionality to launch processes in each node and to synchronise processes through barriers before the start and the end of the parallel computing phase. DLML is entirely based on MPI.

An implementation based on bare MPI is likely to show better performance out of data being moved directly between processing nodes without the cache lookup that is used in DSM systems. However, programming in MPI is much more involved out of the need for explicit communication patterns between *senders* and *receivers*, more so for varying communication patterns as required by some forms of adaptivity such as dynamic load balancing and fault tolerance.

On the other hand, our current implementation serves only as a proof of concept. An implementation intended for wide-spread use ought to be efficient in terms of performance and relatively easy to program with, to reconfigure and to extend. One option is to extend MPI with programming abstractions similar to those provided by our middlewares, and make them easy to reconfigure and extend. Another option is to use middleware which has gained wide-spread use and supports similar abstractions to those provided by our middlewares, such as Global Arrays [3]; such middlewares usually evolve into versions that are easy to reconfigure and extend out of their use by many users.

Our DSM operates on data blocks, which correspond to rows in arrays, through an interface similar to that of files: `DDS_Read(arrid,rownum,size,&ptr)` and `DDS_Write()` gain access to one or more rows in an array for reading and writing, and `DDS_Release()` relinquishes data access. Parallel files can be mapped to the shared addres space and are used through the same interface [4]; hence the programming of in-core and out-of-core applications is practically the same. The management of parallel data lists provided by DLML greatly simplified the implementation of load balancing.

Section 1 presents our compiler support. Section 2 presents our run-time support for algorithm selection and load balancing. Section 3 presents empirical results on the performance benefit of run-time algorithm selection and load balancing. Section 4 presents related work and Section 5 our conclusions.

1. Compiler Support

Figure 1 shows examples of the source code (left) and the object code processed by our compiler. Only the declarations of _shared matrices (arrays), high-level matrix operations on them, and reads and writes to individual elements in them, are processed by our compiler. Other source lines are written into the C *object* file unmodified. The

```
1 /* Matrix declaration */                    1 #include _sh_base_defs.h        /* _FLOAT ... */
2 _shared float A[10000][10000];              2 /* Matrix declaration */
3 _shared float B[10000][10000];              3 typedef struct {
4 _shared float C[10000][10000];              4     int _shtype,              /* int, float, double */
                                              5     int _shndim,              /* num. of dimensions */
                                              6     int _shdim1,              /* # elements in dim1 */
                                              7     int _shdim2,              /* # elements in dim2 */
                                              8     int _shdim3,              /* # elements in dim3 */
                                              9     int _shaddr               /* initial shared add */
                                             10 } _sh_attr;
                                             11 _sh_attr _shattributes[ 3 ] = {
                                             12     _FLOAT,2,10000,10000,0,0,   /* 1st matrix */
                                             13     _FLOAT,2,10000,10000,0,0,   /* 2nd matrix */
                                             14     _FLOAT,2,10000,10000,0,0    /* 3rd matrix */
                                             15 };
5 main() {                                   16 main() {
6   int i,j,k;                               17   int i,j,k;
7   float pi = 3.1416;                       18   float pi = 3.1416;
8                                            19
                                             20   _shInit(3) ;
9   A = B * C;                               21   _shMult_shm_shm_shm(0,1,2);

10  B = B * (C[1][1]/pi);                    22   _shMult_shm_shm_esc(1,1,(_shReadF(2,1,1)/pi));

11 /* typical mat. multiplication code */    23 /* typical mat. multiplication code */
12 for (i=0; i < 10000; i++)                 24 for (i=0; i < 10000; i++)
13   for (j=0; j < 10000; j++)               25   for (j=0; j < 10000; j++)
14     for (k=0; k < 10000; k++)             26     for (k=0; k < 10000; k++)
15       A[i][j]= A[i][j]+B[i][k]*C[k][j];   27       _shWriteF(0,i,j, _shReadF(0,i,j)+\
                                             28                        _shReadF(1,i,k)*\
                                             29                        _shReadF(2,k,j));
16 ]                                         30 _shFinished();
                                             31 }
```

Figure 1. Examples of source C code (left) and object C code of the compiler.

entire object file is then processed by the C compiler and linked to relevant libraries, including our library with adaptive parallel matrix operations.

Matrices to be used in high-level matrix operations are declared using the keyword _shared preceding their data type, either int, float or double (source lines 2-4 in Figure 1). This _shared keyword means that data in these matrices is to be shared between processors/nodes in a cluster in order to profit from parallelism under the SPMD model. Our compiler translates matrix declarations into code that both declares and initialises the structure _shattributes with the attributes of each matrix: data type, number of dimensions (up to 3 in the example), number of elements in each dimension, and initial shared address. Object lines 3-10 declare this structure, and lines 11-15 initialise it. The initialisation of each initial shared address to 0 is temporary; we discuss it further below.

The structure _shattributes is shared between the user program (e.g., that in Figure 1) and each module in our run-time library, where it is declared with the object lines 3-10 followed by the line extern _sh_attr _shattributes[]. Our library modules get to know the actual size of this structure until run time, through the call to the procedure _shInit(3) (object line 20), which is in charge of initialising various C global variables whithin each node (*cf.* SPMD model); the constant 3 is the number of entries in that structure (i.e., the number of _shared matrices declared). The call to _shInit follows any variable declaration following main(). In our current implementation, _shInit also calls in each node the initialisation procedure of our DSM, which allocates _shared matrices to the *shared addess space* and accordingly updates their initial shared address attribute in the structure _shattributes.

A=B*C (source line 9) is translated into _shMult_shm_shm_shm(0,1,2) (object line 21); numbers 0, 1 and 2 refer to the entries in the structure _shattributes that correspond to matrices A, B and C, respectively (they also refer to the order in which they were declared as _shared). For C=A*B, the parameters would be ..._shm(2,0,1). The suffix _shm_shm_shm means that the three parameters refer to _shared matrices. In object line 22, the suffix _shm_shm_esc means the parameters are two _shared matrices and a single escalar value.

Reads and writes to individual elements in _shared matrices are exemplified in source lines 10 and 15; the corresponding object lines are 22 and 27-29, respectively, where a read has been translated into a call to _shReadF and a write into a call to _shWriteF. The letter F in the names _shReadF and _shWriteF stands for float data type; our library includes similar procedures for int and double data types. For all of them, the first parameter identifies the relevant _shared matrix, the following two parameters identify the individual matrix element to read or write and, for a write, the last parameter is the value to write. Clearly, it is very inefficient to use individual reads and writes to code a matrix operation as exemplified in source lines 12-15, as both each individual element is accessed through a read function or a write procedure and writes to individual elements are carried out sequentially by the master processor only. Such read and write functionality is only provided for completeness of our approach.

2. Run-time Support

Our run-time support is a library comprising the procedures that carry out high-level matrix operations and read/write individual elements in shared matrices. Matrix operations run in parallel and are adaptive, currently in two ways: i) in selecting one of two algorithms based on a cost model that considers various platform and application characteristics, and ii) in adapting to load imbalance.

2.1. Algorithm Selection based on Performance Modelling

The performance of parallel algorithms depends on various factors such as level of parallelism, amount of available memory, level of synchronization and size of the problem. These factors can be characterised within a cost model, which can be refined with results of actual runs of algorithms. The cost model can then be used to estimate the execution time of various equivalent algorithms for particular values of those factors prevailing at run time, and select the fastest algorithm according to those estimates. Using this approach we have explored the performance benefit of run-time algorithm selection using two matrix multiplication algorithms. We outline our cost model in this subsection. In Section 3.1 we compare its performance estimates to the performance of actual runs.

Our cost model estimates the execution time of each matrix multiplication algorithm, T_{exec_alg}, considering the size of the problem S, the level of parallelism P, the amount of available memory M, the memory requirements of the algorithm AM, and an overhead factor O due to factors such as contention and synchronisation:

$$T_{exec\_alg}(S, P, M, AM) = T_{comp}(S, P) + T_{comm}(S, P, M, AM) + O(P) \quad (1)$$

T_{comp} is computation time and T_{comm} is communication time. Our cost model assumes for the time being that the target platform is a homeogeneous cluster and the workload is partitioned and assigned equally to processors; hence each processor makes the same amount of work. Under this assumption, the time it takes for a processor to make its work is the execution time of the algorithm running on P processors. Accordingly, T_{comp} computes the computation time for the size of the problem S (i.e., number of instructions times the time to execute each instruction), and divides it into the number of processors P. For instance, for matrix multiplication involving three matrices of size $N \times N$, we use $S = N^3$ multiplication instructions.

T_{comm} works in a similar way to T_{comp} in that it computes the communication time of a single processor, and this time is considered the communication time of the algorithm. However, T_{comm} is more specific both to the algorithm and to the middleware being used. It uses S, P and the access pattern of the algorithm to determine the amount of data D that each processor will access (see Section 3.1). Using M and AM it is determined if D will fit in the memory of each processor or swapping will occur, but the latter is not yet modelled in our cost model; our results correspond to D fitting in memory. With D determined, the number of messages $NumMsg$ to fetch D into the memory of each processor is determined. Then $T_{comm} = NumMsg \times msg\_trans\_time$. Note that $NumMsg$ depends on the middleware used. In our DSM, data is initially allocated by rows among nodes in round robin fashion. Our cost model considers this to estimate how many accesses will be local and how many will be remote which involve messages.

Finally, $O(P)$ characterises cost due to factors such as contention and synchronisation that may be inherent in an algorithm, see Section 3.1.

2.2. Load balancing

Load balancing is a key factor for good performance of parallel applications in unpredictable environments. Its implementation mostly depends on the parallel computing model used to solve the problem. Using the master-slave (task-farming) model, the workload is initially partitioned into smaller parts that are assigned to slave processors *on demand* by one or a few master processors. This model implicitly implements load balancing, as slaves make requests for more work according to their processing capacity.

Under the SPMD model, the workload is typically partitioned and assigned equally to processors at start of computation. This practice is suitable when: i) processing nodes have the same hardware-software configuration and thus deliver fairly equal performance; and ii) nodes are allocated to applications exclusively from start to finish. In unpredictable environments, or if the application dynamically generates more workload, load imbalance is likely to occur, and when so, performance will degrade unless a load balancing mechanism *adapts* the (initial) processor load assignments to match the observed processing capacity of each processor. This type of load balancing is rather involved; it requires: monitoring progress of computation in each processor, a communication protocol to adapt processor load assignments, a cost model to estimate adaptation overhead, and a criterion to decide *when* and *to what* to adapt processor load assignments. The cost model and the decision making criterion are used to help identify useful adaptations that should improve performance; an adaptation near the end of computation may delay completion further than the load imbalance it attempts to correct.

In Section 3.2 we describe the addition of the master-slave model to a matrix multiplication algorithm initially designed for the SPMD model, combining two middlewares.

3. Performance Evaluation

To evaluate the performance benefit of run-time algorithm selection and load balancing in our approach, we carried out various experiments in a homogeneous 32-node cluster configured as follows. Each node has a 3GHz Intel Pentium IV Hyper-Threading processor, 1 GB memory and one 80GB hard disk drive, running Linux Fedora 6 in 64-bit mode; all nodes are interconnected through one gigabit ethernet switch.

Our results correspond to the parallel computing phase only, there is no I/O in this phase, and each processor can hold all the data it uses in its memory. In our DSM, before entering this phase, each processor initialises its lookup directory so that data blocks (rows in all arrays) are allocated to nodes in round-robin fashion: node 0 is allocated the first row, node 1 the 2nd row and so on. (In MPI, this corresponds to the initialisation of arrays by the master processor.) Each processor then goes into a global barrier.

When processors go out of the barrier, timing of the parallel phase begins. Processors access data according to the access pattern of the algorithm, fetching data blocks from remote nodes as determined by the initial round-robin distribution. A read *replicates* the relevant data in the local memory of a processor, residing there until the end of the parallel computing phase because there is enough memory. A write *migrates* the relevant data to the local memory of a processor. (In MPI, the master processor sends data to other processors as determined by the access pattern of the algorithm.) All processors then go into a global barrier; when they go out the timing of the parallel phase stops.

3.1. Run-time Algorithm Selection: Experimental Setting and Results

We ran two matrix multiplication algorithms with different levels of parallelism and with different problem sizes. In one algorithm, each processor computes the result of several rows of the results matrix A ($A = B \times C$). The number of rows in A is divided and assigned equally among the processors. We refer to this algorithm as *traditional* (as it derives from the traditional sequential algorithm). In *traditional*, each processor accesses matrix C in its entirety for each row of A and B that is accessed, one at a time. Matrix C is kept in the memory of each processor.

In the other algorithm, each processor computes a *partial* result of each element in A. For $N \times N$ matrices and p processors, processor 0 uses the first N/p elements of the corresponding row in B and the first N/p elements of the corresponding column in C, processor 1 does the same using the second N/p elements ..., etc. Each processor computes the partial results of an entire row in A locally in one go, and then adds the results to the elements in A. This algorithm requires less memory than *traditional* at any time: one row from A, one row from B, and N/p rows from C. However, it requires synchronisation in reading and writing rows in A. We call it *synchronised*.

Figure 2 shows the execution times of *traditional* and *synchronised* for different levels of parallelism and problem sizes, both of actual runs (left) and computed using our cost model. The execution times of actual runs show that *traditional* performs better than *synchronised* for problem size $N = 1000$ to 4000. This is because of the synchronisation overhead of *synchronised*. However, as the problem size grows, the communication overhead incurred by *traditional* for each node to read matrix C entirely becomes higher than the synchronisation overhead of *synchronised*.

Our cost model is not precise (Figure 2, right). But it does follow the performance trend of each algorithm. Still, it should help to identify a substantial performance differ-

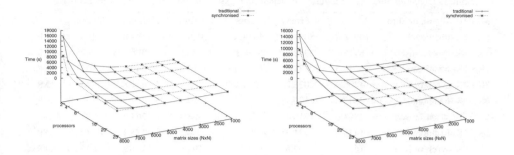

Figure 2. Execution times of *traditional* and *synchronised* matrix multiplication, from actual runs (left) and computed using our cost model.

ence between equivalent algorithms. If there is no substantial gain in performance, there is no substantial loss either.

The actual performance difference between both algorithms can be significant, but cannot be appreciated in Figure 2. Table 1 shows the numerical values of execution times plotted in Figure 2, of actual runs (AR) and computed using our cost model (CM). For actual runs, for problem size $N = 5000$ to 8000, *synchronised* performs increasingly better than *traditional* as both problem size and parallelism level grow. For the largest problem size (8K×8K) and parallelism level (25), *traditional* is $1305.4/405.3 = 3.22$ times slower than *synchronised* (a difference of $1305.4 - 405.3 = 900.1$ seconds).

3.2. Load Balancing: Experimental Setting and Results

We have extended the *traditional* matrix multiplication algorithm to include load balancing based on the master-slave model using the Data List Managment Library (DLML), a middleware for parallel processing of data in lists [2]. In DLML, each processor has a local list from which it gets data to process. When a local list becomes empty, DLML fetches data from other (remote) lists transparently to the user, thus balacing the workload. For *traditional*, the master processor initialises its list with the numbers of all the rows in the results matrix (each number in an item list), and the granularity of each request is set to a single list item. Slaves request the *id* of rows to process, one at a time, according to their processing capacity. After each request (within a *while* loop), *traditional* computes the result for the entire row of the result matrix A.

Figure 3 shows the execution times of *traditional* with and without load balance on 4 (left) and 8 processors for different problem sizes. The runs labelled **no_imbalance-loadBalancing_OFF** are the base case, as no overhead is incurred by the load balancing mechanism. This overhead is relatively small, as shown by the runs labelled **no_imbalance-loadBalancing_ON**. The extra load in the runs with imbalance, **imbalance-loadBalancing__ON** and **imbalance-loadBalancing_OFF**, is as follows. On 4 processors, the overloaded nodes were the master and one slave, and on 8 processors the master and three slaves. In each overloaded processor, 4 more processes are run which continuously make floating point operations. The results show that the use of load balancing can substantially improve performance, reducing execution time by more than half the execution time of runs with no load balance.

Table 1. Execution times (s) of Figure 2, of actual runs (AR) and computed with cost model (CM).

MatrixSizes–algorithm	2-Procs	4-Procs	8-Procs	16-Procs	20-Procs	25-Procs	
8K×8K–traditional	16058.8	8093.7	4048.1	2039.6	1634.8	1305.4	AR
8K×8K–synchronised	8915.1	2972.7	1450.1	738.5	598.1	405.3	AR
7K×7K–traditional	6070.3	3073.2	1555.0	811.8	649.8	537.8	AR
7K×7K–synchronised	4206.4	2028.2	1024.4	533.4	431.8	349.7	AR
6K×6K–traditional	3040.6	1530.7	769.5	394.3	311.8	253.1	AR
6K×6K–synchronised	2398.6	1210.5	617.3	323.4	264.5	234.2	AR
5K×5K–traditional	1479.9	731.3	392.8	204.7	175.1	125.0	AR
5K×5K–synchronised	1425.4	732.6	377.1	199.9	165.1	132.9	AR
4K×4K–traditional	638.4	314.1	166.1	88.8	71.4	60.0	AR
4K×4K–synchronised	689.8	351.2	184.0	97.0	79.5	67.6	AR
3K×3K–traditional	281.1	145.9	76.0	40.7	33.8	32.8	AR
3K×3K–synchronised	301.4	156.8	86.1	47.4	38.5	32.4	AR
2K×2K–traditional	75.1	30.2	22.5	13.2	11.1	9.9	AR
2K×2K–synchronised	85.3	47.7	27.6	16.4	14.6	12.9	AR
1K×1K–traditional	10.9	6.6	4.5	3.2	2.8	2.7	AR
1K×1K–synchronised	12.4	7.9	5.7	4.5	4.1	3.9	AR
8K×8K–traditional	15161.1	7586.4	3799.0	1905.3	1526.6	1223.6	CM
8K×8K–synchronised	9980.7	6299.4	3486.2	1836.5	1487.1	1202.9	CM
7K×7K–traditional	6339.4	3174.5	1592.0	800.8	642.5	515.9	CM
7K×7K–synchronised	4780.7	2791.6	1503.7	786.1	637.2	516.3	CM
6K×6K–traditional	2945.9	1476.8	742.2	374.9	301.5	242.8	CM
6K×6K–synchronised	2490.4	1368.4	721.1	376.0	305.2	248.2	CM
5K×5K–traditional	1437.7	721.8	363.9	184.9	149.2	120.5	CM
5K×5K–synchronised	1310.3	694.2	361.7	189.2	154.3	126.2	CM
4K×4K–traditional	676.3	340.4	172.4	88.4	71.6	58.2	CM
4K×4K–synchronised	643.4	335.3	174.7	92.7	76.1	62.9	CM
3K×3K–traditional	276.1	139.6	71.3	37.2	30.3	24.9	CM
3K×3K–synchronised	268.9	140.0	73.9	40.4	33.7	28.3	CM
2K×2K–traditional	82.8	42.3	22.1	11.9	9.9	8.3	CM
2K×2K–synchronised	81.9	43.5	23.9	14.0	12.0	10.4	CM
1K×1K–traditional	11.9	6.3	3.5	2.2	1.9	1.7	CM
1K×1K–synchronised	12.1	7.0	4.4	3.1	2.8	2.6	CM

4. Related and Future Work

The purpose of our work is to hide the complexity of parallelism and adaptivity issues from the programmer through the use of sequential programming extended with high-level matrix operations. The approaches in [5,6] use skeletons (structured programming) as high-level operations for the same purpose. For data-intensive applications, *mapreduce* is a middleware [7] to develop applications that are both fault tolerant and load balancing. Programmers only specify one or more pairs of mapper-reducer sequential functions which the mapreduce framework runs both in parallel and in pipelined fashion: first mapper copies and then reducer copies.

A promising extension to our compiler is static program analysis to identify patterns in sequential source code that may be replaced with calls to an equivalent procedure

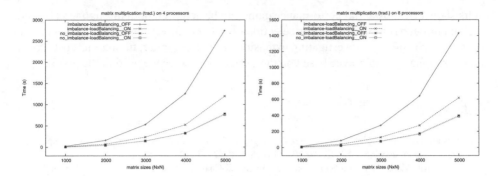

Figure 3. Execution times of *traditional* matrix multiplication with and without load balance on 4 (left) and 8 processors.

in our run-time library [8,9,10]. The signatures of the procedures in our library will correspond to sequential code to facilitate pattern matching, but the actual procedure to invoke at run time will be parallel and adaptive, and can be fine-tuned for a particular platform. In other words, our compiler will identify the typical matrix multiplication code in Figure 1 (left) and will replace it with the call `_shMult_shm_shm_shm(0,1,2)`.

Load balancing based on the master-slave model is implicit; and with adequate task granularity, its overhead can be relatively little. Load balancing which dynamically adapts processor load assignments is much more involved (Section 2.2). It is a form of self-tuning/optimisation which may or may not improve performance because there is no reliable way of predicting future trends in load imbalance; still, it involves the cost of tuning, i.e., the time spent in reconfiguring the system. Many computational systems operate in comparably uncertain settings, and the term *online algorithm* has been coined to refer to a solution to a problem where a sequence of requests is processed as each request arrives without knowledge of future requests [11]. Examples include paging in virtual memory systems [12,13], cache memory management [14] and dynamic selection of component implementations [15]. The term *competitive algorithm* is used of algorithms that seek to make decisions online that can be characterized by how well they compete with an optimal offline algorithm. The algorithm in [15] is 3-competitive, i.e., it cannot perform worse than 3 times the optimal algorithm. In [16], we used a modified version of this algorithm to improve the decision as to *when* and *to what* to adapt processor load assignments under parallel query processing; in [17] we used a probabilistic decision making approach for the same purpose and context. Cost-benefit analysis and control theory were used in [18] to adapt the allocation of memory to different tasks within a database system. In essence, the above systems must make decisions as to which configuration to use in future on the basis of previous performance.

5. Conclusions

This paper has presented an approach to adaptive parallel matrix computing based on compiler and run-time support that simplifies programming and allows instrumenting run-time decisions and freedom of choice in implementing matrix operations. Using existing middleware, we showed that the actual implementation can be simple and efficient but requires non-trivial knowledge of the middleware and the target platforms. Our results show that substantial performance gains can be achieved both through load balancing and through run-time algorithm selection on account of various factors present at run time. We are currently investigating extensions to our compiler, tuning our cost model, and designing fault tolerance based on the same middleware we used in this work.

References

[1]   J. Buenabad-Chávez and S. Domínguez-Domínguez. The data diffusion space for parallel computing in clusters. In Proceedings of *Euro-Par 2005*, LNCS 3648 (2005), 61–71.

[2]   G. Román-Alonso, J.R. Jiménez-Alaniz, J. Buenabad-Chávez, M.A. Castro-García and A.H. Vargas-Rodríguez, Segmentation of brain image volumes using the data list management library. In Proceedings of *EMBC 07*, 29th Conf. of IEEE Engineering in Medicine and Biology Society, 2007, 2085–2088.

[3]   Global Arrays. Web site: http://www.emsl.pnl.gov/docs/global/

[4]   J. Buenabad-Chávez and S. Domínguez-Domínguez. Comparing Two Parallel File Systems: PVFS and FSDDS. In Proceedings of *ParCo 2005*, 507-514. Edited by John von Neumann Institute for Computing (NIC), Germany, NIC Series Volume 33, ISBN 3-00-017352-8, 2006.

[5]   M. Alt, J. Müller, and S. Gorlatch. Towards high-level grid programming and load-balancing: A barnes-hut case study. In Proceedings of *Euro-Par 2005*, LNCS 3648 (2005), 391–400.

[6]   H. González-Vélez and M. Cole. An adaptive parallel pipeline pattern for grids. In Proceedings of *IPDPS 2008*, 1–11.

[7]   J. Dean and S. Ghemawat. Mapreduce: Simplifed data processing on large clusters. *Operating Systems Design and Implementation* (2004), 137–149.

[8]   C. Alias and D. Barthou. Deciding where to call performance libraries. In Proceedings od *Euro-Par 2005*, LNCS 3648 (2005), 336–345, 2005.

[9]   R. Metzger and Z. Wen. Automatic Algorithm Recognition and Replacement: A New Approach to Program Optimization. The MIT Press, 2000.

[10]   L.M. Wills. *Automated program recognition by graph parsing*. PhD thesis, Cambridge, MA, USA, 1992.

[11]   M.S. Manasse, L.A. McGeoch and D.D. Sleator. Competitive Algorithms for On-line Problems. In Proceedings of the twentieth annual ACM symposium on Theory of Computing, 1988, 322–333.

[12]   A. Fiat, R.M. Karp, M. Luby, L.A. McGeoch, D.D. Sleator and N.E. Young. Competitive Paging Algorithms. *J. Algorithms* 12 (1991), 685–699.

[13]   T. H. Romer, W. H. Ohlrich, A. R. Karlin and B. N. Bershad. Reducing TLB and Memory Overhead Using Online Superpage Promotion. In Proceedings of the 22nd Annual International Symposium on Computer Architecture, 1995, 176–187.

[14]   S. J. Eggers and R. H. Katz. Evaluating the performance of four cache coherency protocols. In Proceedings of the 16th International Symposium on Computer Architecture, 1989, 2–15.

[15]   D. M. Yellin. Competitive algorithms for the dynamic selection of component implementations. IBM Systems Journal 42 (2003), 85–97.

[16]   N.W. Paton, J. Buenabad-Chávez, M. Cheng, V. Raman, G. Swart, I. Narang, D.M. Yellin and A.A.A. Fernandes. Autonomic Query Parallelization using Non-dedicated Computers: An Evaluation of Adaptivity Options. Very Large Data Bases Journal 18 (2009), 119-140.

[17]   D.M. Yellin, J. Buenabad-Chávez and N.W. Paton. Probabilistic adaptive load balancing for parallel queries. In Proceedings of the 24th International Conference on Data Engineering (ICDE) Workshops, 2008, pages 19–26.

[18]   A.J. Storm, C. García-Arellano, S.S. Lightstone, Yixin Diao and M. Surendra. Adaptive self-tuning memory in DB2. In Proceedings of the 32nd International Conference on Very Large Data Bases, 2006, 1081–1092.

Parallel I/O

Parallel Computing: From Multicores and GPU's to Petascale
B. Chapman et al. (Eds.)
IOS Press, 2010
© 2010 The authors and IOS Press. All rights reserved.
doi:10.3233/978-1-60750-530-3-371

High-Throughput Parallel-I/O using SIONlib for Mesoscopic Particle Dynamics Simulations on Massively Parallel Computers

Jens FRECHE [a], Wolfgang FRINGS [a] and Godehard SUTMANN [a,1]

[a] *Institute for Advanced Simulation (IAS)*
Jülich Supercomputing Centre (JSC)
Research Centre Jülich, D-52425 Jülich, Germany

Abstract. The newly developed parallel Input/Output-libray SIONlib is applied to the highly scalable parallel multiscale code MP2C, which couples a mesoscopic fluid method based on multi particle collision dynamics to molecular dynamics. It is demonstrated that for fluid-benchmark systems, a significant improvement of scalability under production conditions can be achieved. It is shown that for the BlueGene/P architecture at Jülich a performance close to the bandwidth capacity of $4.7\ GByte/sec$ can be obtained. The article discusses the ease of use of SIONlib from the point of view of application.

Keywords. Parallel computing, molecular dynamics, mesoscopic particle simulations, parallel input/output

Introduction

Mesoscale simulations of hydrodynamic media have attracted great interest during the last years in order to bridge the gap between mircoscopic simulations on the atomistic level on the one side and macroscopic calculations on the continuum level on the other side. Various methods have been proposed which all have in common that they solve the Navier-Stokes equations in different types of discretizations, e.g. Lattice-Boltzmann simulations [1,2] on a spatial grid or Multi-Particle Collision Dynamics (MPC) — also called Stochastic Rotation Dynamics (SRD) — using discrete particles [3,4]. In the latter approach, pseudo-particles are considered to carry both hydrodynamic information and thermal noise. Specifying a small set of parameters, i.e. fluid particle density, scattering angle, mean free path of a particle, it is possible to reproduce a variety of hydrodynamic phenomena. In particular, the regime of small Reynolds numbers has been investigated in detail, e.g. Poiseuille flow, shear flow, vortices or hydrodynamic long time tails, to name a few [4,5]. The method itself is relatively simple and consists basically of two steps: (i) a streaming step, where particles are propagated in space according to their actual

---

[1] Corresponding author, e-mail: g.sutmann@fz-juelich.de

velocity and the applied time step; (ii) a collision or momentum transfer step, where, for the case of SRD, the velocity relative to the center-of-mass velocity inside a locally defined collision cell is rotated by a given angle α around a stochastically chosen axis.

Although the fluid itself is represented as a coarse grained medium, i.e. simulated particles do not correspond to individual particles, but to groups of fluid particles, representing the characteristic behavior of the hydrodynamic medium, the number of degrees of freedom may become very large. Considering the collision cell in MPC as a basic length scale, below which molecular chaos and no hydrodynamics is observed, one often needs to simulate hundreds of basic length units, in order to capture the collective behavior of the fluid. This is even enforced, when the fluid is coupled to macromolecules, which determine the length of the system or when turbulence comes into play which has to be considered on a cascade of length scales. Considering simulation systems of size $L = 100, \ldots, 1000$ this implies a number N of fluid particles $N = 10^7, \ldots, 10^{10}$, when realistic density of $\rho = 10$ particles/collision cell is considered. If one is interested in trajectories of fluid particles, this is a challenge for the input/output routines in a program and it must be implemented most efficiently, for not being limited in scalability of the program due to I/O-bottlenecks in the program. On the other hand, even the handling of restart configurations may already cause a significant bottleneck in performance, when not using parallel I/O-libraries. E.g. organizing the I/O via a master process, which writes out/reads in data to/from disk, limits the number of particles to moderate sizes of several million particles. Otherwise the time for the setup- and final-phase in a program dominates in such a way that it does not justify the usage of > 10000 processors.

In the present paper the newly developed mesoscopic fluid code MP2C [6] is combined with the recently developed parallel I/O-library SIONlib [7]. It is shown that the use of SIONlib enables the highly scalable MP2C code to run most efficient in production mode. This is demonstated by simulating systems of up to $N = 10^{10}$ particles. In the following a short description of the basic principles of MP2C as well as the parallel implementation is presented. Then the coupling to SIONlib is described and compared with the original master-process based implementation. Differences to a possible MPI-IO implementation are given as well.

1. Coupling of Mesoscopic Hydrodynamics to Molecular Dynamics

An advantage of the MPC method is that a coupling to atomistic simulations can be established in a simple way. The main characteristic of MPC is that particles are sorted into cubic cells (with lattice constant a) of a randomly positioned collision grid. Different variants of MPC vary in the way how the momentum exchange between particles within a collision cell is performed. In the SRD-version of MPC, relative velocities are rotated randomly by a given angle around a randomly chosen direction, which mimics collisions between solvent molecules. If coupled to atomistic simulations of solute particles, e.g. by molecular dynamics (MD), the MD-particles are sorted together with fluid particles into collision cells and their velocities are included into the stochastic rotation step. Because atomistic time scales are typically smaller than hydrodynamic time scales, MD-particles are basically simulated according to their force-fields. In order to establish a coupling to the hydrodynamic medium, they are included every n-th step into a stochastic rotation together with the solvent particles.

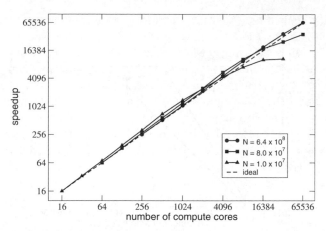

Figure 1. Strong scaling benchmark for the MPC part of MP2C for systems of fluid particles composed of $N = 1.0 \times 10^7, 8.0 \times 10^7, 6.4 \times 10^8$ particles.

Since in typical simulations of colloidal suspensions or semi-diluted polymer systems, fluid particles are $1 - 5$ orders of magnitude more numerous than MD-particles, system sizes get very large in simulations of $10^4 - 10^6$ MD-particles. Therefore, although mesoscale hydrodynamics techniques are algorithmically simple, the computational demand to study large system sizes on long time scales requires an efficient parallel implementation of the simulation code.

2. Scalable Particle Simulation Code

The current version of MP2C is based on MPI and uses a domain decomposition approach, where geometrical domains of the same volume are distributed onto the processors. For convenience, a decomposition of $N_p = 2^n$ is chosen and domains are organised in such a way that in x, y, z-direction that the surface of the rectangular domains gets minimal.

The 3RD part of the program requires basically only nearest neighbor communication to calculate center of mass velocities uniquely for domain overlapping cells and to distribute a unique set of random numbers to define a random rotation axis for the collision step. In addition, particles have to be imported/exported according to their spatial coordinate after the streaming step. The MD part is implemted via an eigth shell (ES) communication for the force computation [8,9] and a minimum transfer scheme for the particle export/import [10]. As it is demonstrated in Fig. 1 MP2C scales up to 65536 compute cores on the BlueGene/P architecture at JSC. This particle based multiscale implementation, including various types of boundary conditions, offers the large scale simulation of microscopic systems coupled to a mesoscopic flow model on extended time scales.

3. Parallel Input/Output

Although the basic algorithm of MPC/MD was shown to scale up to thousands of processors, a limiting factor in production runs is often met in input/output operations. In

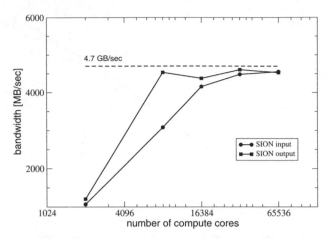

Figure 2. Benchmark for SIONlib, where I/O is measured for the input/output of 2 TBytes of data which are distributed over the processors.

principle, the number of degrees of freedom in the simulations will often be scaled up with number of processors. Since the spatial coordinates and velocities of the particles are distributed over all processors, the storage of trajectory information requires an efficient way to enable input/output-operations. The first approach, realized in the program was to use a master-slave principle, where all processors sent their data to a master process, which opened a file and wrote data to disk. Since for big physical systems, the size of the arrays is larger than the total available memory, processors sent sequentially their data to the master process. In that way, the I/O-operations are of serial type and the problem, arising with this method gets worse (also for a constant global amount of data) when increasing the number of processors, since one adds up latency and buffer filling time. A possible solution could be that every processor writes into an own file. This could be an acceptable solution, if the files need only to be opened in the beginning and to be closed at the end of the simulation. Otherwise, the time to open thousands of files would be a similar overhead. On the other side, this method simply shifts part of the problem to the post-processing step, since data in thousands of files have to be rearranged and sorted, since the output of data will be non-deterministic as particles change their processor identity and consequently data of a given particle will be written in as many different files as the particle has visited different processors. Therefore, the requirement for an efficient, scalable I/O is a consistent parallel implementation, i.e. every processor writes independently from other processors into one single file or in a small set of files.

A solution for this approach may be found with MPI-I/O or other parallel libraries, like Parralel netCDF [11]. In the current version of the program a recently developed library, called SIONlib [7,12] is applied. Using this library, enables the user to access nearly the full possibilities of the network capabilities, i.e. I/O is only limited by the bandwidth capacity of the network. Other features of SIONlib are the support of C, C++ and Fortran interfaces, the parallel open/close of files and POSIX-I/O. The library was run successfully on different platforms like CRAY-XT4, IBM BlueGene/P or Linux based PC clusters. The advantage to use SIONlib compared with other libraries is a considerably reduced time for creation and opening of files, a simple file handling and that no performance penalty has to be paid for read/write operations, i.e. full usage of bandwidth capabilities.

The performance differences between MPI-I/O and SIONlib might be found in different reasons. SIONlib is organised in such a way that a fixed chunk size is used which corresponds to the block size of the underlying file system. Therefore, writing data from one processor, guarantees alignment, i.e. no conflicts between processors, accessing the file system block, may occur. Especially for small data sizes, this removes a serious source of conflicts, resulting in a performance bottleneck. By default, MPI-I/O is non-aligned. A partial solution to this alignment problem with MPI on IBM BlueGene/P may be achieved by setting the switch `IBM_largeblock_IO = true`, which collects data to a small number of proceesors and then writes out relatively large data sets on these processors. This reduces on the one hand the problem of non-alignment of data, since the probability of conflicts increases with the number of processors involved in the output operation, but on the other hand this introduces a serialization, since data have to be sent to this subset of processors, which causes a load-imbalance between the processors.

It is not only an improved performance, which is advantageous when using SIONlib, but also its ease of use. Advantages come into play when data are written out and read in on the same number of processors. SIONlib uses meta data which describe, how many data items were written out on a given processor and how many processors were involved in the I/O. In that way a one-to-one mapping between written data and those which are read in is achieved. This organisation of data is done automatically by SIONlib. Within an MPI environment, there are e.g. basically three calls to SION routines necessary, i.e. `fsion_paropen_mpi`, which opens the output file, `fsion_write`, which writes out the data and finally `fsion_parclose_mpi`, which closes the file. On contrast, using MPI-I/O needs to specify data types for the I/O-procedure, to define a so called view and to define a procedure how to combine different data types. Also there are no meta data by default. The effort from the application point of view of implementing an optimised version of MPI-I/O seems to be larger than using SIONlib. The advantage of using MPI-I/O is, however, that data may be organised contigously in the output file, making it easy to read them, e.g. on a different number of processors than they were produced.

Fig. 2 shows a benchmark (not MP2C) on BlueGene/P, where a fixed data size of 2 TBytes was distributed over the processors and read in/written out from/to disk. The asymptotic value, i.e. the bandwidth of the file system, is shown for comparison, which is for the IBM BlueGene/P at Jülich $\approx 4.7\,GByte/sec$. It is found that for $P \geq 16384$ processors, which correspond to 4 racks of the machine, a bandwidth for I/O is obtained which corresponds close to the maximum capacity. In order to achieve the full bandwidth for output, data were written out on 16 files (see below). Due to the configuration of BlueGene/P racks it is not possible to achieve the full I/O capacity from the file system for a single or small number of racks. Therefore, the full bandwidth can only be achieved if using a larger number of racks. This also avoids that a single user running a job with heavy output on a single rack on such a machine slows down all other processes on the machine, because of saturated bandwidth capacity of the file system. From the benchmark it is found that $P \geq 16384$ cores, a realistic rate of $4.5\,GByte/sec$ for write- and $4.5\,GByte/sec$ for read-operations of aligned data can be achieved.

Although the performance of SIONlib is optimized by a fixed chunksize, guaranteeing alignment of data, this might be a drawback in memory usage, since for every processor which is involved in output operations, a minimum of a chunksize (2 MBytes) is written out. In the case that only data of size $<< 2$ MBytes are written out every step,

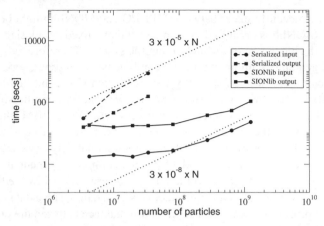

Figure 3. Comparison between conventional I/O and SIONlib for fluid systems of increasing size, simulated on $P = 1024$ processors. The linear curves are a guide to the eye, showing the scaling of the time with numbers of processors between conventional I/O and SIONlib.

the file size might increase very strongly. In this case, a compromise could also be to define a subset of processors, which collect data from other processors to write out data. This would also imply a serialization, but aligned output is guaranteed, nevertheless. This shows that SIONlib is mainly designed for applications, requiring I/O of large data from every processor.

4. Results

In order to demonstrate the capabilities of SIONlib, benchmark runs were carried out for fluid systems with MP2C. The MPC parameters for the benchmark system were chosen as $\alpha = 130^o$, $\lambda_c = 0.1\,a$, $\rho_c = 10$. The number of particles were chosen to give system sizes up to $n_\alpha = 1000$ collision cells in each cartesian direction, i.e. particle numbers up to $N_{mpc} = 1.0 \times 10^{10}$. For this system size it is not convenient to write out trajectory files for every particle in a production run. Simulations are analysed merly during a simulation or data are coarse grained, i.e. densities of coarser chosen volumes are written out. However, it is necessary to save configurations for a restart of the simulation. Therefore it is essential to have a very fast method to write out all coordinate and velocity information of the system.

Benchmark runs were performed on the IBM BlueGene/P architecture at Jülich Supercomputing Centre. As a first test, the conventional I/O is compared to SIONlib. In Fig. 3 the times are compared for I/O with and without SIONlib for a fluid systems of different size, simulated on 1024 processors. Measured is the time, which is spent for reading in and writing out restart configurations, containing particle indices, stored as 8 Byte integers, 3-dimensional particle coordinate- and velocity-vectors, stored in double precision, i.e. the amount of data is $56 \times N$ bytes. The conventional I/O is organized in a way that all processors send their data to a master process, which writes out the data to one file. In that way, the I/O is serialized, which is not favorable for massively parallel applications. The input is organized in such a way that first the complete file is read once and particle coordinates are tested, to which geometrical domain they belong. In such a

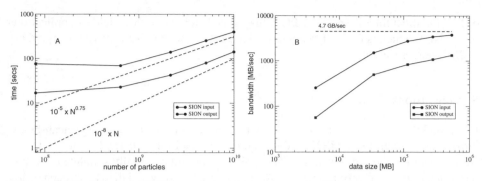

Figure 4. Scaling behavior of SIONlib on $P = 16384$ processors for fluid systems composed of different numbers of particles. A: measured time as a function of particle number. The dashed lines are drawn as a guide for the eye. B: bandwidth as function of data size. As a limiting line, the maximum bandwidth capacity of the file system is shown (4.7 GBytes/sec).

way the maximum number of particles/processor is evaluated and the appropriate memory size is allocated. In a second step the file is read once again and the particle data are sent to the processors, administrating the proper domain. For relatively small data sets, this method might be tolerated. However, for increaing number of particles and increasing number of processors, the serialization introduces a significant bottleneck, which might cost a substantial part of time, reserved for the simulation on the parallel machine. In Fig. 3, conventional I/O is compared to SIONlib. As a guide to the eye, linear curves are shown, which are close to the asymptotic functional behavior of both I/O types. As might be expected, the linear curve of the conventional I/O procedure has a prefactor 3 orders of magnitude larger than the one corresponding to SIONlib, i.e. the number of processors. It is obvious that for applications, running on >10000 processors, this type of I/O introduces a serious bottleneck, even if restart configurations are stored only less frequent.

In Fig. 4 the scaling of SIONlib I/O is shown for fluid systems of increasing size. Simulations were performed on $P = 16384$ processors on BlueGene/P. Results are presented for I/O from/to one single file. This is chosen here for convenience from the application point of view, in order to have one restart file for one simulation. As it is found, in this way the input operations outperform the output operations. Nevertheless, the performance is still quite satisfactory. On the other hand, this behavior might be improved, if more than one physical file is used for I/O operations. As it was shown in Ref. [7], depending on the system architecture, it might be more favorable to use more than one physical file for I/O. For the case of BlueGene/P, use of 8 or 16 files significantly improves the output performance and reaches nearly peak performance, as it is the case for the input.

It needs to clarified, why the maximum bandwidth is only reached asymptotically. Indeed, as Fig. 4 shows, the time required for system sizes composed up to $N = 10^9$ particles, is close to be constant. The reason for this is the fixed chunk size of 2 MBytes. This implies that every process writes at least 2 MBytes in every output operation, regardless of the array size, allocated in the program. Taking into account that every particle corresponds to 56 Bytes of output in the restart file (index, coordinates, velocities), the chunksize of 2 MBytes is reached on $P = 16384$ processors for approximately $N \approx 6 \times 10^8$ particles. This means that for smaller systems and the same number of processors a more or less identical time is spent for I/O. This immediately shows the field of applications of SIONlib, which is found if really large data sets are written from every processor, i.e. $\geq$ 2MBytes/processor.

5. Conclusions

It is found that the use of SIONlib as a tool for parallel I/O-operations significantly improves the scalability of MP2C under production conditions for large systems. It was shown that only the use of parallel I/O enables the program to really simulate large systems on a large number of processors. As it was shown, every serialized approach of I/O gets a prefactor, which is proportional to the number of processors and therefore strongly restricts I/O operations to small and moderate numbers of PEs. This certainly does not allow for a use of > 10000 processors. It was discussed that SIONlib outperforms MPI-I/O because of aligned data output, which avoids conflicts between processors, writing into the same block of the file system. For input operations it could be shown that the bandwidth capacity of the file system is nearly reached. Output performance may be improved by using multiple output files (8 to 16) which will also lead to a performance close to the peak bandwidth. This strategy is planned for MP2C for the near future.

Acknowledgements

The authors are grateful to fruitful discussions with M.A. Hermanns about MPI-IO.

References

[1] S. Succi. *The Lattice Boltzmann Equation: For Fluid Dynamics and Beyond*. Oxfor University Press, Oxford, 2001.

[2] B. Dünweg and A.J.C. Ladd. Lattice Boltzmann Simulations of Soft Matter Systems. *Adv. Polym. Sci.*, 221:89–166, 2009.

[3] A. Malevanets and R. Kapral. Mesoscopic model for solvent dynamics. *J. Chem. Phys.*, 110:8605–8613, 1999.

[4] G. Gompper, T. Ihle, D.M. Kroll, and R.G. Winkler. Multi-Particle Collision Dynamics: A Particle-Based Mesoscale Simulation Approach to the Hydrodynamics of Complex Fluids. *Adv. Polym. Sci.*, 221:1–87, 2009.

[5] R. Kapral. Multiparticle Collision Dynamics: Simulation of Complex Systems on Mesoscales. In S.A. Rice, editor, *Adv. Chem. Phys.*, volume 140, page 89. Wiley, 2008.

[6] G. Sutmann, R. Winkler, and G. Gompper. Multi-particle collision dynamics coupled to molecular dynamics on massively parallel computers. (in preparation), 2009.

[7] W. Frings, F. Wolf, and V. Petkov. SIONlib: Scalable parallel I/O for task-local files. Proceedings of Supercomputing 2009, Portland, Oregon, accepted for publication, 2009.

[8] D. Brown, J. H. R. Clarke, M. Okuda, and T. Yamazaki. A domain decomposition parallel processing algorithm for molecular dynamics simulations of polymers. *Comp. Phys. Comm.*, 83:1, 1994.

[9] D.E. Shaw. A fast, scalable method for the parallel evaluation of distance limited pairwise particle interactions. *J. Comp. Chem.*, 26:1318–1328, 2005.

[10] S. Plimpton. Fast parallel algorithms for short range molecular dynamics. *J. Comp. Phys.*, 117:1, 1995.

[11] J. Li, W.-K. Liao, A. Choudhary, R. Ross, R. Thakur, W. Gropp, R. Latham, A. Siegel, B. Gallagher, and M. Zingale. Parallel netCDF: A High-Performance Scientific I/O Interface. In *Proc. SC'03*, pages 1–11, 2003.

[12] http://www.fz-juelich.de/jsc/sionlib.

Parallel Computing: From Multicores and GPU's to Petascale
B. Chapman et al. (Eds.)
IOS Press, 2010
© 2010 The authors and IOS Press. All rights reserved.
doi:10.3233/978-1-60750-530-3-379

Tracing Performance of MPI-I/O with PVFS2: A Case Study of Optimization

Yuichi TSUJITA [a], Julian KUNKEL [b], Stephan KREMPEL [b], Thomas LUDWIG [c]

[a] *Kinki University*
1 Umenobe, Takaya, Higashi-Hiroshima, Hiroshima 739-2116, Japan
[b] *Ruprecht-Karls-Universität, Heidelberg*
Im Neuenheimer Feld 348, 69120 Heidelberg, Germany
[c] *Universität Hamburg & German Climate Computing Centre (DKRZ)*
Bundesstraße 45a, 20146 Hamburg, Germany

Abstract. Parallel computing manages huge amounts of data due to a dramatic increase in computing scale. The parallel file system PVFS version 2 (PVFS2) realizes a scalable file system for such huge data on a cluster system. Although several MPI tracing tools can check the behavior of MPI functions, tracing PVFS server activities has not been available. Hence, we have missed chances to optimize MPI applications regarding PVFS server activities although effective usage of limited resources is important even in PVFS servers. An off-line performance analysis tool named PIOviz traces both MPI-I/O calls and associated PVFS server activities to assist optimization for MPI applications. Besides, tracing statistical values of PVFS servers such as CPU usage and PVFS internal statistics assists optimization of MPI applications. In this paper, we demonstrate two performance evaluation tests of the HPIO benchmark, and carry out off-line analysis by using PIOviz. The evaluation shows effectiveness of PIOviz in detecting bottlenecks of MPI-I/O.

Keywords. cluster computing, tracing tool, MPI-I/O, PVFS, performance optimization

Introduction

The Parallel Virtual File System (PVFS) [1] was developed to realize parallel file systems on a cluster environment by deploying metadata and data servers on cluster nodes. Each data server has a data storage space to store chunks of striped data, while metadata servers hold information of a cluster-wide consistent name space and file distributions associated with the striped data. The file system is accessible from POSIX I/O and MPI-I/O APIs.

In parallel computing, there is a variety of I/O patterns in both contiguous and non-contiguous data accesses provided by the MPI-I/O. One of the implementations is the ROMIO in MPICH2 [2]. In independent operations with a non-contiguous access pattern, each client process might carry out a large number of small data accesses. In contrast, collective operations adopt the two-phase I/O protocol [3] to improve performance. Data exchanges and synchronizations among client MPI processes are carried out to make large contiguous data accesses on file domains.

Performance optimization is carried out by measuring throughput for example. However, it is difficult to examine reasons for inefficient operation. Variety of data access patterns such as non-contiguous accesses also makes optimization rather difficult. Furthermore, utilization of a parallel file system such as PVFS brings complexity in optimization. However, there is not sufficient research work to reveal effects of PVFS activities under complex I/O patterns. PIOviz [4] is developed to assist such application optimization. In this paper, several measurements for PVFS server statistics were carried out by using the HPIO benchmark [5] with PIOviz.

The rest of this paper is organized as follows. Section 1 provides brief overview of related work. Section 2 describes functionality of PIOviz, followed by short explanations of MPI-I/O access patterns in the HPIO benchmark in section 3. Section 4 discusses performance evaluation of MPI-I/O operations using the HPIO benchmark with the help of PIOviz. Conclusions and future work are discussed in Section 5.

1. Related Work

Jumpshot [6] and Vampir [7] are well-known tracing tools for MPI applications. Jumpshot works in cooperation with the MPICH2 library. It supports analysis of MPI functions for data communications and parallel I/Os. Vampir visualizes MPI calls and records performance data according to the Open Trace Format [8]. Recently it supports MPI-I/O tracing [7]. Another framework SCALASCA [9] supports runtime summarization of measurements during execution and event trace collection for postmortem trace analysis. TAU [10] provides robust, flexible, and portable tools for tracing and visualization of applications. It can also generate trace information which can be displayed with the Vampir. The Paraver toolset [11] provides fruitful analysis tools such as hardware counter and system activity monitor in addition to profiler for applications. However, these tools do not support tracing activities within parallel file systems such as PVFS.

Our project PIOviz is an off-line trace-based environment for MPI operations. It extends existing tracing implementation by incorporating PVFS instrumentation to support tracing PVFS activities in conjunction with MPI-I/O calls. As data format of the trace file is based on SLOG2 format [6], a user can analyze trace information with Jumpshot.

2. PIOviz

PIOviz traces MPI calls and typical PVFS server activities such as network communications (effected by the BMI layer) and disk accesses (Trove layer) in conjunction with MPI-I/O calls. In addition, it also collects statistics of CPU usage and PVFS internal statistics [12]. As PIOviz uses standard PMPI APIs, an application user can utilize it without modification in source codes. Once a user executes a program, trace files are generated by PIOviz in both client and server sides. Correspondence of trace information between client and server sides is analyzed, and then a combined trace file is generated from the trace files through several merging stages. A user can analyze all the MPI and MPI-I/O calls in conjunction with associated PVFS activities with Jumpshot.

3. HPIO Benchmark

The MPI-I/O benchmark HPIO reveals performance statistics about non-contiguous data access patterns in collective and independent operations. For the non-contiguous data

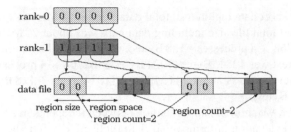

Figure 1. Example of a derived data type in the HPIO benchmark

accesses, derived data types are created with an ensemble of region size, region count, and region space, where region stands for a data area. Figure 1 illustrates an example of a data pattern for two processes. Here we assume that data is stored in a memory contiguously and in a data file non-contiguously. Gaps between data regions are specified by region space of this benchmark. According to a file view created by a derived data type, each client process accesses the data file.

4. Performance evaluation

We used a cluster of 9 PC nodes for our performance measurement. All nodes, DELL PowerEdge 830 PCs, were interconnected via a Gigabit Ethernet switch, 3Com Super-Stack 3 3824. Table 1 summarizes specifications of the cluster system. Since a 64 bit operating system was used, all the libraries in this test were built as 64 bit applications. A PVFS file system was prepared on five nodes. A head node was configured as a metadata server and four computation nodes as data servers. Data storage on each data server was prepared on an ext3 file system configured on a RAID-1 volume. The remainder of the nodes (four nodes) was used for client MPI processes. PIOviz incorporated MPICH2 version 1.0.5p4 and PVFS version 2.6.2, and it was used to build the HPIO.

In the following experiments, we used a contiguous access pattern in a memory (client MPI application side) and a non-contiguous access pattern on a PVFS file system. We arranged short and long data region tests with 32 Bytes and 1024 Bytes for region size, respectively. In both cases, region count was 32768 and region space was

Table 1. Specifications of the test cluster system

CPU	Intel Pentium-D 3.2 GHz, 2×2 MBytes L2 cache	
Chipset	Intel E7230	
Memory	1.5 GBytes DDR2 667 SDRAM	
Disk system (system)	Western Digital WD1600JS-75N (available in each node)	
Disk system (storage space)	RAID-1 (data nodes)	RAID controller: 3ware Escalade 9550SX-4LP
		Disk: $2 \times$ Seagate Barracuda 7200.9 160 GBytes
Network I/F	Broadcom NetXtreme BCM5721 (on-board)	
Linux kernel	2.6.9-42.ELsmp (CentOS 4.4 for x86_64)	
C compiler	gcc version 3.4.6	
Ethernet driver	Broadcom tg3 version 3.52	

128 Bytes. In the short data region test, total data size was 4 MBytes (32 Bytes × 32768 × 4 processes) and total file size including data gaps was about 20 MBytes ((32 Bytes + 128 Bytes) × 32768 × 4 processes - 128 Bytes). On the other hand, total data size in the long data region test was 128 MBytes (1024 Bytes × 32768 × 4 processes) and total file size including data gaps was about 144 MBytes ((1024 Bytes + 128 Bytes) × 32768 × 4 processes - 128 Bytes).

In this chapter, we show (1) an evaluation between independent and collective operations and (2) an evaluation in terms of sizes for collective buffer (hereafter CB) in the two phase I/O. In both cases, mean values of traced statistics obtained by PIOviz were calculated through 10 iterations. For reference, mean values of throughput (including `MPI_File_sync()`) calculated by the HPIO are included. Note that we set the HPIO to compute the mean throughput values by excluding the highest and lowest value.

4.1. Independent and collective I/O

`MPI_File_write()` and `MPI_File_write_all()` were used in the independent and collective cases, respectively. Here `MPI_File_write()` accessed only data regions, while `MPI_File_write_all()` accessed data regions and data gaps because of the two-phase I/O protocol. Table 2 shows mean statistical values of four data servers. Note that BMI load is higher than Trove load if the network is a bottleneck due to many network transfer, and vice versa if there are many disk I/Os. From a user perspective, utilization of available server resources is important, thus a high load is preferable. However, evaluation of the load values together is essential to assess efficient utilization. In the default configuration, a PVFS server issues an I/O operation for a maximum of 256 KBytes. In our case, the write-behind of the Linux kernel can combine multiple small requests into one. It is desirable to issue as much large I/O operations as possible to the kernel to allow efficient write-back. Consequently, it is also important to check Trove size as close to the maximum size.

We can see that BMI load in collective operations is higher than that in independent operations. This was due to the two-phase I/O protocol. On the other hand, Trove load and Trove access in independent operations are higher than those in collective operations due to large number of small data accesses in independent operations.

Table 2. Statistics of data servers obtained by PIOviz in collective (C) and independent (I) I/O operations of the HPIO benchmark

Region size (Bytes)	I/O mode	BMI load (ops/s)	Trove load (ops/s)	Trove access (ops)	Trove size (B/op)	CPU usage (%)	Throughput (MB/s)
32	C	0.425	10	800 (read, write)	262137.6 (read,write)	2.03	15.842
	I	0	49.9	30719 (write)	1365.4 (write)	11.55	5.352
1024	C	0.875	10.3	5760 (read,write)	262143.1 (read,write)	5.02	71.169
	I	0.3	59.4	81919 (write)	16384 (write)	15.135	92.954

In the case of 32 Bytes in a region size, collective operation outperformed independent one. By focusing on CPU usage, the value in the independent case is higher than that in the collective one. This was caused by many small Trove accesses in the independent case. So, the independent case was not efficient in this configuration from the viewpoint of throughput and CPU usage.

On the other hand, independent operation outperformed collective operation with region size of 1024 Bytes. In the collective case, we found inefficient operations of the two-phase I/O in screenshots of trace files generated by PIOviz. Later, this will be discussed in 4.2. Although higher throughput is preferable, users need to pay attention to CPU usage in the independent mode. The high Trove load value is caused by many small I/O operations. As a result, CPU usage is higher than that in the collective mode. If many users share a PVFS file system, performance of independent case might be degraded due to short of CPU resources. As there is a trade-off between throughput and other factors such as CPU usage due to limited computing resources, PIOviz can help to select preferable operation pattern.

4.2. Effects of collective buffer size in the two-phase I/O

We also measured statistical values of the PVFS servers in `MPI_File_write_all()` with changing CB size. Note that default CB size of the ROMIO is 4 MBytes. Table 3 shows measured values from trace files in the case of 32 Bytes in region size. In this test, 16 MBytes was desirable for CB size regarding small CPU usage and higher throughput values. Here, a CB with this size could store the whole data (~ 5 MBytes per process). Trove load, Trove access, and Trove size are almost constant with more than 4 MBytes for CB size. This means that a CB with 4 MBytes was sufficient for PVFS servers to achieve its peak performance. However, throughput in the case of 4 MBytes was smaller than that of 16 MBytes due to larger overhead caused by the two-phase I/O.

Measured throughput values sometimes showed high variance in 10 iterations runs. Four screenshots in Figure 2 show what was going on in client MPI applications and PVFS servers. In every screenshot, the upper 4 time-lines show activities of client MPI applications, while the first line in the lower 5 lines shows activities of a PVFS metadata server and the rest of them shows those of PVFS data servers.

Fig. 2 (a) shows an effective iteration in the case of 4 MBytes in CB size. We can see consecutive operation by Trove read, BMI, and Trove write on every PVFS data server twice for the two-phase I/O protocol. When the MPI I/O function was called, data on a file domain was read by Trove read. The data was transferred to a CB of each client

Table 3. Statistics of data servers with different collective buffer (CB) size in collective operations with region size of 32 Bytes

CB size (MBytes)	BMI load (ops/s)	Trove load (ops/s)	Trove access (ops)	Trove size (B/op)	CPU usage (%)	Throughput (MB/s)
0.5	0.2	10.275	1600 (read,write)	131068.8 (read,write)	2.605	14.962
4	0.425	10	800 (read,write)	262137.6 (read,write)	2.0325	15.842
16	0.5	10.5	800 (read,write)	262137.6 (read,write)	2.0675	23.571

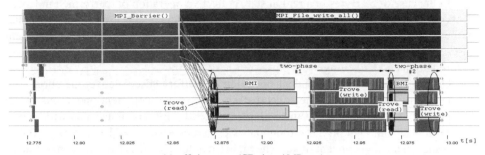

(a) efficient case (CB size: 4 MBytes)

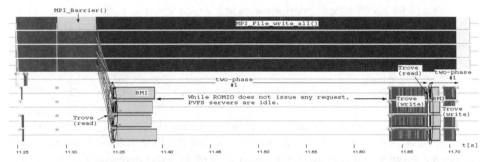

(b) inefficient in client (CB size: 4 MBytes)

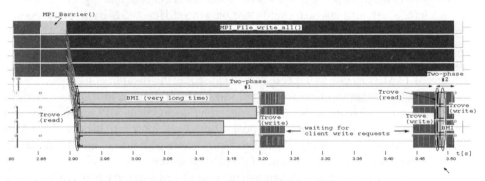

(c) inefficient in network transfer (CB size: 4 MBytes)

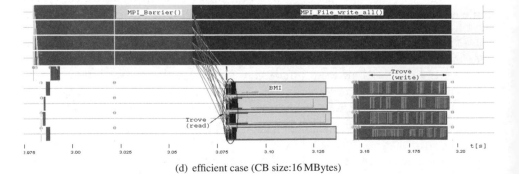

(d) efficient case (CB size: 16 MBytes)

Figure 2. Screenshots of one iteration in the HPIO benchmark

Table 4. Statistics of data servers with different CB size in collective operations with region size of 1024 Bytes

CB size (MBytes)	BMI load (ops/s)	Trove load (ops/s)	Trove access (ops)	Trove size (B/op)	CPU usage (%)	Throughput (MB/s)
0.5	0.4	10.475	11520 (read,write)	131071.6 (read,write)	5.3475	46.955
4	0.875	10.325	5760 (read,write)	262143.1 (read,write)	5.02	71.169
16	2.025	10.7	5760 (read,write)	262143.1 (read,write)	5.355	96.138
64	2.6	10.5	5760 (read,write)	262143.1 (read,write)	5.38	114.634

process by using BMI. Later on, data to be written was exchanged among client processes and overwritten in each CB non-contiguously. Finally data in each CB was transferred to a PVFS data server by using BMI. Then it was written back to an assigned file domain by using Trove write.

Figs. 2 (b), and (c) show typical inefficient cases. In the case (b), PVFS servers were idle for a long time (~ 240 ms) because ROMIO did not issue any request. Note that the waiting time was about 7 ms in Fig. 2 (a). It is considered that network transfer among client applications took a long time. The case (c) shows long network transfer by BMI between client applications and PVFS servers. Here, there could be inefficient network transfer or inefficient MPI communications inside ROMIO. From both examples, it is considered that MPI operations inside ROMIO had some inefficient parts. However we could not examine the network transfer and MPI calls inside ROMIO in detail because the PIOviz could not trace them this time.

In the case of 16 MBytes in CB size, the number of the consecutive operation in the two-phase I/O was one due to enough CB size as shown in Fig. 2 (d). Thus, the screen-shots from trace files of PIOviz are useful for off-line analysis of bottleneck detection.

Table 4 summarizes measured statistics with region size of 1024 Bytes. A 64 MBytes CB provided the best throughput. Here, BMI load values raised up with an increase in CB size. This means that network throughput between client processes and PVFS servers raised up with an increase in CB size. However, Trove load, Trove access, and Trove size are constant with more than 4 MBytes for CB size. A 4 MBytes CB is considered to be enough to achieve peak performance of PVFS servers. By increasing CB size to 64 MBytes, each client process could store whole data (~ 36 MBytes per process) in a CB. As a result, throughput was improved.

5. Summary

MPI-I/O and a PVFS file system provide scalable I/O operations on a cluster system. In order to optimize resource usage of MPI applications, it is helpful to trace relevant performance data. This is composed of not only application related information but also other statistics like e.g. CPU and network usages. PIOviz traces PVFS server activities in conjunction with MPI-I/O calls. Besides, it traces performance statistics and PVFS internal statistics. We demonstrated how PIOviz was used for application optimization. In our experiments of the HPIO benchmark, collective operations were better than independent ones with short data regions regarding both throughput and CPU usage. Independent operations outperformed collective ones with longer data regions. However, we should pay attention to CPU usage because CPU utilization in the independent operations was higher than that in the collective ones.

We also demonstrated tracing of collective operations in terms of collective buffer size in the two-phase I/O protocol. Obviously we could obtain higher throughput by increasing the buffer size. Other statistics such as CPU usage, Trove load, and the number of Trove accesses informed by PIOviz were useful in application optimization. PIOviz is expected to be helpful for tuning MPI applications with paying much attention to effective resource usage of PVFS servers. In our experiments, we showed examples which have inefficient aspects in client applications or network communications. However, we could not find reasons for the inefficient operation because PIOviz could not trace statistics of network transfer and MPI communications inside ROMIO in client applications at this moment. As a future work, implementation of functions to trace performance statistics and MPI calls used inside ROMIO is considered.

Acknowledgments

This research was partially supported by MEXT, Grant-in-Aid for Young Scientists (B), 21700063. The authors would like to thank Olga Mordvinova for her useful advice to improve this paper.

References

[1] PVFS2. http://www.pvfs.org/pvfs2/.
[2] W. Gropp, E. Lusk, N. Doss, and A. Skjellum, "A high-performance, portable implementation of the MPI Message-Passing Interface standard," *Parallel Computing*, vol. 22, no. 6, pp. 789–828, 1996.
[3] R. Thakur, W. Gropp, and E. Lusk, "Optimizing noncontiguous accesses in MPI-IO," *Parallel Computing*, vol. 28, no. 1, pp. 83–105, 2002.
[4] T. Ludwig, S. Krempel, M. Kuhn, J. M. Kunkel, and C. Lohse, "Analysis of the MPI-IO optimization levels with the PIOViz jumpshot enhancement," in *Recent Advances in Parallel Virtual Machine and Message Passing Interface*, vol. 4757 of *LNCS*, pp. 213–222, Springer, 2007.
[5] A. Ching, A. Choudhary, W. keng Liao, L. Ward, and N. Pundit, "Evaluating I/O characteristics and methods for storing structured scientific data," in *Proceedings 20th IEEE International Parallel and Distributed Processing Symposium*, p. 49, IEEE Computer Society, April 2006.
[6] A. Chan, W. Gropp, and E. Lusk, "An efficient format for nearly constant-time access to arbitrary time intervals in large trace files," *Scientific Programming*, vol. 16, no. 2-3, pp. 155–165, 2008.
[7] Vampir. http://www.vampir.eu/.
[8] A. Knüpfer, R. Brendel, H. Brunst, H. Mix, and W. E. Nagel, "Introducing the open trace format (OTF)," in *Computational Science - ICCS 2006, Part II*, vol. 3992 of *LNCS*, pp. 526–533, Springer, 2006.
[9] Z. Szebenyi, B. J. N. Wylie, and F. Wolf, "SCALASCA parallel performance analyses of SPEC MPI2007 applications," in *Performance Evaluation: Metrics, Models and Benchmarks*, vol. 5119 of *LNCS*, pp. 99–123, Springer, 2008.
[10] S. S. Shende and A. D. Malony, "The tau parallel performance system," *The International Journal of High Performance Computing Applications*, vol. 20, pp. 287–311, Summer 2006.
[11] J. Labarta, J. Giménez, E. Martínez, P. González, H. Servat, G. Llort, and X. Aguilar, "Scalability of visualization and tracing tools," in *Proceedings of the International Conference ParCo 2005*, vol. 33 of *NIC Series*, pp. 869–876, John von Neumann Institute for Computing, Jülich, 2006.
[12] J. M. Kunkel and T. Ludwig, "Bottleneck detection in parallel file systems with trace-based performance monitoring," in *Euro-Par 2008 - Parallel Processing*, vol. 5168 of *LNCS*, pp. 212–221, Springer, 2008.

Communication Runtime

Parallel Computing: From Multicores and GPU's to Petascale
B. Chapman et al. (Eds.)
IOS Press, 2010
© 2010 The authors and IOS Press. All rights reserved.
doi:10.3233/978-1-60750-530-3-389

A Historic Knowledge Based Approach for Dynamic Optimization

Saber FEKI [a,1], and Edgar GABRIEL [a]

[a] *Department of Computer Science,*
University of Houston, Houston, TX 77204, USA

Abstract. Dynamic runtime optimization is a means to tune the performance of operations on a given platform while executing the application itself. However, most approaches discussed in literature so far fail for applications which have an adaptive and irregular behavior. In this paper, we present an algorithm which is able to incorporate knowledge gathered from previous optimizations to speed up the dynamic tuning procedure. We present the integration of the algorithm within a dynamic runtime optimization library along with a smoothing mechanism of the historic data entries to deal with outliers and inaccuracies in the knowledge base. The approach is evaluated for two separate parallel adaptive application kernels on three different platforms.

Keywords. adaptive communication library, historic learning, adaptive applications

Introduction

The complexity of today's clusters and high end resources mandate significant efforts by end users and application developers to tune their code for each particular platform. Processor and node-architecture, network interconnect and the software stack all expose a significant number of parameters which influence the performance of an application. Furthermore, these parameters are often correlated, which further complicates the predictability of the performance of any application. Many projects tackle the performance problem by applying a static tuning prior to the execution of the application, i.e. the performance of different versions of the same operation is evaluated for certain problem sizes and the best performing version is chosen for the subsequent executions of the application. This approach has been applied by projects such as ATLAS [1].

Alternatively, dynamic runtime optimization such as used within FFTW [2], PhiPac [3], STAR-MPI [4] and ADCL [5] has been used to tune an operation while executing the application itself. The main advantage of this approach is that it allows to incorporate parameters that can only be determined at runtime, such as process placement by the batch scheduler due to non-uniform network behavior [6], resource utilization due to the fact that some resources such as the network switch or file systems are shared by multiple applications, operating system jitter leading to slow-down of a subset of pro-

---

[1]Corresponding Author

cesses utilized by a parallel job [7] and application characteristics (e.g., communication volume and frequencies).

Dynamic runtime optimization works well for iterative applications working on a fixed problem size, since the same operations is executed repeatedly for exactly the same process count and problem size. Thus, the library has the opportunity to test which version of the according operation works best. This condition is however not given for an adaptive application, where the problem size might change frequently, e.g. by locally refining the computational mesh based on a given error criteria. In fact, the runtime optimization library might not be able to perform the optimization before the problem size changes, and thus the application will typically not benefit at all from the runtime tuning. For these type of applications, a different runtime tuning approach is required.

We have recently presented an algorithm for incorporating results gathered in previous executions, historic data, into an adaptive communication library called ADCL (Abstract Data and Communication Library) [8], which allows to overcome the disadvantages of runtime optimization libraries as described above. In this paper we demonstrate an actual implementation of the algorithm described previously, present some improvements to the algorithm itself and evaluate the performance costs and benefits when using our new approach for two adaptive applications on three different platforms.

The remainder of the paper is organized as follows: Section 1 gives a brief overview of the Abstract Data and Communication Library (ADCL). In section 2 we describe the notion of historic learning and its implementation details in ADCL. Section 3 presents the performance evaluation of this technique for two adaptive application kernels. Finally, section 4 summarizes the work and gives an overview about the currently ongoing research.

1. The Abstract Data and Communication Library

The Abstract Data and Communication Library (ADCL) [5] enables the creation of self-optimizing applications by allowing them to register alternative versions of a particular function. The alternative code versions are grouped in an ADCL function-set, one of the main objects in the ADCL notation. ADCL incorporates predefined function-sets for some highly popular communication patterns such as the n-dimensional neighborhood communication. The library uses the initial iterations of the application to determine the fastest available code version. Once performance data on a sufficient number of versions is available, the library makes a decision on which alternative to use throughout the rest of the execution.

ADCL introduces the notion of attributes, which can be used to describe characteristics of a particular implementation. Examples of attributes characterizing an implementation for communication operations are: the communication pattern used to implement an operation (e.g. binary tree, flat tree, etc.), methods for handling non-contiguous data items (pack/unpack vs. derived data types), and data transfer primitives (synchronous, asynchronous, one-sided). An advantage of annotating code versions using attributes is that the library can use more efficient optimization algorithms internally during the selection phase, resulting in lower overall execution times of the applications.

ADCL has been used successfully to tune the neighborhood communication in CFD codes [5], parallel matrix-matrix multiply operations [10], and the InfiniBand parameters of Open MPI [11].

2. Historic Learning

Dynamic optimization techniques as described in the previous sections can not be applied directly to adaptive applications such as CFD simulations using adaptive mesh refinements. The main restriction of current approaches stems from the fact, that traditional tuning techniques take too long to evaluate various alternatives and determine the best performing version for an operation. Adaptive applications on the other hand work on a fixed problem size for a very short time frame, e.g. a couple of time-steps. We describe here an algorithm which can incorporate performance data of previous executions to speed up the decision logic (Historic Learning).

The motivation behind this approach lies in the fact, that once an operation has been tuned for a particular problem size, the same 'optimal solution' can be applied for many other problem sizes which are close to the originally tuned problem size. The challenge lies in determining how to define a distance measure for various operations, and how to determine the maximum distance where the decision of the result of the previous optimization still applies.

Data Gathering Once a particular operation/function-set has been evaluated for a given problem size, the dynamic run-time tuning library stores *problem characteristics* as well as the corresponding *performance data* for that problem in a history file. The Characterization of the problem consists of the operation which has been optimized, the set of alternative versions which have been explored for that operation, and optionally the attributes and attribute values for each version. Furthermore, it identifies the logical process topology used by the application which contains information about the number of processes used and the logical relation between them in and finally the problem size.

The problem size is an operation specific characterization of the dimensions utilized by the application. For a regular n-dimensional neighborhood communication, the problem size can be described by the length of the messages used to communicate with each of the neighboring processes. The focus of the algorithms presented in the subsequent paragraphs will be on identifying similar problems based on varying problem sizes, which will require a meaningful distance measure between two problem sizes for a given function set.

The second component in the history file contains performance data for a successfully tuned operation. This contains the execution time of the fastest version found in the function-set and the according optimal attribute values. Furthermore, the history file includes the performance data for all other versions tested.

Data Analysis The starting point for the historic data analysis is a given number of entries (N) in the history file for a particular operation. We define the *acceptable performance window* p_{max} as the relative maximum tolerable performance deviation compared to the best performing version of the operation. For each entry in the history file, the algorithm determines the *top cluster*, i.e. the group of alternative versions whose execution time is within $p_{max}\%$ of the execution time of the version which achieved the best performance for that problem size.

The next step requires the definition of a distance metric between two problems. Although in its most general notion the distance will be an operation specific measure, for many operations it is straight forward to use the euclidean distance by using for instance the dimensions of the problem size per process. For each entry E_k we determine the distance to all other entries E_i, $i=1..N$, $i \neq k$ in the history file, and whether the winner version of the entry E_k is in the top cluster of the entry E_i. If this relationship is verified, a flag in a boolean array is marked as *true* for the entry E_i. Once the relationship of all entries to the entry E_k has been evaluated, the boolean array is sorted according to the distance of the entries to E_k. The result of this analysis step is the maximum distance D_{max} for the data entry E_k of the history file which is defined as the distance to the last entry in the boolean array, until which *all* entries are marked as *true*.

The maximum distance quantifies for a given entry, that the winner version of a problem size within this distance leads to an acceptable performance, acceptable being defined as not more than $p_{max}\%$ above the optimal performance. The algorithm outlined above could be run in a post-processing analysis step or at the end of each optimization step. The maximum distance for each entry in the history file is stored along with all the other information outlined in the previous subsection to be reused for next optimizations.

Data Smoothing   In our experiment using historic learning, we noticed the sensitivity of the algorithm to even a single outlier. As a result, a data entry which has a completely different solution than its neighbors can significantly reduce the maximum distance for a given problem size and therefore, the contribution of the according data entry to the selection logic using historic learning will be limited. To overcome this problem, we extended the original algorithm presented in [8] by a smoothing operation of the problems relationship array described in the previous subsection. The smoothing operation will be based on a sliding window, similarly to morphological smoothing operations often applied in digital image processing and flips a 0 to 1 if most of the neighbors within the window have a value of 1.

Historic Data Entries										
0	1	2	3	4	5	6	7	8	9	Maximum Distance D_{max}
Initial Relation Array										
1	1	1	0	1	1	1	0	0	0	Distance(0,2)
Smoothed Relation Array										
1	1	1	1	1	1	1	0	0	0	Distance(0,6)

Figure 1. Smoothing Operation and Maximum Distance.

Figure 1 shows an example of 10 data entries and the corresponding relationship array in which data entry 3 is an outlier. The resulting maximum distance is then equal to the distance between the data entries 0 and 2 although all data entries from 4 to 6 are marked as *true* as well. However, after applying the smoothing operation, the maximum distance is extended significantly to the distance between the data entries 0 and 6 omitting the outlier data entry 3.

Runtime Selection Logic utilizing Historic Data   In the following we outline the alternative algorithms which can be used to predict the best performing version for an new problem based on historic data and the outcome of the analysis described above. We suggest two different prediction algorithms using some computationally inexpensive heuristics. Given a new problem size PSNew, the first algorithm *PredictFromClosest* predicts the code version by taking the winner version of the closest problem size in the history file, if PSNew is within the maximum distance determined for the closest problem size.

Alternatively, algorithm *PredictFromSimilar* suggests to use the winner of a weighted majority vote from the similar problem sizes available in the history file, considering again only the problem sizes for which PSNew is within their defined maximum distance as a result of the historic data analysis. The weight attributed to the winner of a valid entry is proportional to its distance from PSNew. Note, that the algorithm as presented in [8] also contains conditions for skipping historic data, which we omit here due to space restrictions.

2.1. Implementation Details

If the application uses the ADCL API to register its own function-set for optimization, it has to provide some additional functions and information in order to utilize the historic learning feature. However, for predefined function sets supported by ADCL, the library provides all required details and functionalities to use this novel feature. The input to be provided to the library are basically two data structures.

The first one contains four function pointers as follow: (I) two functions for reading and writing an entry from/to the history file, (II) a filtering function that identify which entries from the history are relevant for the historic learning, (III) a distance function in order to provide a proximity measure between two entries in the history file.

The second structure contains the criteria to be used by the filtering function and a pointer to a function which initializes it from the information stored in the main ADCL object.

3. Evaluation

The goal of this section is to evaluate the new concept of historic learning and the accuracy of the proposed prediction algorithm using a weighted majority vote of similar problem sizes. We determine its potential performance benefit especially in the case of an adaptive application. We used in our experiments three different platforms: a cluster consisting of 24 nodes, each having a dual core AMD Opteron processor, using either a 4xInfiniBand (Shark-IB) or a Gigabit Ethernet network interconnect (Shark-GE), and a 648 processors SiCortex system.

3.1. Historic Learning Prediction Accuracy

In this part, we assess the prediction accuracy of the historic learning feature integrated in ADCL. We first generated the history file using a simple benchmark optimizing a large set of problem sizes for the three dimensional neighborhood communication using ADCL. 42 different problem sizes, from 32x32x32 to 64x64x64 mesh points per process, are evaluated with the ADCL brute force selection algorithm. For each implementation we executed 100 iterations in order to get more accurate performance data.

The performance of two applications has been evaluated using ADCL and the history file described above. The first application is *solversys*. This application solves a set of linear equations that stem from discretization of a Partial Differential Equation (PDE) using center differences using an iterative solver. The second application is *parheat* [12], which solves the heat equation using an explicit scheme. In order to evaluate the historic learning capability to dynamically optimize applications with an adaptive behavior,

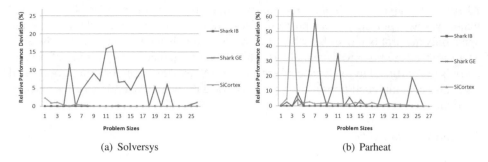

(a) Solversys   (b) Parheat

Figure 2. Performance Deviation according to the Historic Learning prediction accuracy for different applications on different platforms.

both applications have been extended to execute consecutively with 26 different problem sizes, emulating the behavior of an adaptive application. However, while *solversys* executes for each problem exactly the same number of fixed iterations, the execution time of *parheat* increases with the number of grid points.

Both applications use ADCL for the 3-D neighborhood communication, which is a pre-defined function-set within ADCL. Thus, all the necessary data structures related to historic learning are already implemented by the library. The distance measure used is the Euclidean distance between the message lengths to be transferred in each direction.

We first executed each of the 26 problem sizes using each of the available implementations of the neighborhood communication individually with both applications, bypassing the dynamic tuning logic of ADCL. We refer to these executions as the verification runs. We executed afterward the simulated adaptive application with the historic learning feature enabled and using the history file generated as described previously using 2 different applications on 3 different platforms. In the figures 2(a) and 2(b), we show for each problem size the relative performance gap between the implementation selected by the prediction algorithm and the best one according to the verification runs. In most cases, the prediction algorithm chooses the best performing function. Otherwise, most of the selected implementations (except in few problem sizes) show a performance within the acceptable performance window. In average, the performance deviation due to the accuracy of the predictions is ranging from 0.23 % to 7.72%, which is quiet good taking into account that we specified the acceptable performance window to be 10% (a reasonable value a typical user might set). We notice however two major peaks with parheat which result from inaccuracies in the prediction due to the fact, that the corresponding problem size was on the boundaries of a transition from one winner function to another. Note the effect of the smoothing operation, which lead to an improvement of the performance of solversys by 4.53% and of parheat by a 2.66% on Gigabit Ethernet. This improvement is due to a better predicted implementation in a couple of problem sizes when using a smoothing window of size 5 that eliminate any outlier from the history data.

3.2. Historic Learning Performance Benefit

As of now, we have demonstrated that the algorithms presented in the previous section can automatically predict with a reasonable accuracy the version to be used for a new scenario. In this second part of this section, we show the overall performance benefit of using the historic learning feature integrated in ADCL for an adaptive application.

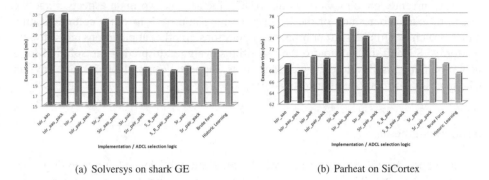

(a) Solversys on shark GE   (b) Parheat on SiCortex

Figure 3. Performance Comparison of an adaptive application utilizing the the ADCL implementations, the Brute Force Search and Historic Learning on different platforms.

We evaluate the overall execution time of the application using all available implementations of the 3D neighborhood communication in ADCL. Furthermore, we evaluate the performance of the application when using the the brute force search algorithm and finally when using a historic knowledge base generated as in the previous subsection.

Fig. 3(a) show the results obtained using 48 processes on the same cluster using the Gigabit Ethernet/Infiniband interconnects. The results for the Solversys application indicate, that the brute force search approach is performing better than many implementations. We notice however the overhead of using this tuning approach, mostly due to the fact that for each of the 26 problem sizes, the selection algorithm is restarted and the evaluation might include executing and evaluating implementations which are inefficient for the platform/problem size. As has been shown in [9] excluding these implementations at all is problematic, due to the fact that very different implementations lead to the best performance in different platforms and for different problem sizes.

The performance of the application is improved by using the historic learning capability within ADCL, which skips testing the under-performing implementations. This version of the code outperforms any static alternatives, which would use a single implementation for the neighborhood communication, due to its ability to switch between different "'best versions'" that vary according to the problem size. Note that the results were also very similar for the Parheat application as in Fig. 3(b) on 256 processors of the SiCortex system as well as in the other platforms.

4. Conclusion

We presented in this paper, a novel technique to speed up the dynamic tuning procedure within ADCL using the historic knowledge gathered from previous optimizations. We described the implementation details of our approach within ADCL and demonstrated that the performance of two parallel applications showing a dynamic behavior is significantly improved using this feature. The results indicates that after applying the smoothing operation that handle nosy data, the prediction algorithm using a weighted majority vote from relevant data entries succeeds to select in most case a solution whose performance is within an acceptable performance window. The overall execution time of the adaptive applications is even better than the best possible using a single implementation.

The currently ongoing work within ADCL focuses on two main aspects. First, we intend to extend our study of the historic learning approach to other communication patterns such as circular shift or broadcast operations, to other applications and different platforms. Second, in addition to the algorithms designed to predict the solution for a new problem, classification techniques such as Support Vector Machines and Baysian Classifier are currently being investigated.

Acknowledgments

Partial support for this work was provided by the National Science Foundation's gunder award no. CNS-0846002. Any opinions, findings, and conclusions or recommendations expressed in this material are those of the authors and do not necessarily reflect the views of the National Science Foundation.

References

[1]   R. C. Whaley and A. Petite, "Minimizing development and maintenance costs in supporting persistently optimized BLAS," *Software: Practice and Experience*, vol. 35, no. 2, pp. 101–121, 2005.

[2]   M. Frigo and S. G. Johnson, "The Design and Implementation of FFTW3," *Proceedings of IEEE*, vol. 93, no. 2, pp. 216–231, 2005.

[3]   R. Vuduc, J. W. Demmel, and J. A. Bilmes, "Statistical Models for Empirical Search-Based Performance Tuning," *International Journal for High Performance Computing Applications*, vol. 18, no. 1, pp. 65–94, 2004.

[4]   A. Faraj, X. Yuan, and D. Lowenthal, "STAR-MPI: self tuned adaptive routines for MPI collective operations," in *ICS '06: Proceedings of the 20th Annual International Conference on Supercomputing*. New York, NY, USA: ACM Press, 2006, pp. 199–208.

[5]   E. Gabriel, S. Feki, K. Benkert, and M. Chaarawi, "The Abstract Data and Communication Library," *Journal of Algorithms and Computational Technology*, vol. 2, no. 4, pp. 581–600, 2008.

[6]   J. J. Evans, C. S. Hood, and W. Gropp, "Exploring the relationship between parallel application run-time variability and network performance in clusters," in *28th Annual IEEE Conference on Local Computer Networks (LCN 2003)*, 2003, pp. 538–547.

[7]   F. Petrini, D. J. Kerbyson, and S. Pakin, "The Case of the Missing Supercomputer Performance: Achieving Optimal Performance on the 8,192 Processors of ASCI Q," in *SC '03: Proceedings of the 2003 ACM/IEEE conference on Supercomputing*.   Washington, DC, USA: IEEE Computer Society, 2003, p. 55.

[8]   S. Feki and E. Gabriel, "Incorporating Historic Knowledge into a Communication Library for Self-Optimizing High Performance Computing Applications," in *SASO '08: Proceedings of the 2008 Second IEEE International Conference on Self-Adaptive and Self-Organizing Systems*.   Venice, Italy: IEEE Computer Society, October 2008, pp. 265–274.

[9]   E. Gabriel, S. Feki, K. Benkert, and M. M. Resch, "Towards Performance and Portability through Run-time Adaption for High Performance Computing Applications," in *International Supercomputing Conference*, Dresden, Germany, June 2008.

[10]   S. Huang, "Applying Adaptive Software Technologies for Scientific Applications," Master Thesis, Department of Computer Science, University of Houston, 2007.

[11]   M. Chaarawi, J. M. Squyres, E. Gabriel, and S. Feki, "A tool for optimizing runtime parameters of open mpi," in *Proceedings of the 15th European PVM/MPI Users' Group Meeting on Recent Advances in Parallel Virtual Machine and Message Passing Interface*.   Berlin, Heidelberg: Springer-Verlag, 2008, pp. 210–217.

[12]   M. Resch, and B. Sander, "A comparison of OpenMP and MPI for the parallel CFD test case", in *Proceedings of the 1st European Workshop on OpenMP (EWOMP'99)*, pp. 71-75, 1999

Parallel Computing: From Multicores and GPU's to Petascale
B. Chapman et al. (Eds.)
IOS Press, 2010
© 2010 The authors and IOS Press. All rights reserved.
doi:10.3233/978-1-60750-530-3-397

Evaluation of Task Mapping Strategies for Regular Network Topologies

Sebastian RINKE [a], Torsten MEHLAN [a] and Wolfgang REHM [a]

[a] *Chemnitz University of Technology*
Computer Architecture Group
Strasse der Nationen 62
09107 Chemnitz
{rinke, tome, rehm}@cs.tu-chemnitz.de

Abstract. The Message Passing Interface (MPI) standard defines virtual topologies for optimizing the placement of processes onto processors in order to reduce communication time. That means, processes with their main communication paths represent a graph that has to be cost efficiently mapped onto the actual communication network. In this context, focusing on regular topologies, state-of-the-art mapping strategies that can be applied to any combination of process/network topology are compared in a two stage approach. First, mapping quality is assessed by a theoretical communication cost measure. Second, based on these results, the most promising methods, which were implemented in Open MPI, are practically compared regarding gain in communication time using MPI's topology mechanism. Finally, a close correspondence between theoretical measure and actual communication time is shown. Additionally, benchmark results prove that optimized process-to-processor mappings can improve communication time by up to 40%, compared to the default linear mapping in many MPI implementations. The findings in this paper can serve as reference not only for MPI implementors, but also for researchers investigating static process-to-processor mappings, in general.

Keywords. Network topologies, MPI, graph mapping, virtual topology

Introduction

The execution time of a parallel program is determined by two factors: Time required for (i) computation and (ii) communication. In MPI [1] the user is responsible for distributing load equally across processors so as to reduce computation time. Regarding communication, MPI defines a topology mechanism which may assist the runtime system in mapping processes onto the underlying sytem architecture, efficiently. That means, the user provides the communication pattern of their processes in form of an undirected graph (virtual topology) to the MPI runtime environment. The result is an assignment of those processes onto processors taking the physical network topology into account in order to reduce communication time. However, in many MPI implementations, this mapping mechanism is trivially implemented by consecutively assigning chunks of processes to processors (linear mapping), regardless of the physical topology. Most authors dealing with task mapping either introduce algorithms for specific process/network topology combinations or do not correlate their results to those of others. Hence, this work compares existing mapping strategies, that accept any combination of process/network topology, in respect of their suitability for optimizing the MPI topology mechanism. However, due to that process/network topologies are mostly regular in practice and the increase of multicore processors, we consider mappings of regular process topologies (m processes) onto regular network topologies (n processors), $m > n$. The next section introduces the mapping problem more formally and discusses cost functions for evaluating the quality of mappings theoretically. Then, a brief overview about the most promising mapping strategies under consideration is given. Section 3 discusses theoretical and practical benchmark results. Finally, the last section concludes.

1. The Mapping Problem

This section describes the form of the mapping problem as it is dealt with in the following. The virtual topology of an MPI program can be represented as a graph $G_v = (V_v, E_v)$, where V_v is the set of processes and E_v the pairs of primarily communicating processes. Similarly, the underlying network topology is described by a graph $G_n = (V_n, E_n)$, where V_n are the processors and E_n the network links between them. Note that the number of processes $|V_v|$ is assumed to be greater than the number of processors $|V_n|$. Furthermore, two functions are given: $w_n: V_n \rightarrow \mathbb{N} \setminus \{0\}$ and $c_n: V_n \times V_n \rightarrow \mathbb{R}$. The former, $w_n(v)$, denotes how many processes have to be assigned to processor v, and the latter, $c_n(u,v)$, the cost to communicate between the processors u and v. Finally, the objective is to find a mapping $\pi: V_v \rightarrow V_n$ which satisfies the size constraints given by w_n and minimizes a mapping cost function.

1.1. Mapping Cost Functions

In order to reduce communication time, the mapping cost function must be chosen carefully. In general, communication time is mainly determined by: (*i*) Network latency, bandwidth, contention, (*ii*) size, frequency of the messages sent, (*iii*) number of hops each message has to travel. Given a fixed application to be run on a fixed architecture, the only two parameters from those above that can be influenced is network contention and number of hops per message. Hence, the following metrics seem to be suitable for a mapping cost function. For the sake of completeness, a new measure $c_v(s,t)$ is introduced. It represents the amount of communication required between two processes s and t.

1.1.1. Edge Cut (Φ)

In its most general form, the edge cut Φ is the total weight of cut edges, i.e., communication requirements between processes that are mapped onto different processors.

$$\Phi = \sum_{\substack{\{u,v\} \in E_v \\ \pi(u) \neq \pi(v)}} c_v(u,v), \quad \tilde{\Phi} = \sum_{\substack{\{u,v\} \in E_v \\ \pi(u) \neq \pi(v)}} 1$$

Hence, it accounts for the success of hiding communication in processors (intra-node communication). On the other hand, the edge cut does not consider differences in communication cost between processors. Thus, it is only suitable for modelling uniform communication cost. In connection with the MPI mapping problem, the edge cut measure is reduced to $\tilde{\Phi}$. This is due to the fact that the virtual topology graph, as defined in MPI, is unweighted. For that reason, in this context, the edge cut counts the number of edges from the virtual topology graph G_v whose vertices are assigned to different processors under a mapping π.

1.1.2. Weighted Edge Cut (Γ)

An extension of the edge cut Φ leads to the weighted edge cut. That means, every communication requirement between two processes is weighted by a factor denoting the cost to communicate between the two processors which the two processes are mapped onto. In other words, the weighted edge cut measure favours intra-node communication and considers non-uniform network communication cost. Thus,

$$\Gamma = \sum_{\substack{\{u,v\} \in E_v \\ \pi(u) \neq \pi(v)}} c_v(u,v) \cdot c_n(\pi(u), \pi(v)),$$

and in terms of the MPI mapping problem,

$$\tilde{\Gamma} = \sum_{\substack{\{u,v\} \in E_v \\ \pi(u) \neq \pi(v)}} c_n(\pi(u), \pi(v)),$$

since G_v is unweighted and c_n is not in the scope of the MPI standard (i.e., an MPI library may consider non-uniform communication cost in an interconnection network during process-to-processor mapping optimization).

1.1.3. Conclusion

Based on the discussion above, the weighted edge cut Γ is the cost function of choice. [2] and [3] also adopted this measure and [2] showed its practical relevance to modelling communication time. Finally, that means, mappings for the MPI mapping problem are theoretically evaluated in the following according to $\tilde{\Gamma}$.

1.2. Formalization

Based on the information given so far, it is possible to give a more formal description of the MPI mapping problem. Considering networks with uniform communication cost leads to a variant of the k-way graph partitioning problem ($k = |V_n|$): Given a graph $G_v = (V_v, E_v)$ with $|V_v|$ vertices, the number of subsets $k \in \mathbb{N}\setminus\{0\}$, and k subset sizes $s_1, \ldots, s_k \in \mathbb{N}\setminus\{0\}$ with $\sum_{i=1}^{k} s_i = |V_v|$. Find a partition π, $\pi: V_v \to \{V_1, \ldots, V_k\}$, of V_v into k disjoint sets $V_1, \ldots, V_k$ such that (i) $|V_i| = s_i$, $i = 1, \ldots, k$, and (ii) $\tilde{\Phi} \longrightarrow$ min. Here, (i) reflects the size constraints of the processors and (ii) denotes the minimization of the edge cut $\tilde{\Phi}$. The graph partitioning problem is known to be NP-complete [4].

Regarding networks with non-uniform communication cost, the MPI mapping problem can be summarized as: Given a graph $G_n = (V_n, E_n)$ with $|V_n|$ vertices, a function $w_n: V_n \to \mathbb{N}\setminus\{0\}$, and a second function $c_n: V_n \times V_n \to \mathbb{R}$. Given a second graph $G_v = (V_v, E_v)$ with $|V_v|$ vertices. The objective is to find a function π, $\pi: V_v \to V_n$, that assigns every vertex in V_v to any vertex in V_n such that (i) $|\{j \in V_v \mid \pi(j) = i\}| = w_n(i)$, $i = 1, \ldots, |V_n|$, and (ii) $\tilde{\Gamma} \longrightarrow$ min. Similarly as above, (i) guarantees to satisfy the size constraints of the processors, and (ii) stands for the minimization of the weighted edge cut $\tilde{\Gamma}$. This is a generalization of the graph partitioning problem and thus NP-complete,

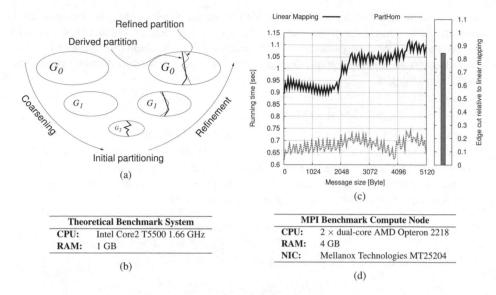

Figure 1. (a) Multilevel graph bipartitioning approach (b) Theoretical results benchmark system (c) Mapping with uniform communication cost: 8×6 2D torus $\rightarrow$ fully connected network (d) MPI benchmark node type

as well. As consequence, mapping heuristics which approximate good solutions in polynomial time are needed.

2. Mapping Strategies

This section describes a subset of the algorithms under consideration, i.e., the reference method and the most promising strategies. For details about all the methods listed in the benchmark results, see [5]. Note that some implementations of algorithms are part of so-called graph partitioning packages such as CHACO [6], METIS [7], JOSTLE [8], and SCOTCH [9]. Hence, the names of the respective packages appear in the strategy names, if necessary. For the sake of convenience, all the methods below are assumed to get the same input, i.e., a virtual topology graph $G_v = (V_v, E_v)$ with the processes numbered $0, \ldots, |V_v| - 1$, and a network topology graph $G_n = (V_n, E_n)$ with the processors $0, \ldots, |V_n| - 1$.

2.1. CHACO *Linear*

The linear scheme, implemented in CHACO [6], is used as reference method, since it is the most common mapping strategy among MPI implementations. Let $|V_v|/|V_n|$ be an integer k, and the processes to be distributed equally across the processors, then $\pi(i) = i \, DIV \, k$, $i \in V_v$. In other words, the first k processes are assigned to processor 0, the next k to processor 1, etc. This yields a mapping that is not aware of any topology information. The complexity is in $O(|V_v|)$.

2.2. CHACO *MLRB*

CHACO multilevel recursive bisectioning (MLRB) is a k-way graph partitioning method that partitions the graph G_v into $|V_n|$ parts by means of recursive bipartitioning (bisectioning) of G_v. That means, starting with the graph G_v, in every step a subgraph of G_v is partitioned into two parts by a multilevel graph bipartitioning algorithm (see below). Finally, CHACO MLRB stops if $|V_n|$ parts were created. The idea of multilevel graph bipartitioning is described in three phases. First – *coarsening phase*, a sequence of increasingly smaller graphs approximating the original graph is created. This is accomplished by contracting edges, i.e., combining vertices. Second – *initial partitioning phase*, the smallest graph is partitioned into two parts. One way to do this is to simply assign half of the vertices to one part and the rest to the other part. Third – *refinement phase*, based on the bipartitioning of the smallest graph and the information about which edges were contracted in the coarsening phase, bipartitionings for all the intermediate (smaller) graphs from the coarsening phase are derived on the path from the smallest up to the original graph. Additionally, the bipartitionings derived on that path are further refined to improve partition quality. Finally, the result is a bipartitioning of the original graph. Figure 1a illustrates the three phases of multilevel graph bipartitioning. More details can be found in [10]. The complexity of CHACO MLRB is $O(|E_v| \log |V_n|)$.

2.3. Tarun Agarwal

This strategy [11], named after the author, is based on a two phase approach. First, in the partitioning phase, the processes V_v are partitioned into $|V_n|$ sets such that heavily communicating processes are placed in the same set. This stage does not consider the actual network topology. Second, in the mapping phase, the $|V_n|$ sets are mapped onto the $|V_n|$ processors such that frequently communicating sets are assigned to nearby processors. Hence, information about non-uniformity in network communication cost is used. Our implementation uses PartHom [5], an implementation based on CHACO MLRB, in the partitioning phase, and, the algorithm proposed by T. Agarwal et al. [11] in the mapping phase, whose complexity is, according to [11], in $O(|V_n||E_v|)$. Hence, the total running time is $O(|E_v| \log |V_n| + |V_n||E_v|) = O(|V_n||E_v|)$.

2.4. Takanobu Baba

The approach by T. Baba et al. [12] considers non-uniform communication cost and proceeds as follows. In each step, a process from the process graph G_v is chosen and allocated to a processor of G_n. Thereby, once allocated, a process is not migrated to a different processor. The most important aspect of this method are the different allocation selection criteria for processes and processors. Selection criteria for processes are, for example, the number of links with already allocated processes and the number of links with all the other processes. Similarly, a processor is selected by total communication cost with already allocated processes and the number of processes that have been allocated to other processors, for instance. More details about those selection criteria can be found in [12]. The complexity of our implementation is $O(|V_v|^2 \log |V_v|)$.

3. Results

This section evaluates mapping strategies in terms of mapping quality. First, mappings are compared according to the (weighted) edge cut. Then, based on this, the most promising techniques are examined regarding reduction in communication time. Finally, a

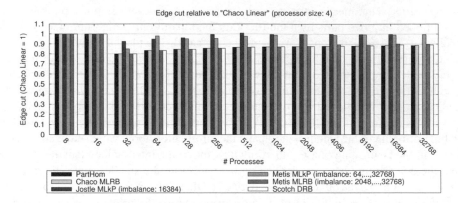

Figure 2. Mapping with uniform communication cost: 3D grid → fully connected network

close correspondence between (weighted) edge cut and communication time is shown. Throughout this section, $|V_v| = 4|V_n|$ and perfect load balance is required, i.e., a valid mapping assigns four processes to each processor. Furthermore, regarding the topologies under consideration, processes/processors are distributed among the dimensions in a balanced way.

3.1. Theoretical Results

In the following, the linear mapping, implemented in CHACO Linear, is used as reference algorithm. Thus, values less than one denote an improvement over the linear mapping. Note that some results are missing for larger process counts. The reason is that mappings were computed for running times < 1 min on the system in Fig. 1b. Fig. 2 shows the results of mapping 3D grid process topologies onto fully connected networks. Since communication cost is uniform in this network, the edge cut Φ is used as quality measure. As it can be seen, especially, the strategies based on recursive bisectioning (MLRB) yield an improved edge cut of about $10 - 20\%$ compared to the linear mapping. Regarding networks with non-uniform communication cost, the weighted edge cut $\tilde{\Gamma}$ is used for quality assessment. The first example is mappings of 2D grids onto 2D grids. It seems obvious that such a combination offers much room for optimization. Fig. 3a shows this with a reduction in the weighted edge cut of about 50% for allmost all strategies. Especially, T. Agarwal's approach yields good results, even for larger problem sizes, in an acceptable amount of time (≈ 1 min). Another example is that of mapping hypercubes onto 3D tori (Fig. 3b). Generally, all but two algorithms yield results that are equal to or worse than the linear mapping. These two, T. Agarwal and T. Baba, have similar results although they use substantially different approaches.

3.2. Practical Results

The basis for this section is the integration of the most promising mapping strategies into Open MPI's process topology mechanism. That means, we consider the effect of the choice of the mapping algorithm on communication time. The corresponding benchmark first creates a new communicator with `MPI_Cart_create()` for the process topology under consideration. In this step the mapping strategy which is to be evaluated is executed

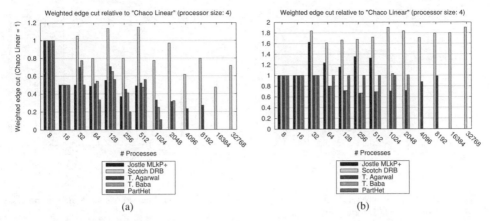

Figure 3. Mappings with non-uniform communication cost: (a) 2D grid → 2D grid (b) Hypercube → 3D torus

to reorder process ranks for an optimized process-to-processor mapping. Then, for each message size, time is taken while each process in that new communicator exchanges 5000 messages with each of its neighbours as depicted in Listing 1. The benchmark system consists of 24 nodes (Fig. 1d), 12 per crossbar switch, that are part of a 530 nodes 2-stage Infiniband fat tree network. Fig. 1c shows the benchmark running times for a 2D torus virtual topology on 12 processors (one switch). As it can be seen PartHom reduces communication time by about 36%, which is also indicated by a reduction in the edge cut measure. Fig. 4a depicts the results for a 3D grid virtual topology. In this case, a benefit in communication time of about 40% can be observed for both PartHom and T. Agarwal. The reason is that PartHom is executed as part of the T. Agarwal method. The last example, however, (Fig. 4b) demonstrates how mapping quality (weighted edge cut) can become even worse with non-trivial mapping algorithms. In particular, the PartHet method yields a mapping whose weighted edge cut is about 10% worse compared to that of the linear mapping. As conseqeuence, communication time increases by 24%. Nevertheless, this also shows that the weighted edge cut is appropriate to assess the impact of different process-to-processor mappings on communication time.

```
1   /* Data exchange along each dimension */
    for (dim = 0; dim < ndims; dim++) {
        MPI_Cart_shift(comm_cart, dim, 1, &rank_pred, &rank_succ);
4       MPI_Sendrecv(sbuffer, size, MPI_CHAR, rank_succ, 1,
                     rbuffer, size, MPI_CHAR, rank_pred, 1,
                     comm_cart, &status);
7       MPI_Sendrecv(sbuffer, size, MPI_CHAR, rank_pred, 1,
                     rbuffer, size, MPI_CHAR, rank_succ, 1,
                     comm_cart, &status);
10  }
```

Listing 1 Data exchange with neighbours in virtual topology

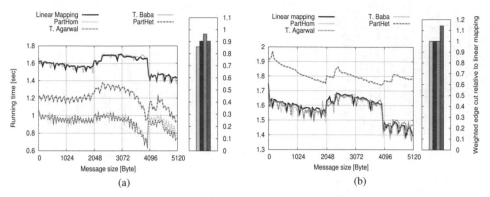

Figure 4. Influence of process-to-processor mapping on communication time: (a) $6 \times 4 \times 4$ 3D grid process topology (b) $6 \times 4 \times 4$ 3D torus process topology

4. Conclusion

We showed that an optimized MPI topology mechanism can improve communication time by up to 40%. However, if and to what extent a benefit can be achieved clearly depends on the mapping strategy. That means, future work could deal with how to decide which strategy to use. One factor was already given, the weighted edge cut, which was shown to be closely related to actual communication time. More details and results can be found in [5]. In order to obtain our extension of Open MPI, please contact the authors.

References

[1]   Marc Snir, Steve W. Otto, Steven Huss-Lederman, David W. Walker, and Jack Dongarra. *MPI: The Complete Reference. Volume 1, The MPI-1 Core*. MIT Press, Cambridge, MA, USA, 1998.
[2]   Gyan Bhanot, Alan Gara, Philip Heidelberger, Eoin Lawless, James C. Sexton, and Robert Walkup. Optimizing task layout on the blue gene/L supercomputer. *IBM Journal of Research and Development*, 49(2-3):489–500, 2005.
[3]   Sangman Moh, Chansu Yu, Hee Yong Youn, Ben Lee, and Dongsoo Han. Mapping strategies for switch-based cluster systems of irregular topology. In *ICPADS*, pages 733–740, 2001.
[4]   M. R. Garey and D. S. Johnson. *Computers and intractability; a guide to the theory of NP-completeness*. W.H. Freeman, 1979.
[5]   Sebastian Rinke. Analysis and adaption of gaph mapping algorithms for regular graph topologies. http://archiv.tu-chemnitz.de/pub/2009/0145, April 2009. Master's thesis.
[6]   Bruce Hendrickson and Robert Leland. *The Chaco User's Guide Version 2*. Sandia National Laboratories, Albuquerque NM, 1995.
[7]   George Karypis and Vipin Kumar. *METIS: Unstrctured Graph Partitioning and Sparse Matrix Ordering System, Version 4.0*, September 1998.
[8]   Chris Walshaw. *The serial JOSTLE library user guide: Version 3.0*. London, UK, July 2002.
[9]   François Pellegrini. *SCOTCH 5.0 Users Guide*, August 2007.
[10]   Bruce Hendrickson and Robert Leland. A multilevel algorithm for partitioning graphs. Technical Report SAND93-1301, Sandia National Laboratories, 1993. appeared in Proc. Supercomputing 95.
[11]   T. Agarwal, A. Sharma, and L. V. Kalé. Topology-aware task mapping for reducing communication contention on large parallel machines. In *Proc. IEEE International Parallel & Distributed Processing Symposium (20th IPDPS'06)*, Rhodes Island, Greece, April 2006. IEEE Computer Society.
[12]   Takanobu Baba, Yoshifumi Iwamoto, and Tsutomu Yoshinaga. A network-topology independent task allocation strategy for parallel computers. In *Proceedings Supercomputing'90*, pages 878–887, New York, November 1990. IEEE. Utsunomiya U.

Benchmark & Performance Tuning

Parallel Computing: From Multicores and GPU's to Petascale
B. Chapman et al. (Eds.)
IOS Press, 2010
© 2010 The authors and IOS Press. All rights reserved.
doi:10.3233/978-1-60750-530-3-407

Automatic Performance Tuning of Parallel Mathematical Libraries [1]

Ihab SALAWDEH[2], Anna MORAJKO, Eduardo CÉSAR, Tomàs MARGALEF,
Emilio LUQUE

*Departament d'Arquitectura de Computadors i Sistemes Operatius,
Universitat Autònoma de Barcelona, 08193 Bellaterra, SPAIN*

Abstract. Scientific and mathematical parallel libraries offer a high level of abstraction to programmers. However, their use involves a large number of decisions, such as choosing partitioning strategies, pre-conditioners, and solving strategies, which have a great impact on the performance of resulting applications. This work proposes a performance methodology for automatic tuning of applications written with the PETSc library. This methodology consists of strategies for: choosing the appropriate data representation and solving algorithms based on historical performance information and data mining techniques, distributing the workload among application processes, and taking advantage of the library memory pre-allocation capacities.

Keywords. Performance Models, Mathematical Libraries Performance.

Introduction

Writing a parallel program from the scratch to solve a mathematical problem is difficult because of the algorithms' complexity and the big effort and expertise needed. Consequently, parallel mathematical libraries [1-4] are used because they provide pre-implemented algorithms and interfaces for the linear system solvers that can be helpful in application development by scientists from different fields. They provide high level APIs that let the programmer to reuse these algorithms in the development of scientific applications without concerning the communication policies between the processors or the inner details of the algorithms. Such libraries support a large number of algorithms and users must provide many parameters to determine the algorithm and the data structures involved. Developing high performance libraries to solve mathematical problems is essential, since these problems needs massive computation and resources. The performance of these algorithms may vary according to the input data or the selection of the correct parameters. In addition, users should be aware of the data distribution among application processes to achieve the proper load balance.

Automatic performance tuning could help the scientists to develop high performance applications without delving into the complexity of the mathematical algorithms and the technical details of parallel programming. Thus, we have developed

---

[1] This research has been supported by the MEC-MICINN Spain under contract TIN2007-64974.

[2] Corresponding Author. Ihab Salawdeh, Departament d'Arquitectura de Computadors i Sistemes Operatius, Universitat Autònoma de Barcelona, 08193 Bellaterra, SPAIN; E-mail: Ihab.Salawdeh@caos.uab.es

a methodology for automatically tuning the selection between the different algorithms provided by the PETSc [3-4] library, in order to improve performance. This methodology aims to help the developer in choosing the most suitable algorithms and parameters depending on the problem characteristics and the input data provided by the user. Moreover, the methodology will also take into account workload balancing among the application processes.

Consequently, the methodology provides automatic identification of the structure and significant characteristics of the input data. Then, it compares the output of this recognition process against a comprehensive set of known cases. At the same time, it also has to include a mechanism to tune the data distribution to avoid load imbalances.

This paper is organized as follows: in section 1 the performance methodology is detailed. Next, in section 2, we show certain experimental results. Then, in section 3, the related efforts are discussed. Finally, our conclusions are presented in section 4.

1. Performance methodology

In order to develop the methodology to improve the performance of the PETSc library, we studied the behavior of applications written with this library and the effects on the performance of the input data and the algorithms' parameters provided by the user. The methodology, presented on figure 1, is based on:

- *A performance knowledgebase*, which contains historical information about previous executions of huge sets of algorithms, with different input data and data representations (e.g. sparse data structure, block diagonal data structures).
- *A data analysis module*, which is responsible for classifying the input data, and comparing it with the data patterns in the historical knowledgebase.
- *A mathematical constraint module*, which is the module responsible for checking mathematical restrictions on the input data. It is known that several solving methods can only be applied if the input data meets certain mathematical restrictions.
- *An application control module*, which is responsible for reconfiguring the application parameters with the parameters suggested by the data analysis component, controlling the solving process and validating the solution.
- *A load balancing module*, which is responsible for distributing the input data across the processors and for efficiently managing the memory allocation.

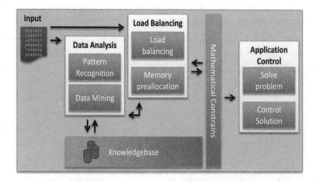

Figure 1. Automatic performance tuning methodology

1.1. Knowledgebase

The knowledgebase contains comprehensive performance information of linear algebraic problem executions. It contains results for different input data representations and all the available parallel solvers and pre-conditioners provided by PETSc. Every case was executed using different number of processors. Then, a reference patterns list was built and stored in the knowledgebase. Table 1 summarizes the input matrices, their sizes and the parameters on which they were executed.

Table 1. The Knowledgebase creating execution parameters.

Input Matrix	No. Processors	Matrix Size	Memory Representations	KSP Solvers	Preconditioners
Diagonal Tri-Diagonal Distributed Zero-Diagonal Lower-Triangular Around-Diagonal	1 8 16 32	1000 10000 20000	Sparse Dense Block Sparse Block Diagonal	BiCGStab BiCGStab(L) BiConjugate Gradient Conjugate Gradient Conj. Grad. Squared Chebychev Conjugate Residuals FGMRES GMRES LSQR Richardson TFQMR	Jacobi Bjacobi ASM

1.2. Data Analysis

The pattern recognition engine makes wide steps in finding the most suitable solving parameters by recognizing the data and summarizing its characteristics. This engine creates a pattern for each input matrix and classifies them by applying density calculation and structural analysis algorithms [5].

The number and the percentage of the nonzero entries in each of its pattern blocks represent the matrix density. The pattern recognition engine uses the City-Block (Manhattan) distance algorithm to calculate the density distance between the input matrix pattern and each knowledgebase pattern. A masking algorithm compares the distribution of the data inside the matrix without concerning about the data density or size; the only factor that affects this algorithm is the presence or the absence of a nonzero entry in the pattern blocks. It also compares matrices diagonal.

Therefore, the data mining engine starts searching for the most suitable solving parameter set in the knowledgebase. Beside the pattern information, the data mining engine takes into consideration other factors such as the real size of the matrix and the number of processors.

Then, the solver prediction component chooses the proper configuration according to the distance factors and the least execution time. If the solving process did not reach a correct solution using this configuration set, the last step will be repeated using the next best configuration until the correct solution reached.

1.3. Load balancing

Load balancing problem is one of the most common and important problems in parallel programming. Especially in mathematical applications because of the huge amount of data involved. The data structure creation, the data distribution and the memory allocation are very time-consuming, as much as the problem solving process in most parallel mathematical applications.

In a mathematical library like PETSc the default data distribution does not provide automatic load balancing policies. The library's default distribution spreads the data between the processors based on the real dimension of the matrix assigning approximately the same number of rows per processor; which, particularly in case of sparse matrices, may lead to a poor performance.

We propose an automatic data distribution where the data is distributed between the processors based on the number of nonzero values of the matrix, not on the matrix number of rows, according to expressions 1 and 2. Moreover, we define performance as the reduction in execution time, the improvement of the memory utilization and the allocation efficiency.

$$values\ per\ processor = \frac{Total\ values}{number\ of\ processors} \tag{1}$$

$$rows\ per\ processor = r_p - r_{p-1}\ \forall\ p\ [1 - P]$$

$$When\ \sum_{i=r_p-1}^{r_p} n_i > values\ per\ processor$$

$$Where\ r_0 : Zero$$
$$P : Number\ of\ Processors$$
$$r_p : The\ last\ row\ assigned\ to\ p$$
$$n_i : Number\ of\ nonzeros\ in\ row\ i$$

$$\tag{2}$$

This method works well for sparse matrices, but it is not feasible to be applied over dense matrices because in this case all the entries are relevant. Table 2 shows an example of two 8x8 sparse matrices distributed between 4 processors. This example compares the size of memory blocks needed to store the matrix entries with the row-based distribution and the value-based distribution.

1.4. Memory pre-allocation

When having an imbalance between the processors the degradation of performance can occur because of two factors: first, the imbalance of computation and communication between the processes; and second, having huge matrices and significant imbalance or bad use of memory increases the possibility of memory swap.

We take advantage of the fact that we read the input matrix, for extracting its pattern and decide the data distribution among application processes, to pre-allocate the memory that would be needed to store it. In table 3 we describe the four methods available in PETSc to allocate memory for different matrix data structures. It shows the memory blocks allocated, the number of memory access needed to allocate this memory and the number of memory blocks allocated for the zero entries.

Table 2. Comparison between row-based and value-based distributions over four processors showing the number of values to be stored per processor

Matrix	Row-based distribution	Values per proc.	Value-based distribution	Values per proc.
		5 5 7 7		5 5 7 7
		15 11 7 3		8 7 11 10

Firstly, with no pre-allocation or the default method each processor allocates a memory location for each loaded nonzero value separately. This method leads to good memory utilization. However, it needs too many memory accesses as the number of memory allocation calls is equal to the number of nonzero values in the matrix. Secondly, dense pre-allocation, each processor allocates its local memory depending on the size of its corresponding rows and columns. The memory allocation function is called once. This method is suitable for dense or small matrices, but unfeasible for sparse matrices. Thirdly, densest row pre-allocation, each processor allocates its local memory based on the densest local row. This method needs only one memory allocation call per processor. However, the size of memory allocated may vary according to the matrix size and its nonzero entries. Another method to allocate memory is the row-based pre-allocation where the number of nonzero values per row is calculated and each processor allocates locally its correspondent rows. This method optimizes the memory utilization but needs higher set-up cost in case of big matrices.

Table 3. Methods to allocate memory for matrix data structures

Memory allocation way	Memory blocks used (floating point)	Memory accesses (mallocs)	Lost memory blocks (floating point)
No prealloc	Nonzero entries	Nonzero entries	$\cong 0$
Dense prealloc	M * N	1	M * N – No. nonzeros
Densest row	$\geq$ Nonzero entries $\leq$ M * N	Number of processors	$\sum_{p=0}^{p=n-1} (m_p * MaxLine_p) - nonzeros$
Row prealloc	Nonzero entries	M	$\cong 0$

When dealing with big matrices, the relation between memory utilization and allocation efficiency is important. After comparing between the four methods we chose for our methodology the row pre-allocation method, because it shares with the no pre-allocation method almost the best memory utilization, and a relatively acceptable number of memory allocation calls. The set-up time needed for the row pre-allocation depends on the matrix number of rows and number of nonzero values.

2. Methodology validation

In order to validate our methodology and to test its efficiency we performed a set of experiments using different solving parameters on different input matrices. As an example, in figure 2 we show the execution times for a Shareman5 3312x3312 matrix contains 20793 nonzero entries (downloaded from the matrix market [6]) on 8 processors and every possible parameter combination (i.e. matrix memory representation, pre-conditioner, and solver). It can be seen that the parameters chosen by the methodology led to a performance very close to the best possible one.

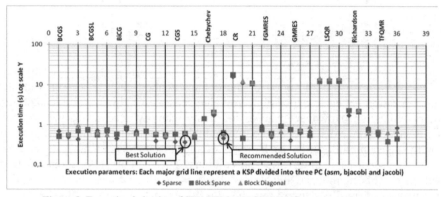

Figure 2. Execution behavior of SHAREMAN5 3312x3312 matrix on 8 processors

In order to validate the load balancing and the memory pre-allocation policies, we show the executions times for a squared banded matrix with 1916928 uniformly distributed nonzero entries and a dimension of 49152x49152 executed on 8 processors. Differentiating the data structure creation time, input file reading time, setting time, assembly time (i.e. the time needed to distribute the data to its corresponding processor if needed) and, finally, the solving time. Figure 3 shows the matrix pattern while table 4 demonstrates both row-based and value-based matrix distributions. It can be noticed that both distributions have the same number of values and rows per processor which guarantees the load balance for both policies.

In order to see the effect of the load balancing and the memory pre-allocation on the execution time, this matrix has been solved using four different configurations: the PETSc default row-based distribution, the value-based distribution, the row-based distribution with memory pre-allocation and the value-based distribution with memory pre-allocation. Figure 4 shows the execution time of matrix row-based distributed. Figure 2 shows the execution time of the matrix value-based distributed. It can be noticed that the performance behavior between these two distribution policies is nearly the same, because in this case both distributions led to the same number of nonzero values and rows per processor and the overhead of the second policy is small. However, the memory pre-allocation improved the performance by reducing the execution time nearly 60% in both row-based distribution and value-based distribution, as shown in figures 6 and 7 correspondently.

Table 4. Comparison between row-based distribution and value-based distribution of a 49152x49152 around-diagonal matrix

Procs	Row-Based Balance		Value-Based Balance	
	Num. Rows	Num. Values	Num. Rows	Num. Values
1 – 8	6144	239616	6144	239616
Total	49152	1916928	49152	1916928

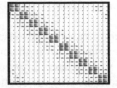

Figure 3. Banded 49152 square matrix pattern

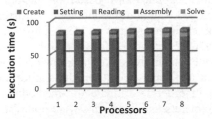

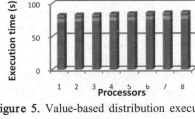

Figure 4. Row-based distribution execution time

Figure 5. Value-based distribution execution time

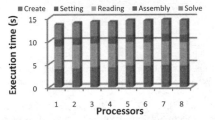

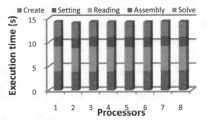

Figure 6. Row-based distribution with memory pre-allocation execution time

Figure 7. Value-based distribution with memory pre-allocation execution time

3. Related Efforts

Different investigations have been carried out to improve the application performance and load balancing. ATLAS [7] project is an approach for the automatic generation and optimization of numerical software concentrated on the widely used linear algebra kernel BLAS. In ATLAS the algorithms are chosen while installing the library based on the architecture, while our approach in addition to the environmental parameters it is based on the input data. More limited ATLAS like functionality was included in PHiPAC[8], and more dynamic solutions are provided by SANS[9] and SALSA[10]. Active Harmony [11] is an infrastructure that allows applications to become tunable. Its tuning points range from parameters such as the size of a read-ahead buffer to what algorithm is being used. To improve performance during a single execution based on the observed performance, Active Harmony needs to apply minimal changes to the application and library source code. Our automatic performance tuning methodology deals with the user application as a black-box. Zoltan [12] is a collection of data management services for parallel, unstructured, adaptive, and dynamic applications. It provides different classes of parallel partitioning algorithms. Zoltan allows an application to switch between partitioning algorithms via a function call. Thus the user may compare between different algorithms easily. This enables users to try several algorithms and find the best ones for their applications.

4. Conclusions

Performance is a key issue in parallel programming and mathematical libraries provide a vast number of high performance parallel mathematical algorithms. From the study of the performance information of the mathematical libraries it was noticed that the performance of the application may vary dynamically according to the input data and the solving environment. In this work we defined a performance methodology for automatic and dynamic tuning of mathematical applications based on historical performance information. Thus, we have developed a tuning methodology consisting of: pattern recognition engine that classifies and characterizes the problem, a historical knowledgebase that was filled with plenty of PETSc's library performance information for a wide set of data, and the data mining engine which dives into the knowledgebase in order to get the recommended configuration and tuning points in the application. Additionally, we planned real case problems in order to validate the methodology making a full execution for all the possible parameters and the results were optimistic. Moreover, it was noticed that the knowledgebase can be adapted by including more performance information for different types of problems.

References

[1] Blackford, S., Chol, J., Cleary, A., D'azevedo, E., Demmel, J., Dhillon, I., Dongarra, J., Hammarling, S., Henry, G., Petitet, A., Stanley, K., Walker, D., and Whaley, R.C.: Scalapack users' guide. Philadelphia, PA, Society for Industrial and Applied Math. (1997)
[2] Balay, S., Eijkhout, V., Gropp, W.D., Mcinnes, L.C., Smith, B.F.: Efficient Management of Parallelism in Object Oriented Numerical Software Libraries. In: Modern Software Tools in Scientific Computing. Arge, E., Bruaset, A.M., Langtangen, H.P.,(eds). Birkh, pp.163--202.
[3] PETSc Web page, http://www.mcs.anl.gov/petsc
[4] Balay, S., Buschelman, K., Eijkhout, V., Gropp, W. D., Kaushik, D., Knepley, M. G., Mcinnes, L. C., Smith, B. F., Zhang, H.: PETSc Users Manual. Argonne National Laboratory, Anl-95/11 - revision 2.1.5, (2004)
[5] Salawdeh, I., César, E., Morajko, A., Margalef, T., Luque, E.: Performance Model for Parallel Mathematical Libraries Based on Historical Knowledgebase. In: Luque, E., Margalef, T., Benitez, D. (Eds.): Euro-Par 2008. LNCS, vol. 5168, pp. 110--119. Springer, Las Palmas de Gran Canaria, Spain (2008)
[6] Boisvert, R. F., Pozo, R., Remington, K., Barrett, R., Dongarra, J. J.: The Matrix Market: A web resource for test matrix collections. In R. F. Boisvert, editor, Quality of Numerical Software, Assessment and Enhancement, pages 125--137, London, Chapman and Hall (1997), http://math.nist.gov/MatrixMarket/
[7] Whaley, R. C., Petitet, A., Dongarra, J. J.: Automated empirical optimizations of software and the ATLAS project. Parallel Computing, vol. 27, pp. 3--35 (2001)
[8] Bilmes, J., Asanovic, K., Chin, C., Demmel J.: Optimizing matrix multiply using PHiPAC: a portable, high-performance, ANSI C coding methodology. In Proceedings of the 11th International Conference on Supercomputing, pp. 340--347, (1997)
[9] Dongarra, J., Bosilca, G., Chen, Z., Eijkhout, V., Fagg, G. E., Fuentes, E., Langou, J., Luszczek, P., Pjesivac-Grbovic, J., Seymour, K., You, H., Vadhiyar, S. S.: Self-adapting numerical software (SANS) effort. IBM J. Res. Dev., vol. 50, pp. 223--238. IBM Corp, NJ, USA (2006)
[10]Demmel, J., Dongarra, J., Eijkhout, V., Fuentes, E., Petitet, A., Vuduc, R., Whaley, R.C., Yelick, K.: Self Adapting Linear Algebra Algorithms and Software. Proceedings of the IEEE , vol.93, no.2, pp.293--312, (2005)
[11]Chung, I.-H. Hollingsworth, J. K.: A Case Study Using Automatic Performance Tuning for Large-Scale Scientific Programs. In: 15th IEEE International Symposium on High Performance Distributed Computing, pp. 45--56, Paris, (2006)
[12]Devine, K., Boman, E., Heaphy, R., Hendrickson, B., Vaughan, C.: Zoltan Data Management Service for Parallel Dynamic Applications. Computing in Science and Engineering, vol. 4, no. 2, pp. 90--97, (2002)

Parallel Computing: From Multicores and GPU's to Petascale
B. Chapman et al. (Eds.)
IOS Press, 2010
© 2010 The authors and IOS Press. All rights reserved.
doi:10.3233/978-1-60750-530-3-415

Automatic Performance Tuning Approach for Parallel Applications Based on Sparse Linear Solvers [1]

Vasiliy Yu. VORONOV [2], Nina N. POPOVA

Department of computational mathematics and cybernetics
Lomonosov Moscow State University
VMK department, MSU, Leninskie Gori, Moscow 119992, Russia
e-mail: basrav@angel.cmc.msu.ru, popova@cmc.msu.ru

Abstract. Approach of automatic selection of parallel sparse linear solver and tuning its parameters is discussed. Performance of linear solver is considered as function of sparse matrix features, selected sparse solver and its settings, hardware platform. Supervised learning is used to create this function and is based on gathering of empirical performance data and the following use of the support vector regression. After creating complexity function, a genetic algorithm is used to find its minimum across the solver types and settings to find locally optimal solver. Results of experiments with PETSc linear solvers are presented for several classes of sparse problems from different applications.

Keywords. Sparse linear solver, automatic performance tuning, PETSc, genetic algorithm, support vector machines.

Introduction

Solvers of sparse linear systems of equations are core part of many scientific applications, performance and scalability of parallel application is affected by performance of linear solver, as it might consume 50%-90% of total runtime.

Creation of near-optimal linear solver for problem with sparse matrix structure requires both careful theoretical studies and experiments on target parallel platforms. For applied scientists who may use linear solvers from scientific libraries for their applications, this problem is somewhat reduced to selection of proper solver from the set of available solvers and tuning its settings in order to get robust, accurate and efficient results for specific task class. Many existing experimental studies of parallel scientific packages [1,2,3,4,5] show that the performance of linear solver significantly relates to the considered parallel platform and features of considered task class.

---

[1]This work was partially supported by the Russian Foundation for Basic Research under grants N08–07–00445a, N08–07–12081.

[2]Corresponding author: Vasiliy Voronov, Department of computational mathematics and cybernetics, Lomonosov Moscow State University, Leninskie Gori, Moscow 119992, Russia; E-mail: basrav@angel.cmc.msu.ru

This leads to creation of automatic performance tuning algorithms. These algorithms are intended to make better utilization of platform resources and support users with proper selection of solver for his problems.

1. Related work

There are particularly two main approaches for creating automatic performance tuning algorithms for scientific computing. They are mainly based on experimental evaluation and selection. First group of algorithms is based on modification of algorithm to match platform specific. This approach was probably pioneered in [6] by introducing polyalgorithm. Here sub algorithm selection was driven by evaluating conditions and comparing them with values, entered by experts. Modern algorithms and projects which implement tuning approach of this type include ATLAS [7], FFTW [8], PHiPACK [9], OSKI [10] and many others. In ATLAS, instances of BLAS functions are generated from templates to match platform specific. It uses experimental evaluation of same functions with adjusted settings. FFTW package has adaptive algorithm of Fourier transform that consists of sequence of codelets. Optimal codelet is inserted in final transform algorithm after experimentally evaluating its performance. PHiPACK is a methodology of tuning sparse matrix kernels by experimental searching. It searches for best settings of kernel by generating set of candidate kernels and experimentally evaluating their performance. OSKI package provides adaptively tuned sparse kernels for matrix-vector operations. It use matrix transformations cache utilization on specific platform. This package could use a priori information about input data from user. It is also able to provide resulting transformation in reusable form to use in external codes.

Another approach is tuning based on input data analysis. This approach is implemented in SALSA [11] package, IPRS [12,13]. SALSA introduces a framework for tuning preconditioner of iterative solver. Tuning process is based on data mining techniques over features of sparse linear system. IPRS has data mining algorithms for selecting solver from the set of available.

In our work, we address the problem of selecting and tuning settings of parallel iterative solvers from mathematical packages for specific users sparse matrices and specific parallel platform. Since particular task class leads to specific matrix structure with numerical properties, selection of proper solver scheme requires much theoretical efforts. It is also known that experimental studies should be done in addition realize performance and stability of selected iterative solver [14,15]. We propose the algorithm of automatic linear solver selection from the given set of mathematical libraries for a given parallel platforms. It is intended to choose best platform, package and tuned linear solver for particular user's input data. The algorithm is based on machine learning approach, where linear solver performance model is built on statistical knowledge of solving flow of linear systems of equations.

2. Proposed solver tuning approach

Performance model of parallel sparse linear solver for user's input $Ax = b$ is introduced as complexity function

$$\mathbf{C}(n, F, S, X) = P,$$

where n is number of processes, $F = (f_1, \ldots, f_n)^T$ is a feature space (set of scalar values extracted from the problem $Ax = b$), $S = (s_1, \ldots, s_m)^T$ encodes type of selected linear solver and values of its settings, X is set of implicit parameters which also affect performance of linear solver. P here is specific performance metric of parallel sparse solution, in this particular case it is defined as product of solver runtime by peak RAM consumption of one process.

2.1. Construction of complexity function

First, the following problem statement of tuning linear solvers is considered in this work: given a user's sparse linear system $Ax = b$, accuracy requirements and number of processes n, find solver S^* which minimize complexity function

$$S^* = \arg \min_{S_j \in S} \mathbf{C}(n, F, S_j, X) \tag{1}$$

Note that many problem statements may be considered, this particular problem statement corresponds to problem of better utilization of machine time when specific number of processors is available for the solver and has to be used efficiency.

Proposition of explicit algorithm for constructing function $\widehat{\mathbf{C}}$ for specific linear solver and parallel platform is very difficult problem for many reasons. It requires deep understanding of linear algebra software performance for specific parallel architecture and probably may be done for specific matrix class. Here more general approach is proposed by building approximation function $\widehat{\mathbf{C}}$ so that

$$\mathbf{C}(n, F, S, X) \approx \widehat{\mathbf{C}}(n, F, S) + error$$

This approximation is built using the set of values $T = \{(n, F_i, S_j, (C)(n, F_i, S_j, X))\}$. T corresponds to set of training problems $\{A_i = b_i\}$ with are solved for different combinations of solvers. Particular approximation $\widehat{\mathbf{C}}$ is built using the support vector regression [16].

2.2. Support vector regression

Support vector regression (i.c. C-SVR) requires solving quadratic optimization problem

$$\min_{w,b,\xi,\xi^*} \frac{1}{2}\mathbf{w}^{\mathbf{T}}\mathbf{w} + C\sum_{i=1}^{l}\xi_i + C\sum_{i=1}^{l}\xi_i^*,$$

$$\mathbf{w}^{\mathbf{T}}\phi(\mathbf{x_i}) + b - z_i \le \epsilon + \xi_i,$$

$$z_i - \mathbf{w}^{\mathbf{T}}\phi(\mathbf{x_i}) - b \le \epsilon + \xi_i^*, \xi_i, \xi_i^* \ge 0, i = 1, \ldots, l.$$

Stated in dual form, it allows to represent $\widehat{\mathbf{C}}$ in the form

$$\widehat{\mathbf{C}}(\mathbf{x}) = \sum_{i=1}^{l}(-\alpha_i + \alpha_i^*)K(\mathbf{x_i}, \mathbf{x}) + b,$$

where l is size of training set, $(\alpha, \mathbf{b})$ is solution of C-SVR. We consider different kernel functions, particularly sigmoid and radial basis functions.

Similar to C-SVR, ν-SVR algorithm is introduced. Different types of SVR are exist since they implement various regularization technique for regression problem. It means that values of regularization parameters affect model accuracy and therefore should be selected carefully.

2.3. Genetic algorithm for finding solver selection

After $\widehat{\mathbf{C}}$ is constructed, S^* from (1) can be found using optimization method.

Since S has parameters of mixed types (categorial, integers, real) and the corresponding optimization problem is likely to be constrained mixed-integer problem, we use genetic algorithm to solve it. It is stochastic method of solving optimization problems. Particularly, genetic algorithm with islands is used [17]. It consists of the following steps:

1. Randomly seed N sets (islands) of candidate species, where each specie encodes candidate solver and its parameters S_i
2. crossover, mutation and downhill operators are introduced and applied at each iteration for each island.
3. Population is estimated with respect to function $\widehat{\mathbf{C}}$, species with minimal values are selected as elite, and once per M iterations exchanged with species from the other islands. Replace "worst" species with new randomly generated.
4. At the last iteration of the algorithm, choose best specie from all islands as the solution S^*

Note that this model is parallel in its nature, since each island may be assigned to specific process and synchronize with the other processes at migration stages.

2.4. Methods of improving accuracy of the tuning algorithm

Since function (2.2) is built to fit given values of training set T, an additional efforts are needed in order to raise generalization properties of $\widehat{\mathbf{C}}$ for problems out of T. Since this problem is not solved in general case, a heuristics are used to construct accurate models. First, score of regression model is performed with respect to 5-fold cross-validation. Since (2.2) returns $\widehat{\mathbf{C}}$ as parameterized function of regularization parameters C, ν kernel parameter γ, it is possible to train several SVR instances for different values and select one with best selection score. Selection criteria we use is mean square error of $\widehat{\mathbf{C}}$ for the training set with subject to cross-validation. Note that model selection is easily parallelized since model evaluation may be done for subsets of hyperparameters.

Another approach to increase accuracy is to decompose solver parameters space S into a set of disjoint subspaces

$$S = S^1 \times S^2 \times \cdots \times S^m,$$

where each subspace S^i corresponds to set of parameters of one of m sparse solver types (particularly, each S^i corresponds to one preconditioner type with different iterative solvers). This allows instead of solving (2.2) solve m tasks of smaller dimension. It allows to reduce both computational complexity of building $\widehat{C}$ and improve its generalization accuracy.

Summary of the proposed solver selection and tuning algorithm is listed in 1.

Algorithm 1 Main stages of proposed linear solving algorithm

Require: User provides input problem $Ax = b$ and desired search space $\mathcal{S}$, training set of tasks T is required

get training tasks set T and collect $Tr = \{n, F, S, \widehat{\mathbf{C}}(n, F, S)\}$ by solving on desired platforms

extract features F from user's task

for each solver subtype $S \in \mathcal{S}$ **do**

    build complexity function $\widehat{\mathbf{C}}(n, F, S)$ from Tr (including hyperparameters search)

    apply genetic algorithm iterations with goal function $\min_{S_i \in S} \widehat{\mathbf{C}}(n, F, S_i)$, get S^* as result

end for

get best S over all found S^* and return it to the user

---

3. Experimental results

Proposed solver selection algorithm was implemented in form of expanded software framework. It has distributed structure and consists of core unit, which reside on user's platform, and platform units, which reside on the parallel platforms. Core unit includes:

1. Database of experiments ran through the system (Matrix features, selected solver & platform, performance results)
2. User interface (Inputs spec. for desired search details, outputs solver selection found)
3. Module for building complexity function (uses LibSVM package [18], (including threaded hyperparameters search algorithm)
4. Genetic algorithm module for minimizing complexity function (threaded implementation)

Platform unit includes:

1. Interaction with the parallel packages installed on platforms (currently PETSc, HYPRE are supported)
2. Extraction of matrix features, interaction with job schedulers, collection of performance and output results

In order to extract features F from linear system of equations, we use the AnaMod package [19]. It extracts from the matrix 5 groups of scalar features related to different numerical properties of matrix (structural, spectral, nonzero-distributions, departure from normality). Note that different features has different computational complexity, not all features are reliable for different matrix classes. Based on several experiments, we have excluded group of features which were not often computed, and worked with the subset of 39 features.

In the experiments we used iterative solvers and preconditioners from the parallel mathematical package PETSc [20]. Two different types of experiments were performed in order to evaluate proposed tuning approach. In the first experiment, we have assumed that training set is collected during the operation of our software system by the user. It is equivalent to training on arbitrary set of problems $\{A_i x = b_i\}$. Second experiment corresponded to case when training set consists of problems of related nature. This case was studied at the example of parallel simulation of large-scale power distribution grids.

3.1. Solver tuning results for arbitrary set of tasks

Training set of linear systems was gathered from the University of Florida's sparse matrix collection [21]. 35 matrices were selected from this collection to constitute training set (30 matrices) and testing set (5 matrices).

Solver search space was constructed from GMRES iterative solver and preconditioners of block Jacobi and additive Schwarz types with incomplete LU-factization for each block. Additional settings were restart rate of GMRES and ILU settings (ILU type, fill-in rate, levels, threshold). Experiment was performed on cluster of 8-cored Intel 5472 nodes with 4-8 Gb RAM. Core unit of the software was running on 8-cores Intel 5472 server.

Comparison of best and worst selected solvers S^* and the default PETSc solver are shown in the table 1a. Performance results are listed in the table 1b. Note that since

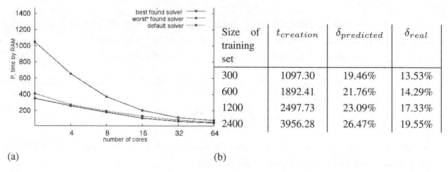

(a)   (b)

Size of training set	$t_{creation}$	$\delta_{predicted}$	δ_{real}
300	1097.30	19.46%	13.53%
600	1892.41	21.76%	14.29%
1200	2497.73	23.09%	17.33%
2400	3956.28	26.47%	19.55%

Table 1. Average P for best, worst found and default solvers for different number of processors(a), average tuning method time ($t_{creation}$), relative error between the performance of default solver and predicted performance of S^* ($\delta_{predicted}$), relative error between the performance of default solver and real performance of S^* (δ_{real}) for experiments with different sizes of training set (b)

size of training set grows, quality of solver selection grows too. Time requirements for constructing complexity function and run genetic algorithm are adequate since parallel genetic algorithm and parallel model selection both scale well. Low percentage rates here primarily related to arbitrary nature of training set.

3.2. Tuning solver for power grid simulation problem

Second experiment is related to problem of power grid simulations [22]. It leads to numerical solution of system of ordinary differential equations for specific time interval. Runtime and scalability results are shown for GMRES + Block Jacobi, stopping $||r_n||_{\inf} < 10^{-5}$ at the each time step in table 2a,b. Experiment was performed on Blue-

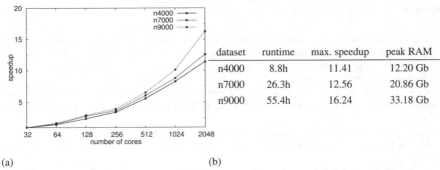

dataset	runtime	max. speedup	peak RAM
n4000	8.8h	11.41	12.20 Gb
n7000	26.3h	12.56	20.86 Gb
n9000	55.4h	16.24	33.18 Gb

(a)   (b)

Table 2. Scalability chart for different power grid sizes (a), runtime and RAM consumption for the same experiment (b)

Gene/P platform for up to 2048 nodes. Note that this is an example of large-scale application, for this problem 94% of runtime is in sparse linear solver, thus tuning linear solver here may lead to significant reduction of runtime. Another important feature of this problem is that simulations are required for many power grids of different structure and size. It gives here natural way of collecting performance statistic and maintaining training set without running additional solves.

For this problem the following experiment was performed: 5 power grids of different size were used as the training set, and testing was performed for 1 larger power grid with the same structure. Moreover, feature space of complexity function for this problem was expanded with 12 scalar features. These features are obtained from the geometrical and physical properties of specific power grid. Their computation costs nothing since the specification of power grid is known.

Solver search space in the experiment the same as for the previous experiment. Results of the experiment are listed in table 3 (with the same layout as for table 1). Here,

Size of training set	$t_{creation}$	$\delta_{predicted}$	δ_{real}
55	401.29	11.23%	6.64%
200	496.55	12.81%	7.49%
400	676.14	11.56%	8.26%
1000	1419.27	11.63%	9.28%

Table 3. Results of tuning solver for power grid simulation problem

9% of runtime improvement over default solver selection reduced simulation time for over 5 thousand node-hours when all 2048 nodes are used.

4. Future work

Proposed approach should be used for choosing best solver for specific class of sparse linear systems in order to get higher prediction accuracy. Moreover, this approach may reduce computation time in large-scale application where sparse linear solvers are used.

Our further work includes study of feature space construction. It requires both study of different sources of features for linear systems of equations and feature selection algorithms for reducing method time.

References

[1] Fukui, Y., Hasegawa, H.: Test of Iterative Solvers on ITBL. HPCASIA '05: Proceedings of the Eighth International Conference on High-Performance Computing in Asia-Pacific Region (2005) 422

[2] Kumbhar, A., Chakravarthy, K., Keshavamurthy, R., Rao, G.: Utilization of Parallel Solver Libraries to solve Structural and Fluid problems. Tech. Rep. Cranes Software International Ltd., Bangalore (2005)

[3] Gould, N.I.M., Scott, J.A., Hu, Y.: A numerical evaluation of sparse direct solvers for the solution of large sparse symmetric linear systems of equations. ACM transactions on mathematical software **33**(2) (2007)

[4] Gupta, A., George, T., Sarin, V.: An Experimental Evaluation of Iterative Solvers for Large SPD Systems of Linear Equations. Technical Report RC 24479, IBM T. J. Watson Research Center, Yorktown Heights, NY (2008)

[5] Oliker, L., Canning, A., Carter, J., Iancu, C., Lijewski, M., Kamil, S., Shalf, J., Shan, H., Strohmaier, E., Ethier, S., et al.: Scientific Application Performance on Candidate PetaScale Platforms. (2007)

[6] Rice, J.R., Rosen, S.: NAPSS. A numerical analysis problem solving system. Proceedings of the 1966 21st national conference (1966) 51–56

[7] Whaley, R., Petitet, A., Dongarra, J.: Automated empirical optimizations of software and the ATLAS project. Parallel Computing **27**(1-2) (2001) 3–35

[8] Frigo, M., Johnson, S.: FFTW: an adaptive software architecture for the FFT. Proceedings of the 1998 IEEE International Conference on Acoustics, Speech, and Signal Processing, 1998. ICASSP'98. **3** (1998)

[9] Bilmes, J., Asanovic, K., Chin, C.W., Demmel, J.: Optimizing Matrix Multiply Using PHiPACK: A Portable, High Performance, ANSI C Coding Methodology. Proceedings of International Conference on Supercomputing 1997 (1997) 340–347

[10] Vuduc, R., Demmel, J., Yelick, K.: OSKI: A library of automatically tuned sparse matrix kernels. Journal of Physics: Conference Series **16**(1) (2005) 521–530

[11] Demmel, J., Dongarra, J., Eijkhout, V., Fuentes, E., Petitet, A., Vuduc, R., Whaley, R., Yelick, K.: Self-adapting linear algebra algorithms and software. Proceedings of the IEEE **93**(2) (2005) 293–312

[12] Xu, S., Lee, E.J., Zhang, J.: An interim analysis report on preconditioners and matrices. Technical Report 388-03, University of Kentucky, Lexington; Department of Computer Science (2003)

[13] Xu, S., Zhang, J.: A Data Mining Approach to Matrix Preconditioning Problem. Proceedings of the 8th Workshop on Mining Scientific and Engineering Databases (MSD05), in conjunction with the 5th SIAM International Conference on Data Mining, Newport Beach, CA, Apr (2005)

[14] Nachtigal, N., Reddy, S., Trefethen, L.: How fast are nonsymmetric matrix iterations? SIAM Journal on Matrix Analysis and Applications **13** (1992) 778

[15] Greenbaum, A., Strakos, Z.: Any nonincreasing convergence curve is possible for GMRES. SIAM Journal of Matrix Analysis Applications (1996)

[16] Chen, P., Fan, R., Lin, C.: A Study on SMO-Type Decomposition Methods for Support Vector Machines. IEEE Transactions on Neural Networks **17**(4) (2006) 893–908

[17] Whitley, D., Rana, S., Hechendorn, R.B.: The island Model Genetic algorithm: On separability, population size and convergence. CIT. Journal of computing and information technology **7**(1) (1999) 33–47

[18] Chang, C.C., Lin, C.J.: LIBSVM: a library for support vector machines. (2001) Software available at http://www.csie.ntu.edu.tw/ cjlin/libsvm.

[19] Eijkhout, V., Fuentes, E.: A proposed standard for numerical metadata. Innovative Computing Laboratory, University of Tennessee, Tech. Rep. ICL-UT-03-02 (2003)

[20] Balay, S., Buschelman, K., Gropp, W.D., Kaushik, D., Knepley, M.G., McInnes, L.C., Smith, B.F., Zhang, H.: PETSc Web page. See http://www. mcs. anl. gov/petsc

[21] Davis, T.: University of Florida sparse matrix collection. NA Digest **97**(23) (1997) 7

[22] Voronov, V.Y., Popova, N.N.: Use of Threaded Numerical Packages for Parallel Power Grid Simulation. In: Proceedings of International Conference on High Performance Computing, Networking and Communication Systems (HPCNCS-09). (2009) 39–45

Parallel Computing: From Multicores and GPU's to Petascale
B. Chapman et al. (Eds.)
IOS Press, 2010
© 2010 The authors and IOS Press. All rights reserved.
doi:10.3233/978-1-60750-530-3-423

423

A Flexible, Application- and Platform-Independent Environment for Benchmarking

Wolfgang Frings, Alexander Schnurpfeil, Stefanie Meier, Florian Janetzko, Lukas Arnold

Jülich Supercomputing Centre (JSC), Forschungszentrum Jülich, Germany
{w.frings,a.schnurpfeil,st.meier,f.janetzko,l.arnold}@fz-juelich.de

Abstract. This paper introduces the new benchmarking environment JuBE. It is a stand-alone framework independent of the underlying benchmark applications and supports all steps of performing and analyzing benchmark runs on different computer systems. These steps are fully recorded to allow a consistent administration and analysis of the runs. JuBE is the benchmarking environment chosen by the European Projects DEISA and PRACE.

Introduction

Benchmarking is used for objective comparison of different computer architectures and is therefore a key issue in procurements of new computer systems. The task of benchmarking a computer system usually consists of numerous steps, which involve several runs of different applications. Configuring, compiling, and running a benchmark suite on several platforms with the accompanied tasks of result verification and analysis needs a lot of administrative work and produces a huge amount of data. These data have to be analyzed and collected. Without a benchmarking environment all these steps have to be handled individually and manually. Therefore, a software is desirable which supports the user in performing, administrating and analyzing benchmark runs.

1. Related Work

In this section we shortly introduce some frameworks developed for the tasks of benchmarking and show the differences to the concepts of JuBE. The most outstanding characteristic of JuBE is the independence of the framework from the underlying benchmark programs (the benchmark suite). In most benchmarking environments the applications and the framework are tightly coupled. Examples for this approach are the benchmark suites from SPEC [5] and NAS [6]. SPEC provides a huge amount of different applications to measure and compare cpu-performance as well as OpenMP or MPI performance. Also the NAS benchmarks are designed for comparison of parallel supercomputers. Both organizations assure that the users of their benchmark suites do not need to perform all the steps regarding the benchmarking process described above by hand and provide benchmarking frameworks for their suites in which the applications are included. The advantage of this approach is that the user of one suite can start the measurements immediately following the instructions given with the framework. It is not necessary to know the applications in detail because they are already fully accessible through the framework. However, on the other hand the user has to get familiar with different frameworks if he wants to use benchmark programs of the different organizations and it is not possible to use the framework for other, e.g. self-written, codes.

The Technical University of Dresden uses another approach in their benchmarking environment *BenchIT* [7]. The environment consists of a graphical user interface for running and analyzing measurements. The main characteristic of *BenchIT* is that the measurements are not performed via real application programs but via kernels. These kernels for performing measurements are also directly coupled to the framework program. The advantage here is the possibility to measure single components of the computer with high accuracy. But this advantage is accompanied by the fact that *BenchIT* can not be used for complex user applications (which is of course not the domain it was developed for).

The approach of JuBE is a different one. Instead of linking applications and framework, it provides a general and stand-alone framework suitable for any application. The advantage is that it is possible to integrate any application or kernels of applications into JuBE, i.e. making them accessible from JuBE, and administrate all runs via a single interface. The time needed for the setup might be a little higher compared to a less general approach but once one is acquainted with JuBE, self-written programs or applications which do not already belong to any benchmark suite can be integrated also. In describing the benchmark process in an abstract way it is possible to support application benchmarks as well as synthetic benchmarks and additionally, the benchmark runs do not depend on a specific platform, the system on which the measurements shall be performed can be described in an abstract way as well.

2. General Strategy

To outline the general strategy of JuBE in a few words, the approach of JuBE is

- to provide templates for the application and the target platform in order to allow application- and platform-independence,
- to span a multi-dimensional parameter space in one step, that means to prepare and process benchmark runs for each point in this space, i.e. for each combination of specified parameter values,
- to record all relevant information of the benchmark process to make it possible to reproduce the runs later on.

To achieve these goals JuBE makes great effort to generalize the benchmarking procedure.

A typical benchmark run with JuBE involves two steps: First, the user invokes the benchmark runs:

```
jube -start bench.xml
==>
...
--->     processing bench.xml ...
--->     processing $PWD/compile.xml ...
--->     processing $PWD/prepare.xml ...
--->     processing $PWD/execute.xml ...
--->     processing $PWD/../platform/platform.xml ...
...
  -> submit job command: [debug] llsubmit ibm_llsubmit.job
----------------------------------------------------------
 JUBE: used id:                              1
----------------------------------------------------------
```

Second, the user retrieves the results via the run identifier assigned by JuBE using the option -result. The option -update scans for results of finished jobs:

```
jube -update -result 1
==>
...
--->     processing $PWD/verify.xml ...
--->     processing $PWD/analyse.xml ...
...
```

In the given example the result table could look like the following one:

```
Subid               nodes    tasks    particle    walltime
----------------    -------  -------- ----------- -----------
n1p16t1_t001_i01        1       16    3000000     4800.00
n1p32t1_t001_i01        1       32    3000000     2400.00
...
n4p16t1_t001_i01        4       16    5000000     1000.00
n4p32t1_t001_i01        4       32    5000000      500.00
```

These kind of tables can also be used as input for tools like *gnuplot* to create diagrams of the results.

This example shows that JuBE performs automatically all relevant steps related to the setup, namely compilation, preparation and execution of the applications as well as the verification and analysis of the results. These steps are organized separately using standardized descriptions via XML configuration files.

As it can be seen in Figure 1, all configurations are described uniformly via definitions in XML. The first level of abstraction is to define the underlying platforms on which the benchmarks should run in a general way. All platform-specific library paths and configuration switches used by applications in the benchmark suite given for a specific platform are stored in one file (*platform.xml*). JuBE is able to distinguish between the different platform definitions by using the concepts of XML: For each platform a certain XML-section defines the environment.

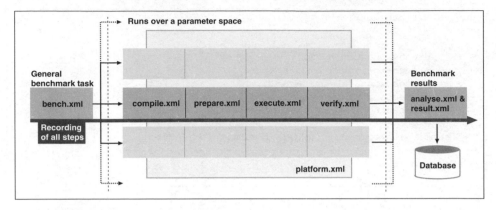

Figure 1. Benchmark runs with JuBE spanning a multi-dimensional parameter space

As a second level of abstraction the desired runs and the application steps have to be generally described. The top level configuration file of a benchmark (in Fig.1 *bench.xml*) defines the benchmark runs, subsequent files organize the compilation and execution as well as the analysis of the results. Additionally it is possible to define some preparation steps and to verify the results after the measurements.

According to the definitions in the XML files, the underlying submission scripts and the compile procedures (like configure scripts, Makefiles or whatever the application's compile routines are) of the application have to be generalized via placeholder in template files. To explain this strategy in more detail we give a short example which shows the generalized compilation of a program.

First the user adapts his compile environment, e.g. the Makefile definitions:

```
. . .
MAKE          = #MAKE#
F90           = #F90#
F90FLAGS      = #F90FLAGS#
. . .
                                                          Makefile.def.in
```

On the right side you see the placeholder characterized by #...#. In *compile.xml* the user can now specify the values, which are used to substitute the placeholder:

```
. . .
<substitute infile="Makefile.defs.in" outfile="Makefile.defs">
   <sub from="#MAKE#"          to="$make" />
   <sub from="#F90#"           to="$f90" />
   <sub from="#F90FLAGS#"      to="$f90flags -qsuffix=cpp=F90" />
. . .
                                                          compile.xml
```

The user can provide actual flags as shown for the substitution of F90FLAGS and also variables marked with a $ which JuBE can find in the general platform description file. In this way it is possible to take advantage of the generic description of the platform environment.

```
...
make             =  "gmake"
f90              =  "xlf90_r"
f90flags         =  "-q64 -qtune=pwr6 -qarch=pwr6"
...
```
platform.xml

JuBE substitutes the placeholder and generates the following Makefile.def file:

```
...
MAKE         =  gmake
F90          =  xlf90_r
F90FLAGS     =  -q64 -qtune=pwr6 -qarch=pwr6 -qsuffix=cpp=F90
...
```
Makefile.def

The procedure for the other XML files is very similar to the example described above. Therefore, it is also possible to perform a generic submission of the job: Using *prepare.xml* one can e.g. define copying of files before execution, in *execute.xml* one specifies all values for the job submission script. The user can benefit from variables already known by JuBE as $taskspernode or also define variables by himself. In the file *verify.xml* it is possible to perform a verification step to test the correctness of the runs.

The generalized presentation of results is defined in *result.xml*. Here, one specifies which values should be shown in the result tables. The file *analyse.xml* is tightly coupled to the result presentation. The user can specify search patterns based on regular expressions to scan the output files and retrieve the data that should be shown in result tables.

One of JuBE's major advantages is the possibility to span a parameter space in a single step. The file for the benchmark definitions (*bench.xml*) plays a decisive role here. In this file the application-dependent parameters as well as runtime parameters are specified. The following example shows parts of a possible configuration:

```
...
<tasks    threadspertask="1" taskspernode="16,32" nodes="1,2,4" />
<param    particles="3000000,5000000" />
...
```
bench.xml

In the <tasks> section all information are set which are needed to let the executable run on the platform. This piece of information will automatically be included in the job file when JuBE starts its work. In the example shown the executable shall run on different numbers of nodes n (1,2,4) with different numbers of tasks per node for each n (16,32). Therefore, the example settings of <tasks> alone would result in six different benchmark runs. The <params> section is dedicated to settings concerning the integrated application. The example application depends on numbers of particles and as can be seen the runs should be performed for 3 million and 5 million particles, so we have in fact not only six but twelve runs in total. These runs build up the parameter space and are consistently managed by JuBE.

After the runs, depending on the parameter space the user is confronted with quite a large number of files and data which have to be administrated and therefore must be labeled in a unique way. JuBE solves this problem by taking the benchmark name, that means the application's name to be exact, the name of the corresponding platform, the number of processors, tasks and threads and combines them with a counter. This information is also used to create a directory structure in which all information are hosted in an ordered, unique manner.

Once the runs are finished the user has the possibility to get the results in form of tables which are defined in the analysis configuration files. In this way, JuBE can parse the stdout and stderr files according to the user's specifications as well as any other additional output files. The user obtains an overview of the results of the runs covering the whole parameter space.

Finally, the third goal of JuBE is to record all steps of a benchmark run, which is realized through a corresponding XML-based log file for each run. We also provide an XSL template and a CSS file for this log, so it is possible to view the log files with a browser in a formatted manner. Fully recorded means that all information about the benchmark environment, compiler versions, compiler flags and so on are stored. Furthermore, it is planned to add system information like the kernel version as well. So it is possible to understand the full run by just investigating this log file.

In Figure 1 the possibility of storing the results in a database is shown. A database interface would help to perform cross-platform analyses and sharing of the results. This is part of the future work on JuBE and will be discussed below.

3. Use Cases

Whatever the motivations for benchmarking runs are, they usually have the necessity of launching a large number of different jobs with different parameters. Because of the general structure described above, JuBE helps to maintain these jobs, labels them uniquely, and records all parameters used. The requested parameter space is defined in the configuration file of the benchmark and will be spanned within one step. To show these features we discuss two of several typical application scenarios of JuBE.

1. The first use case is the task of the evaluation of different computer platforms. This task especially occurs in the procurement process for a new computer system. For such a process, not only a large number of runs of different benchmarks is needed, but they also have to run on a large variety of different platforms. This is easily possible through the described features of JuBE. One has to define the platform definition once and afterwards all different benchmark applications based on this definition can be launched without changing any other configuration step or application parameter.

   Once a decision for a platform is made, JuBE helps in the acceptance phase of the supercomputer. Here, it is quite important to be able to comprehend all steps of the benchmark process and to know the detailed configuration of the runs later on which is guaranteed by JuBE's log functionality.

2. In the early development, JuBE had been considered as a benchmarking environment only. Step by step it appeared not only to be suitable just for the dedicated task as a benchmarking tool but it also became a versatile instrument for monitoring tasks and software production runs as well. It can also be used in a smooth way for detection of changes in the runtime environment of supercomputers. Computers always experience changes over time and this can often result in unexpected behavior. For example, applications are slowed down in perfor-

mance or software which functioned well before does not work anymore. With the feature of logging all parameters and actions during a benchmark run, JuBE can serve as a longtime system- and software-monitoring application as well.

Further use cases will become clear when we have a look at the role of JuBE in the European projects DEISA and PRACE.

4. JuBE's role in the European Projects DEISA and PRACE

JuBE has gained high acceptance in the European projects DEISA and PRACE. In DEISA the comparison of different computer architectures is a major issue. Benchmarking is used for example to find suitable performance conversion factors between the different systems belonging to the project. These factors are needed for accounting purposes because users in DEISA are entitled to run their applications on different platforms of the infrastructure. One aim of PRACE is to set up tier-0 systems in Europe. Therefore PRACE has a need for benchmarking in order to prepare the procurement of new supercomputers. This means that both projects require to perform detailed runs of their benchmark suites on fundamental different computer systems which represent present and future computer architectures. JuBE enables the maintenance of the different benchmark programs in both suites and allows to perform runs and to collect of the resulting data in a consistent way.

Through these projects, about forty applications and several synthetic benchmarks have now already been integrated in the JuBE environment. Among these benchmarks are widely accepted applications from various research areas. In the Core PRACE Application Benchmark Suite are codes from computational chemistry like CPMD [8], codes from computational fluid dynamics like Code_Saturne, GADGET [9] from the field of astronomy, five QCD-kernels from particle physics, TORB [10] from plasma physics, and NEMO [11] from ocean modeling, just to name some of them. DEISA additionally supports RAMSES [12] from astrophysics, Fenfloss [13] from CFD, IFS [14] from earth modeling, QuantumESPRESSO [15] from materials science, PEPC [16] from plasma physics and parts from the HPCC benchmark suite [17] to name also synthetic benchmarks.

In addition, these projects helped in the creation of several generalized platform definitions and batch submission scripts for different platforms like IBM Power6 and IBM BlueGene/P with LoadLeveler, CRAY XT4/5 with PBS, Intel Nehalem with Torque, or Cell with PBS to mention examples of them. Out of this achievement it is very likely that a new user of JuBE can already use existing platform definitions and does not need to create them himself.

Additionally, the usage of JuBE in these projects helped to develop the environment further on. Also some requests occurred which will be considered in the work on JuBE in the next future.

5. Future Work

As described above, JuBE is used within the projects DEISA and PRACE. From the experiences made in these projects further developments have been motivated and are planned for the near future. At the moment the administration of the results is feasible for the owner of the benchmark runs via the analysis configuration. JuBE internally uses the unique identifier of each run and is able to collect and present the results in clearly arranged tables and views. But the analysis and comparison of runs of different users or sharing the results with e.g. project partners is more difficult. Therefore, one major goal is the integration of a database interface which can be used to collect and store all results from the benchmark runs automatically. This work has already been started and denotes a significant step towards the simplification of results maintenance and comparison as well as further analyses of the data. In fact, this database will make it possible to also perform analyses across numerous applications and different platforms.

Additionally, in a following major version, we plan even more generalized and unified views of the different configuration files to allow a completely flexible control over the benchmark runs. Also a generic interface to the batch system for automatically checking the status of the benchmark jobs is part of the work planned. In this context it is also worth thinking about a connection to *Unicore* [18] which is in fact developed for making distributed computing, data, network, and software resources available in a seamless and secure way.

6. Summary

In this paper the new benchmarking environment JuBE has been introduced. The key features of JuBE were shown. The first key concept is the independence of the framework from the underlying applications realized through template files for the whole benchmarking procedure starting from compiling up to retrieving the results. The second concept is the possibility to easily create large sets of benchmark runs spanning a multidimensional parameter space. The third concept covers the recording of all relevant data during the benchmarking process. Use cases were discussed and the relevance of JuBE in big European projects like DEISA and PRACE was described.

References

[1] Jülich Benchmarking Environment: http://www.fz-juelich.de/jsc/jube
[2] Jülich Supercomputing Centre: http://www.fz-juelich.de/jsc
[3] D. Henty et al.: Benchmarking Activity Status Report, *eDeisa-D-eSA4-B4, 2008*, http://www.deisa.eu
[4] Partnership for Advanced Computing in Europe: http://www.prace-project.eu
[5] R. Lieberman, M. S. Müller, T. Elken: SPEC MPI2007 Benchmarks for HPC Systems *Talk, SPEC Benchmark Workshop, 2007*, http://www.spec.org
[6] R. F. van der Wijngaart: NAS Parallel Benchmarks Version 2.4, *NAS Technical Report NAS-02-007, 2002*, http://www.nas.nasa.gov/Resources/Software/npb.html
[7] R. Schöne, G. Juckeland, W.E. Nagel, St. Pflüger, R. Wloch: Performance Comparison and Optimization: Case Studies using BenchIT, *Proceedings of PARCO 2005*, 877–884, http://www.benchit.org
[8] http://www.cpmd.org, Co. IBM Corp 1990-2008,Co. MPI Festkörperforschung Stuttgart 1997-2001.
[9] V. Springel, N. Yoshida, S.D.M. White, *New Astronomy 6* (2001), 79
[10] R. Hatzky, T.M. Tran, A. Könies, R. Kleiber, S.J. Allfrey: *Physics of Plasmas 9* (2002), 898
[11] G. Madec: NEMO ocean engine, *Note du Pole de modélisation, IPSL*, 2008, 27, ISSN No 1288-1619
[12] R.Teyssier: Cosmological hydrodynamics with adaptive mesh refinement - A new high resolution code called RAMSES, *Astronomy and Astrophysics 385* (2002), 337-364
[13] Fenfloss: http://www.ihs.uni-stuttgart.de/116.html?L=1
[14] The ECMWF Integrated Forecast System: http://www.ecmwf.int/research/
[15] P. Giannozzi et al., http://arxiv.org/abs/0906.2569
[16] P. Gibbon, W. Frings, B. Mohr: Performance analysis and visualization of the N-body tree code PEPC on massively parallel computers, *Proceedings of Parallel Computing* (2005).
[17] J.Dongarra, P.Luszczek: Introduction to the HPCChallenge Benchmark Suite, *ICL Technical Report, ICL-UT-05-01* (2005)
[18] A. Streit et al.: UNICORE 6 - A European Grid Technology, *L. Grandinetti, G. Joubert, W. Gentzsch (Eds.), Trends in High Performance and Large Scale Computing, IOS Press, to be published*

Fault Tolerance

Parallel Computing: From Multicores and GPU's to Petascale
B. Chapman et al. (Eds.)
IOS Press, 2010
© *2010 The authors and IOS Press. All rights reserved.*
doi:10.3233/978-1-60750-530-3-433

Optimized Checkpointing Protocols for Data Parallel Programs [1]

Carlo BERTOLLI [a,2] and Marco VANNESCHI [a]

[a] *Dept. of Computer Science, University of Pisa, Italy*

Abstract. A main issue of fault tolerance techniques for High-Performance applications, based on checkpointing and rollback recovery, is related to the feasibility of statically analyzing the induced overhead. In this paper we show that, under the hypothesis of a general unstructured parallelism model (e.g. MPI, OpenMP), it is difficult, where not impossible, to achieve such an analysis. To overcome this issue we propose an approach to fault tolerance based on structured parallel programming (e.g. divide-and-conquer and parallel sort). We show which are the gains of assuming such a programming model in the case of data parallel programs: we introduce an optimized checkpointing protocol and we compare it with a Communication-Induce-Checkpointing (CIC) protocol, representing one of the most advanced solution for general "unstructured" parallelism models.

Keywords. Fault Tolerance, Structured Parallel Programming, Performance Analysis

Introduction

Fault tolerance for High-Performance applications has been traditionally introduced by means of checkpointing and rollback recovery protocols [6]. These are designed to support general parallel computations, essentially featuring nondeterminism. This means that causal dependencies between processes (or implementation modules) are built dynamically: we have a full knowledge of causal dependencies only after the computation has been executed.

Checkpointing and rollback recovery protocols must take into account this issue. Classical solutions are based on coordinating the behavior of processes during checkpointing or by logging messages onto stable storage. These solutions can induce large overheads, which are possibly not known in advance. In Communication-Induced-Checkpointing (CIC) protocols causal dependencies are dynamically tracked and exchanged between processes: they are used to evaluate special predicates, telling each process if it has to checkpoint, avoiding to build inconsistent states [6]. A main issue for CIC protocols is represented by the fact that the number of checkpoints performed during the computation (i.e. the protocol overhead) cannot be statically known [7]: this is especially critical for High-Performance applications.

[1] This work has been partially funded by the italian FIRB In.Sy.Eme. project RBIP063BPH-05.

[2] This author would like to thank the Barcelona Supercomputing Center (BSC) for its proficuos collaboration and its hospitality.

In this paper we propose to attack the issue of building consistent system states by using structured parallelism models. Unlike general parallelism models, this paradigm is based on common parallelism forms (or structures), which include some information about causal dependencies. Examples of parallel structures are divide-and-conquer, parallel sort and, in more general terms, algorithmic skeletons [4]. A main property of these paradigms is represented by the possibility of statically analyzing their performance.

Past research works shown how the structural information of these paradigms can be used to introduce optimized dynamicity supports and adaptivity aspects [9]. In this paper we show how this information can be used to derive optimized checkpointing protocols, based on consistency definition defined at the level of the programming model. Our final goal is to show how it is possible to define a static performance analysis of induced overheads.

We focus our study on data parallel programs, which represent a large class of complex parallel computations. In the data parallel model we replicate the evaluation of a programmer-defined function F on each element of a state. The evaluation of F is iterated for a given number of times or until some condition is satisfied. Function evaluations for elements can be inter-dependent: to compute the next value at step i for an element, we need the values of some neighbor elements computed at the previous step $i-1$. This functional relation is called *stencil* and it characterizes, along with F, a specific data parallel program. A stencil can be equal for all steps (fixed stencil) or it can change (variable stencil). We consider fixed and variable static stencil data parallel programs. Several parallel applications can be modeled according to this model: the re-solution of linear systems (e.g. for heat transfer [8]); the re-solution of tridiagonal systems (e.g. [5]); computation and communication patterns (e.g. reduce).

We show how to derived optimized checkpointing protocols for data parallel programs, which performance impact can be statically analyzed, and we show a possible instantiation. The described protocol is performed locally on each process without online coordination. Each process locally counts its computation steps derived from the abstract programming model. At each step it checks if it has reached some statically defined threshold, equal for all processes, and it possibly performs a checkpointing operation. To assess our research contribution, we perform experiments on bechmarks of data parallel programs. We compare the number of performed checkpoints by an advanced CIC protocol [7] with the one performed by our protocol.

The paper is organized as following: Section 1 presents a critical description of checkpointing and rollback recovery protocols. Section 2 introduces a novel way of describing data parallel programs, used to derive optimized checkpointing. Section 3 describes a fault tolerance implementation of data parallel programs, based on a checkpointing protocol derived from the defined consistency property. Section 4 shows the experimental results and Section 5 synthesizes the conclusions.

1. Related Work

Checkpointing and rollback recovery protocols [6] achieve consistency for global states in different ways:

- by coordinating processes during checkpointing. This can be obtained by either:
  (i) synchronizing them and flushing message buffers and in-transit messages, or

(ii) logging messages onto stable storage during the checkpointing operations, without the need of any synchronization.

- by logging messages onto stable storage and allowing processes to take independent checkpoints. Messages are replayed during recovery to obtain consistent states.
- by allowing processes to take checkpoints uncoordinately and by tracking the causal dependencies between processes. Causal dependency is used to evaluate a predicate, independently on each process, at each message-receive event. The predicate is different for each protocol and it states if a checkpoint is to be locally performed. These *forced* checkpoints avoid the building of inconsistencies between the uncoordinated checkpoints taken by processes. These protocols are denoted with *Communication-Induced-Checkpointing* (CIC), and they represent the most advanced design solution in checkpointing and rollback recovery.

All these protocols feature the same performance analysis issue: the induced overhead on the computation cannot be statically analyzed nor controlled. As a consequence, *it is difficult to select the best protocol between these, given also the information that the programmer has on the application.*

The performance impact of a CIC protocol depends on the number of local and forced checkpoints. While the programmer can control the frequency of local checkpoints (e.g. by means of a timeout), it cannot impose any control over the frequency of forced checkpoints. As discussed in [7] it is not possible to statically know the number of checkpoints taken by processes during the computation. This happens because the conditions inducing a forced checkpoint depend on the causal dependencies between processes, which are dynamically built. These causal dependencies depend on nondeterministic factors, such as the relative speed of processes and their communications.

In this paper we notice that the number of forced checkpoints actually represents the main uncontrolled overhead over the application performance. In Sect. 4 we compare the number of checkpoints performed by our checkpointing protocol with the ones of a representative of CIC protocols.

2. A Novel Data Parallel Model Targeting Fault Tolerance

We introduce a tool for modeling structured parallel programs and we apply it to describe data parallel programs. The tool is inspired by an existing data structure, defined for data-flow languages: the *Incomplete Structures*[1], or I-Structures. An I-Structure can be defined as a collection of typed elements, possibly of unlimited size. Elements in an I-Structure have a unique position (or index). Two operations are defined to access an I-Structure:

- *put*: stores a given element in a given position. The prototype of this operation is *put(position, element)*.
- *get*: given a position, it returns the element that is contained, or will be contained, in that position. The prototype of this operation is: *get(position, element)* (element as output).

These operations are characterized by two main properties, which give the actual semantics of interactions that can be expressed with I-Structures:

```
1    int step = 0;
2    while(!termCondition) {
3        get(step, .., element-1);
4        get(step, .., element-N);
5        result = F(element-1, .., element-N);
6        put(step+1, .., result);
7        step++;
8    }
```

Figure 1. Pseudo-code of a virtual processor implementing a generic data parallel program.

Property 1 *No more than one put can be performed on the same position.*

Property 2 *The get operation on an empty position blocks until a put operation is performed on that position.*

We exploit I-Structures to model the state variables of data parallel programs. This allows us to introduce *sequence identifiers* to model the relationship between control- and data-flow. Sequence identifiers can be used to introduce high-level consistency definitions and to design checkpointing and rollback recovery logics.

We exemplify a generic data parallel program: we model its state S with a single I-Structure. Each I-Structure position includes a set of elements $e_0, \ldots, e_{N-1}$, which corresponds to a value assumed by S at each data parallel loop. Each virtual processor (or VP) is assigned an element e on which it iteratively evaluates **F**. It can access the state with *put* and *get* operations. We assume the owner-computes rule: each VP can perform both *put* and *get* on its element, but only *get* ones on neighbor elements. Accessing operations are used to express the functional dependencies (i.e. the stencil).

Figure 1 we show the pseudo-code of a VP implementing a generic data parallel program. The *step* variable is used to count logical steps: without loss of generality, we map sequence identifiers of I-Structures into integer numbers. At each iteration each VP collects the needed elements (according to the stencil), it applies **F** to the obtained elements, and it puts the result in the proper field of the next I-Structure position.

2.0.1. Consistency Definition for State

We provide and abstraction of the consistency definitions described in [6,3] at the level of the data parallel model. The consistency property can be defined as:

Definition 1 *A consistent state for a data parallel program is one for which all its element values are results of the same number of computing steps.*

That is, all element values are result of the same number of evaluations of the **F** function. Clearly, the states characterized by our definition are only a subset of all possible consistent states (e.g. for map programs all states are consistent). On the other hand, this definition is sufficiently general to cover all possible static stencil data parallel programs.

In this paper we focus on the experimental comparison between CIC protocols and I-Structure ones. Consequently, we avoid all the proofs of correctness. The interested reader can refer to [2] for full proofs.

3. Implementation and Checkpointing Protocol

We implement data parallel programs with distributed processes interacting through message passing. Each process is assigned a state partition: it sequentially applies **F** on the assigned elements. That is, VPs are uniquely assigned to processes. Stencils are implemented as communications between processes. We extend this implementation with a simple checkpointing protocol derived from our I-Structure model of data parallel programs.

Figure 2 shows the pseudo-code of a generic process i for a generic data parallel program during its steady-state. The loop is executed until some *term* condition is verified. The I-Structure positions are counted by means of an integer variable (**step**), which

```
partition  localPart;
partitions  ghosts;
int  step = 0;


while (! term ) {
   chInList = stencilInNeighChannels (step ,  myid );
   int  i = 0;
   for each  ch  in  chInList  do  receive (ch,  &ghosts [ i ++], step );

   myPart =  F( myPart ,  ghosts );

   step ++;

   if ( step  %  DELTA–CHK  == 0) {
      stst –checkpoint ( myPart ,  step );
   }

   chOutList = stencilOutNeighChannels ( step ,  myid );
   for each  ch  in  chOutList  do  send ( ch ,  ghost ( myPart ,  ch ),  step );
}
```

Figure 2. VPM pseudo-code of a generic data parallel program. The *partition* data structure implements a process local partition. The *partitions* data structure implements a container of *partition* data structures.

is incremented at each program loop.

The actions performed by each process are:

- receive neighbour subpartitions: the channel list is obtained by applying the **stencilInNeighChannels** function, which implements the stencil definition and the mapping of VPs onto processes;
- evaluation of the function **F** on each element of the local partition, also using ghost neighbor elements (**F** is overridden for elements and partitions);
- increment of the step;
- checkpointing protocol: check if the step variable has reached some predefined **DELTA-CHK**, and possibly perform a checkpoint;
- send of local sub-partitions to neighbours according to the stencil. The **stencilOutNeighChannels** function returns the channels on which to send the sub-partitions, and the **ghost** function returns the required sub-partition;

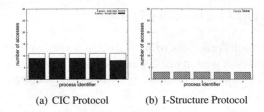

(a) CIC Protocol   (b) I-Structure Protocol

Figure 3. Num. of checkpoints for 5 processes *North-and-South* in CIC (left) and I-Structure (right).

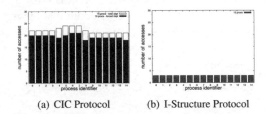

(a) CIC Protocol   (b) I-Structure Protocol

Figure 4. Num. of checkpoints for 15 processes *North-and-South* in CIC (left) and I-Structure (right).

The current step value, passed to send and receive operations, enables the elimination of duplicated messages during rollback recovery.

Thus, the checkpointing protocol includes two main actions: each process periodically performs a checkpointing operation (point 4 above). We require that **DELTA-CHK** is equal on all processes. That is, it is a constant or a variable which can be atomically modified. By assuming this, we guarantee that checkpointing operations taken at the same step, independently by each process without any online coordination, form a consistent recovery line according to definition 1.

During rollback recovery we will need to discard duplicated messages. To do so, we can make use of the property of data parallel programs for which each message sent by a process while performing step i must be received from the corresponding receiver while executing the same step i. We piggyback each application message with the step at which it is sent. We pass the current step value to the receive operation in such a way that the support can select the correct messages and possibly discard duplicated ones.

Finally notice that we are not enforcing a step-synchronous behavior and we are implementing data parallel programs by means of asynchronous communications. As a consequence, the last checkpoint of a process could be different from the last one of another process. For this reason, while performing rollback, we will need to select amongst the last checkpointing steps of all participating processes.

4. Experiments

We have performed experiments on a set of data parallel benchmarks. For brevity we show the results of only a subset of them:

- *North-and-South*: at each step each VP sends and receives ghost partitions from its north and south neighoburs. The functional dependecies are toroidal.
- *Odd-North-Even-South*: at odd steps each VP sends its information to the north neighbour and receives the one of its south neighbour; at odd steps each VP sends

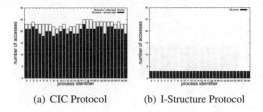

(a) CIC Protocol   (b) I-Structure Protocol

Figure 5. Num. of checkpoints for 30 processes *North-and-South* in CIC (left) and I-Structure (right).

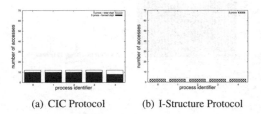

(a) CIC Protocol   (b) I-Structure Protocol

Figure 6. Num. of checkpoints for 5 processes *Odd-North-Even-South* in CIC (left) and I-Structure (right).

its information at south and receives from north. The functional dependecies are *not* toroidal.

We support both benchmarks with the CIC protocol [7] and with the I-Structure one. We measure the number of checkpoints taken by each protocol during an execution of 30 minutes with parallelism degrees equal to 5, 15 and 30. The configuration parameters of the protocols follow: T_F is the time needed to evaluate F on a local process partition; N is the number of data parallel steps; L_{com} is the average communication latency; T_{stst} is the average stable storage access time for a checkpoint; $T_{\Delta_{ckpt}}$ is the checkpointing timeouts; The only difference between the configuration of the two protocols resides in the local checkpointing interval: in the CIC protocol it is a causally generated number between a fixed interval (60 and 180 secs. and 300 and 900 secs.); in our protocol it is fixed to the mean value of these intervals.

Figures 3, 4 and 5 show the comparison for the *North-and-South* benchmark. For the CIC protocol it can be noticed that the number of forced checkpoints (black section) dominates the total number of checkpoints (w.r.t. local checkpoints). Moreover, the number of forced checkpoints changes between different processes and it increases with the parallelism degree, given by the increasing of the diameter of the toroidal stencil. Unlike this behavior, notice that the I-Structure protocol performs the exactly selected number of checkpoints.

Figures 6, 7 and 8 show the comparison for the *Odd-North-Even-South* benchmark. By comparison with the previous benchmark, notice that the stencil highly influences the number of forced checkpoints. Also in this case the number of checkpoints increases with the parallelism degree. The I-Structure protocol performs the very same number of checkpoints.

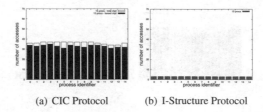

(a) CIC Protocol   (b) I-Structure Protocol

Figure 7. Num. of checkpoints for 15 processes *Odd-North-Even-South* in CIC (left) and I-Structure (right).

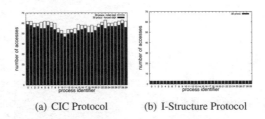

(a) CIC Protocol   (b) I-Structure Protocol

Figure 8. Num. of checkpoints for 30 processes *Odd-North-Even-South* in CIC (left) and I-Structure (right).

5. Conclusions

In this paper we have introduced fault tolerance based on checkpointing and rollback recovery for data parallel programs. We have shown the gain of exploiting a structured parallel programming model for fault tolerance. We have introduced a modeling tool, based on I-Structures, to define consistency properties at the abstraction level. We have instantiated our methodology to define a simple checkpointing protocol, and we have compared it with an advanced CIC protocol. Experimental results show that exploiting a "structure-unaware" programming model induces checkpointing overheads which cannot be statically analyzed. Unlike this, our methodological approach enables programmers to statically and precisely select the frequency of checkpointing operations.

References

[1]   Arvind, R. S. Nikhil, and K. K. Pingali. I-structures: data structures for parallel computing. *ACM Trans. Program. Lang. Syst.*, 11(4):598–632, 1989.

[2]   C. Bertolli. *Fault Tolerance for High-Performance Applications - A Model-Driven Approach*. VDM Verlag, 2009.

[3]   K. M. Chandy and L. Lamport. Distributed snapshots: determining global states of distributed systems. *ACM Trans. Comput. Syst.*, 3(1):63–75, 1985.

[4]   M. Cole. *Algorithmic skeletons: structured management of parallel computation*. MIT Press, USA, 1991.

[5]   Iain S. Duff and Henk A. van der Vorst. Developments and trends in the parallel solution of linear systems. *Par. Comp.*, 25(13-14):1931–1970, 1999.

[6]   E. N. (Mootaz) Elnozahy, L. Alvisi, Y.-M. Wang, and D. B. Johnson. A survey of rollback-recovery protocols in message-passing systems. *ACM Comp. Surv.*, 34(3):375–408, 2002.

[7]   J.-M. Helary, A. Mostefaoui, R. H. B. Netzer, and M. Raynal. Communication-based prevention of useless checkpoints in distributed computations. *Distrib. Comput.*, 13(1):29–43, 2000.

[8]   I.V. Singh and P.K. Jain. Parallel efg algorithm for heat transfer problems. *Adv. in Eng. Softw.*, 36, 2005.

[9]   M. Vanneschi and L. Veraldi. Dynamicity in distributed applications: issues, problems and the assist approach. *Par. Comp.*, 33(12):822–845, 2007.

Parallel Computing: From Multicores and GPU's to Petascale
B. Chapman et al. (Eds.)
IOS Press, 2010
© 2010 The authors and IOS Press. All rights reserved.
doi:10.3233/978-1-60750-530-3-441

Constructing Resilient Communication Infrastructure for Runtime Environments

George BOSILCA [a], Camille COTI [b], Thomas HERAULT [b], Pierre LEMARINIER [a]
and Jack DONGARRA [a]

[a] *University of Tennessee Knoxville*
[b] *University of Tennessee Knoxville, Universite Paris Sud, INRIA*

Abstract. High performance computing platforms are becoming larger, leading to scalability and fault-tolerance issues for both applications and runtime environments (RTE) dedicated to run on such machines. After being deployed, usually following a spanning tree, a RTE needs to build its own communication infrastructure to manage and monitor the tasks of parallel applications. Previous works have demonstrated that the Binomial Graph topology (BMG) is a good candidate as a communication infrastructure for supporting scalable and fault-tolerant RTE. In this paper, we present and analyze a self-stabilizing algorithm to transform the underlying communication infrastructure provided by the launching service into a BMG, and maintain it in spite of failures. We demonstrate that this algorithm is scalable, tolerates transient failures, and adapts itself to topology changes.

Keywords. Self-stabilization, binomial graph, scalability

1. Introduction

Next generation HPC platforms are expected to feature millions of cores distributed over hundreds of thousands of nodes, leading to scalability and fault-tolerance issues for both applications and runtime environments dedicated to run on such machines. Most parallel applications are developed using a communication API such as MPI, implemented in a library that runs on top of a dedicated runtime environment. Notable efforts have been made in the past decades to improve the performance, scalability and fault-tolerance at the library level. The most recent techniques propose to deal with failures locally, to avoid stopping and restarting the whole system. As a consequence, fault-tolerance becomes a critical property of the runtime environment.

A runtime environment (RTE) is a service of a parallel system to manage and monitor applications. It is deployed on the parallel system by a launching service, usually following a spanning tree to improve the scalability of the deployment. The first task of the RTE is then to build its own communication infrastructure to synchronize the tasks of the parallel application. A fault-tolerant RTE must detects failures, and coordinates with the application to recover from them. Communication infrastructures used today (e.g. trees and rings) are usually built in a centralized way and fail at providing the necessary support for fault-tolerance because a few failures lead with a high probability to disconnected components. Previous works [2] have demonstrated that the Binomial Graph topology (BMG) is a good candidate as a communication infrastructure for supporting both scalability and fault-tolerance for RTE. Roughly speaking, in a BMG, each process is the root of a binomial tree gathering all processes.

In this paper, we present and analyze a self-stabilizing algorithm[1] to transform the underlying communication infrastructure provided by the launching service into a BMG, and maintain it in spite of failures. We demonstrate that this algorithm is scalable, tolerate transient failures, and adapt itself to topology changes.

2. Related Work

The two main open source MPI library implementations, MPICH [4] and Open MPI [13] focus on performance, portability and scalability. For this latter purpose, both libraries manage on-demand connections between MPI processes, via their runtime environments. MPICH runtime environment, called MPD [9], connects runtime daemons processes through a ring topology. This topology is scalable in term of number of connection per daemon, but has two major drawbacks: two node failures are enough to divide the dae-mons in two separate groups that cannot communicate with one another, and communi-cation information circulation does not scale well. The Open MPI runtime environment project, ORTE [10], deploys runtime daemons connected through various topologies, usually a tree. Recently, some works have proposed the integration of a binomial graph in ORTE [2]. However, the deployment of this topology inside ORTE is done via a spe-cific node to centralize the contact information of all the other nodes and decide of the mapping of the BMG topology over ORTE daemons. This current implementation pre-vents scalability, and does not reconstruct the BMG upon failures. Our work focuses on the deployment and maintenance of a BMG topology in a distributed and fault-tolerant way, exhibiting more scalability.

Self-stabilization [15,11] is a well known technique for providing fault tolerance. The main idea of self-stabilization is the following: given a property P on the behavior of the system, the execution of a self-stabilizing algorithm eventually leads from *any* start-ing configuration, to a point in the execution in which P holds forever (assuming no out-side event, such as a failure). A direct and important consequence of this fault tolerance technique is that self-stabilizing algorithms are also self-tuning. No particular initializa-tion is required to eventually obtain the targeted global property. Some self-stabilizing algorithms already exist to build and maintain topologies. Most of them address ring [5] and spanning tree topologies [12], on top of a non-complete topology. They are usually designed in a shared memory model in which each node is assumed to know and be able to communicate with all its neighbors [1]. To the best of our knowledge, our work addresses for the first time building and maintaining a complex topology such as BMG. The classical shared memory model does not fit the actual systems we target in which connections are opened based on peer's information, thus we designed our algorithm using a message passing, knowledge-based, model [14].

---

[1] Self-stabilization systems [11] are systems that eventually exhibit a given global property, regardless of the system state at initialization

3. Self-Adaptive BMG Overlay Network

We present in this section a self-stabilizing algorithm to build and maintain a binomial graph topology inside a runtime environment. This BMG construction supposes that every process in the system knows the connection information of a few other processes, at most one to be considered as its parent, such that the resulting complete topology is a tree of any shape. This assumption comes from the fact that the start-up of processes will usually follow a deployment tree. The connection information can be exposed to processes along their deployment, by giving to each process its parent's connection information according to the tree deployment. Each process then contact the parent to complete the tree topology connectivity information.

The algorithm we propose is silent: in the absence of failure during an execution, the BMG topology does not change. This property is mandatory for being able to use this topology to route messages. We also focus on obtaining an optimal convergence time, in terms of number of synchronous steps, for underlying *binomial* trees, as the runtime environment [8] we envisioned to implement this algorithm will usually deploy processes among such topology.

The construction of the BMG is done by the composition of two self-stabilizing algorithms. The first one builds an oriented ring from the underlying tree topology, while the second one builds a BMG from the resulting ring. In the next subsections we present both algorithms, the key ideas of their proof of correctness and an evaluation of the time to build a BMG from different tree shape by simulation.

3.1. Model

System model   Our algorithms are written for an asynchronous system in which each process has a unique identifier. In the rest of the paper, although process identifiers and actual processes are two different notions, we will refer to a process by its identifier. We assume the existence of a unidirectional link between each pair of processes. Each link has a capacity bounded by an unknown constant, and the set of links results in a complete connected graph. As in the knowledge network model, a process can send messages to another process if and only if it knows its identifier. When a process receives a message, it is provided with the sender's identifier. The process's identifiers can be seen as a mapping of IP addresses in a real-world system, and the complete graph as the virtual logical network connecting processes in such a system.

Algorithms are described using the guarded rules formalism. Each rule consists in a guard and a corresponding action. Guards are Boolean expressions on the state of the system or (exclusively) a reception of the first message available in an incoming link. If a guard is true, its action can be triggered by the scheduler. If the guard is a reception, the first message of the channel is consumed by the action. An action can modify the process's local state and/or send messages.

The state of a process is the collection of the values of its variables. The state of a link is the set of messages it contains. A configuration is defined as the state of the system, i.e. the collection of the states of every process and every link. A transition represents the activation of a guarded rule by the scheduler. An execution is defined as an alternate sequence of configurations and transitions, each transition resulting from the activation of a rule whose guard held on the previous configuration.

We assume a centralized scheduler in the proof for the sake of simplicity. As no memory is shared between processes so that no two processes can directly interact, it is straightforward to use a distributed scheduler instead. We only consider fair schedulers, i.e. any rule whose guard remains true in an infinite number of consecutive configurations is eventually triggered.

Fault model   We assume the same fault model as in the classical self-stabilization model: transient arbitrary failures. Thus, faults can result in node crash, message loss, message or memory corruption. The model of transient failures leads to consider that during an execution, there exists time intervals large enough so the execution converges to a correct state before the next sequence of failure. The consequence on the execution model is to consider no failure will happen after any initial configuration.

3.2. Algorithms

We denote $\mathcal{ID}$ the identifiers of a process ; $List(c)$ a list of elements of type c, on which the operation $First(L)$ is defined to return the first element in the list L, and $next(e, L)$ is defined to return the element following e in the list L. Each of these functions return $\perp$ when the requested element cannot be found. $\perp$ is also used to denote a non-existing identifier.

Algorithm 1: Algorithm to build an oriented ring from any tree

Constants:
 $Parent : \mathcal{ID}$
 $Children : List(\mathcal{ID})$
 $Id : \mathcal{ID}$
Output:
 $Pred : \mathcal{ID}$
 $Succ : \mathcal{ID}$
1 - $Children \neq \emptyset \rightarrow$
    $Succ = First(Children)$
    Send $(F\_Connect, Id)$ **to** $Succ$

2 - **Recv** $(F\_Connect, I)$ **from** $p \rightarrow$
    if $p = Parent$ **then** $Pred = I$

3 - $Children = \emptyset \rightarrow$
    Send $(Info, Id)$ **to** $Parent$

4 - **Recv** $(Info, I)$ **from** $p \rightarrow$
    if $p \in Children$ **then**
        let $q = next(p, Children)$
        if $q \neq \perp$ **then**
            Send $(Ask\_Connect, I)$ **to** q
        else
            if $Parent \neq \perp$ **then**
                Send $(Info, I)$ **to** $Parent$
            else
                $Pred = I$
                Send $(B\_Connect, Id)$ **to** I

5 - **Recv** $(Ask\_Connect, I)$ **from** $p \rightarrow$
    $Pred = I$
    Send $(B\_Connect, Id)$ **to** I

6 - **Recv** $(B\_Connect, I)$ **from** $p \rightarrow$
    $Succ = I$

Algorithm 2: Algorithm to build a BMG from a ring which size is known

Input:
 $Pred : \mathcal{ID}$
 $Succ : \mathcal{ID}$
 $N : integer$ size of the ring
 $Id : \mathcal{ID}$
Output:
 /* Clockwise links   */
 $CW : Array[\mathcal{ID}]$
 /* Counterclockwise links */
 $CCW : Array[\mathcal{ID}]$
1 - $\perp \rightarrow$
    $CW[0] = Succ$
    $CCW[0] = Pred$
    Send $(UP, CCW[0], 1)$ **to** $Succ$
    Send $(DN, CW[0], 1)$ **to** $Pred$

2 - **Recv** $(UP, ident, nb\_hop)$ **from** $p \rightarrow$
    $CCW[nb\_hop] = ident$
    if $(2^{nb\_hop+1} < N)$ **then**
        Send $(UP, ident, nb\_hop + 1)$
        to $CW[nb\_hop]$
        Send $(DN, CW[nb\_hop], nb\_hop + 1)$
        to $ident$

3 - **Recv** $(DN, ident, nb\_hop)$ **from** $p \rightarrow$
    $CW\_links[nb\_hop] = ident$
    if $(2^{nb\_hop+1} \leq N)$ **then**
        Send $(DN, ident, nb\_hop + 1)$
        to $CCW[nb\_hop]$
        Send $(UP, CCW[nb\_hop], nb\_hop + 1)$
        to $ident$

3.3. Building a ring from a tree

The first step to build a binomial graph on top of a tree network consists in building a ring. This section defines a ring topology in our model and describes the proposed algorithm to build one from any tree. The last part of this section proposes a proof of correctness of this algorithm.

3.3.1. Topology description

Tree topology Let $\mathcal{P}$ be the set of all the process identifiers of the system, $|\mathcal{P}| = N$ be the size of the system. For every process $p \in \mathcal{P}$, let $Parent_p$ be a process identifier in $\mathcal{P} \cup \{\bot\}$ that p knows as its parent. Let $Children_p$ be a list, possibly empty, of process identifiers from $\mathcal{P}$ that p knows as its children. We define $anc_p(Q)$, the ancestry of the process p in the set of processes Q as a subset of Q such that $q \in anc_p(Q) \Leftrightarrow q \in Q \wedge (q = Parent_p \vee \exists q' \in anc_p(Q)$ s.t. $Parent_{q'} = q)$. A process p such that $Children_p = \emptyset$ is called a leaf. When $Children_p \neq \emptyset$, the first element of $Children_p$ is called first child of p, the last element of $Children_p$ is called the last child of p. We define the *rightmost leaf* of the set Q, noted 'rl_Q' as the unique leaf that is a last children process such that all processes in its ancestry in Q are last children processes.

A set of processes Q builds a tree rooted in r if and only if all processes of Q verify the three following properties: 1) $\forall p, q \in Q : parent_p = q \Leftrightarrow p \in Children_q$, 2) $Parent_r = \bot$, and 3) $\forall p \neq r \in Q, r \in anc_p(Q)$.

For the rest of the paper, we consider that for all configurations of all executions of the system, the collection of variables $Parent_p, Children_p$ for all processes builds a single tree holding all processes in the system. We call *root* the process that is the root of this tree.

We define the subtree rooted in $r \in \mathcal{P}$, as the subset T_r of $\mathcal{P}$, such that $r \in T_r \wedge \forall p \in \mathcal{P}, r \in anc_p(\mathcal{P}) \Leftrightarrow p \in T_r$. Note that $T_{root} = \mathcal{P}$ is the largest subtree. The depth of a subtree T_r, noted $depth(T_r)$, is defined as the size of the largest ancestry in this subtree: $depth(T_r) = max\{|anc_p(T_r)|, p \in T_r\}$.

Ring topology For every process $p \in \mathcal{P}$, let $Pred_p$ and $Succ_p$ represent its knowledge of two processes it considers as respectively its predecessor and its successor in the ring:

Definition 3.1. Consider the relation $\circled{S} : \mathcal{P} \times \mathcal{P}$ such that $p\circled{S}p'$ if and only if $Succ_p = p'$. We define $\mathcal{SU}_p$ as a subset of T_p such that $q \in \mathcal{SU}_p \Leftrightarrow q = p \vee p\circled{S}q \vee \exists q' \in \mathcal{SU}_p$ s.t. $q'\circled{S}q$.

Definition 3.2. Each process of the system is connected through a ring topology in a configuration C iff the following properties are verified: 1) $\mathcal{P} = \mathcal{SU}_{root}$, 2) $\forall p \in \mathcal{P}, \exists q \in \mathcal{P}$ s.t. $Succ_p = q \wedge Pred_q = p$, and 3) $Pred_{Succ_{root}} = Succ_{Pred_{root}} = root$.

3.3.2. Algorithm description

We describe in this section the silent self-stabilizing algorithm 1 that builds an oriented ring from any kind of tree topology. Each process except the root of the tree knows a *Parent* process identifier. Every process also has an ordered list of *Children* process identifiers, possibly empty. The basic idea of this algorithm is to perform two independent and parallel tasks: the first one consists in coupling parents with their first child in order to build a set of chains of processes. The second one consists in coupling endpoints of every resulting chain.

The first task is performed by guarded rules 1 and 2. Rule 1 can be triggered by every process that have at least a child. When triggered, the process considers its first child as the next process in the ring by setting its $Succ$ variable to its first child identifier. It then sends a message to this first child to make it set up its $Pred$ variable accordingly. Rule 2 is triggered by reception of this information message and sets up the $Pred$ variable using the identifier contained in the message. Note that each resulting chain eventually built by the first two rules has a tree leaf as one endpoint, and that every leaf of the tree is an endpoint of such a chain.

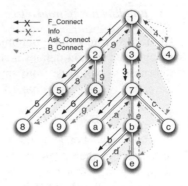

Figure 1.: Message exchanged for building a ring on top of a tree

The second task consists in finding for each leaf a process among the tree, the first free sibling, to pick up as its successor in the ring. Rule 3 can only be triggered by leaf processes and sends a message $Info$ to their parent to find a process. Rule 4 describes what happens upon reception of such $Info$ message. When receiving $Info$ from a child c and c is not the last element of its $Children$ list, it looks for the process identifier c' that is the next element of c' in its $Children$ list. Then it sends an $Ask\_Connect$ message to c' containing the identifier c so that these two processes address each other (Rules 5 and 6). If c is the last element of the $Children$ list, then the process forwards $Info$ to its own parent if it has one, or acts as the process looked for if it is the root of the tree.

3.3.3. Idea of the proof

Due to lack of space, we present here the main idea of the proof. The complete formal proof can be found in the appendices of this paper, and in the Technical Report [7]. As for any self-stabilizing algorithm, we first define a set of legitimate configurations, then demonstrate that any execution starting from a legitimate configuration remains in legitimate configurations (closure), and builds and maintain a ring (correctness), and that any execution starting from any configuration eventually reaches a legitimate configuration (convergence).

Legitimate configurations are defined by exhibiting a property on the state of processes (the succession of the $Succ$ variables starting at the root builds a chain holding all processes, and the $Pred$ variables are symmetrical to the $Succ$ variables), and a property on the messages in the communication channels. We prove first that every message initially present in any initial configuration has a finite impact on the other messages in the rest of the execution and on the state of the processes, because all messages have an effect on neighbors only, except $Info$ messages, which flow upstream in the tree, thus have a finite time to live in the system.

Then, we prove correction by induction on the subtrees of the system, and closure by analyzing all possible actions of the algorithm, assuming that all channels verify the properties of legitimate configurations. Finally, we prove that starting from any configuration, each channel holds a single message repeatedly, depending only on the shape of the tree, and that as a consequence the channels property of legitimate configurations is eventually verified. Using the fairness of the scheduler and following the action associated with each message identified for each channel, we demonstrate that the state-related property of legitimate configurations is also eventually verified.

3.4. building a binomial graph from a ring

The next and final step to build a binomial graph on top of a tree overlay network consists in, starting from the ring topology constructed by algorithm 1, expanding the knowledge of every process with the process identifiers of its neighbors in the BMG to be obtained.

3.4.1. Topology description

As described in [3], a binomial graph is a particular circulant graph [6], i.e. a directed graph $G = (V, E)$, such that $|V| = |\mathcal{P}|$, $\forall p \in V$, $p \in \{0, 1, \ldots, |\mathcal{P}| - 1\}$. $\forall p \in V, \forall k \in \mathbb{N}$ s.t. $2^k < |\mathcal{P}|, \exists (p, (p \pm 2^k) mod\ |\mathcal{P}|) \in E$. It means that every node $p \in V$ has a clockwise (CW) array of links to nodes $CW_p = \lfloor (p + 1)\ mod\ |\mathcal{P}|, (p + 2)\ mod\ |\mathcal{P}|, \ldots, (p + 2^k)\ mod\ |\mathcal{P}| \rfloor$ and a counterclockwise (CCW) array of links to nodes $CCW_p = \lfloor (p - 1)\ mod\ |\mathcal{P}|, (p - 2)\ mod\ |\mathcal{P}|, \ldots, (p - 2^k)\ mod\ |\mathcal{P}| \rfloor$. It is important to note that by definition, $\forall k > 0$ s.t. $2^k < |\mathcal{P}| : q = (p + 2^k)\ mod\ |\mathcal{P}| \in CW_p \Leftrightarrow q = (p + 2^{k-1} + 2^{k-1})\ mod\ |\mathcal{P}| \in CW_{p+2^{k-1}}$.

3.4.2. Algorithm description

The proposed algorithm uses the property of the BMG topology. Every node regularly introduces its direct neighbors to each other with rule 1. When a process is newly informed of its neighbor at distance 2^i along the ring, it stores this new identifier to the targeted list of neighbors, depending on the virtual direction, using either rule 2 or 3. Then it sends the identity of the processes at distance 2^i in both directions to introduce the two processes that are at distance 2^{i+1} along the ring to each other, unless $2^{i+1} \geq |\mathcal{P}|$.

3.4.3. Idea of the proof

Complete proof of the self-stabilizing property can be found in the technical report [7]. Due to lack of space, we give here a simple sketch of the proof: correctness and closure are deduced straightforwardly from the algorithm. For convergence, we reason by induction: assuming that the finger table (CW and CCW variables) is correct on the first i elements, we demonstrate that any execution eventually builds the level $i + 1$. Then, stating that level 0 is the ring that has been demonstrated self-stabilizing previously, we conclude that any execution eventually builds a full BMG.

4. Evaluation of the protocols

In this section, we present some simulations of the tree to ring and ring to BMG algorithms to evaluate the convergence time and communication costs of these protocols. The simulator is an ad-hoc, event-based simulator written in Java for the purpose of this evaluation. The simulator features two kinds of scheduling: a) a synchronous scheduler, where in each simulation phase, each process executes fully its spontaneous rule if applicable, then consumes every messages in incoming channels, and executes the corresponding guarded rule (potentially deposing new messages to be consumed by the receivers in the next simulation phase), and b) an asynchronous scheduler, where for each simulation phase, each process either executes the spontaneous rule if applicable, or consumes one (and only one) message in one incoming channel, and executes the corresponding guarded rule (again, potentially deposing new messages to be consumed by receivers in another simulation phase). The asynchronous scheduler is meant to evaluate upper bound on convergence time, working under the assumption that although every process will work in parallel, the algorithms are communication-bound, and the total convergence time should be dominated by the longest dependency of message transmission. The simulator also features three kinds of trees: 1) binary trees, fully balanced and having depth as a parameter; 2) binomial trees, fully balanced and having depth as a parameter; and 3) random trees having both depth and maximal degree (each process of depth less than the requested depth having at least one child, and at most degree children) as parameter. For all simulations, every node starts with an underlying tree already defined (following the algorithms assumptions), and no other connection established ($Succ_p = Pred_p = CW_p[i] = CCW_p[i] =\perp, \forall p \in \mathcal{P}, \forall 0 \leq i \leq \log_2(N)$). Self-stabilizing algorithms cannot stop communicating, because a process could be initialized in a state where it believes that its role in the distributed system is completed. However, real implementations would rely on timers to circumvent this problem and use less resources when convergence is reached and no fault has been detected. To simulate this behavior, each process in our simulation becomes quiet (it deactivates its local spontaneous rule, but continues to react to message receptions) as soon as its local state is correct ($Succ$, $Pred$, $CW[0]$ and $CCW[0]$ are correctly set).

Figure 2(b) presents the convergence time of the tree-to-ring and ring to BMG algorithms under a synchronous scheduler, for the case of binary and binomial trees, as function of the size of the trees. The x-axis is represented on a logarithmic scale, and one can see that in the case of an underlying binomial tree, the convergence time of the tree-to-ring algorithm is 4 synchronous phases (each $Info$ message originated at one leaf needs only to go up once to reach the parent of the tree this leaf is the rightmost leaf, then is forwarded to the parent that will step down to the next children which exist and create a $Ask\_Connect$ then a $B\_Connect$ message, hence 4 phases). For the case of a balanced binary tree, the longest path of $Info$ message has to go from one leaf in the "left" side of the tree up to the root, then two more messages to create the ring, hence $O(\log_2(N) + 2)$ phases. Until the ring has completely converge, exists at least one process in the system which can not start building one of its list of neighbors for the binomial graph. Thus it adds a $O(\log_2(N))$ more synchronous phases just after the ring is converged.

However, some nodes have to handle multiple communications during each phases, and communication-unbalance can happen. The consequence of this communication-unbalance is expressed in figure 2(a), that represents the same experiment under an asynchronous scheduler. With this scheduler, each simulation step consists of at most one message reception per process. Thus, if more messages have to be handled by some processes, the algorithms take significantly more time to reach convergence. To express convergence in time, we assume that each message takes 50 microseconds to be sent from one node to another (this time has been taken after measuring the communication latency of messages of 32 bytes between two computers through TCP over gigabit ethernet). As one can see on the figure, even if the projected convergence time remains very low for reasonably large trees (less than 1/50 of seconds for 64k nodes), the binomial tree presents a non-logarithmic convergence time, while in the case of binary tree, conver-

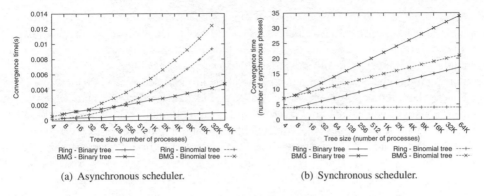

(a) Asynchronous scheduler.   (b) Synchronous scheduler.

Figure 2. Convergence Time for Binary and Binomial Trees.

gence time remains logarithmic. This is explained by figure 3, which presents the maximal number of messages received by a single process during the convergence period for the Binary and the Binomial tree of same size. One can see that the number of messages received by a single process on a Binomial tree is much larger than for a Binary tree. Because a process removes one and only one message at a time from its message queue in the asynchronous scheduler, the size of the queue grows linearly with the number of direct neighbors and with time (as long as processes deposit new messages in the waiting

queue). Thus, the waiting queue of the root in the binomial tree grows of $\log_2(N) - 1$ messages at each phase (until all leafs have ended generating $Info$ Messages), whereas it grows of 2 messages at each phase for a binary tree. Thus, convergence time of the binomial tree in this model is impacted by a factor $\log_2(N)$, and we can see in figure 2(a) that the convergence time for the binomial tree is indeed $\log_2^2(N)$, while it is $\log_2(N)$ for the binary tree.

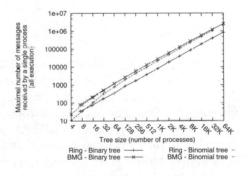

Figure 3.: Maximal number of messages received by a single process for Binary and Binomial Trees under an asynchronous scheduler

The last two figures 4(a) and 4(b) present the convergence times (in number of phases, or in seconds for the asynchronous scheduler) as functions of the tree size and depth, for random trees. The synchronous version presents a logarithmic progression of the convergence time for the ring construction and for the binomial graph construction. The convergence time of the ring construction algorithm is not modified by the number of nodes in the tree, only by the depth of the tree itself. It presents an increase logarithmic in the depth of the tree, which is consistent with the theoretical analysis of the algorithm. Similarly, the BMG construction algorithm highly depends on the number of nodes in the tree: each process has to exchange $2\log_2(N)$ messages when the tree is built to build the finger table of the BMG, and this is represented in the figure. However, this progression remains logarithmic with the number of nodes. The asynchronous case is more

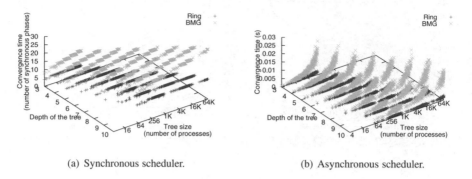

(a) Synchronous scheduler.   (b) Asynchronous scheduler.

Figure 4. Convergence Time for Random Trees.

complex to evaluate: because leafs become quiet only when their successor has received the $Ask\_Connect$ message causally dependent of their $Info$ Message, they introduce a lot of unnecessary $Info$ messages in the system. The asynchronous scheduler of the simulator takes one message after the other, following a FIFO ordering, and this introduces a significant slowdown of the $Info$ message, put in waiting queues. The projected time still remains very low, with less than 1/33 second for a 100k nodes tree. However, these results must be validated on a real implementation, to evaluate if the observed trend is due to simulation effects, or will be confirmed in a real-world system.

5. Conclusion

In this work, we present algorithms to build efficient communication infrastructures on top of existing spawning trees for parallel runtime environments. The algorithms are scalable, in the sense that all process memory, number of established communication links, and size of messages are logarithmic with the number of elements in the system. The number of synchronous rounds to build the system is also logarithmic, and the number of asynchronous rounds in the worst case is square logarithmic with the number of elements in the system. Moreover, the algorithms presented are fault-tolerant and self-adaptive using self-stabilization techniques. Performance evaluation based on simulations predicts a fast convergence time (1/33s for 64K nodes), exhibiting the promising properties of such self-stabilizing approach. The algorithm will be implemented in the STCI [8] runtime environment to validate the theoretical results.

References

[1]   Y Afek and A Bremler. Self-stabilizing unidirectional network algorithms by power supply. *Chicago Journal of Theoretical Computer Science*, 4(3):1–48, 1998.
[2]   T. Angskun, G. Bosilca, and J. Dongarra. Binomial graph: A scalable and fault-tolerant logical network topology. In *Parallel and Distributed Processing and Applications, ISPA 2007*, volume 4742/2007 of *Lecture Notes in Computer Science*, pages 471–482. Springer Berlin / Heidelberg, 2007.
[3]   T. Angskun, G. Bosilca, B. Vander Zanden, and J. Dongarra. Optimal routing in binomial graph networks. pages 363–370, December 2007.
[4]   Argonne National Laboratory. MPICH2. http://www.mcs.anl.gov/mpi/mpich2.

[5]   A Arora and A Singhai. Fault-tolerant reconfiguration of trees and rings in networks. *High Integrity Systems*, 1:375–384, 1995.

[6]   J.-C. Bermond, F. Comellas, and D. F. Hsu. Distributed loop computer networks: a survey. *Journal of Parallel and Distributed Computing*, 24(1):2–10, January 1995.

[7]   George Bosilca, Camille Coti, Thomas Herault, Pierre Lemarinier, and Jack Dongarra. Constructing resiliant communication infrastructure for runtime environments. Technical Report ICL-UT-09-02, Innovative Computing laboratory, University of Tennessee, http://icl.eecs.utk.edu/publications/, 2009.

[8]   Darius Buntinas, George Bosilca, Richard L. Graham, Geoffroy Vallée, and Gregory R. Watson. A scalable tools communication infrastructure. In *Proceedings of the 6th Annual Symposium on OSCAR and HPC Cluster Systems*, June 2008.

[9]   R. Butler, W. Gropp, and E. Lusk. A scalable process-management environment for parallel programs. In Jack Dongarra, Peter Kacsuk, and Norbert Podhorszki, editors, *Recent Advances in Parallel Virutal Machine and Message Passing Interface*, number 1908 in Springer Lecture Notes in Computer Science, pages 168–175, September 2000.

[10] R. H. Castain, T. S. Woodall, D. J. Daniel, J. M. Squyres, B. Barrett, and G .E. Fagg. The open run-time environment (OpenRTE): A transparent multi-cluster environment for high-performance computing. In *Proceedings, 12th European PVM/MPI Users' Group Meeting*, Sorrento, Italy, September 2005.

[11] S Dolev. *Self-Stabilization*. MIT Press, 2000.

[12] Felix C. Gärtner. A survey of self-stabilizing spanning-tree construction algorithms. Technical Report IC/2003/38, EPFL, Technical Reports in Computer and Communication Sciences, 2003.

[13] Richard L. Graham, Galen M. Shipman, Brian W. Barrett, Ralph H. Castain, George Bosilca, and Andrew Lumsdaine. Open MPI: A high-performance, heterogeneous MPI. In *Proceedings, Fifth International Workshop on Algorithms, Models and Tools for Parallel Computing on Heterogeneous Networks*, Barcelona, Spain, September 2006.

[14] Thomas Herault, Pierre Lemarinier, Olivier Peres, Laurence Pilard, and Joffroy Beauquier. A model for large scale self-stabilization. In IEEE International, editor, *Parallel and Distributed Processing Symposium. IPDPS 2007*, pages 1–10, march 2007.

[15] M Schneider. Self-stabilization. *ACM Computing Surveys*, 25(1):45–67, march 1993.

Industrial Papers

Parallel Computing: From Multicores and GPU's to Petascale
B. Chapman et al. (Eds.)
IOS Press, 2010

© 2010 The authors and IOS Press. All rights reserved.

doi:10.3233/978-1-60750-530-3-455

Optimizing Performance and Energy of High Performance Computing Applications

Luigi BROCHARD[a1], Raj PANDA[b], Don DESOTA[b],
Francois THOMAS[a] and Rob BELL Jr.[b]

[a]*Systems and Technology Group, IBM, France*
[b]*Systems and Technology Group, IBM, Austin*
[1] *luigi.brochard@fr.ibm.com*

Abstract. Power consumption is a critical consideration in high performance computing systems and it's becoming the limiting factor to build and operate Petascale and Exascale systems. When studying the power consumption of existing systems running HPC workloads, we find power, energy and performance are closely related leading to the possibility to optimize energy without sacrificing (much or at all) performance.

This paper starts by analyzing the power consumption of different HPC workloads at various levels of the server (processor, memory, io) across different blade systems using different processor micro-architectures (IBM Power6 blades, Intel Hapertown and Nehalem blades). It proposes a model to predict the power consumption of real workloads based on their performance characteristics measured by hardware performance counters (HPM). It shows the power estimation model achieves less than 2% error versus actual measurements. It shows the impact of over clocking and down clocking processor frequency on both power, performance and energy on the same set of HPC workloads and platforms as above.

Keywords. Energy, Performance, Power consumption

Introduction

Recently, power consumption has become a serious concern to managers of HPC data centers due to the rising cost of power and cooling. While data center managers are interested in optimal management of server system power allocation to minimize total operational cost of the data center, a typical HPC user is interested in the best turnaround time of his job. Realizing the importance of power management, hardware vendors are building more and more dynamic power management capabilities into microprocessors and server systems as well as providing software tools to obtain and view the power consumption data from the server systems. Some of the available tools can also be used to set limits on the power delivered to the server systems and thus help data center managers in the management of power and cooling costs. However, these software tools are not targeted to parallel applications and do not predict the impact of processor frequency scaling on total energy consumption, where energy is defined as the product of power consumption * elapsed time. For example, cases are described in this paper in which decreasing the processor frequency increases the energy consumed by the application while power consumption is decreasing.

Recognizing the HPC application community's need, we study performance and power consumption on a selection of HPC applications. Our objective is to experimentally obtain generalized power-performance correlations for HPC applications that can be used to estimate the power consumption and energy of an application, on any platform, and at any frequency. We use IBM POWER6 and Intel Harpertown and Nehalem server results and analysis to carry out these tasks.

Floyd et al. [2] and McCreary et al. [3] describe the system power management support in the POWER6 processor. Techniques such as core throttling and power and temperature monitoring capabilities are discussed. Allarey et al. [5] describe idle and multi-core dynamic power reduction features in Intel's 65nm cores, and they introduce a deep power-down idle state and power-performance tradeoffs for single threads, as well as enhanced sleep states. Rajamani et al. [6] propose real-time power and performance prediction capabilities that can be used for dynamic control of system resources such as DVFS and clock throttling to improve power-performance. They extend prior work related to average power prediction to predicting instantaneous processor power to enable applications such as operating system scheduling. Lee et al. [7] dynamically predict performance and power using regression models and apply them to controlling DVFS for program regions of 100M instructions. Our work is distinguished from prior work by a generalized power consumption model which predicts the power consumption at any frequency based on the application characteristics at nominal frequency as well as the large variety of platforms we tested. The rest of the paper is organized as follows.

Section 1 gives a brief description of the machines used in the power-performance experiments performed for this paper. Section 2 gives a description of the performance data gathering process for both Power6 and Core 2 micro-architectures and the derived metrics used in the models. Section 3 presents the tools used to measure power consumption. Section 4 presents the applications used for this study. Section 5 presents the performance and power measurements gathered on the various platforms, the model used for power and performance projections and the impact of frequency scaling on power and energy for each application on the various platforms.

1. Experimental Systems

The systems used in our experiments are an IBM JS22 blade, an IBM HS21-XM Harpertown blade, and a Nehalem "white box" described below. Table 1 shows configuration details for the systems used in the current work. JS22 is a blade that has two POWER6 modules running at 4.0 GHz. Each module has two cores capable of running in either single threaded (ST) mode or simultaneous multi-threaded (SMT) mode, with two threads per core. The POWER6 chip is a high frequency, in-order superscalar processor with 8MB of L2 cache, an L3 controller, an on-board fabric with controller, and integrated memory controller. In the blade, each POWER6 chip is a single-chip module without an L3, one memory controller, with only two channels attached to the memory DIMMs through buffer chips [1]. The POWER6 core pipeline has two binary floating-point units each capable of two floating-point operations per cycle, for a total of 4 floating-point operations per cycle per chip.

A number of JS22 blades can be inserted into the IBM BladeCenter-H chassis, which modularizes the blade power supplies, switch bays, and point-to-point wiring through the backplane [4]. Each blade contains four angled DIMM slots of 8GB

Table 1. Benchmark systems

System	Processor	Frequency (GHz)	Memory/speed (MHz)	System Power (Watts)	Power Measurement Tools
HS21-XM	Intel Harpertown	2.86	8 x 2GB 667	333	Amester
JS22	IBM Power6	4.0	4 x 4GB 667	417	Amester
Whitebox "Nehalem"	Intel Nehalem	2.93	12 x 4GB 1066	466	Power meter

DDR2-533 DIMMs or 1GB, 2GB, or 4GB DDR2-667 DIMMs, for up to 32GB of memory, supporting ECC, chip-kill and redundant bit steering. The blade also integrates the peripheral chips. Linux RHEL 4.6 and AIX 53L operating systems are supported. The BladeCenter integrates a management module with support for tools such as IBM Director, Power Executive, and the Active Energy Manager (AEM).

The IBM HS21-XM blade (characteristics listed in Table 1) is also deployed in the IBM BladeCenter-H chassis, and is managed by the same tools as the JS22. It has two sockets of Intel Hapertown Core 2 quad-core processors running at 2.8 GHz. The Hapertown processor cores also execute 4 floating point operations per cycle giving a total of 16 floating point operations per cycle per chip. The Hapertown processor is an MCM (Multi-Chip-Module) consisting of two dual core processor chips. The two cores share a common 6MB L2 cache. The MCMs connect to a central memory controller chip via a "front side bus" running at 1333 Mhz.

The Nehalem system is a 2U "white box" server with 2 sockets, each socket with one quad-core Nehalem processor running at 2.93GHz and 12 direct-attach 2GB DIMMs running at 1066MHz. It has private L1 and L2 caches per core and a shared 8MB L3 cache. Nehalem also features an integrated memory controller and QPI (Intel QuickPath Interconnect) interconnect.

2. Applications

For an effective analysis of power-performance, a set of floating point benchmarks was chosen that stress either the processor or the memory in the system, or both. A subset of 8 out of a possible 17 of the SPEC CPU2006 benchmarks was chosen in order to speed up the data collection and analysis tasks and to represent different benchmarks that are important to HPC as well as for their different performance characteristics in terms of CPI (cycles per instruction) and memory bandwidth. These are not true parallel applications but measurements show little difference in power consumption between the parallel versions of these workloads and the SPEC FP counterpart. Table 2 shows the selected applications.

3. Performance Metrics

To carry out our experiments, performance counter data from all three machines was collected.

Table 2. List of applications and HPC areas

Benchmark	Area
416.gamess	Quantum Chemistry
433.milc	Physics
435.gromacs	Molecular Dynamics
437.leslie3d	Fluid Dynamics
444.namd	Molecular Dynamics
454.calculix	Structural Analysis
459.GemsFDTD	Electromagnetics
481.wrf	Weather Forecasting

Table 3. Applications and their performance characteristics on the different systems

	HS21-XM		Nehalem		JS22	
Benchmark	CPI	BW(GB/s)	CPI	BW(GB/s)	CPI	BW(GB/s)
416.gamess	0.58	0.02	0.55	0.07	1.35	0.03
433.milc	11.00	6.23	1.44	39.52	6.84	16.30
435.gromacs	0.63	1.17	0.58	1.73	1.49	0.68
437.leslie3d	9.67	6.27	2.22	36.21	2.61	16.48
444.namd	0.69	0.23	0.63	0.36	1.37	0.27
454.calculix	0.60	2.18	0.52	4.85	1.04	1.89
459.GemsFDTD	10.66	6.10	2.38	37.10	5.10	15.78
481.wrf	5.71	6.12	1.17	34.61	1.53	12.74

For gathering the counter data, we used hpmcount tool on JS22, oprofile on HS21-XM and perfmon on the Nehalem platforms. Performance metrics like CPI (cycles per instruction) and memory bandwidth were computed for each of the SPEC benchmarks based on the hardware counter data collected using these tools. We ran the SPEC benchmarks in the throughput mode to assess the capability of each system. A number of copies of each of the benchmarks in Table 1 were on each platform for gathering the hardware counter data. On JS22 and the Nehalem platforms, we used the systems in SMT (simultaneous multi-thread) mode which implies that we would run twice the number of copies as the number of cores in the system. In other words, we ran one copy of the benchmark for each logical CPU in the system. Based on the elapsed time for the throughput benchmarks to complete on a system, one can also compute the throughput performance called "rate" according to SPEC benchmark rules. In Table 3, CPI and memory bandwidth metrics are shown for each of the benchmarks on each of the three systems.

Significant differences between these applications are apparent. Life Science applications like 416.games (see Table 2, 3rd entry), 435.gromacs 444.namd are very core intensive and have very little memory bandwidth. 454.calculix which is a structural analysis application is also core dominant. The remaining applications 433.milc, 437.leslie3d, 459.GemsFDTD and 481.wrf have high memory bandwidth requirements. Low CPI/Core Intensive applications are highlighted in grey and High CPI/ Memory bound applications in white.

4. Tools for Power Measurement

Two system management tools were used to collect the power data used in our experiments. Amester is a tool that is internal to IBM that we have used to measure power at a component level in the blade server while AEM (Active Energy Manager) is a commercially available product that can be used to measure power at the server level as well as power at chassis level.

The POWER6 processor supports multiple voltage domains on the chip. The circuits are grouped into four classes: analog clock generation circuits, analog off-chip interface circuits, arrays (on-chip SRAMs), and logic, each with its own voltage. By default, all logic, including most latches, operates at the Vdd voltage. The arrays are provided with a separate higher voltage (Vcs) than the standard Vdd logic voltage in order to support higher-performance SRAMs and increase manufacturing yield while allowing the other logic devices to be set to the lower Vdd value. The analog circuits used in the off-chip interface devices require a higher and invariant voltage, which is named Vio, for between-chip signaling.

The Autonomic Management of Energy (AME) project was started at the IBM Research Lab in Austin in 2004 with the goal of controlling server or blade power-performance to within a specified power and temperature budget [2]. JS22 and HS21-XM blades were provided with on-board power-measurement circuits and firmware additions to monitor the circuit outputs. An AME circuit places a very low impedance resistor in series with a power rail. Circuits are placed on the various rails feeding the VRMs(voltage regular modules) that power the system. The on-blade temperature and power management device (TPMD) then converts the voltage drop on each resistor to digital form, which allows it to project the current and power at the rails. The Blade Center management module can then interface digitally to the TPMD through the service processor to read the power and other information coming from the rails and control the behavior of the POWER6 through actuators positioned on the die [2].

The rails that are accessible readily are denoted in this paper in the following way:

1) *Core Power* (or Vdd): Power to the on-chip cores, internal fabric, memory controller, L2 cache controller, and other internal chip logic except for the L2 cache arrays (Vcs), I/O pins (Vio), and standby logic (Vsb).

2) *Total Power* (or 12V Power Supply): Power to the entire blade, including the POWER6 chip, L2 cache arrays, I/O pins, standby circuitry, blade service processor, and TPMD.

3) *DIMM Power* (or Vdram): Power to the memory DRAM and DIMM subsystem.

In the following paragraphs, one additional category of power dissipation, *Other*, consists of the blade components, other than the chips and memory subsystem, that have relatively static power dissipation (except for the L2 cache arrays, I/Os, and standby logic). This is computed as:

Other (Static) Power = Total Power – 2*Core Power – DIMM Power

The power dissipation in the L2 cache arrays and I/Os can vary with the benchmark, but the swing in power is small relative to the overall power of the POWER6 chips and the rest of the system, usually less than 6W, or 2% of the *Total Power*. Amester is executed from a remote machine and passes control commands

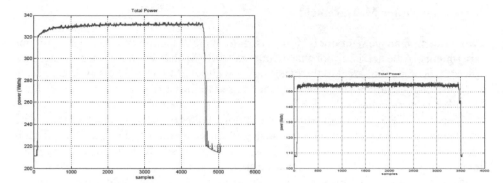

Figure 1. Total power measured on JS22 and HS21-XM for 437.leslie3d.

through the BladeCenter management module to each blade it monitors. The service processor executes the commands by interfacing to the TPMD and returns the requested data. Amester can sample the power dissipation at intervals from 1ms on up, but 32ms to 256ms gives a good tradeoff between resolution and data volume collected. In the following experiments a sampling interval of 256ms to collect power measurements of blade total power, core power, and DIMM power as described above.

Active Energy Manager (AEM) provides management and control of the chassis and individual blade energy use [1]. It supports analysis and control such as power trending and capping, thermal trending, and CPU trending at the chassis or individual blade levels. It's part of IBM Tivoli Director.

5. Power and Performance Data and Models

The Amester tool was used to measure overall power consumption, core power consumption and DIMM power consumption as explained in Section 3. Figure 1 shows a typical total power consumption graph for JS22 and HS21-XM. Note that idle power sits at about 210 Watts for the JS22 and 107 Watts for HS21-XM, which is about two-thirds of the power consumed when the benchmark 437.leslie3D is running.

The tables below summarize the different components of power consumption per benchmark by platform. The different components are the processor sockets (labeled Proc 0 and Proc 1 for JS22 and HS21-XM), the memory DIMMS (labeled Memory for JS22 and HS21-XM) and Others for JS22 and HS21-XM which include the IO chip, off-chip memory controller and off-chip cache if they exist.

Due to the recent availability of Nehalem systems, we did not have sufficient time to port Amester on Nehalem. Thus we have only the total power consumption data for the Nehalem system gathered using a power meter (Table 6).

As expected, processor power consumption accounts for the majority of the total power consumption. Coming in second, off-chip cache and IO chips consume a large amount of power regardless of the application execution characteristics.

We now derive a model to predict the power consumption of a given benchmark at frequency f_n given its characteristics measured at frequency f_0 and the platform characteristics measured at frequency f_n:

$$PWR(f_n) = A_n * GIPS(f_0) + B_n * GBS(f_0) + C_n \qquad (1)$$

Table 4. Power and performance on JS22 @ 4GHz

Benchmark	Performance (Rate)	Elapse Time (s)	Power (Watts)	Proc0 (Watts)	Proc1 (Watts)	Memory (Watts)	Other (Watts)
416.gamess	78.7	1991	299	91	91	14	103
433.milc	49.6	1482	316	80	80	51	104
435.gromacs	66.0	865	298	90	90	15	103
437.leslie3d	58.4	1288	331	88	88	51	105
444.namd	102.6	626	294	89	89	14	102
454.calculix	88.0	750	308	93	93	18	103
459.GemsFDTD	45.5	1866	314	80	80	50	104
481.wrf	81.0	1104	325	89	89	43	104

Table 5. Power and performance on HS21-XM @ 2.8 GHz

Benchmark	Performance (Rate)	Elapse Time (s)	Power (Watts)	Proc0 (Watts)	Proc1 (Watts)	Memory (Watts)	Other (Watts)
416.gamess	167	939	183	54	53	15	62
433.milc	20	3712	160	32	32	30	66
435.gromacs	143	399	181	51	50	17	63
437.leslie3d	22	3380	164	35	33	30	67
444.namd	118	543	178	51	49	15	64
454.calculix	115	574	190	54	52	20	64
459.GemsFDTD	20	4256	162	34	32	29	66
481.wrf	42	2112	165	36	33	29	66

Table 6. Power and performance on Nehalem @ 2.93 GHz

Benchmark	Performance (Rate)	Elapse Time (s)	Power (Watts)
416.gamess	167	939	183
433.milc	20	3712	160
435.gromacs	143	399	181
437.leslie3d	22	3380	164
444.namd	118	543	178
454.calculix	115	574	190
459.GemsFDTD	20	4256	162
481.wrf	42	2112	165

where, PWR, GIPS and GBS are respectively power consumption, Giga instructions per second, Giga bytes per second at a given frequency. GIPS(f_0) and GBS(f_0) are application characteristics measured at the nominal frequency (f_0). A_n, B_n and C_n are coefficients for a given platform at frequency f_n. They are calculated for each frequency with a multiple linear regression analysis using the method of least squares for determining the total power consumption over all workloads at a given frequency to fit Eq. (1). This model over the total power consumption provides a better fit than using separate models for the specific core power, memory power, and other power, and then adding them up. The physical meaning is less evident in the combined model, but it is designed specifically to serve the purpose of projecting power at some frequency f_n based on the nominal frequency f_0, thereby hiding the dependency of GIPS and GBS on clock frequency for a given benchmark. In Table 7, we present the resulting values of

Table 7. Power equation coefficients calculated for all platforms

System	Frequency (GHz)	Model Coefficients		
		An	Bn	Cn
Nehalem	2.93	10.66	1.67	329.4
JS22	3.5	1.41	2.46	224.0
JS22	3.8	1.90	2.55	248.4
JS22	4	2.36	2.62	268.3
HS21	2	0.64	3.61	112.7
HS21	2.67	1.11	3.92	129.7
HS21	2.8	1.20	3.75	135.9

Table 8. CPI and bandwidth measured on JS22

	3.5 GHz		3.8 GHz		4.0 GHz	
Benchmark	CPI	BW (GB/s)	CPI	BW (GB/s)	CPI	BW (GB/s)
416.gamess	1.35	0.03	1.35	0.03	1.35	0.03
433.milc	6.04	16.09	6.47	16.19	6.84	16.30
435.gromacs	1.50	0.61	1.50	0.65	1.49	0.68
437.leslie3d	2.34	16.09	2.48	16.35	2.61	16.48
444.namd	1.37	0.23	1.37	0.25	1.37	0.27
454.calculix	1.04	1.66	1.04	1.79	1.04	1.89
459.GemsFDTD	4.60	15.35	4.83	15.65	5.10	15.78
481.wrf	1.45	11.68	1.49	12.31	1.53	12.74

Table 9. CPI and bandwidth measured on HS21-XM7

	2.0 GHz		2.67 GHz		2.8 GHz	
Benchmark	CPI	BW (GB/s)	CPI	BW (GB/s)	CPI	BW (GB/s)
416.gamess	0.58	0.02	0.59	0.02	0.58	0.02
433.milc	7.00	6.27	9.30	6.27	11.00	6.23
435.gromacs	0.64	0.86	0.64	1.19	0.63	1.17
437.leslie3d	6.17	6.25	8.09	6.25	9.67	6.27
444.namd	0.70	0.17	0.70	0.21	0.69	0.23
454.calculix	0.57	1.66	0.58	2.14	0.60	2.18
459.GemsFDTD	6.79	6.11	8.93	6.10	10.66	6.10
481.wrf	3.69	6.08	4.87	6.10	5.71	6.12

the A, B and C coefficients for the power equation. The average error using this model on all benchmarks over all machines is less than 1.6%.

In Tables 8 and 9, we present CPI and total memory bandwidth measured for all workloads on JS22 and HS21-XM at different frequencies.

We now present the impact of frequency scaling on power and energy for the various benchmarks and platforms. Table 10 shows the power and energy effects of down clocking, or reducing frequency, on the JS22. Tables 11 through 12 show the effects of down clocking and over clocking on the HS21-XM. In all the following tables, energy is defined as Power * Elapsed Time in KWatt.

Table 10. Down clocking from 4.0 to 3.8 GHz on JS22

Benchmark	4.0 GHz			3.8 GHz			Perf delta	Savings	
	Elapse Time (s)	Power	Energy	Elapse Time (s)	Power	Energy		Power	Energy
416.gamess	1991	299	20.7	2104	274	20.0	-5.7%	8.5%	3.3%
433.milc	1482	316	16.2	1490	293	15.2	-0.6%	7.0%	6.5%
435.gromacs	865	298	8.9	917	273	8.7	-5.9%	8.3%	2.9%
437.leslie3d	1288	331	14.8	1302	307	13.9	-1.0%	7.3%	6.4%
444.namd	626	294	6.4	663	268	6.2	-6.0%	8.7%	3.2%
454.calculix	750	308	8.0	794	280	7.7	-5.9%	8.9%	3.5%
459.GemsFDTD	1865	314	20.3	1884	292	19.1	-1.0%	7.1%	6.2%
481.wrf	1103	325	12.5	1142	300	11.9	-3.4%	7.8%	4.6%

Table 11. Down clocking from 2.8 to 2.0 GHz on HS21-XM

Benchmark	2.8 GHz			2.0 GHz			Perf delta	Savings	
	Elapse Time (s)	Power	Energy	Elapse Time (s)	Power	Energy		Power	Energy
416.gamess	939	183	6.0	1329.5	138.2	6.4	-41.6%	24.4%	-7.1%
433.milc	3712	160	20.7	3718.3	135.5	17.5	-0.2%	15.5%	15.4%
435.gromacs	399	181	2.5	559.2	138.6	2.7	-40.3%	23.6%	-7.2%
437.leslie3d	3380	164	19.2	3361.2	138.7	16.2	0.6%	15.4%	15.9%
444.namd	543	178	3.4	756.5	135.6	3.6	-39.3%	23.9%	-6.1%
454.calculix	574	190	3.8	783.5	143.8	3.9	-36.4%	24.2%	-3.5%
459.GemsFDTD	4256	162	23.9	4258.0	136.2	20.1	-0.1%	15.7%	15.6%
481.wrf	2112	165	12.1	2126.0	138.6	10.2	-0.6%	15.8%	15.3%

Table 12. Over clocking from 2.66 to 2.8 GHz on HS21-XM

Benchmark	2.67 GHz			2.8 GHz			Perf delta	Savings	
	Elapse Time (s)	Power	Energy	Elapse Time (s)	Power	Energy		Power	Energy
416.gamess	999	174	6.0	938.7	182.8	6.0	6.0%	-5.2%	1.1%
433.milc	3716	155	20.0	3712.4	160.4	20.7	0.1%	-3.4%	-3.3%
435.gromacs	424	173	2.5	398.6	181.4	2.5	6.0%	-5.0%	1.3%
437.leslie3d	3362	159	18.5	3380.0	164.0	19.2	-0.5%	-3.2%	-3.8%
444.namd	572	168	3.3	543.1	178.1	3.4	5.1%	-5.8%	-0.4%
454.calculix	605	180	3.8	574.2	189.6	3.8	5.1%	-5.3%	0.1%
459.GemsFDTD	4259	157	23.1	4255.6	161.5	23.9	0.1%	-3.2%	-3.1%
481.wrf	2117	159	11.7	2112.5	164.7	12.1	0.2%	-3.4%	-3.2%

From the tables, it can be seen that down clocking frequency on some platforms like the JS22 always saves power and energy regardless of the benchmark, while on other machines like the HS21-XM, down clocking always saves power but increases energy on the benchmarks with low memory bandwidth, as, for example, on 416.gamess, 435.gromacs, 444.namd, and 454.calculix. This behaviour arises when power saving is less than the performance degradation. This may happen for low memory bandwidth applications as the performance of these benchmarks is directly affected by CPU frequency. On the other hand, power saving on HS21-XM is less than power saving on JS22 since HS21 has a lower frequency processor. In other words down clocking has a bigger payback on high frequency platforms since the core power consumption is much higher (see Tables 4 and 5). Therefore, for platforms like the HS21-XM, over clocking can be an option for optimizing energy on low memory bandwidth applications.

Conclusions

This paper proposes a generalized power consumption model that can optimize power and energy consumed by clusters when running HPC applications. The method uses a multiple regression model to predict the power consumed of a particular application at any frequency knowing a few parameters characterizing the application at nominal frequency.

Experimental data measured on different systems, including IBM Power6 and Intel Hapertown and Nehalem microprocessor based systems, have validated the model with an error less than 2% versus measured power consumption.

References

[1] H.Q. Le, W.J. Starke, J.S. Fields, F.P. O'Connell, D.Q. Nguyen, B.J. Rochetti, W.M. Sauer, E.M. Schwarz, M.T. Vaden, "IBM POWER6 microarchitecture," J. Res. & Dev., Vol. 51, No. 6, November 2007, pp. 639–662.

[2] M.S. Floyd, S. Ghiasi, T.W. Keller, K. Rajamani, F.L. Rawson, J.C. Rubio, and M.S. Ware, "System power management support in the IBM POWER6 microprocessor," J. Res. & Dev., Vol. 51, No. 6, November 2007, pp. 733–746.

[3] H.-Y. McCreary, M.A. Broyles, M.S. Floyd, A.J. Geissler, S.P. Hartman, F.L. Rawson, T.J. Rosedahl, J.C. Rubio, and M.S. Ware, "EnergyScale for IBM POWER6 microprocessor-based systems," J. Res. & Dev., Vol. 51, No. 6, November 2007, pp. 775–786.

[4] IBM Corporation, IBM BladeCenter, http://www.ibm.com/servers/eserver/bladecenter.

[5] J. Allarey, V. George, S. Jihagirdar, "Power Management Enhancements in the 45nm Intel Core Microarchitecture," Intel Technology Journal, Vol. 12, Issue 3, 2008, pp. 169–178.

[6] K. Rajamani, H. Hanson, J.C. Rubio, S. Ghiasi, F.L. Rawson, "Online Power and Performance Estimation for Dynamic Power Management," IBM Research Technical Report, RC 24007, July 14, 2006.

[7] S.J. Lee, H.K. Lee, and P.C. Yew, "Runtime Performance Projection Model for Dynamic Power Management," in ACSAC 2007, 2007, pp. 186–197.

Mini-Symposium
"Adaptive Parallel Computing: Latency Toleration, Non-Determinism as a Form of Adaptation, Adaptive Mapping"

Parallel Computing: From Multicores and GPU's to Petascale
B. Chapman et al. (Eds.)
IOS Press, 2010
© 2010 The authors and IOS Press. All rights reserved.
doi:10.3233/978-1-60750-530-3-467

An Operational Semantics for S-Net

Frank PENCZEK [a,1] Clemens GRELCK [a,b] Sven-Bodo SCHOLZ [a]

[a] *University of Hertfordshire, School of Computer Science, United Kingdom*
[b] *University of Amsterdam, Institute of Informatics, The Netherlands*

Abstract. We present the formal operational semantics of S-NET, a coordination language and component technology based on stream processing. S-NET turns conventional (sequential) functions/procedures into asynchronous components interacting with each other through a streaming network; it defines network topologies inductively by a small combinator language that captures essential forms of concurrency. Our formal semantics allows us to reason about program properties and defines the design space for alternative implementation strategies.

1. Introduction

Today's hardware trend towards multi-core/many-core chip architectures [1,2] places immense pressure on software manufacturers: For the first time in history software does not automatically benefit from new generations of hardware. Today, software must become parallel in order to benefit from future processor generations! However, existing software is predominantly sequential, and writing parallel software is notoriously difficult. So far, parallel computing has been confined to supercomputing. Now, it must go mainstream. This step requires new tools and techniques that radically facilitate parallel programming.

S-NET [3] is such a novel technology. Our key design principle is the separation of concerns between *application engineering* and *concurrency engineering*. The former applies domain-specific knowledge to provide application building blocks of suitable granularity using a familiar sequential programming environment. The latter applies expert knowledge of target architectures and concurrency in general to orchestrate sequential building blocks into a parallel application.

S-NET turns conventional functions/procedures into asynchronous, state-less components named *boxes*. Each box has a single input and a single output stream. This restriction is motivated by our guiding principle: The concern of a box is mapping input values into output values, whereas its purpose within a streaming network is unknown to the box itself. Concurrency concerns like synchronisation and routing that immediately arise if a box had multiple input streams or multiple output streams are thus kept away from boxes.

It is a distinguishing feature of S-NET that streams are no explicit objects. Instead, we use algebraic formulae to define the connectivity of boxes. We have

---

[1]Corresponding Author: Frank Penczek, University of Hertfordshire, Science and Technology Research Institute, Hatfield, Herts, AL10 9AB, United Kingdom, e-mail: f.penczek@herts.ac.uk

identified four fundamental construction principles for streaming networks: *serial composition* of two components, *parallel composition* of two components where some routing oracle determines the branch to take, *serial replication* of one component where data is streamed through consecutive instances of the component, and *indexed parallel replication* where an index attached to the data determines which branch (i.e. which replica) to take. Network construction preserves the SISO property: any network, regardless of its complexity, again is a SISO component. We build S-NET on these construction principles because they are pairwise orthogonal, each represents a fundamental principle of composition beyond the concrete application to streaming networks (i.e. serialisation, branching, recursion, indexing), and they naturally express the prevailing models of parallelism (i.e. task parallelism, pipeline parallelism, data parallelism).

The contribution of this paper is a formal operational semantics of S-NET. Defining the meaning of language constructs in a rigorous formal nomenclature will allow us to reason about properties of programs. Equally important, it precisely defines the design space of implementations. This is of particular interest as different implementations of S-NET with orthogonal design philosophies are currently under development [4,5].

The remainder of this paper is structured as follows: Section 2 introduces S-NET in greater detail. In Section 3 we present our operational semantics. We discuss some related work in Section 4 and conclude in Section 5.

2. S-Net at a glance

S-NET structures messages between components as non-recursive records, i.e. sets of label-value pairs. Labels are subdivided into *fields* and *tags*. Fields are associated with values from the box language domain that are opaque to S-NET. Tags are associated with integer numbers that are accessible both on the S-NET and the box language level. Tag labels are distinguished from field labels by angular brackets. For example, `{a,b,<t>}` is the record type (set of labels) of messages containing fields a and b and tag t.

In S-NET, we define a box using the key word `box` followed by the box name and a *type signature*, i.e. a mapping from an *input type* to a disjunction of *output types*. For example,

`box foo ({a,<b>} -> {c} | {c,d,<e>})`

declares a box named `foo` that expects records with a field labelled a and a tag labelled b. The box responds with a number of records that either have just a field c or fields c and d as well as tag e. Both the number of output records and the choice of variants are at the discretion of the box implementation alone. As soon as a record is available on the input stream, the box consumes that record, applies the associated function to the record elements and emits the resulting records on its output stream. S-NET boxes are stateless by definition, i.e., the mapping of an input record to a stream of output records is free of side-effects.

In fact, the above type signature makes box `foo` accept *any* input record that has *at least* field a and tag b, but may well contain further fields and tags. The formal foundation of this behaviour is *structural subtyping* on records: Any record type t_1 is a subtype of t_2 $(t_1 \preccurlyeq t_2)$ iff $t_2 \subseteq t_1$. This subtyping relationship extends nicely to multivariant types, e.g. the output type of box `foo`: A multivariant type x is a subtype of y if every variant $v \in x$ is a subtype of some variant $w \in y$. Subtyping on the input type of a box means that a box may receive input records that contain more fields and tags than the box is supposed to process. Such fields and tags are retrieved from the record before the box starts processing and are added to each record emitted by the box in response to this input record, unless the output record already contains a field or tag of the same name. We call this behaviour *flow inheritance*. In conjunction, record subtyping and flow inheritance prove to be indispensable when it comes to making boxes that were developed in isolation to cooperate with each other in a streaming network.

In S-NET, we define streaming networks using the key word **net** followed by the network name. For example,

net bar connect *expr*

defines the network **bar**. Following the key word **connect**, an expression built out of previously defined box and network names and four network combinators determines the network topology.

Let A and B be the names of two S-NET networks or boxes. Serial composition (denoted `A..B`) constructs a new network where the output stream of A becomes the input stream of B while the input stream of A and the output stream of B become the input and output streams of the compound network. Parallel composition (denoted `(A|B)`) constructs a network where all incoming records are either sent to A or to B and the resulting record streams are merged to the compound output stream. Type inference [6] associates each network with a type signature similar to the type signatures of boxes. Any incoming record is directed towards the branch whose input type matches the type of the record best. Serial replication (denoted `A*type`) constructs an unbounded chain of serially composed instances of A with exit pattern *type*. At the input stream of each instance of A, we compare the type of an incoming record (i.e. the set of labels) with *type*. If the record's type is a subtype of the specified type (we say, it matches the exit pattern), the record is routed to the compound output stream, otherwise into the instance of A. Indexed parallel replication (denoted `A!<tag>`) replicates instances of A in parallel. Unlike in static parallel composition routing is value dependant on a tag specified as right operand. All incoming records must feature this tag; its value determines the instance of the left operand the record is sent to. Output records are non-deterministically merged into a single output stream.

Parallel composition (`|`), serial replication (`*`) and indexed parallel replication (`!`) involve non-deterministic merging of output streams. While S-NET guarantees the order of records communicated over individual streams, very few guarantees on record ordering can be given in these three cases. For many applications the concrete record order is irrelevant, but for others we need stronger guarantees. Therefore, S-NET features deterministic variants of these combinators, written `||`, `**` and `!!`, respectively. Deterministic combinators maintain the *causal order* of records between their input and their output stream, i.e. any record that is an offspring of an earlier record on the input stream is guaranteed to leave the network before any offspring of a later record on the input stream.

Last but not least, S-NET features a synchronisation component that we call *synchrocell*; it takes the syntactic form [| *type, type* |]. Types again act as patterns for incoming records. A record that matches one of the patterns is kept in the synchrocell. As soon as a record arrives that matches the other pattern, the two records are combined into one, which is forwarded to the output stream. Incoming records that only match previously matched patterns are immediately sent to the output stream. Indeed, after successful synchronisation a synchrocell becomes an identity component and may be removed by a runtime system. This extremely simple behaviour of synchrocells captures the essential notion of synchronisation in the context of streaming networks. More complex synchronisation behaviours, e.g. continuous synchronisation of matching pairs in the input stream, can easily be achieved using synchrocells and network combinators. See [7] for more details on this and on the S-NET language in general.

3. Operational Semantics

In order to precisely define the meaning of a program, we provide a formal operational semantics for all entities of S-NET in the form of deduction rules. These rules allow us to construct inductive proofs about the result of a given program and given input that is valid wrt. the program's type. Rules of the form

$$(p, M) \rightarrow (M', q)$$

describe state transitions of our abstract machine: The program M is evaluated on input p and produces output q. As the program M potentially changes during this evaluation, the right-hand-side of the above rule contains M' rather than M. We use this notation in the following formalisation to capture input-dependant transformations, i.e. synchronisation and dynamic unfolding, of the original program. Furthermore, we use the following notation: A single italic letter, as for example p, denotes a single record. A single letter with an arrow on top denotes a stream of records, e.g. $\vec{p}$. The concatenation of two streams is denoted by $\vec{p} ++ \vec{q}$ (appending $\vec{q}$ to $\vec{p}$). An n-fold concatenation, denoted by $++_{i=1}^{n}(\vec{p_i})$, expands to $\vec{p_1} ++ \vec{p_2} ++ ... ++ \vec{p_n}$. As some of the presented rules are defined on single input records, we provide the following map rule in order to apply these rules to streams:

$$\text{MAP} \quad : \quad \frac{\forall i \in \{1, ..., n\} : (p_i, M_i) \rightarrow (M_{i+1}, \vec{q_i}) \quad \vec{s} = ++_{i=1}^{n}(\vec{q_i})}{(\vec{p}, M_1) \rightarrow (M_{n+1}, \vec{s})}$$

The box construct in S-NET allows us to execute user-defined functions, denoted f in the BOX rule. Note here that the semantics of f are not captured in this framework.

$$\text{BOX} \quad : \quad \frac{f(p) = \vec{q}}{(p, \text{box} f) \rightarrow (\text{box} f, \vec{q})}$$

The serial combination is defined in rule SER. The combinator's behaviour is broken down into two independant evaluation steps of the operands:

$$\text{SER} \quad : \quad \frac{(\vec{p}, M) \to (M', \vec{p'}) \quad (\vec{p'}, N) \to (N', \vec{q})}{(\vec{p}, M..N) \to (M'..N', \vec{q})}$$

The non-deterministic choice combinator analyses inbound records in order to dispatch these to the most appropriate operand network. To do this,

$$\text{NDCHOICE} \quad : \quad \frac{\vec{p_l}, \vec{p_r} = \text{lrsplit}(\vec{p}, \tau_M, \tau_N) \quad (\vec{p_l}, M) \to (M', \vec{q_l}) \quad (\vec{p_r}, N) \to (N', \vec{q_r})}{(\vec{p}, M|N) \to (M'|N', \text{ndmerge}(\vec{q_l}, \vec{q_r}))}$$

the inbound stream $\vec{p}$ is divided into two sub-streams $\vec{p_l}, \vec{p_r}$ using algorithm lrsplit which is shown at the end of this section. The algorithm splits the inbound stream up such that records on $\vec{p_l}$ match the left operand of the combinator and the records on $\vec{p_r}$ match the right operand. These result streams are non-deterministically merged, i.e. both streams may be arbitrarily interleaved.

$$\text{DCHOICE} \quad : \quad \frac{(\vec{p_{l_i}}, \vec{p_{r_i}})_{i \in \{1,..,n\}} = \text{lrpsplit}(\vec{p}, \tau_M, \tau_N) \quad \forall i \in \{1,..,n\} : (\vec{p_{l_i}}, M_i) \to (M'_{i+1}, \vec{q_{l_i}}) \quad (\vec{p_{r_i}}, N_i) \to (N'_{i+1}, \vec{q_{r_i}})}{(\vec{p}, M_1||N_1) \to (M_{n+1}||N_{n+1}, ++_{i=1}^n(\vec{q_{l_i}} ++ \vec{q_{r_i}}))}$$

In order to maintain record order for the deterministic variant of the choice combinator (DCHOICE), the inbound stream $\vec{p}$ is divided into pairs of sub-streams $(\vec{p_{l_i}}, \vec{p_{r_i}})$ such that each (potentially empty stream) $\vec{p_{l_i}}$ (resp. $\vec{p_{r_i}}$) contains records matching the input type of the left (resp. right) operand network. The algorithm to do this is shown at the end of this section. The pairs are processed by the operand networks and produce streams $\vec{q_{l_i}}$ and $\vec{q_{r_i}}$ as result. The output streams are concatenated to a result stream and represent the result for one input pair. The overall outbound stream is constructed by concatenating result streams of all input pairs.

The feed-forward semantics of the star combinator is made prominent by the STAR rules. An unrolling of the operand network is reduced to a serial composition and a recursive application of the rules. The non deterministic variant of this combinator is defined by NDCHOICE, the order preserving variant by DCHOICE. As can be seen from DSTAR, record order in the deterministic case is only preserved with respect to the outermost level. The $[\sigma \text{->} \sigma]$ component that appears in the rules is a typed ID component. Its type σ ensures that records matching the exit pattern are attracted to the branch of the ID component.

$$\text{NDSTAR} \quad : \quad \frac{(\vec{p}, (M..M *\{\sigma\})|[\sigma \ \text{->} \ \sigma]) \to (M', \vec{q})}{(\vec{p}, M *\{\sigma\}) \to (M', \vec{q})}$$

$$\text{DSTAR} \quad : \quad \frac{(\vec{p}, (M..M *\{\sigma\})||[\sigma \ \text{->} \ \sigma]) \to (M', \vec{q})}{(\vec{p}, M **\{\sigma\}) \to (M', \vec{q})}$$

The split combinator uses a special form of the choice combinator, syntactically distinguishable from the standard choice combinator by two parameters on top of the bar, which we introduce only informally: This combinator uses value dependant routing rather than purely type directed routing. It examines the value of a given tag name κ and checks it against given value j. If the values match, the combinator routes the record to its left operand and to its right operand otherwise.

$$\text{NDSPLIT} \quad : \quad \frac{(p, N \overset{\kappa=j}{\mid} N!\kappa) \to (N', \vec{q})}{(p, N!\kappa) \to (N', \vec{q})} \qquad\qquad \text{DSPLIT} \quad : \quad \frac{(p, N \overset{\kappa=j}{\parallel} N!!\kappa) \to (N', \vec{q})}{(p, N!!\kappa) \to (N', \vec{q})}$$

We use multiple rules to capture synchro cell semantics: If a record matches a previously unmatched pattern, i.e. the type τ_p of a record p is subtype of pattern σ, the pattern is marked as matched (rule SYNCS). An index at the lower-right corner of the synchro cell indicates this. The SYNCN rule captures the case for a matched first pattern. We will ommit symmetric cases concerning the second pattern. Merging and conversion to an identity component is described by the SYNCM rule. If a record immediately matches both patterns, the record passes unmodified and the synchro cell again will act as an identity component (rule ID), as shown by the SYNCI rule.

$$\text{SYNCS} \quad : \quad \frac{\tau_{p_a} \preccurlyeq \sigma_a \wedge \neg(\tau_{p_a} \preccurlyeq \sigma_b)}{(p_a, [\![\sigma_a, \sigma_b]\!]) \to ([\![\sigma_a, \sigma_b]\!]_{p_a}, \epsilon)}$$

$$\text{SYNCN} \quad : \quad \frac{\tau_p \preccurlyeq \sigma_a \wedge \neg(\tau_p \preccurlyeq \sigma_b)}{(p, [\![\sigma_a, \sigma_b]\!]_{p_a}) \to ([\![\sigma_a, \sigma_b]\!]_{p_a}, p)}$$

$$\text{SYNCI} \quad : \quad \frac{\tau_p \preccurlyeq \sigma_a \wedge \tau_p \preccurlyeq \sigma_b}{(p, [\![\sigma_a, \sigma_b]\!]) \to (\text{id}, p)} \qquad\qquad \text{ID} \quad : \quad \frac{}{(p, \text{id}) \to (\text{id}, p)}$$

The following code samples show the implementation of some algorithms that are used within the inference rules. Due to space limitations we have chosen to present only those algorithms here which we deem to be the most interesting. In the code below, `ndsel` denotes non-deterministic selection and `bestmatch` choses those patterns that have the most labels in common with a given record.

```
prefix :: stream → pattern → pattern → (stream, stream)
prefix p⃗ σl σr =
case p⃗ of
  ε → (ε,ε)
  p : ps⃗ | ndsel (bestmatch p σl σr) == σl → (p:q⃗, r⃗)
  p : ps⃗ | otherwise → (ε, p⃗)
where (q⃗, r⃗) = prefix ps⃗ σl σr

splitOnePair :: stream → pattern → pattern → (stream, stream, stream)
splitOnePair p⃗ σl σr =
case p⃗ of
  ε → (ε, ε, ε)
  p : ps⃗ → (q⃗l, q⃗r, r⃗)
where (q⃗l, t⃗) = prefix p⃗ σl σr
      (q⃗r, r⃗) = prefix t⃗ σr σl

lrpsplit :: stream → pattern → pattern → (streams, streams)
lrpsplit p⃗ σl σr =
```

```
case p⃗ of
    ε → (ε⃗, ε⃗)

    p : p⃗s → (l⃗ₚ : l⃗ₚₗ , r⃗ₚ : r⃗ₚₗ)
where (l⃗ₚ, r⃗ₚ, q⃗) = splitOnePair p⃗ σₗ σᵣ
        (l⃗ₚₗ , r⃗ₚₗ) = lrpsplit q⃗ σₗ σᵣ


lrsplit :: stream → pattern → pattern → (stream, stream)
lrsplit p⃗ σₗ σᵣ = let (p⃗ₗ , p⃗ᵣ) = lrpsplit p⃗ σₗ σᵣ
                   in (map concat p⃗ₗ , map concat p⃗ᵣ)


merge :: record → record → record
merge p q = p ∪ (q \ (p ∩ q))
```

4. Related Work

Due to space limitations we only give a very brief account of selected formalisation approaches for stream processing languages. For a survey on these languages in general see [8], for a thorough formal treatment of the subject [9] and [10]).

Some early works in the area of stream processing did not propose concrete languages as such, but specified computational models instead. In [11] the authors set out to provide a model for queue-based parallel computations and formalised their approach on graph-theoretical foundations. A function-based approach is presented in [12], where stream functions are introduced as a means for structured programming. A concrete language developed in the 1970s is Lucid [13]. Its semantics is rooted in temporal logic.

A more recent development is the language Eden [14], that extends Haskell with process abstraction and instantiation facilities. The formalisation of its semantics [15] uses a layered approach and distinguishes between the computational layer and coordination layer, but still describes both in the same framework.

Another functionally-based language is Hume, which combines a Haskell-like box language with synchronous data flow. The language provides detailed cost and space analysis, and so its operational semantics focus strongly on those issues A formalisation may be found in [16].

Formalisation of the semantics for Streamit [17] mainly focuses on the implemented messaging system and captures constraints on the execution schedule for a program. The aim here is to be able to reason about guarantees on message delivery and latency of Streamit programs.

5. Conclusion

We have developed a high-level coordination language and presented its formal semantics. This formal specification is the foundation for any implementation of the language. In fact, we have implemented a complete, portable tool chain [4] that enables users to harness the computational power of modern multi-core architectures while at the same time they can stick to their familiar (sequential) programming environment for the bulk of an application.

In the setting of S-NET it is rather natural to separate the formalisation of operational semantics of the coordination layer from the actual computation inside the boxes. Nevertheless, it is an intriguing objective to provide a comprehensive formal system that would allow simultaneous reasoning about the embedded box language and the coordination layer. In [18], Matthews *et.al.* present approaches for such a system. We leave this as interesting future work.

Acknowledgments

We would like to thank Alex Shafarenko for many fruitful discussions on S-NET and the anonymous reviewers for their valuable comments.

References

[1]   Sutter, H.: The free lunch is over: A fundamental turn towards concurrency in software. Dr. Dobb's Journal **30** (2005)

[2]   Held, J., Bautista, J., Koehl, S.: From a few cores to many: a Tera-scale computing research overview. Technical report, Intel Corporation (2006)

[3]   Grelck, C., Scholz, S.B., Shafarenko, A.: A Gentle Introduction to S-Net: Typed Stream Processing and Declarative Coordination of Asynchronous Components. Parallel Processing Letters **18** (2008) 221–237

[4]   Grelck, C., Penczek, F.: Implementation Architecture and Multithreaded Runtime System of S-Net. In Scholz, S., Chitil, O., eds.: IFL'08, Hatfield, United Kingdom. LNCS, Springer-Verlag (2009)

[5]   Bousias, K., Jesshope, C., Thiyagalingam, J., Scholz, S.B., Shafarenko, A.:   Graph Walker: Implementing S-Net on the Self-adaptive Virtual Processor. In: Proceedings of AMWAS'08, Lugano, Switzerland. (2008)

[6]   Cai, H., Eisenbach, S., Grelck, C., et.al., F.P.: S-Net Type System and Operational Semantics. In: Proceedings of AMWAS'08, Lugano, Switzerland. (2008)

[7]   Grelck, C., Shafarenko, A. (eds):, Penczek, F., Grelck, C., Cai, H., Julku, J., Hölzenspies, P., Scholz, S.B., Shafarenko, A.: S-Net Language Report 1.0. Technical Report 487, University of Hertfordshire, School of Computer Science, Hatfield, United Kingdom (2009)

[8]   Stephens, R.: A survey of stream processing. Acta Informatica **34** (1997) 491–541

[9]   Broy, M., Stefanescu, G.: The algebra of stream processing functions. Theoretical Computer Science (2001) 99–129

[10] Stefanescu, G.: Network Algebra. Springer-Verlag (2000)

[11] Karp, R.M., Miller, R.E.: Properties of a model for parallel computations: Determinancy, termination, queueing. SIAM Journal on Applied Mathematics **14** (1966) 1390–1411

[12] Burge, W.H.: Stream processing functions. j-IBM-JRD **19** (1975) 12–25

[13] Ashcroft, E.A., Wadge, W.W.: Lucid, a nonprocedural language with iteration. Communications of the ACM **20** (1977) 519–526

[14] Loogen, R., Ortega-Mallén, Y., Peña-Marí, R.: Parallel functional programming in Eden. Journal of Functional Programming **15** (2005) 431–475

[15] Hidalgo-Herrero, M., Ortega-Mallén, Y.: An operational semantics for the parallel language eden. Parallel Processing Letters **12** (2002) 211–228

[16] Hammond, K.: The dynamic properties of hume: a functionally-based concurrent language with bounded time and space behaviour. In: IFL 2000 Aachen, Germany, September 4-7, 2000, Selected Papers. Volume 2011 of LNCS., Springer (2001) 122–139

[17] Thies, W., Karczmarek, M., Amarasinghe, S.P.: Streamit: A language for streaming applications. In: Computational Complexity. (2002) 179–196

[18] Matthews, J., Findler, R.B.: Operational semantics for multi-language programs. SIGPLAN Not. **42** (2007) 3–10

Mini-Symposium
"DEISA: Extreme Computing in an Advanced Supercomputing Environment"

Parallel Computing: From Multicores and GPU's to Petascale
B. Chapman et al. (Eds.)
IOS Press, 2010
© 2010 The authors and IOS Press. All rights reserved.
doi:10.3233/978-1-60750-530-3-477

DEISA Mini-Symposium
on Extreme Computing
in an
Advanced Supercomputing Environment

Wolfgang GENTZSCH and Hermann LEDERER

Rechenzentrum Garching der Max-Planck-Gesellschaft
Max Planck Institute for Plasma Physics, 85748 Garching, Germany
E-mail: {Gentzsch, Lederer} @rzg.mpg.de

Abstract.
The DEISA Mini-Symposium held in conjunction with the ParCo 2009 Conference was devoted to ŞExtreme Computing in an Advanced Supercomputing EnvironmentŤ. For a representative overview of the application related key areas involved, the Mini-Symposium was structured into three sessions devoted to the description of the DEISA Extreme Computing Initiative DECI and the Science Community support, the application oriented support services, and examples of scientific projects performed in the Distributed European Infrastructure for Supercomputing Applications (DEISA) both from the DECI and the fusion energy research related science community behind the EU FP7 project EUFORIA.

Introduction

A consortium of the major supercomputing centres in Europe is operating the Distributed European Infrastructure for Supercomputing Applications [1]. Initiated in 2002 and started as an EU FP6 project in 2004, operation and further development of the HPC infrastructure is continued with EU FP7 support from 2008 to 2011. DEISA2 focuses on the provisioning and operation of infrastructure services which allow its users to work efficiently within a distributed high performance computing environment. Through these services and the continued operation of this infrastructure with global importance, DEISA2 contributes to the effective support of world-leading computational science in Europe [2,3].

1. The DEISA Extreme Computing Initiative and its Science Community Support

The DEISA Extreme Computing Initiative [4,5] was launched in May 2005 by the DEISA Consortium, as a way to enhance its impact on science and technology. The main purpose of this initiative is to enable a number of grand challenge applications in all areas of science and technology. These leading, ground breaking applications must deal with complex, demanding and innovative simulations that would not be possible without the DEISA infrastructure, and which benefit from the exceptional resources provided by the Consortium. The DEISA applications are expected to have requirements that cannot be fulfilled by the national HPC services alone.

A European Call for Extreme Computing Proposals is published regularly. By selecting the most appropriate supercomputer architectures for each project, DEISA is opening up the currently most powerful HPC architectures available in Europe for the most challenging projects. This mitigates the rapid performance decay of a single national supercomputer within its short lifetime cycle of typically about 5 years, as implied by Moore's law.

The number of DECI proposals and accepted projects increases from year to year. Supercomputing resources are awarded for scientific projects on the fastest supercomputers in Europe, accompanied by application enabling services which are distributed over all partner sites, with access to the application specialists' knowledge of each site.

In DEISA2 the consortium has extended its service provisioning model from individual project support, as in the DEISA Extreme Computing Initiative, to persistent service provision to specific European user communities. A call for expressions of interest, published at the end of 2008 [6], resulted in expressions of interest of important communities from the science areas of fusion energy research, cosmology and space science, climate research, and life sciences.

2. Application-Oriented DEISA Infrastructure Services

The applications submitted to DECI consist of complex and innovative simulations requiring the advanced European supercomputer infrastructure DEISA. Therefore DEISA provides a broad spectrum of advanced and integrated services for challenging applications, such as:

- Common global high performance file system, to greatly facilitate data management across Europe;
- Uniform access methods common to the entire infrastructure, such as the UNICORE middleware;
- DEISA Common Production Environment (DCPE) to unify the heterogeneous software environments of the different partner sites;
- A team of European system operation specialists handling the system services operations;
- An Applications Task Force team at the service of the scientists both for user support and enabling of complex applications to utilise DEISA services efficiently.

The various heterogeneous software environments to deal with applications, especially the compilers, libraries, pre-installed applications and tools, have been unified into one homogeneously appearing environment, the DCPE. Together with documentation available to all DEISA users, it dramatically eases application portability from one site to another. DCPE is accessed in an identical way from each site and provides users with a uniform environment, independent of the underlying architecture. There is a particular advantage for the user if the required application is part of the DCPE; in this case the enabling effort required to exploit the DEISA infrastructure will be small because there will already be a compiled and optimized version of the program ready for the user to execute on the target platform. This is often the case in computational chemistry or life sciences where increasing use is made standard codes rather than writing own codes from scratch.

An Applications Task Force team at the service of the scientists has been established both for user support and enabling of complex applications to utilise DEISA services efficiently. Examples of application enabling include scaling of parallel programs for the efficient usage of thousands of processors, architecture dependent code optimizations, management of loosely coupled applications, multi-site task farms and complex work-flows. The process of application enabling for, say a DECI project, involves the researcher who wrote or wishes to use the application, the technical support from the DEISA site which is physically closest to the principle researcher, and the support personnel of the DEISA sites who will provide the computing cycles, who give advice on how best to execute the code on their local architecture. The application enabling effort is an important component of the DEISA infrastructure and is estimated and taken into account for every project proposal or related activity.

3. Science Project: Direct Numerical Simulation of Turbulent Development of a Round Jet at Reynolds Number 11,000

In his talk Christophe Bogey described how a Direct Numerical Simulation (DNS) of a round jet at a Reynolds number of 11,000 has been performed in the framework of the DECI project JetTurb using 755 million mesh points. The turbulent statistics in the region of flow establishment was calculated, and databases of 3-D unsteady fields are now available for further analyses of the jet physics.

The DNS has been performed using an in-house solver of the full 3-D Navier-Stokes equations, based on low-dissipation and low-dispersion explicit finite-difference methods. The jet simulated is round and isothermal, at a Mach number of 0.9 and a Reynolds number of 11,000. The DNS was carried out at the HLRS Centre in Stuttgart, on 36 processors of the NEC SX-8. The overall CPU speed obtained was 212 Gflops (i.e. 5.9 Gflops per processor), and 30,000 CPU hours have been required.

The achievement of the present project is clearly illustrated by preliminary results. The flow development, from the initially laminar to turbulent shear layers, then to the turbulent jet, is spectacular. As expected from a DNS at the Reynolds number considered, fine turbulent scales are visible. First insights into the flow properties are also given by the variations of the terms in the turbulent energy budget. Along the centreline for instance, molecular dissipation, turbulence diffusion and mean flow convection are dominating. In addition, the convergence of the energy terms appears satisfactory, and their sum is nearly nil, which supports that the present DNS is accurately resolved.

4. Science Project: Chemical Characterization of Superheavy Elements on Gold Clusters by 4Component Full Relativistic DFT

The presentation by Leonardo Belpassi was related to the chemical characterization of super heavy elements (SHE), achieved by studying their adsorption on a heavy metal surface, currently being of fundamental importance for the placement of new elements in the periodic table. Relativistic effects on SHE chemistry are known to alter expectations dramatically. Full relativistic 4-component Dirac-Kohn-Sham (DKS) theory has been used in order to gain an accurate understanding of the chemical properties of the element 112 (E112) bound to several gold clusters and extend this approach to the next candidate to experimental characterization: E114. Cluster calculations, analyzing the energetics and electronic structure of the interaction, and assessing convergence with respect to the basis set size and number of atoms have been carried out using the full relativistic density functional theory code BERTHA.

The large numbers of heavy atoms that need be considered, the peculiar structure in the DKS calculations and the large basis set adopted required an extreme computational effort, demanding the development and implementation of highly effective parallelization scheme. The parallelization has been performed using MPI and ScaLAPACK. One peculiar aspect of the approach is that only the master process needs to allocate all the arrays, that is the DKS matrix, the overlap matrix and eigenvectors one. Each slave process allocates only some temporary small arrays when needed.

With this new parallel implementation of the DKS method, the electronic structure and interaction energy of E112 and E114 with several gold clusters up to Au_{34} were accurately computed. The chemical characterization of these SHE has been carried out comparing the energetics, electronic structure and charge transfer with the results obtained for their homologues Hg and Pb and the inert noble gas atom Rn. All the calculations (i.e. 350,000 CPU hours) have been performed, within the DECI project, on the SGI Altix 4700 at Leibniz Rechenzentrum (LRZ), Germany.

5. Science Project: EUFORIA: Exploring E-Science for Fusion

The science community activities related to the EU FP7 project EUFORIA were described by David Coster. In preparing for ITER [7], a number of computational challenges need to be overcome: individual parts of the problem are "grand challenge" problems in their own right, but they also need to be combined to prepare for simulations that encompass all the relevant space and time scales.

ITER is the next generation of fusion devices and is intended to demonstrate the scientific and technical feasibility of fusion as a sustainable energy source for the future. To exploit the full potential of the device and to guarantee optimal operation for the device, a high degree of physics modelling and simulation is needed already in the current construction phase of the ITER project. The detailed modelling tools that are needed for an adequate description of the underlying physics cover both a wide range of time scales and spatial orderings and are in general very demanding from a computational point of view.

The project will enhance the modelling capabilities for ITER sized plasmas through the adaptation, optimization and integration of a set of critical applications for edge and core transport modelling targeting different computing paradigms as needed (serial and parallel grid computing and HPC). Deployment of both a grid service and a High Performance computing service are essential to the project. A novel aspect is the dynamic coupling and integration of codes and applications running on a set of heterogeneous platforms into a single coupled framework through a workflow engine. This strongly enhances the integrated modelling capabilities for fusion plasmas and will at the same time provide new compute tools to the fusion community in general.

Acknowledgments

The authors are deeply grateful to the following colleagues for their contribution to the DEISA Mini-Symposium at ParCo 2009: Alison Kennedy EPCC; Giovanni Erbacci, CINECA; Denis Girou, IDRIS; Gavin J. Pringle, EPCC; Mariano Vazquez, BSC; Juha Fagerholm, CSC; Christophe Bogey and Oliver Marsden, Laboratoire de Mécanique des Fluides et dŠAcoustique, Ecole Centrale de Lyon; Leonardo Belpassi, Loriano Storchi, and Francesco Tarantelli, Department of Chemistry, University of Perugia; David Peter Coster, Max Planck Institute of Plasma Physics, Garching; Par Strand, Chalmers University, Gotcborg; Michael Martinez, Vlad Cojocaru, Paolo Mereghetti, and Rebecca C. Wade, Molecular and Cellular Modelling Group, EML Research gGmbH, Heidelberg; Kia Balali-Mood and Mark Sansom, Dept. of Biochemistry, University of Oxford.

The DEISA Consortium thanks the European Commission for support through contracts RI-508830, RI-031513, and RI-222919.

References

[1] DEISA, 2009, see http://www.deisa.org
[2] Lederer, H.: DEISA2: Supporting and developing a European high-performance computing ecosystem, Journal of Physics: Conference Series 125 (2008) 011003; doi:10.1088/1742-6596/125/1/011003
[3] Supercomputing gets its own superhero, see http://cordis.europa.eu/ictresults/ index.cfm/section/news/tpl/article/BrowsingType/Features/ID/90477
[4] DECI, 2009, see www.deisa.org/deci/
[5] Lederer, H.: DECI - The DEISA Extreme Computing Initiative, inSiDE, Vol 6 No 2, Autumn 2008, eds. H-G. Hegering, Th. Lippert, M. Resch; Gauss Centre for Supercomputing, 2008
[6] DEISA Announces Virtual Community Support Initiative, HPCwire 2008, see http://www.hpcwire.com/industry/government/ DEISA-Announces-Virtual-Community-Support-Initiative-36014839.html
[7] ITER, 2009, see http://www.iter.org

482

Parallel Computing: From Multicores and GPU's to Petascale
B. Chapman et al. (Eds.)
IOS Press, 2010
© 2010 The authors and IOS Press. All rights reserved.
doi:10.3233/978-1-60750-530-3-482

DEISA Extreme Computing Initiative (DECI) and Science Community Support

Alison KENNEDY [a,1]
and Hermann LEDERER [b,2]

[a] *EPCC, The University of Edinburgh, UK*
[b] *Rechenzentrum Garching der Max-Planck-Gesellschaft, Germany*

Abstract.

The DEISA Consortium continues its work in the DEISA2 project with EU FP7 support from 2008 to 2011. DEISA2 focuses on the provisioning and operation of infrastructure services which allow its users to work efficiently within a distributed high performance computing environment. DEISA supports both single projects (via DECI) and Virtual Communities.

Introduction

DEISA is a consortium of leading European national supercomputing centres, founded with the purpose of "fostering and advancing computational science in Europe" in the area of High Performance computing by providing researchers with CPU, applications support and user services [1,2]. The consortium is currently funded through the DEISA2 project with EU support from 2008 to 2011 [3,4]. Researchers have two ways to apply for access to the DEISA infrastructure - via the single-project access route known as the DEISA Extreme Computing Initiative (DECI) or as a Virtual Community. This paper describes these two opportunities and the types of research communities who have availed themselves of DEISA's services.

1. DEISA Extreme Computing Initiative

The DEISA Extreme Computing Initiative (DECI) is a scheme through which European scientists can apply for single-project access to world-leading computational resources in the European HPC infrastructure for a period of up to 12 months per project [5].

DECI was introduced in 2005 to enable world-leading European computational scientists to obtain access to the most powerful national computing resources in Europe regardless of their country of origin or work, and to enhance DEISA's impact on European science and technology at the highest level. Through an annual call, a number of capability computing projects are selected by peer-review on the basis of innovation and sci-

---

[1] Corresponding Author; E-mail: A.Kennedy@epcc.ed.ac.uk
[2] E-mail: Lederer@rzg.mpg.de

entific excellence. The consortium has designed, deployed and operates a complex, heterogeneous supercomputing environment with an aggregate peak performance in excess one PetaFlop/s.

Successful projects are given access to the exceptional resources in the DEISA infrastructure (on HPC architecture selected for its suitability) and are offered applications support to enable them to use it productively. The number of proposals received and the number of CPU cycles requested by applicants has grown year on year since DECI's inception, showing that there is a continuing demand from European researchers for a single-project access scheme. DECI will continue to operate until 2011 through FP7 DEISA2 funding, as one of a range of access initiatives offered by DEISA to the European HPC user community.

DECI is of key importance in continuing to build a European HPC user community, supported in their use of top-level HPC facilities by applications experts from leading European HPC centres. More than 500 different researchers from 25 European countries have participated in the scheme to date as Investigators or related scientific users, along with collaborators from four other continents. The scheme aims to enhance Europe's international standing in science .

DECI also aims to facilitate a better understanding of the likely requirements of future users of the Tier-0 systems (European leadership-class supercomputers) by collecting real use-case information about what European computational scientists want and about the differences between usage of national and European resources and facilities.

DECI-4 call attracted 66 proposals for challenging European computational science projects, requesting over 134 million processor(-core)-hours and asking for significant application support. The call was oversubscribed by a factor of around 3, both in requests for CPU and for applications enabling effort. 49 million processor(-core)-hours were available for distribution, and these were allocated to 42 projects, which have been given access to the infrastructure between 1 January 2009 and 31 December 2009 [6].

The most recent call (DECI-5) attracted 75 proposals, requesting 220 million processor(-core) hours. The 69 million hours available have been awarded to 50 projects [7].

Figure 1 shows how the demand for CPU is increasing at a faster rate than supply. Each partner commits 5% of their CPU to DEISA (although some partners contribute additional resources) so the annual increase in CPU available via DEISA broadly reflects the average increase in CPU available at the partner sites.

Figure 2 shows how the average and the median amount requested has grown during the lifetime of DECI. From this we can see that while the median amount requested has increased broadly in line with the increase in availability of CPU, the average amount requested has seen a very sharp increase. This indicates an increase in the number of projects requesting a large amount of CPU cycles.

1.1. Overview of DECI-4 Projects

The following section gives an overview of the projects running on the DEISA infrastructure during 2009 to show the range of science supported.

1.1.1. Projects by Applications Area

The 42 DECI projects selected for DECI-4 were self-categorised (by the PIs) into six broad scientific disciplines - Astronomical Sciences, Biological Sciences, Earth Sci-

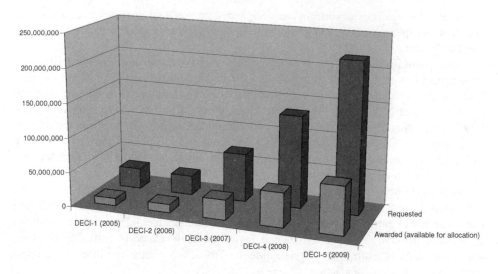

Figure 1. CPU in DEISA is increasing at a faster rate than supply

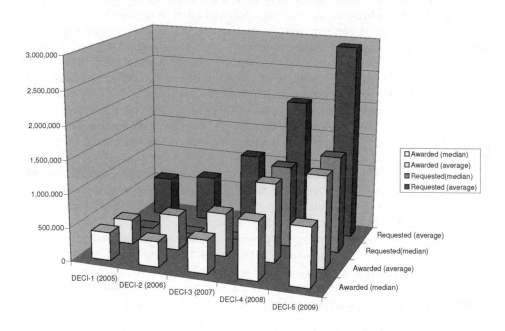

Figure 2. Average and median amount requested during the lifetime of DECI

ences, Engineering, Materials Science and Plasma/Particle Physics. The number of awards by discipline is shown in Figure 3. Overall, about two thirds of the proposals were accepted, although the amount of resources awarded to a number of projects was scaled back to enable as many projects as possible to be supported.

Number of awards by discipline

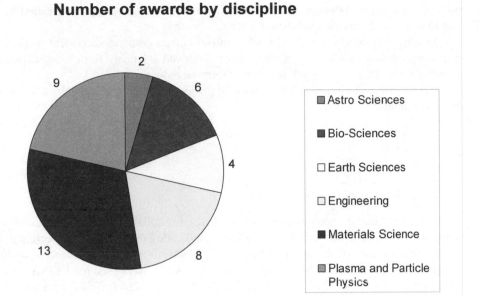

Figure 3. Number of CPU awards by discipline for the DECI-4 projects

1.1.2. Projects by Nationality of Applications

There were 115 investigators named in the 42 accepted DECI-4 projects - an average of 2.7 investigators per project. Of these investigators, 88 (77%) came from countries with a DEISA partner site, 19 (17%) from other European countries and 8 (7%) from large counties outside of Europe (China, Japan, USA). This suggests that successful project proposals were generally based on collaborative European science. All of the 44 PIs (two projects had two PIs) were Europeans, offering further proof that the research being undertaken focuses on European research priorities, with 39 (89%) of the PIs coming from countries with DEISA sites and 5 (11%) coming from other European countries.

As many of the countries with large computational research communities are DEISA partners, it is to be expected that a large majority of the PIs and CoIs will continue to come from countries with DEISA sites. However, we are working to ensure that future calls are publicised extensively throughout Europe. The figures from the latest call (DECI-5) indicate that we are being successful in this respect, showing an increase in the number of investigators from non-DEISA European countries to 20% of the total.

In an effort to find out more about the degree of co-operation and collaboration within DECI projects which were accepted, we analysed the information on investigators in further detail. The number of investigators varied from one to eight, with the median number of investigators being three. During the five years in which DECI has been operating, the average number of investigators per project has risen steadily, year-on-year from 1.03 to 2.96.

A similar analysis was undertaken of the number of institutes involved in each project. This revealed that the number of institutes involved in each project varied from one to six, with the median number of institutes being two.

Finally, we looked at the number of countries collaborating in successful proposals. This showed that 23 (54.8%) of the projects involved scientists from more than one country, with 19% involving scientists from three or more countries.

Here is the evolution of the proportion of projects involving researchers from three or more countries:

- DECI-1: 0%
- DECI-2: 21.4%
- DECI-3: 21.7%
- DECI-4: 19.0%
- DECI-5: 26.0%

This shows that the proportion of projects involving collaborations of scientists from three or more countries in increasing every year, indicating that DECI is supporting pan-European scientific collaboration, and that the DEISA infrastructure is attractive to European researchers. Of the 364 scientific investigators who have used the DEISA infrastructure via DECI, 281 (77%) have been involved in one project to date with a further 83 (23%) involved in two or more projects. These figures indicate that DEISA is being successful in reaching out to new groups and collaborations. But they also show that scientists who have used the infrastructure recognise its value and often apply to use it subsequently for appropriate collaborative projects.

Overall, the statistics which we have collected suggest that DECI is being successful in attracting high quality collaborative proposals involving scientists from more than one European country, and in involving partners from outside Europe where this is appropriate.

1.1.3. CPU awarded

As can be seen from Figure 4, the average number of standard core hours awarded to a DECI project was 1,178,955. The median award was 867,792. Astronomical science, earth science and plasma physics projects on average were awarded more resources than average per project while biological sciences, engineering and materials science were awarded fewer resources than average per project.

However, as can be seen from Figure 3, the largest amount of resources went to materials science projects (27%) closely followed by plasma and particle physics (also 27%). The remaining 48% of the resources were shared between the other four scientific areas.

1.1.4. Scientific codes used

In all projects accepted so far 180 different codes have been specified for usage in DEISA.

The big majority (150 codes or 83%) consists of pure MPI codes, followed by hybrid OpenMP/MPI codes (21 codes or 12%). There has also been a very small number of pure OpenMP codes (six codes or 3%), one pthread-parallel code and two serial codes for pre- and post-processing purposes only.

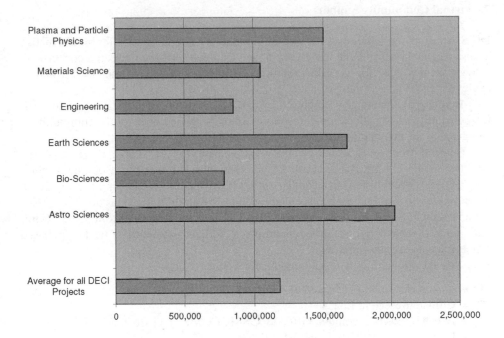

Figure 4. Average number of standard CPU hours by project by discipline

This large number of codes used in DEISA also can provide some insight into the codes used per science area. Since some codes are used in different science areas, the sum will be larger than the total number of codes of 180. The field is led by Plasma and Particle Physics with 43 codes (24%), followed closely by Materials Science with 41 codes (23%). The next three close groups are Engineering (27 codes or 15%), Life Sciences (26 codes or 15%), and Astronomical Sciences (25 codes or 14%). Earth Sciences have been represented with 19 different codes (11%). In addition, Informatics, not shown in Figure 3, was represented with three codes.

Top ranking codes with highest usage over several projects include: NAMD (Materials and Life Sciences, 19 times), CPMD (Materials and Life Sciences, 18 times), CP2K (Materials and Life Sciences, 15 times), GROMACS (Materials and Life Sciences, 12 times). In Astronomical Sciences, GADGET has been used most frequently (four times), in Earth Sciences ECHAM and derivatives (seven times), in Plasma and Particle Physics ELMFIRE, EUTERPE, GENE and ORB5 four times each.

In particular, the large number of different codes used by DECI projects indicates the wide variety of science being undertaken via DECI and reinforces the need for close partnership with users in applications enabling and code tuning to help them achieve their objectives. There is obviously a strong demand for the sort of complementary computing support offered by DECI.

Thus a remarkable high number of codes and their respective projects were able to benefit from the BlueGene/P systems equipped with large numbers of processor-cores for the use of which good scalability to at least 1024 or 2048 cores was mandatory.

2. Virtual Community Support

DEISA has no set definition of a Virtual Community but seeks to offer an alternative access mechanism for larger, loosely or closely coupled European research consortia to provide them with access to DEISA facilities for a longer period of time than the annual cycle of a DECI project can guarantee.

Any Virtual Community supported by DEISA is given an allocation of resources. Responsibility for the allocation of resources amongst the members of the community is delegated to the community itself.

This initiative by DEISA has given a strong impetus to HPC support to Virtual Communities within Europe. An open call for "Expressions of Interest for Community Support" (EoIs) was published in December 2008 [8]. By the closing date in February 2009, seven Expressions of Interest had been received from four different areas of science (Climate Research; Fusion Research; Astro Sciences; and Life Sciences) from Virtual Communities with undisputed scientific reputations as well as a scientific critical mass based across many European countries.

The Virtual Communities who submitted EoIs were as follows:

- Fusion Research: EFDA and EUFORIA
- Climate Research: ENES
- Astrophysics/Cosmology: VIRGO/COSMOCOMP and LFI-PLANCK
- Life Sciences: VPH NoE and VIROLAB

Their motivation for applying to DEISA resources and support is discussed in the following section.

2.1. Fusion Research

DEISA has a tradition in supporting fusion energy research in the field of supercomputer simulations and has now started with direct community support [9].

2.1.1. European Fusion Development Agreement - EFDA

The decision to proceed with ITER - a joint international research and development project that aims to demonstrate the scientific and technical feasibility of fusion power as a viable future energy option -

has focussed EU attention on its own need to have sufficient theory and modelling capabilities to adequately support and exploit the ITER project. This implies having to develop appropriate physics-based models and having adequate computational facilities to apply these models to key ITER-scale problems.

EFTA looked to DEISA to provide High Performance Compute resources, access to state-of-the-art HPC architectures, and application enabling assistance to support physics research in areas such as turbulence, fast particle physics, nonlinear MHD and extended MHD, edge physics, scrape-off-layer (SOL) and plasma wall interactions (PWI), radio-frequency heating and current drive and physical modelling of materials.

2.1.2. EUFORIA

EUFORIA is an FP7 project with 14 countries involved which aims to enhance the modelling capabilities for ITER-sized plasmas through the adaptation, optimization and integration of a set of critical applications for edge and core transport modelling that targets different computing paradigms. Code porting and optimization was undertaken by the EUFORIA partners who then asked DEISA for access for production runs to supercomputing resources, access to state-of-the-art supercomputers, and technology support for accessing DEISA from their gateway machine in Italy.

2.2. Climate Research

2.2.1. European Network for Earth System Modelling - ENES

A major challenge for the climate research community is the development of comprehensive Earth system models capable of simulating natural climate variability and human-induced climate changes. Such models need to account for detailed processes occurring in the atmosphere, the ocean and on the continents including physical, chemical and biological processes on a variety of spatial and temporal scales. They have also to capture complex nonlinear interactions between the different components of the Earth system and assess how these interactions can be perturbed as a result of human activities.

An important task is to develop an advanced software and hardware environment in Europe, under which the most advanced high resolution climate models can be developed, improved, and integrated. The European Network for Earth System Modelling (ENES), comprising about 50 public and private institutions involved in Earth system and climate research, was initiated in 2001.

ENES has asked for High Performance Compute resources, access to state-of-the-art HPC architectures, community data repository, application enabling, and technology support.

2.3. Astro Sciences

2.3.1. LFI-PLANCK

Planck is a European Space Agency satellite that will be launched in 2009 to study the cosmic microwave background. LFI-PLANCK is a project within the ESA PLANCK mission to study the birth of the universe; six European countries are involved.

Planck will have a major impact in cosmology and will be valuable for astrophysics also. Planck data analysis is a complicated and computationally demanding task, where simulation work and Monte Carlo studies play a crucial role.

Planck LFI Virtual Community has requested High Performance Compute resources, a Community data repository (with associated technical support for managing large amounts of disk and data) and application enabling assistance for porting applications.

2.3.2. VIRGO/COSMOCOMP

The Virgo Consortium (founded 1994) is an international group which combines computer, software and personnel resources to carry out top-end simulations of the formation of cosmic structure. It has repeatedly pushed the envelope in this field by carrying out the largest simulations ever of major problems of interest. With respect to the following services: High Performance Compute resources, Access to state of-the-art HPC architectures, Community data repository, Application enabling, Technology support, VIRGO has expressed potential interest in all of them, but the last three are of particular interest for the data archive facility of the Virgo Consortium.

2.4. LIFE Sciences

2.4.1. Virtual Physiological Human - VPH

VPH is an FP7 Network of Excellence with 7 European countries involved.

Virtual Physiological Human lists, as its main target outcome, patient-specific computer models for personalised and predictive healthcare and ICT-based tools for modelling and simulation of human physiology and disease-related processes. The initiative consists of various projects with a need to access compute resources on an EU wide basis, in order to support their scientific objectives.

The following services have been asked by the VPH Consortium to be supported by DEISA: HPC resources, data storage resources, Grid Interfaces (Unicore 6/Globus 4) - OGSA BES interfaces, advanced reservation capabilities (HARC), computational steering (RealityGrid steering library), emergency computing tools (SPRUCE), application deployment support, and user support.

2.4.2. VIROLAB

The mission of the EU FP6 project ViroLab is to develop a virtual laboratory for infectious diseases. In future years, genetic information is expected to become increasingly significant in many areas of medicine. This expectation comes from the recent and anticipated achievements in genomics expected to be of use for the prevention, diagnosis and treatment of diseases.

To continue the HIV drug binding affinity simulation work undertaken by the project, for which DEISA community support was started in 2008, a continuation of the support with additional compute resources was requested until the end of the project in 2009.

2.5. Summary for Virtual Communities

DEISA requested the EoIs to specify the requirements of their community as follows:
What types of DEISA services and resources will be of community interest for the collaboration?

1. High Performance Compute resources,
2. Access to state-of-the-art HPC architectures
3. Community data repository,
4. Application enabling,
5. Technology support

According to the answers we received, all communities expressed needs for multiple services, but no one community had immediate need of all of the services offered by DEISA. However, the flexible support model on offer allows the mix of services to be tailored to the specific requirements of a Virtual Community and to be altered over time.

Conclusions

DEISA has established two complementary and effective ways for challenging super-computing projects in Europe: The classic project-oriented DEISA Extreme Computing Initiative DECI and the support of Virtual Science Communities in the HPC domain. Both ways have found a high user acceptance and thus significantly contribute to the advancement of computational sciences in Europe.

Acknowledgments

The authors thank the European Commission for support through contract RI-222919

References

[1] Lederer, H.: DEISA - towards a persistent European HPC Infrastructure, in: eStrategies: Projects, 2009 (ISSN 1758-2369), 29-31, 2009
[2] Supercomputing gets its own superhero, see http://cordis.europa.eu/ictresults/index.cfm/section/news/tpl/article/BrowsingType/Features/ID/90477
[3] Lederer, H.: DEISA2: Supporting and developing a European high-performance computing ecosystem, Journal of Physics: Conference Series 125 (2008) 011003; doi:10.1088/1742-6596/125/1/011003
[4] For further details see http://www.deisa.eu
[5] Lederer, H.: DECI - The DEISA Extreme Computing Initiative, inSiDE, Vol 6 No 2, Autumn 2008, eds. H-G. Hegering, Th. Lippert, M. Resch; Gauss Centre for Supercomputing, 2008
[6] DEISA Announces Extreme Computing Awards, see http://www.hpcwire.com/offthewire/DEISA-Announces-Extreme-Computing-Initiative-Awards35540714.html
[7] DEISA Announces Extreme Computing Initiative Awards, see http://www.hpcwire.com/offthewire/DEISA-Announces-Extreme-Computing-Initiative-Awards-63714257.html
[8] DEISA Announces Virtual Community Support Initiative, see http://www.hpcwire.com/industry/government/DEISA-Announces-Virtual-Community-Support-Initiative-36014839.html
[9] Commission puts Europe's supercomputers on the path to sustainable energy sources, see http://europa.eu/rapid/pressReleasesAction.do?reference=IP/09/117&format=HTML&aged=0&language=EN&guiLanguage=en

492   *Parallel Computing: From Multicores and GPU's to Petascale*
B. Chapman et al. (Eds.)
IOS Press, 2010
© *2010 The authors and IOS Press. All rights reserved.*
doi:10.3233/978-1-60750-530-3-492

Application oriented DEISA Infrastructure Services

Andrew P J EMERSON [a,1], Giovanni ERBACCI [a], Juha FAGERHOLM [b],
Denis GIROU [c], Gavin J PRINGLE [d] and Mariano VÁZQUEZ [e]

[a] *CINECA Supercomputing Center, Casalecchio di Reno, Italy*
[b] *CSC – IT Center for Science, Finland*
[c] *Institut du Développement et des Ressources en Informatique Scientifique
(CNRS-IDRIS), France*
[d] *EPCC, The University of Edinburgh, UK*
[e] *BSC-CNS, Barcelona, Spain*

Abstract. DEISA is a consortium of leading national supercomputing centres, deploying and operating a persistent production-quality distributed supercomputing environment in Europe, aiming to foster pan-European world-leading computational science research. The DEISA national HPC systems are linked by dedicated networking and an advanced environment for services. The computational scientists access this continental infrastructure via the DEISA Extreme Computing Initiative (DECI) and DEISA's Virtual Communities. The main objective of DECI is to identify, enable and run a number of ground breaking applications in various fields of science and technology. These applications consist of complex and innovative simulations, impossible to realise without the DEISA Infrastructure. To achieve this objective the DEISA Infrastructure provides a broad spectrum of advanced and integrated services. In this paper we explain in detail the features and implementation of these services.

Keywords. DEISA, grid, HPC, middleware, DCPE, UNICORE, DESHL, Globus

1. Introduction

In order to support and perform the most advanced and challenging applications, DEISA has developed, and continues to develop, a wide range of integrated services. In this paper we describe the technologies and software components used to implement these services which can be broadly categorised in three main areas: those involved in providing access to the infrastructure, facilities and tools for the user environment and the various support mechanisms available to researchers. The role played by the expert technical staff of DEISA is illustrated by three case studies from the DEISA Extreme Computing Iniative (DECI).

---

[1]Corresponding Author: Andrew Emerson, CINECA, Supercomputing Center, via Magnanelli 6/3, 40033 Casalecchio di Reno, Italy

2. Accessing the infrastructure

DEISA provides a wide variety of methods which researchers can use for accessing the grid infrastructure. These can generally be divided into two classes:

1. Grid middleware services such UNICORE, DESHL, AHE or Globus.
2. "Direct methods" such as Globus gsissh.

In general, a user will need a Grid Certificate from a certification authority of the EUGridPMA to use these services.

The list of the possible ways in which a user can utilize the DEISA grid infrastructure is under constant review and current users, or potential DEISA users, are often polled to understand their preferences. Thus, from a review of the technical evaluations of the DECI-5 proposals it was found that most researchers preferred gsissh or ssh, unsurprising given that access to most computer centre hardware is generally via these routes. But there was also significant interest in middleware services such as UNICORE or DESHL and these are described in the sections below.

Note that in the remainder of this document we will often refer to the typical connection procedure of a DECI project where the user connects from the *Home Site*, usually the DEISA site closest geographically to the user, to the *Execution Sites*, the centres which will provide the computer resources.

2.1. UNICORE

UNICORE (UNified INterface to COmputing REsources) is an WS-RF based, OGSA-compliant technology which provides a platform independent way of running applications [1]. Originally developed in Germany in the late 1990s, it has since become one of the most used grid middlewares in Europe. UNICORE was adopted early in DEISA and is one of the principal methods of accessing the project's resources. Full details of the implementation are described elsewhere, but essentially each site hosts a UNICORE server which processes requests from UNICORE clients, running on users' local workstations, and interacts with the site's local services to run the user application. This normally involves first verifying that the user has permission to use the resource by comparing the credentials sent with the request with the registered certificate in its database. Then it will translate the user's resource requirements, usually in the form of a SAGA script [2], into a format suitable for the target batch scheduler, such as LoadLeveler or PBS. When requested by the client, UNICORE will poll the batch system for the status of the job and will return the results to the client after job completion.

Job applications can be created and submitted via the graphical UNICORE standalone client, a java application which can be freely downloaded and installed on a user's workstation. Once the user certificate has been installed into the client, it is then possible to view the UNICORE infrastructure of DEISA and see the resources to which the user has access. The user can then submit a simple job by means of a form, or create a more advanced multi-site, multi-job submission or analysis by means of the in-built workflow editor.

2.2. DESHL

An alternative to the graphical UNICORE client is DESHL (DEisa Services Heterogeneous Layer), a middleware developed within DEISA which allows users to manage jobs
and files within the DEISA infrastructure [3]. The important feature of DESHL is that
it can be invoked as a command-line interface or as an API which means that DESHL
commands can be scripted or embedded in other applications, such as graphical clients
or even web portals. Thus it is possible for a developer to create a UNICORE-accessible
client, but with an interface or functionality appropriate to a particularly user community. An example is the user portal of the European FP7 funded project, Immunogrid [4],
which was designed with a graphical interface to reflect the needs of immunologists or
other medical researchers, but capable of submitting jobs to DEISA or other UNICORE
resources[5]. Within DEISA itself, DESHL is often used to create Task Farms. Such
Task Farms, which are not possible using UNICORE, enable users to employ the entire
DEISA infrastructure as a single, vast resource.

2.3. Direct methods

As mentioned above many researchers access the DEISA environment via Globus gsissh
and DEISA has implemented a number of procedures which facilitate its use. Thus the
deisa_service command allows DEISA users to switch between the project sites
without having to remember or look up addresses and port numbers:

```
gsissh 'deisa_service -i -s csc'
```

The gsissh command is normally invoked from the user's Home Site but can also be used
from a non-DEISA site or even from a standalone client.

3. User Environment

On connection to the Execution Site, the user will find himself within a specially designed and common environment and have access to services to facilitate the transfer of
data from one site to another. These are now described below.

3.1. Deisa Common Production Environment (DCPE)

The unified DEISA Common Production Environment (DCPE) is a major feature in
DEISA, as in all distributed infrastructures of this kind, defining a coherent set of software accessible on the various sites of the infrastructure. It offers a common interface
to the users, independent of the target platform employed. Of course, the level of coherence is not the same everywhere in the infrastructure, ranging from very high inside each
subgroup of homogeneous computers to a lower level across the other subgroups.
    The main components of the DCPE are:

- a coherent set of software packages for each architecture, called *the Software
  Stacks*;
- uniform interface to access the software on all the platforms, provided by the
  Modules tool [6] ;
- a framework to monitor the software, provided by the Inca tool [7].

3.1.1. The Software Stacks

They are divided into six categories:

1. the environment, which does not include any software, but defines the environment needed by a DEISA user;
2. the shells (currently only Bash and Tcsh);
3. the compilers;
4. the numerical and graphical libraries (both from the manufacturers and from the public domain);
5. the tools to help the users with various tasks (editing of files, development of scripts, parallel debugging, etc.);
6. the applications, which are executable codes or whole packages available to run simulations in some specialised fields.

The contents of the Software Stacks for the different architectures are similar, but some differences exist between them. In all, the general core software (shells, compilers, generic common numerical and graphical libraries and generic tools) are always included, but some others in the core architecture based software, depend of the architecture, such as the libraries and tools provided by the manufacturers, and some additional specific software (commercial, special libraries and tools and third party applications), may be available or not depending on the site.

Also, each software among the core general and core architecture-based software, has a minimum guaranteed version, commonly agreed between the sites, even if some sites operating a computer of the same architecture can offer an higher version and also different alternative versions in addition to the default one.

3.1.2. The Modules user interface

Each component of the DCPE is accessible by using a dedicated interface based on the Modules tool and called a *modulefile*. Each supported version of each piece of software available to be run on a platform has a corresponding modulefile which defines internally the specific characteristics of the installation of this software (especially the location of the internal components and files) but offer a uniform interface to the users, across all the systems. This is a very useful and important for all users, as they can execute commands and define scripts in a portable way, without having to adapt them from one site to the other according to the local procedures chosen to install the software.

The usage of this framework has been defined to be as simple and straightforward as possible for the users, but with the acceptance of some additional complexity in its development. The robustness of the system has also been emphasized, in order to prevent users from defining incompatible choices that would later create unexpected problems that may be difficult to diagnose.

Originally implemented in 2005, the DEISA Modules environment framework has been revised in 2008 to take account of the experience and feedback received during its first years of usage, both from the staff members of the project and from the users. Accordingly, some important changes have been introduced to enhance the environment, although care has been taken to minimise the changes in the user interface only.

The next step of revision, again to take in account the feedback received and to try and improve further our framework, is planned at the beginning of 2010.

It must be emphasized that this environment has been fully appreciated by the users and has motivated several sites to offer locally a DEISA-like Modules Environment on their platforms for all their users.

3.1.3. The Inca monitoring framework

In a distributed hardware and software infrastructure like DEISA, it is essential that the administrators, the user support services, and in some aspects the users themselves, have an updated view and a detailed status of the software environment. The monitoring of such a distributed software environment has become a requirement in all important grid projects, even if the necessities are rather high and sometimes difficult to handle, especially in a heterogeneous context.

Various monitoring tools are available, but to address the special needs of giving an overview of the status of a distributed software environment like the DCPE, showing not only the status of each software on each platform but also the version available, we chose four years ago the Inca tool (Test Harness and Reporting Framework) [7], initially developed by the San Diego Supercomputer Center for the TeraGrid project [8]. Inca is specifically designed to periodically run a collection of validation scripts, called *reporters*, with the purpose of collecting two different kinds of information:

1. the version of the software installed (version reporters);
2. the availability and the correct operation of this software (unit reporters).

The information collected is stored on a dedicated server and is displayed through a Web interface with different views, including one accessible to the users which shows all the relevant information for them, and these data are also archived to allow statistics to be produced (see Figure1).

Thus a green square indicates that a particular resource is available and is working as expected while red indicates a problem requiring the intervention of DEISA staff who also receive notification of problems via email.

3.2. Data Management

Much of a researcher's time is spent in organizing data and in a distributed environment such as DEISA this usually means uploading input data to the Execution Site followed by downloading the results or other output to the Home Site and eventually the researcher's private facilities. To facilitate data transfer between sites, DEISA provides two main services:

1. A Global High Performance Filesystem (GPFS) linking the major sites and
2. GridFTP - an optimized and parallel version of the FTP protocol

The DEISA GPFS was introduced early on in the DEISA project and is built mainly on 10 Gbit/s network links, although real data transfer rates will generally be lower this.

GridFTP, which is part of the Globus toolkit, is also widely used within DEISA, providing fast but secure file transfers.

Libraries	BSC	CSC	ECMWF	EPCC	FZJ JUGENE	FZJ JUMP	IDRIS	LRZ	RZG GENIUS	RZG VIP	SARA
cluster.library.acml.version	n/a	3.6.1	n/a	n/a	n/a	n/a	n/a	n/a	n/a	n/a	n/a
cluster.library.blacs.version	3.3.1	3.0	3.2.0.0	3.3.0.2	1.1	3.3.0.2	3.3.0.2	n/a	1	3.3.0.2	3.3.0
cluster.library.blacssmp.version	3.3.1	n/a	3.2.0.0	3.3.0.2	n/a	3.3.0.2	3.3.0.2	n/a	n/a	3.3.0.2	3.3.0
cluster.library.compilelink1.unit	pass	n/a	pass	pass	n/i	pass	pass	pass	n/i	pass	pass
cluster.library.essl.version	4.4.0	n/a	4.2.0.4	4.3.0.3	4.4.1	4.3.0.2	4.3.0.3	n/a	4.4.1	4.3.0.3	4.3.1
cluster.library.esslsmp.version	4.4.0	n/a	4.2.0.4	4.3.0.3	n/a	4.3.0.2	4.3.0.3	n/a	n/a	4.3.0.3	4.3.1
cluster.library.fftw.version	2.1.5	2.1.5	2.1.5	2.1.5	2.1.5	2.1.5	2.1.5	2.1.5	2.1.5	2.1.5	2.1.5
cluster.library.gmalloc.version	n/a	1	n/a	n/a	n/a	n/a	n/a	n/a	n/a	n/a	n/a
cluster.library.hdf5.version	1.6.5	1.6.7	1.6.5	1.6.5	1.8.1	1.8.1	1.8.1	1.6.9	1.6.6	1.6.6	1.6.5
cluster.library.hydro.unit	pass	n/a	pass	pass	n/i	pass	pass	pass	n/i	pass	pass
cluster.library.iobuf.version	n/a	1.0.2	n/a	n/a	n/a	n/a	n/a	n/a	n/a	n/a	n/a
cluster.library.lapack.version	3.0	3.0	3.0	3.0	3.1	3.0	3.0	3.0	3.0	3.0	3.0
cluster.library.libsci.version	n/a	10.0.1	n/a	n/a	n/a	n/a	n/a	n/a	n/a	n/a	n/a
cluster.library.mass.version	5.0.0	n/a	5.0.0.0	4.4.0.1	4.4.0	5.0.0.0	5.0.0.0	n/a	4.4.0	5.0.0.0	5.0.0
cluster.library.mkl.version	n/a	n/a	n/a	n/a	n/a	n/a	n/a	9.1.1	n/a	n/a	n/a
cluster.library.nag.version	n/a	n/a	21	n/i	n/i	21.1	21	21	n/i	21.1	21
cluster.library.netcdf.version	3.6.0	3.6.2	3.6.1	3.6.2	3.6.2	3.6.2	3.6.3	3.6.1	3.6.3	3.6.3	3.6.2
cluster.library.pessl.version	3.3.1	n/a	3.2.0.0	3.3.0.2	n/a	3.3.0.2	3.3.0.2	n/a	n/a	3.3.0.2	3.3.0
cluster.library.pesslsmp.version	3.3.1	n/a	3.2.0.0	3.3.0.2	n/a	3.3.0.2	3.3.0.2	n/a	n/a	3.3.0.2	3.3.0
cluster.library.scalapack.version	1.7.0	1.7.0	1.7.0	1.7.0	1.8.0	1.8.0	1.7.0	1.7.0	1.7.0	1.7.0	1.7.0
cluster.library.scalapack.unit	pass	n/a	pass	pass	n/i	pass	pass	pass	n/i	pass	pass
cluster.library.tmqcd.unit	pass	n/i	pass	pass	n/i	pass	pass	pass	n/i	pass	n/i
cluster.library.uw.unit	pass	n/a	pass	pass	n/i	pass	pass	pass	n/i	pass	pass
cluster.library.wsmp.version	n/a	n/a	6.2.28	4.8.5	n/a	9.1.21	9.1.21	n/a	n/a	9.5.24	n/i

Shells	BSC	CSC	ECMWF	EPCC	FZJ JUGENE	FZJ JUMP	IDRIS	LRZ	RZG GENIUS	RZG VIP	SARA
cluster.shell.bash.version	3.1.17(1)	3.1.17(1)	3.1.0(3)	2.05a.0(1)	3.1.17(1)	3.00.16(1)	3.2.0(1)	3.1.17(1)	3.1.17(1)	4.0.10(1)	3.1.17(1)
cluster.shell.tcsh.version	6.14.00	6.14.00	6.14.00	6.11.00	6.14.00	6.11.00	6.15.00	6.14.00	6.14.00	6.11.00	6.14.00

Tools	BSC	CSC	ECMWF	EPCC	FZJ JUGENE	FZJ JUMP	IDRIS	LRZ	RZG GENIUS	RZG VIP	SARA
cluster.tool.compilelink2.unit	pass	n/a	pass	pass	n/i	pass	pass	n/a	n/i	pass	pass
cluster.tool.corba.unit	pass	n/a	pass	pass	n/i	pass	pass	n/a	n/i	pass	pass
cluster.tool.craypat.version	n/a	3.2.3	n/a	n/a	n/a	n/a	n/a	n/a	n/a	n/a	n/a
cluster.tool.emacs.version	21.3.1	21.3.1	21.4	21.3.1	21.3.1	21.3.1	21.3.1	21.3.1	20.2.1	21.3.1	
cluster.tool.gmake.version	3.80	3.80	3.80	3.80	3.80	3.80	3.80	3.80	3.80	3.80	3.80
cluster.tool.hpm.version	n/a	n/a	n/i	3.1.5	n/a	3.2.1	3.2.2	n/a	n/a	3.2.2	3.2.1
cluster.tool.nedit.version	5.5	5.5	5.5	5.5	n/i	5.5	5.5	5.5	n/i	5.5	5.5
cluster.tool.omniorb.version	4.1.0	4.1.0	4.0.6	4.0.6	n/i	4.0.6	4.1.3	n/a	n/i	4.0.6	4.1.1
cluster.tool.openssh.version	4.2p1	4.2p1	4.1p1	5.0p1	5.2p1	4.3p2	5.0p1	4.2p1	4.2p1	5.0p1	4.2p1
cluster.tool.perl.version	5.8.8	5.8.8	5.8.7	5.8.2	5.8.8	5.8.2	5.8.2	5.8.8	5.8.8	5.8.2	5.8.8
cluster.tool.python.version	2.4.2	2.4.3	2.4.2	2.4.4	2.4.2	2.4.3	2.6	2.4.2	2.4.2	2.6.2	2.5.1
cluster.tool.tcl.version	8.4.12	8.4.12	8.4.12	8.4.12	8.4.12	8.4.12	8.5.5	8.4.12	8.4.12	8.4.15	8.4.12
cluster.tool.tk.version	8.4.12	8.4.12	8.4.12	8.4.12	8.4.12	8.4.12	8.5.5	8.4.12	8.4.12	8.4.15	8.4.12
cluster.tool.totalview.version	n/a	8.6.0-1	8.2.0-1	8.1.0-0	8.7.0-2	8.6.1-1	8.6.2-3	n/a	n/i	8.3.0-1	n/i

Figure 1. Excerpt of the Inca monitoring status of the DCPE

4. Support Services

Software and hardware solutions such as those described above can be extremely helpful in aiding the progress to completion of a project, but there is no doubt that many researchers value considerably the availability of expert support. In this section we describe how researchers can request support for their projects and we give some examples of *project enabling*, i.e. getting applications to work in an efficient way on a particular resource, and to employ relevant middlware, i.e. UNICORE.

4.1. Helpdesk and documentation

Although researchers may contact local DEISA staff for advice and assistance, a centralised service called the DEISA Trouble Ticket System has been set up to manage support requests. This is based on the TTS software [9] and records support requests and the responses to them by means of *tickets*, essentially entries in a database with id numbers to which the requestor can refer. A support request thus results in the "creation" of a ticket. The preferred method of creating a ticket is via the web interface (https://tts.deisa.eu/UserSupport/), although an email address is also available support@deisa.eu. If the requestor includes a particular suffix in the subject line, the ticket is automatically created on receipt of the email. Experience within DEISA has shown that managing support requests this way, greatly facilitates the detection of common problems and allows the solution process to be monitored effectively.

DEISA documentation is freely available via the main website with the most important document for new users being the *DEISA Primer*, although there are also separate documents for more specific topics such as the DCPE, UNICORE, DESHL, interactive access and so on. Within DEISA, documentation is kept in a central repository where there is a unique version for each document. Project staff maintain the documents via the website using the Plone tool, thus allowing the possibility of instant publication. PDF versions of some documents are planned.

4.2. Enabling complex applications

An important resource of DEISA is the *Applications Task Force* which is available to scientists and virtual communities for user support and enabling of complex applications for effective use of DEISA resources. The term *Application enabling* includes:

- porting code and architecture dependent optimization
- benchmarking and optimization of parallel scaling
- management of loosely coupled applications, task farms, etc
- providing an interface to the technical staff of the execution or local sites.

The application enabling effort is an important concept in DEISA and is estimated and quoted (usually in terms of person months) for every project or proposal. Due to the heterogeneity of the European transnational supercomputing resources, any enabling effort must be coordinated among all the partners in an efficient way, according to the platform (or platforms) where a given application is due to run. Below we give three examples of application enabling performed by the Task Force within the DECI initiative, where this collaborative effort is clearly shown:

Project UnBLAMD (DECI 2007)
Title Urea-induced unfolding of bovine beta-lactoglobulin by molecular dynamics
Enabling Description permit a very long MD simulation (1 microsecond) of a small
  protein to study the mechanisms influencing protein structure.
DEISA Home site CINECA
DEISA Execution site BlueGene, Julich Supercomputing Center (FZJ).
Work undertaken CINECA helped create the configuration files necessary for NAMD
  and set up the system (the Principal Investigator (PI) had no experience of this
  application). A customised script was also written to automate the batch process.
  FZJ worked to provide an optimised version of NAMD for the BlueGene and suggested parameters for the batch submission which resulted in significant increases
  in performance.

Project QEXX4ROS (DECI 2007e)

Title Exact Exchange and Hybrid Functionals in the Quantum-ESPRESSO package for Research on Reducible Oxides Surfaces

Enabling Description to parallelise a component of the Quantum-ESPRESSO package for simulating the chemistry and reactivity of oxide surfaces

DEISA Home site CINECA

DEISA Execution site RZG

Work undertaken The team had implemented a subroutine into the Quantum-ESPRESSO package for the calculation of the HF exact-exchange potential. However, this subroutine was serial and so prevented the parallel execution of the code. CINECA modified the source code to permit parallel execution for calculations involving this potential. This task took about 2 person months. The RZG team compiled the code and tested it on the Power6 architecture at RZG.

Project HHG (DECI 2007)
Title Hierarchical Hybrid Grids
Description CFD solver for unstructured meshes
DEISA Home site LRZ
DEISA Execution sites FZJ, RZG, EPCC
DEISA Architectures BlueGene, IBM Power 6, Cray XT4
Work undertaken Staff at FZJ and EPCC worked with the PI to improve the single processor performance and to port the code to the machines at their sites. Both sites agreed to make special arrangements for the PI when the full machine was to be used. LRZ helped to coordinate and manage the PI's request to use the full machine at respective sites.

Most of the enabling effort of DEISA is put into adapting applications to run efficiently on new architectures. However, some cases are specially selected for so-called *performance enhancement*. This involves assessing the parallel behaviour of the applications during enabling by probing them with performance analysis tools. Thanks to the considerable experience gained over the years, DEISA technical staff can detect opportunities for efficiency improvements in many cases. When the effort is reasonable according to the man power available, these improvements are implemented in collaboration with the code developers. This is the mission of a special workpackage within DEISA, called the *Enhancing Scalability* workpackage. It should be emphasised that every improvement is transferred to the next release of the enhanced code.

5. Concluding Remarks

The DEISA consortium provides the most advanced supercomputers in Europe, but these facilities must be made available in a reliable, secure and user-friendly environment in order for them to be used effectively by researchers. DEISA has thus invested heavily in its application infrastructure and continues to monitor its effectiveness, often polling researchers and making modifications when necessary. The success of the infrastructure is evident not only from the feedback obtained from users, but also from the observation that many centres in Europe have adopted many of the features of DEISA approach, such as the TTS ticket system or the modules environment, for their local research communities. Indeed, the application infrastructures now being designed for the the next generation of supercomputers to be installed in Europe and elsewhere will rely heavily on the experience and technologies which have been developed for DEISA users.

References

[1] See, for example, http://www.unicore.eu.

[2] http://saga.cct.lsu.edu/

[3] T. M. Sloan, R. Menday, T. P. Seed, M. Illingworth and A. S. Trew, DESHL–Standards Based Access to a Heterogeneous European Supercomputing Infrastructure, *Proceedings of the Second IEEE International Conference on e-Science and Grid Computing*, 91, 2006.

[4] http://www.immunogrid.eu

[5] M.D Halling-Brown, D.S. Moss, A.J Shepherd, Towards a lightweight generic computational grid framework for biological research, *BMC Bioinformatics*, (2008), 407.

[6] http://modules.sourceforge.net/

[7] Inca (Test Harness and Reporting Framework): http://inca.sdsc.edu/

[8] http://www.teragrid.org/

[9] http://bestpractical.com/rt

Parallel Computing: From Multicores and GPU's to Petascale
B. Chapman et al. (Eds.)
IOS Press, 2010
501
© 2010 The authors and IOS Press. All rights reserved.
doi:10.3233/978-1-60750-530-3-501

Chemical Characterization of Super-Heavy Elements by Relativistic Four-Component DFT

Francesco Tarantelli [a,1], Leonardo Belpassi [a] and Loriano Storchi [a]

[a] *Dipartimento di Chimica and I.S.T.M.-C.N.R., Università di Perugia, 06123, Italy*

Abstract. The chemical characterization of super heavy elements (SHE), achieved by studying their interaction with a heavy metal surface, is currently of fundamental importance for the placement of new elements in the periodic table. Effects described by relativity theory on SHE chemistry are known to alter expectations dramatically. We use the 4-component Dirac-Kohn-Sham (DKS) theory in order to gain an accurate understanding of the chemical properties of the element 112 (E112) interacting with large gold clusters. The large number of heavy atoms that have to be considered in the DKS calculations require an extreme computational effort. An important enabling phase, in particular aimed at overcoming the diagonalization bottleneck of DKS calculations and reducing memory usage per processor, took advantage of the expertise available within Distributed European Infrastructure for Supercomputing Applications (DEISA) in a project of the DEISA Extreme Computing Initiative (DECI). We have thus been able to show that all-electron relativistic four-component Dirac-Kohn-Sham (DKS) computations, using G-spinor basis sets and state-of-the-art density fitting algorithms, can be efficiently parallelized and applied to large chemical systems such as those mentioned above.

Keywords. Super-Heavy elements, Relativistic Density Functional Theory, Gold Clusters

Introduction

The production of super-heavy elements (SHE) is a challenge for experimental physics that raises fundamental questions about nuclear structure, stability and chemistry. Clearly, in parallel with their synthesis, the chemical characterization of the heaviest elements is a fundamental step and a crucial tool for their identification and for understanding their properties. Probably the current most important goal of these chemical studies may be summarized as establishing the arrangement of the transactinide elements in the periodic table. In the conclusions of his review about SHE, Schädel wrote that "Most challenging and most fascinating will be the upcoming gas-phase studies of metallic transactinides beyond Group 8. Because of their relativistic stabilized, inert, closed-shell ($7s^2$ and $7s^2 7p_{1/2}^2$), which puts elements 112 and 114 into a unique position among the SHE, chemical studies of these elements have the highest priority in the near future" [1].

---

[1]Corresponding Author. E-mail: franc@thch.unipg.it.

Eichler et al. [2,3] have recently reported a chemical characterization of element 112. Their experiment is based on the detection of the alpha-decay of E112 nuclei adsorbed on a gold surface in a gas-thermocromatography experiment. They observed very few events and, by directly comparing the adsorption characteristics of E112 to those of mercury and the noble gas radon, the authors found that the element 112 is very volatile and, unlike radon, displays a metallic interaction with the gold surface. This cutting-edge experimental work has prompted further investigations and will continue to do so. Indeed, other works have been published, also very recently, aimed at investigating the nature of E112 and, in particular, if it is a metal-like atom with the chemical properties of Group 12 or noble-gas-like [4,5,6]. Experiments in this field are clearly very difficult. The question arises whether ab-initio theoretical work and computational simulations can cast light on the important unresolved issues, make reliable predictions and guide the experiments. The basic requirements here are sufficiently clear and configure a challenging, extremely demanding, task. Simulating the interaction of SHEs with heavy-element surfaces like gold imposes the adoption of theoretical models incorporating all-electron relativistic effects and electron correlation to high order for a very large number of heavy atoms.

The main idea of the present work is to use the full relativistic 4-component Density Functional Theory (DFT) in its Dirac-Kohn-Sham (DKS) form in order to gain accurate insight into the characteristic of the E112-gold chemical interaction. We have attacked this challenging problem through molecular cluster simulations. The calculations have been carried out using our particularly efficient 4-component DFT code, BERTHA (described in Ref. [7] and references therein). We have analyzed the energetics and electronic structure of the interaction, carefully assessing convergence with respect to the basis set size and the number of cluster atoms.

The full four-component DKS calculations have an intrinsically greater computational cost than analogous non-relativistic approaches or less rigorous quasi-relativistic approaches, mainly because of the four-component structure in the representation of the DKS equation, the complex matrix representation that usually arises as a consequence, the increased work involved in the evaluation of the electron density from the spinor amplitudes, and the intrinsically larger basis sets usually required. A significant step forward in the effective implementation of the four-component DKS theory, is based on the electron-density fitting approach that is already widely used in the non-relativistic context. Recently we have implemented the variational Coulomb fitting approach in our DKS method [8], with further enhancements resulting from the use of the Poisson equation in the evaluation of the integralsl [9,10,11], and also from the extension of the density fitting approach to the computation of the exchange-correlation term [7]. The above algorithmic advances have represented a leap forward of several orders of magnitude in the performance of the 4-component DKS approach and have suddenly shifted the applicability bottleneck of the method towards the conventional matrix operations (DKS matrix diagonalization, basis transformations, etc.) and, especially, to the associated memory demands arising in large-system/large-basis calculations. One powerful approach to tackle these problems and push significantly further forward the applicability limit of all-electron 4-component DKS is parallel computation with memory distribution. The purpose of the present paper is to describe the successful implementation of a comprehensive parallelization strategy for our DKS BERTHA code and present the results obtained for the chemical characterization of the super-heavy element E112 on the basis of the study of the nature of its interaction with a large gold cluster.

In Sec. 1 we briefly mention the DEISA framework within which the research activity has been carried out. In Sec. 2 we describe in detail the parallelization strategies adopted here and we discuss the efficiency of the approach presenting the results from some large all-electron test calculations performed on several gold clusters. In Sec.3 we will show the actual chemical application of the method for the all-electron relativistic study of the electronic structure of E112-Au_{20} with a large basis set.

1. DECI framework

The project leading to the results that we present here was awarded a grant within the 2007 call for proposals of the DEISA Extreme Computing Initiative (DECI). The project has required an important enabling phase, in particular aimed at reducing the memory consumption and overcoming the diagonalization bottleneck of DKS calculations. During the algorithmic and computational development phase, the work has been actively supported by the special applications task force (ATASKF) provided by DEISA. The particular computer architecture targeted for the project, an SGI Altix 4700 (1.6 GHz Intel Itanium2 Montecito Dual Core) equipped with the NUMAlink interconnection [12] at LRZ Garching, has turned out ideally suited for optimal performance. The whole project consumed 300 kCPUh.

2. Parallelization strategy and results

One of the peculiar aspects of the DKS implementation in the code BERTHA is that the computational burden of the construction of the Coulomb and exchange-correlation contributions to the DKS matrix has been greatly alleviated with the introduction [8,11] of some effective density fitting algorithms based on the Coulomb metric, which use an auxiliary set of HGTF (Hermite Gaussian Type Functions) fitting functions. In our implementation, we take advantage of a relativistic generalization of the J-matrix algorithm [13,14,15] and an additional simplification arising from the use of sets of primitive HGTFs of common exponent and spanning all angular momenta from 0 to the desired value. (for details see Refs. [7,8]). We have showed that the reduction of the computational cost afforded by the above density fitting scheme is dramatic. Besides reducing the scaling power of the method from $O(N^4)$ to $O(N^3)$, it reduces enormously the prefactor (up to two orders of magnitude) without appreciable effects on the accuracy [7]. However, the application of the method to really large systems is still impeded, first of all, by the big memory requirements imposed by huge basis sets and the consequent enormous matrices. A truly helpful parallelization scheme must inevitably tackle this aspect.

By taking a brief look at the time analysis of a typical serial SCF iteration of our DKS program, we see that three steps dominate the computation, with the DKS matrix diagonalization taking up about half of the time. The J+K matrix computation, which takes about a third of the time, involves essentially the calculation of the three-index two-electron repulsion integrals. The remaining sixth of the time is used almost entirely in the level-shifting phase, which involves the double matrix multiplication transforming the DKS matrix from basis function space to spinor space. Clearly, the parallelization effort must necessarily start from these three time-consuming phases. A small part of the density fitting procedure, together with the HGTF expansion of the density, makes up the portion we will refer to as "serial", because we have left it unparallelized in the work described here. The remaining computation, which we shall label "Density", involves essentially the matrix multiplication necessary to obtain the density matrix from the occupied positive-energy spinors.

In the parallelization of the DKS module of BERTHA we used the SGI implementation of the Message Passing Interface (MPI [16]) and the ScaLAPACK library [17]. The overall parallelization scheme we used can be classified as master-slave. In this approach only the master process carries out the serial portion of the SCF. All the concurrent processes share the burden of the other calculation phases. We decided to use this approach because it is the easiest to code in order to make memory management especially convenient and favorable. Only the master process needs to allocate all the large arrays, that is the overlap, density, DKS, and eigenvector matrices. Each slave process allocates only some temporary small arrays when needed. In using this approach to tackle big molecular systems it is crucial to be able to exploit the fast memory distribution scheme offered by the hardware. In particular, the SGI Altix 4700 is classified as a cc-NUMA (cache-coherent Non Uniform Memory Access) system. The SGI NUMAflex architecture [18] creates a system that can "see" up to 128TB of globally addressable memory, using the NUMAlink [12] interconnect. The master process is thus able to allocate as much memory as it needs, regardless of the actual amount of central memory installed on each node, achieving good performances in terms of both latency and bandwidth of memory access.

To parallelize the **J+K** matrix construction, the most elementary and efficient approach is based on the assignment of matrix blocks computation to the available processes. The optimal integral evaluation algorithm, exploiting HGTF recurrence relations on a single process, naturally induces a matrix block structure dictated by the grouping of G-spinor basis functions in sets characterized by common origin and angular momentum (see also Ref. [19]). At the outset of the computation, the master process broadcasts the small vector representing, in the basis of the fitting functions, the electronic density and exchange-correlation potential. After this, an on-demand scheme is initiated. Each slave begins the computation of a different matrix block, while the master sets itself listening for messages. When a slave has finished computing one block, it returns it to the master and receives the sequence number identifying the next block to be computed. The master progressively fills the global DKS array with the blocks it receives from the slaves. A slave only needs to temporarily allocate the small blocks it computes.

The parallelization of the matrix operations which make up the bulk of the level-shifting, diagonalization, and density construction phases has been performed using the ScaLAPACK library routines [17]. The ScaLAPACK routines we used for the DKS program are PZHEMM in the level-shifting phase, PZGEMM in the density phase and finally PZHEGVX to carry out the complex DKS matrix diagonalization. The workflow is extremely simple. Initially the DKS matrix is distributed to all processors. After this the "Level Shift", "Diagonalization" and "Density" steps are performed in this order, exploiting the intrinsic parallelism of the ScaLAPACK routines. At the end we collect on the master both the density matrix and the eigenvectors. Thus, apart from the internal communication activity of the ScaLAPACK routines, there are just four explicit communication steps, namely the initial distribution of the DKS and overlap matrices, and the final gathering of the resulting eigenvectors and density matrices.

An important aspect of ScaLAPACK diagonalization is that the PZHEGVX routine permits the selection of a subset of eigenvalues and eigenvectors to be computed. In the DKS computation it is only essential, in order to represent the density and carry out the SCF iterations, to compute the "occupied" positive-energy spinors. This clearly introduces great savings in eigenvector computation, both in time and memory, because the size of such subset is a small fraction (about 10% in our tests) of the total. Adopting this approach raises the problem that the computed eigenvectors may not be strictly orthogonal to the remaining ones. However, orthogonality to the negative-energy part of the spectrum is guaranteed in practice by the very nature of the spinors and the very large energy gap that separates them. To ensure orthogonality to the virtual spinors we have always included a number of lowest lying ones in the computed spectrum. The number of virtuals explicitly calculated was set at 10% of the occupied ones. In all cases, the choice of parameters and conditions for the parallel calculations described here ensured exact reproduction of the serial results.

We performed several test computations for the gold clusters Au_2, Au_4, Au_8, Au_{16}, and Au_{32}. To achieve fully comparable results throughout, we used neither integral screening techniques nor molecular symmetry in the calculations. The large component of the G-spinor basis set on each gold atom (22s19p12d8f) is derived by decontracting the double zeta quality Dyall basis set [20]. The corresponding small component basis was generated using the restricted kinetic balance relation [15]. The density functional used is the Becke 1988 exchange functional (B88) [21] plus the Lee-Yang-Parr (LYP) correlation functional [22] (BLYP). As auxiliary basis set we use the HGTF basis called *B20* optimized previously by us [8]. A numerical integration grid has been employed with 61200 grid points for each gold atom. The five Au clusters chosen offer testing ground for a wide range of memory requirements and double-precision complex array handling conditions: the DKS matrix sizes were 1560 for Au_2 (37.1 MB), 3120 for Au_4 (148.5 MB), 6240 for Au_8 (594.1 MB), 12480 for Au_{16} (2.3 GB) and 24960 for Au_{32} (9.3 GB).

Fig. 1 shows the corresponding speedup for the various cases. We see that with some exceptions, the speedup generally tends to increase with the size of the system under study. In particular, the time for the construction of the DKS matrix scales extremely well for large systems, reaching 91% and 95% of the theoretical maximum with 128 processors for Au_{16} and Au_{32}, respectively. The other phases of the calculation scale less satisfactorily, reflecting the performance limitations of the underlying ScaLAPACK implementation. Globally, the total speedup for the SCF DKS iterations appears to converge, for the larger Au clusters on 128 processors, to more than 80% of the theoretical value derived from Amdahl's law [23] and 60% of the limit value for an infinite number of processors (when the execution time reduces to that of the unparallelized portion) [24]. Considered together with the great step forward represented by the memory distribution scheme, we deem this result a very satisfactory one, practically opening the way for previously unfeasible applications.

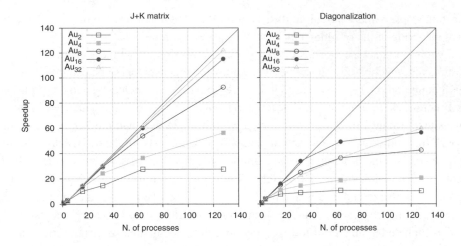

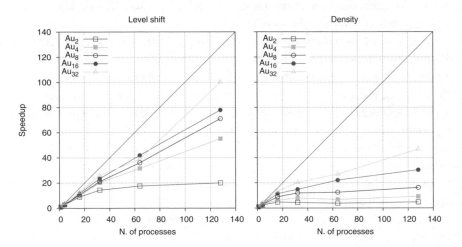

Figure 1. Speedup of the DKS computation steps for the gold clusters studied in the present work.

3. The interaction of E112 with an Au$_{20}$ cluster

Understanding the nature of the interactions involving the super heavy element E112 [25, 26], and in particular its interaction with gold clusters and surfaces, is of high current interest and a challenging task (see for instance Refs. [4,27] and references therein). Herein we want to show the practical effectiveness of our new parallel implementation by applying it to the characterization of the interaction of the mercury atom with the Au$_{20}$ cluster. In particular, besides the determination of some spectroscopic parameters like equilibrium bond length (R) and dissociation energy (D_e), we would like to analyze in detail the modification of the full relativistic all-electron density of E112 and Au$_{20}$ which leads to the formation of the E112-Au$_{20}$ bond.

3.1. Description of the calculations

While the determination of the global equilibrium structure of gold clusters is itself a topic of great current interest (see for instance Ref. [28] and references therein), the structure of the neutral Au_{20} cluster appears to be well established, having been successfully identified in a gas phase vibrational spectroscopy experiment combined with quantum chemical calculations [29]. These confirmed that the neutral cluster retains the symmetric pyramidal geometry established for the anion [30]. We have preliminarily optimized this Au_{20} structure using the Zero Order Relativistic Approximation (ZORA) with small core and a QZ4P basis set as implemented in the ADF package [31,32,33,34] We have then placed an Hg atom above the Au_{20} pyramid vertex, which was found to be a preferred position for an interacting noble-gas atom [29], and further fully optimized the whole adduct with the same method. Using then our parallel DKS program, as described in the previous sections, we substitute the Hg with E112 and re-optimized the sole E112-Au distance, keeping the Au cluster structure fixed. The interaction energy was determined as the difference between the total energy of $E112\text{-}Au_{20}$ and that of the separate fragments E112 and Au_{20}. The large component of the G-spinor basis set that we used was obtained by decontracting the Dyall basis set of triple zeta quality on both gold and E112 atoms [20]. This is a larger basis set than that used in the Au_2–Au_{32} test calculations. The corresponding small component basis was generated using the restricted kinetic balance relation [15]. This results in a DKS matrix of dimension 24584 (9 GB double-precision complex numbers). The density functional used is the Becke 1988 exchange functional (B88) [21] plus the Lee-Yang-Parr (LYP) correlation functional [22] (BLYP). All calculations were carried out with a total energy convergence threshold of 10^{-7} hartree. The Au-E112 bond length was determined iteratively using a quadratic fit to the energy, requiring several DKS single points. The calculations have been performed on the SGI Altix 4700 described above, using 64 processors.

3.2. Discussion

The $E112\text{-}Au_{20}$ bond length resulting from our calculations is 2.87 Å and the corresponding interaction energy is 0.286 eV (27.6 kJ/mol). These results suggest the presence of a chemically relevant interaction. A first qualitative insight into the nature of this interaction is provided by the graphical representation of the electronic density difference between the complex and the non-interacting fragments placed at the same geometry. In Fig. 2 we show a 3D contour plot of such DKS/BLYP electron density difference. A surprising feature of this is its very rich and complex structure, reaching the most remote regions of the Au cluster far away from the interaction zone. Another quite remarkable general feature, which is brought to light thanks to the all-electron nature of our calculations, is that the valence electron rearrangement upon bond formation has large repercussions in the core-electron region closer to the nuclei. The density accumulation is particularly pronounced in the E112-Au internuclear region and in the zone between the first two gold layers (i.e., between the gold atom bound to Hg and the three neighbors below it). Some density depletion zone is observed instead on the far side of the E112 atom, opposite to the E112-Au bond.

It is common to investigate the changes in charge density that result from the binding of an adsorbate to a surface by computing the density difference along the binding direction z, $\Delta\varrho(z)$ [35]. This is given by

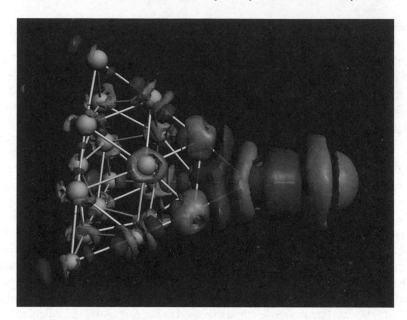

Figure 2. DKS/BLYP contour plot of the electron density difference upon bond formation between the atom E112 and the Au_{20} cluster. Red isodensity surfaces identify zones of density decrease, blue ones of density increase. The density value at the surfaces is ± 0.00008 e/a.u.^{3}.

$$\Delta\varrho(z) = \int_{-\infty}^{\infty} dx \int_{-\infty}^{\infty} dy \, \Delta\varrho(x, y, z) \tag{1}$$

where $\Delta\varrho(x, y, z)$ is the electron density of the complex minus that of the two isolated fragments. $\Delta\rho(z)$ for the Hg-Au_{20} system is shown in the top panel of Fig. 3. Here the z axis is that passing through the positions of the E112 atom and the Au atom nearest to it. Positive values of the function denote accumulation of charge, while negative values indicate regions where the charge density is depleted. Inspection of this plot makes clearly more detailed the qualitative information obtained from Fig. 2. Note in particular the marked density accumulation in the E112-Au bond region and in the vicinity of the second gold layer, accompanied by density depletion around the Hg atom, especially on the far side, and to the left side of the nearest Au atom. There are evident oscillations in the density difference around E112 and the nearest Au which may be put in relation with the structure of the electronic density of the atoms along z.

A more immediately informative picture of the bonding may be obtained by a progressive integration of Eq. (1) along the internuclear axis, i.e., by the function [36]

$$\Delta q(z) = \int_{-\infty}^{\infty} dx \int_{-\infty}^{\infty} dy \int_{-\infty}^{z} \Delta\varrho(x, y, z') \, dz' \tag{2}$$

This measures the actual electron displacement taking place upon bond formation, i.e. the amount of electron charge transferred into the integration region up to z as one moves from left to right along the axis. In other words, $\Delta q(z)$ is the charge displaced from the right to the left side of the plane perpendicular to the axis in z. Thus a negative value indicates a charge transfer of that magnitude from left to right and, similarly, the difference between two Δq values gives the net electron influx into the region delimited by the corresponding planes.

The plot of $\Delta q(z)$ for E112-Au_{20} is shown in the lower panel of Fig. 3. The most immediately eye-catching feature of the plot is that $\Delta q(z)$ is appreciably positive everywhere in the cluster region. This means that there is a shift of charge from the Hg atom towards gold which does not stop at the nearest Au layers but, surprisingly, extends appreciably even beyond the fourth layer. The Δq function shows two peaks, one corresponding to the already observed charge fluctuation between the first and second Au layers, and the second corresponding to the charge accumulation in the E112-Au region. If one defines an arbitrary boundary separating the E112 atom from the gold cluster, a corresponding effective charge-transfer value between the two fragments may be quantified. In Fig. 3 we have shown one plausible such boundary (already usefully proposed in other cases [36,37]), corresponding to the point along z where equal isodensity surfaces of the non-interacting fragments become tangent. Remarkably, this point almost coincides with the peak of density accumulation (maximum of $\Delta \varrho(z)$ or maximum slope of Δq). The charge transfer value at this point is 0.02 e. As noted above, in spite of the weakness of the E112-Au interaction, this transferred charge is delocalized surprisingly far away in the gold cluster. The Δq curve is indeed quite flat between the second and third Au layers, meaning that electrons do not accumulate here, so that nearly half of the total charge transferred is still found beyond the third Au layer.

4. Conclusions

In this work we presented an effective, essentially complete, parallelization of a relativistic all-electron four-component Dirac-Kohn-Sham program called BERTHA. We used MPI, for all data communication of the parallel routines, and the ScaLAPACK library to perform the most demanding matrix operations. The main aim of the parallelization scheme adopted was the effective reduction of memory requirements per processor through array distribution, enabling the handling of the DKS matrices arising in large-scale calculations on chemical systems containing several heavy and super-heavy atoms, using large basis sets. The global performance of the DKS calculation in large test cases was very satisfactory, reaching over 80% of the theoretical limit dictated by Amdahl's law.

As chemically significant application of the new all-electron DKS parallel code, we have studied the interaction of the super-heavy element E112 with a gold cluster of 20 atoms, using a triple-zeta basis set (DKS matrix of about 9 GB). A detailed study of the electronic density modification caused by the interaction shows clearly is characterized by a significant charge transferred from E112 to the gold cluster (about 0.02 electrons). We were able to show the rather unexpected and interesting fact that the charge transferred is significantly delocalized over the whole cluster, about half of it to be found as far away from the interaction site as the third and fourth gold atom layers. Similar ab-initio simulations involving larger gold clusters and the super heavy element E114, have also been performed and will be reported soon.

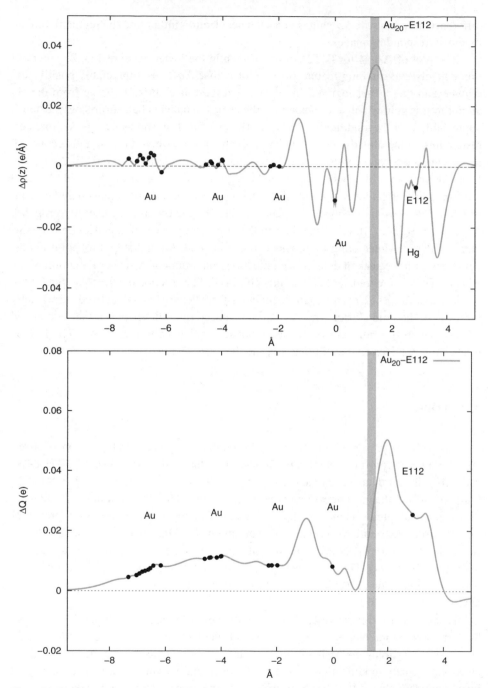

Figure 3. Upper plot: DKS electron density change along the E112-Au bond direction [Eq. (1)] upon formation of the E112-Au$_{20}$ system. The circles on the curve mark the projection of the position of the indicated atoms. The vertical gray strip marks a region of width equal to 10% of the E112-Au distance centered about the z position (vertical line) at which the densities of the non-interacting fragments cross (see the text for more details). Lower plot: Electron charge displacement function $\Delta q(z)$ [Eq. (2)] for the same system.

Acknowledgments

This work has been carried out as part of an Extreme Computing Initiative project of the Distributed European Infrastructure for Supercomputing Applications (DEISA). We thank I. Girotto and G. Erbacci of CINECA and the staff of Leibniz Rechenzentrum (Garching, Germany) for continuous assistance, in particular: S.H. Leong, A. Block, and M. Allalen.

References

[1] M. Schädel, *Angew. Chem. Int. Ed.* **45** (2006), 368.
[2] R. Eichler, *Nature* **447** (2007), 72.
[3] R. Eichler, *Angew. Chem. Int. Ed.* **47** (2008), 3262.
[4] C. Sarpe-Tudoran et al., *Eur. Phys. J.* **D 24** (2003), 65.
[5] V. Pershina and T. Bastuně, *Chem. Phys.* **311** (2005), 139.
[6] N. Gaston, I. Opahle, H. W. Gaggeler, and P. Schwerdtfeger, *Angw. Chem. Int. Ed.* **46** (2007), 1663.
[7] L. Belpassi, F. Tarantelli, A. Sgamellotti, and H. M. Quiney, *Phys. Rev. B* **77** (2008), 233403.
[8] L. Belpassi, F. Tarantelli, A. Sgamellotti, and H. M. Quiney, *J. Chem. Phys.* **124** (2006), 124104.
[9] J. W. Mintmire and B. I. Dunlap, *Phys. Rev. A* **25** (1982), 88.
[10] F. R. Manby and P. J. Knowles, *Phys. Rev. Lett.* **87** (2001), 163001.
[11] L. Belpassi, F. Tarantelli, A. Sgamellotti, and H. M. Quiney, *J. Chem. Phys.* **128** (2008), 124108.
[12] Silicon Graphics, Sgi numalink, White Paper 3771, Silicon Graphics, 2005.
[13] M. Challacombe, E. Schwegler, and J. Almlöf, *J. Chem. Phys.* **104** (1996), 4685.
[14] G. R. Ahmadi and J. Almlöf, *Chem. Phys. Lett.* **246** (1995), 364.
[15] I. P. Grant and H. M. Quiney, *Phys. Rev. A* **62** (2000), 022508.
[16] Message Passing Interface Forum. University of Tennessee, *MPI: A Message-Passing Interface Standard. Version 2.2*, 2009, http://www.mpi-forum.org.
[17] L. S. Blackford et al., *ScaLAPACK Users' Guide*, Society for Industrial and Applied Mathematics, Philadelphia, PA, 1997.
[18] Silicon Graphics, Powering the real-time enterprise, White Paper 3935, Silicon Graphics, 2006.
[19] L. Belpassi, L. Storchi, F. Tarantelli, A. Sgamellotti, and H. M. Quiney, *Future Gener Comp. Sym.* **20** (2004), 739.
[20] K. G. Dyall, *Theor. Chem. Acc.* **112** (2004), 403.
[21] A. D. Becke, *Phys. Rev. A* **38** (1998), 3098.
[22] C. Lee, W. Yang, and R. G. Parr, *Phys. Rev. B* **37**(1988), 785.
[23] G. Amdahl, Validity of the single processor approach to achieving large-scale computing capabilities, in *AFIPS Conference Proceedings, (30)*, 483–485, 1967.
[24] L. Storchi, L. Belpassi, F. Tarantelli, A. Sgamellotti, H. M. Quiney, Development of a parallel all-electron 4-component Dirac-Kohn-Sham method using distributed matrix to calculate the electronic structure of large clusters containing heavy elements, *to be published*.
[25] R. C. Barber, H. W. Gaageller, P. J. Karol, H. Nakahara, and E. Vardaci, *IUPAC, Pure and Applied Chemistry* **81** (2009), 1331.
[26] *Nature Chemistry* **1** (2009), 333.
[27] E. A. Rykova, A. Zaitsevskii, N. S. Mosyagin, T. A. Isaev, and A. V. Titov, *J. Chem. Phys.* **125** (2006), 241102.
[28] B. Assadollahzadeh and P. Schwerdtfeger, *J. Chem. Phys.* **131** (2009), 064306.
[29] P. Gruene et al., *Science* **321** (2008), 674.
[30] J. Li, X. Li, H.-J. Zhai, and L.-S. Wang, *Science* **299** (2003), 864.
[31] G. te Velde et al., *J. Comput. Chem.* **22** (2001), 931.
[32] C. Fonseca Guerra, J. G. Snijders, G. te Velde, and E. J. Baerends, *Theor. Chem. Acc.* **99** (1998), 391.
[33] SCM, Theoretical Chemistry, Vrije Universiteit, Amsterdam, The Netherlands, *ADF User's Guide. Release 2008.1*, 2008, http://www.scm.com.
[34] R. van Leeuwen, E. van Lenthe, E. J. Baerends, and J. G. Snijders, *J. Chem. Phys.* **101** (1994), 1272.
[35] J. A. Steckel, *Phys. Rev. B* **77** (2008), 115412.

[36]   L. Belpassi, I. Infante, F. Tarantelli, and L. Visscher, *J. Am. Chem. Soc.* **130** (2008), 1048.
[37]   L. Belpassi, F. Tarantelli, F. Pirani, P. Candori, and D. Cappelletti, *Phys. Chem. Chem. Phys.* (2009), DOI: 10.1039/b914792f.

Parallel Computing: From Multicores and GPU's to Petascale
B. Chapman et al. (Eds.)
IOS Press, 2010
© 2010 The authors and IOS Press. All rights reserved.
doi:10.3233/978-1-60750-530-3-513

Direct Numerical Simulation of the turbulent development of a round jet at Reynolds number 11,000

Christophe BOGEY [a,1] and Olivier MARSDEN [a,2]

[a] *Laboratoire de Mécanique des Fluides et d'Acoustique, UMR CNRS 5509, Ecole Centrale de Lyon, 69134 Ecully Cedex, France*

Abstract. A Direct Numerical Simulation (DNS) of a round jet at a Reynolds number of 11,000 has been performed using a grid containing 755 million points, within the DEISA (Distributed European infrastructure for Supercomputing Applications) framework. The flow statistics, including mean and turbulent properties as well as the energy budget, have been calculated in the region of jet establishment, and databases of three-dimensional unsteady fields are now available for further analyses of the jet physics. First results support the convergence and the accuracy of the simulation.

Keywords. Direct Numerical Simulation, turbulence, jet, parallel computing

1. Introduction

The study of turbulent jets is both of fundamental and practical interests in fluid dynamics and aeroacoustics. However the mechanisms responsible for flow mixing and noise generation are still only partially described and understood [1,2]. Some uncertainties indeed remain in experimental works because of the limitations of the measurement techniques, preventing direct and accurate access to some turbulent quantities [3,4,5,6,7]. Similar difficulties may be encountered in numerical simulations because of possible insufficient discretization and the use of turbulence modellings. In configurations in which all the turbulent scales cannot be calculated, subgrid-scale (SGS) modellings are for instance used to perform Large-Eddy Simulations (LES). The effects of the SGS modellings on the flow features are however to be examined carefully [8,9]. To obtain reference solutions, one possibility is to perform Direct Numerical Simulations (DNS), in which all the turbulent scales are theoretically computed, implying that there is no need of a turbulence model, but they were restricted, up to recently, to low Reynolds numbers below 3600 because of the computing resources available [10,11].

In the present work, a DNS of a round jet at Reynolds number $Re_D = u_j D/\nu = 11,000$ is carried out, where u_j and D are the jet velocity and diameter, and ν is the kinematic molecular viscosity. A simulation of this magnitude is made possible thanks to the

---

[1] Corresponding Author; E-mail: christophe.bogey@ec-lyon.fr
[2] E-mail: olivier.marsden@ec-lyon.fr

DEISA (Distributed European infrastructure for Supercomputing Applications) framework. The objective is to provide a complete and reference description of a turbulent jet at the significant Reynolds number of 11,000 considered, in the region of flow establishment, which would be the first time to the knowledge of the authors. The DNS is performed by solving the full three-dimensional Navier-Stokes equations, using low-dissipation and low-dispersion numerical methods [12,13], which were recently employed successfully to compute a self-similar round jet at the same Reynolds number of 11,000 by LES [14]. During the DNS, mean and turbulent flow statistics including second and fourth order velocity moments and the budgets for the turbulent kinetic energy are estimated. Databases of three-dimensional unsteady fields are also built.

The present paper is organized as follows. The DEISA framework will be first mentioned. The computational approach using a parallelized version of an in-house solver is then briefly described, and parameters of the simulation are provided. Preliminary results are finally shown to assess the quality of the simulation.

2. DECI Framework

Among the numerous achievements and activities of the Distributed European Infrastructure for Supercomputing Applications consortium, or DEISA, the DEISA Extreme Computing Initiatve (DECI) aims to enable a number of "grand challenge" computational applications in all areas of science and technology. Computational means substantially larger than those offered on a national scale are granted to research projects with exceptional computational requirements. The present work was awarded a grant following a research proposal submitted to the 2007 call for proposals. The proposal was put together with the help of the french national computing centre IDRIS regarding computational requirements. The NEC vector architecture was specifically targeted in the proposal, because of its very good match with the computational code structure. Sustained performance results presented in the next section reflect this point. DECI offers the possiblity of receiving help in porting applications to large HPC environments, via the ATASKF. The code used in this work had already been used in production on large parallel machines, so no help from the ATASKF was requested. DEISA recommends that computations performed at distant sites be managed via Unicore or DESHL software. Unicore was tested during this work, but rejected due to incompatibilities with specific queue parameters at the HPC site. Computational runs were instead launched via the local batch queuing system. GlobusFTP was used to transfer the large amount of recorded data obtained over the duration of the project.

3. Computational approach

The DNS has been performed using an in-house F90 solver of the full 3-D Navier-Stokes equations, using low-dissipation and low-dispersion numerical methods. Fourth-order 11-point finite differences are implemented for spatial discretization, and a second-order 6-stage low-storage Runge-Kutta algorithm is applied for time integration [12]. A high-order/spectral-like relaxation filtering is applied to the flow variable with a constant strength, every second iteration, using an explicit six-order 11-point filter [13] designed to damp only the shortest waves resolved by the grid, discretized by fewer than four points per wavelength.

The simulation have been done using the NEC SX-8 Cluster at the HLRS Centre in Stuttgart, Germany. This was particularly interesting, because our high-order explicit finite-differences code is particularly well suited to vector processing architectures with very high memory bandwidth. Indeed, for single processor SX-8 computations using the same code, we regularly obtain sustained performance rates of around 9 GFlops, to be compared to less than 1 GFlop on a recent x86 type processor. The F90 code used in this work has been run on single vector machines for a number of years. It was parallelized by ourselves [15] using the MPI interface specifically for this study, and great care was taken to maintain highly vectorized code. Thus the overall computation, including the substantial amounts of IO, ran at a speed of 5.9 GFlops per processor, or a total aggregated speed of 212 GFlops, and consumed a total of 250 GB of memory. An amount of 30,000 CPU hours was also required. Over the duration of the simulation, a large amount of time-dependent flow data was recorded, for future processing and analysis. A total of 4 terabytes of flow data was generated, and transferred from the HLRS to the IDRIS Centre in Paris, France, thanks to the GLOBUS fast ftp. A transfer of this magnitude would not have been possible without a fast ftp service. Transfer rates of around 35 megabytes per second were regularly obtained.

4. Simulation parameters

The jet simulated is round, isothermal, at a Mach number of $M = u_j/c_{amb} = 0.9$ (c_{amb} is the ambient speed of sound) and at a Reynolds number of 11,000. Laminar mean flow profiles are specified at the inflow conditions. The initial shear layer is in particular characterized by a momentum thickness of $\delta_0 = r0/100$ ($r_0 = D/2$ is the jet radius), which is sufficiently thin to correspond to experimental conditions in initially laminar jets. Finally random, low-magnitude, vortical disturbances are introduced in the shear layer ar $x = r_0$ to seed the turbulence transition [1,14] .

The computational grid is Cartesian, and contains $n_x \times n_y \times n_z = 2010 \times 613 \times 613$ points allowing the accurate computation of the smallest turbulent scales. The grid has been indeed designed so that the DNS requirement $k_c\eta \simeq 1.5$ in which k_c is the grid cut-off wave number and η is the Kolmogorov scale that can be evaluated using classical expressions for isotropic turbulence, is satisfied. The mesh spacing in the jet is uniform, and is equal to $\Delta x = \Delta y = \Delta z = r_0/68$, and the grid extends up to 28 radii in the axial direction. Thus we focus on the region of jet establishment. To obtain converged turbulent statistics, 295,000 iterations have been performed, corresponding to a normalized time of $3,000 r_0/u_j$.

During the DNS, the flow properties, namely the velocity moments up to the fourth-order, are computed in the plane at $z = 0$. As successfully done in a previous LES study [14], all the terms in the budget for the turbulent kinetic energy, are also explicitly calculated from the unsteady DNS fields. The dissipation is in particular the sum of the viscous dissipation and of the subgrid-scale dissipation taken into account by the relaxation filtering, which will enable us to check *a priori* that the present simulation is a well-resolved DNS.

5. Preliminary results

The processing and the analysis of the DNS data have not been completed. Preliminary results are however presented to assess the accuracy of the simulation. Snapshots of the vorticity norm are shown in figure 1. The development of the jet, from the initially laminar to turbulent shear layers, then to the turbulent jet, can be seen in the top view of the full jet. The two other views represent zooms by factors of ×4 and ×16, respectively. Fine vortical scales are visible, as expected from a DNS at the Reynolds number considered. These scales appear in addition very well resolved by the mesh. The axial extend in the bottom figure, that is $27.5r_0/16$, is for instance discretized by 116 grid points.

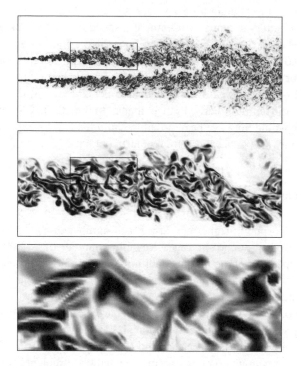

Figure 1. Snapshots of the vorticity norm $|\omega|$ in the plane $z = 0$. The gray scale is defined for levels from 0 to $6u_j/r_0$, $8u_j/r_0$, and $1.05u_j/r_0$, from top to bottom. The top view represents the full jet ($0 \leq x \leq 27.5r_0$), the other views show zooms into the boxes defined in the views respectively above.

The mean properties of the jet flow are illustrated in figure 2 by the variations of the centerline mean axial velocity u_c and the jet half-width $\delta_{0.5}$. The end of the potential core, observed for instance when $u_c = 0.95u_j$, is around $x = 15r_0$, which is more than 10 radii upstream of the outflow boundary, and corresponds roughly the experimental findings. Upstream this axial location, only the shear layers develop, and the jet half-width vary slowly. Downtream, the shear layers have merged, and the jet spreading is important.

The increase of the turbulence intensities along the jet centerline and the lip line is shown in figure 3. As expected, they become significant on the centerline only from the end of the potential core. Along the lip line, they grow rapidly as the laminar-turbulent transition occurs around $x = 3_0$, then do not vary much as the shear layers are fully developed.

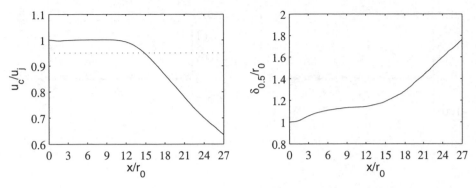

Figure 2. Variations of the centerline mean axial velocity u_c/u_j (left), and of the jet half-width $\delta_{0.5}/r_0$ (right).

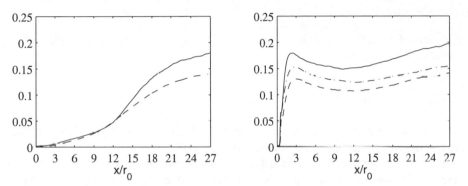

Figure 3. Variations along the jet centerline (left) and along the lip line (right), of the axial, radial and azimuthal turbulence intensities: ———— $[u'u']^{1/2}/u_c$, — — — $[v'v']^{1/2}/u_c$, and — · — · $[w'w']^{1/2}/u_c$.

First insights into the flow physics are finally given in figure 4 with the variations of the main terms in the turbulent energy budget along the jet centreline and the lip line. Five terms are dominating: mean flow convection, production, dissipation, turbulence diffusion and pressure diffusion. The convergence of these terms appears satisfactory. As mentioned previously, the dissipation is the sum of the viscous dissipation and of the subgrid (filtering) dissipation. The latter contribution is however found to be very small, lower than 1%, which indicates that the present simulation is a well-resolved DNS, namely that all the energy-dissipating scales are discretized. The sum of the energy terms is finally also represented in figure 4. It is nearly nil, which suggests that the energy budget is accurately calculated, without additional numerical artefact.

6. Concluding remarks

The first results obtained for the present DNS of a turbulent jet at Reynolds number 11,000 support the convergence and the quality of the simulation. The DNS seems in particular well discretized, and no undesirable numerical artefact has been detected. Comparisons of DNS results with available data of the literature are now required. The present results should in particular complement the measurements obtained by Sami [3,4]. Then

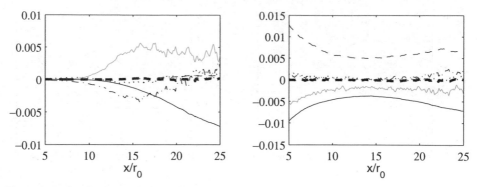

Figure 4. Budget for the turbulent kinetic energy along the jet centerline (left) and along the lip line (right): — · — · mean flow convection, — — — production, ——— dissipation, ——— turbulence diffusion, ······· pressure diffusion; and — — — sum of all the energy terms. The terms are normalized by $\rho_c u_c^3 \delta_{0.5}$ (ρ_c: centerline mean density).

the physics of the jet flow and the turbulence modellings used in previous studies will be discussed.

Acknowledgements

This work has been performed in the framework of the DECI (DEISA Extreme Computing Initiative) project *Simulation of jet turbulence in the region of flow establishment* (project acronym: JetTurb), using the NEC SX-8 Cluster at the HLRS Centre in Stuttgart, Germany. The authors are also grateful to the assistance of the *Institut du Développement et des Ressources en Informatique Scientifique* of the French National Centre for Scientific Research (CNRS), and especially to Jean-Michel Dupays.

References

[1] C. Bogey and C. Bailly, Large Eddy Simulations of transitional round jets : influence of the Reynolds number on flow development and energy dissipation, *Phys. Fluids* **18** (2006), 065101.

[2] C. Bogey and C. Bailly, An analysis of the correlations between the turbulent flow and the sound pressure fields of subsonic jets, *J. Fluid Mech.* **583** (2007), 71–97.

[3] S. Sami, T. Carmody and H. Rouse, Jet diffusion in the region of flow establishment, *J. Fluid Mech.* **27**(2) (1967), 231–252.

[4] S. Sami, Balance of turbulence energy in the region of jet-flow establishment, *J. Fluid Mech.* **29**(1) (1967), 81–92.

[5] I. Wygnanski and H. Fiedler, Some measurements in the self-preserving jet, *J. Fluid Mech.* **38**(3) (1969), 577–612.

[6] N.R. Panchapakesan and J.L. Lumley, Turbulence measurements in axisymmetric jets of air and helium. Part 1. Air jet, *J. Fluid Mech.* **246** (1993), 197–223.

[7] H.J. Hussein, S.P. Capp and W.K. George, Velocity measurements in a high-Reynolds-number momentum-conserving axisymmetric turbulent jet, *J. Fluid Mech.* **258** (1994), 31–75.

[8] B. Vreman, B. Geurts and H. Kuerten, Large-eddy simulation of the turbulent mixing layer, *J. Fluid Mech.* **339** (1997), 357–390.

[9] C. Bogey and C. Bailly, Large eddy simulations of round jets using explicit filtering with/without dynamic Smagorinsky model, *Int. J.Heat Fluid Flow* **27** (2006), 603–610.

[10] J.B. Freund, Noise sources in a low-Reynolds-number turbulent jet at Mach 0.9, *J. Fluid Mech.* **438** (2001), 277-305.

[11]   S.A. Stanley, S. Sarkar and J.P. Mellado, A study of the flow-field evolution and mixing in a planar turbulent jet using direct numerical simulation, *J. Fluid Mech.* **450** (2002), 377–407.

[12]   C. Bogey and C. Bailly, A family of low dispersive and low dissipative explicit schemes for noise computation, *J. Comp. Phys.* **194**(1) (2004), 194–214.

[13]   C. Bogey, N. de Cacqueray and C. Bailly, A shock-capturing methodology based on adaptative spatial filtering for high-order non-linear computations, *J. Comp. Phys.* **228**(5) (2009), 1447–1465.

[14]   C. Bogey and C. Bailly, Turbulence and energy budget in a self-preserving round jet: direct evaluation using large-eddy simulation, *J. Fluid Mech.* **627** (2009), 129–160.

[15]   O. Marsden, C. Bogey and C. Bailly, Direct noise computation of the turbulent flow around a zero-incidence airfoil, *AIAA Journal* **46**(4) (2008), 874–883.

Parallel Computing: From Multicores and GPU's to Petascale
B. Chapman et al. (Eds.)
IOS Press, 2010
© 2010 The authors and IOS Press. All rights reserved.
doi:10.3233/978-1-60750-530-3-520

EUFORIA: Exploring E-Science for Fusion

D.P. Coster [a,1], P. Strand [b] and Contributors to the EUFORIA Project [c]

[a] *Max-Planck-Institut für Plasmaphysik, GERMANY*
[b] *Chalmers University of Technology, SWEDEN (Coordinator)*
[c] *CSC - Tieteellinen laskenta Oy, FINLAND*
Åbo Akademi University, FINLAND
CEA - Commissariat à l'énergie atomique, FRANCE
Université Louis Pasteur , FRANCE
Forschungszentrum Karlsruhe GmbH, GERMANY
Max-Planck-Institut für Plasmaphysik, GERMANY
ENEA, ITALY
University of Ljubljana, SLOVENIA
Poznan Supercomputing and Networking Centre, POLAND
Barcelona Supercomputing Center - Centro Nacional de Supercomputación, SPAIN
Centro de Investigaciones Energéticas Medio Ambientales y Tecnológicas, SPAIN
Consejo Superior de Investigaciones Científicas, SPAIN
Chalmers University of Technology, SWEDEN
The University of Edinburgh, UK

Abstract. The European participation in the next step fusion energy research project, ITER, is very broad with interests from all EU member states. To support the needed physics understanding and predictive capability for ITER discharges, a strong need to promote modelling technologies and access to computing resources on a pan-European basis exists. The EUFORIA project, EU Fusion for ITER Applications, sets out to support these needs by creating an e-Science environment, building on the existing European infrastructure and middleware environments and specifically introducing the developments towards a modelling platform for fusion being advanced within the European fusion community. The aim is to advance the physics modelling capability for ITER on a broadened European Scale. The EUFORIA approach and its different components are discussed here.

Keywords. Grid, HPC, Workflows, Visualization

Introduction

EUFORIA[1], EU Fusion for ITER Applications, is a FP7 project funded by the European Commission which has the aim of working with the European fusion modelling community to provide a comprehensive framework and infrastructure for core and edge transport and turbulence simulation, linking grid and high performance computing.

---

[1]Corresponding Author: David.Coster at ipp.mpg.de

Simulating a full fusion tokamak requires a range of codes and applications which address different aspects of the plasma and at specific ranges of space and time scales to be brought into a single simulation framework. EUFORIA supports fusion modellers in this simulation work by providing programming expertise for porting and optimizing codes on a range of computing platforms, providing grid and HPC resources, and providing the tools required to orchestrate the range of simulation codes necessary to simulate the full fusion reactor.

In particular, EUFORIA has adapted Kepler[2], a workflow orchestration tool, to enable fusion modellers to submit simulations to grid or HPC resources from their desktop and visualize the results they produce. The project also provide support and training for a large range of European scientists, and collaborate with projects such as DEISA[3], GOTiT[4], and HPC-EUROPA[5].

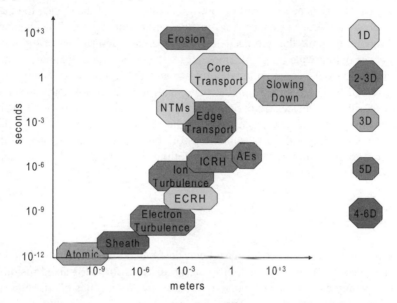

Figure 1. Schematic showing the multi-scale aspects of the ITER physics in time, in linear dimensions and in the dimensionality of the problem.

ITER[6] is the next generation of fusion devices and is intended to demonstrate the scientific and technical feasibility of fusion as a sustainable energy source for the future. To exploit the full potential of the device and to guarantee optimal operation for the device, a high degree of physics modelling and simulation is needed already in the current construction phase of the ITER project. The detailed modelling tools that are needed for an adequate description of the underlying physics cover both a wide range of timescales and spatial orderings (figure 1) and are in general very demanding from a computational point of view.

Current modelling activities rely on local or national computational resources and an improved access to computing infrastructures will be instrumental in advancing a pan-European modelling activity for ITER to a competitive status in relation to the ITER partners.

The project will enhance the modelling capabilities for ITER sized plasmas through the adaptation, optimization and integration of a set of critical applications for edge and core transport modelling targeting different computing paradigms as needed (serial and parallel grid computing and HPC). Deployment of both a grid service and a High Performance Computing service are essential to the project. A novel aspect is the dynamic coupling and integration of codes and applications running on a set of heterogeneous platforms into a single coupled framework through a workflow engine a mechanism needed to provide the necessary level integration in the physics applications. This strongly enhances the integrated modelling capabilities of fusion plasmas and will at the same time provide new computing infrastructure and tools to the fusion community in general.

Simulations are crucial to develop attainable experimental scenarios and modelling the experimental design points as well as estimate heat loads and device stresses. This modelling capability is needed well before the deployment of the device to ensure sufficient understanding of the underlying physics and detailed control mechanisms. The detailed modelling tools that are needed for an adequate description of the underlying physics cover both a wide range of timescales and spatial orderings and are in general very demanding from a computational point of view. ITER operations and experimental campaigns will be based on a comparatively small number of discharges compared to today's experimental devices. Experimental time will be allocated to the ITER partners based on a competitive review process. The high costs associated with a single discharge require very solid proposals to be submitted for consideration - it is expected that proposal incorporating full scale predictive modelling will be essential to succeed in the competitive selection process.

1. Infrastructure Needs

A range of applications and codes have been developed throughout Europe addressing different aspects of ITER plasmas. Full scale predictions for ITER sized fusion devices are currently only available at a comparatively low level of physics fidelity and advancement in this area is needed and requires improved access to computing facilities. The aim of this project is thus to bring local code developments and modelling activities together into a single infrastructure expanding the user base of the modelling codes and at the same time bringing Grid- and High Performance Computing to the fusion modelling community. This will in turn help advance the level of physics refinement and increase the modelling capabilities.

The European participation in ITER is very broad with interests from all EU member states. However, access to computing resources and high level physics codes varies largely across the different member states. Consequently, the different physics applications and modelling codes that forms the basis for full scale predictive modelling is based on different programmatic backgrounds and spans over an equally broad diversity in computational science maturity. This is reflected in the range of computational resources and code optimization needs addressed within the EUFORIA call to fulfill the overall objective of an advancement of the physics modelling capability for ITER on a broadened European Scale.

Focusing on the edge and core physics, including the coupling of the two regions, allows for deployment of a suite of modelling tools addressing a range of critical issues for ITER relating to the performance and optimization of the machine. The coupling between the edge and core region is quite natural as it poses a distinct change in topology of the fusion plasma. The core resides in a region with closed magnetic field lines whereas the edge region has open field lines- leading to a separation in timescales between the two regions. It is therefore quite natural that different approaches have been pursued for the modelling of the two regions with different set of numerical tools and with computational resources ranging from single workstations to HPC computers. The separation in timescales can be utilized to promote an edge-core integration scheme where separate core and edge simulations are sharing only boundary conditions in an iterative fashion.

As a heterogeneous range of computational resources are required this approach relies heavily on the existence and guaranteed availability of the needed computational infrastructures and the organization and transfer of data between applications. To support this structured integration of codes, a workflow orchestration tool is envisaged for scheduling applications, transferring data, integrating results and visualization tools transparently for the end user. A common ontology for the edge and core simulations will be developed based on ongoing European developments towards a mark up language for fusion simulations, data access and storage. Access to the EUFORIA core-edge simulation tool will be through three-tiered approach where an access portal is used to launch the workflow orchestration tool and access to data where simulation arc run on distributed set of resources ranging from grid services to HPC computing platforms.

An important issue for the integration and utilization of a whole range of different codes is to provide tools for natural and efficient processing and visualization of the generated data in order to be able to interpret the results and compare with experimental data. In addition to codes generating 1D or 2D data for which there are now standard visualization tools available, many of the codes involved generate massive and complex 3D data or even 4D or 5D data for the distribution function computed in gyrokinetic codes. Hence visualization support will rely on at least two aspects. First a unique compressed data format that can be handled efficiently needs to be defined, then a single visualization environment should to be included both in the workflow to enable monitoring of the simulation and for post-processing of the compressed data that have been saved during the simulation. This environment should be able to produce in an easy and natural manner line plots, contour plots and other simple plots and also enable the user to generate more sophisticated specific plots when needed.

2. EUFORIA Objectives

The EUFORIA project sets out to achieve the following:

- Deployment of a grid service
- Deployment of an HPC infrastructure
- Development of a portal for general user access
- Adaptation of a standard ontology for edge-core simulations
- Adaptation and optimization of fusion simulation tools and codes targeting

  * Serial grid applications
  * Parallel grid applications
  * High Performance Computing

- Development of a framework or code platform tool providing

  * Dynamic workflow orchestration
  * High quality visualization
  * Data mining capabilities

- Middleware development needed for deployment of computational resources from framework tools

In addition there are a number of outreach and dissemination activities planned to introduce the fusion community at large to the developed infrastructure and make contact with other infrastructure and research projects with similar or associated orientations.

As can be seen from the list above, the project consists of a set of related work packages. A high level of coordination and monitoring is needed to ensure the timely delivery of the different components and emphasis have been put on providing sufficient management structures and resources at the different levels of the project.

3. Implementation

The EUFORIA project consists of two different phases that are partly being developed in parallel from the start of the project to become fully integrated in the later stages. The first is a development and deployment phase consisting of the adaptation and optimization of a selection of codes covering both edge and core physics for grid and HPC environments as appropriate. Inherent within this activity is the deployment of the computational infrastructure where access to grid computing and high performance computing is being developed for the project members. Thus, this stage is mainly directed towards code developers and application developers as it focuses on the detailed implementation and code structures of the physics codes. To carry this effort beyond the Project members and to the broader Fusion modelling community general tutorials on the different aspects of the code adaptation will be provided. The "lessons learned" from the development work done on the fusion codes will be made publicly available and direct user support will be provided to new users bringing their codes to the EUFORIA platform. This activity alone will provide a significant step forward in the modelling capacities and capabilities of the fusion modelling community. The second phase is a standardization and integration activity and has one technology driven part which develops the technologies and tools to provide user transparent methods for resource allocation and scheduling and dynamic coupling of physics codes and on user and physics driven component where a technology for building complex workflows with the optimized codes as components and standardized data structures and transfer methods are being utilized to expand the physics cases for ITER development. Key components here are the adaptation of a common project wide data structure for edge and core simulations, the adaptation of a workflow orchestration tool and generic tools for data exploration and visualization. This second part of the project is mainly directed towards providing the means for building a broader user community for the code packages residing on the platform and in the somewhat longer perspective provides the start for the adaptation of a suite of community operated tools.

4. Grid and HPC infrastructure

EUFORIA maintains and develops infrastructure to support grid computation as well as targeted High Performance Computations. The installed grid services are based on gLite[7] to support serial batch jobs and data management amended by the middleware developments of Interactive European Grid[8]. The extensions over gLite allow users to run MPI parallel jobs and start interactive sessions on their local desktop on remote grid-enabled clusters. EUFORIA has also deployed several Roaming Access Servers dedicated to the users of Migrating Desktop[9], which will be used within to make the connection between the simulation workflow orchestration tool and the grid infrastructure. In order to gather extra resources for simple batch serial jobs we have also installed the support for the Fusion VO[10] of the EGEE[11] project on the EUFORIA user interfaces.

Site	CPUs and type	Intranet interconnection	Online Storage
CSIC	1605 (Intel Xeon)	Infiniband (114 x 4 cores), Gigabit Ethernet the rest	50 TB
FZK	452 (Intel Xeon)	Gigabit Ethernet	4 TB
Chalmers University	640 (Intel Xeon)	Gigabit Ethernet	-
IISAS (Bratislava)	32 (Intel Xeon)	Gigabit Ethernet	-

Table 1. EUFORIA GRID SERVICE

The Grid infrastructure (table 1) has been setup keeping in mind that sustainability and long term perspectives will be a real issue. In particular we take into account the ongoing developments at the level of EGI and National Grid Initiatives in the countries participating in the deployment of the services that keep the EUFORIA Grid up and running.

The European High Performance Computing (HPC) ecology is much more diverse than the existing Grid infrastructure and in order to support access to HPC resources EUFORIA has secured a programming environment for the code developers involved in EUFORIA. Hence, EUFORIA have provided users with the appropriate tools to utilize the available HPC resources. Access to run time on the three centres involved (table 2) in the EUFORIA is provided, free of charge, to such an extent that can be motivated for testing of the optimized codes. Accesses to production run time for participating codes have been provided by collaborative agreements with DEISA (2 MCpuHours in each of 2008 and 2009).

Site	Hardware Resources
CSC	[1] Cray Supercomputer: Cray XT4 (2024 cores, performance 10,5 Tflops). This system is known as Louhi. [2] HP XC-Super cluster, 2048 cores, peak performance 10.6 Tflops.
EPCC	Cray Supercomputer: the XT4 comprises 5664 quad-core AMD 2.3 GHz Opteron, giving a total of 22,656 cores, and a theoretical peak performance of the system of 208 Tflops. Each quad-core processor shared 8 GB of memory, giving a total of 45.3 TB over the whole system. This system is known as HECToR.
BSC	IBM BladeCenter JS21 Cluster, 10240 PPC 970 processors @ 2.3 GHz. Peak performance 94 Tflops, 20 TB of memory.

Table 2. HPC resources

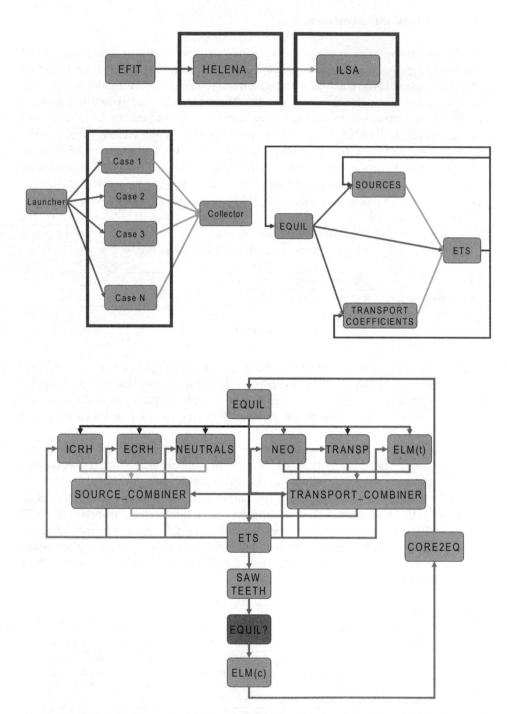

Figure 2. Possible workflows: a simple linear workflow, a parameter scan, a workflow with a simple loop, the simplified version of one of the planned physics workflows

5. Code adaptation and optimization

EUFORIA is set up to help fusion modellers to utilize modern infrastructure in an efficient manner. From the start of the project, a selection of codes relating to edge and core transport and turbulence in fusion plasmas was promoted as candidate EUFORIA codes. These codes were firstly selected because of their potential to enhance the fusion modelling activities in a vital area for the development of a predictive capability. A second reason was the foreseen gains in porting to new infrastructure or optimizing for an architecture they were already running on. Code adaptation and optimization for both grid and HPC infrastructures is undertaken within EUFORIA. The selection of the codes to be ported to the grid and HPC plays a crucial role in achieving high levels of scientific excellence. Provided that all these codes are relevant for ITER exploitation, the selected ones must allow the construction of combined workflows of applications to reproduce more advanced physics.

Eleven candidate codes have been ported to the HPC environment and a subset of three of these codes have been further optimized reaching significant performance gains and improved scaling in some cases even promoted from sequential codes running on several hundred processors in a DEISA environment. In addition, to supporting the code set on HPC several have been ported or are in the process of being installed in the EUFORIA grid environment. Three different teams have been active in porting applications for the grid including a gyro-fluid turbulence code with the aim of exploring the EUFORIA grid for parallel applications.

The selected codes have all benefited from the work in the form of error corrections and performance improvements. Furthermore, there is now also a better understanding of how the codes behave and what factors limits the performance of the codes. All selected HPC codes are now capable of running simulations of ITER size and efficiently utilizing the systems that are at the disposal of the EUFORIA project

6. Workflows, visualization and middleware amendments

EUFORIA has been developing an integrated environment for fusion modelling on the supported infrastructure. The toolset employed in this venture is based on a number of existing tools already developed in support of the European Infrastructure (Migrating Desktop[9], Roaming Access Server, gLite[7], UNICORE[12], Vine Toolkit[13]) and coupling these to modelling tools adapted and developed within the Fusion community (Kepler[2], Universal Access Layer[14]) in addition to this the integration effort is also covering Visualization tools, monitoring middleware, authentication and authorization technology). Since the overall architecture covers support for number of different systems and solutions it is a challenging task. The outcome is a significant improvement of the architecture which simplifies the connection between the workflow engine based on Kepler and the various GRID/HPC infrastructures. Examples of workflows are shown in figure 2.

In order to perform an end-to-end numerical simulation of a Tokamak discharge, several complex codes will need to be coupled and integrated as actors in the scientific workflow package chosen for the project, Kepler. There will in addition also be the need for unified visualization support so that scientists can use it without having to learn to use

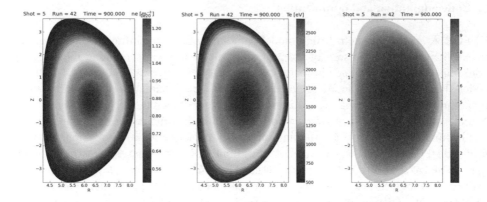

Figure 3. Electron density, electron temperature and safety factor profiles for simulations of ITER with the new European Transport Solver (a 1D core transport code) under development in the Integrated Tokamak Modelling Task Force[15,16] using the visualization tools developed by EUFORIA.

specific tools for each code that has been integrated. The visualization support consists of two aspects. On the one hand, the visualization tools must be able to read the data formats generated by the codes. On the other hand, some specific visualization tools must directly be inserted in the computational workflow in order to be able to monitor ongoing simulations. This last aspect will be addressed during the second year of the project. The first year of the project was devoted to the first aspect in order to demonstrate the integration of open source tools as Python and VisIt to show fusion dataset coming from fusion codes. An example of using the EUFORIA developed visualization tools can be seen in figure 3.

7. Dissemination and training

EUFORIA develops training material and companion guides (documentation) for Grid and HPC infrastructures, and are providing a set of weeklong training courses together with some shorter activities. The target audience for this is the fusion community with the particular aim of bringing new users onto the available infrastructures. To support this courses on Kepler, MPI and Message Passing Programming was given in addition to introductory courses on Grid usage. In collaboration with DEISA a course on MPI Programming was given focusing on MPI I/O. Evaluation and further requirements were solicited from attendees, and the results used to improve future work in training in EUFORIA. Based on the successful implementation of the EUFORIA training programme invitations to promote training in other Fusion programmes have been received.

For the first year of the project, the main objective was to establish a Global Dissemination Strategy for the project as a whole including the project intra-communication channels. A web site has been created to progress Project information and Wikipedia have been used for additional communication channels.

In addition, EUFORIA has created links and collaborative activities with a range of projects supporting the European infrastructure: DEISA[3], PRACE[17], EGEE[11] in particular and a stronger collaboration is foreseen in coming years.

Acknowledgment

The research leading to these results has received funding from the European Community's Seventh Framework Programme FP7 (2007-2013) under grant agreement № 211804 (EUFORIA) and № 222919 (DEISA2).

References

[1] http://www.euforia-project.eu/.
[2] http://kepler-project.org/.
[3] http://www.deisa.eu/.
[4] http://solps-mdsplus.aug.ipp.mpg.de/GOTiT/.
[5] http://www.hpc-europa.eu/.
[6] http://www.iter.org/.
[7] http://glite.web.cern.ch/glite/.
[8] http://www.i2g.eu/.
[9] http://desktop.psnc.pl/.
[10] http://grid.bifi.unizar.es/egee/fusion-vo/.
[11] http://www.eu-egee.org/.
[12] http://www.unicore.eu/.
[13] http://vinetoolkit.org/.
[14] G. Manduchi, F. Iannone, F. Imbeaux, G. Huysmans, J. Lister, et al., Fusion Engineering and Design 83 (2008) 462 , Proceedings of the 6th IAEA Technical Meeting on Control, Data Acquisition, and Remote Participation for Fusion Research.
[15] http://www.efda-itm.eu/.
[16] http://portal.efda-itm.eu/.
[17] http://www.prace-project.eu/.

Mini-Symposium
"EuroGPU 2009"

Parallel Computing: From Multicores and GPU's to Petascale
B. Chapman et al. (Eds.)
IOS Press, 2010
© 2010 The authors and IOS Press. All rights reserved.
doi:10.3233/978-1-60750-530-3-533

Parallel Computing with GPUs

Anne C. ELSTER [a,1] and Stéphane REQUENA [b]

[a] *Norwegian University of Science and Technology (NTNU), Trondheim, Norway*
[b] *Genci, Paris, France*

Abstract.
　　The success of the gaming industry is now pushing processor technology like we have never seen before. Since recent graphics processors (GPU's) have been improving both their programmability as well as have been adding more and more floating point processing, it makes them very appealing as accelerators for general-purpose computing. This minisymposium gives an overview of some of these advancements by bringing together experts working on the development of techniques and tools that improve the programmability of GPU's as well as the experts interested in utilizing the computational power of GPU' scientific applications. This first EuroGPU Minisymposium brought together severl experts working on the development of techniques and tools that improve the programmability of GPU's as well as the experts interested in utilizing the computational power of GPU's for scientific applications. This short summary thus gives a very useful, but quick overview of some of the major recent advancement in modern GPU computing.

The minisymposium started with a short history and overview as seen by Anne C. Elster, one of the organizers. Her talk went directly into her work with her graduate student Rune J. Hovland on *Thoughput Computing on Future GPUs*, both overview papers included here. The rest of the minisymposium was divied into two parts, an industrial track described below and an academic track which 4 papers are included here.

1. Industry related track

This track contained several interesting talks that will be summarized, but not be published here. However, copies of the slides from each can be found on the web at:
　　`http://www.eurogpu.org/eurogpu09` and
　　`http://www.idi.ntnu.no/~elster/pubs/eurogpu09`.

OpenCL, a new standard for GPU programming by Francois Bodin(Caps Enterprice) generated a lot of interest. His presentation gave an overview of OpenCL for programming Graphics Processing Units (GPUs). OpenCL is an initiative launched by Apple to ensure application portability across various types of GPUs. It aims at being an open standard (royalty free and vendor neutral) developed by the Khronos OpenCL working group (`http://www.khronos.org`). OpenCL which is based on the ISO C99, shares many features with CUDA and exposes data and task parallelism.

---

[1] 1A big thank you to Guillaume Colin de Verdiere from CEA for stepping in for Stephane Requena at the last minute at the ParCo 2009 conference!

Heterogeneous Multicore Parallel Programming by Stephane Bihan (Caps Entreprise, Rennes) presented HMPP, a Heterogeneous Multicore Parallel Programming workbench with compilers, developed by CAPS entreprise, that allows the integration of heterogeneous hardware accelerators in a non-intrusive manner while preserving legacy codes.

Cosmological Reionisation Powered by Multi-GPUs by Dominique Aubert (Universite de Strasbourg and Romain Teyssieer(CEA) took the simulated distribution of gas and stars in the early Universe and modelled the propagation of ionising radiation and its effect on the gas. This modeling will help to understand the radio observations in a near future and the impact of this first stellar light on the formation of galaxies. Their code explicitely solves a set of conservative equations on a fixed grid in a similar manner to hydrodynamics and it follows the evolution of a fluid made of photons. However due to typical velocities close to the speed of light, the stringent CFL condition implies that a very large number of timesteps must be computed, making the code intrinsically slow. However, they ported it to a GPU architecture using CUDA which accelerating their code by a factor close to 80. Furthermore, by using an MPI layer, they also expanded it to a multi-GPU version. CUDATON is currently running on 128 GPUs installed on the new CCRT calculator of the French atomic agency (CEA). The code is able to perform 60 000 timesteps on a 10243 grid in 2.5 hours (elapsed). For comparison, the largest calculation made so far on the same topic involved a 4003 grid and required 11 000 cores to be run. Such a boost in the performance demonstrates the relevance of multi-gpu calculations for computational cosmology. It also opens bright perspectives for a systematic exploration of the impact of the physical ingredients on high resolution simulations since the these calculations are extremely fast to complete.

Efficient Use of Hybrid Computing Clusters for Nanosciences by Lugi Genovese (ESFR, Grenoble), Matthieu Ospici (BULL, UJF/LIG, CEA, Grenoble), Jean Francois Mehaut (UJF/INRIA, Grenoble), and Thierry Deutsch (CEA, Grenoble) included their study of the programming and the utilization of hybrid clusters in the field of computational physics. These massively parallel computers are composed of a fast network (Infiniband) connecting classical nodes with multicore Intel processors and accelerators. In our case, the accelerators used are GPUs from NVIDIA. They first analyzed some ways to use with efficiency CPUs cores and GPUs together in a code (BiGDFT, http://inac.cea.fr/L_Sim/BigDFT\) without hotspot routines. Starting from this analysis, they have designed a new library: S_GPU, used to share GPUs between the CPU cores of a node. The implementation and the usage of S_GPU was described. They then evaluated and compared performances between S_GPU and others approaches to share GPUs with CPUs. This performance evaluation was based on BigDFT, an ab-initio simulation software designed to take advantage of massively hybrid parallel clusters as the Titane cluster (CCRT). Their experiments was performed on both one hybrid node as well as on a large number of nodes of their hybrid cluster.

Accelerating a Depth Imaging Seismic Application on GPUs: Status and Perspectives by Henri Calandra(TOTAL, Pau) described how the extraordinary challenge that the oil and gas industry must face for hydrocarbon exploration requires the development of leading edge technologies to recover an accurate representation of the subsurface. Seismic modeling and Reverse Time Migration (RTM) based on the full wave equation discretization, are tools of major importance since they give an accurate representation of complex wave propagation areas. Unfortunately, they are highly compute intensive. He first presented the challenges in O&G and the need in terms of computing power for solving seismic depth imaging problems. He then showed how GPUs can be part of the solution and the the solutions developed at TOTAL.

Debugging for GPUs with DDT, David Lecomber (Allinea Ltd, Bristol, UK) described how evelopers are experimenting with CUDA, OpenCL and others to port (or rewrite) their code to take advantage of this technology, but are discovering there is more to programming than writing code. Finding bugs and optimizing performance are essential tasks - particularly so with a new complex model of program execution. He reveiwed the state of play - exploring what is possible now, and what is being done by Allinea and others to improve the lot of GPU developers who need to debug or optimize their codes.

2. Academic track

The above talks were followed by a more academic track the following day whose corresponding papers along with the introductory papers by Elster and her students, are included in proceedings. The secoond day GPU papers include two papers looking at GPU solvers:

- **Porus Rock Simulations and Lattice Boltzmann on GPUs** by Erik Ola Aksnes and Anne C. Elster (both NTNU, Norway) which looked at using the Lattice Boltzman Method on large 3D datasets on GPUs for fluid similations, and

- **An efficient multi-algorithms sparse linear solver for GPUs** by Stéphane Vialle; Thomas Jost and Sylvain Constassot-Vivier (all from Supé lec Campus de Metz, Franc) which discussed how to implement a sparse solver on GPUs.

The EuroGPU 2009 workshop/minisymposium was rounded off by two GPU modeling presentationo:

- **Abstraction of Programming Models Across Multi-Core and GPGPU Architectures** by Ian Grimstead and David R. Walker (Cardiff University, UK) , and

- **Modeling Communication on Modern GPU Systems** by Anne C. Elster, Daniele G. Spampinato and Thorvald Natvig (all from NTNU, Norway).

The last two papers should provide tools for those who want to get a good feel for the performance potential CPU and multi-core CPU versus GPU and multi-GPU systems.

The overview presentation and presentation on throughout computing on GPU resulted, along with the four academic presentations, in the following papers. These publications together with the on-line PDF files of the presentations from the industrial track should provide a great resource for those who want to take a closer look at how one can harness the great computational power of modern GPUs.

Parallel Computing: From Multicores and GPU's to Petascale
B. Chapman et al. (Eds.)
IOS Press, 2010
© 2010 The authors and IOS Press. All rights reserved.
doi:10.3233/978-1-60750-530-3-536

Porous Rock Simulations and Lattice Boltzmann on GPUs [1]

Eirik O. AKSNES [a] and Anne C. ELSTER [a]

[a] *Norwegian University of Science and Technology (NTNU), Trondheim, Norway*

Abstract.
Investigating how fluids flow inside the complicated geometries of porous rocks is an important problem in the petroleum industry. The lattice Boltzmann method (LBM) can be used to calculate porous rockst' permeability. In this paper, we show how to implement this method efficiently on modern GPUs. Both a sequential CPU implementation and a parallelized GPU implementation is developed. Both implementations were tested using three porous data sets with known permeabilities. Our work shows that it is possible to calculate the permeability of porous rocks of simulations sizes up to 368^3, which fit into the 4 GB memory of the NVIDIA Quadro FX 5800 card. Our single floating-point precision simulation resulted in respectbale 0.95-1.59 MLUPS whereas our GPU implentation achieved remarkable 180+ MLUPS for several lattices in the 160^3 to 368^3 range allowing calculations that would take hours on the CPU to be done in minutes on the GPU. Techniques for reducing round-off errors are also discussed and implemented.

Keywords. Lattice Boltzmann Method, Permeability, GPU, Porous Rocks

1. Introduction

To solve the most complex problems in computational fluid dynamics (CFD), powerful computer systems are necessary. State-of-the-art GPUs can provide computing power equal to small supercomputers since a larger portion of their transistors are used for floating-point arithmetic, sicne they have higher memory bandwidth than modern CPUs. In this paper, we investigate the use of GPUs for computing porous rocks' ability to transport fluids (permeability) using the *Lattice Boltzmann Method* (LBM) [10]. This is a very important, but computationally challenging problem for the petroleum industry. major influences on permeability. The LBM has several desirable properties for fluid flows through porous media, particularly the ability to deal with complex irregular flow geometries without significant penalty in speed and efficiency. The LBM is also particularly suitable for GPUs, since it only requires neighbor interactions.

An overview of our research group's GPU programming experiences can be found in [8]. The models analysed in this work may be generated using CT scans [4]. Extended versions of this paper with added color figures, are provided in [2,3].

[1]The authors would like to thank Numerical Rocks AS for their collaborations and access to test samples, Dr. Pablo M. Dupuy, NTNU, for introducing us to the LBM method, and NVIDIA for supporting Dr. Elster and her HPC-lab.

2. The Lattice Boltzmann Method (LBM)

Historically, the LBM is an outcome from the attempts to improve the Lattice Gas Cellular Automata (LGCA). However, the LBM can be derived directly from the Boltzmann equation formulated by Ludwig Boltzmann, [10], uses classical mechanics and statistical physics, to describe the evolution of a particle distribution function. The LBM solves the Boltzmann equation in a fixed lattice. Instead of taking into consideration every individual particle's position and velocity as in classical microscopic models (molecular dynamics), the particle distribution function in the LBM gives the probability of finding a fluid particle located at the location x, with velocity e, at time t [5]. The statistical treatment in the LBM is necessary because of the large number of particles interacting in a fluid [15]. However, it leads to substantial gain in computational efficiency.

In the LBM, fluids flows are simulated by calculating the streaming and collision of particles within the lattices, often together with some boundary conditions that must be fulfilled for each time step. The discrete lattice locations correspond to volume elements that contain a collection of particles, and represents a position in space that holds either fluid or solid. In the streaming phase, particles move to the nearest neighbor along their path of motion, where they collide with other arrived particles. The outcome of the collision is designed to be consistent with the conservation of mass, energy and momentum. After each iteration, only the particle distribution changes, while the particle distribution function in the center of each lattice locations remains unchanged. The underlying lattice must have enough symmetry to ensure isotropy, and typically lattices are D2Q9, D3Q13, D3Q15, and D3Q19, where Da is the number of dimensions and Qb is the number of distinct discrete lattice velocities $\vec{e}_i$. The discrete Boltzmann equation can be written as Eq.(1) [5]:

$$f_i(\vec{x} + \vec{e}_i, t + 1) - f_i(\vec{x}, t) = \Omega \qquad (1)$$

where $\vec{e}_i$ are discrete lattice velocities, Ω is the collision operator, and $f_i(\vec{x}, t)$ is the discrete particle distribution function in the i direction. The macroscopic kinematic viscosity of the fluid is $v = \frac{2\tau - 1}{6}$. Other macroscopic properties of the fluids – such as the mass density $\rho(\vec{x}, t)$, momentum $\rho(\vec{x}, t)u(\vec{x}, t)$ and velocity $\vec{u}(\vec{x}, t)$ of a fluid particle – can be computed from the particle distribution functions, as seen in the first step of the collision phase in Figure 1. More details and references can be found in [2,3].

Boundary Conditions: The standard boundary condition applied at solid-fluid interfaces is the no-slip boundary condition (a.k.a. bounce-back boundary condition), Eq.(2) [12]:

$$f_i^{in}(\vec{x} + \vec{e}_i, t + 1) = f_i^{out}(\vec{x}, t) = f_i^{in}(\vec{x}, t) \qquad (2)$$

Here the particles close to solid boundaries do not move at all, resulting in zero velocity. The particles at the solid-fluid interfaces are reflected [16], as illustrated in Figure 2. Periodic boundary conditions are also common, and allows particles to be circulated within the fluid domain. With the periodic boundary conditions, outgoing particles at the exit boundaries will come back again into the fluid domain through the entry boundaries on the opposed side. For a more comprehensive overview, see [15] and [19].

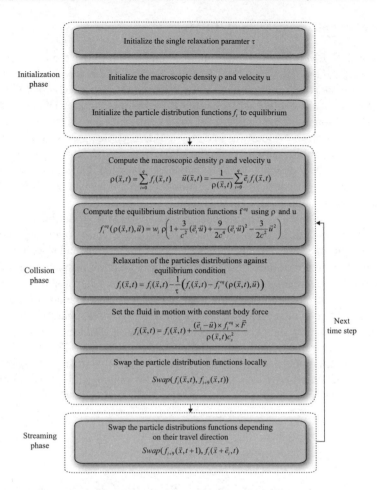

Figure 1. The main phases of the simulation model used. Based on [12].

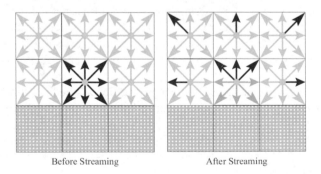

Figure 2. Bounce-back boundary of lattice nodes before (left) and after (right) streaming. Based on [16].

The LBM has been implemented on CPUs for fluid flows through porous media to determine the permeability of porous media [1]. See [18] for a comprehensive overview of efficient CPU implementations of the LBM, in view of the fact that the architecture of the GPU is quite different. See [9,6,17] for recent GPU-based LBMs.

3. Our Simulation Model

The main phases of our LBM simulation model can be seen in Figure 1. In this model, the collisions of particles are evaluated first, and then particles streams to the lattice neighbors along the discrete lattice velocities. Two types of boundary conditions are implemented: the standard bounce back boundary condition to handle solid-fluid interfaces, and periodic boundary condition to allow fluids to be circulated within the fluid domain. The periodic boundary condition is built into the streaming phase, and the bounce back boundary condition is built into the streaming and collision phase. The different phases of our simulation model accompanied by pseudo-code is described in more detail in [2].

Effcient storage: Our simulation model makes use of the D3Q19 lattice. For every node in the lattice, implementations using the D3Q19 model often store and use 19 values for the particle distribution functions and 19 temporary values for the streaming phase, so that the particle distribution functions are not overwritten during the exchange phase between neighbor lattice nodes. The LBMs using such temporary storage thus require gigabytes of memory for lattices sizes of 256^3 and larger [2] and [3].

Instead of duplicating the particle distribution functions to temporary storage in our streaming phase, we use another approach described by Latt [13] for both implementations. Here the source and destination particle distribution functions are instead swapped between neighbor lattice nodes. This approach reduces the memory requirements by 50 %, compared to using temporary storage.

Permeability calculations: Figure 3 shows the expansion of the simulation model for the calculation of permeability of porous rocks. The permeability is obtained directly from the generated velocity fields of the lattice Boltzmann method, together with using Darcy's law for the flow of fluids through porous media. The fluid flow is driven by some external force in the simulation model, but it could also be driven by pressure on the boundaries. The external force is expected to give the same change in momentum as the true $\frac{\Delta P}{L}$, which is the total pressure drop along the sample length L. Note that in Figure 3, a is the node resolution equivalent to the lattice spacing. Driven by some external force, the permeability is always obtained when the velocity field is at steady state. Our simulations is considered to have converged if the change of the average velocity is less than 10^{-9} between time-steps.

Floating-point precision and round-off errors: In the collision phase, the equilibrium distribution function needs to be computed with a mixture of large and small numbers which may lead to lserious rounding errors [11]. To reduce the rounding error when using single floating-point precision, we used an approach taken from [7]. It has been left out from the previous descriptions, due to readability, but can be found in [2].

4. Implementations and further optimizations

Current NVIDIA GPUs support thousands of threads running concurrently, to hide the latency under uneven workloads in programs. In our GPU implementation, every thread created during execution is responsible for performing the collision and streaming for

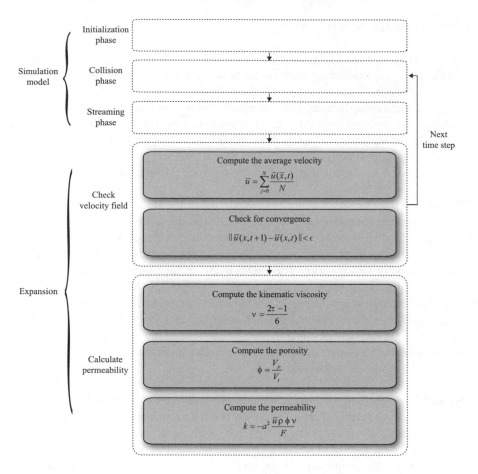

Figure 3. Expansion of the simulation model for permeability calculations.

a single lattice node. To get high utilization of global memory bandwidth, the access pattern to the global memory must be correctly aligned to achieve coalescing.

A structure-of-arrays is useful to achieve coalescing. Threads access the arrays in contiguous memory segments to obtain coalescing. This enables efficient reading and writing of particle distribution functions. Each array contains one discrete direction of the particle distributions functions. Arrays in the structure are three-dimensional, allocated as contiguous memory on the device using cudaMalloc3D. This function takes the width, height, and depth of simulations as input, and pads the allocation to meet the alignment requirements to achieve coalescing. The function returns a pitch (or stride), which is the width in bytes of the allocation. Two-dimensional grids were necessary in order to simulate large lattices, due to NVIDIA's restriction of the maximum number of threads blocks being 65535 in one direction of the grid on our test bench. Note thateven simulation sizes of 512^3 without using temporary storage and with single floating-point precision would alone result in a memory consumption of 9.5 Gigabyte!

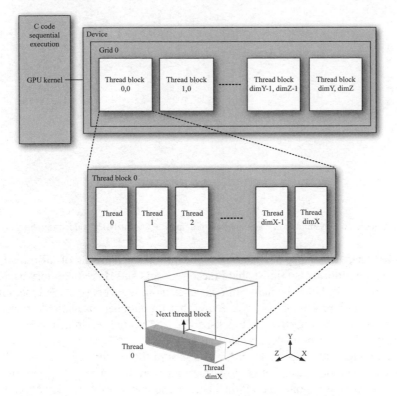

Figure 4. The configurations of grids and thread blocks in kernels.

5. Benchmarks

Our test-bed, the NVIDIA Quadro FX 5800 GPU has 4 GiB of memory. provides high memory bandwidth and 4 GiB of memory. Performance is, like [6], measured in MLUPS (million lattice nodes updates per second).

In **Poiseuille Flows** the analytical solutions of the velocity profile are known. To validate the numerical correctness and exactness of our two implementations, the numerical velocity profile of fluid flow between two parallel plates with lattice dimension 32^3 were compared to known analytical solutions. Two types of boundary conditions were used: bounce back boundaries along the two parallel plates and periodic boundaries in the x, y, and z direction for conservation of fluid particles. The values of the single relaxation parameter and the external force used in the calculations of the permeability of the three datasets used were τ=0.65 and F_x=0.00001 with $F_y = F_z = 0$. Both single and double precision Poiseuille Flow tests were performed. In Figure 5, the solid lines show the analytical solution, and the circles are the numerical results obtained from the Poiseuille Flow simulations. The measured deviations between the numerical and analytical solutions were only $1.680030e - 006$ for both CPU and GPU 32, and $1.622238e - 006$ for both CPU and GPU 64 [3].

Simulation Size Restrictions: The most memory demanding parts of the implementations is the structure-of-arrays used to store the particle distribution functions, together with the array used to store the porous rocks models. The GPU used has 16384 registers

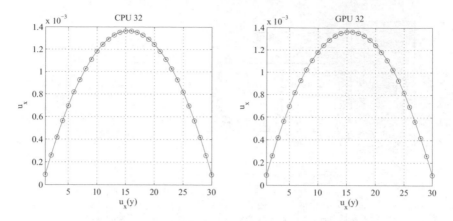

Figure 5. Poiseuille Flows: Comparison of numerical and analytical velocity profiles.

and 16 KB shared memory available per multiprocessor. Threads of all thread blocks running on a multiprocessor must share these registers and shared memory during execution. Kernels will fail to launch if threads uses more registers or shared memory than available per multiprocessor [14]. We found that the number of available registers per thread varies from 64 registers for blocksizes of 256, to only 21 registers available for blocksizes of 768. For more details, see [3].

Performance Measurements: In order to measure the performance of our CPU and GPU implementation, cubic lattice sizes ranging from 8^3 up to 368^3 were used. The cubic lattices were filled only with fluid elements, so that no extra work was required for solid-fluid interfaces. Figure 6 shows arithmetic means over 25 iterations.

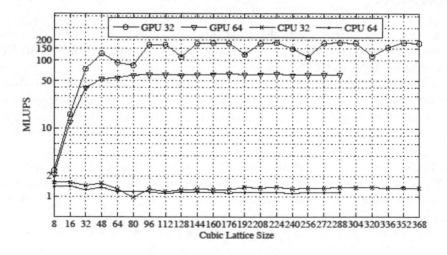

Figure 6. Performance results in MLUPS.

Here our GPU implementation clearly outperforms the CPU implementation. Using single floating-point precision, CPU 32 and GPU 32 achieved the maximum performance equal to 1.59 MLUPS and 184.30 MLUPS. CPU 64 and GPU 64 achieved maximum performance equal to 1.40 MLUPS and 63.35 MLUPS. Highest performance of the CPU 32 and CPU 64 was with lattice sizes smaller than 64^3 and 48^3, since these lattices fit into cache memory. The performance difference between the GPU 32 and GPU 64 is because our NVIDIA GPUs have more single precision cores than double precision cores, and because the GPU 32 and GPU 64 have some differences in occupancy. More details regarding our occupancy calculations and experiments can be found in [2,3]. The turbulent performance of the GPU 32 is caused by the changes in occupancy of the collide kernel, due to changes in thread block sizes.

6. Porous Rock Measurements

In order to evaluate our implementations ability to calculate the permeability of porous rocks, three porous datasets with known permeability provided by Numerical Rocks AS were used. Porosity that reflects only the interconnected pore spaces within the three porous datasets calculated by Numerical Rocks AS was also used. The values of the single relaxation parameter and the external force used in the calculations of the permeability of the three datasets were $\tau = 0.65$, $F_x = 0.00001$ and $F_y = F_z = 0.0$

In our simulations, the configurations of the boundaries parallel to the flow direction were made solid, and with bounce back boundary conditions. The entry and exit boundaries were given periodic boundary conditions. There were also 3 empty layers of void space added at both the entry and exit boundaries. Simulations were run until velocity fields reached a steady state, before calculating the permeability of the three porous datasets. Due to space considerations, we include only the results from our Fontainebleau, the most realistic and interesting dataset here. The results from the two simplest datasets, symmetrical cube and square cube, can be found in [3].

The *Fontainebleau* dataset has a lattice size of 300^3, with the known permeability equal to 1300 mD. The dataset's porosity is 16 %. Note that the dataset is too large to allocate with double precision on our NVIDIA Quadro FX5800 GPU. Table 1 shows the results of our performance measurements and computed permeability. GPU 32 was the fastest of the implementations with the total simulation time equal to 38.0 seconds. All of the implementations calculated the permeability within deviation, with the relative error equal to 4.0% and the absolute error equal to 53. GPU 32 obtained the highest average performance equal to 58.81 MLUPS.

Table 1. Fontainebleau performance and computed permeability results.

Implementation	Average MLUPS	Maximum MLUPS	Total Time	Number Of Iterations	Permeability Obtained
CPU 32	1.03	1.04	2152 s	445	1247.80 mD
GPU 32	58.81	59.15	38.0 s	445	1247.81 mD
CPU 64	0.94	0.94	2375.4 s	445	1247.80 mD

Figure 7 shows the first 4 iteration of fluid flow inside our Fontainbleau. See [3] and [2] for more detailed results.

Figure 7. The first 4 iterations of fluid flow inside Fontainebleau.

7. Conclusions and future work

Modern *Graphics Processing Units* (GPUs) are used to accelerate a wide range of scientific applications which earlier required large clusters of workstations or large expensive supercomputers. Since it would be very valuable for the petroleum industry to analyze petrophysical properties of porous rocks, such as the porosity and permeability, through computer simulations, the goal of this work was to see if such simulations could benefit from GPU acceleration. LBM was used to estimate porous rock's ability to transmit fluids. In order to better analyze our results, both parallel CPU and GPU implementations of the LBM were developed and benchmarked using three porous datasets provided by Numerical Rocks AS where the permeability of each dataset was known. This also allowed us to evaluate the accuracy of our results.

Our development efforts showed that it is possible to simulate fluid flow through the complicated geometries of porous rocks with high performance on modern GPUs. Our GPU implementations clearly outperformed our CPU implementation, in both single and double floating-point precision. Both implementations achieved their highest performances when using single floating-point precision, resulting in their maximum performance equal to 1.59 MLUPS and 184.30 MLUPS, respectively for datsets of size 8^3 by 352^3, where MLUPS is the measurement of million lattice nodes updates per second (indicating the number of lattice nodes that is updated in one second). Suggestions for improving and extending our results inculde:

1. Maximum simulation lattice size in the simulations is limited by the 32-bit architecture of current GPUs which limits memory to 4 GiB. One way to compensate for this is to use multiple GPUs.
2. Use of grid refinement for the improved analysis of the fluid flow inside the narrow pore geometry of the porous rocks.
3. Storing only fluid elements, this will reduce memory usage, since the porous rocks of interest often have small pore geometries.
4. Extenting the LBM to perform multiphase fluid dynamics.

Given the importance for the petroleum industry of getting good fluid simulations of porous rocks, we expect that this will continue to be a great area of research. Flows through porous materials are also be of interest to other fields, including medicine.

Since our ParCo 2009 presentation, NVIDIA annouced in November 2009 their new Fermi GPU architecture that should also be investigated when it becomes available.

References

[1]   Urpo Aaltosalmi. Fluid Flows In Porous Media With The Lattice-Botlzmann Method, 2005.
[2]   Eirik Ola Aksnes. Simulation of Fluid Flow Through Porous Rocks on Modern GPUs , July 2009. Masters thesis, NTNU, Norway.
[3]   Eirik Ola Aksnes and Anne C. Elster. Fluid Flows Through Porous Rocks Using Lattice Boltzmann on Modern GPUs , December 2009. IDI Tech report no. 03-10, ISSN 1503-416X, NTNU, Norway.
[4]   Eirik Ola Aksnes and Henrik Hesland. GPU Techniques for Porous Rock Visualization, January 2009. Masters project, IDI Tech report no. 02-10, ISSN 1503-416X, Norwegian University of Science and Technology.
[5]   Usman R. Alim, Alireza Entezari, and Torsten Möller. The Lattice-Boltzmann Method on Optimal Sampling Lattices. *IEEE Transactions on Visualization and Computer Graphics*, 15(4):630–641, 2009.
[6]   Peter Bailey, Joe Myre, Stuart D. C. Walsh, David J. Lilja, and Martin O. Saar. Accelerating Lattice Boltzmann Fluid Flow Simulations Using Graphics Processors. 2008.
[7]   Bastien Chopard. How to improve the accuracy of Lattice Boltzmann calculations.
[8]   Anne C. Elster. Gpu computing: History and recent challenges. in this ParCo2009 Proceedings.
[9]   J Habich. Performance Evaluation of Numeric Compute Kernels on nVIDIA GPUs, June 2008. Friedrich-Alexander-Universität.
[10] Xiaoyi He and Li-Shi Luo. Theory of the lattice Boltzmann method: From the Boltzmann equation to the lattice Boltzmann equation. *Phys. Rev. E*, 56(6):6811–6817, Dec 1997.
[11] Nicholas J. Higham. *Accuracy and Stability of Numerical Algorithms*. Society for Industrial and Applied Mathematics, Philadelphia, PA, USA, second edition, 2002.
[12] C. Korner, T. Pohl, U. Rude, N. Thurey, and T. Zeiser. Parallel Lattice Boltzmann Methods for CFD Applications. *Numerical Solution of Partial Differential Equations on Parallel Computers*, 51:439–465, 2006.
[13] Jonas Latt. Technical report: How to implement your DdQq dynamics with only q variables per node (instead of 2q), 2007.
[14] NVIDIA. *NVIDIA CUDA Compute Unified Device Architecture. Programming Guide.* V2.0, 2008.
[15] Michael C. Sukop and Daniel T. Thorne Jr. *Lattice Boltzmann Modeling, An Introduction for Geoscientists and Engineers.* Springer, Berlin, Heidelberg, 2007.
[16] Nils Thurey. A single-phase free-surface Lattice Boltzmann Method, 2002. Friedrich-Alexander-Universität.
[17] J Tolke. Implementation of a Lattice Boltzmann kernel using the Compute Unified Device Architecture developed by nVIDIA. *Computing and Visualization in Science*, July 2008.
[18] G. Weillein, T. Zeiser, G. Hager, and S. Donath.
[19] Dieter A. Wolf-Gladrow. *Lattice-Gas, Cellular Automata and Lattice Boltzmann Models, An Introduction.* Lecture Notes in Mathematics. Springer, Heidelberg, Berlin, 2000.

Parallel Computing: From Multicores and GPU's to Petascale
B. Chapman et al. (Eds.)
IOS Press, 2010
© 2010 The authors and IOS Press. All rights reserved.
doi:10.3233/978-1-60750-530-3-546

An efficient multi-algorithms sparse linear solver for GPUs

Thomas JOST [a], Sylvain CONTASSOT-VIVIER [a,b] and Stéphane VIALLE [a,c]

[a] *AlGorille INRIA Project Team, Nancy, France*
[b] *Université Henri Poincaré, Nancy, France*
[c] *SUPELEC, Metz, France*

Abstract. We present a new sparse linear solver for GPUs. It is designed to work with structured sparse matrices where all the non-zeros are on a few diagonals. Several iterative algorithms are implemented, both on CPU and GPU. The GPU code is designed to be fast yet simple to read and understand. It aims to be as accurate as possible, even on chips that do not support double-precision floating-point arithmetic. Several benchmarks show that GPU algorithms are much faster than their CPU counterpart while their accuracy is satisfying.

Keywords. GPU, CUDA, linear solver, sparse matrix, Jacobi algorithm, Gauss-Seidel algorithm, biconjugate gradient algorithm

Motivations and objectives

Nowadays, many research areas rely on simulation. As a consequence, software simulations are expected to continuously become faster, more accurate, and to be able to handle new, bigger, more complex problems. A widely adopted solution to help building such software is to use supercomputers and grids where a large and scalable number of powerful processors are available. This can however be very expensive, both for the hardware and for the energy required to run a large number of processors.

Recent GPUs can be used for general purpose computing using dedicated libraries such as CUDA (for NVIDIA cards) or OpenCL. They are based on a SIMD architecture that makes it possible to handle a very large number of hardware threads concurrently, and can be used for various purposes, including scientific computing. Thanks to the video game industry, GPUs have become very powerful yet quite cheap. They are now able to handle massively parallel problems that require a huge amount of data, which makes them interesting for modern software simulations. Moreover, it is possible that a GPU cluster both computes faster and consumes less energy than a CPU cluster [1]. This makes GPU clusters very attractive for High Performance Computing.

Many physical problems can be modeled by a system of PDEs. A common solution to simulate the phenomenon is to discretize and linearize these equations, and then to solve the resulting linear system using a linear solver. However, solving a huge linear system is not an easy task and it often requires a lot of computational power. GPUs may therefore be of great interest for solving linear systems quickly and efficiently as soon as a SIMD algorithm can be deduced from the sequential scheme.

This article introduces a new linear solver for GPUs, specially designed to solve sparse structured systems. It aims to work on all CUDA-compatible cards, but it was developed using an entry-level board which does not support double-precision arithmetic.

Floating-point precision and memory accesses were therefore given a special attention in order to be as fast and accurate as possible. Finally, several iterative algorithms have been implemented to solve linear problems both on CPU and GPU.

This work takes place in a larger project concerning the adaptation of asynchronous iterative algorithms on a cluster of GPUs. Asynchronous algorithms are a very general class of parallel algorithms in which iterations and communications are asynchronous and overlap. This way, all idle times between iterations are suppressed, which often leads to faster execution times even if more iterations may be necessary. More details can be found in [2]. The two levels of communications present in a cluster of GPUs, the ones between a GPU and its hosting CPU, and the ones between CPUs, should yield representative communication times according to computation times. This represents a particularly good context of use of asynchronous algorithms and this is why we aim at developing asynchronous algorithms on clusters of GPUs.

1. Related works

Several different libraries already exist in the field of linear algebra on GPUs. Most of them use CUBLAS, an implementation of the BLAS on CUDA made by NVIDIA that is shipped with the CUDA SDK [4]. CUBLAS only provides with the most basic linear algebra operations, which are then used by other libraries to develop more or less complex algorithms.

There are many different libraries for dense linear algebra. Some of them seem to be quite interesting, like MAGMA [5], which "aims to develop a dense linear algebra library similar to LAPACK but for heterogeneous/hybrid architectures, starting with current 'Multicore+GPU' systems". Others have more restrictive goals, such as cudaztec [6] (GMRES solver) or GPUmatrix [7] (solver using LU, QR or Cholesky decomposition). However, none of these is interesting for us: they focus on dense linear algebra whereas we deal with sparse structured matrices. Besides, many of these libraries are ongoing research works: no source code is available at the moment for MAGMA, cudaztec seems to have very poor performances (GPU code slower than CPU code), and GPUmatrix does not compile on our Linux machines. Another interesting library is *Concurrent Number Cruncher*, a general sparse linear solver [8]. It is efficient and powerful, but restricted to *general* sparse matrices, while we need support for *structured* sparse matrices. Even though CNC would work fine for our problem, it would be very sub-optimal: for instance memory access patterns would be unaligned or uncoalesced, and would be slow.

So, implementing a new linear solver is the only way to get a code working at top efficiency on GPUs with our structured sparse matrices.

2. Choice of the linear method

For readers not familiar with linear solvers, a description of the ones mentioned here can be found in [3]. The most obvious constraint in the choice of the linear solver to develop is that it must contain a sufficient amount of potential parallelism. This discards intrinsically sequential methods such as Gauss-Seidel. Also, as we are in the context of sparse matrices and according to the limited memory available on GPU boards, iterative methods will be preferred to direct ones, which are more memory consuming. So, methods like GMRES are also discarded. Finally, the linear solver we aim at developing on the GPU is to be used in general scientific problems, most of them being non-linear. Hence, that solver will be a key part of more general solvers. In that context, it must be able to handle as many kinds of matrices as possible. So, simple methods like Jacobi are interesting for matrices with absolute diagonal dominance but cannot be used with more complex ones. Also, the conjugate gradient is interesting for sparse systems but only works on symmetric positive-definite matrices. In the end, a more general method satisfying all the GPU constraints is the biconjugate gradient method. This method is a generalization of the conjugate gradient. However, for symmetric problems, it requires twice more computations than the simpler conjugate version. In the same way, the Jacobi method will be faster with the adequate matrices. So, an interesting approach is to develop several linear solvers on GPU and compare them to each other. This will allow us to decide whether it is sufficient to always use the same solver for any kind of matrices or if it is interesting to dynamically choose the most adapted solver among a small set according to the type of matrices to process.

3. Design and implementation

According to the limited length of the paper and the focus of our work, we only present here the design of the GPU version of the most complex method chosen in our study, i.e. the biconjugate gradient algorithm, which is known to have a very wide range of applications. Although the other methods discussed above are not detailed here, they have been implemented and their results in terms of accuracy and performance are presented in section 4.

3.1. Sequential algorithm

As said above, the biconjugate gradient, given on the right, is an extension of the conjugate gradient algorithm. It produces two mutually orthogonal sequences of vectors in place of the orthogonal sequence of residuals generated in the conjugate gradient algorithm. This implies a modification of the behavior of the iterative process and especially that the minimization is no more ensured. Moreover, it requires the use of the transpose of the matrix to compute one of the two sequences. However, although few theoretical results are known on this method, it has been proved that it is comparable to GMRES for non-symmetric matrices [9].

Biconjugate Gradient algorithm

Compute $r^0 \leftarrow b - A.x^0$
Compute $\widetilde{r}^0 \ (= r^0$ for example)
$i = 1$
repeat
$\quad \rho_{i-1} \leftarrow r^{i-1}.\widetilde{r}^{i-1}$
$\quad$ **if** $\rho_{i-1} = 0$ **then**
$\quad\quad$ method fails
$\quad$ **end if**
$\quad$ **if** $i = 1$ **then**
$\quad\quad p^i \leftarrow r^{i-1}$
$\quad\quad \widetilde{p}^i \leftarrow \widetilde{r}^{i-1}$
$\quad$ **else**
$\quad\quad \beta \leftarrow \frac{\rho_{i-1}}{\rho_{i-2}}$
$\quad\quad p^i \leftarrow r^{i-1} + \beta p^{i-1}$
$\quad\quad \widetilde{p}^i \leftarrow \widetilde{r}^{i-1} + \beta \widetilde{p}^{i-1}$
$\quad$ **end if**
$\quad q^i \leftarrow A.p^i$
$\quad \widetilde{q}^i \leftarrow A^t.\widetilde{p}^i$
$\quad \alpha \leftarrow \frac{\rho_{i-1}}{\widetilde{p}^i.q^i}$
$\quad x^i \leftarrow x^{i-1} + \alpha p^i$
$\quad r^i \leftarrow r^{i-1} - \alpha q^i$
$\quad \widetilde{r}^i \leftarrow \widetilde{r}^{i-1} - \alpha \widetilde{q}^i$
$\quad i \leftarrow i + 1$
until stopping criteria is reached

3.2. Sparse matrix storage

As in the scope of our study the matrix A is sparse, we had to choose a storage scheme providing a good compromise between memory saving and structure regularity. The first point is obvious in the context of the GPU use as the amount of available memory is strictly limited. The second point comes from the way the memory accesses are performed on the GPU board. In order to obtain efficient accesses to the memory from numerous concurrent threads, those accesses have to be as regular as possible.

So, the structure used is similar to the DIA scheme described in [10] and consists in storing only the diagonals containing non-zero values. Hence, the matrix is represented by a two-dimensional array of the non-zero diagonals in which each row contains one diagonal of A. The ordering of the diagonals in that array follows the horizontal order from left to right. An additional one-dimensional array is needed to get the link between a row number in the array and its corresponding diagonal in A.

3.3. GPU scheme

According to the hardware design and functioning scheme of the GPU, the parallel algorithm to produce must follow the SIMT programming model (single-instruction, multiple-thread), which is a slightly more flexible variant of the SIMD paradigm [4]. Our GPU version of the biconjugate gradient algorithm is not fully deported on the GPU. In fact, the main loop controlling the iterations is kept on the CPU but all the computations inside it are performed on the GPU, using either standard CUBLAS functions for classical operations such as dot products, or specific kernels for the more complicated operations. So, the algorithm is divided into three main steps:

- The first one is the initialization of the solver. It mainly consists in allocating the memory on the GPU and transferring the data, the matrix A and the vector b.
- The second step corresponds to the iterative computations of the algorithm. That part is fully detailed below.
- Once the algorithm has converged, the third and last step takes place, which performs the transfer of the result vector x from the GPU to the CPU and the memory deallocation on the GPU.

The middle part of that scheme is decomposed in order to be easily and efficiently implemented on the GPU. The `cublasSdot` function is used to compute the scalar products taking place in the computations of ρ and α. The copies of vectors r and $\widetilde{r}$ respectively in p and $\widetilde{p}$ at the first iteration are directly performed with the `cudaMemcpy` function. Finally, four specific kernels have been designed to implement the computations of:

- p and $\widetilde{p}$: kernel `update_p(Real` β`)`
  as the vectors involved in those computations are already in the GPU memory, the only parameter required by this function is the β value.
- q and $\widetilde{q}$: kernel `update_q()`
  for the same reason as above, that function takes no parameter.
- x, r and $\widetilde{r}$: kernel `update_xr(Real` α`)`
  that function takes the value of α involved in the three updates.
- residual error : kernel `delta(Real* newDelta)`
  the residual is the maximal absolute value in the vector $b - A.x$.

All those kernels are mapped in the same way on the GPU, that is in one-dimensional blocks of 256 threads. This is usually an optimal number of threads per block when scheduling a large number of blocks. In all those computations performed on the GPU, the only transfer between GPU and CPU is the residual error (only one scalar real) which is required on the CPU for the control of the main iterative loop.

As programming in CUDA is quite a recent exercise and since it is not yet an usual task to write a kernel from a high level description of an algorithm, we provide below the two most complex kernels codes.

```
__global__ void update_q() { // ------------------------- Kernel update_q
// Compute q <- A.p and qt <- A.pt. Each thread: 1 element of q and qt.
extern __shared__ int diags[];
int i = blockIdx.x * BLOCKSIZE + threadIdx.x;
Real qi = 0., qti = 0.;

// Fetch the diagonals <-> rows array to shared memory (faster access)
if (threadIdx.x < g.diags)
   diags[threadIdx.x] = g.la[threadIdx.x];
__syncthreads();

if (i < g.size) {          // Avoids out-ranging indices in the last block
   for (int d=0; d < g.diags; d++) {     // For each diagonal...
      int k = diags[d];                  // Row d is diagonal k in A
      int kt = g.size - k;               // and diag. kt in transpose(A)
      if (kt >= g.size) kt -= g.size;

      int j = i + k;                      // Column of the element in A
      if (j >= g.size) j -= g.size;
      int jt = i + kt;                    // Column in transpose(A)
      if (jt >= g.size) jt -= g.size;

      Real a = g.ad[d*g.row_size + i];    // Coalesced read
      Real at = g.ad[d*g.row_size + jt];  // Uncoalesced read
      Real pj = g.p[j];                   // Uncoalesced read
      Real ptj = g.pt[jt];                // Uncoalesced read

      qi += a * pj;        // Perform needed additions and multiplications
      qti += at * ptj;
   }
   g.q[i] = qi;           // Once computation is over, save qt and qti (fast
   g.qt[i] = qti;         // local registers) to the GPU global memory (slow)
}
}


__global__ void delta(Real* dst) { // -------------------- Kernel delta
// Compute dst <- b-A.x. Each thread computes one element of dst.
extern __shared__ int diags[];
int i = blockIdx.x * BLOCKSIZE + threadIdx.x;

// Fetch the diagonals <-> rows array to shared memory (faster access)
if (threadIdx.x < g.diags)
   diags[threadIdx.x] = g.la[threadIdx.x];
__syncthreads();

if (i < g.size) {          // Avoids out-ranging indices in the last block
   Real di = g.b[i];
   for (int d=0; d < g.diags; d++) {     // For each diagonal...
      int k = diags[d];                  // Row d is diagonal k in A
      int j = i+k;                       // Column of the element in A
      if (j >= g.size) j -= g.size;

      Real x = g.x[j];                   // Uncoalesced read
      Real v = g.ad[d*g.row_size + i] * x;  // Coalesced read
      di -= v;
   }
   dst[i] = di;           // Save local register to the GPU global memory
}
}
```

This code shows that our data structure is easy to use and well adapted to the GPU. In these kernels, the most common access scheme is implemented: we iterate over the diagonals (i.e. the lines of the two-dimensional array called g.ad), and for each diagonal we iterate over all of its elements. It is then easy to deduce the corresponding (i, j) coordinates in the "actual" matrix using the diagonal identifier k which is defined as $k = j - i$. Coordinates in the transposed matrix are a bit more difficult to deduce, but this can easily be done too. Textures may then be used to read memory, thus avoiding uncoalesced memory accesses.

The actual code of our solver is a bit more complicated that this one in several ways:

- Textures are used to avoid uncoalesced memory reads. They allow faster access to the memory by hiding latency using a small local cache.
- FMAD (Fused Multiply-Add) opcodes are avoided using the __fmul_rn() intrinsic function. This has a small (non-measurable) performance cost, but it improves accuracy since the GPU FMAD performs aggressive rounding in the multiplication.
- Some additions are made using the Kahan summation algorithm [11] to improve precision.

These modifications make the code more difficult to read, but slightly enhance both accuracy (especially using single-precision arithmetic) and performances.

4. Experiments

According to our study, we have considered three pairs of algorithms for our benchmarks, running on GPU and CPU (mono-core only):

- Jacobi (GPU) and Gauss-Seidel (CPU). We use Gauss-Seidel on the CPU because it is faster and it requires less memory than Jacobi while having quite the same convergence domain. Therefore, it is relevant to compare these algorithms as they are respectively better suited to the tested platforms.
- Biconjugate gradient (BiCG) on CPU and GPU, as described in section 3.1.
- BiCG-Stab, a stabilized variant of the regular BiCG algorithm [12].

We first tested these algorithms on *artificial matrices*, built in a reproducible way, for sizes varying between 100 and 3,000,000 (maximum size before getting out of memory errors on the GPU cards); secondly we ran tests using *real matrices* from a collection of real-world sparse matrices [13]. The tests were made in single precision on a NVIDIA GeForce 8800GT card, and in double precision on a more recent NVIDIA G200 card which includes about 30 IEEE 754R double units over a total of 240 units. On GPU, the time measures include CPU-GPU data transfer time and GPU computation time. The compilers used were nvcc 2.1 (CUDA compiler) and gcc 4.1.

Tests made with artificial matrices in single precision are presented in Figures 1 and 2. Here are the main results:

- GPU algorithms run faster than their CPU counterparts by a factor 20 to 25.
- The absolute error ($\|b - Ax\|_\infty$) is usually higher on GPU than on CPU, but the difference is quite low and both of them are sufficient (around 10^{-6}).

Tests made with artificial matrices in double precision have shown that double precision does not change the factor between CPU and GPU convergence times, and that error

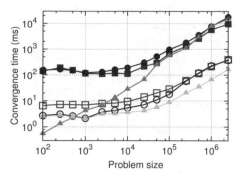

Figure 1. Convergence time in single precision

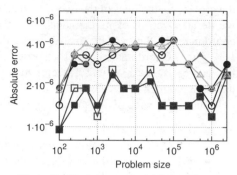

Figure 2. Absolute error in single precision

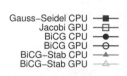

Legend for Figures 1, 2 and 3.

Measures obtained with our set of *artificial matrices*.

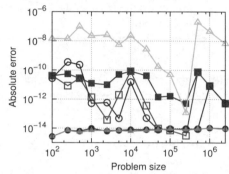

Figure 3. Absolute error in double precision

decreases compared to single precision tests. Figure 3 details the error obtained with double precision; we can observe BiCG and BiCG-Stab errors on CPU are very low (10^{-14}) and close, while corresponding GPU errors are larger (between 10^{-14} and 10^{-6}) and vary a lot. With single precision, BiCG and BiCG-Stab errors were close both on CPU and GPU. Errors of the Gauss-Seidel algorithm on CPU and of the Jacobi one on GPU vary a lot in single precision and still vary in double precision, but are not the lowest errors in double precision. Globally, we observe all errors are lower in double precision, but CPU and GPU algorithms of the same pair have really different behaviors in double precision while they have close behaviors in single precision.

Tests with real matrices, both in single precision (Table 1) and double precision (Table 2), show that BiCG and BiCG-Stab have a wider convergence domain than Jacobi/Gauss-Seidel algorithms (empty and italics cells indicate cases where the algorithm did not converge). They are therefore suitable for a greater variety of problems, which is why we chose them in the first place.

5. Conclusion

Several sparse linear solvers have been designed and implemented on CPU and GPU. The different tested methods have different complexities and applicability ranges.

The first aspect of that work was to compare the performances and accuracies of the GPU and CPU versions of those linear methods. Our experimental results clearly show that problems that only require single-precision arithmetic can be treated using a GPU

Table 1. Absolute error obtained with a set of *real matrices* in single precision

Matrix name	GS CPU	Jacobi GPU	BiCG CPU	BiCG GPU	BiCG-S CPU	BiCG-S GPU
minsurfo	7.15e-7	1.19e-6	8.34e-6	6.32e-6	2.15e-6	2.04e-5
obstclae	7.15e-7	1.19e-6	1.86e-5	7.15e-6	1.91e-6	2.96e-6
wathen100	1.91e-6		1.42e-5	1.60e-5	7.39e-6	7.74e-6
ex1			5.25e-6	4.77e-6	4.77e-6	*1.60e-1*
mcca			6.20e-6	7.63e-6	4.77e-6	*2.16e+0*
dw4096			*1.41e+2*		*4.00e-2*	

Table 2. Absolute error obtained with a set of *real matrices* in double precision

Matrix name	GS CPU	Jacobi GPU	BiCG CPU	BiCG GPU	BiCG-S CPU	BiCG-S GPU
minsurfo	1.33e-15	5.76e-11	1.24e-14	1.05e-7	6.07e-11	6.98e-9
obstclae	1.33e-15	1.06e-7	6.66e-15	4.59e-8	3.42e-9	4.61e-9
wathen100	3.55e-15	*3.02e-2*	3.11e-14	1.79e-7	1.42e-14	8.72e-8
ex1			9.33e-15	6.48e-8	9.10e-9	*6.27e-3*
mcca			1.15e-14	3.74e-8	1.29e-9	*2.55e+1*
dw4096			*3.88e+0*	*6.81e+0*	*3.07e-2*	*1.23e+5*

algorithm, which computes 20 to 25 times faster than its mono-core CPU equivalent. When double precision is required, depending on the really needed accuracy and the acceptable computation time, we have to choose between a CPU and a GPU algorithm.

Finally, comparing every GPU algorithm to each other has allowed us to point out that it would not be efficient to use only one method for all the possible matrices; building a contextual solver should thus be useful.

References

[1]   L.A. Abbas-Turki, S. Vialle, B. Lapeyre and P. Mercier. *High Dimensional Pricing of Exotic European Contracts on a GPU Cluster, and Comparison to a CPU Cluster*, Second Workshop on Parallel and Distributed Computing in Finance (PDCoF 2009). 8 pages. May 29, 2009, Rome, Italy.

[2]   J. Bahi, R. Couturier, K. Mazouzi and M. Salomon, *Synchronous and asynchronous solution of a 3D transport model in a grid computing environment*, Applied Mathematical Modelling, 30(7), 2006.

[3]   J. M. Bahi, S. Contassot-Vivier and R. Couturier, *Parallel Iterative Algorithms: from sequential to grid computing*, Chapman & Hall/CRC, 2007. Numerical Analysis & Scientific Computing Series.

[4]   NVIDIA, *CUDA SDK documentation*, 2009.

[5]   M. Baboulin, J. Demmel, J. Dongarra, S. Tomov and V. Volkov, *Enhancing the performance of dense linear algebra solvers on GPUs*, Poster at Supercomputing 2008, November 18, 2008.

[6]   D. Neckels, *cudaztec*, http://code.google.com/p/cudaztec/.

[7]   N. Bonneel, *GPUmatrix*, http://sourceforge.net/projects/gpumatrix/.

[8]   L. Buatois, G. Caumon and B. Lévy, *Concurrent number cruncher - A GPU implementation of a general sparse linear solver*, International Journal of Parallel, Emergent and Distributed Systems, to appear.

[9]   R. W. Freund and N. M. Nachtigal, *QMR: a Quasi-Minimal Residual Method for Non-Hermitian Linear Systems*, Iterative Methods in Linear Algebra, 151-154. Elsevier Science Publishers. 1992.

[10] N. Bell and M. Garland, *Efficient sparse matrix-vector multiplication on CUDA*, NVIDIA Technical Report NVR-2008-004, NVIDIA Corporation, December 2008.

[11] W. Kahan, *Further remarks on reducing truncation errors*, Comm. of the ACM, 8 (1965), p. 40.

[12] H. A. van der Vorst, *Bi-CGSTAB: A fast and smoothly converging variant of Bi-CG for the solution of nonsymmetric linear systems*, SIAM J. Sci. Comp. 13: pp. 631-644, 1992.

[13] T. A. Davis, *The University of Florida Sparse Matrix Collection*, Technical Report of the University of Florida, http://www.cise.ufl.edu/research/sparse/matrices

554

Parallel Computing: From Multicores and GPU's to Petascale
B. Chapman et al. (Eds.)
IOS Press, 2010
© 2010 The authors and IOS Press. All rights reserved.
doi:10.3233/978-1-60750-530-3-554

Abstraction of Programming Models Across Multi-Core and GPGPU Architectures

Thomas H. BEACH [a], Ian J. GRIMSTEAD [a,1], David W. WALKER [a] and
Nick J. AVIS [a]

[a] *Cardiff School of Computer Science, Cardiff University, Wales, UK*

Abstract. Work in the field of application acceleration devices is showing great promise, but still remains a tool largely for computer scientists with domain knowledge, given the complexity of porting existing algorithms to new architectures or environments. Such porting is hindered by the lack of abstraction available.

   We present our latest work in the development of a novel solution to this abstraction problem; an intelligent semi-automatic porting system. This allows a higher level of abstraction where the user does not have to intervene or annotate their source code, while maintaining reasonable levels of performance. We present comparisons between manual and automatic code ports on two different platforms (NVIDIA CUDA and ClearSpeed C^n), showing the versatility of this approach.

Keywords. Application Acceleration, ClearSpeed, GPGPU, Performance Comparison, Semi-Automatic Porting

Introduction

Application speed-up is moving away from reliance on the increasing clock speed on serial processors (which is beginning to level off and be replaced with multiple cores [1]), and instead alternative approaches are required. Alternative hardware is becoming more popular, ranging from Field Programmable Gate Arrays (FPGA [8]) to Application Specific Integrated Circuits (ASICs) such as General-Purpose Graphics Processing Units (GPGPUs [12]), ClearSpeed accelerators[6] and the CELL Broadband engine[14].

   In this paper we first summarise the current work in using these "application accelerator" devices and the related problems that prevent their wider acceptance in High Performance Computing (HPC). We then present our work in the development of a feasible solution to these problems, an intelligent semi-automatic application porting system. We describe the prototype that has been constructed, the latest results and discuss remaining future work to facilitate the acceptance of application acceleration devices into mainstream HPC.

---

[1]Corresponding Author: Dr. Ian J. Grimstead, Cardiff School of Computer Science, Cardiff University, Queens Buildings, 5 The Parade, Roath, Cardiff, Wales, UK, CF24 3AA; E-mail: I.J.Grimstead@cs.cardiff.ac.uk

1. Background

In recent years various high level tools have been developed to aid programming of application accelerators. To reduce the overhead of the unusual programming model, NVIDIA and AMD/ATI have both released their own high level programming languages for their GPGPUs. However, each of these languages is only compatible with specific series of hardware. There have been several tools developed to aid FPGA development, including Mitrionics who have developed the Mitiron-C language for FPGAs and Nallatech who have developed their DimeC language. To compound this, further application accelerators have been revealed: Intel have announced their Larrabee architecture [15] (a GPGPU consisting of many x86 cores in parallel), and Convey have announced their x86 application coprocessor [7].

Although high level tools have been successful with many applications being accelerated; such as Blast on the FPGA using Mitrion-C[10] and MolPro for Clearspeed[5], there is still a need for compatibility between the various classes of application accelerators and standardisation between languages for a class of device, i.e. FPGA and GPGPU. Brook from Stanford[3] and Rapidmind[13] are two other high level tools that have been developed, these tools enable cross compatibility between the two GPU manufacturers and supports a much wider variety of GPUs. The OpenCL [9] initiative has also been announced to produce a cross-platform programming environment, but still requires detailed knowledge of the abstracted architecture. Overall, the user has to supply explicit annotation within their existing code or to port their code directly to a new language; there is still much work to be done in this field.

2. Research Problem and Aims

We believe the main factor limiting the adoption of these application acceleration devices is the lack of a suitably abstracted programming interface for users of these devices [2]. To successfully port an application to an accelerator expertise is needed not only in the applications domain but the computer science domain also. This limitation is a backwards step from the service orientated view HPC currently takes and will become infeasible in the future.

Our research is working on the development of a solution to this limitation; an intelligent semi-automatic application porting system, we focus particularly on the creation of a programming abstraction layer across a range of acceleration devices and enabling the intelligent selection of an appropriate device based on algorithm characteristics—not the automatic parallelization of sequential code. Our system aims to increase the level of abstraction while maintaining performance and be able to perform the following tasks:

- Locating acceleration devices.
- Selecting an appropriate device.
- Porting the application to the device.
- Allowing additional hand tuning of the code.

3. System Overview

The system is designed to cope with the application accelerators being distributed and not all resident in the host machine, such as more powerful accelerators such as Tesla GPUs[11], ClearSpeed CATS accelerators and FPGAs boards are unlikely to present in commodity workstations; even with data transfer overheads applications will still benefit by utilising these more powerful acceleration devices. Web services were selected to support this distributed environment, as web services are relatively mature and a well-understood and supported tool-set.

The overall compilation flow involved in creating an automatic port to an application accelerator from standard sequential C code is presented in [2]; in summary:

- Parse program code to locate candidate kernels
- Extract kernel features
- Use kernel descriptions to determine the appropriate device for acceleration
- Locate appropriate device (supported by UDDI server)
- Port the code to the accelerator device
- Monitor performance of application

In addition to this standard compilation flow the following features are also supported:

- Full profiling of an application across all application acceleration devices
- Bootstrapping a new application accelerator using stored applications

These tasks are divided between several separate components: UDDI server (for device location), client on user's workstation, program classifier and back-ends to support each type of application accelerator. These components are now described in more detail in the following sections.

3.1. System Client

The client is the front-end of the system, coded in C++. The client is responsible for the analysis and preparation of the program for execution on a acceleration device. Program code passed to the client will go through the following stages of analysis:

1. Syntax Check - A simple syntax check that confirms that the input code is correct.
2. Kernel Formation - Constructs a control flow graph of the input code allowing the location of natural loops within the code[16]. Each natural loop is then marked as a candidate kernel and is separated from the program code, with a placeholder being put in its place. Kernel acceleration feasibility is not yet analysed, as the target acceleration device and its restrictions are not known at this stage.
3. Kernel Analysis - Conducts a code analysis on the kernel code to determine various features of the kernel (such as data flow graph, characteristics of the loops formed, data items to be loaded and/or copied back to/from the device, and various metrics for the program classifier).
4. Initial Kernel Filtering - Performs some initial kernel filtering removing loops that are not suitable for execution, such as infinite loops.
5. Output Phase - The client then outputs a modified version of the input program, with the kernel code separated from the host code. The results of the kernel analysis are output as a kernel description file.

3.2. Program Classifier

The program classifier is a machine learning system, built using the WEKA machine learning workbench [17]. The classifier retains a list of known kernels each with associated metrics to provide a representation of the kernel:

- Required data precision.
- Mathematical intensity of calculations.
- Number of iterations and branches present.
- Amount of data copied to/from the device.

These metrics are generated during kernel analysis by the client, and passed to the program classifier for association with performance data supplied from the back-ends when the kernel is executed.

The program classifier performs decision making based on these data at the kernel level and then the program level. Firstly, if a kernel has sub-kernels (kernels that occur within the code of the kernel) at which level kernel should acceleration take place; secondly, which is the best device to accelerate the kernel in question. These decisions are made using a decision tree algorithm, where the kernel description is analysed to determine which device, based on previous experience, a kernel with those characteristics will perform best on. It is entirely possible at this point for the system to decide the best device to execute the kernel on is the CPU.

The classifier then examines at the overall program level; the optimum device for each kernel is now known, so the significance of each kernel within the program is used to decide which single device will give the best overall performance. If the classifier is unable to make a decision (due to a lack of training data), then the porting system executes the application on all available devices to produce the required data.

Note that the integration of new devices into the system is handled by the classifier. A set of test programs, of which performance data are known, are passed to the new device to enable performance data to be gathered. This will bootstrap the new device into the system and allows its selection as a viable candidate for accelerating programs.

3.3. Back-Ends

Currently three back-ends have been developed, each targeting: single core CPU, NVIDIA CUDA and ClearSpeed C^n. The CPU back-end acts as a control to allow comparison between execution on an acceleration device and on a standard sequential processor. This back-end is fully integrating into the porting system to allow this comparison to be made ignoring communication overheads introduced by the porting system itself.

The NVIDIA CUDA back-end and ClearSpeed C^n back-ends have a common structure, where compilation entails the following steps:

1. Kernel Validation - Validates that each kernel is able to execute on the target device and merges kernels that can not be accelerated back into the host code. This including checking for data dependencies within kernels that will prevent acceleration in their current form.
2. Kernel Code Generation - Generates a CUDA/C^n device function based on the original code for the kernel.

3. Host Code Generation - Generates host code, based on the data from the kernel description, this host code will allocate memory storage on the device and copy data from/to the acceleration device.
4. Creation of Build Scripts - Creation of a build script to handle the CUDA/C^n and C/C++ compilation and the linking of system libraries.

These steps enable the system to abstract the actual compilation of the code, hiding any complexities such as the need to run sections of the device code through multiple compilers. The back-ends also control the execution of the application and provide performance monitoring (through the addition of optional instrumentation code) where kernel execution time can be monitored and stored by the program classifier.

3.4. Other Platforms

The back-end can be ported to support any architecture, as long as it is possible to translate C code into an appropriate language supported by the new architecture. One example is the potential to produce an OpenMP back-end to support multi-core CPUs, or direct hardware support for a Larrabee based accelerator.

4. Results

This section discusses the results obtained by using our prototype system with two applications when executed on the GPGPU, CPU and ClearSpeed. A General Matrix Multiplication (GEMM) and an N-Body simulation were chosen as they fall into a separate dwarf category, based on the seven dwarfs taxonomy of applications[1]. The GEMM is a dense linear algebra problem while the N-Body simulation falls into the N-Body methods category. Both examples were initially developed in C and then passed to the porting system. Once the porting was complete, five test datasets were created to test the performance of the ported code.

To determine how successful the porting system has been in generating efficient code, the generated code was compared against the original C implementation and a manually ported implementation of the examples. Wall clock time was measured, to reveal the overall impact of acceleration with full system overheads taken into account rather than just the accelerated portion of the algorithm.

The CPU tests were carried out on an Intel Xeon E5472 3.0GHz (1600GHz FSB) with 16GB RAM (identical CPUs used with the application accelerators). The GPU Tesla C1060 featuring 240 cores and 4GB of memory, rated at 933 single-precision GFLOPs and 78 double-precision GFLOPS. The ClearSpeed device used was a ClearSpeed e710 card, featuring 2GB of RAM and two CSX700 accelerator processors (each with 96 cores), rated at 96 single-precision GFLOPS, 96 double-precision GFLOPS.

4.1. General Matrix Multiplication

This application utilised the standard GEMM formula $C \leftarrow \alpha AB + \beta C$, where the new matrix C is computed based on the product of two matrices A and B and the old matrix C. The dataset size n signifies the size of matrices A, B and C is $n * n$. The results from these tests are presented in Table 1, showing performance figures from NVIDIA CUDA and ClearSpeed C^n, where "SP" represents Single Precision (i.e. SGEMM), and "DP" represents Double Precision (i.e. DGEMM).

Data	CPU		Execution Time (Seconds)							
Size			Manual GPU Port		Automatic GPU Port		Manual Clearspeed Port		Automatic Clearspeed Port	
	SP	DP	SP	DP	SP	DP	SP	DP	SP	DP
200	0.16	0.16	1.43	1.47	1.47	1.54	0.15	0.19	0.21	0.19
800	4.40	4.46	3.34	3.52	3.42	3.53	3.24	4.45	3.14	4.39
1200	12.91	13.56	6.54	6.98	6.57	7.03	9.79	12.71	9.56	12.75
1600	28.85	29.85	12.48	13.60	12.52	13.71	18.06	25.43	15.25	25.27
2000	53.99	55.78	18.31	21.89	20.99	24.35	28.57	47.43	27.52	47.51
2800	139.94	146.30	45.05	54.26	45.83	67.74	82.95	145.72	77.28	145.51

Table 1. Results of GEMM port to NVIDIA CUDA and ClearSpeed C^n

No.	CPU		Execution Time (Seconds)					
Bodies			Manual GPU Port		Automatic GPU Port		Manual ClearSpeed Port	
	SP	DP	SP	DP	SP	DP	SP	DP
50	0.02	0.02	1.29	1.32	1.31	1.33	0.58	0.60
500	0.76	0.93	1.45	1.64	1.46	1.77	1.02	1.24
1000	3.02	3.77	1.54	2.07	1.56	2.19	2.10	3.21
2000	12.05	15.02	1.71	2.88	1.84	3.00	6.67	10.72
4000	47.97	60.66	2.32	6.09	2.46	6.11	26.08	39.57
8000	189.74	239.86	4.17	16.78	5.27	20.57	102.42	153.33

Table 2. Results of N-Body Simulation Port to NVIDIA CUDA and ClearSpeed C^n

4.2. N-Body Simulation

The N-Body simulation we are using is the all-pairs method outlined in [4], the initial inputs to the problem are a set of n bodies $b_1...b_n$, each body i has mass m_i, velocity v_i and position p_i. The distance between any two bodies is written d_{ij} and the force on body i due to body j is written f_{ij}.

The algorithm then carries out the following steps

- Compute f_{ij} for all pairs of bodies. $f_{ij} = \frac{Gm_i m_j r_{ij}}{|r_{ij}^3|}$ where $i \neq j$
- Compute total force on each body $f_i = \sum_{i,j\neq i} f_{ij}$
- Update the position p_i of each body $p_i = p_i + v_i \Delta t + \frac{\Delta v_i}{2}\Delta t^2$
- Update the velocity v_i of each body $v_i = v_i + \frac{f_i \Delta t}{m_i}$
- In our experiments this algorithm will be carried out for 100 time steps with a varying number of bodies in the system.

Initial results from these tests are presented in Table 2, showing performance figures from NVIDIA CUDA and ClearSpeed C^n. Note that "SP" represents Single Precision and "DP" represents Double Precision variations of the algorithm. Timings of a manual port only were available for ClearSpeed, as the automatic porting is incomplete at present.

4.3. Analysis of Results

The same trends are seen in the results of both examples considered. With the smallest dataset the CPU implementation outperforms the accelerated implementations, this is because the dataset is too small for the speedup achieved to overcome the overhead of moving the dataset into the accelerator's memory.

As the size of the datasets increase the accelerated ports of the applications both begin to outperform the CPU version. The performance for the automatic port compared to the manual port for the GEMM example is very similar, showing the efficiency of the approach. The ClearSpeed accelerator initially ran faster than the GPGPU, then rapidly tailed off at a data size of 800, performed roughly 30% slower than the GPGPU in single precision. This appears to be reasonable given that ClearSpeed device performs double precision at the same speed as single precision (it is designed primarily for double precision).

However, ClearSpeed performed poorly in double precision mode when compared to the GPGPU; this was initially surprising, as a ClearSpeed device should show a slight performance edge given its higher GFLOP rating (96 double-precision GFLOPS compared to 78 GFLOPS on the C1060). It would appear to be caused by on/off device memory bandwidth, as the automatic port and the manual port do not make use of the on-chip swazzle network to reduce off-chip memory accesses (which supports 160Gbyte/sec on-chip, versus 6.4Gb/sec to the accelerator's 2Gb DRAM). For comparison, the NVIDIA C1060 has 102 Gbyte/sec memory bandwidth.

The N-Body problem shows a similar story, where with small datasets the ClearSpeed device performed faster than the GPGPU, but rapidly fell behind. Memory bandwidth would appear to be the issue, given the significant slowdown when moving from single to double precision, yet the raw GFLOP execution rate should be the same for both formats.

Overall, these results are very promising as they show that our porting system is producing code that outperforms the original CPU implementation and furthermore executes at a performance level only slightly depressed from that of manually ported code.

5. Future Work

The above results show the prototype system has performed well and is showing very promising progress towards its goals of increasing the programming abstraction level while maintaining acceptable performance. Future work will focus initially on completing the automatic porting to ClearSpeed devices.

The performance of automatic porting of additional example applications will be investigated and these examples will be selected from each category of the seven dwarfs of applications [1], allowing us to determine for each dwarf category if its applications are generally suitable or unsuitable for acceleration on a particular application accelerator device.

6. Conclusion

We have discussed the background to application accelerators in HPC and the obstacles to their wider adoption in the community. The main obstacle appears to be the lack of a device-agnostic abstraction approach, for which we have presented our proposed solution: a semi-automatic porting system.

Our prototype solution has demonstrated the automatic porting of two C code examples (DGEMM and N-Body) that do not require the user to intervene or annotate their original source code. The results from these tests are promising with the automatically ported code outperforming standard, serial CPU implementations for moderate sized dataset and delivering performance within 15% of manually ported versions of the examples. Our results show that host-device memory bandwidth is a large factor with our two examples; further work aims to investigate other categories of the seven dwarfs to reveal which dwarfs are best suited to which application accelerators.

In summary, our system is a novel tool which has demonstrated promising initial results and as such will be of widespread interest to the HPC community.

References

[1] Krste Asanovic, Ras Bodik, Bryan Catanzaro, Joseph Gebis, Parry Husbands, Kurt Keutzer, David A. Patterson, William Plishker, John Shalf, Samuel Williams, and Katherine A. Yelick. The landscape of parallel computing research: A view from berkeley. Technical report, University of California at Berkeley, 2006.

[2] Thomas H. Beach and Nicholas J. Avis. An intelligent semi-automatic application porting system for application accelerators. In *Proceedings of the ACM International Conference on Computing Frontiers, Workshop on UnConventional High Performance Computing*. ACM, 2009.

[3] Ian Buck, Tim Foley, Daniel Horn, Jeremy Sugerman, Kayvon Fatahalian, Mike Houston, and Pat Hanrahan. Brook for gpus: Stream computing on graphics hardware. *ACM Transactions on Graphics (TOG)*, 23:777–786, 2004.

[4] Francisco Chinchilla, Todd Gamblin, Morten Sommervoll, and Jan F. Prins. Parallel n-body simulation using gpus. Technical report, University of North Carolina at Chapel Hill, 2004.

[5] ClearSpeed. Clearspeed application note: Ground-breaking acceleration quantum chemical calculations using molpro. Technical report, 2007.

[6] ClearSpeed. Csx processor architecture. Technical report, 2007.

[7] Convey Computer Corporation. The convey hc-1 computer: Architecture overview. Technical report, 2008.

[8] Anders Dellson, Goran Sandburg, and Stefan Mohl. Turning FPGAS into supercomputers. Technical report, Cray Users Group, 2006.

[9] Khronos. Khronos launches heterogeneous computing initiative. Technical report, 2008.

[10] Mitrionics. Mitrion accelerated ncbi blast. Technical report, 2007.

[11] NVIDIA. Nvidia tesla computing processor: Solve tomorrows computing problems today. Technical report, 2007.

[12] John D. Owens, David Luebke, Naga Govindaraju, Mark Harris, Jens Kruger, Aaron E. Lefohn, and Timothy J. Purcell. A survey of general purpose computation of graphics hardware. *Eurographics*, 26:80–113, 2005.

[13] Rapidmind. Rapidmind product overview. Technical report, 2006.

[14] M. W. Riley, J. D. Warnock, and D. F. Wendel. Cell broadband engine processor: Design and implementation. *IBM Journal of Research and Development*, 51, 2007.

[15] Larry Seiler, Doug Carmean, Eric Sprangle, Tom Forsyth, Michael Abrash, Pradeep Dubey, Stephen Junkins, Adam Lake, Jeremy Sugerman, Robert Cavin, Roger Espasa, Ed Grochowski, Toni Juan, and Pat Hanrahan. Larrabee: A manycore x86 architecture for visual computing. *ACM Transactions on Graphics*, 27(3):Article 18, 2008.

[16] Jeffrey D. Ullman, Alfred V. Aho, and Ravi Sethi. *Compilers : principles, techniques, and tools*. Wokingham : Addison-Wesley, 1986.

[17] Ian H. Witten and Eibe Frank. *Data Mining : Practical machine learning tools and techniques*. Morgan Kaufmann, 2000.

Parallel Computing: From Multicores and GPU's to Petascale
B. Chapman et al. (Eds.)
IOS Press, 2010
© 2010 The authors and IOS Press. All rights reserved.
doi:10.3233/978-1-60750-530-3-562

Modelling Multi-GPU Systems [1]

Daniele G. SPAMPINATO [a] , Anne C. ELSTER [a] and Thorvald NATVIG [a]

[a] *Norwegian University of Science and Technology (NTNU), Trondheim, Norway*

Abstract. Due to the power and frequency walls, the trend is now to use multiple GPUs on a given system, much like you will find multiple cores on CPU-based systems. However, increasing the hierarchy of resource widens the spectrum of factors that may impact on the performance of the system. The goal of this paper is to analyze such factors by investigating and benchmarking the NVIDIA Tesla S1070. This system combines four T10 GPUs, making available up to 4 TFLOPS of computational power. As a case study, we develop a red-black, SOR PDE solver for Laplace equations with Dirichlet boundaries, well known for requiring constant communication in order to exchange neighboring data. To aid both design and analysis, we propose a model for multi-GPU systems targeting communication between the several GPUs.

The main variables exposed by our benchmark application are: domain size and shape, kind of data partitioning, number of GPUs, width of the borders to exchange, kernels to use, and kind of synchronization between the GPU contexts. We show that the multi-GPU system greatly benefits from using all its four GPUs on very large data volumes. Four GPUs were almost four times faster than a single GPU. The results also allow us to refine our static communication model.

Keywords. GPU computing, multi-gpu, performance modelling, NVIDIA s1070

1. Introduction

GPU computing for high performance computing is generating a lot of interest. In this paper, we investigate multi-GPU systems' performance factors, such as data volume dimensions, data partitioning techniques, number of GPUs, inter-GPU communication methods, and kernel design. In particular, we focus on NVIDIA's S1070 multi-GPU solutions, a system recently deployed at HPC centers world wide. These include Tokyo Technology University's Tsubame supercomputer which was ranked 29th in the world when installed, and the new multi-GPU-based system at GENCI in France. Our methodology and general results should, however, be applicable to most modern multi-GPU systems.

The increasing hierarchy of resources issues new challenges to the developers, widening the spectrum of factors which may impact the performance of a multi-GPU system. The aim of this work is to investigate such factors and consider some important models of parallel systems in order to identify some common properties that can help us in our study. Communication is always a relevant aspect when dealing with distributed resources. By designing a benchmark framework around the SOR PDE solver, an application that constantly requires inter-GPU communication, we are able to develop better a multi-GPU model.

---

[1] A big thank you to NVIDIA for sponsoring our HPC-Lab with cutting-edge GPUs.

2. Current NVIDIA Architecture and Programming Model

The compute unified device architecture (CUDA) environment presents a cutting-edge programming model well-suited for modern GPU architectures [1]. NVIDIA developed this programming environment to fit to the processing model of their Tesla architecture and expose the parallel capabilities of GPUs to the developers.

CUDA maintains a separated view of the two main actors involved in the computation, namely the host (CPU system) and the device (GPU card/system). The host executes the main program, while the device acts like a coprocessor.

Our test bench, the **NVIDIA Tesla S1070 Computing System** is a 1U rack-mount system equipped with four Tesla T10 GPUs (Figure 1).

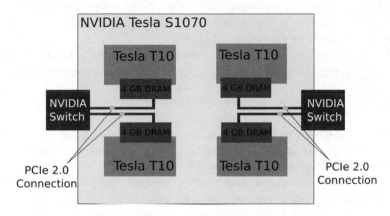

Figure 1. NVIDIA Tesla S1070 Computing System Architecture.

The Tesla T10 has 240 processing cores working either at 1.296 GHz (-400 configuration) or at 1.44 GHz (-500 configuration). The cores are grouped in 30 Streaming Multiprocessors (SMs), each with 8 single-precision cores and a single double-precision core. Each single-precision core is able to issue up to 3 FLOP per cycle, i.e. a *multiply* concurrently to a *multiply-add*, while the double-precision core is able to issue up to 2 FLOP per cycle. This gives a peak theoretical performance of 4 GPUs · 1.44 GHz · 3 FLOP/cycle · 240 cores = 4.147 TFLOP/s in single precision and 4 GPUs · 1.44 GHz · 2 FLOP/cycle · 30 cores = 345 GFLOP/s in double precision.

From a memory point of view, every GPU is connected to 4 GB high speed DRAM, with a bandwidth of 102 GB/s. This gives to the system a total of 16 GB. The connection to the host passes through NVIDIA Switches and PCIe Host Interconnection Cards (HIC). A single PCIe 2.0 16x (or 8x) slot on the host is connected to two GPUs using an NVIDIA Switch and a PCIe HIC. This connection provides a transfer rate of up to 12.8 GB/s between the host node and the computing system.

3. Programming Multiple GPUs

The NVIDIA CUDA Runtime API gives the programmer the possibility to select which device to execute the kernels on. By default device 0 is used, and the devices are enumerated progressively.

To use multiple CUDA contexts, we can associate them to different CPU threads, one for each GPU. For optimal performance, the number of CPU cores should not be less than the number of GPUs in the system. Managing the threads could be done by implementing an ad-hoc communication layer through system libraries, such as NPTL. Otherwise, existing libraries could be used, such as message-passing libraries adapted to perform shared memory communication [2].

4. Parallel Models

As argued in [3], parallel models often lack of connection to the real world, becoming powerless tools in terms of prediction capabilities. Nonetheless, they do not loose their relevance when analyzing new architectures, because they help in focusing on the main characteristics exposed by the systems at issue.

SMP clusters are one such example where the computing platform combines elements from both message-passing multicomputers and shared memory multiprocessors.

4.1. Similarities between SMP Clusters and Multi-GPU Systems

A multi-GPU computing architecture has several characteristics that make it similar to the computing model of an SMP cluster. E.g. Eicker and Lippert [9] sheds some ligtht on the JULI cluster architecture. As shown in Figure 2, every GPU, which in turn is a highly multithreaded system, is linked to every other through the host system. This kind of interconnection, requires communication to setup cooperation in solving a common problem. Because of the difference between a general processor and a graphics processor, some of the concepts need a proper contextualization, posing sometimes new problems to solve.

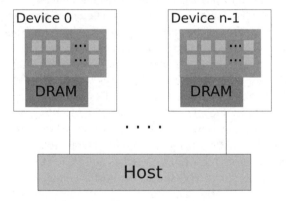

Figure 2. Multi-GPU system as a network of GPUs.

4.2. Synchronization and Consistency

Synchronization is suggested exclusively at thread level. Threadblocks' independence is an important requirements for granting scalability and speed. Also within a threadblock, however, the use of synchronization routines must be carefully controlled and not misused. Mutual exclusions within a threadblock, can be implemented on recent hardware[2] using a combination of barriers and atomic operations, but this goes against the requirement of massive data parallelism required by GPUs to be efficients. Not accidentally, CUDA does not provide any native solution to this kind of approach.

4.3. Memory Performance

Global memory is not cached, and accessing it is an expensive operation, so it is important to design an appropriate access pattern. The datatype must be 4, 8 or 16 bytes large, and must be aligned to a multiple of its size.

There is a separate read-only constant memory, and access to this is cached. Optimal performance is achieved when all the threads of a half-warp read from the same address. Texture memory, which uses the 2D texture unit of the graphics hardware, provide 2D space locality for cache.

4.4. Inter-GPU Communication

We propose a model for a multi-GPU system that extends the Hockney model [5]. Taking into account the description in Section 4, a multi-GPU system is the combination of an interconnection node and a set of GPUs,

$$T_{multi-GPU} = T_{node} + \max_{g \in G} \left(T_{kernel}^g + T_{GPU-GPU}^g \right), \tag{1}$$

where T_{node} models the specific node (e.g. a node of a multicomputer), and the max operator is motivated by the fact that several GPU contexts are executed in parallel. $T_{GPU-GPU}$ expresses the communication between two GPUs, and, supposing identical connections to the host for both the devices, we can define it as

$$T_{GPU-GPU} = T_{GPU-host} + T_{host-host} + T_{host-GPU}$$
$$= 2 \cdot T_{GPU-host} + T_{host-host}. \tag{2}$$

The host to host communication time, $T_{host-host}$, summarizes the time required by all the data movements and synchronization mechanisms part of the communication flow between two GPUs.

The transfer bandwidth between host and device must be carefully considered. Compacting many small transfers into a large one is often much more efficient. A way to increase the bandwidth is to use page-locked memory. This would prevent paging mechanisms from being used on those memory spaces where data have been allocated. Page-locked memory, however, must be used with care. Reducing memory resources may produce system slowdown side effects. Pinned memory introduces a higher startup time relevant for small transfers [4].

Also the $T_{host-host}$ term should be minimized. This can be done exploiting the real parallelism exposed by modern multicore processors. As reported in [2], the use of MPI to communicate between processes on the same node can result in improvable communication overhead. The paper mentions that 2/3 of the communication is spent in buffered

---

[2]Atomic operations are just implemented on devices of compute capability 1.1 or higher.

MPI_Sendrecv. MPI libraries usually are based on inter-process communication. Using threads that share the same address space could turn out more beneficial. Thus, as an alternative to the message-passing approach, multithreading with an appropriate synchronization can be used to implement on-node communication among threads associated to different GPU contexts.

5. Benchmarks

The effect of using more than one GPU is shown in Figure 5 just for the texture based case. The graph underline that involving the most of the GPUs available is always an appropriate decision since from small dimensions of the domain ($N \times N > 3000 \times 3000 \approx 36$ MB). The curve shows that using four GPUs can be up to 3.4X faster than using only one. We have also found that it is 1.8X faster than using two [6].

After $N = 16000$ however, the curves start exhibiting a drastic reduction in performance. We think that this effect can be produced by resource contentions. As described in Section 2, GPUs on the S1070 share pairwise the two PCIe channels. It is possible that, with a relevant traffic ($> 2GB$), the PCIe contention lowers the performance of two parallel transfers almost down to the performance of a single one. As a result, the execution time required by N GPUs gets closer to the time required by a subset of N.

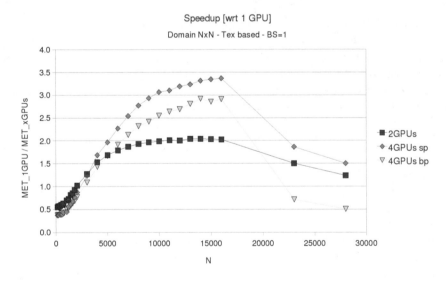

Figure 3. Speedups with respect to one GPU varying number of GPUs.

5.1. Border Size

Elster and Holtet [7,8] have shown that increasing the border size (BS) and doing redundant computation is an effective technique to overcome the latency factor on SMP clusters when solving PDEs numerically. We ran the solver on some representative domains exchanging different borders with width in the range [1-100]. It is reported that, for supercomputers with Infiniband interconnection, some minimal performance improvements were found using values of BS close to one. Since PCIe links are closer in latency to Infiniband interconnections than to Ethernet, we decided to have more test points in the neighborhood of $BS = 1$.

In Figure 4 we report results from the benchmark tests run using strip-partitioned, squared domains and texture-based kernels. Analyzing the graphs, we can deduce that the technique does not boost enough performance. The whole set of results can hardly approach a 10% of improvement (1.1X) with respect to the version based on unitary border width.

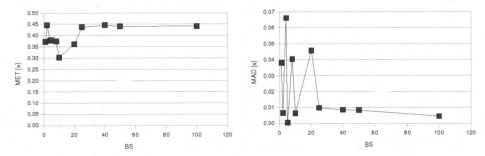

(a) Domain 1024x1024, strip partitioning, texture-based kernels, Median of 3 runs.

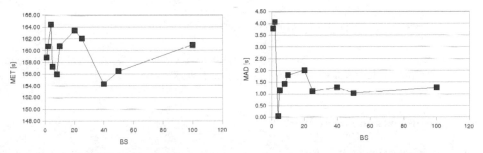

(b) Domain 52000x52000, strip partitioning, texture-based kernels, Median of 3 runs.

Figure 4. Border size influence on performance using four GPUs.

Thus, the empirical results bring us to a similar conclusion as in the supercomputers' case reported in [8], confirming our assumption that PCIe interconnections are fast enough to make the effect of the discussed method vanish.

5.2. Threads Synchronization

During the design phase, we decided to base our communication on POSIX threads synchronization, in order to assess its impact on communication and compare it with the alternative option of message-passing libraries. The latter option was seen to be responsible of around 70% of the communication overhead [2].

Figure 5 shows the impact of both synchronization and data transferring on communication per iteration.

Contrarily to what expected, the impact of synchronization is quite relevant, practically dominating the overall communication. Even though this impact is almost negligible on large scale (the core computation is kernel bound), such an effect must be analyzed and controlled as it may become more relevant in the perspective of more powerful hardware and shorter distances between host and devices.

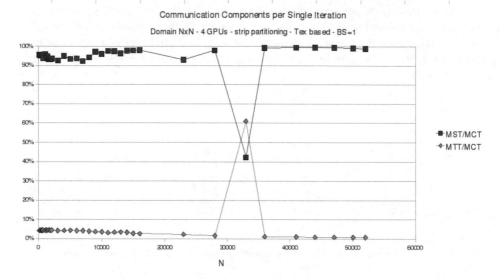

Figure 5. Sinchronization and transfer time over communication time during one iteration.

Profiling, it seems that the delay is due to lock contentions on neighbor domain areas. We plan a deeper investigation in our future work.

6. Conclusions and Future Work

The NVIDIA S1070 multi-GPU system was analyzed based on its specific hardware features and on possible analogies to fundamental parallel models, such as shared memory multiprocessors and multicomputers. The Poisson problem with Dirichlet boundary conditions was picked as our model problem since it does boarder exchanges of information common to a large class of application problems. Based on these analyzes, we defined a test space for the benchmark PDE solver tool we developed.

Varying the domains' dimensions up to 11 GB, we found the application I/O bound. Transferring the domain from host to device memory took always the largest percentage of time, requiring up to three times the kernel time. Excluding the first and the last necessary data transfers, the core computation was instead kernel bound. Exchanging only the essential data during the computation, i.e. the subdomains' borders, required no more than 10% of the total elapsed time.

Since our test system only consisted of four GPUs, vertical strips were more effective than blocked subdomains. However, simple communication models, normally used in parallel computing, were not found suitable for performance prediction on multi-GPU systems. Statistical approaches were found to be more stable and adaptable to slight technological alterations. We found a linear relation between the size of contiguous data expressed in gigabytes and the time required to transfer such data between the host and the device.

Using all four GPUs on the S1070, was always beneficial, performing up to 3.5X and 1.8X speedup on one and two GPUs, respectively. However, performance decreased working with large data volumes possibly due to resource contention.

Synchronizing GPUs through Pthreads condition variables took a relatively large percentage of the communication during the core computation. This is similar to what was previously documented for shared-memory based, message-passing libraries [2].

The framework we developed for our tests can be considered a premature stage of what could become a framework devoted to platform-independent, multi-GPU benchmarking. More attention must be paid to decouple the kernel logic from the synchronization logic, so to allow an easier and more independent design and analysis of both. As described in [4], the use of different precision standards, can also have a certain impact on performance. In a PDE solver context, introducing exit conditions based on proper approximations of the sought solutions can be a possible way to investigate eventual delays introduced by graphics hardware's precision. Our framework could be extended to the third dimension. For example, the requirement of exchanging not only borders but also surfaces introduces asymmetries in communication that would be important to examine.

The next goal should be to analysis GPU clusters composed by several multi-GPU nodes. In such systems, different GPUs may be interconnected through a multi-level communication network. Finally, with the introduction of the Green500 list[3], vendors are challenged to optimize the ratio performance/Watt instead of the only speed factor. This will no doubt lead to new interesting models.

References

[1] *NVIDIA CUDA 2.1 Programming Guide*. NVIDIA Corporation.
http://www.nvidia.com/object/cuda_develop.html.
[2] P. Micikevicius. 3D Finite Difference Computation on GPUs Using CUDA, in *Proceedings of the 2nd Workshop on General Purpose Processing on Graphics Processing Units*, 383, pages 79-84, March 2009.
[3] T. Natvig and A. C. Elster. Using Context-Sensitive Transmission Statistics to Predict Communication Time, in *PARA 2008, LNCS 2010*, A. C. Elster *et al.* editors, Springer, to be published.
[4] D. G. Spampinato and A. C. Elster. Linear Optimization on Modern GPUs, in *Proceedings of the 23rd IEEE International Parallel and Distributed Processing Symposium*, Rome, Italy, May 2009, (CDROM) ISSN: 1530-2075, ISBN: 978-1-4244-3750-4.
[5] R. W. Hockney. The Communication Challange for MPP: Intel Paragon and Meiko CS-2, in *Parallel Computing*, volume 20, issue 3, pages 389-398, March 1994.
[6] D. G. Spampinato. *Modeling Communication on Multi-GPU Systems*. Master thesis, Norwegian University of Science and Technology, July 2009.
http://www.idi.ntnu.no/ elster/master-studs/spampinato/spampinato-master-ntnu.pdf
[7] Anne C. Elster and R. Holtet. *Benchmarking Clusters vs. SMP Systems by Analyzing the Trade-off Between Extra Calculations vs. Computations* SC'02 Poster
[8] R. Holtet. *Communications-reducing Stencil-based Algorithms and Methods* NTNU MS thesis, July 2003. http://www.idi.ntnu.no/ elster/hpc-group/ms-theses/holtet-msthesis.pdf
[9] N. Eicker and T. Lippert. "'Low-level Benchmarking of a New Cluster Architecture"' in emphParallel Computing: Architectures, Algorithms and Applications, Vol. 38, PARCO 2007 Proceedings, Eds. C. Bischof et al., pp 381-388, IOS Press.

---

[3] http://www.green500.org

Parallel Computing: From Multicores and GPU's to Petascale
B. Chapman et al. (Eds.)
IOS Press, 2010
© 2010 The authors and IOS Press. All rights reserved.
doi:10.3233/978-1-60750-530-3-570

Throughput Computing on Future GPUs [1]

Rune J. HOVLAND [a] and Anne C. ELSTER [a]

[a] *Norwegian University of Science and Technology (NTNU), Trondheim, Norway*

Abstract. The focus on throughput and large data volumes separates Information Retrieval (IR) from scientific computing, since for IR it is critical to process large amounts of data efficiently, a task which the GPU currently does not excel at. Only recently has the IR community begun to explore the possibilities, and an implementation of a search engine for the GPU was published recently in April 2009. This paper analyzes how GPUs can be improved to better suit such large data volume applications. Current graphics cards have a bottleneck regarding the transfer of data between the host and the GPU. One approach to resolve this bottleneck is to include the host memory as part of the GPUsŠ memory hierarchy. Benchmarks from NVIDIA ION, 9800m and GTX 240 are included. Several suggestions for future GPU features are also prensented.

Introduction

While the GPU is gaining interest in the HPC community, others are more reluctant to embrace the GPU as a computational device. The field of Information Retrieval is a field with large data volumes and computationally lighter applications than traditional HPC. For this reason the GPU has not yet gained the status as a suited computational platform. However, the WestLab3 research group at the New York University has recently created a fully functional search engine [5] on the GPU with improved performance. While a search engine often contains complex ranking schemes and other calculations, it is still a application bound by the large data volumes stored in a search index.

Handling large data volumes on the GPU is not trivial on current GPUs. A data copy must be performed before the application can start, and the results from the GPU must be copied back to the host after the completed calculations. When handling large data volumes this can cause critical delays which seriously impair the GPUs ability to compete with CPU-only implementations. By introducing full streaming capabilities, the GPU might be able to remove most of these delays and efficiently handle large data volumes.

This paper will suggest improvements that can be made to enable future GPUs to efficiently support large data volumes, and ease the development process of such applications. The NVIDIA Tesla Architecture and the NVIDIA CUDA programming extension will be used as the representative of current GPUs. More detailed models and further references can be found in [3].

---

[1] The authors would like to thank NVIDIA for the donations of the graphic cards benchmarked in this study. This work was done while the first author was a master student at NTNU.

1. GPU performance characteristics

While the GPU allows general-purpose calculations to be performed, it is not a fully general-purpose processor, and thus has a bias towards graphics processing. This bias has made the architectural designers make certain tradeoffs with regard to performance to create the optimal GPU for what NVIDIA considers to be its main markets. This section will shed light on some of these performance characteristics.

1.1. Host to device transfers and GPU global memory

When using a GPU for computations, it usually requires data as input and in most cases produce output data. These data must be copied to and from the GPUs memory, since the GPU is unable to access the host memory while performing the calculations. This copy operation can be costly in many applications, especially for data intensive calculations.

NVIDIA Tesla GPUs have two levels of memory hierarchy [4]. The large storage capacity is provided by the global memory which is currently up to gigabytes. When data is copied from the host memory onto the GPU, it is copied into this memory. An access to this memory is slowed down by a latency between 400 and 600 clock cycles [2], and is thus not able to fulfill the role as high bandwidth memory. To improve performance, global memory allows memory access to adjacent addresses to be grouped together into one read or write operation. This approach is called coalesced read and write operations.

Paging and Direct Memory Access

Modern operating systems allow programs to use more memory than physically available though the use of paging [6]. Paging allows memory to be automatically swapped out to a hard-drive when it is not needed, and thereby freeing physical memory for other uses while still maintaining the integrity of the virtual memory. The main drawback with this technique is that only the operating system knows the exact location of a memory segment since it may be moved around due to memory swapping. In situations where an exact memory location is needed, page-locking can be used. This is mostly used when using Direct Memory Access (DMA), since DMA allows memory copies to be handled by a DMA handler instead of the CPU.

Data transfers to GPU

All copy operations between host memory and device memory on NVIDIA GPUs requires the use of DMA. Since most memory locations are not DMA accessible, there are two techniques which can be used. The first solution is to store all data which will be used on the GPU in page-locked memory locations. This is not always feasible since page-locked memory locations are a scarce resource. The other option is to copy the data to a page-locked memory location before copying it to the GPU. This approach requires an extra memory copy which can be costly. When to use which of the two techniques depends on the usage of the data. For data which will be copied often to the GPU it may be best to use dedicated page-locked memory, while for a one-time copy one may just as well use the second technique [4].

In CUDA, both techniques is supported automatically based on which type of memory location that is given to the copy-instruction [2]. By default, a pageable memory location is given when using the standard C/C++ command malloc, and if such a memory

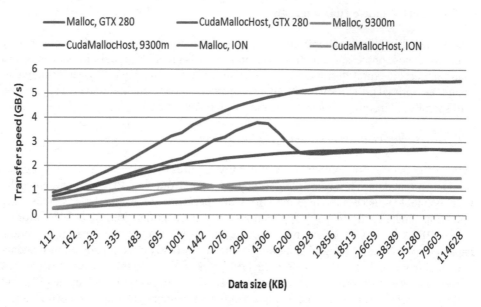

Figure 1. Host-device bandwidths for NVIDIA ION, 9300m, and GTX 280

location is given to the copy instruction in CUDA, it will copy the data to a page-locked memory location before copying it to the GPU. To allocate a page-locked memory location CUDA provides a method cudaMallocHost. Which of the two techniques to use may wary from application to application, but the measured bandwith when using the techniques in a simple test-case on the NVIDIA ION, 9300m adn GTX 280 can be seen in Figure 1.

1.2. Data Access

In large data volume applications, the data may be too large to fit in memory and hard-drives must be used. This means that any data which should be used must be read into main memory before it can be used. If this should be done on the GPU, it is even more cumbersome, since it must first be read into memory, before being copied onto the memory of the GPU. The results calculated at the GPU must also be copied back to the host-memory if it is to be used further by the CPU.

Modern hard-drives are considered to be the bottleneck of any application operating over large datasets. The highest transfer rate12 found for sustainedread for a hard-drive was 171MB/s13 which is fairly low considering the memory bandwidth of the new Intel Core i7 processor14 which is 25.6GB/s. The bandwidth of data transfers to and from the GPU which was found to be close to 6GB/s [4].

This time required can be expressed as a function of the hard-drive latency L_{HD}, size S, and hard-drive bandwidth B_{HD} of the data transfer as given in Equation 1:

$$T = L_{HD} + \frac{S}{B_{HD}} \tag{1}$$

This equation describes the simplest form of data access where the data is stored uncompressed on a single disk. Once read, it is stored directly in the location where it will be used.

2. Compression and GPU off-loading

A search engine [1] can be considered to focus on High-Throughput Computation (HTC) rather than a High-Performance Computation, as long as the latency of a single query is below a certain threshold. This query-latency is the time from the query is given until it is answered. There are many components of this latency, and the retrieval of the index-entry is one of them.

To reduce the impact of the hard-drive transfer rate, one can use compression thereby reducing the size of transferred data. This compression reduces the time required to transfer the data, but introduces a computational step which decodes the data and copies it over to the final memory location.

The new equation for the time required to access the entry which takes into account the time Ccomp required by the added computational step and the compression ratio Rcomp is given in Equation 2:

$$T = L_{HD} + S \cdot \left(\frac{R_{comp}}{B_{HD}} + C_{comp} \right) \tag{2}$$

By offloading the decompression to the GPU, the CPU is free to perform other tasks, and the overall throughput of the system may increase even if the time required to fetch an index-entry may increase.

2.1. Data copy hiding

Current GPUs are incapable of reading directly from the hard-drive, and the hard-drive is unable to write to the GPUs memory. However, it is possible to perform most of the transfer to the GPU parallel with the transfer from the hard-drive to system RAM. This is done by dividing the transfer into n parts, and start copying a part to the GPU asynchronously as soon as it is read from the hard-drive. By choosing the right size to partition the transfer into, the extra time needed to copy datato the GPU would only be equal to the time needed to copy the final part.

The operation of copying of the result to the host-memory is more cumbersome to remove, since it will be used by other parts of the system, and its lifespan may not be known. It is therefore best to free its memory location on the GPU and instead maintain it in host-memory which is more cost-efficient.

2.2. Memory Mapped Files

The last approach which can be considered is to use Memory Mapped Files which is specified in POSIX [20] through mmap(). This is a technique which creates a memory pointer to a Virtual Memory location in which the file is mapped. In this way, the file can be accessed as if it were residing in the memory, and the task of actually supplying the data is left to the operating system. By choosing this approach, the programmer can utilize efficient

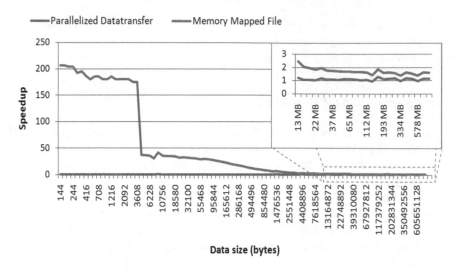

Figure 2. Memory mapped vs. parallel data transfers

2.3. Preliminary Performance Analysis

To determine if either of the two proposed improvements (data copy hiding and memory mapped files) would give improved performance over the basic approach, a test case was developed. By measuring the time each of the three approaches use to read data of various sizes from file and make it accessible on the GPU, an indication on the performance gain by the improved approaches could then be found. In Figure 2, the speedup of the two improvements with regard to the simple approach is given. As one can see, the memory mapped files obtains much better performance than the other two approaches. The hiding of data copy approach does not achieve noticeable speedups. This might be due to an added cost of initializing multiple file reads and data copies.

3. Expanding the memory hierarchy on next-generation GPUs

This section describes how the memory hierarchy of future architecture should be expanded to improve the usability for developers of large data volume application. In this context, a number of suggestions for minor changes to the Tesla Architecture and CUDA are also provided.

3.1. Expanding the Memory Hierarchy

The current Tesla Architecture allows the GPU to have its own dedicated memory or using a part of the host memory as device memory. Any data which is to be used by the GPU must be copied into device memory before a kernel is initialized. Any results from the kernel must be copied back to host memory after execution. These requirements forces any CUDA application to contain three steps; data-copy to device, execution and data-copy from device.

When transferring large amounts of data between the host and device memory, it may be beneficial to start computations before all the data is located on the GPU. The current Tesla Architecture allows this to be done by using streams, where both the data transfers and computations are divided into batches which are performed in an overlapping manner, thus hiding some of the data transfer cost. However, initializing multiple kernels is costly.

Direct host-memory access

Allowing the kernel to directly access the host-memory removes the need for host to device transfers in most cases. Syntactically this would be similar to accessing any other memory location on the GPU, but it would have a higher cost in terms of lower bandwidth and higher latencies. It would therefore be up to the developer to reduce the number of accesses to host-memory to a minimum by pre-fetching data into device memory such as global or shared memory.

For an application with large volumes of data, this possibility to access the host-memory directly would remove the need to divide the calculation into several kernel executions when the data exceeds the size of device memory. With the direct-access approach, the kernel can simply fetch more data into the device memory, while discarding used data without the need to return control to the CPU.

The dedicated GPU memory on the current high-end NVIDIA cards is significantly faster compared to the low-end NVIDIA ION system which uses older DDR2s and also a less powerfull CPU than typcially found on high-end PCs with separate graphics cards. Not surprisingly, the higher-end cards are therefore currently faster, despite the shared CPU-GPU RAM for the ION. This was seen in Figure 1 where the GTX 280 with dedicated memory outperformed the 9300m and ION which use local memory.

Customizing Memory Hierarchy

When allowing direct access to the host-memory from the kernel, it practically adds another level to the GPUs memory hierarchy. This added layer will change the usage of the device-memory since it would allow for more data access patterns. Through the added layer of GPU memory, the need for large device memory locations will be more individual. One can thus envision a more customizable device memory on the GPU to tune the size to the individual needs. Since the GDDR memory used in GPUs is more expensive than DDR memory used for local memory, this customization of memory hierarchy would allow for more cost-efficient installations. It may also allow the GPU access to more memory when computing.

Combining Dedicated and Shared Memory

If enabling customizations of the memory hierarchy is not feasible, there is another approach which seems easier to implement since most aspects needed exists in current GPUs. By allowing the GPU to use both dedicated and local memory as device memory, but dividing them into two distinct levels in the memory hierarchy, the same effect can almost be achieved. It would, however, require that the CPU also has write permissions to the host-memory used as device-memory, and that all data which the GPU will use is stored in this memory location.

Caching Problems

When using either of the two suggested approaches for kernel access to host-memory, there will be issues with CPU caching that must be resolved, since the data stored in the host-memory may not be the valid version due to cache and delayed write-back. These problems are assumed solvable in our study.

Zero-Copy in CUDA 2.2

The Zero-Copyfeature was recently introduced in CUDA version 2.2. Its main purpose is to allow the user to do, to some extent, what is suggested in this section. By allowing the user to access page-locked memory from the GPU, the need for copy prior to and after kernel execution can be eliminated. However, page-locked memory is a scarce resource, so the developer may still be required to do extra copy operations if there is extensive memory usage on the host.

3.2. Additional Improvements

Using CUDA to develop large data volume applications can be a cumbersome process. To increase the usability of CUDA for such applications, we present a number of improvements aimed at simplifying the development process and enable more compact and understandable code.

Caching

While caching is currently not supported for normal data on current Tesla Architecture, there is still a way to have the GPU handle caching. By claiming that the data is a texture, the GPU seizes control of the data access and caches the data using the Texture-memory. One thing that must be noted is that by marking the data as a texture, it is read-only since there is no write-back on the caching. If cached data are altered the result when accessing the data is undefined. While this limitation is unacceptable in many situations, there are applications for which this does not impose a problem. To use data as a texture, it is only necessary to instruct the GPU to treat the data as a texture. Any data may be handled in this manner. However, the syntax for doing so does not resemble the normal way to handle data access, and it may be confusing to use. Therefore CUDA should include functionality to enable caching for data without referencing textures since this may easily be implemented as a syntactic sugar without any alterations to hardware.

Extended Host-Device Synchronization

The CPU and GPU have different objectives and will therefore continue to have different characteristics. To utilize the computational system optimally, calculations should be performed on the processor that gives the best overall performance of the system. This would in many cases require rapid changes between CPU and GPU calculations and data exchange between them. With CUDA, as it is now, this can only be done by stopping the kernel each time the CPU should perform a calculation that the GPU depends on. While this is a solution that enables interaction between CPU and GPU, it is a cumbersome process which complicates the development process. A better solution would be to allow halting the CUDA kernels by synchronizing with the CPU. In this way, there would be a more intuitive interaction between host and device. This can be solved by either actually implementing synchronization in the architecture, or by adding the functionality as syntactic sugar which hides the process of dividing execution into multiple kernels. To efficiently implement the second approach, the cost of initializing a kernel must be reduced so that rapid control changes between GPU and CPU do not affect performance in to large extent. An possibility here is to implement it as syntactical sugar first to see if the developers will use it, and if so implement it in hardware. An approach like this will be less costly as hardware changes are more expensive

3.2.1. Allow File Access

Both search engines and many other applications require large data volumes which are stored on disk. In the current CUDA environment, the GPU cannot access files directly. The CPU must thus regain control and access the file, and copy the data to the GPU before restarting the kernel. Enabling file access from the GPU directly can be difficult, as it would require handling IO between the GPU and the disk. An easier approach could be implemented if local memory access is enabled as described in Section 3.1. This approach is to use memory-mapped files, which enables file access from the GPU by masking the file as a memory location, and giving this memory location to the GPU. By doing so, the operating system ensures that the data in the file is accessible to the GPU trough the virtual memory address that the file is mapped to.

4. Conclusion and Future Work

This paper took a close look at the current NVIDIA GPUs and pointed out the need for certain features which would improve performance for large data volume applications. By including the host-memory in the memory hierarchy of the GPU, like seen on the low-end NVIDIA ION, new ways to access data during calculations can be developed. Other benefits which reduce the complex code of large data volume applications have also been suggested. Further reflections on how likely these features are to be realized, and what work lies ahead in the process of providing these features can be found in [3].

References

[1]   R. Baeza-Yates and B. Ribeiro-Neto. *Modern Information Retrieval*. 1st ed. Addison Wesley Longman Limited, 1999.

[2]   *NVIDIA CUDA 2.1 Programming Guide*. NVIDIA Corporation.
      http://www.nvidia.com/object/cuda_develop.html.

[3]   R. J. Hovland. *Throughput Computing on Future GPUs*. Master thesis, Norwegian University of Science and Technology, July 2009.
      http://www.idi.ntnu.no/ elster/master-studs/runejoho/rune-hovland-master-ntnu.pdf

[4]   R. J. Hovland. *Latency and Bandwidth Impact on GPU-systems* Projet report, December 2008, Department of Computer and Information Science, Norwegian University of Science and Technology.
      http://www.idi.ntnu.no/ elster/master-studs/runejoho/ms-proj-gpgpu-latency-bandwidth.pdf

[5]   S. Ding, J. He, H. Yan, and T. Suel. "Using Graphics Processors for High Performance IR Query Processing," in *Proceedings of the World Wide Web Conference 2009*, Madrid, Spain, April 2009, pp. 421–430.

[6]   J. L. Hennessy and D. A. Patterson. *Computer Architecture: A Quantitative Approach, 4th ed*. Morgan Kaufmann Publishers, 2007.

Mini-Symposium
"ParaFPGA-2009: Parallel Computing with FPGA's"

Parallel Computing: From Multicores and GPU's to Petascale
B. Chapman et al. (Eds.)
IOS Press, 2010
© 2010 The authors and IOS Press. All rights reserved.
doi:10.3233/978-1-60750-530-3-581

ParaFPGA: Parallel Computing with Flexible Hardware

Erik H. D'HOLLANDER [a], Dirk STROOBANDT [a] and Abdellah TOUHAFI [b]

[a] *ELIS Department, Ghent University, Belgium*
[b] *IWT Department, Brussels University Association, Belgium*

Abstract. ParaFPGA 2009 is a Mini-Symposium on parallel computing with field programmable gate arrays (FPGAs), held in conjunction with the ParCo conference on parallel computing. FPGAs allow to map an algorithm directly onto the hardware, optimize the architecture for parallel execution, and dynamically reconfigure the system in between different phases of the computation. Compared to e.g. Cell processors, GPGPU's (general-purpose GPU's) and other high-performance devices, FPGAs are considered as flexible hardware in the sense that the building blocks of one or more single or multiple FPGAs can be interconnected freely to build a highly parallel system. In this Mini-Symposium the following topics are addressed: clustering FPGAs, evolvable hardware using FPGAs and fast dynamic reconfiguration.

Keywords. FPGAs, flexible hardware, dynamic reconfiguration, parallel processing, high performance computing

Introduction

Within the world of parallel computing, FPGAs constitute an attractive option for specialized applications, because of their flexibility, massively parallel framework, relatively low energy consumption and continually expanding features. Due to their inherently parallel electronic components and computation elements, FPGAs can be synthesized into a highly parallel computing architecture. This allows one to construct dataflow architectures and to map an algorithm onto the hardware. FPGAs have been used as accelerators in supercomputers, number crunching for multimedia applications, simulators for new computer architectures and standalone computing platforms. It is clear that no single computing paradigm fits all these applications, and this is reflected in the different topics of this Mini-Symposium: clustering FPGAs, developing evolvable hardware and new techniques for fast dynamic reconfiguration.

The selection and review of the number of papers presented in this Mini-Symposium could not be possible without the extensive help of the program committee. We thank these members for reviewing the submitted papers and selecting the best ones to be presented here. The members of the program committee are listed below.

Abbes Amira, Brunel University, UK
Georgi Gaydadjiev, Delft University of Technology, The Netherlands
Dominique Lavenier, IRISA-INRIA, France
Wayne Luk, Imperial College, UK
Tsutomu Maruyama, University of Tsukuba, Japan
Viktor Prasanna, University of Southern California, USA
Mazen A. R. Saghir, Texas A&M University at Quatar
Donatella Sciuto, Politechnico di Milano, Italy
Alastair M. Smith, Imperial College, UK
Dirk Stroobandt, Ghent University, Belgium, chair
Abdellah Touhafi, Brussels University Association, Belgium, co-chair
Sascha Uhrig, University of Augsburg, Germany
Tom VanCourt, Altera, USA
Steve Wilton, University of British Columbia, Vancouver, Canada
Sotirios G. Ziavras, New Jersey Institute of Technology, USA

We also thank Prof. Jonathan Rose of the University of Toronto for giving a keynote on *Experience, Frustration and Hope with Acceleration of Computation on FPGAs.*

1. Contributions

The first two papers address clustering and communication between FPGAs. In *Software versus Message Passing Implementations for FPGA Clusters* by Creedon and Manzke, a speed-area trade-off was made between the hardware and software implementation of a fast interconnection between FPGAs in a cluster. Interestingly, the authors developed a message passing interface which mimics the well-known MPI standard.

RAPTOR, a Scalable Platform for Rapid Prototyping and FPGA-based Cluster Computing by Porrmann et al., presents the development of a Gigabit-interconnected FPGA cluster used to emulate new multiprocessor hardware architectures. The RAPTOR hardware/software environment has been used to emulate large multiprocessor systems on a chip (MPSoC) and Kohonen self-organizing maps (SOM). In addition, the RAPTOR platform enables the development of powerful hardware accelerators, e.g., to speed-up large scientific simulations.

The next two papers address speeding up the development of evolvable hardware. Evolvable hardware consists of using genetic techniques to develop the optimal or near-optimal implementation of a combinational circuit such as a digital filter, or a complex controller. In *Speeding up Combinational Synthesis in an FPGA Cluster* by Pedraza et al., the computational intensive calculation is delegated to an FPGA in the so-called Fitness Calculation Unit. The speedup over a conventional HPC cluster depends on the search space, and is typically one or more orders of magnitude.

In *A Highly Parallel FPGA-based Evolvable Hardware Architecture* by Cancare et al., another approach is taken, in which the evolution of the candidate solutions is programmed at runtime using partial reconfiguration. This means that in the evolvable region, the quality of the solutions is calculated, while in another part of the evolvable region, new candidates are generated using partial reconfiguration. In this way it is possible to partially or completely hide the reconfiguration time.

Dynamic reconfiguration is the topic of the last three papers. In *Applying Parameterizable Dynamic Configurations to Sequence Alignment* by Davidson et al., an existing algorithm for DNA alignment is reorganized for execution on a smaller FPGA using runtime reconfiguration. In this way, the same application can run on a smaller and cheaper FPGA.

The paper *Towards a More Efficient Runtime FPGA Configuration Generation* Abouelella et al., gives a new insight into generating and minimizing the configuration time for a family of parameterizable bitstreams. A stack machine is presented which allows to compile a parameterizable configuration into configuration bits which are injected into the configuration memory. Parameterizable bitstreams allow a smaller and faster reconfiguration.

Finally, the paper *ACCFS – Virtual Filesystem Support for Host Coupled Run-Time Reconfigurable FPGAs* by Strunk et al., represents a file system for storing runtime reconfigurable modules, which can be loaded on demand by the user. This allows a multitude of compute kernels to be stored in a virtual file system for easy access by a multiple of users in multiple contexts.

2. Conclusion

The contributions presented in this Mini-Symposium show that there exist many opportunities for research and development in the area of parallel computing with FPGAs. Despite the existence of specialized architectures, it is expected that FPGAs will grow in flexibility and performance, and contribute to the parallel computing community in the future.

Parallel Computing: From Multicores and GPU's to Petascale
B. Chapman et al. (Eds.)
IOS Press, 2010
© *2010 The authors and IOS Press. All rights reserved.*
doi:10.3233/978-1-60750-530-3-584

Software vs. Hardware Message Passing Implementations for FPGA Clusters

Eoin CREEDON [a,1], and Michael MANZKE [a]

[a] *Graphics, Vision and Visualisation Group (GV2),*
Trinity College Dublin, Ireland

Abstract A parallel algorithm mapped onto multiple Field Programmable Gate Arrays (FPGAs) and CPUs needs to communicate and synchronise data between the FPGAs' digital logic micro-architectures and the CPU(s). A reconfigurable logic API for the FPGA and the CPU can assist the system programmer with mapping the parallel algorithm across the available resources. This work investigates alternative ways of implementing the reconfigurable logic API.

Keywords. FPGA, Message Passing, Comparison

Introduction

Field Programmable Gate Array (FPGA) based co-processors have demonstrated significant acceleration for a wide range of computationally intensive algorithms e.g. scientific computation [1], linear algebra [2], ray-tracing [3]. A parallelised algorithm executed across multiple FPGAs can assist an application with high computational requirements.

An algorithm that is implemented over several FPGA(s) and CPU(s) requires the exchange of data and synchronisation information between the parallel algorithm components that are implemented as digital logic on the FPGAs and as software on the CPU(s). To achieve this, an Application Programming Interface (API) assists the FPGA programmer to implement the algorithm. This API provides data communication and synchronisation between the micro-architectures that implement the algorithm on the nodes. However, the question arises of how to implement the message passing operations on FPGA logic to meet the parallel algorithm's communication requirements.

This work compares two implementations, a hardware micro-acrhitecture and a software, soft processor solution, each implemented in reconfigurable logic on the FPGA. This allows a programmer to determine which communication solution best matches their hardware and algorithm requirements. As part of this work a Hardware Description Language Message Passing API (HDL MP API) has been developed to abstract the application from the message passing implementation. The HDL MP API mimics the Message Passing Interface (MPI) [4] where appropriate with hardware optimisations applied.

Implementation evaluations, run across an Ethernet interconnect, show which implementation is more appropriate for a given problem's requirements. Experimental results show that a hardware approach achieves the best performance, with software results showing that the use of high speed interconnects may not be required, as processor bottlenecks limit software performance.

---

[1]Corresponding Author: E-mail: eoin.creedon@cs.tcd.ie

1. Background & Related Work

Previous investigations into message passing FPGA clusters have seen both software and hardware approaches used [5,6,7,8,9,10]. Saldaña et al [5], using the TMD-MPI system, implement a lightweight version of MPI running on an FPGA soft processor. Details on performing message sending and receiving using hardware are also discussed however, only software based message passing is demonstrated operating between FPGAs. Inter-FPGA communications use the Off-Chip Communication Controller (OCCC) [6] operating across Multi-Gigabit Transceiver (MGT).

The Reconfigurable Compute Cluster (RCC) [7] is concerned with the requirements for a PetaFLOP FPGA cluster. MGT links provide inter-FPGA point-to-point communications but an Ethernet network is needed to perform collective operations – data distribution, global summation, etc. Message passing is used for inter-node communications across both networks. The use of a processor on each node is discussed but its sole use for inter-FPGA communication is not presented.

Baxter et al [8] have developed Maxwell, an FPGA cluster similar in approach to the RCC. However, unlike the RCC each FPGA is housed in a blade computer with an FPGA processor using MGT links for all point-to-point message passing operations. Collective operations occur through the host blade computer.

Pedraza et al [9], with SMILE, use a message passing processor solution FPGA cluster for content based image recovery. Data communication is performed across MGT links, with the PowerPC on each node used to perform the communication operations. Only message passing send and receive are used in this solution.

Creedon and Manzke [10] present a message passing hardware solution for performing parallel matrix multiplication on an FPGA cluster. They use commodity switched Ethernet with all control logic implemented as dedicated digital logic on the FPGA.

Each solution using MGT links requires the use of FPGA logic for routing operations. To reduce FPGA communication resource utilisation, we look at using Ethernet as the inter-FPGA interconnect. Commodity switches perform data routing between the nodes. However, an Ethernet compliant network controller is required to perform all communications. By using Ethernet on the FPGA, data can be moved from the CPU to the application micro-architectures without traversing bridging logic or host compute nodes where data translation would be required.

2. Message Passing System Requirements

A parallel algorithm running across multiple FPGAs will utilise the FPGA reconfigurable logic for the computations. The exchange of both data and control information will be required to perform the parallel computations. For a parallel algorithm, each FPGA's computations will be asynchronous to the other FPGAs. However, the order of data communications are predefined by the parallel algorithm. To perform the algorithm data exchange, the application uses an API which provides access to communication primitives.

The two main communication operations in a message passing environment are data sending and receiving. To perform the operation correctly, a send/receive pair is required, with one sending data and another receiving data. To achieve this, both sides must maintain state information to perform the appropriate operations, shown in Figure 1 and Figure 2. The state information deals with the message passing protocol and is interconnect independent. The state operations, in an FPGA context, can be implemented with either dedicated reconfigurable hardware state machines or as software running on an FPGA processor. This work evaluates these two configurations by looking at how they perform when run across an appropriate interconnect. The message passing operations are independent of the physical interconnect making a layered implementation approach ideal, similar to MPICH [11] and TMD-MPI [5].

The API is implemented with switched Ethernet allowing for a single system wide interconnect, with both CPUs and FPGAs connected directly to each other. As both the FPGAs and CPU can communicate with each other, this allows for the direct exchange of data between CPU and FPGA nodes without requiring bridging logic. To ensure the correct exchange of data, a software API was developed to run on the CPU nodes which is comparable to the API running on the FPGAs.

Ethernet needs a communication protocol to ensure network operations occur correctly, with a subset of Transmission Control Protocol (TCP) [12] communication protocol used. A sliding window protocol combining selective negative acknowledge, window acknowledge operations is used to improve communication performance. The limited storage resources of the FPGA prevent support for out-of-order packets. If an out-of-order packet is received, it is dropped as are all subsequent out-of-order packets while awaiting the correct packet. Packet resending is controlled by the selective negative acknowledge. An acknowledgment packet signals the correct transfer of that window's data.

3. Message Passing and Communication Configuration

This work presents two implementation solutions for the message passing and communication system, a hardware only and a soft processor only system. The development of these solutions are based on how the computational logic of a parallel application will interact with and exchange data between different parts of a parallel algorithm. A HDL MP API is developed which hides the communication implementation from the application programmer. The HDL MP API is used as the interface between the parts of an algorithm's digital logic that may run on different FPGAs and communicate via an interconnect. Through the use of the HDL MP API, the digital logic is able to exchange both block RAM and node memory with other FPGAs and CPUs that are part of the cluster.

To implement the communication/Ethernet layer, the OpenCores 10/100 Mb Ethernet Media Access Controller (MAC) [13] is used to provide the interconnection functionality for both the hardware and software systems. The controller was modified to provide Gigabit Ethernet functionality, with Figure 3 showing the main modifications that

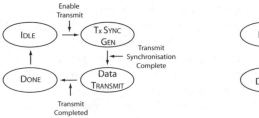

Figure 1. Transmit State Configuration

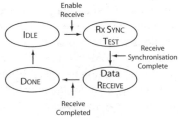

Figure 2. Receive State Configuration

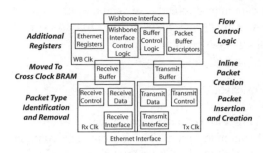

Figure 3. Ethernet Core, showing operational modifications

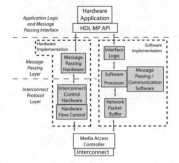

Figure 4. Hardware and Software operational configuration

were applied to the controller. The modifications are written against the appropriate aspect of the controller for where these changes were applied. The operational configurations that are compared in this work are illustrated in Figure 4.

3.1. Software Implementation

The software implementation uses a single MicroBlaze v7.10.d which is configured to perform message passing and communication protocol operations and is not accessible for use performing application computations. Interface translation logic is implemented to convert the HDL MP API message signals into processor accessible data structures. These operations are performed at the processor-HDL MP API interface.

Network buffers store all network data which the software tests to classify received data. Application data is transfered to the HDL MP API data interface while control packets are tested, decoded and discarded once the appropriate operations are complete. To know when new data is in the network buffers, the software continuously polls network status registers. This is required by the asynchronous operations and random arrival pattern of packets between nodes. The software system must also copy and network encapsulate message data before it is placed into the network buffers for communication. To reduce the impact of this operation, all application buffer data copies are 32-bit aligned which reduces the number of transfers that could be required. As a further optimisation, packet pre-buffering is used to hide the copying costs.

3.2. Hardware Implementation

A hardware micro-architecture is implemented to perform all message passing and communication operations as directed by an HDL MP API application. Hardware finite state machines implement the message passing protocol with control packets generated and exchanged to reflect the state, similar to the software operations. Dedicated hardware is used within the communication controller to identify and decode control data with message passing information passed to the message passing state machines. This hardware decode logic tests the network stream directly as it is being received. This is in contrast to the software configuration where the data must be received in the intermediate buffer before the processor can read and test the data.

Along with the control mechanisms, data movement optimisations are investigated. The hardware solution uses zero-copy Direct Memory Access (DMA) operations for all data movements across the network, with data moved directly between the network and application memory. This is in contrast to the software system where the processor copies data between the network buffer and the application memory.

4. Implementation Evaluation and Comparison

The two approaches have been evaluated in order to measure the performance a hardware application can expect for FPGA to FPGA communications. The experimental configuration consists of Xilinx ML402 development boards, hosting a Virtex4Sx35-10 FPGA, interconnected across either a Gigabit Netgear GS608 or 100Mb Netgear FS108 switch. 100Mb Ethernet tests investigate if the use of Gigabit Ethernet is warranted for each approach. All hardware applications operate at 100MHz with results based on experiment elapsed times as recorded by a hardware application counter. The results will first be presented with conclusions drawn after they have been presented.

4.1. Latency Comparison

A ping-pong test measures the latency for exchanging a minimum sized message between two hardware applications. As part of the experiment message passing functionality was controlled to provide additional measurements on the interconnect and communication overheads. Four configurations were looked at

No Flow Control, No MP Synchronisation: Measures the physical interconnect latency by exchanging only data packets.

Flow Control, No MP Synchronisation: Measures the overheads introduced by the communication protocol operations.

No Flow Control, MP Synchronisation: Quantifies the message passing synchronisation overheads in terms of the interconnect performance

Flow Control, MP Synchronisation: The latency to stably exchange a minimum sized packet between two FPGA nodes.

The results, presented in Figure 5 and Figure 6, show that the hardware solution has the lowest latency across all the configurations, which is attributable to its at wire data testing. The various additional operations for exchanging a packet are quantified, with

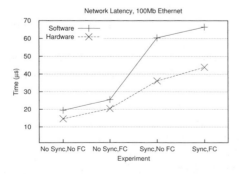

Figure 5. Latency Comparison, 100Mb Ethernet

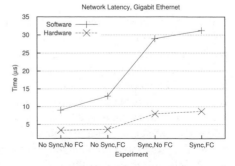

Figure 6. Latency Comparison, Gigabit Ethernet

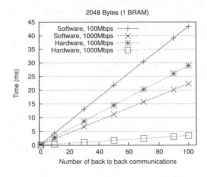

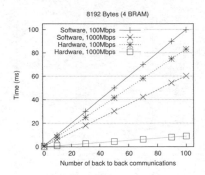

Figure 7. 2048 Bytes, 1 Block RAM   **Figure 8.** 8192 Bytes, 4 Block RAM

synchronisation operations presenting the largest component of a message exchange. This is caused by an inability to utilise the network while awaiting a response packet.

4.2. Block RAM Communication Performance

The HDL MP API is configured to interface with application block RAMs and this experiment measures the time taken to exchange messages when the data is store in these application memories. The experimental configuration is a modified latency experiment using larger message sizes. The experiment does not use the ping-pong style of communication and rather sends a continuous stream of a given size from one node to the other before reversing the process after the number of back to back communications.

Different back to back communication sizes are used across a range of block RAM sizes. The size of the message does not attempt to match efficiently with the network, rather it measures the performance of some possible application block RAM sizes. The one way trip time to send a given block RAM size a given number of times are shown in Figure 7 and Figure 8. Depending on the application requirements, these figures represent the time an application can expect to spend sending the given message sizes.

4.3. Network Bandwidth comparisons

Network bandwidth efficiency measures the time taken to exchange a set amount of data using a defined message size. For the experiment 100,000,000 bytes are exchanged such that a message size of 1,000 bytes requires 100,000 communications, etc. Unidirectional and bidirectional communication bandwidths are measured, with the results presented in Figure 9 and Figure 10. A maximum message size of 95,000 bytes is used as memory is provided by block RAM.

From the results, the hardware setup for both unidirectional and bidirectional communications provides 90% efficient network bandwidth to the HDL MP API when running across the Gigabit network and 95% efficiency across 100 Mb Ethernet network. Quantifying the software efficiency performance however is harder. Its efficiency ranges from 95% on the 100 Mb unidirectional interconnect to 7% on the Gigabit bidirectional interconnect. The software performance drop off equates to only a 5 Mbps difference between the 100Mb bidirectional and Gigabit bidirectional performance.

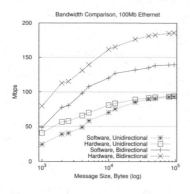
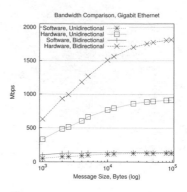

Figure 9. 100Mb Network Bandwidth Comparison   **Figure 10.** Gigabit Network Bandwidth Comparison

4.4. Results Discussion

From the programming perspective, the implementation architecture is not a concern, as the HDL MP API hides the implementation from the digital logic application. However from an algorithm perspective, the hardware message passing approach provides the best performance with the lowest latencies and highest bandwidths.

From the results, the 100Mb unidirectional hardware and software bandwidth efficiencies report equivalent performance, 93Mbps (93% efficient). This is attributable to the software memory aligned copies as to the fact the hardware has saturated the interconnect. The difference in performance between the software 100Mb and Gigabit solutions is also of interest. When looking at raw performance both achieve approximately 140Mbps when performing bidirectional message passing operations. The software performance drop is caused by the limit on-chip interconnect bandwidth of the software solution, i.e. single access vs. burst accesses of the hardware solution. Apart from a lower latency, the use of either interconnect gives the same performance so if cost is a concern, the use of a slower interconnect may be appropriate.

Although the hardware represents the best performance across the range of experiments, this performance comes at great implementation cost with the hardware taking many times longer to implement and test than the software solution. The implementations was designed to remain portable across a range of FPGAs and this is seen from the use of Ethernet which is implemented on the FPGA logic without special dedicated FPGA hardware, MGTs etc., and also through the use of a soft processor which allows the system to run on any FPGA which has the logic to house the software solution.

The FPGA resource utilisation is presented in Table 1, with resource availability

Table 1. Resource utilisation range across the various tests

Resource	Hardware Configuration	Software Configuration
Slices (15360)	4599(30%) - 4646(30%)	4741(31%) - 4827(31%)
Block RAMs (192)	20(10%) - 76(40%)	31(16%) - 87(45%)
DSP48s (192)	0	3(2%)
Frequency	100 MHz	100 MHz
Software	N/A	12,396 Bytes

in brackets. From the results, only a slight difference exists in logic usage between the approaches however the extra storage requirements of the software solution increase its Block RAM usage. The results list the range difference between the experiments.

5. Conclusions and Future Work

Two message passing configurations were evaluated to measure the performance they provide a digital logic application as part of an FPGA cluster, with the evaluation taking the form of microbenchmarks. The evaluation results show that a hardware implementation allows an application to capitalise on the interconnect resources that are available. This is seen by the high bandwidth, low latency results that this approach achieves. Processor based solutions, introduced in the related work would benefit from using a hardware approach to achieve the best use of the available interconnects.

Two dedicated solutions have been investigated but a hybrid solution which uses the hardware DMA operations with the software solution are proposed to see how this affects performance. It would be useful to look at increasing the amount of memory present on each FPGA node. The message size for the bandwidth experiment was limited based on the accessible on-chip memory of the nodes.

References

[1]   F. Belletti, M. Guidetti, A. Maiorano, F. Mantovani, S. F. Schifano, et al.,"Janus: An FPGA-Based System for High-Performance Scientific Computing,"*Computing in Science & Engineering,*vol. 11, 2009.
[2]   Ling Zhuo, Viktor K. Prasanna, "Scalable and Modular Algorithms for Floating-Point Matrix Multiplication on FPGAs," in *18th International Parallel and Distributed Processing Symposium,* 2004.
[3]   Jörg Schmittler, Sven Woop, Daniel Wagner, Wolfgang J. Paul, Philipp Slusallek, "Realtime ray tracing of dynamic scenes on an FPGA chip," in *Proceedings of the ACM SIGGRAPH/EUROGRAPHICS conference on Graphics hardware,* 2004.
[4]   Marc Snir, Steve Otto, Steven Huss-Lederman, David Walker, Jack Dongarra, *MPI-The Complete Reference Volume 1, The MPI Core,* 2nd ed.   The MIT Press, 1998.
[5]   Manuel Saldaña, Paul Chow,"TMD-MPI: An MPI Implementation For Multiple Processors Across Multiple FPGAS,"in *16th International Conference on Field Programmable Logic and Applications,* 2006.
[6]   Christopher John Comis, "A High-speed Inter-process Communication Architecture for FPGA-based Hardware Acceleration of Molecular Dynamics," Master's thesis, University of Toronto, 2005.
[7]   Ron Sass, William V. Kritikos, Andrew G. Schmidt, Srinivas Beeravolu, Parag Beeraka, Kushal Datta, David Andrews, Richard S. Miller, Daniel Stanzione Jr., "Reconfigurable Computing Cluster (RCC) Project: Investigating the Feasibility of FPGA-Based Petascale Computing," in *2007 International Symposium on Field-Programmable Custom Computing Machines,* 2007.
[8]   Rob Baxter, Stephen Booth, Mark Bull, Geoff Cawood, James Perry, Mark Parsons, Alan Simpson, Arthur Trew, Andrew McCormick, Graham Smart, Ronnie Smart, Allan Cantle, Richard Chamberlain, Gildas Genest, "Maxwell - a 64 FPGA Supercomputer," FHPCA, Tech. Rep., 2007.
[9]   Cesar Pedraza, Emilio Castillo, Javier Castillo, Cristobal Camarero, José L. Bosque, José I. Martínez, Rafael Menendez, "Cluster architecture based on low cost reconfigurable hardware," in *18th International Conference on Field Programmable Logic and Applications,* 2008.
[10] Eoin Creedon, Michael Manzke,"Scalable High Performance Computing on FPGA Clusters Using Message Passing," in *18th International Conference on Field Programmable Logic and Applications,* 2008.
[11] "MPICH2:   High-performance   and   Widely   Portable   MPI,"   March   2009, http://www.mcs.anl.gov/research/projects/mpich2/.
[12] Jon Postel, "RFC 793 - Transmission Control Protocol," Tech. Rep., 1981.
[13] "Ethernet   MAC   10/100Mbps,   OPENCORES.ORG,"   May   2009, http://opencores.org/?do=project&who=ethmac.

Parallel Computing: From Multicores and GPU's to Petascale
B. Chapman et al. (Eds.)
IOS Press, 2010
© *2010 The authors and IOS Press. All rights reserved.*
doi:10.3233/978-1-60750-530-3-592

RAPTOR – A Scalable Platform for Rapid Prototyping and FPGA-based Cluster Computing

Mario PORRMANN, Jens HAGEMEYER, Johannes ROMOTH,
Manuel STRUGHOLTZ, and Christopher POHL [1]
Heinz Nixdorf Institute, University of Paderborn, Germany

Abstract. A number of FPGA-based rapid prototyping systems for ASIC emulation and hardware acceleration have been developed in recent years. In this paper we present a prototyping system with distinct flexibility and scalability. The designs will be described from an architectural view and measurements of the communication infrastructure will be presented. Additionally, the properties of the system will be shown using examples, that can be scaled from a single-FPGA-implementation to a multi-FPGA, cluster based implementation.

Introduction

In the process of developing microelectronic systems, a fast and reliable methodology for the realization of new architectural concepts is of vital importance. Prototypical implementations help to convert new ideas into products quickly and efficiently. Furthermore, they allow for the development of hardware and software for a given application in parallel, thus shortening time to market. FPGA-based hardware emulation can be used for functional verification of new MPSoC architectures as well as for HW/SW co-verification and for design-space exploration [1,2,3]. The rapid prototyping systems of the RAPTOR family that have been developed in the System and Circuit Technology group in Paderborn during the last ten years, provide the user with a complete hardware and software infrastructure for ASIC and MPSoC prototyping. A distinctive feature of the RAPTOR systems is that the platform can be easily scaled from the emulation of small embedded systems to the emulation of large MPSoCs with hundreds of processors.

1. RAPTOR-X64 – A Platform for Rapid Prototyping of Embedded Systems

The rapid prototyping system RAPTOR-X64, successor of RAPTOR2000 [4], integrates all key components to realize circuit and system designs with a complexity of up to 200 million transistors. Along with rapid prototyping, the system can be used to accelerate

---

[1]This work was partly supported by the Collaborative Research Center 614 – Self-Optimizing Concepts and Structures in Mechanical Engineering – University of Paderborn.

computationally intensive applications and to perform partial dynamic reconfiguration of Xilinx FPGAs.

RAPTOR-X64 is designed as a modular rapid-prototyping system: the base system offers communication and management facilities, which are used by a variety of extension modules, realizing application-specific functionality. For hardware emulation, FPGA modules equipped with the latest Xilinx FPGAs and dedicated memory are used. Prototyping of complete SoCs is enabled by various additional modules providing, e.g., communication interfaces (Ethernet, USB, FireWire, etc.) as well as analog and digital I/Os. The local bus and the broadcast bus, both embedded in the baseboard architecture, add up to a powerful communication infrastructure that guarantees high speed communication with the host system and between individual modules, as depicted in figure 1. Furthermore, direct links between neighboring modules can be used to exchange data with a bandwidth of more than 20 GBit/s.

For communication with the host system, either a PCI-X interface or an integrated USB-2.0 interface can be used. Both interfaces are directly connected to the local bus, thus creating both a closely coupled, high speed, PCI-X based communication, or a loosely coupled, USB based communication. As configuration and application data can either be supplied directly from the host system or stored on a compact flash card, standalone operation is also supported. Therefore, the system is especially suitable for infield evaluation and test of embedded applications. In addition to these features, RAPTOR-X64 offers several diagnostic functions: besides monitoring of the digital system environment (e.g., status of the communication system), relevant environmental information like voltages and temperatures are recorded. All system clocks are fine-grain adjustable over the whole working range, allowing for running hardware applications at ideal speed.

The latest FPGA module that is currently available for RAPTOR-X64 (called DB-V4) hosts a Xilinx Virtex-4 FX100 FPGA and 4 GByte DDR2 RAM (see figure 1). The FPGAs include two embedded PowerPC processors and 20 serial high-speed transceivers, each capable of transceiving 6.5 GBit/s in full duplex. Utilizing these transceivers, four copper-based data links with a throughput of up to 32.5 GBit/s each are realized on the DB-V4 module. By adapting the cabling between the modules, the communication topology can be changed without affecting the communication via the RAPTOR base system. Serial data transmission at data rates of up to 6.5 GBit/s necessitates techniques to maintain signal integrity between the FPGAs. Utilizing all integrated signal integrity features of the FPGA and providing a sophisticated PCB environment

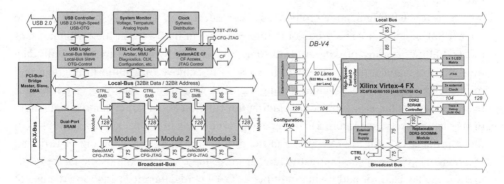

Figure 1. Architecture of the RAPTOR-X64 prototyping system and the FPGA based module DB-V4

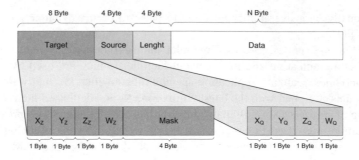

Figure 2. Data-packet format used for communication between the FPGAs.

together with high-end cables and connectors, wire-based communication between the RAPTOR boards is possible up to a distance of two meters at full data-rate.

For easy usage of the high-speed, low-latency communication between the FPGAs, a five-port Rocket-IO switch has been developed and is available as an IP-core. The switch supports non-blocking cut-through operation between Rocket-IO ports, and handles all details of the Rocket-IO based communication such as initialization, channel-bonding, flow-control, error detection, etc. This functionality is built on top of the Xilinx Aurora-protocol. Aurora inherits low-level tasks like bonding multiple Rocket-IOs to a single lane, clock and data recovery, and error detection via 8B/10B encoding mechanisms. It implements an easy to use data and control interface that can be interfaced by the higher layers of the user-protocol.

A generic on-chip interface allows for easy integration of the switch into every design. Futhermore, for integration in a processor-centric design, the switch utilizes a scatter-gather-DMA (SG-DMA) based interface. This implementation enables sending/receiving of packets directly from the processor's main memory (e.g., DDR2-SDRAM), where the processor is only involved in the initialization of the process. The switch implementation is available as an IP-core integrated into the Xilinx EDK. The software libraries allow to access the serial high-speed links similar to other packet-based protocols, e.g., Ethernet, and can easily be integrated into embedded operating systems like Linux.

A custom communication protocol has been developed, which is especially suitable for MPSoC emulation. The protocol is implemented in hardware in the switching fabric, and allows routing of data in up to four dimensions. Switching together with data transmission or reception is executed in parallel to achieve maximum throughput and minimal latency. Besides efficient routing algorithms, a custom data-packet format has been defined for the new protocol, including information about target, source and length of the data packets (see figure 2). Target and source fields in the packet header represent the coordinates of the FPGA-module in the global structure, thus enabling fast routing mechanisms for the desired infrastructure. A mask-field, which extends the target information can be used for addressing multiple FPGA-boards, therefore enabling the use of multicasts or broadcasts.

2. RAPTOR-XPress – A Highly Scalable Rapid Prototyping Platform

RAPTOR-X64 together with the proposed Virtex-4 modules can be used to set up FPGA-based systems with dozens of high-end FPGAs and a high-speed communication infrastructure between the FPGAs. With an increasing number of FPGAs however, the requirements on monitoring and debugging steadily increase, requiring high-bandwidth communication between each individual FPGA and the host computers. Furthermore, in the RAPTOR-X64-based environment, the topology between the FPGAs can only be changed by adapting the cabling. Therefore, the next generation of RAPTOR systems has been developed – RAPTOR-XPress, which will facilitate FPGA-based cluster computing with hundreds of FPGAs connected by a very flexible communication infrastructure. The RAPTOR-XPress base board (see figure 3) can be equipped with up to four daughterboards and provides extensive capabilities for system management and communication. The host connection is realized using eight PCI Express 2.0 channels. Using a dedicated PCI Express switch on the base board, each daughterboard can access the full bandwidth of 32 GBit/s to the host, allowing for a fast, low-latency access of the host CPU to each FPGA in the system. A PCIe to local-bus bridge allows for simple bus access to ease porting legacy FPGA designs and to reuse older modules of the RAPTOR family that do not offer PCIe links. Furthermore, interfaces for USB 2.0 high-speed and Gigabit Ethernet are available.

For communication between FPGA modules, the RAPTOR-XPress base board offers direct connections between adjacent modules. This facilitates a ring topology between all modules on one base board with a bandwidth of 80 GBit/s and a latency of less

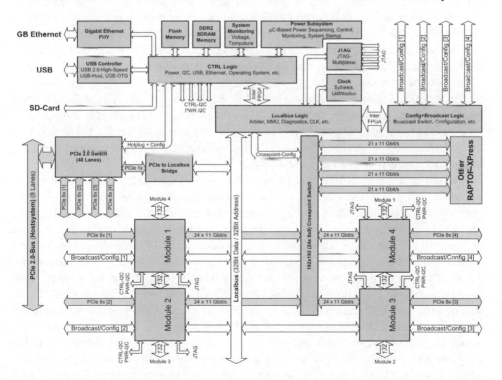

Figure 3. Architecture of the RAPTOR-XPress Baseboard.

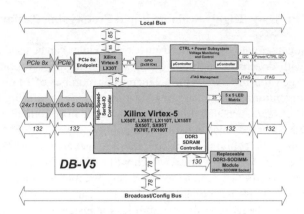

Figure 4. Architecture of the Xilinx Virtex-5-FX-based module DB-V5.

than 10 ns. Furthermore, a central switch, implemented in a dedicated FPGA on the base board, provides the modules with an additional bandwidth of 10 GBit/s in any topology.

For the communication between multiple RAPTOR-XPress base boards four serial high-speed connections are used. The technology is basically the same as for the DB-V4, enabling reuse of the developed protocols and of the switch IPs. The RAPTOR-XPress base board realizes 24 serial high-speed (full duplex) lanes to each module. Each of the four connectors to other RAPTOR-XPress base boards is connected to 21 serial high-speed (full duplex) lanes. Each of these 180 full-duplex lanes offers a bandwidth of 11 GBit/s. The topology of these connections can be changed at runtime using a 180x180 crosspoint switch (1980 GBit/s aggregate bandwidth) on the base board. The first module that realizes the new concepts integrates a Xilinx Virtex-5 FX100T and up to 4 GByte DDR3 memory (see figure 4). The PCIe interface is realized by a dedicated Virtex-5 FX30T on this module.

In addition to the management features of RAPTOR-X64, RAPTOR-XPress integrates advanced temperature monitoring and power management. Supply voltages can be adapted at runtime and power-up sequences for the whole system are controlled by a microcontroller. Voltages are automatically limited to applicable values, to provide maximum compatibility with all existing modules.

Based on the new RAPTOR-XPress system we are currently setting up an FPGA cluster, which will be especially suited for the emulation of large MPSoCs and for high-performance computing since it offers a unique communication infrastructure between the FPGAs and between the FPGAs and the host computers. As depicted in figure 5, the cluster will combine RAPTOR-XPress systems and special FPGA modules with direct connection to the frontside bus (FSB) of the host processor, provided by Nallatech [5]. These FPGA modules can be attached to a socket 604 type CPU socket on an Intel Xeon-based mainboard. This allows to combine the FPGA-module with a normal 7300 (Tigerton) or 7400-series (Dunnington) Intel Xeon CPU on a multi-CPU mainboard. The direct connection to the FSB offers 8.5 GByte/s sustained peak write bandwidth, 5.6 GByte/s sustained peak read bandwidth, and 105 ns latency. Beside the direct connection to the FSB, the FPGAs can communicate with any other FPGA in the cluster using the same serial high-speed links that are used for the connections between multiple Raptor-XPress boards.

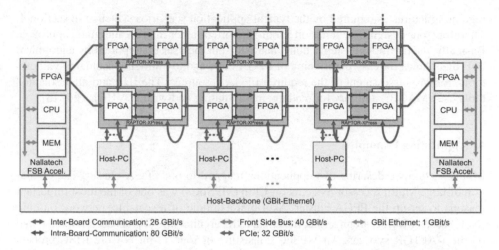

Figure 5. Architecture of the RAPTOR-Xpress-based FPGA cluster, comprising 72 Xilinx Virtex 5 FPGAs

The starting configuration of the cluster consists of 64 Virtex-5 FX100T-2 FPGAs on 16 RAPTOR-XPress systems and 8 Virtex-5 FX200T-2 with FSB-connection. All FPGAs are closely coupled using the proposed high speed serial interfaces, offering a point-to-point bandwidth of 26 GBit/s in a matrix configuration of the crosspoint switch. In total, about 1.3 Million Virtex-5 FPGA slices, 19500 DSP-blocks, 256 GByte DDR3 RAM, 80 MByte BRAM, 12 MByte distributed RAM, 144 integrated PowerPC processors, and 256 GByte of embedded memory are available to the user.

3. Software Environment

For easy and comfortable use of the RAPTOR systems, the software environment Raptor-Suite has been developed, consisting of three layers. The bottom layer, called RaptorLIB, offers a direct interface to the hardware, which is nearly the same for all supported interfaces (USB, PCI, PCI-X, and PCIe, Ethernet), such that an application can easily switch between these protocols. By using the RaptorAPI, remote usage capabilities are added, enabling remote access to the RAPTOR systems using a client/server infrastructure via the local network or the Internet. The graphical user interface RaptorGUI implements comfortable management functionalities and allows basic tests of an application without the need to develop a specific software application based on RaptorLIB/API. Hardware-Software co-verification is further facilitated by a hardware-in-the-loop environment, enabling, e.g., a direct connection between RAPTOR systems and simulators or graphical environments, e.g., Modelsim, Simulink or System Generator [6].

The design-flow for this FPGA based cluster deviates from standard FPGA flows, as an additional partitioning step has to be performed. There are tools available (e.g., Synopsys Certify [7]), which allow for the partitioning of designs for multi-FPGA prototyping environments with a fixed communication infrastructure. For the FPGA cluster, however, this cannot be applied, especially as Certify currently does not support RocketIOs as communication channels. Apart from that, the partitioning algorithm is optimized for prototyping large irregular structures (e.g., singular processors) rather than for regular structures as required by the typical application scenarios sketched in section 4. Therefore, our design-flow relies on a tool-supported rather than an automatic approach. Basically, the partitioning step is done manually, but the user is supported by a graphical IDE that allows for easy partitioning of FPGA code and, by utilizing standard synthesis tools, for easy assessment of the required FPGA resources. The IDE and all associated tools use vMAGIC, a library for reading, manipulating and writing VHDL code [8].

4. Application Examples

In this section we describe two applications mapped to our FPGA cluster. The emulation of large Multiprocessor Systems-on-Chip (MPSoCs) was one of the most important reasons to set up the FPGA cluster. As a first example of a scalable, network on-chip (NoC) based MPSoC architecture, the GigaNetIC architecture [1] has been implemented on the RAPTOR systems. An MPSoC consisting of four 32-bit N-Core RISC processors [1], embedded program and data memory, and the switch box of the NoC can be emulated on the DB-V4. Therefore, GigaNetIC systems with up to 24 embedded processors can be emulated on a single RAPTOR-X64 system. Using simpler NOCs and smaller processors (or processors that are optimized for FPGA implementation like the Xilinx MicroBlaze [2]) the number of processors can easily exceed a hundred.

The second application is an implementation of a neural network based algorithm for hardware accelerated data analysis: Kohonen's self-organizing map (SOM) [9]. SOMs use an unsupervised learning algorithm to form a nonlinear mapping from a given high-dimensional input space to a lower-dimensional (in most cases 2-D) map of neurons. Here, the neurons are emulated by processing elements (PEs), operating in a SIMD (single instruction, multiple data) manner most of the time. The algorithm works as follows:

1. Initialization: The weight vectors $\mathbf{m_i}$ of all neurons N_i need to be initialised, this is often done by assigning random values:

$$\forall_{i,j}\, m_{i,j} = rand[0...1], \tag{1}$$

where j denotes the components of the vector $\mathbf{m_i}$.

2. Search bestmatch: A vector $\mathbf{x}(t)$ is randomly selected from X and the distance between $\mathbf{x}(t)$ and all $\mathbf{m}_i$ is calculated. The neuron with the smallest distance to the input is called bestmatch (BM).

$$\|\mathbf{x} - \mathbf{m}_{bm}\| = \min_{\forall_i} \|\mathbf{x} - \mathbf{m}_i\| \tag{2}$$

3. Adaptation: The weight vectors $\mathbf{m}_i$ are adjusted to the input $\mathbf{m_i}$ according to their distance to the bestmatch in the grid.

$$\forall_i\, \mathbf{m}_i(t+1) = \mathbf{m}_i(t) - |\mathbf{m}_i(t) - \mathbf{x}(t)| \cdot h_{ci}, \tag{3}$$

$$\text{where } h_{ci} = h_{ci}(t, \|N_i - N_{BM}\|) \tag{4}$$

The so called neighborhood function h_{ci} is a function that decreases in space and time, often a Gauss-kernel is chosen.

For an optimal resource utilization on different systems, two different versions of the algorithm have been implemented on the RAPTOR systems. The algorithm itself reveals two inherent degrees of parallelism: all neurons perform the same operations on the same data vectors (neuron-parallel), and all vector components are processed in parallel (component parallel), respectively. For the neuron-parallel approach, up to 512 processing elements can be realized on RAPTOR-X64. The rather more complex and slightly less resource efficient neuron- *and* component-parallel approach is used on the RAPTOR-XPress cluster, mainly for one reason: utilizing all 64 compute FPGAs of the cluster, a total of $128 \times 64 = 8192$ PEs may be instantiated using the cluster. The largest maps currently in use at our department consist of 1600 neurons; therefore, approx. 80% of the cluster could not be utilized using this architecture. The neuron- and component-parallel approach, however, can utilize the complete processing power, because several processing elements can be assigned to the emulation of one neuron. Measurements in comparison with an Intel Core2 Duo processor running at 2.5 GHz show a speed-up of about 10 for RAPTOR-X64 and a speed-up of more than 80 for the RAPTOR-XPress cluster.

5. Conclusion

FPGA-based prototyping systems have been proposed, which offer emulation capacities ranging from typical embedded processor architectures to next-generation high-end MP-SoCs. A tightly integrated cluster of FPGAs, together with a software environment for architecture mapping, monitoring, and debugging enables the fast analysis of MPSoCs with hundreds or even thousands of processors. Furthermore, the close coupling of the cluster to the host PCs via PCIe and especially via the frontside bus of the processors enables the development of powerful hardware accelerators, e.g., to speed-up large scientific simulations.

References

[1] J.-C. Niemann, C. Puttmann, M. Porrmann, and U. Rückert. Resource Efficiency of the GigaNetIC Chip Multiprocessor Architecture. *Journal of Systems Architecture (JSA)*, 53:285–299, 2007.

[2] A. Krasnov, A. Schultz, J. Wawrzynek, G. Gibeling, and P.-Y. Droz. RAMP Blue: A Message-Passing Manycore System in FPGAs. In *Proc. of FPL2007*, pages 54–61, 2007.

[3] Annapolis Micro Systems, Inc. Heterogeneous Processing Platform – FPGA Solutions for the IBM Blade Center, White Paper: 200905.01, 20 May 2009.

[4] Heiko Kalte, Mario Porrmann, and Ulrich Rückert. A Prototyping Platform for Dynamically Reconfigurable System on Chip Designs. In *Proc. of the IEEE Workshop Heterogeneous Reconfigurable Systems on Chip (SoC)*, 2002.

[5] C. Petrie. A review of the FPGA high performance computing industry and the future role of FPGAs within data-centric processing architectures. In *Proc. of the Many-core and Reconfigurable Supercomputing Conference*, 2008.

[6] C. Paiz, C. Pohl, and M. Porrmann. Hardware-in-the-Loop Simulations for FPGA-Based Digital Control Design. *Informatics in Control, Automation and Robotics*, 3:355–372, 2008.

[7] Synplicity. Certify ASIC prototyping solution. online.

[8] Christopher Pohl, Carlos Paiz, and Mario Porrmann. vMAGIC - Automatic Code Generation for VHDL. *International Journal of Reconfigurable Computing*, Special Issue ReCoSoC:7, 2009.

[9] Teuvo Kohonen. *Self-Organizing Maps*, volume 30 of *Springer Series in Information Sciences*. Springer, Berlin, Heidelberg, second edition, 1997.

Parallel Computing: From Multicores and GPU's to Petascale
B. Chapman et al. (Eds.)
IOS Press, 2010
© *2010 The authors and IOS Press. All rights reserved.*
doi:10.3233/978-1-60750-530-3-600

Speeding up combinational
synthesis in an FPGA cluster

César PEDRAZA [a], Javier CASTILLO [a] José Ignacio MARTÍNEZ [a] Pablo HUERTA [a]
José Luis BOSQUE [b] and Javier CANO [a]

[a] *Departamento de ATC y CCIA, Universidad Rey Juan Carlos*
[b] *Departamento de Eletrónica y Computadores, Universidad de Cantabria*

Abstract. One important issue in the evolvable hardware area is speeding up the combinational circuits synthesis. This can be mainly achieved by using genetic programming techniques combined with parallel systems implementations. This paper presents a parallel genetic program for combinational circuits synthesis implemented specifically for an FPGA cluster. This implementation accelerates the computation of the fitness function by a x400 factor. The experiments test the algorithm and the cluster architecture performance in comparison with the Altamira HPC cluster. Results show that the FPGA cluster architecture delivers an interesting high performance for combinational circuit synthesis of systems with more than eight variables. Being able to tune some parameters can greatly help the algorithms to find new optimized implementations in area or speed.

Keywords. FPGA, Combinational Synthesis, Cluster

1. Introduction

The evolutionary algorithms are optimization and search methods based on biological evolution, that use the bio-inspired concepts of mutation, reproduction, recombination and selection. The genetic algorithms (GA) and genetic programming (GP) are common evolutionary algorithms suitable to solve long and non-linear search space problems. This is the case of combinational synthesis, where the goal is to get the best possible digital hardware implementation of a function or truth table for a programmable device or ASIC [1],[2],[3],[4]. Using GP to solve boolean synthesis problems allows the designer to include more restrictions, like area, power consumption and critical path, in order to obtain solutions that could not be reached with traditional synthesis methods. Also related with the boolean synthesis is the evolvable hardware (EH), that can change its internal structure in order to adapt itself to new conditions or to an special environment [5]. Two important topics of this kind of systems are [6]: an evolvable algorithm responsible of establishing the way the hardware should change, and a reconfigurable system that changes its internal hardware modifying the configuration bitstream of a programmable logic device based on the stream obtained with the evolvable algorithm. This paper presents an evolutionary algorithm implemented on an FPGA cluster for solving the combinational on-chip synthesis problem using parallel genetic programming as evolvable algorithm as a part of an evolvable system. Special emphasis is put on showing the performance of the architecture and adapting the algorithm. Section two describes the combinational on-chip synthesis problem. Section three connects concepts related with parallel genetic algorithms with digital hardware synthesis. Section four shows the most relevant facts of the developed FPGA cluster architecture. Finally, sections five and six describe experiments and results, and the conclusions and future work .

2. Combinational synthesis onchip

Combinational synthesis is a design flow process that optimizes and reduces the logic gate networks of a circuit in order to minimize chip area and increase performance. There are many techniques available for combinational synthesis such as the Karnaugh maps, the Quine-McCluskey algorithm, the Reed-Muller algorithm and also heuristic methods. In general terms, these algorithms have disadvantages like exponential growth, lack of restrictions management and multiple solutions for the same problem. On the other hand, genetic algorithms and genetic programming produce new structures for the implementation of combinational blocks that cannot be obtained with the traditional methods [3],[4],[7] and let us add some restrictions to the algorithm such as delay, area, etc. to obtain better results for each problem. When implemented on-chip, the combinational synthesis main problem is the great computational overload of making the circuit to evolve in the design space, especially for embedded systems. There are some intrinsic implementations of combinational synthesis using genetic algorithms (GA) and genetic programming (GP) but with a very low limited number of variables [8] and mainly oriented to obtain a few basic structures. There are also efforts for improving the management of restrictions and increasing the number of variables with GA [5] or GP [3], and mainly suggesting new hardware architectures and representations of the chromosome.

3. Genetic programming and the boolean synthesis

In the evolutive process, the hardware is represented with a chromosome and managed with the Darwinian concept of natural selection [2]. The chromosomes mutates and cross with other chromosomes for creating a population of individuals to evolve. As in nature, a population of individuals is generated. The fitness function evaluates which individuals are suitable for accomplishing the target function requirements and later, a selection process excludes some members whilst the rest mutate and are crossed creating a new next generation. This process is repeated until a population that accomplishes the requirements and restrictions of the target function is obtained. In hardware terms these restrictions usually are 1) getting the appropriate input-output behavior and 2) the minimum number of logic gates. Other restrictions that can be added are propagation delays, type of logic gates available, etc. For hardware synthesis there are some modifications to the evolvable algorithm that has to be done, using a variation of the simple genetic algorithm (SGA) known as genetic programming (GP) . The GP [2][7]is a technique based on genetic algorithms that does not distinguish the search space nor the representation space of the chromosome, and is able to modify the chromosome length and create new mutating and crossing operators. The programs that are evolving can be represented linearly or by trees, being the tree option is the most interesting one for combinational synthesis.

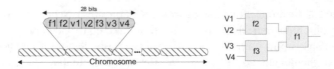

Figure 1. Cell structure and its representation inside the chromosome.

3.1. Chromosome representation

Finding the most appropriate codification for a hardware structure is one of the most important issues in the design process of an EH system. The codification is how a logic circuit is represented using a bit array so that can be managed in the evolution process. There are many conditions that should be fulfilled by a good genetic representation [9]: 1) it must be able to represent all the different solutions of the problem, 2) the crossing and mutating operators should not generate unreal individuals and 3) it must cover all the solution space so the search is really random. There are many different ways of representing combinational hardware for a GP: tree-based representation, 2-D representations, Cartesian representations, PLD-like structure representations and so on [2]. For simplicity, a basic tree structure that allows representing a single boolean function or up to three functions with four input variables coded in binary has been selected. Figure 1 shows the cell structure and the way it is coded inside the chromosome. It has been used 4 bits for representing each boolean function, and 4 bits for representing each input variable. Initially, the chromosome will be composed by one basic cell, after a number of generations if the objective function is not accomplished another cell will be inserted.

It is worth mentioning that the chromosome length has to be variable because the length of the solution to the synthesis problem is unknown. Alander [10] says, based on empirical studies, that a population sized between l and $2l$ is enough for getting the solution for the majority of the evolvable problems, being l the size of the chromosome. This means that if the chromosome length is variable it is probable that the size of the population is also going to be variable. This flexible representation allows to solve up to 5-level minimization problems depending on the complexity of the problem.

3.2. Fitness function.

Finding the appropriate fitness function is another difficult problem in designing evolvable systems because it is the responsible to quantifying the way a chromosome or individual meets the requirements or not. Three parameters have been established for the fitness function: 1) the number of coincidences of the individual X with the target function Y, 2) the number of logic gates of the individual X and 3) the logic circuit levels of the circuit.

$$fitness = \omega_1.\left[\sum_{j=1}^{m}\sum_{i=1}^{n}Y(j,i) - X(j,i)\right] + \omega_2.P(x) + \omega_3.L(x) \tag{1}$$

Equation 1 describes the fitness function for the evolvable systems. The double addition describes the number of n combinations for an individual X that fulfills the objective function Y for m outputs. The $P(X)$ function is used for calculating the number of logic gates of a chromosome taking into account some of the *introns* or segments of the genotype string that will not have any associated function and that do not contribute to the result of the logic circuit they represent. The function $L(X)$ is used to compute the number of levels of the circuit or in other words the number of gates that the critical path crosses. Constants ω_1, ω_2 and ω_3 are used for establishing the weights of each of the parameters that will determine the fitness function.

3.3. Genetic operators.

Selection. It is responsible to identifying the best individuals of the population taking into account the exploitation and the exploration. The first one allows the individuals with better fitness to survive and reproduce more often, and the second one means searching in a wider search space and making possible to find better results. The Boltzman selection method is used for controlling the equilibrium between exploitation and exploration during the execution of the GP by using a temperature factor (T) in a similar way to the simulated annealing method. The equation 2 describes the expected value of an individual as a function of T and the fitness value for an specific iteration or time stamp t.

$$E_{i,t} = \frac{e^{\frac{f(i,t)}{T}}}{\langle e^{\frac{f(i,t)}{T}} \rangle_t} \tag{2}$$

This way an individual is chosen by the number of times its fitness value matches the integer part of the expected value calculated in equation 2.

Mutation. This operator modifies the chromosome randomly in order to increase the search space. It can change: 1) an operator or variable and 2) a segment in the chromosome. Both are executed randomly and with a certain probability. A variable mutating probability during the execution of the algorithm (evolvable mutation) is very appropriate for evolvable systems.

Crossing. This operator combines two selected individuals for obtaining two additional individuals to add to the population. A crossing system with one or two crossing points randomly selected has been implemented because it is more efficient for evolvable systems [1].

3.4. Paralell genetic programming

One of the advantages of evolvable algorithms is its intrinsic parallelism, therefore performance can be increased using more microprocessors, memories and communication systems for the data exchange. A parallel genetic program (PGP) can be implemented in two ways without drastically disturbing its structure: parallelizing the fitness function computation, and executing many evolvable algorithms at a time in different processors, which is equivalent to let many populations evolve in parallel. The performance of the parallel algorithm can be optimized by these three main factors: the topology of the communication infrastructure (ring, completely meshed, master-slave), the ratio of data exchange (the number of the best individuals to exchange increases the probability of finding a better solution) and the migration frequency, because the higher the frequency the individuals are exchanged between nodes in the parallel system the better for finding better solutions in less time.

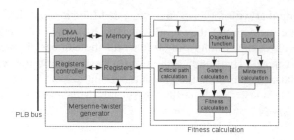

Figure 2. FCU block diagram.

4. Cluster architecture

On previous works [11] the authors have implemented an ad-hoc FPGA cluster called SMILE to accelerate highly demanding computational algorithms. For this new proposal the SMILE cluster has been updated to use the new Xilinx ML507 boards instead of the old VirtexII Pro. This new board includes an XC5VFX70T FPGA with two PowerPC 440 microprocessors. It also has 256MB of DDR2 memory, SystemACE and Gigabit Ethernet connectivity. The custom hardware can be connected to the PowerPC processor through the PLB (Processor Local Bus). The PowerPC processor executes a Linux 2.6 operating system with all the tools and drivers needed to set and manage the system.

Evolutionary Algorithm Acceleration.   The implemented evolutionary algorithm is very intensive from a computational point of view, therefore it demands hardware acceleration on the FPGA fabric. A profiling of the algorithm determined that the most consuming part were the fitness function calculation and the new individual generation (25% and 35% of the execution time, respectively). Therefore, these two has been specifically accelerated with a coprocessor connected to the PowerPC processor. The fitness function is divided into three parts as shown in equation 1 :the minterm coincidence calculation, the number of gates and the number of logic levels (critical path). The FCU (Fitness Calculation Unit) is the element which calculates the three parameters using the objective function, the chromosome and the number of variables as inputs. This coprocessor is connected to the PowerPC 440 processor through the PLB bus using a custom interface. The interface allows register-based and DMA communication to transfer the objective function and the chromosome in an efficient way. Figure 2 shows the FCUs structure. Once the chromosome has been read, each of its basic cells are converted to their equivalent in LUT (Look Up Table) through a ROM based translation and implemented over a virtual-LUT architecture. The next block, computes the minterm value (number of hits of that individual) using the information from the objective function and a counter as inputs. The calculation of the gates number and the logic levels are done in the corresponding blocks and then sent to the fitness calculation block in order to calculate the final fitness value which will be sent back to the PowerPC processor. Finally, in order to accelerate the new generation of individuals, a Mersenne-Twister-based pseudo random number generator were inserted through the registers of the PLB interface, accelerating the generation of new individuals and the mutation process.

5. Experiments and results.

To determine the system performance a 2, 4 and 6-bit comparator have been implemented in two different versions. The first one parallelizes the fitness function, the Evolutionary Engine (EE) is executed in one node (master) and the fitness evaluation is distributed between nodes. The master node is the responsible to generating the population and the mutation and cross operations. The second version executes different algorithms in parallel in 16 SMILE nodes, where the master node sends the objective function and receives the partial solutions. With this information the master node force the selected individuals to migrate to find better solutions. Several tests have been carried out with different populations and different migration rates. The main goals are to calculate the cluster speed-up and to try different number of variables (4, 8 and 12) to be able to compare the results with traditional implementations.

5.1. FCU unit performance.

Figure 3(b) shows the evaluation time on SMILE for different populations with 15 logic gates chromosomes and different number of variables. A significant growth in the evaluation time can be seen for executions with more than 12 variables due to the exponential growth of the input combinations. The SMILE performance is compared with the Altamira HPC made up of 512 processors with a peak performance of 4.5 Gflops. Figure 3(a) shows the response time in Altamira HPC. It is worth mentioning an increment of the evaluation time for 8-bit problems in Altamira when compared with 4-bit problems and to the cluster node evaluation time.

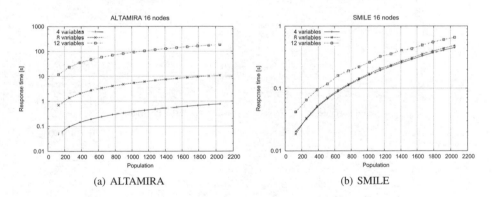

(a) ALTAMIRA   (b) SMILE

Figure 3. Response time for 4, 8 and 12 variables, running 100 generations.

The FPGA resources used by the FCU are 448 slices out of 13696, and the maximum operating frequency is 112 MHz, optimal for the 100 MHz PLB system clock.

5.2. Speed-up and cluster performance.

For the second version of implementation, table 1 shows the response time for Altamira HPC running the genetic program with 8 and 128 individuals, and 100 generations. Table 1 shows the SMILE response time for the same configurations. We can observe a significant difference in response time, more than 2 order of magnitude. The speed-up number was computed for SMILE compared with the Altamira HPC cluster, for 16 nodes with 4, 8 and 12 variables. As shown in figure 4 the SMILE cluster performance is up to 3 times higher than Altamira HPC cluster for 4-variable problems, 40 times higher for 8-variable and 400 times for 12-variable problems with a population of 200 or 600 individuals. A decrease in performance is shown when population increases, because the processing time of the software implemented functions becomes the key factor . Other experiments proved that the speedup for version one is almost 10 times smaller than in version 2, due to the time spent in communication, crossover, individual generation, and other processes not parallelized.

Table 1. Response time in seconds for ALTAMIRA HPC and SMILE (100 generations).

	4 vars		8 vars		12 vars	
ALTAMIRA HPC						
Individuals	1 node	16 nodes	1 node	16 nodes	1 node	16 nodes
128	0.75	0.0488	10.23	0.69	172.91	11.69
2048	11.64	0.77	163.11	10.87	2779.42	186.76
SMILE						
128	0.2855	0.0203	0.2982	0.0186	0.4409	0.0419
2048	30.5697	0.4506	34.6155	0.4860	43.1843	0.6562

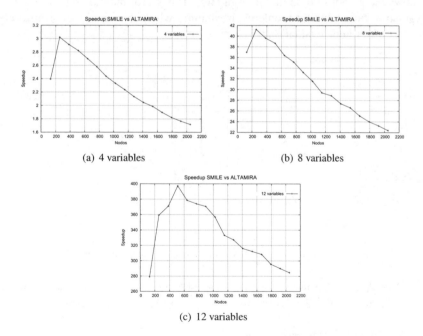

(a) 4 variables

(b) 8 variables

(c) 12 variables

Figure 4. Speed-up for SMILE vs ALTAMIRA with 16 nodes.

Tests with 4 and 6-bit functions were implemented varying the constants ω_2 and ω_3 of the fitness function to obtain synthesis results optimized for number of gates and level of gates. Table 2 shows the results for these different efforts for a 2 and 3-bit comparator.

Table 2. Synthesis results for 2, 3 and 4-bit comparator (4, 6 and 8 bit problems).

	2 bit comparator		3 bit comparator		4 bit comparator	
Effort	Gates	Level Max	Gates	Level Max	Gates	Level Max
Gates	10	3	20	4	97	4
Critical path	15	2	78	3	220	3

6. Conclusions

This paper presented an alternative implementation for the combinational synthesis by using genetic parallel programming. An evolutionary algorithm was implemented in a Virtex5 FPGA cluster and compared in performance with an Altamira HPC cluster. In order to accelerate the process a coprocessor was implemented to calculate the fitness function and to generate random numbers, improving the performance when compared with the Altamira HPC implementation for problems with more than 6 bit. The success of the FCU was due to the use of equivalent LUTs for each combination of functions in the basic cell. Virtual-LUT implementations on conventional memory increased the performance instead of using other slower approaches (PLD-oriented implementations or modifying FPGA configuration memory by dynamic partial reconfiguration). The tests have proven that the algorithm is more effective for 4-bit or 8-bit problems (less variables means processing times similar to communication times, therefore decreasing the performance). There have been some convergence problems for 12-bit functions due to that the space search is too long. This could be solved as future work with some improvements in terms of multiple FCUs inside an FPGA, more nodes and others hardware-accelerated genetic operators. The LUT-oriented solutions of the algorithm can be directly mapped on the Virtex5 thanks to partial reconfiguration techniques via ICAP port, allowing the cluster to change itself. As future work, we are working in an evolvable cluster able to accelerate run-time processes of any algorithm.

References

[1] J Miller and P Thomson. Aspects of digital evolution: Evolvability and architecture. *Lecture Notes in Computer Science*, Jan 1998.
[2] J Koza, F Bennett, D Andre, and M Keane. Genetic programming iii: darwinian invention and problem solving. *Evolutionary Computation*, Jan 1999.
[3] S. Cheang, K. Lee, and K. Leung. Applying genetic parallel programming to synthesize combinational logic circuits. *IEEE Trans on Evolutionary Comput.*, 11:503–520, Aug 2007.
[4] L Jozwiak, N Ederveen, and A Postula. Solving synthesis problems with genetic algorithms. *Euromicro Conf.*, Jan 1998.
[5] T Higuchi and B Manderick. Hardware realizations of evol. algorithms. *Evol. Comp. 1*, Jan 2000.
[6] L Sekanina. Evolvable components from theory to hardware implementations. *Natural computing series*, Jan 2000.
[7] A. Macedo N Nedjah. Genetic syst. programming. *Springer*, Jan 2006.
[8] D Goldberg and J Holland. Genetic algorithms and machine learning. *Machine Learning*, Jan 1988.
[9] Q. Yu, C. Chen, and C. Pan. Parallel genetic algoritms on programmable graphics hardware. *Lecture notes in computer science*, Jan 2006.
[10] J Alander. On optimal population size of genetic algorithms. *Proc. CompEuro'92 Computer Syst. and Software Engineering*, Jan 1992.
[11] C Pedraza, E Castillo, J Castillo, and C Camarero. Cluster architecture based on low cost reconfigurable hardware. *Proc. 18th FPL Conf*, Jan 2008.

Parallel Computing: From Multicores and GPU's to Petascale
B. Chapman et al. (Eds.)
IOS Press, 2010
© 2010 The authors and IOS Press. All rights reserved.
doi:10.3233/978-1-60750-530-3-608

A Highly Parallel FPGA-based Evolvable Hardware Architecture

Fabio CANCARE, Marco CASTAGNA, Matteo RENESTO and Donatella SCIUTO

Dipartimento di Elettronica e Informazione, Politecnico di Milano, Italy

Abstract This work describes a new Evolvable Hardware (EHW) system, based on Xilinx Virtex-4 FPGAs, able to exploit two-dimensional dynamic reconfigurability and direct bitstream manipulation. The focus of this paper is on the performance of this new system. It will be shown how the system components have been designed in order to exploit parallelism and to mask the reconfiguration time. The system is compared to similar solutions in order to show its advantages.

1. Introduction

Evolvable Hardware (EHW) is a new and highly multidisciplinary field concerning the creation or the adaption of physical circuits through evolutionary strategies aiming at improving the circuits behavior with respect to a given specification. EHW systems have been successfully used in the past to create complex controllers, filters and to deal with fault recovery and system adaption. The key elements in Evolvable Hardware are the Evolutionary Algorithms (EA) used (e.g. a canonic genetic algorithm) and the programmable logic devices over which the circuits are deployed (e.g. FPGAs).

Evolvable Hardware was introduced at the beginning of the 1990s in the theoretical works by De Garis [1] and Higuchi et al. [2] and, since then, it has constantly gathered the attention of a large number of researchers. In particular, in the last few years, the number of different approaches developed has become so high that some authors decided to propose rigorous classifications [3,4].

The first important classification concerns the solutions evaluation, which can be retrieved in two ways: the first method is known as *extrinsic evolution* and consists in evolving circuits using a simulation environment; this means that the EA relies on simulated evaluations. Once a suitable solution is found, such solution is downloaded to the programmable logic device. In the second method, called *intrinsic evolution*, each candidate solution is directly mapped and evaluated on the target device; the EA relies on actual evaluations. Obviously, the latter method is more accurate, provides better performance and allows to create self-evolvable hardware systems.

According to the level of solutions representation, the design approaches to EHW can be classified into *Gate Level Evolution* (or fine-grained EHW) and *Function Level Evolution*. Fine-grained EHW maximizes exploration by searching in a large solution space (the space of all electronic circuits composed of some particular types of components) providing very efficient solutions to medium-small problems [5]. On the other hand, function-level EHW generally involves selecting topologies and assembling circuits from high-level functional building blocks. Function-level EHW emphasizes the exploitation of functional building block circuits which are known to the researcher to be necessary and sufficient to solve the problem.

By looking at the nature of the programmable logic devices used it is possible to distinguish between *analog EHW systems*, *mixed analog-digital EHW systems* and *digital EHW systems*; in this paper the focus will be on digital EHW systems based on FPGAs.

Among the possible solutions, the one that is explored in this paper concerns the direct manipulation of the Xilinx Virtex-4 [6] configuration bitstreams. The idea is to create a new EHW system able to exploit the advantages offered by these new devices and, in particular, the possibility to make use of the two-dimensional dynamic reconfiguration mechanism [7]. The aim of this paper is to highlight the advantages offered by this system with respect to other similar solutions. In particular it will be shown how the candidate solutions are mapped over the FPGA resources in the new EHW system, how they can be evaluated in parallel and how to mask the reconfiguration time.

The remaining of this paper is structured as follows: Section 2 describes related work. Section 3 presents the proposed EHW architecture, along with the motivations behind the main design choices. Section 4 shows some experimental results obtained using the new EHW systems. Section 5 wraps up the authors conclusions.

2. State of the Art

A very interesting work summarizing the large variety of architectures, devices, algorithms and parameter settings that can be found in the various experiments performed by researchers in the field of Evolvable Hardware has been presented by Torresen in [3]. Although a number of EHW-oriented platforms have been proposed and created (both analog and digital), up to now the majority of the EHW research work has been carried out using FPGAs; this is due to the low cost and high flexibility provided by these devices. In particular, since the first empirical experiment performed by Thompson [8], Xilinx FPGAs have become the most popular platforms for the EHW systems implementation. The main reason behind this choice is the dynamic reconfiguration support provided by several Xilinx FPGA families.

In the first experiment Thompson used an FPGA belonging to the Xilinx XC6200 device family. This family had a number of features allowing the development of EHW systems: the support for partial reconfiguration , a known bitstream data format and a safe configuration scheme making possible to upload any random configuration without damaging the device [9]. Unfortunately it also had several limits, that is why Xilinx decided to stop the development of the XC6200 and introduced a new device family: the Virtex series. These new chips have many of the properties which made the XC6200 series popular in the EHW research community and other new positive characteristics but they also had two limitations: an almost unknown and undocumented bitstream data format and an unsafe configuration schema. In particular the latter drawback makes possible to physically damage the device by connecting two CLB outputs together. Thus, in order to use the new Virtex devices, researchers had to propose solutions capable to overcome these limitations. The various approaches can be broadly divided in two main categories: the ones based on *Virtual Reconfigurable Circuits* (coarse-grained evolution) and those based on the direct manipulation of the bitstream (fine-grained evolution); in this paper the focus will be on the direct bitstream manipulation.

A fine-grained evolution can be obtained through the direct manipulation of the bit-stream. To perform such operation, it is necessary to know how the information is stored within the configuration bitstreams and how to perform partial internal reconfiguration. The first proposed approaches [9, 10] were based on the JBits API. JBits is a set of Java classes which provides an easy way to read and modify the bitstream data. Even if this library provides some interesting features, there are some major limitations [11]: the de-pendence on (few) supported FPGA families and boards and a limited support from Xil-inx. Thus, Upegui and Sanchez, proposed in [11] three possible methods to implement EHW using a Virtex-II Pro FPGA. The first two methods are based on the Xilinx tools and cannot be used to perform an intrinsic hardware evolution. The third method is based on the direct manipulation of the configuration bitstream. The main idea is to manipulate only the LUT equations while keeping a fixed routing. Each individual is composed of cells which are defined as hard-macros using the Xilinx tools; the connectivity among these computing cells is defined by a HDL description of the full system. The overall idea is valid, however, the cells can be improved reducing the FPGA resource require-ments. Moreover, since the device family used is Virtex-II Pro, the dynamic reconfigura-tion is constrained to be one-dimensional. In all their experiments, Upegui and Sanchez worked with just one candidate solution on the FPGA and thus they did not exploit at all reconfiguration masking and multiple solutions evaluation.

Virtex-4 and Virtex-5 devices enable two-dimensional dynamic reconfiguration, a feature which considerably reduces the reconfiguration time and thus the evolution time. In literature there are few works about EHW systems tailored for Virtex-4 or Virtex-5 devices. In [12] Rafla speaks about an EHW system based on Virtex-4 chips. However, no details about the implementation are given at all. Moreover, the author wrongly states that it is not possible to internally reconfigure the FPGA. Other works, like [13] uses VRCs over Virtex-4 devices, thus introducing all the limits described above.

3. Proposed System

The proposed system works as follows: candidate solutions are mapped over a certain number of FPGA resources. The Evolutionary Algorithm chromosome corresponds to the partial bitstream able to configure such resources. Candidate solutions are evaluated on the device and then their configuration is evolved using the traditional genetic opera-tors, crossover and mutation.

The main system components are:

- the evolvable region, which contains the candidate solutions undergoing to the evolutionary process;
- the PowerPC processor, which executes the Evolutionary Algorithm and generates the information for the dynamic partial reconfiguration of the evolvable region;
- the ICAP controller [14], which performs the device internal reconfiguration pro-cess;
- the EHW interface, which provides access to the evolvable region, thus providing the possibility to retrieve and evaluate the outputs of the candidate solutions.

Such system is similar to the one proposed by Upegui and Sanchez in [11]; however, since the target device family is different (Virtex-4 instead of Virtex-II Pro), the evolvable region and the reconfiguration process must be completely re-defined. The following parts of this Section will describe the reasoning behind the bitstream analysis process; then it will be shown how the evolvable region has been structured and finally how the evolvable region has been interfaced with the remaining system components.

3.1. Virtex-4 Bitstream Analysis

For what concerns the reconfiguration process, since the Xilinx Virtex-4 bitstream format is not documented, an accurate analysis was performed in order to understand how to evolve candidate solutions without downloading illegal configurations to the FPGA. In particular, since the candidate solutions within the evolvable region are LUT-based, it was necessary to:

- understand the relationship between the FPGA slice coordinates (X, Y) and the address of the frame containing the configuration information of that slice;
- understand where to find the LUT configuration bits within the frame structure;
- understand how to change the LUT configuration bits safely.

We have developed a framework for parsing and comparing bitstreams and, starting from a valid design, we were able to retrieve all the necessary information by making small changes to the design and then analyzing the changes at the bitstream level.

When a bitstream needs to change the configuration of a FPGA frame, it writes the frame address in the Frame Address Register (FAR). The FAR is composed of five fields: top/bottom (1 Bit), block type (3 Bits), row address (5 bits), major address (8 bits) and minor address (6 bits); the remaining bits of the 32 bits word are not used at the moment. Since the EHW system needs to change the configuration of one or more LUTs within a slice it is necessary to know how to retrieve the frame address from the slice coordinates. Through the bitstream analysis we have derived the following equations:

$$Major = Major(X) = \left\lfloor \frac{x}{2} \right\rfloor + Adj(X)$$

$$Adj(X) = \begin{cases} 1 & \text{if } 0 \leq X \leq 23 \\ 3 & \text{if } 24 \leq X \leq 31 \\ 4 & \text{if } 32 \leq X \leq 47 \end{cases}$$

$$Minor = Minor(X) = \begin{cases} 21 & \text{if X is even} \\ 19 & \text{if X is odd} \end{cases}$$

$$Row = Row(Y) = \begin{cases} 1 & \text{if } 96 \leq Y \leq 127 \text{ or} \\ & \quad 0 \leq Y \leq 31 \\ 0 & \text{if } 32 \leq Y \leq 95 \end{cases}$$

$$Top/Bottom = Top/Bottom(Y) = \begin{cases} 1 & \text{if } 0 \leq Y \leq 63 \\ 0 & \text{if } 64 \leq Y \leq 127 \end{cases}$$

After specifying the frame address, the bitstream writes in the Frame Data Register, Input (FDRI) the configuration of the resources within the frame. Unfortunately the two LUT configuration bytes have not a fixed starting point within the FDRI data flow, their position depends on the cartesian coordinates of the slice they belong to. The following equations state where the LUT configuration bits start when the top/bottom field in the FAR is set to 1 (the equations are similar for the complementary case):

$$BitStart(Y, LUT) = 8 \cdot ByteStart(Y, LUT) + Adj_{Bit}(Y, LUT)$$

$$Adj_{Bit}(Y, LUT) = \begin{cases} 7 \text{ if } LUT == GLUT \ \& \ Y \geq 64 \\ 1 \text{ if } LUT == GLUT \ \& \ Y \leq 63 \\ 0 \text{ otherwise} \end{cases}$$

$$ByteStart(Y, LUT) = 5 \cdot (Y\%32) + Adj_{LUT}(LUT) + Adj_Y(Y)$$

$$Adj_{LUT}(LUT) = \begin{cases} 0 & \text{if } LUT == \text{"FLUT"} \\ 2 & \text{if } LUT == \text{"GLUT"} \end{cases}$$

$$Adj_Y(Y) = \begin{cases} 4 & \text{if } Y\%32 > 15 \\ 0 & \text{if } Y\%32 \leq 15 \end{cases}$$

$$ByteStart(Y, LUT) = \begin{cases} TopByteStart(Y, LUT) & \text{if } Y \geq 64 \\ 162 - TopByteStart(Y, LUT) \\ \quad - Adj_G(LUT) & \text{if } Y \leq 63 \end{cases}$$

$$Adj_G(LUT) = \begin{cases} 0 & \text{if } LUT == \text{"FLUT"} \\ 1 & \text{if } LUT == \text{"GLUT"} \end{cases}$$

Finally, since there is a central 32 bit checksum word in the FDRI data flow that needs to be changed when altering the frame configuration, we needed to figure out how to compute it. Using the framework we were able to find the necessary information, summarized in the following Python function:

```python
def computeWord(Y, LUT, BitPos):
    CheckWord = 704 + BitStart(Y,LUT)
    #Check if it is necessary to add an offset
    if Y>63  and Y%32>7:
        CheckWord += 32
    if Y<=63 and Y%32<=23:
        CheckWord -= 32
    #Computes the odd parity bit
    if len(filter(lambda x: x == '1',bin(CheckWord))) % 2 == 1:
        CheckWord += 0x800
    return CheckWord
```

3.2. Evolvable Region Design

The proposed evolvable region is composed of a variable number of candidate solutions, is managed by the EHW interface and is dynamically reconfigured by the ICAP. A candidate solution is a 8xN bidimensional array of cells, with an 8 bit datapath (as schematized in Figure 1). Every cell has four inputs and one output; cells are organized in columns, cells belonging to column i are connected to cells belonging to column $i+1$. In other words, this architecture is a Cartesian Genetic Programming [15] schema characterized by a static routing. Every column shares the same clock signal. In order to simplify the deployment of an 8-cell column, a hard macro has been created using the Xilinx design tools and, in particular, FPGA Editor [16].

The structure of the EHW system cell is shown in the right side of Figure 1. A cell is equivalent to a 5-input LUT. The first four LUT inputs are the external inputs,

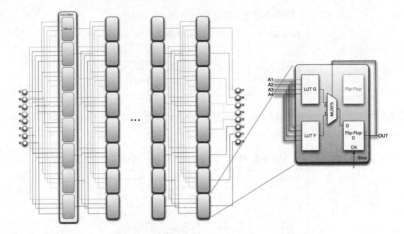

Figure 1. Evolvable Region: structure of a candidate solution

while the last one is represented by the internal flip-flop status. Such 5-input LUT is built using two 4-input LUTs and a multiplexer driven by the flip-flop output. All the needed resources are available in a single Virtex-4 slice (LUT-F, LUT-G and MUXF5). Thus, it is possible to deploy four cells in every FPGA CLB (a CLB contains four slices). In the solution proposed in [11], instead, a single cell, with the same characteristics as the one proposed in this work, needs an entire CLB. By using this new cell structure it is possible to deploy up to 32 cells in the same FPGA frame (a frame contains eight CLBs), that is, it is possible to map a candidate solution composed of four 8-cell columns in a frame.

The number and the size of the candidate solutions within the EHW system depends on the space available on the specific Virtex-4 target device and on the complexity of the aimed functionality. In order to provide flexibility we have decided to create a generator of custom evolvable region. Given the desired number and size of the candidate solutions and the dimension of the target Virtex-4 device the Python script is able to generate the VHDL files allocating the candidate solutions and the EHW Interface IP-core (more details about this component will be given in the next Subsection). Also, the generator produces the system area constraints (in UCF format) for the candidate solutions.

4. Experimental Results

This Section describes the results obtained synthesizing and using the proposed EHW system. In particular, it was decided to create an Evolvable Region characterized by the following parameters:

- number of candidate solutions: **16**
- size of candidate solutions: **8x4 cells**
- number of candidate solutions which can be evaluated in parallel: **4**

The VHDL given as output by the generator described in the previous Section was synthesized using Xilinx ISE [16] for a Virtex-4 XC4VFX12. The maximum frequency of the component is $121 Mhz$ while the occupation data are reported in Table 1.

Then the PLB-based IP-core has been plugged to the PLB bus of a generic system. The other components plugged to the PLB bus are the PPC processor, the DDR con-

Table 1. Evolvable Region occupation data

Resource	Used	Available	% Used
Slice	1,749	5,472	12%
Flip Flops	1,320	10,944	12%
LUT	1,664	10,944	15%

troller, the ICAP controller and the RS-232 controller. The synthesis data of the whole system are reported in Table 2.

Table 2. EHW system occupation data

Resource	Used	Available	% Used
Slice	4,372	5,472	79%
Flip Flops	3,818	10,944	44%
LUT	7,672	10,944	70%

The advantages, in terms of performance, over the most similar solution, the one proposed in [11], can be summarized as follows:

- The resource occupation of the basic cell is reduced to one fourth of the original requirements. The cell expressive power is maintained;
- The introduction of two-dimensional dynamic reconfigurability can reduce reconfiguration time up to one sixteenth. The magnitude of this reduction depends on the number of frames within an FPGA column. In the device used during the experiments there is a 4x improvement;
- The Virtex-4 FPGA family has an Internal Reconfiguration Access Port (ICAP) which can work at $100Mhz$, instead the Virtex-II Pro ICAP can work at most at $66Mhz$;
- Multiple candidate solutions are deployed at the same time within the system. It is possible to evaluate multiple candidate solutions while reconfiguring others candidate solutions. If the evaluation test set is large enough, it is possible to completely mask the reconfiguration time.

It is not possible to provide an analytical performance comparison between this system and other similar solutions because the EHW papers taken into consideration do not report performance data. They just state which kind of circuits they were able to evolve. Using our system we were able to evolve all the applications provided as an example in the reference papers (parity generators, counters, communication channels).

Table 3 shows some analytical data obtained evolving a parity generator. It reports the minimum, maximum and average number of generations created by the Evolutionary Algorithm, the minimum, maximum and average duration of the EA runs, and the percentage of evolution able to converge to a working solution within 10000 generations. If, during the evolution process, no improvements are obtained within 1500 successive generations, the experiment is considered failed.

5. Conclusions

In this work a new Evolvable Hardware system has been described. Such system is able to exploit both the direct manipulation of the configuration bitstreams and the bi-

Table 3. Results obtained evolving parity generators

Bit	Generation Number			Evo. Time [s]			Succ.
	Min	Max	Av.	Min	Max	Av.	
5	86	366	198.5	3.4	14.5	7.9	100%
6	113	581	231.7	8	45.9	18.3	100%
7	117	509	238	18.7	80.5	37.6	100%
8	140	450	243.3	44.2	142	76.8	100%

dimensional reconfiguration mechanism offered by the Virtex-4 FPGA family. Up to now, at the best of our knowledge, there do not exist EHW systems able to take advantage of the 2D reconfiguration capabilities. Plus, none of the current EHW systems based on Virtex-4 devices is able to perform hardware evolution by a direct manipulation of the configuration bitstreams.

References

[1] H. De Garis. Evolvable Hardware: Genetic Programming of a Darwin Machine. In *Artificial Neural Nets and Genetic Algorithms - Proceedings of Int. Conf. on Artificial Neural Nets and Genetic Algorithms*, pages 441–449, 1993.

[2] T. Higuchi, T. Niwa, T. Tanaka, H. Iba, H. de Garis, and T. Furuya. Evolving Hardware with Genetic Learning: A First Step Towards Building a Darwin Machine. In *Proceedings of the second international conference on From animals to animats 2*, pages 417–424. MIT Press, 1993.

[3] J. Torresen. An Evolvable Hardware Tutorial. In *Conference on Field Programmable Logic and Applications*, volume 3203 of *Lecture Notes in Computer Science*, pages 821–830. Springer, 2004.

[4] Ai-Hong Yao, Guo-Yin Zhang, and Lin Guan. A Survey of Dynamically and Partially Reconfigurable FPGA based Self-evolvable Hardware. *CAAI Transactions on Intelligent Systems*, 3(5):436–442, October 2008.

[5] A. Thompson, P. Layzell, and R.S. Zebulum. Explorations in Design Space: Unconventional Electronics Design through Artificial Evolution. *IEEE Trans. Evol. Comp.*, 3(3):167–196, 1999.

[6] Xilinx Inc. Virtex-4 user guide. Technical Report ug070, Xilinx Inc., December 2008.

[7] Xilinx Inc. Virtex-4 configuration user guide. Technical Report ug071, Xilinx Inc., April 2008.

[8] A. Thompson. An Evolved Circuit, Intrinsic in Silicon, Entwined with Physics. In *International Conference on Evolvable Systems*, volume 1259 of *Lecture Notes in Computer Science*, pages 390–405. Springer, 1996.

[9] G. Hollingworth, S. Smith, and A. Tyrrell. Safe Intrinsic Evolution of Virtex Devices. In Jason Lohn, Adrian Stoica, and Didier Keymeulen, editors, *The Second NASA/DOD workshop on Evolvable Hardware*, pages 195–202. IEEE Computer Society, 2000.

[10] Delon Levi and Steve Guccione. GeneticFPGA: Evolving stable circuits on mainstream FPGA devices. In *Evolvable Hardware*, pages 12–17. IEEE Computer Society, 1999.

[11] A. Upegui and E. Sanchez. Evolving Hardware by Dynamically Reconfiguring Xilinx FPGAs. In *International Conference on Evolvable Systems*, volume 3637 of *Lecture Notes in Computer Science*, pages 56–65. Springer, 2005.

[12] N. I. Rafla. Evolvable Reconfigurable Hardare Framework for Edge Detection. In *Circuits and Systems, MWSCAS07. 50th Midwest Symposium on*, pages 65–68, Aug. 2007.

[13] T. Kalganova C. Lambert and E. Stomeo. FPGA-based Systems for Evolvable Hardware. *Transactions on Engineering, Computing and Technology*, 12, March 2006.

[14] Xilinx Inc. Xps hwicap (v1.10.a) product specification. Technical report, Xilinx Inc., October 2007.

[15] J.F. Miller. An Empirical Study of the Efficiency of Learning Boolean Functions Using a Cartesian Genetic Programming Approach. In *Proceedings of the Genetic and Evolutionary Computation Conference*, volume 2, pages 1135–1142, 1999.

[16] Xilinx Inc. *Xilinx ISE 10.1 Design Suite Software Manuals and Help*, 2008.

Parallel Computing: From Multicores and GPU's to Petascale
B. Chapman et al. (Eds.)
IOS Press, 2010
© *2010 The authors and IOS Press. All rights reserved.*
doi:10.3233/978-1-60750-530-3-616

Applying Parameterizable Dynamic Configurations to Sequence Alignment

Tom DAVIDSON [a] , Karel BRUNEEL [a] and Harald DEVOS [a] and
Dirk STROOBANDT [a]

[a] *ELIS, Ghent University, Sint-Pietersnieuwstraat 41, 9000 Gent, Belgium*

Abstract. Hardware acceleration is needed to speed up DNA or protein alignment
while keeping the accuracy of the alignment result high enough. The hardware resources used can be effectively optimized by using a new way of run-time reconfiguration, called parameterizable reconfiguration. In this paper, we show how a
parameterizable configuration can be used to create a run-time reconfigurable implementation of the Smith-Waterman algorithm. This implementation results in a
hardware design that can be implemented on a cheaper FPGA with a performance
penalty due to the reconfiguration overhead.

keywords - DNA Alignment, Run-Time Reconfiguration, FPGA

1. Introduction

In bio-informatics, the comparison of two protein sequences is a prevalent operation to
be performed. It is tackled by the Smith-Waterman algorithm, which selects the region
with the most similarities in both sequences. Due to the huge computation time needed
for the Smith-Waterman algorithm, less accurate heuristic approximations [1] [2] of this
algorithm are used for the alignment of protein sequences. In practice, hardware acceleration significantly improves the runtime and makes the use of the full Smith-Waterman
algorithm viable again. Hence, a more accurate alignment result can be achieved in an
acceptable runtime by using hardware acceleration.

Parameterizable reconfiguration is a method of run-time reconfiguration (RTR) for
FPGAs that was developed within the research group PARIS at Ghent University [3].
Parameterizable reconfiguration enables the design of RTR solutions on a higher abstraction level. Up until now it was only used in proof-of-concept applications. This paper
shows that parameterizable configurations can improve the use of RTR for larger and
real-world applications. In this specific case for the hardware acceleration of the Smith-
Waterman algorithm.

An existing Smith-Waterman algorithm implementation (the FlexWare aligner [4][1])
was converted into an RTR implementation (the RTR aligner) using parameterizable
configurations. Through the usage of RTR, the BRAM usage of the FlexWare aligner
can be reduced. This way cheaper FPGAs with less BRAM become a viable option for
hardware acceleration of the Smith-Waterman algorithm. We compared the RTR aligner
and FlexWare aligner implementations on the Spartan XC3S1600E-4FG484 FPGA. The

---

[1]The FlexWare project is supported by the I.W.T. grant 060068

RTR aligner can instantiate 50 processing elements, 3.57 times more than the FlexWare aligner. This reduces the calculation time by a factor 3.57.

2. Sequence Alignment

Although the Smith-Waterman algorithm can handle both DNA and protein alignments, we will focus our discussion in this paper on DNA alignment, without loss of generality. Deoxyribonucleic acid (DNA) is a helix-structure made out of sequences of nucleotides that have connecting base pairs. These sequences contain genetic data. The information in DNA can be characterized by the sequence of these base pairs. There are four possible base pairs in DNA, each is given a character: adenine (A), cytosine (C), guanine (G) and thymine (T). Comparing two DNA sequences corresponds to comparing the character sequences that characterize these DNA sequences.

The Smith-Waterman algorithm [5] compares two character sequences. The aim of this algorithm is to find similarities, even in the case of insertions, deletions and copying errors. The Smith-Waterman algorithm fills a matrix, the score matrix, that has a character of sequence B assigned to each column and a character of sequence A assigned to each row. The first character of sequence B is B(1), similarly the first character of sequence A is A(1). Sequence B is called the column sequence from now on, similarly sequence A is denoted as the row sequence. Once this matrix is filled, the highest score is selected and trace back is used to find the region with the most similarities in both sequences. The score matrix is filled by solving equation (1) for each score matrix element, $F_{i,j}$. [5]

$$F_{i,j} = Max(F_{i,j}^D, F_{i,j}^V, F_{i,j}^H) \tag{1}$$

where

$$\begin{aligned} F_{i,j}^D &= F_{i-1,j-1} + S(A(i), B(j)) \\ F_{i,j}^V &- \qquad\qquad F_{i-1,j} + \omega \\ F_{i,j}^H &= \qquad\qquad F_{i,j-1} + \omega \end{aligned} \tag{2}$$

F^D takes the matrix element diagonally above and adds a value S. This value S is positive if $A(i)$ and $B(j)$ are the same and negative in case of a mismatch. The values for all possible pairs A(i) and B(j) are described in a substitution matrix. To allow for full protein comparison, the BLOSUM62 substitution matrix was used. The value taken from this matrix is called the substitution cost.

F^V takes the matrix element directly above and adds a gap penalty, ω. F^H does the same but with the element to the left. The maximum of these three values $(F_{i,j}^D, F_{i,j}^V, F_{i,j}^H)$ is then selected and assigned to $F_{i,j}$.

The data dependency of this algorithm (Fig. 1) is clear: to calculate an element of the score matrix one only needs the values left, above and upper left of it. This means that the elements on a antidiagonal of the matrix can be calculated in parallel.

3. Parameterizable Reconfiguration

Parameterizable reconfiguration is a method of FPGA reconfiguration that makes it possible to use RTR from a higher abstraction level in designs. It is suited for applications

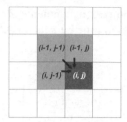

Figure 1. The data dependencies in the Smith-Waterman algorithm [4]

that require a lot of data manipulations where each subsequent manipulation only has a small set of inputs that are different from the previous one.

The inputs that stay constant over a certain time interval can be described as parameters. By not treating these parameters as inputs in the implementation but using their (constant) value in the definition of Look-Up Table (LUT) functions, the implementation can be significantly smaller and also faster than a generic implementation. The LUT configuration bits then become Boolean functions of the parameters and a change in a parameter value results in a (run-time) evaluation of this Boolean function and a reconfiguration of the corresponding LUT configuration bits.

To use parameterizable reconfiguration, a tool flow that allows the design of RTR implementations on a higher abstraction level is needed. The tool chain used here, TMAP flow, was developed by Bruneel et al. [3]. The TMAP flow automatically maps an RTL-design description to an RTR platform. An RTR platform consists of a run-time reconfigurable component, here an FPGA, and a Configuration Manager (CM).

The parameterizable reconfiguration tool flow operates as follows: it starts with a VHDL description at the RTL-level in which some signals are denoted as parameters. From this description, the TMAP flow will then derive a master configuration and a set of special functions, called tuning functions. These functions describe how the master configuration has to be changed to generate an optimized configuration for specific parameter values.

At start up, the CM will use the tuning functions and the master configuration to generate an optimized configuration for the starting values of the parameters. The FPGA will then be configured by the CM. When a parameter changes the CM will use the tuning functions to calculate the new optimized configuration, based on the new parameter values. The tuning functions are Boolean expressions which can be evaluated quickly by the CM.

4. The RTR aligner

4.1. Systolic array

Most hardware acceleration implementations of the Smith-Waterman algorithm are based on systolic arrays. A systolic array is an array of processing elements (PE). Every cycle, each PE takes two inputs from its west neighbor and transfers two outputs to its east neighbor. In detail (Fig. 2), the first PE takes a score of 0 and A(1) as input in the first cycle and calculates $F_{1,1}$ using equation (1). In the next cycle it takes A(2), calculates

$F_{2,1}$, and transfers A(1) and the previously calculated score to the second PE. This PE then uses A(1) and the score of the first PE to calculate $F_{1,2}$.

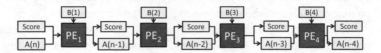

Figure 2. A Systolic array

In this way the complete row sequence is streamed through the systolic array, and every element of the score matrix is calculated. If there are not enough PE's to fully exploit the parallelism, a wrap memory is used to save the output of the last PE. When the first PE finishes its column, it is then started on the first empty column, with the information in the wrap memory as input. The path a PE takes through the score matrix can be seen on Fig 3.

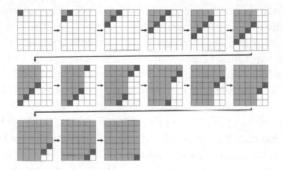

Figure 3. Progress of the PE's in the score matrix during the Smith-Waterman algorithm. [4]

The FlexWare aligner [4] was used as a starting point for the creation of the RTR aligner we propose in this paper. This aligner implements a systolic array as described above; a PE is called SW-Cell in this implementation.

4.2. Our new RTR aligner

The main choice we had to make in our design was the selection of the right parameters in order to obtain a more efficient solution that uses parameterizable RTR. There are several criteria which a parameter must fulfill:

- A parameter has to be a signal that does not change too often. Every time the parameter changes a new configuration is generated and written to the FPGA. Each reconfiguration of the FPGA introduces an overhead, and thus reduces its overall efficiency.
- A second requirement, that is harder to characterize, is that the parameter must have a large enough influence on the design. The optimizations possible because of the parameter having a constant value in between reconfigurations have to result in a design that is small and fast enough to justify the extra CM resources and the possible increase in execution time, caused by the reconfiguration process.

For our RTR aligner, the character from the B sequence or, more accurately, the character that is assigned to a column of the score matrix, is chosen as a parameter for the SW-Cell that calculates that column. This character only changes when the SW-Cell is started on a new column of the score matrix. This can be seen from Fig. 3.

The choice of the column character as a parameter induces a series of design decisions to maximize the impact of this parameter. These are mentioned hereafter.

The column character is only used in the SW-Cell to select the substitution cost from the substitution matrix by using the column and row character as indices. As long as the SW-Cell stays in the same column of the score matrix, only a single row of the substitution matrix will be used. Therefore, it is only necessary to provide a memory containing this row inside the SW-Cell.

Parameterizable configurations do not limit the number of possible parameters, so instead of the column character the whole row of the substitution matrix will be used as a parameter. The CM will select the correct row based on the column sequence. This means the column character is not needed anymore on the level of the SW-Cell, or anywhere else in the design. This reduces the amount of logic needed for every SW-Cell, and removes the memory in which the column sequence is stored from the design.

To facilitate the usage of parameterizable configurations the row of the substitution matrix is implemented in a separate entity. This module accepts the row character and outputs the correct substitution cost for that row character and the column character. The substitution values inside this module are reconfigured every time the SW-Cell is started on a new column. For the SW-Cell this module functions as a sort of ROM memory that is overwritten every time the SW-Cell is reconfigured.

These changes to the FlexWare implementation result in an RTR implementation, the RTR aligner, that uses a lot less BRAMs. The FlexWare aligner needs a BRAM for every SW-Cell and needs two sequence memories. The new SW-Cell does not require any BRAM and adds only a small amount of logic. The RTR aligner only needs to save the row character sequence, thus only one sequence memory is needed, further reducing the total amount of BRAM resources used or needed for a Smith-Waterman implementation.

The current RTR-platform for the RTR aligner is a Xilinx Virtex II Pro FPGA, with the embedded PowerPC used as the CM. The RTR aligner then works as follows.

The PowerPC configures SW-Cells on the FPGA with the row of the substitution matrix as parameter. This row is selected by the corresponding character from the column sequence. When this configuration is finished the PowerPC starts the aligner. The second character sequence, the row sequence, is written to the sequence memory in the FPGA. The aligner will then start every SW-Cell on its own column, every SW-Cell starts comparing his column character with the row characters. When every SW-Cell has finished his column, the aligner will alert the PowerPC. The PowerPC will then reconfigure all the SW-Cells with new rows of the substitution matrix and give a new start signal. This is repeated until the full score matrix has been calculated. Finally, the aligner will output the maximum score and its location to the PowerPC, just as the FlexWare aligner which produces the same output.

5. Results

As we discussed in section 4, the main benefit of using the RTR aligner over the FlexWare aligner is the drastic reduction in the number of BRAMs needed. As the Virtex II Pro

FPGA contains many BRAMs, changing the FlexWare aligner into the RTR aligner does not provide a lot of gain on this component. However, the RTR aligner makes it possible to implement the Smith-Waterman algorithm on much cheaper line of Xilinx FPGAs. The Spartan line of FPGAs has less BRAMs available. These devices are too small for a useful FlexWare aligner implementation, but provide enough resources for an RTR aligner implementation. Therefore, a Spartan XC3S1600E-4FG484 implementation was used to compare both implementations.

Table 1. The resource usage in the FlexWare and RTR aligner

	FlexWare	RTR	Max. Avail.
Slices	3766 (25%)	14708 (99%)	14752
Slice Flip Flops	2635 (8%)	9515 (32%)	29504
4-input LUT's	6967 (23%)	27382 (92%)	29504
BRAM	36 (100%)	19 (52%)	36
SW-Cells	14	50	

Table 1 shows that the resource usage of the RTR aligner on a Spartan device is a lot better than for the FlexWare aligner. It should be noted that only comparing the increase in the number of SW-Cells is not a good comparison. The RTR aligner will be less efficient because it will have to be reconfigured several times.

The data above and the discussion below is based on synthesis data of both aligner implementations. The Spartan FPGA has no on-board PowerPC, so for an actual implementation a different CM would have to be chosen. There are several options, ranging from using an external PowerPC to implementing a stack machine to evaluate the boolean functions. The choice of CM only has an impact on the reconfiguration delay, not on any of the other considerations discussed below.

Both implementations can run at a similar clock frequency: the FlexWare implementation can clock at 46.5 MHz and the RTR aligner clocks at 46 MHz. The column sequence length is m, the row sequence length is n and the amount of SW-Cells is p. $\left\lceil \frac{m}{p} \right\rceil$ describes the number of times each SW-Cell is started on a new column in the FlexWare aligner, or how many times each SW-Cell is reconfigured in the RTR-aligner. If we assume $m, n \gg p$ and $f - \frac{f_{Flex} + f_{RTR}}{2} = 46.25$ MHz, then we can write the difference in calculation time of both implementations as equation (3)

$$t_{Flex} - t_{RTR} \approx \frac{mn}{f} \left(\frac{1}{p_{Flex}} - \frac{1}{p_{RTR}} \right) \tag{3}$$

This result, equation (3), can be used to find an expression for the maximum time allowed for each reconfiguration, so the RTR aligner is at least as efficient as the Flexware aligner. This time is given by equation (4).

$$t_{Max,reconf} \leq \frac{t_{Flex} - t_{RTR}}{\frac{m}{p_{RTR}}} \approx \frac{n}{f} \left(\frac{p_{RTR}}{p_{Flex}} - 1 \right) = \frac{n}{f} \frac{36}{14} \tag{4}$$

These considerations are valid irrespective of sequence length. If we fill in $n = 2^{13} = 8192$, the time allowed for reconfiguration is $455 \ \mu s$. The current implementation of parameterizable reconfigurations is not able to meet these reconfiguration speeds (mainly because the device reconfiguration itself takes in the order of ms). A possible solution for this is to decrease the time needed for reconfiguration. Several improvements are in progress on that part. However, even without changing the implementation of parameterizable reconfiguration there are already improvements possible.

An important part of DNA and protein alignment is the *one vs. all* comparison. In this comparison one sequence is aligned with a database of sequences. For this kind of comparisons a big improvement is possible. It is immediately clear from equation (4) that, if a longer row sequence is aligned, the time allowed for reconfiguration is longer and the efficiency of the RTR aligner increases.

A possible improvement for the *one vs. all* comparison is to set the *one* sequence as the column sequence and make one or several long row sequences out of appended database sequences. To be able to handle these appended sequences, the implementation will need to be slightly altered. This will require some extra logic to keep track of several maxima. Overall, this would lead to a huge performance gain because these changes will make it possible to make the row sequence arbitrarily long.

The overhead introduced by reconfiguration consists of two parts. First, the time needed for the calculation of the new configuration, denoted as *Evaluation* in Fig 4, and second the time needed for writing the new configuration to the FPGA, denoted as *Recon.* in Fig. 4. The relationship between the lengths of the *Evaluation* and *Recon.* tasks are based on estimations, made by extrapolation on simulation data and what is known of parameterizable reconfiguration. The *Execution* task's length is directly dependent on the length of the row sequence.

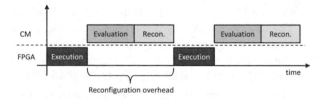

Figure 4. FPGA and CM tasks for the RTR aligner

It is immediately clear from Fig. 4 that the CM is underused in this case, and that a big improvement would be to do the evaluation in parallel with the execution. For this to be possible we have to be able to predict what the new parameter values will be at the start of the second execution. In the case of the RTR aligner, the CM has all the information necessary to start the calculation of the new configuration the moment the current configuration is written to the FPGA. An example of this can be seen in Fig. 5. This change costs essentially nothing, it only takes time the PowerPC would otherwise sit idle, while reducing the reconfiguration overhead significantly. In the worst case scenario, when the evaluation time is longer than the execution time, it will still reduce the reconfiguration overhead with the execution time.

It is possible to further optimize the resource usage. First, we assume that the time needed for writing to the FPGA, *Recon.*, is set and the FPGA will not work when it is reconfigured. We can then deduce from Fig. 5 that the most optimal resource usage occurs when the evaluation time and the execution time take exactly the same time. In

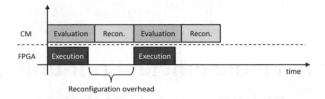

Figure 5. Improved FPGA and CM tasks for the RTR aligner

that case, the PowerPC is in use all the time, and the reconfiguration overhead is only as long as the time needed to write the new configuration to the FPGA.

With the current implementation the biggest problem is that the execution time is less than the evaluation time. The optimization suggested for *one v. all* comparisons can be used to even greater effect here. This adjustment will enable us to increase the execution time at will, since the execution time is dependent on row sequence length.

Another way to improve is to search for new, more efficient ways to write the configuration to the FPGA. The system used here is a proof-of-concept system that can be greatly improved upon. Within the research group PARIS, where the method of parameterizable dynamic reconfiguration has originated there is already an improved method available.

6. Conclusions and Future work

The RTR aligner improves on the FlexWare aligner by optimizing its resource usage in return for reconfiguration overhead. It opens the way to the usage of cheaper FPGAs to implement the Smith-Waterman algorithm. An example is the line of Spartan FPGAs whose BRAM to logic ratio is low. Since the RTR aligner only requires a fixed amount of BRAMs that does not increase with the amount of SW-Cells, it is a lot more suitable for implementation on these FPGAs.

Using TMAP, a parameterizable RTR implementation of the Smith-Waterman algorithm was created. The only design decision directly related to the RTR implementation was the selection of the parameters, which is an RTL-level design decision.

The current method of reconfiguration, with the HWICAP, is too slow to have a performance increase. There are, however, several ways to increase the efficiency of the current RTR aligner. The most obvious one being to optimize for one vs. all comparisons.

References

[1] W. R. Pearson and D. J. Lipman, "Improved tools for biological sequence comparison.," *Proc Natl Acad Sci U S A*, vol. 85, no. 8, pp. 2444–2448, April 1988.
[2] S. F. Altschul, W. Gish, W. Miller, E. W. Myers, and D. J. Lipman, "Basic local alignment search tool.," *J Mol Biol*, vol. 215, no. 3, pp. 403–410, October 1990.
[3] Karel Bruneel and Dirk Stroobandt, "Reconfigurability-aware structural mapping for LUT-based FP-GAs," *Reconfigurable Computing and FPGAs, International Conference on*, pp. 223–228, 2008.
[4] FlexWare, "Deliverable 2.6: Report on the process of the implementation of the Smith-Waterman algorithm on the FPGA architecture," November 2007.
[5] T.F. Smith and M.S. Waterman, "Identification of common molecular subsequences," 1981.

Parallel Computing: From Multicores and GPU's to Petascale
B. Chapman et al. (Eds.)
IOS Press, 2010
© *2010 The authors and IOS Press. All rights reserved.*
doi:10.3233/978-1-60750-530-3-624

Towards a more efficient run-time FPGA configuration generation

Fatma ABOUELELLA [a], Karel BRUNEEL [a] and Dirk STROOBANDT [a]

[a] *ELIS, Ghent University, Sint-Pietersnieuwstraat 41, 9000 Gent, Belgium*

Abstract.

Parameterizable configurations are regular FPGA configurations in which some of the configuration bits are expressed as a Boolean function of a set of parameters. These configurations can rapidly be transformed to a specialized configuration by evaluating the Boolean functions for a specific set of parameter values and are therefore ideal for use in run-time reconfigurable systems. In this paper, the concept of Parameterizable Bitstream (PBS) is introduced to accommodate the use of parameterizable configurations in commercial FPGAs. A stack machine system is implemented that can efficiently transform a PBS to a specialized configuration.

Keywords. FPGA, Parameterizable Bitstream, Stack Machine.

1. Introduction

The functionality of FPGAs is set by configuring them. Configuration is the process of loading the FPGA's internal configuration memory by sending a bitstream to the FPGA's configuration port. This process customizes the functionality implemented by the FPGA fabric.

In some applications, a piece of the implemented hardware should dynamically be changed to adapt the functionality of the application at run-time for some parameter values. To implement such applications on an FPGA, configurations should be generated each time the parameter values change. Conventional tools generate FPGA configurations from scratch. This approach leads to long generation and reconfiguration times, since we have to place and route the design and reconfigure the whole FPGA each time. Partial reconfiguration techniques can be used in such applications, to reduce the generation and reconfiguration times. In this case, a master configuration should be generated first to configure the whole FPGA. Optimized configurations should be later generated or selected to reconfigure a certain piece of the implemented hardware. However, designing for partial reconfiguration using the existing tools is a complex exercise [1].

In [2], the authors have introduced a new form of FPGA configurations which leads to smaller and faster implementations, the so-called parameterizable configurations. These configurations are FPGA configurations, in which some of the configuration bits are expressed as a Boolean function of a set of inputs, the parameters.

Run-time specialization of these configurations means evaluating the Boolean functions according to one specific set of parameter values and thus generating specialized

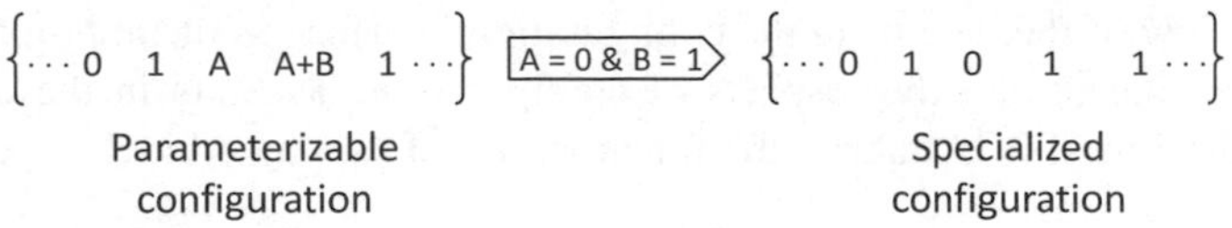

$$\left\{\cdots 0 \quad 1 \quad A \quad A{+}B \quad 1 \cdots\right\} \quad \boxed{A = 0 \,\&\, B = 1} \quad \left\{\cdots 0 \quad 1 \quad 0 \quad 1 \quad 1 \cdots\right\}$$

Parameterizable
configuration

Specialized
configuration

Figure 1. An example of the specialization of the parameterizable configuration

configurations. Figure 1 shows an example of a parameterizable configuration, which has two parameters A and B, and the resulting specialized configuration for A = 0 and B = 1.

This Run-time specialization process is several orders of magnitude faster than using the conventional tools to generate regular configurations [2]. Moreover, the specialized configuration results in an implementation that uses less area and runs faster than a generic FPGA implementation with the same functionality, while maintaining full flexibility of assigning values to the parameters [3]. Also because the reconfiguration is only needed for the parameterizable bits of the parameterizable configuration and all other reconfiguration bits can retain their value, the reconfiguration time is reduced.

Another advantage of this technique is the availability of a fully automated tool chain that generates parameterizable configurations with parameterizable LUT truth tables [3]. This tool chain takes a parameterizable HDL descripion as input. The description can be done on the RTL level. So in contrast to other dynamic reconfiguration techniques [4] no low-level design is needed.

In order to exploit the advantages of the parameterizable configuration in commercial FPGAs, we introduce the concept of the parameterizable bitstream (PBS). This bitstream is a series of configuration commands and data, just as the regular bitstream, but the configuration bits are expressed as Boolean functions of some parameters.

We also introduce a representation for a PBS that is compact and allows efficient evaluation. The definition and advantages of the PBS are presented in section 2.1. A front-end system to the configuration control logic of the FPGA is introduced in section 2.2. This system processes the incoming PBS and produces a specialized bitstream according to a specific set of parameter values.

The stack machine architecture presented in section 3.2 is used to design the front-end system. The speed and simplicity of such a machine are exploited to speed up the evaluation of the PBS and reduce the size of the overall system. In section 4, the experimental results are presented, the memory resources that are needed to store the PBS as well as the generation and reconfiguration times are measured. With this, we propose, for the first time, a truly efficient and easy to use run-time reconfigurable system.

2. Parameterizable Bitstream

An FPGA configuration bitstream is a series of configuration commands and configuration data. This stream tells the FPGA how to use its resources to implement a certain function. The interpretation of the bitstream is an essential process in the FPGA.

Figure 2 shows the architecture of the FPGA from the viewpoint of the configuration designer. The configuration control logic is the part of the FPGA which is responsible for processing the incoming bitstream and for writing the configuration data to the right place in the configuration memory. It consists of a packet processor, a set of registers, and global signals that are controlled by the configuration registers. The packet processor controls the flow of the data from the configuration interface to the appropriate register. The registers control all other aspects of configuration. The bits in the configuration memory control the FPGA fabric: the functionality of the logic blocks and the routing resources.

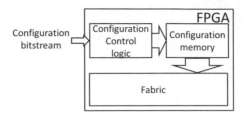

Figure 2. FPGA architecture

2.1. Regular and Parameterizable Bitstreams

A regular bitstream is a series of configuration commands and data, represented as a stream of Boolean values (0, 1). These Boolean values are forming data packets. Each packet targets a specific configuration register to set configuration options, program configuration memory, or toggle internal signals.

In order to benefit from the advantages of the parameterizable configurations mentioned in section 1, it is necessary to find a way to represent these configurations, to be implemented in commercial FPGAs. Therefore, we introduce the concept of a PBS to accommodate the parameterizable reconfigurations. The PBS can be considered a parameterizable version of the regular bitstream, where each bit is expressed as a Boolean function of a set of inputs, the parameters.

An efficient representation of the concept of the PBS is the main goal of this work. To achieve this target, the area and the speed of a PBS implementation should be taken into account. The area of a system is closely related to the way of storing the PBS. The speed of the system is related to the way of evaluating the Boolean functions. Therefore, these two issues are investigated in following sections.

2.2. Configuring an FPGA with a PBS

The question now is how to use the concept of PBS in applications implemented on FPGAs and how to evaluate this bitstream in an efficient way. As explained at the beginning of section 2, the FPGA configuration control logic is responsible for processing the configuration bitstream, and updating the configuration memory with the new configurations. Our solution is to build a front-end system Figure 3 that processes the PBS and uses the parameter values as inputs to generate a specialized bitstream that can be later processed using the existing FPGA configuration control logic in the same way as the regular bitstream.

In our design this front-end is implemented in the FPGA fabric, but it could also be hardwired on the chip.

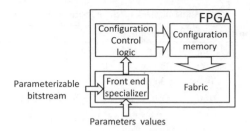

Figure 3. FPGA with a front-end specializer

3. Using a stack machine to evaluate a Parameterizable Bitstream

The aim of this work is to build a fast specialization system, while keeping the size of the system and the size of the PBS representation as small as possible. For this reason, we propose to design the front-end specializer as a stack machine.

In the following subsections, we will start by discussing the reasons for choosing the stack machine as a computation model. Then the architecture of the stack machine, the essential part of the system, is presented. Finally the compilation process that enables the execution of the PBS is explained in detail using a simple example.

3.1. Advantages of stack machines

Apart from the mere fact that a stack machine is capable of evaluating Boolean functions. It has a lot of advantages over other architectures.

Stack machines are simpler than other machines, and provide very good computational power using little hardware. A particularly favorable application area for stack machines is in real time embedded control applications, which require a combination of small size and high processing speed [5]. Therefore, stack machines are achieving our target of building a system with a large speed and small area.

Since the main objective of the stack machine in our intended system is to evaluate Boolean functions with limited number of operations, the instruction set which is needed to represent the PBS is that of a Minimal Instruction Set Computer (MISC). This MISC architecture enables a smaller and faster instruction decode unit, therefore facilitating overall faster operation of the individual instructions.

In addition to its speed and simplicity, the stack machine can achieve higher code density [5,6] compared to the accumulator machine and other machines, since the instructions executed by the stack machines are small and simple. Therefore, we can say that using the stack machine to evaluate the PBS is a good choice to minimize the area of the memory resources needed to store the PBS, as it is represented as a sequence of simple encoded instructions.

3.2. Stack machine architecture

The main purpose of our stack machine is to evaluate Boolean functions with limited Boolean operations (OR, AND and NOT). In our system we have 8 different instructions necessary to evaluate the PBS and output the result, table 1 shows these instructions, their operation code (opcode) and description. All instructions have zero operands, except the PUSH instruction, which has one operand, the parameter input index.

Table 1. Stack machine instructions

Instruction	Opcode	Description
AND	000	Bitwise and
OR	100	Bitwise or
NOT	010	Complement
PUSH	110	Push parameter value to the top of the stack
POP	001	Pop top of the stack
NOP	101	No operation
OUT0	011	Output constant 0
OUT1	111	Output constant 1

The AND and OR instructions perform bitwise operations between the first and the second values on the Top Of the Stack (TOS), while the NOT instruction inverts the top value of the stack. The PUSH instruction followed by an index, stores the value of the parameter pointed by the index to the TOS. The POP instruction is needed to output the evaluation result of a Boolean function. This instruction always ends the group of instructions that evaluate a Boolean function. The OUT0 and OUT1 instructions are needed to directly output a constant value in case of a Boolean constant function (0, 1).

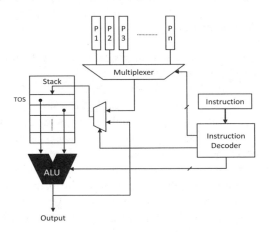

Figure 4. Stack machine architecture

Figure 4 shows the architecture of the stack machine. The design contains a stack as operand memory, an ALU, an instruction decoder and an array of registers that stores the current values of the system parameters. The ALU performs logic operations (OR, AND and NOT) and three individual jobs. In the case of the AND and OR instructions the first and the second top values of the stack are popped, and used as inputs to the ALU, the output of the ALU is pushed to the TOS. While in the case of the NOT instruction only the top of the stack value is popped, inverted and pushed back to the TOS.

The first extra job of the ALU is to pop the TOS and output this value in case of the POP instruction. The second and the third jobs are to output a constant value (0, 1) in case of the OUT0 and OUT1 instructions.

The instruction decoder controls the functions performed by the ALU, determines the stack input path and generates the right address of the parameter value (specified by the PUSH instruction) to be pushed to the stack. For instance, the Boolean function $A\overline{B}$ is evaluated using 5 instructions, these instructions are decoded one after the other by the instruction decoder. Figure 5 shows the evaluations steps, when A=1 and B=0.

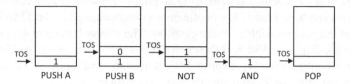

Figure 5. $A\overline{B}$ evaluation steps using stack machine when A=1 and B=0 (TOS Top Of Stack)

The stack machine specializes the PBS. However, to represent this PBS in a suitable form for the stack machine, a compilation for the PBS should take place once off-line first.

3.3. The compilation process

In this section the compilation process is explained using the following PBS example { ..., 0, 1, $A\overline{B}$, 1, ...}, where A and B are the parameters.

For the sake of clarity, we will define three different representations for the PBS: the first is the conceptual PBS which is a stream of Boolean functions, the second is the instruction PBS, a stream of instructions and the last one is the encoded PBS, a stream of machine codes.

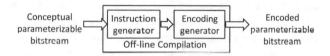

Figure 6. Compilation system

Figure 6 shows the compilation process of the conceptual PBS. This process consists of two stages: the instruction generation and the encoding generation, the output of this process is the encoded PBS.

The instruction generation stage, converts the conceptual PBS to an instruction PBS. Each Boolean function in the conceptual PBS is represented as instruction(s), according to table 1, the Boolean const function (0, 1) is represented either by OUT0 or OUT1 instructions, a Boolean function of parameter(s) is converted to postfix notation and represented as explained in section 3.2. In our example, the instruction PBS is {... , OUT0, OUT1, PUSH A, PUSH B, NOT, AND, POP, OUT1, ...}.

The encoding generation stage converts this instruction PBS to an encoded PBS. In accordance to table 1, each instruction is simply replaced by its opcode, while the PUSH instruction is replaced by its opcode and the index of the parameter in the stack machine. This index is represented as a multiple of three bits according to the number of parameters. In our example, the output encoded PBS is { ..., 011, 111, 110000, 110100, 010, 100, 001, 111, ...}.

Finally, the execution of the encoded PBS by the stack machine at run-time results in a specialized bitstream. In our example, when A=1 and B =0, the output stream is { ..., 0, 1, 1, 1, ...}, which is a regular bitstream.

4. Experiments and Results

In this section we present some results on the size and speed of the stack machine system. We validate our stack machine system using an adaptive filtering application (16-taps, 8-bit coefficients and 8-bit input). The application is implemented in the TMAP tool chain [3] to exploit the paramterizable reconfiguration. The master bitstream generated by the tools is used to configure a Virtex-II Pro device when the system starts. As Virtex devices allow partial reconfiguration [7], a partial PBS is used to reconfigure the FPGA each time the values of the filter coefficients -the parameters- change.

A java program is built to off-line generate and compile the partial PBS. The generated partial instruction PBS is executed at run-time by the stack machine system. Our goal is to build a hardware stack machine, but this is not implemented yet. Currently the stack machine is built as a C application running on the PowerPC of the Virtex device. The partial bitstream resulting from the stack machine is used to reconfigure the FPGA through the FPGA's ICAP (Internal Configuration Access Port).

The size of the partial instruction PBS is 236.1 Kbyte and the size of the partial bitstream generated from the stack machine is 16.3 Kbyte. At first glance, it would appear that the memory resources needed to store this instruction PBS stream are too large compared to the resources needed to store the generated partial bitstream. But that is not true because in a general partial reconfiguration flow, there are up to 2^{128} possible sets of coefficients for the 16-tap FIR filter. In comparison to the situation where all different configuration bit streams are stored separately, our PBS is more efficient in terms of memory use when more than 15 coefficient sets are needed.

Moreover, the instruction PBS can be further optimized. One of these optimizations is to represent the stack machine instruction set using known encoding algorithms that provide data compression, for example Huffman encoding. This representation leads to 20% reduction in the size but at the same time an increase in the complexity of the stack machine architecture is expected.

Since our PBS contains large chunks of constant bits, another simple optimization is to add two new instructions to our instruction set, this can lead to 15% reduction in the size and only a slight change in the stack machine architecture. The first instruction OUT32 outputs 32 bits of constant data at once in its argument. This instruction removes 62% of the overhead of representing the 32 bits using 3-bit OUT0 and OUT1 instructions. The second instruction OUTPAD outputs a group of dummy data, called a pad frame. This instruction is inspired by the structure of the partial bitstream: each frame or subsequent frames in the partial bitstream should be followed by a configuration pad frame for pipelining.

Finally, adding a new instruction PUSHC to push the complement of the parameter leads to 7% reduction in the size of the PBS while only a complemented copy of the parameter values should be added to the stack machine architecture.

So there are enough opportunities to reduce the memory resources needed to a level that is not much higher than the regular bitstream.

The maximum size of the stack in our FIR example is 10. This size can be varied according to the number of parameters and the complexity of the Boolean functions.

The reconfiguration time of the FPGA through the ICAP port is measuredas 2.6 ms that are needed to send the partial bitstream generated by the stack machine. However, this time is not the optimal as the minimum theoretical reconfiguration time should be

0.25 ms. Until now we are restricted by the design of the HWICAP IP provided by Xilinx [8]. This time will be further improved in the future. Finally, we have estimated the expected time for generating a regular partial bitstream with the hardware stack machine to be 6.4 ms in case the clock frequency is 100 MHz and one instruction is processed every clock cycle.

5. Conclusion and Future work

In this paper we introduce the concept of Parameterizable Bitstream (PBS) to accommodate the parameterized reconfigurations in commercial FPGAs. This PBS is a parameterizable version of the regular bitstream, where each bit is expressed as a Boolean function of a set of inputs, the parameters.

We have chosen to represent the PBS as a sequence of instructions for a custom stack machine, since stack machines allow a compact representation of the PBS and an efficient evaluation of Boolean functions. The stack machine system is used as a front-end to the configuration control logic of an FPGA and outputs a specialized regular bitstream. We have implemented a proof-of-concept system and validated it on an adaptive filtering example. We show that even for this first non-optimized implementation the PBS can be represented in a compact way and allows fast processing.

In the future we will implement the stack machine in hardware as a front-end to the Xilinx ICAP interface. We will also further optimize the representation of the PBS and the stack machine architecture. This will allow us to use the concept of PBSs in real applications and to measure the impact of PBSs on the full system (specialization time, reconfiguration time, resources used by the stack machine) accurately. Finally, the depth of the stack and the efficiency of evaluating complex Boolean functions will be investigated as well as the consequence of having a fixed number of parameters.

References

[1] Christophe Bobda, *Introduction to Reconfigurable Computing: Architectures, Algorithms, and Applications*, Springer, November 2007.

[2] K. Bruneel, D. stroobandt, *Automatic generation of run-time parameterizable configurations*, Proceedings of the International Conference on Field Programmable Logic and Applications, 2008, 361–366.

[3] K. Bruneel, F. Abouelella, D. stroobandt, *Automatically Mapping Applications to a Self-reconfiguring Platform*, Proceedings of Design, Automation and Test in Europe . Preas, K. 2009. 964-969.

[4] S. Guccione, D. levi, *Run-Time Parameterizable Cores*, Proceedings of the 9th International Workshop on Field Programmable Logic and Applications, pages 215-222, 1999.

[5] Philip J. Koopman, Jr., *Stack Computers: the new wave* California : Ed. Mountain View Press, 1989.

[6] John L. Hennessy, David A. Patterson , *Computer Architecture: A Quantitative Approach*,Morgan Kaufmann Publishers,1990

[7] Xilinx, *Virtex-II Pro and Virtex-II Pro X FPGA User Guide UG012*, pages 339-366, November 2007.

[8] C. Claus, B. Zhang, W. Stechele, L. Braun, M. Hubner, J. Becker, *A multi-platform controller allowing for maximum Dynamic Partial Reconfiguration throughput*, Proceedings of the International Conference on Field Programmable Logic and Applications, 2008, 535-538.

Parallel Computing: From Multicores and GPU's to Petascale
B. Chapman et al. (Eds.)
IOS Press, 2010
© *2010 The authors and IOS Press. All rights reserved.*
doi:10.3233/978-1-60750-530-3-632

ACCFS - Virtual File System Support for Host Coupled Run-Time Reconfigurable FPGAs

Jochen STRUNK [a], Andreas HEINIG [a], Toni VOLKMER [a], Wolfgang REHM [a] and
Heiko SCHICK [b,1]

[a] *Computer Architecture Group, Chemnitz University of Technology, Germany*
[b] *R&D, IBM Deutschland Research & Development GmbH, Germany*

Abstract. In this paper a solution for the integration of FPGAs into host systems is presented. For managing user requests targeting FPGA tasks, including configuration and communication, the software framework ACCFS (ACCelerator File System) is utilized, which is built on a virtual file system (VFS). Such a system can be used for offloading compute kernels on the FPGA. Applying run-time reconfiguration on dynamically and partially reconfigurable (DPR) FPGAs allows to build plug-in FPGA solutions, consisting only of a single FPGA, without the need of external bridges or a second FPGA to handle host communication. Run-time reconfiguration also enables multi user and multi context support on the FPGA based on the VFS approach. Run-time reconfigurable modules (RTRMs) allow FPGA module creation on demand by the user. For the implementation on a HyperTransport (HT) coupled FPGA, the HT cave was extended in such a way that it provides an infrastructure for dealing with multiple run-time reconfigurable modules. In a case study two distinct compute kernel offload functions are implemented as RTRMs. Multiple instances of these RTRMs can be provided to the user on demand during run-time.

Keywords. VFS, FPGA, run-time reconfiguration, dynamic partial reconfiguration

1. Introduction

Using FPGAs for acceleration can lead to a significant reduction of compute time, due to the creation of specialized processing engines utilizing the highly parallel nature of FPGAs. A speedup of more than 50 compared to a CPU was achieved by Woods et al. [1] accelerating a Quasi-Monte Carlo financial simulation. Zhang et al. [2] gained a speedup of 25 for another Monte-Carlo simulation. Utilizing dynamically and partially reconfigurable (DPR) FPGAs on the other hand offers the possibility to reconfigure partially reconfigurable regions (PRR) during run-time. This enables functionality to be altered such as compute kernels on user requests and host coupled FPGA plug-in cards to be built, which manage host communication and user offloading functionality within a single FPGA. To support the user in the handling of a run-time reconfigurable FPGA we

---

[1]The project is performed in collaboration with the Center of Advanced Study Boeblingen, IBM Research & Development GmbH, Germany.

present the software framework ACCFS, which manages the run-time reconfiguration of the FPGA, the host communication and on the same time provides a high abstraction due to the virtual file system approach. Multiple instances of run-time reconfigurable modules (RTRMs) can be created and managed by ACCFS on behalf of the user. Even multi user support of RTRMs is possible. The rest of the paper is organized as follows: Section 2 is devoted to related work. Section 3 describes the run-time reconfiguration support for a FPGA directly connected to AMD's processor bus. The enhancement for a HyperTransport cave implemented as host interconnect is shown. The infrastructure needed on the FPGA for the support of run-time reconfigurable modules and their creation is presented. The software framework provided to the user is explained in section 4. In a case study, presented as proof of concept in section 5, multiple instances of run-time reconfigurable modules are created on demand by a user application using the ACCFS framework. Two distinct compute kernel offload functions have been implemented as RTRM, the first module acts as an offload function, which finds patterns in a bit stream (pattern matcher) and the second module a Mersenne Twister generates pseudo random numbers at high output frequency. Section 6 concludes the results of this paper.

2. Related Work

Utilizing RTR capabilities of FPGAs and building CPU coupled systems have been proposed under various aspects. Some are dealing with internal communication structures while others concentrate more on system integration. A tool-flow for homogeneous communication infrastructure for RTR capable FPGAs was presented by Hagemeyer et al. [3] built upon the Xilinx design flow. In contrast Koch et al. [4] designed a framework named ReCoBus builder without applying Xilinx's partial reconfiguration flow. Only Virtex-II and Spartan-3 FPGA are supported by the builder so far. Switch architectures with routers between RTR modules have been examined also in [5] [6]. The impact on design and speed of a grid with run-time reconfigurable modules and a central controller, symbolizing e.g. a host interconnect, has been presented in [7]. On the matter of integration of FPGA modules or threads for embedded systems different models have been proposed. ReconOS [8], a real time operating system implemented with static FPGA threads, is based on memory mapping and is used in embedded systems. Another model, BORPH [9], is based on the UNIX IPC mechanism and utilizes the integrated PowerPC as host. For the integration of host coupled accelerators we proposed and implemented the Accelerator File System (ACCFS) [10]. This framework is based on the concept of a virtual file system. We have already shown the integration of the Cell/B.E. processor. In this paper we will show that ACCFS is best suited for the integration of FPGAs, even RTR capable FPGAs, into a host system.

3. Run-Time Reconfiguration Support for a HyperTransport Cave

For a single FPGA chip solution connected to a host utilizing HyperTransport as interconnect, it is essential not to lose the link during the time of the reconfiguration of a RTRM. This implies that the HyperTransport IP-core implementing a HT cave must be kept inside the FPGA as static part. Hot plugging is not supported so far by off the shelf systems. Even if the hardware is capable of handling such requests, most operating systems do not support this. Other RTRMs inside the FPGA would suffer also from the link loss. For that reason the HyperTransport cave is kept in the static region. In this section the enhancement of a HT cave is shown which provides an infrastructure for dealing with RTRMs. A run-time reconfigurable infrastructure for a HyperTransport cave has to provide a communication mechanism between the host and the RTRM and perhaps between RTRMs themselves. It also has to comply to the rules of partial reconfiguration and the partial design flow. To ease porting the infrastructure to other interconnects, e.g. PCI Express, the functionality which must be implemented for a RTR infrastructure should be divided into two parts. One covers the host interconnect specific functions and the other the host interconnect independent portions. The infrastructure designed for a HyperTransport cave supporting RTRMs consists of two host interface specific, i.e. HT Cave Core and HT Packet Engine, and four host independent parts, an Internal Routing Unit, a RTRM Controller, a Reconfig Unit and one or more RTRMs. The HT cave design for the HyperTransport interconnect originates from [11]. The task of the HT Package Engine is to decode the HT packets coming from the host and to convert these into appropriate actions targeting the units inside the FPGA. This includes the creation of responses to requests from the host by injecting valid packets to the HT Cave Core. The Internal Routing Unit routes requests to and from internal units, e.g. RTRM Controller and Reconfig Unit. For fast run-time reconfiguration of RTRMs it is recommended to make use of an internal reconfiguration port. This is done by the Reconfig Unit which controls the internal configuration access port (ICAP) for Xilinx FPGAs. The Reconfig Unit itself is controlled by the vendor specific driver on the host, which validates if requests concerning the creation of new RTRMs can be served. The allocation of RTRMs to available RTR regions is also decided by the host system.

Each RTRM has its virtual address space which is implemented 32 bits wide. This means that a global address space is not divided between the RTRMs using fixed addresses. It would be very difficult to resolve a request when two RTRMs demand the same fixed physical address for their memory regions which are exported to the user application using an entry in the virtual file system implemented on the host system. The interface (entity) of a RTRM serves as an interconnect to the RTRM controller. Communication in both directions, i.e. controller requests (crq) and module requests (mrq), are possible using a stop and valid protocol. The RTRM controller handles requests coming from the HT Core originated by the user application or from the RTRM itself. It converts physical addresses for directly accessing the RTRM, e.g. through direct load and store operations from the host to virtual RTRM addresses. The controller can also be used for RTRM to RTRM communication if desired.

For generating the static part, i.e. the HT cave with RTR support, and the dynamical RTR modules, scripts are provided. The intention is to ease the creation of RTRMs for an application developer who is not so familiar with FPGA IP-core designs and run-time reconfiguration. The top VHDL module is synthesized with the instantiated HT core, the HT packet engine, the internal routing unit, the RTRM controller and the Reconfig Unit by the `build_static` script. The RTRM module is only instantiated as a black box module. Then the static part is implemented with the partial flow option. While the user constraints file (ucf) normally contains location (LOC) constraints for external IO pins, this file must also contain additional LOC constraints for the PR flow covering all clock resources, in particular clock buffers and digital clock managers (DCMs). The resulting placed and routed design represents the basis for creating the dynamic configuration bit stream. For the dynamic part, the user must supply an interface-compliant RTR module with the top entity name 'rtrm' and a description of the file entries which should be exported by ACCFS. This description consists of the type, the size and the virtual address which are essential to export the functionality to the user application. This additional information is added later to the final ACCFS configuration bit stream as a part of the header. Using the `build_dynamic` script the user-supplied RTRM module is implemented with the partial flow option. Next, the Xilinx tools `PR_verify` and `PR_assemble` are used to build the partial bit stream file. Then the ACCFS RTRM bit stream file is created by adding header information containing the HT cave version, the FPGA board version and the user-supplied module description. Due to this header information, it is possible to transfer ACCFS RTRM bit stream files to other hosts which contain the same FPGA accelerator board and use the identical HT cave version.

4. ACCFS for Host System Integration

Different solutions exist for operating system integration of a FPGA. For example, BORPH [9] or ReconOS [8] provide a hardware process/thread abstraction which coexist beside 'normal' software processes. However, deep modifications of the Linux kernel are necessary to implement them. Furthermore, it is required to run Linux on the processing unit of the FPGA. Due to the mentioned disadvantages we proposed and implemented the Accelerator File System (ACCFS) [10]. In this section we describe the major aspects of ACCFS for the integration of FPGAs into a host system. We start with a brief overview in subsection 4.1. Subsection 4.2 depicts the concepts of ACCFS. Thereafter, we present the integration steps for the HT-coupled Virtex-4 card in subsection 4.3.

4.1. Overview

ACCFS is an open generic system interface for the integration of different accelerator types into the Linux operating system. It is based on SPUFS (Synergistic Processing Unit File System) [12] which is used to access the Synergistic Processing Units of the Cell/B.E. processor. The goal of ACCFS is to replace the different character device based interfaces with a generic file system based interface . In the case of character devices the hardware functionalities are usually exported through the `ioctl` system call. However, this system call has the disadvantage of a non-standardized interface. Hence, the usage differs from one vendor to another. In contrast, ACCFS defines a well structured `ioctl`-free interface based on a Virtual File System (VFS) approach. To be customizable when integrating new hardware ACCFS was split into two parts. Part one ('accfs'), provides the user interface, and the other parts ('device handlers') integrate the hardware. Device vendors as well as library programmers benefit from ACCFS. Only the lowest abstraction levels have to be implemented inside the device handlers. The whole user interface is already provided by accfs. Thus integrating a new accelerator requires less device driver programming costs. The library programmer benefits from basic design concepts introduced in the next subsection.

4.2. Basic Concepts

In the previous subsection we already described the concept of **functionality separation** which eases the integration of new hardware. Another concept was the usage of a

VFS which maps the accelerator to normal files. This enables us to implement a `ioctl` free and hence a nearly standard conform approach. All supported file I/O operations are POSIX conform with some exceptions. For example, it is not possible to write beyond the end of a file or to change the position of the current file pointer on some files. ACCFS is designed to support the **virtualization** of the accelerators. We abstract the *physical accelerator* with an *accelerator context*. The context is the operational data set of the accelerator. It includes all information which are necessary to describe the current hardware state in such a way that the operation can be interrupted and resumed later without data loss. During the interruption another context is able to utilize the physical hardware. Virtualization optimizes the resource usage of the accelerators. Contexts which do not make use of the hardware at a given time are not scheduled on the physical accelerator. Each context is bounded on a directory inside the VFS under the ACCFS mount point. The files inside this directory represent the functionalities of the accelerator. To support reconfigurable hardware the file set is **dynamically exported** and can change during runtime. For example, an additional memory can be exported due to reconfiguration of the FPGA with a new RTR module. To interact with the accelerator several methods are feasible. One is the simple memory mapped IO with standard load/store machine instructions. In this direct memory access (DMA) method the host is the active part who issues a read/write for every memory access. Another method is DMA-bulk transfer. Here the accelerator needs a DMA unit capable of moving the data asynchronously to the host processor execution. In cases where the accelerator is able to initiate these transfers by itself, the DMA unit has to handle virtual memory managing issues, too. However, not every accelerator supports virtual memory. For this reason we restrict our solution to **host initiated DMA**, where the host setups the memory management unit and initializes the data transfer. The actual data movement is done asynchronously by the accelerator. Finally, ACCFS supports **asynchronous context execution** based on an explicit synchronization primitive. This concept eases the software development because multi-threading is not required when using multiple accelerator units. Every context runs asynchronously to the host system. The finish status can be read through a 'status' file.

4.3. FPGA Support

To support HyperTransport coupled FPGA boards within ACCFS a new device handler has to be written. This device handler has to provide the structure *accfs_vendor* . The first four entries has to be set and the others are optional. For example, if the callback function for the DMA-bulk transfer is not set (`memory_sdma`), accfs will use the internal routines to copy the data from/to the FPGA. Further details of the device handler implementation are described in the rest of this subsection.

4.3.1. Create Context

ACCFS enforces an accelerator based programming model. The main program is running on the host system and executes the compute kernel on the accelerator. To outsource such a kernel the application has to create a context by invoking the `acc_create` system call. Currently our device handler does not support virtualization hence we can only exclusively provide the FPGA to one application.

4.3.2. Configuration

Loading the design is triggered by a `write` system call on the 'config' file. The data has to be a valid ACCFS bit stream. To ensure that the RTRM matches the RTR infrastructure we provide a tool chain which generates such a bit stream file by writing a special header before the bit stream data. The header contains all necessary information describing the bit stream such as the RTR capable core and FPGA board version. If the validation is successful, the FPGA is programmed with the configuration bit stream file using the internal reconfiguration port ICAP for Xilinx FPGAs or through an external JTAG programming device, e.g. Xilinx USB platform cable. After a successfully configuration the exported memories of the FPGA design are visible in the context directory.

4.3.3. Data Exchange

The access of FPGA memory is possible with the `read` and `write` system calls. In a later development stage these calls start a host initiated DMA-bulk transfer. If the memory is exported as memory mapped IO, the `mmap` system call will map the memory into the address space of the application. The 'data exchange' operation is always possible after the configuration no matter whether the context is in execution or not.

4.3.4. Execute Design

To start the RTR module the application has to invoke the `acc_run` system call. The execution happens asynchronously, meaning that `acc_run` returns immediately. This enables the application to execute more than one context in parallel without using threads. When the application needs to check the execution status, e.g. if the FPGA has finished its work, the 'status' file can be read. Unless this file was opened with *O_NONBLOCK* the `read` system call will block until the RTRM inside the FPGA has finished its task.

4.3.5. Destroy Context

When the application closes the file handle returned by `acc_create` the context gets destroyed.

5. Case Study of using ACCFS with a FPGA supporting multiple RTRMs

As proof of concept we present a case study in which two different compute kernels are utilized as RTRMs in a multi-user and multi-context mode. As FPGA accelerator a HyperTransport coupled Xilinx Virtex-4 FPGA plug-in card [13] was chosen. Multiple users are able to create multiple instances (multiple contexts) of RTRMs as long as sufficient logic area is available on the FPGA. The first RTRM acts as an offload function which finds patterns in a byte stream (pattern matcher) and the second module, a Mersenne Twister, generates pseudo random numbers at high output frequency. As hardware for the host system an Iwill DK8-HTX motherboard with two Opteron processors is utilized. The pre-installed BIOS is replaced by a customized LinuxBios version to get the HTX-card enumerated by the host system. The FPGA on the HTX card is a Xilinx Virtex-4 XC4VFX60.

5.1. RTRMs - Pattern Matcher and Mersenne Twister

Two RTRMs have been implemented, which are described in this subsection, a pattern matcher and a Mersenne twister based on the MT19937 algorithm [14]. The latter uses the MT32 [15] implementation, which is able to provide a new 32 bits pseudo random number each clock cycle. When the host performs a read request on an arbitrary RTRM address, a new 32 bits number is provided. The RTRM pattern matcher simultaneously compares several 32 bits patterns against a search database. The module consists of a finite state machine (FSM), four 32 bits comparators for each pattern, one control register, one status register as well as dual-port block RAMs for the search database, the search patterns and the results. Additionally, a 56 bits window is superimposed over the search database. The registers and memories are mapped into the lower 27 bits addresses of the RTRM's address space and can be accessed by the host. After the host has set the start bit in the control register, the FSM reads the search patterns from the pattern memory, the window is set to the beginning of the search database and the comparators are enabled. Then, the first comparator of each search pattern tests the first 32 bits of the window, the second one 32 bits shifted by one byte, the third one 32 bits shifted by two bytes and the fourth the last 32 bits of the window against the search pattern. Hereby, the window can be shifted by 32 bits each clock cycle. When the end of the search database has been reached, the results are written to the results memory. Afterwards, the 'finished' bit is set in the status register. Next, the host can read the matcher results from the results memory.

5.2. Multi User and Multi Context Support with ACCFS

Multi user and multi context abstraction is provided by ACCFS. Each user can create isolated contexts by invoking the `acc_create` function call. For each context, ACCFS occupies the required logic area on the FPGA. Thereby, a context is only accessible by the user who created it. The mapping of virtual user addresses to physical addresses of the FPGA interconnect is provided by the vendor-specific part of ACCFS, the resolution of these physical addresses to virtual addresses of a specific RTRM is performed by the RTRM controller inside the HT cave with RTR support. Since each RTRM uses its own virtual address space, it is guaranteed that concurrently on the FPGA operating modules do not influence each other. For accessing the RTRMs on the FPGA, e.g. the offloading functions Mersenne twister and pattern matcher, the user has to create at least one application which utilizes the necessary ACCFS function calls in the appropriate order. The user function `matcher_run` demonstrates the usage of the RTRM pattern matcher. First, this function creates a new context and partially reconfigures the FPGA by the function `configure_fpga`. Then, the search database and search patterns are written to the RTRM's database and patterns memory using the `pwrite` system call. Next, the matcher is started using `acc_run` and the user function waits until the execution has finished. After that, the results are read from the FPGA into the buffer `results_out` by the `pread` system call. The user function `run_compute_kernel` uses the pseudo random numbers generated by the RTRM Mersenne twister for the computation kernel `c_kernel_function`. This RTRM is initialized using the same functions like in the previous example. In contrast to the previous one, the random numbers are not read using file handles, but can be accessed by the computation kernel via the memory-mapped buffer `mt32_numbers`.

6. Conclusion and Future Work

The software framework ACCFS and the infrastructure of a host coupled FPGA with run-time reconfiguration support were presented, which ease the way of user applications for run-time reconfigurable computing. ACCFS offers a smooth and fast integration of new FPGA hardware with its vendors specific part for system designers and a dynamic run-time management for application developers due to its generic virtual file system approach. Multi user and multi context creation of run-time reconfigurable FPGA offloading modules are possible. The implementation was done for FPGAs coupled directly to the HyperTransport processor bus of the host system. The concepts provided are applicable to other processor and peripheral bus coupled FPGAs.

To support more common FPGA accelerator plug-in cards, we want to add a reference design for a PCI Express coupled FPGA.

References

[1] N. A. Woods and T. VanCourt, "FPGA Acceleration of Quasi-Monte Carlo in Finance," in *Proceedings of the 2008 IEEE International Conference onField-Programmable Logic, FPL 2008, 8-10 September, Heidelberg.* IEEE, 2008, pp. 335–340.

[2] G. L. Zhang, P. H. W. Leong, C. H. Ho, K. H. Tsoi, C. C. C. Cheung, D.-U. Lee, R. C. C. Cheung, and W. Luk, "Reconfigurable Acceleration for Monte Carlo Based Financial Simulation," in *FPT,* G. J. Brebner, S. Chakraborty, and W.-F. Wong, Eds. IEEE, 2005, pp. 215–222.

[3] J. Hagemeyer, B. Kettelhoit, M. Koester, and M. Porrmann, in *Design of Homogeneous Communication Infrastructures for Partially Reconfigurable FPGAs (ERSA).* CSREA Press, 2007.

[4] D. Koch, C. Beckhoff, and J. Teich, "ReCoBus-Builder a Novel Tool and Technique to Build Statically and Dynamically Reconfigurable Systems for FPGAs," in *Proceedings of the 2008 IEEE International Conference onField-Programmable Logic, FPL 2008, 8-10 September, Heidelberg.* IEEE, 2008.

[5] J. Surisi, C. Patterson, and P. Athanas, "An efficient run-time router for connecting modules in FPGAs," in *Proceedings of the 2008 IEEE International Conference onField-Programmable Logic, FPL 2008, 8-10 September, Heidelberg.* IEEE, 2008.

[6] T. Pionteck, C. Albrecht, K. Maehle, E., Hübner, M., and Becker, J., "Communication Architectures for Dynamically Reconfigurable FPGA Designs," in *Proceedings of IEEE International Parallel and Distributed Processing Symposium,* IPDPS USA, 2007.

[7] J. Strunk, T. Volkmer, K. Stephan, W. Rehm, and H. Schick, "Impact on Run-Time Reconfiguration on Design and Speed - A Case Study Based on a Grid of Run-Time Reconfigurable Modules inside a FPGA," in *proceedings of the Reconfigurable Architectures Workshop (RAW) / IPDPS,* 2009.

[8] E. Lübbers and M. Planner, "ReconOS: An RTOS Supporting Hard-and Software Threads," in *Proceedings of the 2007 IEEE International Conference on Field-Programmable Logic and Applications.* Amsterdam: IEEE, 27-29 August 2007, pp. 441–446.

[9] H. K.-H. So and R. Bordersen, "File System Access From Reconfigurable FPGA Hardware Processes In BORPH," in *Proceedings of the 2008 IEEE International Conference onField-Programmable Logic, FPL 2008, 8-10 September, Heidelberg.* IEEE, 2008.

[10] A. Heinig, R. Oertel, J. Strunk, W. Rehm, and H. Schick, "Generalizing the SPUFS concept - a case study towards a common accelerator interface," in *Proceedings of the Many-core and Reconfigurable Supercomputing Conference,* Belfast, 1-3 April 2008.

[11] D. Slogsnat, A. Giese, and U. Bruening, "A versatile, low latency HyperTransport core," in *Fifteenth ACM/SIGDA International Symposium on Field-Programmable Gate Arrays,* 2007.

[12] A. Bergmann, "The Cell Processor Programming Model," IBM Corporation, Tech. Rep., June 2005.

[13] M. Nuessle, H. Fröning, A. Giese, H. Litz, D. Slogsnat, and U. Brning, "A Hypertransport based low-latency reconfigurable testbed for message-passing developments," in *KiCC'07,* 2007.

[14] M. Matsumoto and T. Nishimura, "Mersenne twister: a 623-dimensionally equidistributed uniform pseudo-random number generator," *ACM Trans. Model. Comput. Simul.,* vol. 8, no. 1, pp. 3–30, 1998.

[15] "Mersenne Twister, MT32. Pseudo Random Number Generator for Xilinx FPGA," Website, 2007. [Online]. Available: http://www.ht-lab.com/freecores/mt32/mersenne.html

Mini-Symposium
"Parallel Programming Tools for Multi-Core Architectures"

Parallel Computing: From Multicores and GPU's to Petascale
B. Chapman et al. (Eds.)
IOS Press, 2010

643

© 2010 The authors and IOS Press. All rights reserved.
doi:10.3233/978-1-60750-530-3-643

Parallel Programming Tools for Multi-core Architectures

Bernd MOHR [a], Bettina KRAMMER [b] and Hartmut MIX [c]

[a] *Forschungszentrum Jülich, Jülich Supercomputing Centre (JSC), Germany*
[b] *University of Versailles Saint-Quentin-en-Yvelines (UVSQ), France*
[c] *Tech. Universtät Dresden, Center for Information Services and High Performance Computing (ZIH), Germany*

1. Introduction

The improvement of the processor performance by increasing the clock rate has reached its technological limits. Increasing the number of processor cores rather than clock rates can give better performance and reduce problems such as energy consumption, heat dissipation and design complexity. We are witnessing the emergence of multi-core processors in all markets - from laptops and game consoles to servers and supercomputers. At the same time, architectures are becoming heterogeneous and memory hierarchies and interconnection networks are increasingly complex.

Multi-core architectures present new opportunities as well as challenges to software that will run on computer systems built up on such multi-core chips. To keep pace with the evolution from dual-, quad-, to large many-core systems, the keys to unleashing significant performance enhancements for such multi-core systems are well-defined parallel programming models and robust, easy-to-use tools supporting the parallelization process. Compared to sequential applications, software engineers require a more powerful, well matched repertoire of development tools and methods for costeffectively achieving highly optimized, reliable, fault tolerant and robust parallel applications.

2. Papers and Presentations

The purpose of this mini-symposium was to bring together researchers and practitioners with diverse backgrounds in order to advance the state of the art in software engineering for multi-core parallel applications. In this spirit, many of the papers do not only present parallel programming tools and methods, but demonstrate their usefulness on real-world industrial applications.

The paper "Parallel Programming for Multi-core Architectures" by Jean-Marc Morel gives an overview on the European ParMA project (2007-2010). This project targets the development and extension of programming methods, tools, libraries and Linux operating system, to enable parallel applications to exploit fully the power of multi-core architectures, both for High-Performance and Embedded Computing.

Andres Charif-Rubial et al. present a "Methodology for Application Performance Tuning". This methodolgy combines static assembly analysis using the MAQAO tool and dynamic hardware performance monitoring and memory tracing. Applying it to an iterative linear solver developed by Dassault Aviation, a speed-up of almost up to 2.5 could be achieved.

Another success story of applying different tools to an industrial use-case is presented by Benedetto Risio et al. in "How to Accelerate an Application: a Practical Case Study in Combustion Modelling". The tool-chain comprises both low-level (MAQAO) and high-level (VAMPIR, SCALASCA) analysis of the application: optimising memory access, cache utilisation and MPI synchronisation leads to a significant performance improvement.

Alejandro Duran et al. gave a presentation on "Supporting OpenMP in a heterogeneous world". Efficiently programming heterogeneous architectures with accelerator devices (e.g. graphics processors, vector units) is currently a complex task. They present a series of extensions to OpenMP, inspired in the work of the StarSs programming model, that allow developers to easily write portable codes for a number of different platforms, relieving them from developing the specific code to off-load tasks to the accelerators and the synchronization of tasks.

Daniel Millot et al. present the STEP tool in "From OpenMP to MPI: first experiments of the STEP source-to-source transformation". STEP can transform OpenMP code into MPI code, thus allowing easy transition from shared to distributed memory systems. Some benchmark results are presented.

The paper "Using Multi-Core Architectures to Execute High Performance-Oriented Real-Time Applications" by Christophe Aussaguès et al. describes the OASIS design, compilation and execution framework for embedded real-time systems that execute High-Performance oriented applications on multi-core architectures. OASIS is demonstrated on the example of a 2D-tracking algorithm from Dassault Aviation.

Allen D. Malony et al. report early experiences of "Performance Tool Integration in Programming Environments for GPU Acceleration: Experiences with TAU and HMPP". They describe the design approach of integrating the TAU parallel performance system, the TAUcuda accelerator performance tool and the HMPP workbench for programming GPU accelerators using CUDA. Two case studies are presented.

Tobias Hilbrich et al. present UniMCI, "An Interface for Integrated MPI Correctness Checking". This interface provides functionality for coupling performance analysis frameworks and correctness checking tools in a generic way. First results of a prototype implementation using the Marmot correctness checker and the VampirTrace performance analysis tool are shown.

Last not least, Thomas William et al. describe an approach of "Enhanced Performance Analysis of Multi-core Applications with an Integrated Tool-chain". In this case, the VAMPIR and SCALASCA performance analysis tools are connected through a common bus system, which allows users to identify and locate performance problems quickly with SCALASCA and to use the powerful VAMPIR visualistaion tool to dive into the execution history. The usefulness and effectiveness of this integrated tool-chain is demonstrated with the INDEED metal forming simulation software.

Parallel Computing: From Multicores and GPU's to Petascale
B. Chapman et al. (Eds.)
IOS Press, 2010
© 2010 The authors and IOS Press. All rights reserved.
doi:10.3233/978-1-60750-530-3-645

Parallel Programming for Multi-core Architectures

Jean-Marc MOREL [a] for the ParMA Project Partners [b]

[a] *Bull SAS, France*
[b] *France, Germany, Spain, UK*

Abstract. This paper gives an overview of the European ITEA2 project named ParMA ("Parallel Programming for Multi-core Architectures"), which aims at developing advanced technologies for exploiting multi-core architectures both for conventional High Performance Computing (HPC) and for Embedded Computing. It presents the main components of the ParMA technology and describes how application developers applied it and improved the performance of their applications.

Keywords. parallel programming, multi-core, performance analysis, code optimization, (embedded) high-performance computing.

1. Introduction

The ParMA project has been proposed in 2006 when it was acknowledged that the "free lunch was over" as Herb Sutter stressed it in his famous article [1]: "because the microprocessor serial processing speed is reaching a physical limit, processor manufacturers will turn en masse to hyperthreading and multi-core architectures, forcing software developers to develop massively multithreaded programs to harness the power of such processors". Indeed, the number of cores per chip doubles every 18 months, instead of clock frequency as shown in Figure 1.

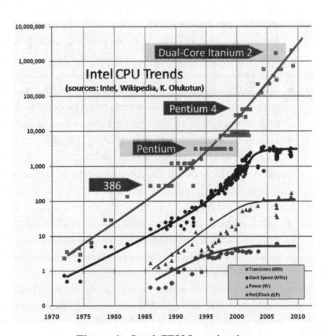

Figure 1.: Intel CPU Introductions

On the other hand, research and industry do need more powerful and more cost effective technical and scientific computing systems either to solve big challenges (e.g. global warming studies, bio-informatics) or to design new products in a more effective manner (e.g. using car crash simulation to spare the cost of hardware prototypes). Efficient parallel computing appears to be paramount to meet these challenges.

Therefore, the ParMA project (see http://www.parma-itea2.org/) has been launched mid-2007 to develop and leverage parallel programming techniques and tools enabling to take advantage of multi-core architectures. The aim is to build a software development environment intended, on the one hand, to significantly improve the performance of HPC applications (thus the modelling and simulation of more complex models) and, on the other hand, to prepare to develop power- intensive embedded applications that could not be envisaged so far.

In the following sections, we present the ParMA approach, the main components of the ParMA technology (focusing on the elements that are not presented in the companion papers [2,3,4,5,6,7]), and the first results obtained on industrial applications, while the list of partners with their main contribution is given in Table 1 on the last page.

2. The ParMA Approach

The advent of various types of massively and multilevel parallel architectures presents several real challenges:

- Since most existing HPC applications are designed as a set of independent processes communicating and synchronising through calls to MPI (Message Passing Interface) primitives with each process being bound to a processor, programming paradigms and tools must be developed to help restructure these applications so that they can fully benefit from the multilevel parallelism offered by new architectures;
- Due to the huge number of threads that multi-core processors will be able to run in parallel, dramatic improvements must be achieved in the way threads are allocated and monitored to minimise memory access – i.e. data exchanges between threads;
- Because of the increased complexity resulting from the huge number of threads, more powerful programming, debugging and performance analysis tools are needed . They should also be more easy to use, and should help optimize applications using different forms of parallel architectures in various contexts (e.g. SMP, NUMA, MPSoC).
- Since embedded systems will also be built with multi-core processors, multilevel parallel design, programming and execution models must be defined and tools must be developed accordingly; including tools to design efficient interconnecting networks for MPSoC.
- Because each domain – simulation, virtual reality, avionics, etc. – has its own characteristics and specific constraints, the proposed approaches must be experimented and validated with different applications from various domains.

To meet the above challenges, ParMA proposed a holistic approach and we split the technical work into four inter-connected work packages as shown in Figure 2.

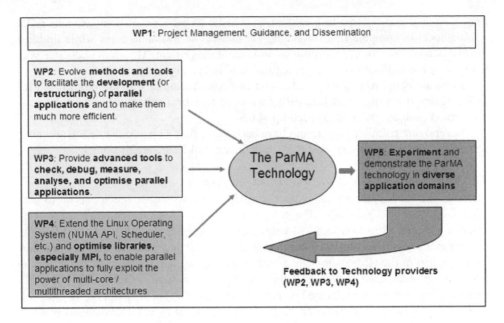

Figure 2. The ParMA cooperation schema

3. The ParMA Technology

As it is acknowledged that there is no silver bullet to port a compute-intensive application on a multi-core architecture and get better performance, several key enablers need to be combined and leveraged that include:

- Algorithms that are more accurate and converge faster
- Methods and tools to detect and extract parallelism (thread extraction),
- New parallel programming models and extended directives to express parallelism,
- Easy to use and scalable performance-analysis tools,
- Powerful correctness checker and debugger,
- Code optimization tools,
- Optimized libraries for multithread / multi-core, and
- Enhanced software infrastructure with optimized thread management, job scheduling, etc.

Thus, the ParMA project organized to advance the state-of-the-art in these various aspects:

3.1. Algorithms that are more accurate and converge faster

Several partners recognized the need to start by identifying critical algorithms that could not take advantage from parallelism or could not scale properly and to replace them by new ones which can well exploit multi-core architectures thereby yielding faster and more accurate results. CEA- LIST for instance, developed innovative algorithms of collision detection (based on Bounding Volume Hierarchy) and object motion management.

They designed and tested a task calibration scheme to get a set of homogeneous tasks (with respect to compute time) matching the number of available cores while limiting the overhead to pay for synchronisation and task management. The main challenge was to organize the tasks (threads) to get optimal load balancing.

In an industrial test case carried out on an 8 core machine with an initial speed-up of 1.7, their extraction parallelism (using a mix of temporal coherency and geometrical properties) enabled to deliver a speed-up of 6.9.

Several other similar experiences have been made that, in particular, led to adopting solvers that are more efficient and more scalable on multi-core architectures.

3.2. Methods and tools to detect and extract parallelism

Methods and tools to detect and extract parallelism are of course much needed to parallelize a sequential application. Therefore CAPS (http://www.caps-entreprise.com/) developed a thread extraction tool that helps identify possible threads using profiling information: hot paths and memory transfers (data size and dependencies). This extraction facility is part of the HMPP tool which enables to map domain specific and critical computations on specialized processors (hardware accelerators such as GPU or FPGA) while generic computations are allocated on generic cores (CPUs). This mapping is specified by mean of OpenMP-like compiler directives that are used to generate codelets that encapsulate hardware-specific code, while determining which data are local or shared to minimize data transfers.

3.3. New parallel programming models and enriched directives to express parallelism

Evolving parallel programming models to help application developers express parallelism to get optimal binary code on multi-core architectures is also an important research path in ParMA. In addition to HMPP directives mentioned above, two extensions have been designed and are being implemented:

- The STEP approach [4] to transform an OpenMP program to an MPI program so that it can be executed on distributed-memory platforms.
- The introduction of data parallelism in the OASIS parallel time-triggered programming and execution model for embedded system, evaluated with an intense-computing application provided by Dassault Aviation [5].

3.4. Easy to use and scalable performance-analysis tools

Easy to use and scalable performance-analysis tools are of the utmost importance to help developers understand how their parallel application behaves on a given multi -core architecture. These tools point out the performance bottlenecks, and help identify how to remove these bottlenecks and more generally how to optimize the code or reduce the time spent in inter- processes communications. See [7] for more details about the performance toolset (Scalasca + Vampir) that has been extended, enhanced, and integrated in ParMA.

3.5. Powerful correctness checker and debugger

Powerful correctness checker and debugger is also a much needed category of tools when dealing with highly parallel code, in particular when this code must execute in various contexts (on different platforms, using different MPI libraries, etc.). Whereas various tools exist that address different problems (for instance DDT from Allinea to debug the code and Marmot from HLRS and TU Dresden to check MPI correctness), it appears tedious for the user to run them separately. ParMA enabled to efficiently integrate and combine these tools to ease their use. In particular, an "Interface for Integrated MPI Correctness Checking" [6] was designed, allowing to easily combine any MPI correctness checker with performance analysis tools.

3.6. Code optimisation tools

Parallelism enables to distribute the work on different processors but optimal performance cannot be obtained without code optimisation. First, the developer needs facilities to identify which resources are saturated (e.g. the memory bandwidth) and which part of the code should be changed. Then, guidance is needed to find out what should be changed (e.g. the algorithm, the data layout, the directives, or the compiler options) and in which way. UVSQ designed a semi- automated methodology to analyze performance and guide the optimization process [2] using both static analysis (with the MAQAO tool) and dynamic analysis (with Hardware Performance monitoring and memory traces).

3.7. Optimized libraries for multithread / multi-core

As an important part of the executing time is spent in functions from various libraries, for instance the BLAS[1] library that contains routines for performing basic vector and matrix operations, optimizing performance-critical and complex routines such as DGEMM (matrix-matrix multiply) is both challenging and rewarding. So, UVSQ explored the impact of data prefetching on multi core Xeon platform and devised efficient workarounds that led to an optimized parallel version of two building block functions, `matrix_init` and `memcpy2D` which perform significantly better than the Intel£s implementation. Thus, these functions can be used to replace the corresponding routines of the Intel MKL when there is an important need of them, typically in iterative solvers.

3.8. Optimized software infrastructure

An optimized software infrastructure is more than needed to ensure efficient communications (data exchanges) among interrelated processes and threads that execute concurrently. For example, an optimized implementation of MPI (Message Passing Interface) must be topology- aware in order to use the most efficient way of moving data between two threads depending on their relative position in the hierarchical architecture (an HPC cluster being usually composed of several groups / islands of computing nodes, each node containing several sockets, each socket containing several cores, and each core being possibly multithreaded). For intra-node communication for instance, Bull designed an efficient shared and cache memory management that minimizes buffer copy and optimizes bandwidth. To be optimal, different protocols depending on the size of the message to be transmitted are implemented. Other optimizations include (1) improved scheduling policies, (2) synchronisation of daemons on all nodes to reduce their disturbances thus improving MPI collective operations, and (3) enhanced resources and job management to ensure that all cores of a cluster are consistently and optimally exploited.

The need for efficient communications also exists in embedded systems where multi-core processors are making their way. As traditional bus-based interconnects prove to be insufficient to support the increasing volume of data exchange between the multiple processors on a MPSoC (Multi-Processor System-on-Chip), inter-processors communi-

---

[1] BLAS stands for Basic Linear Algebra Subprograms. It is part of the Intel Math Kernel Library (MKL)

cations in embedded systems should now be based on the Network-on-Chip (NoC) concept. UAB developed the NoCMaker tool that helps NoC developers to design an efficient network for a given embedded system architecture and the set of applications that will run on it. NoCMaker enables to simulate and analyze not only the performance of the designed NoC but also its area and energy consumption because those who embrace the manycore wave also expect superior energy efficiency (MOPS/mW).

Finally, to enable Indra to develop a custom on-chip SDR (Software Defined Radio, an example of power-intensive embedded application), Robotiker designed and implemented a NoC-based MPSoC platform using a FPGA[2].

It has the following components:
– Soft-core IP processors (P_i)
  Xilinx Microblaze soft-core processor
– Distributed memory subsystem (M_i)
– Network Interface Controller (NICi)
– Driver for Network Interface Controller
– NoC communication architecture
– On-Chip Message Passing Interface
  (ocMPI)

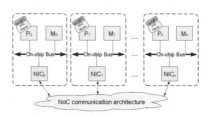

Note that this on-chip message passing interface implements a subset of the MPI standard which has been adapted to the embedded system environment [8].

The embedded system developers also adopted OTF (the Open Trace Format) which has been designed as the common trace format for the performance analysis tools (e.g. Vampir), thereby enabling to also benefit from these tools.

4. First Results Obtained on Industrial Applications

ITEA projects being industry-driven, the validation and uptake of the developed technology by industrial partners is quite important. As such, the ParMA project includes several numerical simulation software editors and several compute-intensive application developers who started to experiment with the initial version of the ParMA tools. They run a series of performance measurements to identify performance bottlenecks, understand the behavior of their code on multi-core architecture, assess its scalability, and when possible compare the performance of MPI versus OpenMP code version. Most often, these results were analyzed with the help of HPC experts from the labs who in addition gave some hints on how the code should be restructured or the compilation options changed to get better performance. Of course several cycles (measure, analyze, optimize the code) are generally needed to obtain satisfactory results. Hereafter are some examples.

CEA-LIST / LSI developed an efficient parallel dose exposure simulation and, using Vampir and Scalasca to identify bottlenecks, succeeded to reach 0.4s response time on a 16-core platform (instead of 5s on a scalar machine), thus enabling user interactivity. However, scalability can be further improved.

GNS GNS restructured the assembly phase of its metal forming simulation application INDEED (INnovative DEEp Drawing) and got improved performance (30%) by minimizing the sequential code in the assembly phase and by a better load balancing.

---

[2]An FPGA (Field-Programmable Gate Array) is a semiconductor device containing programmable logic components called "logic blocks", and programmable interconnects.

Besides, the combined use of Scalasca and Vampir enabled GNS to optimize the adaptive mesh refinement and load balancing phases. See more details in [7].

MAGMA had two versions of its MAGMAsolid solver: (1) A SMP version (i.e. for shared-memory architecture only) that did not scale well (speedup limited to 3.5 on 8 or 16 cores) and (2) an MPI version that scaled well on distributed memory architecture with a large number of processors (speedup ~45x using 64 cores) but was about four times slower than the SMP version on a 1- to 8-core shared memory architecture. Thus, MAGMA application developers carried out a detailed performance analysis of the MPI version to get a unique and efficient product. They first identified that they should switch from a CG (Conjugate Gradient) based solver to an ADI (Alternating Direction Implicit) based solver (~2x faster). Then, they found out that they could improve the cache efficiency by reorganizing the data structures (eliminating 6 temporary arrays) and enable the compiler to better optimize the code by removing function calls in inner loops. Still with the help of the performance analysis tools, MAGMA also obtained 3.5x performance increase for its MAGMAfill module by redesigning central communication routines using asynchronous communication and by optimizing the checkpointing strategy. As a result, MAGMA customers are now provided with a unique scalable solution (2x to 4x faster) on whatever architecture they use.

RECOM's objective in ParMA was to adopt a hybrid parallel programming model, allowing for the combination of distributed memory parallelization across nodes and data parallel execution within the nodes. For this, an OpenMP- and MPI-Implementation, as well as a hybrid parallel version using a combined MPI- and OpenMP-parallel programming model was implemented and installed on the project platform where detailed performance analysis could be carried out using different combinations of MPI processes and OpenMP threads in each MPI process. For instance, using Vampir, RECOM application developers identified and removed a synchronization bottleneck, obtaining a 10% performance improvement. They also studied with the help of the MAQAO tool how to improve memory access as well as memory utilisation for some memory-intense routines, and could achieve performance gains of about 34% for the entire application. See more details in [3].

5. Conclusion and Future Work

In this paper we described the overall approach of the ParMA team to consistently advance the various techniques and tools that are needed to speed-up compute-intensive applications and to get them scalable on modern multi-core architectures. Efficient teamwork between HPC application developers and performance tools providers enabled to find out pr oblems, their cause, and most often a solution that significantly improves the performance of the application, up to 4x faster in some cases. So, from now on, application partners can provide their customers with new, very efficient and scalable solutions. Besides, embedded applications developers started to experiment with parallelization of their code, taking advantage from the experience, the techniques, and the tools from the HPC world: they designed ocMPI after MPI, adopted OTF (Open Trace Format), and can benefit from the performance analysis tools such as Vampir. Our plan is to consolidate these early results and to further disseminate them during the few months before the end of the project.

Acknowledgments

This work has partially been supported by the French Ministry of Industry (DGCIS), the German Ministry for Research and Education (BMBF), and the Spanish Ministry of Industry through the ITEA2 project "ParMA" (No 06015, June 2007 – May 2010).

The ParMa Consortium

Ctry	Partner	Category (Industrial, Lab, University)	Main contribution
FR	Bull	I: HPC platform provider	Provide common HPC platform
FR	CAPS	I: Accelerate HPC code using GPU	Develop thread extraction tool
FR	CEA-LIST	L: Safety real-time embedded system	Extend programming model
FR	Dassault Aviation	I: Aircraft design	Experiment with critical code
FR	IT SudParis	U: Institut Telecom Sud Paris	Transform OpenMP to MPI
FR	UVSQ	U: University of Versailles St-Quentin	Optimize code with MAQAO
DE	GNS	I: Metal forming simulation software	Experiment with INDEED
DE	GWT	I: HPC software tool editor	Develop Vampir with TUD
DE	HLRS	U: University of Stuttgart	Develop MPI correctness tool
DE	JSC	L: Jülich Supercomputing Center	Develop Scalasca
DE	MAGMA	I: Casting process simulation software	Experiment with MAGMASoft
DE	RECOM	I: 3D combustion modeling software	Experiment with AIOLOS
DE	TU Dresden	U: Technische Universität Dresden	Develop Vampir with GWT
ES	INDRA	I: Avionics systems (e.g. SDR)	Experiment with Soft. Radio
ES	Robotiker	L: Embedded Systems	Develop MPSoC platform
ES	UAB	U: Universitat autonoma de Barcelona	Develop NoCMaker tool
UK	Allinea	I: HPC software tools Editor	Develop debugger (DDT)

Table 1. The ParMA consortium.

References

[1] Sutter, H. 2005. The free lunch is over: A fundamental turn toward concurrency in software, Dr. Dobb's Journal, 30(3).

[2] Andres Charif-Rubial, Souad Koliai, William Jalby, Bettina Krammer, Quang Dinh: An Approach to Application Performance Tuning (Proceedings of Parco 2009).

[3] Benedetto Risio, Alexander Berreth, Stephane Zuckerman, Souad Koliai, Mickael Ivascot, William Jalby, Bettina Krammer, Bernd Mohr, Thomas William: How to Accelerate an Application: a Practical Case Study in Combustion Modelling (Proceedings of Parco 2009).

[4] Daniel Millot, Alain Muller, Christian Parrot, Frédérique Silber-Chaussumier: From OpenMP to MPI: first experiments of the STEP source-to-source transformation (Proceedings of Parco 2009).

[5] Christophe AUSSAGUES, Emmanuel OHAYON, Karine BRIFAULT, Quang V. DINH: Using Multi-Core Architectures to Execute High Performance-Oriented Real-Time Applications (Proceedings of Parco 2009).

[6] Tobias Hilbrich, Matthias Jurenz, Hartmut Mix, Holger Brunst, Andreas Knüpfer, Matthias S. Müller, Wolfgang E. Nagel : An Interface for Integrated MPI Correctness Checking (Proceedings of Parco 2009).

[7] Thomas William, Hartmut Mix, Bernd Mohr, Felix Voigtländer, René Menzel: Enhanced Performance Analysis of Multi-core Applications with an Integrated Tool-chain (Proceedings of Parco 2009).

[8] Jaume Joven, David Castells-Rufas: a lightweight MPI-based programming model and its HW support for NoC-based MPSoC. DATE'09 (Design Automation and Test in Europe), April 2009, Nice, France.

Parallel Computing: From Multicores and GPU's to Petascale
B. Chapman et al. (Eds.)
IOS Press, 2010

© 2010 The authors and IOS Press. All rights reserved.

doi:10.3233/978-1-60750-530-3-653

An Approach to Application Performance Tuning

Andres CHARIF-RUBIAL [a], Souad KOLIAI [a], Stéphane ZUCKERMAN [a],
Bettina KRAMMER [a], William JALBY [a] and Quang DINH [b]

[a] *University of Versailles Saint-Quentin-en-Yvelines, France*
[b] *Dassault-Aviation, France*

Abstract. Current hardware trends place increasing pressure on programmers and tools to optimize scientific code. Numerous tools and techniques exist, but no single tool is a panacea; instead, an assortment of performance tuning utilities are necessary to best utilize scarce resources (e.g., bandwidth, functional units, cache). This paper describes an optimization strategy combining static assembly analysis using the MAQAO tool with dynamic information from hardware performance monitoring (HPM) and memory traces. A new technique, decremental analysis (DECAN), is introduced to iteratively identify the individual instructions causing performance bottlenecks. We present a case study on an industrial application from Dassault Aviation on a Xeon Core 2 platform. Our strategy helps discover and fix problems related to memory access locality and loop unrolling, which leads to a sequential and parallel speedup of up to 2.5.

Keywords. code optimization, performance analysis, static analysis, dynamic analysis

1. Introduction

In High Performance Computing (HPC), there is a constant hunger for more resources (e.g., CPU, RAM, I/O). With finite limits on these resources, it is the responsibility of the programmer, interacting with the compiler, to optimize an application for peak performance. Optimization consists of gathering data about a program's behavior, diagnosing the problem by identifying resources that are saturated and the instructions at fault, and prescribing a solution which entails applying a change to the code's algorithm, structure, or data layout.

The first step, data collection, involves an array of different analysis techniques to examine different aspects of application performance. Typically, a code is deemed optimal if it approaches the peak numerical throughput of the processor; this implies that only an algorithmic change could further improve performance.

In this paper, we address optimization of HPC applications, specifically CPU- and memory-bound ones. We describe a semi-automated methodology to analyze performance and guide the optimization process. Both static analysis (with MAQAO and visual inspection) and dynamic analysis (of memory access patterns) of the code are performed. Information from these analyses guides us to the regions of code furthest from peak performance. Using this information, we introduce a new approach to identify the

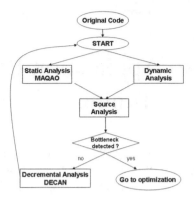

Figure 1. Methodology diagram

specific set of instructions that are responsible for increased computation latency: decremental analysis (DECAN). DECAN involves systematically changing instructions' behavior in a particular region to identify the runtime contribution of each instruction or set of instructions. DECAN is useful in those cases where the static and dynamic analyses do not give enough information about the program's behavior.

This methodology has been applied to several industrial HPC codes, among them ITRLSOL (ITeRative Linear SOLver) from Dassault-Aviation, which is presented in this paper and where we achieved a speedup of nearly 2.5.

Section 2 presents the tools and techniques in our analysis approach. Section 3 describes a case study (ITRLSOL) on which our methodology was applied leading to significant performance improvements. Section 4 discusses other approaches to performance tuning. Finally, Section 5 concludes.

2. Toward a better evaluation process

This section provides a high-level description of each step of the methodology. Figure 1 shows a flow diagram of the process with the following performance analysis techniques being intended to identify the root cause of a performance bottleneck. It is assumed that the targets of optimization are significant contributors to program execution time as reported by tools such as gprof [7] or Intel PTU [1].

2.1. Static Analysis: MAQAO

MAQAO [5] is a static analysis tool which aims at analyzing assembly code produced by the compiler, extracting key characteristics from it and detecting potential inefficiencies. MAQAO was originally developed for the Intel Itanium architecture, and was recently extended to support x86 programs using Intel Core 2 processors as well. Figure 2 shows the graphical interface for browsing compiled programs. It can provide the user with many metrics derived from the assembly code analysis:

1. **Vectorization Report Analysis:** provides individual measures on vector instruction usage (load, store, add, multiply). These metrics are essential to evaluate the quality of the vectorizing capabilities of the compiler and therefore try to palliate some of its deficiencies by inserting appropriate pragmas or directives.

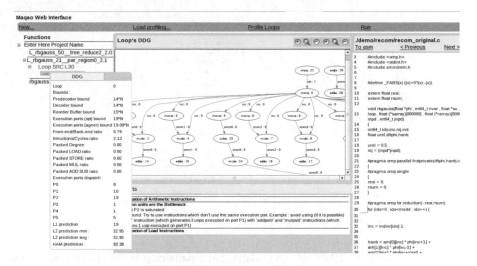

Figure 2. MAQAO interface

2. **Execution Port Usage:** for each of the independent execution ports, MAQAO computes an estimate of the number of cycles spent for one iteration of the loop. This metric is essential to measure the amount of parallelism exploitable between the key functional units: add, multiply, load and store units.

3. **Performance Estimation in L1:** taking into account all of the limitations of the pipeline front end (decoder and permanent register file access limitations, special microcoded instructions) and the pipeline back end, MAQAO provides an estimate of the amount of cycles necessary to execute one loop iteration assuming all operands are in L1. As previously mentioned, this bound is most useful as an optimal lower bound representing peak execution.

4. **Performance Estimations in L2/RAM:** MAQAO computes an estimate for the execution time of a loop iteration, assuming all operands are in L2 or RAM and are accessed with stride 1. This estimation relies on memory access patterns detected at the assembly level and micro benchmarking results on the same memory patterns. The drawback of both of these estimates is twofold: they ignore the stride problem (which in RAM will be essential), and they do not take into account the mixture of hits and misses which is typical of real applications.

5. **Performance Projections for Full Vectorization:** In cases where the code is partially or not vectorized, MAQAO computes performance estimations for full vectorization. This is performed by replacing the scalar operations by their vector counterparts and updating the timing estimate due to the use of these instructions.

6. **Loop Attribute Profiling:** provides important metrics such as the number of iteration of the loop body and the number of instructions per iteration. This concept will be further developed in Section 2.2.

2.2. Dynamic Analysis - Hardware Counters and Memory Traces

2.2.1. Hardware Counters

Using hardware performance counters can provide us with very useful information on the program execution and, in particular, on how resources are used. Tools such as Intel's

```
Thread 1                                    #pragma omp for schedule (static,chunk)
for i0 = 0 to 7                             for (j=0; j<NCB; j++)
  for i1 = 0 to 63                          {
    for i2 = 0 to 63                          for(i=0; i<NRA; i++)
      val 0x62cd5a0 + 64*i0 + 512*i1         {
Thread 2                                        for (k=0; k<NCA; k++)
for i0 = 0 to 7                                 {
  for i1 = 0 to 63                                c[i*NRA+j] += a[i*NRA+k] * b[k*NCA+j];
    for i2 = 0 to 63                           }
      val 0x62cd5a8 + 64*i0 + 512*i1        }
Thread 3                                    }
for i0 = 0 to 7
  for i1 = 0 to 63                                      Thread 8
    for i2 = 0 to 63                                    for i0 = 0 to 7
      val 0x62cd5b0 + 64*i0 + 512*i1                      for i1 = 0 to 63
                                        ........            for i2 = 0 to 63
                                                              val 0x62cd5d8 + 64*i0 + 512*i1
```

Figure 3. DGEMM 128x128 with 8 Threads and MAQAO trace results

PTU [1], PerfMon [6], PAPI [9], and others make gathering HPM (High Performance Monitoring) information relatively easy. However, even though hundreds of events can be monitored through hardware counters, most of the counters give information that is either too arcane or too esoteric to be useful.

2.2.2. Memory Traces

Memory accesses can dramatically slow down the execution of a program, particularly when it is memory bound. The MAQAO tool is able to provide us with information on the memory behavior of an application. It can track down inefficient memory access behavior in a program by instrumenting instructions dealing with memory. It is also able to catch strides when accesses are done in a regular fashion thanks to the built-in nested loop recognition algorithm. Resulting traces are analyzed to report issues such as false sharing or thread load balancing when using OpenMP. Figure 3 illustrates a typical false sharing issue when misusing the OpenMP schedule type (for directive).

If the chunk is sufficiently small - assume we set chunk to 1 - then the schedule will lead to a false sharing issue because threads are all writing on the same cache line. We can see in the traces that the threads' start address (dark hexadecimal values) have only a 1-element distance. Using higher chunk values leads to load issue balancing between threads, only a reduced number of the available threads will be used.

2.3. Decremental Analysis: DECAN

DECAN is an added technique of performance analysis which is used when the static and dynamic analyses are not sufficient to pinpoint the bottleneck. Actually, DECAN is performed manually and consists in: first measuring the original version of the code, and then measuring a version of code modified by removing one or more expressions or instructions. This will of course result in incorrect output of the program, and instructions that will result in a crash or alternate control flow are not removed. Once an instruction is removed, the program is again profiled to account for the contribution of the removed instruction. Timing differences and deltas in L1 and L2 miss rates indicate an individual instruction's effect on a loop's overall performance. DECAN is performed on two levels:

Source Level: here, removing an expression, or more precisely an operand, in an arithmetic expression is simpler and allows a direct correlation between a given source instruction and its impact on performance. However, care has to be taken to make sure that the compiler still performs the same optimizations in both versions.

Assembly level: here the corresponding instruction is replaced by a nop instruction of equivalent size. This case is simpler because we are sure the compiler will not optimize the code differently. However, it is more tedious to reason about the dependences and relate the changes to source instructions.

3. Case study

Here we apply our methodology to a real-life application from Dassault-Aviation.

3.1. Experimental Setup

The experimental platform consists of a computation node equipped with four Xeon X7350 (Tigerton). Each Xeon processor is a quad-core chip cadenced at 2.93 GHz, equipped with two 4 MB L2 caches (two cores share one L2 cache), and 32 kB L1 data cache (private to each core). There are 48 GB of RAM available on this node.

The Intel C and Fortran Compilers (icc and ifort v10.1) are used to generate all our assembly codes and also OpenMP parallel regions when appropriate. Intel's Performance Tuning Utility (PTU) is used to access hardware counters and perform part of the dynamic analysis.

3.2. Iterative Solver for the Navier-Stokes Equation

Brief description The ITRLSOL (ITeRative Linear SOLver) [4] application provided by Dassault-Aviation is the linear solver kernel of AcTHER, a larger Computational Fluid Dynamics (CFD) simulation code for the solution of Navier-Stokes equations, discretized on unstructured meshes. ITRLSOL is based on an iterative algorithm where the most time-consuming part is located in the EUFLUXm subroutine, which implements a sparse matrix-vector product.

EUFLUXm contains two groups of 4-level-nested loops (2 identical 4-level-nested loops in each group). The following code snippet displays one of the most time-consuming 4-level-nested loops:

```
        do cb=1,ncbt
           igp = isg
           isg = icolb(icb+1)
           igt = isg + igp
c$OMP   PARALLEL DO DEFAULT(NONE)
c$OMP&  SHARED(igt,igp,nnbar,vecy,vecx,ompu,ompl)
c$OMP&  PRIVATE(ig,e,i,j,k,l)
           do ig=1,igt
              e = ig + igp
              i = nnbar(e,1)
              j = nnbar(e,2)
cDEC$ IVDEP
              do k=1,ndof
cDEC$ IVDEP
                 do l=1,ndof
                    vecy(i,k) = vecy(i,k) + ompu(e,k,l)*vecx(j,l)
                    vecy(j,k) = vecy(j,k) + ompl(e,k,l)*vecx(i,l)
                 enddo
              enddo
           enddo
        enddo
```

Static analysis   The MAQAO vectorization report indicates that no vectorization is performed (no use of SSE instructions). The loads cannot be vectorized due to the non unit stride on the two vectors but the multiplications and the additions could have been vectorized by the compiler. However, the Execution Port Usage report clearly indicates that the vectorization of additions and multiplications will improve P0 and P1 ports (execution units ports) but not the P2 port (loads port) which is the bottleneck.

Dynamic analysis   Loop attribute profiling allows to detect that the main specific feature in the 4-level-nested loops is that the two innermost loop bounds (ndof) are small ($4 \leq$ ndof ≤ 10). The two outermost trip counts are larger and vary throughout execution.

Memory tracing shows that the two innermost loops are accessing all of the arrays along the wrong dimension (row-wise) leading to poor spatial locality. Moreover, the values of indexes used for accessing the first dimension of all arrays are not regular and lead to indirect addressing.

In the EUFLUXm code, cache behaviour is interesting. PTU allows to detect that for every iteration, a quarter of a cache line, i.e. $64\,B/4 = 16\,B = 2$ double precision elements, are brought into L2. This confirms the fact that the two bi-dimensional vectors are most likely kept into L2 while the two 3-dimensional arrays are streamed from RAM.

Decremental analysis   No decremental analysis is performed on Eufluxm. The static and dynamic analyses are significant enough to detect the key performance bottleneck.

Optimization   Since the key performance bottleneck for this routine is a poor spatial locality (accesses on the wrong dimension), various transformations are performed. Over the various code transformations that were performed on the code, two have a significant impact on performance: hardwiring ndof and loop interchange.

Value specialization consists in replacing a variable whose value is unknown by the compiler ndof by its proper value (in our case 4) to help the compiler in particular for unrolling. The compiler fully unrolls the two innermost loops inside the loop nest. As no SIMD instructions were generated, MAQAO is fooled by the fact that the innermost loop is not the one it used to be. Hence no direct comparison with the previous reports can be made, except that according to MAQAO no loop vectorization occurred. A speedup of 1.5 is observed for sequential executions.

The second transformation consists in interchanging the second loop on ig and the two innermost loops (the ig loop becomes the innermost loop). All of the arrays are now accessed column-wise. The static analysis of this transformation with MAQAO shows that indirect accesses still prevent the compiler from vectorizing the loop. However, dynamic analysis shows that interchanging loops substantially increases the data traffic into L1 but drastically improves performance. The L2 traffic remains the same but the hardware prefetch behavior is vastly improved. This optimization improves the single core performance by a speedup of 1.5.

In a multicore environment the same optimizations are applied. Variable specialization has an impact on the overall execution of ITRLSOL, but interchanging loops gives even better results, with a speedup of almost up to 2.5, see Fig. 4.

4. Related work

Automatic static analysis of code source generally leads to optimization performed directly inside the compiler [3].

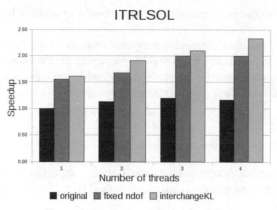

Figure 4. ITRLSOL speedups on multicore.

When it comes to performance analysis, dynamic analysis is a natural choice. Efforts have been made to identify the bottlenecks (such as memory contention, communication imbalance leading to idle tasks, etc.) that occur in HPC software [12], as well as a methodology to better understand parallel applications [2]. It introduces a methodology which aims at a better understanding of large-scale HPC applications through the case study of an application which is part of the SPEChpc benchmark suite.

Tallent and Mellor-Crummey propose to measure three metrics to evaluate how well a parallel, multithreaded program performs (parallel idleness, parallel overhead, and logical path profiling) [13]. These criteria then help the programmer to see when to coarsen or refine concurrency granularity, focus on serial performance optimization, or even switch parallelization strategies.

This leads to the design of performance tools dealing with static and dynamic analysis, such as HPCTOOLKIT. It is able to perform binary analysis on an executable (rebuilding loop nests and call graphs, identifying inlined routines) and do a call path profiling at runtime. LoopProf and LoopSampler [8] also work on binary files and focus on loop profiling, with information such as loop properties, nesting, self/total count, trip count, etc. Another framework for instrumentation and measurement of applications is presented by Shande et al. [11]. It describes a suite of performance analysis tool based on PAPI and TAU [10] tools. The profiling with IIPM and a tracing tool are applied to extract various types of measurements on Matrix-Multiply and PETSc benchmarks.

5. Conclusion and future work

The methodology presented here provides a semi-automatic way of analyzing and understanding performance issues in the case of High-Performance applications. It combines different tools (MAQAO , hardware counters, value profiling, etc.) used to perform static and dynamic analysis, and possibly decremental analysis for uncovering hidden bottlenecks. Better execution times are achieved in the case of kernels used in real-life applications, with speedups of at least 2.

Nevertheless, there still remains a lot of work to get a better analysis process. Memory traces are analyzed and interpreted by a human being. Detecting the wrong strided accesses due to the wrong loop ordering (such as what was found in the ITRLSOL application) is automatable to a certain point, and should ultimately be performed by the machine.

Moreover, performing decremental analysis is tedious work best left to a machine. Work is under way to automate DECAN at the binary level. That way, the user will have more control upon what must be suppressed, and what are the consequences, without fearing external intervention (e.g. an optimizing compiler).

Acknowledgments

The research presented in this paper has partially been supported by the French Ministry for Economy, Industry and Employment through the ITEA2 project "ParMA" [17] (June 2007 – May 2010).

References

[1]   A. Alexandrov, S. Bratanov, J. Fedorova, D. Levinthal, I. Lopatin, and D. Ryabtsev. Parallelization made easier with Intel Performance-Tuning utility, 2007.

[2]   B. Armstrong and R. Eigenmann. A methodology for scientific benchmarking with large-scale applications. pages 109–127, 2001.

[3]   K. D. Cooper and L. Xu. An efficient static analysis algorithm to detect redundant memory operations. *SIGPLAN Not.*, 38(2 supplement):97–107, 2003.

[4]   Q. V. Dinh, A. Naïm, and G. Petit. Projet fame2: rapport final de synthèse sur l'optimisation des logiciels de simulation numérique de l'aéronautique, 2007.

[5]   L. Djoudi, D. Barthou, P. Carribault, C. Lemuet, J.-T. Acquaviva, and W. Jalby. Exploring application performance: a new tool for a static/dynamic approach. In *Los Alamos Computer Science Institute Symp.*, Santa Fe, NM, Oct. 2005.

[6]   S. Eranian. Perfmon2: a flexible performance monitoring for linux, 2006.

[7]   S. L. Graham, P. B. Kessler, and M. K. Mckusick. Gprof: A call graph execution profiler. In *SIGPLAN '82: Proceedings of the 1982 SIGPLAN symposium on Compiler construction*, pages 120–126, New York, NY, USA, 1982. ACM.

[8]   T. Moseley, D. A. Connors, D. Grunwald, and R. Peri. Identifying potential parallelism via loop-centric profiling. In *Proceedings of the 2007 International Conference on Computing Frontiers*, May 2007.

[9]   P. J. Mucci, S. Browne, C. Deane, and G. Ho. Papi: A portable interface to hardware performance counters. In *In Proceedings of the Department of Defense HPCMP Users Group Conference*, pages 7–10, 1999.

[10]   S. S. Shende and A. D. Malony. The TAU parallel performance system. *The International Journal of High Performance Computing Applications*, 20:287–331, 2006.

[11]   S. Shende, A. Malony, S. Moore, P. Mucci, and J. Dongarra. Integrated tool capabilities for performance instrumentation and measurement. 2007.

[12]   D. Skinner and W. Kramer. Understanding the causes of performance variability in hpc workloads. In *In International Symposium on Workload Characterization*, 2005.

[13]   N. R. Tallent and J. M. Mellor-Crummey. Effective performance measurement and analysis of multi-threaded applications. In *PPoPP '09: Proceedings of the 14th ACM SIGPLAN symposium on Principles and practice of parallel programming*, pages 229–240, New York, NY, USA, 2009. ACM.

[14]   N. R. Tallent, J. M. Mellor-Crummey, and M. W. Fagan. Binary analysis for measurement and attribution of program performance. In *PLDI '09: Proceedings of the 2009 ACM SIGPLAN conference on Programming language design and implementation*, pages 441–452, New York, NY, USA, 2009. ACM.

[15]   AMD. Software optimization guide for AMD family 10h processors.

[16]   Intel. Intel 64 and IA-32 architectures optimization reference manual.

[17]   ParMA: Parallel Programming for Multi-core Architectures - ITEA2 Project (06015). http://www.parma-itea2.org/

Parallel Computing: From Multicores and GPU's to Petascale
B. Chapman et al. (Eds.)
IOS Press, 2010
661
© 2010 The authors and IOS Press. All rights reserved.
doi:10.3233/978-1-60750-530-3-661

How to Accelerate an Application: a Practical Case Study in Combustion Modelling

Benedetto RISIO [a,1], Alexander BERRETH [a], Stéphane ZUCKERMAN [b],
Souad KOLIAI [b], Mickaël IVASCOT [b], William JALBY [b], Bettina KRAMMER [b],
Bernd MOHR [c], and Thomas WILLIAM [d]
[a] *RECOM Services GmbH, Germany*
[b] *Université de Versailles Saint-Quentin-en-Yvelines, France*
[c] *JSC Jülich, Germany ;* [d]*GWT-TUD GmbH Dresden, Germany*

Abstract. Developing parallel high-performance applications is an error-prone and time-consuming challenge. Performance tuning can be alleviated considerably by using optimisation tools, either by simply applying a stand-alone tool or by applying a tool chain with a number of more or less integrated tools covering different aspects of the optimisation process. In the present paper, we demonstrate the benefits of the latter approach on the industrial combustion modelling software RECOM-AIOLOS. The applied tool chain comprises both low-level and high-level analysis of the application: using the MAQAO tool, the assembly code generated by the compiler can be analysed statically, aiming at possible optimisations on a loop level. Another important aspect is identifying and optimising bottlenecks in memory access and cache utilisation. On a higher level, efficient usage of parallel programming paradigms (MPI, OpenMP) is verified by the VAMPIR and SCALASCA frameworks. Combining the different optimisation strategies leads to a significant overall performance improvement.

Keywords. performance analysis, optimization, application, combustion

1. Introduction

The 3D-combustion modeling software RECOM-AIOLOS is a tailored application for the mathematical modelling of industrial firing systems ranging from several hundred kW to more than 1000 MW. In-depth validation using measurements from industrial power plants, the extension of chemical reaction models and the rapid development of computer technology have made RECOM-AIOLOS a well proven and reliable tool for the prediction of industrial furnace efficiency. The software solves approx. 100 conservation equations (mass, momentum, energy, species concentrations, radiation) on a 10-15 million cells finite volume grid, leading to high computational demands. Originally being designed for high-performance computing on parallel vector-computers and massively parallel

---

[1] RECOM Services GmbH, Nobelstrasse 15, D-70569 Stuttgart, Germany,
Fax: +49-711-6868 9149, E-mail: info@recom-services.de

systems, the software has been ported to low-cost multi-core systems to expand the hardware base. In the present work a suite of optimization tools (MARMOT [1], VAMPIR [2], SCALASCA [3], MAQAO [4]) was used for performance tuning to identify execution bottlenecks and potential improvements in a systematic way.

2. Applied Workflow for Performance Tuning

The applied workflow for performance tuning consists of a combination of high-level and low-level performance analysis. The total workflow for performance tuning was executed in the following sequence:

1.) An optimized massively parallel execution across nodes was achieved by a high-level analysis of the existing MPI-Parallelization. The tool MARMOT was used to check the MPI-Implementation. Furthermore, the MPI-parallel execution was analysed with the tools VAMPIR & SCALASCA.

2.) An optimized execution on individual cores was achieved by a low-level performance analysis for single and multi-core execution within the node. The tools VAMPIR & MAQAO were used to assess single and multi-core execution on a subroutine level using performance counters. Furthermore, the tool MAQAO was also used to identify performance bottlenecks on a loop level within critical subroutines.

3.) An optimized shared memory parallel execution within the multi-core node has been achieved by a high-level performance analysis of hybrid parallelism. The work focused on the investigation of the benefits of using hybrid (OpenMP and MPI) parallel execution within the node.

3. High Level Performance Analysis of MPI-Parallelization

The MPI-performance of the RECOM-AIOLOS code on multi-core systems was analyzed using the tools VAMPIR & SCALASCA. The performance analysis of the original MPI-communication for a portion of the code covering 0.25 s is shown in Fig. 1. The red zones in Fig. 1 indicate that the MPI-communication generates an unexpectedly large number of wait events at the synchronisation points of the application. A deeper analysis of the problem revealed, that the MPI-processes were forced to synchronize in a prescribed sequence by using the MPI_WAIT subroutine for synchronisation. This led to a significant overhead in the synchronisation because some of the MPI-processes were still in computation while others were ready for synchronisation, but because of the prescribed synchronisation sequence had to wait for other MPI-processes to finish their computation. The problem was solved by replacing the MPI_WAIT subroutine with MPI_WAITALL, thus allowing the MPI-processes to synchronize as they finish their computation.

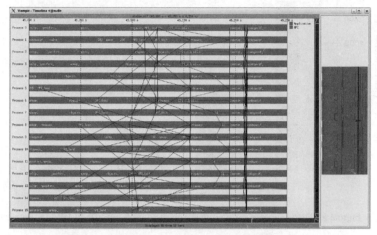

Figure 1: Performance analysis of original MPI-communication

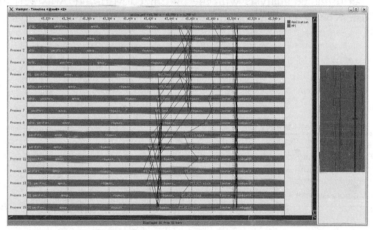

Figure 2. Performance analysis of modified MPI-communication

The modified MPI-communication for the same portion of the code covering 0.25 s is shown in Fig. 2. Fig. 2 shows a significant lower amount of red zones indicating that the MPI-communication now generates a significant lower number of wait events at the synchronization points of the application.

The savings in execution time achieved with the modified MPI-communication (MPI_WAIT versus MPI_WAITALL) are summarized in the Fig. 3. The results indicate, that the performance improvements increase with increasing number of cores. Execution time savings in the order of 10 % were measured for 128 cores.

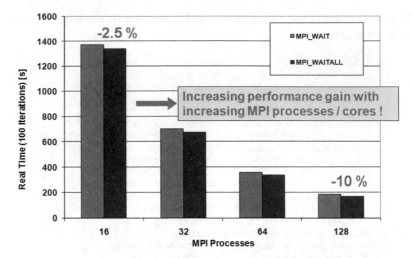

Figure 3. Performance improvements achieved with modified MPI-communication

An MPI-performance analysis with the optimized MPI-code was performed on a Xeon-Cluster (NOVA) using up to 128 cores. The result of this analysis is shown in Fig. 4.

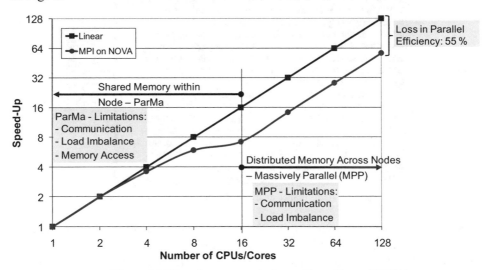

Figure 4. MPI-performance analysis on a Xeon-Cluster (NOVA)

The results shown in Fig. 4 indicate an almost linear scaling for the massively parallel (MPP) execution across the nodes. However, a performance breakdown can be observed within the node. A closer look at this so-called Parallel Multi-Core (ParMa) region reveals good scaling up to four cores and a continuous breakdown for 8 and 16 cores. The total loss in parallel efficiency when using the entire node is 55%. The performance loss within the node is hereby the critical factor for the entire multi-core system.

4. Low Level Performance Analysis for Single and Multi-Core

In order to analyze the performance breakdown within the node more deeply the tools VAMPIR & MAQAO were used to assess the general sustained performance in terms of MFlops achieved. The results of the performance measurements for single core and full node utilisation are summarised in Figs. 5 and 6. The analysis shown in Figs. 5 and 6 reveals, that the subroutines Combgasif and Combedc (calculation of the homogeneous gas-phase and the heterogeneous particle chemistry) that perform a large number of floating point operations in relation to the data that is required from the memory achieve almost 930-970 MFlops of computational speed on a single core, and the computational speed drops only slightly to 820-910 MFlops when using 16 cores simultaneously. On the other hand the subroutines Rbgauss and Apmsp that do a smaller number of floating point operations in relation to the required data from the memory achieve only a reduced computational speed of 400-410 MFlops on a single core, and the computational speed severely drops to 100-110 MFlops when using 16 cores simultaneously.

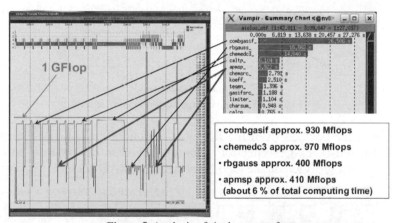

Figure 5. Analysis of single core performance

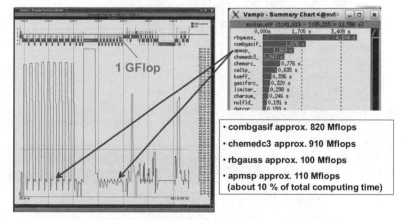

Figure 6. Analysis of full node performance (16 cores)

The analysis of the parallel performance on subroutine level summarized in Fig. 7 shows, that the memory-intense routines Rbgauss and Apmsp also exhibit a severe breakdown in parallel performance when using more than two cores simultaneously, while scaling is almost linear for the compute-intense subroutines Combgasif and Combedc. The function powL (power law system function) scales ideally with increasing number of CPUs/Cores because it only performs floating point operations without any memory access. This is somehow misleading, because this function is called mostly within the Combgasif and Combedc subroutine that contains the required memory access time. Taking this into account these both routines would even scale better.

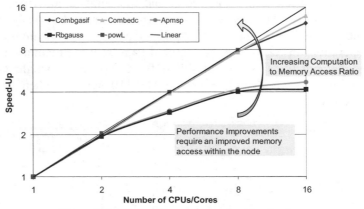

Figure 7. Parallel performance on subroutine level

The performance breakdown of the Rbgauss subroutine, which is a Gauss-Seidl Solver with Red-Black-Ordering for resolving the data dependency within the loop, was further analysed on the loop-level with the MAQAO tool.

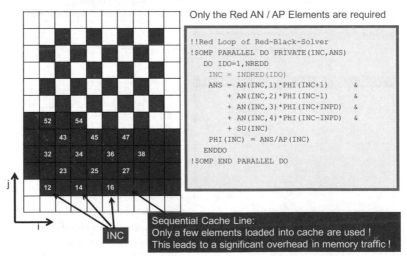

Figure 8. Original implementation in Rbgauss subroutine

The outcome of this analysis showed, that due to the internal data structure within the code, only a few elements of the sequential cache line were used for calculation (see Fig. 8). This led to a significant overhead in memory traffic. The majority of the memory traffic was hereby generated through the loading of the array AN and AP (see Fig. 8) using an indirection array. The remedy was a reorientation of the load intensive data stream. The arrays AN and AP were stored linearly in the memory and accessed via a direct access (see Fig. 9), leading to a full utilisation of the data that was loaded into the cache. The reoriented arrangement is shown in Fig. 9. The resulting performance improvement due to the restructuring of the Rbgauss subroutine is 38 % on a subroutine level and around 13.6 % on 16 cores for the entire application.

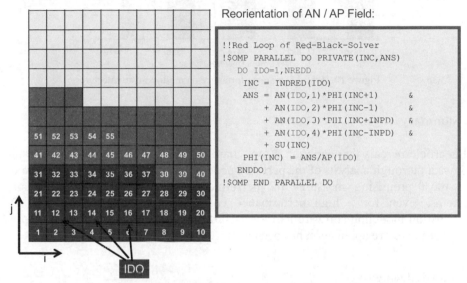

Reorientation of AN / AP Field:

```
!!Red Loop of Red-Black-Solver
!$OMP PARALLEL DO PRIVATE(INC,ANS)
   DO IDO=1,NREDD
      INC = INDRED(IDO)
      ANS = AN(IDO,1)*PHI(INC+1)       &
          + AN(IDO,2)*PHI(INC-1)       &
          + AN(IDO,3)*PHI(INC+INPD)    &
          + AN(IDO,4)*PHI(INC-INPD)    &
          + SU(INC)
      PHI(INC) = ANS/AP(IDO)
   ENDDO
!$OMP END PARALLEL DO
```

Figure 9. Reoriented data arrangement in Rbgauss subroutine

5. High Level Performance Analysis of Hybrid Parallelism

Another approach for better using the available memory bandwidth on a multi-core systems was found by adapting the parallel programming model to the given memory architecture. The adaption was done by varying the number of MPI-processes and OpenMP threads in the parallel execution (hybrid approach). A comparison of the performance achieved with hybrid parallel execution on Itanium versus Xeon X7350 (Tigerton) and Nehalem is shown in Fig. 10. The results in Fig. 10 show, that memory degradation is so severe on the Xeon system that a variation of the number of MPI-processes and OpenMP threads hardly effects the parallel performance, while the Itanium and the Nehalem system take advantage from using 4 OpenMP threads on a single logical memory block. Fig. 10 demonstrates the superiority of the memory access in a NUMA architecture compared to a conventional bus system. Performance improvements of roughly 15% were achieved through the usage of a hybrid parallel approach.

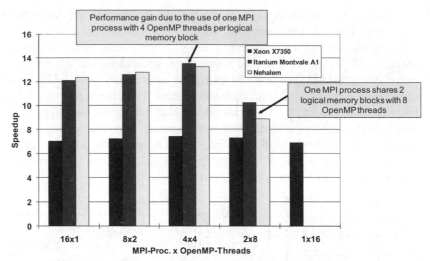

Figure 10. Hybrid parallel performance on multi-core architectures

6. Summary

This article reveals that applying a tool chain of well selected optimization tools allows a thorough analysis of the performance bottlenecks and the identification of the most promising measures for performance improvements on multi-core systems. Even for a high performance computing application like the 3D-combustion modeling software RECOM-AIOLOS a performance gain of roughly 34% for the entire application has been achieved.

Acknowledgements

The research presented in this paper has partially been supported by the German Ministry for Research and Education (BMBF), and the French Ministry for Economy, Industry and Employment (DGCIS) through the ITEA2 project "ParMA" [5] (June 2007 – May 2010).

References

[1] Krammer, B.; Bidmon, K.; Müller, M.S.; Resch, M.M.: MARMOT: An MPI Analysis and Checking Tool. In Joubert, G.R., Nagel, W.E., Peters, F.J., Walter, W.V., eds.: PARCO. Volume 13 of Advances in Parallel Computing., Elsevier (2003) 493–500

[2] Müller, M.S.; Knüpfer, A.; Jurenz, M.; Lieber, M.; Brunst, H.; Mix, H.; Nagel, W.E.: Developing Scalable Applications with Vampir, VampirServer and VampirTrace, Advances in Parallel Computing, Volume 15, ISSN 0927-5452, ISBN 978-1-58603-796-3 (IOS Press), 2008.

[3] Geimer, M.; Wolf, F.; Wylie, B. J. N.; Abraham, E.; Becker, D.; Mohr, B. (2008): The SCALASCA Performance Toolset Architecture, Proceedings of the International Workshop on Scalable Tools for High-End Computing (STHEC), Kos, Griechenland / ed.: M. Gerndt, J. Labarta, B. Miller. - 2008. - pp. 51 – 65

[4] Djoudi, L.; Barthou, D.; Carribault, P.; Lemuet, C.; Acquaviva, J-T.; Jalby, W.: MAQAO: Modular Assembler Quality Analyzer and Optimizer for Itanium 2, Workshop on EPIC architectures and compiler technology, San Jose, 2005.

[5] ParMA: Parallel Programming for Multi-core Architectures - ITEA2 Project (06015). http://www.parma-itea2.org/

Parallel Computing: From Multicores and GPU's to Petascale
B. Chapman et al. (Eds.)
IOS Press, 2010
© 2010 The authors and IOS Press. All rights reserved.
doi:10.3233/978-1-60750-530-3-669

From OpenMP to MPI: first experiments of the STEP source-to-source transformation tool

Daniel MILLOT [a] Alain MULLER [a] Christian PARROT [a]
Frédérique SILBER-CHAUSSUMIER [a]

[a] *Institut TELECOM, TELECOM SudParis, Computer Science Department,
91011 Évry, France* [1]

Abstract. The STEP tool allows source-to-source transformation of programs, from OpenMP to MPI, for execution on distributed-memory platforms. This paper describes tests of STEP on popular benchmarks, and analyses the results. These experiments provide both encouraging feedback and directions for improvement of the tool.

Keywords. source-to-source transformation, parallel execution, OpenMP, distributed execution of OpenMP programs, MPI

1. Introduction

In order to have good performance, HPC applications must be tuned to the target platform, be it a multicore, a cluster of multicores or a computation grid. When an end-user wants to adapt his sequential application for execution on a particular multiprocessor platform, he has to choose between two programming paradigms: shared variables or message-passing, which usually means OpenMP directives or calls to MPI communication primitives. As multiprocessor architectures nowadays tend mainly to use distributed memory, for scalability reasons, message-passing programming appears more suitable at first sight. Yet, as the distribution of both data and computation among the nodes of the target platform must be made explicit, this is reserved to expert parallel programmers. The resulting code is also generally much more intricate and fragmented, thus less easy to maintain and evolve securely, whereas OpenMP only requires high-level expression of parallelism, which does not corrupt the given code too much.

The STEP tool [1] is an attempt to reconcile the relative simplicity of OpenMP programming with the effectiveness of MPI programs that can be tuned further by experts. Based on the PIPS [2] workbench for program analysis and transformation, STEP generates MPI source code from a code annotated with OpenMP directives, thanks to the powerful inter-procedural array region analyses of PIPS. Being a source-to-source transformation tool, STEP enables the

---

[1] {daniel.millot, alain.muller, christian.parrot, frederique.silber-chaussumier}@it-sudparis.eu

programs of legacy applications to evolve easily and reliably without the burden
of restructuring the code so as to insert calls to message passing API primitives.

This paper is organized as follows: section 2 recalls the main decisions for the
design of STEP and gives some details on how it works. Section 3 then describes
the experiments we have made with different scientific applications and comments
on the results. Section 4 suggests some directions for improvement of the STEP
tool and concludes.

2. The STEP tool

The state of the art section of the IWOMP'08 paper presenting STEP [1] describes several other attempts to provide distributed execution of OpenMP programs [3,4,5,6,7,8]. The STEP tool has been developed in the PIPS (Inter-
procedural Parallelisation of Scientific Programs) workbench [2], which provides
powerful code transformations and analyses of Fortran codes (inter-procedural
analyses, array regions analyses, etc). For a first prototype, we chose a simple
parallel execution model, as shown in Figure 1: each MPI process executes the sequential code (between parallel sections) together with its share of the workshare
constructs; all data are allocated for all processes and updated at the end of each
workshare construct by means of communications, so as to be usable later on.

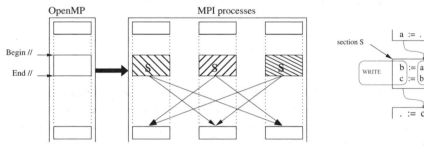

Figure 1. Execution model

Figure 2. *READ, WRITE, IN* and *OUT* tags

The STEP OpenMP-to-MPI transformation is achieved through three successive phases: outlining (directed by OpenMP directives), computation of array
regions to communicate (through region analysis) and MPI parallel code generation.

2.1. Outlining

This first phase prepares for the execution of the code of parallel sections in different contexts by the MPI processes: the code of each parallel section is replaced
by a call to a procedure with the section code as its body (one procedure per such
section). This code transformation keeps the semantics of the original program.
For instance, the code of the loop labelled 20 in Listing 1 is outlined and replaced
by a call to a new subroutine (called *P1_DO*20 in Listing 2).

Listing 1: Before outlining

```
PROGRAM P1
INTEGER I,N,F1
PARAMETER (N=10)
INTEGER T(N,2), A(N-1)
  ...
!$OMP PARALLEL DO
  DO 20 I = 1, N-1
    A(I) = F1(T, I)
20 CONTINUE
!$OMP END PARALLEL DO
  ...
  END
```

Listing 2: After outlining

```
PROGRAM P1
INTEGER I,N,F1
PARAMETER (N=10)
INTEGER T(N,2), A(N-1)
  ...
!$OMP PARALLEL DO
  CALL P1_DO20(I, 1, N-1, N, A, T)
!$OMP END PARALLEL DO
  ...
  END

  SUBROUTINE P1_DO20(I, I_L, I_U, N, A, T)
  INTEGER I, I_L, I_U, N, F1
  INTEGER A(1:N-1), T(1:N, 1:2)
  DO 20 I = I_L, I_U
    A(I) = F1(T, I)
20 CONTINUE
  END
```

The parameters of the new procedure are composed of:

- loop parameters that is to say the loop index and the loop bounds (see parameters I, I_L and I_U in Listing 2),
- variables, arrays and parameters used in the outlined statements (see parameters N, A and T in Listing 2).

2.2. Region analysis

The purpose of this second phase is to determine the data that processes must exchange at the end of each parallel section, in order to build the corresponding MPI messages. It is based on PIPS array regions analyses.

For each array accessed in a parallel section, PIPS associates a convex polyhedron (or region) which it tags as $READ$ (resp. $WRITE$) [9] containing all the array elements which are read (resp. written) by statements of the parallel section (see $READ/WRITE$ tags in Figure 2). Furthermore, PIPS associates also an array region tagged as IN (resp. OUT) containing imported elements that are read in the parallel section after having been written previously by another code section (resp. exported elements used afterwards in the program continuation). As they are inter-procedural, PIPS analyses apply not only to the code of the parallel section under analysis, but also to procedures called in the section. The $READ$, $WRITE$, IN or OUT region tag is exact when all the elements of the region can themselves be tagged in the same way. Otherwise, the region is an over-approximation.

Combining tags, generated thanks to the previous analyses, STEP can minimize the size of the $COMM(A)$ region to be communicated between processes at the end of a given workshare construct for a given array A, in order to ensure data coherency. $COMM(A)$ is necessarily a subregion of $OUT(A)$, and should be restricted to $WRITE(A)$:

$$COMM(A) = OUT(A) \cap WRITE(A).$$

As it is an intersection of convex polyhedrons, a $COMM$ region itself is a convex polyhedron. To make the message construction simpler, we use a rectangular hull of $COMM$ regions as the message payload.

When at the end of a parallel section a process receives an array region which it has not altered at all during the execution of the section, the region is copied into the array straightforwardly. Otherwise, a comparative scan of both a resident copy and the received region of the array allows to decide which part of the data in the received message should be copied into the array. This time consuming operation must be done at runtime and reduces performance.

2.3. MPI code generation

Using the source code resulting from the outlining phase and the $COMM$ regions provided by the analysis phase, STEP finally generates MPI code. For instance, a new procedure (with a name suffixed by $\_MPI$) is created to replace the procedure generated from a "parallel do" directive when outlining. Listing 3 shows that the call to procedure $P1\_DO20$ of Listing 2 is replaced by a call to procedure $P1\_DO20\_MPI$. The new procedure successively:

- splits the loop, in order to distribute work between the MPI processes according to their rank (lines 15 to 17);
- determines $COMM$ regions for the different arrays accessed in the loop, according to the loop splitting (line 20);
- calls the initially outlined procedure with bounds adapted to the loop slice of each process (lines 23 to 26);
- exchanges $COMM$ regions with other processes (line 29).

Listing 3: MPI source file generated by STEP

```
 1       PROGRAM P1
 2       include "step.h"
 3    C     declarations
 4       CALL STEP_Init
 5       ...
 6       CALL P1_DO20_MPI(I, 1, N-1, N, A, T)
 7       ...
 8       CALL STEP_Finalize
 9       END
10
11       SUBROUTINE P1_DO20_MPI(I, I_L, I_U, N, A, T)
12       include "step.h"
13    C     declarations
14
15    C     Loop splitting
16       CALL STEP_SizeRank(STEP_Size, STEP_Rank)
17       CALL STEP_SplitLoop(I_L, I_U, 1, STEP_Size, I_STEP_SLICES)
18
19    C     SEND region computing
20       CALL STEP_Compute_Regions(A_STEP_SR, I_STEP_SLICES,...)
21
22    C     Where the work is done
23       I_IND = STEP_Rank+1
24       I_LOW = I_STEP_SLICES(LOWER, I_IND)
25       I_UP = I_STEP_SLICES(UPPER, I_IND)
26       CALL P1_DO20(I_IND, I_LOW, I_UP, N, A, T)
27
28    C     Regions communications
29       CALL STEP_AllToAllRegion(A_STEP_SR, STEP_Rank, ...)
30       END
```

3. Using STEP on scientific computations

In this section, we give results of experiments conducted in order to identify the conditions for a relevant usage of the STEP tool and point up its benefits and drawbacks. Different types of executions are compared for a collection of applications. They are denoted as follows:

- *SER* is execution of the serial code;
- *OMP* is execution of an OpenMP version of the code;
- *STEP* is execution of the code generated by STEP from the OpenMP version;
- *KMP* is execution of the OpenMP version through usage of the Intel Cluster OpenMP suite [10]. Cluster OpenMP is based upon a software layer implementing a distributed shared memory (DSM) which allows an OpenMP application to run on a cluster of multiprocessors (without any modification in the case of a Fortran code, which is our case);
- *MPI* is execution of a hand-written MPI version of the code.

The performance of the execution denoted *STEP* is compared with executions *SER* and *OMP* systematically, with *MPI* when available, and with *KMP* when this can give workable results.

Some of the applications have been selected because they are reference benchmarks while others have because they illustrate properties of STEP. First we have chosen two reference NAS benchmarks [11]: *FT* solves the PDE system of the 3D heat equation by using FFT; *MG* solves the Poisson equation with periodic boundary conditions by a multigrid method. These two applications differ in their communication patterns: all computing nodes need to communicate in FT whereas only some need to in MG. *SER*, *OMP* and *MPI* are applicable for both benchmarks. We selected also the molecular dynamics simulation application *MD*, for which an OpenMP version is available [12], because of its high computation/communication (comp/comm) ratio. Finally we chose the standard matrix product of square matrices *Matmul* which allows to adjust the comp/comm ratio.

The execution platform was a cluster with 20 GB/s Infiniband interconnect and 14 nodes available, with 48 GB RAM memory each and 4 Xeon-1.6 GHz quadcores (thus making it 16 cores per node). For the distributed memory executions (*MPI*, *KMP* and *STEP*), only one core per node is used, other cores being inactive. For shared-memory executions (*OMP*), the applications run on cores of the same node. For optimal execution of the NAS benchmarks (*MG* and *FT*), the number of computing nodes we used was a power of 2, which meant respectively two, four and eight nodes on our target cluster. For both benchmarks, *KMP* did not succeed (dead lock for one and false results for the other) and is thus not compared to the other executions. *KMP* also produced large standard deviations of the execution time for benchmarks for which it could compute correct results, probably due to some cache effect of the DSM system. The execution time for each execution type is the average of the execution times over ten runs.

An in depth study of the code generated by STEP for all the selected benchmarks shows that the array region analysis optimizes the size of the MPI messages sufficiently (no over-approximation) to avoid any time consuming comparative scan at runtime, a benefit of minimising the size of messages.

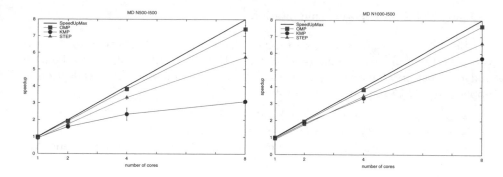

Figure 3. Speedup for MD

Figure 3 shows that *STEP* is very efficient for *MD* which has a high comp/comm ratio. In contrast to *MD*, for both *MG* and *FT*, although the MPI and OpenMP expressions of parallelism are rather similar for the former and different for the latter, the results of *STEP* are worse than those of *SER*. The performance analysis tool Vampir [13] has shown how small the comp/comm ratio of these benchmarks is for *STEP*, which is the reason for this result.

In the case of *MG*, the volume of data communicated could be reduced, thus the comp/comm ratio increased. Indeed, with the current execution model, data can be tagged *COMM* and communicated but not accessed by the next code section; worse, it can even be communicated many times uselessly, i.e. without being used. To get around this problem, STEP could use another execution model with "producer" and "consumer" parallel sections being tied more closely. Such a model would require a more in depth array region analysis, not only computing $OUT(A) \cap WRITE(A) = COMM_O(A)$, but also $IN(A) \cap READ(A) = COMM_I(A)$ to determine whether a section consumes data from array A or not (a code section producing $COMM_O$ regions and consuming $COMM_I$ ones). This would relax synchronisation of memory updates, delaying communication of data until required, and allow overlap of communication by computation. It could also be effective for *FT*, with a slight simplification of the given source code in order to ease the work of STEP.

The influence of the comp/comm ratio over the efficiency of *STEP* can be assessed by means of *Matmul*, the ratio increasing with the matrix size. Figure 4 shows that the speedup increases faster with the comp/comm ratio for *STEP* and *KMP* than for *OMP*. The *STEP* speedup is also better than the *KMP* one for the smallest value of the comp/comm ratio (N=1000). Fewer memory pages means more competition for access when the number of client processes of the Cluster OpenMP DSM system increases.

All these experiments confirm that STEP is relevant for applications with high comp/comm ratio. Of course, STEP performance cannot compete with those of MPI code written by an expert MPI programmer. On the contrary, the use of STEP has been shown to lead to interesting speedups, compared to that of OMP or KMP, for a certain class of applications.

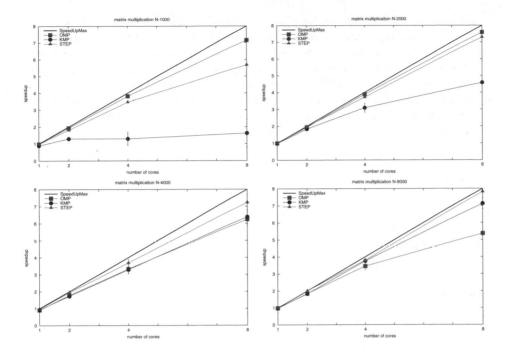

Figure 4. Speedup for matrix multiplication

4. Conclusion and future work

We have presented the source-to-source transformation tool called STEP which generates MPI source code, from a program annotated with OpenMP directives. We have also presented the results of experiments with STEP on typical scientific applications. STEP relies on PIPS inter-procedural region analyses, the quality of which allows STEP to reduce both the volume of data that need to be communicated and the extent of time consuming scan at runtime when updating arrays at the end of parallel sections. The experiments have shown that STEP is relevant for applications with a high enough comp/comm ratio and given some hints for future work.

Namely, the current execution model of STEP requires systematic data updates, that may be very expensive for some applications. As illustrated by *MD*, a high comp/comm ratio can compensate for these updates and lead to interesting speedups. The execution model of STEP could then evolve as suggested in the previous section with more complete region analyses in order to optimize the volume of communicated data.

Besides, in the short term, we plan to allow STEP to deal with multilevel parallelism and generate hybrid MPI/OpenMP code. Coarse-grain parallelism could be dealt with by means of calls to MPI primitives, and exploited across distributed memory nodes, whereas fine-grain parallelism could be expressed through OpenMP directives, and exploited within each multicore node. The resulting parallel code should be relevant for clusters of multicores. As PIPS analyses could compute the comp/comm ratio for each parallel section, STEP could decide the best execution mode for a parallel section, either distributed or shared memory.

Since it simplifies the production of a parallel code adapted to distributed memory architectures, STEP can be used by the designer of an application straightforwardly. Therefore, an objective of STEP in the long term is to build on the designer's expertise to guide STEP in certain decisions, in order to improve the quality of the source code it produces.

5. Acknowledgements

The research presented in this paper has partially been supported by the French Ministry for Economy, Industry and Employment (DGCIS) through the ITEA2 project "ParMA" [14] (No 06015, June 2007 – May 2010).

References

[1] D. Millot, A. Muller, C. Parrot, and F. Silber-Chaussumier. STEP: a distributed OpenMP for coarse-grain parallelism tool. In *Proc. International Workshop on OpenMP '08, OpenMP in a New Era of Parallelism, Purdue University, USA, IWOMP*, 2008.

[2] C. Ancourt, B. Apvrille, F. Coelho, F. Irigoin, P. Jouvelot, and R. Keryell. PIPS — A Workbench for Interprocedural Program Analyses and Parallelization. In *Meeting on data parallel languages and compilers for portable parallel computing*, 1994.

[3] M. Sato, S. Satoh, K. Kusano, and Y. Tanaka. Design of OpenMP Compiler for an SMP Cluster. In *Proceedings of First European Workshop on OpenMP (EWOMP)*, 1999.

[4] A. Basumallik, S.J. Min, and R. Eigenmann. Towards OpenMP Execution on Software Distributed Shared Memory Systems. In *International Workshop on OpenMP: Experiences and Implementations, WOMPEI'2002*, 2002.

[5] R. Eigenmann, J. Hoeflinger, R. H. Kuhn, D. Padua, A. Basumallik, S.J. Min, and J. Zhu. Is OpenMP for Grids. In *NSF Next Generation Systems Program Workshop held in conjunction with IPDPS*, 2002.

[6] Y.S. Kee, J.S. Kim, and S. Ha. ParADE: An OpenMP Programming Environment for SMP Cluster Systems. In *Conference on High Performance Networking and Computing*, 2003.

[7] T. Boku, M. Sato, M. Matsubara, and D. Takahashi. OpenMPI - OpenMP like tool for easy programming in MPI. In *Sixth European Workshop on OpenMP*, 2004.

[8] A. Basumallik, S.J. Min, and R. Eigenmann. Programming Distributed Memory Systems Using OpenMP. In *12th International Workshop on High-Level Parallel Programming Models and Supportive Environments*, 2007.

[9] B. Creusillet. *Array region analyses and applications*. PhD thesis, École Nationale Supérieure des Mines de Paris, 1996.

[10] J. Hoeflinger. Extending OpenMP to Clusters. Technical report, Intel Corporation, 2006.

[11] NAS parallel benchmarks. http://www.nas.nasa.gov/Resources/Software/npb.html.

[12] B. Magro. OpenMP samples. Kuck and Associates Inc. (KAI), http://www.openmp.org/samples/md.f.

[13] A. Knüpfer, H. Brunst, J. Doleschal, M. Jurenz, M. Lieber, H. Mickler, M. S. Müller, and W. E. Nagel. The vampir performance analysis tool-set. In *Tools for High Performance Computing*, 2008.

[14] ParMA: Parallel Programming for Multi-core Architectures. ITEA2 Project (06015) http://www.parma-itea2.org.

Parallel Computing: From Multicores and GPU's to Petascale
B. Chapman et al. (Eds.)
IOS Press, 2010
© 2010 The authors and IOS Press. All rights reserved.
doi:10.3233/978-1-60750-530-3-677

Using Multi-Core Architectures to Execute High Performance-Oriented Real-Time Applications

C. AUSSAGUES[a,1], E. OHAYON[a], K. BRIFAULT[a] and Q. DINH[b]

[a] *CEA LIST, Embedded Real Time Systems Laboratory*
[b] *Dassault Aviation, DGT/DPR (General Technical Dir. / Future Research Business)*

Abstract. This paper presents a method and the associated tools to design and implement embedded real-time systems that execute high-performance-oriented applications on multi-core architectures. After presenting the OASIS design, compilation and execution framework, the paper focuses on the principles of the modifications performed on the safety-oriented real time kernel to execute transparently and consistently multitasking applications on multi-cores. It then gives the first results of benchmarking performed on a Dassault Aviation's HPC application called "2D-tracking algorithm". It concludes on the future works towards the introduction of data-parallelism in the OASIS parallel time-triggered programming and underlying execution models.

Keywords. Embedded high-performance computing, real-time, multi-cores.

Introduction

Recently, major processor manufacturers introduced support for multi-processors on a single chip (Multi-Core), and many hardware vendors started to develop and market Multi-processor system-on-chip (MPSoC). These multiprocessors become fairly popular and attractive for embedded systems as they bring more performance in offering higher parallel computation capability and lower power consumption [1].

This tendency accelerates the emergence of high-performance embedded applications and emphasizes the use of parallel programming models integrating different levels of parallelism where a trade-off between expressed parallelism and automatic parallelization is necessary. So, embedded real-time (RT) applications are starting to run on Symmetric Multi-Processing (SMP) systems. But, extending an existing Operating System (OS) to support SMP systems is not a trivial task [2]. To take advantage of a SMP architecture, an OS needs to take into account the shared memory facility, the migration & load-balancing between processors, and the communication between tasks. Besides, implementing all the SMP mechanisms and considering how they interfere is particularly laborious when the chosen OS is a hard real-time one [3], raising the issues of synchronization and predictability. For embedded real-time

---

[1] CEA LIST, Embedded real time systems laboratory, Point Courrier 94, Gif-sur-Yvette, F-91191 France, E-mail: christophe.aussagues@cea.fr

applications, a key problem is to be able to bridge the gap between parallelism expressed in design (*modularity*) and those available in multi-core based architecture (*performance*). Use of multi-core architectures in embedded systems should impact as less as possible the software design and the run-time behaviour, especially when real-time constraints are at stake. Like in High-Performance Computing (HPC), the concern for embedded high-performance real-time systems is to allow increasing performance from single-core architectures to multi-core ones. But, it means that executing embedded applications on single-core or multi-core systems should provide the same results/outputs in real time and that it should be possible to add new functionalities (e.g. real-time tasks) to existing embedded applications with all real-time constraints still fulfilled.

After reviewing in section 1 related work on several common Real-Time Operating Systems (RTOS) and their extensions to multi-core architectures, we present our research work to extend the OASIS (see section 2) hard real-time kernel for HPC-oriented embedded systems. The design of the OASIS kernel to take full advantage of SMP multi-cores will then be presented in section 3. Before concluding and addressing future works, section 4 will provide the results of the first experiments with an HPC-based 2D-object tracking application provided by Dassault Aviation and ported to OASIS-SMP.

1. Related works

Several approaches exist to design a SMP RTOS. A first idea consists in proposing a monolithic kernel, in which the entire operating system is run in kernel space as supervisor mode. All OS services run along with the main kernel thread, residing in the same memory area. An example is VxWorks, where the kernel and tasks run in one address space. This allows tasks switching to be very fast and eliminates the need for system call traps. Monolithic systems are easier to design and implement than other solutions, and are extremely efficient when well written. However, the main disadvantages of monolithic kernels are the dependencies between system components, and the fact that large kernels become very difficult to maintain (lack of modularity).

A second approach consists in running the RTOS on top of a micro-kernel, which only implements core services such as process scheduling, inter-process communication, low-level network communication, and interrupt dispatching. All other services, such as device drivers or file systems, are implemented as user processes making the kernel smaller and faster. Some examples are the QNX Neutrino or L4Linux. These user-space implementations are easier to debug, while memory accesses violations can be detected and isolated. Another advantage is scalability. However, performance can be a weak point since micro-kernel architectures place an heavy load on inter-process communication and context switching.

A third idea consists in modifying a SMP kernel to dedicate some processors to real-time tasks. Those asymmetric kernels, such as APRIX[4], ASMP-Linux [8] or ARTiS [5], consider real-time processes and related devices as privileged and shield them from other system activities. Piel et Al. [6] extend a standard SMP Linux kernel with a real-time scheduler, and propose a migration mechanism in order to allow flexibility in the processor allocation. Even though their work provides a comprehensive performance evaluation, it considers an event-driven real-time system, not suitable for hard real-time operations, while simultaneously addressing the cohabitation matter (i.e. mixing real-time and generic purpose tasks within the same system).Both problems addressed jointly raise major resource management issues such as the denial of service problem, not resolved in their approach.

A fourth approach is based on virtualized clusters, where each processor runs a modified version of the Linux kernel, and where the kernels cooperate in a virtual high-speed and low-latency network. An example is Adeos nano-kernel [7]. In a similar approach Kagström et Al. [9] address the SMP extension of an existing OS. A micro-kernel is added to every slave processor and the main single-processor system is kept almost unchanged. Benchmarks results along with a minimal kernel hacking are provided. Their work is close to our, as they consider asymmetric SMP OS.

2. OASIS Principles

OASIS [10][12] defines a method and a set of tools to design and implement multitasking deterministic real-time systems. It consists in a programming language, named ψC and an execution environment, for the hard real-time embedded systems, that uses a fully parallel time-triggered execution model beyond the classical TT paradigm [13]. ψC allows a formal description of the different real-time tasks (called agents) in an application, where pure algorithmic parts written in ANSI C are combined with an observable temporal behaviour described in a declarative way. The execution environment offers a safety-oriented real-time kernel (for single-core architectures) and an associated tool chain for the implementation of the OASIS model.

The OASIS model brings some novelties in comparison with the classical so-called TT approach: it allows asynchronism by the coexistence of different time scales between the agents in order to make the application design easier. It facilitates the decomposition of the application into parallel agents defined in elementary activities (see [12]). Time management in the OASIS kernel is entirely lock-free to avoid the overhead, contention problems, deadlocks and the possibility of processes priority inversion.

The OASIS communication model is composed of two mechanisms: periodic data flows (called temporal variables), and message boxes. These non-blocking communication mechanisms are completely described in an interface that links the programming model to the underlying execution environment.

The OASIS model implies no assumptions on the scheduling algorithm. As it has a TT approach, there are neither precedence constraints nor resource protocols, and only temporal constraints are required. The Earliest Deadline First (EDF) algorithm [17] can be used as it is a simple, sufficient and optimal one [11].

3. Design of OASIS-SMP

3.1. Objectives – Target architecture

The aim of the OASIS-SMP extension is to allow the programmer to benefit *transparently* from the computation power increase supplied by the multi-processors. The OASIS time-triggered execution model is preserved, and the issue of task dispatching between execution cores is hidden from the programmer: *no modification is required to the OASIS programming model, and therefore to the application ΨC source code.* Ultimately, the new kernel is even able to run on different CPUs multiple agents of an OASIS application that was compiled for the original single-core version. The IA-32 OASIS kernel has been modified to be able to run on Intel SMP 32bit platform. This is a very popular architecture in the mass-market of personal computers, where the different identical cores share a single memory bus for a Uniform Memory Access topology. The choice was motivated by the commonness of the architecture, and the fact that a robust IA-32 single-core version of OASIS is already available.

3.2. Scheduling policy

Obviously, the choice of the scheduling algorithm is critical when designing a "hard" real-time operating system. In order to map automatically and transparently the different agents of an application to the available cores, the chosen scheduling policy for the SMP version is a fairly intuitive extension of EDF – Global-EDF [18]. The priority index of a task is still defined by the time remaining before its deadline[2], only if *n* cores are available, then the *n* first tasks with the highest priority are distributed among the CPUs.

In the general case, Global-EDF is *not* an optimal multi-processor algorithm [19]. Although other algorithms may be later considered (see [16]), it provides a fast, easy to implement policy, and it is totally transparent to the user.

3.3. Software parallelization analysis

The following figure shows the general software architecture of an OASIS system, separated in three layers.

The user agents: each agent is a real-time task defined by the programmer. The OASIS execution model forbids memory sharing: inter-task communications are "services" handled only by the kernel (see below). Therefore, synchronization between agents –e.g. resource sharing– is ensured by their temporal behaviour: no locks are allowed. The OASIS design ensures that agents may safely be executed simultaneously (or interleaved, on the single-core version). This also explains why the application source code requires no modification for execution on the SMP version.

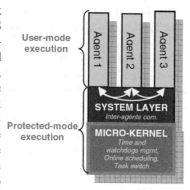

The system layer: this part of the OASIS kernel ensures safety-oriented sanity checks and inter-agents communication. The system layer and especially the communication mechanisms were originally written to be entirely interruptible. Therefore, executing instances of the system layer for different agents on different cores simultaneously does not raise any new problem[3].

---

[2] The lower the priority index, the more the task is priority.

[3] This property is true thanks to the memory consistency model of the Intel processors, which is strong enough for this application.

The micro-kernel: it includes among other things the scheduler and the context-switcher. It also updates the global real-time clock and handles the watchdogs for time-triggered events. All these modules may not be executed simultaneously and require atomic execution to ensure the consistency of the micro-kernel data structures. This property is implemented by a fair active-waiting spinlock protecting the whole micro-kernel.

3.4. Time management – Asymmetric kernel architecture

Global time management and time-triggered events are handled by a specific CPU, chosen arbitrarily at boot-time, referred further as CPU0. Conversely, software system calls (or "traps") may happen on any CPU, leading to the execution of the scheduler. A re-scheduling arms a new watchdog that will be handled by CPU0. Therefore, most of the micro-kernel code – the scheduler and the context switcher – may be executed on any CPU. Only time management parts run on CPU0.

The SMP architecture is made asymmetric by this choice, since CPU0 suffers from a micro-kernel execution overhead. However this choice is a fair compromise between:
- a symmetric architecture, where each CPU would update its local time, requiring a synchronization protocol;
- a completely asymmetric architecture, where one control-CPU would be devoted to handling all micro-kernel operations for the other computation-CPUs.

4. Running a HPC application on OASIS-SMP

4.1. Parallelizing Dassault Aviation's tracking algorithm

The HPC application provided by Dassault Aviation is a sequential implementation of a tracking algorithm, relying on Bayesian's probabilistic methods to detect moving objects in a two-dimensional field based on real-time radar data. The implementation consists of a global loop refining iteratively a cloud of particles, used for objects detection. The application is so compute-intensive on single-core architectures that its present usage is only as a background computation, i.e. to be run only when there are enough computer resources left. On the other hand, this code is locally and globally highly parallelizable.

OASIS provides a safe and real-time execution environment for this application, where parallelism can be expressed at a task level in order to improve performances.

Therefore, porting Dassault's implementation to a ΨC application basically requires:
1. Defining a temporal behaviour of the application, i.e. splitting the code into different elementary activities with an associated deadline;
2. Expressing task-parallelism by defining several communicating agents that share the computation load and are executed simultaneously on different cores by the OASIS-SMP kernel.

A master-slave approach was used to split the application into different agents: one master agent runs the code, discharging punctually a part of its work to one or more slave agents. As seen before, the OASIS kernel requires that communication between the master and its slaves go through specific kernel mechanisms, which ensure memory isolation between the agents. Since shared memory is prohibited, all communications require copying data between source and destination buffers. For that reason, communication overheads are expected. In order to minimize them, only the heaviest computation section within the loop is parallelized, while the sole master agent executes the rest sequentially.

The ΨC version of Dassault Aviation's application defines 5 temporal synchronization points and 2 actual data exchanges between the master and its agents. The deadlines associated to each time window are based on performance measurement of the original C code executed in a Linux environment. The sum of each of these deadlines defines a global end-to-end real-time constraint inferior to 1 second per iteration, following Dassault's requirements.

Note that when the master is executing sequential portions of the code, the slave agents have basically nothing to do, and are automatically put at rest by the scheduler. See *Figure 1 – Architecture of the ΨC application.*

4.2. Benchmarks results

The OASIS-SMP micro-kernel implements utility system calls to retrieve easily the *actual* CPU time used by an agent during its last temporal slot (independently from the associated deadline). In order to compare relevant execution times, Dasssault Aviation's application was ported into two ΨC versions:

a) a first task-parallelized version following the master/slave software architecture described in the previous section, with one master agent and one slave agent.

b) A sequential version made of a single agent, with the same temporal behaviour as the master agent of the previous application (i.e. defining the same temporal synchronization points).

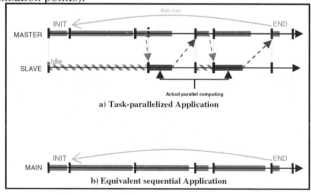

Figure 1 – Architecture of the ΨC application

A first observation is that both applications have the exact same real-time behaviour, as expected with the OASIS runtime environment.

The following figure 2 (left chart) shows the global speedup of the master/slave version against the sequential version for the first loop iterations. It appears that performances are globally not impacted by parallelization. The slight performance variations are due mainly to cache filling effects for the first iterations, then to the fluctuant complexity of the floating-point computations.

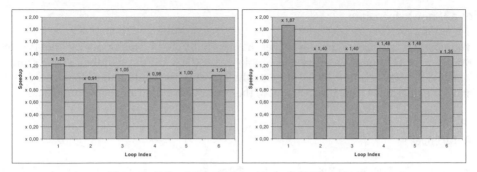

Figure 2 – **Left**: global speedup with parallel ΨC application
Right: local speedup, focusing on parallelized sections only – communication are not considered

The figure 2 (right chart) shows a measured speedup comparison on purely parallelized elementary activities, i.e. on time slots where no communication is made between the master and the slave, only computation (parallel versus sequential). The parallel version shows significant performances improvement, close to optimum (x2).

In conclusion, communications between the master and the slave show overheads, as expected: indeed, one OASIS communication system call requires three memory moves or more and two MMU switches. However, the performance improvement observed on purely parallel section is very promising and opens the road to more efficient parallelization methods.

5. Conclusions and future works towards data-parallelism

This paper presented the principles of extending a safety-oriented real-time kernel, OASIS, to take full advantage of multi-processors on a single chip in terms of performances. The extension of OASIS runtime environment to exploit parallelism at the kernel level allows supporting the execution of multitasking embedded applications on multi-cores in a transparent and consistent way: the same application is running on single- and multi-cores with the same real-time behaviour, but allowing the integration of more real-time tasks in an efficient manner. The modifications of the micro-kernel were presented, as well as the first results of the OASIS-SMP kernel use on a high-performance oriented real-time application provided by Dassault Aviation.

The results presented in section 4 are consistent with the expectations, in both temporal behaviour and global performances perspectives. They also show that task-parallelism is not always sufficient to take fully advantage of a multi-core architecture.

Due to their safeness based on memory isolation, OASIS's inter-agents communication mechanisms are also costly. In order to workaround this limitation, an agent should be able to split into several execution threads sharing the same memory context. A single agent, splitting on demand into multiple memory sharing execution threads, would then replace the master-slave software architecture.

A new extension of the OASIS-SMP kernel implementing such capability is currently being tested and already shows very promising results. Future directions to improve performances include implementing the extension of the ΨC language to express and take advantage of the data-parallelism. Another direction could be the evaluation of the performance impacts of OASIS-SMP on specific embedded parallel applications from the points of view of cache/memory accesses or inter-processor interrupts.

6. Acknowledgements

The research presented in this paper has partially been supported by the French Ministry for Economy, Industry and Employment (DGCIS) through the ITEA2 project "ParMA"[4] (n°06015, June2007--May 2010). The authors would like to thank V. David and M. Lemerre for their involvement in these works and their relevant comments.

References

[1]   R. Sasanka, S.V. Adve, Y-K. Chen and E. Debes, The energy efficiency of CMP vs. SMT for multimedia workloads, *in ICS'04: Proc. of the 18th annual international conference of Supercomputing* (2004), 196—206.

[2]   W. Wolf, The future of Multiprocessor Systems-on-Chips, *in DAC'04: Proceedings of the 41st annual conference of Design Automation* (2004), 681—685.

[3]   J. A. Stankovic, R. Rajkumar. *Real-Time Operating Systems*. Kluwer Academic Publishers, 2004.

[4]   M. Seo, H. Seok Kim, J. Chan Maeng, J. Kim and M.Ryu, An Effective Design of Master-Slave Operating System Architecture for Multiprocessor Embedded Systems, in *Advances in Computer Systems Architecture*, Lecture Notes in Computer Science, Berlin, vol. 4967 (2007).

[5]   P. Marquet, E. Piel, J. Soula and J-L. Dekeyser, Implementation of ARTiS, an asymmetric real-time extension of SMP Linux, *in Proc. of the 6th Real-time Linux Workshop* (2004).

[6]   E. Piel, P. Marquet, J. Soula, J-L. Dekeyser, Real-time systems for multiprocessor architectures, *in IPDPS'06 : Proc. of the 20th international parallel and distributed processing Symposium* (2006), 8—16.

[7]   K. Yaghmour, A practival approach to Linux Clusters on SMP hardware, *Tech. report of ADEOS Project* (2002), 1—12.

[8]   E. Betti, D.P. Bovet, M. Cesati, and R. Gioiosa, *EURASIP Embedded Systems Journal*, Hard real-time performances in multiprocessor-embedded systems using ASMP-Linux, Hindawi Publishing Corp. 2008.

[9]   S. Kagström, H. Grahn, L. Lundberg, *Softw. Pract. Exper. Jounral*, The application kernel approach – a novel approach for adding SMP support to uniprocessor operating systems, John Wiley & Sons Inc., 2006.

[10] V. David, C. Aussaguès, C. Cordonnier, M. Aji and J. Delcoigne, OASIS: a new way to design safety critical applications", in *21st IFAC/IFIP Workshop on Real-Time Programming* (WRTP'96), 1996.

[11] C. Aussaguès. V. David, A method and a technique to model and ensure timeliness in safety critical real-time systems, *in Intl Conference of Engineering of Complex Computer Systems* (1998), 2—12.

[12] D. Chabrol, G. Vidal-Naquet, V. David, C. Aussaguès, and S. Louise, OASIS: a chain of development for safety-critical real-time systems, *in Proc. of Embedded Real-Time Software Conference (ERTS'04),* (2004).

[13] H. Kopetz, The Time-Triggered Model of Computation, *in RTSS'98: Proc. of the 19th real-time Systems Symposium* (1998), 168—178.

[14] H. Kopetz, The Time-Triggered Architecture, *in ISORC'98: Proc. of the 1st IEEE International Symposium on Object-Oriented Real-Time Distributed Computing* (1998), 22—29.

[15] C. Liu, J. Layland. *Journal of the ACM*, Scheduling algorithms for multiprogramming in a hard real-time environment, ACM Publisher, 1973.

[16] Lemerre, M., David, V., Aussaguès, C., and Vidal-Naquet, G. 2008. Equivalence between Schedule Representations: Theory and Applications. *In Proceedings of the 2008 IEEE Real-Time and Embedded Technology and Applications Symposium - Volume 00* (April 22 - 24, 2008). RTAS. IEEE Computer Society, Washington, DC, 237-247.

[17] Lamport, L. 1990. Concurrent reading and writing of clocks. *ACM Trans. Comput. Syst.* 8, 4 (Nov. 1990), 305-310

[18] John Carpenter, Shelby Funk, Philip Holman, Anand Srinivasan, James Anderson, and Sanjoy Baruah. A categorization of real-time multiprocessor scheduling problems and algorithms. *In Hand-book on Scheduling Algorithms, Methods, and Models*. Chapman Hall/CRC, Boca, 2004.

[19] Cynthia A. Phillips, Cliff Stein, Eric Torng, and Joel Wein. Optimal time-critical scheduling via resource augmentation (extended abstract). *In STOC '97: Proc. of the 29th annual ACM symposium on theory of computing, pages 140–149*, New York, NY, USA, 1997. ACM

---

[4]   http://www.parma-itea2.org/

Parallel Computing: From Multicores and GPU's to Petascale
B. Chapman et al. (Eds.)
IOS Press, 2010
© 2010 The authors and IOS Press. All rights reserved.
doi:10.3233/978-1-60750-530-3-685

Performance Tool Integration in a GPU Programming Environment: Experiences with TAU and HMPP

Allen D. MALONY[1,3] , Shangkar MAYANGLAMBAM[1] , Laurent MORIN[2] ,
Matthew J. SOTTILE[1] , Stephane BIHAN[2] , Sameer S. SHENDE[1,3] , and
Francois BODIN[2]

[1] *Dept. of Computer & Information Science, University of Oregon, Eugene, OR 97403*
[2] *CAPS Entreprise, 35000 Rennes, France*
[3] *ParaTools, Inc., Eugene, OR 97405*

Abstract. Application development environments offering high-level programming support for accelerators will need to integrate instrumentation and measurement capabilities to enable full, consistent performance views for analysis and tuning. We describe early experiences with the integration of a parallel performance system (TAU) and accelerator performance tool (TAUcuda) with the HMPP Workbench for programming GPU accelerators using CUDA. A description of the design approach is given, and two case studies are reported to demonstrate our development prototype. A new version of the technology is now being created based on the lessons learned from the research work.

1. Introduction

Multi-core systems with GPU acceleration offer a high performance potential to application developers. Unfortunately, achieving performance improvements with accelerators is challenging due to complexity of the multi-core hardware and their low-level device interface. Programming environments targeting GPU accelerators attempt to hide this complexity by allowing the application developer to work with libraries, special language constructs, or directives to a compiler. The benefit for the programmer is a higher-level abstraction for accelerator programming and protection of their software investment, since the environment takes the responsibility for translating the program to work with different acceleration backends. The challenge for accelerator programming environments is to provide high-level support and flexibility without sacrificing delivered performance. Traditionally the use of performance tools for measurement and analysis allows developers to identify performance inefficiencies and inform optimization strategies. For optimization of GPU-accelerated applications, these tools must 1) be able to measure performance of GPU computations, and 2) be integrated with the high-level programming framework to generate important performance events and meta data for representing performance results to the user. Furthermore, when used in large-scale parallel environments, it is important to understand the performance of accelerators in the context of whole parallel program's execution. This will require the integration of accelerator measurements in scalable parallel performance tools.

This paper discusses our initial efforts to integrate the TAU Performance System® [4] and the HMPP Workbench [2]. We focus on the use of the prototype TAU CUDA measurement interface (TAUcuda [5] within HMPP and the model for inserting TAU instrumentation in the HMPP-translated code to best present a performance picture of the resulting application execution. Two case studies are presented to demonstrate the approach.

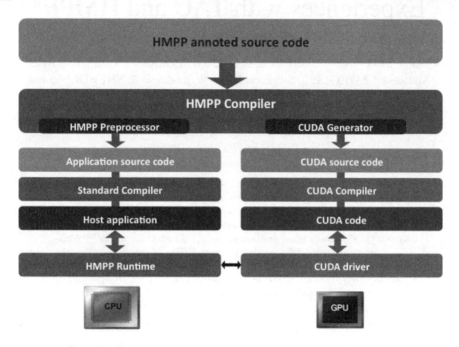

Figure 1. HMPP Workbench compilation for applications targeting CUDA.

2. Design Approach

The objective of a high-level programming environment is to insulate the developer from dealing with low-level concerns. In the case of accelerator programming, the HMPP Workbench offers a directive-based approach for C and Fortran languages to specify *codelets* for execution on accelerator devices and *callsites* in the host program where codelets will be invoked. HMPP operates as a source-to-source translator, adding all the necessary host-side code to interface with the accelerator, and generating target-specific code depending on accelerator type. Figure 1) shows the two compilation paths needed to build HMPP applications with CUDA as the target accelerator. The HMPP execution model allows for asynchronous CPU/GPU execution and managed data transfers, utilizing the functionality provided in the CUDA driver interface.

To evaluate the performance of an HMPP application, it is necessary to make measurements of important execution events and to relate the performance data back to the

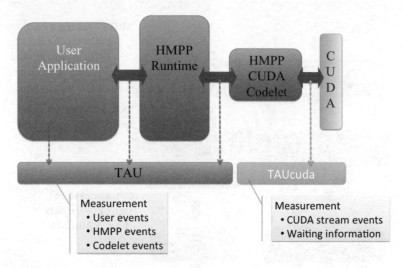

Figure 2. Integration of HMPP, TAU, and TAUcuda instrumentation and measurement support.

HMPP programming abstractions. As shown in Figure 2, there are three levels in the HMPP framework to instrument to capture the full picture of application execution: application code, HMPP runtime, and CUDA codelets. Although HMPP is a source-to-source translator, the application developer is ill-equipped for performance instrumentation on their own, much less knowledgable of the event semantics between levels. The advantage HMPP brings for performance integration is in the automation of instrumentation, designed specifically to capture necessary event information to present a full performance view.

Instrumentation relies on an underlying measurement infrastructure. We chose the TAU Performance System for HMPP performance measurements, given its robust capabilities for profiling and tracing of parallel applications. However, TAU only solves the problem of CPU-side measurements. Some other technology was needed for CUDA measurements. Luckily, our concurrent work on the prototype TAUcuda system offered the missing piece. (See [5] for more information on TAUcuda.)

Figure 2 identifies which performance events are measured by TAU and TAUcuda, respectively. HMPP is responsible for placing all instrumentation appropriately in the generated code and in the HMPP runtime system. The application build chain with instrumentation included is shown in Figure 3. Notice that TAU's instrumentation tool can be used at the start to generate events for (non-HMPP) application-level routines. Measurements of these events are important because they provide an application-level *context* for HMPP-related and CUDA-related events. We use the term *HMPP-TAU* to refer to entire integrated performance tool chain.

Having integrated the different instrumentation and measurement facilities, the goal for HMPP performance analysis was to track the events unfolding during codelet execution and reconstruct a high-level view to highlight performance problems. One of the challenges introduced was HMPP's support for asynchronous codelet execution as well as memory transfers. This exposed the need for new mechanisms to be developed in TAU to correctly maintain performance data from concurrent tasks. A workaround using virtual threads was developed by CAPS Entreprise to deal with problem, but a more robust solution will be necessary for going forward.

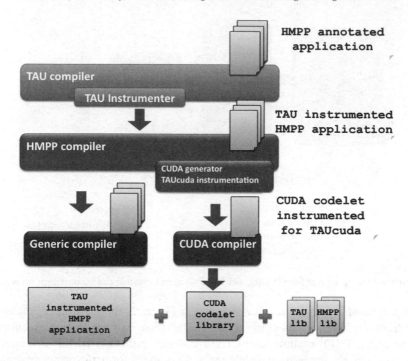

Figure 3. HMPP application build chain with instrumentation enabled.

The issue had to do with HMPP's model of computation and how its runtime system maintained the codelet abstraction during execution. Effectively, it uses a single thread to interface to a GPU device, but manages codelets separately on GPU streams. TAU requires a dinstinguishable thread ID to separate HMPP codelet-specific events. However, since only one real thread is used, a virtual thread ID needed to be provided for TAU events when the HMPP runtime is working on behalf of a specific codelet.

3. Case Studies

Two benchmarks were used as case studies to test the functionality of HMPP-TAU. The first was a implementation of Conway's *Game of Life* [3] (GoL) using HMPP. Figure 4 lists the entire HMPP program, showing the codelet callsite in the main routine on the left panel and the codelet specification with two parallel loop kernels on the right. We used HMPP-TAU to instrument the GoL application and ran several experiments with different problem sizes (number of cells) to see the performance effects. The results are shown in Figure 5. Notice there are different TAU events listed representing different (CPU-side) HMPP instrumention points. Those prefixed by `hmpp` correspond to the HMPP runtime layer, while those prefixed by `codelet_` correspond to the codelet interface. Because the HMPP codelet is launched synchronously, the `codelet_wait` event effectively contains the execution time of the two kernels. The `hmppStartCodelet` event is the HMPP runtime library event encapsulating the `codelet_wait`. The reults show how the increasing problem size results in larger kernel execution times, as well as larger times for data transfer.

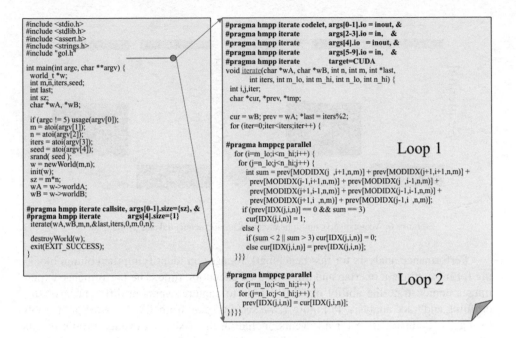

Figure 4. Game of Life HMPP source code.

TAU Event	calls	Computation time(ms) for varying input matrix size				
		1000X1000	2000X2000	3000X3000	4000X4000	5000X5000
hmppStartCodelet	1	7931	25506	95711	152348	345741
hmppGetAvailableHWA	1	2765859	2702177	2705051	2769246	2714853
hmppReleaseDevice	1	50235	2732	2831	44236	2923
hmppWriteDataToHWA	10	1318	1596	2064	2694	3488
hmppAllocateInputOnHWA	7	1234	1235	1234	1241	1277
hmppReadDataFromHWA	3	1718	3261	5648	8894	12811
hmppAllocateInOutOnHWA	3	1218	1357	1256	1302	1277
hmppStartHMPP	1	9	11	11	12	11
codelet_wait	1	5566	22925	93184	149688	343263
codelet_readDataFromHWA	3	590	2021	4320	7522	11534
codelet_writeDataToHWA	10	121	371	808	1430	2235
codelet_allocateInOutOnHWA	3	81	88	99	117	138
codelet_start	1	104	107	104	131	131
codelet_allocateInputOnHWA	7	0	0	1	1	1

Figure 5. Game of Life scaling results.

The second benchmark is a standard vector matrix multiplication used to demonstrate the advantage of overlapping GPU kernel computation with data input/output transfers. Consider the two cases portrayed in Figure 6. The *Sequential* case requires Vin vector and the Min matrix to be first uploaded to the GPU device (upper part of picture) before the kernel computation can begin (lower part of picture). Only a single HMPP codelet would be used. Writing back of results (Vout) can be pipelined with the kernel execution to a limited extent in the codelet. The *Overlapped* case breaks up the Min data transfer into columns and overlaps it with vector-column multiplication and Vout results transfer. The result is more efficient pipelined execution with greater performance. However, two HMPP codelets are required to make this happen.

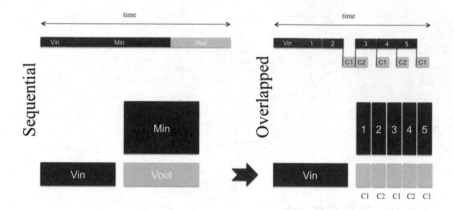

Figure 6. Vector-matrix multiplication benchmark: sequential and overlapped.

Performance analysis for this benchmark focuses on identifying the column blocking for most efficient overlap and minimal total execution time. The performance experiments demonstrate the ability of HMPP-TAU to capture events at different levels for profiling and trace analysis. In Figure 7, we see a display from TAU's ParaProf [1] tools listing the exclusive time for all events, including the TAUcuda events. Profile results allows event time ratios to be compared to determine optimal blocking parameters. Para-Prof can conduct an analysis across multiple experiments with different parameters and display the results to the developer.

TAU is also able to capture the HMPP-TAU events in an execution trace. This enables the temporal behavior of the events to be observed in order to highlight event relationships and ordering. However, we needed to do a little hand massaging of the performance data to separate the events into virtual thread traces. Figure 8 uses the Jumpshot [6] tool to display events from the HMPP runtime and codelet levels for the overlapped vector matrix benchmark. One can see the main HMPP thread at the top setting up the computation and kicking off the codelets. Each codelet executes asynchronously of the other, but their execution is coordinated by the main HMPP thread. The trace visualization allows us to see the data transfer of one codelet overlap with the kernel execution of the other. Of course, profile and trace analysis tools can be used together in performance investigation, as shown in Figure 9.

4. Conclusion

We developed the early HMPP-TAU prototype reported on here in just a few weeks of efforts, after the first version of the TAUcuda tool became functional. While the results are quite encouraging, the integration of the three components – HMPP, TAU, and TAUcuda – exposed several issues that need more consideration. It is important that the HMPP programming abstraction and execution model be reflected in the performance views being delivered by HMPP-TAU. The support for asynchronous modes in the HMPP runtime system and codelet execution (not to mention CUDA's over nuances) was a challenge to merge with TAU's way of handling events in a multi-threaded program. We used retrofits to get things working successfully, but a better designed and more robust solution is re-

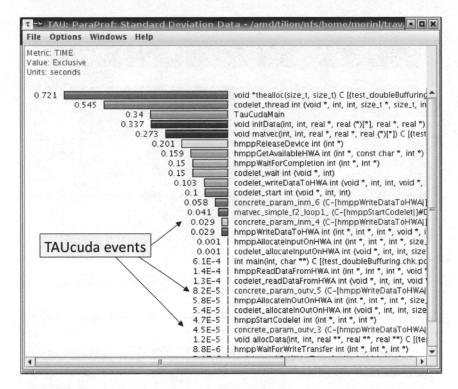

Figure 7. Profile of multiplication benchmark showing events from all instrumentation levels.

quired. The good news is that the experience gained in identifying HMPP events, automating instrumentation, and using TAU's measurement API will all translate forward into future developments.

Our plan is to re-engineer HMPP-TAU in the coming months. The TAUcuda tool is being re-developed presently to use new technology from NVIDIA for access to CUDA library, driver, and kernels execution events. HMPP-TAU will benefit directly from this work. Although the benchmarks shown here are basic, HMPP can be used for parallel applications targeted to large GPU clusters. We intend to HMPP-TAU to be used in such scenarios.

Acknowledgments

This research was supported by the U.S. Department of Energy, Office of Science, under contract ER25933 and the NVIDIA Professor Partnership grant at the University of Oregon.

References

[1]   R. Bell, **A. Malony**, and S. Shende. A Portable, Extensible, and Scalable Tool for Parallel Performance Profile Analysis. In *European Conference on Parallel Processing (EuroPar)*, volume LNCS 2790, pages 17–26, September 2003.

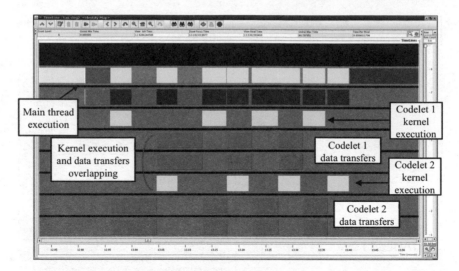

Figure 8. Trace of multiplication benchmark showing temporal events relationships.

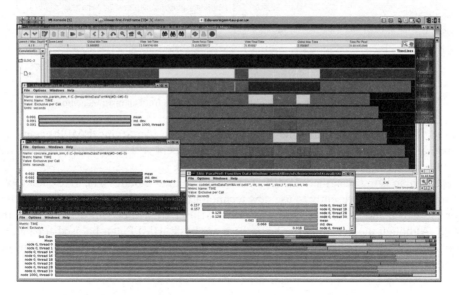

Figure 9. Combined HMPP-TAU performance analysis environment.

[2]   R. Dolbeau, S. Bihan, and F. Bodin. HMPP: A Hybrid Multi-core Parallel Programming Environment. In *Workshop on General Purpose Processing on Graphics Processing Units (GPGPU 2007)*, 2007.

[3]   M. Gardner. Mathematical Games: the Fantastic Combinations of John Conway's New Solitaire Game "Life". *Scientific American*, 223:120–123, October 1970.

[4]   A. Malony, S. Shende, A. Morris, S. Biersdorff, W. Spear, K. Huck, and Aroon Nataraj. Evolution of a Parallel Performance System. In M. Resch, R. Keller, V. Himmler, B. Krammer, and A. Schulz, editors, *2nd International Workshop on Tools for High Performance Computing*, pages 169–190. Springer-Verlag, July 2008.

[5]   S. Mayanglambam, A. Malony, and M. Sottile. Performance Measurement of Applications with GPU cceleration using CUDA. In *Parallel Computing (ParCo)*, September 2009. To appear.

[6]   O. Zaki et. al. Toward scalable performance visualization with Jumpshot. *The International Journal of High Performance Computing Applications*, 13(3):277–288, Fall 1999.

Parallel Computing: From Multicores and GPU's to Petascale
B. Chapman et al. (Eds.)
IOS Press, 2010
© 2010 The authors and IOS Press. All rights reserved.
doi:10.3233/978-1-60750-530-3-693

An Interface for Integrated MPI Correctness Checking

Tobias HILBRICH [a], Matthias JURENZ [b], Hartmut MIX [b], Holger BRUNST [b],
Andreas KNÜPFER [b], Matthias S. MÜLLER [b], and Wolfgang E. NAGEL [b]

[a] *GWT-TUD GmbH*
Chemnitzer Straße 48b, 01187 Dresden, Germany
tobias.hilbrich@zih.tu-dresden.de

[b] *Center for Information Services and High Performance Computing (ZIH)*
Technische Univeristät Dresden, D-01062 Dresden, Germany
{matthias.jurenz, hartmut.mix, . . . }@tu-dresden.de

Abstract. Usage errors of the widely accepted Message-Passing Interface
(MPI) are common and complicate the development process of parallel
applications considerably. Some of these errors are hard to track, especially when they only occur in certain application runs or on certain
platforms. Runtime correctness checking tools for MPI simplify the detection of these errors. However, they usually need the MPI profiling
interface for their analysis. This paper addresses two issues related to
correctness tools: First, due to the exclusive usage of the MPI profiling
interface, it is not possible to use such tools in conjunction with other
MPI tools, which are also based on the profiling interface. Second, correctness checking tools usually lack the ability to provide a detailed history of the events leading to an error, whereas such a history is provided
naturally by tracing frameworks. We introduce the Universal MPI Correctness Interface (UniMCI) to overcome the first problem. This interface provides functions that invoke correctness checking and return detected errors in a manner that is independent of the correctness checker
in use. Furthermore, we demonstrate the applicability of UniMCI with
an implementation that uses the Marmot correctness checker and an exemplary integration of the interface into the VampirTrace performance
analysis framework. As a result, we can provide a history for detected
correctness events, which provides detailed information for debugging.
Finally, we present a study using the SPEC MPI2007 benchmark to
demonstrate the feasibility and applicability of our approach.

Keywords. Correctness checking, Message-Passing Interface, Tools,
Marmot, Vampir

Introduction

Usage of the widely accepted Message-Passing Interface (MPI) standard [1] is
simplified by a variety of tools for performance optimization, debugging, or other
tasks. Using multiple tools simultaneously can help pinpoint issues faster, e.g.,
the combination of a tracing and a correctness tool can provide the history that
leads to a correctness event and add further details to a detected error. Thus, it
simplifies the identification of the root cause of an error.

Such runtime tools usually employ the MPI profiling interface (PMPI), which
enables an interception of MPI calls along with an associated analysis of these

(a) Integrations without UniMCI   (b) Integrations with UniMCI

Figure 1. Integrating a host tool with correctness checking tools.

calls. The usage of the profiling interface is exclusive, therefore, a simultaneous usage of two tools is not immediately possible. The P^nMPI [2] tool already solves this problem by allowing multiple tools to intercept MPI calls. Further problems of combining two tools are: First, the output of both tools should be merged into one combined output. And second, tools incorporating correctness outputs should not depend upon a specific MPI correctness tool, but rather use a generic interface that works with any correctness tool.

Our contribution is the design and implementation of the so called Universal MPI Correctness Interface (UniMCI) that addresses these problems. This paper is structured as follows: Section 1 introduces UniMCI and its design. Section 2 presents a tool combination of the correctness checker Marmot [3] and the tracing tool VampirTrace [4], to show the applicability of UniMCI. Section 3 provides an example application that demonstrates some of the benefits of this tool combination. We present a performance study for the VampirTrace-Marmot combination in Section 4, as such tool combinations have an impact on performance. Finally, we present related work and our conclusions in Sections 5 and 6.

1. UniMCI

Tool integration is necessary to incorporate MPI correctness checking functionality into another MPI tool, e.g., into a performance tool. We refer to the tool using the functionality of a correctness tool as the *host* tool, whereas the tool being used for correctness checking is referred to as the *guest* tool. One possible solution to combine a host and a guest tool is an integration that is specific to these two tools, e.g., a certain performance tool is integrated with a certain correctness tool. However, this direct approach would require the host tool to provide one integration for each guest tool. To avoid these extensive development costs and to simplify tool integration, we present the Universal MPI Correctness Interface (UniMCI). It provides correctness checking functionality independent of the actual correctness tool that is used. As a result, the host tool only needs one UniMCI integration to utilize any correctness checking tool that implements UniMCI. This is illustrated in Figures 1(a) and 1(b).

UniMCI is designed to be as portable and as independent of other tools as possible. As the MPI profiling interface can only be used by one tool at a time, a method is needed that allows both the host and the guest tool to analyze each MPI call. UniMCI offers two distinct solutions for this problem: first, name-shifted functions to pass MPI call arguments to the guest tool, and second, a prototype solution with P^nMPI [2]. The P^nMPI based solution will be released with a future UniMCI version and simplifies the tool coupling. However, it requires that a P^nMPI installation is present and that both the host and the guest tool support P^nMPI, which usually requires both tools to be available as a shared library. We will only present details for the name-shifted interface due to space considerations.

```
/*Wrapper for MPI_Send*/
int MPI_Send(void* buf, int count, MPI_Datatype type, int dest, int tag,
    MPI_Comm comm)
{
  ...
  UNIMCI_check_pre_MPI_Send(buf, count, type, dest, tag, comm, FILE, LINE, ID);
  check_unimci_return();
  PMPI_Send(buf, count, type, dest, tag, comm);
  UNIMCI_check_post_MPI_Send(buf, count, type, dest, tag, comm, FILE, LINE, ID);
  check_unimci_return();
  ...
}

/*Error evaluation function*/
void check_unimci_return()
{
  UNIMCI_MSG *msg;
  while (UNIMCI_has_msg())
  {
    UNIMCI_pop_msg(&msg);
    /*Do something with msg, e.g., log it into output*/
    UNIMCI_msg_free(&msg);
  }
}
```

Figure 2. Host tool using UniMCI, with name-shifted interface.

The name-shifted interface provides two functions for each MPI call: one to analyze the initial arguments of the MPI call, called *pre* check, and one to analyze the results of the MPI call, called *post* check. All runtime MPI checkers will need an analysis of the initial MPI call arguments to detect errors in the given arguments, which is invoked with the pre check function of UniMCI. The post check is usually needed for MPI calls that create resources, e.g., `MPI_Isend`, which creates a new request. MPI correctness tools have to add these new resources to their internal data structures, in order to be aware of all valid handles and their respective state. By splitting the analysis of the MPI call into two parts it is possible to return check result to the host tool before the actual MPI call is issued, which is important to guarantee that errors are handled before the application might crash.

Results of checks are returned with additional interface functions that have to be issued after each check function. A simple correctness message record is used to return problems detected by the guest tool. Figure 2 provides an example of how a host tool can use UniMCI in its MPI wrappers. Note that even though the number of additional source lines needed for UniMCI seems high, most MPI wrappers are created by wrapper generators, which simplifies the integration of the extra code. The additional arguments *FILE*, *LINE*, and *ID* are used to provide source information to the guest tool. *FILE* and *LINE* identify the source code location of the wrapped MPI call. The *ID* argument is used to pass an identifier to the guest tool that is used in correctness messages resulting from this call. This functionality may be used by the host tool to correlate correctness events with past MPI calls. Future versions of the interface will contain extensions and rules to handle asynchronous correctness checking tools and multi-threaded applications.

2. Marmot-VampirTrace with UniMCI

This section presents details on a first correctness tool that supports UniMCI and a first host tool that utilizes the interface. As a guest tool, we use Marmot [3], a portable MPI checker, which is already integrated into various tools, IDE's, and debuggers. As a host tool, we choose VampirTrace [4], a performance event tracing tool.

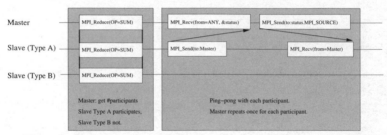

Figure 3. Communication pattern for master and slaves in example 4.

Marmot executes various local checks to detect MPI usage errors and non-portable constructs. Further, one of the MPI processes is used to execute global checks, e.g., a timeout based deadlock detection. This process is also informed about each MPI call, which causes significant overhead. As tool combinations with performance tools will become impractical if the execution of the guest tool is too expensive, a low overhead version of Marmot was used for the implementation of UniMCI by disabling this global process. This does not affect Marmot's powerful local checks.

Marmot's implementation of UniMCI is mostly straightforward. As a first step, Marmot's core functionality was refactored in order to clearly separate pre checks from post checks. Further, a new logger was introduced to store MPI messages for retrieval by the host tool. In order to provide the necessary functions to retrieve Marmot's messages, we extended Marmot's external interface. The name-shifted interface is implemented with generated functions that are very similar to Marmot's regular MPI wrappers. Marmot's global process is disabled to remove its performance bottleneck.

The first host tool that uses UniMCI is VampirTrace. It detects the presence of a UniMCI installation during its *configure* step. If an installation is available it queries the provided *unimci-config* tool for the libraries and flags needed to compile and link with UniMCI. VampirTrace uses the name-shifted interface in its MPI wrappers. This is an optional feature of VampirTrace and is controlled with environmental variables.

VampirTrace stores UniMCI correctness events in a separate *marker* file. Each marker is associated with a timestamp and a process. Further, each marker has a type, a name, and a textual message. This data is used during visualization with *VampirServer* [5]. Each marker is added to the global timeline at its respective process and timestamp. Detailed information can be retrieved by clicking on the visualized marker.

3. Example

To demonstrate the benefits of a VampirTrace and Marmot combination, we present an artificial example with an MPI usage error. The usual synthetic MPI usage error is simple to solve and becomes obvious when the error is detected by a correctness tool. However, some errors are more complex and result from a series of MPI calls. VampirTrace is able to visualize such a history of calls, which simplifies debugging in its presence. As a result, here we present an error which is more complicated to track.

For space considerations we can't present the full example code here, rather we will highlight the parts that are related to the correctness error. The exam-

```
33   for  (i = 0;  i < num_participating_slaves;  i++)
34   {
35     MPI_Recv  (&buf,  1,  MPI_INT,  MPI_ANY_SOURCE,  tag,  MPI_COMM_WORLD,  &status);
36     MPI_Send  (sendbuf[buf],  1,  type[buf],  status.MPI_SOURCE,  tag,  MPI_COMM_WORLD);
37   }
```

Figure 4. Example of a complex potential MPI error (master process).

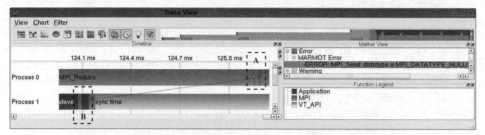

(a) Global timeline for processes 0 and 1, zoomed into the error region.

(b) Detail information for process 1, zoomed into the area labeled B in (a).

Figure 5. Vampir visualization for the example from Figure 4

ple uses a master slave communication were the communication pattern is repeated in multiple iterations. The communication used for each of the iterations is schemed in Figure 3. Each slave computes whether it is going to participate in this iteration's communication or not. Slaves that participate are of *type A* and will do a ping-pong communication with the master process, whereas slaves that do not participate are of *type B*. An MPI_Reduce is used to determine the total number of slaves that are going to participate in an iteration. The master repeats a wildcard receive and a send, in order to implement the ping-pong communication with each of the participating slaves. Figure 4 presents the lines of code that are used by the master process to implement the ping-pong communication. Note that the send uses a datatype and a buffer based on the value received in the preceding wildcard receive. Finally, an additional communication is started after all the iterations ended. During this final communication each slave sends one message to the master, whereas the master calls MPI_Recv once for each slave.

This code contains a potential MPI error, which manifests for some, but not all runs. The application is likely to crash if the error manifests. When Marmot is used without any other tool and the error manifests, it is able to detect the MPI call that causes the application crash. Marmot detects the usage of an invalid datatype(MPI_DATATYPE_NULL) in the MPI_Send call of line 36 on the master process. However, this output is only of limited use, as the datatype used in this call depends on the value received in the MPI_Recv call of line 35. As this is a wildcard receive, it is unclear which value was received there.

When using the UniMCI based Marmot and VampirTrace integration, it is possible to analyze the series of events that lead to this situation. Figure 5(a) shows a VampirServer visualization for a trace file that contains the error. It shows a global timeline of the process activities. The light gray bars represent MPI calls, whereas the dark gray areas represent the execution of the actual application.

Depicted is a zoomed-in part of the area in which the error occurred. The Marmot messages are represented with little triangles on the respective MPI calls that caused the message. Two areas of the timeline are highlighted as A and B in the figure. The second triangle in area A is the marker that points to the detected error. The error text is displayed to the right of the timeline. The line from area B to area A in Figure 5(a) shows the message that was received by the MPI_Recv call of line 35. As discussed above, this call determines which datatype is used by the MPI_Send call that causes the error. Figure 5(b) shows details for the area B from the timeline in Figure 5(a). It identifies the individual activities of the process that sends this message (process 1). The presence of the MPI_Finalize call after the send call reveals that this send call should not have matched the receive of the master process. It is not a send call from one of the iterations, but rather the send call from the final communication that is executed after all the iterations have ended. This reveals the source of the error, a slave of type B, which does not participate in the ping-pong communication of the last iteration, may already enter the final communication. Thus, the master process may receive a wrong message in line 35.

Solutions to this problem are either synchronization calls, e.g., usage of a MPI_Barrier or different tags for the communications.

4. Performance Results

This section presents a performance study for the VampirTrace and Marmot combination introduced in this paper. Both tools incur an overhead at runtime to perform their respective analyses, of interest is whether the combined overhead limits the applicability of the tool combination. We use the SPEC MPI2007 [6] benchmark as a challenging test suite. It contains 13 different application codes from various fields of science. The benchmark uses three different sizes for its data sets, from which we use the largest one (mref). All applications are strong scaling, which allows us to analyze the impact of message sizes on the total tool overhead. For our experiments we use 32, 64, and 128 MPI processes with three different versions of the benchmarks. One version without any tools, one version that only uses VampirTrace, and one version with the VampirTrace-Marmot integration from this paper. As all of the codes in the SPEC MPI2007 benchmark are widely used production codes, the presence of MPI usage error is very unlikely. We use an SGI Altix 4700 to run our experiments.

Figure 6 presents the slowdown of VampirTrace and the VampirTrace-Marmot combination for all of the SPEC MPI2007 applications at different scales. Both VampirTrace and the tool combination incur an overhead of less than 10% for all applications when using 32 processes. Only *121.pop* is an exception that is known to be very challenging for MPI runtime tools, as it uses a very high amount of small messages.

For the applications *113.GemsFDTD*, *115.fds4*, *122.tachyon*, and *126.lammps*, the tool combination still has a low overhead at a scale of 128 processes. For the remaining applications the overhead increases with scale. As these are strong scaling problems it is expected that the tool overhead increases with scale. This results from a decreased average message size. As intercepting and analyzing MPI calls with VampirTrace and Marmot is independent of the message size, the overhead per MPI call increases, as the actual communication takes less time. Both

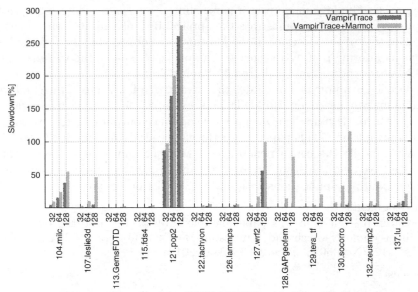

Figure 6. Slowdown for SPEC MPI2007 with 32 to 128 tasks.

104.milc and *137.lu* cause VampirTrace and Marmot to incur a higher overhead at increased scale. Whereas for *107.leslie3d*, *128.GAPgeofem*, *129.tera_tf*, *130.socorro*, and *132.zeusmp2* the increase in Marmot's overhead is dominating. This results from increased complexity of correctness checks. A common case where this happens is the usage of one or multiple MPI request for each process. With increased scale, the total number of concurrently existing requests increases, which adds complexity to the verifications of *MPI_Request* arguments. These overheads may be reduced in future Marmot releases as its performance was – up to now – only of second concern, as long as its usage was still feasible.

5. Related Work

Employing UniMCI as an interface for MPI correctness checking is a reliable and portable way of integrating correctness data into other tools. Future versions of the interface will also offer a P^nMPI [2] based interface that further simplifies the usage of UniMCI. Additional guest tools that might implement this interface are MPI-Check [7], Umpire [8], and ISP [9]. Some of these tools provide more powerful global checks, e.g., Umpire and ISP. As a result, an UniMCI implementation from these tools would provide UniMCI users with a larger set of correctness features.

Usage of UniMCI may also affect a variety of different host tools. Other performance tools, besides VampirTrace, that might use UniMCI are Scalasca [10] and Tau [11]. With a UniMCI integration, these tools may provide MPI correctness checking to users that are not aware of the underlying guest tools. Especially an integration of UniMCI into Scalasca is very promising, as both Scalasca and Marmot use the same output format.

6. Conclusions

This paper presents UniMCI, a universal interface for incorporating runtime MPI correctness checking functionality into host tools such as tracing frameworks. Two distinct modes of usage provide a straightforward integration of UniMCI into existing tools. The first mode uses a name-shifted interface, whereas the second mode uses P^nMPI. We demonstrate the applicability of UniMCI with a sample implementation of the interface in the Marmot correctness checker and the VampirTrace monitoring tool. Extensions to VampirServer enable the visualization of identified correctness events collected by VampirTrace.

A detailed example demonstrates the advantage of a VampirTrace and Marmot combination based on UniMCI. This example shows that understanding source code errors is simplified when using a combined output of these two tools. A further contribution of this paper is a performance study for the SPEC MPI2007 benchmark. While the concurrent usage of Marmot and VampirTrace adds up their respective overheads, we demonstrate the applicability of this tool combination for multiple applications with up to 128 MPI processes.

Acknowledgments

The research presented in this paper has partially been supported by the German Ministry for Research and Education (BMBF) through the ITEA2 project "ParMA" [12] (No 06015, June 2007 – May 2010).

References

[1]   Message Passing Interface Forum. MPI: A Message-Passing Interface Standard, Version 2.1. http://www.mpi-forum.org/docs/mpi21-report.pdf, September 2008.

[2]   M. Schulz and B.R. de Supinski. P^{N}MPI Tools A Whole Lot Greater Than the Sum of Their Parts. In *Supercomputing 2007 (SC'07)*, 2007.

[3]   B. Krammer, K. Bidmon, M.S. Müller, and M.M. Resch. MARMOT: An MPI Analysis and Checking Tool. In G. R. Joubert, W. E. Nagel, F. J. Peters, and W. V. Walter, editors, *PARCO*, volume 13 of *Advances in Parallel Computing*, pages 493–500. Elsevier, 2003.

[4]   A. Knüpfer, H. Brunst, J. Doleschal, M. Jurenz, M. Lieber, H. Mickler, M.S. Müller, and W.E. Nagel. The Vampir Performance Analysis Tool-Set. In *Tools for High Performance Computing*, pages 139–155. Springer Verlag, July 2008.

[5]   H. Brunst, D. Kranzlmüller, and W.E. Nagel. Tools for Scalable Parallel Program Analysis - Vampir NG and DeWiz. *The International Series in Engineering and Computer Science, Distributed and Parallel Systems*, 777:92–102, 2005.

[6]   SPEC MPI2007 Benchmark Suite for MPI.
      http://www.spec.org/mpi2007/.

[7]   G. R. Luecke, Y. Zou, J. Coyle, J. Hoekstra, and M. Kraeva. Deadlock detection in MPI programs. *Concurrency and Computation: Practice and Experience*, 14(11):911–932, 2002.

[8]   J.S. Vetter and B.R. de Supinski. Dynamic Software Testing of MPI Applications with Umpire. *Supercomputing, ACM/IEEE 2000 Conference*, pages 51–51, 04-10 Nov. 2000.

[9]   S.S. Vakkalanka, S. Sharma, G. Gopalakrishnan, and R.M. Kirby. ISP: A Tool for Model Checking MPI Programs. In *PPoPP '08: Proceedings of the 13th ACM SIGPLAN Symposium on Principles and practice of parallel programming*, pages 285–286, New York, NY, USA, 2008. ACM.

[10] F. Wolf, B. Wylie, E. Abraham, D. Becker, W. Frings, K. Fuerlinger, M. Geimer, M. Hermanns, B. Mohr, S. Moore, and Z. Szebenyi. Usage of the SCALASCA Toolset for Scalable Performance Analysis of Large-Scale Parallel Applications. In *Tools for High Performance Computing*, pages 157–167. Springer Verlag, July 2008.

[11] D. Brown, S. Hackstadt, A. Malony, and B. Mohr. Program Analysis Environments for Parallel Language Systems: The TAU Environment. In *In Proceedings of the 2nd Workshop on Environments and Tools for Parallel Scientific Computing*, pages 162–171, 1994.

[12] ParMA: Parallel Programming for Multi-core Architectures - ITEA2 Project (06015). http://www.parma-itea2.org/.

Parallel Computing: From Multicores and GPU's to Petascale
B. Chapman et al. (Eds.)
IOS Press, 2010
© 2010 The authors and IOS Press. All rights reserved.
doi:10.3233/978-1-60750-530-3-701

701

Enhanced Performance Analysis of Multi-core Applications with an Integrated Tool-chain

Using Scalasca and Vampir to Optimise the Metal Forming Simulation FE Software INDEED

Thomas WILLIAM [a], Hartmut MIX [b] Bernd MOHR [c], René MENZEL [d]
Felix VOIGTLÄNDER [c]

[a] *GWT-TUD GmbH Dresden, Germany*
[b] *Technische Universität Dresden, ZIH, Germany*
[c] *Jülich Supercomputing Centre, Germany*
[d] *GNS mbH Braunschweig, Germany*

Abstract. Programming and optimising large parallel applications for multi-core systems is an ambitious and time consuming challenge. Therefore, a number of software tools have been developed in the past to assist the programmer in optimising their codes. Scalasca and Vampir are two of these performance-analysis tools that are already well established and recognised in the community. While Scalasca locates, quantifies, and presents performance flaws (defined as event patterns) in a compact and simple to use tree representation, the Vampir framework visualises all details of the function call sequences and communication patterns in a great variety of timeline or statistic displays. Scalasca locates and presents the problems found and their severity but gives limited practical hints on the case history to find a solution. Looking at the huge amount of detailed data in Vampir can make it hard to find the interesting spots in spatial and temporal resolution for identification of problems and selection for further investigation. This observation led to the combination of these tools resulting in a more productive tool-chain. In this paper we present our approach to connect Scalasca and Vampir through a common bus system. A practical real-world example is provided and the beneficial impact of the integration on the work-flow is shown by optimising the adaptive mesh refinement and load balancing phases of the metal forming simulation FE software INDEED.

Keywords. MPI, OpenMP, performance optimisation, tools integration, Scalasca, Vampir

Introduction

Performance analysis and optimisation of applications are important phases of the development cycle. Like testing and debugging it should be imperative. It is an important precondition to guarantee efficient usage of expensive and limited computing resources.This means obtaining the results with minimum resource usage and cost. Furthermore, it is important for scalability, i.e. being able to achieve the next larger simulation with the given resources. For that, it is particularly important to exploit as much of the theoretically available performance as possible.

The task of the analysis phase is to measure the actual performance on a given platform in terms of computing speed or throughput as well as resource consumption in regard to run-time or memory requirement or storage space. Secondly, performance analysis has to identify opportunities for performance improvement or reduction of resource usage. Tracing requires the modification of the target application in order to detect event occurrences, this step is also known as instrumentation. The events gathered during tracing are simply points of interest in the course of program execution. The most common event types are entering and leaving a program region, sending or receiving messages, collective operations, and performance counter samples which provide a scalar value at a point in time. The tracing records all individual events along with general properties like exact time stamp and the originating process or thread as well as further event type specific properties. Thereby, tracing allows to investigate single events. Information about events permit to infer about application flow like function calls (or general basic blocks), communication or other activities relative to individual processes or threads. This enables trace-based tools to identify variations in the dynamic behaviour of the program over many iterations.

In this paper we will show the benefit that can be gained by combining two tracing tools which provide different but complementary functionality. The paper is structured in the following way: At first we introduce the two tool-chains Scalasca and Vampir and show how we integrated them. Then the application INDEED which we analysed to demonstrate our new integrated tool-set is described. This is followed by the optimisations we achieved. Finally we refer to related work and draw a conclusion.

Scalasca / KOJAK

Scalasca is an automatic performance evaluation system for C/C++ or Fortran parallel applications. It is developed by Forschungszentrum Jülich, Germany. The Scalasca framework generates event traces from running applications and automatically searches them off-line for execution patterns indicating inefficient application behaviour. These patterns are used during the analysis process to recognise, classify, and quantify the inefficiencies in the application. The performance problems recognised by Scalasca include inefficient use of the parallel programming models MPI, OpenMP, and SHMEM as well as low CPU and memory performance. The analysis process automatically transforms the traces into a compact call-path profile that includes the execution time penalties caused by the different patterns broken down by call path and process or thread. The predecessor tool, called KOJAK, searched the patterns sequentially. The new Scalasca tool performs the search in parallel which allows to efficiently analyse parallel programs running on many thousand cores (see figure 1, lower part). For a detailed description of KOJAK including a complete list of all patterns see [4,5]. Scalasca is described in detail in [6].

The call-path profile produced by the analysis can be viewed using the CUBE presenter. CUBE is a generic tool for displaying a multidimensional performance space consisting of the dimensions (i) metric, (ii) call path, and (iii) system resource. Each dimension is represented as a tree browser that can be collapsed or expanded to achieve the desired level of granularity or specialisation. The tree browsers are coupled such that

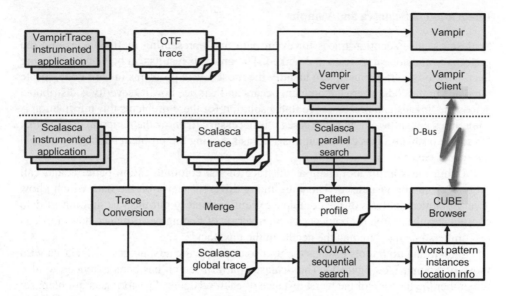

Figure 1. Combined workflow of the Vampir (top) and Scalasca (bottom) toolsets as of Fall 2009. Stacked boxes indicate parallel execution or multiple files. Work is under way to extend the Scalasca parallel search to also produce the "worst pattern instances location information" (replacing the inefficient old merge and sequential search facilities) and to design and implement a common Vampir/Scalasca measurement system and trace format, both simplifying the future work flow tremendously.

the penalty caused by a particular performance problem can be identified for each call path and process or thread (see figure 3).

Vampir

The Vampir tool family [10] consists of the instrumentation and measurement component VampirTrace [11] and the visualisation applications Vampir and VampirServer [9]. It is developed by the Technische Universität Dresden for analysing the runtime behaviour of parallel MPI/OpenMP programs and visualises the program execution by means of event traces (see figure 1, upper part).

The visualisation takes place after the monitored program has been completed, using traces recorded during its execution. VampirServer introduces parallel performance data evaluation concepts which are implemented in a client-server framework. The server component can be executed on a segment of the parallel production environment. The corresponding client can run on a remote desktop computer to visualise the performance results graphically. This has the advantages that performance data which tends to be bulky is kept where it was created, that parallel processing significantly increases the scalability of the analysis process, and that very large trace files can be browsed and visualised interactively. The visualisation client translates the condensed performance data into a variety of graphical representations providing developers with a good understanding of performance issues concerning their applications. This allows for quick focusing on appropriate levels of detail which provide the detection and explanation of various performance bottlenecks such as load imbalances and communication deficiencies.

Integration of Scalasca and Vampir

Scalasca scans execution traces for event patterns representing inefficiencies and the patterns found are categorised and ranked. The analysis results can be visualised using the CUBE browser. The users can identify the most severe problems in their code, locate the place in the code where the problem occurs and can see how its severity is distributed across the threads and processes. To find a solution for these problems this information is sometimes not sufficient. In some cases it is necessary to know the temporal context that led to the problem. This can be summarised as knowing the problem but having no real hint on its cause.

Using the Vampir tool chain a full trace of the communication patterns and call sequences can be visualised. There are many different views on the data which allow a very detailed analysis of the complete execution history but the vast amount of data complicates the search for bottlenecks. So in terms of finding performance flaws this can be cumbersome like "finding the needle in the haystack".

Integrating both tools enables the user to combine the advantages of Scalasca with those of Vampir (see figure 1). The Scalasca pattern search has been extended to also remember the location of the worst instance of each recognised performance problem for every call-path effected by the problem. The CUBE browser now features a new option in the file-menu to connect to Vampir. If this is selected, starting the Vampir client and server as well as connecting the two, and the loading of the necessary trace-file are all handled automatically. This is more user-friendly because the latest Vampir version can now also load and interpret Scalasca traces directly. CUBE then opens the global timeline as a default view in Vampir. Right clicking a pattern in CUBE reveals a new option "Max severity in trace browser" with which Vampir is instructed to zoom into that portion of the trace where the worst instance of this pattern occurred. Now the user can leverage all the possibilities available in Vampir to explore the trace to further investigate the history which led to the problem located.

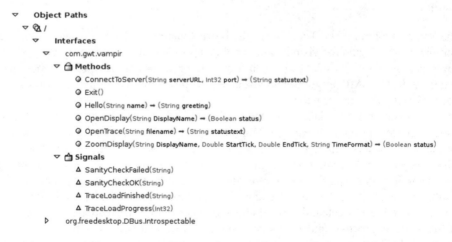

Figure 2. D-Bus interface

The remote control of Vampir through the CUBE browser or any other program is realised with the D-Bus protocol (see [12]). Using the D-Bus interface exposed by Vampir is fairly simple. The developer can implement it using the mechanism provided by Qt, C or C++. Figure 2 shows the interface of Vampir as it can be seen on the D-Bus using introspection.

INDEED

INDEED (INnovative DEEp Drawing) is an implicit finite element software for the numerical simulation of sheet metal forming processes like deep drawing, roll forming, crash forming, hydro forming of tubes and welded blanks and hydro mechanical deep drawing [1]. The main characteristics of INDEED are summarised as follows :

- an implicit integration scheme based on a total Lagrangian formulation with contact and equilibrium iterations fulfilled at the end of each increment.
- specially developed thick shell elements based on the so-called director shell theory [2] with 21 degrees of freedom per element
- fast contact-search algorithm based on an "active-set-strategy" and taking locally smoothed second-order contact-surfaces into account
- adaptive mesh refinement accounting for tool radii and local blank curvature

The requirements for metal forming simulation software are increasing steadily: on one hand, more time consuming sophisticated material models, element and contact formulations are necessary to obtain accurate results of complex phenomena like spring-back prediction or surface defects detection, while on the other hand a cost effective manufacturing process with a short development time is the main focus. To meet these requirements, a parallelization of the software was inevitable. At first, the most time consuming routines were parallelized with OpenMP directives, but currently a domain decomposition approach based on the message-passing interface (MPI) is also under development to benefit from massively parallel cluster technology. Special care must be taken in this case in an adaptive mesh refinement step. To allow for a correct mesh connectivity, some information has to be exchanged across sub-domain boundaries. Furthermore, the independent mesh refinement of each sub-area might result in an imbalance of the computational load of the processors in subsequent steps. That problem is solved in a second phase via a revaluation of the domains. For this purpose the PARMETIS[3] library can be used, but also own coordinate-based repartitioning algorithms were developed. The following section gives an example for the analysis and optimisation of both phases with the approach described in this paper.

Optimisation

INDEED uses an adaptive mesh refinement accounting for the tool radii and the local blank curvature. The recently developed parallel version based on domain decomposition induced new challenges during the rezoning step. The algorithm has to safeguard the correct element connectivity across adjacent sub-domains while rezoning. An update of the information concerning the neighbouring sub-domains has to be performed. Additionally the repartitioning of the blank has to be taken into account as the computational load of the domains becomes too unbalanced. With these background information it is now possible

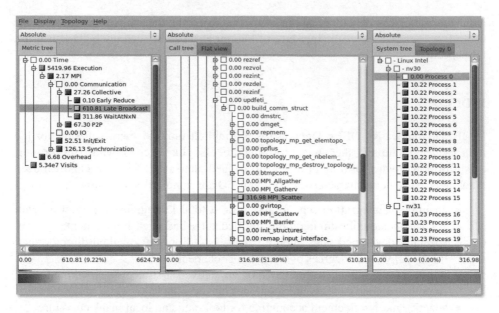

Figure 3. CUBE view showing the severity of the *Late Broadcast* pattern located at the MPI_SCATTER call in the build_comm_struct function

to investigate the performance problems located by Scalasca in the CUBE browser (see figure 3). Most of the time is lost in the MPI part of the application due to the pattern called *Late Broadcast*. Stepping down into the call-tree reveals an inefficient MPI_Scatter in the function build_comm_struct to be the main reason for this problem. The system tree on the right shows that process 0 seems to be the root-node of the broadcast operation providing the information too late. This knowledge alone is not enough as we have no indication of why process 0 took so long to enter MPI_Scatter. Using our new approach described above it is possible to investigate the history of this problem directly in Vampir (see figure 4). The figure reveals that process 0 is still computing while all the other processes are already waiting for data in the MPI_Scatter. The function only called by process 0 is find_neighbour_coor (see figure 4)and is responsible for the update of neighbour relationships during the rezoning or repartitioning. Although this function only takes a small amount of time to finish it has to be called for all edge-nodes of each zone or partition. Therefore the coordinates of all edge nodes are collected and send from each process to the process 0 were the recalculation takes place. As can be seen in the Vampir timeline display, this behaviour leads to the *Late Broadcast* pattern. The solution in this particular case is fairly easy as this type of coordinate matching can be done in parallel. Implementing this (and a few other optimizations) and rerunning the application results in a decrease of time lost in the *Late Broadcast* pattern from 610 seconds down to 28 (see figure 5). A positive side effect is that also the synchronisation time dropped down from 126 to 16 seconds as well as the *WaitAtNxN* pattern (311 down to 233) while the peer-to-peer communication time slightly increased from 67 to 74. So, by parallelizing this single function and thereby restructuring the load-balancing and rezoning steps an overall benefit to the runtime could be accomplished.

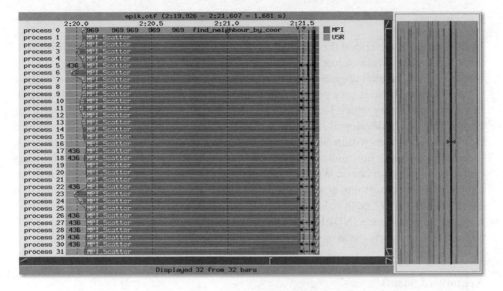

Figure 4. Same *Late Broadcast* Pattern shown in global timeline of Vampir

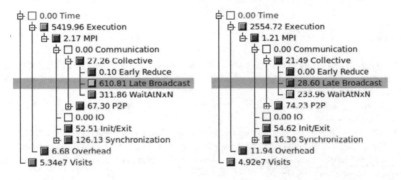

Figure 5. Different severity values before and after the optimization step

Related Work

Parallel performance tools so far were typically only very loosely coupled, for example by providing performance data (profiles, traces) converters. While this allows the use of another tool to analyse the same data in a different way, it was left to the users to find the corresponding data or displays in the second tool for a problem they found in the first tool. Also, it is often the case that information gets lost in the conversion. In our approach, the tools are very tightly coupled via a modern inter-process communication mechanism.

The latest version of the Paraver visualization tool [7] provides a remote control interface [8] that allows coupling Paraver with other tools comparable to what we did. However, the inter-process communication is based on the (unreliable and unportable) UNIX signal mechanism, and is not yet documented and published, which makes a more detailed comparison impossible.

Conclusions

In this paper we described the integration of the well-established parallel performance tools Vampir and Scalasca into a coherent integrated tool-set. Scalasca allows to quickly locate and rank parallel programming model related performance problems in application codes. Vampir provides very powerful visualisation and analysis functions to investigate the execution history which led to these problems and therefore find a potential solution easily. The newly developed integration allows to automatically start Vampir with the right trace data from within Scalasca and to display the execution history of problems located by Scalasca in timeline displays of Vampir with one mouse click streamlining the whole analysis process. We demonstrated the usefulness and effectiveness of these new features by describing how we used these tools for the optimisation of the adaptive mesh refinement and load balancing phases of the industrial metal forming simulation finite-element software INDEED. While the example used in this paper only used MPI, our software supports the same features also for hybrid OpenMP/MPI applications.

Acknowledgments

This work has partially been supported by the German Ministry for Research and Education (BMBF) through the ITEA2 project "ParMA"(No 06015, June 2007 – May 2010).

References

[1] Mathematical Modelling of the Sheet Metal Forming Process with INDEED. El Rifai Kassem, K. et al. (J.-L. Chenot, R. D. Wood. ed.). Numerical Methods in Industrial Forming Processes. NUMIFORM 92. Balkema. 1992

[2] Schalenelement mit 6 kinematischen Freiheitsgraden bei großen Verschiebungen. H. Schoop. ZAMM 67. 4 : 237-239, 1987

[3] PARMETIS Parallel graph partitioning and sparse matrix ordering library Version 3.1. George Karypis and Vipin Kumar, University of Minnesota, Department of Computer Science and engineering, 2003

[4] F. Wolf, B. Mohr: Automatic performance analysis of hybrid MPI/OpenMP applications, *Journal of Systems Architecture*, Vol. 49, No. 10-11, 421–439, 2003.

[5] F. Wolf, B. Mohr, J. Dongarra, S. Moore: Automatic analysis of inefficiency patterns in parallel applications, *Concurrency and Computation: Practice and Experience*, Vol. 19(11), 1481–1496, 2007.

[6] M. Geimer, F. Wolf, B. J. N. Wylie, B. Mohr: A scalable tool architecture for diagnosing wait states in massively parallel applications, *Parallel Computing*, Vol. 35, 375–388, 2009.

[7] J. Labarta, J. Giménez, E. Martinez, P. González, H. Servat, G. Llort, X. Aguilar: Scalability of visualization and tracing tools, in: Proceedings of Parallel Computing (ParCo), Málaga, Spain, 2005.

[8] Private communication with Paraver developer, 2009.

[9] M. Müller, A. Knüpfer, M. Jurenz, M. Lieber, H. Brunst, H. Mix, W. E. Nagel: Developing Scalable Applications with Vampir, VampirServer and VampirTrace *In C. Bischof, M. Bücker, P. Gibbon, G. Joubert, T. Lippert, B. Mohr, F. Peters: "Parallel Computing: Architectures, Algorithms and Applications"*, Vol. 15, pp. 637-644, ISBN: 978-1-58603-796-3, IOS Press, 2007

[10] A. Knüpfer, H. Brunst, J. Doleschal, M. Jurenz, M. Lieber, H. Mickler, M. S. Müller, W. E. Nagel: The Vampir Performance Analysis Tool-Set, *In Tools for High Performance Computing, Proceedings of the 2nd International Workshop on Parallel Tools*, Pages 139-155, Springer, 2008

[11] A. Knüpfer, R. Brendel, H. Brunst, H. Mix, W. E. Nagel: Introducing the Open Trace Format (OTF) *In Vassil N. Alexandrov, Geert Dick van Albada, Peter M. A. Sloot, Jack Dongarra (Eds): Computational Science - ICCS 2006: 6th International Conference, Reading, UK, May 28-31, 2006, Proceedings, Part II*, Springer Verlag, ISBN: 3-540-34381-4, pages 526-533, Vol. 3992, 2006

[12] D-Bus Specification and Documentation *http://www.freedesktop.org/wiki/Software/dbus*

Mini-Symposium
"Programming Heterogeneous Architectures"

Parallel Computing: From Multicores and GPU's to Petascale   711
B. Chapman et al. (Eds.)
IOS Press, 2010
© 2010 The authors and IOS Press. All rights reserved.
doi:10.3233/978-1-60750-530-3-711

Mini-symposium on Programming Heterogeneous Architectures

Lei Huang[a] Eric Stotzer[b] and Eric Biscondi[b]
[a] *University of Houston, USA*
[b] *Texas Instruments, USA*

Introduction

Modern computer architectures have evolved from homogeneity to heterogeneity by integrating specialized processing elements into a single system. Heterogeneous processing elements allow developers to maximize application performance by efficiently deploying software components to different processing elements based on their needs. What is lacking is a comprehensive programming model for these systems. There are vast opportunities to improve the performance and portability of software developed for heterogeneous systems and the productivity of the programmers working on these systems.

The mini-symposium included presentations from industry and universities with presentations on the challenges and opportunities of programming heterogeneous systems. Included here are three of the best papers presented.

Parallel Computing: From Multicores and GPU's to Petascale
B. Chapman et al. (Eds.)
IOS Press, 2010
© 2010 The authors and IOS Press. All rights reserved.
doi:10.3233/978-1-60750-530-3-712

Parallelization exploration of wireless applications using MPA

Martin PALKOVIC , Praveen RAGHAVAN, Thomas J. ASHBY, Andy FOLENS,
Hans CAPPELLE, Miguel GLASSEE, Liesbet VAN DER PERRE and
Francky CATTHOOR

Kapeldreef 75, B-3001 Leuven, Belgium

Abstract. Digital wireless communication has played a key role in our lives for more than one decade. Over the last decade we have observed rapid increase of the variability within and in the number of standards in the wireless domain and rapidly increasing computational demand for those applications. Embedded solutions for those systems require highly flexible programmable multi-core low power Software Defined Radio (SDR) platforms. Such platforms exist, however an efficient mapping flow from the algorithmic specification towards the implementation of the algorithm is lacking.

In this paper we present a complete mapping flow from algorithmic specification to parallel implementation on an SDR platform. The flow is supported by industrial and in-house tools for the critical parts of the mapping path. Local loops in the flow are avoiding global iterations and allow fast exploration at different stages. Results obtained by applying the flow on an industrial-strength test-vehicle, namely a 40 MHz MIMO SDM-OFDM baseband subsystem are discussed at the end of the paper.

Keywords. Parallelization, Mapping Flow, Wireless Systems, Software Defined Radio, 40 MHz MIMO SDM-OFDM

Introduction

Nowadays, sophisticated electronic products on the market tend to communicate with their environment via a wireless communication protocol. Usually, the communication is not restricted to one standard, but several communication standards are present in the device. This is going to be crucial especially in future cognitive radio devices that "intelligently" choose the appropriate protocol based on a free slot in the spectrum and the content that needs to be transferred. Those requirements cannot be achieved by a direct Very-Large-Scale Integration (VLSI) implementation [16], which still is a challenging task when going to modes with higher bandwidth anyhow. Thus, more promising in this area are the SDR solutions [18], even though they have much more stringent constraints compared to the VLSI implementation. Because of the high computational requirements of the current wireless standards, an SDR platform typically hosts multiple embedded processors. To achieve good performance of those multi-processor programmable solutions compared to the VLSI custom implementation, the wireless applications have to be implemented optimally on those devices whilst still meeting the development time constraints. To achieve this goal a systematic design flow starting with sequential specification and ending with parallel implementation on the platform is needed. Nowadays, even when multi-processor SDR platforms are present, the complementary design flow is often lacking. In this paper we contribute to mitigate parts of this gap by providing a design flow for a baseband subsystem.

The paper is structured as follows; in Section 1 we discuss the related work in parallelization, which is a crucial part of our approach. In Section 2 we describe a typical SDR platform and provide an example of our BEAR SDR platform. In Section 3 we explain our design flow and in Section 4 we discuss more in detail the parallelization exploration using our MPA tool. In Section 5 we provide the results obtained by our design flow on our heterogeneous multi-processor platform running the 40 MHz MIMO SDM-OFDM baseband processing application and in Section 6 we draw the conclusions.

1. Related work

There exist many alternative approaches to parallel programming and the mapping of sequential programs to parallel architectures. In the embedded context, the most relevant are probably the following: programming by hand with message passing [14] or threads [6], design using a dataflow graph formalism [9], and SPRINT [2] (and similar approaches). Much work on parallel programming and mapping has also been done in the scientific computing domain. Auto-parallelizing compilers mostly target only loop-level/data parallelism [1,5], although there has been some tertiary work on functional parallelism [7,8]. However, the most popular methodologies are probably programming using MPI [13] and annotating sequential programs using OpenMP [3].

Programming by hand or using threads is tedious, error prone and requires a lot of effort if the original code was sequential. The result is also usually specific to the number of threads chosen (and possibly even the specific architecture) and so causes problems for keeping multiple code versions up to date when retargeting an application or targeting multiple architectures, as opposed to keeping one code and multiple mapping schemes. Dataflow formalisms are related to our MPA approach in that the output of the tool can be informally viewed as a type of dataflow graph. However, MPA has neither the model restrictions of most dataflow models, nor the behavioral guarantees on the end mapping. Also, dataflow formalisms are more concerned with how to model a code that has already been mapped into different functional parts (actors) rather than enabling a mapping from sequential code in the first place. SPRINT (when compared to MPA) did not handle coarse grain data parallelism and was not integrated with the profiling framework. Compared to auto-parallelizing compilers for homogeneous platforms, MPA can be used for heterogeneous platforms if there is not a need to change input code for different cores.

2. Software Defined Radio Platforms

Nowadays, almost all handheld devices ensure wireless connectivity via one or combination of more wireless standards such as GSM, WLAN, Bluetooth etc. To implement those standards both, from hardware and software perspective is a challenging task. In the past, custom hardware was used to achieve needed efficiency. This limited the flexibility and reconfigurability of such a device. When it started to be crucial for features demanded by the customers such as quick time-to-market, flexibility and reusability, programmable solutions have been introduced in the last decade. Nowadays, the options are spanning from full custom to fully programmable SDR solutions [17].

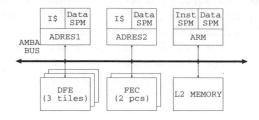

Figure 1. The IMEC BEAR platform.

An example of fully programmable SDR solution is the IMEC BEAR chip [4]. The high level block diagram of the platform is depicted in Figure 1. The platform consists of 2 in-house fixed point ADRES processors [11] running at 400 MHz with their own L1 data Scratch-Pad Memory (SPM) and L1 instruction cache, an ARM processor with its separate L1 data and instruction SPM, 3 Digital Front-End (DFE) tiles, 2 Forward Error Correction (FEC) decoders and an L2 memory. The platform is heterogeneous, consisting of different programmable processing elements such as DFE tiles and ADRES processors and custom hardware such as FEC. All the components are communicating via the 32 bit AMBA bus running at 200 MHz.

The BEAR chip design ensures flexibility and programmability due to its fully or partly programmable parts and also good energy efficiency due to energy efficient design of individual parts and separation of functionality based on duty cycles to DFE, ADRES and FEC.

3. Design flow for baseband processing

In this section we explain our design flow for baseband processing of wireless applications which is instantiated in [15] for 40 MHz MIMO SDM-OFDM application. The DFE processing is directly coded in assembly and the FEC is custom hardware. The block diagram of the design flow for baseband processing is depicted in Figure 2.

In our design flow we start from the algorithmic specification described in MAT-LAB. Wireless algorithmic designers prefer MATLAB because of the fast algorithm prototyping possibilities. However, MATLAB is not suited for the implementation on an embedded platform. After algorithmic exploration, the MATLAB specification is fixed and the MATLAB code is converted into C code using the Agility ^{TM} tool [19]. To produce a code suitable for the rest of the design flow, some optimizations are required already at the MATLAB level based on the result of the MATLAB to C conversion. Those optimizations include array constant propagation and code pruning, rewriting MATLAB specific features that cannot be translated to C (such as dynamic array extension), inlining of MATLAB function calls, intermediate buffers removal, loop transformations etc. The MATLAB code is compiled and profiled using a representative testbench. Based on the results the range of the variables is determined and the code is quantized, i.e. converted

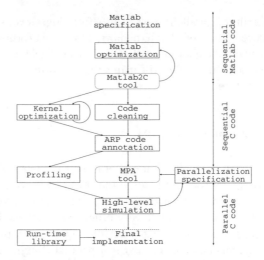

Figure 2. IMEC design flow for baseband processing.

to fixed point. After the MATLAB optimization and quantization which will happen in the local loop *MATLAB optimization* ↔ *MATLAB2C tool*, the final C code of this stage is generated. This code contains no more floating-point variables and is compliant with our instruction set.

The final code generated by Agility ^{TM} MATLAB to C conversion contains Agility ^{TM} runtime library calls that are replaced by C library calls in the code cleaning phase. Then the individual kernels are identified in the code. *Kernel* in this context means a sequence of code which is usually surrounded by a loop and which represents certain functionality (e.g. FFT, channel estimation, MMSE matrix computation etc.). Those kernels are exlined (opposite of inlined) to functions and each kernel is optimized individually for the processors we use at the platform. For each kernel a test bench is created which can verify functional correctness of the kernel after the optimizations. Optimization of the kernel is an iterative process. After optimization, the kernel is placed into a library. The optimized kernels are plugged back to the skeleton code which remains after exlining the kernels. Such a sequential optimized quantized code is used for the parallelization exploration.

The input to the parallelization exploration is the sequential optimized quantized code and the parallelization specification which determines how the individual kernels (functional split) and loop iterations (data split) are distributed over the different threads. To enable the parallelization specification the kernels in the sequential code have to be annotated by labeling the corresponding blocks of code. Also, the sequential code has to be profiled using an instruction-set simulator to obtain the cycle counts for each kernel in each iteration. During the parallelization several parallelization options are rapidly explored by simply changing the parallelization specification file. Those options are also rapidly evaluated using the high-level simulator that takes as an input the parallel code produced by the MPA tool [12] and profiling information of the individual kernels in individual iterations. The parallelization exploration with MPA creates also a local loop in the design flow. As mentioned before, in this local loop the different strategies described in parallelization specification files are automatically applied and quickly evaluated using high-level simulator.

When satisfied with the parallelization results from high-level simulation, the final parallel code is produced. This code has to be ported to the platform which means bridging the MPA tool API with the platform API. This is achieved by creating a light-weight RT library that implements the MPA API using the platform API. After this step, the code can run on the platform.

4. Parallelization exploration using MPA

In this section we focus on parallelization exploration using our MPA tool for 40 MHz MIMO SDM-OFDM application. We assume that MATLAB code was optimized and quantized and the C code was generated. Kernels were exlined and optimized for DLP and ILP. For DLP optimization we utilize very efficient specialized instructions (intrinsics) of our processor such as *C4mult* that is performing complex multiplication of two complex numbers (e.g., antenna one and two) in parallel (Single Instruction Multiple Data (SIMD)). For ILP optimization the *for* loops are optimally compiled using modulo scheduling on our processor with a large array of functional units (in the Coarse Grain Array (CGA) mode) so that different iterations of multiple operations (such as *pack* or *C4mult*) can be performed in parallel. The details about modulo scheduling and CGA mode of ADRES architecture are out of the scope of this paper and can be found in [10,11].

Except of the kernels, the application contains also the skeleton code (everything except the kernels) that has to be prepared for parallelization. This means removing or simplifying the pointer arithmetic, identifying the variables and iterators with unique name and moving the variables to its real scope in the code. We call this preparation process cleaning.

After kernel optimizations and cleaning of the skeleton code, the preamble processing which is performed once per burst, consumes 14.4 kcycles (12.6 kcycles, i.e. 87.5% are on CGA), which corresponds to 36 μs on a 400 MHz ADRES processor. In total the data processing requires 2320 cycles (1776 cycles, i.e. 76.6% are on CGA) to process one symbol of input data (note that one symbol has 160 samples which means for 40 MHz the receive time 4 μs for a symbol). This corresponds to a processing time of 5.80 μs on a 400 MHz ADRES. Splitting the computation load on two processors as we will discuss in this section and thus exploiting the Task Level Parallelism (TLP) ability of our platform, is crucial to enable to process the incoming symbols real-time. When we compare the optimized sequential code to the C code directly generated by Agility ^{TM}, the optimized sequential code is 88.7× faster.

In sequel we explain the parallelization exploration using MPSoC Parallelizing Assistant (MPA) tool and provide one example of possible parallelization. The input for the tool is the C code and the *par.spec* file (see Figure 3a) which specifies the parallelization. In the *par.spec* file we specify the block of code that is target for our parallelization (*OFDMParsec* label) and the distribution of different parts of the code within the parsection into individual threads. The distribution for our parallelization example is as following: *preamble* label into thread *preamble*, *symbol_kernel* label for iterations of *j2* from 0 to 4 into thread *symbol_odd* and *symbol_kernel* label for iterations of *j2* from 4 to 8 into thread *symbol_even*. We use also one shared variable *out_out* for which synchronization is left to the designer.

The tool analyzes the dependencies in the C code, performs the parallelization and inserts First-In First-Out (FIFO) buffers at the points where communication between the threads is needed. The schematic graph of parallelized code (which is part of the tool's output) is depicted in Figure 3b. Note that this is just one example of the possible parallelizations and multiple parallelization options can be generated and explored rapidly by simply changing the *par.spec* file.

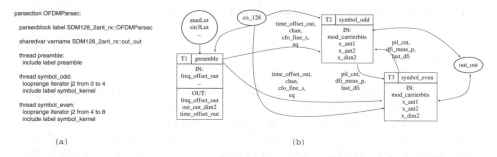

(a)   (b)

Figure 3. Parallelization of the 40 MHz MIMO SDM-OFDM Baseband Processing with the MPA tool: (a) Parallelization specification file, (b) Schematic graph of parallel code.

The rectangles in Figure 3 represent the three threads: the preamble thread (T1), the odd group of symbol thread (T2) and the even group of symbol thread (T3). Thread T1 uses a bunch of constants (*atanLut, sin3Lut, ...*) to compute the time and frequency offset and the channel compensation matrix. Those are going to be used in T2 and T3. T2 uses information about time and frequency offset and the channel from T1 via the FIFOs. The T2 thread processes the input stream of the odd group of symbols (continuous data processing) passing the necessary information to T3 via FIFOs (*pil_cnt, dfi_meas_p, last_dfi*). The output of the thread is written to a shared variable *out_out*. T3 works in the same way as T2, but for the even group of symbols.

Except for the parallelization itself, the MPA tools part called high-level simulator is also able to provide parallel timing, if the input code is ATOMIUM Record-Playback (ARP) call annotated and the sequential code is profiled as depicted in the flow on Figure 2. The parallel code output of MPA tool can be compiled with a *hlsim* library and together with the kernel timing information previously recorded and stored in the *data.arp* file can provide parallel timing of the application. The result of the parallel timing can be printed into a waveform.

As mentioned in Section 3 the MPA Application Programming Interface (API), e.g. FIFOs, have to be implemented using the platform resources in a Run-Time (RT) library when going to the final implementation . For our platform, the *FIFO put* is implemented as the Very Long Instruction Word (VLIW) interrupt of the ADRES baseband engine. This interrupt does not halt the processor, it is just calling the VLIW Interrupt Service Routine (ISR) of the given ADRES. In the VLIW ISR the actual copying of the data from local memory of a given ADRES to the local memory of the other ADRES. The *FIFO get* is implemented via the halt interrupt which is halting the ADRES. In the halt ISR we have implemented that the ADRES is released if the data are in its local memory. Otherwise it is released immediately after the data are copied from the other ADRES. The comparison of the high-level simulation and the actual platform results will be worked out in Section 5.

	Total execution time [s]			Waiting time [%]			
	10 bursts	Preamble	Payload	BBE1	BBE1	BBE2	BBE2
	(18 symb)		(1 symb)	HALT	VLIW	HALT	VLIW
MPA model	934.2μs	35.98μs	3.19μs	0%	0%	20%	0%
TLM platform	1153.0μs	43.00μs	4.00μs	9%	8%	20%	7%
Difference [%]	23.6%	19.5%	25.4%	9%	8%	0%	7%

Table 1. Comparison of total execution time and waiting time in MPA high-level modeling (zero delay model) and in the actual run on the TLM platform.

5. Results

In this section we compare the high-level simulation results with actual platform results and show that the final implementation can reach the real-time throughput.

Total execution time columns in Table 1 compare the MPA high-level modeling with the results on the Transaction Level Model (TLM) of our platform. The real TLM run is 23.6% worse than the MPA high-level model. This is caused by several factors which we are going to discuss below.

For the MPA we used a zero delay model, thus we assumed zero delay for the FIFO communication. On the platform this is not true. The communication is implemented via interrupts and the data are communicated to the other ADRES memory in the VLIW ISR, when they are ready. In the MPA model the zero delay can be changed to non zero delay. However, before running the code on the TLM platform, we did not have an exact idea how long the communication would take.

The interrupt itself also takes a certain amount of time. The percentage of time spent in waiting for the different interrupts is listed in the second line of *Waiting time* columns in Table 1. This overhead counts all delays: the actual waiting time when the data is not ready yet, the communication time and the interrupt time. It is largely not considered in the MPA model as can be seen in the first line of *Waiting time* columns. From Table 1 we can see an additional 17% non-active time on BBE1 due to halt and VLIW interrupts and an additional 7% non-active time on BBE2 due to VLIW interrupt when comparing MPA and TLM model.

Last but not least, the MPA model considers only the kernel timing (because only the kernels were profiled in the profiling) and does not count the cycles for the code that is outside those kernels. Thus there still is some wrapper code, which is counted for the TLM model and is not considered in the MPA model. However, this is only 2.5% of the total cycle count. Still, it is contributing to the difference between the MPA model and the TLM platform timing.

When we compare the sequential continuous (symbol) processing timing (5.8 μs per symbol) with the parallel timings from Table 1 (*Payload* column) we see the speedup of 1.81× for the MPA modeling (without communication, interrupt and wrapper function overhead) and 1.45× for the TLM platform. Together with the 88.7× speedup from kernel optimizations it speeds the application by 128.6× for TLM platform compared with the non-optimized sequential code directly generated form MATLAB, and thus achieves the real-time behavior. The big difference between speed-up due to the Instruction Level Parallelism (ILP) and Data Level Parallelism (DLP) and the TLP is because in ILP we work with 16 functional units, in DLP we work with 4-way SIMD but in TLP we work just with 2 processor cores.

6. Conclusions

In this paper we have shown a design flow starting from a MATLAB specification and producing a parallel code for an MPSoC SDR platform. The automatically generated parallel code exploits TLP and can be evaluated quickly using the high-level simulator. The optimized kernels exploit DLP via specialized SIMD instructions and allow good ILP via an optimized CGA mapping. The consolidated design flow with unique combination of parallelization at different granularities allows us to run critical parts of highly computational demanding wireless modes such as the 40 MHz MIMO SDM-OFDM baseband processing in real-time.

References

[1]   P.Banerjee, J.A.Chandy, M.Gupta, et al., "The Paradigm Compiler for Distributed-Memory Multicomputers", *Computer, IEEE Computer Society Press*, Vol. 28(10), pp.37–47, 1995.

[2]   J.Cockx, K.Denolf, B.Vanhoof, R.Stahl, "SPRINT: a tool to generate concurrent transaction-level models from sequential code", *J. on Applied Signal Processing*, Vol. 2007(1), pp.213–228, Jan. 2007.

[3]   L.Dagum, R.Menon, "OpenMP: An Industry-Standard API for Shared-Memory Programming", *Journal of Computing in Science and Engineering*, Vol. 5(1), pp.46–55, Jan. 1998.

[4]   V.Derudder, B.Bougard, A.Couvreur, et al., "A 200Mbps+ 2.14nJ/b Digital Baseband Multi Processor System-on-Chip for SDRs", *Proc. of VLSI Symposum*, Kyoto, Japan, June 2009.

[5]   M.W.Hall, J.M.Anderson, S.P.Amarasinghe, et al., "Maximizing Multiprocessor Performance with the SUIF Compiler", *Computer, IEEE Computer Society Press*, Vol. 29(12), pp.84–89, 1996.

[6]   ISO/IEC/JTC 1/SC 22, "ISO/IEC 9945-1:1996, Portable Operating System Interface (POSIX) – Part 1: System Application Program Interface (API)", Nov. 1996.

[7]   I.Karkowski, H.Corporaal, "FP-Map - An Approach to the Functional Pipelining of Embedded Programs", *HIPC '97: Proceedings of the Fourth International Conference on High-Performance Computing*, Washington, DC, pp.415, 1997.

[8]   B.Kienhuis, E.Rijpkema, E.Deprettere, "Compaan: deriving process networks from Matlab for embedded signal processing architectures", *CODES '00: Proceedings of the eighth international workshop on Hardware/software codesign*, San Diego, CA, pp.13–17, 2000.

[9]   E.A.Lee, T.M.Parks, "Dataflow process networks", *Proc. of the IEEE*, Vol. 83(5), pp.773–801, 1995.

[10] B.Mei, S.Vernalde, D.Verkest, H.De Man, R.Lauwereins, "Exploiting loop-level parallelism on coarse-grained reconfigurable architectures using modulo scheduling", *Proc. 6th ACM/IEEE Design and Test in Europe Conf.(DATE)*, Munich, Germany, pp.296-301, March 2003.

[11] B.Mei, S.Vernalde, D.Verkest, H.De Man, R.Lauwereins, "ADRES: an architecture with tightly coupled VLIW processor and coarse-grained configurable matrix", *Proc. IEEE Conf. on Field Programmable Logic and its Applications (FPL)*, Lisbon, Portugal, pp.61–70, Sep. 2003.

[12] The MPSoC Team, "MPSoC Parallelizing Assistant 4.0.2 User's Manual", *Imec internal user documentation*, March 2007.

[13] Message Passing Interface Forum, "MPI: A Message-Passing Interface Standard", June 1995.

[14] The Multicore Association, "Multicore Communications API Specification V1.063", March 2008.

[15] M.Palkovic, A.Folens, H.Cappelle, M.Glassee, and L.Van der Perre, "Optimization and Parallelization of 40 MHz MIMO SDM-OFDM Baseband Processing to Achieve Real-Time Throughput Behaviour," *Proc. ICT-MobileSummit 2009 Conference*, Santander, Spain, June 2009.

[16] P.Petrus, Q.Sun, S.Ng, et al., "An Integrated Draft 802.11n Compliant MIMO Baseband and MAC Processor", *Proc. IEEE Intl. Solid-State Circuits Conf. (ISSCC)*, San Francisco, CA, pp.266-269, Feb. 2007.

[17] U. Ramacher, "Software-Defined Radio Prospects for Multistandard Mobile Phones", *IEEE Computer Magazine*, vol. 40, no. 10, pp. 62–69, Oct. 2007.

[18] L.Van der Perre, B.Bougard, J.Craninckx, et al., "Architectures and Circuits for Software-Defined Radios: Scaling and Scalability for Low Cost and Low Energy", *Proc. IEEE Intl. Solid-State Circuits Conf. (ISSCC)*, San Francisco, CA, pp.568–569, Feb. 2007.

[19] *http://www.agilityds.com/products/matlab_based_products/default.aspx*

Parallel Computing: From Multicores and GPU's to Petascale
B. Chapman et al. (Eds.)
IOS Press, 2010

© 2010 The authors and IOS Press. All rights reserved.

doi:10.3233/978-1-60750-530-3-720

Prototyping and Programming
Tightly Coupled Accelerators

Eric STOTZER [a,b,1], Ernst L. LEISS [b], Elana GRANSTON [c], and David HOYLE [d,2]

[a] *Texas Instruments*
[b] *University of Houston*
[c] *Cutting Edge Consulting*
[d] *Qualcomm*

Abstract. A tightly coupled accelerator is specialized hardware attached to and controlled by a host processor. In this paper, we will discuss the features of tightly coupled accelerators and describe our programming model. We will show that our approach allows for the rapid prototyping and development of tightly coupled accelerators, using a worked out example on a Texas Instruments processor.

Keywords. accelerators, instruction level parallelism, software pipelining

Introduction

A tightly coupled accelerator is specialized hardware attached to and controlled by a host processor. In our work, the host processor is a statically scheduled very long instruction word (VLIW) with an unprotected pipeline [2]. I/O between the host processor and the accelerator is explicitly managed by specialized instructions that are scheduled on the host processor. The accelerator has an unprotected pipeline that executes synchronously with the host processor's pipeline. Because both the host processor and accelerator have unprotected pipelines, instruction scheduling must be statically determined before program execution. The host processor implements a small set of accelerator interface instructions. The accelerator is defined and programmed using a symbolic resource and dependency description language. The compiler translates the accelerator description language to resource and dependency constraints, and then uses software pipelining [1] to statically schedule the parallel execution of the host processor and accelerator. In this paper, we will discuss the features of tightly coupled accelerators and describe our programming model. We will show that our approach allows for the rapid prototyping and development of tightly coupled accelerators.

The motivation for developing hardware accelerators is efficiency improvement with respect to power, performance, and silicon area [6]. High performance applications are characterized by dynamic compute intensive regions. Optimizing the compute intensive parts of the application is highly desirable. Often these parts of the application contain

---

[1] Corresponding Author: Eric Stotzer, Texas Instruments, Stafford TX, USA; E-mail: estotzer@ti.com.
[2] This work was done while Elana Granston and David Hoyle were employed at Texas Instruments.

loops with high degrees of parallelism. One way to dramatically improve the overall performance of the application is to execute the compute intensive parts of the application on a hardware accelerator. Since the hardware accelerator is specialized for a specific function, it eliminates non-essential circuitry that must be present on a general purpose processor. This enables the accelerator to use less power to execute the same function. With respect to area, specialized accelerator hardware tends to be much smaller than the number of general purpose processors that would be required to execute the accelerated code block in the same amount of time.

The trade off for developing and using an accelerator is the development cost and the programming model. There is a spectrum between totally non-programmable hardwired and flexible programmable accelerators. Programmability is attractive because it allows for adaptability as software and standards change, which allows the accelerator to be used for more than one function. However, programmability requires some type of regular programming model, which is often difficult to implement on the irregular hardware features of accelerators. In addition, the more flexible the accelerator gets, there tends to be a reduction in the efficiency gains in power and area.

1. Tightly Coupled Accelerators

Our approach uses a host processor + tightly coupled accelerator. A tightly coupled accelerator is specialized hardware attached to and controlled by a host processor. The accelerator operations and host instructions are mixed in the same program. This leverages the host eco-system such as the debugger and the compiler. For example, in Figure 1 the accelerators are connected to the host processor via shared switch fabric. The accelerators can also send data to each other.

The host and accelerator have an unprotected pipeline. Static instruction scheduling is performed before program execution. Software pipelining is used to exploit instruction level parallelism. The hardware pipelines of the host and the tightly coupled accelerator execute synchronously. The host processor implements a small set of accelerator interface instructions. These are basically I/O management commands to move data to and from the accelerator, and an instruction to issue accelerator commands. All of these instructions are issued from the host processor.

2. Software pipelining

Finding a valid software pipeline is an instruction scheduling problem. A component of the compiler must perform instruction scheduling by examining data dependencies to determine which operations may execute in parallel [4]. In order to extract instruction level parallelism from a program, the relationships between operations must be completely understood. Since only independent operations may execute in parallel, operation dependencies must be determined first.

In order to comprehend operation dependencies, a data dependency graph (DDG) is constructed where nodes represent operations and the edges express data precedence relations between the operations. Cyclic dependency graphs contain back edges caused by loops in the control flow such that results from values computed in one loop iteration are

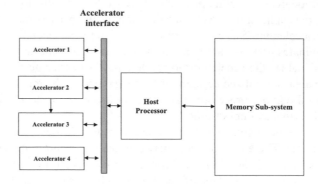

Figure 1. Tightly coupled accelerators.

used as inputs in successive iterations. This type of dependency is called a recurrence or loop carried dependency (LCD). The edges in a cyclic dependency graph are augmented with an iteration difference, which is the number of iterations separating the output and input operations of the dependency.

Modulo scheduling is motivated by the development of pipelined hardware functional units. The rate at which new loop iterations are started is called the Initiation Interval (II) [3]. The Minimum Initiation Interval (MII) is the smallest II for which a valid schedule can be found. The resource bound (ResMII) is determined by the total resource requirements of the operations in the loop. The recurrence bound (RecMII) is determined by loop carried data dependencies. The MII is thus determined as MAX(ResMII, RecMII). Methods for finding the ResMII and the RecMII can be found in [3,4].

The schedule for a single iteration is divided into a sequence of stages each with a length of II. In the steady state of the execution of the software pipelined loop, each of the stages will execute in parallel. The instruction schedule for a software pipelined loop has three components: a prolog, a kernel, and an epilog. The kernel is the instruction schedule that will execute the steady state. In the kernel, an instruction scheduled at cycle k will execute in parallel with all instructions scheduled at cycle k modulo II. The prolog and epilog are the instruction schedules that setup and drain the execution of the loop kernel.

3. Accelerator instructions

The programming model is built upon a set of accelerator interface instructions. The accelerator interface is the small set of instructions that the host uses to communicate with the accelerator. These instructions fall into three categories: send data, receive data, and command (see Figure 2). The send and receive I/O instructions store and load data to and from the accelerator respectively. The I/O functions have a command operand that specifies a destination or source resource in the accelerator. The accelerator command operation directs the accelerator to execute internal functions.

Send data to the accelerator
ACCSTW src,ucst32
ACCSTDW src1:src2,ucst32
Receive data from the accelerator
ACCLDW dst,ucst32
ACCLDDW dst1:dst2,ucst32
Send command to the accelerator
ACCCMD ucst32

Figure 2. Accelerator commands

4. Accelerator intrinsic functions

The accelerator instructions are exposed to the programmer via C/C++ intrinsic functions. This enables the programmer to control the accelerator behavior by using a high level language and a compiler. The compiler translates the intrinsic functions directly into the accelerator interface instructions. The intrinsics have an extra attribute argument that is used to indicate to the compiler the accelerator operation's latencies and dependencies. The intrinsic functions are shown in Figure 3.

Send data to the accelerator from the host processor
void acc_send(**const char** * attributes , **int** data, **int** dst);
void acc_sendll (**const char** * attributes , **long long** data, **int** dst);
Copy data from the accelerator to the host processor
int acc_recv(**const char** * attributes , **int** src);
long long acc_recvll (**const char** * attributes , **int** src);
Send a command to the accelerator
void acc_cntrl (**const char** * attributes , **int** cmd);

Figure 3. General accelerator intrinsic functions

The accelerator attribute string is used to express the dependence and resource requirements of the accelerator operations (see Figure 4). The attribute string is a comma separated list of reference descriptors. A reference descriptor includes a name resource reg and an optional reference type $reftype$ and $cycle$. The $reftype$ is either u or d for use or definition respectively. A u $reftype$ uses the reg, and a d $reftype$ defines the reg. The $cycle$ indicates when in time relative to the start of the accelerator instruction the reference occurs. The default $reftype$ and $cycle$ is $u0$ or a use on the same cycle that the operation executes. The reg ref is used to represent both logical and physical resources in the accelerator.

"ref=<reg>(<reftype><cycle>)[,<reg>(<reftype><cycle>),] "

Figure 4. Accelerator operation attributes string

The following examples demonstrate how to use the attribute string to program an accelerator. The $acc\_send()$ function *writes* data from the host processor to an accelerator resource that is specified in the destination argument. Likewise, the $acc\_recv()$ function *reads* data from an accelerator resource encoded in the source argument and returns it to the host. The attribute string describes the behavior of the accelerator with respect to when the reads and writes of the resources occur in the accelerator hardware pipeline. The *acc_cmd*() function is used to issue a command to the accelerator. Any side-effects of an accelarator function on a resource are encoded in the attribute string. The accelerator pipeline behavior is determined by the accelerator hardware. The attribute string is used by the compiler to schedule the accelerator interface instructions. For correct execution, the attribute string must reflect the behavior of the accelerator hardware pipeline.

Examples of using the accelerator attribute string are shown in Figure 5. In the first example, the attribute strings are used to specify a dependence between accelerator command and receive operations. The *DECOMP* command writes (*defs*) the register $r3$ four cycles after the command issues. The receive command reads (*uses*) $r3$ one cycle after it issues. This indicates that $S2$ must be scheduled at least four cycles after $S1$. In the second example, because there is no common *reg* named int the attribute strings of $S3$ and $S4$, there is no dependence between the two operations.

Specify a four cycle dependence from S1 to S2
#**define** DECOMP 0x10
S1: acc_cmd("ref=r3(d4)", DECOMP);
S2: x = acc_recv("ref=r3(u1)");
No dependence between S3 and S4
S3: acc_cmd("ref=r3(d5)", DECOMP);
S4: x = acc_recv("ref=r5(u1)");

Figure 5. Programming accelerator behavior

The accelerator attribute string enables experimentation with different accelerator designs. Developing a prototype using the accelerator intrinsics does not require changes in the compiler. The compiler uses the information in the attribute string to schedule the accelerator interface instructions. Listing 1 presents a simple $filter()$ function that has a a doubly nested loop where the inner loop accumulates into sum the function $F(X[i+j], H[j])$. To keep the example simple assume that $F(x, h) = x * h$.

```
1
2    filter(float X[], float H[], float Y[], int N, int NCOEF)
3    {
4        int i,j;
5        for (i=0; i<N; i++) {
6            float sum = 0.0
7            for (j=0; j<NCOEF; j++)
8                sum += F(X[i+j], H[j]);
9            Y[i] = sum;
10        }
11   }
```

Listing 1 Host+accelerator code

Listing 2 is a version of the $filter()$ function where the inner loop is performed on a tightly coupled accelerator. The accelerator implements a parallel floating point multiply accumulate (MAC) operation. The maximum number of parallel MAC operations is determined by the specific accelerator implementation. The accelerator has two FIFO buffers $F1$ and $F2$. A write to a FIFO buffer shifts all elements in the buffer and an element is dropped from the end of the buffer. An initialization command sets the number of parallel MAC operations and the size of the FIFO's.

In Listing 2, the MAC_INIT command initializes the accelerator, sets the number of parallel MACS to $NCOEF$, and initializes the FIFO's. The first loop loads $F1$ with $NCOEF$ values from $H[]$, and $F2$ with the first $NCOEF - 1$ values from $X[]$. The compute loop streams a new value of $X[]$ into $F2$, issues the MAC_DO command to perform the MAC, and then reads the result from the accelerator resource register SUM and stores it into $Y[i]$.

```
1    /* Filter accelerator interface */
2    #define MAC_INIT 0x01 /* accelerator commands */
3    #define MAC_DO    0x02
4    #define F1      0x00 /* accelerator resource */
5    #define F2      0x01
6    #define SUM    0x02
7    #define TAPS 0x03
8
9    filter_acc(float X[], float H[], float Y[], int N, int NCOEF)
10   {
11       int i;
12       acc_send("ref=TAPS(d)", NCOEF, TAPS);
13       acc_cmd("ref=TAPS,F1(d),F2(d)", MAC_INIT);
14       for (i=0; i<NCOEF-1; i++) {
15           acc_send("ref=F1,F1(d)", H[i], F1);
16           acc_send("ref=F2,F2(d)", X[i], F2);
17       }
18       acc_send("ref=F1,F1(d)", H[i], F1);
19
20       for (i=0; i<N; i++) {
21           acc_send("ref=F2,F2(d)", X[i+NCOEF-1], F2);
22           acc_cmd("ref=F1,F2,SUM(d)", MAC_DO);
23           Y[i] = acc_recv("ref=SUM", SUM);
24       }
25   }
```

Listing 2 Host+accelerator code

Programmers can build higher level functionality using macros or inline functions. This enables abstractions that hide the accelerator intrinsics. In Listing 3 the lower level commands to program the accelerator $filter()$ function are hidden in inlined functions.

5. Software pipelining host+accelerator code

The host processor we used is a Texas Instruments TMS320C674x (C674x) VLIW processor [5] with the addition of an accelerator interface port. The $filter()$ function and supporting accelerator interface code are input to the C/C++ compiler.

```
1    inline void mac_init(float X[], float H[], int NCOEF) {
2        int i;
3        acc_send("ref=TAPS(d)", NCOEF, TAPS);
4        acc_cmd("ref=TAPS,F1(d),F2(d)", MAC_INIT);
5        for (i=0; i<NCOEF-1; i++) {
6            acc_send("ref=F1,F1(d)", H[i], F1);
7            acc_send("ref=F2,F2(d)", X[i], F2); }
8        acc_send("ref=F1,F1(d)", H[i], F1);
9    }
10
11   inline float mac_do(float Xi[], float H[], int NCOEF) {
12       acc_send("ref=F2,F2(d)", Xi[NCOEF-1], F2);
13       acc_cmd("ref=F1,F2,SUM(d)", MAC_DO);
14       return acc_recv("ref=SUM", SUM);
15   }
16
17   filter_acc(float X[], float H[], float Y[], int NCOEF, int N)
18   {
19       int i;
20       mac_init(X, H, NCOEF);
21       for (i=0; i<N; i++)
22           Y[i] = mac_do(&X[i], H, NCOEF);
23   }
```

Listing 3 Abstracted Host+accelerator code

The compiler generates machine instructions and builds a dependency graph for the instructions that form the loop of the $filter()$ function. The compiler then uses modulo scheduling to generate the software pipelined loop shown in Figure 6. For the sake of brevity the branch instruction is not shown. The resulting schedule has an II of one with ten iterations executing in parallel in the kernel. A new result is produced every cycle.

For a basic performance analysis, the critical measurement is the number of multiplies performed per cycle. The C674x can perform 2 floating point multiplies per cycle. The original loop executes $N * NCOEF$ floating point multiplies. The best case performance for the C674x on this loop is $(N * NCOEF/2)$ cycles. The accelerator is designed to execute $NCOEF$ multiplies per cycle. With the accelerator the best case performance is reduced to $(N * NCOEF)/NCOEF$ or N cycles. The speedup factor for the accelerator is $NCOEFS/2$. For example, assuming 32 coefficients, the speedup factor is 16x.

In regards to power and area, the qualitative assumption is that because the accelerator is designed for a specific case, it can eliminate hardware that would be required for a general purpose implementation. In other words, adding 30 more general purpose floating point multiply units to the C674x would not not only be impractical, but would significantly increase the processor size and power usage.

6. Conclusion

Accelerators have efficiency advantages that improve performance, reduce power consumption, and reduce cost. However, the challenge is to present a usable programming

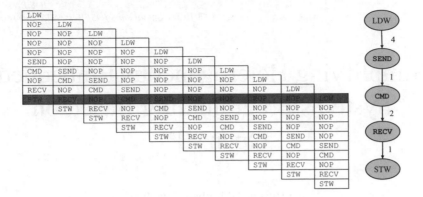

Figure 6. Software pipeline and dependence graph

model. For tightly coupled accelerators, the host and accelerator work together. We have presented an accelerator interface that includes a set of basic instructions, which are basic elements that can be put together in a flexible programming model. We have presented accelerator intrinsics that offer a higher level interface and enable a simple programmable model. Our model includes a programming language for specifying scheduling constraints between these basic operations. In this way higher level complex operations are constructed from these elements. These higher level abstractions can hide complexity behind macros and inline functions. We have shown a simple example the demonstrates how this approach can be used to accelerate a program region. For this example with 32 coefficients, the accelerator provides a 16x performance improvement. In addition, the programming model is a simple extension to an existing high level language.

Acknowledgments

We would like to acknowledge our colleagues at Texas Instruments who have worked with us on various aspects of this research.

References

[1] V. H. Allan, R. B. Jones, R. M. Lee, and S. J. Allan, "Software pipelining," *ACM Comput. Surv.*, vol. 27, no. 3, pp. 367–432, 1995.

[2] J. A. Fisher, P. Faraboschi, and C. Young, *Embedded Computing : A VLIW Approach to Architecture, Compilers and Tools*. Morgan Kaufmann, December 2004.

[3] B. R. Rau, "Iterative modulo scheduling: an algorithm for software pipelining loops," in *MICRO 27: Proceedings of the 27th Annual International Symposium on Microarchitecture*. New York, NY, USA: ACM, 1994, pp. 63–74.

[4] E. Stotzer and E. Leiss, "Modulo scheduling for the tms320c6x vliw dsp architecture," in *LCTES '99: Proceedings of the ACM SIGPLAN 1999 Workshop on Languages, Compilers, and Tools for Embedded Systems*. New York, NY, USA: ACM, 1999, pp. 28–34.

[5] *TMS320C674x DSP CPU Instruction Set User's Guide*, sprufe8 ed., Texas Instruments, Inc., October 2008.

[6] W. Wolf, *High-Performance Embedded Computing: Architectures, Applications, and Methodologies*. Morgan Kaufman, 2006.

Parallel Computing: From Multicores and GPU's to Petascale
B. Chapman et al. (Eds.)
IOS Press, 2010
© 2010 The authors and IOS Press. All rights reserved.
doi:10.3233/978-1-60750-530-3-728

Simplifying Heterogeneous Embedded Systems Programming Based on OpenMP[1]

Lei Huang and Barbara Chapman[2]

University of Houston, 4800 Calhoun Rd, Houston, TX, USA;

Abstract. Modern computer architectures have increased their paces to move into heterogeneity by integrating specialized processing elements such as GPUs, FPGAs, DSPs into a single system together with general processors. The integration allows developers to maximize their applications performance by mapping the different modules to different processing elements based on the characteristics. However, the current programming models are not comprehensive, portable or expressive enough to support developers' needs. In this paper, we are exploring the current programming approach on heterogeneous embedded systems, as well as studying the popular shared memory programming model OpenMP for how to adapt it to heterogeneous systems. We present our initial design of OpenMP extensions to support work distribution and data communication between different processing elements.

Keywords. OpenMP, Heterogeneous Systems, High Performance Computing

1. Introduction

As the computing industry turns to parallelism as the predominant source of higher performance, it is becoming increasingly important to provide systems that can exploit the different kinds of parallelism present in a variety of applications. In addition to the creation of homogeneous processors consisting of a number of cores that access shared memory (possibly in a non-uniform manner), several different flavors of coprocessors, or hardware accelerators, have been designed and incorporated into laptops, desktops, supercomputers and embedded systems. Such accelerators are often particularly efficient at processing very specific kinds of workloads, sometimes offering several orders of magnitude in performance enhancements over general-purpose processors where these are present, yet rather limited in their applicability. As a result, their deployment must be carefully considered during application development to ensure that they are used to maximum benefit.

Heterogeneous systems, consisting of general-purpose as well as one or more such specialized processing units, thus offer an attractive path to meeting increased computa-

[1]This work is sponsored by NSF CCF-0833201 and Texas Instrument.
[2]Corresponding Author: Lei Huang, University of Houston, 4800 Calhoun Rd, Houston, TX, USA; E-mail: leihuang@cs.uh.edu.

tional demands in a flexible manner. A portion of a workload that cannot be executed efficiently on a general-purpose unit may be much more efficiently processed on a configured accelerator that is amenable to its specific set of instructions and data types. Many conventional systems and high-end platforms already routinely provide one or more accelerators, whether in the form of a vector coprocessor, a specialized high-end floating coprocessor, a general-purpose graphics programming unit (GPU), a field programmable gate array (FPGA) or a digital signal processor (DSP), and are thus heterogeneous. It is currently expected that there will be a great increase in heterogeneous architectures in conventional and high-end systems, partly as a result of the low cost of some accelerators, but also as the result of systems under construction at both Intel and AMD. The extent of the heterogeneity is also likely to increase.

Embedded systems are frequently heterogeneous. They are usually designed to perform a very specific set of tasks and the configured devices will have been carefully designed or chosen to best meet the requirements and operating constraints of those tasks. The overall system may today include several processing cores, FPGAs, DSPs and other devices. The use of multicore technology is leading to the creation of new and powerful embedded devices and provide new opportunities for deploying data and compute intensive applications.

2. Background

Heterogeneous computing is not new, but the range of devices and the extent of their deployment is. Many accelerators are widely used today in the form of coprocessors that are able to enhance the performance of suitable computations, sometimes providing several orders of magnitude better performance than a conventional processor. Hybrid systems such as the IBM's Cell Broadband Engine have been used both for games as well as for technical computing. Low-cost GPGPUs are likely to become ubiquitous in the near future. With plans by Intel and AMD to introduce general-purpose chips that are heterogeneous [30], they are poised to enter the mainstream. We briefly review current hardware and programming practices.

2.1. Hardware for Heterogeneous Systems

Heterogeneous platforms may include any combination of conventional processors, including multicores, and DSPs, application specific instruction processors (ASIPs), FPGAs, stream processors, SIMD processors, high-end floating point accelerators, GPGUs and more. Heterogeneous systems abound in the marketplace, especially for embedded applications. Many desktops and laptops include GPPGUs, and some high-end systems incorporate special-purpose accelerators or FPGAs. ARM's ARM11 MPCore [7] and Analog Device's ADSP-BF561 [11] are multi-core RISC based architectures. Texas Instruments DaVinci [17] and OMAP 3 (Open Multimedia Application Platform) [16] are examples of RISC + DSP configurations. Texas Instruments TNETV3020 [15] and TMS320TCI6488 [14], Freescale Semiconductor's MSC8144 [12], and picoChip's PC20x [29] family are examples of multi-core DSP based architectures. Cradle Technologies CT3600 [22] incorporates 8 to 16 DSPs along with 4 to 8 RISC processors. The Cell Broadband Engine [20] contains a single PowerPC core along with eight "synergistic processing elements" which are SIMD based processors.

2.2. Programming Models for Heterogeneous Systems

Accelerator boards are hard to program. In addition to the task of identifying regions of code that will benefit from deployment on a given device, the code must be adapted to this task. Since memory is generally not shared between accelerators and a host platform, it is necessary to carefully determine how much data needs to be transferred and when and how this may best occur. Since most accelerators require a high ratio of computation to data, reorganization of loop nests for data reuse is essential. Unfortunately, custom language features must then be used to express the computation in a form suitable for a given accelerator.

Several vendors have provided programming interfaces for acceleration. Most of these have adapted the C programming language to fit the strict requirements of applications on their platform. GPUs were originally programmed using OpenGL. Domain-specific lanuages for graphics programming like GLSL (OpenGL Shading Language), HLSL(high level shader language), Cg (C for graphics) from NVIDIA are also available. With their growing usefulness for compute-intensive functions in general-purpose applications, a number of programming interfaces (mostly based on C) have been provided to facilitate the development of application kernels for them. These include StreamIt [5], Sh [25], Brook [8], and CUDA [26]. CUDA in particular has become popular for general-purpose programming on NVIDIA GPUs. CUDA code is embedded in the host code and translated by a preprocessor. Although it does not require the user to explicitly declare and use threads, it does expect the programmer to divide the data among the thread processors, who will then execute the same instructions on their portion of data. A block of threads can operate on the same data. The application developer must determine the best number of threads and size of such blocks for their code. Clearspeed has defined Cn [3], an extension of C to support their data-parallel floating-point accelerator architecture by providing the definitions of mono (scalar) and poly (parallel, or replicated) data types. RapidMind [2] provides APIs to adapt the computation to a mixture of multicores, GPUs and Cell by managing communication, data flow and load balancing between the host processor and target device(s). It uses SPMD data parallelism programming model with streaming data access to efficiently use memory. Ct [19] is a new data parallel programming model designed by Intel to address both CPU and GPU programming. At the time of writing, the OpenCL [1] 1.0 specification has just been released by a group of vendors.

2.2.1. Stream Programming Model

The stream programming model represents a program by multiple actors that are connected via point-to-point data streams. A large class of emerging processors directly support the stream based programming model [10,21,4,24,32,28]. Stream Processors, Inc. has commercialized stream processing for DSP applications. It is well suited to the programming of accelerators, since it can be used to specify the identical processing of a sequence of data sets. AMD has developed extensions to Brook+ to support stream programming on their GPGUs. The StreamIt [5] language represents a program as a set of autonomous actors communicating through FIFO data channels. StreamFlex [31] enables stream programming by combining streams with objects through extensions to Java. Researchers have proposed extensions to OpenMP [27] to facilitate the expression of streaming applications by enabling the expression of pipelined computations [13].

2.2.2. Hybrid Shared Memory and Message Passing Model

Research on parallel programming models in the high performance embedded space has considered both shared memory and message passing parallel programming paradigms due to the heterogeneity in memory interconnects for MPSoCs. The MultiFlex system maps an application to heterogeneous parallel components utilizing a distributed system object component (DSOC) object oriented message passing model (similar to a subset of CORBA) and a symmetrical multiprocessing (SMP) model using shared memory (similar to the POSIX threads standard). It provides an efficient implementation by supporting low overhead hardware-assisted message passing, context scheduling and dynamic scheduling. The MESCAL system defines concurrency primitives in the shared address space (e.g. support for thread creation and synchronization) and a subset of the MPI standard. SMM (Shared Messaging Model) integrates message passing and shared memory models to improve the communication latency of message passing.

3. OMAP DSP Systems

In the early 1980s, programmable digital processors were developed with specialized hardware features for implementing signal-processing algorithms (for example, the Fast Fourier Transform (FFT) or the Finite Impulse Response (FIR) filter). Offering high performance, programmability, and low cost, DSP processors enabled embedded real-time applications that previously had only run on supercomputers. The DSP field has grown today to include such applications as antilock braking systems, disk drive controllers, digital filtering, image compression and transmission, radar processing, cellular base stations and telephony, video conferencing, speech recognition, multi-channel modems, and much more.

The OMAP35x (Open Multimedia Application Platform) [18] is a family of heterogeneous MPSoCs with the capability to have very high performance general purpose processing, video / multimedia processing, graphics acceleration, and a highly integrated peripheral set all in one very small package. The OMAP35x has an ARM based general purpose processor, a high performance digital signal processor, a graphics accelerator, a video accelerator, and set of highly integrated peripherals. The OMAP35x family includes configurations that add or remove various processing elements to match performance, power, and cost requirements.

The general purpose processor present on all OMAP35x platforms is the ARM based architecture with enhancements for reduced code size and multimedia SIMD extensions. The ARM processor is capable of running up to 600Mhz and is an in-order dual-issue, superscalar with hardware support for branch dynamic prediction. The Arm processor has an MMU and is capable of running general purpose applications and operating systems such as Linux.

The C64+ digital signal processor (DSP) on the OMAP35x is capable of running up to 430 MHz. The C64+ is a Very Long Instruction Word (VLIW) capable of issuing eight instructions in parallel. The C64+ is statically scheduled by the compiler. It has specialized instructions for signal processing such as saturation, normalization, and complex multiplication. Combined with the C64+ is a video hardware accelerator. The C64+ based video system is capable of processing up to 720 HD resolution video.

The graphics accelerator on the OMAP35x platform is a PowerVR SGZ, which is a tile based architecture capable of up to 10 MPoly/sec. It includes a scalable shader engine with a multi-threaded pixel and vertex functionality. The graphics accelerator implements industry standard support for OpenGLES and OpenVG1.0.

Finally, all of these processing elements are combined on one chip with memory and programmable peripherals that enable communication, synchronization, and power saving technologies.

3.1. Programming on OMAP3X

As described in last section, the OMAP3X series architectures consist of one general processing processor ARM Cortex, and one special processing unit TMS320C64X+ DSP. An OS, typically Linux, is running on ARM processor to handle general resource management, graphic interfaces, database, event handling, and so on. It is quite similar as programming on regular PC if we do not consider to use DSP. In order to use DSP, it starts becoming quite complicated to program since DSP is not managed by OS and it is programmer's responsibility to start, manage, and stop the DSP device and synchronize with GPP side program.

DSPLINK/BIOS is a foundation software for the inter-processor communication across the GPP-DSP boundary. DSP is running a simple real-time OS called BIOS that manages its resources. DSPLINK provides a generic API that abstracts the characteristics of the physical link connecting GPP and DSP from the applications. While it simplifies the programmer's work in providing detailed hardcore code to communicate GPP and DSP, it is still quite complex to control, manage and synchronize DSP from GPP code.

As a result, the current programming approach on OMAP is to write two separate, complete programs for both ARM and DSP sides, and compile them using a ARM-based compiler and TI DSP compiler respectively. It may require to use a Windows host to compile and debug DSP code and a Linux host to compile GPP part of code. The DSPLINK library is linked with them to handle communications and synchronizations between them, as well as I/O operations at DSP side. A simple functionality program requires quite large amount of management code to handle all of these events and debugging on such systems is much more complicated. In this work, we are exploring an unified programming model based on OpenMP to simplify the programming efforts on such heterogeneous systems.

4. Proposed OpenMP Extensions

OpenMP is a widely-adopted shared memory parallel programming interface providing high level programming constructs that enable the user to easily expose an application's task and loop level parallelism in an incremental fashion. Its range of applicability was significantly extended recently by the addition of explicit tasking features [6]. OpenMP has already been proposed as the starting point for a programming model for heterogeneous systems by Intel, ClearSpeed, The Portland Group and CAPS SA.

We believe that OpenMP is a suitable programming model for the internal programming of components of an embedded application, for multicores and accelerators, but do not plan to rely on shared virtual memory for performance reasons. It is our vision that a unified shared memory programming model will be proved to be an efficient and popular programming model in MPSoCs. OpenMP is one of the candidates and it is worth exploring its evolution on MPSoCs due to its distinguish features to adapt existing programs incrementally to MPSoCs.

Our goals of the work are to provide high level programming primitive to speed up development based on OpenMP; to create a single program that can run on both general processor and accelerators (ARM + DSP); and to simplify the data communication and management. In this section, we briefly introduce our initial ideas for extending OpenMP to heterogeneous embedded systems.

4.1. Target Clause in OpenMP

On heterogeneous systems, application developers need the capability to specify where a fragment of code may be executed on the host, DSPs, or other accelerators. We propose to provide an extension "target" clause to OpenMP task construct to allow developers to specify a task/kernel to be executed on a target hardware. Task "target" syntax is as follows.

#pragma omp task *target(DSP)*

The "target" clause is potentially able to apply to other OpenMP worksharing constructs, but we limit its application at this moment to OpenMP task due to the complete data environment for a task. It may be used to target different hardware, and it is possible to provide a generic hardware descriptor handle to achieve portability. A compiler will generate object code based on the targeted hardware and its descriptor. This feature will allow developers to partition and allocate the application components on different hardware devices to maximize performance. The developers is able to work on one source code for both GPP and DSP using this feature, which will greatly simplify the programming efforts and code maintenance.

4.2. Data Streaming Attribute

The streaming programming model has the advantages of increasing parallelism via pipelined execution and data locality. However, it may suffer from limitations on pipelining as well as load imbalance. The stream size and data transfer granularity has a big impact on performance. We propose to introduce data streams into OpenMP and pay particular attention to overcoming these limitations. Data stream in and out attribute syntax is as follows.

#pragma omp task target(DSP) *stream_in(var[,var]) stream_out(var[,var])*

The stream_in and stream_out indicates that the input stream data and output stream data, as well as the data access pattern is following FIFO fashion. The compiler will generate data communication code between the GPP and targeted DSP and handle their synchronization transparently. It will eliminate the programming efforts to use DSPLINK explicitly to communicate between GPP and DSP in such applications. However, it is still necessary to use DSPLINK in complex communication cases if the data access pattern is not FIFO.

The following code sample is a simple example illustrating the usage of both "target" and "stream" clauses associated with OpenMP task. In this case, the nested loop calculation is offloaded on DSP side and array b and c are streamed into DSP local memory, while the results is streamed out to array "a" memory location at GPP side.

```
#pragma omp task target(DSP) stream_in(b,c) stream_out(a)
  {
    for (int i=0; i<N; i++)
      for (int j=0; j<N; j++)
        a[i,j] = b[i][j] * c[i][j];
  }
```

5. Conclusion and Future Work

This paper describes our initial experience and ideas of extending OpenMP on heterogeneous embedded systems in order to simplify the programming efforts. It is still at an early stage for language design and our experimental implementation is currently under development based upon our OpenUH [23] compiler, a branch of the open source Open64 compiler suite for C, C++, and Fortran 95 and the IA-64 Linux ABI and API standards. OpenUH is currently connected with TI C64X DSP compiler to generate OpenMP executables for DSP[9]. We are working on compiler and runtime implementation of the proposed features and are experimenting them with medical imaging applications to demonstrate its productivity and performance. Further research in language extension, compiler and runtime optimizations are critical to ensure the success of this work.

References

[1] OpenCL 1.0 Specification. http://www.khronos.org/opencl/.
[2] Rapidmind. http://www.rapidmind.net/.
[3] The ClearSpeed Software Development Kit.   http://support.clearspeed.com/resources/documentation/sdk_preliminary_programming.pdf.
[4] Daniel J Abadi, Yanif Ahmad, Magdalena Balazinska, Ugur Cetintemel, Mitch Cherniack, Jeong-Hyon Hwang, Wolfgang Lindner, Anurag S Maskey, Alexander Rasin, Esther Ryvkina, Nesime Tatbul, Ying Xing, and Stan Zdonik. The Design of the Borealis Stream Processing Engine. In *Second Biennial Conference on Innovative Data Systems Research (CIDR 2005)*, Asilomar, CA, January 2005.
[5] Saman Amarasinghe, Michael I. Gordon, Michal Karczmarek, Jasper Lin, David Maze, Rodric M. Rabbah, and William Thies. Language and compiler design for streaming applications. *Int. J. Parallel Program.*, 33(2):261–278, 2005.
[6] OpenMP ARB. OpenMP Application Programming Interface. http://www.openmp.org/drupal/mp-documents/spec30_draft.pdf, October 2007.
[7] ARM. *ARM11 MPCore Processor*, r1p0 edition, August 2006.
[8] Ian Buck, Tim Foley, Daniel Horn, Jeremy Sugerman, Kayvon Fatahalian, Mike Houston, and Pat Hanrahan. Brook for GPUs: stream computing on graphics hardware. In *SIGGRAPH '04: ACM SIGGRAPH 2004 Papers*, pages 777–786, New York, NY, USA, 2004. ACM.
[9] Barbara Chapman, Lei Huang, Eric Biscondi, Eric Stotzer, Ashish Shrivastava, and Alan Gatherer. Implementing openmp on a high performance embedded multicore mpsoc. In *IPDPS '09: Proceedings of the 2009 IEEE International Symposium on Parallel&Distributed Processing*, pages 1–8, Washington, DC, USA, 2009. IEEE Computer Society.

[10]   William J. Dally, Francois Labonte, Abhishek Das, Patrick Hanrahan, Jung-Ho Ahn, Jayanth Gum-
       maraju, Mattan Erez, Nuwan Jayasena, Ian Buck, Timothy J. Knight, and Ujval J. Kapasi. Merrimac:
       Supercomputing with streams. In *SC '03: Proceedings of the 2003 ACM/IEEE conference on Super-
       computing*, page 35, Washington, DC, USA, 2003. IEEE Computer Society.

[11]   Analog Devices. *ADSP-BF561 Blackfin Processor Hardware Reference*, February 2007.

[12]   Freescale Semiconductor. *MSC8144 Reference Manual*, 2 edition, November 2007.

[13]   M. Gonzalez, E. Ayguade, X. Martorell, and J. Labarta. Exploiting pipelined executions in OpenMP. In
       International Conference on Parallel Processing, pages 153 – 160, 2003.

[14]   Texas Instruments.   TMS320TCI6488 DSP Platform.   `http://focus.ti.com/lit/ml/`
       `sprt415/sprt415.pdf`.

[15]   Texas Instruments. TNETV3020 Carrier Infrastructure Platform. `http://focus.ti.com/lit/`
       `ml/spat174/spat174.pdf`.

[16]   Texas Instruments. OMAP 3 family of multimedia applications processors. `http://focus.ti.`
       `com/pdfs/wtbu/ti_omap3family.pdf`, 2007.

[17]   Texas Instruments. *TMS320DM6467 Digital Media System-on-Chip*, December 2007.

[18]   Texas Instruments.   OMAP35x Technical Reference Manual (Rev. B). Literature num-
       ber SPRUF98B.   `http://focus.ti.com/dsp/docs/dspsupporttechdocsc.tsp?`
       `sectionId=3\&tabId=409\&abstractName=spruf98b`, September 2008.

[19]   Intel. Ct: A Flexible Parallel Programming Model for Tera-scale Architectures. Technical report, 2007.

[20]   J.A. Kahle, M.N. Day, H.P. Hofstee, C.R. Johns, T.R. Maeurer, and D. Shippy.   Introduction to the
       Cell multiprocessor. `http://researchweb.watson.ibm.com/journal/rd/494/kahle.`
       `html?S_TACT=105AGX16&S_CMP=LP`, September 2005.

[21]   Ujval Kapasi, William J. Dally, Scott Rixner, John D. Owens, and Brucek Khailany. The Imagine Stream
       Processor. In *Proceedings 2002 IEEE International Conference on Computer Design*, pages 282–288,
       Freiburg, Germany, September 2002.

[22]   David Lammers.   Architectures: Vendors flex MPU tech.   `http://www.eetimes.com/`
       `showArticle.jhtml?articleID=160400535`, April 2005.

[23]   Chunhua Liao, Oscar Hernandez, Barbara Chapman, Wenguang Chen, and Weimin Zheng. OpenUH:
       An optimizing, portable OpenMP compiler. In *12th Workshop on Compilers for Parallel Computers*,
       2006.

[24]   Ken Mai, Tim Paaske, Nuwan Jayasena, Ron Ho, William J. Dally, and Mark Horowitz. Smart memo-
       ries: a modular reconfigurable architecture. *SIGARCH Comput. Archit. News*, 28(2):161–171, 2000.

[25]   M. McCool and S. Toit. Metaprogramming GPUs with Sh. A K Peters, Ltd., 2004.

[26]   NVIDIA. CUDA. `http://www.nvidia.com/object/cuda_home.html`.

[27]   OpenMP: Simple, portable, scalable SMP programming. `http://www.openmp.org`, 2006.

[28]   Pier S. Paolucci, Ahmed A. Jerraya, Rainer Leupers, Lothar Thiele, and Piero Vicini. SHAPES: a
       tiled scalable software hardware architecture platform for embedded systems. In *CODES+ISSS '06:
       Proceedings of the 4th international conference on Hardware/software codesign and system synthesis*,
       pages 167–172, New York, NY, USA, 2006. ACM.

[29]   picoChip. Practical, programmable multi-core DSP. Technical Report 1.1, April 2007.

[30]   Larry Seiler, Doug Carmean, Eric Sprangle, Tom Forsyth, Michael Abrash, Pradeep Dubey, Stephen
       Junkins, Adam Lake, Jeremy Sugerman, Robert Cavin, Roger Espasa, Ed Grochowski, Toni Juan, and
       Pat Hanrahan. Larrabee: A many-core x86 architecture for visual computing. *ACM Trans. Graph.*,
       27(3):1–15, 2008.

[31]   Jesper H. Spring, Jean Privat, Rachid Guerraoui, and Jan Vitek. Streamflex: high-throughput stream
       programming in java. *SIGPLAN Not.*, 42(10):211–228, 2007.

[32]   Michael Bedford Taylor, Jason Kim, Jason Miller, David Wentzlaff, Fae Ghodrat, Ben Greenwald, Henry
       Hoffman, Paul Johnson, Jae-Wook Lee, Walter Lee, Albert Ma, Arvind Saraf, Mark Seneski, Nathan
       Shnidman, Volker Strumpen, Matt Frank, Saman Amarasinghe, and Anant Agarwal. The raw micro-
       processor: A computational fabric for software circuits and general-purpose programs. *IEEE Micro*,
       22(2):25–35, 2002.

Parallel Computing: From Multicores and GPU's to Petascale
B. Chapman et al. (Eds.)
IOS Press, 2010
© 2010 The authors and IOS Press. All rights reserved.

737

Author Index

Abouelella, F.	624	Castro-García, M.A.	359
Aguilar-Cornejo, M.	359	Catalyurek, U.	299
Aksnes, E.O.	536	Catthoor, F.	712
Aldinucci, M.	265, 273	Cecilia, J.M.	331
Aliaga, J.I.	125	César, E.	407
An Mey, D.	249	Chapman, B.	v, 728
Aoyagi, M.	220	Charif-Rubial, A.	653
Arnold, L.	423	Cicotti, P.	83
Asenjo, R.	351	Ciechanowicz, P.	169
Ashby, T.J.	712	Contassot-Vivier, S.	546
Atenekeng Kahou, G.-A.	51	Corbera, F.	351
Aussagues, C.	677	Coster, D.P.	520
Avis, N.J.	554	Coti, C.	441
Baden, S.B.	83	Creedon, E.	584
Barbieri, D.	307	D'Amore, L.	185
Beach, T.H.	554	D'Hollander, E.H.	581
Bell Jr., R.	455	Danelutto, M.	265, 273
Belpassi, L.	501	Davidson, T.	616
Berreth, A.	661	Desota, D.	455
Bertolli, C.	433	Desprez, F.	v
Bihan, S.	685	Devos, H.	616
Biscondi, E.	711	Dinh, Q.	653, 677
Bodin, F.	685	Domínguez-Domínguez, S.	359
Bogey, C.	513	Dongarra, J.	441
Bollhöfer, M.	125	Dupros, F.	67
Bosilca, G.	441	Dzhosan, O.	177
Bosque, J.L.	600	Elster, A.C.	533, 536, 562, 570
Brifault, K.	677	Emerson, A.P.J.	492
Drochard, L.	433	Erbacci, G.	492
Bruneel, K.	616, 624	Erhel, J.	51
Brunst, H.	693	Essafi, A.	205
Buenabad-Chávez, J.	359	EUFORIA Project Contributors	520
Cancare, F.	608	Fagerholm, J.	492
Canning, A.	107	Feki, S.	389
Cano, J.	600	Filippone, S.	307
Canot, É.	51	Folens, A.	712
Cappelle, H.	712	Fortin, P.	323
Cardellini, V.	307	Freche, J.	371
Carissimi, A.	67	Frings, W.	371, 423
Casaburi, D.	185	Gabriel, E.	389
Castagna, M.	608	Gajbe, M.	107
Castillo, J.	600	Gallopoulos, E.	238
Castillo, R.	351	Gara, A.	3

Garbey, M.	212	Krempel, S.	379
García, J.M.	331	Krusche, P.	158
Gentzsch, W.	477	Kuchen, H.	169
Georgiou, K.	238	Kunkel, J.	379
Ghoting, A.	289	Lamotte, J.-L.	323
Gibbon, P.	35	Lankamp, M.	16
Giorgi, P.	315	Lederer, H.	477, 482
Girou, D.	492	Lefèvre, L.	228
Glassee, M.	712	Leiss, E.L.	720
Gorlatch, S.	169	Lemarinier, P.	441
Granston, E.	720	Li, X.S.	83
Grelck, C.	467	Lichnewsky, A.	v
Grimstead, I.J.	554	Lieber, M.	281
Grützun, V.	281	Linel, P.	75
Gupta, A.	289	Ludwig, T.	379
Hagemeyer, J.	592	Lumsdaine, A.	289
Hartley, T.D.R.	299	Luque, E.	407
Heinig, A.	632	Machida, M.	91
Herault, T.	441	Mahjoub, A.	205
Hicks, M.	16	Maki, J.	220
Hilbrich, T.	693	Malony, A.D.	341, 685
Hoffmann, M.	35	Manzke, M.	584
Hovland, R.J.	570	Marcellino, L.	185
Hoyle, D.	720	Margalef, T.	407
Huang, L.	711, 728	Marsden, O.	513
Huerta, P.	600	Martín, A.F.	125
Igual, F.	299	Martínez, J.I.	600
Iliopoulos, C.S.	150	Mayanglambam, S.	341, 685
Imamura, T.	91	Mayo, R.	299
Inadomi, Y.	220	Méhaut, J.-F.	67
Ivascot, M.	661	Mehlan, T.	397
Izard, T.	315	Meier, S.	423
Jalby, W.	653, 661	Meneghin, M.	273
Janetzko, F.	423	Menzel, R.	701
Jesshope, C.	16	Merkulow, I.	249
Jost, T.	546	Millot, D.	669
Joubert, G.	v	Mix, H.	643, 693, 701
Jurenz, M.	693	Mohr, B.	643, 661, 701
Kambadur, P.	289	Morajko, A.	407
Kapinos, P.	249	Morel, J.-M.	645
Kegel, P.	169	Morin, L.	685
Kennedy, A.	482	Mouchard, L.	150
Kilpatrick, P.	265, 273	Mounié, G.	205
Knüpfer, A.	693	Muller, A.	669
Kobayashi, T.	220	Müller, M.S.	281, 693
Koliai, S.	653, 661	Murli, A.	185
Kollias, G.	238	Nagel, W.E.	281, 693
Korzh, A.	177	Nair, R.	3
Krammer, B.	643, 653, 661	Nakajima, K.	99

Natvig, T.	562	Shalf, J.	107
Navarro, A.	351	Shende, S.S.	685
Ngoko, Y.	43	Silber-Chaussumier, F.	669
Nguyen, V.H.	212	Smaoui Feki, M.	212
Nuentsa Wakam, D.	51	Sottile, M.J.	341, 685
Ohayon, E.	677	Spampinato, D.G.	562
Orgerie, A.-C.	228	Speck, R.	35
Palkovic, M.	712	Spezzano, G.	195
Panda, R.	455	Storchi, L.	501
Papatheodorou, T.S.	257	Stotzer, E.	711, 720
Papuzzo, G.	195	Strand, P.	520
Parrot, C.	669	Stroobandt, D.	581, 616, 624
Pedraza, C.	600	Strugholtz, M.	592
Penczek, F.	467	Strunk, J.	632
Peralta, J.C.	359	Sutmann, G.	371
Peters, F.	v	Takami, T.	220
Pissis, S.P.	150	Tarantelli, F.	501
Pohl, C.	592	Terboven, C.	249
Popova, N.N.	177, 415	Thomas, F.	455
Porrmann, M.	592	Tiskin, A.	158
Poss, R.	16	Tisserand, A.	315
Pousa Ribeiro, C.	67	Torquati, M.	273
Pringle, G.J.	492	Touhafi, A.	581
Priol, T.	v	Tromeur-Dervout, D.	75
Quintana-Ortí, E.S.	125	Trystram, D.	43, 205
Raghavan, P.	712	Tsujita, Y.	379
Rauber, T.	117	Ujaldón, M.	299, 331
Rehm, W.	397, 632	Van der Perre, L.	712
Renesto, M.	608	Vanneschi, M.	433
Requena, S.	533	Vázquez, M.	492
Rinke, S.	397	Venetis, I.E.	257
Risio, B.	661	Vialle, S.	546
Roman, J.E.	133	Voigtländer, F.	701
Romero, E.	133	Volkmer, T.	632
Romoth, J.	592	Voronov, V.Yu.	415
Rosales-Camacho, R.A.	359	Walker, D.W.	554
Ruiz, A.	299	Wang, L.-W.	107
Rünger, G.	117	Wasserman, H.	107
Salawdeh, I.	407	William, T.	661, 701
Salnikov, A.N.	143	Wolke, R.	281
Schellmann, M.	169	Yamada, S.	91
Schick, H.	632	Zanella, R.	59
Schleiden, C.	249	Zanni, L.	59
Schnurpfeil, A.	423	Zapata, E.L.	351
Scholz, S.-B.	467	Zhang, L.	16
Sciuto, D.	608	Zuckerman, S.	653, 661
Serafini, T.	59		